THE JERUSALEM TALMUD
THIRD ORDER: NAŠIM
TRACTATES *GIṬṬIN* AND *NAZIR*

STUDIA JUDAICA

FORSCHUNGEN ZUR WISSENSCHAFT DES JUDENTUMS

HERAUSGEGEBEN VON
E. L. EHRLICH UND G. STEMBERGER

BAND XXXIX

WALTER DE GRUYTER · BERLIN · NEW YORK

THE JERUSALEM TALMUD
תלמוד ירושלמי

THIRD ORDER: NAŠIM
סדר נשים
TRACTATES *GIṬṬIN* AND *NAZIR*
מסכתות גיטין ונזיר

EDITION, TRANSLATION, AND COMMENTARY

BY

HEINRICH W. GUGGENHEIMER

WALTER DE GRUYTER · BERLIN · NEW YORK

ISBN 978-3-11-068123-9
e-ISBN (PDF) 978-3-11-089889-7

This volume is text- and page-identical with the hardback published in 2007.

Library of Congress Control Number: 2020942817

Bibliographic information published by the Deutsche Nationalbibliothek
The Deutsche Nationalbibliothek lists this publication in the
Deutsche Nationalbibliografie;
detailed bibliographic data are available on the Internet at http://dnb.dnb.de.

© 2020 Walter de Gruyter GmbH, Berlin/Boston

Printing and binding: CPI books GmbH, Leck

www.degruyter.com

Preface

The present volume is the ninth in this series of the Jerusalem Talmud, the third in a four volume edition, translation, and Commentary of the Third Order of this Talmud. The principles of the edition regarding text, vocalization, and Commentary have been spelled out in detail in the Introduction to the first volume. The text in this volume is based on the manuscript text of the Yerushalmi edited by Professor Sussman for the Academy of the Hebrew Language, Jerusalem 2001. The author has exercised his own independent judgment on what may or may not be corrupt in the text.

The text contains many passages which are repeated in other Tractates of this Talmud. It is "general knowledge" that parallel passages in the Jerusalem Talmud are copies of one another. In the present edition, parallel passages are considered as parallel sources and a full list of variant readings is given in every case. These readings show that in fact parallel passages are to be considered witnesses to the same original text, but it appears that a number of deviations cannot be explained as copyists' errors and that the scribe of the Leiden ms. copied different tractates from different mss. representing different histories of transmission and different stages of adaptation of Palestinian spelling (as represented by most Geniza fragments) to the Babylonian spelling with which the scribes were familiar.

The extensive Commentary is not based on emendations; where there is no evidence from manuscripts or early prints to correct evident scribal errors, the proposed correction is given in the Notes. As in the preceding volume, for each paragraph the folio and line numbers of the text in the Krotoschin edition are added. It should be remembered that these numbers may differ from the *editio princeps* by up to three lines. It seems to be important that a translation of the Yerushalmi be accompanied by the text, to give the reader the possibility to compare the interpretation with other translations.

Again I wish to thank my wife, Dr. Eva Guggenheimer, who acted as critic, style editor, proof reader, and expert on the Latin and Greek vocabulary. Her own notes on some possible Latin and Greek etymologies are identified by (E. G.).

Contents

Introduction to Tractate Giṭṭin   1

Giṭṭin Chapter 1, המביא
- Halakhah 1   5
- Halakhah 2   25
- Halakhah 3   33
- Halahkah 5   34
- Halakhah 6   43

Giṭṭin Chapter 2, המביא בתרא
- Halakhah 1   55
- Halakhah 2   62
- Halakhah 3   66
- Halakhah 4   78
- Halakhah 5   82
- Halakhah 6   84
- Halakhah 8   86

Giṭṭin Chapter 3, כל גט
- Halakhah 1   89
- Halakhah 2   101
- Halakhah 3   105

Halakhah 4	109
Halakhah 5	111
Halakhah 6	114
Halakhah 7	117
Halakhah 8	123

Giṭṭin Chapter 4, השולח

Halakhah 1	132
Halakhah 2	134
Halakhah 3	143
Halakhah 4	147
Halakhah 5	160
Halakhah 6	164
Halakhah 7	170
Halakhah 8	173
Halakhah 9	175

Giṭṭin Chapter 5, הניזקין

Halakhah 1	180
Halakhah 3	193
Halakhah 4	206
Halakhah 5	216
Halakhah 6	222
Halakhah 8	232
Halakhah 9	233
Halakhah 10	243

Giṭṭin Chapter 6, האומר התקבל

Halakhah 1	247
Halakhah 2	259
Halakhah 3	256
Halakhah 5	267
Halakhah 7	269

Halakhah 8	275
Halakhah 9	280

Giṭṭin Chapter 7, מי שאחזו

Halakhah 1	285
Halakhah 2	295
Halakhah 3	297
Halakhah 4	304
Halakhah 5	311
Halakhah 6	314
Halakhah 8	319
Halakhah 10	322

Giṭṭin Chapter 8, הזורק גט

Halakhah 1	325
Halakhah 2	331
Halakhah 3	334
Halakhah 4	342
Halakhah 5	343
Halakhah 6	346
Halakhah 8	348
Halakhah 10	350
Halakhah 11	352
Halakhah 12	355

Giṭṭin Chapter 9, המגרש

Halakhah 1	365
Halakhah 2	374
Halakhah 3	377
Halakhah 4	379
Halakhah 5	381
Halakhah 6	383

Halakhah 7	384
Halakhah 8	389
Halakhah 9	396
Halakhah 10	398
Halakhah 11	404

Introduction to Tractate Nazir 409

Nazir Chapter 1, כל כינויי נזירות

Halakhah 1	411
Halakhah 2	419
Halakhah 3	431
Halakhah 4	435
Halakhah 6	437

Nazir Chapter 2, הריני נזיר

Halakhah 1	441
Halakhah 2	449
Halakhah 3	452
Halakhah 5	457
Halakhah 6	460
Halakhah 7	462
Halakhah 8	462
Halakhah 9	464
Halakhah 10	469

Nazir Chapter 3, מי שאמר

Halakhah 1	476
Halakhah 2	479
Halakhah 3	484
Halakhah 4	486
Halakhah 5	488

Halakhah 6	497
Halakhah 7	499

Nazir Chapter 3, מי שאמר

Halakhah 1	476
Halakhah 2	479
Halakhah 3	484
Halakhah 4	486
Halakhah 5	488
Halakhah 6	497
Halakhah 7	499

Nazir Chapter 4, מי שאמר בתרא

Halakhah 1	504
Halakhah 2	508
Halakhah 3	511
Halakhah 4	516
Halakhah 5	527
Halakhah 6	530

Nazir Chapter 5, בית שמאי

Halakhah 1	538
Halakhah 4	555
Halakhah 5	561
Halakhah 6	566

Nazir Chapter 6, שלשה מינין

Halakhah 1	570
Halakhah 2	594
Halakhah 3	598
Halakhot 4-5-6	606
Halakhah 7	609

Halakhah 8	612
Halakhah 9	615
Halakhah 10	617
Halakhah 11	620
Halakhah 12	627

Nazir Chapter 7, כהן גדול

Halakhah 1	632
Halakhah 2	650
Halakhah 3	664
Halakhah 4	674

Nazir Chapter 8, שני נזירין

Halakhah 1	682
Halakhot 2-10	697

Nazir Chapter 9, הגוים אין להם

Halakhah 1	713
Halakhah 2	722
Halakhah 3	735
Halakhah 4	743
Halakhah 5	745
Halakhah 6	751

Indices

Index of Biblical Quotations	753
Index of Talmudic Quotations	
Babylonian Talmud	755
Jerusalem Talmud	757
Mishnah	759
Tosephta	760
Midrashim	761

Rabbinical Literature	761
Index of Greek, Latin, and Hebrew words	761
Author Index	762
Subject Index	762

Introduction to Tractate Giṭṭin

The word גט (plural גִּיטִין) appears in Accadic as a Sumerian loan word *giṭṭum* (plural *giṭṭāni*) meaning "tablet, written document, note." The second meaning is the one adopted in rabbinic Hebrew. *Geṭ* without a modifier always means "bill of divorce" since divorce is the only legal action impossible without a written document. Other documents may also be called *geṭ*, e. g., a bill of manumission for a slave; this has to be called *geṭ of freedom*, since manumission may be effected without a written document. Similarly, an IOU may be called a *geṭ of indebtedness*; the existence of a debt may also be established by the testimony of witnesses. Tractate *Giṭṭin* deals with divorce documents but also contains the rules of other documents.

The rules for divorce mainly derive from *Deut.* 24:1,3, which repeatedly emphasizes that the husband has to "write her a document of separation, deliver it to his wife, and send her away from his house." This makes the divorce uniquely an act by the husband which requires a written document delivered to the wife and a permanent separation of the parties. Most of the Tractate deals with the implementation of these rules, especially the rules of delivery by an agent. Most of the rules of agency are valid for all kinds of documents.

The Tractate starts with a discussion of how the bill of divorce can be delivered to the wife if the husband is far away; there are different rules depending on whether the transaction takes place in the Land of Israel, under the supervision of a complete system of rabbinical courts, or involves another country, where some questions of authenticity may arise. The discussion of the boundaries of the Land echoes the corresponding texts in *Ševi'it*, Chapter 6. Since the delivery of the bill is an intrinsic part of the divorce proceedings, it needs the presence of at least two witnesses. The same is true for a bill of manumission, whose delivery turns the slave into a full member of the Jewish people. This leads to a discussion of the similarities and dissimilarities of bills of divorce as compared to bills of manumission.

The second Chapter begins and ends with the topic of the first but in between turns to the writing of the document, the writing materials, and the persons empowered to write.

The third Chapter concentrates on the biblical requirement that the divorce document be written "for the wife". A scribe may not prepare forms in advance where he only enters the essential data in case of need, although he may do so for commercial contracts. Returning to the topic of delivery of the bill, there follows a general discussion of the presumption of the permanence of the *status quo*, based on the case of a bill of divorce which an agent may deliver assuming that the far-away husband is still alive.

The fourth Chapter starts with the possibilities open to the husband to retract a divorce once the bill was handed to an agent. That possibility, quite unrestricted in biblical law, was severely restricted by rabbinic practice. This leads to an enumeration of rabbinic practices in several other fields, the settlement of payments from an estate to a widow, redemption of kidnapped slaves and their manumission. The Chapter ends with cases in which a man is rabbinically forbidden to remarry his divorcee even if she had not contracted another marriage in the meantime.

The fifth Chapter mostly deals with money matters, starting with the liquidation of debts arising from judgments for torts, with real estate obtained by improper means, and ending with rules of civilized behavior known as "ways of peace" (mostly repetitions from *Ševi'it* 4:3, 5:9).

Chapter Six again deals with aspects of the rules of agency. Chapter Seven starts with the possibility of divorce for a man temporarily incapacitated and then turns to various possibilities of conditional divorces, including the relaxed rules for emergency divorce of a childless sick husband who wants to free his wife from levirate marriage.

Chapter Eight deals with questions of doubtful delivery of a bill of divorce and related questions concerning delivery of a marriage gift or liquidation of a debt, followed by a discussion of the validity of a bill of divorce if the parties do not terminate sexual relations, and divorce by a bill of questionable validity. The Halakhah includes a discussion of the legal status of lesbian women. The Chapter ends with a rule about sealed contracts, relevant mostly for commercial transactions.

The last Chapter continues the subject of irregular bills of divorce, whether through fault of the scribe, conditions imposed by the husband, or caused by the signing witnesses. Since in the biblical text a divorce is a unilateral act by the husband, the question arises whether the court can force the husband to divorce, either because the marriage is sinful or because the wife complains of abuse by the husband. The final Mishnah addresses the basic underlying question, *viz.*, whether divorce is really a voluntary act. According to the House of Shammai, divorce is permitted only if the husband has reason to suspect his wife of adultery or otherwise immoral behavior. This seems to imply that marriages are concluded in Heaven[1] and can be dissolved only if required by Heaven's Law[2]. According to the House of Hillel, stated in particular by R. Aqiba, divorce is an option always available.

It seems clear that the scribe of the Leiden ms., the only source available for this Tractate, did copy different Tractates from different sources (or his source already was collected from different sources). The text of *Gittin*, at least Chapters One to Eight, is copied from a text whose adaptation to Babylonian spelling is much more pronounced than in other Tractates. For example, Chapter One (Note 118) even contains a present participle construed with a prefix ק.

---

1   Babli *Sanhedrin* 22a, Yerushalmi *Beṣah* 5:2, 63a l. 66; *Mark* 10:9.
2   *Matth.* 19:9.

המביא פרק ראשון

(fol. 43a) **משנה א**: הַמֵּבִיא גֵט מִמְּדִינַת הַיָּם צָרִיךְ שֶׁיּאמַר בְּפָנַי נִכְתַּב וּבְפָנַי נִתְחַתֵּם. רַבָּן גַּמְלִיאֵל אוֹמֵר אַף הַמֵּבִיא מִן הָרְקַם וּמִן הַחֶגֶר. רִבִּי אֱלִיעֶזֶר אוֹמֵר אֲפִילוּ מִכְּפַר לוּדִים לְלוּד. וַחֲכָמִים אוֹמְרִין אֵינוֹ צָרִיךְ שֶׁיּאמַר בְּפָנַי נִכְתַּב וּבְפָנַי נִתְחַתֵּם אֶלָּא הַמֵּבִיא מִמְּדִינַת הַיָּם וְהַמּוֹלִיךְ וְהַמֵּבִיא מִמְּדִינָה לִמְדִינָה בִּמְדִינַת הַיָּם צָרִיךְ שֶׁיּאמַר בְּפָנַי נִכְתַּב וּבְפָנַי נִתְחַתֵּם. רַבָּן שִׁמְעוֹן בֶּן גַּמְלִיאֵל אוֹמֵר אֲפִילוּ מֵהֶגְמוֹנְיָיא לְהֶגְמוֹנְיָיא.

Mishnah 1: Somebody who brings a bill of divorce from overseas[1] must be able to say: "It was written and signed before me." Rabban Gamliel says, even somebody who brings from Reqam[2] and Ḥeger[3]; Rebbi Eliezer says, even from Kefar Ludim to Lydda[4]; but the Sages say that the only one who has to be able to say that it was written and signed before him is one who brings from overseas or to overseas. One who brings from one province[5] to another overseas has to say that it was written and signed before him; Rabban Simeon ben Gamliel says, even from one district to the next.

1   "Overseas" stands for all places who do not have a rabbinic authority ordained by the Patriarchate in the Land of Israel or the two Academies acting on the authority of the Prince of the Diaspora in Babylonia. If one cannot be sure that all fine points of the rules of bills of divorce were followed, the court must have the possibility of examining the messenger about the details of the writing and signing of the document.

2   Two places "Reqam" are mentioned as border towns in

Transjordan in the description of the borders of the Land of Israel; cf. *Ševi'it* 6:1, Notes 47, 51.

3   This place has not been identified; it is conjectured to be on the Southern border of the Land of Israel.

4   Which were close to one another but in different court districts.

5   While in Biblical Hebrew מדינה means "province", in Talmudic usage the word often has the late hieroglyphic, and Arabic, meaning of "capital".

6   The district under the command of a ἡγεμών "general", a word used in the Roman Empire even for the Emperor, but mostly for the *praeses provinciae*. The usual interpretation given in this Mishnah is "administrative district".

(43a line 30) **הלכה א**: הַמֵּבִיא גֵט מִמְּדִינַת הַיָּם כול'. וְקַשְׁיָא. אִילוּ הַמֵּבִיא שְׁטָר מַתָּנָה מִמְּדִינַת הַיָּם שֶׁמָּא חָשׁ לוֹמַר. בְּפָנַיי נִכְתַּב וּבְפָנַיי נֶחְתַּם. רְבִּי יְהוֹשֻׁעַ בֶּן לֵוִי אָמַר. שַׁנְיָיא הִיא שֶׁאֵינָן בְּקִיאִין בְּדִיקְדּוּקֵי גִיטִּין. אָמַר רְבִּי יוֹחָנָן. קַל הֵיקֵלוּ עָלֶיהָ שֶׁלֹּא תְהֵא יוֹשֶׁבֶת עֲגוּנָה. וְהַיְינוּ קַל. אֲנוּ אֶלָּא חוֹמֶר. שֶׁאִילוּ לֹא אָמַר לָהּ. בְּפָנַיי נִכְתַּב וּבְפָנַיי נֶחְתַּם. אַף אַתְּ אֵין מַתִּירָהּ לְהִינָּשֵׂא. אָמַר רְבִּי יוֹסֵי. חוֹמֶר שֶׁהֶחֱמַרְתָּהּ עָלֶיהָ מִתְּחִילָּה שֶׁיְּהֵא צָרִיךְ לוֹמַר. בְּפָנַיי נִכְתַּב וּבְפָנַיי נֶחְתַּם. הֵיקַלְתָּהּ עָלֶיהָ בְּסוֹף שֶׁאִם בָּא וְעִירְעֵר עֲרָרוֹ בָטֵל. רְבִּי מָנָא סְבַר מֵימַר. בְּעָרָר שֶׁחוּץ לְגוּפוֹ. אֲבָל בְּעָרָר שֶׁבְּגוּפוֹ כְּעָרָר שֶׁאֵין בּוֹ מַמָּשׁ. אֲפִילוּ כְּעָרָר שֶׁיֵּשׁ בּוֹ מַמָּשׁ. אָמַר רְבִּי יוֹסֵי בֵּי רְבִּי בּוּן. מִכֵּיוָן דְּתֵימַר דְּטַעֲמָא חוֹמֶר שֶׁהֶחֱמַרְתָּהּ עָלֶיהָ מִתְּחִילָּה שֶׁיְּהֵא צָרִיךְ לוֹמַר. בְּפָנַיי נֶחְתַּם. הֵיקַלְתָּהּ עָלֶיהָ בְּסוֹף שֶׁאִם בָּא וְעִירְעֵר עֲרָרוֹ בָטֵל. הֲוֵי לֹא שַׁנְיָיא. הוּא עָרָר שֶׁחוּץ לְגוּפוֹ הוּא עָרָר שֶׁבְּגוּפוֹ. הוּא עָרָר שֶׁאֵין בּוֹ מַמָּשׁ הוּא עָרָר שֶׁיֵּשׁ בּוֹ מַמָּשׁ. וְחָשׁ לוֹמַר. שֶׁמָּא חֲתָמוּ בְעֵדִים פְּסוּלִין. אָמַר רְבִּי אָבוּן. אֵינוֹ חָשׁוּד לְקַלְקְלָהּ בִּידֵי שָׁמַיִם. בְּבֵית דִּין הוּא חָשׁוּד לְקַלְקְלָהּ. שֶׁמִּתּוֹךְ שֶׁהוּא יוֹדֵעַ שֶׁאִם בָּא וְעִרְעֵר עֲרָרוֹ בָטֵל אַף הוּא מַחְתְּמוֹ בְּעֵדִים כְּשֵׁירִין.

Halakhah 1: "Somebody who brings a bill of divorce from overseas," etc. This is difficult. If somebody brings a gift document from overseas, would you require him to say, it was written and signed[7] before me? Rebbi Joshua ben Levi said, there is a difference because they are not conversant with the fine points of bills of divorce[8]. Rebbi Joḥanan said, that is a leniency lest she sit abandoned[9]. Is that a leniency? It is only a restriction, for if he does not say to her, it was written and signed before me, you do not permit her to remarry. Rebbi Yose said, the difficulty which you impose upon her at the beginning, that he is required to say, it was written and signed before me, makes it easy for her at the end. For if [the husband] would come and protest, his protest would be void. Rebbi Mana wanted to say, a protest other than the text of the bill[10]. But is a protest about the text of the bill a protest which has no validity[11]? Even for a protest which has validity, said Rebbi Yose ben Rebbi Abun, since you say that the reason for the difficulty which you impose upon her at the beginning, that he is required to say, it was signed before me, is to make it easy for her at the end, that if [the husband] would come and protest, his protest would be void; this means that there is no difference whether it is a protest not about the text of the bill or about the body of the bill, a protest which has no validity, or a protest which does have validity[12]! But should you worry that maybe be gave the bill to disqualified witnesses to sign[13]? Rebbi Abun said, he is not suspect to damage her before Heaven[14]. Before the court he is suspect to damage her. But since he knows that if he comes and protests his protest is void, he will choose qualified witnesses to sign.

7   The form נחתם is that of most Mishnah mss. and of the Babli. The form נחתמו in the Mishnah is that of several Palestinian Mishnah mss.

8   In the Babli, 2a/2b, it is pointed out that a bill of divorce has to be

written for the woman to be divorced since the verse says (*Deut.* 24:1): "He shall write *for her*". While the text of the bill must mention the names of husband and wife, it cannot be ascertained from the text whether the scribe was instructed to write the text specifically for that woman; there must be a live witness available who can be examined about this point. A second opinion notes that the signatures of the witnesses themselves would need confirmation.

9 In the Babli, 3a, this is an anonymous (unanimous) opinion. As explained in the sequel, if the husband could come later and claim the the bill of divorce was fake, no woman could ever remarry on a bill of divorce written far away for fear that her children from a second husband could retroactively be declared to be bastards; cf. Mishnah *Yebamot* 10:1.

10 E. g., if the husband claims that he had attached a condition to the bill not provided for in the bill and that the condition was not satisfied. Since the condition was not presented to the court which oversaw the delivery of the document, it cannot be considered.

11 He claims that the entire bill is fake or that there is an intrinsic defect which makes the entire document invalid.

12 Since there was a witness who was cross-examined about the validity of the bill, the husband cannot be admitted to testify since when he claims to be still the husband of his divorcee he declares himself a relative by marriage who is barred from acting as a witness for or against his wife.

13 The messenger who delivers the bill might not know that the witnesses either were relatives of one of the parties or convicted felons; their signatures would invalidate the document.

14 For if both the local court and the wife act in good faith, Heaven will absolve her but he has sinned. Cf. *Yebamot* 15:4, Notes 92-93.

(43a line 46) הָיָה כָּתוּב בּוֹ מַתָּנָה. וְאָמַר. בְּפָנַיי נִכְתַּב וּבְפָנַיי נֶחְתַּם. מֵאַחַר שֶׁעֲרָרוֹ בָּטֵל אֵצֶל הַגֵּט עֲרָרוֹ בָּטֵל אֵצֶל הַמַּתָּנָה. אוֹ מֵאַחַר שֶׁעֲרָרוֹ בָּטֵל אֵצֶל הַגֵּט עֲרָרוֹ קַיָּים אֵצֶל הַמַּתָּנָה. תַּנִּינָן דְּבָתְרָהּ. אֶחָד גִּיטֵּי נָשִׁים וְאֶחָד שִׁיחְרוּרֵי עֲבָדִים שָׁוִין בְּמוֹלִיךְ וּבְמֵבִיא. הָיָה כָּתוּב בּוֹ מַתָּנָה. וְאָמַר. בְּפָנַיי נִכְתַּב וּבְפָנַיי נִתְחַתָּם. מֵאַחַר שֶׁעֲרָרוֹ בָּטֵל אֵצֶל הַגֵּט עֲרָרוֹ קַיָּים אֵצֶל הַמַּתָּנָה. אוֹ מֵאַחַר

שֶׁעֲרָרוֹ קַיָּים אֶצֶל הַמַּתָּנָה עֲרָרוֹ קַיָּים אֶצֶל הַגֵּט. כָּתַב כָּל נְכָסָיו לְעַבְדּוֹ. אַתְּ אָמַר. הוּא גִיטוֹ הוּא מַתְּנָתוֹ. מָה אַתְּ עָבַד לָהּ. בְּגֵט הוּא וְעֲרָרוֹ בָּטֵל אוֹ בַמַּתָּנָה הוּא וְעֲרָרוֹ קַיָּים. וְיֵיבָא כְהָדָא. כָּתַב כָּל־נְכָסָיו לִשְׁנֵי בְנֵי אָדָם כְּאַחַת וְהָיוּ עֵדִים כְּשֵׁירִין לָזֶה וּפְסוּלִין לָזֶה. רִבִּי אִילָא בְשֵׁם רִבִּי אַמִּי. אִיתְפַּלְגוּן רִבִּי יוֹחָנָן וְרֵישׁ לָקִישׁ. חַד אָמַר. מֵאַחַר שֶׁהֵן פְּסוּלִין לָזֶה פְּסוּלִין לָזֶה. וְחָרָנָה אָמַר. כְּשֵׁירִין לָזֶה וּפְסוּלִין לָזֶה. רִבִּי מָנָא לֹא מְפָרֵשׁ. רִבִּי אָבִין מְפָרֵשׁ. רִבִּי יוֹחָנָן אָמַר. מֵאַחַר שֶׁהֵן פְּסוּלִין לָזֶה פְּסוּלִין לָזֶה. וְרֵישׁ לָקִישׁ אָמַר. כְּשֵׁירִין לָזֶה וּפְסוּלִין לָזֶה. אָמַר רִבִּי אֶלְעָזָר. מַתְנִיתָא מְסַיְּיעָא לְרִבִּי יוֹחָנָן. מָה הַשְּׁנַיִם נִמְצָא אֶחָד מֵהֶן קָרוֹב אוֹ פָסוּל עֵדוּתָן בְּטֵילָה אַף הַשְּׁלֹשָׁה נִמְצָא אֶחָד מֵהֶן קָרוֹב אוֹ פָסוּל עֵדוּתָן בְּטֵילָה. רִבִּי יַעֲקֹב בַּר אָחָא אָמַר. אִיתְפַּלְגוּן רִבִּי חֲנַנְיָה חֲבֵרִין דְּרַבָּנִין וְרַבָּנִין. חַד אָמַר. יָאוּת אָמַר רִבִּי לֶעְזָר. וְחָרָנָה אָמַר. לֹא אָמַר רִבִּי לֶעְזָר. מָאן דְּאָמַר. יָאוּת אָמַר רִבִּי אֶלְעָזָר. נַעֲשִׂית עֵדוּת אַחַת וּבְאִישׁ אֶחָד כְּעֵדוּת שֶׁבְּטֵלָה מִקְצָתָהּ בְּטֵלָה כּוּלָּהּ. וּמָאן דְּאָמַר. לֹא אָמַר רִבִּי לֶעְזָר יָאוּת. נַעֲשָׂה כִּשְׁתֵּי כִיתֵּי עֵדִים כְּשֵׁרִין לָזֶה וּפְסוּלִין לָזֶה.

If [the bill of divorce] contained documentation of a gift and [the messenger] said, it was written and signed before me, is [the husband's] protest about the gift void since it is void about the divorce[15]? Or, since his protest is void [only] about the divorce, is it valid about the gift[16]? We have stated later: "Bills of divorce for wives and documents of manumission are equal in the rules of carrying and bringing." If [the document of manumission] contained documentation of a gift and [the messenger] said, it was written and signed before me, is [the master's] protest about the gift void since it is void about the manumission? Or since his protest is void [only] about the manumission, is it valid about the gift[17]? If somebody signed all his property over to his slave[18], you say that the gift is the document of manumission[19]. How do you treat this?

Is it a document of manumission and his protest is void or is it a gift and his protest is valid? This can be compared to the following: [20]If somebody signed all his property over to two persons in one document and the testimony of the witnesses was valid for one but invalid for the other. Rebbi Ila in the name of Rebbi Immi[21]: Rebbi Joḥanan and Rebbi Simeon ben Laqish disagreed; one said, since it is invalid for one it is invalid for the other, but the other said, it is valid for one and invalid for the other. Rebbi Mana did not specify; Rebbi Abin specified: Rebbi Joḥanan said, since it is invalid for one it is invalid for the other; but Rebbi Simeon ben Laqish said, it is valid for one and invalid for the other. Rebbi Eleazar said, a Mishnah supports Rebbi Joḥanan: "Since testimony of two [witnesses] is invalid if one of them turns out to be related or disqualified, so also of three [witnesses] it is invalid if one of them turns out to be related or disqualified". Rebbi Jacob bar Aḥa said, Rebbi Ḥanina the colleague of the rabbis and the rabbis disagree. One says, the argument of Rebbi Eleazar is correct, but the other says, Rebbi Eleazar is not correct. For him who says, the argument of Rebbi Eleazar is correct, it is a testimony about one person; as testimony it is totally invalid if it is partially invalid. For him who says, the argument of Rebbi Eleazar is not correct, it is as if two groups of witnesses came, valid for one and disqualified for the other.

15 The question presupposes that one follows R. Joḥanan's opinion in the preceding paragraph. The messenger who delivers the bill of divorce is a single witness who cannot validate a monetary claim. But since by tradition he has the power to validate a bill of divorce and the delivery of the bill implies authorization of the divorcee to collect her *ketubah*, it follows that in matters of bills of divorce the single messenger has the power to validate

money claims as long as they are included in or dependent upon the bill of divorce.

16 Since annulment of the special gift from the husband to his divorcee will not hinder her from remarrying, there seems to be no special reason why a single witness should make a money claim definitive.

17 If the document of manumission was accepted by the local court at the point of delivery, the slave upon immersion in a *miqweh* became a full Jew. A Jew cannot be enslaved by a fellow Jew (*Lev.* 25:42). The reason why the master's protest is void has nothing to do with monetary claims; there seems to be no reason why the master cannot disclaim the gift.

18 This seems to have been a common occurrence in Roman society.

19 The essence of freedom is that a person is master of himself; the gift document transfers mastership of the slave to himself.

20 The following is from *Ketubot* 11:5, explained in Notes 97-102, and *Makkot* 1:16. The variant readings are given in *Ketubot*. The messenger who delivers the document of manumission, which in this case is a document about money matters, is believed as if he were a group of two in regard of the manumission but is disqualified for the money part. All the questions asked up to this point can be answered if one decides whether to follow R. Joḥanan or R. Simeon ben Laqish.

21 In *Ketubot*: R. Yasa. Since rabbis Yasa (Assi) and Immi (Ammi) form a permanent pair in the Babli, there is no real difference in the attributions.

(43a last line) עַד שֶׁיֹּאמַר. בְּפָנַי נִכְתַּב בַּיּוֹם וְנֶחְתַּם בַּיּוֹם. עַד שֶׁיֹּאמַר. נִכְתַּב לִשְׁמָהּ וְנֶחְתַּם לִשְׁמָהּ. בָּעָא קוֹמֵי רִבִּי יוֹחָנָן. צָרִיךְ שֶׁיְּהֵא מַכִּיר שְׁמוֹתָן שֶׁל עֵדִים בִּשְׁעַת חֲתִימָתָן. אָמַר לוֹן. גּוֹיִם לוּקְיָן חֲתוּמִין עָלָיו. וְאַתֶּם אוֹמְרִין אָכֵין. מַתְנִיתָא מְסַייְעָא לְרִבִּי יוֹחָנָן. כָּל־הַגִּטִּין הַבָּאִין מִמְּדִינַת הַיָּם אַף עַל פִּי שֶׁשְּׁמוֹתָן כְּשֵׁם גּוֹיִם הֲרֵי אֵילוּ כְשֵׁירִין מִפְּנֵי שֶׁיִּשְׂרָאֵל שֶׁבְּחוּצָה לָאָרֶץ שְׁמוֹתָן כִּשְׁמוֹת הַגּוֹיִם. לֹא אָמַר אֶלָּא שֶׁבְּחוּצָה לָאָרֶץ. הָא שֶׁבָּאָרֶץ יִשְׂרָאֵל לֹא. מַאי כְדוֹן. רִבִּי בֵּיבֵי בְשֵׁם רִבִּי אַסִּי. עַד שֶׁיִּכְתּוֹב. בְּמָקוֹם יְהוּדָאִיקֵי. אִם אֵין שָׁם יְהוּדָאִיקֵי. בְּבֵית הַכְּנֶסֶת. אִם אֵין שָׁם בֵּית הַכְּנֶסֶת מְצָרֵף עֲשָׂרָה בְּנֵי אָדָם.

אָמַר רִבִּי אָבִין. נוֹחַ לִי לְקַיְּימוֹ בְּחוֹתְמָיו וְלֹא לְצָרֵף עֲשָׂרָה בְּנֵי אָדָם. מָאי כְּדוֹן. אֲפִילוּ בַחֲנוּתָן שֶׁלְיִשְׂרָאֵל.

Only if he says, it was written before me during the day and signed during the day[22]; only if he says, it was written before me especially for her and signed expressly for her[23]. It was asked before Rebbi Joḥanan: Does he have to know the names of the witnesses at the moment of their signing? He said to them, did the Gentiles Luciani sign it[24]? And you say so? A *baraita* supports Rebbi Joḥanan: "All bills of divorce coming from overseas are valid even if their names sound Gentile since Jews outside the Land of Israel bear Gentile names.[25]" He said only, outside the Land; therefore not in the Land of Israel[26]. What about this? Rebbi Bevai in the name of Rebbi Issi: unless he writes, at a Jewish place[27]. If there is no Jewish place, in the synagogue. If there is no synagogue, he assembles there ten people[28]. Rebbi Abun said, it would be better to certify the signatures[29] than to assemble there ten people. What about this? Even in a Jewish store[30].

22 "The day" means the day written as date in the document. Mishnah 2:2 notes that a pre-dated bill of divorce is invalid like all pre-dated documents. The bill may have been written in the night and signed the following day since the rabbinic day is counted from sundown to sundown; it cannot have been written during daytime and signed the following night since that would make it pre-dated.

23 The messenger must have heard the husband tell the scribe to write a bill of divorce for his wife, mentioning her by name. The Babli agrees, 3a.

24 If the names sound Roman, it does not mean anything. In the Babli, 11b, R. Joḥanan notes that if a Gentile name is known to be used by Jews, the matter does not have to be investigated. Examples given in the Babli are Λύκος "wolf", a frequent substitute for Benjamin (*Gen.* 49:27), and Λίς "lion" (in epic poetry, cf.

Semitic ליש), a substitute for Jehudah (*Gen.* 49:9). Cf. E. and H. Guggenheimer, J*ewish Family Names and their Origins: An Etymological Dictionary* (Ktav, 1992; German edition *Etymologisches Wörterbuch der jüdischen Familiennamen,* Saur 1996), Introduction: Sobriquets, Animal Names.

25   Babli 11b, Tosephta 6:4.

26   It should not be assumed that Jewish people with Gentile names cannot sign a bill of divorce in the Land of Israel; there are a number of rabbis with Gentile names such as Eudaimon, Pappos, Antigonos. But in case such a name appears, an inquiry has to be made about the identity of the witness, wheras in documents coming from outside the Land, all names are accepted without inquiry.

27   Greek Ἰουδαϊκός, -ή, -όν "Jewish". If the names of the witnesses are Gentile, some indication of this being a purely Jewish document is needed since all documents executed in a Gentile court are valid except bills of divorce.

28   All of whom have to sign as witnesses even if most of them are related to the couple, if only two of the witnesses are acceptable in law; it is to be assumed that not all of their names will be characteristically Gentile. Cf. Tosephta 7:11; M. A. Friedman, *Jewish Marriage in Palestine*, Vol. 1, p. 489.

29   After the document was duly signed, the local court could append a certification that the witnesses were known to the court and in good standing. Such a certification would have to be accepted by every rabbinic court anywhere (Mishnah 1:3).

30   The document must mention the place where it was written. One might add that it was written in a Jewish store to emphasize the Jewish character of the document, implicitly validating the Gentile-sounding signatures.

(43b line 10) וְלֹא אָמַר. נִכְתַּב בַּיוֹם וְנֶחְתַּם בַּיוֹם נִכְתַּב לִשְׁמָהּ וְנֶחְתַּם לִשְׁמָהּ. נֵימַר מַה דְשָׁאִיל אֲמוֹרָא. אָמַר לֵיהּ. וְיֵידָא דְּאָמַר רָבִין בַּר רַב חִסְדָּא. אַיְיתֵי גִּיטָא וּנְתָנוֹ לָהּ. וְלֹא אָמַר לָהּ. בְּפָנַיי נִכְתַּב וּבְפָנַיי נֶחְתָּם. אָתָא עוֹבְדָא קוֹמֵי רַבִּי יוֹחָנָן. אָמַר לֵיהּ. טְלֵיהוּ מִמֶּנָּה וֶאֱמוֹר לָהּ בִּפְנֵי שְׁנַיִם. בְּפָנַיי נִכְתַּב וּבְפָנַיי נֶחְתָּם. וְרַבִּי יוֹחָנָן כְּרַבִּי שִׁמְעוֹן בֶּן אֶלְעָזָר. דְּרַבִּי שִׁמְעוֹן בֶּן אֶלְעָזָר אָמַר. אֵינוֹ

גֵּט עַד שֶׁיֹּאמַר לָהּ בִּשְׁעַת מַתָּנָה. שֶׁהוּא גִיטֵיךְ. דְּרִבִּי יוֹחָנָן יָיבֹא מִן רִבִּי שִׁמְעוֹן בֶּן אֶלְעָזָר. וְלֹא מוֹדֶה רִבִּי שִׁמְעוֹן בֶּן אֶלְעָזָר שֶׁאִם אָמַר לָהּ בִּשְׁעַת מַתָּנָה. שֶׁהוּא גִיטֵיךְ. שֶׁאֵינוֹ גֵט. וְהָכָא אֲפִילוּ אִם אָמַר לָהּ בִּשְׁעַת מַתָּנָה. שֶׁהוּא גִיטֵיךְ. אֵינוֹ גֵט עַד שֶׁיֹּאמַר לָהּ בִּפְנֵי שְׁנַיִם. בְּפָנַיי נִכְתַּב וּבְפָנַיי נֶחְתַּם. אֶלָּא מִיסְבּוֹר סָבַר רִבִּי יוֹחָנָן דְּאֵין הָאִשָּׁה נֶאֱמֶנֶת לוֹמַר. הִתְקַבַּלְתִּי גִיטִי מִשְּׁלוּחֵי בַעֲלִי. וְהָא תַּנִּינָן. הָאִשָּׁה עַצְמָהּ מְבִיאָה גִיטָהּ. וְחָשׁ לוֹמַר שֶׁמָּא מִשְּׁלוּחֵי הַבַּעַל קִבְּלָהּ. מַאי כְדוֹן טַעֲמָא דְּרִבִּי יוֹחָנָן. כְּדֵי לְהַחֲזִיקָהּ גְּרוּשָׁה בִּפְנֵי שְׁנַיִם.

If he did not say: "it was written and signed before me"? Should not an Amora have asked this question? He said to him[31], that is what Rabin ben Rav said: If he brought a bill of divorce, gave it to her, but did not tell her: "It was written and signed before me"[32]? There came a case before Rebbi Johanan, who said to him[33], take it from her and say in front of two [witnesses]: "It was written and signed before me.[34]" Does Rebbi Johanan follow Rebbi Simeon ben Eleazar, since Rebbi Simeon ben Eleazar said[35], it is no bill of divorce unless he tells her at the moment of delivery that it is her bill of divorce? Can the position of Rebbi Johanan be derived from Rebbi Simeon ben Eleazar? Would Rebbi Simeon ben Eleazar agree that if he told her at the moment of delivery that it was her bill of divorce it would not be a bill of divorce[36]? But here, even if he tells her at the moment of delivery that it is her bill of divorce, it is no bill of divorce unless he tells her in front of two [witnesses]: "It was written and signed before me." But Rebbi Johanan might hold that a woman cannot be believed if she says, I received a bill of divorce from my husband's agents[37]. But we did state[38]: "The wife herself can bring her bill of divorce." Would you not have to be afraid that she might have received the bill from a representative of the husband[39]? How is it? The reason of Rebbi Joḥanan is to make her known as divorcee in front of two [witnesses]⁴⁰.

31 It is unclear to whom this refers; the text seems defective.

32 Is the bill of divorce invalid in this case? In the Babli, 5b, Rabin bar Rav Ḥisda brought a bill of divorce before R. Joḥanan, who instructed him to deliver the bill in the presence of two witnesses and to make the required declaration. The question here can be interpreted to mean that Rabin asked whether the formality was really necessary in view of the fact, reported in the next paragraph, that R. Joshua ben Levi, of the generation of R. Joḥanan's teachers, did not require the declaration. In the Babli, which is edited according to strict historical principles, R. Joshua ben Levi is mentioned before R. Joḥanan.

33 The messenger who had delivered the bill of divorce without making the required declaration.

34 It is understood that the Mishnah requires the declaration to be made either in the presence of two witnesses or at the local court. Tosephta 2:1 permits the declaration to be made "even after three years" if the bill of divorce can be returned to the messenger.

35 Tosephta 6:1; a different version Babli 78a, 84b. The statement refers to Mishnah 8:2: "If he said to her, take this bond, or she took it out from his belt, and when she read it she realized that it was her bill of divorce, it is not a bill of divorce unless he says to her: This is your bill of divorce." The reason is that *Deut.* 24:1 requires that in a divorce the husband deliver the bill into the wife's hand. The question arises whether the required declaration is valid after the bill is already in the wife's hand. In the Babli 78a, Rebbi is quoted as holding that the bill is invalid unless given as a bill of divorce; R. Simeon ben Eleazar permits the husband to reclaim the bill from his wife and deliver it a second time accompanied by the required declaration. In the Tosephta, Rebbi is reported not to require the declaration, R. Simeon ben Eleazar requires that the declaration accompany the delivery. The language of the Tosephta is that of the Yerushalmi; it is not clear whether R. Simeon ben Eleazar permits taking the document back.

36 The answer to this rhetorical question clearly is no; the only condition imposed by R. Simeon ben Eleazar is that the wife be informed of the nature of the document at the moment of delivery.

37 Therefore, the delivery of the document characterized as a bill of divorce must be made before two witnesses in good standing. It seems that in his case, the document was delivered in private; the main reason of R. Joḥanan was not the recitation of the formula but the delivery in front of witnesses.

38 Mishnah 2:7. If the husband delivers the document to her on condition that it should not become effective until she presents it to the court which has to preside over the payment of her *ketubah,* she can bring it herself and declare before the court that "it was written and signed before me."

39 Why should she be believed if she brings the document from abroad when she is not believed if the document is delivered to her in private? It is implied here that the act which makes the document valid is its *signing* by two reliable witnesses, not its *delivery*.

40 He holds that the requirement of the declaration mentioned in the Mishnah is prescriptive but its omission does not invalidate the divorce.

(43b line 22) אָתָא עוֹבְדָא קוֹמֵי רבִּי יְהוֹשֻׁעַ בֶּן לֵוִי. אָמַר לֵיהּ. לֵית צָרִיךְ. מִחְלְפָה שִׁיטָתֵיהּ דְּרִבִּי יְהוֹשֻׁעַ בֶּן לֵוִי. תַּמָּן אָמַר רבִּי יְהוֹשֻׁעַ בֶּן לֵוִי. שַׁנְיָיא הִיא שֶׁאֵינָן בְּקִיאִין בְּדִיקְדּוּקֵי גִיטִּין. וְהָכָא אָמַר אָכֵן. חַבְרַיָּיא בְּשֵׁם דְּרִבִּי יְהוֹשֻׁעַ בֶּן לֵוִי. הָדָא דְּאַתְּ אָמַר בָּרִאשׁוֹנָה שֶׁלֹּא הָיוּ חֲבֵירִים מְצוּיִין בְּחוּצָה לָאָרֶץ. אֲבָל עַכְשָׁיו שֶׁחֲבֵירִים מְצוּיִין בְּחוּצָה לָאָרֶץ בְּקִיאִין הֵן. וְהָא תַּנִּינָן וְהַמּוֹלִיךְ. וַאֲפִילוּ תֵימַר. אֵין חֲבֵירִים מְצוּיִין בְּחוּצָה לָאָרֶץ. אֲנָן מְצוּיִין בְּאֶרֶץ יִשְׂרָאֵל. שֶׁלֹּא לַחֲלוֹק בְּגִיטִּין בְּחוּצָה לָאָרֶץ. מֵעַתָּה הַמֵּבִיא גֵט מִמְּדִינַת הַיָּם לֹא יְהֵא צָרִיךְ לוֹמַר. בְּפָנַיי נִכְתַּב וּבְפָנַיי נֶחְתַּם. שֶׁלֹּא לַחֲלוֹק בְּגִיטֵּי אֶרֶץ יִשְׂרָאֵל. מַאי כְדוֹן. מַחְמִירִין בַּקַּל מִפְּנֵי הֶחָמוּר וְאֵין מַקִּילִין בֶּחָמוּר מִפְּנֵי הַקַּל. רבִּי יַעֲקֹב בַּר אָחָא בְּשֵׁם רבִּי שִׁמְעוֹן בַּר אַבָּא. מֵהָדָא דְּאָמַר רבִּי יְהוֹשֻׁעַ בֶּן לֵוִי. לְשֶׁעָבַר. אֲבָל בִּתְחִילָּה אוֹף רבִּי יְהוֹשֻׁעַ בֶּן לֵוִי מוֹדֶה.

A case came before Rebbi Joshua ben Levi[41]. He said to him, it is unnecessary. The opinion of Rebbi Joshua ben Levi seems inverted. There, Rebbi Joshua ben Levi said, there is a difference because they are not conversant with the fine points of bills of divorce[8], but here, he says so? The colleagues in the name of Rebbi Joshua ben Levi: What you said was in earlier times when no Fellows[42] were found outside the Land, but now that there are Fellows found outside the Land, they are competent[43]. But did we not state, "and one who brings there[44]"? And even if you say that no Fellows are found outside the Land, are we not found in the Land of Israel? In order not to make a distinction in the bills of divorce from outside the Land[45]. But then one who brings from overseas should not have to say: "It was written before me and signed before me." Not to make a distinction in the bills of divorce in the Land of Israel. What about it? One is restrictive in a simple case because of the complicated one and one is not permissive in the complicated because of the easy one[46]. Rebbi Jacob bar Aḥa in the name of Rebbi Simeon bar Abba: This[47] of Rebbi Joshua ben Levi, if it was done. But from the start even Rebbi Joshua ben Levi agrees[48].

41   In the Babli, 5b, it was R. Simeon bar Abba, a recognized scholar, who brought the document.

42   Here, "Fellow" does not have the technical meaning of "person who observes the rules of food purity" but means "person learned in the law."

43   In the Babli, this is R. Joshua ben Levi's explanation given to R. Simeon bar Abba the Babylonian.

44   In the Mishnah, the duty to declare that the document was written in the presence of the messenger is extended to bills of divorce written in the Land and delivered abroad.

45   There otherwise would be no reason to require a declaration for bills originating in the Land.

46   It is preferable to require a declaration for documents originating

in Palestine (the easy case) rather than to eliminate the declaration for documents originating outside the Land (the complicated case).

47 The statement that the declaration was unnecessary.

48 In that, R. Joshua ben Levi agrees with R. Joḥanan. The Babli, 5b, disagrees since in its version R. Simeon bar Abba asked R. Joshua ben Levi whether he had to make the declaration when delivering the bill of divorce.

(43b line 33) רִבִּי בָּא בְשֵׁם רַב רִבִּי זְעִירָא בְשֵׁם אַבָּא בַּר חָנָה. שְׁנַיִם שֶׁהֵבִיאוּ אֶת הַגֵּט אֵינוֹ צָרִיךְ לוֹמַר. בְּפָנֵינוּ נִכְתַּב וּבְפָנֵינוּ נֶחְתַּם. רִבִּי יוֹסֵי בֶּן יוֹסֵי בְּשֵׁם רִבִּי יוֹחָנָן. צָרִיךְ. הוּא עַצְמוֹ שֶׁהֵבִיא אֶת הַגֵּט אֵינוֹ צָרִיךְ לִיתְּנוֹ לָהּ בִּפְנֵי שְׁנַיִם כְּדֵי לְהַחֲזִיקָהּ גְּרוּשָׁה בִּפְנֵי שְׁנַיִם. נָתַן לָהּ גֵּט. נָטְלוֹ מִמֶּנָּה וְהִשְׁלִיכוֹ לַיָּם אוֹ לַנָּהָר. לְאַחַר זְמָן אָמַר לָהּ. נְיָיר חָלָק הָיָה וּשְׁטָר פָּרוּעַ הָיָה. לֹא הַכֹּל מִמֶּנּוּ לְפוּסְלָהּ. רִבִּי בּוּן בַּר חִיָּיה בְּעָא קוֹמֵי רִבִּי זְעִירָא. הוּא אֵינוֹ פּוֹסְלָהּ מִי פּוֹסְלָהּ. אָמַר לֵיהּ. מִכֵּיוָן שֶׁהוּחְזַק גְּרוּשָׁה בִּפְנֵי שְׁנַיִם לֹא הַכֹּל מִמֶּנּוּ לְפוֹסְלָהּ. נָתַן לָהּ גִּיטָהּ. אַשְׁכְּחוּנֵיהּ גֵּט בְּפָסוּל. כְּפוּנְיָה וִיהַב לָהּ חוֹרָן. אָתָא עוֹבְדָא קוֹמֵי רַבָּנִין וְאַכְשְׁרוּן. וְלֹא כֵן אִיתָּמַר. לֹא הַכֹּל מִמֶּנּוּ לְפוֹסְלָהּ. תַּמָּן לֹא הוּכַח פָּסוּל. הָכָא הוּכַח פָּסוּל. כְּהָדָא חִינָנָה בְּרֵיהּ דְּרִבִּי אָסִי הֲוָה מֵיסַן וְזָרַק גִּיטָא לְאִתְּתֵיהּ. אָמַר לָהּ. הֲרֵי גִיטֵּךְ. צְוָחַת. וַעֲלוֹן מְגִירָתָהּ חַטְפֵיהּ מִינָהּ. וִיהַב לָהּ נְיָיר חָלָק. אָתָא עוֹבְדָא קוֹמֵי רַבָּנִין וְחָשׁוּן. וְלֹא כֵן אָמַר רִבִּי יָסָא בְשֵׁם רִבִּי יוֹחָנָן. נִבְדַּק הַשֵּׁם וְנִמְצָא מִפִּי נָשִׁים וּמִפִּי קְטַנִּים בָּטֵל הַשֵּׁם. תַּמָּן לֹא הוּזְכַּר הַשֵּׁם. בְּרַם הָכָא הוּזְכַּר שֵׁם הַגֵּט. וְאִית דְּבָעֵי מֵימַר. אִם אָמַר. גֵּט כָּשֵׁר הָיָה. וְכֵיוָן דְּצָוְוחַת וַעֲלוֹן מְגִירָתָהּ חַטְפֵיהּ מִינָהּ. וִיהַב לָהּ נְיָיר חָלָק.

Rebbi Abba in the name of Rav, Rebbi Ze'ira in the name of Abba bar Ḥana: Two who brought a bill of divorce do not have to declare: It was written before us and signed before us[49]. Rebbi Yose ben Yose in the name of Rebbi Joḥanan: They have to[50]. He himself who brought the bill of divorce does not have to deliver the bill in the presence of two [witnesses][51] in order to declare her a divorcee in the presence of two. "If he gave her the bill[52], took it from her, and threw it into the sea or into a river[53]. If later he says to her that it was an empty papyrus or a paid bond, he cannot be believed to disqualify her."[54] Rebbi Abun bar Ḥiyya asked before Rebbi Ze'ira: If he[55] cannot disqualify her, who can? He said to him, since she was declared a divorcee in the presence of two [witnesses], he cannot be believed to disqualify her[56]. If he gave her a bill of divorce which was found to be invalid, they[57] forced him to give her a replacement. This case came before the rabbis and they declared it valid. Did we not say, he cannot be believed to disqualify her? There, the flaw was not proved; here the flaw was proved[58]. As the following: Ḥinena, the son of Rebbi Asi, was a medical doctor and threw a bill of divorce to his wife[59]. She cried. Her neighbor came, grabbed it from her, and gave her an empty papyrus. The case came before the rabbis and they took it into account[60]. But did not Rebbi Yasa say in Rebbi Joḥanan's name: If the designation was checked and found to be based on [the testimony of] women or children, the designation is invalid[61]? There, the designation was not mentioned. But here the name "bill of divorce" was mentioned. And some want to say, if he asserted that it was a valid bill of divorce[62], but she cried, her neighbor came, grabbed it from her, and gave her an empty papyrus.

49   In the Babli, 5a, this opinion is attributed to Rav Huna, Rav's student.

50   In the Babli, 16a/b, he is quoted in the opposite sense.

51   In the Babli, a fundamental question is whether a bill of divorce is validated by the signatories of the bill or the witnesses to the delivery. The first opinion is attributed in the Babli to R. Meïr; it is generally accepted in the Yerushalmi. The second opinion is R. Eleazar's in both Talmudim

(Mishnah 9:4). The Babli considers R. Eleazar the dominant author in matters of divorce; the Yerushalmi considers his a minority opinion. Accordingly, the Yerushalmi permits private delivery from husband to wife. Nevertheless, since marriage is a public affair, the divorcee cannot remarry unless her divorce is made public. The husband therefore has to publicly declare her a divorcee after his private delivery.

52   In the presence of witnesses.

53   Where it cannot be retrieved.

54   Tosephta 6:2, quoted in Babli 19b.

55   Since the preceding sentence deals with the husband, the question is whether it extends to everybody else.

56   Since there are two witnesses to the delivery, the divorce could be put in doubt only by a proof that the witnesses are false. In the interpretation of the Babli, 55a, the divorce is valid if the witnesses knew that the document was a bill of divorce, but the wife did not. It is possible to read the Yerushalmi 5:5 in the same sense.

57   The court supervising the divorce. A forced divorce is valid if forced and executed by a rabbinic court, Mishnah 9:10. However, the power of a court to force divorces is severely circumscribed, Halakhah 9:10. In a case of forced divorce, it has to be ascertained whether the court remained within the limits of his authority. It seems clear that the court has the authority to force a divorce if the giver of the invalid bill was a Cohen since even an invalid divorce forbids the wife to return to her priestly husband; but without a valid divorce she cannot marry any other man or collect the sums due her.

58   The husband cannot invalidate a bill of divorce which is not available for inspection; the court can invalidate a document in its possession.

59   Under certain circumstances, a bill of divorce can be delivered by depositing it in the wife's domain, Chapter 8.

60   She was "divorced and not divorced." Since the document is not available for inspection, it cannot be declared invalid. Since the delivery was irregular, it cannot be declared valid. The husband has to be forced to deliver a second bill.

61   Halakhah 9:11. The Mishnah states that if a woman is generally said to have received a bill of divorce, one can accept the divorce as a fact. R. Joḥanan notes that if an investigation

reveals that nobody who might appear as a formal witness in criminal cases is the source of the opinion, one has to disregard the "general knowledge" of the population. If it is known that she received a document from her husband, it does not necessarily mean that it was a bill of divorce.

In the Babli, 89a, it is a matter of dispute between Babylonian authorities whether a "general opinion" must be traced to a person who might appear as witness in good standing before a criminal court.

62   The husband himself is the source of the rumor. If he is a person of good standing, Mishnah 9:11 requires that his information be trusted. According to this interpretation, the wife is divorced and does not need a second bill in order to collect her *ketubah* and remarry.

(43b line 49) רִבִּי יִרְמְיָה בָּעֵי. כְּתָבוֹ בְּאֶרֶץ יִשְׂרָאֵל וַחֲתָמוֹ בְּחוּצָה לָאָרֶץ וְהָלַךְ לִיתְּנוֹ לָהּ בְּחוּצָה לָאָרֶץ וְלֹא מְצָאָהּ בְּחוּצָה לָאָרֶץ. וּבָא וּמְצָאָהּ בְּאֶרֶץ יִשְׂרָאֵל. צָרִיךְ שֶׁיֹּאמַר לָהּ בְּפָנַיי נִכְתַּב וּבְפָנַיי נֶחְתַּם. מִפְּנֵי שֶׁכְּתָבוֹ לָאָרֶץ וַחֲתָמוֹ בְּחוּצָה לָאָרֶץ. אֲבָל נִכְתַּב בְּאֶרֶץ יִשְׂרָאֵל וְנֶחְתַּם בְּאֶרֶץ יִשְׂרָאֵל וְהָלַךְ לִיתְּנוֹ לָהּ בְּחוּצָה לָאָרֶץ וְלֹא מְצָאָהּ. וּבָא וּמְצָאָהּ בְּאֶרֶץ יִשְׂרָאֵל. אֵינוּ צָרִיךְ שֶׁיֹּאמַר. בְּפָנַיי נִכְתַּב וּבְפָנַיי נֶחְתַּם. נָתַן לָהּ אֶת גִּיטָהּ וְאַחַר כָּךְ אָמְרָה. תִּזְכֶּה לִי חֲצֵירִי שֶׁבְּעַכּוֹ. אָמַר רִבִּי חִינֶנָא. נַעֲשֵׂית כְּמִי שֶׁהָיְתָה יָדָהּ אֲרוּכָה. אִילּוּ מִי שֶׁהָיְתָה יָדָהּ אֲרוּכָה וְהוֹשִׁיטָה אֶת יָדָהּ וּנְטָלַתּוּ שֶׁמָּא אֵינוֹ צָרִיךְ לוֹמַר. בְּפָנַיי נִכְתַּב וְנֶחְתַּם. אָמַר רִבִּי אַבָּא מָאן אָמַר דְּלֹא.

Rebbi Jeremiah asked: If he wrote it in the Land of Israel, signed it outside the Land, went to deliver it to her outside the Land but did not find her outside the Land, returned and found her in the Land of Israel. He must say, "it was written and signed before me," because he wrote it in the Land of Israel and signed it outside the Land But if it was written and signed in the Land of Israel, he went to deliver it to her outside the Land but did not find her outside the Land, he need not say, "it was written and signed before me."[63] If he gave her bill of divorce to her when she said, my courtyard at Acco[64] shall acquire it for me, Rebbi Ḥinena said, it is as if she had a long arm. If she had a long arm, she stretched it out and took it from there, does he not have to say "it was written and signed before me"[65]? Rebbi Abba said, who would deny it[66]?

63 This seems to refer to a tannaïtic statement similar to Tosephta 2:2: "If he wrote it in the Land and had it signed outside the Land, one has to say 'it was written and signed before me.' If it was written outside the Land but signed in the Land, one does not have to say 'it was written and signed before me.'" Since a document must be signed on the date indicated in it, writing and signing must take place at a border point.

64 The border of the Land of Israel passes through Acco, cf. Halakhah 2 and *Ševi'it* 6:1, Note 30. The bill of divorce was presented to her in the Israeli part of Acco, but she desired it to be deposited in her courtyard which was outside the Land. A bill of divorce can be legally delivered by being deposited in a house or walled courtyard which is the woman's property (even if it was part of her dowry, which becomes the husband's property but reverts to her at the moment of divorce.)

65 Because the delivery took place outside the Land.

66 R. Ḥinena's statement is trivial; the nontrivial part is that a delivery in a courtyard is valid even if the wife is far away at the moment of delivery; cf. Rashba, *Novellae to Giṭṭin* 77b. In the Babli, 77b, delivery from a distance is a matter of contention and prohibited by Ulla; there nobody accepts the notion of an "extended arm."

(43b line 58) רִבִּי עֶזְרָא בְּעָא קוֹמֵי רִבִּי מָנָא. אִישׁ וְאִשָּׁה שֶׁהָיוּ תְפוּשִׂין בַּגֵּט. הִיא אוֹמֶרֶת. זָכִיתִי. וְהוּא אָמַר. לֹא זָכִיתָהּ. תַּפְלוּגְתָּא דְּרִבִּי וּדְרַבָּן שִׁמְעוֹן בֶּן גַּמְלִיאֵל. דְּאִיתְפַּלְגוּן. הַמַּלְוֶה וְהַלֹּוֶה שֶׁהָיוּ תְפוּשִׂין בַּשְּׁטָר. הַמַּלְוֶה אוֹמֵר. שֶׁלִּי הוּא שֶׁאָבַד מִמֶּנִּי. וְהַלֹּוֶה אוֹמֵר. שֶׁלִּי הוּא שֶׁפְּרַעְתִּיו לָךְ. יִתְקַיֵּים הַשְּׁטָר בְּחוֹתְמָיו. דִּבְרֵי רִבִּי. דְּרַבָּן שִׁמְעוֹן בֶּן גַּמְלִיאֵל אוֹמֵר. יַחֲלוֹקוּ. אָמַר רִבִּי לְעָזָר. הַכֹּל הוֹלֵךְ אַחַר הַתְּפוּשׂ בְּעֵדִים. מַה פְּלִיגִין. כְּשֶׁכְּתָבוֹ לְאוֹרֶךְ וּשְׁנֵיהֶן תְּפוּשִׂין

בְּעֵדִים. אָמַר לֵיהּ. דִּבְרֵי הַכֹּל הִיא. הָכָא אֲפִילוּ כּוּלָהּ בְּיָדָהּ וְחוּט אֶחָד בְּיָדוֹ אֵינוֹ גֵט. דִּכְתִיב וְנָתַן בְּיָדָהּ. עַד שֶׁיְּהֵא כּוּלוֹ בְּיָדָהּ.

Rebbi Ezra asked before Rebbi Mana: If a man and his wife held on to a bill of divorce; she says, I acquired it, but he says, you did not acquire[67]. Does this refer to the disagreement between Rebbi and Rabban Simeon ben Gamliel? Since they disagreed[68]: If creditor and borrower both hold on to the bond; the creditor says it is mine; I had lost it. The borrower says, it is mine because I paid it off. The document should be verified by its signatories, the words of Rebbi[69]. Rabban Simeon ben Gamliel says, they should split[70]. Rebbi Eleazar said, everything depends on who actually holds the signatures of the witnesses[71]. Where do they disagree? If it was written lengthwise[72] and both hold part of the signatures of the witnesses. He said to him, it is everybody's opinion that it is not a bill of divorce if all is in her hand but a thread is in his hand, for it is written: "He shall deliver it into her hand," not unless all be in her hand[73].

67 He demands some money from her before he is willing to give her a divorce.

68 *Baba Meṣi'a* 1:1, Babli *Baba Meṣi'a* 7a.

69 In the interpretation of the Babli, a private bond is valid only if its signatures have been notarized in court. Rebbi permits late notarizing, so the creditor can claim half.

70 Following Symmachos that "money in doubt shall be split," Mishnah *Baba Meṣi'a* 1:1; cf. *Ketubot* 2,

Note 9, 10, Note 62.

71 Since only the signatures validate the document.

72 In computer printers this is called "landscape format". The writing parallels the long side of the paper; it is possible for both parties to hold on to part of the lines used for signatures.

73 In the Babli, 78b Rav Ḥisda formulates: If the bill is in her hands and a thread is in his hand: if he can draw it back to himself, she is not divorced, otherwise she is divorced.

The Babli bases its ruling on the meaning of the word כריתות "divorce" which requires complete physical separation.

(43b line 66) מְתִיב רִבִּי לְעָזָר לְרַבָּנָן. כְּמָא דְאִית לְכוֹן הַמֵּבִיא גֵט מִמְּדִינָה לִמְדִינָה בִּמְדִינַת הַיָּם צָרִיךְ שֶׁיֹּאמַר. בְּפָנַיי נִכְתַּב וּבְפָנַיי נֶחְתַּם. אַף אֲנָא אִית לִי הַמֵּבִיא גֵט מִמְּדִינָה לִמְדִינָה בְּאֶרֶץ יִשְׂרָאֵל צָרִיךְ שֶׁיֹּאמַר. בְּפָנַיי נִכְתַּב וּבְפָנַיי נֶחְתַּם. אָמַר רִבִּי יַעֲקֹב בַּר זַבְדִי. מַעֲשֶׂה בְּאֶחָד שֶׁהֵבִיא אֶת הַגֵּט מִלְּמֵינָה שֶׁלְּקֵיסָרִין. אָתָא עוֹבָדָא קוֹמֵי רִבִּי אַבָּהוּ. אָמַר לֵיהּ. אֵין צָרִיךְ לוֹמַר. בְּפָנַיי נִכְתַּב וּבְפָנַיי נֶחְתַּם. וְאֵין לְמֵינָה שֶׁלְּקֵיסָרִין כְּקֵיסָרִין. אָמַר רִבִּי אָבִין. סְפִינָה מַפְרֶשֶׁת הָיְיתָהּ. וְתַנֵּי כֵן. הַמֵּבִיא גֵט מִן הַסְּפִינָה כְּמֵבִיא מְחוּצָה לָאָרֶץ. וְצָרִיךְ שֶׁיֹּאמַר. בְּפָנַיי נִכְתַּב וּבְפָנַיי נֶחְתַּם.

Rebbi Eliezer objected to the rabbis: Just as you hold that one who brings a bill of divorce from one province to another overseas has to say, "it was written and signed before me," so I hold that one who brings a bill of divorce from one province to another in the Land of Israel has to say, "it was written and signed before me." Rebbi Jacob bar Zavdi said, it happened that one brought a bill of divorce from the harbor of Caesarea[74]. The case came before Rebbi Abbahu who said yes, he has to say that it was written and signed before him. But is the harbor of Caesarea not part of Caesarea? Rebbi Abin said, it was from a departing ship, and it was stated thus: One who brings a bill of divorce from a ship is like one who brings from outside the Land and has to say that it was written and signed before him[75].

74 He delivered it in the city of *Caesarea maritima,* formerly called Straton's Tower, which was not part of the Land of Israel; cf. *Ševi'it* 6:1, Note 32.

75 In the Babli, 7b, there are *baraitot* quoted either that the declaration is needed or not needed,

but there the reference is to a person who brings a bill of divorce *in* a ship connecting places in the Land, rather than *from* a ship sailing overseas.

(43b line 74) הָיְתָה הֶגְמוֹנְיָיא אַחַת וְנַעֲשֵׂית שְׁתַּיִם. אֵינוֹ צָרִיךְ לוֹמַר. בְּפָנַיי נִכְתַּב וּבְפָנַיי נֶחְתַּם. וְכֵן שְׁתַּיִם וְנַעֲשׂוּ אַחַת.

If there was one district which was subdivided into two, one does not have to say it was written and signed before me. Similarly if two were combined to form one.

(fol. 43a) **משנה ב**: רִבִּי יְהוּדָה אוֹמֵר מֵרֶקָם וְלַמִּזְרָח וְרֶקָם כְּמִזְרָח. מֵאַשְׁקְלוֹן וְלַדָּרוֹם וְאַשְׁקְלוֹן כְּדָרוֹם מֵעַכּוֹ וְלַצָּפוֹן וְעַכּוֹ כְּצָפוֹן. רִבִּי מֵאִיר אוֹמֵר עַכּוֹ כְּאֶרֶץ יִשְׂרָאֵל לַגִּיטִין.

Mishnah 2: Rebbi Jehudah says, from Reqam[2] to the East and Reqam belongs to the East, from Ascalon to the South and Ascalon belongs to the South, from Acco to the North and Acco belongs to the North. Rebbi Meïr says, Acco belongs to the Land of Israel in matters of bills of divorce[77].

76 The list in this Mishnah mentions border towns from where the messenger has to affirm that the document was written and signed in his presence. The basic reference is the *baraita* on the borders of the Land of Israel, *Ševi'it* 6:1, Notes 32-51.

77 He agrees that in matters of ritual purity and Sabbatical laws, most of Acco is outside the Land.

(43b line 75) **הלכה ב**: רִבִּי יְהוּדָה אוֹמֵר. מֵרֶקָם וְלַמִּזְרָח כול׳. רִבִּי יוֹחָנָן אָמַר לְצִיפּוֹרָיָיא. אַתּוּן אָמְרִין בְּשֵׁם רִבִּי יוֹחָנָן. אַף הַמֵּבִיא מִבָּבֶל לְכָאן אֵינוֹ צָרִיךְ

לוֹמַר. בְּפָנַיי נִכְתַּב וּבְפָנַיי נֶחְתַּם. וַאֲנִי אוֹמֵר שֶׁהוּא צָרִיךְ. דְּהִיא מַתְנִיתָא. מֵרָקָם וְלַמִּזְרָח וְרָקָם כְּמִזְרָח. וַאֲפִילוּ תֵּימַר. חֲלוּקִין עַל רַבִּי יְהוּדָה שֶׁאֵין רֶקֶם כַּמִּזְרָח. שֶׁמָּא מִבָּבֶל לְכָאן. רַב אָמַר. עָשִׂינוּ עַצְמֵינוּ כְּאֶרֶץ יִשְׂרָאֵל לַגִּיטִּין. וּשְׁמוּאֵל אָמַר. אֲפִילוּ מִשְּׁכוּנָה לִשְׁכוּנָה. בָּעָא קוֹמֵי מִיחְזוֹר בֵּיהּ. אָמַר לֵיהּ כַּהֲנָא. וּמַה נַּעֲשֶׂה לָרִאשׁוֹנוֹת שֶׁנִּישְּׂאוּ. אָמַר לֵיהּ. וּמַה בְיָדָךְ. דְּהוּא סָבַר כְּהָדָא דְרִבִּי דְּתַנֵּי. הַמֵּבִיא גֵט מִמְּדִינַת הַיָּם לֹא נִכְתַּב לְפָנָיו וְלֹא נֶחְתַּם לְפָנָיו. תֵּצֵא בִּשְׁלֹשָׁה עָשָׂר דָּבָר. דִּבְרֵי רִבִּי. אֲבָל חֲכָמִים לֹא הוֹדוּ לַדָּבָר.

Halakhah 2: "Rebbi Jehudah says, from Reqam to the East," etc. Rebbi Joḥanan told the people of Sepphoris: You say in the name of Rebbi Joḥanan[78], even a person who brings a bill of divorce from Babylonia does not have to say "it was written and signed before me." But I am saying that it is necessary, for there is a Mishnah: "Rebbi Jehudah says, from Reqam to the East and Reqam belongs to the East." And even if you say that they disagree with Rebbi Jehudah and say that Reqam does not belong to the East, what about from Babylonia to here[79]? Rav said, we consider ourselves as in the Land of Israel in the matter of bills of divorce. But Samuel said, even from one city quarter to another[80]. He asked before him to change his opinion[81], when Cahana told him, what would we do with the earlier cases of women who remarried[82]? He said to him, what do you have in your hand? For he was of Rebbi's opinion as it was stated: If somebody brings a bill of divorce from overseas which was neither written nor signed in his presence, she has to leave under the thirteen penalties[83], the words of Rebbi. But the Sages did not agree in this matter[84].

78 This name is obviously incorrect; it is impossible to determine what was in its place or whether the name should simply be deleted.

79 In the Babli, 6a, the argument is attributed to R. Jeremiah.

80 In the Babli, 6a, Rav is quoted as he is here; Samuel says that Babylonia is like any other place outside the Land, Rav Sheshet requires confirmation from one city quarter to another and Rav Ḥisda requires an attestation in all cases in which the witnesses are unknown to the court in whose district the bill is delivered.

81 Samuel convinced Rav that he should change his opinion.

82 Cahana pointed out that if Rav changed his practice, he would attach a presumption of illegitimacy to any children of women who had remarried according to his previous standard.

83 All the disabilities enumerated in Mishnaiot 8:5 about a woman remarrying after an invalid divorce, and *Yebamot* 10:1 regarding a woman who remarried thinking that her husband was dead when he was alive and later returned.

84 Since the absence of the provision about writing and signing does not invalidate the bill, cf. Notes 32 ff.

(43c line 9) הַכֹּל מוֹדִין שֶׁאִם בָּא וְעִירֵר עִרְעוּרוֹ בָּטֵל. עַד כְּדוֹן בְּשֶׁעִירֵר מִשֶּׁנִּישֵּׂאת. עִירֵר עַד שֶׁלֹּא נִיסֵּאת וְנִישֵּׂאת. נִישְׁמְעִינָהּ מִן הָדָא. מַעֲשֶׂה בְּאֶחָד שֶׁהֵבִיא אֶת הַגֵּט לִפְנֵי רִבִּי יִשְׁמָעֵאל. אָמַר לֵיהּ. מְנַיִין אַתְּ. אָמַר לֵיהּ. מִכְּפַר סַמַּיי שֶׁבִּתְחוּם עַכּוֹ. אָמַר לֵיהּ. אַף אַתְּ צָרִיךְ לוֹמַר. בְּפָנַיי נִכְתַּב וּפָנַיי נֶחְתַּם. וְאַל תִּזְקֵק לְעֵדִים. וּכְשֶׁיָּצָא אָמַר לוֹ רִבּוּ אִילְעַאי. רִבִּי. וַהֲלֹא כְּפַר סַמַּיי מֵאֶרֶץ יִשְׂרָאֵל הִיא קְרוֹבָה לְצִיפּוֹרִין יוֹתֵר מֵעַכּוֹ. אָמַר לֵיהּ. הוֹאִיל וְיָצָא הַמַּעֲשֶׂה בְּהֶיתֵר יָצָא. מָהוּ הוֹאִיל וְיָצָא הַמַּעֲשֶׂה בְּהֶיתֵר יָצָא. אָמַר רִבִּי זְעִירָא. שֶׁאִם בָּא וְעִירֵר עִרְעוּרוֹ בָּטֵל. אִילּוּ הַמֵּבִיא מֵאֶרֶץ יִשְׂרָאֵל לְאֶרֶץ יִשְׂרָאֵל שֶׁמָּא הָאוּ צָרִיךְ לוֹמַר. בְּפָנַיי נִכְתַּב וּפָנַיי נִתְחַתֵּם. הֲוֵי לֹא שַׁנְיָיה. הוּא עֲרֵר מִשֶּׁנִּישֵּׂאת הוּא עֲרֵר עַד שֶׁלֹּא נִישֵּׂאת וְנִישֵּׂאת.

Everybody agrees that if [the husband] comes and protests, his protest is invalid[9,12]. That is, if he protested after she remarried. If he protested before she remarried and then she remarried[85]? Let us hear from the following[86]: It happened that somebody brought a bill of divorce before Rebbi Ismael. He asked him, from where are you? He answered, from Kefar Simai[87] in the region of Acco. He said to him, then you have to say, "it was written and signed in my presence;" you do not need witnesses[88]. After [that person] left, Rebbi Ilai said to him, my teacher, is not Kefar Simai in the Land of Israel, closer to Sepphoris than to Acco? He answered, since the matter was resolved in a permissive way; it stands. What means "since the matter was resolved in a permissive way; it stands"? Rebbi Ze'ira said, that if [the husband] came and protested, his protest would be invalid. But does a person who brings a bill of divorce from the Land of Israel for delivery in the Land of Israel have to say, "it was written and signed in my presence"? Therefore, there cannot be any difference whether he protested after she remarried or before she remarried and then she remarried[89].

85   Should one require that she not remarry before the matter has been decided by the local court?

86   The same story is in the Babli, 6b.

87   Probably Kafr Sumeïa on the road from Acco to Safed, in the border region described in Ševi'it 6:1. In the Tosephta, 1:3, the place is mentioned as סאסאי or ססי.

88   The signatures on the bill do not have to be notarized by the court, which would have been difficult in the court of R. Ismael in the far South on the border of Idumea.

89   It does not depend on the declaration by the messenger; no bill of divorce delivered under the supervision of a court can be attacked.

(43c line 18) רִבִּי יַעֲקֹב בַּר אָדָא בַּר עַתְלַיי בְּשֵׁם רִבִּי לְעָזָר. הֲלָכָה כְּרִבִּי מֵאִיר בְּגִיטִּין. וַהֲוָה רִבִּי זְעִירָא מִסְתַּכֵּל בֵּיהּ. אָמַר לֵיהּ. לָמָה אַתְּ מִסְתַּכֵּל בִּי.

דְּאִיתְמַר הֲלָכָה כְּמִי שֶׁהוּא מֵיקַל בְּדִבְרֵי סוֹפְרִין. סָבְרִין מֵימַר בְּיָחִיד אֵצֶל יָחִיד. אֲבָל בְּיָחִיד אֵצֶל חֲכָמִים לֹא. וְהָכָא אֲפִילוּ יָחִיד אֵצֶל חֲכָמִים.

Rebbi Jacob bar Ada, Bar Athlay in the name of Rebbi Eleazar: Practice follows Rebbi Meïr in matters of bills of divorce[90]. Rebbi Zeʿira was looking at him[91]. He asked him, why do you look at me? Was it not said that practice follows the lenient opinion in rabbinic matters? They thought, that is a single opinion against a single opinion, but not a single opinion against the Sages, and here even a single opinion against the Sages[92].

90 This opinion is not mentioned in the Babli.
91 Disapproving.
92 They hold that Acco is split in matters of divorce as it is split in matters of impurity, as explained later in the Halakhah.

(43c line 22) רִבִּי חִייָה רִבִּי בָּא אָמַר. הַמּוֹכֵר עַבְדּוֹ לְעַכּוֹ יָצָא לְחֵירוּת. רִבִּי יִשְׁמָעֵאל אֲבוּהּ דְּרִבִּי יוּדָן בָּעֵי. וַאֲפִילוּ מֵעַכּוֹ לְעַכּוֹ. וְאַתְיָיא כַּיי דָּמַר רִבִּי יַעֲקֹב בַּר אָחָא בְּשֵׁם רִבִּי אִמִּי. מִן תְּרֵין עוֹבְדוֹי דְּרִבִּי אֲנָן יֶלְפִין. עַכּוֹ יֵשׁ בָּהּ אֶרֶץ יִשְׂרָאֵל וְיֵשׁ בָּהּ חוּצָה לָאָרֶץ. רִבִּי הֲוָה בְעַכּוֹ. חֲמָתוּן אָכְלוֹן פִּיתָּה נְקִייָא. אָמַר לוֹן. מַה אַתּוּן לָתִין. אָמְרוּ לֵיהּ. תַּלְמִיד אֶחָד בָּא לְכָאן וְהוֹרָה לָנוּ עַל מֵי בֵיצִים שֶׁאֵינֵן מַכְשִׁירִין. וַאֲנַן שָׁלְקִין בֵּיעִין וְלָתָן בְּמֵיהוֹן. סָבְרִין מֵימַר מֵי שֶׁלָק שֶׁלְּבֵיצִים. וְלֹא אָמַר אֶלָּא שֶׁלְּבֵיצִים עַצְמָן. אָמַר רִבִּי יַעֲקֹב בַּר אִידִי. מֵאוֹתָהּ שָׁעָה גָּזְרוּ שֶׁלֹּא יְהֵא תַלְמִיד מוֹרֶה הוֹרָיָיה. רִבִּי חוּנָה בְּשֵׁם רִבִּי הוּנָא אָמַר. תַּלְמִיד שֶׁהוֹרָה אֲפִילוּ כַּהֲלָכָה אֵין הוֹרָייָתוֹ הוֹרָייָה.

3 אמי | ש אימי   6 שאינן | ש שאין   - | ש סברין מימר   7 שלביצים | ש מי ביצים
8 חונה | ש חייה   9 הורייתו | ש הוראתו

Rebbi Ḥiyya [bar] Abba said: If one sold a slave into Acco, the latter was set free[93]. Rebbi Ismael, the father of Rebbi Yudan, asked: Even from Acco to Acco? [94]This follows what Rebbi Aḥa bar Jacob said in the name of Rebbi Immi: From two actions of Rebbi we learn that Acco is partly of the Land of Israel and partly outside the Land. Rebbi was in Acco when he saw them eating clean bread; he asked them, how did you knead [the dough]? They said to him, a student came here and instructed us that egg water does not prepare. We are boiling eggs and use their water to knead. They thought he was talking about cooking water of eggs when he spoke only of the eggs themselves. Rebbi Jacob bar Idi said, at that moment they decreed that a student may not render decisions. Rebbi Ḥiyya in the name of Rebbi Ḥuna: If a student gives instructions even according to practice, his instructions are no instructions.

93   In the Babli, 8a, he is quoted pointing out that R. Meïr declares all of Acco to be of the Land only for bills of divorce; therefore not for the laws of slaves. It is forbidden to sell slaves from the Land to places outside the land; any such sale frees the slave.

94   From here to the end of the Halakhah, the text is from *Ševi'it* 6:1, explained there in Notes 23-30. Variant readings from there are noted ♥. All indications are that the text in *Ševi'it* is the original.

(43c line 32) תַּנֵּי. תַּלְמִיד שֶׁהוֹרָה הֲלָכָה לִפְנֵי רַבּוֹ חַיָּיב מִיתָה. תַּנֵּי בְשֵׁם רבִּי אֱלִיעֶזֶר. לֹא מֵת נָדָב וַאֲבִיהוּא אֶלָּא שֶׁהוֹרוּ הֲלָכָה לִפְנֵי מֹשֶׁה רַבָּן. מַעֲשָׂה בְּתַלְמִיד אֶחָד שֶׁהוֹרָה לִפְנֵי רַבּוֹ רִבִּי לִיעֶזֶר. אָמַר לְאִימָּא שָׁלוֹם אִשְׁתּוֹ. אֵינוֹ מוֹצִיא שַׁבָּתוֹ. וְלֹא יָצְאַת שַׁבָּתוֹ עַד שֶׁמֵּת. אָמְרוּ לוֹ תַלְמִידָיו. רִבִּי נָבִיא אַתָּה. אָמַר לָהֶן. לֹא נָבִיא אָנֹכִי וְלֹא בֶן נָבִיא אָנֹכִי. אֶלָּא כָךְ אֲנִי מְקוּבָּל שֶׁכָּל־תַּלְמִיד מוֹרֶה הֲלָכָה לִפְנֵי רַבּוֹ חַיָּיב מִיתָה. תַּנֵּי אָסוּר לְתַלְמִיד לְהוֹרוֹת הֲלָכָה לִפְנֵי רַבּוֹ עַד שֶׁיְּהֵא רָחוֹק מִמֶּנּוּ שְׁנֵים עָשָׂר מִיל כְּמַחֲנֵה יִשְׂרָאֵל. וּמַה טַעַם. וַיַּחֲנוּ עַל הַיַּרְדֵּן מִבֵּית הַיְשִׁימוֹת עַד אָבֵל הַשִּׁטִּים בְּעַרְבוֹת מוֹאָב. וְכַמָּה

הֵן. שְׁנֵים עָשָׂר מִיל כְּמַחֲנֵה יִשְׂרָאֵל. כְּהָדָא רִבִּי תַּנְחוּם בַּר יִרְמְיָה הֲוָה בְחֶפֶר. וַהֲווֹן שְׁאָלִין לֵיהּ וְהוּא מוֹרֶה. אָמְרִין לֵיהּ. וְלֹא כֵן אוּלְפָן רִבִּי שֶׁאָסוּר לְתַלְמִיד לְהוֹרוֹת הֲלָכָה לִפְנֵי רַבּוֹ עַד שֶׁיְּהֵא רָחוֹק מִמֶּנּוּ שְׁנֵים עָשָׂר מִיל כְּמַחֲנֵה יִשְׂרָאֵל. וְהָא רִבִּי חָנָא רַבָּךְ יָתִיב בְּצִיפּוֹרִין. אָמַר לוֹן יֵיתֵי עָלַי דְּלָא יָדַעִית. מִן הַהִיא שַׁעְתָּא לָא אוֹרֵי.

2 אליעזר | ש ליעזר   מת | ש מתו   הלכה | ש -   לפני | ש בפני   3 רבו ר' אליעזר |
ש ר' ליעזר רבו   4 מוציא | ש יוצא   יצאת | ש יצא   6 מורה | ש המורה   לפני | ש
בפני   7 לפני | ש בפני   8 בערבות מואב | ש -   9 כמהנה ישראל | ש -   9
ירמיה | ש חייה   - | ש שאלון ליה והוא מורה   12 חנא | ש מנא

It was stated: A student who gave instructions about practice in front of his teacher has committed a deadly sin. It was stated in the name of Rebbi Eliezer: Nadab and Abihu died only because they determined practice in the presence of their teacher Moses. It happened that a student gave instructions about practice in front of his teacher Rebbi Eliezer. The latter said to his wife Imma Shalom: That one will not live out his week. The week was not completed when he died. His students said to him: Rebbi, you are a prophet. He said to them (*Amos* 7:14) "I am neither a prophet nor the disciple of a prophet" but I have received a tradition that any student who gives instructions about practice in front of his teacher has committed a deadly sin. It was stated: A student is forbidden to give instructions about practice during the lifetime of his teacher unless he be at a distance of at least 12 *mil* from him, [the breadth of] the camp of Israel. What is the reason? (*Num.* 33:49) "They encamped along the Jordan from Bet Hayyešimot to Abel Haššiṭṭim in the plains of Moab"; how far is this? Twelve *mil*. Like this: Rebbi Tanḥum ben Jeremiah was in Ḥefer; they asked him and he gave instructions about practice. They said to him, did the Rabbi not teach us that a student may not give instructions about practice during the lifetime of his teacher unless he be at a distance of at least 12 *mil* from him, [the breadth of] the camp of Israel; and your teacher Rebbi Ḥana sits at Sepphoris! He said to them, so it should come over me that I did not know! From that moment on he did no longer give instructions.

(43c line 45) רִבִּי הֲוָה בְעַכּוֹ. חָמָא חַד בַּר נָשׁ מִכֵּיפְתָא וּלְעֵיל. אָמַר לֵיהּ. לֵית אַתְּ בְּרֵיהּ דְּפַלָּן כַּהֲנָא וְלֹא הֲוָה אָבוּךְ כֹּהֵן. אָמַר לֵיהּ. עֵינָיו שֶׁלְאַבָּא הָיוּ גְבוֹהוֹת וְנָשָׂא אִשָּׁה שֶׁאֵינָהּ הוֹגֶנֶת לוֹ וְחִילֵּל אוֹתוֹ הָאִישׁ.

1 - 1 ש סלק   מכיפתא ש מן כיפתא   2 ולא ש לא   3 את ש -

Rebbi was in Acco when he saw a man on the rock. He said to him, "are you not the son of the Cohen X, was your father not a Cohen?" He said to him, "the eyes of my father were high, but he married a woman unfit for him and profaned this man."

(43c line 45) עֲיָירוֹת שֶׁבִּתְחוּם צִיפּוֹרִין הַסְּמוּכוֹת לְעַכּוֹ. עֲיָירוֹת שֶׁבִּתְחוּם עַכּוֹ הַסְּמוּכוֹת לְצִיפּוֹרִין. מַה אַתְּ עֲבַד לוֹן. כְּעַכּוֹ. כְּצִיפּוֹרִין.

The villages in the territory of Sepphoris close to Acco, the villages in the territory of Acco close to Sepphoris, what do you do with them? Like Acco, like Sepphoris[95]?

95 If practice follows R. Meïr, it does not make any difference in the rules of bills of divorce. Therefore, no answer is needed.

(fol. 43a) **משנה ג:** הַמֵּבִיא גֵט בְּאֶרֶץ יִשְׂרָאֵל אֵינוּ צָרִיךְ שֶׁיֹּאמַר בְּפָנַי נִכְתַּב וּבְפָנַי נֶחְתַּם. אִם יֵשׁ עָלָיו עוֹרְרִים יִתְקַיֵּים בְּחוֹתְמָיו. הַמֵּבִיא גֵט מִמְּדִינַת הַיָּם וְאֵינוֹ יָכוֹל לוֹמַר בְּפָנַי נִכְתַּב וּבְפָנַי נֶחְתַּם אִם יֵשׁ עָלָיו עֵדִים יִתְקַיֵּים בְּחוֹתְמָיו.

Mishnah 3: Somebody who brings a bill of divorce from the Land of Israel does not have to say: "It was written and signed before me." If the document is contested, it should be confirmed by its signers[96]. If somebody brings a bill of divorce from overseas and is unable to say: "it was written and signed before me," it should be confirmed by its signers.

96 The court at the place of origin can confirm that the signatures are genuine. A document bearing two certified signatures cannot be attacked. Since courts in the Land of Israel are usually competent, a bill of divorce which is not contested does not have to be certified.

(43c line 50) **הלכה ג:** הַמֵּבִיא גֵט בְּאֶרֶץ יִשְׂרָאֵל כול׳. מִי עִירֵר. רַב חִסְדָּא אָמַר. הַבַּעַל עִירֵר. אָמַר רִבִּי יוֹסֵי. הַלְּקוּחוֹת עוֹרְרִין שֶׁלֹּא תִּיטָּרֵף מִיָּדָן. רִבִּי יוּדָן בָּעֵי. עַד כְּדוֹן בְּעֵרֶר שֶׁחוּץ לְגוּפוֹ. עֵרֶר שֶׁבְּגוּפוֹ תַּפְלוּגְתָּא דְּרִבִּי יוֹחָנָן וְרַבָּנִין דְּתַמָּן. עַל דַּעְתֵּיהּ דְּרַבָּנִין דְּתַמָּן לֹא שַׁנְיָיה. הוּא עֵרֶר שֶׁחוּץ לְגוּפוֹ. הִיא עֵרֶר שֶׁבְּגוּפוֹ. עֵרֶר שֶׁחוּץ לְגוּפוֹ עֵרְרוֹ בָּטֵל. וְעֵרֶר שֶׁבְּגוּפוֹ עֵרְרוֹ קַיָּים.

Halakhah 3: "Somebody who brings a bill of divorce from the Land of Israel," etc. Who protests? Rav Ḥisda said, the husband protests[97]. Rebbi Yose said, the buyers protest, lest she repossess from them[98]. Rebbi asked: So far a protest which does not concern the text of the bill[10]. A protest which concerns the text of the bill[11] is in dispute between Rebbi Joḥanan and the rabbis there[99]. In the opinion of the rabbis there, there is no difference to a protest concerning or not concerning the body of the bill. [100]A protest not concerning the text of the bill is void, a protest concerning the text of the bill is valid[101].

97 It is the position of the Babli, 9a, that in the absence of witnesses to fraud only the husband has standing to question the validity of a bill of divorce. Tosaphot 9a, *s. v.* אלא, read R. Yose's statement in the argument of the Babli; this does not seem to be justified.

98 If the husband had real estate at the place of his wife which he sold and then sent a bill of divorce to his wife from far away without the payment due her upon divorce, the divorcee can reclaim any real estate sold after the date of her definitive marriage up to the value of the *ketubah* payment due her.

99 Their dispute is in *Yebamot* 10:4 (Notes 97-102) and *Ketubot* 2:2. The Babylonian rabbis hold that a document whose signatures have been notarized as genuine by a court cannot be attacked.

100 A clause is missing here: "In the opinion of R. Johanan".

101 A claim that a document is forged must always be investigated.

(43c line 55) דְּתַנֵּי. הַמֵּבִיא גֵט מִמְּדִינַת הַיָּם וְלֹא נִכְתַּב לְפָנָיו וְלֹא נֶחְתַּם לְפָנָיו. הֲרֵי מַחֲזִירוֹ לִמְקוֹמוֹ. וְעוֹשֶׂה עָלָיו בֵּית דִּין וּמְקַיְּימוֹ בְחוֹתְמָיו וְאֵינוֹ צָרִיךְ שֶׁיֹּאמַר. בְּפָנַיי נִכְתַּב וּבְפָנַיי נֶחְתָּם. אֶלָּא אוֹמֵר. שְׁלִיחַ בֵּית דִּין אָנִי.

As it was stated[102]: "If somebody brings a bill of divorce from overseas which was not written and signed in his presence, he returns the bill to its place of origin, presents it to a court and has its signatures notarized. Then he does not have so say, 'it was written and signed before me', but he says, 'I am deputized by the court.'"

102 Tosephta 1:1.

(fol. 43a) **משנה ד**: אֶחָד גִּיטֵּי נָשִׁים וְאֶחָד שִׁיחֲרוּרֵי עֲבָדִים שָׁוִין לַמּוֹלִיךְ וְלַמֵּבִיא. וְזוֹ אֶחָד מִן הַדְּרָכִים שֶׁשָּׁווּ גִּיטֵּי נָשִׁים לְשִׁיחֲרוּרֵי עֲבָדִים.

Mishnah 4: Bills of divorce and slaves' bills of manumission are equal in [the requirement] about those who carry and bring[103]. This is one of the aspects in which bills of divorce have the same rules as bills of manumission[104].

משנה ה: כָּל־גֵּט שֶׁיֵּשׁ עָלָיו עֵד כּוּתִי פָּסוּל חוּץ מִגִּטֵּי נָשִׁים וְשִׁיחֲרוּרֵי עֲבָדִים. מַעֲשֶׂה שֶׁהֵבִיאוּ לִפְנֵי רַבָּן גַּמְלִיאֵל לִכְפַר עוֹתְנַי גֵּט אִשָּׁה וְהָיוּ עֵידָיו עֵידֵי כוּתִים וְהִכְשִׁירוֹ. כָּל־הַשְּׁטָרוֹת הָעוֹלִין בְּעַרְכָּאוֹת שֶׁלַּגּוֹיִם אַף עַל פִּי שֶׁחוֹתְמֵיהֶן גּוֹיִם כְּשֵׁירִים חוּץ מִגִּטֵּי נָשִׁים וְשִׁיחֲרוּרֵי עֲבָדִים. רְבִּי שִׁמְעוֹן אוֹמֵר כּוּלָּן כְּשֵׁירִין לֹא הוּזְכְּרוּ אֶלָּא בִּזְמַן שֶׁנַּעֲשׂוּ בַּהֶדְיוֹט.

Mishnah 5: Any document signed by a Samaritan is invalid[105], except bills of divorce and bills of manumission. It happened that they brought before Rabban Gamliel at Kefar Othnay[106] a bill of divorce whose witnesses were Samaritans and he declared it valid. All documents confirmed by a Gentile recorder's office[107] are valid, even if they are signed by Gentiles[108], except bills of divorce and bills of manumission[109]. Rebbi Simeon says, all are valid[110]; they said it only when they were made by private persons.

103 They have to be written and signed before the messenger when executed or delivered outside the Land, or have to be confirmed by a court before being delivered to a messenger.

104 This is an introduction to a series of Mishnaiot on the same subject. Since the slave of a Jew becomes a full member of the Jewish endogamous society upon his manumisson, strict rules are justified.

105 Since Samaritans, as a Sadducee sect, explain *Lev.* 19:14 to mean that it is forbidden to put a stone in the path of a blind man, but not, as Pharisees do, as a prohibition to do damage to the inadvertent, there is no biblical prohibition for a Samaritan to sign false monetary documents as long as he does not swear or appears as witness in a court. The literal interpretation of *Lev.* 19:14 in Philo (*The Special Laws*

IV, xxxviii, 198) is probably sufficient to characterize him as Alexandrian Sadducee. Bills of divorce or manumission become valid only by the signature of the witnesses (in contrast to a bond, where "the debtor's signature is worth a hundred witnesses"); the Samaritan himself would be the guilty party in an adulterous remarriage by the wife served with a fake bill of divorce or the marriage of a slave with a free Jewish woman, forbidden to him as long as he is a slave. Since "those rules which they keep (including marriage taboos), the Samaritans keep more strictly than do the rabbinic Jews" (Babli 10a, Yerushalmi *Pesaḥim* 1:1, 27b l. 58), there is no reason to disqualify Samaritans from witnessing documents regarding marriage.

106 *Kafr 'Uthnay*, a village near Megiddo on the Southern border of Jewish Galilee (Mishnah 7:7). While the Mishnah speaks only of *a Samaritan* witness, Rabban Gamliel accepted *two Samaritans*.

107 The Gentile court usually is ערכי, Greek τὰ ἀρχεῖα "public records, archives." For ערכאות compare τὸ ἀρχεῖον "town hall".

108 While Gentiles cannot be required to be honest, Gentile courts can be trusted to be jealous of their reputation.

109 The Gentile court is unable to determine who can or cannot marry in Jewish law.

110 If executed by Jews and notarized by a Gentile court.

(43c line 58) **הלכה ה**: כָּל־גֵּט שֶׁיֵּשׁ עָלָיו עֵד כּוּתִי פָּסוּל כּוֹל'. עַל הַמָּמוֹן נֶחְשְׁדוּ וְעַל הַמָּמוֹן נִפְסְלוּ. לֹא נֶחְשְׁדוּ עַל הָעֲרָיוֹת. וְעֵידֵי נְפָשׁוֹת כְּעֵידֵי עֲרָיוֹת. מֵעַתָּה אֲפִילוּ שְׁנֵיהֶן כּוּתִים. שַׁנְיָיא הִיא שֶׁאֵינָן בְּקִיעִין בְּדִיקְדּוּקֵי גִיטִּין. מֵעַתָּה אֲפִילוּ כּוּתִי אֶחָד יְהֵא פָסוּל. אָמַר רִבִּי אָבִין. תִּיפְתָּר שֶׁחָתַם יִשְׂרָאֵל בַּסּוֹף. אָמַר רִבִּי יוֹסֵי. אַתְיָיא כְּמָאן דְּאָמַר. עֵדִים חוֹתְמִין זֶה שֶׁלֹּא כְּנֶגֶד זֶה. בְּרַם כְּמָאן דְּאָמַר. אֵין עֵדִים חוֹתְמִין אֶלָּא זֶה בִּפְנֵי זֶה. אֲפִילוּ חָתַם כּוּתִי בַּסּוֹף כָּשֵׁר.

Halakhah 5: "Any document signed by a Samaritan is invalid," etc. They are suspected about money; about money they were disqualified.

They are not suspected about incest and adultery. And testimony in capital criminal cases has the same status as testimony about incest and adultery. Then even if both of them are Samaritans[111]? There is a difference, for they are not conversant with the fine points of bills of divorce[112]. Then even one Samaritan witness should be disqualified! Rebbi Abin said, explain it if a Jew signed last[113]. Rebbi Yose said, that is according to the opinion that the witnesses may sign separately, not in the presence of each other. But according to him who says that witnesses may sign only in the presence of each other[114], it is valid even if the Samaritan signed last.

111 Why does the Mishnah mention only a single Samaritan witness?

112 If both witnesses are Samaritans, one has to assume that the scribe also was Samaritan and that the rabbinic rules of writing a bill of divorce were not followed. A bill of divorce can be written only on the explicit demand of the husband; an infraction of this rule cannot be discovered by examination of the bill.

113 He would not sign if the bill was invalid. The Babli, 10a, considers this to be R. Eleazar's authoritative opinion (cf. Note 51).

114 Accepted in the Babli, 10b, for bills of divorce and manumission only.

(43c line 65) שְׁטָר שֶׁחוֹתְמוֹ בְּאַרְבָּעָה עֵדִים וְנִמְצְאוּ שְׁנַיִם הָרִאשׁוֹנִים קְרוֹבִים אוֹ פְּסוּלִים כָּשֵׁר וְתִתְקַיֵּים הָעֵדוּת בַּשְּׁאָר. רִבִּי אִילָא בְשֵׁם רִבִּי רִבִּי יָסָא. אַתְיָיא כְּמָאן דְּאָמַר. אֵין הָעֵדִים חוֹתְמִין אֶלָּא זֶה בִּפְנֵי זֶה. בְּרַם כְּמָאן דְּאָמַר. עֵדִים חוֹתְמִין זֶה שֶׁלֹּא בִּפְנֵי זֶה. אֲפִילוּ חָתַם יִשְׂרָאֵל בַּסּוֹף פָּסוּל. וְיַעֲשֶׂה בְּהַרְחֵק עֵדוּת וִיהֵא פָּסוּל. לֵית יְכִיל. דְּקָאָמַר רִבִּי יָסָא בְשֵׁם רִבִּי יִרְמְיָה. עֵדִים פְּסוּלִין אֵינָן נַעֲשִׂין כְּהַרְחֵק עֵדוּת. שֶׁלֹּא בָאוּ אֶלָּא לְהַכְשִׁירוֹ שֶׁלַּגֵּט.

If a bond was signed by four witnesses and it turned out that the first two were relatives or disqualified, it is valid and is confirmed by the remaining testimony[115]. Rebbi Ila in the name of Rebbi Yasa: This follows him who says that witnesses sign only in the presence of each other. But following him who says that witnesses may sign without being in the presence of each other, even if the Jew signed last it is invalid[116]. And would it not be remote testimony[117]? That one cannot say since Rebbi Yasa said in the name of Rebbi Jeremiah[118] that disqualified witnesses do not constitute remote testimony since they came only to support the document's validity[119].

115 A similar text (5 signatures, 3 of them invalid) is in Tosephta 7:11 and Babli *Baba batra* 162b. In the text here, "disqualified" are people who cannot be admitted to be witnesses in money matters, such as Samaritans, gamblers, and fences. Relatives of either lender or borrower are disqualified for the particular document in question. Two of the signatures must belong to witnesses who can certify the document in court.

116 This refers to the problem discussed in the preceding paragraph about a bill signed by a Samaritan and a Jew.

117 Tosephta 7:11 notes that a document whose signatures are so far removed from the text of the document that a sentence could have been added between text and signatures is invalid; it might be that there was a different text and the witnesses signed to that. In practice, this means that exactly one line must be empty between the text and the first signatures. If the qualified witnesses signed two lines below the text, it is admissible to have two unqualified witnesses sign on the line above to fill in the space between the document text and the signatures of the witnesses.

118 This means, R. Yasa in the name of Rav Jeremiah (who in the Yerushalmi frequently has the title of Rebbi, as a Babylonian authority predating the creation of the Title of "Rav"). In Halakhah 9:8: R. Abba in the name of Rav Jeremiah. Note the pure Babylonian Aramaic spelling דקאמר.

119 In the Babli, 18b, invalid signatures do not diminish the validity of a document if the signatories were

invited to sign for any reason other than being witnesses. This probably is understood here also. In particular, it was customary to have relatives sign on all marriage documents. In *Baba batra* 162b, the statement of R. Yasa is quoted in the name of Ḥizqiah. Cf. also Halakhot 8:12, 9:8.

(43c line 71) כּוּתִים מִפְּנֵי מַה הֵן פְּסוּלִין. אָמַר רִבִּי יוֹחָנָן. מִשּׁוּם גִּיּוּרֵי אֲרָיוֹת. וְקַשְׁיָא. אִילוּ מִי שֶׁלֹּא נִתְגַּיֵּיר לְשׁוּם שָׁמַיִם וְחָזַר וְהִתְגַּיֵּיר לְשׁוּם שָׁמַיִם שֶׁמָּא אֵין מְקַבְּלִין אוֹתוֹ. רִבִּי יוֹחָנָן בְּשֵׁם רִבִּי אֶלְעָזָר. מִשּׁוּם גּוֹי וְעֶבֶד הַבָּא עַל יִשְׂרְאֵלִית הַוָּלָד מַמְזֵר. וְהָאָמַר רִבִּי עֲקִיבָה. גִּיּוּרֵי צֶדֶק הֵן. עַל שֵׁם שֶׁהֵן מְיַיבְּמִין אֶת הָאֲרוּסוֹת וּמוֹצִיאִין אֶת הַנְּשׂוּאוֹת. וְהָא רַבָּנִין אָמְרִין. אֵין מַמְזֵר בִּיבָמָה. עַל שֵׁם שֶׁאֵין בְּקִיעִין בְּדִיקְדּוּקֵי גִיטִּין. הָא רַבָּן גַּמְלִיאֵל מַכְשִׁיר בְּגִיטֵּיהֶן. רִבִּי יַעֲקֹב בַּר אִידִי בְּשֵׁם רִבִּי יוֹחָנָן. עַל שֶׁנִּתְעָרְבוּ בָּהֶם כֹּהֲנֵי בָמוֹת. וַיַּעַשׂ כֹּהֲנִים מִקְצֹת הָעָם. אָמַר רִבִּי אִילָא. מִן הַקּוֹצִים שֶׁבָּעָם וּמִן הַפְּסוּלִים שֶׁבָּעָם.

Why are Samaritans disqualified[120]? Rebbi Joḥanan said, because they are lions' proselytes[121]. But if somebody converted not for Heaven's sake and then converted for Heaven's sake, does one not accept him[122]? Rebbi Joḥanan in the name of Rebbi Eleazar[123]: Because the child is a bastard if a Gentile or a slave have intercourse with a Jewish woman[124]. But did not Rebbi Aqiba say, they are genuine proselytes[125]? Because they require levirate marriage from the preliminarily married and free the definitively married[126]. But do not the rabbis say, there is no bastard from a sister-in-law[127]? Because they are not conversant with the fine points in writing bills of divorce[128]. But does not Rabban Gamliel accept their bills of divorce[106]? Rebbi Jacob bar Idi in the name of Rebbi Joḥanan: Because they intermingled with the priests of the High Places: "He chose priests from the borderline of the people,[129]". Rebbi Ila said, from the "thorns" of the people, i. e., from the disqualified of the people.

120   Why does one not intermarry with Samaritans?

121   The originally Gentile part of the population of Samaria adopted the worship "of the local god" because they were attacked by lions, *2K.* 17:24-41. In the Babli, *Qiddušin* 75b, this is identified as the teaching of R. Ismael.

122   That argument may have had validity in the first few generations after the destruction of Samaria, but in talmudic times the Samaritans had been monotheists for at least 700 years.

123   In *Jebamot* 7:6 (Note 129), "R. Ismael". In the Babli, *loc. cit.*, identified as teaching of R. Aqiba.

124   Assuming that the deportees from Cutha and Media who were resettled in Samaria were mostly male. When they intermarried with local Jewish women, in this opinion the children were all bastards.

125   Even if the preceding opinion were generally accepted, which it is not, it would be irrelevant concerning Samaritans. Agreed to in the Babli, *loc. cit.*

126   *Jebamot* 1, Notes 192-196. Pharisaic tradition frees the preliminarily married woman and obligates the definitively married one. The Samaritan ruling had its partisans among the rabbinic school of Shammai (*Jebamot* 1:6, Note 193.)

127   Even if a childless widow flouts the rules and marries an unrelated man without ḥaliṣah, the child is not a bastard and can marry in the congregation (Mishnah *Jebamot* 4:15). Therefore even a Samaritan who is the offspring of a rabbinically forbidden marriage should be an acceptable marriage partner.

128   There could be women divorced according to Samaritan rules who would not be considered divorced by rabbinic rules and, therefore, their children in a second marriage would be bastards not eligible for marriage with Jews.

129   *1K.* 12:31. The root קצה "to be distant, of the elite" of מקצת is identified with קוץ, קצץ "to cut, to chop off", one of whose derivatives is קוֹץ "thorn". (The same explanation is in the Babli, *loc. cit.*, of R. Joḥanan following R. Ismael.) In any case, there is no reason to exclude marriages with Samaritans other than general convention; but cf. *Demay* 3:4, Note 98.

HALAKHAH 5

(43d line 4) אָמַר רִבִּי אֲחָא. קוֹל יוֹצֵא בָּאַרְכִּיִּים. מֵעַתָּה אֲפִילוּ שְׁנֵיהֶן כּוּתִים. שֶׁהֲיָה הוּא אוֹמֵר. שֶׁאֵינָן בְּקִיעִין בְּדִיקְדּוּקֵי גִיטִּין. וְהָא רִבִּי שִׁמְעוֹן מַכְשִׁיר בְּגִיטֵּיהֶן. רִבִּי בָּא בְשֵׁם רִבִּי זְעֵירָא. אַתְיָיא דְרִבִּי שִׁמְעוֹן כְּרִבִּי אֶלְעָזָר. כְּמָה דְרִבִּי לֶעָזָר אָמַר. אַף ל פִּי שֶׁאֵין עָלָיו עֵדִים. כָּשֵׁר. כֵּן רִבִּי שִׁמְעוֹן אָמַר. אַף עַל פִּי שֶׁאֵין עָלָיו עֵדִים כָּשֵׁר. מֵעַתָּה אֲפִילוּ נַעֲשָׂה בְהֶדְיוֹט. הֲוֵי צוֹרְכָא לְהַהוּא דָמַר רִבִּי יַעֲקֹב בַּר אֲחָא. קוֹל יוֹצֵא בָּאַרְכִּיִּים. שְׁטַר יוֹצֵא בְּבֵית שְׁאָן וְהָיוּ עֵדָיו עֵידֵי גוֹיִם. רִבִּי יוֹסֵי אוֹמֵר. אִיתְפַּלְגוּן רִבִּי יוֹחָנָן וְרֵישׁ לָקִישׁ. חַד אָמַר. פָּסוּל. וְחַד אָמַר. כָּשֵׁר. רִבִּי אַבָּהוּ מְפָרֵשׁ. רִבִּי יוֹחָנָן אָמַר. פָּסוּל. וְרֵישׁ לָקִישׁ אָמַר. כָּשֵׁר. וּמַה טַעֲמָא דְּרֵישׁ לָקִישׁ. שֶׁלֹּא לְהַפְסִיד לְיִשְׂרָאֵל מָמוֹן. וַאֲפִילוּ דְּלֵית מַפְסִיד לְדֵין מַפְסִיד לְדֵין. אָמַר רִבִּי יוּדָן. אֶלָּא כְּדֵי שֶׁלֹּא לִנְעוֹל הַדֶּלֶת לִפְנֵי בְנֵי אָדָם. שֶׁלְּמָחָר הוּא מְבַקֵּשׁ לִלְווֹת וְהוּא אֵינוֹ מוֹצֵא.

Rebbi Aḥa[130] said, the acts of a Gentile court are public knowledge[131]. Then even if both [witnesses] are Samaritan? Did one not say that they are not conversant with the fine points in writing bills of divorce[128]? But Rebbi Simeon validates their bills of divorce! Rebbi Abba in the name of Rebbi Ze'ira: It turns out that Rebbi Simeon agrees with Rebbi Eleazar. Just as Rebbi Eleazar said, even if no witnesses signed on it, it is valid[132], so Rebbi Simeon said, even if no witnesses signed on it, it is valid. But then even if it was made by private persons[133]? This shows that it was necessary that Rebbi Jacob bar Aḥa said, the acts of a Gentile court are public knowledge. A bond[134] was executed in Bet Shean[135], whose witnesses were Gentiles. Rebbi Yose says, Rebbi Joḥanan and Rebbi Simeon ben Laqish[136] disagree, one said it is invalid, the other said it is valid. Rebbi Abbahu explained: Rebbi Joḥanan said it is invalid, Rebbi Simeon ben Laqish said it is valid. What is Rebbi Simeon ben Laqish's reason? That a Jew should not lose money[137]. But if that one would not lose money, the other would lose money[138]! Rebbi Yudan said, it must be in order not to close the door before people, for tomorrow one would look to borrow but does not succeed[139].

130   Later in the paragraph he is quoted as R. Jacob bar Aḥa. The latter attribution is correct since R. Jacob bar Aḥa was one of the teachers of R. Ze'ira quoted later, while R. Aḥa lived after R. Ze'ira.

131   If a document of indebtedness is not valid as a court document, it will be valid as being witnessed in public.

132   Mishnah 9:4. R. Eleazar (the Tanna, ben Shamua') holds that the essence of divorce is the delivery of the bill of divorce to the wife (*Deut.* 24:1). Therefore, he requires that the delivery be certified by two witnesses in good standing. They have to verify that the document contains the language which makes it a bill of divorce from the specified husband to the specified wife and that it was delivered into the hands of the wife either by the husband or by his duly appointed agent. Any signatures on the document are irrelevant. By contrast, R. Meïr holds that a bill of divorce not certified by two witnesses is invalid.

133   Why does R. Simeon in the Mishnah invalidate bills of divorce signed by Gentiles not in a court of law?

134   A document of indebtedness, containing a mortgage clause.

135   A Gentile city in Mishnaic times.

136   ריש לקיש is the Babylonian version of ר' שמעון בן לקיש

137   That the creditor should be able to enforce the terms of the loan in a rabbinic court.

138   Any gain of the lender is a loss for the borrower if both parties to the bond were Jewish.

139   If mortgages could not be foreclosed, nobody would lend money and all economic activity would come to a standstill. Therefore, R. Joḥanan's opinion cannot be considered even though he can point to *Ps.* 144:8,11 invalidating Gentile witnesses.

(fol. 43a) **משנה ו:** הָאוֹמֵר תֵּן גֵּט זֶה לְאִשְׁתִּי וּשְׁטָר שִׁיחְרוּר זֶה לְעַבְדִּי אִם רָצָא לַחֲזוֹר בִּשְׁנֵיהֶן יַחֲזוֹר דִּבְרֵי רבִּי מֵאִיר. וַחֲכָמִים אוֹמְרִים בְּגִיטֵּי נָשִׁים אֲבָל לֹא בְשִׁיחְרוּרֵי עֲבָדִים לְפִי שֶׁזָּכִין לוֹ לְאָדָם שֶׁלֹּא בְּפָנָיו וְאֵין חָבִין לוֹ אֶלָּא בְּפָנָיו שֶׁאִם יִרְצֶה שֶׁלֹּא לָזוּן אֶת עַבְדּוֹ רַשַּׁאי וְשֶׁלֹּא לָזוּן אֶת אִשְׁתּוֹ אֵינוֹ רַשַּׁאי. אָמַר לָהֶן וַהֲרֵי הוּא פוֹסֵל אֶת עַבְדּוֹ מִן הַתְּרוּמָה כְּשֵׁם שֶׁהוּא פוֹסֵל אֶת אִשְׁתּוֹ. אָמְרוּ לוֹ מִפְּנֵי שֶׁהוּא קִנְיָינוֹ. הָאוֹמֵר תֵּן גֵּט זֶה לְאִשְׁתִּי וּשְׁטָר שִׁיחְרוּר זֶה לְעַבְדִּי וָמֵת לֹא יִינָּתְנוּ לְאַחַר מִיתָה. תְּנוּ מָנֶה לְאִישׁ פְּלוֹנִי וָמֵת יִתְּנוּ לְאַחַר מִיתָה.

Mishnah 6: If one says, "give this bill of divorce to my wife or this document of manumission to my slave," if he wants to change his mind in either case he can retract[140], the words of Rebbi Meïr. But the Sages say, only for women's bills of divorce[141] but not for slaves' documents of manumission[142] because one may bestow benefit on a person in his absence but put a detriment on him only in his presence; for if one chooses not to sustain his slave, he has the right not to do so, but not to sustain his wife he has no right. He said to them, but he[143] disqualifies his slave for heave the same way he disqualifies his wife! They answered him, because he is his property[144]. If one says, "give this bill of divorce to my wife or this document of manumission to my slave" and dies, they shall not be delivered after his death[145]; "give this *mina* to Mr. X" and dies, they shall deliver it after his death[146].

140 Before the delivery of the bill or the document. The husband can appoint an agent for delivery of the document; he cannot appoint the agent as receiver of the document on behalf of wife or slave, as explained in the Mishnah.

141 It is held that any divorce other than one which the wife can enforce in court is to the wife's detriment.

142 The Sages hold that for a slave the benefits of freedom (and with it the status of a full Jew) always outweigh any possible material

detriment attached to manumission.

143 If the husband or owner is a Cohen, all members of his household share in his sanctified food; unless the household members are born of priestly status they lose the access to sanctified food the moment they leave his household. In contrast to Roman law, a freedman is not part of his patron's *familia*.

144 The slave's ability to eat heave is not intrinsic; it is derivative from his servile status. The slave can eat heave even if his master, the Cohen, refuses to support him.

145 The Sages who do not permit retraction of a document of manumission agree that both divorce and manumission become effective only at the moment of delivery of the document into the hands of the recipient by the agent representing his employer. But a dead person can neither divorce nor manumit. In Chapter 7 it is explained how a terminally ill childless person can divorce his wife to spare her (or prevent her from entering) a levirate marriage to his brother without divorcing her in case he recovers from his sickness.

146 If the gift was given when the giver was aware of his impending death, the heirs are bound to respect the wishes of the deceased.

(43d line 16) **הלכה ו**: הָאוֹמֵר תֵּן גֵּט זֶה לְאִשְׁתִּי כול׳. כָּל־אָתָר אַתְּ אָמַר. תֵּן כְּהוֹלֵךְ. וְהָכָא אַתְּ אָמַר. תֵּן כִּזְכֵה. תֵּן כִּזְכֵה. כֵּינִי מַתְנִיתָא. זְכֵה גֵּט זֶה לְאִשְׁתִּי. זְכֵה שְׁטָר שִׁחְרוּר זֶה לְעַבְדִּי. לְשָׁם מַתְנִיתָא אֲמָרָה כֵן. לְפִי שֶׁזְּכִין לוֹ לְאָדָם שֶׁלֹּא בְּפָנָיו וְאֵין חָבִין לְאָדָם אֶלָּא בְּפָנָיו. רִבִּי מֵאִיר אוֹמֵר. חוֹבָה הוּא בֵין לַזֶּה בֵּין לַזֶּה. וְרַבָּנִין אֲמָרִין. זְכוּת הוּא לָעֶבֶד וְחוֹבָה הִיא לָאִשָּׁה. רִבִּי חִייָה בַּר בָּא אָמַר. רִבִּי יוֹחָנָן בָּעֵי. הֲגַע עַצְמָךְ שֶׁהָיָה עַבְדּוֹ שֶׁלְּקָצִין. הֲרֵי חוֹבָה הוּא לָעֶבֶד. חֲבֵרַיָּיא אֲמְרוּ. רִבִּי יוֹחָנָן בָּעֵי. הֲגַע עַצְמָךְ שֶׁהָיְתָה אִשְׁתּוֹ שֶׁלְּמוּכֵּי שְׁחִין. הֲרֵי זְכוּת הוּא לְאִשָּׁה. לֵית לָךְ אֶלָּא כְהָדָא. אִילוּ הַמּוֹכֵר אֶת עַבְדּוֹ שֶׁלֹּא מִדַּעְתּוֹ שֶׁמָּא אֵינוֹ מָכוּר. וְהַמְגָרֵשׁ אֶת אִשְׁתּוֹ שֶׁלֹּא מִדַּעְתָּהּ שֶׁמָּא מְגוֹרֶשֶׁת הִיא מִפְּנֵי שֶׁהִיא קִנְיָינוּ. אָמַר רִבִּי אָבִין. קִנְיָינוּ הוּא אֶלָּא שֶׁהוּא פוֹסְלוֹ מִן הַתְּרוּמָה..

Halakhah 6: If one says, "give this bill of divorce to my wife," etc. Elsewhere you say that "give" means "bring", but here you say that "give" means "acquire"[147]! So is[148] the Mishnah: "Acquire this bill of divorce for my wife; acquire this document of manumission for my slave." The formulation[149] of the Mishnah says so: "Because one may bestow benefit on a person in his absence[150] but put a detriment on a person only in his presence." Rebbi Meïr says, it is a detriment for either of them, but the Sages say it is a benefit for the slave but a detriment for the wife. Rebbi Hiyya bar Abba said, Rebbi Johanan asked: Think of it, if he was the slave of a rich person, would it not be a detriment for the slave[151]? The colleagues said, Rebbi Johanan asked: Think of it, if she was the wife of a man suffering from boils[152], would it not be a benefit for the woman? You have only the following: If one sells his slave without the latter's knowledge, is the sale of the slave not valid[153]? If one divorces his wife without her knowledge, is the divorce valid[154] because she[155] was acquired by him? Rebbi Abin said, he is his property but he disqualifies him for heave[156].

147 If the messenger was appointed only as an agent for delivery, there would be no question that the sender has the right to retract his instructions. It does not seem reasonable to assume that a charge to deliver something lets the addressee acquire an interest in the document to be delivered at the moment it is given to the agent since "a person's agent represents him in every respect" [*Qiddušin* 2:1 (62a l.41), Babli 43a]. Since a person can do what he wishes with a document still in his possession, why can he not do the same with the document in his agent's hand?

148 It is not so, but must be interpreted in this way. In the Babli, 11b, R. Jeremiah is reported to hold that "give to" really means "accept for".

149 לשם is dialectal version of לשן, Aramaic equivalent of Hebrew לשון, cf. S. Lieberman, לשם לשן *Tarbiz* 6 (1935),

p. 235; J. N. Epstein, מבוא לנסח המשנה[2], Jerusalem-Tel Aviv 1964, p. 475.

150   This argument would be futile if the owner had not bestowed freedom on his slave by handing the document to the messenger. Therefore, the rule of the Mishnah applies only if the owner had given some indication that the messenger also acted as the slave's agent.

151   Who as a free man probably never would eat as well as he did as a slave.

152   In which case the wife can force a divorce, Mishnah *Ketubot* 7:10.

153   Therefore, the slave can be manumitted without his consent and the owner can appoint the messenger as the slave's agent without that latter's knowledge.

154   Nobody can represent the wife without her consent; even if the husband would appoint a person to be his wife's agent, the appointment would be invalid and the delivery of the bill of divorce by the agent to the wife would be illegal.

155   That is the ms. version, copied in *editio princeps*. But it seems preferable to follow the commentators and read this clause as a quote from the Mishnah מִפְּנֵי *שֶׁהוּא* קְנְיָינוֹ "because he (the slave) is his property", asking what is the relevance of this fact to the problem in hand, i. e., whether manumission is a benefit or a detriment to the slave.

156   Since the Cohen owner can sell his slave to an Israel any time he wishes, the slave has no intrinsic right to heave that would be eliminated by the document of manumission. This explanation is given in the Babli, 13a, in the name of Rava (Rav Abba bar Rav Josef bar Ḥama).

(43d line 26) הָאוֹמֵר. טַבִּי עַבְדִּי עָשִׂיתִי בֶּן חוֹרִין. עוֹשֶׂה אֲנִי אוֹתוֹ בֶּן חוֹרִין. הֲרֵי זֶה בֶּן חוֹרִין. זָכָה. רִבִּי אִינְיָיא בְּשֵׁם רִבִּי יוֹחָנָן. וּבִלְבַד בִּשְׁטָר. יַעֲשֶׂה בֶּן חוֹרִין. רִבִּי אוֹמֵר. זָכָה. וַחֲכָמִים. לֹא זָכָה. תְּנוּ שְׁטָר שִׁיחְרוּר זֶה לְעַבְדִּי. וָמֵת. רִבִּי אוֹמֵר. לֹא זָכָה. וַחֲכָמִים אוֹמְרִים. זָכָה. כּוֹפִין אֶת הַיּוֹרְשִׁין לְקַיֵּים דִּבְרֵי הַמֵּת. אָמַר רִבִּי זְעִירָא. בִּסְתָם חֲלוּקִין. מָה אֲנָן קַיָּימִין. אִם בְּאוֹמֵר. שִׁחְרְרוּ. אַף רִבִּי מוֹדֶה. אִם בְּאוֹמֵר. כִּתְבוּ וּתְנוּ. אַף רַבָּנִין מוֹדוּ. אֶלָּא כֵן אֲנָן קַיָּימִין. בְּאוֹמֵר. תְּנוּ. רִבִּי אוֹמֵר. הָאוֹמֵר. תְּנוּ. כְּאוֹמֵר. כִּתְבוּ וּתְנוּ. וְרַבָּנִין אָמְרִין. הָאוֹמֵר. תְּנוּ. כְּאוֹמֵר. שִׁחְרְרוּ.

[157]"If somebody says, I freed my slave Ṭabi[158], I shall free him, he is free, he acquired[159]." Rebbi Inaia[160] in the name of Rebbi Joḥanan: But only by a document[161]. "He should be freed[162], Rebbi says, he acquired, but for the Sages he did not acquire. Give this document of manumission, and he died, Rebbi says, he did not acquire but the Sages say, he did acquire; one forces the heirs to fulfill the instructions of the deceased." Rebbi Ze'ira said, they disagree[163] if he did not specify. How do we hold? If he said, "free him", Rebbi will agree[164]. If he said, "write and deliver," the Sages will agree[165]. But we deal with the case that he said "give". Rebbi says, one who says "give" is like one who said "write and deliver," but the Sages say, one who says "give" is like one who said "free him".

157   This *baraita* also appears in *Baba Batra* 8:9, 16c.

158   For Ṭabi (m.), Ṭabitha (f.) as names of slaves cf. *Niddah* 1:5, Note 103.

159   The slave acquired the right to be freed.

160   In *Baba Batra*: R. Ḥiyya.

161   The slave cannot acquire freedom by the simple declaration of his owner; he only can acquire the right to a document of manumission.

162   The owner said that the slave should be freed, but did not say it in the context of a last will and testament. The Sages hold that this is a not binding promise; Rebbi holds that this kind of promise is binding.

163   In the case of the owner who gave instructions to write a document for his slave.

164   Since the heirs are required to follow the wishes of the testator, they have to free the slave.

165   This is the case of the Mishnah; if the owner instructed to write the document and deliver it in his name, the instruction becomes void at his death.

(43d line 35) הָאוֹמֵר. יִנָּתְנוּ כָּל־נְכָסָיו לִפְלוֹנִי. וְהוּא כֹהֵן. וְהָיוּ שָׁם עֲבָדִים. אַף עַל פִּי שֶׁאָמַר. אִי אֶיפְשִׁי בָהֶן. הֲרֵי אֵילוּ אוֹכְלִין בַּתְּרוּמָה. רַבָּן שִׁמְעוֹן בֶּן

גַּמְלִיאֵל אוֹמֵר. מִכֵּיוָן שֶׁאָמַר. אִי אִיפְשִׁי בָהֶן. זָכוּ בָהֶן הַיוֹרְשִׁין. אָמַר רבִּי זְעִירָא. בִּסְתָמָן חֲלוּקִין. מָה אֲנַן קַיָּימִין. אִם מִשֶּׁקִּיבֵּל עָלָיו מִשָּׁעָה רִאשׁוֹנָה אַף רַבָּן שִׁמְעוֹן בֶּן גַּמְלִיאֵל מוֹדֶה. אִם בְּשֶׁלֹּא קִיבֵּל עָלָיו מִשָּׁעָה רִאשׁוֹנָה אַף רַבָּנָן מוֹדוּ. אֶלָּא כֵן אֲנַן קַיָּימִין בִּסְתָמָן. רִבִּי אוֹמֵר. לֵית בַּר נָשׁ אָמַר. אִי אֶיפְשָׁר. אֶלָּא מִכֵּיוָן שֶׁקִּיבֵּל עָלָיו. רַבָּן שִׁמְעוֹן בֶּן גַּמְלִיאֵל אוֹמֵר. מִכֵּיוָן שֶׁאָמַר. אִי אֶיפְשָׁר. הוֹכִיחַ סוֹפוֹ עַל תְּחִילָתוֹ.

[166]"If somebody said that all his property should be given to X, a Cohen, and [the estate] contained slaves, even if [the Cohen] said 'I cannot have them' they eat heave[167]. Rabban Simeon ben Gamliel said, since he said 'I cannot have them', the heirs[168] acquired them." Rebbi Ze'ira said, they disagree if he[169] did not specify. How do we hold? If he accepted at the first moment, Rabban Gamliel will agree[170]. If he did refuse at the first moment, the rabbis will agree[171]. But we deal with the case that he did not specify. Rebbi says, nobody says 'it is impossible' unless he had accepted[172]. Rabban Simeon ben Gamliel said, since he said 'it is impossible', the end is proof for the start[173].

166 Tosephta *Baba Batra* 8:1; Yerushalmi *Baba Batra* 8:8 16b; Babli *Baba Batra* 138a, Ḥulin 39b, *Keritut* 24b.

167 Since the transfer of possession is automatic, the slaves belong to the Cohen until he disposes of them.

168 The legal heirs who would have inherited in the absence of a will.

169 The recipient.

170 If the Cohen was owner of the slaves for one moment, he cannot dispose of them except by sale or manumission.

171 Nobody is forced to accept a bequest against his will.

172 And had time to inspect what he received.

173 Since he was noncommittal at the start, his later rejection has retroactive power. The same explanation is given in the Babli in the name of R. Joḥanan.

(43d line 42) הָאוֹמֵר. תֵּן מָנֶה זֶה לִפְלוֹנִי שֶׁאֲנִי חַייָב לוֹ. הוֹלֵךְ מָנֶה זֶה לִפְלוֹנִי בְּפִקָּדוֹן שֶׁיֵּשׁ לוֹ בְיָדִי. אִם רָצָה לְהַחֲזִיר לֹא יַחֲזִיר. וְחַייָב הָאִישׁ בְּאַחֲרָיוּתוֹ עַד שֶׁיְּקַבֵּל אוֹתוֹ הָאִישׁ אֶת שֶׁלּוֹ. אָמַר רִבִּי אִילָא. הַמַּתָּנָה כְחוֹב. תֵּן מָנֶה זֶה לִפְלוֹנִי. הוֹלֵךְ מָנֶה זֶה לִפְלוֹנִי. תֵּן זֶה שְׁטַר מַתָּנָה לִפְלוֹנִי. הוֹלֵךְ שְׁטַר זֶה מַתָּנָה לִפְלוֹנִי. אִם רָצָה לְהַחֲזִיר (לֹא) יַחֲזִיר. הָלַךְ וּמְצָאוֹ שֶׁמֵּת יַחֲזִיר לַמְשַׁלֵּחַ. וְאִם מֵת יִתֵּן לְיוֹרְשָׁיו. זְכֵה מָנֶה זֶה לִפְלוֹנִי. קַבֵּל מָנֶה זֶה לִפְלוֹנִי. זְכֵה שְׁטָר זֶה מַתָּנָה לִפְלוֹנִי. קַבֵּל שְׁטָר זֶה מַתָּנָה לִפְלוֹנִי. אִם רָצָה לְהַחֲזִיר לֹא יַחֲזִיר. הָלַךְ וּמְצָאוֹ שֶׁמֵּת יִתֵּן לְיוֹרְשָׁיו. וְאִם לְאַחַר מִיתָה זָכָה יַחֲזִיר לַמְשַׁלֵּחַ. שֶׁאֵין אָדָם זוֹכֶה בִכְתָב לְאַחַר מִיתָה. מִי שֶׁאָמַר. מָנֶה זֶה לִפְלוֹנִי. טוֹל מָנֶה זֶה לִפְלוֹנִי. יְהֵא מָנֶה זֶה לִפְלוֹנִי בְּיָדָךְ. אִם רָצָה לְהַחֲזִיר לֹא יַחֲזִיר. וְהָדֵין זָכָה לְחַבְרֵיהּ לָא יְכִיל חֲזוֹר בֵּיהּ.

"If somebody says, give this *mina* to X because I owe it to him, bring this *mina* to X for the pledge which he has from me, if he wants to change his mind he cannot do so but he himself is responsible until X receives his due[174]." Rebbi Ila said, a gift is like a debt. [175]"Give this *mina* to X, bring this *mina* to X, give this gift document to X, if he wants to change his mind he can(not)[176] do so. If he went and found that X had died, he should return it to the sender[177], and if that one had died he should give it to the latter's heirs." [178]"Acquire this *mina* for X, accept this mina for X, acquire this gift document for X, accept this gift document for X, if he wants to change his mind he cannot do so. If he went and found that X had died, he should deliver it to his heirs. But if he acquired after [X's] death[179] he should return it to the sender since nobody can acquire documents after his death." [179]"If somebody says, this *mina* is for X, take this *mina* for X, this *mina* shall be in your hand for X, if he wants to change his mind he cannot do so" because if somebody acquires for another person it cannot be changed.

174 While the agent can accept the payment for the creditor (which is to the creditor's benefit), the debt is not paid until the creditor receives it; without the creditor's instructions the responsibility for the money cannot be transferred to the creditor since that would be a detriment; Tosephta 1:6. In the Babli 14a, Samuel disputes the ruling and holds that there is no acquisition without consent; the possibility of a detriment invalidates the benefit.

175 Tosephta 1:7.

176 "Not" is in the ms. but not in the Tosephta. All Medieval authors who quote this Yerushalmi mention it in the version of the Tosephta: *Sefer Miṣwot Gadol* 2, 161d, #82; Rashba *ad* 14a, Tosaphot haRosh *ad* 13a, *s. v.* והוא (col. 99 in the edition of H. B. Ravitz, Jerusalem 2004). Aviezri (Eliezer ben Joel, Ravia) is quoted in Mordechai *Giṭṭin* 532 as having seen in one Tosephta ms. the reading "cannot"; he rejects that since then the Tosephta could have been formulated together with the following one. This argument is accepted by S. Lieberman, *Tosefta ki-Fshutah Giṭṭin* p. 793, but it does not seem conclusive since the treatment of the case that the recipient died is different in the two cases. Therefore, the reading לא should be provided with a question mark but cannot be rejected out of hand.

177 Not deliver to the recipient's heirs since it was not intended for them.

178 Tosephta 1:8.

179 If it turned out that the recipient was already dead at the time the messenger was intended to become an agent for him, there was no transaction since nobody can become an agent for a dead person. The messenger was not appointed as agent for the deceased's estate.

180 Tosephta 1:9.

(43d line 54) דְּלֹמָא. רִבִּי דּוֹסְתַּי בֵּירִבִּי יַנַּאי וְרִבִּי יוֹסֵי בֶּן כִּיפֵּר נַחְתּוֹן מִיגְבֵּי לְחַבְרֵיהּ תַּמָּן וְאִיתְאָמְרַת עֲלֵיהוֹן לְשָׁן בִּישׁ. אָתוֹן בָּעֵיי מִיפְקָא מִינֵּיהּ. אָמְרִין לוֹן. כְּבָר זָכִינָן. אָמְרִין לוֹן. אֲנָן בְּעֵי תְקִימִינּוֹן טָבָאת. אָמְרִין. שׁוֹמֵר חִינָם

אֲנַחְנוּ. אָתוֹן לְגַבֵּי רִבִּי דּוֹסְתַּי בֵּירִבִּי יַנַּאי. אָמַר לוֹן. הֲהֵנוּ כּוּלָהּ. נַסְבוּן לְרִבִּי יוֹסֵי בֶּן כִּיפָּר וּפָטְרוֹי וְאַפְקוֹן מִינֵּיהּ. כַּד סַלְקוֹן לְהָכָא אֲתָא לְגַבֵּי אֲבוּי. אָמַר לֵיהּ. לֵית אַתְּ חֲמֵי מָה עֲבַד לִי בְּרָךְ. אָמַר לֵיהּ. מָה עֲבַד לָךְ. אָמַר לֵיהּ. אִילּוּ אַשְׁוְויֵי עִימִּי לָא הֲווֹן מַפְקִין מִינָן כְּלוּם. אָמַר לֵיהּ. מָה עֲבַדְתְּ כֵּן. אָמַר לֵיהּ. רָאִיתִי אוֹתָן בֵּית דִּין שָׁוֶה וְכוֹבָעֵיהֶן אַמָּה וּמְדַבְּרִין מַחֲצָיִים. וְיוֹסֵה אָחִי כָּפוּת וּרְצוּעָה עוֹלָה וְיוֹרֶדֶת. וְאָמְרִית. שֶׁמָּא דוֹסְתַּאי אַחֵר יֵשׁ לְאַבָּא. אָמַר רִבִּי חַגַּיי. הָדָא דְּתֵימַר בְּהוּא דְלָא יְכִיל מִיקָמָה טַבְאוּת. בְּרַם הַהוּא דְּיָכִיל מִיקָמָה טַבְאוּת מֵיפַק לוֹן מִן הָדָא וְיִטְלוֹן לְדֵין.

1 ינאי | ג יניי   כיפר | ג כופר   מיגבי | ק לגבי   2 לחבריה | ק לחבריא   ואיתאמרת | ק איתאמר   לישן ביש | ק לישנא בישא   - ק הוון בעיין דלא יהיביין כלום   בעיי | ק בעין   מיניה | ק מינהון   3 זכינן | ק זבנן   - ק אמרין לו. ומנן.   אנן | ק מנן   תקימינון | ק תקמינונן   טבאות | ק טבאות   שומר | ק שומרי   4 אתון | ק אזלון   ההנו | ק אהן הוא   כולה | ק כולא   5 ופטרוי | ק וכפתון   6 לית את | ק -   7 אשוויי | ק אשוי   מפקין | ק מפקה   8 מחציים | ק מחציין   9 ואמרית | ק ואמרתי   10 דתימר | ק דאת אמר   בהוא | ק בההוא   טבאות | ק גרמיה טביות   11 טבאות | ק גרמיה טבאות   מיפק | ק נסב   ויטלון | ק ויהב

[181] Rebbi Dositheos ben Rebbi Yannai and Rebbi Yose ben Kipper descended[182] to collect there for a colleague[183] when they were slandered[184]. They[185] came and wanted to take it back from them. They answered, we already acquired it[186]. They[185] said, we wish for you to accept it in good faith[187]; they answered, we are unpaid trustees[188]. They[185] approached Rebbi Dositheos ben Rebbi Yannai who told them, there it is, all of it[189]. They[185] took Rebbi Yose ben Kipper, whipped him with ropes, and took it[190] from him. When they returned here, he[191] went to his father and told him, look what your son did to me! He asked him, what did he do to you? He answered, if he had taken my position, they could not have taken anything from us. He asked him[192], why did you act in such a way? He said, I saw that they were a unanimous court,[193] their

hats were a cubit wide[194], they were directing blows, my brother Yose was bound[195] and the whip ascended and descended. I said, does my father have another Dositheos[196]? Rebbi Ḥaggai said, you say that for somebody who cannot give a warranty in good faith. But if somebody gives a warranty in good faith, one takes from this one and gives to the other[197].

181   A parallel, in somewhat better shape, is in *Qiddušin* 3:3, 64b l. 37. The readings of the Leiden ms. are given by ק, those of one half line in a Geniza fragment (*Qiddušin*) by ג.

182   "To descend" everywhere means: To travel from Galilee to Babylonia.

183   In the parallel story in the Babli, 14a/b, R. Aḥai ben R. Joshia asked them to bring him a silver vessel which was owed to him in Nahardea. According to the story in *Qiddušin*, they went to collect money for the Galilean Academy.

184   After they had collected the debt, a rumor was spread that they were dishonest.

185   The debtors, afraid of losing their money, being responsible if it was stolen by the messengers.

186   Since we are empowered by the creditor, the money became the creditor's the moment it was given to us.

187   They wanted a declaration by the rabbis that they would be responsible for any loss in transit.

188   An unpaid trustee is only responsible for losses incurred because of his negligence but not for losses through robbery or other events beyond his control (Mishnah *Baba Meṣi'a* 7:8).

189   He returned the money, against the rules.

190   The part of the money which he had.

191   R. Yose ben Kipper went to complain to R. Yannai.

192   R. Yannai interrogated his son Dositheos.

193   They had made up their minds; it was impossible to argue with them.

194   Perhaps wide-rimmed hats were the uniform of violent people.

195   Following the text in *Qiddušin*. It seems that the word פטרוי, which in other contexts means "they freed him",

is a scribal corruption and should be removed from the dictionaries. Before correction, the scribe wrote ופרכוי "and they forced him", which may be correct.

196 He was afraid for his life; this justifies his breaking the rules.

197 If the messenger is empowered to sign a receipt for the money which shields the debtor from any claim of the creditor's under any circumstances, he cannot ask the money back.

(43d line 66) דִּין דְּמָחַל שְׁטָר לְחַבְרֵיהּ. רִבִּי חֲנַנְיָה וְרִבִּי מָנָא. חַד אָמַר. מָחַל. וְחָרָנָה אָמַר. לֹא מָחַל עַד דְּמָסַר לֵיהּ שְׁטָרָא.

דין דמחל | ק וימחול   מחל | ק מחיל   2 דמסר | ק דחזר

If somebody forgave a bond to another person. Rebbi Ḥanania and Rebbi Mamal: one said it is forgiven[198]; the other said it is not forgiven unless he handed over the bond[199].

198 An oral declaration by which the creditor engages himself not to claim a debt is valid without any act of acquisition by the debtor. This is the decision of Šulḥan ʿArukh Ḥošen Mišpaṭ Chapter 12 §8, based on inferences from the Babli.

199 The debtor has to take possession of the bond directly or by an indirect act of acquisition.

(43d line 67) תֵּן מָנֶה זֶה לִפְלוֹנִי. וָמֵת. אִם רָצוּ הַיּוֹרְשִׁין לְעַכֵּב אֵינָן יְכוֹלִין. אֵין צָרִיךְ לוֹמַר בְּאוֹמֵר. זְכֵה לוֹ. כְּאוֹמֵר. הִתְקַבֵּל לִי. הֵן. אָמַר רַבָּא בַּר מָמָל. בְּשָׁכִיב מְרַע הִיא מַתְנִיתָא. אִם בְּשָׁכִיב מְרַע בְּהָדָא אֵין צָרִיךְ לוֹמַר. זְכֵה לוֹ. הִתְקַבֵּל לוֹ. אָמַר רִבִּי מָנָא. קַיְימוּתֵיהּ מִדְּאָמַר רִבִּי בָּא בַּר רַב הוּנָא בְּשֵׁם רַב. עָשׂוּ דִּבְרֵי שְׁכִיב מְרַע כִּבְרִיא שֶׁכָּתַב וְנָתַן. וְהוּא שֶׁמֵּת מֵאוֹתוֹ חוֹלִי. הָא אִם הִבְרִיא לֹא. אֵין צָרִיךְ לוֹמַר בְּאוֹמֵר. זְכֵה לוֹ. הִתְקַבֵּל לוֹ.

"'Give this *mina* to X,' then he died. If the heirs want to hinder [the delivery] they are powerless. It is unnecessary to say that it is so if he said, acquire for him, if he said, accept by my orders.[200]" Rebbi Abba bar

Mamal said, this *baraita* refers to a sick person. If he is sick, does he not have to say: acquire for him, accept for him? Rebbi Mana said, I confirmed this by what Rebbi Abba bar Rav Huna said in the name of Rav: They treated verbal instructions by a sick person as if they were written and delivered[201]. But only if he died from that sickness, not if he recovered, he did not have to say: acquire for him, accept for him.

200   In a slightly different wording, this is Tosephta 1:9.

201   In the Babli (13a, 15a, *Baba Batra* 121a, 175a) this is a statement of Rav Naḥman, universally accepted. Cf. *Ketubot* 11:1, Note 22.

(43d line 74) תְּנוּ מָנָה לְאִישׁ פְּלוֹנִי. וָמֵת. יִתְּנוּ לְאַחַר מִיתָה. רִבִּי אָבִין בְּשֵׁם רִבִּי בָּא בַּר מָמָל. בִּשְׁכִיב מְרַע הִיא מַתְנִיתָא.

"'Give this *mina* to Mr. X' and he dies, they shall deliver it after his death"[146,202]. Rebbi Abin in the name of Rebbi Abba bar Mamal: The Mishnah refers to a sick person.

202   The last clause of the Mishnah is essentially identical with the Tosephta discussed in the preceding paragraph.

המביא בתרא פרק שיני

(fol. 44a) **משנה א**: הַמֵּבִיא גֵט מִמְּדִינַת הַיָּם וְאָמַר בְּפָנַיי נִכְתַּב אֲבָל לֹא בְּפָנַיי נֶחְתַּם בְּפָנַיי נֶחְתַּם אֲבָל לֹא בְּפָנַיי נִכְתַּב בְּפָנַיי נִכְתַּב כּוּלוֹ וּבְפָנַיי נֶחְתַּם חֶצְיוֹ בְּפָנַיי נִכְתַּב חֶצְיוֹ וּבְפָנַיי נֶחְתַּם כּוּלוֹ פָּסוּל. אֶחָד אוֹמֵר בְּפָנַיי נִכְתַּב וְאֶחָד אוֹמֵר בְּפָנַיי נֶחְתַּם פָּסוּל. שְׁנַיִם אוֹמְרִים בְּפָנֵינוּ נִכְתַּב וְאֶחָד אוֹמֵר בְּפָנַיי נֶחְתַּם פָּסוּל. וְרִבִּי יְהוּדָה מַכְשִׁיר. אֶחָד אוֹמֵר בְּפָנַיי נִכְתַּב וּשְׁנַיִם אוֹמְרִים בְּפָנֵינוּ נֶחְתַּם כָּשֵׁר.

Mishnah 1: If somebody brings a bill of divorce from overseas and says, "it was written before me," but not "it was signed before me," or "it was signed before me" but not "it was written before me", "it was written before me but signed only partially before me", "it was partially written before me but signed completely before me", it is invalid[1]. If one said "it was written before me" and another "it was signed before me", it is invalid; if two people say, "it was written before us" but only one[2] says, "it was signed before me," it is invalid; but Rebbi Jehudah declares it valid[3]. If one says, "it was written before me" but two say, "it was signed before us," it is valid[4].

---

[1] The rule of Mishnah 1:1 is not followed.

[2] A third person.

[3] R. Jehudah declares a bill of divorce valid if one witness testifies to the writing and one to the signing; he does not require that both be the same person.

[4] Any document is valid which is witnessed by two persons whose signatures are validated by two witnesses.

הלכה א: (44a line 31) הַמֵּבִיא גֵט מִמְּדִינַת הַיָּם כול'. נִיחָא בְּפָנַיי נִכְתַּב אֲבָל לֹא בְּפָנַיי נֶחְתַּם. בְּפָנַיי נֶחְתַּם אֲבָל לֹא בְּפָנַיי נִכְתַּב. כְּלוּם קִיּוּמוֹ שֶׁלַגֵּט אֶלָּא בְּחוֹתְמָיו. אֶלָּא כְרַבִּי יוּדָה. דְּרַבִּי יוּדָה פּוֹסֵל בַּטוֹפְסִין. וּדְרַבִּי יוּדָה בְּחוּצָה לָאָרֶץ כִּמְגָרֵשׁ בְּאֶרֶץ יִשְׂרָאֵל. וְיֵשׁ טוֹפְסֵי גִיטִּין בְּחוּצָה לָאָרֶץ כִּמְגָרֵשׁ בְּחוּצָה לָאָרֶץ. עַד שֶׁיֵּדַע שֶׁהוּא גֵט אִשָּׁה עַד שֶׁיֵּדַע שֶׁהוּא נַעֲשָׂה שָׁלִיחַ. וְלֹא הָיָה יוֹדֵעַ שֶׁהוּא גֵּט אִשָּׁה. עַד שֶׁיִּכְתּוֹב כּוּלּוֹ בְּפָנָיו עַד שֶׁיִּתְחַתֵּם כּוּלּוֹ בְּפָנָיו. תַּנֵּי רַבִּי חָנִין. אִם הָיָה נִכְנָס וְיוֹצֵא מוּתָּר.

"If somebody brings a bill of divorce from overseas," etc. One understands "it was written before me" but not "it was signed before me", but "it was signed before me" but not "it was written before me"? Is not a bill of divorce validated by its signatures? That must follow Rebbi Jehudah, for Rebbi Jehudah invalidates forms[5]. Following Rebbi Jehudah outside the Land as for one who divorces in the Land of Israel[6]. Are there forms of bills of divorce outside the Land for divorces outside the Land? It is necessary for him to know that it is a bill of divorce[7] and that he be appointed as an agent; he would not know that it was a bill of divorce unless it was written completely before him. Rebbi Ḥanin stated: It is permitted that he enter and leave[8].

---

5 In Mishnah 3:2, the anonymous majority permit the routine production of forms of bills of divorce where everything is written in advance and only the names of husband and wife, the date, and the statement of divorce are then inserted for the particular couple involved in the divorce; but R. Jehudah holds that the requirement that "he write for her" (*Deut.* 24:1) can only be fulfilled if the bill was written specifically for that wife from the first letter to the last.

6 In Halakhah 3:2, practice is declared as following R. Jehudah.

7 Since the agent is to be interviewed about the writing of the bill, it is obvious that he could not answer if the bill was a form in which only the names of husband and wife

and the time were inserted. Even the anonymous majority of Mishnah 3:2 must agree that forms are possible only in the Land.

8   In all matters of supervision, it is possible for the supervisor to leave the place occasionally as long as he can return at any moment and the person to be supervised, in this case the scribe, does not know in advance when the supervisor will return. The same *baraita* is accepted in the Babli, 6a.

(44a line 37) רִבִּי יוֹסֵי בָּעֵי. אָמַר. בְּפָנַיי נִכְתַּב וּבְפָנַיי נֶחְתַּם אֶלָּא נִתְיַיחֵד בִּרְשׁוּת הַבְּעָלִים בֵּין כְּתִיבָה לַחֲתִימָה. נִישְׁמְעִינָהּ מִן הָדָא. אֶחָד אוֹמֵר. בְּפָנַיי נִכְתַּב. וְאֶחָד אוֹמֵר. בְּפָנַיי נֶחְתַּם. פָּסוּל. מִפְּנֵי שֶׁאֶחָד אוֹמֵר. בְּפָנַיי נִכְתַּב. וְאֶחָד אוֹמֵר. בְּפָנַיי נֶחְתַּם. אֲבָל אִם אָמַר בְּפָנַיי נִכְתַּב וּבְפָנַיי נֶחְתַּם אֶלָּא שֶׁנִּתְיַיחֵד בִּרְשׁוּת הַבְּעָלִים בֵּין כְּתִיבָה לַחֲתִימָה. כָּשֵׁר. רַב חִסְדָּא בָּעֵי. חֶצְיוֹ מִתַּקָּנָה וְחֶצְיוֹ מִדְּבַר תּוֹרָה. אָמַר בְּפָנַיי נִכְתַּב וּבְפָנַיי נֶחְתַּם אֶלָּא שֶׁנִּתְיַיחֵד בִּרְשׁוּת הַבְּעָלִים. נִישְׁמְעִינָהּ מִן הָדָא. אֶחָד אוֹמֵר בְּפָנַיי נִכְתַּב וְאֶחָד אוֹמֵר בְּפָנַיי נֶחְתַּם. פָּסוּל. מִפְּנֵי שֶׁאֶחָד אוֹמֵר. בְּפָנַיי נִכְתַּב. וְאֶחָד אוֹמֵר. בְּפָנַיי נֶחְתַּם. אֲבָל אִם אָמַר. בְּפָנַיי נִכְתַּב וּבְפָנַיי נִתְחַתֵּם אֶלָּא שֶׁנִּתְיַיחֵד בִּרְשׁוּת הַבְּעָלִים שָׁעָה אַחַת. כָּשֵׁר.

Rebbi Yose asked: If he said, "it was written and signed before me, but it was in the sole possession of the husband between writing and signing"[9]? Let us hear from the following: "If one said 'it was written before me' and another 'it was signed before me', it is invalid." That is, because one said, "it was written before me" and another, "it was signed before me"; this implies[10] that if one said, "it was written and signed before me, but it was in the sole possession of the husband between writing and signing", it is valid. Rav Ḥisda asked: half of an institution and half as biblical decree[11]? If he said, "it was written and signed before me, but it was in the sole possession of the husband between writing and signing"? Let us hear from the following: "If one said 'it was written before me' and another 'it was signed before me', it is invalid." That is, because one said "it was written before me" and another "it was signed before me"; this implies that if one said, "it was written and signed before me, but it was in the sole possession of the husband for an hour," it is valid.

9   In the meantime, the husband could have substituted an invalid document for the valid one which was written in the presence of the agent.

10   The fact that the case is not mentioned in the Mishnah; neither here nor in Mishnah 1:1 is there any mention that the document has to be seen by the agent between writing and signing.

11   The requirement that the bill be written specifically for that wife is biblical, the requirement that the agent be present at writing and signing is purely rabbinical. It was stated in Halakhah 1:1 (Note 14) that the husband is not suspected of doing anything which would make the divorce recognized by the court when it is invalid in the eyes of Heaven (since then he would commit a sin without hurting his ex-wife). Therefore, the answer given to R. Yose's question is reasonable.

(44a line 47) רִבִּי אֶלְעָזָר אָמַר. רִבִּי אָבִין בָּעִי. אָמַר. בְּפָנַיי נִכְתַּב וּבְפָנַיי נֶחְתַּם בְּעֵד אֶחָד. וּשְׁנַיִם מְעִידִין עַל חֲתִימַת הָעֵד הַשֵּׁינִי. אָמַר רִבִּי אִמִּי בַּבְלָייָא. אֵין כָּשֵׁר אֶלָא זֶה. רִבִּי אַבָּא לֹא אָמַר כָּךְ אֶלָא. אָמַר. בְּפָנַיי נִכְתַּב וּבְפָנַיי נִתְחַתֵּם בְּעֵד אֶחָד וַאֲנִי הוּא הָעֵד הַשֵּׁינִי. נַעֲשָׂה כְנוֹגֵעַ בְּעֵדוּתוֹ.

Rebbi Eleazar said, Rebbi Abun asked: If he said "it was written and one witness signed before me," and two[12] testify about the signature of the second witness. Rebbi Immi the Babylonian said, nothing can be more valid than this. Rebbi Abba did not say[13] so but: If he said "it was written and one witness signed before me, and I am the second witness." He is like a party interested in his testimony[14].

12 Two other witnesses.

13 R. Abin's question was trivial.

14 He becomes party and can no longer be a witness. In the Babli, 15b, the reason is given that a bill of divorce can be validated either as a document, by the independent testimony about the signature of the witnesses, or by the special rule of divorces which allows an agent to declare that it was written and signed before him, but not by a combination of both because then the witness would validate himself.

(44a line 51) הָיָה מְתוּתָם בְּאַרְבָּעָה וְאָמַר. בְּפָנַיי נִכְתַּב וּבְפָנַיי נִתְחַתֵּם בִּשְׁנֵי עֵדִים. אִילֵין תְּרֵין חוֹרָנָא לִינָא יָדַע מָה עִיסְקֵיהוֹן. תַּפְלוּגְתָּא דְּרִבִּי יוֹחָנָן וְרִבִּי שִׁמְעוֹן בֶּן לָקִישׁ. דְּאִיתְפַּלְגוֹן. אָמַר לַעֲשָׂרָה. חִתְמוּ בַגֵּט. וְהוּחְתְּמוּ מִקְצָתָן הַיּוֹם וּמִקְצָתָן לְמָחָר. רֵישׁ לָקִישׁ אָמַר. כָּשֵׁר. וְהַשְּׁאָר עַל תְּנַאי. רִבִּי יוֹחָנָן אָמַר. פָּסוּל עַד שֶׁיַּחְתְּמוּ בּוֹ בַּיּוֹם.

If there were four signatures and he said, "it was written and signed by two witnesses before me; I do not know anything about the other two." That is the disagreement of Rebbi Johanan and Rebbi Simeon ben Laqish, who disagreed: If he said to ten people, sign the bill of divorce, and some signed on that day and some the next day. Rebbi Simeon ben Laqish said, it is valid, for the remainder are only because of the condition[15]. Rebbi Johanan said it is invalid unless all sign on the same day[16].

15 The first two witnesses validate the document as a bill of divorce The others only sign because he made a condition that the bill be valid only with ten signatures, to make a public statement that he would no longer be responsible for his wife's debts.

16 One cannot split the conditions; all ten signatures are needed to validate and, therefore, must be affixed on the date specified in the document. Otherwise the document would be invalid as predated.

In the Babli, 18b, the attributions are switched. This means that the Babli, which always prefers R. Johanan to R. Simeon ben Laqish, follows what is declared here to be R. Simeon ben Laqish's opinion. The Yerushalmi does not decide between the opinions.

(44a line 51) אָמַר רְבִּי אִמִּי. מַה פְּלִיגִין. בְּיוֹצֵא מִתַּחַת יָדוֹ. אֲבָל בְּיוֹצֵא מִתַּחַת יְדֵי אַחֵר אַף רַבָּנָן מוֹדוֹי שֶׁהוּא כָשֵׁר. רְבִּי חֲנַנְיָה דְּרְבִּי אִמִּי אָמַר רְבִּי זְעִירָא. מַה פְּלִיגִין. בְּיוֹצֵא מִתַּחַת יְדֵי אַחֵר. אֲבָל בְּיוֹצֵא מִתַּחַת יָדוֹ אַף רְבִּי יְהוּדָה מוֹדֶה שֶׁהוּא פָּסוּל. מָתִיב רְבִּי זְעִירָא לְרְבִּי אִימִּי. אִם בְּיוֹצֵא מִתַּחַת יְדֵי אַחֵר רְבִּי יוּדָה מַכְשִׁיר אֲפִילוּ בְּקַמַּיְיתָא. אַייְתֵי רְבִּי אִמִּי לְרְבִּי יוֹנָה חֲמוֹי וְתַנָּה לֵיהּ. אֶחָד אוֹמֵר. בְּפָנַיי נִכְתַּב וּבְפָנַיי נֶחְתַּם. פָּסוּל. רְבִּי יוּדָן מַכְשִׁיר. אָמַר רְבִּי אָבִין. לִישָׁן מַתְנִיתָא מְסַיְּיעָא לְרְבִּי זְעִירָא. בְּזֶה רְבִּי יוּדָן מַכְשִׁיר. וְקַשְׁיָא עַל דְּרְבִּי זְעִירָא. אִם בְּיוֹצֵא מִתַּחַת יְדֵי אַחֵר כְּהָדָא לֹא עָשׂוּ אוֹתוֹ כִשְׁנַיִם. אֵימָתַי עָשׂוּ אוֹתוֹ כִשְׁנַיִם. בִּזְמַן שֶׁהוּא מֵעִיד עַל הַכְּתִיבָה וְעַל הַחֲתִימָה.

Rebbi Immi said, where do they disagree? If the document is presented by him personally. But if it is presented by another person, even the rabbis will agree that it is valid[17]. Rebbi Ḥananiah agrees with Rebbi Immi. Rebbi Zeʿira said, where do they disagree? If the document is presented by another person. But if it is presented by him personally, even Rebbi Jehudah will agree that it is invalid[18]. Rebbi Zeʿira objected to Rebbi Immi: If the document is presented by him personally, does Rebbi Jehudah declare it valid even in the first case[19]? Rebbi Immi brought his father-in-law Rebbi Jonah who stated for him: If one said "it was written before me" and another "it was signed before me", it is invalid, but Rebbi Jehudah declares it valid[20]. Rebbi Abin said, the formulation of a *baraita* supports Rebbi Zeʿira: *In that case*, Rebbi Jehudah declares it valid[21]. But it is difficult following Rebbi Zeʿira: If the document is presented by another person, that is when they do not treat the messenger as two. When do they treat him as two? When he testifies to both writing and signing[22].

17 This refers to the clause in the Mishnah where two people say that the bill was written in their presence and a third person testifies that it was signed in his presence. R. Immi holds that the rabbis declare the bill invalid if it is presented by the single person who saw the signing, whose testimony is incomplete, whereas R. Jehudah accepts the bill as valid if two people testify to any state of the writing of the bill. But if the bill was delivered by one of the witnesses to the writing, then he and the witness to the signing are two and the rabbis will agree that two messengers who bring a bill of divorce do not have to declare that it was written and signed before them.

18 According to R. Ze'ira, R. Jehudah agrees that the bill is invalid if writing and signing are attested to by different persons. In the Babli, 17a, both opinions are recorded in the name of R. Immi, held at different times.

19 In the Mishnah, the bill is unanimously declared invalid if writing and signing are attested to by different persons. One has to assume that R. Jehudah agrees.

20 A *baraita* shows that R. Jehudah accepts the bill if different people testify to writing and signing, showing that R. Ze'ira's objection is unjustified.

21 Tosephta 2:2; only in one case does R. Jehudah accept the bill as genuine.

22 Since in that case, any later protest by the husband is disregarded (Chapter 1, Note 9), it must be that the messenger who testifies to both writing and signing of the bill has the status of two witnesses whose testimony cannot be attacked.

(44a line 63) רִבִּי יָסָא בְּשֵׁם רִבִּי יוֹחָנָן. וּבְיוֹצֵא מִתַּחַת יָדוֹ. וַהֲוָה רִבִּי זְעִירָא מִסְתַּכֵּל בֵּיהּ. אָמַר לֵיהּ. לָמָּה אַתְּ מִסְתַּכֵּל בִּי. וַאֲפִילוּ יוֹצֵא מִתַּחַת יְדֵי אַחֵר. אַתְיָיא דְּרִבִּי יוֹסֵי כְּרִבִּי אִימִּי עַד לֹא יַחֲזוֹר בֵּיהּ. אָמַר רִבִּי מָנָא. אֲפִילוּ מִן דְּחָזַר בֵּיהּ אַתְיָיא הִיא. שַׁנְיָיה הִיא כְּתִיבָה בִּשְׁנַיִם וַחֲתִימָה בִּשְׁנַיִם. חֲתִימָה בִּשְׁנַיִם כּוֹחָהּ מְיוּפֶּה וּכְתִיבָה בִּשְׁנַיִם אֵין כּוֹחָהּ מְיוּפָּה.

Rebbi Yasa said in the name of Rebbi Joḥanan: If it is presented by him personally[23]. Rebbi Ze'ira was looking at him[24]. He asked, why are you looking at me? Even if it is presented by another person[25]. It means that Rebbi Yasa before he changed his mind followed Rebbi Immi[26]. Rebbi Mana said, even after he changed his mind it can be explained following him. There is a difference between two witnesses to the writing and two witnesses to the signing. Signing before two [witnesses] is empowered[27], writing before two is not empowered[28].

23 This refers to the last clause of the Mishnah, where one witness has seen the writing and two the signing. The singular implies that the person presenting the bill of divorce is alone; he is the person attesting to the writing.

24 Disapprovingly.

25 He changed his mind and accepts that two witnesses to the signature make any other witnesses superfluous.

26 In the preceding paragraph.

27 Any document is confirmed by two signatures if the latter can be notarized in court.

28 Except for bills of divorce, the circumstances of writing a document are irrelevant.

(fol. 44a) **משנה ב:** נִכְתַּב בַּיּוֹם וְנֶחְתַּם בַּיּוֹם בַּלַּיְלָה וְנֶחְתַּם בַּלַּיְלָה בַּלַּיְלָה וְנֶחְתַּם בַּיּוֹם כָּשֵׁר. בַּיּוֹם וְנֶחְתַּם בַּלַּיְלָה פָּסוּל רִבִּי שִׁמְעוֹן מַכְשִׁיר שֶׁהָיָה רִבִּי שִׁמְעוֹן אוֹמֵר כָּל הַגִּיטִין שֶׁנִּכְתְּבוּ בַּיּוֹם וְנֶחְתְּמוּ בַּלַּיְלָה פְּסוּלִין חוּץ מִגִּטֵּי נָשִׁים.

If it was written during daytime and signed during daytime, in the night and signed in the night, in the night and signed during daytime, it is valid[29]. During daytime and signed in the night it is invalid[30]. Rebbi Simeon declares it valid since Rebbi Simeon says that all documents which were written during daytime and signed at night are invalid except for women's bills of divorce[31].

29 Since the Jewish calendar day starts at nightfall, all these documents are signed on the day indicated as date in it.

30 Since every night belongs to the next day in the calendar, the document is predated.

31 He holds that the date of the writing of a divorce document has no monetary consequences; the duty of the husband to pay the *ketubah* and to return the dowry to his wife starts with the date of delivery of the bill.

(44a line 68) **הלכה ב:** נִכְתַּב בַּיּוֹם וְנֶחְתַּם בַּיּוֹם כול׳. אָמַר רִבִּי יוֹחָנָן. פָּסוּל מִפְּנֵי אֲכִילַת פֵּירוֹת. אָמַר לֵיהּ רֵישׁ לָקִישׁ. מֵעַתָּה תָחוּשׁ לַגִיטִּין הַבָּאִין מִמְּדִינַת הַיָּם שֶׁמָּא נִכְתְּבוּ בַיּוֹם וְנֶחְתְּמוּ בַלַּיְלָה. אָמַר לֵיהּ. זֶה זִיּוּפוֹ מִתּוֹכוֹ וְזֶה זִיּוּפוֹ מִדָּבָר אַחֵר.

Halakhah 2: "If it was written during daytime and signed during daytime," etc. Rebbi Joḥanan said, it is invalid because of the usufruct[32]. Rebbi Simeon ben Laqish told him, then you should also be suspicious of the bills of divorce brought from overseas; maybe they were written during daytime and signed in the night[33]! He answered him, there the forgery is intrinsic[34], here it is extrinsic[34].

32 He holds that the husband's right to the yield of his wife's property ends with the signing of the bill of divorce, not with its delivery. A predated bill of divorce is a predated document about money and, therefore, invalid automatically.

The Babylonian theory, given in Halakhah 4:3, requires a date as a matter of criminal law. In the Babli, 17a/b, both opinions are attributed either to R. Joḥanan or to R. Simeon ben Laqish; cf. *Sefer Ha'iṭṭur* 1, 6d, Note 26.

33 The messenger has to testify that he was present at the writing and signing of the bill, so he can be asked whether the document was written and signed specifically for the woman to be divorced. Why does he not have to testify that it was signed on the date of writing?

34 If the bill was not written specifically for the woman for whom it

is intended, it is worthless. If the writing and the signing are done for the correct purpose, the document is executed correctly. It becomes unenforceable by an outside circumstance.

(44a line 71) אָמַר רִבִּי יוֹחָנָן. לֹא אָמַר רבי שמעון אֶלָּא בַּלַּיְלָה. אֲבָל לְמָחָר אוֹף רִבִּי שמעון מוֹדֶה. רֵישׁ לָקִישׁ אָמַר. לֹא שַׁנְיָיא. הוּא לַיְלָה הוּא מָחָר הוּא לְאַחַר כַּמָּה. הֵיי דֵין הוּא לְמָחָר. רִבִּי חֲנַנְיָה וְרִבִּי מָנָא. חַד אָמַר. לְמָחָר. וְחָרְנָא אָמַר. מְחָרָא דְמָחָר. וְקַשְׁיָא דְרִבִּי יוֹחָנָן עַל דְּרֵישׁ (לָקִישׁ). כֵּן אָמַר רִבִּי בָּא בְשֵׁם רִבִּי זְעִירָא. אַתְיָא דְרִבִּי שמעון (בֶּן לָקִישׁ) כְּרִבִּי אֶלְעָזָר. כְּמָה דְרִבִּי אֶלְעָזָר אָמַר. אַף עַל פִּי שֶׁאֵין עָלָיו עֵדִים כָּשֵׁר. כֵּן רִבִּי שמעון אוֹמֵר. אַף עַל פִּי שֶׁאֵין עָלָיו עֵדִים כָּשֵׁר. אָמַר רִבִּי שְׁמוּאֵל אַחֵי דְרִבִּי בְּרֶכְיָה. כָּאן בְּרוֹצֶה לְחַתְּמוֹ וְכָאן בְּשֶׁאֵינָהּ רוֹצָה לְחַתְּמוֹ. אָמַר לַעֲשָׂרָה. חִתְמוּ בַגֵּט זֶה. וְחָתְמוּ מִקְצָתָן הַיּוֹם וּלְמָחָר מִקְצָתָן. רִבִּי שמעון בֶּן לָקִישׁ אָמַר. כָּשֵׁר. וְהַשְׁאָר עַל תְּנַאי. רִבִּי יוֹחָנָן אָמַר. פָּסוּל עַד שֶׁיַּחְתְּמוּ כּוּלָּן בּוֹ בַיּוֹם. רִבִּי יַעֲקֹב בַּר אִידִי בְשֵׁם רִבִּי יְהוֹשֻׁעַ בֶּן לֵוִי. מַעֲשֶׂה בְּאֶחָד שֶׁאָמַר לַעֲשָׂרָה. חִתְמוּ בַגֵּט. וְחָתְמוּ מִקְצָתָן הַיּוֹם וּמִקְצָתָן לְמָחָר. אָתָא עוֹבְדָא קוֹמֵי רַבָּנִין וְכַשְׁרוּן וְחָשׁוּן. הָדָא מְסַיְּיעָא לְרִבִּי יוֹחָנָן מִן דְּרַבָּנִין וּפְלִיגָא עֲלוֹי דְּרִבִּי שמעון. הָדָא מְסַיְּיעָא לְרִבִּי שמעון בֶּן לָקִישׁ מִן דְּרִבִּי שמעון וּפְלִיגָא עֲלוֹי מִן דְּרַבָּנִין.
13 הדא מסייעא | ג הדה משייעה   ופליגא עלוי | ג ופליגה עלוי על   הדא | ג הדה

Rebbi Joḥanan said, Rebbi Simeon stated this only for the night; but on the next day even Rebbi Simeon will agree[36]. But Rebbi Simeon ben Laqish said, there is no difference, whether night, or the next day, or after many days[37]. What is the next day? Rebbi Ḥanania and Rebbi Mana, one said the next day, the other said the day after the next[38]. The statement of Rebbi Joḥanan about Rebbi Simeon (ben Laqish)[39] is difficult! [40]So says Rebbi Abba in the name of Rebbi Ze'ira: It turns out that Rebbi Simeon (ben Laqish)[39] agrees with Rebbi Eleazar. Just as Rebbi Eleazar said, even if there are no witnesses signed on it, it is valid, so Rebbi Simeon said, even if there are no witnesses signed on it, it is valid. Rebbi Samuel, the brother of Rebbi Berekhiah, said: Here, if he wants the document to be signed, there if she does not want the document to be signed. If he said to ten people, sign the bill of divorce, and some signed today and some the next day. Rebbi Simeon ben Laqish said, it is valid for the remainder [are signing] only because of the condition[15]. Rebbi Johanan said it is invalid unless all sign on the same day[16]. Rebbi Jacob bar Idi in the name of Rebbi Joshua ben Levi: There was a case that one said to ten people, sign the bill of divorce, and some signed on that day and some the next day. The case came before the rabbis who reluctantly declared it valid[42,43]. This supports Rebbi Johanan from the position of the rabbis[44] and disagrees with Rebbi Simeon. This supports Rebbi Simeon ben Laqish from the position of Rebbi Simeon and disagrees with the rabbis.

36 Since R. Simeon accepts documents from a Gentile court (Mishnah 1:5), he must accept Gentile dating for which the night follows the day. But the next day is a different date even in the Gentile calendar.

37 He holds that for R. Simeon the date of a bill of divorce is irrelevant.

38 This opinion is difficult to understand.

39 Clearly, "ben Laqish" is a copyist's error since the reference is to the Tanna, ben Iohai. Cf. *Sefer Ha'ittur* 7c, Note 62.

40 This is a quote from Chapter 1:5, Note 132.

41 It is not obvious that the argument of Halakhah 1:5 can be transferred to the case here. There, R. Simeon accepts a document from a Gentile court whose Gentile signatures are not considered by the rabbinic court; it is obvious that R. Simeon must follow R. Eleazar's opinion that the only witnesses who count are those of the delivery of the bill. But here it is

not obvious that if the husband wants valid signatures on the bill one does not have to follow all the rules exactly. That certainly eliminates the interpretation of "tomorrow" as "day after tomorrow".

42   The case is mentioned in the Babli, 18b, as coming before R. Joshua ben Levi's court where the latter declared that "R. Simeon is important enough that one may follow him in an emergency"; the husband had disappeared and it was impossible to obtain a replacement bill from him.

43   From here on there exists a Geniza fragment whose readings are given by ג.

44   Since they permitted a bill signed on two different dates only in order to save the wife from being married to a husband who had disappeared, they agree with him that his rule represents the normal case.

משנה ג: בַּכֹּל כּוֹתְבִין בַּדְּיוֹ בַּסִּיקְרָא וּבַקּוֹמוֹס וּבַקַּלְקַנְתּוֹם וּבְכָל דָּבָר (fol. 44a) שֶׁהוּא רוֹשֵׁם. אֵין כּוֹתְבִין לֹא בַּמַּשְׁקִין וְלֹא בְּמֵי פֵירוֹת וְלֹא בְּכָל־דָּבָר שֶׁאֵינוֹ שֶׁל קַיָּימָא. עַל הַכֹּל כּוֹתְבִין עַל הֶעָלֶה שֶׁלַזַּיִת וְעַל הַקֶּרֶן שֶׁלַפָּרָה וְנוֹתְנִין לָהּ אֶת הַפָּרָה. וְעַל הַיָּד שֶׁלָעֶבֶד וְנוֹתְנִין לָהּ אֶת הָעָבֶד. רַבִּי יוֹסֵי הַגְּלִילִי אוֹמֵר אֵין כּוֹתְבִין לֹא עַל דָּבָר שֶׁיֵּשׁ בּוֹ רוּחַ חַיִּים אַף לֹא עַל הָאוֹכְלִין.

Mishnah 3: One writes with anything, with ink, with vermilion, with gum, and with copper sulfate[44], and anything that leaves a record. One does not write with drinks, or fruit juice, or anything not permanent. One writes on anything, on a leaf of the olive tree, on a cow's horn if one delivers the cow to her[45], on a slave's hand if one delivers the slave to her. Rebbi Yose the Galilean says, one does not write on anything living nor on food.

44   These words are explained in *Soṭah* 2:5,6, Notes 147,152.

(44b line 12) **הלכה ג:** בַּכֹּל כּוֹתְבִין כול'. וְכָתַב לֹא חָקַק. וְכָתַב לֹא מַטִיף. כָּתַב לֹא הַשׁוֹפֵךְ. כָּתַב לֹא חוֹקֵק. אִית תַּנָּיֵי תַנֵּי. אֲפִילוּ חוֹקֵק. אָמַר רַב חִסְדָּא. מָאן דְּאָמַר. לֹא חוֹקֵק. בְּפוֹלֵט מְקוֹם הַכְּתָב. כְּגוֹן הָדֵין דֵּינָרָא. מָאן דְּאָמַר. אֲפִילוּ חוֹקֵק. כְּגוֹן הָדֵין פִּינְקְסָא. כָּתַב לֹא הַמַּטִיף. רִבִּי יוּדָן בַּר שָׁלוֹם וְרִבִּי מַתַּנְיָה. חַד אָמַר. שֶׁלֹּא עֵירַב אֶת הַנְּקוּדוֹת. וְחָרָנָה אָמַר. אֲפִילוּ עֵירַב אֶת הַנְּקוּדוֹת. כָּתַב לֹא הַשּׁוֹפֵךְ. אָמַר רִבִּי חִיָּיה בַּר בָּא. אִילֵּין בְּנֵי מָדִינְחָא עֲרִימִין סַגִּין. וְכַד חַד מִינְהוֹן בָּעֵי מִשְׁלְחָה כְּתַב מִיסְטִירִין לְחַבְרֵיהּ הוּא כָתֵב בְּמֵי מִילִין. וְהַהּ דִּמְקַבֵּל כְּתָבֵיהּ שָׁפִיךְ דְּיוֹ שֶׁאֵין בּוֹ עֲפַץ וְהוּא קוֹלֵט מְקוֹם הַכְּתָב. עָשָׂה כֵן בַּשַּׁבָּת מָהוּ. תַּמָּן תַּנֵּינָן. כָּתַב עַל גַּבֵּי כְתָב פָּטוּר. רִבִּי יוֹחָנָן וְרִבִּי שִׁמְעוֹן בֶּן לָקִישׁ דְּאָמְרֵי תְּרַוַייְהוּ. וְהוּא שֶׁכָּתַב דְּיוֹ עַל גַּבֵּי דְיוֹ וְסִיקְרָא עַל גַּבֵּי סִיקְרָא. אֲבָל אִם כָּתַב דְּיוֹ עַל גַּבֵּי סִיקְרָא וְסִיקְרָא עַל גַּבֵּי דְּיוֹ חַיָּיב. רִבִּי יִצְחָק בַּר מְשַׁרְשְׁיָא בְּשֵׁם רַבָּנִין דְּתַמָּן. חַיָּיב שְׁתַּיִם. מִשּׁוּם מוֹחֵק וּמִשּׁוּם כּוֹתֵב.

1 בכל כותבים כול' | ש - כול' | ג - וכתב | ש כתב (2 times) מטיף | ש המטיף 2 כתב | ש וכתב 2-3 אמר רב חסדא ... פינקסא | ג כגון הדין פינקסא בפולט | ש בבולט 4 כתב | ש וכתב בר | גש ביר' 5 שלא | ג בשלא את הנקודות | ש הנקודות (2 times) וחרנה | ש וחרונה 6 כתב | ש וכתב 7 ערימין | ש ערומין כתב | ש מילה מיסטירין | גש מיסטריקון 8 מילין | ג מלין והד | ג והן ש והן כתביה | ש כתבייא הוא שפיך | ג שפך ש שופך עפץ | ג חפץ 9 מהו | ג מהוא 10 דאמרי תרויהו | ג תריהון אמרין ש תרווייהון אמרין על גבי | ג על 11 סיקרא | ג סיקרה (4 times) 12 משום מוחד ומשום כותב | ג משם כתב ומשם מוחק

Halakhah 3: "One writes with anything," etc. [45]"He shall write[46]", not engrave. "He shall write", not dropping points. "He shall write", not pouring. "He shall write", not engrave; some Tannaïm state, he even may engrave. Rav Ḥisda[47] said, he who says not to engrave, if the writing stands out as on a denar. He who says even to engrave, as on a writing tablet[48]. "He shall write", not dropping points; Rebbi Yudan bar Shalom and Rebbi Mattaniah: One said, if he did not connect the points; the other said, even if he connected the points[49]. "He shall write", not pouring. Rebbi Ḥiyya bar Abba said, those Orientals are very sophisticated. If one of them wants to write a secret[50] letter to another, he writes with juice of gall-nuts[51]. The recipient pours ink without gall over it, which is absorbed at the place of the writing[52]. If one did that[53] on the Sabbath, what? There, we have stated[54]: "Writing on top of writing is not prosecutable." Rebbi Joḥanan and Rebbi Simeon ben Laqish both said, only if he wrote ink on ink or vermilion on vermilion[55]. But if he wrote ink on vermilion or vermilion on ink, he is guilty. Rebbi Isaac bar Mesharshia in the name of the rabbis from there: He is doubly guilty, once for erasing and once for writing[56].

45 This paragraph is paralleled in *Šabbat* 12:5 (13d l. 29); the readings from there are noted ⱽ.

46 *Deut.* 24:1: "He shall write her a scroll of divorce and deliver it into her hand."

47 In the Babli, 20a, this statement of the Babylonian Rav Ḥisda is in the name of the Galilean R. Eleazar.

48 On a wax-covered writing tablet (πίναξ), one writes by engraving. The same is true for writing cuneiform on clay tablets. Therefore, engraving can be called "writing".

49 Even though one can produce letters that look as if written, they are not written.

50 Greek μυστήριον "mystery or secret rite". In the parallel sources the word is more appropriately the adjective μυστηρικός "of or for mysteries".

51 This is the meaning of the expression in the Babli, 19a. But the word might also mean "apple juice, fruit juice", from Greek μῆλον "apple, or other fruit".

52 If the ink is washed off the paper, the writing becomes visible.

53 Is pouring a fluid over a paper to make invisible writing visible an act of writing, which is forbidden on the Sabbath?

54 Mishnah *Šabbat* 12:5.

55 In that case, the writing has no visible effect.

56 In the Babli, 19a, this is quoted as the common opinion of R. Joḥanan and R. Simeon ben Laqish.

עֵדִים שֶׁאֵינָן יוֹדְעִין לַחְתוֹם. רֵישׁ לָקִישׁ אָמַר. רוֹשֵׁם לִפְנֵיהֶן בַּדְּיוֹ (44b line 25)
וְהֵן חוֹתְמִין בַּסִּיקְרָא. בַּסִּיקְרָא וְהֵן חוֹתְמִין בַּדְּיוֹ. אָמַר לֵיהּ רִבִּי יוֹחָנָן. מִפְּנֵי
שֶׁאֵינֲנוּ עֲסוּקִין בְּהִילְכוֹת שַׁבָּת אָנוּ מַתִּירִין אֶת אֵשֶׁת אִישׁ. אֶלָּא מֵבִיא נְיָיר
חָלָק וּמְקָרְעַ לִפְנֵיהֶן וְחוֹתְמִין. וְלֹא כְּתַב יָדוֹ שֶׁלָּרִאשׁוֹן הוּא. אֶלָּא מַרְחִיב לָהֶן
אֶת הַקֶּרַע. רִבִּי מָנָא בָעֵי. וְלָמָּה לִינָן אָמְרִין. רוֹשֵׁם לִפְנֵיהֶן בַּמַּיִם. אִם בָּא
וְעִירְעֵר עִרְעוּרוֹ קַייָם. הַקּוֹרֵעַ עַל הָעוֹר כְּתַבְנִית כְּתָב כָּשֵׁר. הָרוֹשֵׁם עַל הָעוֹר
כְּתַבְנִית כְּתָב פָּסוּל.

1 ריש לקיש | גש ר' שמעון בן לקיש   2 והן | ג והם   2-1 רושם לפניהן בדיו . . . . | בדיו |
ג רושם לפניהן בדיו והן רושמין בדיו   3 שאינן | ש שאנו   מתירין | ג מתירים   את |
ש -   4 וחותמין | ש והן חותמין   ומקרע | ג ומקורע   לפניהן | ג לפניהם   אלא | גש -
לחן | ג לפניהם   6 קיים | ש בטל   העור | ג הצור   כשר | ש חייב   העור | ג העיר
7 פסול | ש פטור

If the witnesses do not know how to sign. Rebbi Simeon ben Laqish said, one sketches for them in ink and they sign with vermilion, or with vermilion and they sign in ink. Rebbi Joḥanan told him, because we are occupied[57] with the rules of the Sabbath, should we permit a married woman[58]? But he brings an blank sheet of paper and cuts it before them[59]. Would it not have been the first person's handwriting[60]? One has to widen the cuts. Rebbi Mana said, why do we not say that one sketches for them with water? If he would come and protest, his protest would be accepted[61]. If somebody tears into skin[62] in the form of writing it is valid. If somebody sketches on skin[63] in the form of writing it is invalid.

57 Following the reading in *Šabbat*. The reading of the two texts in *Giṭṭin*, "because they are not occupied", does not make sense. The meaning is also

58 Because writing with ink on vermilion is a desecration of the Sabbath, it does not follow that if illiterate witnesses draw their signatures in ink over vermilion letters that this is valid testimony. As the sentence after the next points out, the witnesses in that case paint the first writer's letters; they do not sign in a way that could be notarized.

59 They draw with a pen along the lines cut into the paper. In the Babli, 19a, this method is attributed to Rav.

60 The objection raised against R. Simeon ben Laqish can also be raised against R. Johanan. But for his method, the objection can be overcome by not cutting lines into the paper but cutting out small strips where the witness has some leeway where to draw his lines which spell his name.

61 If the witnesses just wrote over the letters, irrespective of how these were drawn, the signatures could not be notarized and the husband could claim that there are no signatures. The method indicated by R. Johanan is the only acceptable one.

62 Before it was turned into leather which was used as writing material in those times. Since it is permitted to write with a stylus, a permanent inscription can be made on hide and this is valid.

63 Writing on untanned skin can simply be wiped off; this is not permanent writing and therefore is invalid as stated in the Mishnah. The parallel in *Šabbat* deals with the laws of Sabbath and characterizes the first writing as incurring guilt, because permanent, and the second as not prosecutable, because not permanent.

In the Tosephta, *Giṭṭin* 2:4, *Šabbat* 11:8, the terms "valid, invalid" and "guilty, not prosecutable" are switched.

(44b line 32) הֲרֵי זֶה גִּיטֵיךְ עַל מְנָת שֶׁתִּתְּנֶהוּ לִי. פָּסוּל. עַל מְנָת שֶׁתַּחֲזִירֵהוּ לִי. כָּשֵׁר. וְלֹא דָא הִיא קַדְמָיְיתָא. אָמַר רִבִּי יוֹסֵי. לִכְשֶׁתַּדִּינִי. אָמַר רִבִּי יוֹסֵי בֵּירִבִּי בּוּן. לִכְשֶׁתִּזָּקֵף בּוֹ וּבְמִצְוָתוֹ תַּחֲזֵרֵהוּ לִי. כְּהָדָא תֵּרוּנְגָּא הֲווֹן מְצַפְצְפִין תַּמָּן. וַהֲוָה רַב נַחְמָן בַּר יַעֲקֹב יָהַב תֵּרְנְגָּא מַתָּנָה לִבְרֵיהּ וַאֲמַר לֵיהּ. לִכְשֶׁתִּזָּקֵף בּוֹ וּבְמִצְוָתוֹ תַּחֲזֵרֵהוּ לִי.

1 זה | ג -   2 דא | ג דאמ'   יוסי | ג יוסה   לכשתדיני | ג לכשתרצה   3 בון | ג בין

HALAKHAH 3

לכשתזכה | ג לכשתזכי   ובמוותו | ג ובמצוותיו   כהדא | ג כהדה   תרונגא | ג תרונגיה
4 והוה | ג והווה   תרנגא | ג תרונגה   ואמ' | ג א'

"This is your bill of divorce on condition that you give it to me," is invalid[64]. "On condition that you return it to me," is valid. Is that not the prior case? Rebbi Yose said, after you went to court[65]. Rebbi Yose ben Rebbi Abun said, "after you have acquired all the rights for which it was made, return it to me.[66]" Similar to that: *Etrogim*[67] were scarce over there. Rav Naḥman bar Jacob gave an *etrog* to his son and said to him, if you have acquired it and fulfilled its obligation, return it to me[68].

64 If the bill of divorce has to be returned immediately, there is no divorce. *Deut.* 24:1 requires that the bill of divorce be "given into her hand", i. e., be legally in her power.

65 Once the document has served its purpose, it may be returned without invalidating the divorce. In the Babli, 20b, the formulation is: "'This is your bill of divorce but I remain the owner of the paper' is invalid; 'this is your bill of divorce on condition that you return the paper to me' is valid." Here also it is understood that the paper will be returned only when it is no longer needed.

The Geniza text reads: "after you acquired it." The Leiden text is preferable since for the Geniza text the explanation which follows is unnecessary.

66 He agrees with R. Yose; he only gives the legal formula for what the Babli calls "a transfer of ownership on condition that it be returned." This is everywhere considered a valid transfer of ownership and, therefore, satisfies *Deut.* 24:1.

67 Persian *turungān* (a word of Indian origin) designates all citrus fruits. It was used for *citrus medica*, rabbinic Hebrew *etrôg*, which was identified as the "fruit of the tree of splendor" mentioned in *Lev.* 23:40 together with palm branches, brook willows, and a branch of the thick-leaf tree (traditionally the myrtle).

68 *Lev.* 23:40 reads: "You shall take *for yourselves* on the first day palm branches...". The prescribed ritual can only be fulfilled if the four kinds mentioned are the personal

property of the celebrant. Therefore, if a person gives his "four kinds" to another person for the celebration, it cannot be a loan but must be "a transfer of ownership on condition that it be returned." In Babylonian sources (*Sukkah* 41b, Tosephta *Sukkah* 2:11) the conditional transfer of ownership is a tannaïtic institution.

(44b line 36) רִבִּי יִרְמְיָה בָּעֵי. כְּתָבוֹ עַל כּוֹס שֶׁלְּזָהָב וְאָמַר לָהּ. מְקוֹם הַכְּתָב שֶׁלִּיךְ וּבֵין הַשִּׁיטִים שֶׁלִּי. וְיֵשׁ כְּתָב. עוֹר הַנִּקְרָע הֲרֵי זֶה כָשֵׁר. נִתְקְרַע הֲרֵי זֶה פָסוּל. בְּשֶׁלֹּא נִתְקְרַע קֶרַע בֵּית דִּין. אֲבָל אִם נִקְרַע כְּקֶרַע בֵּית דִּין. אֵי זֶהוּ קֶרַע שֶׁלְּבֵית דִּין. בֵּין כְּתָב לָעֵדִים.

1 לה | ג ליה   2 שלי | ג שלו   כתב | ג כתב פורח   הרי זה | ג הרי   3 בשלא נתקרע | ג נקרע הרי זה פסול בשלא נקרע   בית דין | ג בית דין פסול   אי זהו | ג איזה הוא

Rebbi Jeremiah asked: If he wrote it on a golden cup and said, the writing is yours but the space between the lines belongs to me? Is that writing[69]? Torn leather is valid, if it was torn it is invalid. If it was not torn by the tear of a court, but if it was torn by the tear of a court[70]. What is the tear of a court? Between the text and the witnesses.[71]

69   In the Geniza text: "Does the text fly?" There is no text if there is no space between the letters. In Babylonian sources (Babli 20b, Tosephta 2:5) the formulation is: If he retains ownership of the paper, the bill is invalid.

70   This text clearly is defective. In the Tosephta, 7:11, the text reads: נקרע כשר נתקרע פסול נקרע בו קרע של בית דין פסול "torn is valid, if it was torn it is invalid; if the tear is that of a court it is invalid." The Geniza text is similar. In the opinion of most commentators, the meaning is that a bill of divorce written on a piece of leather that has a tear is valid but if it was torn after the document was written and signed but before it was delivered, it is invalid. In the opinion of S. Lieberman, נתקרע means that the piece of leather had many tears before it was used.

71   If the *ketubah* was paid under

the supervision of the court, the court will tear the bill of divorce to make sure that the divorcee cannot use the bill to collect the *ketubah* a second time in the jurisdiction of another court. Since the witnesses have to sign immediately after the text, to avoid the fraudulent insertion of additional text, a document in which the signatures are separated from the text is automatically invalid.

(44b line 40) עַל הֶעָלֶה שֶׁלַּזַּיִת. וְלֹא כִמְקוּרָע הוּא. אָמַר רִבִּי זְעִירָא. תַּנָּא בִּינָה שִׁילוֹח. אֲפִילוּ כּוֹתֵב. אֲנִי פְלוֹנִי מְגָרֵשׁ אֶת אִשְׁתִּי. כָּשֵׁר. וְאַתְיָיא כֵיי דְּמַר רִבִּי אִילָא. אִם פֵּירֵשׁ פָּסוּל. וְאִם לֹא פֵירֵשׁ כָּשֵׁר.

1 תנא | ג תנה   2 שילוח | ג בר שילה   3 פירש | ג פרש

"On a leaf of the olive tree." Is that not like torn[72]? Rebbi Zeʿira said, Bina bar Shila[73] stated: Even if he only wrote: "I X am divorcing my wife,[74]" it is valid. This follows what Rebbi Ila said, if he detailed it is invalid[75], if he did not detail[76] it is valid.

72 The leaf is much to small for the text of the bill, even if written in miniature letters.

73 Text of the Geniza ms. and the Constantinople print.

74 The name of the wife must be mentioned, the fact that she is his wife then need not be mentioned; the fact of the divorce must be mentioned.

75 If the full text is written it must comply with all rules to be valid.

76 If he only wrote his and her names and the fact of the divorce.

(44b line 43) עַל הַקֶּרֶן שֶׁלַּפָּרָה. מַתְנִיתָא כְּשֶׁאָמַר לָהּ. הֲרֵי גִיטִּיךְ. אֲבָל אִם אָמַר לָהּ. הֲרֵי גִיטִּיךְ וְהַשְׁאָר לִכְתוּבָּתֵיךְ. נִתְקַבְּלָה גִיטָּהּ וּכְתוּבָתָהּ כְּאַחַת. אָמַר לָהּ. הֲרֵי גִיטִּיךְ וּכְתוּבָּתֵיךְ כְּאַחַת. רִבִּי זְעִירָא בָעֵי רִבִּי מָנָא. מָסַר לָהּ בִּמְסִירָה מַהוּ. מִיַּדַּת הַדִּין אַתְּ אָמַר נִקְנֶה הַמָּקַח. וְהָכָא אַתְּ אָמַר הָכֵין. אוֹ שַׁנְיָיא הִיא. דִּכְתִיב וְנָתַן בְּיָדָהּ. עַד שֶׁיְּהֵא כוּלּוֹ בְּיָדָהּ.

1 כשאמר | ג בשאמר   2 לכתבתיך | ג לכתובתך   3 לה | ג ליה   וכתובתיך | ג

וכתובה   זעירא | ג עזרא   בעי | ג באה קומי   4 במוסירה מהו | ג במוסרה מהוא
המקח | ג המקנה   והכא | ג והכה   הכין | ג אכין

"On a cow's horn." The Mishnah[77] in case he says to her, here is your bill of divorce. But if he says to her, here is your bill of divorce and the remainder is for your *ketubah*, her bill of divorce and the payment of her *ketubah* were received together[78]. If he said to her, here is your bill of divorce and the payment of your *ketubah* together[79]? Rebbi Ezra[80] asked before Rebbi Mana: If he delivered the halter to her, what[81]? In commercial law, the buy is acquired, do you say so here[79]? Or is it a difference since it is written: "he shall deliver into her hand," until it is completely in her hand[82]!

77   Which requires that the cow be delivered to the wife as bill of divorce.

78   The moment she accepts the horns carrying the bill of divorce, she acquires the animal as part payment of the *ketubah*. There is a small problem here which is not mentioned in either Talmud: A bill of divorce can be given to a wife against her will but the *ketubah* can be delivered in merchandise, instead of coin, only with her consent. Since transfer of property of an animal *always* requires an act of acquisition, the husband who writes the bill of divorce on the horns of a cow gives up his right to unilateral divorce.

79   In the first case, the payment of the *ketubah* was a consequence of the delivery of the bill of divorce. As it is explained at the end of the paragraph, one may interpret the verse as meaning that the bill of divorce has to come into the wife's hand unconditionally, not as part of an acquisition of anything else. In this opinion, the requirement that the payment of the *ketubah* be simultaneous with the divorce, not a consequence of the divorce, invalidates the proceedings. In the Babli, 20b, the example is a bill of divorce engraved on a plate of gold and Rav Naḥman states that the simultaneous delivery of divorce document and *ketubah* is valid, in contrast to the conclusion of the Yerushalmi.

80 Reading of the Geniza. The reading of the Leiden ms., R. Ze'ira, cannot refer to R. Ze'ira, the head of the Academy of Tiberias, who lived in the second generation after R. Mana I and two generations before R. Mana II. A R. זְעוּרָה, student of R. Mana I, is quoted a few times in other places in the Yerushalmi.

81 A bridled animal can be acquired by the buyer by taking the halter in his hand and causing the animal to walk one step at his command.

82 The bill of divorce has to come into the wife's hand by being delivered by the husband, not by an active act of acquisition on her part. The formulation of this paragraph implies that this delivery of a bill of divorce is classified as invalid.

(44b line 48) וּמָה טַעֲמָא דְרִבִּי יוֹסֵי הַגְּלִילִי. סֵפֶר. מַה סֵפֶר מְיוּחָד שָׁאֵין בּוֹ רוּחַ חַיִּים אַף כָּל־דָּבָר שָׁאֵין בּוֹ רוּחַ חַיִּים. מַה סֵפֶר שָׁאֵינוֹ אוֹכֵל אַף כָּל־דָּבָר שָׁאֵינוֹ אוֹכֵל. מַה טַעֲמָא דְרַבָּנִין. סֵפֶר. מַה סֵפֶר שֶׁהוּא בְתָלוּשׁ אַף כָּל־דָּבָר שֶׁהוּא בְתָלוּשׁ. עַל דַּעְתֵּיהּ דְּרִבִּי יוֹסֵי הַגְּלִילִי יָדוֹת הָאוֹכְלִין כְּאוֹכְלִין. נִשְׁמְעִינָה מִן הָדָא. כְּתָבוֹ עַל קֶרֶן צְבִי גְרָדוֹ וַחֲתָמוֹ וּנְתָנוֹ לָהּ כָּשֵׁר. מִפְּנֵי שֶׁגְּרָדוֹ וְאַחַר כָּךְ חֲתָמוֹ. הָא אִם חֲתָמוֹ וְאַחַר כָּךְ גְּרָדוֹ לֹא. רִבִּי בָּא בְשֵׁם רִבִּי מְיָישָׁא. וְהוּא שֶׁכָּתַב עַל זִכְרוּתוֹ שֶׁלַּקֶּרֶן. אֲבָל אִם כָּתַב עַל נַרְתֵּיקוֹ כְּפָרוּשׁ הוּא וְכָשֵׁר. רִבִּי יוֹנָה בָּעֵי. אַף לְהַכְשֵׁר זְרָעִים כֵּן. חָשַׁב שֶׁיֵּרְדוּ עַל הַבְּהֵמָה וּמִן הַבְּהֵמָה עַל הָאוֹכְלִים. תַּמָּן אָמַר רִבִּי יוֹסֵי הַגְּלִילִי. סֵפֶר. מַה סֵפֶר מְיוּחָד שָׁאֵין בּוֹ רוּחַ חַיִּים אַף כָּל־דָּבָר שָׁאֵין בּוֹ רוּחַ חַיִּים. וְהָכָא הוּא אָמַר אָכֵן. אוֹ שַׁנְיָיא הִיא. דִּכְתִיב וְכָל־מַשְׁקֶה אֲשֶׁר יִשָּׁתֶה בְּכָל־כְּלִי יִטְמָא. מֵעַתָּה אֲפִילוּ חִישֵׁב שֶׁיֵּרְדוּ לְבוֹרוֹת שִׁיחִין וּמְעָרוֹת. שַׁנְיָיא הִיא הָכָא. דִּכְתִיב כְּלִי.

3 טעמא דרבנין | ג טעם ודרבנין   4 האוכלין כאוכלין | ג האוכלים כאוכלים   5 הדא | ג הדה   גרדו | ג גררו (3 times)   וחתמו | ג וחיתמו (3 times)   6 בא | ג אחא   7 זכרותו | ג זיכרותו   כפרוש | ג כפירוש   8 להכשר | ג לעינין הכשר   9 האוכלים | ג האכלים   10 והכא | ג והכה   שנייא היא | ג שנייה   11 וכל משקה . . . | כלי טמא | ג ומשקה שכל טמא   חישב | ג חשב   12 לבורות שיחין | ג לבירות לשיחין   שנייא היא הכא | ג שנייה היא הכה

What is Rebbi Yose the Galilean's reason? "Scroll." Since a scroll is special in not being a living being, so no living being. Since a scroll is not food, so no food[83]. What is the rabbis' reason? "Scroll." Since a scroll is detached, so everything detached[84]. Are stalks of food in Rebbi Yose the Galilean's opinion like food[85]? Let us hear from the following: If he wrote it on a deer's antlers[86], shaved it off, had it signed, and gave it to him[87], it is valid. Because he shaved it off before he had it signed. Therefore, not if he had it signed and afterwards shaved it off[88]. Rebbi Abba[89] in the name of Rebbi Miasha: Only if he wrote on the male horn[90]. But if he wrote on the sheath[91] it is as if separated[92] and is valid. Rebbi Jonah asked: Is that the same for preparation of produce[93]? If he desired that it should rain on an animal and [the rain] dropped from the animal on food[94]. There, Rebbi Yose said "a scroll", since a scroll is special in not being a living being, so no living being; and here, does he say so[95]? There is a difference since it is written[96], "any drinkable drink in any vessel shall be impure". Then also if it rained into cisterns, ditches and caves? There is a difference here, for it is written: "a vessel"[97].

83 The same argument in the Babli, 21a. The interpretation of the rabbis' position is quite different in the Babli.

84 This refers to Mishnah 4 where it is stated that a bill of divorce cannot be written on anything connected to the ground. The bill of divorce cannot be written on the walls of a house and the house given to the wife.

85 The stalks of fruits which usually are harvested together with the fruits have the status of fruits in the laws of impurity; this is the theme of Tractate *Uqeṣin*. The question is whether R. Yose the Galilean will forbid these inedible stalks as materials for bills of divorce since they are subject to the impurities of foodstuffs.

86 This *baraita* must be attributed to R. Yose the Galilean since for the rabbis the entire deer could have been given to the wife. The antlers are

inedible bony structures attached to the living deer just as stalks are inedible wooden structures attached to fruits.

87   This should be "her", correctly in the Geniza text. As explained in the next Halakhah, "signing" covers not only the signatures of the witnesses but also the insertion of the necessary data into the formulaic text; cf. Note 100.

88   This proves that the antler is an integral part of the deer for R. Yose the Galilean. It is reasonable to assume that a stalk for him is an integral part of the fruit.

This rule also follows the rabbis of Mishnah 4 whose position is explained in the Babli (21b) from *Deut.* 24:1: "he writes and hands over to her" that no necessary action may intervene between signing and delivery of the document.

89   In the Geniza text: Aḥa. While it is known that R. Aḥa was a student of R. Miasha's, the reading of the Leiden ms. cannot be rejected out of hand since Rabbis Abba and Aḥa were contemporaries.

90   This refers to horns of cattle and goats rather than deer. These horns consist of a horny sheath (the female horn) over a bony spur (the male).

91   Greek νάρθηξ; cf. *Berakhot* 5:2, Note 67.

92   The rabbis of Mishnah 4 would certainly object and require that the entire animal be handed over to the wife; cf. Note 88.

93   While food is under rules of impurity that are much stricter than those for vessels, etc., harvesting alone does not transform produce into food for these rules; only intentional moistening will have that effect, cf. *Demay* 2:3, Note 136-141.

94   In this case, the moistening was desired by him for the animal but not for the food. Mishnah *Makhširin* reads: Any fluid which at the start is desired, even if at the end it is not desired, or if at the end is desired, even if at the start it was not desired, fulfills the condition "that it be given" (i.e., it prepares for impurity by the terms of *Lev.* 11:38: "If water be given on seeds . . . it shall be impure for you".) For the anonymous rabbis it is obvious that drops from water which was desired for the animal will prepare food for impurity by this Mishnah. But R. Yose the Galilean, who disqualifies animals as writing materials for bills of divorce, might equate animals to things connected to the soil which are disqualified for bills of divorce in Mishnah 4, and for objects of desire

which act in impurity as explained in the following.

95   Does he exclude animals from the category of objects which prepare for impurity if watered? There seems to be no reason why this should be so.

96   Lev. 11:34.

97   A similar text is in *Sifra Šemini Parašah* 8(2): "I could think also [if it rained] into cisterns, ditches and caves? It is written: 'a vessel'; since one of the characteristics of a vessel is that it is separated from the ground, so only things separated from the ground." Everybody agrees that water collected in cisterns, etc., does not prepare for impurity; the reason for this has nothing to do with the controversy over writing materials.

(fol. 44a) **משנה ד**: אֵין כּוֹתְבִין בִּמְחוּבָּר לַקַּרְקַע. כְּתָבוֹ בִּמְחוּבָּר תְּלָשׁוֹ וַחֲתָמוֹ וּנְתָנוֹ לָהּ כָּשֵׁר. וְרִבִּי יְהוּדָה פּוֹסֵל עַד שֶׁתְּהֵא כְּתִיבָתוֹ וַחֲתִימָתוֹ בְּתָלוּשׁ. רִבִּי יְהוּדָה בֶּן בָּתִירָא אוֹמֵר אֵין כּוֹתְבִין לֹא עַל הַנְּיָיר מָחוּק וְלֹא עַל הַדִּיפְתְּרָא מִפְּנֵי שֶׁהוּא יָכוֹל לְהִזְדַּיֵּיף וַחֲכָמִים מַכְשִׁירִין.

Mishnah 4: One does not write on anything connected to the ground. If he wrote on anything connected, detached it, signed,[98] and delivered it, it is valid, but Rebbi Jehudah declares it invalid unless both writing and signing took place when it was detached. Rebbi Jehudah ben Bathyra says, one writes neither on erased papyrus nor on διφθέρα[99] because these can be falsified but the Sages declare valid.

98   Not only affixed the signatures of the witnesses but also inserted the essential data of the document; cf. Note 100.

99   In Mishnaic usage, hide incompletely tanned; cf. *Soṭah* 2:6, Note 151. The hide does not absorb the ink which can be wiped off without leaving a trace.

(44b line 61) **הלכה ד:** אֵין כּוֹתְבִין בִּמְחוּבָּר לַקַּרְקַע כול'. לֵית הָא פְּלִיגָא עַל רִבִּי יוֹחָנָן. דְּרִבִּי יוֹחָנָן אָמַר. כָּתַב תָּרְפּוֹ בַּטוֹפֶס כָּשֵׁר. רֵישׁ לָקִישׁ אָמַר. כָּתַב תָּרְפּוֹ כַּטוֹפֶס פָּסוּל. שְׁמוּאֵל בַּר אַבָּא בָּעֵי. כְּתָבוֹ וַחֲתָמוֹ בְּתָלוּשׁ. חִיבְּרוֹ וּתְלָשׁוֹ וּנְתָנוֹ לָהּ. מַה אָמַר בָּהּ רִבִּי יוּדָה. רִבִּי אֶלְעָזָר אָמַר. רִבִּי אָבִין בָּעֵי. כְּתָבוֹ וַחֲתָמוֹ בְּתָלוּשׁ חִיבְּרוֹ וַחֲתָמוֹ תְּלָשׁוֹ וּנְתָנוֹ לָהּ. מַה אָמְרִין בָּהּ רַבָּנִין.

1 לקרקע כול' | ג - פליגא | ג פליגה | - ג ר' זעירה אמ' בהדה פליגין ר' יוחנן א' | 2
כתב תרפו בטפס כשר ריש לקיש | ג ר' שמעון בן לקיש 3 כטופס | ג בטרפס אבא |
ג אבה כתבו וחתמו | ג כיתבו וחיתמו 4 ותלשו | ג ותילשו אלעזר | ג ליעזר וחתמו
| ג וחיתמו (2 times)

Halakhah 4: "One does not write on anything connected to the ground," etc. This does not disagree with Rebbi Joḥanan, since Rebbi Joḥanan said, writing the essential text with the formula is valid[100,101]. Rebbi Simeon ben Laqish said, writing the essential text with the formula is invalid. Samuel bar Abba asked: If he wrote and signed it when detached, then he connected it again, detached it, and delivered it to her; what does Rebbi Jehudah say[102]? Rebbi Eleazar said, Rebbi Abin asked: If he wrote and signed it when detached, then he connected again, signed, and detached it, and delivered it to her; what do the rabbis say[103]?

100 This refers to Mishnah 3:2, in which permission is given to scribes to prepare the formulaic text of divorce documents, so that only the names of husband and wife and the date have to be inserted, without violating the commandment that the document be written specifically for the woman concerned. It is not mentioned in the Mishnah whether the text which turns the document into one of divorce, "this is your bill of divorce and you are permitted to every man" is part of the formulaic text or has to be written with that particular woman in mind. R. Joḥanan permits this sentence to be written as a formula, R. Simeon ben Laqish prohibits. (In the Babli, 21b, the attributions are switched, probably because the Babli insists that practice

follow R. Johanan.) In the interpretation of the Babli, the divorce formula may be prepared in advance for R. Eleazar, for whom only the witnesses to the delivery of the text are important, but not for R. Meïr, for whom the witnesses signing the document are those who validate the divorce. It is impossible to know whether the Yerushalmi would agree to this interpretation.

101 The Geniza text has a longer sentence: "R. Ze'ira said, they disagree in this, R. Johanan said, writing the essential text with the formula is valid, R. Simeon ben Laqish said . . . " This text adds no new information.

102 Since the bill was written according to the rules, does a later unnecessary action invalidate the document? No answer is given; it is difficult to see why the answer should be "valid".

103 This text seems to be self-contradictory since "signing" is mentioned twice. It is difficult to amend the text against the concurrent testimony of the ms. sources available. *Sefer ha'Ittur* I 26a, quotes an identical text for both questions, one addressed to R. Jehudah and one to the rabbis. Rashba (*Novellae ad* 21b, end) reads in the question addressed to the rabbis: If he wrote it when detached, attached, signed, detached, and delivered it, what do the rabbis say? In this case the obvious answer is: invalid. The text as it stands can be interpreted to mean that the bill was written when detached, including date, both names, and the statement that it was a divorce document which freed the wife to marry any man, but that the witnesses signed when it was attached to the ground. Then it would be invalid for R. Meïr and valid for R. Eleazar the Tanna.

(44b line 66) אָמַר רִבִּי אֶלְעָזָר. מַה פְּלִיגִין. בְּגִיטִין. אֲבָל בִּשְׁטָרוֹת אוּף רִבִּי יוּדָה מוֹדֶה. דִּי פָתַר לָהּ שְׁטָר עַל הֶחָלָק וְעֵדִים עַל הַמַּחַק. רִישׁ לָקִישׁ אָמַר. לֹא שַׁנְיָיה הִיא. בֵּין בְּגִיטִין בֵּין בִּשְׁטָרוֹת הִיא הַמַּחֲלוֹקֶת. דִּי פָתַר לָהּ שְׁטָר עַל הֶחָלָק וְעֵדִים עַל הַמַּחַק. וְקַשְׁיָא. אָמַר לוֹ. עַל דְּרִבִּי לִיעֶזֶר. אִם בְּעֵדִים עַל הַמַּחַק בְּדָא חֲכָמִים מַכְשִׁירִין. אָמַר רִבִּי זְעִירָא קוֹמֵי רִבִּי מָנָא. חֲכָמִים שֶׁהֵן בְּשִׁיטַת רִבִּי אֱלִיעֶזֶר. דִּי פָתַר לָהּ שְׁטָר עַל הַמַּחַק וְעֵדִים עַל הֶחָלָק. שְׁמוּאֵל

אָמַר. זֶה וָזֶה עַל הַמַּחַק. יָאוּת אָמַר רִבִּי יְהוּדָה. וּמַה טַעֲמָא דְרַבָּנִין. אָמַר
רִבִּי אַבָּא. נִיכָּר הוּא אִם נִמְחַק פַּעַם אַחַת וְאִם נִמְחַק שְׁתֵּי פְעָמִים.

1 אלעזר | ג ליעזר   2 די | ע דו   ריש לקיש | גע ר' שמעון בן לקיש   4 וקשיא | ג
וקשיה   אמ' לח | גע -   ליעזר | ג לעזר ע אלעזר   5 בדא הכמים מכשירין | ג בדה
חכמים מכשירים   6 אליעזר | ג לעזר ע אלעזר   7 יהודה | ע יוסי   ומה | ג ומאי
8 שתי | גע שני

[104]Rebbi Eleazar[105] said, where do they disagree? About bills of divorce. But for contracts even Rebbi Jehudah will agree[106]. He explains it if the document is on a smooth surface and the witnesses on the erasure[107]. Rebbi Simeon ben Laqish said, it makes no difference; they disagree both about bills of divorce and contracts[108]. He explains it if the document is on a smooth surface and the witnesses on the erasure. It is difficult for Rebbi Eleazar: If the witnesses [sign] on the erasure, do the Sages declare it valid[109]? Rebbi Ze'ira[80] said before Rebbi Mana: The Sages follow the argument of Rebbi Eleazar[110], for he explains that the document is on the erasure and the witnesses on a smooth surface[111]. Samuel said, everything is on the erasure[112]. Does not Rebbi Jehudah say it correctly? Rebbi Abba said, it is recognizable whether there was an erasure once or twice[113].

104 This paragraph is also in *Sefer ha'Ittur* 26d (Note 52); the variant readings are given by ע. While medieval authors cannot be expected always to quote exactly, the text is quoted as support for the Geniza readings.

105 The Amora.

106 In the Babli, 22b, R. Eleazar says that the Sages agree with R. Jehudah that contracts may not be written as palimpsests or on erasable leather.

107 Then the document cannot be forged and one hopes that the signatures can be verified either by the signers or by comparing the signatures with those on other known documents.

108 In the Babli, 22b, this is

attributed to R. Joḥanan.

109   It is difficult to agree that the signatures cannot be forged.

110   The Tanna who dismisses the signatures on the bill of divorce as irrelevant and requires delivery of the bill in the presence of witnesses to the delivery. This is the explanation of the Babli in the name of the Amora R. Eleazar.

111   The witnesses to the delivery must read the document before delivery to verify that it is what it is declared to be. They would detect a forgery.

112   The entire document is a palimpsest. This explanation is implied by the language of the Mishnah; such a document is declared valid in the Babli (*Baba batra* 163a) in the name of Rav.

113   The editors of the Babli agree, *Baba batra* 164a.

(fol. 44a) **משנה ה:** הַכֹּל כְּשֵׁירִין לִכְתּוֹב אֶת הַגֵּט אֲפִילוּ שׁוֹטֶה חֵרֵשׁ וְקָטָן. הָאִשָּׁה כּוֹתֶבֶת אֶת גִּיטָהּ וְהָאִישׁ כּוֹתֵב אֶת שׁוֹבְרוֹ שֶׁאֵין קִיּוּם הַגֵּט אֶלָּא בְחוֹתְמָיו. הַכֹּל כְּשֵׁרִין לְהָבִיא אֶת הַגֵּט חוּץ מִשּׁוֹטֶה חֵרֵשׁ קָטָן וְסוֹמָא וְנָכְרִי.

Mishnah 5: Everybody is acceptable to write the bill of divorce, even an insane, a deaf-and-dumb, or a minor[114]. The wife may write her bill of divorce[115] and a man his receipt[116], for the certification of the bill of divorce is only effected by its signatures. Everybody is acceptable to bring the bill of divorce except an insane, a deaf-and-dumb, a minor, a blind person[117], or a Gentile.[118]

114   As explained in the Halakha, they may write only the formulaic text which does not have to be written specifically for the divorcing couple. This justifies the inclusion of the deaf-and-dumb.

115   She has to hand the completed bill to her husband who must have it signed by the witnesses and return it to her in front of witnesses.

155   The debtor who pays his debt may present the creditor with a receipt

which the latter signs. The text of the receipt does not have to be in the creditor's hand.

117 It is explained in the Babli that the blind person is disqualified only for bills of divorce transported across the border since he cannot affirm that he saw its writing and signing.

118 Since the rules of divorce are biblical, they can be fulfilled only by a person subject to the biblical rules.

(44b line 74) **הלכה ה:** הַכֹּל כְּשֵׁירִין לִכְתּוֹב אֶת הַגֵּט כּוֹל'. רַב הוּנָא אָמַר. וְהוּא שֶׁהָיָה פִּיקֵחַ עוֹמֵד עַל גַּבָּיו. רִבִּי יוֹחָנָן אָמַר. וְהִכְתִיב וְכָתַב לָהּ. לִשְׁמָהּ. שְׁמוּאֵל אָמַר. צָרִיךְ שֶׁיַּנִּיחַ תָּרְפּוֹ שֶׁלַּגֵּט עִמּוֹ. וְאַתְיָיא כַּיי דָּמַר רֵישׁ לָקִישׁ. כָּתַב תָּרְפּוֹ בַּטּוֹפֶס פָּסוּל.

1 כשירין | ג כשרים   לכתוב את הגט כול' | ג -   2 והוא | ג והא   אמר | ג בעי   והכת'
| ג והא הוא   3 עמו | ג עימו   ריש לקיש | ג ר' שמעון בן לקיש   4 בטופס | ג בטפס

Halakhah 5: "Everybody is acceptable to write the bill of divorce," etc. Rav Huna said, only if a sane person watches over them[119]. Rebbi Johanan asked[120]: But is it not written: "He shall write for her," in her name[5]? Samuel said, it is necessary that one reserve the essential text for him[121]. This follows what Rebbi Simeon ben Laqish said, writing the essential text with the formula is invalid[100].

119 If an incompetent person (insane, deaf-and-dumb, or minor) writes the text, they must be directed by a person who knows for what they write. The same statement is in the Babli, 22b/23a.

120 The translation follows the Geniza text and *Sefer ha'Iṭṭur* (27b).

121 The essential text must be written by a responsible person under the husband's direction. The Babli agrees, 23a.

(fol. 44a) **משנה ו**: קִבֵּל הַקָּטָן וְהִגְדִּיל. חֵרֵשׁ וְנִתְפַּקֵּחַ. סוֹמָא וְנִתְפַּתֵּחַ. שׁוֹטֶה וְנִשְׁתַּפָּה נָכְרִי וְנִתְגַּיֵּיר פָּסוּל.

Mishnah 6: If the minor received it and became an adult, the deaf-and-dumb and started talking, the blind and became seeing, the insane and became sane, the Gentile and converted, it remains invalid[122].

משנה ז: אֲבָל פִּיקֵּחַ וְנִתְחָרֵשׁ וְחָזַר וְנִשְׁתַּפָּה פִּיתֵּחַ וְנִסְתַּמָּא וְחָזַר וְנִתְפַּתֵּחַ שָׁפוּי וְנִשְׁתַּטָּא וְחָזַר וְנִשְׁתַּפָּה כָּשֵׁר. זֶה הַכְּלָל כָּל־שֶׁתְּחִילָּתוֹ וְסוֹפוֹ בְּדַעַת כָּשֵׁר.

Mishnah 7: But if a hearing person became deaf-and-dumb, then regained his hearing, a seeing person became blind, then regained his vision, a sane person became insane, then regained his sanity, it is valid. This is the principle: Whenever the beginning and the end was in full competence, it is valid[123].

122 Since *Deut.* 24:1 requires that the husband hand the divorce document over to his wife, he can be represented in this transaction only by a duly appointed representative. But since an incompetent person cannot be a representative, nor a Gentile be an agent in a Jewish religious transaction, any such delivery could not be considered as the husband's.

123 Even if there was an interval in which delivery could not be made, on condition that the responsible person remember his appointment as the husband's representative.

(44c line 2) **הלכה ו**: קִיבֵּל הַקָּטָן וְהִגְדִּיל כול׳. אָתָא עוֹבְדָא קוֹמֵי רִבִּי אִימִּי בְּעֶבֶד שֶׁהֵבִיא אֶת הַגֵּט כָּשֵׁר. אָמַר לֵיהּ רִבִּי אַבָּא. וְהָתַנֵּי רִבִּי חִייָה. עֶבֶד שֶׁהֵבִיא אֶת הַגֵּט פָּסוּל. אָמַר רִבִּי אַסִי. אִילוּלֵי רִבִּי בָּא כְּבָר הָיִינוּ לְהַתִּיר אֶת אֵשֶׁת אִישׁ. וַאֲפִילוּ תֵימַר. לֹא שְׁמִיעַ רִבִּי אַסִי הָא דְּתַנֵּי רִבִּי חִייָה. לֹא שְׁמִיעַ מִילֵּיהוֹן דְּרַבָּנִין. נִישְׁמְעִינָהּ מִן הָדָא דְּאָמַר רִבִּי זְעִירָא רִבִּי חִייָה בְּשֵׁם רִבִּי יוֹחָנָן. נִרְאִין דְּבָרִים שֶׁיְּקַבֵּל הָעֶבֶד גֵּט שִׁיחְרוּר וְאַל יְקַבֵּל כְּווֹתֵיהּ. סָבְרִין מֵימַר. לֹא אָמַר אֶלָּא אַל יְקַבֵּל. הָא אִם עָבַר וְקִיבֵּל כָּשֵׁר. רִבִּי יַעֲקֹב בַּר אָחָא בְּשֵׁם רַב הוֹשַׁעְיָה. מַעֲשֶׂה הָיָה וְכֹהֶנֶת הָיְיתָה וְלֹא חָשׁוּ לָהֶן מִשּׁוּם רֵיחַ פָּסוּל.

3 אסי | ג אמי 4 אסי | ג אימי 5 הדא | ג הדה 6 נראין | ג נראים שיקבל | ג
שקיבל שיחרור | ג שחרור כותיך | ג גט כותין 7 אלא | ג - 8 הייתה | ג היית
להן משום | ג להם משם

Halakhah 6: "If the minor received it and became an adult," etc. There came a case before Rebbi Immi that a slave brought a bill of divorce; [he declared it] valid[124]. Rebbi Abba said to him, did not Rebbi Hiyya[125] state that if a slave brought a bill of divorce, it would be invalid? Rebbi Assi[126] said, if not for Rebbi Abba, we would have permitted a married woman[127]! Even if you say that Rebbi Assi did not accept what Rebbi Hiyya stated, did he not accept what the rabbis said? Let us hear from the following which Rebbi Ze'ira, Rebbi Hiyya[128] said in the name of Rebbi Johanan: It is reasonable that a slave could accept a bill of manumission [for delivery][129] but he should not accept [a bill of divorce] as we do[130]. They thought, he formulated "he should not accept," therefore, if he transgressed and accepted, it would be valid[131]. Rebbi Jacob bar Aha in the name of Rav Hoshaiah: It happened that she was a Cohen's wife[132] and they were not afraid of a hint of invalidity[133].

124 In the Babli, 23a, this was a theoretical question and R. Assi was the opponent.

125 R. Hiyya the Elder.

126 This is the Babylonian name of R. Yasa, the constant companion of R. Immi. The version of the Geniza ms. which reads "R. Immi" for all occurrences of "R. Assi" is preferable.

127 A woman who receives an invalid bill of divorce remains married to her husband.

128 R. Hiyya bar Abba, student of R. Johanan and teacher of R. Ze'ira. In the Babli, 23b, this is quoted by Rav Samuel bar Jehudah in the name of R. Johanan.

129 He can bring another slave's bill of manumission since he himself may be manumitted. In the Babli this is restricted to another owner's slave.

130 Translation of the Geniza text,

supported by the Leiden ms. in *Qiddušin* 1:3, 60a l. 50. Since a slave cannot legally marry, he cannot divorce and like a Gentile is barred from acting in a divorce proceeding. R. Immi, who initially accepted the bill of divorce, must have held with R. Meïr that the slave's hand is his master's hand (*Qiddušin* 1:3, 60a l. 49).

131   It is not formulated as an absolute impossibility.

132   Since a Cohen may not be married to a divorcee (*Lev.* 21:7), in all cases in which there may be the slightest doubt about the validity of a divorce given by a Cohen, the court will force the husband to give a second, unquestionably valid divorce.

133   They declared the bill of divorce in the hand of the slave as non-existent and permitted the wife to stay married to her Cohen husband.

(fol. 44a) **משנה ח:** אַף הַנָּשִׁים שֶׁאֵינָן נֶאֱמָנוֹת לוֹמַר מֵת בַּעְלָהּ נֶאֱמָנוֹת לְהָבִיא אֶת גִּיטָהּ חֲמוֹתָהּ וּבַת חֲמוֹתָהּ וְצָרָתָהּ וִיבִמְתָּהּ וּבַת בַּעְלָהּ. מַה בֵּין גֵּט לְמִיתָה. שֶׁהַכְּתָב מוֹכִיחַ. הָאִשָּׁה עַצְמָהּ מְבִיאָה אֶת גִּיטָהּ וּבִלְבַד שֶׁיְּהֵא צְרִיכָה לוֹמַר בְּפָנַי נִכְתַּב וּבְפָנַי נִתְחַתֵּם.

Mishnah 8: Even women who cannot be believed if they say that [a woman's] husband died are trustworthy to bring her bill of divorce: Her mother-in-law, her mother-in-law's daughter, her co-wife, her sister-in-law, and her husband's daughter[134]. What is the difference between divorce and death? The writing is the proof. A woman may herself bring her own bill of divorce, but she still is required to say that it was written and signed before her.

134   These are presumed to hate her, Mishnah *Yebamot* 15:4; it is assumed that they would not mind tricking her into adultery.

(44c line 10) **הלכה ח:** אַף הַנָּשִׁים שֶׁאֵינָן נֶאֱמָנוֹת לוֹמַר. מֵת בַּעֲלָהּ כול'. אֲפִילוּ נִכְתַּב וְלֹא נֶחְתַּם מַאֲמִינִים אוֹתָהּ. שֶׁאִילוּ לֹא אָמְרָה. בְּפָנַיי נִכְתַּב וּבְפָנַיי נֶחְתַּם. אַף אַתָּה מַתִּירָהּ לְהִינָּשֵׂא. אָמַר רִבִּי יוֹסֵי בֵּירִבִּי בּוּן. כַּיי דָּמַר רִבִּי אָבִין. אֵינוֹ חָשׁוּד לְקַלְקְלָהּ בִּידֵי שָׁמַיִם. בְּבֵית דִּין הוּא חָשׁוּד לְקַלְקְלָהּ. שֶׁמִּתּוֹךְ שֶׁהוּא יוֹדֵעַ שֶׁאִם בָּא וְעִירֵר עֲרָרוֹ בָּטֵל אַף הוּא מַחְתִּמוֹ בְעֵדִים כְּשִׁירִים.

2 נכתב ולא נחתם | ג ובכתב ולא מיפים י ולא מפיה   3 אתה | ג אין את י את שמא   ר' יוסי ביר' בון | ג ר' יוסה בר' בין   כיי | י כההיא   5 ועירר עררו | ג וערר עררו י ועדיו עמו   6 כשירים | ג כשרין

Halakhah 8: "Also those women who cannot be believed if they say that [a woman's] husband died," etc. [135]Would you believe her if it was written but not signed [in her presence]? If she did not say 'it was written in my presence, it was signed in my presence', would you permit her to remarry[136]? Rebbi Yose ben Rebbi Abun said, that parallels what Rebbi Abun said, he is not suspect to damage her before Heaven. Before the court he is suspect to damage her. But since he knows that if he comes and protests, his protest is void, he will choose qualified witnesses to sign[137].

135 This paragraph is also in *Yebamot* 15:4, explained there in Notes 91-94. The variants are denoted by י.
136 Therefore, it is not the text which allows the wife to remarry but the other woman's testimony.

137 An additional sentence, extant in *Yebamot*, is missing here to the effect that if one of these women would recant her testimony she also would not be believed.

(44c line 15) הַגַּע עַצְמָךְ שֶׁעָשְׂתָה עֶשֶׂר שָׁנִים בְּרוֹמִי וְנִישֵּׂאת. אָמַר רִבִּי יוֹחָנָן. מַתְנִיתָהּ כְּשֶׁאָמַר לָהּ. אַל תִּיגָּרְשִׁי אֶלָּא בְּמָקוֹם פְּלוֹנִי.

2 כשאמ' | ג בשא'   תיגרשי | ג תגרשי בו

Think of it, if she stayed in Rome ten years and remarried[138]! Rebbi Joḥanan said, the Mishnah if he said to her, you shall only be divorced [by this document] at place X[139].

138 Since the woman is divorced once the bill is delivered into her hands, does the Mishnah mean that a woman married for the second time has to keep her bill of divorce and show it to the local court any time she moves to a new location? This is impossible since the bill is torn up by the court once the *ketubah* was paid to her in full.

139 She is divorced as soon as she declares at her place of destination that the bill was written and signed in her presence. The Babli, 24a, agrees after a lengthy and tortuous discussion.

כל גט פרק שלישי

משנה א: כָּל־גֵּט שֶׁנִּכְתַּב שֶׁלֹּא לְשֵׁם אִשָּׁה פָּסוּל. כֵּיצַד הָיָה עוֹבֵר (fol. 44c) בַּשּׁוּק וְשָׁמַע קוֹל הַסּוֹפְרִים מַקְרִים אִישׁ פְּלוֹנִי מְגָרֵשׁ אֶת אִשְׁתּוֹ פְּלוֹנִית מִמָּקוֹם פְּלוֹנִי. וְאָמַר זֶה שְׁמִי וְזֶה שֵׁם אִשְׁתִּי פָּסוּל מִלְּגָרֵשׁ בּוֹ. יוֹתֵר מִיכֵּן כָּתַב לְגָרֵשׁ אֶת אִשְׁתּוֹ וְנִמְלַךְ מְצָאוֹ בֶּן עִירוֹ וְאָמַר לוֹ שְׁמִי כִשְׁמָךְ וְשֵׁם אִשְׁתִּי כְשֵׁם אִשְׁתְּךָ פָּסוּל מִלְּגָרֵשׁ בּוֹ. יוֹתֵר מִיכֵּן יֵשׁ לוֹ שְׁתֵּי נָשִׁים וּשְׁמוֹתֵיהֶן שָׁוִין כָּתַב לְגָרֵשׁ בּוֹ אֶת הַגְּדוֹלָה לֹא יְגָרֵשׁ בּוֹ אֶת הַקְּטַנָּה. יוֹתֵר מִיכֵּן אָמַר לַלִּיבְּלָר כְּתוֹב לְאֵיזוֹ שֶׁאֶרְצֶה אֲגָרֵשׁ פָּסוּל מִלְּגָרֵשׁ בּוֹ.

Mishnah 1: Every bill of divorce which was not written for a particular wife[1] is invalid. How? If one was walking in the market and heard the scribes dictating[2] "Mr. X divorces his wife Y from place Z" and said, these are mine and my wife's names, it is invalid and cannot be used to divorce by. In addition, if he wrote [a bill] to divorce his wife but had second thoughts, and a fellow townsman came and said to him, my name is identical with yours and my wife's name is identical with your wife's, it is invalid and cannot be used to divorce by. In addition, if he had two wives with identical names and wrote a document to divorce the older one by, he cannot use it to divorce the younger. In addition, if he said to the scribe: write that I may divorce either one[3] I wish, it is invalid and cannot be used to divorce either one.

1 If the scribe did not intend to write for one particular woman. As will be clear from the sequel, the scribe not only has to know the wife's

name but her identity as well.

2 A school of scribes and the teachers were dictating a text as example of a bill of divorce. At the end of the course, every student would have forms available for all situations.

3 Of the two who have identical names.

(44c line 57) **הלכה א:** כָּל־גֵּט שֶׁנִּכְתַּב שֶׁלֹּא לְשֵׁם אִשָּׁה כול'. מַהוּ מַקְרִין. מְלַמְּדֵי תִינוֹקוֹת. מַהוּ יוֹתֵר מִיכֵּן. תַּמָּן לֹא נִכְתַּב לְשֵׁם גֵּט. בְּרַם הָכָא נִכְתַּב לְשֵׁם גֵּט. מַהוּ יוֹתֵר מִיכֵּן. תַּמָּן (תַּנִּינָן)⁴ לֹא נִכְתַּב לֹא לִשְׁמוֹ וְלֹא לִשְׁמָהּ. בְּרַם הָכָא נִכְתַּב לִשְׁמוֹ וְלֹא נִכְתַּב לִשְׁמָהּ. מַהוּ יוֹתֵר מִכָּאן. תַּמָּן לֹא נִכְתַּב לִשְׁמוֹ וְלֹא נִכְתַּב לִשְׁמָהּ. בְּרַם הָכָא נִכְתַּב לִשְׁמוֹ וְלִשְׁמָהּ אֶלָּא שֶׁלֹּא הָיָה לָהּ כְּרוּת לִשְׁמָהּ מִשָּׁעָה רִאשׁוֹנָה.

3 תנינן | ג - ·   4 מיכאן | ג מיכן   5 ולשמה | ג ושמה   לה | ג -

Halakhah 1: "Every bill of divorce which was not written for a particular wife," etc. Who is dictating? School teachers⁵. ⁶What means "in addition"⁷? There it was not written as a bill of divorce but here it was written as a bill of divorce. What means "in addition"⁸? There it was written neither in his name nor in her name but here it was written in his name but not in her name. What means "in addition"? There it was written in his name but not in her name but here it was written in his name and in her name but it was not written for divorce from the start⁹.

4 The expression תַּמָּן תַּנִּינָן is the standard reference to a Mishnah (other than the one under discussion). Since the reference is to a clause in the Mishnah under discussion, the word תנינן is a learned scribe's slip of the pen; it is missing in the Geniza text.

5 In the Babli, 24b, "a training course for scribes."

6 From the Babli, 24b, it appears that the remainder of this paragraph is a *baraita*.

7 In what is the case of the man who wants to use somebody else's bill different from the case of the bill written as a writing exercise?

8   The question is what is the difference between the bill destined for the older one and the bill destined for either one of the two.

9   *Deut.* 24:1 requires that the husband "write her a scroll of divorce"; it must be written from the start for one and only one divorce.

(44c line 63) רַב אָמַר. כּוּלְּהֶם אֵינָן פְּסוּלִין חוּץ מִן הָאַחֲרוֹן שֶׁהוּא פָּסוּל. אִיסִי אָמַר. כּוּלָּן פְּסוּלִין חוּץ מִן הָרִאשׁוֹן שֶׁאֵינוֹ פָּסוּל. רִבִּי בָּא בַּר חִינְנָא אָמַר. כּוּלָּן פְּסוּלִין. מִילְתֵיהּ דְּרֵישׁ לָקִישׁ אָמְרָה. כּוּלָּן פְּסוּלִין. דְּרֵישׁ לָקִישׁ אָמַר. כָּתַב תָּרְפוֹ בַּטוֹפֶס פָּסוּל. מִילְתֵיהּ דְּרִבִּי יוֹחָנָן אָמְרָה. כּוּלָּן אֵינָן פְּסוּלִין. דְּרִבִּי יוֹחָנָן אָמַר. כָּתַב תָּרְפוֹ בַּטוֹפֶס כָּשֵׁר. מִילְתֵיהּ דְּרִבִּי אֶלְעָזָר אָמְרָה. כּוּלָּן אֵינָן פְּסוּלִין. רִבִּי אֶלְעָזָר שָׁאַל. כְּתַב קִידּוּשִׁין שֶׁכְּתָבוֹ שֶׁלֹּא לִשְׁמוֹ מַהוּ שֶׁיִּתְפְּסוּ בָהּ קִידּוּשִׁין. מִן מַה דְּצְרִיכִין לָהּ בְּגִיטִּין שֶׁאֵינָן פְּסוּלִין לְפוּם כֵּן שָׁאַל לָהּ בְּקִידּוּשִׁין. אִין תֵּימַר. צְרִיכִין לָהּ בְּגִיטִּין. לֹא יִשְׁאֲלִינָּהּ בְּקִידּוּשִׁין. מָה אִם גִּיטִּין עַל יְדֵי שֶׁהוּא צָרִיךְ לִשְׁמָהּ וְכָתַב שֶׁלֹּא לִשְׁמָהּ לֹא נָגְעוּ בָהּ גֵּירוּשִׁין. קִידּוּשִׁין שֶׁאֵינוֹ צָרִיךְ לִשְׁמָהּ וְכָתַב שֶׁלֹּא לִשְׁמָהּ אֵינוֹ דִין שֶׁיִּתְפְּסוּ בָהּ קִידּוּשִׁין. וּתְהֵא פְּשִׁיטָה לֵיהּ הָא. כֵּן הוּא פְּשִׁיטָא לֵיהּ. הוֹאִיל וְלֹא לְמַדּוּ כְּתַב קִידּוּשִׁין אֶלָּא מִגֵּירוּשִׁין. מַה בְּגֵירוּשִׁין אֵינָהּ מְגוֹרֶשֶׁת אַף בְּקִידּוּשִׁין אֵינָהּ מְקוּדֶּשֶׁת.

2 כולן | ג כולם   (4 times)   ר' בא בר חיננא | ג זעור בר חננא   4-3 מילתיה דריש לקיש ... פסול | ג -   4 דר' יוחנן אמ' | ג דמר ר' יוחנן   5 כתב תרפו בטופס כשר | ג תרפו בטפס פסול   ר' אלעזר | ג ר' לעזר   6 לשמו | ג לשמה   שיתפסו | ג שייתפסו   7 דצריכין | ג דצריכה   (2 times)   לפום כן | ג לפם כן הוא   לה | ג ליה   8 ישאלינה | ג ישאלנה   9-10 שאינו צריך לשמה וכתב שלא לשמה | ג שאינו צריך לשמה שלא לשמה נגעו בה קידושין ותהא כן לית יכיל מה אם גיטין על ידי שהוא צריך לשמה שלא לשמה נגעו בה גירושין קידושין שאינו צריך לשמה וכתב שלא לשמה   10 שיתפסו | ג שייתפסו   11 ליה הא כן פשיטא ליה | ג פשיטא ליה הא כן היא צריכה ליה

Rav said, none of these are invalid[10] except for the last which is invalid[11]. Issi[12] said, all are invalid[13] except for the first which is not invalid. Rebbi Abba bar Ḥinena[14] said, all are invalid[15]. The word of Rebbi Simeon ben Laqish implied that all are invalid since Rebbi Simeon ben Laqish said, if he wrote the essential text with the formula, it is invalid[16]. The word of Rebbi Joḥanan implied that none are invalid since Rebbi Joḥanan said, if he wrote the essential text with the formula, it is valid[17]. Does the word of Rebbi Eleazar imply that none are invalid? Since Rebbi Eleazar asked: if one wrote a bill of preliminary marriage[18] not for a specific name[19], does preliminary marriage take hold? If he had a problem with divorce, would he ask about preliminary marriage[20]? Since in the case of divorce, where the document is required to be for a specific name and he did not write for a specific name, divorce will not touch her, is it not logical that in the case of preliminary marriage, where a specific name is not required and he did not write for a specific name, preliminary marriage take hold with her[21]? That should be obvious to him. Really, the following is obvious to him: Since one inferred the bill of preliminary marriage only from divorce[22], and in the case of divorce she is not divorced, in the case of preliminary marriage she is not preliminarily married[23].

10   As explained in Chapter 2, Note 132, if a Cohen divorces his wife with a document which is found to be invalid but which possibly might have been valid, (the technical term is: the document has the "smell" of a bill of divorce) one forces the Cohen to deliver a valid divorce document to his wife and he is prohibited from changing his mind and not divorce her. Rav states that all the bills of divorce mentioned in the Mishnah except the last do not have a "smell" of a bill of divorce; they are pieces of paper, not bills of divorce, neither valid nor invalid.

11   The bill written for two wives with identical names is invalid but if the husband is a Cohen he is forced to divorce the wife to whom the bill was delivered.

12   In the Babli, 24b/25a, Rav's opinion is atributed to Rav Assi (= Issi) and vice versa.

13   And force a definitive divorce if made by a Cohen. In the Babli, 24b, this position is attributed to Rav.

14   An Amora of this name is not otherwise known. In the Geniza text, the name is Ze'ur bar Ḥinena, known from both Talmudim as the name of a third-Century Amora who almost was killed by Queen Zenobia of Palmyra.

15   In the Babli, 24b, this appears as Samuel's opinion.

16   The sentence about R. Simeon ben Laqish is missing in the Geniza text. R. Simeon ben Laqish considers the statement that the document is one of divorce so important that its writing without the explicit instruction by the husband invalidates the bill; cf. Chapter 2, Notes 100,101. But his choice of the word "invalid", not that "there is no 'smell' of a divorce", shows that in all cases he holds that any material expression of the husband's desire to divorce prohibits the Cohen to remain married to his wife.

17   R. Joḥanan strictly follows the Mishnah that only the names of husband and wife and the date have to be written by the explicit instruction of the husband. Therefore, he also follows the language of the Mishnah, not that the bills of divorce are simply invalid but are "invalid to be used in divorce", meaning that the use of any of these documents cannot imply any divorce in any form. (The classical commentators all feel obliged to switch the positions attributed to R. Simeon ben Laqish and R. Joḥanan; this position cannot be sustained against the testimony of both mss.) The Babli, 25a, quotes R. Joḥanan in the sense given here but explains his disagreement with the position attributed here to Rav by the fact that he never admits retroactive validation of documents; therefore, he cannot admit that the husband has the power to decide after the writing of the document to which wife it shall apply.

18   Mishnah *Qiddušin* 1:1 states that a preliminary marriage can be effected either by a transfer of valuables, or a contract, or sexual relations. It is then explained [*Qiddušin* 1:1 (58c l. 29), Babli 9a] that the contract is a written statement by the groom declaring his future bride to be his wife; the marriage is effected by the acceptance of the letter by the adressee (or, if she is underage, her father).

19   Meaning: not for a specific woman; since no name has to be written in the statement, it may simply read: By accepting this document, you are my wife. The document contains

no formulaic text.

20   If he thought that any of the bills of divorce mentioned in the Mishnah would possibly count as active for a Cohen's wife, he would have to ask about circumstances of divorce, where the problems are real and grave.

21   The Geniza text has a longer argument: "Since he has a problem with divorce where [the documents] are not invalid; therefore he asks about preliminary marriage. If you say he has a problem with divorce, he should not ask about preliminary marriage. Since in the case of divorce, where it is required that the document be for a specific name and he did not write for a specific name, divorce did not touch her; in the case of preliminary marriage, where a specific name is not required, if it was not for a specific name preliminary marriage should take hold of her. It should be so. That is impossible. Since in the case of divorce, where it is required to be for a specific name, if it was not for a specific name, divorce did touch her; in the case of preliminary marriage, where a specific name is not required and he did not write for a specific name, preliminary marriage should take hold of her." It is difficult to make coherent sense of this text.

22   The validity of a preliminary marriage by a symbolic bride purchase is given biblical status by reading *Deut.* 24:1 "if a man take a wife" as "if a man buy a wife" since in Mishnaic Hebrew the verb לקח means "to buy" [*Qidduŝin* 1:1 (58b l.35), Babli 4b]. The possibility of marriage by document is inferred from *Deut.* 24:2: "She [the divorcee] left his house, went and became another man's." Since "becoming a man's" means to marry him, the verse connects leaving (divorce) with becoming (marriage). Since leaving is effected by a document, so becoming can be effected by a document [*Qidduŝin* 1:1 (58b l.33), Babli 9b]. Therefore, a document invalid for leaving must be invalid for becoming.

23   The Babli agrees, *Qidduŝin* 9b. There, the question is attributed to R. Simeon ben Laqish; the argument agrees with the latter's position as given here.

(44d line 6) רִבִּי לְעָזָר בַּר יוֹסֵי בָּעָא קוֹמֵי רִבִּי יוֹסֵי. הָדָא דְתֵימַר. גֵּט אֶחָד פָּסוּל בִּשְׁתֵּי נָשִׁים. וְדִכְוָותָהּ וְהֵן שְׁנֵי גִיטִין פְּסוּלִין בִּשְׁתֵּי נָשִׁים. אָמַר לֵיהּ.

בָּעוּ. אָמַר לֵיהּ. וְהָתַנִּינָן שְׁנֵי גִיטִּין שֶׁשִּׁילְחוּ שְׁנַיִם וְנִתְעָרְבוּ נוֹתֵן שְׁנֵיהֶן לָזוֹ וּשְׁנֵיהֶן לָזוּ. תַּמָּן זֶה כָרוּת לִשְׁמָהּ וְזֶה כָרוּת לִשְׁמָהּ. תַּעֲרוֹבֶת הִיא שֶׁגָּרְמָה. בְּרַם הָכָא לֹא זוֹ כָרוּת לִשְׁמָהּ וְלֹא זוֹ כָרוּת לִשְׁמָהּ.

1 יוסי | ג יוסה (2 times)   הדא דתימר | ג דתמר   2 פסולין | ג פוסלין   3 והתנינין | ג תנינין   שנים | ג שני גיטין שווים   שניחן | ג שניהם (2 times)   4 זו | ג זה (2 times)

Rebbi Eleazar bar Yose asked before Rebbi Yose: Concerning what you say that one bill of divorce is invalid for two women[24], should not two bills of divorce be invalid for two women? He asked him, what is the question? He answered, did we not state[25]: "If two people sent two [identical][26] bills of divorce which were intermingled[26], he gives both documents to both women." There, it is a divorce for this one and a divorce for the other one; the mix-up caused {the problem}[27]. But here, neither this one is divorced in her name nor is that one divorced in her name.

24 This refers to the last clause in the Mishnah, when the husband, married to two identically named women, orders a bill of divorce in their name without specifying to whom it will refer.

25 Mishnah 9:5.

26 Added from the Geniza text. The same messenger carries two bills of divorce from two men, both called X ben Y, to two wives, both called Z bat U.

26 The messenger can no longer say which bill is addressed to which wife.

27 If each wife receives both bills it is certain that each one received the one intended for her.

(44d line 11) מִכֵּיוָן שֶׁנְּתָנוֹ לָהּ יֵעָשֶׂה כְּמוֹ שֶׁהָיָה כָרוּת לִשְׁמָהּ מִשָּׁעָה רִאשׁוֹנָה. רִבִּי יוֹסֵי בְּשֵׁם דְּרַבִּי ביבון. דְּרִבִּי שִׁמְעוֹן הִיא דְּתַנֵּי. אָמַר לְאוּמָן עֲשֵׂה לוֹ שְׁנֵי זוּגִין. אֶחָד לַקַּרְקַע וְאֶחָד לַבְּהֵמָה. עָשָׂה לוֹ שְׁנֵי מַחֲלָצוֹת. אַחַת לִישִׁיבָה וְאַחַת לְאוֹהָלִים. עָשָׂה לוֹ שְׁנֵי סְדִינִין. אֶחָד לִשְׁכִיבָה וְאֶחָד לָעוֹרוֹת. עַד שֶׁיְּפָרִישֵׁם

בְּטָהֳרָה. רִבִּי שִׁמְעוֹן מְטַהֵר עַד שֶׁיְפָרִישֵׁם בְּטוּמְאָה. כְּמָה דְהוּא אָמַר תַּמָּן. עַד שֶׁיְהֵא כְּלִי מִשָּׁעָה רִאשׁוֹנָה. כָּךְ הוּא אָמַר. עַד שֶׁיְהֵא כְרוּת לִשְׁמָהּ מִשָּׁעָה רִאשׁוֹנָה.

2 יוסי | ג יוסה   דר' ביבון | ג ר' בין בר' חייה   לו | ג לי   (3 times)   4 סדינין | ג סדינים   לעורות | ג לצורות   בטהרה | ג בטהרם   6 כך | ג כן   - | ג הכח

After it was delivered to her[24], could it not be considered as if written in her name from the start[28]? Rebbi Yose in the name of Rebbi [Abin bar Ḥiyya][29]: It follows Rebbi Simeon, as it was stated[30]: "If one said to a craftsman, make me two bells, one for the ground[31] and one for an animal, make me two mats, one to sit on and one for a tent[32], make me two sheets[33], one to lie on and one for [a pattern][34], [35]only if he designated them in purity. Rebbi Simeon declares them pure unless he designated them for impurity[36]." As he said there, only if it was a utensil from the start, so he says, unless it was a divorce in her name from the start[37].

28   Since the bill was written for one of two women, can one not say that the delivery made it clear that from the start it was written for the recipient?

29   Text of the Geniza.

30   Tosephta *Kelim Baba Meṣi'a* 1:14.

31   In the Tosephta: For the door. "For the ground" means the same, i. e., to be affixed to a structure connected to the ground. A cowbell can become impure (Tosephta *Kelim Baba Meṣi'a* 1:13) but a doorbell cannot become impure.

32   A mat to sit on can become impure in many ways; a mat used as part of a tent cannot become impure.

33   Textile sheets.

34   The translation follows the Geniza text, supported by the Tosephta. A bed sheet can become impure like a mat; a sheet on which a picture is embroidered to serve as a pattern to be copied is not a utensil and is pure (Mishnah *Kelim* 24:13; concurrent

explanation by *Arukh*, Maimonides, and R. Simson of Sens, based on a Gaonic source.) The Leiden ms. text, "for hides" is difficult to understand since a sheet used as wrapping is an implement and subject to the impurity of utensils.

35   In the Tosephta the text reads: "All these accept impurity up to the moment when he spells out;" if a utensil is made which can serve a dual purpose, it can become impure (once finished) unless it is clearly designated for a use which shields it from impurity. The common testimony of both ms. texts leaves no room for the addition of the Tosephta but its interpretation is similar: All these utensils are subject to impurity unless he spells out which one is pure, i. e., is shielded from impurity.

36   Since a manufactured item only accepts impurity if it is used as a vessel or a tool, R. Simeon rejects any retroactivity in the designation of dual use items and declares that impurity can affect the item only in the future, after it was designated as tool or utensil, even if it was exposed to impurity beforehand (cf. D. Pardo, Commentary on the Tosephta, Part 4-1, ed. S. Lieberman, New York - Jerusalem 1970, p. 84). In the Tosephta, R. Simeon agrees that if an item is manufactured for sale as a utensil it is subject to impurity up to the moment a buyer designates it for a protected use.

37   He rejects any retroactivity, cf. Note 17.

(44d line 18) רִבִּי חֲנַנְיָה בְּשֵׁם רִבִּי ביבון בַּר חִייָה. אָמַר רִבִּי יוֹחָנָן וְתַגֵּי כֵן. כָּל־הַתִּנָּאִים פּוֹסְלִין בַּגֵּט. דִּבְרֵי רִבִּי. וַחֲכָמִים אוֹמְרִים. אֶת שֶׁהוּא פוֹסֵל בַּפֶּה פוֹסֵל בִּכְתָב. וְאֶת שֶׁאֵינוֹ פוֹסֵל בַּפֶּה אֵינוֹ פוֹסֵל בִּכְתָב. הֲרֵי אַתְּ מוּתֶּרֶת לְכָל־אָדָם חוּץ מִפְּלוֹנִי. הוֹאִיל וְהוּא פוֹסֵל בַּפֶּה פוֹסֵל בִּכְתָב. הֲרֵי זֶה גִיטִיךְ עַל מְנָת שֶׁתִּתְּנִי לִי מָאתַיִם זוּז. הוֹאִיל וְאֵינוֹ פוֹסֵל בַּפֶּה אֵינוֹ פוֹסֵל בִּכְתָב. אָמַר רִבִּי יוּדָן. מַה פְּלִיגִין. בְּשֶׁבִּיטֵּל תְּנָאוֹ. אֲבָל אִם לֹא בִיטֵּל תְּנָאוֹ אַף רִבִּי מוֹדֶה. הֲרֵי הוּא אָמַר. כָּל־הַתְּנָאִין שֶׁהִתְנִינוּ בַגִּיטִּין דְּלֹא כְרִבִּי. אָמַר רִבִּי חִינְּנָא. תַּמָּן בַּכּוֹתֵב עַל מְנָת כֵּן. בְּרַם הָכָא בַּנּוֹתֵן עַל מְנָת כֵּן. רִבִּי עֶזְרָא בְּעָא קוֹמֵי רִבִּי[38] מָנָא. הָדָא אָמְרָא אֵין תּוֹפְשִׂין כְּרִבִּי. אָמַר לֵיהּ. מָן אַתְּ בָּעֵי. מִן רִבִּי.

כְּרַבִּי יוּדָה. דְּרַבִּי יוּדָה פּוֹסֵל בַּטּוֹפְסִין. רֵישׁ לָקִישׁ אָמַר. כָּל־הַתְּנָאִין פּוֹסְלִין בַּגֵּט. דִּבְרֵי הַכֹּל. אֲתָא עוֹבְדָא קוֹמֵי רִבִּי יִרְמִיָה וַעֲבַד כְּרֵישׁ לָקִישׁ. אֲמַר לֵיהּ רִבִּי יוֹסֵי. שֶׁבְקִין רִבִּי יוֹחָנָן וְעָבְדִין כְּרֵישׁ לָקִישׁ. אֲמַר לֵיהּ. הוֹרָיוֹתֵיהּ דְּרִבִּי יוֹחָנָן הוֹרָיָיה וְהוֹרָיָיתָא דְּרֵישׁ לָקִישׁ לָאו הוֹרָיָיה. אָמַר רִבִּי יַעֲקֹב בַּר אָחָא. לֹא רֵישׁ לָקִישׁ פְּלִיג עַל רִבִּי יוֹחָנָן אֶלָּא מַתְנִיתָא שָׁמַע וְעָמַד עָלֶיהָ. אָמַר רִבִּי יוֹסֵי בֵּירִבִּי בּוּן. לֹא דְּרֵישׁ לָקִישׁ מַתְרִיס לָקֳבֵל רִבִּי יוֹחָנָן בְּגִין דְּאִיתְפְּלִיג עֲלֵהּ אֶלָּא בְּגִין מַפְקִין עוֹבַד מִנֵּיהּ. כַּד שָׁמַע מַתְנִיתָא הוּא סָמַךְ עֲלֵיהּ. כַּד דְּלָא שָׁמַע מַתְנִיתָא הוּא מְבַטֵּל דַּעְתֵּיהּ מִקּוֹמֵי דַעְתֵּיהּ דְּרִבִּי יוֹחָנָן.

1 ביבון | ג בין   חייה | ג חייא. דר' היא   2 פוסלין | ג פסולין   4 פוסל בפה | ג פסל בפה   5 שתתני | ג שתתן לי   6 תנאו | ג תנויין   תנאו | ג תניין   7 הרי הוא אמ' | ג הרחי אמרי   שהתנינו | ג שתנינן   8 חיננא | ג חננא   9 עזרא | ג עזרה   בעא | ג בעה

Rebbi Ḥanania in the name of Rebbi Abin bar Ḥiyya, [this is Rebbi's opinion.][39] Rebbi Joḥanan said, and it was stated so[40]: "All conditions[41] invalidate a bill of divorce, the words of Rebbi[42]. But the Sages say, what invalidates orally invalidates in writing, and what does not invalidate orally does not invalidate in writing." "You are permitted to marry anybody except Mr. X," because this invalidates orally it invalidates in writing[43]. "This is your bill of divorce on condition that you give me 200 *zuz*"; because this does not invalidate orally it does not invalidate in writing[44]. Rebbi Yudan said, when do they disagree? If he rescinded his condition. But if he did nor rescind his condition, even Rebbi agrees[45]. Otherwise, we would have to say that all conditions which were stated for bills of divorce do not follow Rebbi[46]. Rebbi Ḥinena said, there when he writes "on condition," here if he gives "on condition.[47]" Rebbi Ezra[48] asked before Rebbi Mana: Does this imply that Rebbi does not recognize formulaic texts[49]? He answered him, about whom do you ask? About

Rebbi! He follows Rebbi Jehudah, for Rebbi Jehudah invalidates formulaic texts[50]. Rebbi Simeon ben Laqish said, everybody agrees that all conditions invalidate a bill of divorce[51]. There came a case before Rebbi Jeremiah and he acted following Rebbi Simeon ben Laqish[52]. Rebbi Yose said to him, does one neglect Rebbi Joḥanan[53] and act following Rebbi Simeon ben Laqish? He answered him, is Rebbi Joḥanan's instruction an instruction but Rebbi Simeon ben Laqish's instruction not an instruction[54]? Rebbi Jacob bar Aḥa said, it is not that Rebbi Simeon ben Laqish[55] disagrees with Rebbi Joḥanan, but he understood a *baraita*[56] and acted accordingly. Rebbi Yose ben Rebbi Abun said, not that Rebbi Simeon ben Laqish fights against Rebbi Joḥanan when he disagrees with him only to extract a ruling from him. If he finds a *baraita*, he depends on it; if he does not find a *baraita*, he retracts his opinion before Rebbi Joḥanan's opinion.

38   Here ends the Geniza ms.

39   From the Geniza text, missing in the Leiden ms. but confirmed by Naḥmanides (*Milḥamot Hashem*, on Alfasi #556). One still discusses the case of the man with two wives whose names are identical; Rebbi rejects the bill of divorce since he holds that its meaning must be clear before it is delivered; cf. Note 45.

40   The same *baraita* is quoted in the Babli, 84b.

41   The bill of divorce is called סֵפֶר כְּרִיתוּת "a scroll of cutting" in *Deut.* 24:1. This is interpreted to mean that all ties between husband and wife have to be cut; a divorce in which the husband retains any influence in his wife's life is invalid.

42   Any condition written into the bill invalidates the bill. If the husband wants to attach a condition to the divorce he has to negotiate this separately with his wife before delivering the bill.

43   This reserves an influence of the husband's for the rest of the wife's life and clearly invalidates the divorce.

44   The divorce becomes valid immediately; the wife accepts a

monetary obligation which the husband eventually could enforce by foreclosure. If the stipulation had read: on condition that you pay me 200 *zuz* within 30 days, then the divorce would become valid if and only if the money had been paid within 30 days. If it had read: only if you pay me 200 *zuz*, the divorce would be invalid since without a time limit there is no separation. The Babli's concerns, whether the stipulation was written in the declaration of divorce or attached to it, are unknown to the Yerushalmi and all explanations of the Yerushalmi text based on the Babli have to be rejected, as noted by Naḥmanides (Note 39).

45   In this interpretation, Rebbi agrees with the Sages on what is or is not an acceptable condition. He differs in that (a) he does not permit any erasures in a bill of divorce and (b) he stipulates that there cannot be any change in conditions after the delivery of the bill.

46   It is unreasonable to assume that Rebbi formulated an entire series of Mishnaiot about conditions attached to divorce documents (Chapter 7) if he himself held that these are impossible.

47   The previous argument is invalid; the Mishnaiot are about conditions attached to, but no written in, the bill of divorce.

48   Cf. Chapter 2, Note 80.

49   Since he does not admit any conditions to be written in the text of the bill, he does not make any distinction between the formulaic text and the essential entries. Does this imply that he prohibits the scribe from preparing bills where only the names, the date, and the declaration of the divorce can be entered with a specific couple in mind?

50   In Mishnah 3:2.

51   No condition can be written in the bill; if written it would have to be a separate codicil.

52   Since the condition was written in the bill, he declared it invalid.

53   Who permitted written conditions under certain cirsumstances.

54   The Babli would take this as a statement of fact.

55   Who only was No. 2 in R. Joḥanan's court.

56   The text is not spelled out.

(fol. 44c) **משנה ב:** הַכּוֹתֵב טוֹפְסֵי גִיטִּין צָרִיךְ שֶׁיַּנִּיחַ מְקוֹם הָאִישׁ וּמְקוֹם הָאִשָּׁה וּמְקוֹם הַזְּמָן. שְׁטָרֵי מִלְוָה צָרִיךְ שֶׁיַּנִּיחַ מְקוֹם הַמַּלְוֶה וּמְקוֹם הַלּוֶֹה וּמְקוֹם הַמָּעוֹת וּמְקוֹם הַזְּמָן. שְׁטָרֵי מֶקַח וּמִמְכָּר צָרִיךְ שֶׁיַּנִּיחַ מְקוֹם הַלּוֹקֵחַ וּמְקוֹם הַמּוֹכֵר וּמְקוֹם הַמָּעוֹת וּמְקוֹם הַשָּׂדֶה וּמְקוֹם הַזְּמָן מִפְּנֵי הַתַּקָּנָה. רִבִּי יְהוּדָה פּוֹסֵל בְּכוּלָּן. רִבִּי אֶלְעָזָר מַכְשִׁיר בְּכוּלָן חוּץ מִגִּיטֵּי נָשִׁים שֶׁנֶּאֱמַר וְכָתַב לָהּ לִשְׁמָהּ.

Mishnah 2: If somebody[57] writes formulaic texts of bills of divorce he has to leave space for the man, the woman, and the time. For bonds, he has to leave space for the lender, the borrower, the sum, and the time. For commercial deeds, he has to leave space for the buyer, the seller, the sum, the field[58], and the time[59], because of good order[60]. Rebbi Jehudah invalidates all of these. Rebbi Eleazar validates all of them except women's bills of divorce, for it is said[61]: "He shall write for her", in her name.

57   A scribe.

58   The descriptions of the boundaries of the parcel.

59   All predated documents having financial implications are invalid; cf. Chapter 2, Note 16.

60   There is a dispute between the Talmudim about the meaning of this clause.

60   *Deut.* 24:1.

(44d line 36) **הלכה ב:** הַכּוֹתֵב טוֹפְסֵי גִיטִּין כול'. רִבִּי יוֹחָנָן אָמַר. כָּתַב תָּרְפּוֹ בְּטוֹפֶס כָּשֵׁר. רֵישׁ לָקִישׁ אָמַר. כָּתַב תָּרְפּוֹ כַטּוֹפֶס פָּסוּל. מַתְנִיתָא פְלִיגָא עַל רִבִּי יוֹחָנָן. הַכּוֹתֵב טוֹפְסֵי גִיטִּין צָרִיךְ שֶׁיַּנִּיחַ מְקוֹם הָאִישׁ וּמְקוֹם הָאִשָּׁה וְהַזְּמָן. פָּתַר לָהּ וְתוֹרְפּוֹ עִמּוֹ. וְקַשְׁיָא עַל דְּרִבִּי יוֹחָנָן. אִם בְּשֶׁכָּתַב תּוֹרְפוֹ בְּטוֹפֶס בְּדָא חֲכָמִים מַכְשִׁירִין. רִבִּי יִרְמְיָה בְּשֵׁם רִבִּי זְעִירָה. מִפְּסוּלוֹ אַתְּ לָמֵד הֶכְשֵׁירוֹ. אִילוּ כָתַב כּוּלּוֹ לִשְׁמָהּ וְשֵׁם הָאִישׁ וְשֵׁם הָאִשָּׁה לֹא לִשְׁמָהּ שֶׁמָּא אֵינוֹ פָסוּל. וְדִכְוָותָהּ כָּתַב כּוּלוֹ שֶׁלֹּא לִשְׁמָהּ וְשֵׁם הָאִישׁ וְשֵׁם הָאִשָּׁה לִשְׁמָהּ כָּשֵׁר. רִבִּי יוֹסֵי

שָׁאַל לְרִבִּי יִרְמְיָה. הַגַּע עַצְמָךְ שֶׁזִּיוֵוג. אָמַר לֵיהּ. כֵּן אָמַר לֵיהּ רִבִּי זְעִירָא רַבּוֹ. מִכֵּיוָן שֶׁאֵינוֹ מָצוּי לְזַגֵּיג אֲפִילוּ כְּמִי שֶׁלֹּא זִיוֵוג. וְקַשְׁיָא עַל רֵישׁ לָקִישׁ. אִם בְּשֶׁלֹּא כָתַב בַּטּוֹפֶס תּוֹרְפּוֹ בְּדָא רִבִּי יוּדָה פּוֹסֵל. רִבִּי יוֹסֵי בְּרִבִּי זְעִירָא. לְעִנְיָין אַחֵר עֲבַד לָהּ רִבִּי יוּדָה. וַתְיָיא כַּיי דְּאָמַר שִׁמְעוֹן בַּר בָּא בְּשֵׁם רִבִּי יוֹחָנָן. חָלָק מָקוֹם שְׁנֵי שִׁיטִין לְעִנְיָין אֶחָד אֲפִילוּ כָּל־שֶׁהוּא פָּסוּל.

Halakhah 2: "If somebody writes formulaic texts of bills of divorce," etc. Rebbi Johanan said, writing the essential text with the formula is valid. Rebbi Simeon ben Laqish said, writing the essential text with the formula is invalid[61]. The Mishnah disagrees with Rebbi Johanan: "If somebody writes formulaic texts of bills of divorce he has to leave space for the man, the woman, and the time.[62]" He explains it, with the essential text[63]. It is difficult for Rebbi Johanan: Do the Sages declare valid in case he wrote the essential text with the formulaic text? Rebbi Jeremiah in the name of Rebbi Ze'ira: From its invalidity you learn its validity. If he wrote everything[64] in her name but the husband's and the wife's names not in her name, would that be valid? Similarly, if he wrote everything not in her name but the husband's and the wife's names in her name, it is valid. Rebbi Yose asked Rebbi Jeremiah: Think of it, if it was paired[65]? He said, so said his teacher Rebbi Ze'ira to him: Since pairing is infrequent, even if there was pairing it is as if there was no pairing[66]. Then it is difficult for Rebbi Simeon ben Laqish: Even if he did not write the essential text in the formula, Rebbi Jehudah declares invalid[67]! Rebbi Yose ben Rebbi Ze'ira: Rebbi Jehudah refers to something else; it follows what Simeon bar Abba said in the name of Rebbi Johanan: An empty space of two lines[68] about one subject[69] is invalid in any case.

61 Cf. Chapter 2, Note 100. The Babli, 26a, reports only R. Simeon ben Laqish's opinion, in the name of Samuel.

62 It is assumed by the questioner that the text to be written for that woman only includes the sentence that by the document she is divorced.

63 The Mishnah has to be explained in a restrictive way: Only the spaces mentioned in the Mishnah have to be left blank.

64 Including the divorce sentence.

65 If there were two couples in town, in both cases the husband was called X ben Y and the wife Z bat U, would this not require a special characterization such as "X ben Y who dwells in house W", and the space left blank would not suffice for the characterizations..

66 Even if there were two couples with identical names, if the bill of divorce is written without special characterizations it is valid since one assumes that the bill was intended for the woman who presents it together with her *ketubah* to collect her due.

(The Babli permits only in emergencies to divorce such a couple without due characterization or in the presence of the other couple; 66a.).

67 The opinion of R. Simeon ben Laqish has no basis in the Mishnah which either does not permit prepared forms or requires only the personal data and the date to be filled in.

68 The witnesses have to sign on the second line after the end of the text; not directly after the text in order to show the difference between the text and the witnesses nor two lines apart because then the document could be falsified: a line could be added after the witnesses signed. A document signed by witnesses at a distance of more than one line is invalid in all cases (Halakhah 9:8, 50c l. 10; Babli *Baba Batra* 162b; Tosephta *Giṭṭin* 7:11).

69 The Venice printer read אחר instead of אֶחָד, this led the commentators into difficulties. (The ms. text has אחר in *Baba batra* 10:1; this belongs to another editorial team. Cf. Halakhah 9:8.)

(44d line 49) מָהוּ מִפְּנֵי הַתַּקָּנָה. רִבִּי שַׁבְּתַי בְּשֵׁם חִזְקִיָּה. מִפְּנֵי תַּקָּנַת בְּנוֹת יִשְׂרָאֵל שֶׁלֹּא יְהוּ מְצוּיוֹת לְהִתְגָּרֵשׁ. רִבִּי שְׁמוּאֵל בַּר רַב יִצְחָק שָׁאַל לְרִבִּי חִיָּיה

בַּר בָּא. כָּשֵׁר וְאַתְּ אָמַר אָכֵן. אִין תֵּימַר פָּסוּל וְיָאוּת. מַאי כְדוֹן. אָמַר רִבִּי אָבוּן. מִפְּנֵי תַקָּנַת הַלִּיבְלָר. כְּדֵי שֶׁיְּהוּ חַיָּיו מְצוּיִין לוֹ.

What is "the good order"? Rebbi Sabbatai in the name of Ḥizqiah: Because of the good order of Jewish women, lest they frequently be divorced[70]. Rebbi Samuel ben Rav Isaac asked Rebbi Ḥiyya bar Abba: It is valid, and you say so? If it were invalid, then [the explanation] would be acceptable[71]. Rebbi Abun said, for the good order of the scribe, that his livelihood be guaranteed[72].

70 The forms must contain blank spaces to introduce an artificial complication forcing the husband to go to a scribe to get a bill of divorce.

71 The answer given fits the position of R. Jehudah who prohibits the preparation of forms.

72 All legal formalities contain an element of protection for lawyers, to make sure their services are needed. This is the only explanation given in the Babli, 26a.

(44d line 54) רִבִּי זְעִירָא רַב הוּנָא בְשֵׁם רַב. הֲלָכָה כְרִבִּי יוּדָה בַּגִּיטִּין וּכְרִבִּי אֱלִיעֶזֶר בַּשְּׁטָרוֹת. נֹאמַר הֲלָכָה כְרִבִּי אֱלִיעֶזֶר. רִבִּי בָּא בְשֵׁם רַב. הֲלָכָה כְרִבִּי לִיעֶזֶר בַּגִּיטִּין וּכְרִבִּי יוּדָה בַּשְּׁטָרוֹת. נֹאמַר הֲלָכָה כְרִבִּי יְהוּדָה. אֶלָּא בְגִין דְּרַב וּשְׁמוּאֵל תְּרַוַויְיהוּ אֱמָרִין. הֲלָכָה כְרִבִּי לְעָזָר. וְלֹא תִיסְבַּר מֵימַר אַף הָכָא כֵן. צָרַךְ מֵימַר. הֲלָכָה כְרִבִּי יוּדָה בַּגִּיטִּין וּכְרִבִּי אֶלְעָזָר בַּשְּׁטָרוֹת.

Rebbi Ze'ira, Rav Huna in the name of Rav: Practice follows Rebbi Jehudah for bills of divorce and Rebbi Eleazar[73] in commercial documents. Could we not say, practice follows Rebbi Eleazar[74]? Rebbi Abba in the name of Rav: Practice follows Rebbi Eleazar for bills of divorce and Rebbi Jehudah in commercial documents. Could we not say, practice follows Rebbi Jehudah? But because Rav and Samuel both say that practice follows Rebbi Eleazar[75]; in order not to let you think that here it is the same, it was necessary to state that practice follows Rebbi Jehudah for bills of divorce and Rebbi Eleazar in commercial documents[76].

73 Both in Mishnah 3:2 and in 9:4 the name is R. Eleazar, but in Mishnah 9:4 in the Babli (*editio princeps* and Munich ms.) as well as in the Cambridge ms. of the Mishnah the reading is Eliezer. In Tosephta 2:10, two sources read Eliezer, one Eleazar. Since "Eleazar" is the reading of all Medieval commentators of the Babli, it is accepted here.

74 Since he agrees with R. Jehudah about bills of divorce.

75 That the witnesses to the delivery of the bill effectuate the divorce. The Babli agrees, 86b.

76 The reason for the rejection of divorce documents based on prepared forms is that of R. Jehudah, i. e., that both writing and signing are part of the biblical requirement of "writing for her". The statement of R. Abba is rejected.

(fol. 44c) **משנה ג:** הַמֵּבִיא גֵט וְאָבַד מִמֶּנּוּ מְצָאוֹ עַל אֲתָר כָּשֵׁר וְאִם לָאו פָּסוּל. מְצָאוֹ בַּחֲפִיסָה אוֹ בְדלוֹסְקְמָא אִם מַכִּירוֹ כָּשֵׁר. הַמֵּבִיא גֵט וְהִנִּיחוֹ זָקֵן אוֹ חוֹלֶה נוֹתְנוֹ לָהּ בְּחֶזְקַת שֶׁהוּא קַיָּים. בַּת יִשְׂרָאֵל שֶׁנִּשֵּׂאָה לְכֹהֵן וְהָלַךְ בַּעֲלָהּ לִמְדִינַת הַיָּם אוֹכֶלֶת בַּתְּרוּמָה בְּחֶזְקַת שֶׁהוּא קַיָּים. הַשּׁוֹלֵחַ חַטָּאתוֹ מִמְּדִינַת הַיָּם מַקְרִיבִין אוֹתָהּ בְּחֶזְקַת שֶׁהוּא קַיָּים.

Mishnah 3: If somebody transports a bill of divorce and loses it, if he finds it on the spot it is valid[77], otherwise it is invalid. If he finds it in a small bag or in a box[78], if he recognizes it, it is valid. If somebody transports a bill of divorce from an old or sick man, he delivers it to her under the presumption that the man is alive[79]. The daughter of an Israel who is married to a Cohen[80] and whose husband went overseas, may eat heave under the presumption that he is alive. If somebody sends his purification offering from overseas, it is sacrificed under the presumption that he is alive[81].

77 One does not fear that the bill might be written for another couple with identical names from identical places.

78 Greek γλωσσόκομον "case, box, chest".

79 If the husband died childless, the widow is freed from *ḥaliṣa* or levirate marriage as long as the husband's death was not known at the moment of delivery of the bill.

80 And who is childless at the moment of her husband's departure. At the moment of her husband's death she loses her right to priestly food.

81 A dead person's purification offering cannot be sacrificed since "the dead are free" (from obligations) (*Ps.* 88:6). The last two statements are included to illustrate the principle that in matters of ritual law one may always act on the assumption of the permanence of the *status quo ante*.

(44d line 59) **הלכה ג:** הַמֵּבִיא גֵט וְאָבַד מִמֶּנּוּ כול'. אִי זֶהוּ עַל אָתָר. רִבִּי יוֹחָנָן אָמַר. כָּל־שֶׁלֹּא עָבַר שָׁם בְּרִייָה. רִבִּי יַעֲקֹב בַּר אִידִי רִבִּי שִׁמְעוֹן בַּר אַבָּא בְשֵׁם רִבִּי יְהוֹשֻׁעַ בֶּן לֵוִי. כָּל־שֶׁלֹּא עָבְרוּ שָׁם שְׁלֹשָׁה בְנֵי אָדָם. עָבַר גּוֹי. נִישְׁמְעִינָהּ מִן הָדָא. אַבָּא בַּר בַּר חָנָה אַייְתֵי גִיטָּא וָבַד מִינֵּיהּ וְאַשְׁכְּחֵיהּ חַד סִירְקָיי. אָתָא עוֹבָדָא קוֹמֵי רִבִּי יוֹחָנָן וְאַכְשְׁרוּן. הָדָא אֲמָרָה. עָבַר גּוֹי כָּשֵׁר. נֵימַר. סִימָן הֲוָוֹ לֵיהּ בֵּיהּ. וְלֹא כֵן תַּנֵּי. אֵין סִימָן בַּגִּיטִּין. וְהוּא דָמַר תְּרֵין תְּלַת שׁוּרִין. חֶרֶם הָכָא ה"א שֶׁבּוֹ הָיָה נָקוּד. רִבִּי עֶזְרָא בְּעָא קוֹמֵי רִבִּי מָנָא. הָכָא לָמָּה הוּא פָסוּל. אֲנִי אוֹמֵר. אַחֵר הָיָה שָׁם וְהָיָה שְׁמוֹ כִשְׁמוֹ. הַגַּע עַצְמָךְ שֶׁבָּדְקוּ כָּל־אוֹתוֹ הַמָּקוֹם וְלֹא מָצְאוּ אָדָם שֶׁשְּׁמוֹ כִשְׁמוֹ. אֶלָּא מִשּׁוּם חוֹמֶר הוּא בַּעֲרָיוֹת. וְהָא תַנִּינָן. הָלְכוּ וְלֹא מָצְאוּ שָׁם אָדָם וְהִשִּׂיאוּ אֶת אִשְׁתּוֹ. הָלְכוּ וְלֹא הִכִּירוּהוּ וְהִשִּׂיאוּ אֶת אִשְׁתּוֹ. אָמַר לֵיהּ רִבִּי מָנָא. כֵּן אָמַר רִבִּי שְׁמוּאֵל בַּר אָחָא. הָאִישׁ הַזֶּה שְׁנֵי גִיטִּין הָיוּ בְיָדוֹ. אֶחָד כָּשֵׁר וְאֶחָד פָּסוּל. אִיבֵּד אֶת הַכָּשֵׁר וְהִשְׁלִיךְ אֶת הַפָּסוּל. בְּשָׁעָה שֶׁיִּמָּצֵא אֲנִי אוֹמֵר. הַפָּסוּל מָצָא.

2-3 כל שלא עבר ... שלשה בני אדם | י כל שלא עברו שם שלשה בני אדם 3 גוי | י גוי
מהו 4 ובד | י ייבד 5 קומי ר' יוחנן | י קומי רבנין נימר | י נאמר 6 הוה ליה
בה | י היה לו בה סימן | י סימנין והוא דמר | י בההוא דאמר 7 ר' עזרא בעי | י ר'
זעירא בעא[48] 8 כל אותו המקום | י אותו מקום 11 ר' שמואל בר אחא | י ר' שמי
ר' אחא בשם ר' בון בר חייה

Halakhah 6: "If somebody transports a bill of divorce and loses it," etc. [82]What means "on the spot"? Rebbi Joḥanan said, as long as nobody passed by there[83]. Rebbi Jacob bar Idi, Rebbi Simeon bar Abba in the name of Rebbi Joshua ben Levi: as long as three people did not pass by there. If a Gentile passed by there? Let us hear from the following: Abba bar bar Ḥana transported a bill of divorce; he lost it and a Saracen found it. The case came before Rebbi Joḥanan[84]; they declared [the bill] valid. This means that if a Gentile passed by it is valid. Could we say that he had a mark to identify it? But was it not stated: There are no marks for bills of divorce. That is, if he said, two or three lines. But here, the ה in it had a spot. Rebbi Ezra asked before Rebbi Mana: Why is it invalid here? I say, it was another [husband] whose name was like his name. Think of it, if they checked out that entire place and did not find another man whose name was like his name! But it is because of the severity of adultery. But did we not state[85]: "They went and found nobody but let his wife remarry; they went there, did not recognize him, and let his wife remarry"? Rebbi Mana told him: This man had two bills of divorce in his hand, one valid, the other invalid. He lost the valid one and threw away the invalid. When he found it, I say that what he found was the invalid bill[86].

82 The paragraph also appears as Halakhah 16:6 in *Yebamot*, explained there in Notes 133-144. The readings from there are noted י.

83 This statement is missing in *Yebamot*. In the Babli, it is attributed to the Tanna R. Simeon ben Eleazar and the Amora R. Abba bar bar Hana (27b,28a); there it is declared as practice. It is also the only explanation offered in Tosephta 2:11.

84 The reading of *Yebamot*, "before the rabbis" is preferable since the verb is in the plural.

85 Mishnah *Yebamot* 16:6

86 The Mishnah is explained away, as referring to a most unlikely hypothetical case. In the Babli, the Mishnah is accepted practice; the contrast between the two Talmudim is noted in *Sefer Ha'ittur* 36a.

(44d line 73) תַּנֵּי בַּר קַפָּרָא. אֲפִילוּ הִינִיחוֹ בֶּן מֵאָה שָׁנָה וְעָשָׂה בַדֶּרֶךְ עוֹד מֵאָה שָׁנָה נוֹתְנוּ לָהּ בְּחֶזְקַת שֶׁהוּא קַיָּים.

Bar Qappara stated: Even if he left [the man] when he was 100 years old and spent another 100 years on the way, he delivers it to her under the presumption that he is alive[87].

87 The Babli, 28a, explains this *baraita* away, that a person who has reached 100 years of age might go on to live much longer, and implies that a person between the ages of 81 and 99 can be presumed to die soon. Since the Yerushalmi quotes the statement without commentary, it appears that it endorses an unrestricted application of the permanence of the *status quo ante* until further notice.

(44d line 75) וְלֹא כֵן תַּנֵּי. מִנַּיִין הָאוֹמֵר לְאִשְׁתּוֹ. הֲרֵי זֶה גִיטֵיךְ לִפְנֵי מִיתָתִי שָׁעָה אַחַת. וְכֵן הָאוֹמֵר לְשִׁפְחָתוֹ. הֲרֵי שְׁטָר שִׁחְרוּרֶיךָ לִפְנֵי מִיתָתִי שָׁעָה אַחַת. שֶׁהִיא אֲסוּרָה לוֹכַל בַּתְּרוּמָה מִיָּד. תַּמָּן מִשָּׁעָה רִאשׁוֹנָה נִתְקַלְקְלָה. בְּרַם הָכָא לִכְשֶׁיָּמוּת הִיא מִתְקַלְקֶלֶת

But did we not state[88]: From where that "if somebody[89] says to his wife[90], this is your bill of divorce one hour before my death, or he says to his slave girl, this is the document of your manumission one hour before my death, each would be immediately forbidden to eat heave?" There, she is disabled immediately[91], but here she will only be disabled when he has died[92].

88 A similar text is in Tosephta 4:12, quoted in the Babli 28a, *Yebamot* 69b.

90 She is childless.

91 Since the bills were executed in the expectation of his death, whose time is unknown, it has to be expected immediately.

92 Since the husband expects to return from his trip overseas, the wife does not have to expect his death and can apply the principle of permanence of the *status quo ante*. The Tosephta does not contradict the principle.

The explanations of the Babli in *Gittin* and *Yebamot* are inconsistent with one another and the Yerushalmi.

משנה ד: שְׁלֹשָׁה דְבָרִים אָמַר רִבִּי אֶלְעָזֶר בֶּן פַּרְטָא לִפְנֵי חֲכָמִים (fol. 44c) וְקִייְמוּ אֶת דְּבָרָיו עַל עִיר שֶׁהִקִּיפוּהָ כַּרְקוֹם וְעַל הַסְּפִינָה הַמִּיטָּרֶפֶת בַּיָּם וְעַל הַיּוֹצֵא לִידוֹן שֶׁהֵן בְּחֶזְקַת קַיָּימִין. אֲבָל עִיר שֶׁכְּבָשָׁהּ כַּרְקוֹם וּסְפִינָה שֶׁאָבְדָה בַיָּם וְהַיּוֹצֵא לֵיהָרֵג נוֹתְנִין עֲלֵיהֶן חוּמְרֵי חַיִּים וְחוּמְרֵי מֵתִים. בַּת יִשְׂרָאֵל לְכֹהֵן וּבַת כֹּהֵן לְיִשְׂרָאֵל לֹא תֹאכַל בַּתְּרוּמָה.

Mishnah 4: Rebbi Eleazar ben Parṭa said three things before the Sages and they confirmed his words: [People in] a city which was surrounded by palisades[93], on a ship in emergency at sea, or a person about to be judged[94], are presumed to be alive[95]. But on [people in] a city conquered from palisades, a ship lost at sea, or a person led to execution, one puts the restrictions of the living and the dead: neither an Israel's daughter[96] married to a Cohen[97] nor a Cohen's daughter[96] married to an Israel[98] may eat heave.

93 Besieged by a hostile army.	husband's death.
94 In a capital case.	97 She has to assume that her husband is dead and she has lost the right to priestly food.
95 The wife of a man in one of these situations has to assume that her husband is alive.	
96 If she is childless; otherwise she remains in her husband's clan after the	98 She has to assume that her husband is alive and she has not regained the right to priestly food.

(45a line 3) **הלכה ד:** שְׁלֹשָׁה דְבָרִים אָמַר רבי לְעָזָר בֶּן עֲזַרְיָה לִפְנֵי חֲכָמִים בַּכֶּרֶם בְּיַבְנֶה. עַל עִיר שֶׁהִקִּיפוּהָ כַרְקוֹם. אֵי זֶהוּ כַרְקוֹם. רִבִּי בָּא בְשֵׁם רַב חִייָה בַּר אַשִׁי. כְּגוֹן זוּגִין וְשַׁלְשְׁלָיוֹת וּכְלָבִים וַאֲוָוזִין וְתַרְנְגוֹלִים וְאִסְטְרָטִיּוֹת הַמַּקִּיפִין אֶת הָעִיר. וְאָמַר רִבִּי בָּא בְשֵׁם רַב חִייָה בַּר אַשִׁי. מַעֲשֶׂה הָיָה וּבָרְחָה מִשָּׁם סוּמָא אַחַת. הָיָה שָׁם פִּירְצָה אַחַת מַצֶּלֶת אֶת הַכֹּל. הָיוּ שָׁם מַחְבּוּיָיה צְרִיכָה. רִבִּי זְעִירָא רִבִּי בָּא בַר זַבְדָּא רִבִּי יִצְחָק בַּר חֲקוּלַאי בְּשֵׁם רִבִּי יוּדָן נְשִׂייָא. וּבִלְבַד כַּרְקוֹם שֶׁלְּאוֹתוֹ מַלְכוּת. אֲבָל כַּרְקוֹם שֶׁלְּמַלְכוּת אֲחֶרֶת כְּלִיסְטִים הֵן.

3 זוגין | **כ** דוגין   כלבים | **כ** כבלים   ואסטרטיות | **כ** וארטוטוט   4 חייה | **כ** חמא
סומא | **כ** סומה   5 מחבויייה | **כ** מחבויים   6 זעירא | **כ** זעירה   חקולאי | **כ** חקולא
7 כליסטים | **כ** כליסטיס

"Rebbi Eleazar ben Azariah said three things before the Sages in the vineyard at Jabne: About [people in] a city which was surrounded by palisades."99 100What are palisades? Rebbi Abba in the name of Rav Ḥiyya bar Ashi: For example if bells, chains, and dogs, and geese, and chickens, and soldiers surround the town. And Rebbi Abba in the name of Rav Ḥiyya bar Ashi said, it happened that a blind woman was able to flee from there. If there was one breach, it saved all. If there were hiding places, it is questionable. Rebbi Ze'ira, Rebbi Abba bar Zavda, Rebbi Isaac bar Ḥaqula, in the name of Rebbi Yudan the Prince: Only if there were palisades of that government. But palisades from another government are like robbers.

99 This is not a quote from the Mishnah; it might be from a *baraita* which seems to have disappeared from Tosephta 2:12 (quoted in the next paragraph) which is missing an introduction.

100 This is from *Ketubot* 2:10 (noted כ), explained there in Notes 163-171. (Note the spelling ליסטים, the final ם representing ס, a sure sign of Babylonian spelling.)

(45a line 11) וְעוֹד שְׁלֹשָׁה הוֹסִיפוּ עֲלֵיהֶן. אֶת שֶׁגְּרָרַתּוֹ חַיָה וְאֶת שֶׁשְּׁטָפוֹ נָהָר וְאֶת שֶׁנָּפְלָה עָלָיו מַפּוֹלֶת. נוֹתְנִין עָלֶיהָ חוּמְרֵי חַיִּים וְחוּמְרֵי מֵתִים. בַּת יִשְׂרָאֵל לְכֹהֵן וּבַת כֹּהֵן לְיִשְׂרָאֵל לֹא תֹאכַל בַּתְּרוּמָה.

[101]They added three additional cases: One who was dragged away by a wild animal, one who was swept away by a river, and one buried by a collapse[102]. One puts the restrictions of the living and the dead on her[103]: neither an Israel's daughter[96] married to a Cohen[97] nor a Cohen's daughter[96] married to an Israel[98] may eat heave.

101 Tosephta 2:12.
102 Collapse of a house or a landslide.

103 The wife of a man who is the victim of one of these accidents.

(fol. 44c) **משנה ח:** הַמֵּבִיא גֵט בָּאָרֶץ יִשְׂרָאֵל וְחָלָה הֲרֵי זֶה מְשַׁלְּחוֹ בְּיַד אַחֵר. אִם אָמַר לוֹ טוֹל לִי מִמֶּנָּה חֵפֶץ פְּלוֹנִי לֹא יְשַׁלְּחֶנּוּ בְּיַד אַחֵר שֶׁאֵין רְצוֹנוֹ שֶׁיְּהֵא פִּקְדוֹנוֹ בְּיַד אַחֵר.

Mishnah 5: If somebody is transporting a bill of divorce in the Land of Israel when he falls sick, he may send it by somebody else[104]. If [the husband] had told him, take from her such and such[105], he cannot send it by somebody else since he[106] does not want to see his valuables in somebody else's hand.

104 Since the messenger does not have to declare that the bill was written and signed before him, there is no reason why the original messenger would have to deliver the bill.

105 If the wife wants the divorce, the husband can require to be paid for it.

106 The husband. A person entrusted to handle valuables cannot transfer his responsibilities to another person without becoming liable for any damages that may occur; cf. *Ketubot* 9:5, Note 144.

(45a line 14) **הלכה ה:** הַמֵּבִיא גֵט בְּאֶרֶץ יִשְׂרָאֵל וְחָלָה כול׳. מִפְּנֵי שֶׁחָלָה. הָא לֹא חָלָה לֹא.

Halakhah 5: "If somebody is transporting a bill of divorce in the Land of Israel when he falls sick," etc. Because he falls sick; therefore not if he did not fall sick[107].

107 Without special authorization, the messenger who transports the bill of divorce cannot appoint a substitute. In Babylonian sources (Babli 29a, Tosephta 2:13) any messenger is empowered to deliver the bill to a substitute unless the husband explicitly restricted his powers.

(45a line 15) לֵית הָדָא פְּלִיגָא עַל רִבִּי יוֹחָנָן. דְּרִבִּי יוֹחָנָן אָמַר. שׁוֹמֵר שֶׁמָּסַר לְשׁוֹמֵר הָרִאשׁוֹן חַיָּיב. רִבִּי בָּא בְּרֵיהּ דְּרִבִּי חִייָה. מִשּׁוּם תְּנַאי גִיטִין. מַה נָּפַק מִבֵּינֵיהוֹן. קִידֵּם הַבַּעַל וּנְטָלָהּ. אִין תֵּימַר מִשּׁוּם תְּנַאי גִיטִין. יָאוּת. אִין תֵּימַר שֶׁאֵין רְצוֹנִי שֶׁיְּהֵא פִקְדוֹנִי בְּיַד אַחֵר. הֲרֵי אֵין פִּקְדוֹנוֹ בְּיַד אַחֵר. אַף בְּקִידּוּשִׁין

כֵּן. מַה בֵּין גִּיטִּין מַה בֵּין קִידּוּשִׁין. בְּיַד כָּל־אָדָם מָצוּי לְגָרֵשׁ. לֹא בְיַד כָּל־אָדָם מָצוּי לְקַדֵּשׁ.

This does not disagree with what Rebbi Joḥanan said, since Rebbi Joḥanan said, if an agent handed over to another agent, the first one is responsible[108]. Rebbi Abba the son of Rebbi Ḥiyya: Because of a condition of the divorce[109]. What is the difference between them? If the husband came earlier and took it[110]. If you say, because of a condition of the divorce, that is understandable[111]. If you say, because I do not want to see my valuables in somebody else's hand, his valuables are not in somebody else's hand[112]. Is it the same for preliminary marriages[113]? What is the difference between divorces and preliminary marriages? One can divorce through the agency of anybody[114]. One cannot preliminarily marry through the agency of anybody[115].

108 Unless the principal gave his prior agreement. The main source is *Qiddušin* 1:4 (60b l.48). In the Babli (*Baba Qama* 11b, 56b; *Baba Meṣiʿa* 36a) the matter is in dispute. In this opinion, the messenger who chooses a substitute if there are valuables involved accepts responsibility for any accidents that may befall the substitute for his mishandling of the matter.

109 He reads the Mishnah as stating that the divorce shall become valid only if (a) the bill of divorce was delivered and (b) the valuables were delivered by the wife to the designated messenger. A substitute can fulfill (a) but not (b), invalidating the divorce.

110 The valuable he wanted from the wife.

111 The Mishnah which states that the messenger *cannot* appoint a substitute, meaning that the appointment of a substitute invalidates the divorce.

112 In this case, one has to read the Mishnah as stating that the messenger *should not* appoint a substitute, but such an appointment does not invalidate the divorce.

113 According to R. Joḥanan, can an

agent appointed to conclude a preliminary marriage by proxy appoint a substitute agent?

114   Since the divorce does not need the consent of the wife, the choice of the agent is the husband's and is irrelevant.

115   An agent not approved by the prospective bride is useless.

(fol. 44c) **משנה ו:** הַמֵּבִיא גֵט מִמְּדִינַת הַיָּם וְחָלָה עוֹשֶׂה בֵית דִּין וּמְשַׁלְּחוֹ וְאוֹמֵר לִפְנֵיהֶם בְּפָנַי נִכְתַּב וּבְפָנַי נֶחְתַּם. וְאֵין הַשָּׁלִיחַ הָאַחֲרוֹן צָרִיךְ שֶׁיֹּאמַר בְּפָנַי נִכְתַּב וּבְפָנַי נֶחְתַּם אֶלָּא אוֹמֵר שָׁלִיחַ בֵּית דִּין אֲנִי.

Mishnah 6: If somebody transports a bill of divorce overseas and falls sick, he assembles a court to send it and declares before them: "it was written and signed before me." The later messenger does not have to say: "it was written and signed before me," but he says: "I am an agent of the court.116"

116   This implies that if the original bill of divorce was certified by a court, no messenger has to say that it was written and signed before him but that he is a court appointee, or, in modern terms, that a bill of divorce certified by a competent court can even be sent by mail to the court which has jurisdiction over the wife.

(45a line 21) **הלכה ו:** הַמֵּבִיא גֵט מִמְּדִינַת הַיָּם וְחָלָה כול׳. אָמַר רִבִּי מָנָא. לָכֵן צְרִיכָה. וְהוּא שֶׁבָּא לְאֶרֶץ יִשְׂרָאֵל. שֶׁלֹּא תֹאמַר. הוֹאִיל וּבָא לְאֶרֶץ יִשְׂרָאֵל יֵעָשֶׂה כְגִיטֵי אֶרֶץ יִשְׂרָאֵל. וְגִיטֵי אֶרֶץ יִשְׂרָאֵל אֵין צָרִיךְ לוֹמַר. בְּפָנַיי נִכְתַּב וּבְפָנַיי נֶחְתַּם.

If somebody transports a bill of divorce overseas and falls sick," etc. Rebbi Mana said, this117 is only necessary if he already has arrived in the

Land of Israel. Lest you say, since he arrived in the Land of Israel it should be treated as a bill of divorce from the Land of Israel[118], and for bills of divorce from the Land of Israel one does not have to say: "it was written and signed before me.[119]"

117 His problem is, if the second messenger is an agent of the court, why does he have to declare anything (in front of two witnesses at the moment he hands over the bill of divorce)?

118 Since it had been certified by a court in the Land of Israel.

119 Nor does he have to say: I am an agent of the court.

(45a line 23) חָלָה הַשָּׁלִיחַ. אָמַר רִבִּי חֲנִינָה. בְּרֵיהּ דְּרִבִּי אַבָּא הֲוָה לֵיהּ עוֹבְדָא וְשָׁאַל וְשָׁלַח לְרִבִּי חִייָה וּלְרִבִּי יָסָא וּלְרִבִּי אִימִּי וְהוֹרוֹן לֵיהּ. אֵין הַשָּׁלִיחַ הָרִאשׁוֹן צָרִיךְ שֶׁיֹּאמַר. בְּפָנַיי נִכְתַּב וּבְפָנַיי נֶחְתָּם. אֶלָּא אוֹמֵר. שָׁלִיחַ בֵּית דִּין אֲנִי.

If the messenger[120] fell sick. Rebbi Ḥanina said, a case came before the son of Rebbi Abba and he sent to ask Rebbi Ḥiyya, Rebbi Yasa and Rebbi Immi[121]. They instructed him that the first messenger[122] does not have to say: "it was written and signed before me[123]," but he says, "I am an agent of the court.[124]"

120 The one appointed by the dying first messenger.

121 The three successors of R. Joḥanan.

122 He is called "first" because he appoints a new messenger but really he is a second or later messenger to whom the bill was entrusted. The problem is that the Mishnah only empowers the original messenger to appoint a new one; nothing is said about successive later messengers.

123 Since he is a substitute, he could not say that.

124 He can say that and appoint a new messenger by the local court. The Babli, 29b, reads the expression in the Mishnah: "the later messenger" as "any

later messenger", to the effect that the appointment of successive messengers is explicitly authorized by the Mishnah.

There, the main actor is the son of R. Abba*hu*.

(45a line 27) צָרִיךְ לִמְסוֹר לוֹ כָּל־שְׁלִיחוּתוֹ. רִבִּי יִרְמְיָה אָמַר. צָרִיךְ לִמְסוֹר לוֹ כָּל־שְׁלִיחוּתוֹ. רִבִּי אָבִין בַּר כַּהֲנָא אָמַר. אֵין צָרִיךְ לִמְסוֹר לוֹ כָּל־שְׁלִיחוּתוֹ. מַייתֵי לָהּ דְּרִבִּי אָבִין בַּר כַּהֲנָא מִן הָדָא. אֵין הַשָּׁלִיחַ הָאַחֲרוֹן צָרִיךְ שֶׁיֹּאמַר. בְּפָנַיי נִכְתַּב וּבְפָנַיי נֶחְתַּם. אֶלָּא אוֹמֵר. שָׁלִיחַ בֵּית דִּין אֲנִי. אָמַר רִבִּי יִרְמְיָה. חָזַר בֵּיהּ רִבִּי אָבִין בַּר כַּהֲנָא מִן הָדָא. אֵין הַשָּׁלִיחַ הָאַחֲרוֹן צָרִיךְ שֶׁיֹּאמַר. בְּפָנַיי נִכְתַּב וּבְפָנַיי נֶחְתַּם. אֶלָּא אוֹמֵר. שָׁלִיחַ בֵּית דִּין אֲנִי.

Does he have to deliver the entire agency to him[125]? Rebbi Jeremiah said, he has to deliver the entire agency to him. Rebbi Abin bar Cahana said, he need not deliver the entire agency to him. Rebbi Abin bar Cahana brought it from this: "The later messenger does not have to say: 'it was written and signed before me,' but he says: 'I am an agent of the court.'[126]" Rebbi Jeremiah said, Rebbi Abin bar Cahana retracted this, because of: "The later messenger does not have to say: 'it was written and signed before me,' but he says: 'I am an agent of the court.'[127]"

125 If the husband had entrusted the first messenger not only with the bill of divorce but charged him with additional messages, is the transfer of agency valid if only the delivery of the bill is given to a subsequent messenger or is the agency one and indivisible? This is a new question since its protagonist, R. Jeremiah, was a student of R. Ḥiyya (bar Abba)'s student R. Ze'ira.

126 He reads the Mishnah as stating that the later messenger has only to identify himself as an agent of the court for the delivery of the bill without further comment.

127 The same Mishnah can be read in the opposite sense: Since obviously no substitute messenger can say that the bill was written and signed before

him, the mention of writing and signing for a later messenger can only mean that he stands for the first in all respects.

משנה ז (fol. 44c): הַמַּלְוֶה מָעוֹת אֶת הַכֹּהֵן וְאֶת הַלֵּוִי וְאֶת הֶעָנִי לִהְיוֹת מַפְרִישׁ עֲלֵיהֶן מֶחֶלְקָן מַפְרִישׁ עֲלֵיהֶן בְּחֶזְקַת שֶׁהֵן קַיָּימִין וְאֵינוֹ חוֹשֵׁשׁ שֶׁמָּא מֵת כֹּהֵן אוֹ לֵוִי אוֹ הֶעֱשִׁיר הֶעָנִי. מֵתוּ צָרִיךְ לִיטוֹל רְשׁוּת מִן הַיּוֹרְשִׁין. אִם הִלְוָום בִּפְנֵי בֵית דִּין אֵינוֹ צָרִיךְ לִיטוֹל רְשׁוּת.

Mishnah 7: If somebody[128] lent money to a Cohen, a Levite, or a poor person to separate on their account, he can proceed on the assumption that they are alive and does not worry whether the Cohen or Levite died or the poor person became rich[129]. If they died, he has to receive permission from the heirs[130]; if the loan was executed in court he does not need permission[131].

128 A farmer gave a loan to potential recipients of his heave and tithes with the understanding that they do not have to repay the loan but that the farmer will separate both heaves for the account of the Cohen, sell the heaves to another Cohen, and credit the receipt to the Cohen's account with him, reducing the amount owed. Similarly, he will separate first tithe on the Levite's account and tithe of the poor for the poor man, deduct the fair value of the produce from his account and eat the tithes himself with his family, since tithes are permitted food for anybody.

129 Once the poor person becomes disqualified for public assistance, he has to inform the farmer.

130 They might want to pay off the outstanding balance to establish a record of good credit.

131 If the setup was part of a public document, the heirs would have to negotiate with the farmer to change its terms.

(45a line 33) **הלכה ז**: הַמַּלְוֶה מָעוֹת אֶת הַכֹּהֵן כול'. רִבִּי אַבָּהוּ בְשֵׁם רֵישׁ לָקִישׁ. דְּרִבִּי יוֹסֵי הִיא. דְּתַנִּינָן תַּמָּן. רִבִּי יוֹסֵי אוֹמֵר. כָּל־שֶׁיֵּשׁ לוֹ חֲלִיפִין בְּיַד כֹּהֵן פָּטוּר מִן הַמַּתָּנוֹת. וְרִבִּי מֵאִיר מְחַיֵּיב. כְּלוּם אָמַר רִבִּי יוֹסֵי לֹא בְקַיָּים. בְּרַם הָכָא עַד כְּדוֹן בָּעֵי מִיזְרַע. רִבִּי אַבָּהוּ בְשֵׁם רִבִּי יוֹחָנָן. בְּמַכָּרֵי כְהוּנָּה וּלְוִיָּה הִיא מַתְנִיתָא. וְהָא תַּנִּינָן עָנִי. וְיֵשׁ מַכָּר לְעָנִי. אֲתָא עוֹבְדָא קוֹמֵי רִבִּי אִימִּי. כֹּהֵן לֵוִי שֶׁהָיָה חַיָּיב לְיִשְׂרָאֵל מָעוֹת וְאָמַר לוֹ. הַפְרֵשׁ עָלֵיהֶם מֵחֶלְקִי. אָמַר לֵיהּ. וְלֹא תַּנִּינָן אֶלָּא. הַמַּלְוֶה מָעוֹת אֶת הַכֹּהֵן וְאֶת הַלֵּוִי וְאֶת הֶעָנִי לִהְיוֹת מַפְרִישׁ עֲלֵיהֶן מֵחֶלְקוֹ. כְּשֶׁהִלְוָהוּ עַל מְנָת כֵּן. הָא לֹא הִלְוָהוּ עַל מְנָת כֵּן לֹא. רִבִּי זְעִירָא אָמַר. אֲפִילוּ לֹא הִלְוָהוּ עַל מְנָת כֵּן. חֵילֵיהּ דְּרִבִּי זְעִירָא מִן הָדָא. וְכֵן בֶּן לֵוִי שֶׁהָיָה חַיָּיב לְיִשְׂרָאֵל מָעוֹת. הַפְרֵשׁ עָלֵיהֶם מֵחֶלְקִי. וְלֹא יְהֵא גוּבָה וּמַפְרִישׁ. שֶׁאֵין לֵוִי עוֹשֶׂה לֵוִי. שֶׁלֹּא אָמַר אֶלָּא. לֹא יְהֵא מַפְרִישׁ. הָא מִשֶּׁלּוֹ מַפְרִישׁ.

Halakhah 7: "If somebody lent money to a Cohen," etc. Rebbi Abbahu in the name of Rebbi Simeon ben Laqish: This follows Rebbi Yose; as we have stated there[132]: "Rebbi Yose says, anything whose replacement is in the Cohen's hand is freed from the gifts, but Rebbi Meïr obligates." Did Rebbi Yose not speak only if it did exist? But here, he still needs to sow[133]! Rebbi Abbahu in the name of Rebbi Johanan: The Mishnah speaks of acquaintances of Cohanim or Levites[134]. But did we not state "a poor person"? Does a poor person have acquaintances[135]? There came a case before Rebbi Immi: A Cohen or Levite who owed money to an Israel and told him[136], separate from my part for my account. He said to him, did we not state: "If somebody lent money to a Cohen, a Levite, or a poor person to separate on their account." When the loan was given under these conditions. Therefore, not if it was not a condition of the loan! Rebbi Ze'ira said, even if it was not a condition of the loan. Rebbi Ze'ira's force is from the following[137]: "Similarly, a Levite who owed money to an Israel and said to him, separate on my account; only he should not collect and separate because no Levite makes a Levite." He only said, he should not separate[138], but from his own he may separate.

132 Mishnah *Bekhorot* 2:8. The Mishnah speaks of a rancher whose ewe gave birth to twin lambs, one of which is a firstling but it is not known which. A firstling has to be given to a Cohen (*Deut.* 15:19); it may not be shorn (or, if a calf, used for work). The rancher can fulfill his monetary obligation by giving one of the two lambs to the Cohen; the other lamb has to be put out to graze until it develops a defect; then it can be eaten by its owner (*Deut.* 15:21-22). If it was known which lamb was a firstling, that one would have to be given to the Cohen and if the other lamb were slaughtered, some parts would have to be given to a Cohen (*Deut.* 18:3). But in the case under consideration, R. Yose holds that no gifts to the Cohen are due since potentially the lamb was the Cohen's and a Cohen who slaughters does not have to give away anything. He equates potential possession and real possession. The application to the Mishnah here is that the Cohen can dispose of the heave as if he had received it.

R. Meïr holds that the gifts are due since they would be due if it was known which one was the firstling.

In the Babli, 30a, this is Ulla's opinion.

133 Since nobody can acquire anything nonexistent (*Ketubot* 5:5, Note 113), R. Yose's argument cannot be applied to our case.

134 The expression is Biblical (*2K.* 12:6,8); it refers to people who regularly give all their priestly gifts or tithes to the same Cohen or Levite. Then heave and tithes have the status of annuities and cannot be said to be nonexistent.

In the Babli, 30a, this is Rav's opinion. Samuel requires that heave or tithes be actually given to a third party Cohen or Levite, acting as recipient for the debtor, who then returns the produce to the farmer. That opinion has no parallel in the Yerushalmi.

135 The tithe of the poor has to be

given to the first poor person who applies.

136 After the loan was given, the debtor then asked to be excused from repayment using the method outlined in the Mishnah.

137 Tosephta *Demay* 7:15. The Levite cannot tell the Israel to arrange with other farmers that they pay him to give tithes for them and deduct the sum from the Levite's debt, since no Levite can dispose of another Levite's tithes.

138 Missing in the text: Other people's tithes.

(45a line 45) לֵית כָּאן אֵינוֹ חוֹשֵׁשׁ. אֲבָל חוֹשֵׁשׁ הוּא שֶׁלֹּא יַעֲשִׁיר הֶעָנִי. וְתַנֵּי כֵן. הַמַּלְוֶה מָעוֹת אֶת הֶעָנִי וְאֶת הֶעָשִׁיר אֵין מַפְרִישִׁין עֲלֵיהֶן. שֶׁאֵין מַפְרִישִׁין עַל הָאָבוּד.

There is no "he does not worry," since he has to worry lest the poor became rich. It was stated so[139]: "If somebody lends money to a poor and rich person he cannot separate for him, for one does not separate for what was lost."

139 It seems that the text is slightly corrupt; the translation follows the text of Tosephta 3:1: הַמַּלְוֶה מָעוֹת אֶת הֶעָנִי וְהֶעָשִׁיר אֵין מַפְרִישִׁין עָלָיו. שֶׁאֵין מַפְרִישִׁין עַל הָאָבוּד. This is also the Yerushalmi text quoted in many medieval authors, cf. *Tosefta ki-Fshuta Giṭṭin* p. 824, Note 16. The last clause means that if the poor person temporarily became rich (i. e., was ineligible for public welfare as defined in *Peah* 9:9) and then poor again, the lender cannot use the tithe of the poor of the time of ineligibility but must give it away to another poor person since that tithe was lost for the borrower. The Yerushalmi text considers poor and rich as different persons residing in the same body since they fall in different legal categories.

(45a line 47) רִבִּי חִייָה בַּר עוּקְבָּה בְּשֵׁם רִבִּי יוֹסֵי בְּשֵׁם רִבִּי חֲנִינָה. בְּיוֹרְשֵׁי כְהוּנָּה וּלְוִייָה הִיא מַתְנִיתָא. אֲבָל בְּיוֹרְשֵׁי עָנִי אֵין לְעָנִי נַחֲלָה. תַּנֵּי בַּר קַפְּרָא. אֵין לָךְ אָדָם שֶׁאֵינוֹ בָא לִידֵי מִידָה זוֹ. אִם לֹא הוּא בְנוֹ. אִם לֹא בְנוֹ בֶּן בְּנוֹ.

הָדָא אָמְרָה. יָכוֹל הוּא לַחֲזוֹר בּוֹ. הַמַּלְוֶה מַהוּ שֶׁיַּחֲזוֹר בּוֹ. נִשְׁמְעִינָהּ מִן הָדָא. הַמַּלְוֶה מָעוֹת אֶת הֶעָשִׁיר וְאֶת הֶעָנִי אֵין מַפְרִישִׁין עֲלֵיהֶן. שֶׁאֵין מַפְרִישִׁין עַל הָאָבוּד. וְזָכָה הֶעָנִי בְּמַה שֶּׁיֵּשׁ בְּיָדוֹ. הָדָא אָמְרָה הַמַּלְוֶה אֵינוֹ יָכוֹל לַחֲזוֹר בּוֹ.

Rebbi Ḥiyya bar Uqba in the name of Rebbi Yose in the name[139a] of Rebbi Ḥanina: The Mishnah speaks of the heirs in priesthood and Levitic status[140]. But concerning the poor, the poor has no inheritance. Bar Qappara stated: No person is immune from this[141]; if not he then his son, if not his son then his grandson. This[142] means, he can change the terms. Can the creditor change the terms? Let us hear from the following: "If somebody lends money to a first rich and then poor person he cannot separate for him, for one does not separate for what was lost and the poor acquired what is in his hand.[143]" This implies that the creditor cannot change the terms[144].

139a This probably should read "son of".

140 The creditor has to renew the contract if the heirs are priests or Levites. This excludes the poor from this rule, as well as cases in which a Cohen or Levite has only daughters married to Israel husbands.

141 Poverty.

142 "This" is not Bar Qappara's homily but the Tosephta stated earlier and repeated later, that the poor debtor who became rich cannot continue the arrangement but must pay off the debt. This means that if the circumstances change, the debtor can change the terms to terms less favorable to him.

143 The last sentence is also in the Tosephta, Note 139, quoted in the Babli, 30b. If the poor remains rich, the creditor has no way to recoup his money.

144 In the Tosephta, 3:1, this is an explicit statement. In the Babli, 30a, both the statement that the debtor can change the arrangement but the creditor cannot are attributed to the late Amora Rav Papa; both Talmudim are unaware of the Tosephta.

(45a line 54) לֵית הָדָא פְּלִיגָא עַל דְּרַב. דְּרַב אָמַר. יוֹרֵשׁ כִּמְשׁוּעְבָּד. כְּשֵׁם שֶׁאֵין מִלְוֶה בְּעֵדִים נִגְבֵּית מִן הַמְשׁוּעְבָּדִין כָּךְ אֵינָהּ נִגְבֵּית מִן הַיּוֹרְשִׁין. פָּתַר לָהּ בְּמִלְוֶה בִשְׁטָר. רִבִּי אַבָּהוּ בְשֵׁם רִבִּי יוֹחָנָן. מִלְוֶה בְּעֵדִים נִגְבֵּית מִן הַיּוֹרְשִׁין וּבִלְבַד יוֹרְשִׁין שֶׁיָּרְשׁוּ קַרְקַע. כְּהָדָא אִילֵּין דְּרַב נְחֶמְיָה אַשְׁאֲלוֹן לְצִיבּוּרַיָּיא פְרִיטִין. אָתָא עוֹבְדָא קוֹמֵי רַבָּנִין אָמְרִין לֵיהּ. לֵית צִיבּוּר כּוּלֵּיהּ עָתַר לֵית צִיבּוּר כּוּלֵּיהּ מֵיעָנִי.

Does this[145] not disagree with Rav? Since Rav said, an heir is like a holder of encumbered property. Just as a loan given before witnesses cannot be collected from encumbered property[146], so it cannot be collected from heirs. He explains it for a documented loan[147]. Rebbi Abbahu in the name of Rebbi Johanan: A loan given before witnesses can be collected from heirs, on condition that they inherited real estate[148]. As[149] those from the house of Rav Nehemiah, who lent money to the public[150]. The case came before the rabbis who said, the public is neither all rich nor all poor.

145 The statement that after the Cohen's death the creditor has to renew the agreement with his heirs.

146 In rabbinic practice, mortgages are not written on specified parcels but are liens on all real estate the debtor owned at the time the loan was given. If such real estate is later sold, the lien of the mortgage holder is not removed; if the debtor cannot pay, the creditor can foreclose from the buyer. A loan arrangement made orally before witnesses is not a mortgage; the loan can be foreclosed neither from any buyer nor from debtor's property subject to another person's lien. If the loan cannot be foreclosed, there seems to be no reason why the creditor can ask anything from the heirs.

147 A mortgage.

148 He agrees that a loan cannot be foreclosed from encumbered property, but if the debtor has unencumbered property, free of any lien, it can be foreclosed on the testimony of the witnesses. Therefore, as long as the

heirs inherit any real estate (in the language of the Babli, 30b, at least the area covered by a needle), the oral loan remains in force and the creditor has reason to approach the heirs.

149 This is an illustration of the Mishnah, not of the preceding rules.

150 They advanced money to the public welfare fund, to be repaid from future collections. The question was raised whether money collected for the relief of the poor can be diverted to repay the capitalists. The answer is positive since the committee overseeing charity always will have clients on whose behalf they took the money in the first place and on whose behalf they may repay.

(fol. 44c) **משנה ח:** הַמַּנִּיחַ פֵּירוֹת לִהְיוֹת מַפְרִישׁ עֲלֵיהֶן תְּרוּמָה וּמַעְשְׂרוֹת מָעוֹת לִהְיוֹת מַפְרִישׁ עֲלֵיהֶן מַעֲשֵׂר שֵׁנִי מַפְרִישׁ עֲלֵיהֶן בְּחֶזְקַת שֶׁהֵן קַיָּימִין. אִם אָבְדוּ הֲרֵי זֶה חוֹשֵׁשׁ מֵעֵת לָעֵת דִּבְרֵי רִבִּי לֶעְזָר. רִבִּי יְהוּדָה אוֹמֵר. בִּשְׁלֹשָׁה פְרָקִים בּוֹדְקִין אֶת הַיַּיִן בְּקָדִים שֶׁלְּמוֹצָאֵי הֶחָג וּבְהוֹצָאַת סְמָדַר וּבִשְׁעַת כְּנִיסַת מַיִם בַּבּוֹסֶר.

Mishnah 8: If somebody sets aside[151] produce to be used for future heave and tithes, or money to be used for Second Tithe[152], can refer to them on the presumption that they exist. If they were lost, one worries about them for 24 hours back[153], the words of Rebbi Eleazar[154]. Rebbi Jehudah says, three times a year one has to check the wine[155]: At the time of East wind after Tabernacles[156], when the vines blossom, and when fluid starts to enter unripe grapes.

151 At the beginning of the harvest he sets aside a quantity of produce so that for the remainder of the harvest he simply can declare that all heave and tithes due at the moment of declaration should be taken from a certain spot of the set-aside. He can do that from a distance and does not have

actually to go to the produce and separate heave and tithes for the next batch. For the rules of heave, see Tractate *Terumot*.

152 To redeem the Second Tithe the moment it becomes due; cf. Introduction to Tractate *Ma'aser Šeni*.

153 Any heave and tithes which were supposed to be referred to the produce set aside earlier than within 24 hours of the discovery that they were missing are still considered in good order; only produce referred to in the last 24 hours before discovery has to be tithed a second time.

154 The Tanna, ben Shamua.

155 That it remained wine and did not turn into vinegar, since vinegar cannot be used to tithe wine.

156 A fall *ḥamsīn* wind.

(45a line 60) **הלכה ח:** הַמַּנִּיחַ פֵּירוֹת כול'. רִבִּי אֶלְעָזָר בֶּן אַנְטִיגְנָס בְּשֵׁם רִבִּי לֶעְזָר בֶּן יַנַּאי. זֹאת אוֹמֶרֶת שֶׁאֵין לָךְ מְקוּלְקָל מֵעַת לְעֵת אֶלָּא יוֹם הָאַחֲרוֹן בִּלְבָד. אָמַר רִבִּי יוֹחָנָן. אֵין לָךְ מְתוּקָּן מֵעַת לְעֵת אֶלָּא יוֹם רִאשׁוֹן בִּלְבָד. דְּתַנִּינָן תַּמָּן. מִקְוֶה שֶׁנִּמְדַד וְנִמְצָא חָסֵר. חִינָנָא בְּרֵיהּ דְּרַב אַסִּי בַּר מָמָל בְּשֵׁם רִבִּי לֶעְזָר. זוֹ לְהוֹצִיא מִדִּבְרֵי רִבִּי לֶעְזָר. דְּתַנִּינָן. אִם אָבְדוּ הֲרֵי זֶה חוֹשֵׁשׁ מֵעַת לְעֵת. דִּבְרֵי רִבִּי לֶעְזָר.

Halakhah 8: "If somebody sets aside produce," etc. Rebbi Eleazar ben Antigonos in the name of Rebbi Eleazar ben Yannai: This means that nothing is in disorder for 24 hours but the last day[153]. Rebbi Joḥanan said: Nothing is in order for 24 hours but the first day[157], as we have stated there[158]: "If a *miqweh* was measured and found deficient." Ḥinena the son of Rav Assi bar Mamal in the name of Rebbi Eleazar[159]: That is to negate the words of Rebbi Eleazar[154], as we have stated: "If they were lost, one worries about them for 24 hours back, the words of Rebbi Eleazar.[160]"

157 He reads the words of R. Eleazar meaning that one worries about all the times except the first 24 hours; all produce processed later than that

date have to be tithed again. Both opinions are also reported in the Babli, 31a, with the Babli leaning towards the interpretation of R. Joḥanan as the correct one.

158 Mishnah *Miqwa'ot* 2:2: If a *miqweh* was measured and found deficient (containing less than 40 *se'ah* of water), all things and persons purified by immersion in the *miqweh* after the last preceding check are considered impure. As pointed out by M. Margalit, R. Joḥanan proves too much since by his reason everything should have to be re-tithed, even what was put in order during the first 24 hours.

159 The Amora, ben Pedat.

160 The Mishnah in *Miqwa'ot* is inconsistent with that in *Giṭṭin*. This proves that the Mishnah here, which is formulated in the name of a single person, represents a minority opinion. The Mishnah in *Miqwa'ot* is from the anonymous majority. The same argument is quoted in R. Eleazar's name in the Babli, 31b.

(45a line 66) תַּמָּן תַּנִּינָן. הַלּוֹקֵחַ יַיִן מִבֵּין הַכּוּתִים. תַּנֵּי רִבִּי יוֹסֵי וְרִבִּי שִׁמְעוֹן אוֹסְרִין. שֶׁמָּא תִּבָּקַע הַנּוֹד וְנִמְצָא שׁוֹתֵהּ טְבָלִים לְמַפְרֵעַ. וְהָדָא מַתְנִיתָא לֹא כְרִבִּי יוֹסֵי וּכְרִבִּי שִׁמְעוֹן. אָמַר רִבִּי זְעִירָה. תַּמָּן לְמַפְרֵעַ נִתְקַלְקְלָה. בְּרַם הָכָא מִיכָּן וְהֵילַךְ נִתְקַלְקְלוּ.

There, we have stated[161]: "If someone buys wine from Samaritans." It was stated[162]: "Rebbi Yose and Rebbi Simeon prohibit to do so, for the wine bag might spring a leak and it may turn out retroactively that he drank *ṭevel*[163]." Does the Mishnah here not follow Rebbi Yose and Rebbi Simeon[164]? Rebbi Ze'ira said, there[165] it was not in order from the start. But here it is not in order from now to the future.

161 Mishnah *Demai* 7:5; Notes 60-62. The Mishnah states that one may drink Samaritan wine (which is kosher but certainly not tithed) immediately on condition that one declare that one will take a stated amount from it as heave and tithe as soon as the wine is in storage.

162 Halakhah *Demai* 7:5, Note 63.

163 *Ṭevel* is untithed produce, whose

consumption at times other than during the harvest is a deadly sin.

164 Since the Mishnah permits to tithe by relying on produce stored elsewhere, and which might have disappeared in the meantime.

165 RR. Yose and Simeon may agree with the Mishnah here. In the case of Samaritan wine, it was known that the wine was not tithed, but here there is a presumption following the *status quo ante* that everything is in order.

(45a line 70) יַיִן מִגִּיתּוֹ מַפְרִישִׁין עָלָיו בְּחֶזְקַת שֶׁהוּא יַיִן עַד אַרְבָּעִים יוֹם. רַבִּי יְהוּדָה אוֹמֵר. עַד הַפֶּרֶק. אַשְׁכְּחַת אָמַר קוּלָּא וְחוּמְרָא עַל רַבִּי יְהוּדָה קוּלָּא וְחוּמְרָא עַל רַבָּנִין. קוּלָּא עַל רַבִּי יוּדָה. שֶׁאִם בָּא עַד הַפֶּרֶק וְלֹא בָאוּ אַרְבָּעִים יוֹם. וְחוּמְרָת. שֶׁאִם בָּאוּ אַרְבָּעִים יוֹם וְלֹא בָא הַפֶּרֶק אֵינוֹ תוֹרֵם. קוּלַּת עַל דְּרַבָּנִין. שֶׁאִם בָּאוּ אַרְבָּעִים יוֹם וְלֹא בָא הַפֶּרֶק אֵינוֹ תוֹרֵם. וְחוּמְרָת. שֶׁאִם בָּא הַפֶּרֶק וְלֹא בָאוּ אַרְבָּעִים יוֹם אֵינוֹ תוֹרֵם. רַבִּי סִימוֹן בָּעֵי. הִגִּיעַ אַרְבָּעִים יוֹם וְלֹא בָדַק. נִתְעַצֵּל שְׁנַיִם שְׁלֹשָׁה יָמִים וּבָא וּמְצָאוֹ חוֹמֶץ. לְמַפְרֵעוֹ הוּא נַעֲשֶׂה חוֹמֶץ אוֹ מִיכָּן וּלְהַבָּא. מַה נָפִיק בֵּינֵיהוֹן. עָבַר וְתָרַם. אִין תֵּימַר. לְמַפְרֵעַ נַעֲשָׂה חוֹמֶץ. תְּרוּמָתוֹ תְרוּמָה. אִין תֵּימַר. מִיכָּן וּלְהַבָּא. אֵין תְּרוּמָתוֹ תְרוּמָה. בָּדַק חָבִית לִהְיוֹת מַפְרִישׁ עָלֶיהָ וְהוֹלֵךְ. וּבָא וּמְצָאָהּ חוֹמֶץ. רַבִּי סִימוֹן בְּשֵׁם רַבִּי יְהוֹשֻׁעַ בֶּן לֵוִי. שְׁלֹשָׁה יָמִים הָרִאשׁוֹנִים וַדַּאי יַיִן וְהָאַחֲרוֹנִים חוֹמֶץ. וְהָאֶמְצָעִיִּים סָפֵק. אָמַר רַבִּי אַבָּהוּ. אֲנִי שְׁמַעְתִּיהָ מֵרַבִּי יְהוֹשֻׁעַ בֶּן לֵוִי. וְרַבִּי יוֹחָנָן לֹא אָמַר כֵּן אֶלָּא. שְׁלֹשָׁה יָמִים הָרִאשׁוֹנִים וַדַּאי יַיִן. מִיכָּן וְאֵילָךְ סָפֵק. מַה וּפְלִיג סָפֵק. מַה דְּאָמַר רַבִּי יוֹחָנָן בְּשֶׁמְּצָאוֹ חוֹמֶץ דֶּהָא. מַה דְּאָמַר רַבִּי יְהוֹשֻׁעַ בֶּן לֵוִי בְּשֶׁמְּצָאוֹ חוֹמֶץ בָּרוּר. וְאַתְיָין אִילֵּין פְּלוּגָתָא כְּאִילֵּין פְּלוּגָתָא. דְּתַנִּינָן תַּמָּן. מַחַט שֶׁנִּמְצֵאת חֲלוּדָה אוֹ שְׁבוּרָה טְהוֹרָה. תַּנֵּי. הִנִּיחָהּ שִׁיפָה וּבָא וּמְצָאָהּ חֲלוּדָה. רַבִּי סִימוֹן בְּשֵׁם רַבִּי יְהוֹשֻׁעַ בֶּן לֵוִי. שְׁלֹשָׁה הָרִאשׁוֹנִים וַדַּאי טְמֵאָה. אַחֲרוֹנִים טְהוֹרָה. אֶמְצָעִיִּים סָפֵק. אָמַר רַבִּי אַבָּהוּ. אָמַר רַבִּי יְהוֹשֻׁעַ בֶּן לֵוִי. וְרַבִּי יוֹחָנָן לֹא אָמַר כֵּן אֶלָּא. שְׁלֹשָׁה יָמִים הָרִאשׁוֹנִים וַדַּאי טְמֵאָה. מִיכָּן וָאֵילָךְ סָפֵק. רַבִּי אִילָא וְרַבִּי אַבָּא וְרַבִּי אֶלְעָזָר בְּשֵׁם כָּל־רַבָּנִין דְּעָלִין לְבֵי מִדְרָשָׁא. בְּיַיִן וּבְמַחַט הֲלָכָה כְּרַבִּי יְהוֹשֻׁעַ בֶּן לֵוִי.

For freshly pressed wine one can allow for up to forty days presuming that it is wine[166]; Rebbi Jehudah says, up to a break point[167]. You find that there is a leniency and a restriction following Rebbi Jehudah, and a leniency and a restriction following the rabbis. [168]A leniency following Rebbi Jehudah, if a break point arrived before forty days had passed, and a restriction if forty days passed without break point that he cannot give heave. A leniency following the rabbis, if forty days passed without break point that he cannot give heave, and a restriction, if a break point arrived before forty days had passed that he cannot give heave. Rebbi Simon asked: If the fortieth day arrived and he did not check. He was lazy for two or three days, then he came and found it to be vinegar. Is it retroactively considered to be vinegar or only from there on to the future? What is the difference? If he had transgressed and given heave. If you say that retroactively it is considered to be vinegar, his heave is heave[169]. From there on to the future it is not heave. [170]If he had checked an amphora to continuously give heave from it[171]. When he returned, he found it to be vinegar. Rebbi Simon in the name of Rebbi Joshua ben Levi: The first three days it certainly is wine, the last vinegar, and the middle ones are in doubt. Rebbi Abbahu said, I heard that from Rebbi Joshua ben Levi; Rebbi Joḥanan did not say so but the first three days it certainly is wine, after that it is in doubt[172]. Do they differ in the treatment of doubt? What Rebbi Joḥanan said refers to the case that he came and found it to be stale vinegar[173]. What Rebbi Joshua ben Levi said refers to the case that he came and found it to be strong vinegar[174]. Or their difference equals another difference, for what we have stated there[175]: "A rusty or broken needle is pure[176]." It was stated: He put it down smooth, then he came and found it rusty. Rebbi Simon in the name of Rebbi Joshua ben Levi: The first three days it certainly is impure, the last pure, and the middle ones are in doubt. Rebbi Abbahu said, that is what Rebbi Joshua ben Levi said; Rebbi Joḥanan did not say so but the first three days it certainly is impure, after that it is in doubt. Rebbi Ila, Rebbi Abba and Rebbi Eleazar in the name of all rabbis who are frequenting the House of Study: Concerning wine and needle practice follows Rebbi Joshua ben Levi[177].

166 It is difficult to judge whether fermenting freshly pressed cider will turn out to be wine or vinegar. Since in most cases one obtains wine, the fermenting juice can be considered to be wine and if a vessel full of fermenting cider was set apart to serve as heave for the entire harvest, one may declare parts of it to be heave for successive batches up to 40 days.

167 One of the three meteorologically dangerous dates listed by him in the Mishnah when wine is apt to turn into vinegar.

168 The following two sentences are garbled. One should read: A *restriction* following Rebbi Jehudah, if a break point arrived before forty days had passed, *he cannot give heave*, and a *leniency* if forty days passed without break point that he *can* give heave. A *restriction* following the rabbis, if forty days passed without break point that he cannot give heave, and a *leniency*, if a break point arrived before forty days had passed that he *can* give heave.

Since wine and vinegar are considered two different products for the purpose of heave, it is forbidden to give heave for wine from vinegar and vice-versa (Mishnah *Terumot* 3:1).

169 The previous paragraph shows that in this sentence one has to read: His heave is no heave. In the next sentence, one has to read: His heave is heave. The text already was corrected in *editio princeps*.

170 From here to the end of the Halakhah there exists a parallel text in *Baba Batra* 6:1 (15b/c) edited differently. The first part also has a parallel in the Babli, *Baba Batra* 96a.

171 Since heave has to be given from the finished agricultural product,

it is in order to set aside a small amphora of the first wine of the season to be used to provide heave for the entire harvest. From the moment the first small volume of wine is declared as heave, the entire contents of the amphora can be consumed only by a ritually pure Cohen. This does not alter the fact that most of the contents are still profane and can be used for future declarations of heave; cf. Note 151.

172   In the Babli, R. Joḥanan's opinion is supported by a *baraita*. There it is explained that they differ in the analysis of the process which turns wine into vinegar. This cannot be the background of the Yerushalmi since then the comparison to the status of the needle would be impossible.

173   It was exposed to oxydation for a prolonged period after turning into vinegar.

174   Turned into vinegar only recently.

175   Mishnah *Tahorot* 3:5. There, "pure" means "cannot be impure" and "impure" "can become impure". The only items which can become impure are humans, food, vessels, and tools. An impure tool or vessel is purified when it becomes unusable.

176   In this state it is not usable. It is stated in Tosephta *Kelim Baba Meṣi'a* 3:10 that if it was impure, rusted and became pure, then was rubbed clean, it returned to its original impurity.

177   In *Baba Batra* 6:1, practice is decided following R. Joshua ben Levi only in the case of the needle. The Babli *Baba Batra* 96a implies that practice follows R. Joḥanan in the case of the amphora (understood in this sense by Maimonides and R. Moses of Coucy.)

(45b line 17) רִבִּי קְרִיסְפָּא בָּעֵי. כָּל־שָׁנָה וְשָׁנָה הוּא בוֹדֵק אוֹ אַחַת לְשָׁלֹשׁ שָׁנִים. נִשְׁמְעִינָהּ מִן הָדָא. הַמּוֹכֵר יַיִן לַחֲבֵירוֹ סְתָם חַיָּיב בְּאַחֲרָיוּתוֹ עַד הֶחָג. אָמַר רִבִּי יוּדָה. תִּיפְתָּר בְּאִילֵין בְּנֵי גְלִילָא דְּאִינוּן קֵטְפִין בָּתַר קַדְמִיתָא דְּחַגָּא. וְלֵית שְׁמַע מִינָהּ כְּלוּם. וְהָדָא אֲמָרָה. יָשָׁן מִשֶּׁלְּאֶשְׁתָּקַד וּמְיוּשָּׁן מִן שָׁלֹשׁ שָׁנִים. נֵימַר מִשּׁוּם הָדָא מַטְעוּמִיתָא. הָדָא אֲמָרָה דְּאֵי מָתַי יָשָׁן חַיָּיב בְּאַחֲרָיוּתוֹ. שְׁתֵּי שָׁנִים. הָדָא אֲמָרָה מְתִייָּשָׁן חַיָּיב בְּאַחֲרָיוּתוֹ עַד הֶחָג. הָדָא אֲמָרָה בְּכָל־שָׁנָה וְשָׁנָה הוּא בוֹדֵק. כֵּיצַד הוּא בוֹדֵק. בּוֹדֵק חָבִית אַחַת וְכוּלָּן תְּלוּיוֹת בָּהּ וְאֵינָן

מַחֲמִיצוֹת. אָמַר רִבִּי שַׁמַּי. אִית בְּנֵי נָשׁ מַקְשִׁין עַל גַּרְבָּא מִלְּבַר וְאִינּוּן יָדְעִין מָה אִית בָּהּ מִלְּגָיו.

Rebbi Crispus asked: Does he check every year or only once every three years[178]? Let us hear from the following[179]: If somebody sells unspecified wine to another person, he has to warrant it until after Tabernacles. Rebbi Yudan[180] said, explain it for those Galileans who harvest only after the beginning of Tabernacles[181] and you cannot deduce anything. That which was said, "old from the preceding year, very old aged three years[182]", should we say because of the tasting? This means that any time it is declared old he has to warrant it for two years[183]. This means that very old [wine] has to be warranted until Tabernacles. This means that he has to check every year[184]. How does he check? May one check one amphora on which all others depend that they would not become vinegar? Rebbi Shammai said, there are people who knock on the barrel from the outside and know what is inside[185].

178 This question is asked only for R. Jehudah who identifies times dangerous for wine.

179 This belongs to trade rules, one of the topics of *Baba Batra*. If wine turns into vinegar before Tabernacles, usually in October, the buyer can declare the transaction as executed under false pretenses, return the wine, and request restitution of his money.

180 This is the name in *Baba Batra*. There is no Amora called "R. Judah" without additional qualifier.

181 Since harvesting is forbidden on Tabernacles, they harvest overripe grapes to make sweet wine after the end of the holiday (for Tokay wine this is called *Ausbruch*). This wine has to be guaranteed until the next Tabernacles and automatically has to be checked at R. Jehudah's three break points.

182 Mishnah *Baba Batra* 6:3. Wine sold as old is warranted to be aged at least a full 12 months.

183 The year it was made and the

next.

184 The seller who does not check all his wine after Tabernacles cannot sell his wine without risking to have to take it back. The entire paragraph only deals with money matters, not with heave since it is forbidden to give heave from one year's produce for that of another year.

185 Vintners do not have to open the amphoras and taste; they learn how to check quickly and accurately; the rules of warranty do not require an undue amount of work.

השולח פרק רביעי

(fol. 45b) **משנה א:** הַשׁוֹלֵחַ גֵּט לְאִשְׁתּוֹ וְהִגִּיעַ בַּשָּׁלִיחַ אוֹ שֶׁשָּׁלַח אַחֲרָיו שָׁלִיחַ וְאָמַר לוֹ גֵּט שֶׁנָּתַתִּי לָךְ בָּטֵל הֲרֵי זֶה בָּטֵל. קָדַם אֵצֶל אִשְׁתּוֹ אוֹ שֶׁשָּׁלַח אֶצְלָהּ שָׁלִיחַ וְאָמַר לָהּ גֵּט שֶׁשָּׁלַחְתִּי לֵיךְ בָּטֵל הוּא הֲרֵי זֶה בָּטֵל. אִם מִשֶּׁהִגִּיעַ הַגֵּט לְיָדָהּ שׁוּב אֵינוֹ יָכוֹל לְבַטְּלוֹ.

Mishnah 1: If somebody sent a bill of divorce to his wife and caught up with the agent, or he sent another agent after him and said: the bill of divorce I gave you is annulled, it is annulled[1]. If he met his wife or he sent an agent to her and said: the bill of divorce I sent to you is annulled, it is annulled. After the bill of divorce came into her possession, he no longer can annul it.

1 It is not active and cannot be reactivated. If the husband changed his mind again, he would have to write a new bill.

(45c line 2) **הלכה א:** הַשׁוֹלֵחַ גֵּט לְאִשְׁתּוֹ כול'. הָדָא פְּלִיגָא עַל רִבִּי יוֹחָנָן. דְּרִבִּי יוֹחָנָן אָמַר. אָדָם מְבַטֵּל שְׁלִיחוּתוֹ בִּדְבָרִים. פָּתַר לָהּ מִשּׁוּם חוֹמֶר הוּא בַּעֲרָיוֹת. עָשָׂה שָׁלִיחַ לְהוֹלִיךְ אֶת הַגֵּט צָרִיךְ לִתְּנוֹ לָהּ בִּפְנֵי שְׁנַיִם. וְאֵין הַשָּׁלִיחַ עוֹלֶה לוֹ מִשּׁוּם שְׁנַיִם. הָלַךְ הַשָּׁלִיחַ לְבַטֵּל אֶת הַגֵּט צָרִיךְ לְבַטְּלוֹ בִּפְנֵי שְׁנַיִם. וְהַשָּׁלִיחַ עוֹלֶה מִשּׁוּם שְׁנַיִם. הָלַךְ לְבַטֵּל אֶת הַגֵּט. אַשְׁכְּחֵיהּ בְּאִיסְטְרָטָא. אָמַר לֵיהּ. הַהוּא גִיטָא דִיהָבַת לָהּ. אָמַר לֵיהּ. יְכִילִי לָהּ. מִי מִישְׁתָּעֵי שְׁמָא נָפַל מִינֵּיהּ. אָמַר לֵיהּ. לֹא אָמַרְתָּ לִי יְכִילִית לָהּ. אָמַר לֵיהּ. יְכִילִי לָהּ וְאָמְרַת לִי. יְהֵי לִי בְיָדֶיךָ. מָה. מֵאַחַר שֶׁיֵּשׁ בְּיָדוֹ לְגָרֵשׁ נֶאֱמָן. אוֹ מֵאַחַר שֶׁנִּמְצָא בְיָדוֹ אֵינוֹ

נֶאֱמָן. חָלָה הַשָּׁלִיחַ. מָה אַתְּ עֲבַד לָהּ. כְּגִיטִּין כְּקִידּוּשִׁין. אֵין תַּעֲבְדִינָהּ כְּגִיטִּין. בְּיַד כָּל־אָדָם מָצוּי לְגָרֵשׁ. אֵין תַּעֲבְדִינָהּ כְּקִידּוּשִׁין. לֹא בְיַד כָּל־אָדָם מָצוּי לְקַדֵּשׁ.

Halakhah 1: "If somebody sent a bill of divorce to his wife," etc. This disagrees with Rebbi Joḥanan, since Rebbi Joḥanan said that a person invalidates the agent appointed by him by a declaration². He explains it by the stringency of the rules of incest³. If he appointed an agent to deliver the bill of divorce, the latter has to deliver it in the presence of two [witnesses]; the agent is not counted as one of the two⁴. If another agent went to invalidate the bill of divorce, he has to invalidate it in the presence of two [witnesses] and the agent is counted as one of the two⁵. If he met him on the road and asked him, what about the bill of divorce I gave you? He answered, I delivered it to her⁶. While they were talking there, he dropped it⁷. He said, did you not tell me that you delivered it to her? He explained, I delivered it to her and she said, keep it for me. What? Can he be believed since it is in his power to divorce, or can he not be believed because it is in his hand⁸? If the agent⁹ fell sick, how do you treat this? By the rules of divorces or the rules of preliminary marriages? By the rules of divorces one can divorce through the agency of anybody. By the rules of preliminary marriages one cannot preliminarily marry through the agency of anybody¹⁰.

2   If a person can declare the agency void by a declaration at his place without informing the agent, why does the Mishnah accept voiding the agency only if either the agent for delivery or the recipient of the bill is informed of the annulment? R. Joḥanan's statement is also in *Qiddušin* 4:9; in the parallel in the Babli, *Qiddušin* 59a, his reason is that words can be invalidated by words; he is opposed by R. Simeon ben Laqish. As

an Amora, R. Johanan should not have the authority to contradict a Mishnah.

3   Adultery is always included under the rules of incest. R. Johanan may hold his opinion in matters of agency in civil law, but marriages and divorces are also matters of criminal law since as long as a woman is married, she is forbidden by criminal law to have relations with men other than her husband. Therefore, agency for delivery of a bill of divorce has to follow the standards of criminal law.

4   Since the agent represents the husband, he is party and cannot be a witness under the rules of criminal procedure.

5   This follows the rules of civil procedure since the husband could have invalidated the agency alone and without witnesses.

6   The husband cannot invalidate the divorce retroactively.

7   The bill of divorce fell from the agent's hand. This seems to indicate that it was not delivered and the husband still can invalidate it.

8   The question is not answered; it can easily be resolved by asking the (ex-)wife.

9   The second agent, sent to inform the first that his agency was terminated. It already was stated in Chapter 3 that the original agent can appoint successor agents.

10   Cf. Chapter 3, Notes 114-115.

משנה ב: בָּרִאשׁוֹנָה הָיָה עוֹשֶׂה בֵית דִּין בְּמָקוֹם אַחֵר וּמְבַטְּלוֹ. הִתְקִין (fol. 45b) רַבָּן גַּמְלִיאֵל הַזָּקֵן שֶׁלֹּא יְהוּ עוֹשִׂין כֵּן מִפְּנֵי תִּיקּוּן הָעוֹלָם. בָּרִאשׁוֹנָה הָיָה מְשַׁנֶּה שְׁמוֹ וּשְׁמָהּ שֵׁם עִירוֹ וְשֵׁם עִירָהּ וְהִתְקִין רַבָּן גַּמְלִיאֵל הַזָּקֵן שֶׁיְּהֵא כוֹתֵב אִישׁ פְּלוֹנִי וְכָל־שֵׁם שֶׁיֵּשׁ לוֹ אִשָּׁה פְלוֹנִית וְכָל־שֵׁם שֶׁיֵּשׁ לָהּ מִפְּנֵי תִּיקּוּן הָעוֹלָם.

Mishnah 2: In earlier times, he could go to a court at another place and annul [the bill of divorce]; Rabban Gamliel the Elder[11] instituted that one should not do that because of the public good[12]. In earlier times, his name and her name and the names of his and her towns could change[13]; Rabban Gamliel the Elder instituted that one should write Mr. X and all his names, Mrs. Y and all her names, because of the public good[14].

11 Hillel's grandson, the grandfather of Rabban Gamliel of Jabneh.

12 If it was not assured that both the agent and the wife were informed of the annulment, all kinds of complications could arise which are described in the Halakhah.

13 For example, if he lived in the city where the bill was written under a name different from the one he used earlier in the city where his wife still lives, the court in his wife's city will not recognize the bill as valid for divorce of the wife.

14 It is not clear, and there were different interpretations given in rabbinic practice, whether the Mishnah requires that a bill enumerate correctly all names under which either party ever lived, or only a statement that the parties (or the town) also were known by other names.

(45c line 14) **הלכה ב:** בָּרִאשׁוֹנָה הָיָה עוֹשֶׂה בֵּית דִּין כּוּל׳. לֵית הָדָא פְּלִיגָא עַל רֵישׁ לָקִישׁ. דְּרֵישׁ לָקִישׁ אָמַר. אֵין אָדָם מְבַטֵּל שְׁלִיחוּתוֹ בִּדְבָרִים. פָּתַר לָהּ בְּבֵית דִּין שָׁכוֹחוֹ מְרוּבָּה.

Halakhah 2: "In earlier times, he could go to court," etc. Does this[15] not disagree with Rebbi Simeon ben Laqish, since Rebbi Simeon ben Laqish said that nobody can annul an agency by speech[2,16]. Explain it in a fully constituted court[17].

15 This question is based on the interpretation of the term "court" in the Mishnah as an *ad hoc* court, that the husband was able *ad hoc* to assemble three people as a court, and declare before them that he was revoking the agency given to the agent. This is the explanation accepted in the Babli in the name of Rav Naḥman, 32b.

16 For money transactions, this is credited to R. Joḥanan in the Babli, 32b.

17 He will hold that even in earlier times the agency could be revoked only by a public act of the local court who was presumed to transmit a copy of the document to the court at the wife's place of residence.

(45c line 16) מִפְּנֵי תִיקוּן הָעוֹלָם. אָמְרִין בְּשֵׁם רֵישׁ לָקִישׁ. שֶׁלֹּא תָבוֹא לִידֵי מַמְזֵירוּת. וְאָמְרִין בְּשֵׁם רֵישׁ לָקִישׁ. שֶׁלֹּא תְהֵא יוֹשֶׁבֶת עֲגוּנָה. מָאן דְּאָמַר. שֶׁלֹּא תְהֵא יוֹשֶׁבֶת עֲגוּנָה. סְבוּרָה שֶׁבִּיטְלָהּ וְהוּא לֹא בִיטֵל וְנִמְצֵאת יוֹשֶׁבֶת עֲגוּנָה. וּמָאן דְּאָמַר. שֶׁלֹּא תָבוֹא לִידֵי מַמְזֵירוּת. סְבוּרָה שֶׁלֹּא בִיטֵל וְהוּא בִיטֵל. וְהִיא הוֹלֶכֶת וְנִישֵּׂאת בְּלֹא גֵט. וְנִמְצְאוּ בָנֶיהָ בָאִין לִידֵי מַמְזֵירוּת. סְבוּרָה שֶׁבִּיטֵל וְהוּא לֹא בִיטֵל וּבָא אַחֵר וְקִידְּשָׁהּ תּוֹפְסִין בָּהּ קִידּוּשִׁין. וְהִיא סְבוּרָה שֶׁלֹּא תוֹפְסִין בָּהּ קִידּוּשִׁין. וְהִיא מַמְתֶּנֶת עַד שֶׁיָּמוּת בַּעֲלָהּ הָרִאשׁוֹן וְהִיא הוֹלֶכֶת וְנִישֵּׂאת. וְנִמְצָא בָנֶיהָ בָאִין לִידֵי מַמְזֵירוּת. אָמַר רִבִּי מָנָא. סַלְקִית לְשִׁייָרָא וְשָׁמְעִית לְרִבִּי יַעֲקֹב בַּר אָחָא וְרִבִּי אִימִּי בְּשֵׁם רֵישׁ לָקִישׁ. שֶׁלֹּא תָבוֹא לִידֵי מַמְזֵירוּת. אָמַר רַב הוּנָא. אֲפִילוּ כְּמָאן דְּאָמַר. שֶׁלֹּא תְהֵא יוֹשֶׁבֶת עֲגוּנָה אִית לֵיהּ שֶׁלֹּא תָבוֹא לִידֵי מַמְזֵירוּת.

"Because of the public good." They say in the name of Rebbi Simeon ben Laqish: That she should not risk bastardy[18]. Some say in the name of Rebbi Simeon ben Laqish: That she should not remain anchored[19]. He who said, that she should not remain anchored, [is afraid that] she turns out to be anchored if she thought that he annulled[20] when he did not annul. He who said, that she should not risk bastardy, [is afraid that] her children will be bastards if she thought that he did not annul when he annulled[21], she goes and marries without a bill of divorce. If she thought that he annulled when he did not annul, another man comes and marries her preliminarily; the preliminary marriage is valid but she thinks it is invalid[22]. She waits until her first husband dies, then she goes and marries [another man][23]; the result is that her children will be bastards. Rebbi Mana said, I went with a caravan and heard Rebbi Jacob bar Aḥa and Rebbi Immi in the name of Rebbi Simeon ben Laqish: That she should not risk bastardy. Rav Huna said, even the one who said that she should not remain anchored also agrees that she should not risk bastardy.

18 In the Babli, 33a, this is R. Johanan's opinion.

19 This is a technical term. Just as an anchored ship cannot move, so an abandoned woman without a clear bill of divorce cannot move into another man's house.

In the Babli, 33a, this is R. Simeon ben Laqish's opinion.

20 That the bill of divorce delivered to her was worthless since the husband could have annulled it at a place unknown to her.

21 She received the bill in due form in the presence of two witnesses. The husband can later reappear when she is remarried and declare her divorce void and her children from the second husband bastards born in adultery.

22 Any adulterous or incestuous marriage is null and void (cf. *Yebamot* 1:1, Note 64).

23 Then in reality she is [preliminarily] married to the man to whom she thinks she is not married; her new [definitive] marriage is adulterous and her children bastards. In all these cases, the adultery is unknown to her and the world; the children are bastards only in the eyes of Heaven; it is the duty of the judicial system to see to it that such cases do not occur.

(45c line 27) עָבַר וּבִיטְּלוֹ. נִישְׁמְעִינָהּ מִן הָדָא. אִם בִּיטְּלוֹ הֲרֵי זֶה מְבוּטָּל. דִּבְרֵי רִבִּי. רַבָּן שִׁמְעוֹן בֶּן גַּמְלִיאֵל אוֹמֵר. אֵינוֹ יָכוֹל לְבַטְּלוֹ וְלֹא לְהוֹסִיף עַל תְּנָאוֹ. יָאוּת אָמַר רַבָּן שִׁמְעוֹן בֶּן גַּמְלִיאֵל. מַאי טַעֲמָא דְּרִבִּי. דְּבַר תּוֹרָה הוּא שֶׁיְּבַטֵּל וְהֵן אָמְרוּ שֶׁלֹּא בִיטֵּל. וְדִבְרֵיהֶן עוֹקְרִין דִּבְרֵי תוֹרָה. וְכִי שֶׁמֶן עַל זֵיתִים וַעֲנָבִים עַל הַיַּיִן לֹא תוֹרָה הוּא שֶׁיִּתְרוּם מִפְּנֵי גֶּזֶל הַשֵּׁבֶט. וְהֵם אָמְרוּ שֶׁלֹּא יִתְרוֹם. וְלֹא עוֹד אֶלָּא שֶׁאָמְרוּ. עָבַר וְתָרַם אֵין תְּרוּמָתוֹ תְּרוּמָה. רִבִּי אוֹשַׁעְיָה בַּר אַבָּא אָמַר לְרִבִּי יוּדָן נְשִׂייָא. בְּאַגָּדָה דְּסַבָּךְ מָאן דַּייֵּיק לָן.

If he transgressed and annulled? Let us hear from the following[24]: "If he annulled it is annulled, the words of Rebbi. Rabban Simeon ben Gamliel says, he can neither annul it nor add to his condition." Rabban Simeon ben Gamliel says it correctly[25]. What is the reason of Rebbi? It is the word of the Torah that he has the power to annul[26] but they[27] said, he shall not annul. Can their word uproot the words of the Torah? But is it not from the Torah that one may [give as heave] olives for oil and grapes for wine, but because of robbing the tribe[28] they said not only that one may not give heave [in this way] but if he transgressed and gave, his heave is not heave. Rebbi Oshaia bar Abba said to Rebbi Yudan the Prince: Who could tell exactly what your ancestor[29] meant?

24 Tosephta 3:3, Babli 33a. Did Rabban Gamliel the Elder decree that any annulment not in the presence of agent or wife was null and void?

25 It seems that the names of Rebbi and Rabban Simeon ben Gamliel are switched here and in the next sentence. The Babli, 33b, decides practice following Rebbi.

26 The biblical text decrees that the husband has to hand his wife a bill of divorce if he has decided to divorce her. The text contains no hints to any restriction as to the exercise of his free will.

27 In this case, the rabbinic authorities of the first half of the first century C. E.

28 *Terumot* 1:4, Mishnah and Note 137. Biblical heave is due only for "grain, cider, and oil". The prohibition to satisfy the tithing duty with unprocessed grapes and olives is strict only according to the House of Hillel; they hold that if olives were given as heave for olive oil then both the olives and the oil remain *ṭevel*, untithed, by rabbinic decree and their consumption is a deadly sin.

29 In modern Hebrew, סבא means "grandfather". In the Talmudim, generally it means "old man"; since "grandfather" usually is formulated as סַבָּא אֲבִי אַבָּא can also mean "great-grandfather". The interpretation of the word depends on the reading of the names in this discussion.

(45c line 33) אִישׁ פְּלוֹנִי וְכָל־שֵׁם שֶׁיֵּשׁ לוֹ. הַגַּע עַצְמָךְ דַּהֲוָה שְׁמֵיהּ רְאוּבֵן וְאַפִּיק שְׁמֵיהּ שִׁמְעוֹן. אֶלָּא אֲנִי פְלוֹנִי וְכָל־שֵׁם שֶׁיֵּשׁ לִי. יוֹתֵר מִכֵּן אָמְרוּ. הָיוּ לוֹ שְׁתֵּי נָשִׁים אַחַת בִּיהוּדָה וְאַחַת בַּגָּלִיל. וְלוֹ שְׁנֵי שֵׁמוֹת אֶחָד בִּיהוּדָה וְאֶחָד בַּגָּלִיל. וְכָתַב זֶה שֶׁבִּיהוּדָה לְגָרֵשׁ זוֹ שֶׁבַּגָּלִיל וְשֶׁבַּגָּלִיל לְגָרֵשׁ זוֹ שֶׁבִּיהוּדָה. אֵינָהּ

HALAKHAH 2

מְגוּרֶשֶׁת. מַתְנִיתָא שֶׁהָיָה מִיהוּדָה וְכָתַב לְגָרֵשׁ בַּגָּלִיל. מִגְּלִיל וְכָתַב לְגָרֵשׁ בִּיהוּדָה. אֲבָל אִם הָיָה מִיהוּדָה וְכָתַב לְגָרֵשׁ בִּיהוּדָה. מִגָּלִיל וְכָתַב לְגָרֵשׁ בַּגָּלִיל. הֲרֵי זוֹ מְגוּרֶשֶׁת. אָמַר רִבִּי אִילַי. כַּתְּחִילָה צָרִיךְ לוֹמַר. אֲנִי פְלוֹנִי שֶׁמִּיהוּדָה עִם כָּל־שֵׁם שֶׁיֵּשׁ לִי בַּגָּלִיל. אִם הָיָה שָׁרוּי בַּמָּקוֹם אֶחָד מְגָרֵשׁ לְאֵי זֶה שֶׁיִּרְצֶה. אָמַר רִבִּי יוֹסֵי. הָדָא דְאַתְּ אָמַר לְשֶׁעָבַר. אֲבָל לְכַתְּחִילָה צָרִיךְ לְמֵיעֲבַד כְּהָדָא דְרִבִּי אִילַי. אָמַר רִבִּי אָבִין. אִם יָצָא לוֹ שֵׁם בְּמָקוֹם אַחֵר צָרִיךְ לְהַזְכִּיר שְׁלָשְׁתָּן.

[30]"Mr. X and all his names." Think of it, if his name was Reuben and he went away[31] under the name of Simeon. But: "I am X and[32] every other name which I have." [33]"In addition, they said if he had two wives, one in Judea and one in Galilee, and he is known by two names, one in Judea and one in Galilee. He used [his name] in Judea to divorce the one in Galilee and [his name] in Galilee to divorce the one in Judea. Neither one is divorced." This *baraita* if he was in Judea[34] and wrote to divorce in Galilee or in Galilee and wrote to divorce in Judea. But if he was in Judea and wrote to divorce in Judea, or in Galilee and wrote to divorce in Galilee, she is divorced[35]. Rebbi Ilai said, according to the rules he has to say: "I am X with every other name which I have in Galilee.[32]" If he was at another place, he can divorce either one he wishes[36]. Rebbi Yose said, one says that if he did it[37]. But to start out[38] he has to follow Rebbi Ilai. Rebbi Abin said, if he is known by (another) name at another place, he has to mention all three.

30 This paragraph is quoted by R. Nissim Gerondi in his commentary to Alfassi (#456). While his spelling is still more babylonized than the ms. text and it is not clear that his deviations from our text are from his text or are his interpretation, his text is very clear in its meaning and is followed in the commentary.

31 R. Nissim: אפיך "he changed it

32   R. Nissim: עם כל שם "with every name", i.e., all the names have to be spelled out. This is the ms. text later in the name of R. Ilai, so probably the ms. text here is original.

33   Similar texts are in the Babli, 34b, and Tosephta 6:5.

34   The translation uses the text of R. Nissim: בשהיה ביהודה. The ms. text could be read as: If he used the name from Judea,

35   If only the local name was used. The divorce is valid only if both the witnesses signing the document and the witnesses to the delivery are able to identify the husband; therefore, both names (possibly with an indication where which name is being used) are required.

36   R. Nissim: באיזה מהם שירצה "with any [name] he chooses". If he is not known locally, he can identify himself in any way he chooses (as long as the name is recognized as his at the place of delivery of the bill.)

37   If the bill was written without asking for rabbinical advice. This is quoted in Tosaphot 34b, *s. v.* והוא.

38   If he asks for instructions, he has to be told to enumerate all names under which he is known. (It is not clear whether the reference, in the edict on Jewish names by the German Emperor Joseph II, to Jews having different names at different places, refers to a reality in the 18th Century or to the talmudic discussion.)

(45c line 45) תַּמָּן תַּנִינָן. כּוֹתְבִין גֵּט לָאִישׁ אַף עַל פִּי שֶׁאֵין אִשְׁתּוֹ עִמּוֹ. וְשׁוֹבֵר לְאִשָּׁה אַף עַל פִּי שֶׁאֵין בַּעֲלָהּ עִמָּהּ. וּבִלְבַד שֶׁיְהֵא מַכִּירָם. וְהַבַּעַל נוֹתֵן אֶת הַשָּׂכָר. אָמַר רִבִּי אַבָּא. צָרִיךְ שֶׁיְהֵא מַכִּיר אֶת שְׁנֵיהֶן. אָמַר רִבִּי לָא. צָרִיךְ שֶׁיְהֵא מַכִּיר לָאִישׁ בַּגֵּט וְלָאִשָּׁה בְּשׁוֹבְרָהּ. רִבִּי אָבוּן בַּר חִיָּיה בָּעֵי קוֹמֵי רִבִּי. הַגַּע עַצְמָךְ שֶׁהֵבִיא אִשָּׁה אַחֶרֶת וְגֵירֵשׁ בָּהּ. אָמַר לֵיהּ. לִכְשֶׁיָּבוֹאוּ וְיָעִידוּ הָעֵדִים. וְלֹא כֵן אָמַר רֵישׁ לָקִישׁ. עָשׂוּ עֵדִים הַחֲתוּמִים עַל הַשְּׁטָר כְּמִי שֶׁנֶּחְקְרָה עֵדוּתָן בְּבֵית דִּין. תַּמָּן בְּשֶׁאָמְרוּ. לֹא חָתַמְנוּ כָּל־עִיקָּר. בְּרַם הָכָא בְּאוֹמְרִים. בָּזֶה חָתַמְנוּ וְלֹא חָתַמְנוּ עַל זֶה. מַתְנִיתָא פְּלִינָא עַל רִבִּי אַבָּא. בָּרִאשׁוֹנָה הָיָה מְשַׁנֶּה שְׁמוֹ וּשְׁמָהּ שֵׁם עִירוֹ וְשֵׁם עִירָהּ. אִם בַּמַּכִּירָהּ בָּזֶה צָרִיךְ לְשַׁנּוֹת אֶת שְׁמוֹתָם. אִית בַּר נָשׁ דְּחַכְמִין לְחַבְרֵיהוֹן בְּאַפִּין וְלָא יָדְעִין

שְׁמְהַתְהוֹן. מַתְנִיתָא פְּלִיגָא עַל רִבִּי אִילַי. הִתְקִין רַבָּן גַּמְלִיאֵל בֶּן גַּמְלִיאֵל שֶׁיְּהוּ כּוֹתְבִין. אִישׁ פְּלוֹנִי וְכָל־שֵׁם שֶׁיֵּשׁ לוֹ. אִשָּׁה פְּלוֹנִית וְכָל־שֵׁם שֶׁיֵּשׁ לָהּ. מִפְּנֵי תִיקּוּן הָעוֹלָם. מַתְנִיתָא בִּמְגָרֵשׁ בְּעַל כּוֹרְחוֹ. מַה דְּאָמַר רִבִּי אִילָא בִּמְגָרֵשׁ בִּרְצוֹנוֹ. וְאִית דְּבָעֵי מֵימַר בִּמְגָרֵשׁ בִּמְקוֹמוֹת אֲחֵרִים. מַה דְּאָמַר רִבִּי אִילַי בִּמְגָרֵשׁ בְּאוֹתוֹ מָקוֹם.

There, we have stated[39]: "One writes a bill of divorce for a man even if his wife is not with him, and a receipt[40] for a woman even if her husband is not with her, and the husband pays the fee[41]." Rebbi Abba said, he[42] has to know both of them. Rebbi La[43] said, he has to know the husband for the bill of divorce and the wife for her receipt. Rebbi Abun bar Ḥiyya asked before Rebbi [[44]]: Think of it, if he brought another woman and divorced by means of her[45]. He said to him, let the witnesses come and testify. But did not Rebbi Simeon ben Laqish say[46] that they considered witnesses who signed a document as if their testimony had been cross-examined in court? There, if they said, we did not sign at all. But here if they say, we signed this but not that[47]. The Mishnah disagrees with Rebbi Abba: "In earlier times, his name and her name and the names of his and her towns could change." If he knows them, why would he change their names[48]? There are people who know others by sight but do not know their names. The Mishnah disagrees with Rebbi Ilai: "Rabban Gamliel the Elder instituted that one should write Mr. X and all his names, Mrs. Y and all her names[49], because of the public good." The Mishnah about one who is forced to divorce[50], Rebbi Ila speaks about one who divorces on his initiative; some want to say if he divorces at another place[51].

39 Mishnah *Baba Batra* 10:4. The statements of rabbis Abba and La (Ilai) are also quoted there in Halakhah 10:4.

40 A receipt for the amount of the

ketubah due her at her divorce.

41   The scribe's fee.

42   The scribe.

43   He is R. Ilai. In the Babli, *Baba Batra* 167b, his statement is attributed to Rav.

44   Clearly, a name is missing. R. Abun bar Ḥiyya is known to have asked questions of R. Ilai (*Yoma* 3:5).

45   Can the agent of an absent husband not fraudulently give the bill of divorce to another woman, not the wife, and have that woman foreclose the *ketubah* from the husband's local property?

46   Cf. *Ketubot* 2:3, Note 56, *Ševi'it* 10:5, Note 96 (*Baba Batra* 10:16, 14d l.26); Babli 3a, *Ketubot* 18b. Signatories of documents cannot claim that they never signed unless they claim that the signatures are forgeries.

47   The witnesses can identify the persons for whom they signed; this is not a second testimony.

48   If the scribe knew all persons involved, he could not be tricked into writing a misleading document.

49   The Mishnah treats husband and wife on an equal footing but R. Ilai does not.

50   One of those cases in which the wife can force a divorce (cf. *Ketubot* 7:10) when the husband's cooperation cannot be taken for granted.

51   Where he has to prove his and his wife's identities to the scribe.

(45c line 60) כְּחָדָא דּוֹשׁוֹ אֲחֵוֵי דְדוֹדוֹ הֲוָה מַשְׁבָּק אִיתְּתֵיהּ. אָתָא עוֹבְדָא קוֹמֵי רַבָּנִין אָמְרִין. הִיא תִּתֵּן אַגְרָא. וְהָתַנִּינָן. הַבַּעַל נוֹתֵן אֶת הַשָּׂכָר. רִבִּי אִילַי בְּשֵׁם שְׁמוּאֵל. בְּמוֹחֶלֶת לוֹ כְּתוּבָתָהּ.

[52]For example Doso, Dodo's brother, divorced his wife. The case came before the rabbis who said that she should pay the fee[53]. But did we not state: "the husband pays the fee"? Rebbi Ilai in the name of Samuel: If she forgives him her *ketubah*[54].

52   This discusses the statement of the Tosephta that the husband has to pay the expenses for the divorce document. The statement that the husband cannot change the conditions of the divorce once the document is no longer in his hands was discussed in Chapter 3, Note 45.

53   The Babli, *Baba Batra* 168a, agrees that current rabbinic practice requires the wife to pay the scribe to prevent the husband from dragging his feet once the couple has decided on a divorce.

54   If he makes money out of the divorce, he will not drag his feet and one can make him pay.

(fol. 45b) **משנה ג:** אֵין אַלְמָנָה נִפְרַעַת מִנִּכְסֵי יְתוֹמִין אֶלָּא בִשְׁבוּעָה. נִמְנְעוּ מִלְהַשְׁבִּיעָהּ הִתְקִין רַבָּן גַּמְלִיאֵל הַזָּקֵן שֶׁתְּהֵא נוֹדֶרֶת לַיְתוֹמִים כָּל־מַה שֶׁיִּרְצוּ וְגוֹבָה אֶת כְּתוּבָּתָהּ וְהָעֵדִים חוֹתְמִין עַל הַגֵּט מִפְּנֵי תִיקּוּן הָעוֹלָם. הִלֵּל תִּיקֵּן פְּרוֹזְבּוֹל מִפְּנֵי תִיקּוּן הָעוֹלָם.

Mishnah 3: A widow can be paid from the orphans' property only by an oath[55]. When they avoided letting her swear[56], Rabban Gamliel the Elder instituted that she should make a vow[57] on the instruction of the orphans for anything they would decide on and collect her *ketubah*, and that witnesses sign the bill of divorce because of the public good. Hillel instituted *prozbol* for the public good[58].

55   If the widow continued to live in her husband's house, she is suspected to have taken from her husband's property more than was necessary for her guaranteed support and, therefore, if she decides to leave that house she cannot collect her *ketubah* without swearing that nothing of her *ketubah* already came into her hand, similar to a woman who had received a down payment on her *ketubah*, cf. *Ketubot* 9:8,9.

56   The rabbis became worried that the widow while caring for the orphans took things which she thought were payment for her work but which legally should be counted as part payment of the *ketubah*; if she then swore that she had received nothing, the widow involuntarily transgressed the prohibition of false oaths and the rabbis the prohibition of "putting a

stone in the path of the blind."

57   A vow that she would prohibit on herself the use of anything (food, vessel, place) chosen by the orphans if she had received any down payment for her *ketubah*. For these "vows of mortification", see Introduction to Tractate *Nedarim*.

58   *Prozbol* is a document which turns a private debt (subject to the laws of revocation in the Sabbatical year) into a public debt (exempt from these laws) in order to maintain an operating banking system; cf. *Ševi'it* 10:3 ff.

(45c line 63) **הלכה ג:** אֵין אַלְמָנָה נִפְרַעַת מִנִּכְסֵי יְתוֹמִין כול'. בָּרִאשׁוֹנָה הָיוּ נִשְׁבָּעוֹת לַשֶּׁקֶר וְקוֹבְרוֹת אֶת בְּנֵיהֶם. שֶׁנֶּאֱמַר לַשָּׁוְא הִכֵּיתִי אֶת בְּנֵיכֶם. וְעוֹד שֶׁאֵימַת נְדָרִים עֲלֵיהֶן יוֹתֵר מִן הַשְּׁבוּעוֹת. עָבְרָה וְנִשְׁבְּעָה. רַב הוּנָא אָמַר. אִם נִשְׁבְּעָה נִשְׁבְּעָה. רַב אָמַר לְכַלָּתֵיהּ. אִילוּלֵיהּ דַּאֲנָא וַתְּרָן אֲפִילוּ קְלוֹסִיתֵיהּ דְּעַל רֵישָׁךְ דִּידִי הוּא. שְׁמוּאֵל אָמַר. זָכַת בַּכֵּלִים שֶׁעָלֶיהָ. מַתְנִיתָא מְסַיְּיעָא לֵיהּ לִשְׁמוּאֵל. אֵין לוֹ לֹא בִכְסוּת אִשְׁתּוֹ וְלֹא בִכְסוּת בָּנָיו.

Halakhah 3: "A widow can be paid from the orphans' property only," etc. Earlier they swore falsely and buried their children, since it is written[59]: "For vain [vows] I smote your children." In addition, they fear vows more than oaths[60]. If she transgressed and swore? Rav Huna said, if she swore, she swore[61]. Rav said to his daughter-in-law: If I were not a person readily making concessions, even the cover on your head would be my property. Samuel said, she acquires the garments which she is wearing[62]. A Mishnah supports Samuel: "Neither his wife's garments nor his children's are his property[63]."

59   *Jer.* 2:30. For the statement that children die for the parents' sins of vows cf. *Ketubot* 7:7, Note 66.

60   For example, there is an annual revocation rite, *Kol Nidre*, for vows with oaths only mentioned as an afterthought; cf. introduction to Tractate *Nedarim*, Note 4.

61 If she swears on her own initiative to expedite the process, it is valid and she has to be paid. The same statement in the Babli, 35a.

62 The same disagreement, whether or not garments, which the husband has to supply during the marriage, are counted against the *ketubah*, is in the Babli *Ketubot* 54a.

63 *'Arakhin* 6:5. The family's clothing cannot be counted as the husband's property in bankruptcy proceedings. In the Babli, nevertheless practice is decided following Rav, against the Yerushalmi.

(45c line 69) רַב הוּנָא אָמַר. מִפְּנֵי מָה הִתְקִינוּ זְמַן בַּגֵּט. מִפְּנֵי מַעֲשֶׂה שֶׁאֵירַע. מַעֲשֶׂה בְּאֶחָד שֶׁהָיָה נָשׂוּי אֶת בַּת אֲחוֹתוֹ וְזִינַּת עַד שֶׁהִיא אֵשֶׁת אִישׁ. הָלַךְ וְהִקְדִּים זְמַנּוֹ בַּגֵּט. אָמַר. מוּטָב שֶׁתִּידוֹן כִּפְנוּיָה וְאַל תִּדּוֹן כְּאֵשֶׁת אִישׁ.

Rav Huna said, why did they require a date on the bill of divorce? Because of an actual case. It so happened that a man was married to his sister's daughter who committed adultery when she was still married. He predated the bill of divorce and said, it is better she should be judged as single rather than as a married woman[64].

64 In the Babli, 17a/b, R. Joḥanan refers to this story; the editors of the Babli assumed that this Yerushalmi was generally known.

(45c line 72) אָמַר רַב הוּנָא. קַשִׁיתָא קוֹמוֹי רַב יַעֲקֹב בַּר אָחָא. כְּמַאן דְּאָמַר. מַעְשְׂרוֹת מִן דִּבְרֵיהֶן. בְּרַם כְּמַאן דְּאָמַר. מַעְשְׂרוֹת מִן הַתּוֹרָה. וְהִילֵּל מַתְקִין עַל דְּבַר תּוֹרָה. אָמַר רִבִּי יוֹסֵי. וְכִי מִשָּׁעָה שֶׁגָּלוּ לְבָבֶל כְּלוּם נִפְטְרוּ אֶלָּא מִמִּצְוֹת הַתְּלוּיוֹת בָּאָרֶץ. וְהַשְׁמֵט כְּסָפִים נוֹהֵג בֵּין בָּאָרֶץ בֵּין בְּחוּצָה לָאָרֶץ. חָזַר רִבִּי יוֹסֵי וְאָמַר. זֶה דְּבַר הַשְׁמִיטָה שָׁמוֹט. בְּשָׁעָה שֶׁהַשְׁמִיטָה נוֹהֵג בָּאָרֶץ מִדְּבַר תּוֹרָה הַשְׁמֵט כְּסָפִים נוֹהֵג בֵּין בָּאָרֶץ בֵּין בְּחוּצָה לָאָרֶץ דְּבַר תּוֹרָה. בְּשָׁעָה שֶׁהַשְׁמִיטָה נוֹהֵג בָּאָרֶץ מִדְּבְרֵיהֶן הַשְׁמֵט כְּסָפִים נוֹהֵג בֵּין בָּאָרֶץ בֵּין בְּחוּצָה לָאָרֶץ מִדִּבְרֵיהֶן. תַּמָּן אָמְרִין. אֲפִילוּ כְּמַאן דְּאָמַר. מַעְשְׂרוֹת מִדִּבְרֵי

תוֹרָה. מוֹדֶה בִּשְׁמִטָּה שֶׁהִיא מִדִּבְרֵיהֶן. וְזֶה דְּבַר הַשְּׁמִטָּה שָׁמוֹט. רִבִּי אוֹמֵר.
שְׁנֵי שְׁמִטִּין שְׁמִטָּה וְיוֹבֵל. בְּשָׁעָה שֶׁהַיּוֹבֵל נוֹהֵג הַשְּׁמִטָּה נוֹהֶגֶת מִדִּבְרֵי תוֹרָה.
פָּסְקוּ הַיּוֹבִילוֹת נוֹהֶגֶת שְׁמִטָּה מִדִּבְרֵיהֶן. אֵימָתַי פָּסְקוּ הַיּוֹבִילוֹת.
לְכָל־יוֹשְׁבֶיהָ. בִּזְמַן שֶׁיּוֹשְׁבִין עָלֶיהָ לֹא בִּזְמַן שֶׁגָּלוּ מִתּוֹכָהּ. הָיוּ עָלֶיהָ וְלֹא הָיוּ
מְעוּרְבָּבִין שֵׁבֶט יְהוּדָה בְּבִנְיָמִין וְשֵׁבֶט בִּנְיָמִין בִּיהוּדָה יָכוֹל יְהֵא הַיּוֹבֵל נוֹהֵג.
תַּלְמוּד לוֹמַר יוֹשְׁבֶיהָ. לְכָל־יוֹשְׁבֶיהָ. נִמְצֵאתָ אוֹמֵר. כֵּיוָן שֶׁגָּלוּ שֵׁבֶט רְאוּבֵן וְגָד
וַחֲצִי שֵׁבֶט מְנַשֶּׁה בָּטְלוּ הַיּוֹבִילוֹת.

1 רב הונא | **לר** ר' חונא   קשיתא | **ל** קשייתה   קומי | **ל** קומוי   רב יעקב | **לר** ר' יעקב
2 מן דבריהן | **ל** - **ר** מדבריהם   כמאן דאמ' | **ל** - **ר** כמן דא'   מן התורה | **לר** מדבר תורה
והילל | **לר** והלל   3 שגלו | **לר** שגלו ישראל   כלום נפטרו אלא | **ל** לא נפטרו   4
לארץ | **ל** דבר תורה **ר** בדר תורה משום דחובת הגוף הן⁶⁵   5 נוהג בארץ מדבר תורה |
לר נוהגת בארץ דבר תורה   7 בשעה | **לר** ובשעה   נוהג בארץ | **לר** נהגת   נוהג | **לר**
נוהגת   8 מדברי | **לר** דבר   9 וזה | **לר** דתני וזה   10 שני שמיטין | **ל** שני שמיטין
הללו **ר** שתי פעמים שמיטות   השמיטה | **לר** שמיטה   מדברי תורה | **לר** דבר תורה
11 נוהגת שמיטה | **לר** שמיטה נוהגת   12 לכל | **ל** - **ר** כל   שיושבין | **לר** שיושביה
שגלו מתוכה | **ר** שאין עליה   ולא | **לר** אבל   13 יהא היובל נוהג | **לר** יהו היבילות
נוהגין   15 מנשה | **לר** המנשה

⁶⁶Rav Huna⁶⁷ said, I asked before Rebbi Jacob ben Aḥa: Following him who says tithes are from their words. But following him who says tithes are from the Torah, does Hillel institute anything against the words of the Torah? Rebbi Yose said, from the moment that Israel was exiled to Babylonia, did they not become free from all commandments connected with the Land, but the remission of debts applies both in the Land and outside the Land from the words of the Torah? Rebbi Yose turned and said, (*Deut.* 15:2) "this is the word of the abandonment, remit" as long as abandonment is followed in the Land as a word of the Torah, remission of debts applies both in the Land and outside the Land from the words of the Torah, but when abandonment is followed in the Land as their word,

remission of debts applies both in the Land and outside the Land from their word. There, they say that even one who holds that tithes are from the Torah will hold that the Sabbatical is from their word. (*Deut.* 15:2): "This is the word of the remission, remit!" Rebbi says, two remissions are the Sabbatical and the Jubilee. As long as the Jubilee is operative, the Sabbatical is from words of the Torah. If the Jubilees are abolished, the Sabbatical is operative from their words. When were the Jubilees abolished? (*Lev.* 25:10) "For all its inhabitants." In the time when they lived on it, not when they went from it into exile. If they lived on it but did (not)[68] intermingle, the tribe of Judah in Benjamin, and the tribe of Benjamin in Judah, I could think that the Jubilee was operative. The verse mentions its inhabitants, "All its inhabitants;" you find that when the tribes of Reuben, Gad, and half the tribe of Manasseh went into exile, the Jubilees were disestablished.

65   This looks like a gloss using the language of the Babli.

66   *Ševi'it* 10:3, explained there in Notes 83-88. The Leiden ms. is denoted by ל, the Rome ms. by ר.

67   The readings from *Ševi'it*, "*Rebbi* Ḥuna", "*Rebbi* Jacob", are the only ones which make sense in place and time.

68   This clearly is a scribal error; see the variant readings.

משנה ד: עֶבֶד שֶׁנִּשְׁבָּה וּפְדָאוּהוּ אִם לְשׁוּם עֶבֶד יִשְׁתַּעְבֵּד אִם לְשׁוּם בֶּן (fol. 45b) חוֹרִין לֹא יִשְׁתַּעְבֵּד. רַבָּן שִׁמְעוֹן בֶּן גַּמְלִיאֵל אוֹמֵר בֵּין כָּךְ וּבֵין כָּךְ יִשְׁתַּעְבֵּד. עֶבֶד שֶׁעֲשָׂאוֹ רַבּוֹ אַפּוֹתִיקֵי לַאֲחֵרִים וְשִׁיחְרְרוֹ שׁוּרַת הַדִּין אֵין הָעֶבֶד חַיָּיב כְּלוּם אֶלָא מִפְּנֵי תִּיקוּן הָעוֹלָם כּוֹפִין אֶת רַבּוֹ וְעוֹשֶׂה בֶּן חוֹרִין וְכוֹתֵב שְׁטָר עַל דָּמָיו. רַבָּן שִׁמְעוֹן בֶּן גַּמְלִיאֵל אוֹמֵר אֵינוֹ כוֹתֵב אֶלָּא מְשַׁחְרֵר.

Mishnah 4: If a slave was kidnapped and ransomed[69], if it was as a slave[70] he shall serve[71], if as a free person he shall not serve[72]; Rabban Simeon ben Gamliel says, in any case he shall serve[73]. A slave whom his master gave as mortgage to others and then freed[74] in strict law does not owe anything[75], but for the public good[76] one forces the master to formally manumit him and he[77] writes a bond for his own value. Rabban Simeon ben Gamliel says, only the one who manumits writes[78].

69   A Jewish community at another place ransomed him. Since he is under the laws of the Torah, any Jewish community is obligated to ransom him.

70   If they knew that he was a slave and ransomed him as such.

71   His former master, who has to indemnify the community which provided the ransom.

72   A person who was a free Jew even for one moment cannot be enslaved.

73   He holds that a slave can be freed only by a formal act of manumission, otherwise he will be forbidden to marry a Jewish woman. Since the act of ransom does not change the slave's status in marriage law, it cannot change it in civil law.

74   The act of manumission breaks the chattel mortgage; this is declared as a general principle in the Babli, 40b.

75   Since the evil act was his master's, not his own.

76   Lest the creditor come and enslave a free person.

77   The slave, who owns no money.

78   The slave is free and free from debt.

(45d line 15) **הלכה ד:** עֶבֶד שֶׁנִּשְׁבָּה וּפְדָאוּהוּ כול'. רִבִּי אַבָּהוּ בְשֵׁם חִזְקִיָּה. בְּדִין הָיָה שֶׁאֲפִילוּ לְשֵׁם עֶבֶד לֹא יִשְׁתַּעְבֵּד. וְלָמָּה אָמְרוּ יִשְׁתַּעְבֵּד. שֶׁלֹּא יְהֵא עֶבֶד מַבְרִיחַ עַצְמוֹ מִן שַׁבּוּיָין. אָמַר רִבִּי זְעִירָא. מַתְנִיתָא אָמְרָה כֵן. רַבּוֹ נוֹתֵן אֶת דָּמָיו וּמְשַׁחְרְרוֹ. לֹא אָמְרוּ אֶלָּא רַבּוֹ. הָא אַחֵר לֹא. רִבִּי אִילָא בְשֵׁם רִבִּי יָסָא. בְּדִין הָיָה אֲפִילוּ לְשֵׁם בֶּן חוֹרִין יִשְׁתַּעְבֵּד. וְלָמָּא אָמְרוּ לֹא יִשְׁתַּעְבֵּד. שֶׁלֹּא לְהוֹצִיא לוֹזָה עַל בְּנֵי חוֹרִין. אָמַר רִבִּי יוֹסֵי. אִם כֵּן. רַבָּן שִׁמְעוֹן בֶּן

גַּמְלִיאֵל אוֹמֵר. בֵּין כָּךְ וּבֵין כָּךְ יִשְׁתַּעְבֵּד. כְּשֵׁם שֶׁיִּשְׂרָאֵל מְצוּוִין לִפְדּוֹת בֶּן חוֹרִין כָּךְ הֵן מְצוּוִין לִפְדּוֹת אֶת הָעֲבָדִים. אָהֵן תַּנָּיָיא קַדְמָייָא סָבַר מֵימַר. מְצוּוִין הֵן לִפְדּוֹת בְּנֵי חוֹרִין וְאֵין מְצוּוִין לִפְדּוֹת אֶת הָעֲבָדִים. רבי יַעֲקֹב בַּר אִידִי בְשֵׁם רֵישׁ לָקִישׁ אָמַר. הֲלָכָה כְּרַבָּן שִׁמְעוֹן בֶּן גַּמְלִיאֵל.

"If a slave was kidnapped and ransomed," etc. Rebbi Abbahu in the name of Ḥizqiah: It would be logical that even as a slave he should not have to serve[79]. And why did they say, he has to serve? That a slave should not run away to the kidnappers[80]. Rebbi Ze'ira said, a *baraita*[81] implies this: "His master pays his ransom and frees him.[82]" They said that only about his master, not anybody else[83]. Rebbi Ila in the name of Rebbi Yasa: It would be logical that even as a free person he should have to serve[84]. Why did they say that he does not have to serve? Not to damage the reputations of free persons[85]. Rebbi Yose said, but it is so: "Rabban Simeon ben Gamliel says, in any case he shall serve; just as Israel are obligated to ransom free persons so they are obligated to ransom slaves.[81]" The first Tanna is of the opinion that they are obligated to ransom free persons but they are not obligated to ransom slaves[86]. Rebbi Jacob bar Idi in the name of Rebbi Simeon ben Laqish: Practice follows Rabban Simeon ben Gamliel[87].

79 In the Babli, 37b, Ḥizqiah is quoted in a discussion whether the ransom mentioned in the Mishnah occurred when the owner still had hope to recover his slave or whether he had given up this hope. Since the case that the owner had given up hope and therefore relinquished his claim to ownership is discussed later, the Yerushalmi must hold that the Mishnah deals with the case that the slave still was a slave in fact, not only in name, i.e., that the original owner had not given up hope to recover him. As R. Yose explains later, the slave should not have to serve since he was

ransomed as a Jew.

80   Offer himself to kidnappers as a sure way to gain his freedom.

81   Tosephta 3:4; Babli 37b.

82   If the master wishes, he may free him once the community which provided the ransom is reimbursed.

83   It is not clear what is the meaning of the *baraita* clause that the master frees the slave. The Tosephta implies that the community which ransoms the slave sends his master the bill with the slave. No other person has an interest in the slave.

84   Since there was no formal manumission, there seems to be no reason why the slave, redeemed in the erroneous belief that he was a free Jew, should not remain a slave.

85   If it were possible later to enslave a person redeemed as a free person, nobody would be safe.

86   Since Rabban Gamliel has to spell out his opinion in the Tosephta, it follows that the dissenting opinion also applies in this case. The slave of a Jew is obligated to keep the Sabbath and eat only kosher food; since he cannot do that as slave of a Gentile, the Jewish community is responsible for him.

87   In the Babli, it is a Saboraic principle that "practice follows Rabban Simeon ben Gamliel in his statements in the Mishnah" almost always (*Ketubot* 77a); the Babli does not have to state that practice follows him.

(45d line 26) רִבִּי סִימוֹן בְּשֵׁם רִבִּי יְהוֹשֻׁעַ בֶּן לֵוִי אָמַר יֵיסִי בֶּן שָׁאוּל בְּשֵׁם רִבִּי. הַמִּתְיָיאֵשׁ בְּעַבְדּוֹ אֵינוֹ רַשַּׁאי לְשַׁעְבְּדוֹ וְצָרִיךְ לִכְתּוֹב לוֹ גֵּט שִׁיחְרוּר. שָׁמַע רִבִּי יוֹחָנָן וְאָמַר. יָפֶה לִימְּדֵנִי רִבִּי יְהוֹשֻׁעַ בֶּן לֵוִי. כְּלוּם לָמְדוּ גֵּט שִׁיחְרוּר לֹא מֵאִשָּׁה. מָה אִשָּׁה אֵינָהּ יוֹצֵאת מִשּׁוּם יֵיאוּשׁ שֶׁצְּרִיכָה מִמֶּנּוּ גֵּט. אַף עֶבֶד אֵינוֹ יוֹצֵא מִשּׁוּם יֵיאוּשׁ וְצָרִיךְ גֵּט שִׁיחְרוּר.

Rebbi Simon in the name of Rebbi Joshua ben Levi: Yossi ben Shaul said in the name of Rebbi: A person who had given up hope to recover his slave[88] is not entitled to enslave him but has to write him a bill of manumission. Rebbi Joḥanan[89] heard this and said, Rebbi Joshua ben Levi taught us that correctly. Did they not infer the rules of a bill of manumission from women⁹⁰? Just as a woman is not freed if [the husband] has given up hope⁹¹, but she needs a bill of divorce from him, so a slave is not freed if [the master] has given up hope, but he needs a bill of manumission.

88   It is a general rule that anything abandoned becomes ownerless and may be taken by anybody who finds it. If a person gives up hope to recover something he lost, this is abandonment (*Baba meṣi'a* 2:1, first line). It is stated later that an adult slave, being able to become a responsible person, acquires himself if he becomes ownerless. Since then he is a full Jew, if the owner later finds him, he cannot reduce him to slavery. But the former slave cannot marry a Jewish partner without a bill of manumission.

89   In the Babli, 39a, the entire statement is in R. Joḥanan's name.

90   This is nowhere explicit in the Yerushalmi or the halakhic Midrashim; it is found in the Babli (*Giṭṭin* 29b,41b; *Ḥagigah* 10a; *Qidduśin* 23a) from a comparison of the language used for the manumission of a handmaid (*Lev.* 19:20) and the divorce of a wife (*Deut.* 24:1).

91   If a woman left her husband and the latter has given up hope that she ever would return to him, she still cannot remarry without a formal bill of divorce.

(45d line 31) שִׁמְעוֹן בַּר בָּא בְּשֵׁם רִבִּי יוֹחָנָן. עֶבֶד שֶׁבָּרַח מִן הַשַּׁבּוֹיִין אֶצֶל רַבּוֹ אֵין רַבּוֹ רַשַּׁאי לְשַׁעְבְּדוֹ וְצָרִיךְ לִכְתּוֹב לוֹ גֵט שִׁיחְרוּר. רִבִּי אַבָּהוּ בְּשֵׁם רִבִּי יוֹחָנָן אָמַר. הַמַּפְקִיר אֶת עַבְדּוֹ אֵינוֹ רַשַּׁאי לְשַׁעְבְּדוֹ וְאֵינוֹ רַשַּׁאי לִכְתּוֹב לוֹ גֵט שִׁיחְרוּר. אָמַר לֵיהּ רִבִּי זְעִירָא. כָּל־עַמָּא אָמְרִין דְּהוּא צָרִיךְ. וְאַתְּ אוֹמֵר. אֵינוֹ צָרִיךְ. שֶׁמָּא אֵינוֹ מְעַכְּבוֹ מִלּוֹכַל בַּפֶּסַח. כְּהָדָא דְתַנֵּי. וְכָל־עֶבֶד אִישׁ מִקְנַת כֶּסֶף וּמַלְתָּה אוֹתוֹ. בְּשָׁעָה שֶׁהוּא עוֹבֵד אֶת רַבּוֹ הוּא מְעַכְּבוֹ לוֹכַל בַּפֶּסַח. וּבְשָׁעָה שֶׁאֵינוֹ עוֹבֵד אֶת רַבּוֹ אֵינוֹ מְעַכְּבוֹ מִלּוֹכַל בַּפֶּסַח.

Simeon bar Abba in the name of Rebbi Joḥanan: If a slave fled from the kidnappers to his master, the master may not enslave him⁹² but has to write him a bill of manumission[93]. Rebbi Abbahu said in the name of Rebbi Joḥanan: If somebody declares his slave as ownerless he can neither enslave him nor write him a bill of manumission[94]. Rebbi Zeʿira said to him, everybody says that he needs one[95]; do you say that he does not need? Would he hinder him from eating the Passah [sacrifice][96]? As it was stated: "The slave of any man, acquisition of his money, if you circumcise him." Anytime he serves his master, he prevents his master from eating the Passah; if he does not serve his master, he does not prevent his master from eating the Passah[97].

92 Since he was not ransomed, it is as if his owner had given up hope to recover him.

93 In order to permit him to marry a Jewish partner.

94 Since a bill of manumission can be written only by the owner and this master has formally declined ownership, there is nobody who can write a bill of manumission for this slave. The Babli, 39a/b, holds in the name of R. Joḥanan that the owner can only renounce his ownership in money matters; for ceremonial law he can divest himself of ownership only by writing a bill of manumission. The Babli agrees that if the original owner dies before writing the bill of manumission, his children do not inherit any rights to the slave and the latter cannot be rescued from his state *in limbo*, free but unable to marry.

95 In the Babli, 39a, this is a statement of Ulla in the name of R. Joḥanan.

96 A person is prevented from eating the Passah sacrifice if any member of his *familia* is not circumcised (or if a female slave, not inducted into the Jewish faith by immersion in a *miqweh*), *Ex.* 12:43-45.

97 Therefore, the slave declared ownerless is no longer part of his owner's *familia*; the master no longer is a patron.

(45d line 38) סִימֵּא שְׁתֵּי עֵינָיו כְּאַחַת. הִפִּיל שְׁנֵי שִׁינָּיו כְּאַחַת. יוֹצֵא בָהֶן לַחֵירוּת. זוֹ אַחַר זוֹ. יוֹצֵא לַחֵירוּת בָּרִאשׁוֹנָה וְנוֹתֵן לוֹ דָמִים בַּשְּׁנִייָה. רִבִּי אִילָא בְשֵׁם רֵישׁ לָקִישׁ כְּמָאן דְּאָמַר. אֵינוֹ צָרִיךְ לִכְתּוֹב לוֹ גֵט שִׁיחְרוּר. בְּרַם כְּמָאן דְּאָמַר. צָרִיךְ לִכְתּוֹב לוֹ גֵט שִׁיחְרוּר. וְאַתְּ אוֹמֵר. מְשַׁלֵּם לוֹ. אֵין לִי אֶלָּא הַיּוֹצֵא בְשֵׁן וְעַיִן. מְנַיִּין הַיּוֹצֵא בְכִיפָּה ובהרנירק טיאונוס וּבְחֵרוּת שֶׁלַּמְּלָכִים. תַּלְמוּד לוֹמַר. לַחָפְשִׁי יְשַׁלְּחֶנּוּ מִכָּל מָקוֹם. בָּנָיו מָה הֵן. הַיּוֹצֵא בְּשֵׁן וְעַיִן בָּנָיו עֲבָדִים. וְהַיּוֹצֵא מִשּׁוּם יֵיאוּשׁ בָּנָיו בְּנֵי חוֹרִין. אָמַר רִבִּי יוֹסֵי בֵּירִבִּי בּוּן. לֹא מִסְתַּבְּרָא. חִילוּפִין. הַיּוֹצֵא בְּשֵׁן וְעַיִן הוֹאִיל וְשִׁיחְרָרָתוֹ הַתּוֹרָה בָּנָיו בְּנֵי חוֹרִין. וְהַיּוֹצֵא מִשּׁוּם יֵיאוּשׁ הוֹאִיל וְלֹא שִׁיחְרָרָתוֹ הַתּוֹרָה בָּנָיו עֲבָדִים.

If [the master] blinded [the slave's] two eyes simultaneously, or broke two of his teeth simultaneously, the slave thereby obtains his freedom[98]. One after the other, he obtains his freedom from the first [injury] and [the master] has to pay for the second[99]. Rebbi Ila in the name of Rebbi Simeon ben Laqish: Following the opinion that [the master] does not have to write a bill of manumission for him. But following the opinion that [the master] has to write a bill of manumission for him, can you say that he has to pay him[100]? Not only does this[101] apply to one who gains his freedom for a tooth or an eye, from where also that he may gain his freedom by a cap[102], or הרנירק טיאונוס[103], or the king's freedom[104]? The verse says, "he shall send him to freedom", in any way. What is the status of his[105] children? The children of him who leaves for a tooth or an eye are slaves, the children of him who leaves by the loss of hope are free. Rebbi Yose ben Rebbi Abun said, that is unreasonable; it is the other way around. The children of one who leaves for a tooth or an eye are free because the Torah freed him. The children of one who leaves by the loss of hope are slaves because the Torah did not free him.

98 *Ex.* 21:26-27 ordains freedom to a slave whose owner destroys one of his eyes or teeth. By rabbinic interpretation, this is extended to all important body parts.

99 For the second injury, the slave can already require the damages due to a free person.

100 In the Babli, 42a (quoted also *Qiddušin* 24b), this is a dispute among Tannaïm which is resolved by deciding that a bill of manumission is not needed for injury to teeth or eyes since the verse represents the bill of manumission, but is needed for all other body parts whose loss results in freedom to the slave only by rabbinic interpretation. The following sentence shows that this interpretation is not accepted in the Yerushalmi. In case a bill of manumission is required, damages can be claimed only after delivery of the bill.

It seems that the *baraita* in *Mekhilta dR. Ismael, Mišpaṭim* 9, contains a polemic against the argument here since it emphasizes that the verse requires to send the slave to freedom for his tooth or for his eye; the singular implies that the slave can request payment for the second injury independent of his legal status.

101 Even an authority who requires a bill of manumission for the slave freed by the Torah will not insist that the rules of these bills be followed to the letter but all forms of manumission accepted in Gentile courts are acceptable.

102 A Phrygian cap given to the slave by his master as a sign of freedom.

103 These words are unexplained. In the Babli 20a, speaking of manumission in general, not of the slave freed by the Torah, it is stated that a bill of manumission engraved on a writing tablet is valid, but not one written on a cap and אנדוכתרי (var. אנדרכתן, אדוכתן, אנדרוכתרי) explained in *Arukh* as text woven into the cloth (but see next paragraph).

In *Massekhet 'Avadim*, end of Chap. 3, the *baraita* quoted here appears in one ms. as: "If he broke his two teeth simultaneously, or blinded his two eyes simultaneously, the slave goes to freedom and is not paid anything, one after the other he obtains his freedom for the first and is paid for the second. If he cut his flesh or destroyed a tooth which did not come out yet, he is freed by אנטוקטא, a tablet, a writing tablet, but not by קיפה of kings." The word אנטוקטא was read by Pineles, דרכה של תורה, as *vindicta*, a reading accepted by all later lexicographers. It is likely that אנדוכתרי and its variants also represent forms of *vindicta* in Babylonian spelling, which does not show the usual exactness of transliterations in the Yerushalmi, standing for *manumissio per vindictam*, manumission by having the slave touched with a *vindicta*, or staff, by a duly authorized government official. Such a manumission is invalid in any case not ordered by the Torah.

104 The acts of manumission recognized in Roman law, *manumissio per vindictam, inter amicos,* and *per epistulam,* also manumission in Egyptian law by declaration before a notary public and payment of the applicable tax (cf. R. Taubenschlag, *The Law of Greco-Roman Egypt in Light of the Papyri,* New York 1944, p.73).

105 This should read "her" here and in the sequel since a male slave cannot marry and has no family relationship with his children.

(45d line 48) גֵּר שֶׁמֵּת וּבִזְבְּזוּ יִשְׂרָאֵל אֶת נְכָסָיו. וְהָיוּ שָׁם עֲבָדִים בֵּין גְּדוֹלִים בֵּין קְטַנִּים. יָצְאוּ לְחֵירוּת. אַבָּא שָׁאוּל אוֹמֵר. גְּדוֹלִים יָצְאוּ לְחֵירוּת. קְטַנִּים לֹא יָצְאוּ לְחֵירוּת. לָמָּה. שֶׁהֵן יָצְאוּ בְּמִיתַת רַבָּן. מֵעַתָּה אֲפִילוּ גְדוֹלִים. אָמַר רִבִּי בָּא. גְּדוֹלִים עַל יְדֵי שֶׁיֵּשׁ בָּהֶן דַּעַת לִזְכּוֹת אֶת עַצְמָן יָצְאוּ לְחֵרוּת. קְטַנִּים עַל יְדֵי שֶׁאֵין בָּהֶן דַּעַת לִזְכּוֹת לְעַצְמָן לֹא יָצָא לְחֵירוּת. רִבִּי יְהוֹשֻׁעַ בֶּן לֵוִי אָמַר. הֲלָכָה כְּאַבָּא שָׁאוּל. מַחְלְפָה שִׁיטָתֵיהּ דְּרִבִּי יְהוֹשֻׁעַ. תַּמָּן אָמַר רִבִּי סִימוֹן בְּשֵׁם רִבִּי יְהוֹשֻׁעַ בֶּן לֵוִי וְרִבִּי יוֹסִי בֶּן שָׁאוּל בְּשֵׁם רִבִּי. הַמַּתְיָיאֵשׁ מֵעַבְדּוֹ אֵינוֹ רַשַּׁאי לְשַׁעְבֵּד בּוֹ. אָמְרִין. מַה דְּאָמַר רִבִּי יְהוֹשֻׁעַ לְשַׁעְבֵּד. דְּלָא יְהַב לָא יָהֵב. דִּילְמָא הֲלָכָה לְשַׁעְבְּדוֹ וְצָרִיךְ לִכְתּוֹב לוֹ גֵּט שִׁיחֲרוּר וְהָכָא הוּא אָמַר הָכֵין. שָׁמַעְנוּ דְּאָמַר רִבִּי יוֹחָנָן. יָפָה לִימְּדָנִי רִבִּי יְהוֹשֻׁעַ בֶּן לֵוִי. דִּילְמָא הֲלָכָה כְּאַבָּא שָׁאוּל. אָמְתֵיהּ דְּרַבָּא בַּר זוּטְרָא עֲרָקַת. אִיתְיָיאֵשׁ מִינָהּ. אָתָא שָׁאַל לְרִבִּי חֲנִינָה וּלְרִבִּי יְהוֹשֻׁעַ בֶּן לֵוִי. אָמְרוּ. אֵינוֹ רַשַּׁאי לְשַׁעְבְּדָהּ. מַהוּ לִכְתּוֹב לָהּ גֵּט שִׁיחֲרוּר. אָמְרוּ לֵיהּ. אִם כָּתַבְתָּ יָאוֹת אַתְּ עָבַד. רִבִּי חֲנִינָה בְּשֵׁם רִבִּי יִשְׁמָעֵאל בֵּירִבִּי יוֹסֵה. עֶבֶד שֶׁנָּשָׂא בֶּן חוֹרִין לִפְנֵי רַבּוֹ יָצָא לְחֵירוּת. אָמַר רִבִּי יוֹחָנָן. אֶמֶשׁ הָיִיתִי יוֹשֵׁב וְשׁוֹנֶה. הַכּוֹתֵב כְּתַב קִידּוּשִׁין לְעַבְדּוֹ אוֹ כְּתַב נִישׂוּאִין לַאֲמָתוֹ. רִבִּי אוֹמֵר. זָכָה. וַחֲכָמִים אוֹמְרִים. לֹא זָכָה. אָהֵן תַּנַּיָּיא קַדְמַיָּיא סָבַר כְּרִבִּי זָכָה.

If a convert died[106] and Jews plundered his property, if there were slaves, either adult or underage, they gain their freedom[107]. Abba Shaul said, the adults gain their freedom, the minors do not become free. Why? They are no longer property after their owner's death[108]. Then even adults? Rebbi Abba said, since adults are competent to acquire themselves, they gain their freedom. Minors, who are not competent to acquire for themselves, do not gain their freedom. Rebbi Joshua ben Levi said, practice follows Abba Shaul[109]. The opinions of Rebbi Joshua ben Levi are contradictory. There, Rebbi Simon in the name of Rebbi Joshua ben Levi and Rebbi Yossi ben Shaul in the name of Rebbi said: A person who has given up hope to recover his slave[88] is not entitled to enslave him[110]. They said, what Rebbi Joshua said about enslaving, if he did not give, he did not give[111]; perhaps practice would be to enslave him, therefore he has to write him a bill of manumission[112]. And here, he says so! We heard that Rebbi Joḥanan said, Rebbi Joshua ben Levi taught us that correctly, perhaps practice follows Abba Shaul[113]. The slave girl of Rabba bar Zuṭra ran away and he gave up hope to recover her. He went to ask Rebbi Ḥanina and Rebbi Joshua ben Levi. They said, he is not entitled to enslave her[114]. How is it to write her a bill of manumission? They said to him, if you wrote, you did the right thing[115]. Rebbi Ḥanina in the name of Rebbi Ismael ben Rebbi Yose: A slave who married as a free person[116] in the presence of his master gained his freedom. Rebbi Joḥanan said, yesterday I was sitting and formulating: If somebody writes a document of preliminary marriage for his slave or a document of definitive marriage for his girl slave, Rebbi says, they acquired[117], but the Sages say, they did not acquire[118]. The first Tanna[119] follows Rebbi: he acquired.

106 He failed to start a Jewish family. Since he no longer is a member of his Gentile family and did not acquire Jewish heirs, his property becomes ownerless.

107 Since they become ownerless, they go free, cf. Note 94. This Tanna holds that the ownerless slave does not need a bill of manumission. In the Babli, 39a, Rav Naḥman explains that since the rules of bills of manumission are derived from those of bills of divorce, since a widow does not have a bill of divorce, the slave who gains freedom by his master's death does not need a bill.

108 And can be acquired by anybody who takes them.

109 The Babli, 39a/b, agrees and is ambivalent in the matter, as is the Yerushalmi.

110 And he asserts that the master has to write a bill of manumission for the slave. But the adult slave who gains his freedom by his master's death does not need a bill of manumission.

111 The owner cannot be forced to write a bill of manumission for the absconded slave.

112 It may be that any ownerless slave is automatically free without a written document; it also may be that the runaway slave whose master has given up hope of recovery is not free. Therefore, that slave cannot marry in the Jewish community without being formally freed.

113 Practice follows Abba Shaul, not as a necessity but as recommended action.

114 Even if he found her later, he could not bring any action to recover her as a servant.

115 He cannot be forced to write a bill but, since the runaway girl probably will reappear as a Jewish woman in some distant community and marry there, for the benefit of the community it is appropriate that the former owner write her a bill of manumission and appoint a local person to receive it in her stead (since one may give benefits to absent persons without their knowledge) to legitimize the children from any marriage she might contract.

116 The Babli, 39b/40a, and the *editio princeps* read בַּת חוֹרִין "a free woman" instead of בֶּן חוֹרִין "a free man" in the ms. One has to assume that the Venice typesetter was influenced by the Babli since the ms. shows no correction by the editor of the print; the text makes perfect sense as it stands. Since a slave cannot marry, if the master organizes a marriage for

him it is obvious (a) that the owner manumits the slave and (b) that the woman he marries must be free.

117 He accepts the marriage document as a bill of manumission; the slave acquires his own legal personality with the marriage document.

118 Since a slave's hand is his master's hand, a slave cannot acquire a document for himself unless he first was manumitted.

119 R. Ismael ben R. Yose.

(45d line 66) מִי מְשַׁחֲרֵר. רַב אָמַר. בֵּין רַבּוֹ הָרִאשׁוֹן וּבֵין רַבּוֹ הַשֵּׁנִי. אָמַר רַבִּי יוֹחָנָן. אֵין לָךְ מְשַׁחֲרֵר אֶלָּא רַבּוֹ הָרִאשׁוֹן בִּלְבָד. הָתִיב רַבִּי חַגַּיי קוֹמֵי רַבִּי יוֹסֵי. מַתְנִיתָא פְּלִיגָא עַל רַב. יִשְׂרָאֵל שֶׁהִלְוָה אֶת הַנָּכְרִי עַל חָמֵיצוֹ אַחַר הַפֶּסַח מוּתָּר בַּהֲנָאָה. אֵין תֵּימַר. בַּר יִשְׂרָאֵל הוּא וִיהֵא אָסוּר מָה עָבִיד לָהּ רַב. אָמַר רַבִּי יוּדָן. קַל הוּא בְשִׁחְרוּר. כְּהָדָא דְּתַנֵּי. הָעוֹשֶׂה עַבְדּוֹ אֲפוֹתֵיקֵי. מְכָרוֹ אֵינוֹ מָכוּר. שִׁחְרְרוֹ מְשׁוּחְרָר. חֵיילֵיהּ דְּרַבִּי יוֹחָנָן מִן הָדָא. רַבָּן שִׁמְעוֹן בֶּן גַּמְלִיאֵל אוֹמֵר אֵינוֹ כּוֹתֵב אֶלָּא מְשַׁחְרֵר. אִילּוּ הַמְשַׁעְבֵּד שָׂדֶה לַחֲבֵירוֹ וּמְכָרָהּ שֶׁמָּא אֵין בַּעַל חוֹב בָּא וְטוֹרֵף. אָמַר רַבִּי אַבָּהוּ. פָּתַח לָנוּ רַבִּי יוֹחָנָן פֶּתַח (ר') מֵאִיר בְּדָה כְאוֹרָה. לֹא מָצִינוּ עֶבֶד מִשְׁתַּחְרֵר וְחוֹזֵר וּמִשְׁתַּעְבֵּד. מֵעַתָּה לֹא יִכְתּוֹב לוֹ שְׁטָר עַל דָּמָיו. אָמַר רַבִּי אִילָא. מוּטָב שֶׁיֹּאמַר לוֹ. תֵּן לִי מָאתַיִם זוּז שֶׁיֵּשׁ לִי בְיָדָךְ. וְלֹא שֶׁיֹּאמַר לוֹ. עַבְדִּי אַתָּה. רַבָּנִין דְּקַיְסָרִין אָמְרִין בְּשֵׁם רַבִּי בִּיסָא. אַתְיָא דְּרַבָּן שִׁמְעוֹן בֶּן גַּמְלִיאֵל כְּרַבִּי מֵאִיר. כְּמָה דְּרַבִּי מֵאִיר קוֹנֵס בִּדְבָרִים כֵּן רַבָּן שִׁמְעוֹן בֶּן גַּמְלִיאֵל קוֹנֵס בִּדְבָרִים. דְּתַנֵּי. שְׁטָר שֶׁיֵּשׁ בּוֹ רִבִּית קוֹנְסִין אוֹתוֹ וְאֵינוֹ גוֹבֶה לֹא אֶת הַקֶּרֶן וְלֹא אֶת הָרִיבִּית. דִּבְרֵי רַבִּי מֵאִיר. וַחֲכָמִים אוֹמְרִים. גּוֹבֶה אֶת הַקֶּרֶן וְלֹא אֶת הָרִיבִּית.

1 ובין רבו השני | פ בין רבו אחרון   2 חגיי | פ חגי   יוסי | פ יוסה   4 בהנאה | פ בהנייה   בר | פ ברשות   ויהא | פ יהא   עביד | פ עבד   5 בשחרור | פ בשיחרור   6 שחררו | פ שיחררו   משוחרר | פ הרי זה משוחרר   7 ומכרה | פ ומכרה | פ והלך ומכרה   8 ר' | פ   9 בדה | פ -   -   מצינו | פ מצאנו   10 לא | פ -   11 ולא שיאמר | פ ואל יאמר   אמרין בשם רבי ביסא | פ בשם רבי נסא   13 שיש | פ יש   15 ולא | פ ואינו גובה

[120]Who frees[121]? Rav says, either his first or his second master[122]. Rebbi Johanan says, only his first master alone is able to free[123]. Rebbi Haggai objected before Rebbi Yose: Does not a *baraita* disagree with Rav? If a Jew gave a loan to a Gentile on the latter's leavened matter, it is permitted after Passover. If you say that the Jew has property rights[124] in it, it would be forbidden[125]. What does Rav do with this? Rebbi Yudan said, manumission is made easy, as it was stated: If somebody gives his slave as mortgage, if he sold him, he is not sold; if he freed him, he is freed[126]. The strength of Rebbi Johanan is from the following: Rabban Simeon ben Gamliel says, only the manumittor writes[78]. If somebody mortgaged his field to another, then went and sold it, can the creditor not come and foreclose? Rebbi Abbahu said, in this matter Rebbi Johanan opened for us a door to illuminate[124]. We do not find that a slave can again be enslaved after having been freed[127]. If that is so, he should not have to write a bond for his value! Rebbi Ila said, it is better that a person say to him, give me the 200 *zuz* which you owe me than say to him, you are my slave[128]! The rabbis of Caesarea say in Rebbi Nasa's[124] name: Rabban Simeon ben Gamliel follows Rebbi Meïr. Just as Rebbi Meïr imposes a fine for words, so Rabban Simeon ben Gamliel imposes a fine for words. As it was stated: With a bond documenting both principal and interest one can collect neither principal nor interest, the words of Rebbi Meïr[129]. But the Sages say, one collects the principal but not the interest[130].

120 A parallel is in *Pesaḥim* 2:2, l. 24 ff.; variants noted ⁍.

121 Here starts the discussion of the last part of the Mishnah, *viz.*, the mortgaged slave who was manumitted.

122 Both the owner and the

mortgage holder can free the slave (Babli 40a).

123 A mortgage holder is not a proprietor.

124 The translation follows ב.

125 In fact, Mishnah *Pesaḥim* 2:2 states that leavened matter pledged to a Jew is forbidden after Passover. This is explained in both Talmudim to refer to a contract which in case of foreclosure would retroactively transfer property rights to the creditor from the moment the loan was given. If the loan was given before Passover and foreclosed after Passover, the leavened matter was in the Jew's possession during Passover and is permanently forbidden to Jews. In the Yerushalmi *baraita* one assumes that the contract states explicitly that the creditor would acquire property rights only after foreclosure.

126 *Yebamot* 7:1, Notes 23-27.

127 The moment the slave gains his freedom he is a full Jew and is protected by all biblical laws regarding treatment of converts.

128 The only reason the rabbis require the ex-slave to write a bond to the creditor is for his own protection.

129 Cf. *Baba Meṣi'a* 10a l.60; Babli 72a, *Baba Qama* 30b, *Baba Batra* 94b. Rabban Simeon ben Gamliel holds that the manumission of a pledged slave is illegal and therefore the perpetrator has to pay.

130 The bond is valid and those parts which conform to the law can be enforced.

(fol. 45b) **משנה ה:** מִי שֶׁחֶצְיוֹ עֶבֶד וְחֶצְיוֹ בֶּן חוֹרִין עוֹבֵד אֶת רַבּוֹ יוֹם אֶחָד וְאֶת עַצְמוֹ יוֹם אֶחָד דִּבְרֵי בֵית הִלֵּל. בֵּית שַׁמַּאי אוֹמְרִים תִּיקַנְתֶּם אֶת רַבּוֹ וְאֶת עַצְמוֹ לֹא תְקַנְתֶּם. לִישָּׂא שִׁפְחָה אֵינוֹ יָכוֹל בַּת חוֹרִין אֵינוֹ יָכוֹל יִבָּטֵל. וַהֲלֹא לֹא נִבְרָא הָעוֹלָם אֶלָּא לְפִירִיָיה וְרִבִּיָיה שֶׁנֶּאֱמַר לֹא תוֹהוּ בְרָאָהּ לָשֶׁבֶת יְצָרָהּ. אֶלָּא מִפְּנֵי תִיקוּן הָעוֹלָם כּוֹפִין אֶת רַבּוֹ וְעוֹשֶׂה אוֹתוֹ בֶּן חוֹרִין וְכוֹתֵב שְׁטָר עַל חֲצִי דָמָיו. חָזְרוּ בֵית הִלֵּל לְהוֹרוֹת כְּדִבְרֵי בֵית שַׁמַּאי.

Mishnah 5: A person who is half slave and half free works for his master one day and for himself one day, the words of the House of Hillel. The House of Shammai say, you provided for his master but you did not provide for him. He can marry neither a slave woman[131] nor a free woman[132]: shall he be alone? But the world was created only for procreation and increase, as it is said[133]: "He did not create it to be empty, He formed it to be settled." For the public good one forces his master to manumit him and he writes a bond for half his value[134]. The House of Hillel changed and instructed following the House of Shammai.

131 The free part in him is forbidden any sexual relation with a slave.
132 The free woman is forbidden any sexual relation with the slave part in him.
133 *Is.* 45:18.

134 This entered Roman law by a decree of Justinian, c. 1. C. 7,7. Most earlier jurists rejected the idea of partial manumission; cf. R. Taubenschlag (Note 104), p. 75.

(46a line 6) הלכה ה: מִי שֶׁחֶצְיוֹ עֶבֶד וְחֶצְיוֹ בֶּן חוֹרִין כּוּל׳. הֵיאַךְ אֶפְשָׁר חֶצְיוֹ עֶבֶד וְחֶצְיוֹ בֶּן חוֹרִין. תִּיפְתָּר אוֹ כְרַבִּי. דְּרַבִּי אוֹמֵר. אָדָם מְשַׁחְרֵר חֲצִי עַבְדּוֹ. אוֹ דִבְרֵי הַכֹּל בְּעֶבֶד שֶׁלִּשְׁנֵי שׁוּתָּפִין וְעָמַד אֶחָד מֵהֶן וְשִׁיחְרֵר חֶלְקוֹ. מָצָא מְצִיאָה. בְּיוֹם שֶׁל רַבּוֹ שֶׁל רַבּוֹ. בְּיוֹם שֶׁלְּעַצְמוֹ שֶׁלְּעַצְמוֹ. וְלֵית מָחָר בְּעֵי יַעֲבְדָּה לֵיהּ לְמָרֵיהּ. קִידֵּשׁ אִשָּׁה. בְּיוֹם שֶׁל מָרֵיהּ אֵין חוֹשְׁשִׁין לְקִידּוּשָׁיו. בְּיוֹם שֶׁלְּעַצְמוֹ חוֹשְׁשִׁין לְקִידּוּשָׁיו. וְלֹא כֵן אָמַר רִבִּי חִייָה בְּשֵׁם רִבִּי יוֹחָנָן. מִי שֶׁחֶצְיוֹ עֶבֶד וְחֶצְיוֹ בֶּן חוֹרִין קִידֵּשׁ אִשָּׁה אֵין חוֹשְׁשִׁין לְקִידּוּשָׁיו. דִּכְוָותָא גֵּירַשׁ אֵין חוֹשְׁשִׁין לְגֵירוּשָׁיו.

Halakhah 5: "A person who is half slave and half free," etc. How is it possible that anyone be half slave and half free? Explain it either following Rebbi, since Rebbi said that a person can free half of his slave[135], or following everybody in the case of a slave belonging to two partners, when one of them manumitted his part. If he found anything of value, on his master's day it belongs to his master[136], on his own day it belongs to him. But would he not on the next day turn it over[137] to his master? If he entered a preliminary marriage. On his master's day, one would not consider his marriage[138], on his own day one would consider his marriage[139]. But did not Rebbi Ḥiyya say in Rebbi Joḥanan's name: If a person who is half slave and half free entered a preliminary marriage, one does not consider his marriage[140]. In parallel, if he divorced one does not consider his divorce[141].

135 In the Babli (41b, 23b, *Temurah* 25b) one holds that in the opinion of the rabbis opposed to Rebbi a person cannot free half of his slave but the freedom of a slave can be bought in installments.

136 Since at least for R. Meïr a slave's hand is his master's hand (*Ketubot* 6:1, Note 10; *Nedarim* 11:8, Note 70), what he finds belongs to his master.

137 Reading יעברה for יעבדה. Since a slave cannot own property, all he has would be intermittently his owner's. This is legally an impossible situation; even without the argument of the House of Shammai it would be necessary to totally free the partially manumitted person or to declare the partial manumission as void.

138 As a slave, he cannot marry. A woman who receives valuables from a slave for a preliminary marriage is free to marry any other man without a divorce; she is not considered married.

139 While the marriage could not be consummated (Note 132), there seems to be no reason why the preliminary marriage should not be valid according to the House of Hillel, who hold that on alternate days he is a free person.

140 By a rabbinic decree, the half-free person is disqualified from entering a preliminary marriage.

141 If a half-free person entered a preliminary marriage and then, upon being informed that his act was invalid, gave the woman a bill of divorce; the recipient was never either married or divorced and is free to marry a Cohen.

(46a line 15) תַּמָּן תַּנִּינָן. אֵין נוֹשְׂאִין נָשִׁים בְּמוֹעֵד. שִׁמְעוֹן בַּר אַבָּא בְּשֵׁם רִבִּי יוֹחָנָן. מִשּׁוּם בִּיטוּל פְּרִיָּיה וְרִבְיָיה. בְּעוֹן קוֹמֵי רִבִּי יוֹסֵי. עֶבֶד מָהוּ שֶׁיִּשָּׂא אִשָּׁה בְּמוֹעֵד. אָמַר לֵיהּ. נִשְׁמְעִינָהּ מִן הָדָא. לִיבְטִיל. וַהֲלֹא לֹא נִבְרָא הָעוֹלָם אֶלָּא לִפְרִיָּיה וְרִבְיָיה. וְאָמַר רִבִּי שִׁמְעוֹן בַּר אַבָּא בְּשֵׁם רִבִּי יוֹחָנָן. כָּל־שֶׁהוּא מְצוּוֶה עַל פְּרִיָּיה וְרִבְיָיה אָסוּר לוֹ לִישָּׂא אִשָּׁה בְּמוֹעֵד.

There[142], we have stated: "One does not marry women on a holiday[143]." Simeon bar Abba in the name of Rebbi Joḥanan: Because of refraining from being fruitful and increase[144]. They asked before Rebbi Yose: May a slave marry a woman on a holiday[145]? He told them, let us hear from the following: "Shall he be alone? But the world was created only for procreation and increase!" And Rebbi Simeon bar Abba said in the name of Rebbi Joḥanan: Anybody commanded to be fruitful and increase is forbidden to marry on a holiday[146].

142 Mishnah *Mo'ed Qaṭan* 1:7.
143 The intermediate days of the Passover and Tabernacles holidays when acquisitions are permitted and in biblical law the man could acquire a wife and the woman the *ketubah* rights.
144 The prohibition to organize weddings on the intermediate days of a holiday is purely rabbinical, so that people should not refrain from marrying during the rest of the year in order to save money.
In *Mo'ed Qaṭan* 1:7 l. 26ff. and the Babli, 8b/9a, the reason for the prohibition is a matter of disagreement among several authors.
145 The question is difficult to understand since the slave cannot marry as long as he is a slave but is a full Jew subject to all Jewish laws the moment he is manumitted. Maybe the question is about a slave manumitted on the holiday.
146 Even if in this case the marriage has to be postponed for a few days. A slightly different version of this paragraph is in *Mo'ed Qaṭan* 1:7 80d l. 30, quoted by Tosaphot *Ḥagiga* 2b, *Giṭṭin* 41b, *s. v.* לא. Tosaphot point out that in a certain sense a male slave cannot fulfill the commandment to be fruitful because he cannot have any family relationship with his biological children.

(fol. 45b) **משנה ו:** הַמּוֹכֵר אֶת עַבְדּוֹ לַגּוֹיִם אוֹ לְחוּצָה לָאָרֶץ יָצָא בֶּן חוֹרִין. אֵין פּוֹדִין אֶת הַשְּׁבוּיִין יוֹתֵר עַל כְּדֵי דְמֵיהֶן מִפְּנֵי תִיקּוּן הָעוֹלָם. וְאֵין מַבְרִיחִין אֶת הַשְּׁבוּיִין מִפְּנֵי תִיקּוּן הָעוֹלָם. רַבָּן שִׁמְעוֹן בֶּן גַּמְלִיאֵל אוֹמֵר מִפְּנֵי תַקָּנַת שְׁבוּיִים. וְאֵין לוֹקְחִין סְפָרִים תְּפִילִין וּמְזוּזוֹת מִן הַגּוֹיִים יוֹתֵר עַל כְּדֵי דְמֵיהֶן מִפְּנֵי תִיקּוּן הָעוֹלָם.

Mishnah 6: If somebody sells his slave to Gentiles or outside the Land, the slave gains his freedom[147]. One does not ransom kidnap victims for more than the going rate[148] because of the public good. One does not smuggle kidnap victims out because of the public good; Rabban Simeon ben Gamliel says, because of the welfare of the kidnap victims[149]. One does not buy Torah scrolls, phylacteries, and *mezuzot* from Gentiles for more than their worth because of the public good[150].

147 Since a slave is required to obey all of the biblical prohibitions imposed on Jews, a sale to a Gentile is equivalent to the slave's removal from Jewish practice. Also, there are more commandments to be observed in the Land than abroad. In both cases, it is a rabbinic decree that the master has to buy the slave back and then formally manumit him. (In *Sifry Deut.* 259, this is connected to *Deut.* 23:16-17.)

148 If the kidnap victims were sold as slaves on the open market. If it were known that Jews be ready to ransom their co-religionists for any price, no Jew would be safe from kidnapping.

149 The majority holds that one never tries to free kidnap victims without paying because then the robbers would put their next victims in chains and otherwise mistreat them. Rabban Simeon ben Gamliel holds that one may not try to steal the kidnap victims if one cannot free all of them in the hand of a group of kidnappers, because those left behind then would be mistreated. He does not fear an adverse reaction in a larger context.

150 Gentiles should not get the impression that stealing Jewish cult objects might be a particularly profitable business.

(46a line 20) **הלכה ו:** הַמּוֹכֵר אֶת עַבְדּוֹ לַגּוֹיִם כול'. לְגוֹי אֲפִילוּ בְּאֶרֶץ יִשְׂרָאֵל. מִי מְשַׁחְרְרוֹ. רַבּוֹ רִאשׁוֹן נוֹתֵן דָּמָיו וְהַשֵּׁינִי מְשַׁחְרְרוֹ. וּבְחוּצָה לָאָרֶץ אֲפִילוּ יִשְׂרָאֵל. נֵימַר. אִם יָדַע רַבּוֹ הַשֵּׁינִי שְׁנֵיהֶן נוֹתְנִין אֶת דָּמָיו. וְאִם לָאו הָרִאשׁוֹן נוֹתֵן דָּמָיו וְהַשֵּׁינִי מְשַׁחְרְרוֹ. אֲנִי פְּלוֹנִי בֶּן פְּלוֹנִי מוֹכֵר אֶת עַבְדִּי פְּלוֹנִי אַנְטִיוֹכִי. יָצָא לְחֵירוּת. מִשֶּׁהוּא בְלוֹד לֹא יָצָא לְחֵירוּת. תַּנֵּי. יוֹצֵא עֶבֶד עִם רַבּוֹ בְחוּצָה לָאָרֶץ. לְפִיכָךְ אִם מְכָרוֹ לְשָׁם מָכוּר. בָּא מֵחוּצָה לָאָרֶץ עַל מְנַת לַחֲזוֹר כּוֹפִין אוֹתוֹ לְמָחָר לַחֲזוֹר. עַל מְנַת שֶׁלֹּא לַחֲזוֹר אֵין כּוֹפִין אוֹתוֹ לַחֲזוֹר. בָּרַח מֵחוּצָה לָאָרֶץ רַשַּׁאי לְהַחֲזִירוֹ. בָּרַח מֵאֶרֶץ לְחוּצָה לָאָרֶץ. רִבִּי יֹאשִׁיָּה בְּשֵׁם רִבִּי חִייָה רָבָא אָמַר. רִבִּי הוֹשַׁעְיָה רַבָּה אָמַר. מוּתָּר. רִבִּי מָרִינוֹס בְּרֵיהּ דְּרִבִּי הוֹשַׁעְיָה רַבָּה אָמַר. אָסוּר. אָמַר רִבִּי זְעִירָא. לֹא פְלִיגִין. מָאן דְּאָמַר מוּתָּר. בְּלָמוּד לִבְרוֹחַ לְשָׁם. וּמָאן דְּאָמַר אָסוּר. בְּשֶׁאֵינוֹ לָמוּד לִבְרוֹחַ לְשָׁם. אָמַר רִבִּי יוֹסֵי. וְלֹא פְלִיגִין. מָאן דְּאָמַר מוּתָּר. בְּיָכוֹל לַהֲבִיאוֹ מִשָּׁם. וּמָאן דְּאָמַר אָסוּר. בְּשֶׁאֵינוֹ יָכוֹל לַהֲבִיאוֹ מִשָּׁם.

Halakhah 6: "If somebody sells his slave to Gentiles," etc. To a Gentile even in the Land. Who frees him? His original owner pays for him and the second frees him[151]. "Or outside the Land," even to a Jew. Let us say that if the second owner knew[152], both of them split the price[153]; otherwise the first pays for him and the second frees him. "I X ben Y sold my slave Z to Antiochia", he gains his freedom. But if he is in Lydda, he did not gain his freedom[154]. It was stated: A slave goes outside the Land with his master[155]. Therefore, if he sold him there, he is sold[156]. If he[157] came from outside the Land to the Land with the intention to return, one forces him to return. With the intention not to return, one does not force him to return. If he fled from outside the Land to the Land, he[158] may return him. If he fled from the Land to outside the Land, Rebbi Joshia in the name of the Elder Rebbi Ḥiyya said, it is permitted[159]. The great Rebbi Hoshaia said, it is permitted. Rebbi Marinos, the son of the great Rebbi Hoshaia said, it is forbidden[160]. Rebbi Ze'ira said, they do not disagree. He who says, it is permitted, if he is used to flee there. But he who says, it is forbidden, if he is not used to flee there. Rebbi Yose said, they do not disagree. He who says, it is permitted, if he can return him from there; but he who says, it is forbidden, if he cannot return him from there[161].

151 This sentence and the next should be switched since if the slave was sold to a Gentile it is obvious that the Jewish owner has to manumit the slave; Mishnah 1:5 states that the manumission of a Jewish slave by the rules of a Gentile court is invalid. The original text probably was close to Tosephta 'Avodah Zarah 3:18: "If somebody sells his slave to a place outside the Land he gains his freedom and the second master has to write him the bill of manumission." The Babli, 44b, infers from the Tosephta that the sale in itself is valid, otherwise the buyer would not have the power to manumit the slave.

152 That the sale was illegal by rabbinic rules.

153 The seller has to repay only half the sale price.

154 This is much clearer in the Tosephta, loc. cit., in the name of Rabban Simeon ben Gamliel: "'I X ben Y sold my slave to Antiochia', he gains his freedom; 'to Z the Antiochian who dwells in Lydda' he does not gain his freedom." This is qualified in the Babli, 44b, by the statement that the Antiochian has to own an apartment in Lydda.

155 In the Tosephta and the Babli, this is restricted to Syria. There is no indication in the Yerushalmi of any restriction on a person to take his slave with him on a trip as a valet.

156 Since the slave was legally taken on the trip. The sale is only illegal if contracted in the Land.

157 If a diaspora Jew comes to the Land for a visit, his slave cannot refuse to return with him. But if he came to immigrate, the slave acquires the rights of residence. A slightly garbled version is in the Tosephta.

158 The owner of the slave can take

him back. (*Deut.* 23:16,17 refers to the slave of a Gentile owner.

159   To forcibly return the slave to the Land.

160   The question arises how the son can disagree with his father.

161   In that case, the slave gained his freedom when the owner gave up hope to recover him; cf. Note 88.

(46a line 33) נִיתְנֵי. וְאִם הִתְנָה עִמּוֹ מוּתָּר. עַד כְּדוֹן בִּגְדוֹלִים. בִּקְטַנִּים. נִיתְנֵי עִם רַבְּהוֹן. עַד כְּדוֹן בְּשֶׁהָיָה רַבּוֹ יִשְׂרָאֵל. הָיָה רַבּוֹ גּוֹי. רִבִּי טָבְלָא זְבִין עַבְדֵּיהּ וּמַתְנֵי עִם רַבְּהוֹן. רִבִּי יִצְחָק דַּהֲבָן הֲווֹן לֵיהּ עַבְדֵּיהּ עָרְקִין לִבְנוֹתְהוֹן. אָתָא שָׁאַל לְרִבִּי אִימִּי וְהוֹרֵי לֵיהּ. אוֹנִי אָסוּר. אַנְטְרִיס שָׁרֵי. אַפָּרְכוֹרִים צְרִיכָה. אַמְתֵּיהּ דְּרִבִּי אַבָּא בַּר אָדָא עָרְקַת לְקִלִיסְיָיא. אָתָא שָׁאַל לְרִבִּי מָנָא וְהוֹרֵי לֵיהּ כְּרִבִּי אִימִּי. אוֹנִי אָסוּר. אַנְטְרִיס שָׁרֵי. אַפָּרְכוֹרִים צְרִיכָה.

There could be terms[162]. If he entered into terms with him[163], it is permitted. That means, with adults. With minors, the terms can be with their masters. That is, if the master was a Jew. If he was Gentile? Rebbi Tevele sold his slave and entered into terms with his master[164]. Rebbi Isaac the goldsmith had slaves who fled to Bnoton[165]. He came and asked[166] Rebbi Immi who instructed him that a sales contract[167] is forbidden, a loan for use[168] is permitted, a cession[169] is questionable. The slave girl of Rebbi Abba bar Ada fled to Cilicia. He came and asked Rebbi Mana, who instructed him following Rebbi Immi: a sales contract is forbidden, a loan for use is permitted, a cession is questionable.

162   If the slave was bought on condition that he could be resold outside the Land, the deal might be valid.

163   If the condition was stipulated with the slave, it is valid.

164   This could even be a sale within the Land to a Gentile if the buyer guaranteed that the slave could continue following Jewish law, keeping the Sabbath and eating kosher.

165   Name of an unidentified place,

probably a corruption. As a noun, the word means "their daughters".

166 When the slaves were caught outside the Land, he asked how he could dispose of them there within the rules. The explanation of this passage follows J. N. Epstein, *Tarbiz* 8 (1937) 316-318, with a note by I. Ostersetzer, *Tarbiz* 9 (1938) 395-397.

167 Greek ὠνή "sales contract, purchase". The outright sale of the slave outside the Land is forbidden.

168 Greek ἀντίχρησις "loan for use," reading אנטיכריס for אנטריס, which is possible in such a heavily Babylonized text. An antichretic loan is a loan in which the creditor obtains the use of the mortgaged object, and the rental fee, instead of being paid to the borrower, is used to amortize the loan (cf. Taubenschlag, Note 104, p. 218, on antichretic loans of slaves.) Since the slave remains the property of the owner, there is no sale. J. N. Epstein points out that R. Immi in *Baba Meṣi'a* 5:3 (10b 1.20) explicitly states that antichretic mortgages are valid and do not violate interest prohibitions. (In an earlier article, Epstein had read ἀντίδοσις "exchange".)

169 Greek παραχώρησις "cession, surrender, assignment." Rabbinic law accepts the division between possession (*possessio*) and ownership (*dominium*) found in Ptolemaic and Roman law. Parachoresis means handing over the pledge (in this case, the slave) by the debtor to the creditor for possession to be turned into ownership if the debtor fails to repay the loan. It is now stated that the sale of the slave in form of a fictitious chattel mortgage (when the owner of the slave has no intention to repay the sum he received) is of questionable character; it would be valid if the owner had the intention of repaying the loan and taking back his slave since, as antichresis shows, the (temporary) transfer of possessions without transfer of ownership is perfectly legal. Cf. Taubenschlag, pp. 172,316. (In an earlier article, Epstein had read ἐπίχειρον "wages, pay of manual labor".)

(46a line 39) אֵין פּוֹדִין אֶת הַשְּׁבוּיִין יוֹתֵר מִדְּמֵיהֶן מִפְּנֵי תִּיקוּן הָעוֹלָם. רַבָּן שִׁמְעוֹן בֶּן גַּמְלִיאֵל אוֹמֵר מִפְּנֵי תַקָּנַת הַשְּׁבוּיִין. דְּלָא יְהַוּוֹן קְטָרִינוֹן. וְאֵין מַבְרִיחִין אֶת הַשְּׁבוּיִין מִפְּנֵי תִּיקוּן הָעוֹלָם.

"One does not ransom kidnap victims for more than the going rate[148] because of the public good. Rabban Simeon ben Gamliel says, because of the welfare of the kidnap victims." That they should not be put in chains[149]. "One does not smuggle kidnap victims out because of the public good."

(46a line 42) תַּנֵּי. גוֹי מוֹכֵר סְפָרִים תְּפִילִין וּמְזוּזוֹת אָסוּר לִיקַּח מִמֶּנּוּ. וְהָא תַנֵּי. מַעֲשֶׂה בְגוֹי אֶחָד בְּצַיְדָּן שֶׁהָיָה מוֹכֵר תְּפִילִין וּמְזוּזוֹת. וּבָא מַעֲשֶׂה לִפְנֵי חֲכָמִים וְאָמְרוּ. מוּתָּר לִיקַּח מִמֶּנּוּ. רִבִּי שְׁמוּאֵל בַּר נָתָן בְּשֵׁם רִבִּי חָמָא בַּר חֲנִינָה. בְּגוֹי שֶׁחָזַר לְסוּרוֹ הֲוָה.

It was stated: "It is prohibited to buy from a Gentile who sells Torah scrolls, phylacteries, and *mezuzot*[170]." But was it not stated[171]: "It happened that a Gentile in Sidon sold phylacteries and *mezuzot*. The case came before the Sages who said that it was permitted to buy from him." That one was a Gentile who reverted to his error[172].

170 Since probably he is a fence. Babylonian sources in theory (Babli 45b, Tosephta *Avodah Zarah* 3:6) permit to buy from the Gentile if the writing follows all established rules, in practice disapprove, 45b.

171 Babli 45b, Tosephta *Avodah Zarah* 3:7. This Tosephta is a polemic against the Yerushalmi *baraita*.

172 He was a proselyte who had learned to write Jewish sacred texts. Since the status of being Jewish cannot be lost, when he reverted to Gentile ways he remained a Jew. Therefore, he is entitled to write these texts; he is not a fence. The Babli has the same explanation, 45b.

(fol. 45b) **משנה ז:** הַמּוֹצִיא אֶת אִשְׁתּוֹ מִשּׁוּם שֵׁם רַע לֹא יַחֲזִיר מִשּׁוּם נֶדֶר לֹא יַחֲזִיר. רְבִּי יְהוּדָה אוֹמֵר כָּל־נֶדֶר שֶׁיָּדְעוּ בוֹ הָרַבִּים לֹא יַחֲזִיר וְשֶׁלֹּא יָדְעוּ בוֹ הָרַבִּים יַחֲזִיר. רְבִּי מֵאִיר אוֹמֵר כָּל־נֶדֶר שֶׁצָּרִיךְ חֲקִירַת חָכָם לֹא יַחֲזִיר וְשֶׁאֵינוֹ צָרִיךְ חֲקִירַת חָכָם יַחֲזִיר. אָמַר רְבִּי אֶלְעָזָר לֹא אָסְרוּ זֶה אֶלָּא מִפְּנֵי זֶה. אָמַר רְבִּי יוֹסֵי בַּר יְהוּדָה מַעֲשֶׂה בְּצַיְדָּן בְּאֶחָד שֶׁאָמַר לְאִשְׁתּוֹ קוֹנָם שֶׁאֵינִי מְגָרְשָׁהּ וְגֵרְשָׁהּ וְהִתִּירוּ לוֹ חֲכָמִים שֶׁיַּחֲזִירֶנָּה מִפְּנֵי תִיקּוּן הָעוֹלָם.

Mishnah 7: If somebody divorces his wife because of bad reputation[173], he cannot take her back[174]; because of a vow[175], he cannot take her back[174]. Rebbi Jehudah says, for any vow known in public[176], he cannot take her back; not known in public, he can take her back. Rebbi Meïr says, for any vow which needs investigation by a Sage, he cannot take her back; if it does not need investigation by a Sage, he can take her back[177]. Rebbi Eleazar said, they forbade one because of the other[178]. Rebbi Yose ben Jehudah said, it happened in Sidon that one said to his wife, a *qonam*[179] if I do not divorce you, and he divorced her, and the Sages permitted him to take her back[180], for the public good.

173 She has the reputation of an adulteress but he has no proof.

174 As explained in the Halakhah, to protect the wife's children in a subsequent marriage. This is in the public interest.

175 Because of a vow she made.

176 Which according to R. Jehudah cannot be dissolved; cf. *Nedarim* 5:4, Note 56.

177 A vow made in error which never was binding.

178 This is explained in the Halakhah.

179 He forbade certain things on himself if he did not fulfill the conditions he imposed on himself; cf. Tractate *Nedarim*, Introduction.

180 This is unproblematic since he fulfilled his vow. The case is quoted only to show that the prohibition to take her back is due only to a vow of hers, not his.

(46a line 46) **הלכה ז:** הַמּוֹצִיא אֶת אִשְׁתּוֹ מִשּׁוּם שֵׁם רַע כול׳. וְתַנֵּי. מִפְּנֵי מַה אָמְרוּ חֲכָמִים. הַמּוֹצִיא מִשּׁוּם שֵׁם רַע לֹא יַחֲזִיר. שֶׁהֲרֵי הַמּוֹצִיא אֶת אִשְׁתּוֹ מִשּׁוּם שֵׁם רַע וְהָלְכָה וְנִישֵּׂאת לְאַחֵר וְיָלְדָה מִמֶּנּוּ בָנִים. לְאַחַר זְמָן נִמְצְאוּ הַדְּבָרִים בְּדָאִים. אָמַר. אִילּוּ הָיִיתִי יוֹדֵעַ שֶׁהַדְּבָרִים בְּדָאִים אִילּוּ הָיָה אָדָם נוֹתֵן לִי בְּאִשְׁתִּי מֵאָה מָנֶה לֹא הָיִיתִי מְגָרְשָׁהּ. וְנִמְצָא גֵט בָּטֵל וּבָנֶיהָ מַמְזֵירִים. וּמִתּוֹךְ שֶׁהוּא יוֹדֵעַ שֶׁאִם הוּא מְגָרְשָׁהּ שֶׁהִיא אֲסוּרָה לַחֲזוֹר לוֹ אַף הוּא נוֹתֵן לָהּ גֵּט שָׁלֵם מִשָּׁעָה רִאשׁוֹנָה.

"If somebody divorces his wife because of bad reputation," etc. And it was stated[181]: "Why did the Sages say that he who divorces his wife because of bad reputation cannot take her back[182]? For if he divorced his wife because of bad reputation, when she went, married another, and bore him children, after some time it turned out that the accusations were baseless and he said, if I had known that the accusations were baseless, even if somebody had offered me a hundred minas for my wife I would not have divorced her, then the bill of divorce would be invalidated[183] and her children bastards. But since he knows that if he divorces her, she will be forbidden to return to him, from the start he gives her a perfect bill of divorce."

181   Babli 46a, Tosephta 3:5.

182   The court will not let him take her back. While a divorce as a matter of principle is a private affair between husband and wife and needs only two witnesses for the document and two for the delivery, a divorce because of probable cause of adultery is a public affair. The husband can divorce his wife without paying her *ketubah* only if he can show probable cause in court. If he divorces her and pays the *ketubah*, it is not classified as "divorce because of bad reputation".

183   Since *Deut.* 24:1 make the divorce dependent on the husband's will, if later he retracts that will, he retroactively invalidates the divorce. This is also accepted in the Babli; in modern practice the husband has to agree that any later change of heart must be disregarded.

(46a line 43) תַּנֵּי. מִפְּנֵי מָה אָמְרוּ. הַמוֹצִיא אֶת אִשְׁתּוֹ מִשּׁוּם נֶדֶר לֹא יַחֲזִיר. שֶׁהֲרֵי הַמּוֹצִיא אֶת אִשְׁתּוֹ מִשּׁוּם נֶדֶר וְהָלְכָה וְנִישֵּׂאת לְאַחֵר וְיָלְדָה מִמֶּנּוּ וְנִמְצָא נֶדֶר בָּטֵל. אָמַר. אִילּוּ הָיִיתִי יוֹדֵעַ שֶׁהָיָה הַנֶּדֶר בָּטֵל אִילּוּ הָיָה אָדָם נוֹתֵן לִי בְאִשְׁתִּי מֵאָה מָנָה לֹא הָיִיתִי מְגָרְשָׁהּ. וְנִמְצָא גֵּט בָּטֵל וְהַוְולָד מַמְזֵר. וּמִתּוֹךְ שֶׁהוּא יוֹדֵעַ שֶׁאִם הוּא מְגָרְשָׁהּ שֶׁהִיא אֲסוּרָה לַחֲזוֹר לוֹ אַף הוּא נוֹתֵן לָהּ גֵּט שָׁלֵם מִשָּׁעָה רִאשׁוֹנָה. אָמַר רִבִּי זְעִירָה. תֵּדַע לָךְ שֶׁעֵילָה הָיָה רוֹצֶה לְגָרְשָׁהּ. שֶׁהֲרֵי נֶדֶר שֶׁאֵינוֹ צָרִיךְ חֲקִירַת חָכָם הָיָה. אָמַר רִבִּי זְעִירָה. תֵּדַע לָךְ שֶׁעֵילָה הָיָה רוֹצֶה לְגָרְשָׁהּ. שֶׁהֲרֵי נֶדֶר שֶׁלֹּא יָדְעוּ בוֹ רַבִּים הָיָה. אָמַר רִבִּי לֶעְזָר. לֹא אָסְרוּ זֶה אֶלָּא מִפְּנֵי זֶה. בְּדִין הָיָה שֶׁאֲפִילוּ נֶדֶר שֶׁהוּא צָרִיךְ חֲקִירַת חָכָם יַחֲזִיר. שֶׁהַדַּקֶּן עוֹקֵר אֶת הַנֶּדֶר מֵעִיקָרוֹ. מִפְּנֵי מָה אָסְרוּ נֶדֶר שֶׁאֵינוֹ צָרִיךְ חֲקִירַת חָכָם. מִפְּנֵי נֶדֶר שֶׁצָּרִיךְ חֲקִירַת חָכָם.

It was stated[184]: "Why did they say that he who divorces his wife because of a vow cannot take her back? For if he divorced his wife because of a vow, when she went, married another, and bore him children, after some time it turned out that the vow was void and he said, if I had known that the vow was void, even if somebody had offered me a hundred minas for my wife I would not have divorced her, then the bill of divorce would be invalidated and her child a bastard. But since he knows that if he divorces her, she will be forbidden to return to him, from the start he gives her a perfect bill of divorce." Rebbi Ze'ira said, you can see that he was looking for a pretext to divorce her since it must have been a vow which does not need investigation by a Sage[185]! Rebbi Ze'ira said, you can see that he was looking for a pretext to divorce her since it must have been a vow which was not public knowledge[186]! [187]"Rebbi Eleazar said, they forbade one because of the other." The law should be that he can take her back even if it was a vow which needs investigation by a

Sage, for the Elder uproots the vow. Why did they forbid a vow which needs investigation by a Sage? Because of a vow which does not need investigation by a Sage[188].

184 Tosephta 3:5.
185 The only invalid vows are those which do not need an Elder to be nullified. Therefore, the husband could have annulled the vow (*Nedarim* Chapters 10-11).
186 Also for a public vow, the situation described in the Tosephta cannot arise.
187 This is quoted in *Ketubot* 7:9, explained there in Notes 117,118.
188 In which case the situation described in the Tosephta could arise.

משנה ח: הַמוֹצִיא אֶת אִשְׁתּוֹ מִשּׁוּם אַיְילוֹנִית רִבִּי יְהוּדָה אוֹמֵר לֹא יַחֲזִיר וַחֲכָמִים אוֹמְרִים יַחֲזִיר. נִישֵּׂאת לְאַחֵר וְהָיוּ לָהּ בָּנִים מִמֶּנּוּ וְהִיא תוֹבַעַת כְּתוּבָתָהּ. אָמַר רִבִּי יְהוּדָה אוֹמֵר לָהּ שְׁתִיקוּתֵיךְ יָפָה מִדִּיבָּרֵיךְ. (fol. 45b)

Mishnah 8: If somebody divorces his wife because she is a she-ram[189], Rebbi Jehudah says, he cannot take her back, but the Sages say, he may take her back. If she was married to another man, had children by him, and requests her *ketubah*, Rebbi Jehudah says, he tells her: Your silence would be better than your talking[190].

189 A woman lacking secondary female sex characteristics; she is presumed to be infertile. If she was married when very young and then failed to develop, the husband can claim the the marriage and his obligation of *ketubah* was entered into in error. Cf. *Yebamot* 1:1, Note 65; *Ketubot* 7:7, Note 77. R. Jehudah holds that a she-ram should not be married, Mishnah *Yebamot* 6:5.
190 This gives R. Jehudah's rationale. If she was divorced without payment of the sum promised her in

the *ketubah* and it turns out that she is not infertile, the husband tells her that if she goes to court, he will declare that he would never have divorced her, had he known that she was not infertile (or, according to Rashi, that he would have to pay the *ketubah*), and turn her children from the second husband into bastards.

(46a line 66) **הלכה ח:** הַמּוֹצִיא אֶת אִשְׁתּוֹ מִשּׁוּם אַיְילוֹנִית כול'. תַּנֵּי. מִפְּנֵי מָה אָמְרוּ. הַמּוֹצִיא אֶת אִשְׁתּוֹ מִשּׁוּם אַיְילוֹנִית לֹא יַחְזִיר. שֶׁהֲרֵי הַמּוֹצִיא אֶת אִשְׁתּוֹ מִשּׁוּם אַיְילוֹנִית וְהָלְכָה וְנִישֵּׂאת לְאַחֵר וְיָלְדָה מִמֶּנּוּ בָּנִים. וְאָמַר. אִילּוּ הָיִיתִי יוֹדֵעַ שֶׁאִשְׁתִּי יוֹלֶדֶת אִילּוּ הָיָה אָדָם נוֹתֵן לִי בְּאִשְׁתִּי מֵאָה מָנֶה לֹא הָיִיתִי מְגָרְשָׁהּ. וְנִמְצָא גֵט בָּטֵל וְהַוָּלָד מַמְזֵר. וּמִתּוֹךְ שֶׁהוּא יוֹדֵעַ שֶׁאִם הוּא מְגָרְשָׁהּ שֶׁהִיא אֲסוּרָה לַחֲזוֹר לוֹ אַף הוּא נוֹתֵן לָהּ גֵט שָׁלֵם מִשָּׁעָה רִאשׁוֹנָה. אָמַר רִבִּי זְעִירָה. תֵּדַע לָךְ שֶׁעֲיִלָּה הָיָה רוֹצֶה לְגָרְשָׁהּ. שֶׁהֲרֵי כַּמָּה נָשִׁים נְשׂוּאִין אַיְילוֹנִיּוֹת וְעַל יְדֵי שֶׁיֵּשׁ לָהֶן נַחַת רוּחַ מֵהֶן מְקַיְּימִין אוֹתָן.

Halakhah 8: It was stated[184]: "Why did they say that he who divorces his wife as a she-ram cannot take her back? For if he divorced his wife as a she-ram, when she went, married another man, and bore him children, and he said, if I had known that she can have children, even if somebody had offered me a hundred minas for my wife I would not have divorced her, then the bill of divorce would be invalidated and her child a bastard. But since he knows that if he divorces her, she will be forbidden to return to him, from the start he gives her a perfect bill of divorce." Rebbi Ze'ira said, you can see that he was looking for a pretext to divorce her since there are women she-rams who are married and since [their husbands] are satisfied with them they keep them[191].

191 He rejects the Mishnah and its implications. If the court would tell him that he was lying when he claimed that he was divorcing her because of

infertility, it could force him to pay the *ketubah* or let him take her back.

(46a line 73) רִבִּי יְהוּדָה אוֹמֵר לֹא יַחֲזִיר. וְאַתְּ אָמַר כֵּן. אָמַר רִבִּי יוֹחָנָן. לֵית כָּאן רִבִּי יְהוּדָה אֶלָּא רִבִּי מֵאִיר. וְתַנֵּי כֵן מִשּׁוּם רִבִּי מֵאִיר. אוֹמֵר לָהּ. שְׁתִיקוּתֵיךְ יָפָה מִדִּיבָּרֵיךְ.

"Rebbi Jehudah says, he cannot take her back," and you say so[192]? Rebbi Johanan said, there is no Rebbi Jehudah but Rebbi Meïr[193]. It was stated thus in Rebbi Meïr's name: Your silence would be better than your talking.

192 Since R. Jehudah prohibits him to take her back and he knows that the divorce is irrevocable, how can he then claim that he would not have divorced her?

193 Who is represented by the "Sages" in the Mishnah. The Babli, 46b, disagrees and holds that for R. Meïr the bill of divorce is valid and immune from attack by the first husband unless the bill of divorce was delivered with the explicit declaration that it be valid if and only if she is a sterile she-ram.

(fol. 45b) **משנה ט:** הַמּוֹכֵר אֶת עַצְמוֹ וְאֶת בָּנָיו לַגּוֹיִם אֵין פּוֹדִין אוֹתוֹ אֲבָל פּוֹדִין אֶת הַבָּנִים לְאַחַר מִיתַת אֲבִיהֶן. הַמּוֹכֵר אֶת שָׂדֵהוּ לְגוֹי וְחָזַר וּלְקָחָהּ מִמֶּנּוּ יִשְׂרָאֵל הַלּוֹקֵחַ מֵבִיא בִיכּוּרִים מִפְּנֵי תִיקּוּן הָעוֹלָם.

Mishnah 9: If somebody sells himself and his children to Gentiles[194], one does not buy him back[195], but one buys his children back after their father's death. If somebody sold his field[196] to a Gentile and then a Jew bought it back from him[197], the buyer brings first fruits because of the public good[198].

194 As slaves.	from the obligation of First Fruits as Gentile property.
195 With public money.	
196 In the Land of Israel.	198 In order to encourage people to buy agricultural properties in the Land.
197 During the growing season, when the produce already was exempt	

(46a line 66) **הלכה ח:** הַמוֹכֵר אֶת עַצְמוֹ וְאֶת בָּנָיו לַגּוֹיִם כול׳. מַתְנִיתָא בְּשֶׁמָּכַר עַצְמוֹ וְשָׁנָה. אֲבָל אִם מָכַר עַצְמוֹ פַּעַם אַחַת פּוֹדִין אוֹתוֹ. וְאִם מָכַר עַצְמוֹ לְלוּדִים אֲפִילוּ פַּעַם אַחַת אֵין פּוֹדִין אוֹתוֹ. מַעֲשֶׂה בְּאֶחָד שֶׁמָּכַר עַצְמוֹ לְלוּדִים. אֲתָא עוֹבְדָא קוֹמֵי רִבִּי אַבָּהוּ. אָמַר. מַה נַּעֲשֶׂה מִפְּנֵי חַיָּיו עָשָׂה.

Halakhah 9: "If somebody sells himself and his children to Gentiles," etc. The Mishnah, if he sold himself repeatedly. But if he sold himself once, one buys him back[199], but if he sold himself to the games[200], one does not buy him back. There was a case of one who sold himself to the games; the case came before Rebbi Abbahu, who said, what can we do? He did it for his livelihood[201].

199 The Babli agrees, 46b.	with money given for charity. In the Babli, 47a, this scenario is restricted to the case of a gladiator who continues to eat only kosher.
200 As a gladiator.	
201 Otherwise he would have starved. He agreed to buy him back	

(46b line 4) מַתְנִיתִין דְּרִבִּי מֵאִיר. דְּרִבִּי מֵאִיר אָמַר. אֵין קִנְיָין לְגוֹי בְּאֶרֶץ יִשְׂרָאֵל לְפוֹטְרוֹ מִן הַמַּעַשְׂרוֹת. רִבִּי יוּדָן וְרִבִּי שִׁמְעוֹן אוֹמְרִין. יֵשׁ קִנְיָין לְגוֹי בְּאֶרֶץ יִשְׂרָאֵל לְפוֹטְרוֹ מִן הַמַּעַשְׂרוֹת. רִבִּי אִימִּי בְשֵׁם רֵישׁ לָקִישׁ. טַעֲמָא דְּרִבִּי מֵאִיר. וְהִתְנַחַלְתֶּם אוֹתָם לִבְנֵיכֶם אַחֲרֵיכֶם לָרֶשֶׁת אֲחוּזָה. הִקִּישׁ עֲבָדִים לַאֲחוּזָה. מַה עֲבָדִים אַתֶּם קוֹנִין מֵהֶן וְאֵין הֵן קוֹנִין מִכֶּם. אַף אֲחוּזָה אַתֶּם קוֹנִין מֵהֶן וְהֵן אֵינָן קוֹנִין מִכֶּם. אָמַר רִבִּי אֶלְעָזָר בֵּי רִבִּי יוֹסֵי קוֹמֵי רִבִּי יוֹסֵי. וְהָא מְסַיִּיעָא לְרִבִּי מֵאִיר. וְהָאָרֶץ לֹא תִמָּכֵר לִצְמִיתֻת. לְחוּלְטָנוּת. אָמַר לֵיהּ.

כָּל־גְּמָרָא אֲמְרָה דְהִיא מְסַיְּיעָה לְרַבִּי שִׁמְעוֹן. לֹא תִימָּכֵר. הָא אִם נִמְכְּרָה חֲלוּטָה הִיא. רִבִּי הוּנָא דְצִיפּוֹרִי אָמַר. הִנְהִיג רִבִּי חֲנִינָא בְצִיפּוֹרִין כְּהָדָא דְרַבִּי שִׁמְעוֹן.

2 לפוטרו מן המעשרות | ד להפקיעו מיד מעשר   יודן | ד יודה   3 המעשרות | ד המעשר   ריש לקיש | ד ר׳ שמעון בן לקיש   4 אחוזה | עבדים   5 לעבדים | לאחוזה   ואין הן | והן אינן   6 אלעזר | ד לעזר   יוסי | ד יסא   7 והא | ד ודא   לצמיתות | ד לצמיתות כי לי הארץ   לחלטנות | ד לחולטנית   8 גמרא | ד גרמה   תימכר | ד תמכר   9 הונא דציפורי | ד חונא רובא דציפורין

[202]The Mishnah is Rebbi Meïr's, since Rebbi Meïr says that a Gentile may not acquire real estate in the Land of Israel to remove it from tithes; Rebbi Jehudah and Rebbi Simeon say, a Gentile may acquire real estate in the Land of Israel to free it from tithes. Rebbi Immi in the name of Rebbi Simeon ben Laqish: The reason of Rebbi Meïr (*Lev.* 25:46): "You shall transmit them by inheritance to your sons after you, to inherit by the rules of real estate." This brackets slaves with real estate. Just as you may buy slaves from them but they cannot buy from you, so real estate you may buy from them but they cannot buy from you. Rebbi Eleazar ben Rebbi Yose said before Rebbi Yasa[203], the following supports Rebbi Meïr (*Lev.* 25:23): "The land shall not be sold permanently," absolutely. He said to him, that in itself[203] supports Rebbi Simeon. "It shall not be sold", because if it was sold, it would be sold absolutely. Rebbi Huna from Sepphoris said, Rebbi Ḥanina instituted in Sepphoris following Rebbi Simeon.

202 This is from *Demay* 5:9, explained there in Notes 104-109.

Variants are denoted by ד.

203   This is the correct reading in ד.

(46b line 14) רִבִּי זְעוּרָה קוֹמֵי רִבִּי אַבָּהוּ בְּשֵׁם רִבִּי אֶלְעָזָר. אַף עַל גַּב דְּרִבִּי מֵאִיר אָמַר. אֵין קִנְיָין לְגוֹי בְּאֶרֶץ יִשְׂרָאֵל לְהַפְקִיעוֹ מִן הַמַּעֲשְׂרוֹת. מוֹדֶה שֶׁיֵּשׁ לוֹ בָהּ קִנְיָין נְכָסִים. מָהוּ קִנְיָין נְכָסִים. אָמַר רִבִּי אַבָּא. אֲכִילַת פֵּירוֹת וְהָתַנִּינָן. הַלּוֹקֵחַ מֵבִיא בִיכּוּרִים מִפְּנֵי תִיקוּן הָעוֹלָם. וְיָבִיא בִיכּוּרִים דְּבַר תּוֹרָה.

Rebbi Ze'ira said before Rebbi Abbahu in the name of Rebbi Eleazar: Even though Rebbi Meïr said that a Gentile may not acquire real estate in the Land of Israel to remove it from tithes, he agrees that he has property rights. What are property rights? Rebbi Abba said, the usufruct[204]; as we have stated: "the buyer brings First Fruits because of the public good," otherwise he could have brought First Fruits by the word of the Torah[205].

204 All the yield rightfully belongs to the Gentile; the land is not ownerless and taking anything from there would be theft.

205 If the fruits were not the Gentile's, his possession could not have freed the field from the biblical obligation of First Fruits.

(46b line 19) קָנָה שָׂדֶה בַּיּוֹבֵל. רִבִּי אִילָא אָמַר. קָנָה קַרְקַע. אַבָּא בַּר מַמָּל אָמַר. לֹא קָנָה קַרְקַע. מָתִיב רִבִּי אַבָּא בַּר מָמָל לְרִבִּי אִילָא. עַל דַּעְתָּךְ דְּאַתְּ אָמַר. קָנָה קַרְקַע. יַחְפּוֹר בָּהּ בּוֹרוֹת שִׁיחִין וּמְעָרוֹת. אָמַר לֵיהּ. הַתּוֹרָה אָמְרָה וְשָׁב לַאֲחוּזָּתוֹ. בְּעֵיינוּ. אַייְתֵי רִבִּי יַעֲקֹב בַּר אָחָא שְׁמוּעָתָא קֳדָמֵיהוֹן וְלֹא יָדַע דְּעוֹד אִינּוּן פְּלִיגִין. רִבִּי יוֹחָנָן אָמַר. מֵבִיא וְקוֹרֵא. רִבִּי שִׁמְעוֹן בֶּן לָקִישׁ אָמַר. אֵינוֹ מֵבִיא וְקוֹרֵא. אָמַר רִבִּי לָעֶזֶר בֵּירִבִּי יוֹסֵי קוֹמֵי רִבִּי יוֹסֵי. כָּל-עַמָּא מוֹדֵיי שֶׁהוּא מֵבִיא. מַה פְּלִיגִין. בַּקְּרִייָה. רִבִּי יוֹחָנָן אָמַר. מֵבִיא וְקוֹרֵא. רִבִּי שִׁמְעוֹן בֶּן לָקִישׁ אָמַר. מֵבִיא וְאֵינוֹ קוֹרֵא.

If somebody bought a field during a Jubilee period[206]. Rebbi Ila said, he acquired ownership of the ground[207], Abba bar Mamal said, he did not acquire ownership of the ground. Rebbi Abba bar Mamal objected to

Rebbi Ila: In your opinion, since you say that he acquired ownership of the ground, why can he not dig cisterns, ditches, and caves[208]? He said to him, the Torah said[209], "he shall return to his inheritance," as it was. Rebbi Jacob bar Aḥa brought this topic before them and did not know that they still disagreed: Rebbi Joḥanan said, he brings and recites; Rebbi Simeon ben Laqish said, he does not bring and recite[210]. Rebbi Eleazar ben Rebbi Yose said before Rebbi Yose: Everybody agrees that he brings[211]. Where do they disagree? Rebbi Joḥanan said, he brings and recites; Rebbi Simeon ben Laqish said, he brings but does not recite.

206 This discussion is purely theoretical since the institution of the Jubilee was abolished with the exile of the Ten Tribes, not to be re-instated; cf. Note 66; *Ševi'it* 1:1 Note 7, 10:3 Notes 83-88.

207 A sale of ancestral agricultural land in a Jubilee period is really a long-term lease since the land returns to the owner in the Jubilee year. The buyer certainly acquires possession; the question is whether he also acquires ownership (cf. Note 169).

208 The prohibition to alienate agricultural lands from their status is not found otherwise in either one of the Talmudim There may be a hint of this in *Sifra Behar*, *Pereq* 5(7); also *Parašah* 4(6) where it is stated that cisterns, ditches, and caves follow the rules of houses, which sometimes are not returned in the Jubilee year, but not those of agricultural land, which always is returned. The buyer/lessee has no right to change the legal status of the land; this seems to indicate that he has no ownership.

209 *Lev.* 25:28.

210 In the Babli, 47b/48a, it is clearly stated that R. Joḥanan holds that possession is like ownership, R. Simeon ben Laqish holds that possession and ownership are distinct. In this, practice of the Babli strictly follows R. Simeon ben Laqish.

211 Possession of the land is sufficient for the property to be subject to the duty of first fruits but not enough for the farmer to declare (*Deut.* 26:10) "I brought the First Fruits of the land which You gave me, o Eternal"; cf. Mishnah *Bikkurim* 1:2,6.

הניזקין פרק חמישי

(fol. 46b) **משנה א:** הַנִּיזָקִין שָׁמִין לָהֶן בָּעִידִית וּבַעַל חוֹב בַּבֵּינוֹנִית וּכְתוּבַּת אִשָּׁה בַּזִּיבּוּרִית. רַבָּן שִׁמְעוֹן בֶּן גַּמְלִיאֵל אוֹמֵר. אַף כְּתוּבַּת אִשָּׁה בַּבֵּינוֹנִית.

Mishnah 1: For tort victims one estimates with best quality land[1], for a creditor with average quality, and for a woman's *ketubah* with lowest quality. Rabban Simeon ben Gamliel[2] says, also for a woman's *ketubah* with average quality.

1   If a person is due damages and is not paid, he can ask the court for foreclosure. If the guilty party owns several pieces of land, the tort victim is indemnified, up to the value of his claim, from the land which carries the highest value per unit of surface area. A creditor whose mortgage does not specify a particular piece of land is indemnified from land which the court's experts assess to be of average value among all of the debtor's holdings.

2   In all other Mishnah sources mentioned in M. S. Feldblum, *Dikduke Soferim - Gittin* (New York 1966), the name is R. Meïr.

(46c line 2) **הלכה א:** הַנִּיזָקִין שָׁמִין לָהֶן בָּעִידִית כול'. קַל וָחוֹמֶר לְהֶקְדֵּשׁ. אָמַר רִבִּי אַבָּא בַּר פָּפֵּי קוֹמֵי רִבִּי יוֹסֵי. מָה אָנָן קַייָמִין. אִם לְהֶכְשֵׁר נְזָקִין. הָדָא דְתַנִּינָן. שׁוֹר רְעֵהוּ וְלֹא שׁוֹר הֶקְדֵּשׁ. אִם לְנִיזְקֵי גוּפוֹ. הָדָא הִיא דְּתַנֵּי רִבִּי חִייָה. נְזָקִין לְהֶדְיוֹט וְאֵין נְזָקִין לְגָבוֹהַּ. אֶלָּא כֵן אָנָן קַייָמִין בְּאוֹמֵר. הֲרֵי עָלַי מֵאָה מָנָא לְהֶקְדֵּשׁ. וְהָלַךְ שׁוֹרוֹ וְהִזִּיק. שֶׁלֹּא תֹאמַר. יֵעָשֶׂה בַעַל חוֹב וְיִגְבֶּה בְּבֵינוֹנִית. לְפוּם כָּךְ צָרַךְ מֵימַר הַנִּיזָקִין שָׁמִין לָהֶן בָּעִידִית. קַל וָחוֹמֶר לְהֶקְדֵּשׁ.

Halakhah 1: "For tort victims one estimates with best quality land," etc. "By an inference *de minore ad maius*, for Temple property[3]." Rebbi Abba bar Pappaios said before Rebbi Yose, where do we hold[4]? If to qualify as damages, is that not what we stated "his neighbor's ox[5]" but not the ox of Temple property? If for bodily damages, is that not what Rebbi Hiyya stated: A private person can claim damages but not the Temple[6]? But we must deal with one who said, I obligate myself to give 100 minas to the Temple, [7]when his ox went and did damage. You should not say, [the Temple] is a creditor and should collect from average quality land. Therefore, it was necessary to say that "for tort victims one estimates with best quality land, by an inference *de minore ad maius*, for Temple property."

3   A statement by R. Aqiba in *Mekhilta dR. Ismael, Mišpaṭim* 14, also quoted by the Babli, 48b.

4   What does the statement about Temple property mean?

5   *Ex.* 21:35; Mishnah *Baba Qama* 4:3. The rules of damages do not apply to Temple property, not for damages inflicted by Temple animals nor damages done to them. Quoted in the Babli, 49a.

6   The formulation is ambiguous; it also could mean that the Temple never pays damages.

7   The following clause is missing in the quote of the passage by Tosaphot *Giṭṭin* 49a, *s. v.* שור, and in the Constantinople edition of the Yerushalmi. If one accepts the text as it stands, one has to explain that the person making the vow thought that he could pay his vow in cash, but before he could do this, he had to pay damages and now he is short of cash. If one does not read the clause, then there is a straightforward statement that debts to the Temple in all cases are privileged like debts for damages (a statement considered and rejected by the Babli, 49a). The interpretation of the Babli, that damages inflicted on Temple property always must be paid in full, is incompatible with the Yerushalmi.

(46c line 8) תַּנֵּי רְבִּי חִיָּיה. נֶזֶק וַחֲצִי נֶזֶק נִגְבִּין מִן הַמְשׁוּעְבָּדִין. נִיחָא נֶזֶק. חֲצִי נֶזֶק לֹא מִגּוּפוֹ הוּא מְשַׁלֵּם. אָמַר רְבִּי יוֹסֵי. תִּיפְתָּר בְּשׁוֹר תָּם שֶׁהִזִּיק וְהָלַךְ הַבַּעַל וּמְכָרוֹ. כְּבָר נִשְׁתַּעְבַּד גּוּפוֹ לְבַעַל הַנֶּזֶק. רַבָּנִין דְּקַיְסָרִין אָמְרִין. תִּיפְתָּר שֶׁזְּקָפָן עָלָיו מִלְוֶה. מֵעַתָּה לֹא תִגָּבֶה אֶלָּא בְּבֵינוֹנִית. מֵאַחַר שֶׁעִיקָּרוֹ נֶזֶק גּוֹבֶה בַּעִידִית.

Rebbi Ḥiyya stated: "Full and partial damages are collected from encumbered property." One understands full damages[8]. Are partial damages not collected from the animal's body[9]? Rebbi Yose said, explain it when it was a docile ox which did damage and then his owner went and sold it. Its body already was encumbered to the injured party[10]. The rabbis of Caesarea said, explain it if he converted it[11] into a loan. Then it should be foreclosed only by average quality land! Since the debt originated in a damage claim, he may collect from best quality.

8   *Ex.* 21:36 requires the owner of an animal with a history of causing damages to pay all damages in full. If the animal's owner cannot pay cash, the Mishnah decrees that the damages be liquidated by the best available land, even if mortgaged.

9   *Ex.* 21:35 requires the damages inflicted by an animal which never before had caused damage to be paid from proceeds of a sale of the animal itself.

10   The "encumbered property" mentioned in the *baraita* is not mortgaged land but the animal causing the damage, which can be repossessed by the owner of the damaged property from a buyer of the agressive animal.

11   The owner of the injured animal did not insist on immediate payment but agreed that the debt be liquidated *as if it were* a loan.

(46c line 13) שָׂדֵהוּ פְּרָט לַמְשׁוּעְבָּד. כַּרְמוֹ פְּרָט לְהֶקְדֵּישׁ. מָה אֲנָן קַייָמִין. אִם בְּשֶׁהִזִּיק וְאַחַר כָּךְ הִקְדִּישׁ. הָדָא הִיא דְתַנִּינָן. הִקְדִּישׁ תִּשְׁעִים מָנֶה וְהָיָה חוֹבוֹ מֵאָה מָנֶה. אִם בְּשֶׁהִקְדִּישׁ וְאַחַר כָּךְ הִזִּיק. הָדָא הִיא דְתַנִּינָן. שׁוֹר רְעֵהוּ וְלֹא

שׁוֹר הֶקְדֵּשׁ. אָמַר רִבִּי יוּדָן. תִּיפְתָּר בְּשׁוֹר שֶׁלְהֶקְדֵּשׁ שֶׁרָעָה לְתוֹךְ שָׂדֵה הֶדְיוֹט. אָמַר לֵיהּ רִבִּי מָנָא. אֲנָן בָּעֲנִן קַרְקַע הֶקְדֵּשׁ וְאַתְּ אָמַרְתְּ תּוֹךְ שָׂדֵה הֶדְיוֹט. אֶלָּא כֵּן. אֲנָן קַיָּימִין בָּאוֹמֵר. הֲרֵי עָלַי מֵאָה מְנֶה לָהֶקְדֵּשׁ. וְהָלַךְ הוּא וְהִזִּיק. שֶׁלֹּא תֹאמַר. אִילוּ נְזָקִין וּמִלְוֶה בְּעֵדִים הַנִּזָּקִין קוֹדְמִין. וְכָא קוֹדֶם הַנֵּזֶק לָהֶקְדֵּשׁ. לְפוּם כָּךְ צָרַךְ מֵימַר. כַּרְמוֹ פְּרָט לְהֶקְדֵּשׁ.

"His field[12]", except if it was mortgaged[13]. "His vineyard", except Temple property. Where do we hold[14]? If somebody caused damage and then dedicated to the Temple, that is what we have stated[15]: "If he dedicated 90 minas but his debt was 100 minas." If somebody dedicated to the Temple and then caused damage, that is what we have stated: "'His neighbor's ox[5]' but not the ox of Temple property." Rebbi Yudan said, explain it if an ox of Temple property grazed on a private field. Rebbi Mana told him, we require Temple real estate and you say "on a private field"? But we must hold about one who said: I am obligating myself for 100 minas to the Temple; then went and caused damage. You should not say that between damages and a loan given before witnesses[16] damages are privileged, and here damages are privileged against the Temple; therefore it was necessary to say "his vineyard", except Temple property[17].

12 *Ex.* 22:4: "If a person destroys a field or a vineyard through animals by sending his livestock to graze on another's field, *the best of his field or the best of his vineyard* he shall give in payment." This is the basis of the Mishnah requiring that damages be paid with best quality real estate.

13 "*His* field" excludes third-party interests.

14 What relation can Temple property have with damages due from a private person?

15 Mishnah *'Arakhin* 6:2: "If somebody dedicated his property to the Temple while he owed a *ketubah* to his wife or a debt to a creditor, neither the woman nor the creditor can collect from the Temple; but the redeemer redeems on condition to pay the

ketubah to the woman or the debt to the creditor. If he dedicated 90 minas but his debt was 100 minas, [the redeemer] adds another denar and redeems these properties on condition to pay the debt to the creditor." In order to combine two conflicting principles, viz., that vows cannot be used to escape obligations towards third parties, and that Temple obligations override all others, it is decreed that the Temple has to put the dedicated properties up for sale but collects only for the amount by which the value of the properties exceeds the obligation, with the third party buyer accepting the obligation to pay off the liens on the property. (It has to be a third party buyer since the person making the dedication would have to add another 25% to the redemption amount, *Lev.* 27:19.) Claims for damages have to be handled in the same way.

16 Not in documented form; the witnesses do not sign anything. Such a loan is not a mortgage and is not privileged.

17 The statement about Temple property is not to exclude Temple property from damage claims but to privilege Temple property relative to all civil claims.

(46c line 20) שָׂדֵהוּ פְּרָט לְמִטַּלְטְלִין. כַּרְמוֹ פְּרָט לָרָאוּי כְּבַמּוּחְזָק. שָׂדֵהוּ פְּרָט לְמִטַּלְטְלִין. בְּהֶן דְּלָא בָעֵי מִטַּלְטְלִין מִשָּׁעָה רִאשׁוֹנָה. וְהָכָא כְהָדָא דְתַנֵּי. אֵין לִי אֶלָּא קַרְקַע. מִנַּיִין שֶׁאִם רָצָה לִיתֵּן כֶּסֶף. תַּלְמוּד לוֹמַר. כֶּסֶף יָשִׁיב לִבְעָלָיו. מַה בְּעִית מֵימַר קַרְקַע עִיקָר. אִי נֵימַר כֶּסֶף עִיקָר. וְיַחֲלִיטוּ לוֹ מִשָּׁעָה רִאשׁוֹנָה. וְאָנָן חָמֵי רַבָּנִין מַחְלְטִין לוֹ קַרְקָעוֹת. כַּרְמוֹ פְּרָט לָרָאוּי כְּבַמּוּחְזָק. רִבִּי לָעְזָר בְּשֵׁם רִבִּי נִיסָא. בְּשֶׁחָפַר אָבִיו בּוֹר וְהִזִּיק בְּחַיֵּי אָבִיו וְנָפְלוּ לוֹ נְכָסִים אַחַר מִיתַת אָבִיו. הָיִיתִי אוֹמֵר. יִשְׁתַּעְבְּדוּ נְכָסִים לְאוֹתוֹ הַנֵּזֶק. לְפוּם כֵּן צָרַךְ מֵימַר. כַּרְמוֹ. פְּרָט לָרָאוּי כְּבַמּוּחְזָק.

"His field," except movables. "His vineyard," except potential property which is not similar in status to that in possession. "'His field,' except movables." About those who did not claim movables from the start. Is this different from what we stated: There is not only real estate; from where if he wanted to pay money? The verse says: "Money he shall return to its owner[18]." What did you mean to say that real estate is primary? Or[19] should we say that money is primary? Then it should be irrevocably given to [the claimant] from the start! Do we not see rabbis who irrevocably give him real estate! "'His vineyard,' except potential property which is not similar in status to that in possession." Rebbi Eleazar in the name of Rebbi Nisa: If his father dug a cistern[20] which caused injury during his father's lifetime. Property fell to him after his father's death[21]. I might say that this property should be encumbered for that damage; therefore, it was necessary to say "his vineyard" to except potential property which is not similar in status to that in possession.

18   Ex. 21:33, speaking of somebody digging a hole in the public domain which then causes injury to another person's animal. This damage has to be paid in money (or, in the Babli's interpretation, in money's worth). In the Babli, *Baba Qama* 7a, 14b, money is legal tender to liquidate all debts. The Yerushalmi gives the injured party the right to claim real estate in those cases in which the verse prescribed payment in real estate.

19   אי is Babylonian spelling for Galilean אֹו "or", אִין "if", אֵי "not". The first alternative applies here.

20   In the public domain, cf. Note 18.

21   The injury claim was not paid during the father's lifetime. By accepting the inheritance, the son became liable to pay the injury claim. If later he received inheritance from another source, e. g., grandparents, the later inheritance is not liable for claims stemming from a prior inheritance even if the son was the only known heir and therefore the grandparent's property was potentially his.

(46c line 29) מֵיטַב שָׂדֵהוּ וּמֵיטַב כַּרְמוֹ. דִּבְרֵי רִבִּי יִשְׁמָעֵאל. רִבִּי עֲקִיבָא אוֹמֵר. מֵיטַב שָׂדֵהוּ וּמֵיטַב כַּרְמוֹ שֶׁלַּנִּיזָּק. קַשְׁיָא עַל דְּרִבִּי עֲקִיבָא. נִיזּוֹק. וְאַתְּ אָמַר כֵּן. אֶלָּא בֵּית דִּין רוֹאִין אִי זֶהוּ שָׂדֵהוּ יָפָה לִפְנֵי הַנִּיזּוֹק

וְשָׁמָה לָהּ כַּמוֹתָהּ. כְּהָדָא דְּתַנֵּי. יָכוֹל אִם אָכְלָה מִן הָעֵדִית שָׁמִין לוֹ מִן הָעֵידִית. מִן הַזִּיבּוּרִית שָׁמִין לוֹ מִן הַזִּיבּוּרִית. הֵיךְ עֲבִידָא. עֵידִית שֶׁבַּזִּיבּוּרִית טָבָא סַגִּין. אִם אוֹמֵר אַתְּ כֵּן נִמְצֵאת מַשְׁבִּיחַ אֶת הַנִּיזָּק. רוֹאִין אֶת הַשָּׂדֶה כְּאִילוּ מְלֵיאָה עֵידִית וְשָׁמִין לוֹ מִן הָעֵידִית. וְזִיבּוּרִית שָׁמִין לוֹ מִן הַזִּיבּוּרִית. נִמְצָא מְשַׁלֵּם מִן הָעֵידִית עַל הָעֵידִית וּמִן הַזִּיבּוּרִית עַל הַזִּיבּוּרִית. מְנַיִין לְרִבִּי עֲקִיבָא הַנִּיזָּקִין שָׁמִין לָהֶן בָּעֵידִית. לֵיתָהּ מִן הַתּוֹרָה. אִיתָא מִן הַתַּקָּנָה. מִפְּנֵי מָה אָמְרוּ הַנִּיזָּקִין שָׁמִין לָהֶן בָּעֵידִית. מִפְּנֵי הַגַּזְלָנִין. שֶׁיְּהֵא אָדָם אוֹמֵר. מַה בְּיָדִי גָּזֵל מַה בְּיָדִי מַזִּיק. לְמָחָר רוֹאִין בֵּית דִּין שָׂדֶה יָפָה שֶׁלִּי וְנוֹטְלִין אוֹתָהּ מִלְּפָנָיי. וְסוֹמְכִים אוֹתָהּ לַמִּקְרָא. מֵיטַב שָׂדֵהוּ וּמֵיטַב כַּרְמוֹ יְשַׁלֵּם. עַד כְּדוֹן קַרְקָעוֹ. מַשְׁכּוֹנוֹ לָמַד מִקַּרְקָעוֹ. מַה קַּרְקָעוֹ בָּעֵידִית אַף מַשְׁכּוֹנוֹ בָּעֵידִית.

"The best of his field and the best of his vineyard *he* shall pay,[12]" i. e., the party responsible for the damage, the words of Rebbi Ismael[22]. Rebbi Aqiba says, "the best of *his* field and the best of *his* vineyard", of the person suffering the damage. It is difficult for Rebbi Aqiba, he suffered damage, and you say so[23]? But the court see what the field was worth before it was damaged and estimates accordingly. As it was stated, it is possible if the grazing was on best quality land, one estimates from best quality, from lowest quality one estimates from lowest quality. How is this? The best of the lowest quality is quite good. If you say so you provide a windfall for the person suffering the damage[24]. One looks at the field as if it was full of first quality [produce] and estimates for him from the best quality land; least quality one estimates from least quality land. It turns out that he pays with best quality for best quality and from least quality for least quality. From where has Rebbi Aqiba that "for tort victims one estimates with best quality land"[25]? It is not from the Torah, it is a decree. [26]"Why did they say, 'for tort victims one estimates with best quality land"? Because of the robbers[27]. That a man should say, why should I have robbed [land] in my hand, or land subject to a suit for damages on my hand? Tomorrow, the court will see my good field, take it from me, and support it by the verse, 'the best of his field and the best of his vineyard he shall pay.'" So far his real estate. His pledge[28] was inferred from his real estate. Since his real estate [is taken] from the best quality, also his pledge [is taken] from the best.

22 In the Babli, 48a, the attribution of names is switched; the same is implied by *Mekhilta dR. Ismael*, ed. Horovitz-Rabin p. 296; the interpretation of R. Ismael is quoted anonymously in *Mekhilta dR. Simeon bar Iohai*, ed. Epstein-Melamed p. 196, together with the interpretation given later to the opinion of R. Aqiba.

23 Why should the person responsible only pay corresponding to the best remaining parts of a ruined field?

24 According to R. Aqiba, the holdings of the person suffering the damage are graded into best, average, and lowest quality. In each category, the value of the damage is established and paid by the person responsible with his best real estate in the given category, up to the value established in court.

25 Since he reads the verse as referring to the method of estimating the damage, not payment, the Mishnah has no biblical foundation.

26 This is a *baraita*, quoted in the Babli, 49b, in the name of R. Simeon (in some sources, R. Simeon ben Eleazar.) A similar, anonymous, text is in Tosephta *Ketubot* 12:2.

27 Since a robber of land is also inflicting damage on the person robbed.

28 If the person responsible cannot pay directly, any pledge taken should be of his most valuable possessions.

(46c line 43) וּבַעֲלֵי חוֹב בַּבֵּינוֹנִית. מִפְּנֵי הָרַמָּאִין. שֶׁלֹּא יְהֵא אָדָם רוֹאֶה אֶת שְׂדֵה רֵעֵהוּ יָפָה וּמַלְוֶה אוֹתוֹ מָעוֹת וְעוֹקֵף וְנוֹטְלָהּ מִמֶּנּוּ. מֵעַתָּה לֹא יָשׁוּמוּ לוֹ

אֶלָּא בַּזִּיבּוּרִית. אָמַר רִבִּי יוּדָה. וְכֵינִי. אֶלָּא שֶׁלֹּא לִנְעוֹל דֶּלֶת בִּפְנֵי בְנֵי אָדָם. שֶׁלְּמָחָר הוּא מְבַקֵּשׁ לִלְווֹת וְאֵינוֹ מוֹצֵא.

29"'For creditors, average quality,' because of tricksters. That a man should not see a desirable field in his neighbor's hand, lend him money, and contrives to take it from him. Then one should estimate only from the least quality! Rebbi Jehudah said, that is correct; but not to lock the door before people needing to borrow. For tomorrow he may need to borrow and does not find [a lender.]"

29 A continuation of the Tosephta (Note 26). In the Babli, R. Jehudah agrees that loans should be foreclosed only by least quality land but R. Meïr states that to support credit one has to allow loans to be foreclosed from average quality.

(46c line 47) דָּרַשׁ רִבִּי סִימַאי. וְהָאִישׁ. זֶה שָׁלִיחַ בֵּית דִּין. שֶׁאִם נִכְנַס הַמַּלְוֶה הוּא מוֹצִיא אֶת הַיָּפָה. וְִם נִכְנַס הַלֹּוֶה הוּא מוֹצִיא אֶת הָרָע. הָא כֵיצַד. שָׁלִיחַ בֵּית דִּין נִכְנַס וּמוֹצִיא אֶת הַבֵּינוֹנִית. רִבִּי יִשְׁמָעֵאל אוֹמֵר. דְּבַר תּוֹרָה הוּא שֶׁיִּכָּנֵס הַמַּלְוֶה. דִּכְתִיב וְהָאִישׁ אֲשֶׁר אַתָּה נוֹשֶׁה בוֹ יוֹצִיא אֵלֶיךָ אֶת הָעֲבוֹט הַחוּצָה. עַד כְּדוֹן מַשְׁכּוֹנוֹ. קַרְקָעוֹ לָמַד מִמַּשְׁכּוֹנוֹ. מַה מַּשְׁכּוֹנוֹ בַּבֵּינוֹנִית אַף קַרְקָעוֹ בַּבֵּינוֹנִית.

Rebbi Simai preached: "And the man,[30]" that is the agent of the court[31]. For if the creditor enters, he removes the best. If the borrower enters, he removes the worst. How is this? The agent of the court enters and removes from average quality. Rebbi Ismael says, it is a word from the Torah that the creditor[32] should enter, for it is written: "The man whose creditor you are should bring the pledge out for you." That is, his pledge. His real estate was inferred from his pledge. Since his pledge [is taken] from average quality, also his real estate [is taken] from average quality.

30 *Deut.* 24:11, about a creditor taking a pledge, quoted in full later in the paragraph.

31 *Sifry Deut.* 276 seems to read וְהָאִישׁ as "'and any man', to include the agent of the court" since the verse obviously refers to the creditor.

32 The context would require to read "debtor"; this is an Amoraic statement in the Babli, 50a.

(46c line 53) פְּשִׁיטָא דָא מִילְתָא. מִלְוֶה שֶׁהִיא נַעֲשֵׂית בּוֹ כַּפְרָנוּת אֵינָהּ נִשְׁמֶטֶת. כַּפְרָנוּת שֶׁהִיא נַעֲשֵׂית מִלְוֶה מְשַׁמֶּטֶת. רִבִּי יִרְמְיָה בָּעֵי. אַף לְמִידַת הַדִּין כֵּן הִיא. מִלְוֶה שֶׁהִיא נַעֲשֵׂית כַּפְרָנוּת גּוֹבָה. כַּפְרָנִית שֶׁהִיא נַעֲשֵׂית מִלְוֶה גּוֹבָה בְּבֵינוֹנִית.

1 כפרנות | ש כפרנית (in all cases)   נשמטת | ש משמטת   2 אף | ש אם   כן | ש כן היא. לא צורכה דלא   3 כפרנות שהיא נעשית | ש -

[33]This is obvious: A loan that is disputed is not remitted. A loan that was disputed but is now a [confirmed][34] loan, is remitted. Rebbi Jeremiah asked: Is this also true for judgments? A loan that was disputed can be collected. A disputed loan turned into a [confirmed] loan is collected from property of average quality.

33 *Ševi'it* 10:2, explained there in Notes 75-77, variant readings noted ש. The Mishnah notes that court judgments are not subject to the rules of the Sabbatical.

34 By judgment of the court.

(46c line 56) אֵין שָׁם אֶלָּא עִידִּית גּוֹבָה בָּעִידִּית. בֵּינוֹנִית גּוֹבָה בַּבֵּינוֹנִית. זִיבּוּרִית גּוֹבָה בַּזִּיבּוּרִית. עִידִּית וּבֵינוֹנִית. הַנִּיזָּקִין שָׁמִין לָהֶן בָּעִידִּית וּבַעַל חוֹב וּכְתוּבַּת אִשָּׁה בַּבֵּינוֹנִית. בֵּינוֹנִית וְזִיבּוּרִית. הַנִּיזָּקִין וּבַעֲלֵי חוֹב שָׁמִין לָהֶן בַּבֵּינוֹנִית וּכְתוּבַּת אִשָּׁה בַּזִּיבּוּרִית. הָיְתָה עִידִּית שֶׁלּוֹ יָפָה מִשֶּׁלְּכָל־אָדָם עִידִּית הִיא. בֵּינוֹנִית שֶׁלּוֹ יָפָה מִשֶּׁל כָּל־אָדָם בֵּינוֹנִית הִיא. זִיבּוּרִית שֶׁלּוֹ יָפָה מִשֶּׁל כָּל־אָדָם זִיבּוּרִית הִיא. הָיְתָה עִידִּית שֶׁלּוֹ בֵּינוֹנִית שֶׁלְּכָל־אָדָם. רִבִּי זֵירָא וְרִבִּי אִילָא בָּעֵי. נִישְׁמְעִינָהּ מִן הָדָא. בֵּינוֹנִית וְזִיבּוּרִית. הַנִּיזָּקִין וּבַעֲלֵי חוֹב שָׁמִין

לָהֶן בַּבֵּינוֹנִית וּכְתוּבַּת אִשָּׁה בַּזִּיבּוּרִית. וּכְמָה דְאַתְּ בָּעֵי עִידִית וּבֵינוֹנִית נִיזָקִין דּוֹחִין לְבַעֲלֵי חוֹב בַּבֵּינוֹנִית. וְדִכְוָותָהּ. בֵּינוֹנִית וְזִיבּוּרִית יִדְחוּ הַנִּיזָקִין לְבַעֲלֵי חוֹב בַּזִּיבּוּרִית. רִבִּי יוֹסֵי בַּר בּוּן בְּשֵׁם רַב חִסְדָּא. תִּיפָּתָר שֶׁהָיְתָה לוֹ עִידִית וּמְכָרָהּ וּכְבָר נִדְחוּ לְבַעֲלֵי חוֹב לִגְבוֹת בַּבֵּינוֹנִית.

If there is only best quality, one collects from the best quality, [only] average quality one collects from average quality, [only] worst quality one collects from worst quality. Best and average, torts are assessed from best quality, creditors and a woman's *ketubah* from average. Average and worst, torts and creditors are assessed from average, a woman's *ketubah* from worst. If his best quality was like everybody's best quality, it is best quality. If his average quality was like everybody's average quality, it is average quality. If his worst quality was like everybody's worst quality, it is worst quality[35]. If his best quality was like everybody's average? Rebbi Ze'ira and Rebbi Ila asked: Let us hear from the following: Average and worst, torts and creditors are assessed from average, a woman's *ketubah* from worst. But just as you need in the case that you have best and average quality, torts push creditors to the average, so in this case, of average and worst quality, should not torts push creditors to the worst quality[36]? Rebbi Yose bar Abun in the name of Rav Ḥisda: Explain it that he had best quality which he sold, and the creditors were already pushed to average quality[37].

35 The statement up to here is a *baraita*, quoted as such in the Babli, *Baba Qama* 7b. One can foreclose only existing property; the only question which arises is how to classify claims if there are properties of two different qualities but claims for all three. The Babli formulates this as: Do the notions of best, average, and worst refer to the available land or are these general notions used by realtors to classify properties?

36 If his best quality is classified by realtors as average, nevertheless it is his best, reserved for satisfaction of tort judgmens, and creditors should be satisfied with second best quality, even if that is worst in universal classification. This seems to prove that the classifications mentioned in Mishnah and *baraita* are universal, not referring to the debtor.

37 His explanation is also given by Rav Ḥisda in the Babli, *Baba Qama* 8a. As Rashi explains, the loan was taken when there was best quality land; then automatically the average quality land was pledged to the creditor. When later the best quality land was sold, the pledge was not removed. When then a claim for torts was entered, it only could be additional to the existing lien. (The Babli lists three other possible explanations, all agreeing that in a normal case in which only two qualities of real estate are available, the better one is declared best, reserved for the satisfaction of tort claims.)

(46c line 68) וּכְתוּבַּת אִשָּׁה בַּזִּיבּוּרִית. אָמַר רִבִּי יִרְמְיָה. לֹא שָׁנוּ אֶלָּא מָנֶה מָאתַיִם. אֲבָל כְּתוּבַּת אֶלֶף דִּינָר גּוֹבָה בַּבֵּינוֹנִית. וְרִבִּי יוֹסֵי אוֹמֵר. אֲפִילוּ כְתוּבַּת אֶלֶף דִּינָר אֵינָהּ גּוֹבָה אֶלָּא מִן הַזִּיבּוּרִית. וְאַתְיָין אִילֵּין פְּלוּגְוָותָא כְּאִילֵּין פְּלוּגְוָותָא. כָּל־זְמַן שֶׁהִיא בְּבֵית אָבִיהָ גּוֹבָה כְּתוּבָּתָהּ לְעוֹלָם. כָּל־זְמַן שֶׁהִיא בְּבֵית בַּעֲלָהּ גּוֹבָה כְּתוּבָּתָהּ עַד עֶשְׂרִים וְחָמֵשׁ שָׁנָה. רִבִּי סִימוֹן אָמַר רִבִּי יְהוֹשֻׁעַ בֶּן לֵוִי. לֹא שָׁנוּ אֶלָּא כְתוּבַּת מָנֶה מָאתַיִם. אֲבָל הָיְתָה כְּתוּבָּתָהּ אֶלֶף דִּינָר גּוֹבָה כְּתוּבָּתָהּ לְעוֹלָם. אָתָא רִבִּי אַבָּהוּ בְשֵׁם רִבִּי יוֹחָנָן. אֲפִילוּ כְתוּבָּה שֶׁלְּאֶלֶף דִּינָר אֵינוֹ גּוֹבָה אֶלָּא עַד עֶשְׂרִים וְחָמֵשׁ שָׁנָה. וְאַתְיָיא דְרִבִּי יוֹסֵי כְרִבִּי יוֹחָנָן וּדְרִבִּי יִרְמְיָה כְרִבִּי יְהוֹשֻׁעַ בֶּן לֵוִי. דְּתַנִּינָן תַּמָּן. הַכּוֹתֵב נְכָסָיו לְבָנָיו וְכָתַב לְאִשְׁתּוֹ קַרְקַע כָּל־שֶׁהוּא אִבְּדָה כְתוּבָּתָהּ. רַב אָמַר. בְּמוֹכֵר עַל יָדָהּ. וּשְׁמוּאֵל אָמַר בִּמְחַלֵּק לְפָנֶיהָ. רִבִּי יוֹסֵי בַּר חֲנִינָא אָמַר מְקוּלֵּי כְתוּבָה שָׁנוּ כָאן. וְתַנֵּי בַּר קַפָּרָא. מְקוּלֵּי כְתוּבָה שָׁנוּ. אָמַר רִבִּי בָּא. טַעְמָא דְרִבִּי יוֹסֵי בֶּן חֲנִינָא לֹא סוֹף דָּבָר בִּכְתוּבַּת מָנֶה מָאתַיִם. אֶלָּא אֲפִילוּ כְתוּבָה שֶׁלְּאֶלֶף דִּינָר מְקוּלֵּי כְתוּבָה שָׁנוּ.

"For a woman's *ketubah* with lowest quality." [40]Rebbi Jeremiah said, they taught only for a *ketubah* of a mina or 200 [*zuz*], but a *ketubah* of a thousand denar she collects from average quality[41]. Rebbi Yose said, even a *ketubah* of a thousand denar she collects only from lowest quality. It turns out that this disagreement parallels the following disagreement: "While she lives in her father's house, she always can collect her *ketubah*; if she lives in her husband's house, she can collect her *ketubah* for 25 years."[42] Rebbi Simon in the name of Rebbi Joshua ben Levi: One stated this only for the *ketubah* of a mina or 200 [*zuz*]. But a *ketubah* of 1'000 denar she collects forever. Rebbi Abbahu quoted in the name of Rebbi Johanan: Even a *ketubah* of 1'000 denar she can collect only up to 25 years. It turns out that Rebbi Yose follows Rebbi Johanan and Rebbi Jeremiah Rebbi Joshua ben Levi. As we have stated there[43]: "If somebody signs over his property to his sons and signs over some real estate to his wife, she loses her claim to *ketubah*." Rav said, if he sells through her[44]. Samuel says, if he distributes in her presence. Rebbi Yose ben Hanina said, they stated here a relaxation of the laws of *ketubah*. Rebbi Abba said, the reason of Rebbi Yose ben Hanina is that it applies not only to a *ketubah* of a mina or two hundred, but even regarding a *ketubah* of one thousand denar they proclaimed a relaxation of the laws of *ketubah*.

40 This paragraph is a re-arrangement of a paragraph in *Ketubot* 12:5 (Notes 54-59) and one in *Peah* 3:9 (Notes 182-189).

41 The obligatory minimum she collects only from the lowest quality land; any excess she can take from average quality. The Yerushalmi does not give a reason why a woman can collect only from lowest quality real estate; the Babli (49b-50a) after a lengthy discussion decides that this is a

necessary institution to induce men to get married.

42   Mishnah *Ketubot* 12:5.
43   Mishnah *Peah* 3:9.
44   In *Peah*, "if he lets them acquire through her agency." One has to assume that this is meant here also.

משנה ב: אֵין נִפְרָעִין מִנְּכָסִים מְשׁוּעְבָּדִין בְּמָקוֹם שֶׁיֵּשׁ נְכָסִין בְּנֵי חוֹרִין וַאֲפִילוּ הֵן זִיבּוּרִית. אֵין נִפְרָעִין מִנִּכְסֵי יְתוֹמִין אֶלָּא מִן הַזִּיבּוּרִית.

Mishnah 2: One does not collect from encumbered property[45] as long as there is free property, even if the latter is of lowest quality. One may collect from orphans'[46] property only from the lowest quality.

משנה ג: אֵין מוֹצִיאִין לַאֲכִילַת פֵּירוֹת וְלִשְׁבָח קַרְקָעוֹת וְלִמְזוֹן הָאִשָּׁה וְהַבָּנוֹת מִנְּכָסִים מְשׁוּעְבָּדִין מִפְּנֵי תִּיקוּן הָעוֹלָם.

Mishnah 3: One cannot collect for usufruct[47], for improvement of the land[48], or for sustenance of the wife and the daughters[49] from incumbered property, for the public good[50].

45 "Encumbered property" is property sold when there was a lien on it. If the lienholder cannot get satisfaction from the debtor, he can have regress on the buyer. But as long as the debtor has any real estate left in his possession, it has to be foreclosed before any claim can be raised against a buyer.

46 As long as the orphans are underage.

47 If a robber took land by force, had its use for some time, and then sold it, the land itself can be reclaimed from the buyer but payment for the illicit use of the land can be exacted only from the robber himself.

48 If the buyer of some property makes improvements, such as planting fruit trees, and then loses the property through the foreclosure of a prior lien, he can recoup his expenses for the improvements only from the original seller directly.

49 It is a required condition in a *ketubah* that after the husband's death his widow and unmarried daughters be sustained by the estate (*Ketubot* 4:11-12). While the *ketubah* itself is a mortgage lien on all real estate acquired by the husband, the additional conditions cannot be foreclosed as a mortgage.

50 All other Mishnah sources have an additional clause, either as original text or addition: "The finder shall not be made to swear, for the public good." Since the statement is quoted in the Halakhah (Note 88), it should be read here also.

(46d line 7) **הלכה ג:** אֵין מוֹצִיאִין לַאֲכִילַת פֵּירוֹת כול׳. רִבִּי יוֹחָנָן בְּשֵׁם רִבִּי יַנַּאי. אֵין נִפְרָעִין מִנִּכְסֵי יְתוֹמִין קְטַנִּים אֶלָא בִשְׁטַר שֶׁהָרִיבִּית אוֹכֶלֶת בּוֹ. וְיֵשׁ אוֹמְרִים. אַף לִכְתוּבַּת אִשָּׁה. אָמַר רִבִּי אִימִּי. מִפְּנֵי מְזוֹנוֹת. אָמַר רִבִּי מַתַּנְיָה. מָאן חָשׁ לִמְזוֹנוֹת. רִבִּי שִׁמְעוֹן. דְּרִבִּי שִׁמְעוֹן אָמַר. בִּמְגְבָּה הַדָּבָר תָּלוּי. מַאי כְדוֹן. מִפְּנֵי חֵינָה. כְּדֵי שֶׁיְּהוּ קוֹפְצִין הַכֹּל עָלֶיהָ לִישָֹאֲנָהּ. וְיֵשׁ אוֹמְרִים. אַף לִגְזֵילָה וְלַנִּיזָקִין. אָמַר רִבִּי יוֹסֵי בֵּירִבִּי בּוּן. אַף אֲנָן תַּנִּינָן תַּרְתֵּיהוֹן. לִגְזֵילָה מִן הָדָא. אִם הָיָה דָבָר שֶׁיֵּשׁ לוֹ אֲחֵרָיוּת חַייָבִין לְשַׁלֵּם. לַנִּיזָקִין מִן הָדָא. וְאֵין נִפְרָעִין מִנִּכְסֵי יְתוֹמִין אֶלָא מִן הַזִּיבּוּרִית. כֵּינֵי מַתְנִיתָא. אֵין נִפְרָעִין מִנִּכְסֵי יְתוֹמִין לַנִּיזָקִין אֶלָא מִן הַזִּיבּוּרִית. וְהָתַנֵּי. עָמַד הַבֵּן תַּחַת הָאָב. הַנִּיזָקִין שָׁמִין לָהֶן בָּעִדִּית וּבַעֲלֵי הַחוֹב בַּבֵּינוֹנִית וּכְתֻבָּת[51] אִשָּׁה בַּזִּיבּוּרִית. אָמַר רִבִּי יוֹסֵי בֵּירִבִּי בּוּן. כָּאן בְּיָתוֹם גָּדוֹל כָּאן בְּיָתוֹם קָטָן.

Halakhah 3: "One cannot collect for usufruct," etc. [52]Rebbi Johanan said in the name of Rebbi Yannai: One pays from an orphan's property only a document on which interest is due, and some say, also a woman's *ketubah*. Rebbi Yannai said, because of her sustenance. Rebbi Mattaniah said, who is worried about sustenance? Rebbi Simeon! Since Rebbi Simeon said, it depends on the collection. What about it? For attraction, that everybody should be eager to marry her. Some say, also for robbery and torts. Rebbi Yose said, we stated both of these. Robbery from the following: "If it was mortgageable, he has to pay." For torts from the following: "One pays from an orphan's property only from the least valuable." So is the Mishnah: One pays for torts from an orphan's property only from the least valuable. But was it not stated: If the son took his father's place, one estimates torts from the most valuable land, creditors from average quality, and a woman's *ketubah* from the least valuable. Rebbi Yose ben Rebbi Abun said, there about an adult orphan, here[46] about an underage orphan.

51 Vocalization of the ms.
52 This paragraph is from *Ketubot* 9:8, explained in Notes 187-197. The variant readings (including a parallel text in *Šebuot* 5:5) are given in *Ketubot*.

(46d line 20) **הלכה:** אֵין נִפְרָעִין מִנְּכָסִים מְשׁוּעְבָּדִין כול'. אָמַר רִבִּי חֲנִינָא. מִפְּנֵי שֶׁאֵין לָהֶן קִיצְבָּה.

Halakhah: "One does not collect from encumbered property,"[53] etc. Rebbi Ḥanina said, because they have no fixed amount[54].

53 This quote from Mishnah 2 is not in its place. The reference is to Mishnah 3 and the list of items which cannot be subject to foreclosure from a buyer.
54 Mortgage liens are only fixed amounts. The same statement is in the Babli, 50b.

(46d line 21) גָּזַל שָׂדֶה מִשִּׁמְעוֹן וּמְכָרָהּ לְלֵוִי וּבָא שִׁמְעוֹן וּטְרָפָהּ מִלֵּוִי. לֵוִי גּוֹבֶה מִמְּשׁוּעְבָּדִין שֶׁל רְאוּבֵן וְשִׁמְעוֹן גּוֹבֶה אֲכִילַת פֵּירוֹת מִבְּנֵי חוֹרִין שֶׁלְּלֵוִי. עָמַד לֵוִי וְהִשְׁבִּיחַ. לֵוִי גּוֹבֶה אֶת הַקֶּרֶן מִמְּשׁוּעְבָּדִין שֶׁלִּרְאוּבֵן וְגוֹבֶה אֶת הַשֶּׁבַח מִבְּנֵי חוֹרִין שֶׁלְּשִׁמְעוֹן. רִבִּי חִייָה בְשֵׁם רִבִּי יוֹחָנָן אָמַר. וְהוּא שֶׁקָּדַם מִקְחוֹ שֶׁל זֶה לְשִׁבְחוֹ שֶׁל זֶה. אֲבָל אִם קָדַם שִׁבְחוֹ שֶׁל זֶה לְמִקְחוֹ שֶׁל זֶה לֵוִי גּוֹבֶה אֶת הַקֶּרֶן אֲפִילוּ מִמְּשׁוּעְבָּדִין שֶׁל שִׁמְעוֹן. אַף בַּאֲכִילַת פֵּירוֹת כָּךְ הִיא עָבְדָא. אַפִּיק

אַרְבָּעָה דֵינָרִין וְהוּא שְׁבַח אֶשְׁתָּא. לֵוִי גָּבֵי אַרְבַּעְתֵּי דֵינָרַיָּיא מִמְּשׁוּעְבָּדִין שֶׁלִּרְאוּבֵן וְגָבֵי תְּרֵין אוֹחְרָנַיָּיא מִבְּנֵי חוֹרִין שֶׁלְּשִׁמְעוֹן. רִבִּי אָבִין בְּשֵׁם רַבָּנִין דְּתַמָּן. אֵין לָהּ יוֹרֵד בִּרְשׁוּת וְיָדוֹ לְתַחְתּוֹנָה אֵצֶל שִׁמְעוֹן. רִבִּי יוֹסֵי בֵּירִבִּי בּוּן בְּשֵׁם רַבָּנִין דְּתַמָּן. אֵין לָהּ יוֹרֵד בִּרְשׁוּת וְיָדוֹ לָעֶלְיוֹנָה אֵצֶל רְאוּבֵן.

If [Reuben][55] robbed a field from Simeon and sold it to Levi[56], then Simeon came[57] and foreclosed it from Levi; then Levi collects from Reuben's encumbered property and Simeon collects the usufruct from Levi's free property[58]. If Levi in the meantime improved [the property], Levi collects the capital from Reuben's encumbered property and the improvement from Simeon's free property. Rebbi Ḥiyya in the name of Rebbi Joḥanan said, only if a third party's buying preceded the improvement by this one[59]. But if the improvement by this one preceded a third party's buying, Levi can collect the capital even from Simeon's encumbered property[60]. Rebbi Abba, Rebbi Ḥiyya in the name of Rebbi Joḥanan said: With usufruct one proceeds in the same way[61]. If he spent four denars and the improvement is worth six, Levi collects four denars from Reuben's encumbered property and another two from Simeon's free property. Rebbi Abin in the name of the rabbis there: Since he did not enter with permission, his hand is weak against Simeon[62]. Rebbi Yose ben Rebbi Abun in the name of the rabbis there: Since he entered with permission, his hand is strong against Reuben[63].

55 Missing in the text but clearly demanded by the sequel.

56 In all cases discussed, Levi is presumed to be an innocent buyer who did not know that the seller had no title.

57 Who could prove his ownership in court.

58 This follows the Mishnah and is unproblematic.

59 If Simeon sold property before he knew that Levi had improved the

property which he is going to retake, the eventual obligation of Simeon towards Levi is no lien on the real estate sold to the third party. In the Babli, 51b, a similar but tannaïtic statement applies only in case the field was sold by the buyer from the robber to another person, whose innocent purchase is protected.

60   In this opinion, whose problematic aspect is discussed later, Simeon's potential liability is an automatic lien on all his properties.

61   There also, it depends on when the obligation of payment started. The Babli agrees, *Baba Meṣi'a* 14b, where the situation described here is alluded to.

62   Since for Simeon all that Levi did in his field was unauthorized, Simeon does not have to pay at all since he would pay only an amount equal to the smaller of investment or improvement, but since the investment is collected from Reuben, there is no enforceable claim against Simeon. (Cf. also *Yebamot* 15:3, Note 71.)

63   Since Reuben sold the field to Levi, the latter can collect from Reuben the value of the improvement, not only the amount of investment.

(46d line 32) רְאוּבֵן שֶׁגָּזַל שָׂדֶה מִשִּׁמְעוֹן וּמְכָרָהּ לְלֵוִי וְהָלַךְ לֵוִי וּנְתָנָהּ מַתָּנָה לִיהוּדָה וּבָא שִׁמְעוֹן וּטְרָפָהּ מִיהוּדָה. יְהוּדָה לֹא אָזִיל גַּבֵּי לֵוִי דְּהִיא מַתָּנָה. לֵוִי אָזַל גַּבֵּי רְאוּבֵן דְּהִיא מְכִירָה. וְלֹא מַתָּנָה יְהַבְתִּינָהּ. יָכִיל הוּא מֵימַר לֵיהּ. בְּעֵי הֲוֵינָא מִיתַּן לֵיהּ וִישַׁלֵּם לִי טִיבוּ. רְאוּבֵן גָּזַל שָׂדֶה מִשִּׁמְעוֹן וּנְתָנָהּ מַתָּנָה לְלֵוִי וְהָלַךְ לֵוִי וּמְכָרָהּ לִיהוּדָה וּבָא שִׁמְעוֹן וּטְרָפָהּ מִיהוּדָה. יְהוּדָה אָזַל גַּבֵּי לֵוִי דְּהוּא מְכָרָהּ. לֵוִי לֹא אָזַל גַּבֵּי רְאוּבֵן דְּהִיא מַתָּנָה. דָּמַר רִבִּי יוֹסֵי בְּשֵׁם רַבָּנִין. אֵין שִׁיעְבּוּד לְמַתָּנָה.

[64]Reuben robbed a field from Simeon and sold it to Levi; Levi went and gave it to Jehudah as a gift. Then Simeon foreclosed it from Jehudah. Jehudah has no regress on Levi since it was a gift. Levi has regress on Reuben since it was a sale. Did he not give it away as a gift? He can say to him, it was my intention to give it to him so he would return me favors[65]. Reuben robbed a field from Simeon and gave it to Levi as a

gift; Levi sold it to Jehudah. Jehudah has regress on Levi since he sold it; Levi has no regress on Reuben since it was a gift; as Rebbi Yose said in the name of the rabbis: No easement is created by a gift.

64 This paragraph is discussed by Rashba in a letter to Meïri (*Responsa attributed to Naḥmanides*, #96). The text is practically identical with that of the ms.

65 While goodwill cannot be easily quantified in monetary terms, it is of value and can be used in a claim against a robber.

(46d line 39) רְאוּבֵן שֶׁגָּזַל שָׂדֶה מִשִּׁמְעוֹן וּמְכָרָהּ לְלֵוִי. וְלֹא הִסְפִּיק לִכְתּוֹב טָרְפוֹ עַד שֶׁמֵּת. דְּמָאן הִיא. רַב הוּנָא וְחִיָּיה בְּרֵיהּ דְּרַב. חַד אָמַר. אִם כָּתַב שְׁטָר טָרְפוֹ. שֶׁלִּרְאוּבֵן. וְאִם לָאו. שֶׁלְּלֵוִי הִיא. וְחָרָנָה אָמַר. הִיא כָתַב הִיא לֹא כָתַב שֶׁלְּלֵוִי הִיא. אָמַר רִבִּי מָנָא. מִסְתַּבְּרָה דְּלֹא דִּרְאוּבֵן. דְּיָכִיל לְמֵימַר לֵיהּ. מִילָה דְּלָא דִּידִי זְבָנִית לָךְ. אָמַר רִבִּי יוֹסֵי בֵּירִבִּי בּוּן. לֹא מִסְתַּבְּרָה דְּלָא דְּלֵוִי. דִּרְאוּבֵן יָכִיל לְמֵימַר לֵיהּ. הַאי דְּלָא קוֹמֵיךָ אָקוּם לְזַבִּינֵיהּ טָבֵי אַתְּ.

Reuben robbed a field from Simeon and sold it to Levi, and he[66] did not have time to write the foreclosure document before he died: whose is it[67]? Rav Huna and Ḥiyya the son of Rav: One said, if he wrote the foreclosure document, it is Reuben's, if not, it is Levi's. The other one said, whether he wrote or did not write, it belongs to Levi. Rebbi Mana said, it is reasonable that it does not belong to Reuben since he can say to him, I sold you something which was not mine. Rebbi Yose said, it is not reasonable that it should not be Levi's, since Reuben[68] can tell him, is this not before you? You are good to confirm the sale.

66 "He" seems to be Simeon, who has to go to court and obtain a document which gives him the right to take the field from Levi.

67 It should be obvious that the field is Simeon's and after him his

heirs. The paragraph is difficult to understand; the commentators all emend the text to fit their explanations, which can be disregarded. It seems that the question is to whom do the heirs have to address their foreclosure document.

The problem is an old one; Meïri, after Rashi the second most important Medieval commentator, asked Rashba for an explanation (cf. Note 64). Meïri's text read טרפו "his foreclosure document," Rashba's read חרפו "his sales document." This is Rashba's anwer:

"It is my opinion that our text is defective and it should be as follows: Reuben robbed a field from Simeon and sold it to Levi, *then Reuben bought it from Simeon* but before he could write *the sales contract*, he died. That is the case about which Samuel asked Rav in (Babli) *Baba Meṣi'a* (15b), viz., if it turns out that the field was not his, but he went and bought it from the original owners, what are the rules? He told him, the first (the robber) sold to the second (the buyer) any present and future rights to the parcel. ... And this is the explanation of this text according to my understanding: Reuben had robbed a field from Simeon and sold it to Levi who did not realize that it was robbed. Afterwards, Reuben bought the parcel from Simeon, but Simeon had not yet written the sales contract when Reuben died: who is the owner? Rav Huna and Ḥiyya bar Rav: One says if the document was first, if the sale was completed before he died, the sale was final and Reuben did not transfer [the field] to Levi; this shows that Reuben did not intend to leave the field in Levi's hands, ostensibly to leave it to his heirs. He does not spell this out since the sales document was not yet written. The other one said, there is no difference between written and not written, he wants the field to be Levi's since he did not dispose of the field in a will. {The same Rav Huna and Ḥiyya bar Rav disagree in the Babli *Baba Meṣi'a* (16a) about the time available to the robber to act to protect his credit.) Rebbi Mana has a different explanation: He says that in any case the field belongs to Reuben, following Rami bar Ḥama (in the Babli, *Baba Meṣi'a* 16a) who said that Levi's contract was not worth the paper it was written on. But Rebbi Yose bar Abun is of the opposite opinion, since Levi can tell him, is the field not now before you that you can turn the sale into a valid one. This follows Rava (in the Babli, *Baba Meṣi'a* 16a) who told

Rami bar Ḥama that Levi acquired the property by the trust he put in Reuben.

But following your reading, since you read טרפו with ט, it is possible that this refers to a foreclosure document which Levi obtained against the robber after he had lost the field to Simeon, and that is the same disagreement we find there (in the Babli, *Baba Meṣi'a* 16a); how long does a person have credit, Rav says until the start of court proceedings, Ḥiyya bar Rav says, until the foreclosure document was signed, and Rav Papa said, until the public sale."

69 Rashba reads "Levi" as text, not as correction.

(46d line 45) מָהוּ לִגְבּוֹת פַּרְנָסָה מִן הַמְשׁוּעֲבָדִין. אָמַר רַבִּי זְעִירָה. רַבִּי יוֹחָנָן לֹא גָבֵי. מָאן גָּבֵי. רִבִּי חֲנִינָה וְרִבִּי אִילָא גָבֵיי. רִבִּי יָסָא אִיתְפְּקַד מִדַּל דְּיַתְמִין וַהֲווּ תַמָּן בְּעַיָין פַּרְנָסָה. אָעִיל עוּבְדָא קוֹמֵי רִבִּי אֶלְעָזָר וְקוֹמֵי רִבִּי שִׁמְעוֹן בֶּן יָקִים. אָמַר רִבִּי שִׁמְעוֹן בֶּן יָקִים. לֹא מוּטָב שֶׁיִּתְפַּרְנְסוּ מִשֶּׁלָּאֲבִיהֶן וְלֹא מִן הַצְּדָקָה. אָמַר לֵיהּ רִבִּי לְעָזָר. רִבִּי. אִילוּ יָבוֹאוּ לִפְנֵי רַבּוֹתֵינוּ אֵין רַבּוֹתֵינוּ נוֹגְעִין בּוֹ. וְאָנוּ עוֹשִׁין בּוֹ מַעֲשֶׂה. אָמַר רִבִּי יוֹסֵי. אֲנָא יְהִיב. וְאֵין קָמוֹן יַתְמִין וְעָרְרִין אֲנָא יְהִיב לוֹן. אֲפִילוּ כֵן קָמוֹן וְעָרְרוֹן.

1 זעירה | כ זעירא   2 ר׳ חנינה ור׳ אילא | כ ר׳ חניניה לא   גביי | כ גבי   מדל | כ כגביה מדל   והוו | כ והוה   3 תמן | כ תמן יתמין   פרנסה | כ מפרנסא   4 בן יקים | כ בר יקים   5 לעזר | כ אלעזר   רבי. אילו | כ דבר שאילו   יבואו | כ יבוא   אין | כ ואין   6 נוגעין בו | כ נוגעין   עושין בו | כ עושין אותו   7 יהיב | כ יהוב לון   יתמין וערריו | כ יתמי וערון   קמון וערון | כ חמון ולא עירון

Can one collect dowry from encumbered property[70]? [71]Rebbi Ze'ira said that Rebbi Joḥanan does not collect. Who collects? Rebbi Ḥanina and Rebbi Ila collect. Rebbi Yasa was appointed custodian of orphans' property. There were orphan [girls] who asked for dowry. He brought the case before Rebbi Eleazar and Rebbi Simeon bar Yaqim. Rebbi Simeon bar Yaqim said, is it not better to provide for them from their father's estate rather than from charity? Rebbi Eleazar said to him: If such a case came before our teachers, our teachers would not touch it; would we act? Rebbi Yose said, I shall give to them, and if some orphans would get up and complained, I would give it to them. They stood up and complained[72].

70   Since providing a dowry for daughters is one of the obligatory conditions attached to a *ketubah*; cf. *Ketubot* 6:6.

71   This text is from *Ketubot* 6:6 (30d l.59), explained there in Notes 93-97. Variant readings are noted ב.

72   This is the opposite of what is asserted in *Ketubot*.

(46d line 52) גְּזַר דִּין נְפַק. צִיפּוֹר בַּת אַבְשָׁלוֹם. רִבִּי סִימוֹן וְרִבִּי יַעֲקֹב בַּר אִידִי בְּשֵׁם רִבִּי שִׁמְעוֹן בַּר בָּא. אֲנָא וְרַבּוֹתֵינוּ גָּבִינוּ לָהּ מִן הַמִּטַּלְטְלִין כְּמִנְהַג מְקוֹמָהּ.

A judgment was rendered[73] for Ṣippor bat Absalom. Rebbi Simon and Rebbi Jacob bar Idi in the name of Rebbi Simeon bar Abba: I and our teachers collected for her from movables[74], following the custom of her place.

73   In *Ketubot* (6:6, Note 98) it is only asserted that a judgment was given following R. Ḥanina.

74   Following the principle that local custom is the overriding determinant in the judicial interpretation of *ketubah* obligations; cf. *Ketubot* 6:4, Note 67.

(46d line 54) רַב הֲוָה כְּתִיב לְרִבִּי עַבְרוֹן עַל דַּעְתֵּיהּ דְּרִבִּי חִיָּיה רַבָּה. וַהֲוָה רִבִּי חִיָּיה כְּתִיב בֵּינֵי שִׁיטַיָּיא. עָמְדוּ הַיְתוֹמִין וּמָכְרוּ. גּוֹבִין מִן הַפַּרְנָסָה וְאֵין גּוֹבִין מִן הַמְּזוֹנוֹת. עָמְדוּ וְשִׁיעְבְּדוּ. הַשִּׁיעְבּוּד הַזֶּה אֵינִי יוֹדֵעַ מָהוּ. תַּנָּא לֵוִי. אֶחָד שִׁיעְבּוּד הָאָב וְאֶחָד שִׁיעְבּוּד הַבֵּן גּוֹבִין מִן הַפַּרְנָסָה וְאֵין גּוֹבִין מִן הַמְּזוֹנוֹת. אָמַר רִבִּי אַבָּא. לֵית כָּאן בְּשִׁיעְבּוּד הָאָב אֶלָּא בְּשִׁיעְבּוּד הַבֵּן. אִם בְּשִׁיעְבּוּד

הָאָב. אִם בְּחַיֵּי הָאָב אֵינוֹ גוֹבֶה לֹא כָּל־שֶׁכֵּן לְאַחַר מִיתַת הָאָב. רִבִּי חָמָא בַּר עוּקְבָּא בְּשֵׁם רִבִּי יוֹסֵי בַּר חֲנִינָה. נִישְׂאוּ הַבָּנוֹת אַלְמָנָה נִיזוֹנֶת מֵהֶן. רִבִּי בָּא כְדִידֵיהּ וְרִבִּי יוּדָה כְדִידֵיהּ. דְּאַחְתֵּיהּ דְּרִבִּי יוֹסֵי בַּר חֲנִינָה בְּשֵׁם רִבִּי יוֹסֵי בֵּירִבִּי חַגַּיי. אֲפִילוּ מֵתוּ אַלְמָנָה נִיזוֹנֶת מֵהֶן.

Rav wrote to Rebbi, who transferred it to the Elder Rebbi Ḥiyya and Rebbi Ḥiyya wrote between the lines. If the orphans sold against the rules[75], one collects for dowry but one does not collect for sustenance[76]. If they accepted a lien[77]. I do not know what this lien is[78]. Levi stated: Both for a lien made by the father and for a lien made by the son, one collects for dowry[79] but one does not collect for sustenance[80]. Rebbi Abba said, there is no mention of a lien made by the father, only a lien made by the son. If one cannot collect during the father's lifetime[81], not so much less after the father's death? Rebbi Ḥama bar Uqba in the name of Rebbi Yose bar Ḥanina: If the daughters are married, the widow is sustained by them[82]. Rebbi Abba follows his own [opinion] and Rebbi Jehudah[82] follows his own [opinion]. For the sister of Rebbi Yose bar Ḥanina in the name of Rebbi Yose ben Rebbi Ḥaggai: Even if they died, the widow is sustained by them.

75 Since by talmudic rules, all obligations of a *ketubah* are to be satisfied by real estate, any sale while some of the obligations are still open is against the rules.

76 The daughters, who do not inherit if there are sons, have a claim of (in general) 10% of their father's estate as dowry. Cf. *Ketubot* 6:6. Since this claim exists even during the father's lifetime, it has precedence over the widow's claim to sustenance which starts only at her husband's death.

77 This was Rav's question. The lien is a mortgage obligation.

78 This is R. Ḥiyya's note. Was the mortgage taken during the father's lifetime or after his death? In the Babli, *Ketubot* 69a, the question from

the start was about a mortgage the heirs took out on real estate of their inheritance.

79   From real estate sold or pledged.

80   This is also quoted as Rebbi's opinion in the Babli, *Ketubot* 69a.

81   Mishnah *Ketubot* 4:6.

82   In the Babli, *Ketubot* 51a, the question never arises since the claims of the widow and the daughters are accorded equal status; this rule is quoted in *Yebamot* 15:3 (14d l.68), *Ketubot* 4:8 (29a l.25).

82   There is no R. Jehudah quoted in the matter, but in the Babli, *Ketubot* 49b, instead of "the sister of R. Yose ben Ḥanina" one reads "R. Jehudah, the son of the sister of R. Yose ben Ḥanina". One has to assume that the name was omitted by the scribe in the next sentence.

(46d line 64) בְּנֵי בָנִים מָה הֵן. רִבִּי מָנָא אָמַר. בְּנֵי בָנִים הֲרֵי הֵן כְּבָנִים. רִבִּי יוֹסֵי אָמַר. אֵין בְּנֵי בָנִים כְּבָנִים. רִבִּי שְׁמוּאֵל בְּרֵיהּ רִבִּי יוֹסֵי בֵּירִבִּי בּוּן וְרִבִּי מַתַּנְיָיה הֲווֹן יָתְבִין. סָבְרִין מֵימַר. הִיא בְּנֵי בָנִים שֶׁכָּאן הִיא בָנִים שֶׁלְּהַלָּן. אָמַר לוֹן רִבִּי יוֹסֵי בֵּירִבִּי בּוּן. בְּנֵי בָנִים קָפְצָה עֲלֵיהֶן יְרוּשַׁת תּוֹרָה.

[83]What is the situation of grandchildren? Rebbi Mana said, grandchildren are like children. Rebbi Yose said, grandchildren are not like children. Rebbi Samuel, son of Rebbi Yose ben Rebbi Ḥanina and Rebbi Mattaniah were sitting together. They wanted to say, the same situation applies to grandchildren here as there. Rebbi Yose ben Rebbi Ḥanina said to them, inheritance by biblical law jumped on grandchildren.

83   The Text is from *Ketubot* 4:8, Notes 200-201. Variant readings are given there.

(46d line 68) תַּמָּן תַּנִּינָן. מָנֶה לְאַבָּא בְּיָדָךְ אֵין לָךְ בְּיָדִי אֶלָּא חֲמִישִׁים דִּינָרִין. פָּטוּר. מִפְּנֵי שֶׁהוּא כְּמֵשִׁיב אֲבֵידָה. אָמַר רִבִּי לְעָזֵר. תַּקָּנָה תִּיקְנוּ בוֹ כְּדֶרֶךְ שֶׁתִּיקְנוּ בַּמְצִיאָה. דְּתַנִּינָן. הַמּוֹצֵא מְצִיאָה לֹא יִשָּׁבַע מִפְּנֵי תִיקּוּן הָעוֹלָם. אָמַר רִבִּי בָּא. מַתְנִיתָא בְּשֶׁאָמַר לוֹ. שְׁנֵי שְׁוָורִים מָצָאתָ לִי. אֲבָל אִם אָמַר לוֹ. שְׁנֵי

שְׁוָרִים מָצָאתִי לָךְ וְהֶחֱזַרְתִּי לָךְ אֶת שְׁנֵיהֶן. וְהוּא אוֹמֵר לוֹ. לֹא הֶחֱזַרְתָּ לִי אֶלָּא אַחַת. לֹא בָזֶה תִיקְנוּ. רִבִּי פְּדָת בְּשֵׁם רִבִּי יוֹחָנָן. בָּזֶה תִיקְנוּ. אֲבָל בָּרִאשׁוֹנָה דְּבַר תּוֹרָה הִיא. כְּהָדָא דְּתַנֵּי. יָכוֹל אָמַר לוֹ. שְׁנֵי שְׁוָרִים מָצָאתָ לִי. וְהוּא אָמַר. לֹא מָצָאתִי אֶלָּא אֶחָד. יָכוֹל יְהֵא חַיָּב. תַּלְמוּד לוֹמַר אוֹ מָצָא אֲבֵידָה וְכִחֵשׁ בָּהּ. פְּרָט לָזֶה שֶׁלֹּא כִיחֵשׁ. אֲבָל אִם אָמַר לוֹ. עוֹמֵד הָיִיתִי בְּרֹאשׁ גַּגִּי וּרְאִיתִיךָ מוֹשֵׁךְ שְׁנֵי שְׁוָרִים קְשׁוּרִין. שְׁנֵי שְׁוָרִים קְשׁוּרִים מָשַׁכְתָּ לִי. וְהוּא אוֹמֵר. לֹא מָשַׁכְתִּי אֶלָּא אֶחָד. לֹא בָזֶה תִיקְנוּ. וְדִכְוָותָהּ. עוֹמֵד הָיִיתִי עַל אַבָּא בִּשְׁעַת מִיתָתוֹ וְטָעַנְךָ מָנֶה וְהוֹדֵיתָהּ לוֹ. וְהוּא אוֹמֵר. לֹא הוֹדֵיתִי אֶלָּא חֲמִשִּׁים. לֹא בָזֶה תִיקְנוּ.

There[84], we have stated: "You[85] have in your hand a mina of my father's; you[86] have to get from me only 50 denars. He does not have to swear since he is like a person who returns a find[87]." Rebbi Eleazar said, in this case they instituted a regulation as they instituted for a find, as we have stated[50]: "The finder of a lost object shall not swear because of the public good[88]." Rebbi Abba said, this Mishnah [applies] when he said to him, you found my two oxen[89]. But if he[90] said, I found your two oxen and returned both of them, but the other[91] said, you returned only one, in that case they did not institute the rule[92]. Rebbi Pedat in the name of Rebbi Johanan: In this case they did institute[93]. But in the first case[89], it is a word of the Torah, as it was stated: I could think that if he said to him, you found my two oxen[94], but the other said, I found only one, should he be obligated [to swear]? The verse[95] says, "or if he found a find and disowned it;" that excludes this one who did not disown. But if he said to him, I was standing on my roof when I saw you dragging away two tied oxen, two tied oxen you dragged away from me[96], and he says, only one I dragged away; in that case they made no regulation. Similarly: "I was standing with my father when he was dying and he claimed from you a mina and you agreed to it[97]," and the other says, "I agreed only for 50;" in that case they made no regulation.

84 Mishnah *Ševu'ot* 6:1. The subject is the biblical oath imposed on a person who denies an obligation (*Ex.* 22:8). The rabbinic interpretation of the expression אֲשֶׁר יֹאמַר כִּי הוּא זֶה is "if he [the defendant] agrees that there is a case." If the defendant in a civil suit, in which there are no witnesses and no documents, denies the entire claim, he does not have to swear a biblical oath (he may have to swear a rabbinical oath). But if he agrees to part of the claim, he has to swear a biblical oath to free himself from the remainder. Only if the claim is advanced as tentative, then any admission by the defendant is a gift to the claimant and by rabbinic rule no oath of any kind is due.

85 The speaker is the claimant.

86 The speaker is the defendant.

87 The heir is not conversant with all the details of his father's business dealings. Since he cannot swear that the father had not received payment, he has no case if the defendant denies the entire claim. The partial admission of the claim is the equivalent of a gift by the defendant to the claimant.

88 If the owner claims to have lost more than the finder returns, the finder cannot be made to swear that he did not retain anything for himself, since otherwise nobody would return any find.

89 As explained later, one ox was found but the owner claims to have lost two. Returning one ox is not accepting part of a claim of two.

90 The finder.

91 The original owner.

92 He has to swear since both parties claim to be sure of their case.

93 This is a case of returning a find and the finder is protected.

94 This cannot be more than a conjecture; the claimant cannot make a defendant swear about a hypothetical case.

95 *Lev.* 5:22, speaking of the sacrifice required of the person who swears falsely in the situation described in *Ex.* 22:8.

96 The claimant asserts as a certainty that he saw his two oxen in the finder's possession.

97 This is an assertion of a certain claim which falls under the rule of *Ex.* 22:8.

משנה ד: (fol. 46b) יְתוֹמִים שֶׁסָּמְכוּ אֵצֶל בַּעַל הַבַּיִת אוֹ שְׁמִינָה לָהֶן אֲבִיהֶן אֶפִּיטְרוֹפּוֹס חַיָּיב לְעַשֵׂר פֵּירוֹתֵיהֶן. אֶפִּיטְרוֹפּוֹס שֶׁמִּינָהוּ אֲבִי הַיְתוֹמִים יִשָּׁבַע מִינָהוּ בֵּית דִּין לֹא יִשָּׁבַע. אַבָּא שָׁאוּל אוֹמֵר חִילּוּף הַדְּבָרִים. הַמְטַמֵּא וְהַמְדַמֵּעַ וְהַמְנַסֵּךְ אִם שׁוֹגֵג פָּטוּר וְאִם מֵזִיד חַיָּיב. הַכֹּהֲנִים שֶׁפִּיגְּלוּ בַּמִּקְדָּשׁ מְזִידִים חַיָּיבִין.

Mishnah 4: If orphans rely on a property owner[98] or if their father appointed a guardian[99] for them; these are obligated to tithe their produce. A guardian appointed by the orphans' father shall be made to swear[100]; if he was appointed by the court he shall not be made to swear. Abba Shaul says, it is the other way around[101]. If someone causes impurity[102], or *dema'*[103], or libation wine[104], if it was unintentional he is free[105], intentional he is obligated[106]. If Cohanim in the Temple intentionally made [a sacrifice] *piggul*[107], they have to pay.

98 If orphans are adults (older than 13 years) but not able to act in real estate matters (younger than 20 years) and they seek assistence from a relative or acquaintance, that person is not a guardian but by rabbinic usage he has some rights and obligations of a guardian, in particular to see to it that the produce of the orphan's fields is tithed so it becomes available for sale or for their own use. In general, a third person cannot give heave and tithe for others; this is another example of a "regulation for the public good."

99 Greek ἐπίτροπος, cf. *Bikkurim* 1:5, Note 82.

100 At the end of his service, the court shall require him to swear that he retained nothing of the orphan's property for himself.

101 The guardian appointed by the father's will shall not be made to swear, so people will not refuse to serve. The court appointee, who does not have the deceased father's trust, can be made to swear.

102 This and the following cases all concern invisible defects which cannot be detected by inspection. Causing impurity to food can imply a diminution of value, since the food cannot be sold to people eating only in purity, or it can make it unfit for use, if the item was heave or any other sanctified food.

103 *Dema'* is profane food mixed with heave, which is forbidden to lay persons and only permitted to priests, who will pay only a fraction of the value. Cf. *Demay* 1:3, Note 175.

104 Wine used in a pagan libation rite. Such wine is prohibited for all usufruct and makes all food and drinks it comes in contact with forbidden in the most minute amount.

105 Since the damage is invisible, it does not fall under the tort laws.

106 By a rabbinic rule for the public good (Tosephta 3:7), that people should not do damage with impunity.

107 פִּגּוּל by biblical definition (*Lev.* 19:7) is sacrificial meat on the third day after slaughter. The root seems to be preserved in Arabic نجل "to be soft", as in Aramaic פּוּגְלָא "radish", i. e., a soft, edible root. Applied to meat, which starts to decompose, probably a better translation would be "to be mushy".

In rabbinic interpretation, the deadly sin is not to eat the meat when it becomes unsanitary but to slaughter and offer the blood to the altar with the idea of eating the sacrifice after its allotted time. Since the blood is only handled by the Cohen, not the person offering the sacrifice, the Cohen could disqualify the sacrifice and inflict a heavy financial loss on the faithful bringing the sacrifice simply by telling him that he handled the sacrifice with the wrong intention. Since this also is an invisible damage, it is clear that some penalties are in order for the public good (Tosephta 3:8).

(47a line 6) **הלכה ד:** יְתוֹמִים שֶׁסָּמְכוּ אֵצֶל בַּעַל הַבַּיִת כול׳. אַתֶּם פְּרָט לְשׁוּתָּפִין. אַתֶּם פְּרָט לָאֲפִּיטְרוֹפּוֹס. אַתֶּם פְּרָט לְתוֹרֵם שֶׁאֵינוֹ שֶׁלּוֹ. אַתֶּם פְּרָט לְשׁוּתָּפִין. וְהָתַנִּינָן הַשּׁוּתָּפִין שֶׁתָּרְמוּ. אֶלָּא כָּאן בִּתְרוּמָה גְדוֹלָה כָּאן בִּתְרוּמַת מַעֲשֵׂר. כְּלוּם לָמְדוּ תְרוּמָה גְדוֹלָה לֹא מִתְּרוּמַת מַעֲשֵׂר. אֶלָּא כָּאן לַהֲלָכָה כָּאן

לְמַעֲשֶׂה. אַתֶּם פְּרָט לָאֶפִּיטְרוֹפוֹס. וְהָתָנִיָא יְתוֹמִים שֶׁסָּמְכוּ אֶצֶל בַּעַל הַבַּיִת אוֹ שֶׁמִּינָּה לָהֶן אֲבִיהֶן אֶפִּיטְרוֹפוֹס חַיָּיב לְעַשֵּׂר פֵּירוֹתֵיהֶן. חַבְרַיָּיא אָמְרִין. כָּאן לְאֶפִּיטְרוֹפִין לְעוֹלָם כָּאן לְאֶפִּיטְרוֹפִין לְשָׁעָה. רִבִּי יוֹסֵי בָּעֵי. אִם בְּאֶפִּיטְרוֹפִין לְעוֹלָם. וְדָא דְתַנֵּי. מוֹכֵר הוּא עֲבָדִים אֲבָל לֹא קַרְקָעוֹת. אֶלָּא כָן בְּיָתוֹם גָּדוֹל כָּאן בְּיָתוֹם קָטָן.

2 לאפיטרופוס | ת לאפיטרופין שאינו | ת את שאינו פרט לשותפין | ת ולא שותפין
3 והתנינן | ת והתנן[108] השותפין שתרמו | ת שותפין שתרמו זה אחא זה בתרומה | ת
לתרומה בתרומת | ת לתרומת 4 תרומה | ת לתרומה לא | ת אלא[109] 5 פרט
לאפיטרופוס | ת ולא אפיטרופין והתניא[108] | ת והתנינן 6 אפיטרופוס | ת
אפיטרופין חבריא | ת חבריא 7 אפיטרופין | ת אפיטרופוס באפיטרופין | ת
באפיטרופוס 8 ודא | ת כהדא הוא עבדים | ת מטלטלין וזן כן | ת כאן

"If orphans rely on a property owner, etc." [110](*Num.* 18:28) "you" excludes partners, "you" excludes guardians, "you" excludes one who gives heave from what is not his. Did we not state (*Terumot* 3:3): "Partners who gave heave one after the other?" But one must be for Great Heave, the other for heave of the tithe. Did we not infer the laws of the Great Heave from heave of the tithe? But one is for practice, the other for action. "You" excludes guardians; but did we not state: "Orphans dependent on a home owner, or for whom the father had appointed a guardian, must tithe their produce." The colleagues say, here for a permanent guardian, there for a temporary guardian. Rebbi Yose asked, does that apply to: "he may sell slaves but not real estate?" But here one deals with an adult orphan, there with an underage orphan.

108   A Babylonian term.

109   Corrector. The scribe had לא.

110   From *Terumot* 1:1, explained in

Notes 61-69. Variants are denoted by ת.

(47a line 15) אָמַר רִבִּי יוֹחָנָן. בַּתְּחִילָה אֵין מַעֲמִידִין אֶפִּיטְרוֹפוֹס לִיתוֹמִין לְחוֹב לָהֶן אֶלָּא לְזָכוֹת לָהֶן. וְאִם חָבוּ חָבוּ. רִבִּי יוֹסֵי בַּר חֲנִינָה אָמַר. בֵּין בַּתְּחִילָה בֵּין בַּסּוֹף אֵין מַעֲמִידִין בֵּין לְזָכוֹת בֵּין לְחוֹבָה. מַתְנִיתָא פְלִיגָא עַל רִבִּי יוֹסֵי בַּר חֲנִינָה. מַעֲמִידִין לָהֶן אֶפִּיטְרוֹפוֹס. שַׁנְיָיא הִיא בְשׁוֹר שֶׁלֹא יֵלֵךְ וְיַזִּיק. הִזִּיק. מִשֶּׁל מִי מְשַׁלְּמִין. רִבִּי יוֹחָנָן אָמַר. מִשֶּׁל יְתוֹמִין. רִבִּי יוֹסֵי בַּר חֲנִינָה אָמַר. מִשֶּׁל אֶפִּיטְרוֹפוֹס. וַאֲפִילוּ דְלָא יִסְבּוֹר רִבִּי יוֹחָנָן כֵּן לֵית מִילְּתֵיהּ אָמַר כֵּן. לֹא. דְהוּא אָמַר לַבְּסוֹף. אִם חָבוּ חָבוּ.

[111]Rebbi Johanan said, as a matter of principle one does not appoint guardians for orphans to their detriment, only to their profit; but if they are detrimental, they are detrimental[112]. Rebbi Yose bar Hanina said, neither as a matter of principle nor as a reaction, neither for profit not for detriment[113]. A Mishnah disagrees with Rebbi Yose bar Hanina: "One appoints a guardian for them[114]" There is a difference about an ox, lest it continue to cause damage[115]. If it did do damage, from whom does one take payment? Rebbi Johanan said, from the orphans. Rebbi Yose bar Hanina said, from the guardian[116]. And even if Rebbi Johanan never taught this, does not his word imply it since he said if in the end they are detrimental, they are detrimental?

111 There is a different but parallel treatment of the subject of this paragraph in *Baba Qama* 4:5 (4b l.50).

112 If the estate of underage minors is sued, the court does not appoint a guardian to conduct their defense but one tells the claimant to wait until the orphans are adults. But if the estate has a claim to pursue, the court may appoint a guardian to prosecute their case; if the guardian is not successful, the orphans cannot sue him.

113 All suits involving an estate, whether by a defendant or a claimant, have to be postponed until the orphans are adults.

114 Mishnah *Baba Qama* 1:5: If an animal of an irresponsible person (a minor, an insane, or a deaf-and-dumb person) did damage, the court has to

appoint a guardian to take care of the matter. This seems to imply that one appoints guardians for underage orphans who are defendants in a damage suit.

115   The Mishnah does not express a biblical principle but a rabbinic rule for the public good, that a dangerous animal should be slaughtered to prevent more damage.

116   If the animal did additional damage when the guardian already was in charge.

(47a line 22) אֶפִּיטְרוֹפּוֹס שֶׁמִּינָהוּ אֲבִי יְתוֹמִין יִשָּׁבַע. שֶׁאֵין דַּרְכּוֹ לִבָּחֵן. שֶׁמִּינוּהוּ בֵּית דִּין לֹא יִשָּׁבַע. שֶׁדַּרְכּוֹ לִבָּחֵן. אַבָּא שָׁאוּל אוֹמֵר. חִילוּף הַדְּבָרִים. אֶפִּיטְרוֹפּוֹס שֶׁמִּינָהוּ אֲבִי יְתוֹמִין יִשָּׁבַע. מִפְּנֵי שֶׁהוּא כְּנוֹשֵׂא שָׂכָר. שֶׁמִּינוּהוּ בֵּית דִּין לֹא יִשָּׁבַע. דְּיָכִיל מֵימַר לֵיהּ. טָבוֹת הֲוֵינָא עֲבִידְנָא לָךְ. אַתְיָיא דְּרִבִּי יוֹחָנָן כְּרַבָּנִין וּדְרִבִּי יוֹסֵי בַּר חֲנִינָה כְּאַבָּא שָׁאוּל. דְּרִבִּי יוֹחָנָן כְּרַבָּנִין. וַאֲפִילוּ יִסְבּוֹר כְּאַבָּא שָׁאוּל בָּעֵי הוּא בַּר נָשׁ מִיתַּן מְהֵימָן וּמִיקְרַיָּיא מְהֵימָן. וּדְרִבִּי יוֹסֵי בַּר חֲנִינָה כְּאַבָּא שָׁאוּל. אֲפִילוּ דְּיִסְבּוֹר כְּרַבָּנִין אָדָם מַבְרִיחַ עַצְמוֹ מִן הַשְּׁבוּעָה וְאֵין אָדָם מַבְרִיחַ עַצְמוֹ מִן הַתַּשְׁלוּמִין.

A guardian appointed by the orphans' father shall be made to swear, for usually he is not checked out[117]. If he was appointed by the court he shall not be made to swear for usually he was checked out. Abba Shaul says, it is the other way around; a guardian appointed by the orphans' father[118] shall be made to swear, for he is like one who is paid[119]; if he was appointed by the court[120] he shall not be made to swear for for he can say to him, I am doing this as a favor to you. It turns out that Rebbi Johanan follows the rabbis and Rebbi Yose ben Hanina Abba Shaul. Does Rebbi Johanan follow the rabbis? Even if he holds with Abba Shaul, a person acts as a trustee[121] in order to be declared trustworthy[122]. Does Rebbi Yose ben Hanina [follow] Abba Shaul? Even if he holds with the rabbis, a person is apt to slip away from an oath but not from payments[123].

117 A private person usually does not have the ability to judge the honesty of his friends.

118 This should read: "appointed by the court".

119 Even if he is not paid, the reputation he obtains by publicly being trusted by the court may be worth money to him. Therefore, a person will not refrain from serving even if he has to swear in the end. The Babli agrees, 52b.

120 This should read: "appointed by the father."

121 Tosaphot (52b, *s. v.* הלכה) quotes a slightly different text: בעי איניש מיתן זוזי "a person would be ready to pay money".

122 Therefore, he can be made to swear.

123 If people know they will have to swear, they will not be available to be appointed guardians. They will think that they are competent enough not to have to pay; very few people will refrain from becoming guardians because of the potential liability.

(47a line 31) רִבִּי יוּדָן לֹא נָחַת לְבֵית וַעֲדָא. קָם עִם רִבִּי מָנָא אָמַר לֵיהּ. מַה חַדְתִּין יֵימְרוּן. אָמַר לֵיהּ. כֵּן אָמַר רִבִּי יוֹסֵי. הַמְטַמֵּא אֵינוֹ כְעוֹשֶׂה מַעֲשֶׂה. מִן הָדָא תְּרוּמָה וְנִיטְמֵאת. אָמַר לֵיהּ. תִּיפְתָּר שֶׁנִּיטְמֵאת מֵאֵילֶיהָ וְלֵית שְׁמַע מִינָהּ כְּלוּם. דְּהִיא מַתְנִיתָא. דָּן אֶת הַדִּין. זִיכָּה אֶת הַחַיָּיב וְחִייֵב אֶת הַזַּכַּאי. טִימֵּא אֶת הַטָּהוֹר טִיהֵר אֶת הַטָּמֵא. דָּמַר רַב יִרְמִיָה בְּשֵׁם רַב. בְּמַגִּיעוֹ לְיָדוֹ. וּשְׁמוּאֵל אָמַר. בְּמַגִּיעוֹ לְיָדוֹ. רִבִּי יְהוּדָה בֵּירִבִּי אוֹמֵר. בַּדִּין הָיָה שֶׁאָפלוּ בְּמֵזִיד יְהֵא פָּטוּר. לָמָּה אָמְרוּ חַיָּיב. כְּדֵי שֶׁיְּהֵא מוֹדִיעַ. וְרִבִּי יוֹחָנָן אָמַר. בַּדִּין הָיָה אָפלוּ שׁוֹגֵג יְהֵא חַיָּיב. וְלָמָּה אָמְרוּ פָּטוּר. מִשּׁוּם קְנָס. חֵיילֵיהּ דְּרִבִּי יוֹחָנָן מִן הָדָא. הַמְטַמֵּא וְהַמְדַמֵּעַ וְהַמְנַסֵּךְ בְּשׁוֹגֵג פָּטוּר וּבְמֵזִיד חַיָּיב. וְאָמַר רִבִּי יוֹחָנָן. וּמִשּׁוּם קְנָס. מַתְנִיתָא מְסַייְעָא לְרִבִּי יוֹחָנָן. הַנּוֹתֵן עוֹל עַל גַּבֵּי פָרָתוֹ שֶׁלַּחֲבֵירוֹ פָּטוּר מִדִּינֵי אָדָם וְחַיָּיב בְּדִינֵי שָׁמַיִם.

Rebbi Yudan did not go to the assembly. He was standing with Rebbi Mana and asked him, what new was said? He said: So says Rebbi Yose, a person causing impurity does not have the status of a perpetrator[124], from the following[125]: "Heave which became impure." He answered: Explain it, if it became impure by itself[126]; then you cannot infer anything, because of a Mishnah[127]: "If somebody judged, absolved the guilty and obligated the innocent, declared the pure impure and the impure pure." For Rav Jeremiah said in the name of Rav: If he touched it with his hand[128]. Samuel said: If he touched it with his hand. Rebbi Jehudah ben Rebbi says, it should have been logical that even intentionally he should have been free. Why did they say that he is obligated[129]? That he should tell. And Rebbi Joḥanan said, it should have been logical that even unintentionally he should have been obligated. Why did they say that he is free[130]? Because of a fine. The strength of Rebbi Joḥanan comes from this: "If someone causes anything to become impure, or *dema'*, or libation wine, if it was unintentional he is free, intentional he is obligated," and Rebbi Joḥanan said, he pays a fine. A *baraita* supports Rebbi Joḥanan: "A person who puts a yoke on another's cow is free in human law but guilty in Heaven's law.[131]"

124 Because an outside observer could not notice any change in the food which was made impure.

125 Mishnah *Baba Qama* 9:2. If somebody stole heave and it became impure in his possession, he can hand it back to the owner and tell him, this is yours. But pure heave was food and impure heave can only be used as fuel; the difference in value cannot be claimed in court.

126 The passive formulation in the Mishnah invites this interpretation.

127 *Bekhorot* 4:4. The Mishnah is part of R. Yudan's argument since it states that if a person who is not duly ordained exercizes the function of a rabbi or judge, he is personally responsible for any damage he causes by a wrong decision. In the Babli, 53b, the same argument is made by Rav Papa.

128 The obligation to pay in this case is not by the declaration that

something is impure, but by the act of the incompetent judge who handles the material in question when he declares it impure. Since a person can make impure only by an action, either touching or moving, he equally will be responsible under the laws of torts.

129 It is obvious that "free" and "obligated" have to be interchanged. Since the prior argument showed that causing impurity is causing damage under the laws of torts, the person causing unintentional impurity should have to pay. The reason that courts refrain from applying the rules of torts in this case is that the damage is not visible and, in order to guard the owner of the impure food and others from unintentional sin, it is necessary to induce the person causing the damage to come forward and tell by granting him immunity.

130 Here also, it is obvious that "free" and "obligated" have to be interchanged. Since the damage cannot be detected, it cannot be claimed in court. The obligation to pay is not derived from the laws of torts but is a regulation "for the public good" in line with the other rules of this chapter.

131 In the times of the Temple, a red (probably meaning reddish-brown) cow without any black hair was worth millions (as material for the purification from the impurity of the dead, *Num.* 19) provided it never was used for work and never wore a yoke. Putting a yoke on such a cow for the shortest of times robs its owner of an enormous sum of money but, since the damage is not visible, it is not claimable in a human court. This follows the doctrine of R. Johanan that damages which cannot be observed on the object cannot be claimed in court.

(47a line 42) עַד כְּדוֹן כְּסָבוּר שֶׁהוּא חוּלִין. הָיָה יוֹדֵעַ בָּהּ שֶׁהִיא תְרוּמָה וּכְסָבוּר שֶׁמּוּתָּר לְטַמּוֹתָהּ. נִשְׁמְעִינָהּ מִן הָדָא. הַכֹּהֲנִים שֶׁפִּיגְּלוּ בַּמִּקְדָּשׁ מְזִידִין חַיָּיבִין. מָה אֲנָן קַיָּימִין. אִם כְּסָבוּר כֹּהֵן שֶׁהוּא חוּלִין. וְיֵשׁ פִּיגּוּל בְּחוּלִין. אֶלָּא כֵן אֲנָן קַיָּימִין בְּיוֹדֵעַ בָּהֶן שֶׁהֵן קוֹדֶשׁ. וְסָבוּר לוֹמַר שֶׁמּוּתָּר לְפַגֵּל בַּקּוֹדֶשׁ. וְהָכָא בְּיוֹדֵעַ שֶׁהִיא תְרוּמָה וְסָבוּר לוֹמַר שֶׁמּוּתָּר לְטַמּוֹתָהּ.

So far if he thought that it was profane[132]. If he knew that it was heave but he thought that it was permitted to make it impure? Let us hear from the following: "If Cohanim in the Temple intentionally made [a sacrifice] *piggul*, they have to pay.[133]" Could the Cohen think that it was profane? Is there *piggul* of profane things? But we must hold that he knew that it was holy but thought that it was permitted to make *piggul* of sacrifices. And here, if he knew that it was heave but thought that it was permitted to make it impure.

132 This refers to the statement in the Mishnah that the person who inadvertently causes damage by making food impure does not have to pay. The only food where there would be a measurable diminution in value is sanctified food, of which heave is the most common example.

133 Since the Mishnah does not state that "the Cohanim who cause *piggul* in the Temple have to pay", it follows that there must be a scenario in which a Cohen could cause *piggul* inadvertently.

(47a line 47) רַב הוּנָא בְּשֵׁם רַב. בַּתְּחִילָּה וְהוּא נִיסֵּךְ וְעִירְבְּבָהּ. וְהוּא שֶׁעִירֵב. חַייָב מִיתָה וְלַבְּסוֹף בַּתַּשְׁלוּמִין. הָתִיב רִבִּי אַבָּא. הַגַּע עַצְמָךְ שֶׁהָרַג אֶת הַנֶּפֶשׁ וְשִׁיבֵּר אֶת הַצְּלוֹחִית. כַּתְּחִילָּה הוּא חַייָב מִיתָה וְלַבְּסוֹף בַּתַּשְׁלוּמִין. מָתִיב רִבִּי יוֹסֵי. הַגַּע עַצְמָךְ שֶׁהְדְלִיק גְּדִישׁוֹ שֶׁלַּחֲבֵירוֹ בְּיוֹם הַכִּיפּוּרִים. בַּתְּחִילָּה הוּא חַייָב מִיתָה וְלַבְּסוֹף בַּתַּשְׁלוּמִין. הַמְטַמֵּא וְהַמְדַמֵּעַ וְהַמְנַסֵּךְ בְּשׁוֹגֵג פָּטוּר. בְּמֵזִיד חַייָב. וְאָמַר רִבִּי יוֹחָנָן. מִשּׁוּם קְנָס.

Rav Huna in the name of Rav: If he mixed[134]. If he made a libation and then mixed it[135], at the start he committed a capital crime and at the end he has to pay[136]? Rebbi Abba objected: Think of it, if he killed somebody and broke the flask, at the start he committed a capital crime and in the end he has to pay[137]? Rebbi Yose objected: Think of it, if he set fire to somebody's grain stack on the Day of Atonement, at the start he committed a capital crime and in the end he has to pay[138]? "If someone causes anything to become impure, or turn into *dema'*, or libation wine, if it was unintentional he is free, intentional he is obligated," and Rebbi Johanan said, he pays a fine[139].

134 He took wine which was used for a pagan rite and is forbidden for any use by a Jew, and mixed it with permitted wine of the same kind, so that the damage was not visible. In the Babli, 52a, this interpretation of "libation wine" in the Mishnah is attributed to Samuel.

135 In the Babli, this is the interpretation of Rav.

136 Since rabbinic doctrine excludes multiple punishment for one offense (cf. *Terumot* 7:1, Notes 19-70) and idolatry is a capital crime, it seems difficult to understand why the culprit should pay. The Babli, 52b, notes that the argument is faulty in its understanding of the double penalty clause. The libation and the later mixing are two different acts. Even if there is only a libation, not followed by mixing with other wine, the libation can only be performed after the wine was poured into a vessel and the vessel lifted. Since we are speaking of wine belonging to a person other than the perpetrator, the latter becomes liable for all damages by lifting the vessel, some time before he commits the capital crime. It is clear, therefore, that the Yerushalmi view of the double punishment clause does not allow for splitting one action into separate parts.

137 If somebody committed murder by administering poison in another person's flask and in the act broke the flask, nobody will require the murderer to pay for the flask.

138 Everything forbidden on the Sabbath is forbidden on the Day of Atonement (except that the crime will be punished by Heaven, rather than by the earthly court.) Since both making a fire and arson on the Day of Atonement are crimes punishable by Divine extirpation, no money is due (cf. *Terumot* 7:1, Note 62.)

139 Since the payment is a fine, not a judgment following biblical law, the principle of single punishment does not apply. This argument is mentioned in the Babli, 53a.

(fol. 46b) **משנה ה:** הֵעִיד רַבִּי יוֹחָנָן בֶּן גּוּדְגְּדָה עַל הַחֵרֶשֶׁת שֶׁהִשִּׂיאָהּ אָבִיהָ שֶׁהִיא יוֹצְאָה בְגֵט וְעַל קְטַנָּה בַת יִשְׂרָאֵל שֶׁנִּישֵּׂאת לַכֹּהֵן שֶׁאוֹכֶלֶת בַּתְּרוּמָה וְאִם מֵתָה בַּעֲלָהּ יוֹרְשָׁהּ וְעַל הַמָּרִישׁ הַגָּזוּל שֶׁבְּנָאוֹ בַבִּירָה שֶׁיִּטּוֹל אֶת דָּמָיו וְעַל הַחַטָּאת הַגְּזוּלָה שֶׁלֹּא נוֹדְעָה לָרַבִּים שֶׁהִיא מְכַפֶּרֶת מִפְּנֵי תִיקּוּן הַמִּזְבֵּחַ.

Mishnah 5: Rebbi Johanan ben Gudguedah testified about a deaf-mute girl[140] who was married off by her father, that she must be divorced by a bill of divorce[141], and about an underage girl who was married to a Cohen[142], that she may eat heave and her husband inherits from her if she dies, and about a stolen log which was used to build a house[143], that [the owner] has to take the value[144], and about a purification sacrifice of a stolen animal[145] which was not known in public, that it atones because of the order of the altar.

140 She is presumed not to be able to read and write. Since she has no means of communication with the outside world, she is incompetent in law. She herself could not conclude a marriage valid by biblical standards, but her father can marry her off when underage in a biblically valid marriage. Cf. *Yebamot*, Mishnah 14:3, Notes 20-24.

"Testified" usually means a statement of practice from Temple times accepted by the Jabneh Academy as binding.

141 Since a divorce is a unilateral act by the husband as long as she is able to receive the bill. An insane woman, who cannot keep her bill of divorce, cannot be divorced.

142 Even if the father had died and she was married in a rabbinically valid marriage by her mother or brothers, from which she may walk out without formality before she reaches adulthood (cf. *Yebamot* 1:2, Note 38).

143 In Babylonian versions of the Mishnah, it is added "for the benefit of repentant sinners", as explained in the Halakhah.

144 He cannot sue the robber for restitution of the original log.

145 It is a sinful act to use any stolen or robbed animal as a sacrifice. If such a sacrifice would be declared invalid, no Cohen would volunteer to

serve in the Temple for fear of unwittingly committing the sin of eating from an invalid sacrifice.

Therefore, a sacrifice can be rejected only if it is known that it was obtained by illegal means.

(47a line 53) **הלכה ה:** הֵעִיד רבִּי יוֹחָנָן בֶּן גּוּדְגְּדָה כול׳. רִבִּי חֲנִינָה בָּעֵי קוֹמֵי רבִּי אִימִּי. נִרְאִין דְּבָרָיו בְּפִיקַחַת שֶׁיֶּשׁ לָהּ דַּעַת שֶׁהִיא יוֹצֵא בֵּין לְדַעַת בֵּין שֶׁלֹא לְדַעַת. וְחֵרֶשֶׁת שֶׁאֵין לָהּ דַּעַת לֹא תֵצֵא אֶלָּא לְדַעַת. וְלֹא עֵדוּת הִיא. אַף אָבִיו כַּיּוֹצֵא בָהּ. וּמוֹסִיפִין עַל הָעֵדוּת. רבִּי חֲנִינָה סָבַר. בְּפִיקַחַת שֶׁהִשִּׂיאָהּ אָבִיהָ וְאִמָּהּ. רַבִּי יוֹסֵי סָבַר מֵימַר בִּקְטַנָּה שֶׁהִשִּׂיאָהּ אָבִיהָ וְאִמָּהּ וְנִתְגָּרְשָׁה.

1 חנינה ׀ חנניה   בעי ׀ בעא   2 אימי ׀ הילא   דבריו ׀ הדברים   לה ׀ בה
יוצא ׀ יוצאה   3 לה ׀ בה   עדות ׀ עידות   אביו ׀ זו   4 ר׳ חנינה ׀ ור׳ חנניה
סבר ׀ סבר מימר   אביה ואמה ׀ אביה ונתחרשה   5 יוסי ׀ יוסה   אביה ואמה ׀ אביה

Halakhah 5: [146]"Rebbi Johanan ben Guedgedah testified," etc. Rebbi Hananiah asked before Rebbi Immi. His testimony seems reasonable for a hearing woman of sound mind, that she is divorced with or without her acquiescence. But a deaf-mute woman who has no will should not be divorced except with her acquiescence. But is it not testimony "that is an example"[147]; does one add to a testimony? Rebbi Hanania is of the opinion that this refers to a hearing girl who was married off by her father (and mother[148]) and became deaf-and-dumb. Rebbi Yose is of the opinion that this refers to an underage girl who was married off by her father (and mother[148]) and became divorced.

146 This paragraph is from *Yebamot* 14:2, Notes 25-28. The readings from there are noted ׳.

147 This is the text from *Yebamot*. The text here, "his father is the same", does not make any sense; it indicates that the text in *Yebamot* is original.

148 The mention of the mother is an addition here; legally the mother has no authority over her daughter.

(47a line 58) אָמַר רִבִּי יוֹחָנָן. מַה טַעַם אָמְרוּ. קְטַנָּה בַּת יִשְׂרָאֵל אוֹכֶלֶת בַּתְּרוּמָה. מִפְּנֵי שֶׁיְּהוּ הַכֹּל קוֹפְצִים עָלֶיהָ לִישָׂא מִפְּנֵי חִינָּה. אָמַר רִבִּי שַׁמַּי. וְהוּא שֶׁתְּהֵא יוֹדַעַת לִשְׁמוֹר קִידּוּשִׁין. אָמַר רִבִּי אִימִּי. מַתְנִיתָא אָמְרָה כֵן. נִישֵּׂאת לַכֹּהֵן תֹּאכַל בַּתְּרוּמָה. אָמַר רִבִּי חֲנַנְיָה. מִן מַה דְּאָמַר רִבִּי יוֹחָנָן מִפְּנֵי חִינָּה. הָדָא אָמְרָה. אֲפִילוּ לֹא יוֹדַעַת לִשְׁמוֹר קִידּוּשֶׁיהָ.

Rebbi Johanan said, why did they say "an Israel underage girl eats heave," that all should be eager to marry her for her attractiveness[149]. Rebbi Shammai said, only if she knows how to keep her [valuables given for] preliminary marriage[150]. Rebbi Immi said, a Mishnah said so, "married to a Cohen she eats heave.[151]" Rebbi Hananiah said, since Rebbi Johanan said, for her attractiveness, that means, even if she does not know how to keep her [valuables given for] preliminary marriage[152].

149   And not be reluctant to take a very young girl off her parent's hands.

150   He wants to abolish the theoretical age of 3 years and one day for the marriage of girls and requires that she know the difference between something given for a legal obligation and a toy.

151   Since the Mishnah changes the topic from a deaf-mute to a minor it implies that only an Israel underage girl, which will reach understanding, but not a deaf-mute, is able to eat heave. It follows that as long as the girl is like a deaf-mute, having no understanding, she is not included. (A similar Mishnah, *Niddah* 5:4, speaking of a girl 3 years and 1 day old, could be used as counter-argument since such a girl, if married off by her father, is married even if mentally handicapped.)

152   R. Johanan could have said that a minor can eat heave because she has understanding, to emphasize the difference between the minor and the deaf-mute. Since he chose to represent the ruling as rabbinical, to help marrying off underage girls, it follows that he does not require the girl to understand the situation. If the girl is given in marriage by her father, she is married by biblical rule, is part of the priestly clan, and eats heave by biblical law. If she was an orphan married off

by her mother or brothers, if she actually lives with her husband she is part of her husband's household and was acquired by his gift of valuables (*Lev.* 22:11).

(47a line 63) רַב הַמְנוּנָא בְּשֵׁם רִבִּי אַסִי. קְטַנָּה אֵין לָהּ חוּפָּה שֶׁתֹּאכַל בַּתְּרוּמָה. אָמַר רִבִּי אִמִּי. מַתְנִיתָא אָמְרָה כֵן. נִישֵּׂאת לַכֹּהֵן תֹּאכַל בַּתְּרוּמָה. רִבִּי אָבִין בָּעֵי. בְּשֶׁנִּכְנְסָה לַחוּפָּה וְלֹא נִבְעֲלָה וּשְׁלָחָהּ לְבֵית אָבִיהָ וְהִגְדִּילָה. מָהוּ שֶׁתֹּאכַל בַּתְּרוּמָה. נִשְׁמְעִינָהּ מִן הָדָא. עַל גַּב חוּפָּתָהּ הָרִאשׁוֹנָה.

Rav Hamnuna in the name of Rebbi[153] Assi: An underage girl has no definitive marriage to let her eat heave[154]. Rebbi Immi said, a Mishnah said so, "married to a Cohen she eats heave.[155]" Rebbi Abin asked: If she was definitively married but had no intercourse, [the husband] sent her to her father's house and she grew up, may she eat heave[156]? Let us hear from the following: "Based on her earlier definitive marriage.[157]"

153 In the Babli, he always is called Rav Assi.

154 An underage Israel girl married to a Cohen acquires the right to eat heave only by living with her husband, not by the definitive marriage ceremony.

155 *Niddah* 5:4. The Mishnah does not say "by definitive marriage ceremony" but "being married to", i.e., living with her husband.

156 Since an adult married to a Cohen can eat heave immediately, during the wedding meal, before sleeping with her husband.

157 There is a *baraita*, not otherwise attested to, which does not require any additional action to give all her rights to the adult married woman. The Babli (*Yebamot* 58a) quotes dissenting opinions without deciding the matter.

(47a line 67) גָּזַל מָרִישׁ וּבְנָאוֹ בַּבִּירָה. בֵּית שַׁמַּאי אוֹמְרִים. יְקַעְקֵעַ כָּל־הַבִּירָה וְיִתְּנֶנּוּ לוֹ. וּבֵית הִלֵּל אוֹמְרִים. נוֹתֵן לוֹ דָּמָיו בְּשָׁוְויוֹ מִפְּנֵי תַּקָּנַת הַשָּׁבִין. אָמַר רִבִּי לָעְזָר. מַה פְּלִיגִין. בְּשֶׁגְּזָלוֹ מְשׁוּפָּה. אֲבָל אִם גְּזָלוֹ וְשִׁיפָּהוּ דָּמִים הוּא חַיָּיב

לוֹ. גְּזָלוֹ וְשִׁיפָּהוּ עַל גַּב מְקוֹמוֹ מַהוּ. נִישְׁמְעִינָהּ מִן הָדָא. הַיּוֹרֵד לְתוֹךְ חוּרְבָּה שֶׁלַחֲבֵירוֹ וּבְנָיָיהּ שֶׁלֹּא בִּרְשׁוּת שָׁמִין לוֹ וְיָדוֹ עַל הַתַּחְתּוֹנָה. בִּיקֵּשׁ לִיטוֹל עֵצָיו וַאֲבָנָיו אֵין שׁוֹמְעִין לוֹ. רִבִּי יַעֲקֹב בַּר אָחָא בְּשֵׁם רִבִּי יְהוֹשֻׁעַ בֶּן לֵוִי מִשּׁוּם רַב נַחְמָן בַּר יַעֲקֹב בָּעֵי. אִילּוּ הַפּוֹרֵק חֲבִילָתוֹ לְתוֹךְ חוּרְבָּתוֹ שֶׁלַחֲבֵירוֹ וְהָלַךְ לִיטְּלָה שֶׁמָּא אֵין שׁוֹמְעִין לוֹ. וְלֹא שְׁמִיעַ דְּאָמַר רִבִּי יַעֲקֹב בַּר אִידֵי מִשּׁוּם רִבִּי יְהוֹשֻׁעַ בֶּן לֵוִי. מִשּׁוּם יִישּׁוּב. יָאוּת אָמַר רִבִּי יוֹסֵי. הֲוִינָא סָבַר מֵימַר. מַה פְּלִיגִין. בָּאָרֶץ. אֲבָל בְּחוּצָה לָאָרֶץ לֹא. מִן מַה דְּאָמַר רִבִּי יַעֲקֹב בַּר אָחָא מִשּׁוּם יִישּׁוּב. הָדָא אֲמָרָה. הִיא בָּאָרֶץ הִיא בְחוּצָה לָאָרֶץ. בִּיקֵּשׁ לִיטוֹל עֵצָיו וַאֲבָנָיו מָהוּ. אוֹמְרִים לוֹ. הַמְתֵּן עַד שֶׁיִדּוֹר בְּתוֹכָהּ. וּשְׁמוּאֵל אָמַר. נוֹתְנִין לוֹ מִיָּד.

"If somebody stole a log and used it in building. The House of Shammai say, he has to tear down the entire building and return it. But the House of Hillel say, for the benefit of repenting sinners[158], that he has to pay its full value." Rebbi Eleazar said, where do they disagree? If he stole it planed, but if he stole and planed it himself, he owes him money[159]. If he stole and planed it on the spot[160], what is the rule? Let us hear from the following[161]: "If somebody appropriates another person's ruin and rebuilds it without prermission, one appraises it and his hand is weak[162]. If he wants to take his logs and stones[163], one does not listen to him." Rebbi Jacob bar Aḥa in the name of Rebbi Joshua ben Levi: It was asked in the name of Rav Naḥman bar Jacob: If somebody stores his bundle in somebody else's ruin and wants to take it from there, does one not listen to him? He had not heard that Rebbi Jacob bar Idi[164] said in the name of Rebbi Joshua ben Levi: Because of civilisation[165]. Rebbi Yose said, this is correct. We would have thought that they disagree only in the Land, but not outside the Land. Since Rebbi Jacob bar Aḥa said, because of civilisation[166], this implies that there is no difference between the Land

and outside the Land. If he[167] wants to take [the value of] his logs and stones, what is the rule? One tells him, wait until he[168] dwells in it. Samuel said, one pays him immediately.

158 Quoted in *Baba Qama* 9:1, Tosephta *Baba Qama* 10:5, Babli *Giṭṭin* 55a.

159 If he stole a piece of raw wood and turned it into building material, it cannot be returned to its original state. The robber acquired ownership of the material by changing it into something new; at the same time he incurred a debt to the original owner in the value of what he had taken (Mishnah *Baba Qama* 9:2).

160 Does acquisition by changing the object require removing it from the domain of the original owner?

161 Tosephta *Ketubot* 8:10, *Baba Qama* 10:6,7; Yerushalmi *Baba Qama* 9:1 (6d l.28); as an object of controversy Babli *Baba Meṣi'a* 101a.

162 As explained in the Tosephta, the owner of the bundle pays the builder the smaller amount either of the increase in value of his land and the building expenses.

163 Which already form part of the building.

164 This should be "Aha".

165 One does not destroy houses except for an urgent need, either to avoid a collapse or to improve the housing stock. The question (Note 160) is answered in the negative.

166 The formulation is universal יָשׁוּב "civilization", not narrow יִשּׁוּב אֶרֶץ יִשְׂרָאֵל "settlement of the Land of Israel".

167 The illegal builder.

168 The owner of the land.

(47b line 4) עוּלָא בַּר יִשְׁמָעֵאל. בְּדִין הֲוָה אֲפִילוּ [ ] נוֹדְעָה לָרַבִּים לֹא תְכַפֵּר. לָמָה אָמְרוּ תְכַפֵּר. שֶׁלֹּא יְהֵא הַמִּזְבֵּחַ שָׁמֵם. רֵישׁ לָקִישׁ אָמַר. בְּדִין הֲוָה אֲפִילוּ נוֹדְעָה לָרַבִּים תְכַפֵּר. לָמָה אָמְרוּ לֹא תְכַפֵּר. שֶׁלֹּא יְהֵא מִזְבֵּחַ מְקַבֵּל גְּזֵילוֹת. וְכַמָּה הֵם רַבִּים. רִבִּי גּוּרְיוֹן בְּשֵׁם רֵישׁ לָקִישׁ. שְׁלֹשָׁה בְּנֵי אָדָם. רִבִּי אָבִין בְּשֵׁם רִבִּי יוֹחָנָן. וַהֲבֵאתֶם גָּזוּל אֶת הַפִּסֵּחַ וְאֶת הַחוֹלֶה. מַה פִּסֵּחַ וְחוֹלֶה בְּגָלוּי אַף כֹּל בְּגָלוּי.

Ulla bar Ismael: By law, it should not atone even if it was [not] known in public[169]. Why did they say that it atones? Not to let the altar be deserted[145]. Rebbi Simeon ben Laqish[170] said, by law, it should atone even if it was known in public. Why did they say that it does not atone? Not to let the altar accept robberies. How many are "public"? Rebbi Gorion in the name of Rebbi Simeon ben Laqish: Three people. Rebbi Abin in the name of Rebbi Johanan: "You brought robbed goods with the lame and the sick.[171]" Since lame and sick are obvious, so everything must be obvious.

169 Babli 55a. There, Ulla explains that the sacrifice is not acceptable once the original owners have given up hope of recovery, since while abandonment makes a thing ownerless (Chapter 4, Note 88), ownership requires a conscious act of acquisition by the person in actual possession..

170 In the Babli this is attributed to Rav Jehudah and it is explained that abandonment by the former owner makes the object the property of the person in possession.

171 *Mal.* 1:13.

(fol. 46b) **משנה ו:** לֹא הָיָה סִיקָרִיקִין בִּיהוּדָה בַּהֲרוּגֵי הַמִּלְחָמָה. מֵהֲרוּגֵי הַמִּלְחָמָה וְאֵילָךְ יֵשׁ בָּהּ סִיקָרִיקִין. כֵּיצַד. לָקַח מִסִּיקָרִיקִין וְחָזַר וְלָקַח מִבַּעַל הַבַּיִת מִקְחוֹ בָּטֵל. מִבַּעַל הַבַּיִת וְחָזַר וְלָקַח מִסִּיקָרִיקִין מִקְחוֹ קַיָּים. לָקַח מִן הָאִישׁ וְחָזַר וְלָקַח מִן הָאִשָּׁה מִקְחוֹ בָּטֵל מִן הָאִשָּׁה וְחָזַר וְלָקַח מִן הָאִישׁ מִקְחוֹ קַיָּים. זוֹ מִשְׁנָה רִאשׁוֹנָה. בֵּית דִּין שֶׁלְּאַחֲרֵיהֶן אָמְרוּ נוֹתֵן לַבְּעָלִים רְבִיעַ.

Mishnah 6: There was no law of *siqarii*[172] in Judea for those killed in the war[173]. After those killed in the war there was a law of *siqarii*. How is this? If one bought from a *siqarius* and afterwards from the original owner, his acquisition is void[174]; from the original owner and afterwards from the *siqarius*, his acquisition is valid. If one bought from a husband and afterwards from the wife, his acquisition is void[175]; from the wife and afterwards from the husband, his acquisition is valid. This is the earlier Mishnah; a later court said that he who buys from a *siqarius*[176] gives a quarter to the original owner.

משנה ז: אֵימָתַי. בִּזְמַן שֶׁאֵין בְּיָדָן לִיקַח אֲבָל יֵשׁ בְּיָדָן לִיקַח הֵן קוֹדְמִין לְכָל־אָדָם. רִבִּי יְהוֹשֻׁעַ הוֹשִׁיב בֵּית דִּין וְנִמְנוּ שֶׁאִם שָׁהֲתָה בִּפְנֵי הַסִּיקָרִיקִין שְׁנֵים עָשָׂר חוֹדֶשׁ כָּל־הַקּוֹדֵם לִיקַח יִקַּח וְנוֹתֵן לַבְּעָלִים רְבִיעַ.

Mishnah 7: When is this? If they have no means to buy, but if they have the means to buy, they precede everybody else[177]. Rebbi (Joshua) assembled a court who voted that if it was in the *siqarius*'s hand for twelve months, any who wants to buy shall buy[178] and give a quarter to the original owner.

172 סִיקָרִיקִין or סְקָרִיקוֹן (in the Halakhah and everywhere in the Babli) is usually interpreted to refer both to *sicarii* (members of organized crime bands armed with a *sica*, "curved dagger", and the rules promulgated to deal with these.

A. Gulak [*Siqariqon*, Tarbiz 5 (1934) pp. 23-27] objects to the derivation of *siqariqon* from *sicarii* since it is inconceivable that Rebbi's court, in the early years of the third Century C.E. had to deal with the aftermath of the first revolt against the Romans, in the first half of the first Century. He proposes to see in the word a compression of σὺν κήρυκι to *συγκηρυκι "by herold" referring to the public sale of properties confiscated by the government which always was done by publicly announced auction. [While the Babli clearly connects the law of *siqariqon* with the first revolt against the Romans, the Yerushalmi squarely refers it to the revolt of Bar Kokhba. We know of no general confiscation of Jewish land after the first revolt; after the second there was at least the seizure of all Jewish property in and around Jerusalem. Since both Talmudim emphasize the cordial relations of Rebbi with the administration of the Severan dynasty and Rebbi clearly addressed a current problem, it seems rather that the law refers to a problem arising from a breakdown of internal security. Talmudic law certainly authorizes buying of property confiscated for nonpayment of taxes. Gulak's interpretation is difficult to square with Mishnah *Bikkurim* 1:2.}

A forced sale is intrinsically invalid since the seller can hope that in the future, when law and order are re-established, he may have a chance to appeal to a court and regain his property. But if a band of known *sicarii* give a property owner the choice of selling his land for a pittance or be killed together with his family, one may assume that he willingly gives the land to stay alive. In that situation, the land becomes the *siqarii*'s not only in possession but also in ownership, and may be sold by the current owner to any buyer. It is a matter of judgment of the court as to which situation does apply.

173 "The war" refers to the revolt of Bar Kokhba and its aftermath, as shown by the parallel in *Ketubot* to the first sentences in the Halakhah. S. Lieberman (*Tosefta kiFshutah Gittin* p. 844) has noted that the reading "R. Joshua" in Mishnah 7 is clearly a scribal error since Rav, a student of Rebbi, states both in the Yerushalmi (Note 205) and the Babli (58b/59a) that he himself was a member of the court relaxing the *siqariqon* rules. Also, the Halakhah never refers to R. Joshua or any of his contemporaries. Therefore, one has to read in the Mishnah, with all sources other than the Mishnah in the Yerushalmi, "Rebbi assembled a court" in the first quarter of the third Century, to deal with the problem of organized crime in his own day. Together with the rules about kidnappings, this shows that the forces of the Roman Empire (at least starting with the Severan dynasty) were barely able to guarantee the external, but not the internal, security of the Empire.

The Mishnah states that land taken from Jews during the war can be bought by anybody who has the means, without regard to any prior owner. (In this case, *sicarii* is a code name for Roman soldiers.) The Babli connects the Mishnah to a long string of tales about the first war against the Romans; this should not be taken as indication that the Mishnah refers to that war.

174 It was decided that the original owner retains claim to title even though he probably sold the land to save his life. Therefore, a potential buyer must first buy the right to title before buying the land.

175 The husband is not the owner of his wife's (paraphernalia) properties, but their administrator. While the details of the sale must be contracted by the husband, prior consent of the wife is needed; otherwise, the husband is not authorized to deal and anything he agrees to is illegal.

176 Without needing prior consent. This is a regulation "for the public good", to retain as much of the Land as possible in Jewish hands.

177 If the original owner has the cash available, he can pay the full price to the buyer and take back his title to the land.

178 After 12 months, the original owner lost his right to regain the land.

(47b line 10) **הלכה ו:** לֹא הָיָה סִיקָרִיקוֹן בִּיהוּדָה כֹּל׳. בָּרִאשׁוֹנָה גָּזְרוּ שְׁמָד עַל יְהוּדָה. שֶׁכֵּן מְסוֹרֶת בְּיָדָם מֵאֲבוֹתָם. יְהוּדָה הָרַג אֶת עֵשָׂיו. דִּכְתִיב יָדְךָ בְּעוֹרֶף אוֹיְבֶיךָ. וְהָיוּ הוֹלְכִין וּמְשַׁעְבְּדִין בָּהֶן וְנוֹטְלִין שְׂדוֹתֵיהֶן וּמוֹכְרִין אוֹתָן לַאֲחֵרִים. וְהָיוּ בַעֲלֵי בָתִּים בָּאִין וְטוֹרְפִין וְהָיְתָה הָאָרֶץ חֲלוּטָה בְּיַד סִיקָרִיקוֹן. נִמְנְעוּ מִלִּיקַח. הִתְקִינוּ שֶׁלֹּא יְהֵא סִיקָרִיקוֹן בִּיהוּדָה. בַּמֶּה דְּבָרִים אֲמוּרִים. בַּהֲרוּגֵי הַמִּלְחָמָה לִפְנֵי הַמִּלְחָמָה. אֲבָל הֲרוּגִים שֶׁנֶּהֶרְגוּ מִן הַמִּלְחָמָה וְהֵילַךְ אֵין בָּהֶן מִשּׁוּם סִיקָרִיקוֹן. וַהֲרוּגִים שֶׁלִּפְנֵי הַמִּלְחָמָה לֹא כְּלְאַחַר הַמִּלְחָמָה הֵן. תִּיפְּתָר שֶׁבָּא סִיקָרִיקוֹן וְגָזַל וְחָמַס. לֹא הִסְפִּיק תָּרְפוּ עַד שֶׁבָּא סִיקָרִיקוֹן לְכָל־הָעוֹלָם. שֶׁלֹּא תְּהֵא הֲלָכָה לְמֶחֱצָה.

2 על יהודה | **ב** ביהודה   בידם | **ב** להם   יהודה | **ב** שיהודה

Halakhah 5: "There was no law of *siqariqon* in Judea" etc. 179In earlier times they decided on a persecution in Judea because they had a tradition from their forefathers that Jehudah had killed Esaw, as it is written: "Your hand is on your enemies' neck." They went and enslaved them, took their fields and sold them to third parties. The original owners could come and repossess180; therefore the land was left absolutely in the hand of the *siqariqon* since they refrained from buying[181]. "They decreed that the law of *siqariqon* should not apply in Jehudah[182]. When was this said? About war killings before the war[183]. But about anybody killed in and after the war, the notion of *siqariqon* does not apply[184]." But are those killed before the war not like those killed after the war? Explain it that a *siqariqon* came and robbed and suppressed; there was no time left to write the sales contract before murder engulfed the entire world, that practice should not be partial[185].

179 This sentence and part of the next is also in *Ketubot* 1:5 (Notes 196-199). Variants are given by ב.

180 After the Jewish court system was reestablished under R. Jehudah.

181 As long as the court held that a forced sale was invalid.

182 Nobody had the right to reclaim from third parties land he had given away to save his life.

183 In the anarchy between the begin of the revolt and the occupation of the Land by Roman forces.

184 In Tosephta 3:10: "But about anybody killed in and after the war, the notion of *siqariqon* applies." The Yerushalmi text should *not* be corrected based on Tosephta or Babli. Since one refers to the war of Bar Kokhba and the Hadrianic decrees in its aftermath, it is clear that the situation during and after the war was worse than before the war. One does not speak of a forced sale but of the rights of the heirs of a person who was killed and his land taken by Roman soldiers or civilians. It is clear that there was no sale. Since the greater part of the Jewish population of Judea was either killed in the war or deported as slaves, it made no sense for the organizers of the survivors to take notice of prior ownership. One has to assume that "Judea" means the Judean hills, to exclude the settlements in the plain centered around Lydda.

185 Robberies during the anarchy before the Roman invasion cannot be separated from what happened during the war; in both cases no documentation can be recovered.

(47b line 20) גָּלִיל לְעוֹלָם יֵשׁ בּוֹ מִשּׁוּם סִיקָרִיקוֹן. הַמְטַלְטְלִין אֵין בָּהֶן מִשּׁוּם סִיקָרִיקוֹן. תַּנֵּי. חֲכִירֵי בָתֵּי אָבוֹת אֵין בָּהֶן מִשּׁוּם סִיקָרִיקוֹן. הַיּוֹרֵד מִשֵּׁם חוֹב וּמִשֵּׁם אֲנָפָרוֹת אֵין בָּהֶן מִשּׁוּם סִיקָרִיקוֹן. אֲנָפָרוֹת עַצְמָהּ מַמְתֶּנֶת לַבְּעָלִים שְׁנֵים עָשָׂר חוֹדֶשׁ. אָמַר רִבִּי יוּדָה בֶּן פָּזִי. מַכְרִיזִין וְהוֹלְכִין אַרְבַּע שַׁבָּתוֹת לְאַחַר שְׁנֵים עָשָׂר חוֹדֶשׁ. פָּתַר לָהּ תְּרֵין פִּתְרִין. נְסָבָהּ מִן חָכוֹר וִיַיבָהּ לְחָכוֹר. אָתָא בְעָא מִיטְרַף. אָמַר לֵיהּ. וְלָאו חָכוֹר אַתְּ. שְׁבוֹק לִי. וּמָה דְּאַתְּ גָּזֵי גְּזֵי. נְסָבָהּ מִבַּעַל הַבַּיִת וִיַיבָהּ לְחָכוֹר. אָתָא בָעֵי מִיטְרוֹף. אָמַר לֵיהּ. מָה הֲנָייָה לָהּ דְּאַתְּ מְסִיבְנָא מִינֵּיהּ וְהוּא מְנַסְבָא מִינָּךְ. אֶלָּא מַה דְּאִית לִי בְּחַיֵּילִי אֲנָא יְהִיב לָךְ.

"The law of *siqariqon* always applies in Galilee.[186]" The law of *siqariqon* does not apply to movables[187]. It was stated[188]: "The law of *siqariqon* does not apply to foreclosures for a debt[189] and for tenant fees[190]. [A foreclosure for nonpayment of] tenant fees waits twelve months for the owners[191]." Rebbi Judah ben Pazi said, after twelve months one announces on four consecutive Sabbaths[192]. He explained it in two ways. If he[193] took it from a tenant and gave it to a tenant and the first wants to foreclose, he says to him, are you not a tenant? Leave it for me and what you cut, you cut[194]. If he[195] took it from the owner and gave it to a tenant, the [owner] wants to foreclose, he tells him, what use do you have if you take it from me and he will take it from you, but what I can afford I shall give to you.

186 Tosephta 3:10. In Galilee, the Hadrianic decrees were never applied to dispossess Jewish farmers.

187 If one buys movables from an organized crime enterprise, one does not have to give anything to the former owners since these had given up hope to recover (cf. Note 169).

188 Tosephta 3:10.

189 If a Gentile forecloses for a loan, the Jewish buyer does not owe anything to a former Jewish owner.

190 A. Gulak has shown that ἀναφορά ("offering, installment, means of repairing a deficiency") was the equivalent of Roman *vectigal*, the fee due by hereditary farmers of government land (cf. *Ketubot* 10:5, Note 91; *Tosefta kiFshutah Gittin* p. 846). The Babli, 58a, treats ἀναφορά as robbery. It is not clear whether the term was also used for fees payable by hereditary tenants to landlords other than the government.

191 If a hereditary tenant is evicted for non-payment of the *vectigal*, a Jewish farmer cannot apply to fill his place before 12 months after his eviction, to give the original tenant time to settle with the government. {The text is confirmed by *Sefer ha'Ittur* II, 68b; the explanation follows S. Lieberman in his commentary to Tosephta 3:11.}

192 After twelve months, there will be public anouncements that the twelve months' grace period for the property (either one taken by organized crime or foreclosed for non-payment of the tax) has expired without action by the former owner.

193 The *sicarius* did not sell the property but installed a tenant farmer to produce a continuous stream of income.

194 Since the *sicarii* are not interested in selling, the original tenant cannot bid for the property. But during the 12 months accorded to him, he can offer the new tenant (who moved in in violation of the 12 months' rule) not to sue him in rabbinic court, to enter the property under the terms accorded by the *siqariqon*, and let the new tenant keep any yield he already had reaped.

195 A similar situation in which the *sicarii* are not interested in selling, exists where the new tenant can arrange with the original owner to stay in place if and when he manages either to buy from the organized crime group or to recoup his title with government help.

(47b line 29) עַד כְּדוֹן בִּשְׁתֵּי שְׁטָרוֹת. הָיָה שְׁטָר אֶחָד. רִבִּי זְעִירָא וְרִבִּי אִילָא תְּרֵיהוֹן אָמְרִין. כָּל־שֶׁכֵּן מִקְחוֹ בָטֵל. וְהוּא שֶׁלָּקַח מִן הָאִשָּׁה וְחָזַר וְלָקַח מִן הָאִישׁ. רִבִּי חֲנִינָה וְרִבִּי בִּיבוֹן תְּרֵיהוֹן אָמְרִין. כָּל־שֶׁכֵּן מִקְחוֹ קַייָם. וְהוּא שֶׁלָּקַח מִן הָאִישׁ וְחָזַר וְלָקַח מִן הָאִשָּׁה. וְאֵין כָּל־מַה שֶׁיֵּשׁ לָאִשָּׁה מְשׁוּעֲבָד לָאִישׁ. לַאֲכִילַת פֵּירוֹת.

So far, if there were two contracts[196]. If there was one contract[197]? Rebbi Ze'ira and Rebbi Ila both say, certainly the sale is invalid; i. e., if he bought from the wife and then bought from the husband. Rebbi Ḥanina and Rebbi Bevon both said, certainly the sale is valid; i. e., if he bought from the husband and then bought from the wife. But is not all the wife's property administered by the husband? For the yield[198].

196   This refers to the part of the Mishnah in which husband and wife sell from the wife's real estate. It is clear that the Mishnah text underlying the Yerushalmi is not the Mishnah of the ms. (which frequently represents a different tradition) but that of the *editio princeps* of the Mishnah (Napoli) and the Vienna ms. of the Tosephta: "If one bought from a wife and afterwards from her husband, his acquisition is void; from the husband and afterwards from his wife, his acquisition is valid." S. Lieberman (*Tosefta ki-Fshutah Giṭṭin* p. 847) considers this reading as "incomprehensible" and, against his declared intention, does base his text on the Vienna ms. in this case. But it seems that the text can be well understood, since all depends on the legal status of the property, whether it is mortmain or paraphernalia (cf. *Yebamot* 7:1, Note 1). Mortmain is the husband's property; at the dissolution of the marriage the wife is entitled to receive it or its value back; during the marriage all she has is a mortgage lien on her husband's properties. Therefore, if she sells mortmain properties, she sells what she does not have; this is invalid. But if the husband sells, she has a right of regress on the property if it should turn out that the estate is insufficient to cover her *ketubah* claim. A buyer may want to buy insurance against such a possibility by paying the wife for her final assent to the sale. If she receives a consideration for her signature, she cannot claim later that she only signed to please her husband. The Mishnah speaks of paraphernalia property, which is the wife's and of which the husband only has rights of administration.

197   In that case, the buyer might not pay separately for the wife's signature.

198   Of the paraphernalia property.

(47b line 33) רִבִּי חִזְקִיָּה בְּשֵׁם רִבִּי אָחָא. וְכֵינִי. מָכַר לָרִאשׁוֹן וְחָתְמָה לַשֵּׁינִי לַשְּׁלִישִׁי וְחָתְמָה גּוֹבָה מִן הָאַחֲרוֹן. לֹא הִסְפִּיק גּוֹבָה מִשֶּׁלְּפָנָיו. לֹא הִסְפִּיק גּוֹבָה מִשֶּׁלִּפְנֵי פָנָיו. עָלָהּ אָמַר רַב. בִּנְכָסִים שֶׁהִכְנִיסָה לוֹ בִּכְתוּבָתָהּ. אֲבָל בִּנְכָסִים שֶׁהִכְנִיסָה לוֹ פָּרָה פְרָנוֹן גּוֹבָן מֵאֵי זֶה שֶׁיִּרְצֶה.

Rebbi Ḥizqiah in the name of Rebbi Aḥa: So it is: If he sold to a first person and she signed, to a second and a third and she signed, she can collect from the last[199]. If it is insufficient, she collects from the one before the last. If this is insufficient, she collects from the one before the penultimate. On this, Rav said: For property which she brought him in her *ketubah*[200]. But property which she brought to him as paraphernalia[201], she collects from any she wants.

199 She signed on the sales contract after her husband and claims that she did so to please her husband, not as a commercial transaction. The court will uphold this claim. But the earlier buyer can claim that when he bought the real estate, there were left sufficient assets to cover the wife's *ketubah* mortgage and his property should be immune to the wife's claims.

200 *Dos aestimata*, the value of which is written in the *ketubah* document and which establishes a mortgage on all the husband's properties.

201 *Dos non aestimata*, property she inherited or otherwise acquired during the marriage; any sale by the husband is invalid even if the wife signs the sale document after her husband; cf. *Yebamot* 7:1, Note 1.

(47b line 38) **הלכה ח**: חֵרֵשׁ רוֹמֵז וְנִרְמָז. הֵן אוֹמְרִים. בְּיָדֵינוּ לִיקַּח. וְהַלּוֹקֵחַ אוֹמֵר. לָאו. אָמַר רִבִּי יוֹסֵי. לְעוֹלָם הַשָּׂדֶה בְּחֶזְקַת הַבְּעָלִים. שֶׁהַמּוֹצִיא מֵחֲבֵירוֹ עָלָיו הָרְאָיָיה.

(**Halakhah 8**: The deaf-mute communicates by sign language.)[202] They say[203], we had the means to buy; the buyer says, no. Rebbi Yose says, the field is always in the possession of the current owner[204] since the burden of proof is on the claimant.

202 This heading is misplaced; it belongs after the next Mishnah. Probably it should read "Halakhah 7" and quote Mishnah 7.
203 Here starts the discussion of Mishnah 7. Who has to bring proof if the heirs of the original owner say that they had the means to buy back the property but the actual buyer disputes their assertion?
204 In *Sefer ha'Ittur* II, 66d "the buyers". The commentary (Note 176) lists all other authors who copied from there.

(47b line 40) רַב אָמַר. אֲנָא הֲוֵינָא מִמִּנְיָינָא. וְלָאו שַׁנְיָא הִיא. הוּא רְבִיעַ קַרְקַע הוּא רְבִיעַ מָעוֹת. אָמַר רִבִּי יוֹסֵי בֵּירִבִּי בּוּן. קַרְקַע דֵּינָר אַגְרָמָא רְבִיעַ מָעוֹת סְרִימְסִין.

Rav said, I was of the voters[205]. There is no difference between a quarter in real estate or a quarter in money[206]. Rebbi Yose ben Rebbi Abun said, real estate for a denar a γραμμάριον[207], in money a quarter is a *tremis*[208].

205 This refers to the court convened by Rebbi which decreed that after 12 months the original owners or their heirs lost the right of first refusal but retained the right to an indemnity. The Mishnah does not spell out whether a third of the real estate should be returned or one speaks of a payment.
206 The same statement is in the Babli, 58b.
207 Greek γραμμάριον, the equivalent of Latin *scrupulus*, two obols, a third of a denar's (or drachma's) weight. As measures of land, the denar is $1/96$ and the scruple $1/288$ of a *iugerum* of 28'800 Roman square feet. R. Yose ben R. Abun holds that the "quarter" mentioned in the Mishnah is computed from above, a quarter of the total expense which is a third of the price paid to the criminal. The computation from above is that of Samuel in the Babli, 58b.

208 A third of an *aureus*; a large coin mentioned in *Threni rabba* 1(14) as טרימיסיא.

משנה ח: חֵרֵשׁ רוֹמֵז וְנִרְמָז בֶּן בְּתֵירָה אוֹמֵר קוֹפֵץ וְנִקְפָּץ בְּמִטַּלְטְלִין. (fol. 46b)
הַפָּעוֹטוֹת מִקְחָן מֶקַח וּמִמְכָּרָן מִמְכָּר בְּמִטַּלְטְלִין.

Mishnah 8: A deaf-mute communicates in sign language, and Ben Bathyra says, in pantomimes[209], referring to movables. Underage children: their buy is a buy and their sale is a sale, referring to movables.

209 This is Rashi's explanation, based on *Job* 5:10. Maimonides's explanation is based on a meaning "to jump" (*Cant.* 2:8) meaning that the deaf-mute has to bring and handle the object.

(47b line 42) בֶּן בְּתֵירָה אוֹמֵר קוֹפֵץ וְנִקְפָּץ. שׂוֹכֵר וּמִשְׂתַּכֵּר. אַפְּיוֹטוֹת פְּרִייָא.
אָמַר רִבִּי יוֹחָנָן. מִפְּנֵי חַיֵּיהֶן. אָמַר רִבִּי מָנָא. אַף עַל גַּב דְּרִבִּי יוֹסֵי רִבּוֹ גָּבֵי
עִיצוּמִין. מוֹדֶה בְּאִילֵּין דִּיהָבוּן בְּנֵיהוֹן לְאוּמָּנוּתָא דְּאִינּוּן גָּבוֹי עִיצוּמִין מִפְּנֵי
חַיֵּי הַבְּרִיּוֹת.

"Ben Bathyra says, in pantomimes[210]." He hires and is hired[211]. The artless, small children[212]. Rebbi Joḥanan said, because of their livelihood. Rebbi Mana said, even though Rebbi Yose raises difficulties in collecting forfeits[213], he agrees that those who give their children to artisans that they collect forfeits because of the livelihood of people[214].

210 This is the quote from the Mishnah but it is not discussed.
211 The deaf-mute, by sign language.

212 The uncommon Semitic word פָּעוּט is compared to Greek ἀποίητος "artless", παιδία "childhood". (Explanation of H. L. Fleischer.) S.

Lieberman (*Tosephta kiFshutah* p. 847) explains אפיוטות, הפיוטות as Greek ἑπτέτης, ἑπταετής, adj., "seven years old". There is no reason to single out that age.

213   He holds that nobody signs a contract that imposes a fine on himself with the idea that he really will have to pay the fine. Therefore, a contract which contains a forfeit clause for each party may be *asmakhta* and invalid (*Ketubot* 5:5, Note 117); the court is reluctant to enforce such a clause. (In modern Hebrew, עִצּוּמִים are labor union actions just short of a strike.)

214   If an artisan bows out of a contract for an apprentice, he will have to pay a fine since the child needs to learn a trade to be able to make a living.

(fol. 46b) **משנה ט:** אֵילוּ דְבָרִים אָמְרוּ מִפְּנֵי דַרְכֵי שָׁלוֹם. כֹּהֵן קוֹרֵא רִאשׁוֹן וְאַחֲרָיו לֵוִי וְאַחֲרָיו יִשְׂרָאֵל מִפְּנֵי דַרְכֵי שָׁלוֹם. מְעָרְבִין בְּבַיִת יָשָׁן מִפְּנֵי דַרְכֵי שָׁלוֹם. בּוֹר שֶׁהוּא קָרוֹב לָאַמָּה מִתְמַלֵּא רִאשׁוֹן מִפְּנֵי דַרְכֵי שָׁלוֹם. מְצִיאַת חֵרֵשׁ שׁוֹטֶה וְקָטָן יֵשׁ בָּהֶן מִשּׁוּם גֵּזֶל מִפְּנֵי דַרְכֵי שָׁלוֹם. רִבִּי יוֹסֵי אוֹמֵר גֵּזֶל גָּמוּר. מְצוּדוֹת חַיָּה וְעוֹפוֹת וְדָגִים יֵשׁ בָּהֶם מִשּׁוּם גֵּזֶל מִפְּנֵי דַרְכֵי שָׁלוֹם. רִבִּי יוֹסֵי אוֹמֵר גֵּזֶל גָּמוּר. הַמְנַקֵּף בְּרֹאשׁ הַזַּיִת גֵּזֶל מִפְּנֵי דַרְכֵי שָׁלוֹם. רִבִּי יוֹסֵי אוֹמֵר גֵּזֶל גָּמוּר. אֵין מְמַחִין בְּיַד עֲנִיֵּי גוֹיִם בַּלֶּקֶט וּבַשִּׁכְחָה וּבַפֵּיאָה מִפְּנֵי דַרְכֵי שָׁלוֹם.

Mishnah 9: The following was said for communal peace: A Cohen reads first, after him a Levite, after him an Israel, for communal peace[215]. One puts an *eruv* in an old house, for communal peace[216]. A cistern which is close to a water canal is filled first, for communal peace[217]. Finds of a deaf-mute, or an insane person, or a minor[218] fall under the category of robbery, for communal peace; Rebbi Yose says, complete robbery[219]. Traps for wild animals, birds, or fish fall[220] under the category of robbery, for communal peace; Rebbi Yose says, complete robbery. If one knocks off [olives] from high up in the olive tree[221], it falls under the category of robbery, for communal peace; Rebbi Yose says, complete robbery. One does not hinder poor Gentiles [from taking] gleanings, forgotten sheaves, or *peah*[222], for communal peace.

215 In any public reading from the Torah, a Cohen has to be given precedence (if there is one present), followed by a Levite. If there is no Levite present, the Cohen is called for a second reading since all Cohanim are Levites (*Ma'aśer Šeni* 5:5, Note 90).

216 In a common courtyard serving many houses with different owners one cannot carry on the Sabbath unless one symbolically unites all houses by depositing some common food in one of them. This is called עֵרוּב חֲצֵרוֹת "the combination of courtyards". If one house was the depository for some time, one cannot change the place of deposit without insulting the owner of that house; therefore, it is forbidden to change.

217 The order of filling cisterns (or irrigation of fields) is by the length of the side canal used by cistern or field, to avoid quarrels.

218 These cannot legally acquire anything they find since they have no legal standing. But it is forbidden to act on this fact.

219 The Halakhah will explain when taking finds from an incompetent person is a prosecutable offense.

220 If set in the public domain under rules which permit setting up such traps, the catch is private property and protected as such.

221 Olives are harvested by shaking the olive tree and collecting under the tree. Those which did not fall off are left for the poor. The person who climbs into the tree to knock off the remaining olives is a poor person, not the owner of the orchard. What he knocks off and causes to fall under the tree is protected as his property. (The Mishnah in the Babli and in several Mishnah mss. is more explicit in speaking about the poor.)

222 Since one supports the Gentile poor for communal peace.

(47b line 46) **הלכה ט**: אֵילוּ דְבָרִים אָמְרוּ מִפְּנֵי דַרְכֵי שָׁלוֹם כול'. מִילְתֵיהּ דְּרִבִּי שִׁמְעוֹן בֶּן יוֹחַי אָמַר שֶׁהוּא מִדִּבְרֵי תוֹרָה. דְּתַנֵּי רִבִּי שִׁמְעוֹן בֶּן יוֹחַי. וַיִּכְתּוֹב מֹשֶׁה אֶת הַתּוֹרָה הַזֹּאת וַיִּתְּנָהּ אֶל הַכֹּהֲנִים בְּנֵי לֵוִי וגו'. וְאַחַר כָּךְ וְאֶל כָּל־זִקְנֵי יִשְׂרָאֵל. מִילְתֵיהּ דְּרִבִּי יְהוֹשֻׁעַ בֶּן לֵוִי שֶׁהוּא מִדִּבְרֵיהֶן. דְּאָמַר רִבִּי יְהוֹשֻׁעַ. מִיָּמַיי לֹא בֵּירַכְתִּי לִפְנֵי כֹהֵן וְלֹא הִינַּחְתִּי לְבָרֵךְ יִשְׂרָאֵל לְפָנָיו. מִילְתֵיהּ דְּרִבִּי חֲנִינָה אוֹמֵר שֶׁהוּא מִדִּבְרֵיהֶן. דָּמַר רִבִּי חֲנִינָה. עִיר שֶׁכּוּלָּהּ כֹּהֲנִים יִשְׂרָאֵל קוֹרֵא רִאשׁוֹן מִפְּנֵי דַרְכֵי שָׁלוֹם.

"The following was said for communal peace," etc. The saying of Rebbi Simeon ben Ioḥai implies that it is of the words of the Torah, for Rebbi Simeon ben Ioḥai stated: "Moses wrote this Torah and gave it to the Cohanim, the Levites (etc.)" and afterwards "to all the Elders of Israel.[223]" The saying of Rebbi Joshua ben Levi implies that it is of their words, as Rebbi Joshua said, never did I recite the benediction before a Cohen and I did not allow an Israel to do it before him[224]. The saying of Rebbi Ḥanina implies that it is of their words, as Rebbi Ḥanina said, in a city of only Cohanim, an Israel reads first because of communal peace[225].

223 *Deut.* 31:9. The implication is that in all matters of reading the Torah the Cohanim and Levites have precedence over Israel Elders. In the Babli, 58b, the author of the statement is given as the Amora R. Mattaniah.

224 If it were a Torah obligation to give precedence to Cohanim, there would be no reason to point it out as a sign of particular religiosity. In the Babli, *Megillah* 28a, the statement is attributed to the wonder-working R. Perida. In Yerushalmi *Berakhot* 5:5 (9d l.3), the reference is that R. Joshua ben Levi never let any non-Cohen publicly recite Grace in the presence of a Cohen (Halakhah 5:5, Notes 163,164.)

225 If it were a Torah obligation, then even to avoid quarrels it would not be possible to call an Israel.

236　GITTIN CHAPTER FIVE

(47b line 52) רִבִּי אָחָא וְרִבִּי תַּנְחוּם בַּר חִייָה בְּשֵׁם רִבִּי שִׂמְלַאי. עִיר שֶׁכּוּלָּהּ כֹּהֲנִים כּוּלָּן נוֹשְׂאִין אֶת כַּפֵּיהֶן. וּלְמִי הֵן מְבָרְכִין. לַאֲחֵיהֶן שֶׁבַּצָּפוֹן וּבַדָּרוֹם. וּמִי עוֹנֶה אַחֲרֵיהֶן. הַנָּשִׁים וְהַקְּטַנִּים. תַּנֵּי אַבַּיֵּי בַּר בִּנְיָמִין. עִם הָעוֹמֵד אַחֲרֵי הַכֹּהֲנִים אֵינָן בִּכְלָל בְּרָכָה. הָעוֹמְדִים לִפְנֵי הַכֹּהֲנִים. אָמַר רִבִּי חִייָה בַּר בָּא. אֲפִילוּ חוֹמָה שֶׁלְּבַרְזֶל אֵינָהּ מַפְסָקֶת. הָעוֹמְדִים מִן הַצְּדָדִין. נִישְׁמְעִינָהּ מִן הָדָא. נִתְכַּוֵּון לְהַזּוֹת לְפָנָיו וְהִזָּה לְאַחֲרָיו לְאַחֲרָיו וְהִזָּה לְפָנָיו. הַזָּייָתוֹ פְּסוּלָה. לְפָנָיו וְהִזָּה עַל הַצְּדָדִין הַזָּייָתוֹ כְּשֵׁירָה. הָדָא אָמְרָה. הָעוֹמֵד מִן הַצְּדָדִין בִּכְלָל בְּרָכָה הֵן. אָמַר רַב חִסְדָּא. וְצָרִיךְ שֶׁיְּהֵא הַחַזָּן יִשְׂרָאֵל. אָמַר רַב חִסְדָּא. אִם הָיָה כֹּהֵן אֶחָד. אוֹמֵר. כֹּהֵן. לִשְׁנַיִם. אוֹמֵר כֹּהֲנִים. וְרַב הוּנָא אָמַר. אֲפִילוּ לְאֶחָד אוֹמֵר. כֹּהֲנִים. שֶׁאֵינוֹ קוֹרֵא אֶלָּא הַשֵּׁבֶט. שֶׁלֹּא תֹּאמַר. אִי אִישׁ פְּלוֹנִי מְנַלֶּה עֲרָיוֹת וְשׁוֹפֵךְ דָּמִים וְהוּא מְבָרְכֵנוּ. אָמַר הַקָּדוֹשׁ בָּרוּךְ הוּא. וּמִי מְבָרֶכְךָ. לֹא אֲנִי מְבָרֶכְךָ. שֶׁנֶּאֱמַר וְשָׂמוּ אֶת שְׁמִי עַל בְּנֵי יִשְׂרָאֵל וַאֲנִי אֲבָרֲכֵם.

2 כולן | ב - ר כולם   ולמי | ב למי   ובדרום | ב לאחיהן שבדרום לאחיהן שבמזרחלאחיהן שבמערב   3 אחריהן | ב אחריהן אמן   והקטנים | ב והטף   בר | ב ביר׳   עם העומד | ב העומדין   4 העומדים | ב העומדין   בא | ב ווא   5 אינה מפסקת | ב הברכה מפסקתה   הצדדין | ב הצדדים   7 העומד מן הצדדין | ב אף העומדין מן הצדדים   8 אמ׳ רב חסדא | ב רב נחמן בר יעקב אמ׳   9 לשנים או׳ | ב אם היו שנים או׳   ורב הונא אמ׳ | ב אמ׳ רב חסדא   אפילו לאחד | ב אפי׳ כהן אחד   10 השבט | ב לשבט.

From here to the end of the paragraph this passage is missing in *Berakhot*

226Rebbi Aḥa and Rebbi Tanḥum bar Ḥiyya in the name of Rebbi Simai: In a city of only Cohanim, all of them lift their hands. For whom do they recite the blessing? For their brothers to the North and South. Who answers after them? Women and children227. Abbaie bar Benjamin stated: People who stand behind the Cohanim are not included in the blessing. For those in front of them, Rebbi Ḥiyya bar Abba said that even an iron wall does not interrupt. Those who stand to their side? Let us hear from the following: "If he intended to sprinkle before himself but sprinkled behind himself, behind himself but sprinkled before himself; his sprinkling is invalid. Before himself but sprinkled sideways, his sprinkling is valid." This implies that those who stand to their side are included in the blessing. Rav Ḥisda said, it is necessary that the organizer be an Israel. Rav Ḥisda[228] said, if there was one Cohen, he says "Cohen." For two, he says "Cohanim." But Rav Huna said, even for one he says "Cohanim" since he only calls the tribe, lest you say, probably person X is an adulterer or a murderer,[229] and he shall bless us? The Holy, praise to Him, said: Who blesses you? Am not I blessing you? As it was said[230]: "They shall put My name over the Children of Israel and I shall bless them."

226 A parallel is in *Berakhot* 5:5, explained in Notes 167-175. The readings of the Leiden ms. are noted by ב, of the Rome ms. by ר.

227 There may be a material difference between the two texts since קטנים refers to all underage children but טף only to those who still need their mothers. The *Berakhot* text might allow almost adult children to join their fathers in the priestly blessing.

228 The name attributions in *Berakhot* seem preferable since this style of repetition is not usual.

229 This is an exaggeration since a homicide is barred from reciting the priestly blessing. It simply means that people might be offended if others think that they could dispense blessings to them. It has to be emphasized that the Cohen is just fulfilling a hereditary duty; his person is not giving the blessing.

230 *Lev.* 6:27, the verse following the text of the priestly blessing.

(47b line 65) מְעָרְבִין בְּבַיִת יָשָׁן. אָמַר רִבִּי אָבִין. וּבְדִיּוּר יָשָׁן הִיא מַתְנִיתָא.

"One puts an *eruv* in an old house." Rebbi Abin said, the Mishnah speaks of a prior dweller[231].

231 Not the house is offended if the *eruv* is removed from it but the owner of the house. Therefore, if there is a new owner in an old house, one may move the location of the *eruv*. The statement is copied in *Eruvin* 6, 23d l. 40.

(47b line 66) בּוֹר הַקָּרוֹב לָאַמָּא מִתְמַלֵּא רִאשׁוֹן. וְהוּא שֶׁתְּהֵא אַמַּת הַמַּיִם עוֹבֶרֶת עַל גַּבָּיו. שְׁמוּאֵל אָמַר. אֲפִילוּ מִן הַצַּד. תַּמָּן אָמְרִין. דְּרְחִיק וְנִיחָא לְמִישְׁתֵּי קָדִים דְּקָרִיב וְקָשָׁה לְמִישְׁתֵּי.

"A cistern which is close to a water canal is filled first." Only if it passes through it[232]. Samuel said, even if it is close by. There[233], they say what is farther away but easy to drink from precedes one which is close by but difficult to drink from.

232 In the Babli, 60b, this is one interpretation given by Samuel, that the owner of the cistern cannot be forced to install a lock.

233 In Babylonia. This is not mentioned in the Babli, which prefers to have the situation handled without set rules. "Drink" may mean "being irrigated".

(47b line 69) עַל דַּעְתֵּין דְּרַבָּנִין דְּתַמָּן נִיחָא. תַּמָּן אָמְרִין בְּשֵׁם רַב נַחְמָן בַּר יַעֲקֹב. כָּל־שֶׁנּוֹתְנִין לוֹ אֱגוֹז וּמַשְׁלִיכוֹ צְרוֹר וְנוֹטְלוֹ. הַמּוֹצִיא בְּיָדוֹ כְּמוֹצִיא לָאַשְׁפָּה. אֱגוֹז וְנוֹטְלוֹ צְרוֹר וְזוֹרְקוֹ גְּזֵילוֹ גֵּזֶל מִפְּנֵי דַרְכֵי שָׁלוֹם. אֱגוֹז וּצְרוֹר נוֹטְלָן וּמַצְנִיעָן וּמְבִיאָן לְאַחַר זְמָן גְּזֵילוֹ גֵּזֶל גָּמוּר. זוֹכֶה לְעַצְמוֹ אֲבָל לֹא לַאֲחֵרִים. רַב הוּנָא אָמַר. כְּשֵׁם שֶׁזּוֹכֶה לְעַצְמוֹ כָּךְ הוּא זוֹכֶה לַאֲחֵרִים. הַכֹּל מוֹדִין שֶׁאֵין מַתָּנָתוֹ מַתָּנָה. דִּכְתִיב כִּי יִתֵּן אִישׁ. מַתְּנַת אִישׁ מַתָּנָה וְאֵין מַתְּנַת קָטָן מַתָּנָה. דִּבְרֵי חֲכָמִים. רִבִּי יוּדָה בֶּן פָּזִי בְּשֵׁם רִבִּי יוֹחָנָן. לְעוֹלָם אֵין גְּזֵילוֹ מַחֲוִיר עַד שֶׁיָּבִיא שְׁתֵּי שְׂעָרוֹת. רִבִּי אַבָּהוּ בְּשֵׁם רִבִּי יוֹחָנָן. הָדָא דְּאַתְּ אָמַרְתְּ לְהוֹצִיא מִמֶּנּוּ בְּדִין. אֲבָל לְקָרְבָּן וְלִשְׁבוּעָה כָּל־עַמָּא מוֹדֶה. עַד שֶׁתָּבִיא שְׁתֵּי שְׂעָרוֹת. בְּרַם כְּרַבָּנִין דְּהָכָא. רִבִּי יוֹסֵה בָּעֵי. מֵעַתָּה אַף לְעַצְמוֹ לֹא יִזְכֶּה.

HALAKHAH 9

שֶׁנֶּאֱמַר אִישׁ אֶל רֵעֵהוּ עַד שֶׁיְהֵא כְרֵעֵהוּ.   רִבִּי יוֹסֵי בֵּי רִבִּי בּוּן בְּשֵׁם רִבִּי שְׁמוּאֵל בַּר רַב יִצְחָק. וְיָרְדוּ לָהּ בְּשִׁיטַת הַפְעוּטוֹת. דְּתַנִּינָן תַּמָּן. הַפְעוּטוֹת מִקְחָן מֶקַח וּמִמְכָּרָן מִמְכָּר בְּמִטַּלְטְלִין. וְהָא תַנִּינָן תַּמָּן. אֲבָל אֵינוֹ מְזַכֶּה לָהֶן לֹא עַל יְדֵי בְנוֹ וּבִתּוֹ הַקְּטַנִּים וְלֹא עַל יְדֵי עַבְדּוֹ וְשִׁפְחָתוֹ הַכְּנַעֲנִים מִפְּנֵי שֶׁיָּדָן כְּיָדוֹ. רַבָּנִין דְּקֵיסָרִין אָמְרִין. כָּאן בְּתִינוֹק שֶׁיֵּשׁ בּוֹ דַעַת כָּאן בְּתִינוֹק שֶׁאֵין בּוֹ דַעַת.

1 תמן | מ דתמן   2 ונוטלו | מ והוא נוטלו   3 לאשפה | מ באשפה   ונוטלו | מ והוא נוטלו   וזורקו | מ והוא משליכו   נוטלן | מ והוא נוטלן   4 נוטלן | מ והוא נוטלן   זוכה | מ זכה   5 שזוכה | מ שהוא זוכה   7 בן | מ בר   - | מ ר' יעקב בר אחא בשם ר' יוחנן   מחזר | מ גזל גמור   9 דאת אמרת | מ דתימ'   לקרבן ולשבועה | מ להביא קרבן שבועה   10 מודה | מ מודיי   11 יוסה | מ יוסי   שתביא | מ שיביא   אף | מ אפילו   שנא' איש | מ דכת'   13 רבי שמואל | מ שמואל   וירדו | מ פתר   הפעוטות | מ אפיעוטות (2 times)   14 והא תנינן תמן | מ והתנינן להן | מ -   16 תינוק | מ קטן (2 times)

[234]Following the opinion of the rabbis there it is acceptable since there, they say in the name of Rav Naḥman bar Jacob: One to whom one gives a nut and he throws it away, a pebble and he keeps it, what is found in his hand is as if found on a garbage heap; a nut and he keeps it, a pebble and he throws it away, what is robbed from him is robbed because of communal peace; a nut or a pebble he takes, hides them, and produces them later, what is robbed from him is total robbery. He can acquire for himself but not for others. Rav Huna said, just as he can acquire for himself so he can acquire for others. Everybody agrees that his gift is not a gift since it is written (*Ex.* 22:6): "If a man give." The gift of a man is a gift, but the gift of a minor is no gift, the words of the Sages. Rebbi Jehudah bar Pazi in the name of Rebbi Joḥanan, Rebbi Jacob bar Aḥa in the name of Rebbi Joḥanan, robbing from him is not clear[235] unless he grew two pubic hairs. Rebbi Abbahu in the name of Rebbi Joḥanan, that

is, to recover from him by a law suit, but to have to bring a sacrifice for [a false] oath only if he grew two pubic hairs. But following the rabbis here, Rebbi Yose asked that even for himself he should not be able to acquire since it is written (*Ex.* 22:6): "A man to his neighbor", until he be like his neighbor. Rebbi Yose ben Rebbi Abun in the name of Rebbi Samuel ben Rav Isaac explained it by the method of the artless. As we have stated there[236]: "For underage children, their buying is buying and their selling selling, for movables." But did we not state there[237]: "He cannot make them acquire through his minor son or daughter or his Canaanite male or female slave, because their hand is like his hand." The rabbis of Caesarea say, here a minor[238] with knowledge, there a minor without knowledge.

234   The text is from *Ma'aser Šeni* 4:4, Notes 80-90. Variants are noted מ. Cf. Note 236.

235   מחזר is a misspelling for מְחֻוָּר, a Babylonian spelling for Yerushalmi מְחוּבָּר "(logically) connected; clear". It is not derived from the Aramaic root חור "pale". Cf. H. Guggenheimer, *Zur Aussprache des Bet in talmudischer Zeit*, Bulletin des Vereins jüdischer Lehrer und Kantoren der Schweiz 21 (1977), 4-5.

236   Since the Mishnah is from here, this shows that the original is in *Ma'aser Šeni*.

237   Mishnah *Ma'aser Šeni* 4:4.

238   The talmudic expression תִּינוֹקוֹת שֶׁל בֵּית רַבָּן "schoolchildren" shows that the word denotes older children. The root is ינק "to suckle".

(47c line 9) מְצוּדוֹת חַיָּה וְעוֹפוֹת כול'. הָדָא דְאַתְּ אָמַר בְּאִילֵּין רַבְרְבָתָא. אֲבָל בְּאִילֵּין דַּקִּיקָתָא כְּמָאן דְּאִינּוּן בְּגוֹ בֵּייתֵיהּ.

"Traps for wild animals, birds," etc. That is[239], about large ones[250]. But small ones are as if inside his house.

239 The difference of opinion between the Sages, who hold that taking from them is only rabbinically forbidden, and R. Yose, who holds that taking from traps is biblically a sin.

240 Where animals are trapped but not immobilized; they cannot be considered acquired by the owner of the trap, in contrast to small traps which immobilize the prey. In the Babli, 60a/61b, in the interpretation of Rashi and R. Hananel, it is stated similarly that animals or birds trapped in nets are acquired by the trapper but those caught in larger contraptions constructed of planks are subject to the controversy of the Mishnah.

(47c line 11) הֶעָנִי הַמְנַקֵּף בְּרֹאשׁ הַזַּיִת מַה שֶׁתַּחְתָּיו גֶּזֶל מִפְּנֵי דַרְכֵי שָׁלוֹם. רִבִּי יוֹסֵי אוֹמֵר גֶּזֶל גָּמוּר. הָדָא דְאַתְּ אָמַר בְּדְאַרְעָא. אֲבָל הַלּוֹקֵחַ בְּיָד זָכְתָה לוֹ יָדוֹ.

"If *a poor person* knocks off [olives] from high up in the olive tree, *what is under him* falls under the category of robbery[241], for communal peace; Rebbi Yose says, complete robbery." That means, on the earth[242]. But if he plucks with his hand, his hand acquires for him.

241 The longer version of the Mishnah (indicated by *italics*) is close to the text of the Babli and most Mishnah mss.

242 What falls down on the ground is only protected by rabbinic rule. But what the poor person picks and puts in a vessel is his property by biblical standards.

(47c line 13) אֵין מְמַחִין בְּיַד עֲנִיֵּי גוֹיִם בַּלֶּקֶט וּבַשִּׁכְחָה וּבַפֵּיאָה מִפְּנֵי דַרְכֵי שָׁלוֹם. תַּנֵּי. עִיר שֶׁיֵּשׁ בָּהּ גוֹיִם וְיִשְׂרָאֵל. מַעֲמִידִין גַּבָּאֵי גוֹיִם וְגַבָּאֵי יִשְׂרָאֵל. וְגוֹבִין מִשֶּׁלְּגוֹיִם וּמִשֶּׁלְיִשְׂרָאֵל. וּמְפַרְנְסִין עֲנִיֵּי גוֹיִם וַעֲנִיֵּי יִשְׂרָאֵל. וּמְבַקְּרִין חוֹלֵי גוֹיִם וְחוֹלֵי יִשְׂרָאֵל. וְקוֹבְרִין מֵיתֵי גוֹיִם וּמֵיתֵי יִשְׂרָאֵל. וּמְנַחֲמִין אֲבֵילֵי גוֹיִם וַאֲבֵילֵי יִשְׂרָאֵל. וּמְכַבְּסִין כְּלֵי גוֹיִם וּכְלֵי יִשְׂרָאֵל מִפְּנֵי דַרְכֵי שָׁלוֹם.

2 מעמידין גבאי גוים וגבאי יש׳. וגובין | ד הגביים גובין ו הגבאים   3 משלגוים ושל יש׳ |
ד משליש׳ ומשלגוים   ענייי גוים וענייי יש׳ | ד ענייי יש׳ וענייי גוים   4 חולי גוים וחוליי
יש׳ | ד חולי יש׳ וחולי גוים   מיתי גוים ומיתייי יש׳ | ד מיתי יש׳ ומיתי גוים   5 אבילי
גוים ואבילייי יש׳ | ד אבילי יש׳ ואבילי גוים   ומכבסין | ד ומכניסין

[243]"One does not hinder poor Gentiles [from taking] gleanings, forgotten sheaves, or *peah*, for communal peace." It was stated: "In a town where Gentiles and Jews live together, one appoints overseers of charity from Gentiles and Jews; one provides for the Gentile and Jewish poor, visits Gentile and Jewish sick, buries Gentile and Jewish dead, and consoles Gentile and Jewish mourners. Also, one washes Gentile and Jewish clothes for the sake of peaceful coexistence."

(47c line 17) גִּירְדָּאי שָׁאַל לְרִבִּי אִימִי. יוֹם מִשְׁתֶּה שֶׁלְּגוֹיִם מַהוּ. וּסְבַר מִשְׁרֵי
לוֹן מִן הָדָא מִפְּנֵי דַּרְכֵי שָׁלוֹם. אָמַר לוֹן רִבִּי אַבָּא. וְהָתַנֵּי רִבִּי חִייָה יוֹם מִשְׁתֶּה
שֶׁלְּגוֹיִם אָסוּר. אָמַר רִבִּי אִימִי. אִילּוּלֵי רִבִּי אַבָּא כְּבָר הָיִינוּ בָאִין לְהַתִּיר
עֲבוֹדָה זָרָה שֶׁלָּהֶן. וּבָרוּךְ שֶׁהִבְדִּילָנוּ מֵהֶן.

1 שאל | ד שאלון   וסבר | ד סבר   2 הדא | ד הכא   אבא | ד בא   חייה | חייא   3
אבא | ד בא   היינו באין | ד היה לנו   4 שהבדילנו מהן | ד שריחקנו מהם

A weaver asked Rebbi Immi, what about a Gentile wedding feast? He wanted to permit it to them from this: "Because of peaceful coexistence." Rebbi Abba told them, did not Rebbi Ḥiyya state that the holiday of a Gentile wedding feast is forbidden? Rebbi Immi said, if it had not been for Rebbi Abba, we would have come to permit their strange worship; praised be He Who separated us from them.

243   The text, to the end of the Halakhah, is also in *Demai* 4:6, Notes 76-79. Variants from there are noted ד; a (Babylonian spelling) variant from the Venice print by ו. The text there is probably copied from a ms. which underwent fewer changes than the text here.

(fol. 46b) **משנה י**: מַשְׁאֶלֶת אִשָּׁה לַחֲבֶירְתָהּ הַחֲשׁוּדָה עַל הַשְּׁבִיעִית נָפָה וּכְבָרָה רֵיחַיִם וְתַנּוּר. אֲבָל לֹא תָבוֹר וְלֹא תִטְחוֹן עִמָּהּ. אֵשֶׁת חָבֵר מַשְׁאֶלֶת לְאֵשֶׁת עַם הָאָרֶץ נָפָה וּכְבָרָה וּבוֹרֶרֶת וְטוֹחֶנֶת וּמְרַקֶּדֶת עִמָּהּ. אֲבָל מִשֶּׁתַּטִּיל מַיִם לֹא תִגַּע בָּהּ שֶׁאֵין מַחֲזִיקִין יְדֵי עוֹבְרֵי עֲבֵירָה. וְכוּלָּן לֹא אָמְרוּ אֶלָּא מִפְּנֵי דַרְכֵי שָׁלוֹם. וּמַחֲזִיקִים יְדֵי גּוֹיִם בַּשְּׁבִיעִית אֲבָל לֹא יְדֵי יִשְׂרָאֵל. וְשׁוֹאֲלִין בִּשְׁלוֹמָן מִפְּנֵי דַרְכֵי הַשָּׁלוֹם.

3 מים | ש את המים   4 בה | ש אצלה   כולן | ש כולם

244**Mishnah 10**: A woman may lend to her neighbor, whom she suspects in matters of the Sabbatical, a coarse sieve[80], a fine sieve, grindstones, or an oven[81], but she should neither cull nor grind with her. The wife of a Fellow may lend to the wife of a vulgar[82] a coarse sieve and a fine sieve, she may cull, grind, and sift with her, but she may not touch hers once water has been put in[83] because one does not support transgressors[84]. All this has only been said for communal peace. One[85] encourages Gentiles in the Sabbatical year but not Jews. One greets them for communal peace.

244 The entire Halakhah is from Ševi'it 5:9, Notes 80-98. The variant ms. readings from there are noted **ש**. The last two paragraphs are also from Ševi'it 4:3, Notes 50-57.

(47c line 23) **הלכה י**: מַשְׁאֶלֶת אִשָּׁה לַחֲבֶירְתָהּ כול'. רִבִּי זְעִירָא בָּעֵי קוֹמֵי רִבִּי מָנָא. מַתְנִיתָא בִסְתָם. הָא בְּפֵירוּשָׁא לֹא. אָמַר לֵיהּ. וּסְתָמוֹ לָאו כְּפֵירוּשׁ הוּא. אָמַר לֵיהּ. אֲנִי אוֹמֵר נָפָה לִסְפּוֹר בָּהּ מָעוֹת. כְּבָרָה לִכְבּוֹר בָּהּ חוֹל. רֵיחַיִם לִטְחוֹן בָּהּ סַמְמָנִים. תַּנּוּר לְהַטְמִין בּוֹ אוּנִּין שֶׁלְּפִשְׁתָּן.

1 בעי | בעא   2 בפירושא | ש במפרש   כפירוש | ש כפירושו   אמר ליה | ש -   4 להטמין | ש לטמון

Halakhah 10: "A woman may lend to her neighbor," etc. Rebbi Zeïra asked before Rebbi Mana: Does our Mishnah deal with the implicit case, rather than the explicit? He said to him, is the implicit case not explicit? He said to him, I can say a coarse sieve to count coins, a sieve to sift sand, grindstones to grind spices, a stove to put in flax bundles.

(47c line 30) רִבִּי פִינְחָס בָּעֵי. בַּמֶּה קָנְסוּ. בְּמָקוֹם שֶׁזּוֹרְעִין וְאוֹכְלִין אוֹ בְּמָקוֹם שֶׁזּוֹרְעִין וְלֹא אוֹכְלִין. מַה נָּפַק מִבֵּינֵיהוֹן. רָאוּ אוֹתוֹ לוֹקֵחַ מִן הַסִּירְקִי. אָסוּר. וְאִין תֵּימַר בִּמְקוֹם שֶׁזּוֹרְעִין וְאוֹכְלִין רָאוּ אוֹתוֹ לוֹקֵחַ מִן הַסִּירְקִי מוּתָּר.

2 אסור | ש אין תימר. במקום שזורעין ואוכלין. ראו אותו לוקח מן הסירקי   3 ואין | אין   ואוכלין | ש ואין אוכלין

Rebbi Phineas asked: For what did they impose a fine? At a place where they sow and eat or at a place where they sow but do not eat? What is the difference? If one saw him buying from Saracens. [246]It is forbidden; if you say at a place where they sow and eat, if one saw him buying from Saracens it is permitted.

246 See variant readings and the translation in *Ševi'it* for the text that probably was omitted here.

(47c line 30) רִבִּי יוֹסֵי בֵּירִבִּי חֲנִינָה בָּעֵי. עַל כָּל־פִּירְקָא אִיתְּמַר אוֹ עַל הָדָא הִילְכְתָא אִיתְּאָמַר. רַבָּנִין דְּקֵיסָרִין בְּשֵׁם רִבִּי יוּדָה בַּר טִיטֹס. מִן מַה דְּתַנִּינָן בְּגִיטִּין אֶלָּא הָדָא אָמְרָה הָדָא הִילְכְתָא. עַל הָדָא הִילְכְתָא אִיתְּמַר.

1 ביר׳ | בר   איתמר | ש איתאמרת   [247](in all occurrences)   2 דתנינן | ש דלא תנינן   3 אמרה הדא | ש [248]-   על | הדא אמרה על

Rebbi Yose bar Ḥanina asked: Has this been said for all of this chapter or only for this Mishnah? The rabbis of Caesarea in the name of Rebbi

Judah bar Titus: From the fact that we state this Mishnah in *Giṭṭin* it follows that it was said only for this Mishnah.

247 איתמר is standard Babylonian spelling, איתאמרת Galilean.

248 The text is slightly garbled here. The translation follows the *Ševi'it* text.

(47c line 33) תַּמָּן תַּנִּינָן נַחְתּוֹם שֶׁהוּא עוֹשֶׂה בְטוּמְאָה לֹא לָשִׁין וְאֵין עוֹרְכִין עִמּוֹ. וְתַנֵּי עֲלָהּ. לֹא בּוֹרְרִין וְלֹא טוֹחֲנִין עִמּוֹ. וְהָכָא הוּא אָמַר אָכֵן. אָמַר רִבִּי אִילָא. כָּאן לְחוּלִין כָּאן לִתְרוּמָה. וְהָתַנִּינָן נַחְתּוֹם. אִית לְמֵימַר נַחְתּוֹם בִּתְרוּמָה. חֲבֵרַיָּיא אָמְרֵי. כָּאן בְּלוֹתֵת וְכָאן בְּשֶׁאֵינוֹ לוֹתֵת. מַתְנִיתָא מְסַיְּיעָא לַחֲבֵרַיָּיא. אֲבָל מִשֶּׁתַּטִּיל אֶת הַמַּיִם לֹא תִגַּע אֶצְלָהּ.

1 ואין | ש ולא   2 טוחנין עמו | ש טוחנין ולא מרקידין עמו   אכן | ש הכן   3 אילא | ש לא   4 למימר | ש לך מימר   5 את המים | המים   - | ש שאין מחזיקין ידי עוברי עבירה. וכולן לא אמרו אלא מפני דרכי שלום

There, we have stated: One does not knead or form bread with a baker working in impurity. And it was stated additionally: One should neither cull nor grind with him. And here, it says so? Rebbi La said, here for profane [bread], there for heave. Can you say heave at a baker's? The colleagues say, one if he washes, there if he does not wash. The Mishnah supports the colleagues: "But she may not touch hers once water has been put in."

(47c line 39) רִבִּי חִייָה וְרִבִּי אִימִי חַד אָמַר חֲרוֹשׁ בָּהּ טָבָאוֹת וַאֲנָא נְסַב לָהּ מִינָךְ בָּתַר שְׁמִיטְתָא. וְחָרְנָא אָמַר. יַיְשֵׁר. מָאן דְּאָמַר. חֲרוֹשׁ בָּהּ טָבָאוֹת וַאֲנָא נְסַב לָהּ מִינָךְ בָּתַר שְׁמִיטְתָא. מַה שׁוֹאֲלִין בִּשְׁלוֹמָן שֶׁלְּיִשְׂרָאֵל. יַיְשֵׁר. וּמָאן דְּאָמַר לְגוֹי יַיְשֵׁר. דְּלֹא מָא רִבִּי חִינְנָא בַּר פַּפָּא וְרִבִּי שְׁמוּאֵל בַּר נַחְמָן עֲבַרוּן עַל חַד מֵחוֹרְשֵׁי שְׁבִיעִית. אָמַר לֵיהּ רִבִּי שְׁמוּאֵל בַּר נַחְמָן. יִשְׂרָאֵל אַתְּ. אָמַר לֵיהּ רִבִּי חִינְנָא בַּר פַּפָּא. לֹא כֵן אוּלְפָן רִבִּי. וְלֹא אָמְרוּ הָעוֹבְרִים בִּרְכַּת יי עֲלֵיכֶם.

אִילּוּ אוּמוֹת הָעוֹלָם שֶׁהֵן כָּלִין וְעוֹבְרִין מִן הָעוֹלָם. לֹא אָמְרוּ לְיִשְׂרָאֵל בִּרְכַּת יְיָ עֲלֵיכֶם. מַה יִשְׂרָאֵל אוֹמְרִין לָהֶן. בֵּרַכְנוּ אֶתְכֶם בְּשֵׁם יְיָ. לֹא דַיֵּיכֶם שֶׁכָּל־הַבְּרָכוֹת שֶׁבָּאוֹת לָעוֹלָם בִּזְכוּתֵינוּ הֵן בָּאוֹת. וְלֹא דַיֵּיכֶם שֶׁאֵין אַתֶּם אוֹמְרִים לָנוּ בּוֹאוּ וּטְלוּ מִן הַבְּרָכוֹת הַלָּלוּ. אֶלָּא שֶׁאַתֶּם מְגַלְגְּלִין עָלֵינוּ פִּיסִים וְזִימִיּוֹנוֹת גּוּלְגָּלִיּוֹת וְאַרְנוֹנִיּוֹת.

[249]Rebbi Ḥiyya, Rebbi Ammi. One said: "Plough it well then, I will rent it from you after the Sabbatical." The other one said: "May you succeed" For him who says, plough it well, then I will rent it from you after the Sabbatical, what means "one greets them" in a Jewish way? "May you succeed." For him who says to the Gentile "may you succeed"? Explanation: Rebbi Ḥinena bar Pappa and Rebbi Samuel bar Naḥman passed by one of the ploughmen in the Sabbatical. Rebbi Samuel bar Naḥman said to him, are you not Jewish? Rebbi Ḥinena bar Pappa said to him, did not Rebbi teach us (*Ps.* 129:8): "The passers-by did not say, the blessing of the Eternal be on you," these are the nations of the world who pass out of the world, they did not say to Israel "the blessing of the Eternal is on you." What does Israel say to them, "we bless you in the Name of the Eternal." All blessings that come into the world because of us are not enough for you; not only do you not say, come and take from these blessings for yourselves, but you roll over us pro-rated contributions and fines, head taxes and *annonae*.

249 The essence of the paragraph is missing in this copy; cf. the full text in *Sevi'it* 4:3, (Notes 50-57). The paragraph should not be taken as a variant of the text but as a hint to look up the original.

האומר התקבל פרק ששי

משנה א: הָאוֹמֵר הִתְקַבֵּל גֵּט זֶה לְאִשְׁתִּי אוֹ הוֹלֵךְ גֵּט זֶה לְאִשְׁתִּי אִם (fol. 47c) רָצָה לְהַחֲזִיר יַחֲזִיר. הָאִשָּׁה שֶׁאָמְרָה הִתְקַבֵּל לִי גִּיטִי אִם רָצָה לְהַחֲזִיר לֹא יַחֲזִיר. לְפִיכָךְ אִם אָמַר לוֹ הַבַּעַל אִי אֶיפְשִׁי שֶׁתְּתַקַּבֵּל לָהּ אֶלָּא הוֹלֵךְ וְתֵן לָהּ אִם רָצָה לְהַחֲזִיר יַחֲזִיר. רַבָּן שִׁמְעוֹן בֶּן גַּמְלִיאֵל אוֹמֵר אַף הָאוֹמֶרֶת טוֹל לִי גִּיטִי אִם רָצָה לְהַחֲזִיר לֹא יַחֲזִיר.

Mishnah 1: Somebody who says, accept this bill of divorce for my wife, or bring this bill of divorce to my wife, may retract if he wants to retract[1]. If a woman said, accept the bill of divorce for me, he[2] cannot retract even if he wants to retract. Therefore, if the husband said, it is not possible for me that you accept for her but bring and deliver it to her, he may retract if he wants to retract[3]. Rabban Simeon ben Gamliel says, even if she says, take my the bill of divorce for me, he cannot retract even if he wants to retract[4].

1 If the husband appoints an agent, he may annul the agency any time as long as the bill was not delivered.

2 The husband cannot retract the bill of divorce once it has been delivered to the wife's agent whose hand acts for her hand.

3 The husband may refuse to recognize the messenger as the wife's agent but appoint him as his own agent. Then the messenger acts uniquely as the husband's agent.

4 Even if the wife's agency was not spelled out clearly.

(47d line 22) **הלכה א**: הָאוֹמֵר הִתְקַבֵּל גֵּט זֶה לְאִשְׁתִּי כול׳. בְּכָל־אָתָר אַתְּ אָמַר. הִתְקַבֵּל כִּזְכֵה. הָכָא אַתְּ אָמַר. הִתְקַבֵּל כְּהוֹלֵךְ. שַׁנְיָיה הִיא שֶׁזָּכִין לוֹ לְאָדָם שֶׁלֹּא בְּפָנָיו. הָתִיב רִבִּי שַׁמַּי. הַגַּע עַצְמָךְ שֶׁהָיְתָה צוֹוַחַת לְהִתְגָּרֵשׁ. אֲנִי אוֹמֵר. שֶׁמָּא חָזְרָה בָהּ. הָא תַנִּינָן. הִיא עַצְמָהּ מְבִיאָה אֶת גִּיטָהּ. חָשׁ לוֹמַר שֶׁמָּא חָזְרָה בָהּ. תַּמָּן הִיא חָבָה לְעַצְמָהּ. בְּרַם הָכָא חוֹב לָהּ.

Halakhah 1: "Somebody who says, accept this bill of divorce for my wife," etc. Everywhere you say that "accept" is the equivalent of "obtain,"[5] but here you say that "accept" is the equivalent of "bring"[6]? There is a difference, for one can obtain something for a person without him being present[7]. Rebbi Shammai objected: Think of it, if she was shouting to obtain a divorce[8]? I say, maybe she changed her mind. But did we not state[9]: "A woman herself may bring her bill of divorce"? Could you say that she may have changed her mind[10]? There, she is damaging herself[11]; here it is to her detriment.

5   If A says to B: "accept this gift for C", then if B has accepted the gift it is C's property and A cannot retract the gift. Why can the husband annul the bill of divorce when he empowered the agent to receive the bill of divorce for his wife?

6   The divorce takes effect only by delivery of the bill into the woman's hand.

7   In the language of the Babli (11b, *Ketubot* 11a, *Yebamot* 118b, *Qiddušin* 23a, 24a, *Eruvin* 81b, *Baba Meṣi'a* 12a, *Ḥulin* 63a): "One may give a benefit to a person without his knowledge but one cannot put a detriment on him without his knowledge." Since a divorce is considered detrimental to the wife, the husband has no power to appoint an agent to receive the bill for his wife; his instruction has to be re-interpreted to mean that he has to deliver the bill to the wife.

8   Then the divorce would be a benefit to her.

9   Mishnah 2:8, Note 139.

10   If the husband hands the bill of divorce to his wife and stipulates that the divorce become valid only at the

moment she brings the bill to the court at her place of residence which is not his place, can she change her mind, return to her place, and not showing the bill, being then married to her husband without his knowledge?

11 By accepting to be her husband's agent, she accepted the obligation to become divorced; this is with her knowledge and cannot be compared to the agency of a third party. This interpretation is by Rashba (on *Yebamot* 118b), quoted by *Nimmuqe Yosef* (on Alfassi *Yebamot*, end of Chapter 15).

(47d line 28) רַב נַחְמָן בַּר יַעֲקֹב אָמַר. אָמְרָה. הָבֵא לִי גִיטִּי. וְהָלַךְ וְאָמַר לוֹ. אִשְׁתְּךָ אָמְרָה. הִתְקַבֵּל לִי גִיטִּי. אַף עַל פִּי שֶׁהִגִּיעַ לְיָדָהּ אֵינוֹ גֵט. שֶׁהוּא סָבוּר מִדַּעַת הַשָּׁלִיחַ מִתְגָּרֶשֶׁת. וְהִיא אֵינָהּ מִתְגָּרֶשֶׁת אֶלָּא מִדַּעְתָּהּ. הָתִיב רִבִּי הוּנָא בַּר חִיָּיה. וְהָא דְתַנִּינָן. הָאִשָּׁה שֶׁאָמְרָה. הִתְקַבֵּל לִי גִיטִּי. אֵינוֹ גֵט עַד שֶׁיַּגִּיעַ גֵּט לְיָדָהּ. מֵעַתָּה אֲפִילוּ הִגִּיעַ גֵּט לְיָדָהּ אֵינוֹ גֵט. שֶׁהִיא סְבוּרָה שֶׁהִיא מִתְגָּרֶשֶׁת מִדַּעַת הַשָּׁלִיחַ. וְהִיא אֵינָהּ מִתְגָּרֶשֶׁת אֶלָּא מִדַּעְתָּהּ. בְּיוֹדֵעַ הֲלָכָה לוֹמַר. הִתְקַבֵּל וּזְכֵה כְּהוֹלֵךְ. וְהָתַנִּינָן. קְטַנָּה שֶׁאָמְרָה. הִתְקַבֵּל לִי גִיטִּי. אֵינוֹ גֵט עַד שֶׁיַּגִּיעַ גֵּט לְיָדָהּ. מֵעַתָּה אֲפִילוּ הִגִּיעַ גֵּט לְיָדָהּ אֵינוֹ גֵט. שֶׁהִיא סְבוּרָה שֶׁמָּא לְדַעַת הַשָּׁלִיחַ הִיא מִתְגָּרֶשֶׁת. וְהִיא אֵינָהּ מִתְגָּרֶשֶׁת אֶלָּא מִדַּעְתָּהּ. בְּיוֹדֵעַ שֶׁאֵין הַקָּטָן עוֹשֶׂה שָׁלִיחַ.

[12]Rav Naḥman bar Jacob said: If she said, bring me my bill of divorce, but he went and said to him[13], your wife said, accept the bill of divorce for me[14], even after the bill came into her hand it is not a valid bill of divorce, since he[15] thinks that she will be divorced by the acceptance of the agent but she can be divorced only by her own acceptance[16]. Rebbi Huna bar Ḥiyya objected: But did we not state that if a woman said, accept the bill of divorce for me, it is not a valid bill of divorce until it reaches her hand[17]? Then even if the bill came into her hand it should not be a valid bill! For she thinks that she will be divorced by the acceptance

of the agent but she can be divorced only by her own acceptance. If he knows that practice is that "accept" and "obtain" mean "bring"[18]. But did we not state[19]: "If an underage girl said, accept the bill of divorce for me, it is not a valid bill until the bill of divorce reaches her hand." Then it should not be a valid bill even if the bill of divorce reaches her hand. For she thinks that maybe she is divorced by the acceptance of the agent, but she can be divorced only by her own acceptance. If he knows that a minor cannot appoint an agent[20].

12   A similar discussion is in the Babli, 62b-63a, quoting the same authors but in a different setting. (In the Babli, the husband shows that he does not quite believe the agent; here the husband acts on the agent's word.)

13   The wife's agent speaking to the husband.

14   Since the wife can empower an agent to accept the bill of divorce for her, "accept" in this context must mean "acquire". The agent violated the terms of his agency.

15   The husband.

16   Since *Deut.* 24:1 requires that the husband put the bill of divorce into the wife's hand, it is a biblical requirement that both husband and wife know the moment of divorce. In the case before us, the defect of the divorce is biblical and cannot be remedied except by a new bill.

17   The quote is elliptic; most probably it refers to a text close to Tosephta 4:2 where the wife appoints an agent to *receive* her bill of divorce and the husband instructs him to *deliver* the bill into her hand.

18   While the wife can appoint an agent to legally receive the bill in her stead, the husband cannot appoint such an agent and, as explained in the preceding paragraph, for him "receive" means "deliver". The husband is free to interpret the wife's instructions in terms of his own vocabulary. (The Babli, obviously dissatisfied with this solution, holds that the husband's instructions must be followed to the letter but since the wife can be divorced against her will, the husband's instructions override those of the wife and the latter's instructions were given only subject to the husband's approval.)

19 Mishnah 6:3.

20 While an underage girl becomes emancipated from her father's *potestas* by marriage (*Ketubot* 4:2, Note 42), she can become an adult only by reaching the age of puberty. If she is divorced while being underage, she becomes "an orphan during her father's lifetime" and will need an adult guardian to execute legal acts in her behalf. The husband in this case has to empower the agent to deliver the bill; he cannot rely on the underage wife's instructions.

(47d line 38) רַב הוּנָא בְּשֵׁם רַב. אֵין הָאִשָּׁה עוֹשָׂה שָׁלִיחַ לְקַבֵּל גִּיטָּהּ מִשְּׁלוּחוֹ שֶׁלְבַּעֲלָהּ. שְׁמוּאֵל שְׁמָעָהּ מִינֵּיהּ וְלָעֲתָהּ בַּתְרֵיהּ אַרְבָּעִים זִמְנֵי.

Rav Huna said in the name of Rav: A woman cannot appoint an agent to accept her bill of divorce from her husband's agent[21]. Samuel heard this from him and repeated after him forty times.

21 Quoted in the Babli, 63b, and opposed there by the Galilean R. Ḥanina. Rabbinic practice follows R. Ḥanina. The Babli conjectures that a possible reason for Rav's statement is that if the wife refuses to accept the bill from the husband's agent but appoints her agent to receive the bill, she does this only to hinder the husband's agent to fulfill his mission to deliver the bill to her. In that case, the wife would be entitled to appoint her agent if her appointment precedes her husband's. Another conjectured reason is that there is a very remote possibility that things can go wrong if the bill is not actually delivered from hand to hand but deposited on her (or her agent's) property. The basis for the possible complication is a rule which is not alluded to in the Yerushalmi and, therefore, should not be used to explain a statement in that Talmud.

(47d line 40) רִבִּי זְעִירָא בָּעֵי. עַד כְּדוֹן בְּשֶׁאֲמָרָהּ. הֲבָא לִי. וְאָמְרָה לוֹ. הִתְקַבֵּל לִי. אֲמָרָהּ. הִתְקַבֵּל לִי. וְהוּא אָמַר לוֹ. הֲבָא לִי. אַשְׁכָּח תַּנֵּי עַל תְּרַוֵּיהוֹן.[23] הֲרֵי זֶה גֵט וְאִם רָצָה לְהַחֲזִיר לֹא יַחֲזִיר. וְהָא תַנִּינָן. וְנָתַן בְּיָדָהּ. אֵין לִי אֶלָּא

בְּיָדָהּ. מִנַּיִן בְּיַד שְׁלוּחוֹ בְּיַד שְׁלוּחָהּ מִשְׁלוּחוֹ לִשְׁלוּחָהּ מִשְׁלוּחָהּ לִשְׁלוּחוֹ מִנַּיִן. תַּלְמוּד לוֹמַר וְנָתַן וְנָתַן. מָה תַּנֵּי אִי אֶיפְשִׁי. רַבִּי. דְּתַנֵּי. אֶמְרָה. הָבֵא לִי גִיטִּי. וְהָלַךְ וְאָמַר לוֹ. אִשְׁתְּךָ אֶמְרָה. הִתְקַבֵּל לִי גִיטִּי. הוֹלִיכוּ לָהּ וּנְתָנוּ לָהּ זָכָה לָהּ וְנִתְקַבֵּל לָהּ. אִם רָצָא לְהַחֲזִיר לֹא יַחֲזִיר. דִּבְרֵי רַבִּי. רַבִּי נָתָן אוֹמֵר. הוֹלִיכוּ לָהּ וּנְתָנוּ לָהּ. אִם רָצָא לְהַחֲזִיר לֹא יַחֲזִיר עַד שֶׁיֹּאמַר לוֹ. אִי אֶיפְשִׁי שֶׁתְּקַבְּלוֹ לָהּ אֶלָּא שֶׁתּוֹלִיכוּ לָהּ. וְקַשְׁיָא עַל דְּרַבִּי. הֵילָךְ מִן דִּיבּוּרִי אִם רָצָא לְהַחֲזִיר יַחֲזִיר. וְקַשְׁיָא עַל דְּרַבִּי נָתָן. הֵילָךְ לְדִיבּוּרָהּ אִם רָצָא לְהַחֲזִיר יַחֲזִיר. רַב הוּנָא אָמַר. נַעֲשָׂה שְׁלוּחוֹ וּשְׁלוּחָהּ. אַסִּי אָמַר. כָּל הֵיכָא דְּאָמַר. שְׁלוּחוֹ וּשְׁלוּחָהּ. מְגוּרֶשֶׁת וְאֵינָהּ מְגוּרֶשֶׁת.

2 (Ma'aser Šeni 4:7, 55a l. 70) התקבל | ונתקבל   3 אם רצה להחזיר | אם רצה להחזיר יחזיר. זכה לה והתקבל לה אם רצה להחזיר לא יחזיר. ר' או'. בכולן לא יחזיר   4 שתקבלו | שתקבלי   שתוליכו | שתוליכי   הילך²³ | הא לך   5 מן דיבורי | מדיבורי יחזיר | לא יחזיר   וקשיא | וקשייא   הילך²³ | הא לך   לדיבורה | מדיבורא   6 יחזיר | לא יחזיר   רב הונא | ר' חונא   אסי²³ | איסא   כל היכא דאמ' | כולהון דתנינן

אָמַר רִבִּי חַגַּיי קוֹמֵי רִבִּי יוֹסֵי. וְאַתְיָין אִילֵּין פְּלוּגָתָא כְּאִילֵּין פְּלוּגָתָא. דְּתַנִּינָן תַּמָּן. הָיָה מְדַבֵּר עִם הָאִשָּׁה עַל עִסְקֵי גִיטָּהּ וְקִידּוּשֶׁיהָ וְנָתַן לָהּ גִּיטָּהּ וְקִידּוּשֶׁיהָ וְלֹא פֵירַשׁ. רִבִּי יוֹסֵי אוֹמֵר דַּיָּיו. רִבִּי יְהוּדָה אוֹמֵר. צָרִיךְ לְפָרֵשׁ. וְאַתְיָא דְּרִבִּי כְּרִבִּי יוֹסֵי. וּדְרִבִּי נָתָן כְּרִבִּי יוּדָה. אָמַר לֵיהּ וְאַתְּ מַה בְּיָדָךְ. דְּאָמַר רִבִּי זְעִירָא אָמַר רִבִּי חִייָא בַּר אָבִין בַּר אָדָא בַּר תַּחְלִיפָא בְּשֵׁם רִבִּי הוֹשַׁעְיָה. מַה פְּלִיגִין. עַצְמוּ לְעִנְיָינוֹת אֲחֵרִים. אֲבָל אִם הָיָה עוֹסֵק בְּאוֹתוֹ עִנְיָין גֵּט הוּא. וְהָכָא אֲפִילוּ בָּעוֹסְקִין בְּאוֹתוֹ עִנְיָין הִיא מַחֲלוֹקֶת.

1 (Ma'aser Šeni 4:7, 56a l. 4) ואת מה | ומה   דאמר | ואמר   אמר ר' | -   אבין | בון   2 ר' | רב   עצמו לעניינות | כשהפליגו דעתן לעניינות   2-3 היה עוסק | היו עסוקין בעוסקין | הן עסוקין   3 מחלוקת | המחלוקת

²²Rebbi Ze'ira asked: So far if she said, bring me, but [the agent] said [to the husband] "receive for me"²⁴. If she said, receive for me but [the agent] said [to the husband] "bring me"? If was found stated in both cases,

this is a bill of divorce and if he wants to retract he cannot retract[25]. But did we not state[26]: "He shall deliver into her hand," that includes not only her hand, from where through his agent's hand, into her agent's hand, from his agent to her agent, and from her agent to his agent; the verse says, "he shall deliver, he shall deliver." Who said, "it is impossible for me"? Rebbi! [27]As it was stated: "If she said, bring me my bill of divorce, but he said to him, your wife said, accept my bill of divorce for me: If he brought it to her, gave it to her, he acquired it for her, it was received for her; if he wants to retract, he may not[28] retract, the words of Rebbi. Rebbi Nathan says, 'bring it to her, give it to her,' [29][if he wants to retract, he may retract; 'acquire it for her, receive it for her', if he wants to retract, he may not retract. Rebbi says, in any of these cases] he may not retract except if he says, 'It is impossible for me that you accept it for her, but give it to her.'[30]" It is difficult for Rebbi, "here you have it from my word", if he wants to retract, he may retract[31]. It is difficult for Rebbi Nathan, "here you have it from her word", if he wants to retract, he may retract[32]! Rav Huna said, he becomes his and her agent[33]. Assi said, everywhere we have stated "his and her agent", she is both divorced and not divorced.

Rebbi Haggai said before Rebbi Yose: Is not this disagreement the same as that disagreement, as we have stated there[34]: "If a man was talking with a woman about her bill of divorce or her preliminary marriage and gave her the bill of divorce or [some valuable for] preliminary marriage and did not spell it out[35], Rebbi Yose says it is sufficient[36]; Rebbi Jehudah says he has to be explicit." Then Rebbi follows Rebbi Yose and Rebbi Nathan Rebbi Jehudah. He[37] said to him, what do you have in your hand, did not Rebbi Zeïra, Ḥiyya bar Abin, Abba bar Taḥlifa, say in the name of Rebbi Hoshaia, when do they differ? [If they thought about] other things but if he still was on the same subject, it is a bill of divorce[38]. But here, even if they are still on the same subject there is disagreement.

22 The major source of this paragraph and the next is in *Ma'aser Šeni* 4:7, Notes 118-129. Since the introduction is different and some essential passages are missing here, it is clear that this passage is derivative. But since the text has suffered some rearrangement, it cannot be a direct copy (as noted in the Introduction.)

23 A Babylonism.

24 Since the agent was not appointed by the husband, he cannot legally deliver the bill.

25 Probably a text similar to Tosephta 4:2 (Babli 63a) following the three main sources of the Tosephta (a text rejected by S. Lieberman.) While the bill is considered delivered only when the wife receives it, the agent is not empowered to return it to the husband. The Babli, 63a, explicitly states that the divorce is valid from the moment the agent receives the bill.

26 This inference from the repetition of the expression וְנָתַן בְּיָדָהּ in *Deut.* 24:1,3 is missing in other sources;

cf. Halakhah 8:1. The Babli, *Qiddušin* 41a, derives the possibility of divorce by agent (שָׁלִיחַ) from the expression וְשִׁלְּחָהּ in *Deut.* 24:1 For the general principle that "an agent takes the place of a principal" cf. *Qiddušin* 2:1 (62a l. 41), Babli 41b. It is not trivial that a bill of divorce can be delivered by an agent since *ḥalîṣah* cannot be performed by an agent.

27 Here starts the text from *Ma'aser Šeni*, Notes 120 ff. The quote in *Ma'aser Šeni* is from Tosephta *Giṭṭin* 4:1; the text here, while almost identical, has a totally different meaning. In the Tosephta, the husband instructs the agent to act for him; in the text here, the husband does not say anything but gives the bill to the agent who delivers it to the wife. It then is stated that the act of delivery validates the divorce.

28 In the Tosephta mss., "not" is missing.

29 From the text in *Ma'aser Šeni*, missing here but essential for an

understanding of the text. The omission from להחזיר to להחזיר is easily explained.

30 If the husband explicitly appoints the agent as his own.

31 If the husband gives the bill and tells the agent to deliver, it should automatically invalidate the wife's commission and let him retract.

32 If the husband tells the agent to do for him what the wife instructed him to do, he did not accept the agent as her agent and should be able to retract.

33 In either case mentioned here, it is not clear whose agent he is; the divorce is questionable and does not permit the wife to remarry. (Babli 63b, Rav Huna in the name of Rav).

34 Mishnah *Ma'aser Šeni* 4:7.

35 There were two witnesses present but the man did not alert them that he was going to divorce or marry, neither did he warn the woman that he was now going to act on his word.

36 It is sufficient that everybody involved understood what was going on.

37 R. Yose to R. Haggai.

38 Even R. Jehudah will agree that if two witnesses are present during the writing of a bill of divorce they do not have to be alerted for the delivery. But this has no implications for our case where the question is the due form of the appointment of an agent. In the Babli, *Qiddušin* 6a, this is the concurrent opinion of Rav and Samuel.

(47d line 60) רִבִּי זְעִירָא בָּעֵי קוֹמֵי רִבִּי מָנָא. אַף לְעִנְיָין מַתָּנָה כֵן. אָדָם עוֹשֶׂה שָׁלִיחַ לְקַבֵּל דָּבָר שֶׁאֵינוֹ שֶׁלּוֹ. אָמַר לֵיהּ. תַּמָּן הַתּוֹרָה זִיכַּת אוֹתָהּ בְּגִיטָּהּ וְהִיא עוֹשָׂה שָׁלִיחַ לְקַבֵּל דָּבָר שֶׁהוּא שֶׁלָּהּ. אִית לָךְ מֵימַר בְּמַתָּנָה. אָדָם עוֹשֶׂה שָׁלִיחַ לְקַבֵּל דָּבָר שֶׁאֵינוֹ שֶׁלּוֹ. וְעוֹד מִן הָדָא דְּאָמַר רִבִּי יוֹסֵה וְרִבִּי יַעֲקֹב בַּר זַבְדִּי רִבִּי אַבָּהוּ בְּשֵׁם רִבִּי יוֹחָנָן. אָמַר לִיתֵּן מַתָּנָה לַחֲבֵירוֹ וּבִיקֵּשׁ לַחֲזוֹר בּוֹ חוֹזֵר בּוֹ. קָם רִבִּי יוֹסֵי עִם רִבִּי יַעֲקֹב בַּר זַבְדִּי. אָמַר לֵיהּ וְהֵן הוּא הִין צֶדֶק. אָמַר לוֹ. בְּשָׁעָה שֶׁאָמְרוּ הִין צֶדֶק הֲוָה.

1 (Ma'aser Šeni 4:7, 56a l. 7) זעירא | עזרה   4 יוסה | יוסי   ור' | ר'   6 והן הוא | והינו   אמר לו | אמרין

Rebbi Ze'ira asked before Rebbi Mana: Is it the same for a gift? Can a person appoint an agent for anything that is not his? He said to him, there the Torah gave her the right to a bill of divorce and she appoints an agent to receive what is rightfully hers. Can you say in regard to a gift that a person can appoint an agent for anything that is not his? In addition, from what Rebbi Yose and Rebbi Jacob bar Zavdi, Rebbi Abbahu in the name of Rebbi Johanan said, if somebody said to give a gift to another and he wants to retract, he may retract. Rebbi Yose stood near Rebbi Jacob bar Zavdi and said to him, is that a just "yes"[39]? He said to him, at the moment he said it, it was a just "yes".

[39] *Lev.* 19:36: "Your *hîn* shall be just". The הִין is a liquid measure (half a *se'ah*). But since biblical כֵּן "yes" became rabbinic הֵן, the verse is interpreted to mean that in money matters any "yes" has to be honest. The formal argument is that the verse already mentioned the *ephah* as correct measure; therefore the smaller *hîn* requires symbolic interpretation. [This learned pun is in the name of R. Yose ben R. Jehudah in the Babli, *Baba meṣi'a* 49a, *Bekhorot* 13b; *Sifra Qedošim Pereq* 8(7)].

(47d line 69) אָמַר לוֹ. הוֹלֵךְ גֵּט אִשְׁתִּי גֵּט בִּתָּהּ גֵּט אֲחוֹתָהּ. וְהָלַךְ וּנְתָנוֹ לָהּ. אֵינוֹ גֵט. תְּבָעוֹ הַשָּׁלִיחַ וְאָמַר לוֹ. תֵּן גֵּט לְאִשְׁתּוֹ. אָמַר לוֹ. הֵילָךְ גֵּט אִשְׁתִּי גֵּט בִּתָּהּ גֵּט אֲחוֹתָהּ. וְהָלַךְ וּנְתָנוֹ לָהּ. הֲרֵי זֶה גֵט. רִבִּי יוֹסֵי בֵּירִבִּי בּוּן וְרִבִּי אָבִין בְּשֵׁם רִבִּי שַׁמַּי. זוֹ דִּבְרֵי רִבִּי. אֲבָל חֲכָמִים אוֹמְרִים. בְּאוֹמֶרֶת. יְהֵא לִי בְיָדָךְ.

If [the husband] said to [another person]: Bring my wife's bill of divorce, or her daughter's, or her sister's, then he went and delivered it to her, it is no divorce[40]. But if [the other] said: Give a bill of divorce to his wife, and [the husband] said, here is my wife's bill of divorce, or her daughter's, or her sister's, and he went and gave it to her, it is a divorce.

Rebbi Yose ben Rebbi Abun and Rebbi Avin in the name of Rebbi Shammai: These are Rebbi's words. But the Sages say, only if she says, it should be mine in your hand[41].

40 The text is not in good condition. A similarly corrupt text is in Tosephta 4:2, but from both texts the original can be approximated: If the husband said to a third party: Bring my wife's, or (*your* or *his*) daughter's or (*your* or *his*) sister's, and he went and delivered it to her, it is no divorce since the third party was never appointed an agent for delivery. But if a woman appoints an agent, who goes and requests a bill of divorce from her husband and receives the bill without being appointed the husband's agent of delivery, it is a perfectly valid divorce the moment the agent takes possession of the bill. (According to Rav Huna, this situation is preferable to one in which the agent also becomes the husband's agent, unless the husband explicitly invalidates the wife's commission.)

41 Rebbi accepts an implicit commissioning while the rabbis require an explicit statement.

(47d line 73) אָמַר רִבִּי חֲנִינָא. הֲלָכָה כְרַבָּן גַּמְלִיאֵל. וְהוּא שֶׁאָמְרָה לוֹ הִיא טוֹל לִי. יְהֵא לִי בְיָדָךְ. חַד בַּר נַשׁ שָׁלַח גֵּט לְאִיתְּתֵיהּ. אָמְרָה לֵיהּ. יְהֵא לִי בְיָדָךְ. אֲתָא עוֹבְדָא קוֹמֵי רַב. אָמַר. אִם בָּא לְהַחֲזִיר לֹא יַחֲזִיר. מַה וּפְלִיג. שַׁנְיָיא הוּא יְהֵא בְיָדָךְ שַׁנְיָיא הוּא יְהֵא לִי בְיָדָךְ. אָמַר רִבִּי חִזְקִיָּה. אֲנָא יָדַע רֵישָׁא וְסֵיפָא. אִשָּׁה אַחַת עָשְׂת שָׁלִיחַ לְקַבֵּל גִּיטָּהּ מִשְּׁלוּחֵי בַעֲלָהּ. אֲתָא עוֹבְדָא קוֹמֵי רַב. אָמַר. אִם רָצָה לְהַחֲזִיר לֹא יַחֲזִיר. מַחְלְפָה שִׁיטָּתֵיהּ דְּרַב. תַּמָּן אָמַר רַב הוּנָא בְשֵׁם רַב. אֵין הָאִשָּׁה עוֹשָׂה שָׁלִיחַ לְקַבֵּל גִּיטָּהּ מִשְּׁלוּחֵי בַעֲלָהּ. וְהָכָא הוּא אָמַר הָכֵין. אֲנִי אֹמֵר. אַחַר הַדֶּלֶת הָיָה עוֹמֵד וְשָׁמַע אֶת קוֹלָהּ.

Rebbi Ḥanina said, practice follows Rabban Gamliel[42]: if she said "take for me, it should be mine in your hand.[43]" A man sent a bill of divorce to his wife. She told [the agent]: "It should be mine in your hand." The case came before Rav, who said, if he wants to retract he cannot retract[44]. Does he disagree[45]? There is a difference between "it should be in your hand" and "it should be mine in your hand.[46]" Rebbi Ḥizqiah said, I know the beginning and the end. A woman appointed an agent to accept her bill of divorce from the husband's agents. The case came before Rav, who said, if he wants to retract he cannot retract. Rav's opinion has switched! There, Rav Huna said in the name of Rav: A woman cannot appoint an agent to accept her bill of divorce from her husband's agent[21], and here, he says so? I say, he was standing behind the door and heard her voice[47].

42   This should read: Rabban Simeon ben Gamliel.

43   Not only the expression טול לי mentioned in the Mishnah but any equivalent expression is sufficient to appoint an agent for the wife. The Babli agrees, 63b.

44   Since the bill was never delivered into the wife's hand, the husband then claimed that there was no divorce; but Rav decided that the appointment of the husband's agent as the wife's agent represented delivery of the bill.

45   It is not quite clear with what Rav is supposed to disagree. A similar story is told in the Babli, 63b, about a woman whose hands were dirty and who told the husband's agent to keep the bill, that it should be in his hand. Rav Naḥman, in the generation after Rav, decided that this was no delivery.

46   The second version is clearly an acceptance of the bill whereas the first one is not.

47   The relations between husband and wife were so bad that not only did the husband not want to deliver the bill to his wife who was nearby but the wife did not even want to receive it from the husband's agent. Since the appointment of an agent by the husband under these circumstances was intended as an insult to his wife, her appointing her own agent was an adequate response. Since the husband was present during the entire proceedings, he must have agreed with his wife's appointing her own attorney and there could be no reason to invalidate the proceedings. The statement of Rav Huna can be applied only to cases where not both parties are present.

(fol. 47c) **משנה ב:** הָאִשָּׁה שֶׁאָמְרָה הִתְקַבֵּל לִי גִּטִּי צְרִיכָה שְׁנֵי כִתֵּי עֵדִים. שְׁנַיִם שֶׁאוֹמְרִים בְּפָנֵינוּ אָמְרָה וּשְׁנַיִם שֶׁאוֹמְרִים בְּפָנֵינוּ קִבְּלָהּ וּקְרָעָהּ אֲפִילוּ הֵן הָרִאשׁוֹנִים וְהֵן הָאַחֲרוֹנִימד אוֹ אֶחָד מִן הָרִאשׁוֹנִים וְאֶחָד מִן הָאַחֲרוֹנִים וְאֶחָד מִצְטָרֵף עִמָּהֶן. נַעֲרָה מְאוֹרָסָה הִיא וְאָבִיהָ מְקַבְּלִין אֶת גִּטָּהּ. רַבִּי יְהוּדָה אוֹמֵר אֵין שְׁתֵּי יָדַיִם זוֹכוֹת כְּאַחַת אֶלָּא אָבִיהָ מְקַבֵּל גִּטָּהּ בִּלְבַד. וְכָל שֶׁאֵינָהּ יְכוֹלָה לִשְׁמֹר אֶת גִּטָּהּ אֵינָהּ יְכוֹלָה לְהִתְגָּרֵשׁ.

Mishnah 2: A woman who said, accept my bill of divorce for me, needs two groups of witnesses[48]; two who say that she appointed in their presence and two who say that in their presence he received it and tore it up[49], even if the first ones are the latter ones, or one of the first together with one of the latter and a third person is associated with them[50]. A preliminarily married adolescent girl[51], or her father, can accept her bill of divorce. Rebbi Jehudah says, no two hands can acquire together; only her father alone can accept her bill of divorce. Any female[52] who cannot take care of her bill of divorce cannot be divorced.

48 Since a divorce is a public act it must be executed in front of at least two witnesses. The agent certainly needs two witnesses for the delivery since the woman herself must receive the bill in front of two witnesses. It is only natural that the agent needs two witnesses to legitimize his status (or be appointed by a duly witnessed document.)

49 It is not necessary that the bill be torn up after delivery; this clause is added only to show that the divorce is valid even if the document never reaches the wife because it was torn up after delivery. (This has nothing to do with current rabbinic practice to cut up the bill of divorce after delivery in order to prevent outsiders from questioning the validity of the document.)

50 There do not have to be four different people; there may also be two or three.

51 Between the ages of 12 years and 12 years and six months; cf.

Nedarim 10:1, Note 1. Since she is over 12 years of age, she is able to act in law. But since she is not definitively married, she is still under her father's authority.

52 This statement is independent of the preceding one; it deals with an insane woman or an underage girl who was definitively married and, therefore, is emancipated from her father's power. If she is too young to understand the meaning of divorce and the need to keep the document until she has collected all the monies due her, she cannot be divorced and the husband cannot escape the obligation to feed and house her.

(48a line 7) **הלכה ב:** הָאִשָּׁה שֶׁאָמְרָה הִתְקַבֵּל לִי גִּיטִּי כול'. שְׁנַיִם שֶׁאָמְרוּ בְּפָנֵינוּ אָמְרָה. וּשְׁנַיִם שֶׁאָמְרוּ. בְּפָנֵינוּ קִיבֵּל וְקָרַע. וְהוּא מוֹדֶה. יִצְטָרֵף הַשָּׁלִיחַ. תִּיפְתָּר שֶׁהָיָה קָרוֹב. הָדָא אָמְרָה שֶׁהַקָּרוֹב נַעֲשֶׂה שָׁלִיחַ.

Halakhah 2: "A woman who said, accept my bill of divorce for me," etc. Two say that she appointed in their presence and two say that in their presence he received and tore it. But if he[53] agrees, the agent should be able to be added. Explain it, it he was a relative[54]. This implies that a relative can act as agent.

53 The husband. The wife only needs testimony that the bill was delivered in order to be able to remarry. Why does the Mishnah not state that the agent together with another person can testify in her behalf?

54 A close relative who is inadmissible as witness.

(48a line 10) נַעֲרָה מְאוֹרָסָה הִיא וְאָבִיהָ מְקַבְּלִין גִּיטָּהּ. רֵישׁ לָקִישׁ אָמַר. כְּמַחֲלוֹקֶת בְּגִיטִּין כָּךְ מַחֲלוֹקֶת בְּקִידּוּשִׁין. אָמַר רִבִּי יוֹחָנָן. הַכֹּל מוֹדִין בְּקִידּוּשִׁין שֶׁאִמָּהּ מְקַדְּשָׁהּ וְלֹא הִיא. מוֹדֶה רֵישׁ לָקִישׁ בְּנִישׂוּאִין. לֹא הַכֹּל מִמֶּנָּה לְהַשִּׂיא אֶת עַצְמָהּ וּלְהַפְסִיד מַעֲשֵׂה יָדֶיהָ לְאָבִיהָ. עַל דַּעְתֵּיהּ דְּרִבִּי יוֹחָנָן אֵין לָהּ דַּעַת אֵצֶל אָבִיהָ וְאֵינוֹ עוֹשֶׂה שָׁלִיחַ. עַל דַּעְתֵּיהּ דְּרֵישׁ לָקִישׁ יֵשׁ לָהּ דַּעַת

אֵצֶל אָבִיהָ וְהִיא עוֹשָׂה שָׁלִיחַ. מַתְנִיתָא פְּלִיגָא עַל רִבִּי יוֹחָנָן. הָאִישׁ מְקַדֵּשׁ בּוֹ וּבִשְׁלוּחוֹ וְהָאִשָּׁה מִתְקַדֶּשֶׁת בָּהּ וּבִשְׁלוּחָהּ. פָּתַר לָהּ בִּגְדוֹלָה. וְהָתַנִּינָן. קְטַנָּה שֶׁאָמְרָה. הִתְקַבֵּל לִי גִיטִי. אֵינוֹ גֵט עַד שֶׁיַּגִּיעַ גֵּט לְיָדָהּ. פָּתַר בִּיתוֹמָה. וְהָא תַּנִּינָן. אִם אָמַר לוֹ אָבִיהָ. צֵא וְהִתְקַבֵּל לְבִתִּי גִיטָהּ. אִם רָצָה לְהַחֲזִיר לֹא יַחֲזִיר. פָּתַר לָהּ לִצְדָדִין הִיא מַתְנִיתָהּ. רֵישָׁא בִּיתוֹמָה וְסֵיפָא בְּשֶׁיֵּשׁ לָהּ אָב. מַתְנִיתָא פְּלִיגָא עַל רֵישׁ לָקִישׁ. הָאִישׁ מְקַדֵּשׁ אֶת בִּתּוֹ כְּשֶׁהִיא נַעֲרָה בּוֹ וּבִשְׁלוּחוֹ. פָּתַר לָהּ כְּרִבִּי יְהוּדָה. דְּרִבִּי יְהוּדָה אָמַר. אֵין שְׁתֵּי יָדַיִם זוֹכוֹת כְּאַחַת. דְּאָמַר רִבִּי יוֹסֵי. חַד רַב נָפַק מִבֵּית וַעֲדָא אָמַר. נְפַק עוֹבְדָא כְּרִבִּי יוֹחָנָן. וְסָמְכִין עֲלוֹי. לָא הֲוָה צְרִיכָא מִיסְמוֹךְ עֲלוֹי אֶלָּא דַהֲוָת מִן יַמָּא לְטִיגְנֵי.

3 שאמה | ק שאביה   מקדשה | ק מקדשה ולא היא   מודה | ק לא היה מודה   לא | ק שלא   4 את | ק -   ולהפסיד | ק להפסיד   לאביה | ק על אביה   5 ואינו | ק ואינה דריש לקיש | ק דר׳ שמעון בן לקיש   8 פתר | ק פתר לה   והא תנינן | ק והתנינן   10 היא | ק הא   רישא | ק ראשה   וסיפא | ק וסופה   11 ריש לקיש | ק ר׳ שמעון בן לקיש   12 יהודה | ק יודה   (2 times) 13 דאמ׳ ר׳ יוסי | ק אמ׳ ר׳ אסי   מבית | ק מן בית   14 הוה | ק דהוה   צריכא | ק צורכא   מיסמוך | ק מיסמך   15 דהות | ק דהוות לטיגני | ק לטיגנא

[55]"A preliminarily married adolescent girl[51], or her father, can accept her bill of divorce." Rebbi Simeon ben Laqish said, like the disagreement about divorce is the disagreement about preliminary marriage[56]. Rebbi Joḥanan said, everybody agrees about preliminary marriage that [her father][57] contracts but not she herself. Rebbi Simeon ben Laqish agrees about a definitive marriage that she is not empowered to marry herself off and let her father lose her earnings[58]. In the opinion of Rebbi Joḥanan she has no legal standing relative to her father[59] and cannot appoint an agent. In the opinion of Rebbi Simeon ben Laqish she has legal standing relative to her father and can appoint an agent. A Mishnah disagrees with Rebbi Joḥanan: [60]"A man contracts a preliminary marriage by himself

and through his agent and a woman contracts a preliminary marriage by herself and through her agent." He explains it about an adult woman. But did we not state[61]: "If an underage girl said, accept the bill of divorce for me, it is no valid bill until the bill of divorce reaches her hand.[62]" He explains it about an orphan[63]. But did we not state[61]: "If her father[64] said to [an agent]: Go and receive my daughter's bill of divorce, if [the husband] wants to retract he cannot retract." He explains that the Mishnah deals with cases; the first part about an orphan and the second part if she has a father. A Mishnah disagrees with Rebbi Simeon ben Laqish. [60]"A man may contract a preliminary marriage for his adolescent daughter either by himself or by his agent.[65]" He explains that following Rebbi Jehudah[66], since Rebbi Jehudah said, "no two hands can acquire together; only her father alone can accept her bill of divorce." Rebbi Yose said, a rabbi came out from the assembly and said, a case was decided following Rebbi Johanan[67]. Can one rely on that[68]? It was no question of relying on him since it was as from the sea to the frying pan[69].

55 A parallel is in *Qiddušin* 2:1; the readings there are noted ק.

56 The rabbis allow the adolescent girl to contract a preliminary marriage; R. Jehudah reserves this right to the father. The same discussion is in the Babli, *Qiddušin* 43b-44a.

57 Reading from *Qiddušin*. The text here has "mother"; but the mother has no say during the father's lifetime.

58 Since the father has the right to his adolescent unmarried daughter's earnings, Mishnah *Ketubot* 4:6. One must assume that R. Simeon ben Laqish holds that the girl must deliver to her father any valuables she received for her preliminary marriage.

59 But an orphan girl or a definitively married one becomes able to act in law (and appoint agents) once she reaches the age of 12 years and one day.

60 *Qiddušin* 2:1.

61 Mishnah *Gittin* 6:3.

62 While the Mishnah confirms that the girl cannot appoint an agent, it seems to contradict the statement that the adolescent has no standing in law since she is able to accept her bill of divorce.

63 Including an "orphan during her father's lifetime", cf. Note 20.

64 If the Mishnah speaks about an orphan, there could be no father.

65 Since this is a sentence in the same Mishnah which stated that a woman may agree to a preliminary marriage, the absence of any mention of the power of the girl implies that she cannot enter a preliminary marriage on her own.

66 The Babli agrees, *Qiddušin* 44a.

67 The court denied the right of an adolescent girl to marry on her own initiative.

68 There is no name attached to this information; it is impossible to check the standing of the informant in the legal hierarchy.

69 The statement was made immediately after judgment was rendered. For the expression "from the sea to the frying pan" cf. *Berakhot* 4:5, Note 233; Babli *Qiddušin* 44a.

(48a line 26) חֲבֵרַיָּא אָמְרִין. בֶּחָצֵר וּבְאַרְבַּע אַמּוֹת פְּלִיגִין. רִבִּי יוֹחָנָן אָמַר. יֵשׁ לָהּ חָצֵר וְיֵשׁ לָהּ אַרְבַּע אַמּוֹת. רֵישׁ לָקִישׁ אָמַר. אֵין לָהּ חָצֵר וְאֵין לָהּ אַרְבַּע אַמּוֹת. רִבִּי אֶלְעָזָר אָמַר. בֶּחָצֵר פְּלִיגִין וְאֵין לָהּ אַרְבַּע אַמּוֹת. מִי אָמַר רִבִּי יוֹחָנָן בִּפְשׁוּט יָדַיִם. רִבִּי אֶלְעָזָר שָׁאַל. חֲצֵירוֹ שֶׁלַּשָּׁלִיחַ מָהוּ שֶׁתְּיֵעָשֶׂה כְיָדוֹ.

The colleagues said, they[70] disagree about courtyard[71] and four cubits[72]. Rebbi Joḥanan said, she has both courtyard and four cubits. Rebbi Simeon ben Laqish said, she has neither courtyard nor four cubits. Rebbi Eleazar said, they disagree about the courtyard but she has no four cubits. What[73] did Rebbi Joḥanan say about outstretched hands[74]? Rebbi Eleazar asked, does an agent's courtyard act as his hand[75]?

70 R. Joḥanan and R. Simeon ben Laqish disagree about the legal standing of a minor. The corresponding discussion in the Babli is *Baba Meṣi'a* 10b. This paragraph really refers to Mishnah 3.

71 As the Babli, *Baba Meṣi'a* 11a, explains in the name of the Galilean R.

Yose ben R. Ḥanina, a fenced-in property acquires for a person even if he is not aware of it. For example, if somebody lost an article without distinguishing marks on somebody else's fenced-in courtyard, that article becomes automatically the courtyard owner's property since it cannot be reclaimed by the person who lost it. Nobody else is allowed to take it.

In the Babli, the disagreement between R. Joḥanan and R. Simeon ben Laqish is explained to the effect that R. Joḥanan considers the courtyard as an extension of its owner's hand. Since Mishnah 3 states that a minor legally can receive her bill of divorce, she has a "hand" and, therefore, her courtyard acquires for her. R. Simeon ben Laqish holds that the courtyard is its owner's agent and since the minor cannot appoint an agent, her courtyard cannot acquire for her.

71 If a person stands still in the public domain and nobody else is within 8 cubits from her, anything found or delivered to her at a distance of at most 4 cubits belongs to her (cf. Mishnaiot 8:2, *Yebamot* 3:9). The question is whether this rule extends to emancipated underage females (it certainly does not extend to underage males.)

73 מִי is a Babylonian Aramaic particle used as a general question mark. In Galilean Aramaic, it should be מָה.

74 In Halakhah 8:2, R. Joḥanan states that an adult woman standing in the public domain is divorced if the husband throws her the bill (in front of two witnesses) and it lands close enough for her to take it up without moving her feet. According to R. Eleazar, who states that R. Joḥanan agrees that an underage girl has no 4 cubits, it is questionable whether throwing the bill within the reach of the underage wife's hands is delivery in the meaning of the verse. The question is not answered.

75 Following R. Joḥanan, is a woman divorced if the husband throws the bill into her agent's courtyard in the presence of two witnesses? This question is not answered either.

(48a line 30) נִישֵׂאת הִיא לֹא אָבִיהָ. קְטַנָּה אָבִיהָ לֹא הִיא. נִיסֵּית בֵּין הִיא בֵּין אָבִיהָ. אִם יֵשׁ בָּהּ דַּעַת הִיא לֹא אָבִיהָ. אֵי זוֹ הִיא קְטַנָּה שֶׁהִיא צְרִיכָה

לְהִתְגָּרֵשׁ. אָמַר רִבִּי יוֹחָנָן. כָּל־שֶׁנּוֹתְנִין לָהּ גִּיטָּהּ וְדָבָר אַחֵר עִמּוֹ וְהִיא מוֹצִיאָה אוֹתוֹ לְאַחַר זְמָן.

[76]If she is definitively married, she but not her father[77]. An underage girl, her father but not she[78]; if she is definitively married, both she and her father[79]. If she has understanding, she but not her father. Who is an underage girl who needs to be divorced [by herself]? Rebbi Joḥanan said, any female who is given her bill of divorce together with something else and she produces it after some time.

76 This paragraph is explained by R. Nissim Gerondi, Commentary to Alfasi Chapter 6, #510.

77 The Mishnah which gives the father the right to receive the bill of divorce of his adolescent, preliminarily married daughter, excludes the definitively married daughter over which the father has no power and who can be divorced only by direct delivery of the bill to her.

78 To divorce a preliminarily married underage girl, the bill must be delivered to the father.

79 The definitively married underage girl who lacks understanding (as defined in this paragraph by R. Joḥanan) cannot be divorced since her standing is the same as her father's. Since her father cannot receive her bill of divorce because by definitive marriage she became emancipated from him, so she cannot receive her bill of divorce, as explained in the Mishnah.

(fol. 47c) **משנה ג:** קְטַנָּה שֶׁאָמְרָה. הִתְקַבֵּל לִי גִיטִּי. אֵינוֹ גֵט עַד שֶׁיַּגִּיעַ גֵּט לְיָדָהּ. לְפִיכָךְ אִם רָצָה הַבַּעַל לְהַחֲזִיר יַחֲזִיר שֶׁאֵין הַקָּטָן עוֹשֶׂה שָׁלִיחַ. וְאִם אָמַר לוֹ אָבִיהָ. צֵא וְהִתְקַבֵּל לְבִתִּי גִיטָּהּ. אִם רָצָה לְהַחֲזִיר לֹא יַחֲזִיר.

Mishnah 3: If an underage girl said, accept the bill of divorce for me, it is no valid bill until the bill of divorce reaches her hand. Therefore, if the husband wants to retract he can retract since an underage person cannot appoint an agent. But if her father said to [an agent]: Go and receive my daughter's bill of divorce, if [the husband] wants to retract he cannot retract.80

משנה ד: הָאוֹמֵר תֵּן גֵּט זֶה לְאִשְׁתִּי בְּמָקוֹם פְּלוֹנִי וּנְתָנוֹ לָהּ בְּמָקוֹם אַחֵר פָּסוּל. הֲרֵי הִיא בְּמָקוֹם פְּלוֹנִי וּנְתָנוֹ לָהּ בְּמָקוֹם אַחֵר כָּשֵׁר.

Mishnah 4: If somebody says, deliver this bill of divorce to my wife at place X[81] and he delivered it at another place, it is invalid. But if he said, she is at place X, and he delivered it at another place, it is valid.

80 This was explained in the preceding Halakhah.

81 This is formulated as a condition of the appointment. In the next sentence, the place is mentioned only as an indication.

(48a line 34) **הלכה ג**: קְטַנָּה שֶׁאָמְרָה. הִתְקַבֵּל לִי גִיטִּי כול'. מַתְנִיתָא דְלָא כְרִבִּי אֶלְעָזָר. בְּרַם כְּרִבִּי אֶלְעָזָר לְעוֹלָם אֵינָהּ מְגוֹרֶשֶׁת עַד שֶׁיֹּאמַר לוֹ. אַל תְּגָרְשֶׁנָּהּ לִי אֶלָּא בְמָקוֹם פְּלוֹנִי. הֲרֵי הִיא בְּמָקוֹם פְּלוֹנִי. וְהָלַךְ וְגֵירְשָׁהּ בְּמָקוֹם אַחֵר. הֲרֵי זוֹ אוֹף רִבִּי לְעָזָר מוֹדֶה שֶׁאֵינוֹ אֶלָּא כְמַרְאֶה לָהּ מָקוֹם. אוֹף רַבָּנִין מוֹדֵיי שֶׁאֵינוֹ אֶלָּא כְמַרְאֶה לָהּ מָקוֹם.

Halakhah 3: "If an underage girl said, accept the bill of divorce for me,[82]" etc. The Mishnah does not follow Rebbi Eleazar[83]. But following Rebbi Eleazar she is (not)[84] divorced unless [the husband] tells [the agent]: Do not divorce her except at place X[84]. "If he said, she is at place X and he delivered it at another place," Rebbi Eleazar agrees that he only indicates a place; the rabbis agree that he only indicates a place.

82 The reference should be to Mishnah 4, not 3.

83 Who in Mishnah 5 holds that instructions about delivery are not

binding on the agent. The Babli disagrees (65a) and holds that R. Eleazar (the Tanna) considers the husband's instructions as binding, but not the wife's.

84 The context and the parallel about preliminary marriage by agent (*Qiddušin* 2:4) show that this word has to be deleted.

84 Only the formulation as a prohibition prevents the agent from delivering at any place convenient to him.

(fol. 47c) **משנה ה:** הָאִשָּׁה שֶׁאָמְרָה הִתְקַבֵּל לִי גִיטִּי בְּמָקוֹם פְּלוֹנִי וְקִיבְּלָהּ לָהּ בְּמָקוֹם אַחֵר פָּסוּל. וְרִבִּי אֶלְעָזָר מַכְשִׁיר. הָבֵא לִי גִיטִּי מִמָּקוֹם פְּלוֹנִי וֶהֱבִיאוֹ לָהּ מִמָּקוֹם אַחֵר כָּשֵׁר.

Mishnah 5: If a woman says, accept my bill of divorce at place X, and he accepted it at another place, it is invalid, but Rebbi Eleazar[83] declares it valid. Bring my bill of divorce from place X and he brought it from another place, it is valid.

משנה ו: הָבֵא לִי גִיטִּי אוֹכֶלֶת בַּתְּרוּמָה עַד שֶׁיַּגִּיעַ גֵּט לְיָדָהּ. הִתְקַבֵּל לִי גִיטִּי אֲסוּרָה לוֹכַל בַּתְּרוּמָה מִיַּד. הִתְקַבֵּל לִי גִיטִּי בְּמָקוֹם פְּלוֹנִי אוֹכֶלֶת בַּתְּרוּמָה עַד שֶׁיַּגִּיעַ גֵּט לְאוֹתוֹ מָקוֹם. רִבִּי אֶלְעָזָר אוֹסֵר מִיַּד.

Mishnah 6: "Bring my bill of divorce", she may eat heave until the bill is delivered to her. "Receive my bill of divorce," she is immediately forbidden to eat heave. "Receive my bill of divorce at place X," she may eat heave until the bill arrives at that place; Rebbi Eleazar forbids immediately[85].

(48a line 39) **הלכה ה:** הָאִשָּׁה שֶׁאָמְרָה הִתְקַבֵּל לִי גִיטִּי כול׳. מַה טַעֲמָא דְּרִבִּי לְעָזָר. אֲנִי אוֹמֵר. אַחַר הַדֶּלֶת מְצָאוֹ. תַּמָּן תַּנִּינָן. הָאוֹמֵר לְמִי שֶׁאֵינוֹ נֶאֱמָן עַל

הַמַּעְשְׂרוֹת. קַח לִי מִמִּי שֶׁהוּא נֶאֱמָן מִמִּי שֶׁהוּא מְעַשֵּׂר. אֵינוֹ נֶאֱמָן. תַּנֵּי. רִבִּי יוֹסֵי אוֹמֵר. אֲפִילוּ לֹא אָמַר לוֹ. מִפְּלוֹנִי. אֵינוֹ נֶאֱמָן עַד שֶׁיֹּאמַר לוֹ. קַח וַאֲנִי נוֹתֵן מָעוֹת. מַה טַעֲמָא דְּרִבִּי יוֹסֵי. אֲנִי אוֹמֵר. אֶחָד קָרוֹב מְצָאוֹ וְלָקַח מִמֶּנּוּ. אַתְיָא דְּרִבִּי אֶלְעָזָר כְּרִבִּי יוֹסֵי וּדְרִבִּי יוֹסֵי כְּרִבִּי אֶלְעָזָר בֵּירִבִּי יוֹסֵי. וְלֹא מוֹדֶה רִבִּי אֶלְעָזָר שֶׁאִם אָמְרָה לוֹ. אַל תְּקַבְּלֵהוּ לִי אֶלָּא בְּמָקוֹם פְּלוֹנִי. שֶׁהִיא אוֹכֶלֶת בִּתְרוּמָה עַד שֶׁיַּגִּיעַ הַגֵּט לְאוֹתוֹ מָקוֹם. וְהָכָא אֲפִילוּ אָמַר לוֹ. מִפְּלוֹנִי. אֵינוֹ נֶאֱמָן עַד שֶׁיֹּאמַר לוֹ. קַח וַאֲנִי נוֹתֵן מָעוֹת. מַאי טַעֲמָא דְּרִבִּי יוֹסֵי. אֲנִי אוֹמֵר. אֶחָד קָרוֹב מָצָא וְלָקַח מִמֶּנּוּ.

3 ר׳ יוסי אומר | ד אמ׳ ר׳ יוסי   4 לא | ד -   5 מצאו | ד מצא   6 אתייא | ד אתא אלעזר | ד לעזר   (3 times) ביר׳ יוסי | ד דר׳ יוסי ריבה מן דר׳ לעזר   8 הגט | ד גט 9 מעות | לו מעות   מאי | ד מה

Halakhah 5[86]: "If a woman says, accept my bill of divorce," etc. What is the reason of Rebbi Eleazar? I say that he found it behind the door. There, we have stated: "If someone tells a person who is not trustworthy, buy for me from somebody who is trustworthy, or from somebody who tithes, he is not trustworthy. It was stated: "Rebbi Yose said, even if he specified, from **X**, he is not trustworthy unless he said, you buy and I will pay." What is the reason of Rebbi Yose? I say that he found someone close by and bought from him. It turns out that Rebbi Eleazar is like Rebbi Yose and Rebbi Yose is like Rebbi Eleazar (ben Rebbi Yose.)[87] [Rebbi Yose says more than Rebbi Eleazar;][88] does not Rebbi Eleazar agree that if she says to him, do not accept it except at such and such a place, she continues eating until the bill of divorce reaches that place? But here, even if he says, only from **X**, he is not trustworthy, except if he said, you buy and I will pay. What is the reason of Rebbi Yose? I say that he found someone close by and bought from him.

85 As the Halakhah explains, since R. Eleazar permits the agent to pick up the bill anywhere, he might have received it as soon as he left the house.
86 This is essentially Halakhah 4:7 in *Demay* (⇒ Notes 81-85). Except for the omission of a sentence, the differences in readings are explained by the Babylonian spelling in *Giṭṭin*. The reference should be to Mishnah 6.
87 The Tanna R. Eleazar is R. Eleazar ben Šamua'. The addition here is a corruption of the following sentence from *Demay*.
88 From *Demay*, cf. the variant readings.

משנה ז: הָאוֹמֵר כִּתְבוּ גֵט וּתְנוּ לְאִשְׁתִּי גָּרְשׁוּהָ כִּתְבוּ אִגֶּרֶת וּתְנוּ לָהּ הֲרֵי אֵילוּ יִכְתְּבוּ וְיִתְּנוּ. פִּטְרוּהָ פַּרְנְסוּהָ עֲשׂוּ לָהּ כַּנּוֹמוֹס עֲשׂוּ לָהּ כָּרָאוּי לֹא אָמַר כְּלוּם. בָּרִאשׁוֹנָה הָיוּ אוֹמְרִים הַיּוֹצֵא בַקּוֹלָר וְאָמַר כִּתְבוּ גֵט לְאִשְׁתִּי הֲרֵי אֵילוּ יִכְתְּבוּ וְיִתְּנוּ. חָזְרוּ לוֹמַר אַף הַמְפָרֵשׁ וְהַיּוֹצֵא בַּשְׁיָּרָא. רְבִּי שִׁמְעוֹן שְׁזוּרִי אוֹמֵר. אַף הַמְסוּכָּן. (fol. 47d)

Mishnah 7: If somebody says: "Write a bill of divorce and deliver to my wife, divorce her, write a letter[89] and deliver to her", they should write and deliver. "Discharge her, provide for her, treat her according to the law[90], do what is necessary;" he did not say anything[91]. Earlier, they said that if somebody was led away in a neck-iron[92] when he said, write a bill of divorce for my wife, they should write and deliver. They reconsidered and said, also one who leaves on a ship or in a caravan. Rebbi Simeon from Shezur said, also the dangerously sick.

89 In Mishnah 9:3, the bill of divorce is called "letter of abandonment".
90 Greek νόμος.
91 These expressions are unspecific; they do not have to be interpreted as instructions for a divorce.

92 Latin *collare*. While, in general, the instruction to write a bill of divorce does not include an instruction to deliver, it was decided that the court had the authority to wave the separate instruction for delivery in an emergency situation when it is clearly implied.

(48a line 50) **הלכה ז:** הָאוֹמֵר כִּתְבוּ גֵט וּתְנוּ לְאִשְׁתִּי כול'. הָאוֹמֵר. תֵּרְכוּהָ. כְּאוֹמֵר. גֵּירְשׁוּהָ.

Halakhah 7: "If somebody says: "Write a bill of divorce and deliver to my wife," etc. If somebody says in Aramaic "divorce her," it is as if he said in Hebrew "divorce her.[93]"

93 The statement is also quoted in the Babli, 65b. In the Tosephta, 4:5, in a parallel to the Mishnah, תרכו is used as substitute for גרשוה. It should be obvious that the command to write a bill of divorce can be given in any language understood by husband, scribe, and witnesses. The statement implies that in the Aramaized Hebrew of the educated person in Palestine, a mixture of Hebrew and Aramaic terms was completely acceptable.

(48a line 51) פִּטְרוּהָ פַּרְנְסוּהָ עֲשׂוּ לָהּ כַּנֵּימוֹס[94] עֲשׂוּ לָהּ כָּרָאוּי לֹא אָמַר כְּלוּם. אֲנִי אוֹמֵר. לִמְזוֹנוֹת.

"'Discharge her[95], provide for her, treat her according to the law, do what is necessary;' he did not say anything." I say, he meant sustenance.

94 The usual Babylonian form of Galilean נומוס
95 The Babli, 65b, wants to make a difference between the meaning of פטר in *qal*, פְּטָרוּהָ, "discharge (my obligations towards her), provide for her", and *pi'el* פַּטְּרוּהָ "get rid of her, discharge her (from the marriage)".

(48a line 52) אָמַר רִבִּי מָנָא. וְלֹא סוֹף דָּבָר בְּקוֹלָר שֶׁלַּסַּכָּנָה אֶלָּא אֲפִילוּ בְּקוֹלָר שֶׁלְמָמוֹן. שֶׁכָּל־הַקּוֹלָר בְּחֶזְקַת שֶׁלַּסַּכָּנָה. רִבִּי אֶלְעָזָר שָׁאַל. מַתָּנָתוֹ כְּמַתָּנַת

שְׁכִיב מְרַע. רִבִּי נַחְמָן בְּשֵׁם רִבִּי יַעֲקֹב אַרְמֶנַיָּיא. מַה דְהִיא צְרִיכָה לְרִבִּי שִׁמְעוֹן פְּשִׁיטָה לֵיהּ לְרִבִּי יוֹסֵי בַּר חֲנִינָה. דְּתַנִּינָן תַּמָּן. הָאִשָּׁה שֶׁנֶּהֶרְגָה נֶהֱנִין בִּשְׂעָרָהּ. בְּהֵמָה שֶׁנֶּהֶרְגָה אֲסוּרָה בַּהֲנָיָיה. אָמַר רִבִּי יוֹסֵי בַּר חֲנִינָה. בְּאוֹמֶרֶת. תִּינָּתֵן כְּבִינָתִי לְבִתִּי.

Rebbi Mana said, not only a neck-iron of mortal danger[96] but also a neck-iron of money[97]. For every neck-iron is a mortal danger. Rebbi Eleazar asked: Does his gift follow the rules of the gift of a sick person[98]? Rebbi Nahman in the name of Rebbi Jacob the Armenian: That which is a problem for Rebbi Simeon[99] is obvious for Rebbi Yose bar Hanina, as we have stated there[100]: "One may have use for the hair of a woman who was executed[101] but an animal which was executed is forbidden for all use[102]." Rebbi Yose bar Hanina said, if she said, my bonnet should be given to my daughter[103].

96 The chain put on a person condemned to death.

97 If the person arrested can expect to have to pay a fine. The Babli disagrees in the interpretation of Rashi (on the Mishnah, 65b) but not in that of *Sefer ha'Ittur* (I, 28b, Note 154).

98 Some formal rules of gifts are waived for a person on his deathbed. If a sick person directs that gifts should be given and he dies, the gifts are valid even though no act of acquisition was performed for the benefit of the recipients. But if he recovers, his instructions are void in the absence of a formal act of acquisition; cf. *Peah* 3:9;

Babli *Baba batra* 146b ff.

99 It seems that one should read "R. Eleazar"; this is Rashba's reading in his *Novellae* (who reads "R. Jacob the Red" instead of "R. Jacob the Armenian".)

100 Mishnah *'Arakhin* 1:4.

101 Even though a human corpse is forbidden for all usufruct ['*Avodah zarah* 5:12 (45b l.4), Babli 29b], this does not include the hair which is a dead part of the living body.

102 An animal which is stoned because it has killed a human becomes forbidden, together with its hide and hair, not by stoning but by the sentence passed upon it by the court [*Ex.* 21:28;

Mekhilta dR. Ismael (Horovitz-Rabin) p. 282, dR. Simeon ben Iohai (Epstein-Melamed) p. 179].

103   In the Babli (*Arakhin* 7b), R. Yose ben R. Ḥanina is quoted as questioning whether in this case a wig worn by the woman at her execution can be inherited by her daughter.

(48a line 58) כְּהָדָא. גְּנִיבָה אִיתְאַפַּק לְמִקְטְלָא. אָמַר. יָבוֹן לְרִבִּי אֲבוּנָא זוּז מִן חַמְרָא דִכְפַר פַּנְיָיא. וְלֹא יָבוֹן לֵיהּ. חָשִׁין לְהָא דְרָב. דְּרָב אָמַר. הַיּוֹרֵשׁ כִּמְשׁוּעֲבָד. כְּשֵׁם שֶׁאֵין מִלְוֶה בְעֵדִים נִגְבֵּית מִן הַמְשׁוּעֲבָד כָּךְ אֵינָהּ נִגְבֵּית מִן הַיּוֹרְשִׁין. וְלֹא יִתְּנוּן לֵיהּ מִשּׁוּם חוֹב יִתְּנוּן לֵיהּ מִשּׁוּם מַתָּנָה. חָשִׁין לְהָא דְּרִבִּי אֶלְעָזָר. דְּרִבִּי אֶלְעָזָר שָׁאַל. מַתָּנָתוֹ כְּמַתְּנַת שְׁכִיב מְרַע. אַיְיתֵי דְּרִבִּי זְעִירָא לְרִבִּי יִצְחָק עַטוּשָׁיָיא וְתַנּוּן לֵיהּ. אָמַר לֵיהּ רִבִּי בָּא. אוֹ מַה גִּיטִּין אִם לֹא נָתַן בְּחַיָּיו לֹא נוֹתֵן. אַף מַתָּנָה אִם לֹא נָתַן בְּחַיָּיו לָאו שְׁמָהּ מַתָּנָה. אָמַר לֵיהּ. הָכָא אָתָא רִבִּי מַפְקַח חָכְמְתָהּ וּמַפְסְדָא לְרִבִּי אֲבוּנָא זוּזֵי. לֵית יָכִיל. דְּתַנִּינָן תַּמָּן. תְּנוּ מָנֶה לְאִישׁ פְּלוֹנִי. וּמֵת. יִתְּנוּ לְאַחַר מִיתָה. כְּרִבִּי שִׁמְעוֹן. דְּרִבִּי יוֹחָנָן פְּלִיג יָבוֹן לֵיהּ. דָּמַר רִבִּי אַבָּהוּ בְּשֵׁם רִבִּי יוֹחָנָן. מִלְוֶה בְעֵדִים נִגְבֵּית מִן הַיּוֹרְשִׁין וּבִלְבַד יוֹרְשִׁין קַרְקַע. אָמַר רִבִּי יוֹסֵה. הֲדָא דְתֵימַר בְּהֵן דַּהֲוָה קָאִים גַּבֵּיהּ עַד שָׁעָה דְמִית. בְּרַם אִם עָלִיל וּנְפִיק אֲנָא אֲמַר. כְּבָר יְהִיב לֵיהּ. מִילְּתֵיהּ דְּרִבִּי חֲנִינָה אָמַר דְּלָא יְהִיב לֵיהּ. רִבִּי חֲנִינָה הֲוָה מִישְׁתָּעֵי אֲהֵן עוֹבְדָא. לֵוִי פְּרִיסָא הֲוָה עֲבַר מִן אֲתַר לַאֲתַר. נַפְקִין קְרִיבֵיהּ דִּגְנִיבָא מֵיכוּל עִמֵּיהּ. אָמַר. יֵיבוּן לְרִבִּי אֲבוּנָא זוּזֵי וְאִיתְגְּרוּן לַחְמָא.

As the following: Ganiba was lead out to be executed[104]. He said, One should give money[105] to Rebbi Abuna from the wine of Kefar Panaya[107]. They did not give him[107]; they were considering what Rav said, "an heir is like the buyer of encumbered property." Just as a loan before witnesses cannot be collected from encumbered property, so it cannot be collected from heirs[108]. If they did not give it as payment of a debt, they should have given as a gift! They were considering what Rebbi Eleazar said, for

Rebbi Eleazar asked: Does his gift follow the rules of the gift of a sick person[98]? Rebbi Ze'ira[109] brought Rebbi Isaac from Atosha who stated for him: A gift is like a bill of divorce[110]. Rebbi Abba said to him, perhaps like bills of divorce which one cannot deliver if not delivered during his lifetime, so a gift is not called a gift if not delivered during his lifetime? He said to him, here comes the rabbi with sophistication to let Rebbi Abuna lose money! You cannot, for we have stated there[111]: "Give a mina to X; then he died. One shall give after death." Following Rebbi Simeon. For Rebbi Joḥanan disagrees, they should give him, as Rebbi Abbahu said in the name of Rebbi Joḥanan: A loan before witnesses can be collected from the heirs[112] on condition that they inherited real estate. Rebbi Yose said, that is, if somebody was with him until the moment of his death[113]. But if he goes in and out, I am saying that already he gave him. The word of Rebbi Ḥanina implies that it[114] was not given since Rebbi Ḥanina reported this fact: Levi Parisa[115] was going from place to place when Ganiba's relatives came to eat with him. He said, the money should be given to Rebbi Abuna; they started quarelling with him.

104 It seems, by the Persian government as a political trouble maker. (Babli 7a).

105 In the Babli, 65b, 400 *zuz*. It seems that R. Abuna was Ganiba's only student (*Ḥulin* 44a,50b). He also was Rav Huna's student.

106 In the interpretation of the Babli, 66a, neither the wine should be given nor its value, but the wine should serve as guarantee for the payment. This seems to be the background of the opinion which sees in the payment a repayment of a debt.

107 In the Babli, 66a, the heirs were forced to pay by Rav Huna.

108 Cf. Chapter 3, Note 146. The opinion ascribed here [and in 3:7, *Baba qama* 10:1 (7b l. 39), *Baba meṣi'a* 1:6 (8a l.26)] to Rav is quoted as common to Rav and Samuel (i. e., established Babylonian practice) in *Baba batra*

175b.
109 In the Babli, he counsels R. Abina to appeal to Rav Huna.
110 Which is valid without formality if ordered by a person sentenced to death.
111 Mishnah 1:6.
112 Quoted as opinion shared by R. Johanan and R. Simeon ben Laqish (i. e., common Galilean practice) in *Baba batra* 175b.
113 Who can testify that from the moment of the gift to the donor's death nothing was given to the recipient of the gift.
114 Ganiba's gift.
115 In *Šabbat* 3:4 (6a l. 63), he is called Levi Sarisa. He may be Levi ben Sisi, known as a commuter between Galilee and Babylonia.

(48a line 74) תַּנֵּי. אַף הַחוֹלֶה. רִבִּי יַעֲקֹב בַּר אִידִי בְּשֵׁם רִבִּי יוֹנָתָן. הֲלָכָה כְרִבִּי שִׁמְעוֹן שְׁזוּרִי בִּמְסוּכָּן. מַה בֵּין מְסוּכָּן מַה בֵּין חוֹלֶה. חוֹלֶה כְדַרְכָּהּ הָאָרֶץ. וּמְסוּכָּן כָּל שֶׁקָּפַץ עָלָיו הַחוֹלִי. דֶּרֶךְ הָאָרֶץ הַקְּרוֹבִים נִכְנָסִין אֶצְלוֹ מִיַּד וְהָרְחוֹקִים לְאַחַר שְׁלֹשָׁה יָמִים. וְאִם קָפַץ עָלָיו הַחוֹלִי אֵילּוּ וְאֵילּוּ נִכְנָסִין אֶצְלוֹ מִיַּד. דְּלָמָא. רִבִּי הוּנָא רִבִּי פִּינְחָס רִבִּי חִזְקִיָּה סָלְקוּן מְבַקְּרָא לְרִבִּי יוֹסֵי בָּתַר תְּלָתָא יוֹמִין. אָמַר לוֹן. בִּי בָעִיתוּן מְקַייְמָה מַתְנִיתָא.

2 מה בין מסוכן מה בין חולה | ע‎116 מה בין חולה למסוכן   4 לאחר | פ נכנסין לאחר ואם | פ אם   5 מבקרא | פ מבקרה   6 בי | פ 117reading uncertain

It was stated: Also the sick person. Rebbi Jacob bar Idi in the name of Rebbi Jonathan: Practice follows Rebbi Simeon from Shezur about the dangerously ill[118]. What is the difference between a dangerously ill and a sick person? A sick person is a normal case; any who gets sick suddenly is dangerously ill. [119]In a normal case, the relatives visit him immediately; unrelated persons visit him after three days. If he falls ill suddenly, everybody visits him immediately. An example: Rebbi Huna, Rebbi Phineas, and Rebbi Hizqiah went to visit Rebbi Yose after three days. He said to them: Do you want to sustain the *baraita* in my case?

116	Reading from 'Arukh, s. v. מסכן (1).
117	Cf. Peah 3:9, Note 153.
118	The Babli (Ketubot 55a) agrees in the name of R. Jonathan.
119	From here on, the text is from Peah 3:9 (פ), Note 155.

(fol. 47d) **משנה ח:** מִי שֶׁהָיָה מוּשְׁלָךְ בַּבּוֹר וְאָמַר כָּל־הַשּׁוֹמֵעַ אֶת קוֹלִי יִכְתּוֹב גֵּט לְאִשְׁתִּי הֲרֵי אִלּוּ יִכְתְּבוּ וְיִתְּנוּ. הַבָּרִיא שֶׁאָמַר כִּתְבוּ גֵט לְאִשְׁתִּי רָצָה לְשַׂחֵק בָּהּ. מַעֲשֶׂה בְבָרִיא אֶחָד שֶׁאָמַר כִּתְבוּ גֵט לְאִשְׁתִּי וְעָלָה לְרֹאשׁ הַגַּג וְנָפַל וָמֵת. אָמַר רַבָּן שִׁמְעוֹן בֶּן גַּמְלִיאֵל. אָמְרוּ חֲכָמִים אִם מֵעַצְמוֹ נָפַל הֲרֵי זֶה גֵט. אִם הָרוּחַ דְּחָאַתּוּ אֵינוֹ גֵט.

Mishnah 8: If somebody was thrown into a cistern[119] and said, anybody hearing my voice should write a bill of divorce for my wife[120], they should write and deliver[121]. If a healthy person said, write a bill of divorce for my wife, he wants to make fun of her[122]. It happened to a healthy person who had said, write a bill of divorce for my wife, that he went on the roof[123], fell down, and died. Rabban Simeon ben Gamliel said, the Sages said that if he jumped, it is a bill of divorce[124]; if the wind pushed him, it is no bill of divorce.

119	He is injured and has no way to climb out. He may be afraid that his corpse will never be found or, if he is childless, that his wife would have to marry his brother.
120	Naturally, he has to declare his and his wife's full names as well as their place of residence. The people hearing him do not have to ask for further identification.
121	Even though he did not say that the bill should be delivered.
122	Since he did not instruct anybody to deliver the bill, it is invalid.
123	After the bill had been written and (erroneously) been delivered to the

wife when he was still alive.

124 The bill of divorce of the suicide retroactively becomes an emergency bill and is valid.

(48b line 5) **הלכה ח:** מִי שֶׁהָיָה מוּשְׁלָךְ בַּבּוֹר כּוּל'. אָמַר רִבִּי חֲנִינָה. לִימְּדָנוּ רִבִּי יוֹנָתָן. וְהֵן שֶׁרָאוּ בּוּבְיָיה שֶׁלְּאָדָם. תַּמָּן תַּנִּינָן. מְעִידִין לְאוֹר הַנֵּר וּלְאוֹר הַלְּבָנָה וּמַשִּׂיאִין עַל פִּי בַת קוֹל. וָמַר רִבִּי יוֹנָתָן. וְהֵן שֶׁרָאוּ בּוּבְיָיה שֶׁלְּאָדָם. רִבִּי אָחָא בַּר חֲנִינָה בְשֵׁם רִבִּי חֲנִינָה. הָדָא דְתֵימַר בַּשָּׂדֶה. אֲבָל בָּעִיר אֲפִילוּ לֹא רָאוּ בּוּבְיָיה שֶׁלְּאָדָם. וְהָתַנִּינָן. מִי שֶׁהָיָה מוּשְׁלָךְ בַּבּוֹר. וְאָמַר רִבִּי יוֹנָתָן. וְהֵן שֶׁרָאוּ בּוּבְיָיה שֶׁל אָדָם. אָמַר רִבִּי אָבִין. הַמַּזִּיקִין הָיוּ מְצוּיִין בַּבּוֹרוֹת כְּדֶרֶךְ שֶׁהֵן מְצוּיִין בַּשָּׂדוֹת.

1 חנינה | • חנינא (2 times) | • לימדנו | • למדני 2 בובייה | • בוביח (4 times) 4 בר חנינה | • ר' חננא 5 ראו | • - והתנינן | • והן תנינן בבור | • בבור ואמר כל־השומע את קולי תכתוב גט לאשתו. הרי זה יכתבו ויתנו. 6 היו | • - אבין | • אבון

Halakhah 8: "If somebody was thrown into a cistern," etc. [125]Rebbi Ḥanina said, Rebbi Jonathan taught us, only if they saw a man's shadow. There, we have stated: "One testifies by the light of a candle or by the light of the moon and one permits to remarry on the basis of a disembodied voice", and Rebbi Jonathan said, only if they saw a man's shadow. Rebbi Aḥa bar Ḥanina, in the name of Rebbi Ḥanina: That means, in the fields, but in town even without a man's shadow. But did we not state: "If somebody had been thrown into a cistern," and Rebbi Jonathan said, only if they saw a man's shadow? Rebbi Abin said, damaging spirits were[126] as frequent in cisterns as they are frequent on the fields.

125 This text essentially is from *Yebamot* 16:6, Notes 117-124.

126 This disclaimer of the current existence of spirits is not in the *Yebamot* text (which is an insert of the corrector, not a text by the original

scribe), nor in the text quoted by Rashba (*Novellae* to 66a) The Babli definitely believes in evil spirits. The sentence is quoted by Tosaphot (*s. v.* וליחוש, 66a) as מְצוּיִין הֵן בַּשָּׂדוֹת "they are found in the fields." But that text is not usable as witness since it is thoroughly babylonized, using תימא for תימר, בבואה for בובייה.

(48b line 11) סָפֵק מֵעַצְמוֹ נָפַל סָפֵק הָרוּחַ דְּחָתוּ. נִישְׁמְעִינָהּ מִן הָדָא. רַבָּן שִׁמְעוֹן בֶּן גַּמְלִיאֵל אוֹמֵר. אִם עַל אָתָר נָפַל הֲרֵי זֶה גֵט. וְאִם לְאַחַר זְמָן נָפַל אֵינוֹ גֵט. וְהֵן עַל אָתָר וְלֹא סָפֵק הוּא. הָדָא אָמְרָה. סָפֵק מֵעַצְמוֹ נָפַל סָפֵק הָרוּחַ דְּחִיַּתּוּ הֲרֵי זֶה גֵט.

If it was doubtful whether he jumped or the wind pushed him? Let us hear from the following: Rabban Simeon ben Gamliel says, if he fell down immediately, it is a bill of divorce; if he fell after some time it is no bill of divorce. But is "immediately" not a case of doubt whether he jumped or the wind pushed him? This implies that in case of doubt whether he jumped or the wind pushed him, it is a bill of divorce[127].

127 The different versions of the Tosephta seem to disagree with the Yerushalmi (the topic is not treated in the Babli). Tosephta 4:7 (Lieberman) "If a healthy person said, write a bill of divorce for my wife, climbed on a roof, and fell down, one writes and delivers as long as he still is alive. Rabban Simeon ben Gamliel says, if he jumped, it is a bill of divorce; if he fell down after some time, it is no bill of divorce since I may say that the wind pushed him." Tosephta 6:9 (Zuckermandel): "If a healthy person said, write a bill of divorce for my wife, climbed on a roof, and fell down, one writes and delivers as long as he still is alive. If he fell down after some time, it is no bill of divorce since I may say that the wind pushed him." Tosephta (quote of Rashba): "If a healthy person said, write a bill of divorce for my wife, climbed on a roof, and fell down, one writes but does not deliver since I may say that the wind pushed him." A discussion of the different versions is in J. N. Epstein, [2]מבוא לנוסח המשנה, p. 600-601.

(48b line 15) שְׁחָטָהּ לִזְרוֹק דָּמָהּ לַעֲבוֹדָה זָרָה וּלְהַקְטִיר חֶלְבָּהּ לַעֲבוֹדָה זָרָה. רִבִּי יוֹחָנָן אָמַר. הַמַּחֲשָׁבָה פוֹסֶלֶת. רֵישׁ לָקִישׁ אוֹמֵר. אֵין הַמַּחֲשָׁבָה פוֹסֶלֶת. הָתִיב רִבִּי יַעֲקֹב בַּר אִידִי קוֹמֵי רֵישׁ לָקִישׁ. וְהָתַנִּינָן. רִבִּי יוֹסֵי אוֹמֵר. קַל וְחוֹמֶר הַדְּבָרִים. מַה אִם בְּמָקוֹם שֶׁהַמַּחֲשָׁבָה פוֹסֶלֶת בַּמּוּקְדָּשִׁין וכו'. וּפִיגּוּל וְנוֹתָר הַמַּחֲשָׁבָה פוֹסֶלֶת. אָמַר לֵיהּ. פִּיגּוּל וְנוֹתָר אֵין הַמַּחֲשָׁבָה פוֹסֶלֶת. אֲבָל אִם שְׁחָטָהּ לִזְרוֹק אֶת דָּמָהּ לַעֲבוֹדָה זָרָה וְלִקְטוֹר חֶלְבָּהּ לַעֲבוֹדָה זָרָה אֵין הַמַּחֲשָׁבָה פוֹסֶלֶת. שְׁחָטָהּ וְזָרַק דָּמָהּ לַעֲבוֹדָה זָרָה וְהִקְטִיר חֶלְבָּהּ לַעֲבוֹדָה זָרָה. זֶה הָיָה מַעֲשֶׂה בְּקֵיסָרִין וְלֹא אָמְרוּ לֹא לְאִיסוּר וְלֹא לְהֵיתֵר. רִבִּי חֲנִינָה בְשֵׁם רַב חִסְדָּא. זֹאת אוֹמֶרֶת לֹא חָשׁוּ. אִין תֵּימַר חָשׁוּ. הָיָה לָהֶם לְהוֹרוֹת אִיסּוּר. רִבִּי יוֹסֵי בְשֵׁם רַב חִסְדָּא. זֹאת אוֹמֶרֶת שֶׁחָשׁוּ. אִין תֵּימַר לֹא חָשׁוּ. לֹא הָיָה לָהֶן לְהוֹרוֹת.

If somebody slaughtered with the intention of sprinkling [the victim's] blood in idolatry or to burn its fat for idolatry[128], Rebbi Johanan said, the intention invalidates[129], Rebbi Simeon ben Laqish said, the intention does not invalidate[130]. Rebbi Jacob bar Idi objected before Rebbi Simeon ben Laqish: Did we not state[131]: "Rebbi Yose said, that is a matter of a conclusion *de minore ad majus*. Since in a case where thought makes sanctified food unusable, etc.," and thought invalidates for *piggul* and leftover[132]. He said to him, truly thought invalidates for *piggul* and leftover; but if somebody slaughtered with the intention of sprinkling [the victim's] blood in idolatry or to burn its fat for idolatry, the intention does not invalidate[133]. If he slaughtered and then the blood was sprinkled in an idolatrous rite and the fat was burned in an idolatrous rite[134], there was such a case in Caesarea and they pronounced neither prohibition nor permission. Rebbi Hanina in the name of Rav Hisda: This means that they were not apprehensive[135]. If you say that they were apprehensive, they should have taught a prohibition. Rebbi Yose in the name of Rav Hisda: This means that they were apprehensive. If you say that they were not apprehensive, they should not have dealt with the case[136].

128 Any idolatrous sacrifice is forbidden for any use; *Deut.* 13:18.

129 If the slaughter were for idolatry, everybody would agree that the meat is forbidden for consumption. But here the slaughter is not intended for idolatry, only that later part of the blood and fat would be used for idolatrous purposes, for instance, if the animal is a Gentile's property; cf. Note 131.

130 Only an action can trigger the prohibition. If the Gentile takes part of the animal for himself for idolatrous purposes after he had sold most of the meat to Jews, there is no reason why the meat should be forbidden to Jews.

131 Mishnah *Hulin* 2:7: "If somebody slaughters for a Gentile, his slaughtering is valid, but Rebbi Eliezer declares it invalid. Rebbi Eliezer said: Even if he slaughtered it only for the Gentile to eat the appendage of its liver, it is invalid since the Gentile's thoughts are always for idolatry. Rebbi Yose said, that is a matter of a conclusion *de minore ad majus*. Since in a case where thought makes sanctified food unusable, everything is determined by the person who officiates; in the case of profane food which cannot become invalidated by thought, it is only logical that everything depend on the slaughterer."

It is forbidden to eat from a sacrifice after its appointed time (*piggul*) or outside the appropriate sacred precinct. If the slaughterer intends the sacrifice to be eaten at the wrong time or place, the entire sacrifice becomes invalid. But if the owners had the same idea, their intentions are irrelevant; they could invalidate the sacrifice only by actually using it at the wrong time and at the wrong place. R. Yose argues that profane slaughter cannot have rules more strict than sacrificial slaughter. If the owner's intentions are irrelevant for sacrificial slaughter, they must be irrelevant also for profane slaughter.

132 A sacrifice not eaten during its appointed time becomes forbidden as leftover even if it was not intended from the start to be eaten out of its time.

133 He holds that only for Jewish sacrifices does the wrong thought at slaughter invalidate the act; for all others the wrong thought invalidates the act but is not transferable to others. If the slaughter was for idolatry, the entire meat is forbidden. If the slaughter was for using part of the blood or fat for idolatry, that blood or fat becomes forbidden by being used; it has no influence on the other parts. (Babli *Ḥulin* 39a/b).

134 In the Babli (*Ḥulin* 39b): It was slaughtered and after that [the slaughterer] expressed an intention [of idolatry].

135 In the Babli, the reference is to the opinion of Rabban Simeon ben Gamliel in the Mishnah, who holds that a later action indicates a prior thought. If suicide can validate a prior bill of divorce then idolatrous practice can invalidate a prior slaughter. Since this also explains the insertion of the paragraph here, it has to be accepted as explanation.

136 A rabbi could have dismissed the case without bringing it to the attention of the full court. But what they really said was that the scrupulous should not eat from the meat; those who did eat did not sin.

(fol. 47d) **משנה ט:** אָמַר לִשְׁנַיִם תְּנוּ גֵט לְאִשְׁתִּי אוֹ לִשְׁלֹשָׁה כִּתְבוּ גֵט וּתְנוּ לְאִשְׁתִּי הֲרֵי אֵילוּ יִכְתְּבוּ וְיִתְּנוּ. אָמַר לִשְׁלֹשָׁה תְּנוּ גֵט לְאִשְׁתִּי הֲרֵי אֵילוּ יֹאמְרוּ לַאֲחֵרִים כְּתוֹבוּ מִפְּנֵי שֶׁעֲשָׂאָן בֵּית דִּין דִּבְרֵי רַבִּי מֵאִיר. וְזוֹ הֲלָכָה שָׁלַח חֲנַנְיָה אִישׁ אוֹנוֹ מִבֵּית הָאָסוּרִין מְקוּבָּל אֲנִי בָּאוֹמֵר לִשְׁלֹשָׁה תְּנוּ גֵט לְאִשְׁתִּי שֶׁיֹּאמְרוּ לַאֲחֵרִים כְּתוֹבוּ מִפְּנֵי שֶׁעֲשָׂאָן בֵּית דִּין. אָמַר רַבִּי יוֹסֵי נוֹמֵינוּ לַשָּׁלִיחַ אַף אָנוּ מְקוּבָּלִין שֶׁאֲפִילוּ אָמַר לְבֵית דִּין הַגָּדוֹל שֶׁבִּירוּשָׁלֵם תְּנוּ גֵט לְאִשְׁתִּי צָרִיךְ שֶׁיִּלְמְדוּ וְיִכְתְּבוּ וְיִתְּנוּ. אָמַר לַעֲשָׂרָה כִּתְבוּ גֵט לְאִשְׁתִּי אֶחָד כּוֹתֵב וּשְׁנַיִם חוֹתְמִין. כּוּלְּכֶם כִּתְבוּהוּ אֶחָד כּוֹתֵב וְכוּלָּן חוֹתְמִין. לְפִיכָךְ אִם מֵת אֶחָד מֵהֶן הֲרֵי זֶה גֵט בָּטֵל.

Mishnah 9: If one said to two persons, give a bill of divorce to my wife[137], or to three persons, write a bill of divorce and deliver to my wife, they should write and deliver[138]. If he said to three persons, deliver a bill of divorce to my wife, they shall ask others to write since he appointed them as a court, the words of Rebbi Meïr. This instructions for practice did Ḥananiah[139] from Ono send from jail: I know from tradition that if someone said to three persons, deliver a bill of divorce to my wife, they shall ask others to write since he appointed them as a court. Rebbi Yose said, we told the messenger that we also know from tradition that even if he said to the Supreme Court in Jerusalem, deliver a bill of divorce to my wife, they shall learn[140], write, and deliver. If he said to ten persons, write a bill of divorce for my wife, one writes and two sign. All of you shall write, one writes and all sign. Therefore, if one of them died, the bill of divorce would be void.

137 Since the husband did not authorize a scribe, the appointed persons themselves have to write the bill of divorce.

138 Since he specifically asked them to write, they cannot constitute themselves as a court and direct the scribe of the court to write the bill but must write it themselves.

139 In *Sanhedrin* 1:2 (18d last line) he is called Ḥanina; in Babli sources Rebbi Ḥanina.

140 If they do not know how to write a document.

(48b line 25) **הלכה ט:** אָמַר לִשְׁנַיִם. תְּנוּ גֵט לְאִשְׁתִּי כול׳. מַתְנִיתָא דְּרִבִּי מֵאִיר מִן דְּבַתְרָהּ אָמַר לִשְׁלֹשָׁה. וְאָמַר רַב חִסְדָּא. טַעֲמָא דְּרִבִּי מֵאִיר. מַה מָּצִינוּ בְּכָל־מָקוֹם אֲחֵרִים כּוֹתְבִין וּבֵית דִּין חוֹתְמִין. וְהָכָא אֲחֵרִים כּוֹתְבִין וּבֵית דִּין מַחְתִּימִין.

Halakhah 9: "If one said to two persons, give a bill of divorce to my wife," etc. The Mishnah follows Rebbi Meïr[141], from the next sentence: "If he said to three persons;" and Rav Ḥisda said, the reason of Rebbi Meïr is that we find everywhere that others write and the court signs, also here others write and the court affixes their signatures.

141 The problem discussed is hinted at in Halakhah 7:2 but made explicit only in the Babli (66b, also 29a,71b,72b). R. Yose (ben Ḥalaphta, the Tanna of overriding authority) holds that "words cannot be delivered to an agent." Therefore (Mishnah 7:2), if a sick person says to the (at least three) persons attending him, write a bill of divorce to my wife; if they ask a scribe to produce the bill and then they all sign, the bill is invalid since the order to write the bill cannot be delivered through an agent. This contrasts with the Mishnah here, which states that if three persons were appointed, they can be considered a court and have the authority to order the document to be drawn up *as a court*, not as agents. There really is no doubt that the Mishnah is R. Meïr's, since it is stated explicitly. The question is only what is R. Meïr's reason in opposing R. Yose. It seems that R. Yose will agree that a court can cause the bill to be written if the husband in so many words appoints three persons *as a court*; he does not accept R. Meïr's position that the appointment of at least three joint agents automatically constitutes them as a court; he does not admit that a person can appoint others (in any number, but not a formal court) to act as agents to have a document written for him (Babli 66b).

(48b line 29) רִבִּי הִלֵּל בַּר וָלֵס בְּעָא קוֹמֵי רִבִּי. מָה רָאוּ לוֹמַר. הֲלָכָה כְרִבִּי יוֹסֵי. אָמַר לֵיהּ. שֶׁלֹּא רְאִיתִיו. רִבִּי כַּד הֲוָה בְעֵי מַקְשֵׁיי עַל דְּרִבִּי יוֹסֵי אָמַר. אָנָן עֲלִיבַיָּיא מַקְשַׁיָּיא עַל דְּרִבִּי יוֹסֵי. שֶׁכְּשֵׁם לְבֵין קָדָשִׁי הַקֳּדָשִׁים לְבֵין חוּלֵי חוּלִין כָּךְ בֵּין דּוֹרֵינוּ לְדוֹרוֹ שֶׁלְּרִבִּי יוֹסֵי. אָמַר רִבִּי יִשְׁמָעֵאל בֵּירִבִּי יוֹסֵי. כְּשֵׁם שֶׁבֵּין זָהָב לְעָפָר כָּךְ בֵּין דּוֹרֵינוּ לְדוֹרוֹ שֶׁל אַבָּא.

Rebbi Hillel ben Valens asked before Rebbi: What reason did they have to say that practice follows Rebbi Yose[142]? He said to him, because I never met him. If somebody questioned statements of Rebbi Yose, Rebbi said, we miserable ones asked against Rebbi Yose, for as there is a difference between the most holy and the most profane, so is there a difference between Rebbi Yose's generation and ours. Rebbi Ismael ben Rebbi Yose said, the difference between my father's generation and ours is like that between gold and dust.

142 There is no doubt that in the Mishnah, practice has to follow R. Yose even if the opinion of Hanania from Ono might have the authority of R. Aqiba behind it (cf. *Terumot* 3:1, Note 23).

(48b line 34) אָמַר לַעֲשָׂרָה. הוֹלִיכוּ אֶת הַגֵּט הַזֶּה. אֶחָד מוֹלִיךְ עַל יְדֵי כוּלָּן. כּוּלְּכֶם הוֹלִיכוּ. כּוּלָּם מוֹלִיכִין וְאֶחָד נוֹתֵן עַל יְדֵי כוּלָּן. לְפִיכָךְ אִם מֵת אֶחָד מֵהֶן הֲרֵי הַגֵּט בָּטֵל. רִבִּי יוֹחָנָן בְּשֵׁם רִבִּי אֶלְעָזָר דְּמִן רוֹמָא. הַמְזַכֶּה כְּאוֹמֵר. כּוּלְּכֶם.

[143]"If somebody said to ten persons, 'bring this bill of divorce', one transports in the name of all of them. 'All of you shall bring', they all transport and one delivers in the name of all of them; therefore, if one of them died, the bill of divorce becomes invalid." [144]Rebbi Johanan in the name of Rebbi Eleazar from Rome: The one who awards[145] it like one who says "all of you".

143 Tosephta 4:13; Babli 67b.
144 Babli 67b; quoted in the name of the Yerushalmi but in Babli language in *Sefer Ha'Ittur* I, 29d (Note 186).
145 It is difficult to understand what it means to "award" the right to deliver a bill of divorce. The Babli version

(also ascribed to the Yerushalmi, Note 144), reads: "The one who counts is like one who says 'all of you'," which according to Rashi means that the husband says: you, 1, 2, 3, 4 (pointing at persons and counting the number of persons he appointed) shall deliver. One could try to explain the version of the text if the husband is a very well known personality and it is an honor to be his representative. Then, if he appoints his representatives by name without indication of any preferences between them, they all have equal rank and all are appointed jointly but not separately.

מי שאחזו פרק שביעי

(fol. 48b) **משנה א:** מִי שֶׁאֲחָזוֹ קוֹרְדְּיָיקוֹס וְאָמַר כִּתְבוּ גֵט לְאִשְׁתִּי לֹא אָמַר כְּלוּם. אָמַר כִּתְבוּ גֵט לְאִשְׁתִּי וַאֲחָזוֹ קוֹרְדְּיָיקוֹס וְחָזַר וְאָמַר אַל תִּכְתּוֹבוּ אֵין דְּבָרָיו הָאַחֲרוֹנִים כְּלוּם. נִשְׁתַּתֵּק אָמְרוּ לוֹ נִכְתּוֹב גֵט לְאִשְׁתְּךָ וְהִרְכִּין בְּרֹאשׁוֹ בּוֹדְקִין אוֹתוֹ שְׁלֹשָׁה פְּעָמִים. אִם אָמַר עַל לָאו לָאו וְעַל הֵן הֵן הֲרֵי אֵילוּ יִכְתְּבוּ וְיִתְּנוּ.

Mishnah 1: If somebody had an attack of seizures[1] and said, write a bill of divorce for my wife, he did not say anything. If he had said, write a bill of divorce for my wife, and afterwards had an attack of seizures and said, do not write, his later words are nothing. If somebody became paralyzed[2], one asks him, shall we write a bill of divorce for your wife, and he nods his head, one checks him out three times. If he answers no for no, yes for yes[3], they shall write and deliver.

1 The word קורדייקוס is taken as Greek κορδακικός "staggering, making drunken movements," derived from κόρδαξ, Latin *cordax*, "extravagant dance in Greek comedy." The nature of the seizures is not described in either Talmud, but it is implied that during an attack the person is not of sane mind.

2 He is of clear mind but has lost his power of speech.

3 If he repeatedly shakes his head sideways when asked whether not to write the bill but nods if asked whether to write the bill, his intentions and instructions are confirmed.

(48c line 20) **הלכה א:** מִי שֶׁאֲחָזוֹ קוּדְיָיקוֹס כול׳. סִימָן שׁוֹטֶה. הַיּוֹצֵא בַלַּיְלָה וְהַלָּן בְּבֵית הַקְּבָרוֹת וְהַמְקָרֵעַ כְּסוּתוֹ וְהַמְאַבֵּד מַה שֶׁנּוֹתְנִין לוֹ. רִבִּי חוּנָא אָמַר.

וְהֵן שֶׁיְּהוּ כוּלְּהֶם בּוֹ. דְּכֵן הַיּוֹצֵא בַּלַּיְלָה קֵנִיטְרוֹפִיס. וְהַלָּן בְּבֵית הַקְּבָרוֹת הַמְקַטֵּר לַשֵּׁדִים. וְהַמְקָרֵעַ אֶת כְּסוּתוֹ וְהַמְאַבֵּד מַה שֶּׁנּוֹתְנִין לוֹ קִינוֹקוֹס. רִבִּי יוֹחָנָן אָמַר. אֲפִילוּ אֶחָד מֵהֶן. אָמַר רִבִּי אָבִין. מִסְתַּבְּרָא כְּמָה דְּאָמַר רִבִּי יוֹחָנָן. אֲפִילוּ אֶחָד מֵהֶן. וּבִלְבַד בִּמְאַבֵּד מַה שֶּׁנּוֹתְנִין לוֹ. שֶׁאֲפִילוּ שׁוֹטֶה שֶׁבַּשּׁוֹטִין אֵין מְאַבֵּד מַה שֶּׁנּוֹתְנִין לוֹ. קוֹרְדְּיַיקוֹס אֵין בּוֹ אֶחָד מִכָּל אִילּוּ. מָהוּ קוֹרְדְּיַיקוֹס. אָמַר רִבִּי יוֹסֵי. הַמִּים. אָתָא עוּבְדָא קוֹמֵי רִבִּי יוֹסֵי בְּחַד טַרְסִיִּי דַּהֲווֹן יְהָבִין לֵיהּ סִימוּק גּוֹ אָכִים וַהֲוָה לָעֵי. אָכִים גּוֹ סְמִיק וַהֲוָה לָעֵי. זֶהוּ קוֹרְדְּיַיקוֹס שֶׁאָמְרוּ חֲכָמִים.

1 סימן | ת סימני   2 את | ת -   ר' חונא אמר | ת אמ' ר' הונא   3 והן שיהו | ת והוא שיהא   דל כן | ת דלא כן אני אומר   קניטרופיס | ת קניטרוכוס   והלן | ת הלן   4 המקטר לשדים | ת מקטיר לשידים   והמקרע | ת המקרע   - | ת כוליקוס   קינוקוס | ת קודייקוס   ר קיניקוס   5 אחד | ת אחת   (2 times)   אבין | ת בון   כמה | ת תמה   6 ובלבד | ת בלבד   שאפי' | ת אפי'   7 שבשוטין | ת שבשוטים   מה | ת כל מה   שנותנין | ת שנותון   אחד | ת אחת   קורדייקוס | ר קודריקוס   המים | ר המיני   9 אכים | ת אכוס   (2 times)   וחוה | ת והוא   (2 times)   סמיק | ת סימוק   10 זהו | ת אמר דו הוא

"If somebody had an attack of seizures", etc. ⁴The symptoms of an insane person: One who goes out in the night, stays overnight in a graveyard, tears his clothing, and destroys what one gives to him. Rebbi Huna said, only if all of that is in him since otherwise I say that one who goes out in the night is a man-dog⁵; he who stays overnight in a graveyard burns incense to spirits, he who tears up his clothing is [a choleric person]⁶, and he who destroys what one gives to him is a Cynic. Rebbi Joḥanan said, even only one of these symptoms is proof. Rebbi Abun said, what Rebbi Joḥanan said, even only one of these by itself is reasonable for him who destroys what one gives to him; even the greatest idiot does not destroy all one gives to him. The one attacked by seizures does not exhibit any of these signs. What is one attacked by seizures? Rebbi Yose said, a decrepit one. There came a case before Rebbi Yose of a weaver who, when one gave him red on black he was exerting himself, black on red he was exerting himself. This is the *cordiacus* described by the Sages.

4 This text is from *Terumot* 1:1, Notes 38-50. In the variants, ת denotes the Leiden ms. of *Terumot* and ר the Rome ms.

5 Cf. E. Guggenheimer and H. Guggenheimer, *Notes on the Talmudic vocabulary, gndryps-qntrwpys*, Lešonenu 35 (1971) 201-207 (Hebrew); *Talmudic evidence for Greek spelling*, Studi classici in onore di Quintino Cataudella, vol. iv, U. Catania (1972) 1981, 313-314.

6 From the text in *Terumot*, missing here.

פְּעָמִים שׁוֹטֶה פְּעָמִים חָלוּם. בְּשָׁעָה שֶׁהוּא שׁוֹטֶה הֲרֵי הוּא כְּשׁוֹטֶה לְכָל־דָּבָר. וּבְשָׁעָה שֶׁהוּא חָלוּם הֲרֵי הוּא כְּפִיקֵחַ לְכָל־דָּבָר. אָתָא עוּבְדָא קוֹמֵי שְׁמוּאֵל אָמַר. כַּד דְּהוּא חֲלִים יִתֵּן גֵּט. מָה. שְׁמוּאֵל כְּרֵישׁ לָקִישׁ. דְּרֵישׁ לָקִישׁ אָמַר לִכְשֶׁיִּשְׁתַּפֶּה. יֵיבָא דִּשְׁמוּאֵל מֵרֵישׁ לָקִישׁ דּוּ אָמַר. חָלוּם יִתֵּן גֵּט. וְתַחֲלִימֵנִי וְתַחֲיֵינִי.

פְּעָמִים שׁוֹטֶה פְּעָמִים חָלוּם. הֲרֵי הוּא כְּפִיקֵחַ לְכָל־דָּבָר. בְּשָׁעָה שֶׁהוּא שׁוֹטֶה הֲרֵי הוּא כְּשׁוֹטֶה לְכָל־דְּבָרָיו. וּבְשָׁעָה שֶׁהוּא חָלוּם הֲרֵי הוּא כְּפִיקֵחַ לְכָל־דָּבָר. אָתָא עוּבְדָא קוֹמֵי שְׁמוּאֵל אָמַר. בַּר דּוּ חֲלוּם יִתֵּן גֵּט. וְיִשְׁאוֹל כְּרַבִּי שִׁמְעוֹן בֶּן לָקִישׁ. דְּרַבִּי שִׁמְעוֹן בֶּן לָקִישׁ אָמַר לִכְשֶׁיִּשְׁתַּפֶּה. דּוּ בָהּ דִּשְׁמוּאֵל מִן דְּרַבִּי שִׁמְעוֹן בֶּן לָקִישׁ. בַּר דּוּ חֲלוּם אָמַר. דְּהוּא יִתֵּן גֵּט וְתַחֲלִימֵנִי וְהַחֲיֵינִי.

[7] "If sometimes he is insane and sometimes healthy. When he is insane he is insane in all regards, when healthy he is normal in all regards." A case came before Samuel who said, when he is of sound mind he should deliver the bill of divorce. Why? Samuel follows Rebbi Simeon ben Laqish; as Rebbi Simeon ben Laqish said[8], when he regains his sanity. It follows that Samuel acted according to Rebbi Simeon ben Laqish who said, only if he is of sound mind may he deliver the bill of divorce; (Is. 38:16) "make me healthy and let me live![9]"

7 From *Terumot* 1:1, Notes 52-55. The slightly different *Terumot* text is given in the second column.

8 In the next paragraph.

9 The verse is quoted correctly in *Terumot*.

(48c line 35) רִבִּי יַעֲקֹב בַּר אָחָא אָמַר. אִיתְפַּלְגוּן רִבִּי יוֹחָנָן וְרֵישׁ לָקִישׁ. רִבִּי יוֹחָנָן אָמַר. עוֹדֵהוּ קוֹרְדְּיַיקוֹס עָלָיו כּוֹתְבִין גֵּט וְנוֹתְנִין לְאִשְׁתּוֹ. רֵישׁ לָקִישׁ אָמַר. לִכְשֶׁיִּשְׁתַּפֶּה. מִחְלָפָה שִׁיטָתֵיהּ דְּרֵישׁ לָקִישׁ. דְּאִיתְפַּלְגוּן. נִתְחָרֵשׁ אוֹ נִשְׁטָטָה אוֹ נִשְׁתַּמֵּד אוֹ שֶׁהוֹרוּ בֵית דִּין לָאֱכוֹל חֵלֶב. רִבִּי יוֹחָנָן אָמַר. נִדְחֵית חַטָּאתוֹ. רֵישׁ לָקִישׁ אָמַר. לֹא נִדְחֵית חַטָּאתוֹ. רִבִּי יוֹסֵי בֵּירִבִּי בּוּן אָמַר. רִבִּי יוֹחָנָן מֵיחְלַף שְׁמוּעָתָא. דְּלֹא תְהֵא מִילְתֵיהּ דְּרִבִּי יוֹחָנָן פְּלִיגָא עַל מִילְתֵיהּ. דְּאָמַר רִבִּי שְׁמוּאֵל בַּר אַבָּא בְּשֵׁם רִבִּי יוֹחָנָן. הַגּוֹסֵס זוֹרְקִין עָלָיו מִדַּם חַטָּאתוֹ וּמִדַּם אֲשָׁמוֹ. רַבָּנִין דְּקַיְסָרִין אָמְרִין. רִבִּי חִייָה רִבִּי יָסָא חַד כְּהָדֵין וְחַד כְּהָדֵין.

10 1 לאכול חלב | ה מותר לאכול חלב   2 ריש לקיש | ה ר' שמעון בן לקיש   3 ר' יוחנן מיחלף | ה ר' אחא מחלף   4 שמואל בר אבא | ה שמעון בר אבא   5 ר' יסא | ד ור' ה אמי   חד כהדין וחד כהדין | ד חד ה מחלף וחד אמ' כאן תנייה

מַתְנִיתָא פְלִיגָא עַל רֵישׁ לָקִישׁ. אָמַר. כִּתְבוּ גֵט לְאִשְׁתּוֹ. וַאֲחָזוֹ קוֹרְדְּיַיקוֹס וְחָזַר וְאָמַר. אַל תִּכְתְּבוּ. אֵין דְּבָרָיו הָאַחֲרוֹנִים כְּלוּם. פָּתַר לָהּ. לִכְשֶׁיִּשְׁתַּפֶּה אֵין דְּבָרָיו הָאַחֲרוֹנִים כְּלוּם. נָתַן לָהּ אֶת גִּיטָהּ וְאָמַר. לֹא יְהֵא גֵט אֶלָּא לְמָחָר. וְנַעֲשָׂה קוֹרְדְּיַיקוֹס. תַּפְלוּגְתָּא דְּרִבִּי יוֹחָנָן וּדְרֵישׁ לָקִישׁ. זָרַק לָהּ אֶת גִּיטָהּ וְאָמַר. לֹא יְהֵא גֵט אֶלָּא לְמָחָר. תַּפְלוּגְתָּא דְּרִבִּי יוֹחָנָן וּדְרֵישׁ לָקִישׁ. רִבִּי אֶלְעָזָר אָמַר. רִבִּי אָבִין בָּעֵי. תְּרָם אֶת כְּרְיוֹ וְאָמַר. לֹא יְהֵא תְרוּמָה אֶלָּא לְמָחָר. וְנַעֲשָׂה קוֹרְדְּיַיקוֹס. תַּפְלוּגְתָּא דְּרִבִּי יוֹחָנָן וְרֵישׁ לָקִישׁ. אָמַר רִבִּי זְעִירָא. מַתְנִיתָא פְלִיגָא עַל רֵישׁ לָקִישׁ וְלֵית לֵיהּ קִיּוּם. הֲרֵי שֶׁהָיָה צָלוּב אוֹ מְגוּיָּיד וְרָמַז וְאָמַר. כִּתְבוּ גֵט לְאִשְׁתּוֹ. כּוֹתְבִין וְנוֹתְנִין בְּחֶזְקַת שֶׁהַנְּשָׁמָה תְּלוּיָה בוֹ. וְאִיפְשָׁר שֶׁלֹּא נִטְרְפָה דַעְתּוֹ שָׁעָה אֶחָת. הָדָא פְלִיגָא עַל רֵישׁ לָקִישׁ וְלֵית לֵיהּ קִיּוּם.

Rebbi Jacob bar Aḥa said, Rebbi Joḥanan and Rebbi Simeon ben Laqish disagree. Rebbi Joḥanan said, even while he is suffering an attack of seizures, one writes the bill of divorce and delivers it to his wife. Rebbi

Simeon ben Laqish said, when he regains his sanity[11]. The argument of Rebbi Simeon ben Laqish seems to be inverted, since they disagreed: [12]If he became deaf-mute[13], or insane, or became an apostate[14], or the Court ruled that fat may be eaten[15], Rebbi Johanan said, his sacrifice of purification is pushed aside, Rebbi Simeon ben Laqish said, his sacrifice of purification is not pushed aside[16]. Rebbi Yose ben Rebbi Abun said, Rebbi (Johanan) [Aha][17] switches traditions, to avoid that a word of Rebbi Johanan contradict his own word. For Rebbi Samuel[18] bar Abba said in the name of Rebbi Johanan: One sprinkles the blood of a purification sacrifice or a reparation sacrifice for a person terminally ill[19]. The rabbis of Caesarea said, Rebbi Hiyya and Rebbi Yasa[20], one follows the one, the other follows the other[21]. The Mishnah disagrees with Rebbi Simeon ben Laqish: "If he had said, write a bill of divorce for my wife, and afterwards had an attack of seizures and said, do not write, his later words are disregarded." He explains it: After he regains his sanity, his later words are disregarded. If he gave her a bill of divorce saying that it should be valid only the next day and then suffered an attack of seizures, this is the disagreement between Rebbi Johanan and Rebbi Simeon ben Laqish[22]. If he threw her bill of divorce to her saying that it should be valid only the next day and then suffered an attack of seizures, this is the disagreement between Rebbi Johanan and Rebbi Simeon ben Laqish. Rebbi Eleazar said that Rebbi Abin asked: If he separated heave[23] from his grain heap and said, it shall be heave only tomorrow but the next day he suffered an attack of seizures, is this the disagreement between Rebbi Johanan and Rebbi Simeon ben Laqish? Rebbi Ze'ira said, a *baraita* disagrees with Rebbi Simeon ben Laqish and he cannot explain it: If somebody had been crucified or mortally wounded[24] when he signalled to write a bill of divorce to his wife, one writes and delivers on the assumption that his soul hangs on in him[25]. Is it not impossible that his mind should not have been disturbed for an hour? This disagrees with Rebbi Simeon ben Laqish and he cannot explain it.

10 The parallel text is in *Horaiot* 1:2 (45d l. 64). The variants from the Leiden ms. are noted ת, those from the printed Yerushalmi text in the Babli are noted י.

11 In the Babli, 70b, the attributions are switched, following the later argument in this paragraph (Note 17).

12 This quote is incomplete; the text has to be completed from *Horaiot* (Note 10) and a related text in the Babli, *Zebaḥim* 12b. The completed text must read: "If somebody had eaten forbidden fat and already had prepared his separation sacrifice when he became..." A purification sacrifice is personal; if its owner died it cannot be transferred to another owner or another use, nor can it be redeemed. The question is whether insanity makes a person lose his individuality; if the answer is positive then during the period of insanity the sacrificial animal was ownerless and cannot then or afterwards be of any use; it has to be put away until it dies a natural death.

13 The illiterate deaf-mute has lost his legal personality; cf. *Ketubot* Chpater 1, Note 134, *Yebamot* 14:1.

14 *Lev.* 1:2: "If a person *from among you* present a sacrifice..." is interpreted to mean that the rules of obligatory sacrifices apply to converts but exclude apostates [Babli *Ḥulin* 5a, 13b; *Erubin* 69b; *Sifra Wayyiqra Paršata* 2(3)].

15 The High Court in the Temple ruled that the circumstances for which the person brings his purification offering do not imply that a sin was committed. Since a purification offering cannot be brought as a voluntary gift, the offering becomes unusable. It is stated here that if the court later reverses itself, R. Joḥanan holds that the sacrifice is not reinstated.

16 If circumstances change, the sacrifice may be re-instated.

17 It is obvious that the reading from *Horaiot*, R. Aḥa, is correct, since R. Joḥanan, who is quoted in the text here, has no influence over what future generations report in his name. R. Aḥa's tradition is the source of the quote in the Babli (Note 11).

18 Since both R. Samuel bar Abba and R. Simeon bar Abba were students of R. Joḥanan, it is impossible to decide

between the readings here and in *Horaiot*.

19 These sacrifices may not be offered for the deceased. The priest who was informed that the offering was for a terminally ill person can proceed under the assumption that the person is alive at the moment which validates the offering, when the blood of the sacrifice is sprinkled on the wall of the altar.

20 In *Horaiot*: R. Immi, the permanent companion of R. Yasa. It follows that the R. Ḥiyya mentioned here is R. Ḥiyya bar Abba, student and successor to R. Joḥanan.

21 It is not stated who followed R. Joḥanan and who R. Simeon ben Laqish; from the following it seems that the Yerushalmi does not accept R. Aḥa's relabelling of the opinions.

22 For R. Joḥanan, the wife is divorced since the bill was delivered; for R. Simeon ben Laqish the attack of insanity invalidates the delivery. If the husband regains his sanity, he has to take back the bill from his wife and deliver it a second time.

23 The insane person cannot separate heave from grain; his actions are irrelevant in law (Mishnah *Terumot* 1:1).

24 He is slowly but surely dying.

25 A similar formulation is in the Tosephta (5:1): "If somebody had been crucified or mortally wounded when he signalled to write a bill of divorce to his wife, one writes and delivers as long as he is alive."

26 The Tosephta clearly prescribes to deliver the bill while the husband is alive but unconscious.

(48c line 55) תַּנֵּי. חֵרֵשׁ שֶׁתָּרַם אֵין תְּרוּמָתוֹ תְרוּמָה. אָמַר רַבָּן שִׁמְעוֹן בֶּן גַּמְלִיאֵל. בַּמֶּה דְבָרִים אֲמוּרִים. שֶׁהָיָה חֵרֵשׁ מִתְּחִילָּתוֹ. אֲבָל אִם הָיָה פִּיקֵחַ וְנִתְחָרֵשׁ כּוֹתֵב וַאֲחֵרִים מְקַיְּימִין כְּתַב יָדוֹ.

2 שהיה | ת בשהיה | - ת שומע ואינו מדבר הרי הוא כפיקח ר -.

[27]It was stated: "If a deaf-mute person gave heave, it is not heave. Rabban Simeon ben Gamliel said, to what does this refer? If he was born deaf-mute. But if he was normal and became deaf and dumb, he writes and others confirm his signature."

27 This and the following paragraphs are from *Terumot* 1:1 (**ת**), Notes 19-32). The Rome ms. is indicated by **ר**. Variants which are introduced by the hand of the corrector in *Terumot* are indicated by **מ**.

(48c line 57) רִבִּי יַעֲקֹב בַּר אָחָא רִבִּי חִייָה בְּשֵׁם רִבִּי יוֹחָנָן. חֲלוּקִין עַל [הַשּׁוֹנָה הַזֶּה]. אָמְרִין וְהָא מַתְנִיתִין פְּלִיגָא. נִתְחָרֵשׁ הוּא אוֹ נִשְׁתַּטָּה אֵינוֹ מוֹצִיא עוֹלָמִית. וְיִכְתּוֹב וִיקַיְימוּ אֲחֵרִים כְּתַב יָדוֹ. קַיְימָנֵיהּ בְּשֶׁאֵינוֹ יוֹדֵעַ לִכְתּוֹב. הָתִיב רִבִּי בָּא בַּר מָמָל. וְהָא מַתְנִיתָא פְּלִיגָא. הֲרֵי שֶׁכָּתַב בִּכְתַב יָדוֹ. אָמַר לַסּוֹפֵר וְכָתַב וְלָעֵדִים וְחָתְמוּ. אַף עַל פִּי שֶׁכְּתָבוּהוּ וַחֲתָמוּהוּ וּנְתָנוּהוּ לוֹ וְחָזַר וּנְתָנוֹ לָהּ אֵינוֹ גֵט. אָמַר רִבִּי יוֹסֵי. אֱמֹר דְּבַתְרָהּ. וְלֵית הָדָא פְּלִיגָא. אֵינוֹ גֵט עַד שֶׁיִּשְׁמְעוּ קוֹלוֹ. אָמַר לַסּוֹפֵר. כְּתוֹב. וְלָעֵדִים חֲתוֹמוּ. סוֹף דָּבָר עַד שֶׁיִּשְׁמְעוּ אֶת קוֹלוֹ. וְלֹא אֲפִילוּ הִרְכִּין בְּרֹאשׁוֹ. וְאַתְּ אָמַר לֵית כָּאן. אָמַר רִבִּי מָנָא אִית כָּאן. הִיא שְׁמִיעַת הַקּוֹל הִיא הַרְכָּנַת רֹאשׁ.

1 השוטה הוה | **ת** השונה הזה   2 נשתטה | **ת** נשטה   3 ידו | **ת** ידיו   קיימניה | **ת** קיימונה   4 התיב | **ת** מותיב   הרי | **ת** והרי   בכתב | **ת** כתב   ידו | **ת** ידיו   אמ' | **ת** או שאמ'   5 וכתב ולעדים וחתמו | **ת** כתוב. ולעדים. חתומו   כתבוהו וחתמוהו ונתנוהו | **ת** כתבו וחתמו ונתנו   6 יוסי | **ת** יוסה   דבתרה | **ת** סופה   הדא | **ת** היא   7 קולו | **ת** את קולו   אמ' | **ת** שאמ'   סוף ר | **מ** לא סוף   8 ולא | **ת** אלא   ואת | **מ** את   - | **ת** ואף הכא לית כאן

Rebbi Jacob bar Aḥa, Rebbi Ḥiyya, in the name of Rebbi Joḥanan: One disagrees with this Tanna. They say, does not a Mishnah disagree: "If he became deaf-mute or insane, he may never divorce." Why can he not write and have others execute his written instructions? They upheld it, if he was illiterate. Rebbi Abba bar Mamal objected, does not a *baraita* disagree: "If he wrote himself, or told the scribe to write and the witnesses to sign, even though the scribe wrote, the witnesses signed, they gave him [the bill] and he in turn gave it to her, it is no divorce." Rebbi Assi said, complete the sentence and there is no disgreement: "it is no divorce unless they hear his voice." But even if he gave a sign with his head you say it is invalid, (here also it is invalid). Rebbi Mana said, it is valid: hearing the voice has the same status as seeing him nod his head!

(48c line 66) רִבִּי זְעִירָא בְּעָא מִינֵּיהּ דְּרִבִּי מָנָא. כְּמָה דְּתֵימַר. עַד שֶׁיְּרְכִּין בְּרֹאשׁוֹ שָׁלֹשׁ פְּעָמִים. אָמַר לֵיהּ. לִשְׁמִיעַת הַקּוֹל פַּעַם אַחַת. לְהַרְכָּנַת הָרֹאשׁ שְׁלֹשָׁה פְעָמִים. וְדִכְוָותָהּ עַד שֶׁיִּשְׁמְעוּ אֶת קוֹלוֹ שְׁלֹשָׁה פְעָמִים.

1 זעירא | **ת** עזרא   מיניה דר' | **ת** קומי ר'   2 שלש | **ת** שלשה   - | **ת** ודכוותה עד שישמעו קולו שלשה פעמים. (moved to the wrong place in *Giṭṭin*).

Rebbi Ze'ira[28] asked before Rebbi Mana: Just as you say that three times he must give a sign with his head, (must one equally hear his voice three times)? He said to him, hearing his voice once, giving a sign with his head three times.

28 Since R. Ze'ira lived too late to have known R. Mana I and was the teacher of R. Mana II's teacher, the correct reading is that from *Terumot*: R. Ezra.

(48c line 69) אָמַר רִבִּי יוּדָן. בְּאוֹמֵר. כָּךְ וְכָךְ עָשִׂיתִי. בְּרַם הָכָא בְּאוֹמֵר. כָּךְ וְכָךְ עֲשׂוּ. רִבִּי בִּנְיָמִין בַּר לֵוִי בָּעֵי. מָה אֲנָן קַיָּימִין. אִם יֶשׁ בּוֹ דַעַת לָבֹא יֶשׁ בּוֹ דַעַת לְשֶׁעָבַר. אֵין בּוֹ דַעַת לָבֹא. אָמַר רִבִּי אַבָּא מָרִי. בְּחֵרֵשׁ אֲנָן קַיָּימִין. וְאֵין שְׁלִיחוּת לְחֵרֵשׁ. רִבִּי יוֹסֵי בֵּירִבִּי בּוּן אָמַר. בְּבָרִיא אֲנָן קַיָּימִין. לָמָּה אֵינוֹ גֵט. אֲנִי אוֹמֵר. מִתְעַסֵּק בִּשְׁטָרוֹתָיו. וְתַגֵּי כֵן. בַּמֶּה דְּבָרִים אֲמוּרִים. בִּזְמָן שֶׁנִּשְׁתַּתֵּק מִתּוֹךְ בּוּרְיָיו. אֲבָל אִם נִשְׁתַּתֵּק מִתּוֹךְ חָלְיוֹ דַּיּוֹ פַּעַם אַחַת.

1 באו | **ת** תמן באו'   ברם | **ת** -   2 בר | **ת** בן   מה אנן קיימין | **ת** -   אם יש בו דעת לבא יש בו דעת לשעבר. אין בו דעת לבא | **ת** אם יש בו דעת לשעבר יש בו דעת להבא. אם אין בו דעת לשעבר אין בו דעת להבא.   3 אבא מרי | **ת** אבודימי   4 ביר' בון אמ' | **ת** אמ' ר'   למה | **ת** ולמה   5 בשטרותיו | **ת** היה בשטרותיו   שנשתתק | **ת** שפירש   6 מתוך | **ת** מחמת

Rebbi Yudan said, there, if he said I did such and such, here, if he says do such and such. Rebbi Benjamin ben Levi inquired: He should have understanding for the future if he has understanding for the past; (if he has no understanding for the past,) he would not have understanding for the future! Rebbi Abba Mari said, here we deal with a mute; there is no agency for a mute. Rebbi Yose ben Rebbi Abun said, we deal with a sane person. Why is there no divorce? Because I say, he was occupied with his documents. We also stated thus: "When was this said? When he was paralyzed while being healthy. But if he was paralyzed by a prior sickness, once is enough."

(48c line 76) וּבִלְבַד בִּמְסָרְגִין לוֹ. נִכְתּוֹב גֵּט לְאִשְׁתָּךְ. וְהוּא אוֹמֵר. הֵין. לְאִמָּךְ. וְהוּא אוֹמֵר. לָאו. לְאִשְׁתָּךְ. וְהוּא אוֹמֵר. הֵין. לְבִתָּךְ. וְהוּא אוֹמֵר. לָאו. לְאִשְׁתָּךְ. וְהוּא אוֹמֵר. הֵין. לַאֲחוֹתָךְ. וְהוּא אוֹמֵר. לָאו. אַף בְּעֵדִיּוֹת כֵּן. אָתָא רִבִּי אַבָּהוּ בְשֵׁם רִבִּי יוֹחָנָן. אַף בְּעֵדִיּוֹת כֵּן. שֶׁאָדָם מֵעִיד עֵדוּתוֹ מְיוּשָׁב. אַף בִּנְדָרִינָם כֵּן. תַּנֵּי רַב שֵׁשֶׁת. כְּשֵׁם שֶׁבּוֹדְקִין אוֹתוֹ בְגִיטִין ג פְּעָמִים כָּךְ בּוֹדְקִין אוֹתוֹ בִּירוּשׁוֹת וּבְמֶקַח וּמִמְכָּר וּבְמַתָּנוֹת.

But only if it is intermittent[29]. Shall we write a bill of divorce for your wife? And he says, yes. For your mother, and he says, no. For your wife? And he says, yes. For your daughter, and he says, no. For your wife? And he says, yes. For your sister, and he says, no[30]. Is it the same for testimony? Rebbi Abbahu came in the name of Rebbi Johanan: It is the same for testimony, since a person may testify while sitting[31]. The same holds for vows. Rav Sheshet stated: Just as one checks three times for bills of divorce, so one checks for inheritance, commercial transactions, and gifts[32].

29 This refers to the last part of the Mishnah, about the bill of divorce to be written for a paralyzed man. As explained here, one asks questions in which the one which counts is alternating with other questions for

which the answer must be "no" (or shaking of the head).

30 A paraphrase, not a parallel text, is quoted in Tosaphot 70b, *s. v.* בודקין.

31 *Deut.* 19:17 requires only that the parties to a suit stand before the judges, not the witnesses. Therefore there is no biblical impediment to ascertaining testimony from a paralyzed person.

32 A similar text in the Babli, 71a, and Tosephta, 5:1. In both of these texts, testimony is explicitly included.

(fol. 48b) **משנה ב:** אָמְרוּ לוֹ נִכְתּוֹב גֵּט לְאִשְׁתֶּךָ. אָמַר לָהֶם כְּתבוּ אָמְרוּ לַסּוֹפֵר וְכָתַב לָעֵדִים וְחָתְמוּ. אַף עַל פִּי שֶׁכְּתָבוּהוּ וַחֲתָמוּהוּ וּנְתָנוּהוּ לוֹ וְחָזַר וּנְתָנוֹ לָהּ הֲרֵי זֶה גֵּט בָּטֵל עַד שֶׁיֹּאמַר לַסּוֹפֵר כְּתוֹב וְלָעֵדִים חֲתוֹמוּ.

Mishnah 2: If they[33] said to him[34], shall we write a bill of divorce for your wife? If he said to them, write[35], and they told the scribe who wrote, and the witnesses who signed; even though they wrote, signed, and delivered it to him and he delivered it to her, this is an invalid bill of divorce unless he said to the scribe, write, and to the witnesses, sign.

33 An indeterminate plural always means 2.

34 As Rashi points out, he must be either a healthy person or a sick scholar, for whom the special simplified rules for the dangerously ill do not apply.

35 The husband did not appoint the people talking to him as a court since they are only two. Nor did he appoint them as witnesses to his order to the scribe, as explained in the Halakhah.

(48d line 6) **הלכה ב:** אָמְרוּ לוֹ נִכְתּוֹב גֵּט לְאִשְׁתֶּךָ כול'. אָמַר לִשְׁנַיִם. אָמְרוּ לִפְלוֹנִי שֶׁיִּכְתּוֹב וְלִפְלוֹנִי וּפְלוֹנִי שֶׁיַּחְתֹּמוּ. רִבִּי זְעִירָה בְּשֵׁם רִבִּי יִרְמְיָה. מַעֲשֶׂה הָיָה בִּימֵי רִבִּי וְאָמַר. לֹא יֵעָשֶׂה כֵן בְּיִשְׂרָאֵל. שְׁמוּאֵל אָמַר. יֵעָשֶׂה וְיֵעָשֶׂה. רַב יִרְמְיָה שָׁאַל לִשְׁמוּאֵל. אָמַר לִשְׁנַיִם. אָמְרוּ לִפְלוֹנִי שֶׁיִּכְתּוֹב וְאַתֶּם חֲתוֹמוּ.

אָמַר לֵיהּ. הֲרֵי זֶה גֵט אֶלָּא שֶׁהַדָּבָר צָרִיךְ תַּלְמוּד. מִחְלְפָה שִׁיטָתֵיהּ דִּשְׁמוּאֵל. תַּמָּן הוּא אָמַר. יֵעָשֶׂה וְיֵעָשֶׂה. וְהָכָא הוּא אָמַר אָכֵן. שַׁנְיָיא הִיא שֶׁשִּׁינּוּ אֶת עֵדוּתָן.

Halakhah 2: "If they said to him, shall we write a bill of divorce for your wife," etc. If he said to two people, say to **X** that he shall write[36] and to Y and Z that they shall sign. Rebbi Ze'ira in the name of Rebbi[37] Jeremiah, this happened in the days of Rebbi, and he said, such a thing should not be done in Israel[38]. Samuel said, it certainly should be done. Rav Jeremiah asked Samuel[39]: If he said to two people, say to **X** that he write and you sign. He said to him, that is a bill of divorce but it needs study[40]. The opinion of Samuel seems inverted. There, he said, it certainly should be done, and here, he says so? There is a difference, because they changed their testimony[41].

36 As explained in the preceding Note, this legalizes the writing of the bill.

37 He is identical with the Rav Jeremiah mentioned later in this paragraph.

38 The Babli, 67a, which attributes the statement to Rav, explains that the procedure is disapproved of since a wife might hire witnesses to falsely instruct the scribe to write and witnesses to sign.

39 A similar question, in the name of Rav's Academy, is mentioned in the Babli, 66b.

40 The woman is divorced but she cannot remarry based on that bill.

41 The argument is cryptic. It assumes that the question was: "If he said to two people, tell X that he write and you sign; they told the scribe to sign and others to sign." (In the Babli, the question is inverted, with the witnesses being instructed to have others sign but they signed themselves.) The question then arises, is it sufficient that the bill of divorce be written correctly (which it is) but not signed according to instructions? (The arguments of the Babli about this case are irrelevant for the Yerushalmi.)

נִיחָא לָעֵדִים וְחִתְמוּ לַסּוֹפֵר וְכָתַב. לֵית הָדָא פְלִיגָא עַל דְּרִבִּי (48d line 12) יוֹחָנָן. דְּרִבִּי יוֹחָנָן אָמַר. כָּתַב טָרְפוֹ בְּטוֹפֶס כָּשֵׁר. פָּתַר לָהּ כְּרִבִּי יְהוּדָה. דְּרִבִּי יְהוּדָה פּוֹסֵל בְּטוֹפְסִין.

We understand[42], to the witnesses, sign! But to the scribe, write? Does this not disagree with Rebbi Joḥanan, since Rebbi Joḥanan said, if he wrote the essential text with the formula, it is valid[43]. He explains it[44] following Rebbi Jehudah, since Rebbi Jehudah invalidates formulas.

42 This now is a discussion of the Mishnah. The persons asking whether a bill of divorce should be written cannot engage witnesses without special authorization. But why should the scribe not be able to write on a simple order since he is able to write the entire bill of divorce in advance, just leaving blanks for the names and addresses of the parties?

43 The problem of bills written in advance was treated in Chapter 3, Note 17 ff.

44 The Mishnah here follows R. Jehudah who prohibits the scribe from using prepared texts.

מְשָׁנָה ג: זֶה גִיטֵּיךְ אִם מַתִּי זֶה גִיטֵּיךְ אִם מַתִּי מֵחוֹלִי זֶה זֶה גִיטֵּךְ (fol. 48b) לְאַחַר מִיתָתִי לֹא אָמַר כְּלוּם. מֵהַיּוֹם אִם מַתִּי מֵעַכְשָׁיו אִם מַתִּי הֲרֵי זֶה גֵט. מֵהַיּוֹם לְאַחַר מִיתָתִי אֵינוֹ גֵט וְאִם מֵת חוֹלֶצֶת וְלֹא מִתְיַבֶּמֶת.

Mishnah 3: "This is your bill of divorce if I should die, this is your bill of divorce if I should die from this illness, this is your bill of divorce after my death," he did not say anything[45]. "From today if I should die, from now if I should die," that is a bill of divorce. "From today after my death" is no bill of divorce[46]; if he dies[47] she must receive ḥaliṣah but is barred from levirate marriage.

45 Nobody can be divorced after his death. The next sentence makes it clear that a bill of divorce would be valid if given on condition to become

activated one hour before the husband's death. But from that moment he can no longer live with his wife without invalidating the divorce.

46 The husband's intent cannot be determined from this language. Does he want to say that the divorce shall be valid from the moment the bill was handed to his wife if he should die (either from the illness he is currently suffering from, or on a trip overseas he is just starting, or any other foreseeable dangerous situation which causes him to write the bill), or does he really mean that the divorce should become effective only at the time of his death? In the first case, the wife becomes a divorcee after his death, in the second case she becomes a widow.

In some Bablylonian sources, the wording is "it is and is not a bill of divorce."

47 If he dies childless and has a brother, the wife cannot enter levirate marriage since she might be a divorcee; she cannot marry outside the family without *ḥaliṣah* since she might be a widow; cf. Introduction to Tractate *Yebamot*.

(48d line 15) **הלכה ג:** זֶה גִּיטֵיךְ אִם מַתִּי. זֶה גִּיטֵיךְ מֵחוֹלִי זֶה. זֶה גִּיטֵךְ לְאַחַר מִיתָתִי. לֹא אָמַר כְּלוּם. וְרַבּוֹתֵינוּ אָמְרוּ. הֲרֵי זֶה גֵּט. מָנֵי רַבּוֹתֵינוּ. רְבִּי יְהוּדָה הַנָּשִׂיא וּבֵית דִּינוֹ. בִּשְׁלֹשָׁה מְקוֹמוֹת נִקְרָא רְבִּי יְהוּדָה הַנָּשִׂיא רַבּוֹתֵינוּ. בְּגִיטִּין בַּשֶּׁמֶן וּבְסַנְדָּל. וְיִקְרְאוּ לוֹ בֵּית דִּין שָׁרְיָא. שֶׁכָּל־בֵּית דִּין שֶׁהוּא מַתִּיר שְׁלֹשָׁה דְבָרִים הוּא נִקְרָא בֵּית דִּין שָׁרְיָא. אָמַר רְבִּי יוּדָן בֵּירְבִּי יִשְׁמָעֵאל. בֵּית דִּינוֹ חָלוּק עָלָיו בְּגִיטִּין.

Halakhah 3: "'This is your bill of divorce if I should die, this is your bill of divorce from this illness, this is your bill of divorce after my death,' he did not say anything." [48]But our teachers said, it is a bill of divorce[49]. Who are "our teachers"? Rebbi Jehudah the Prince and his court[50]. In three places is Rebbi Jehudah the Prince called "our teachers", about bills of divorce, oil[51], and a sole[52]. They should have called him "permissive court" since any court which permits three [previously forbidden] things is called "permissive court." Rebbi Yudan ben Rebbi Ismael[53] said, his court disagreed with him about the bills of divorce.

48   This paragraph is also in *Niddah* 3, explained there in Notes 93-97. "Rebbi Jehudah the Prince" may be Judah II, Rebbi's grandson; cf. Note 51.

49   The Babli, *Giṭṭin* 72b, reports the same but in 76b refers the decision to Mishnah 7:9: "If he says, this is your bill of divorce if I do not return within 12 months; if he dies in the meantime, the bill of divorce is void." In this case also, he did not specify *from today*. The Babli explains that in both cases they follow R. Yose who holds that "the date of a document is proof of its validity;" a bill of divorce executed before the husband's death is valid (cf. below, Note 67). The Yerushalmi's interpretation is given in the second and third paragraphs following.

50   *Šabbat* 1:1 (3d l.20), *Giṭṭin* 7:3 (48d l.17), *Avodah zarah* 2:8 (41d l.48); obliquely mentioned in the Babli *Giṭṭin* 72b, 76b; *Ketubot* 2b, *Avodah zarah* 37a.

51   Mishnah *Avodah zarah* 2:9. The Mishnah has a list of foods that cannot be taken from Gentiles without kosher supervision since one cannot be sure that no forbidden ingredients were used, but which are not forbidden for usufruct. A first group includes milk, bread, and olive oil, with a note that "our teachers permitted olive oil" [to be used without supervision.] In the Babli, this permission is attributed to Rebbi, not his grandson R. Jehudah the Prince. (The chronology of the House of Hillel in the Third Cent. and the attribution of decrees between Rabbis Jehudah I, II, and III is in dispute.)

52   If a woman has a miscarriage in the shape of a sole (essentially an empty placenta) she is subject to all disabilities of the woman who gave birth to a male and a female. Rebbi Jehudah's court restricted this to the case that a human shape was recognizable.

53   In *Niddah* simply: R. Yudan.

(48d line 21) מָהוּ שֶׁתְּהֵא מוּתֶּרֶת לִינָשֵׂא. רִבִּי חַגַּיי אָמַר. מוּתֶּרֶת לִינָשֵׂא. רִבִּי יוֹסֵי. אֲסוּרָה לִינָשֵׂא. אֲנִי אוֹמֵר. נַעֲשׂוּ לוֹ נִיסִּים וְחָיָה.

May she[54] be allowed to remarry? Rebbi Haggai said, she is allowed to remarry. Rebbi Yose: she is forbidden to remarry; I say that a miracle happened to him and he survived.

54 This cannot refer to the case in the Mishnah here, but must refer to Mishnah 10, about a man going overseas who gave his wife a bill of divorce to be valid if he should not return within 12 months. It is clear that the wife can remary after 12 months. The question is whether she can remarry within 12 months if news was received of her husband's death (meaning that he would not be able to return) but the news was not brought by two witnesses testifying in court.

(48d line 22) מֵהַיּוֹם אִם מַתִּי. מֵעַכְשָׁיו אִם מַתִּי. הֲרֵי זֶה גֵּט. מֵהַיּוֹם וּלְאַחַר מוֹתִי. אֵינוֹ גֵט. אָמַר רִבִּי יוּדָן. רַבָּנִין וְרַבּוֹתֵינוּ. מְתִיבִין רַבּוֹתֵינוּ לְרַבָּנִין. לָמָה אַתּוּן אָמְרִין. הֲרֵי זֶה גֵט. בְּגִין דְּאָמַר. אִם. וְהָא סֵיפָא וְאָם. וְאַתּוּן אָמְרִין. אֵינוֹ גֵט. אֶלָּא בְגִין דְּאָמַר. מֵהַיּוֹם. אוּף אֲנָן כֵּן אִית לָן מֵהַיּוֹם עִיקָּר. מֵתִיב רִבִּי לְרַבָּנִין. לָמָה אַתּוּן אָמְרִין. אֵינוֹ גֵט. בְּגִין דְּאָמַר. מֵהַיּוֹם. וְהָא רֵישָׁא מֵהַיּוֹם. וְאַתּוּן אָמְרִין. הֲרֵי זֶה גֵט. אֶלָּא בְגִין דְּאָמַר. אִם. אוּף אֲנָא אִית לִי אִם עִיקָּר. תַּמָּן מַחְלְפִין. רִבִּי יָסָא בְשֵׁם רִבִּי יוֹחָנָן וְרַב תְּרֵיהוֹן אָמְרִין. דִּבְרֵי רִבִּי תַּמָּן דְּהוּא רַבָּנִין דְּהָכָא. מִכֵּיוָן שֶׁאָמַר. מֵהַיּוֹם. כְּמִי שֶׁאָמַר. עַל מְנָת. רִבִּי זְעִירָא בְעָא קוֹמֵי רִבִּי יָסָא. עַל מְנָת אִם מַתִּי אוֹ עַל מְנָת לְאַחַר מִיתָה. אָמַר לֵיהּ. עַל מְנָת אִם מַתִּי. רִבִּי בָּא בְשֵׁם רַב. דִּבְרֵי רִבִּי הָכָא דְּהוּא רַבָּנִין דְּתַמָּן. מִכֵּיוָן שֶׁאָמַר. מֵהַיּוֹם. כְּמִי שֶׁאָמַר. לְאַחַר מִיתָה.

"'From today if I should die, from now if I should die,' that is a bill of divorce. 'From today after my death' is no bill of divorce." Rebbi Yudan said, the rabbis and our teachers [discussed.] Our teachers objected to the rabbis[55]: Why do you say, it is a bill of divorce? Because he said, "if"[56]! But in the last statement, he said "if" and you say, it is no bill of divorce[57]! But it must be because he said, "from today". We also hold that "from today" is the main point[58]. Rebbi objected to the rabbis. Why do you say, it is not a bill of divorce[59]? Because he said, "from today"! But in the earlier statement[60], he said "from today" and you say, it is a bill of divorce! But it must be because he said, "if". I also am holding that "if" is the main point⁶¹. There⁶², they switch attributions. Both Rebbi Yasa in the name of Rebbi Johanan and Rav say that the words of Rebbi [interpreted] there are the words of the rabbis [interpreted] here: Since he said "from today" it is as if he had said "on condition." Rebbi Ze'ira asked before Rebbi Yasa, "on condition that I die⁶³" or "on condition that it be after my death⁶⁴"? He said to him, "on condition that I die." Rebbi Abba in the name of Rav: The words of Rebbi [interpreted] here are the words of the rabbis [interpreted] there: Since he said "from today" it is as if he had said "after death.⁶²"

55 Since in the sequel Rebbi (who is "our teachers") objects to the rabbis, it follows that here one has to read: The rabbis (of the Mishnah) objected to our teachers (who declare the bills of divorce of the first series as valid.)

56 Our teachers follow R. Yose (Note 67) who declares that "the date of a document is proof", meaning that the date of a document valid under certain conditions is proof of intent that it should be valid from that date on once the condition was satisfied. Therefore, the difference between the first and second series of bills of divorce is irrelevant; all are conditional in the same way.

57 He really did not say "if" but "from today after my death" but this means the same as "from today on condition that I shall have died." In any case, it is a dated document with an implied condition.

58 An undated document, while valid if executed unconditionally and delivered before witnesses at the time it was written, can never be validated after that time.

59 "From today after my death".

60 The first two examples of the second series.

61 That every dated document containing a condition is to be read as valid from the date of execution once the condition is satisfied (unless it is stated otherwise in the document.)

62 In the Babli, 72b, Rebbi is quoted to the effect that "from today after my death" is a valid condition.

63 Retroactively valid now if the husband dies from his current illness.

64 That the divorce be valid only after the husband's death.

(48d line 34) תַּמָּן תְּנִינָן. הַכּוֹתֵב נְכָסָיו לְבָנָיו צָרִיךְ שֶׁיִּכְתּוֹב. מֵהַיּוֹם וּלְאַחַר מִיתָה. דִּבְרֵי רִבִּי יְהוּדָה. רִבִּי יוֹסֵי אוֹמֵר. אֵינוֹ צָרִיךְ. מַה טַעֲמָא שֶׁלְּרִבִּי יוֹסֵי. זְמַנּוּ שֶׁלַּשְּׁטָר מוֹכִיחַ עָלָיו. חֲבֵרַייָא בְּשֵׁם רִבִּי יוֹחָנָן. אֵינָהּ איסרטה. רִבִּי זְעִירָא בְּשֵׁם רִבִּי יוֹחָנָן. אֵינָהּ כְּגִיטִּין אֵינָהּ כְּמַתָּנָה. אָמַר רִבִּי אִילָא. בְּמַתָּנָה מִכֵּיוָן שֶׁאָמַר. מֵהַיּוֹם. מַתָּנָה גְמוּרָה הִיא. לְאֵי זֶה דָבָר כָּתַב בָּהּ. לְאַחַר מִיתָה. לְשַׁיֵּיר לוֹ אֲכִילַת פֵּירוֹת. וּבְגִיטִּין. מִכֵּיוָן שֶׁכָּתַב. מֵהַיּוֹם. בַּגֵּט. כָּרוּת הוּא. לְאֵי זֶה דָבָר כָּתַב בָּהּ. לְאַחַר מִיתָה. לְשַׁיֵּיר לוֹ אֲגוּפָהּ. אָמַר רִבִּי בִּיבוֹן בַּר כַּהֲנָא קוֹמֵי רִבִּי אִילַי. לְשַׁיֵּיר לוֹ מַעֲשֵׂה יָדֶיהָ. אָמַר לֵיהּ. לֹא מָצִינוּ אִשָּׁה נְשׂוּאָה לָזֶה וּמַעֲשֵׂה יָדֶיהָ שֶׁלָּזֶה. וַהֲוָה רִבִּי זְעִירָא מְקַלֵּס לֵיהּ וְצָוַוח לֵיהּ. בְּנֵייהּ דְּאוֹרָיְיתָא.

There[65], we have stated: "If somebody writes his property over to his sons, he has to write: From today and after death[66]. Rebbi Yose says, this is unnecessary." What is Rebbi Yose's reason? The date of the document is its proof[67]. The colleagues in the name of Rebbi Johanan: This is no condition[68]. Rebbi Ze'ira in the name of Rebbi Johanan: It applies neither to bills of divorce nor to gifts[69]. Rebbi Ila[70] said, for a gift; since he said "from today", the gift is irrevocable. Why did he write "after death"? To reserve the yield to himself[71]. But in bills of divorce, since he wrote "from today" in the bill, it would be a separation[72]. Why did he write "after death"? To reserve her body[73] to himself. Rebbi Bibon[74] bar Cahana said before Rebbi Ilai, not to reserve her earnings for himself[75]? He answered, we do not find a woman married to one man and her earnings belonging to another. Rebbi Ze'ira praised him for this and called him "son of the Torah."

65 Mishnah *Baba Batra* 8:7.
66 By a positive biblical rule, an inheritance has to be divided evenly among the male heirs (*Num.* 27:6-11) except that the firstborn male in rabbinic interpretation receives a double portion (*Deut.* 21:17). If the father wants to distribute his property

unevenly, or leave real estate to his daughters, he has to execute a will which has to become valid during his lifetime since nobody can act in law after his death.

67   Since everybody knows that a will has to be activated during the testator's lifetime, the date of the will automatically becomes the date of its validation except if this is disclaimed in the document itself. The same statement is in the Babli, *Baba Batra* 136a.

68   Perhaps compare Greek ὕστερος "later, subsequent" as in combination τῇ ὑστέρῃ προσβολῇ "later, subsequent, conditions added to a document." (E. G.) Less likely is a relation between the *hapax* איסרטה and Arabic شرط "stipulation, clause" which might be Aramaic שטר, Accadic *šeṭrum, šaṭārum* "document".

69   This is a reformulation of the colleague's statement: R. Yose's statement about wills is applicable neither to divorces nor to gifts.

70   He disagrees with R. Ze'ira.

71   During his lifetime.

72   If it is a divorce, the wife will be able to marry another man.

73   The use of prothetic א for על, אל is Babylonian. He wants to prevent his wife from remarrying during his lifetime. Therefore, the mention of "after death" contradicts the statement "from today" and there is no divorce. Rashba (*Novellae ad* 72b) reads: "the bill of divorce is unclear" (He also reads גופה לו לְשַׁיֵּיר, a better Yerushalmi style).

74   Rashba reads: R. Bun. [Compare the Latin adjective *vivus* "alive" as equivalent of חַיִּים, cf. also the Roman name *Bibulus*. (E.G.)]

75   Then the divorce would be absolute and the wife entitled to remarry during her first husband's lifetime.

(48d line 44) אַף בְּגֵט שִׁחְרוּר כֵּן. הֲרֵי גֵט שִׁחְרוּרֶךְ מֵעַכְשָׁיו לְאַחַר ל יוֹם. עַל דַּעְתֵּיהּ דְּרִבִּי הֲרֵי זֶה גֵט. עַל דַּעְתִּין דְּרַבָּנִין אֵינוֹ גֵט. אַף בְּהֶקְבֵּר כֵּן. שָׂדִי מוּבְקֶרֶת מֵעַכְשָׁיו לְאַחַר ל יוֹם. עַל דַּעְתֵּיהּ דְּרִבִּי מוּבְקֶרֶת. עַל דַּעְתִּין דְּרַבָּנִין אֵינָהּ מוּבְקֶרֶת. אַף בְּהֶקְדֵּשׁ כֵּן. כָּל־עַמָּא מוֹדֵיי. אֲמִירָתִי לַגָּבוֹהַּ כִּמְסִירָתִי לְהֶדְיוֹט. אַף בְּקִידּוּשִׁין כֵּן. אַשְׁכַּח תַּנֵּי. רִבִּי אוֹמֵר. מְקוּדֶּשֶׁת קִידּוּשִׁין גְּמוּרִין.

The same situation obtains for bills of manumission. "This is your bill of manumission valid after 30 days from now." In Rebbi's opinion, it is a bill[75]; in the rabbi's opinion, it is no bill[76]. The same situation obtains for abandoning. "My field shall be abandoned after 30 days from now." In Rebbi's opinion, it is abandoned[77]; in the rabbi's opinion, it is not abandoned. Is it the same for dedications[78]? Everybody agrees that "my speaking to Heaven is equivalent to my delivering to a person."[79] Is it the same for preliminary marriage? It was found stated: Rebbi says, she is completely preliminarily married[80].

75 The slave is freed immediately but for the next 30 days has to deliver his earnings to his former patron.

76 The document is self-contradictory and therefore invalid.

77 And freed from some of the obligations imposed by biblical law on agricultural properties in the Land; cf. *Sevi'it* 9:6, Note 85.

78 Donations to the Temple or, in later times, for charitable purposes.

79 Formulated in the third person this is Mishnah *Qiddušin* 1:6. Promises of charitable giving always are absolute and irrevocable.

80 This refers to Mishnah *Qiddušin* 3:1: "'(You are preliminarily married to me) after 30 days from today', if another man married her preliminarily within the thirty days she is married and not married." In the Babli, *Qiddušin* 59b, Rav holds that she is permanently disabled from marrying anyone unless she receives a bill of divorce from both men; Samuel holds that she cannot definitively marry until the 30 day period has passed, when the claim of the second man disappears automatically. In contrast, Rebbi here asserts that the preliminary marriage of the second man never was valid in law.

(fol. 48b) **משנה ד:** זֶה גִּיטַּיךְ מֵהַיּוֹם אִם מַתִּי מֵחוֹלִי זֶה וְעָמַד וְהוֹלֵךְ בַּשּׁוּק וְחָלָה וָמֵת אוֹמְדִין אוֹתוֹ אִם מַחֲמַת חוֹלִי הָרִאשׁוֹן מֵת הֲרֵי זֶה גֵט וְאִם לָאו אֵינוֹ גֵט. לֹא תִתְיַיחֵד עִמּוֹ אֶלָּא בִּפְנֵי עֵדִים אֲפִילוּ עֶבֶד אֲפִילוּ שִׁפְחָה חוּץ מִשִּׁפְחָתָהּ מִפְּנֵי שֶׁלִּיבָּהּ גַּס בְּשִׁפְחָתָהּ. וּמַה הִיא בְּאוֹתָן הַיָּמִים. רַבִּי יְהוּדָה אוֹמֵר כְּאֵשֶׁת אִישׁ לְכָל־דָּבָר. רַבִּי יוֹסֵי אוֹמֵר מְגוֹרֶשֶׁת וְאֵינָהּ מְגוֹרֶשֶׁת.

Mishnah 4: "This is your bill of divorce from today if I should die from this illness;" if he got up, walked on the market[81], fell ill again and died, one estimates whether he died from the original sickness, in which case it is a bill of divorce; otherwise it is no bill of divorce. She may not be alone with him except in the presence of witnesses[82], which may be even a male or a female slave except her personal slave girl since she has no shame in the presence of her personal slave girl. What is her status in those days? Rebbi Jehudah says, she is a married woman in all respects. Rebbi Yose says, she is divorced and not divorced[83].

81   If he got out of bed but never left the house, then fell ill again and died, it is a valid bill of divorce even without an expert opinion on the cause of death.

82   To avoid intimacy. If she has sex with him then either it is married sex and the bill of divorce is automatically invalidated, or it is illicit sex and sinful. In Mishnah 8:4, the House of Hillel invalidate any bill of divorce if husband and wife were alone together at any time between the signing of the document and its date of validation. The House of Shammai do not invalidate the bill. The Mishnah follows the House of Hillel.

83   She is divorced in criminal law but not divorced in civil law.

(48d line 49) **הלכה ד**: הֲרֵי זֶה גִּיטֵּיךְ מֵהַיּוֹם כול׳. אָכַל גְּרִיסִין לְגַסָּה כְּמִי שֶׁמֵּת מֵאוֹתוֹ חוֹלִי. פּוּנְדְּקָאוֹת עַצְמָן וְלֹא עָמַד כְּמִי שֶׁלֹּא מֵת מֵאוֹתוֹ חוֹלִי.

Halakhah 4: "This is your bill of divorce from today," etc. If he overate on groats it is as if he died from that illness, hazelnuts[84] alone and he did not get out of bed it is as if he did not die from that illness[85].

84   Arabic بندق, from Greek κάρυον ποντικόν "Pontic (Black Sea) nut".

85   Overindulging in cereal is not in itself life threatening, but eating hazelnuts without anything else is (since it causes both vomiting and diarrhea at the same time).

(48d line 51) אִם מֵת הַחוֹלִי[86] הַזֶּה. וְנָפַל עָלָיו גַּל אוֹ שֶׁנְּכָשׁוֹ נָחָשׁ. אֵינוֹ גֵט. אֶלָּא מֵת מֵאוֹתוֹ הַחוֹלִי. אִם לֹא עָמַדְתִּי מֵחוֹלִי זֶה. וְנָפַל עָלָיו גַּל אוֹ שֶׁנְּכָשׁוֹ נָחָשׁ. הֲרֵי זֶה גֵט. שֶׁלֹּא עָמַד מֵאוֹתוֹ הַחוֹלִי.

"If he died from that sickness[87]," and a stone heap fell on him, or a snake bit him[88], it cannot be a bill of divorce unless he died of that sickness. "If I should not recover from that sickness[87]," and a stone heap fell on him, or a snake bit him[88] it is a bill of divorce since he did not recover from that sickness[89].

86 *Tosaphot* 73a, s.v. מאי read מֵחוֹלִי. This may or may not be the original reading; cf. H. Guggenheimer, *The Scholar's Haggadah* (Northvale 1995), p. 322.

87 This is the condition on which the bill was delivered.

88 While the patient was still bedridden, he died from another cause.

89 The Babli agrees, 73a.

(48d line 54) תַּנֵּי. אַף הַמְסוּכָּן. אָמַר רִבִּי יַעֲקֹב בַּר אָחָא. מַעֲשֶׂה הָיָה כָהֵן שֶׁבָּעַל מֵת.

It was stated: "Also the one in mortal danger." Rebbi Jacob bar Aḥa said, it happened in such a case that he died during intercourse[90].

90 A terminally ill person is forbidden intercourse not for legal but for medical reasons.

(48d line 55) שֶׁלֹּא עָמַד מֵאוֹתוֹ הַחוֹלִי. וְעֶבֶד וְשִׁפְחָה נֶאֱמָנִין. יוֹדְעִין הֵן הָעֵדִים שֶׁבְּשָׁעָה שֶׁנִּתְיַיחֲדָה עִמּוֹ יָחַד שָׁם עֶבֶד וְשִׁפְחָה. כְּהָדָא. נִתְיַיחֲדָה עִמּוֹ בִּפְנֵי שְׁנַיִם צְרִיכָה הֵימֶנּוּ גֵט שֵׁינִי. בְּאֶחָד אֵינָהּ צְרִיכָה מִמֶּנּוּ גֵט שֵׁינִי. בְּאֶחָד בְּשַׁחֲרִית וּבְאֶחָד בֵּין הָעַרְבַּיִם. זֶה הָיָה מַעֲשֶׂה וְשָׁאַל רִבִּי אֶלְעָזָר בֶּן תְּרַדְיוֹן לַחֲכָמִים וְאָמְרוּ. אֵין זֶה יֵחוּד. נִתְיַיחֲדָה עִמּוֹ כְּדֵי בְעִילָה חוֹשְׁשִׁין לָהּ מִשּׁוּם בְּעִילָה וְאֵין חוֹשְׁשִׁין לָהּ מִשּׁוּם קִידּוּשִׁין. רִבִּי יוֹסֵי בֵּירִבִּי יְהוּדָה אוֹמֵר. אַף חוֹשְׁשִׁין לָהּ מִשּׁוּם קִידּוּשִׁין. רִבִּי יִרְמְיָה פָּתַר מַתְנִיתָא. נִתְיַיחֲדָה עִמּוֹ כְּדֵי

בְּעִילָה חוֹשְׁשִׁין לָהּ מִשּׁוּם בְּעִילַת זְנוּת וְאֵין חוֹשְׁשִׁין לָהּ מִשּׁוּם קִידּוּשִׁין בִּבְעִילָה. לֹא נִתְיַיחֲדָה עִמּוֹ כְּדֵי בְעִילָה אֵין חוֹשְׁשִׁין לָהּ מִשּׁוּם כְּלוּם. רְבִּי יוֹסֵי פָּתַר לָהּ מַתְנִיתָא. נִתְיַיחֲדָה עִמּוֹ כְּדֵי בְעִילָה חוֹשְׁשִׁין לָהּ מִשּׁוּם בְּעִילַת זְנוּת וְאֵין חוֹשְׁשִׁין לָהּ מִשּׁוּם קִידּוּשִׁין בִּבְעִילָה. רְבִּי יוֹסֵי בֵּירְבִּי יְהוּדָה אוֹמֵר. אַף חוֹשְׁשִׁין לָהּ מִשּׁוּם קִידּוּשִׁין בִּבְעִילָה. לֹא נִתְיַיחֲדָה עִמּוֹ כְּדֵי בְעִילָה אֵין חוֹשְׁשִׁין לָהּ מִשּׁוּם קִדּוּשִׁין בְּכֶסֶף. רְבִּי יוֹסֵי בֵּירְבִּי יְהוּדָה אוֹמֵר. אַף חוֹשְׁשִׁין לָהּ מִשּׁוּם קִידּוּשִׁין בְּכֶסֶף. אָמַר רִבִּי אָבִין. אַתְיָא דְבֵית שַׁמַּי כְּרַבָּנִין וּדְבֵית הִלֵּל כְּרִבִּי יוֹסֵי בֵּירְבִּי יְהוּדָה.

"Whether he died from the original sickness." Are male or female slaves trustworthy[91]? The witnesses know that at the time she was alone with him a male or female slave was present[92]. [93]"If she was alone with him with the knowledge of two witnesses, she needs a second bill of divorce from him[94]. One witness, she does not need a second bill of divorce from him[95]. One in the morning and one in the afternoon, that was a case and Rebbi Eleazar bar Thaddeus[96] asked the Sages who said, this is not [testimony of] being alone[97]. If she was alone together with him long enough for intercourse, one suspects her about intercourse but not about preliminary marriage[98]. Rebbi Yose ben Rebbi Jehudah says, one also suspects her about preliminary marriage." Rebbi Jeremiah explains the *baraita*: If she was alone together with him long enough for intercourse, one suspects her about immoral intercourse but not about preliminary marriage. If the time was not long enough for intercourse, one does not suspect anything. Rebbi Yose explains the *baraita*: If she was alone together with him long enough for intercourse, one suspects her about immoral intercourse but not about preliminary marriage by intercourse. Rebbi Yose ben Rebbi Jehudah says, one also suspects her about preliminary marriage by intercourse. If the time was not long enough for intercourse, one does not suspect preliminary marriage by money[99]. Rebbi Yose ben Rebbi Jehudah says, one also suspects her about preliminary marriage by money. Rebbi Abin said, It turns out that the House of Shammai[100] parallels the rabbis and the House of Hillel Rebbi Yose ben Rebbi Jehudah.

91 The validity of the bill of divorce may be the subject of a law suit. Can such a suit be decided on the testimony of slaves? Slaves cannot be witnesses in court because (1) their testimony is subject to the influence of their master and, more importantly, (2) in money matters they are not subject to the laws of perjury (since they do not have personal property) and "the testimony of a person not subject to the laws of perjury is worthless."

92 The slaves do not have to appear in court.

93 A parallel text is in Tosephta 5:4 and Babli 73b; the text is partially quoted in Soṭah 1:1, Note 52.

94 Since two witnesses establish a fact by biblical rules and the House of Hillel invalidate a bill of divorce if the parties were alone together between signing and time of validation, the knowledge of two independent witnesses in itself invalidates the bill.

95 A single witness has no standing in court in matters of validity of marriages or divorces.

96 The name is חַדָּאי "Thaddeus" in Soṭah, the two parallel (and additional) Babylonian sources, against the reading "Tradion" here.

97 Two single witnesses testifying about two different facts can never be considered as two witnesses for a pattern; cf. Soṭah 1:1, Note 52.

98 Preliminary marriage (not intended to be definitive) can be effected by intercourse (Mishnah Qiddušin 1:1); this is biblical standard. A marriage ceremony which is not witnessed is automatically invalid but it is possible to consider the witnesses to their being alone together as witnesses of intercourse. In Mishnah 8:11 the House of Hillel require only minimal standards from witnesses once the parties had been definitively married and living together.

99 This is an extraordinary relaxation of the standards of testimony in the circumstances of Mishnah 8:11. The Babli, 73b, rejects any legal consequences of physical intimacy not confirmed by two eye-witnesses.

100 Mishnaiot 8:4,11.

(48d line 71) לְיֵי דָא מִילָא. רבִּי לָעְזָר אוֹמֵר. לְיוֹרְשָׁהּ. דְּתַנִינָן תַּמָּן. וְזַכַּאי בִּמְצִיאָתָהּ וּבְמַעֲשֵׂה יָדֶיהָ וּבְהֵפֶר נְדָרֶיהָ. אָמַר רבִּי זְעִירָא. זאת אוֹמֶרֶת שֶׁהִיא כְאֶשֶׁת אִישׁ לְכָל־דָּבָר.

For what[101]? Rebbi Eleazar said, to inherit from her[102], as we have stated there[103]: "He has a claim on what she finds and on her earnings, to dissolve her vows." Rebbi Ze'ira said, this is what is implied by "she is a married woman in all respects.[104]"

101 What does R. Jehudah mean when he states that the woman who receives a bill of divorce which becomes valid at an indeterminate point in the future is a married woman in all respects?

102 If the wife dies before her severely ill husband. In the Babli (73b/74a) and the Tosephta (5:4), this is a tannaïtic statement.

103 Mishnah *Ketubot* 4:6. The reference is to the part of the Mishnah which is not quoted, viz., that the husband has the usufruct from the wife's properties (and inherits from her should she die during the marriage.)

104 The husband did not relinquish his right to his wife's properties' yield.

(48d line 73) מִחְלְפָה שִׁיטָתֵיהּ דְּרִבִּי יוּדָה. תַּמָּן הוּא אָמַר. מִיתָה מְצוּיָה. וְהָכָא הוּא אָמַר. אֵין מִיתָה מְצוּיָה. תַּמָּן בַּצִּיבּוּר כָּאן בְּיָחִיד. דְּתַנְיָא. רבִּי יְהוּדָה אוֹמֵר. לֹא הָיָה שׁוֹפָר שֶׁלְּקִינִּין בִּירוּשָׁלַיִם מִפְּנֵי הַתַּעֲרוֹבֶת. שֶׁמָּא תָמוּת אַחַת מֵהֶן וְנִמְצְאוּ דְּמֵי חַטָּאוֹת מֵתוֹת מְעוֹרָבוֹת בָּהֶן.

The opinion of Rebbi Jehudah seems to be inverted. There[105], he says that death is frequent but here, he says that death is not frequent[106]. There in public, here in private, as it was stated[107]: Rebbi Jehudah says there was no chest for nests in Jerusalem because of the mixing, maybe one of them would die and money for purification offerings destined to die would be mixed in with them.

105 Mishnah *Yoma* 1:1. On the Day of Atonement, the High Priest first has to atone for "himself and his house" (*Lev.* 16:6). "His house" is interpreted

to mean "his wife"; an unmarried High Priest is unable to officiate. R. Jehudah requires that the married High Priest preliminarily marry another woman lest his wife die in the week before the Day of Atonement and prevent him from serving. He cannot definitively marry another woman since he alone among all Jews is required to be monogamous (*Lev.* 21:13). The other rabbis consider R. Jehudah's precaution to be excessive.

106   He could not say that the woman who received a bill of divorce "from now if I should die" is married in all respects if at any moment he would expect the husband to die and the wife to be divorced.

107   חניא is Babylonian spelling for Yerushalmi חני. The reference is to *Šeqalim* 6:5 (belonging to Mishnah 6:7). The Mishnah enumerates 13 chests which were maintained at the Temple gate for the public to deposit its contributions. One of the chests was labelled for "nests", the pairs of birds required as a purification sacrifice (*Lev.* 12:8) before a woman after childbirth could partake of family sacrifices. The women would deposit the money in the chest and every day the priests would offer the corresponding number of pairs of birds to purify the women. R. Jehudah holds that there was no such automatic arrangement in the Temple but that every woman after childbirth had to provide the pair of birds and personally hand them to a Cohen. His problem was that one of the birds was a holocaust but the other a purification offering and purification offerings might be presented only for living persons. If a woman died between the time she deposited the money in the chest and the next morning when the money was counted and the number of birds determined, then not only her purification offering would be invalid (it could not be offered, nor could it be released; it had to be kept in isolation until it died) but it would invalidate all other offerings of the same day (cf. Babli *Yoma* 55b/56b). R. Jehudah goes to extraordinary lengths for fear of sudden deaths; his position in the Mishnah here becomes more difficult to understand.

בְּעִילָתָהּ מָהוּ. אִית תַּנָּיֵי תַּנֵּי. בְּעִילָתָהּ בְּרוּרָה. וְאִית תַּנָּיֵי תַנֵּי. בְּעִילָתָהּ סָפֵק. מָאן דְּאָמַר בְּעִילָתָהּ בְּרוּרָה. מֵבִיא אָשָׁם תָּלוּי. וּמָאן דְּאָמַר בְּעִילָתָהּ סָפֵק. מֵת פָּטוּר. לֹא מֵת מֵבִיא חַטָּאת.

What is the status of her intercourse[108]? Some Tannaïm state, her intercourse is certain[109], but some Tannaïm state, her intercourse is in doubt[110]. According to him who says that her intercourse is certain, he brings a "hung" sacrifice[111]. According to him who says that her intercourse is in doubt, if [the husband] dies, he is free; if [the husband] does not die, he brings a purification sacrifice[112].

108 What is the legal status of a woman who had intercourse with another man after she had received a bill of divorce valid "from today when I shall die."

109 It certainly is sinful.

110 If the husband dies, it is clear retroactively that the intercourse was permitted.

111 If the man involved was unaware at the moment of the act that the woman might be married. The "hung" sacrifice is the expiation sacrifice prescribed in *Lev.* 5:17-19 for an unintentional sin whose nature eludes the perpetrator.

112 A regular purification sacrifice (*Lev.* 4:27-35) for unintentional adultery. No sacrifice can ever atone for intentional sin (*Num.* 15:30).

(fol. 48b) **משנה ה:** הֲרֵי זֶה גִּיטֵיךְ עַל מְנָת שֶׁתִּתְּנִי לִי מָאתַיִם זוּז הֲרֵי זוֹ מְגוֹרֶשֶׁת וְתִתֵּן. עַל מְנָת שֶׁתִּתְּנִי לִי מִכָּן וְעַד שְׁלֹשִׁים יוֹם אִם נָתְנָה בְּתוֹךְ שְׁלֹשִׁים יוֹם מְגוֹרֶשֶׁת וְאִם לָאו אֵינָהּ מְגוֹרֶשֶׁת. אָמַר רַבָּן שִׁמְעוֹן בֶּן גַּמְלִיאֵל מַעֲשֶׂה בְצַיְידָן שֶׁאָמַר אֶחָד לְאִשְׁתּוֹ הֲרֵי זֶה גִּיטֵיךְ עַל מְנָת שֶׁתִּתְּנִי לִי אִיצְטְלָיָתִי וְאָבְדָה אִיצְטְלָיָתוֹ וְאָמְרוּ חֲכָמִים תִּתֵּן לוֹ אֶת דָּמֶיהָ.

Mishnah 5: "This is your bill of divorce on condition that you give me 200 *zuz*;" she is divorced and has to pay[113]. "On condition that you give me within thirty days," if she paid within thirty days she is divorced, otherwise she is not divorced. Rabban Simeon ben Gamliel said, it happened in Sidon that someone said to his wife "this is your bill of divorce on condition that you return to me my stole[114]" and it turned out that his stole was lost; then the Sages said, she shall pay him its value[115].

113   She is divorced immediately but she cannot act on the divorce (either claim the *ketubah* or remarry) before she paid up.

114   Greek στολίς, στολή "garment" also "equipment, arms, etc." Can the rabbinic Hebrew כְּלִי "garment" (for biblical "vessel, equipment, arms") be induced by analogy with the Greek (E. G.)?   In Latin *stola* "garment, ceremonial robe".

115   Since this statement is labelled as Rabban Simeon ben Gamliel's, it follows that others either invalidate the divorce if the stole cannot be found or that she has to replace it in kind.

(49a line 5) **הלכה ה:** הֲרֵי זֶה גִּיטֵיךְ עַל מְנָת שֶׁתִּתְּנִי לִי מָאתַיִם זוּז כול׳. תַּנֵּי. לֹא הִסְפִּיקָה לִיתֵּן עַד שֶׁמֵּת. רַבָּן שִׁמְעוֹן בֶּן גַּמְלִיאֵל אוֹמֵר. תִּינָתֵן לְאָבִיו וּלְאָחִיו וְהִיא פְטוּרָה מִן הַחֲלִיצָה וּמִן הַיִּיבּוּם. אַף בְּקִידּוּשִׁין כֵּן. הֲרֵי אַתְּ מְקוּדֶּשֶׁת לִי עַל מְנָת שֶׁאֶתֵּן לֵיךְ מָאתַיִם זוּז. וְלֹא הִסְפִּיק לִיתֵּן עַד שֶׁמֵּת. רַבָּן שִׁמְעוֹן בֶּן גַּמְלִיאֵל אוֹמֵר. אָבִיו וְאָחִיו נוֹתְנִין לָהּ וְהִיא זְקוּקָה לַחֲלִיצָה וּלְיִיבּוּם.

Halakhah 5: "This is your bill of divorce on condition that you give me 200 *zuz*," etc. It was stated[116]: If she did not manage to pay before he died, Rabban Simeon ben Gamliel says, she pays his father or his brother and is free from *ḥaliṣah* and levirate marriage[117]. [118]The same holds for preliminary marriage: "You are preliminarily married to me on condition that I shall give you 200 *zuz*;" if he did not manage to pay before he died, Rabban Simeon ben Gamliel says, his father or his brother pay and she is subject to *ḥaliṣah* or levirate marriage.

116   In the Babylonian sources, Babli 74a (*Qiddušin* 60b), Tosephta 5:5, this is formulated as a dispute: "If he died before she paid, she is subject to levirate marriage; after she paid, she is not subject to levirate marriage; Rabban Simeon ben Gamliel said..."

117   If the husband died childless, cf. Introduction to Tractate *Yebamot*. As the Babli explains, 74a, "anybody who

says 'on condition that' means to say 'valid immediately on condition that'" (Tosephta 5:6). The delay in fulfilling the condition does not change the fact that the divorce preceded the husband's death.

118 While the statement on divorce is also quoted in *Qiddušin* 3:2 (63d line 16) as tannaïtic, the parallel about marriage is presented as amoraic inference. It is obvious that at the moment of preliminary marriage the groom has to give some valuables to the bride.

(49a line 10) אָמַר רִבִּי יוּדָן. בְּשֶׁאָבְדָה בְאוֹנֶס אֲנָן קַייָמִין. עָשׂוּ אוֹתָהּ כְּמַתְנֵה שׁוֹמֵר חִנָּם לִהְיוֹת פָּטוּר מִן הַשְּׁבוּעָה. אָמַר רִבִּי יוֹסֵה. וְכָא אֲתִינֶן מִיתְנֵי שׁוֹמֵר חִנָּם לִהְיוֹת פָּטוּר מִן הַשְּׁבוּעָה. אֶלָּא כְּשֶׁאָבְדָה בִּפְשִׁיעָה אֲנָן קַייָמִין. דָּמִים עָשׂוּ אוֹתָהּ בְּאִיצְטָלִית. רַבָּנָן אָמְרִין. אַחַת זוֹ וְאַחַת זוֹ מִשּׁוּם תְּנָאֵי גִיטִּין.

Rebbi Yudan said, we deal with the case that it was lost by compulsion[119]. They treated her like an unpaid trustee who may stipulate to be free from an oath. Rebbi Yose said, do we state here that the unpaid trustee is free from an oath[120]? But we deal with the case that it was lost by mishandling. They treated the stole according to its value. But the rabbis say that in any case it has to be treated as a case of condition of a bill of divorce[121].

119 The reason Rabban Simeon ben Gamliel does not insist that the condition on which the divorce was given be fulfilled to the letter is that the wife is an unpaid trustee who is not required to pay for damages beyond his control. In contrast to the unpaid trustee who has to swear that it was beyond his control if he does not want to pay, the wife does not have to swear (*Ketubot* 9:4, Note 121).

120 If R. Yudan's explanation were correct, some reference should have been made to the rules of trustees. Since no reference was made, it makes no difference why the stole was lost. Rabban Simeon ben Gamliel from the start treats the request for the stole as a request for money.

121 The rabbis who oppose Rabban Simeon ben Gamliel require fulfillment of the condition to the letter. If the stole cannot be produced for any cause whatever, the divorce is invalid. In the

Babylonian sources (38a, 75a; *Baba qama* 69a, *Baba meṣi'a* 38b, *Baba batra* 174a, *Ketubot* 77a, *Sanhedrin* 31b, *Bekhorot* 24a), practice is decided following the rabbis. This is reported as Babylonian practice in *Baba batra* 10:14 (17d l. 9).

(fol. 48b) **משנה ו:** הֲרֵי זֶה גִּיטֵּיךְ עַל מְנָת שֶׁתְּשַׁמְּשִׁי אֶת אַבָּא עַל מְנָת שֶׁתָּנִיקִי אֶת בְּנִי כַּמָּה הִיא מְנִיקַתּוּ שְׁתֵּי שָׁנִים. רַבִּי יְהוּדָה אוֹמֵר שְׁמוֹנָה עָשָׂר חֹדֶשׁ. מֵת הַבֵּן אוֹ שֶׁמֵת הָאָב הֲרֵי זֶה גֵט.

Mishnah 6: "This is your bill of divorce on condition that you serve my father," "on condition that you breast-feed my son," how long does she have to breast-feed him? Two years[122]; Rebbi Jehudah says, eighteen months. If the son or the father died, it is a valid divorce[123].

משנה ז: עַל מְנָת שֶׁתְּשַׁמְּשִׁי אֶת אַבָּא שְׁתֵּי שָׁנִים וְעַל מְנָת שֶׁתָּנִיקִי אֶת בְּנִי שְׁתֵּי שָׁנִים. מֵת הַבֵּן אוֹ שֶׁאָמַר הָאָב אֵי אֶפְשִׁי שֶׁתְּשַׁמְּשֵׁנִי שֶׁלֹּא בְהַקְפָּדָה אֵינוֹ גֵט. רַבָּן שִׁמְעוֹן בֶּן גַּמְלִיאֵל אוֹמֵר כָּזֶה גֵט. כְּלָל אָמַר רַבָּן שִׁמְעוֹן בֶּן גַּמְלִיאֵל כָּל־עַכָּבָה שֶׁאֵינָהּ מִמֶּנָּה הֲרֵי זֶה גֵט.

Mishnah 7: "On condition that you serve my father for two years," or "on condition that you breast-feed my son for two years;" if the son died or the father said, I cannot stand you serving me (without being offended)[124], it is no divorce[125]. Rabban Simeon ben Gamliel said, that is a divorce. Rabban Simeon ben Gamliel stated a principle: Given any hindrance which is not from her side, it is a divorce.

122 This is R. Meïr's opinion; cf. *Soṭah* 4:4, Notes 55 ff. She does not have to nurse the baby for two years after the divorce but only until he reaches the age of two years (Tosephta 5:6). Since the expenses of child-rearing are the father's responsibility, the mother does not have to nurse her

child if she is divorced before the child is weaned.

123 This may mean that, if the father or the child died immediately after the bill of divorce was handed over, the divorce nevertheless stands. It is a matter of dispute in the Halakhah.

124 She did nothing to offend the father.

125 Since the condition was not satisfied. The Mishnah in the Babli and most Mishnah mss. adds: "or if the father died in the meantime".

(49a line 15) **הלכה ו:** הֲרֵי זֶה גִּיטֵּיךְ עַל מְנָת שֶׁתְּשַׁמְּשִׁי אֶת אַבָּא כול'. אָמַר רִבִּי בָּא. בְּחַיָּיו וְהוּא שֶׁתְּשַׁמְּשִׁינוּ כָּל־צוֹרְכוֹ. וְהוּא שֶׁתְּנִיקִי כָּל־צוֹרְכוֹ. אֲפִילוּ לֹא שִׁימְּשַׁתּוּ כָּל־צוֹרְכוֹ. אֲפִילוּ לֹא הֱנִיקַתּוּ כָּל־צוֹרְכוֹ. אֶלָּא אֲפִילוּ שִׁימְּשַׁתּוּ שָׁעָה אַחַת. אֲפִילוּ הֱנִיקַתּוּ שָׁעָה אַחַת. לְאַחַר מִיתָה אֲפִילוּ לֹא שִׁימְּשַׁתּוּ וְלֹא הֱנִיקַתּוּ כְּלוּם. מַתְנִיתָא פְּלִיגָא עַל רֵישׁ לָקִישׁ. כַּמָּה הִיא מְנִיקַתּוּ. שְׁתֵּי שָׁנִים. רִבִּי יְהוּדָה אוֹמֵר. שְׁמוֹנָה עָשָׂר חוֹדֶשׁ. אָמַר רִבִּי אָבִין. בִּשְׂכַר מֵנִיקָה שָׁנוּ.

Halakhah 6: "'This is your bill of divorce on condition that you serve my father,' etc. Rebbi Abba[126] said: During his lifetime, on condition that she serve all his needs, on condition that she breast-feed all his needs[127]. [128]Even if she did not serve all his needs, even if she did not breast-feed all his needs, but even if she served him for one hour, or breast-fed him for one hour[129]. After death[123,130], even if she never served him or never breast-fed him. The Mishnah disagrees with Rebbi Simeon ben Laqish: "How long does she have to breast-feed him? Two years, Rebbi Jehudah says, eighteen months." Rebbi Abin said, this was taught about the cost of a wet-nurse[131].

126 The scribe first wrote "R. Hiyya bar Abba" and then deleted "R. Hiyya". The *editio princeps* has "R. Hiyya bar Abba". But since the opposite opinion is referred to as R. Simeon ben Laqish's, one of R. Hiyya bar Abba's teachers, the final text of the ms. is the correct one, against the *editio princeps*.

127 His interpretation of Mishnah 6 is that the absence of any time limit in the condition implies that the divorcee has to be the husband's father's

geriatric nurse for the rest of the latter's life or to breast-feed her child for a full 24 months.

128 It seems from the following that a note "Rebbi Simeon ben Laqish said," was omitted here. In the Babylonian sources, Babli 75b, Tosephta 5:6, it is a tannaïtic text.

129 He opts for a minimalist interpretation of the condition. Since no time limit was given, *any* service or *any* breast-feeding satisfies the condition and validates the divorce.

130 It could also mean, "after the husband's death." Cf. S. Lieberman's commentary to Tosephta 5:6.

131 R. Abin reads the condition not as a request that the ex-wife breast-feed her child for 24 months and therefore be forbidden to remarry during all this time (cf. *Soṭah* 4:4, Notes 55 ff.) but that the wife pay for a wet-nurse to care for the child in the husband's house, with the wife being free to remarry 90 days after the divorce.

(49a line 21) אָמַר רִבִּי אַבָּהוּ בְשֵׁם רִבִּי יוֹחָנָן. סֵדֶר סִימְפּוֹן כָּךְ הוּא. אֲנָא פְלָן בַּר פְלָן מְקַדֵּשׁ לִיךְ אַנְתְּ פְלָנִית בַּת פְלָן עַל מְנָת לִיתֵּן לָךְ מִיקְמַת פְלָן וּמִנְכְסִים לְיוֹם פְלָן. דְּאִין אָתָא יוֹם פְלָן וְלָא כְנַסְתֵּיךְ לָא יְהַוִּי לִי עֲלַיִךְ כְּלוּם. אִירַע לוֹ אוֹנֶס. רִבִּי יוֹחָנָן אָמַר. אוֹנְסָא כְּמַאן דְּלָא עֲבַד. רֵישׁ לָקִישׁ אָמַר. אוֹנְסָא כְּמַאן דַּעֲבַד. עַל דַּעְתֵּיהּ דְּרֵישׁ לָקִישׁ אֵין הֲוָה צָרִיךְ לְמֵיעֲבַד. וְאִין אָתָא יוֹם פְלָן וְלָא כְנַסְתָּהּ לִי לֹא יְהַוִּי לִי עֲלַיִךְ כְּלוּם. רִבִּי יוֹחָנָן מִי דָמִיךְ פְּקִיד לִבְנָתֵיהּ דִּי יְהַוְויָן עָבְדָן כְּרֵישׁ לָקִישׁ. אָמַר. שֶׁמָּא יַעֲמֹד בֵּית דִּין אַחֵר וְיִסְבֹּר דִּכְוָתֵיהּ. וְנִמְצְאוּ בָנָיו בָּאִין לִידֵי מַמְזֵרוּת.

1 אמר | ק - סימפון | ק הסימפון 2 ליך | ע אותך את בת | ק בר ליתן | ע מיתן מיקמת | ע מקמת ומנכסים | עק ומיכנסיניך 3 דאין | ק ואין ע אין עליך | ק - ע עלייך 4 ריש לקיש | ק ר' שמעון בן לקיש 5 דריש לקיש | ק דר' שמעון בן לקיש אין הוה | ק היך ואין | ק דאין 6 כנסתה | ק הוויתי כונסה יהוי לי עליך | ק יהא עלייך מי דמיך | ק דמיד 7 די יהווין | ק דיחוין כריש לקיש | ק כר' שמעון בן לקיש

132Rebbi Abbahu in the name of Rebbi Joḥanan: The following is the contract text133: "I, X son of Y, contract a preliminary marriage with you, Z, daughter of U, on condition that I shall give you property A and definitively marry you by day B. If that day should pass without me having taken you in[134], I shall have no claim on you[135]." If anything intervened beyond his control? Rebbi Joḥanan said, matters beyond his control are as if he were inactive[136]. Rebbi Simeon ben Laqish said, matters outside his control are as if he had acted[137]. In the opinion of Rebbi Simeon ben Laqish, what would be necessary? "If that day should pass without you having taken me in, I shall have no claim on you.[138]" When Rebbi Joḥanan was dying, he told his daughters to act following Rebbi Simeon ben Laqish. He said, maybe in the future there might be a court which follows him; then his descendants might be in danger of bastardy[139].

132 The text is also in *Qiddušin* 3:2 (63d l. 20), readings noted ק. The contract text is also in *Erubin* 3 (21b l. 20), noted ע.

133 Greek τὸ σύμφωνον "(written) agreement". In general, a preliminary marriage was concluded by an act of the male, with passive acceptance by the female. Since a preliminary marriage can also be effected by contract (Mishnah *Qiddušin* 1:1), in certain circles in Galilee this was the preferred course of action (it is not mentioned in the Babli.) The main attraction of the contractual marriage for the woman was that it provided insurance against foot-dragging by the groom (cf. Mishnah *Ketubot* 13:5).

134 The translation follows the parallel texts in *Qiddušin* and *Erubin*.

The text here would read: "but not transfer real estate to you".

135 The preliminary marriage is conditional. If the condition is not satisfied, the marriage is non-existent and the woman may marry another man without needing a bill of divorce from the first. She may even marry a Cohen, which would be impossible if the first preliminary marriage had been valid.

136 The condition is absolute. If the definitive marriage did not take place before the contracted date, the preliminary marriage is annulled.

137 If the only reason that the definitive marriage did not take place were circumstances beyond the groom's control, the preliminary marriage is *not* annulled.

138 The condition has to be

formulated not for the male, who actively has to take the woman in and therefore can claim unavoidable circumstances, but for the passive female. Since the contract is σύμφωνον, a mutual agreement, she gives her passive acceptance of the preliminary marriage only on condition that she be definitively married by a fixed date. If she refuses her agreement, no preliminary marriage is possible and no bill of divorce due.

139 If a woman contracts a preliminary marriage by the terms of R. Joḥanan's formulation of the contract and is not married by the time specified because of unavoidable circumstances, and then contracts another marriage without a bill of divorce in the domain of jurisdiction of a court following R. Simeon ben Laqish, her children from the second marriage will be illegitimate if the first groom claims her as his wife.

(49a line 29) חַד בַּר נָשׁ אַקְדֵּם פְּרוּטִין לְאִילְפָּא וּנְגַב נַהֲרָא. אָתָא עוֹבְדָא קוֹמֵי רַב נַחְמָן בַּר יַעֲקֹב. הָא אִילְפָּא. אֵייתֵי נַהֲרָא. אַבָּא בַּר הוּנָא בְּשֵׁם רִבִּי אַבָּא הֲוָה מַצְלֵי דְּיֵינַגְב נַהֲרָא בְּגִין דְּנִיסַּב פְּרִיטוֹי. אָמַר. רִבִּי יוֹחָנָן וְרִבִּי אַבָּא סָבְרִין כְּרַבָּן שִׁמְעוֹן בֶּן גַּמְלִיאֵל. חָתְכָה כְּמִי שֶׁעִיכְּבָה. נֶחְתַּךְ יָדָהּ כְּמִי שֶׁלֹּא עִיכְּבָה.

A person gave money for a ship when the canal dried up[140]. The case came before Rav Naḥman bar Jacob: There is the ship, bring the canal[141]! Abba bar Huna in the name of Rebbi Abba was praying that the canal should dry up and he could recover his money. He said, Rebbi Joḥanan and Rebbi Abba are of the same opinion as Rabban Simeon ben Gamliel[142]. If she cut off, she hindered. If her hand[143] (?) was cut off, it is not as if she hindered.

140 This is in Babylonia, where most transport is by water. A person rented a ship for some future transport and then could not use it since in the meantime the canal had dried up. This shows that the disappearance of the old system of canals between Euphrates and Tigris cannot all be dated to the Arab conquest but that the neglect of the canal system already started early in Sassanid times.

141 Rav Naḥman holds with R. Simeon ben Laqish that circumstances beyond the contracting party's control

do not invalidate the contract.

142   Who holds in the Mishnah that any circumstance beyond the woman's control does not interfere with her having complied with the terms of the divorce. (Rashba, *Novellae ad* 75b, prefers to switch the attributions. He reads אשכחת אמר "it turns out that one has to say", making the sentence an editorial remark, not R. Abba's statement.)

143   In order to make sense of this statement, it is necessary with Rashba (*Novellae ad* 75b) and the commentators to read דד instead of יד "If the woman who was divorced under the condition of breast-feeding her child cut off her breast herself, she violated her contract. If her breast was cut off by others, the hindrance is not her fault and the divorce stands."

(fol. 48b) **משנה ח:** הֲרֵי זֶה גִּיטֵּיךְ אִם לֹא בָאתִי מִכָּן וְעַד שְׁלֹשִׁים יוֹם וְהָיָה הוֹלֵךְ מִיהוּדָה לַגָּלִיל. הִגִּיעַ לְאַנְטִיפַטְרֵס וְחָזַר בָּטֵל הַתְּנַאי. הֲרֵי זֶה גִּיטֵּיךְ אִם לֹא בָאתִי מִכָּן וְעַד שְׁלֹשִׁים יוֹם וְהָיָה הוֹלֵךְ מִגָּלִיל לִיהוּדָה וְהִגִּיעַ לִכְפַר עוֹתְנַי וְחָזַר בָּטֵל הַתְּנַאי. הֲרֵי זֶה גִּיטֵּיךְ אִם לֹא בָאתִי מִכָּן וְעַד שְׁלֹשִׁים יוֹם וְהָיָה הוֹלֵךְ לִמְדִינַת הַיָּם וְהִגִּיעַ לְעַכּוֹ וְחָזַר בָּטֵל הַתְּנַאי. הֲרֵי זֶה גִּיטֵּיךְ כָּל־זְמַן שֶׁאֶעֱבוֹר מִכְּנֶגֶד פָּנַיִךְ שְׁלֹשִׁים יוֹם הָיָה הוֹלֵךְ וּבָא הָיָה הוֹלֵךְ וּבָא הוֹאִיל וְלֹא נִתְיַיחֵד עִמָּהּ הֲרֵי זֶה גֵּט.

Mishnah 8: "This is your bill of divorce if I should not return within thirty days from today;" if he intended to go from Judea to Galilee, came to Antipatris, and returned, it is invalidated following his condition[144]. "This is your bill of divorce if I should not return within thirty days from today;" if he intended to go from Galilee to Judea, came to Kefar Othnay[145], and returned, it is invalidated following his condition. "This is your bill of divorce if I should not return within thirty days from today;" if he intended to go overseas, came to Acco[146], and returned, it is invalidated following his condition. "This is your bill of divorce if I should be absent from you for thirty days;" even if he repeatedly came and left, it is a bill of divorce if he never was alone with her[147].

משנה ט: הֲרֵי זֶה גִּיטֵּיךְ אִם לֹא בָּאתִי מִכָּאן וְעַד שְׁנֵים עָשָׂר חֹדֶשׁ מֵת בְּתוֹךְ שְׁנֵים עָשָׂר חֹדֶשׁ אֵינוֹ גֵט. הֲרֵי זֶה גִיטֵּיךְ מֵעַכְשָׁיו אִם לֹא בָאתִי מִכָּאן וְעַד שְׁנֵים עָשָׂר חֹדֶשׁ מֵת בְּתוֹךְ שְׁנֵים עָשָׂר חֹדֶשׁ הֲרֵי זֶה גֵט.

Mishnah 9: "This is your bill of divorce if I should not return within twelve months," if he died within the twelve months it is no bill of divorce[148]. "This is your bill of divorce *from today* if I should not return within twelve months," if he died within the twelve months it is a bill of divorce[149].

144 The great trade route of the *via maris*, connecting Egypt with Damascus, leaves Judea at Antipatris, near today's Roš Ha'ayin, to enter Samaria. The Mishnah states that a person wanting to leave a country is considered to have left it already when he has reached the border, even if he did not actually cross the border. The person is considered to have left the country; if he then changed his mind and returned, he returned within 30 days and invalidated the bill of divorce.

145 *Kafr 'Uthnay* near the excavations of Megiddo was the border town at which the *via maris*, coming from the South, entered Galilee.

146 By the principle explained in Note 144, if the person reaches a harbor where he could find a ship taking him overseas, he is considered to have gone overseas. The Mishnah also can be read as requiring the husband actually to have left the Land of Israel since Acco is partially inside and partially outside the Land (Chapter 1, Notes 64, 77).

147 Since in the opinion of the Yerushalmi "absent from you" means "not having marital relations with you." In the Babli, 76b, this is the interpretation of Rav Huna, against R. Joḥanan who invalidates the divorce if the wife saw the husband within a 30 day period.

148 After 12 months the woman is a widow, and a widow cannot be divorced.

149 It is a valid bill of divorce the

moment it has been ascertained that the husband will not be able to return within 12 months.

(49a line 33) **הלכה ח:** הֲרֵי זֶה גִּיטֵיךְ כול׳. לְיֵי דָה מִילָּה. רַבִּי לְעָזָר אָמַר. לְבֵיתוֹ. רַבִּי יוֹחָנָן אָמַר. לִמְקוֹמוֹת. מַתְנִיתָא מְסַייְעָא לְמָאן דְּאָמַר לְבֵיתוֹ. הִגִּיעַ לְעַכּוֹ וְחָזַר בָּטֵל הַתְּנַאי. אָמַר רַבִּי חַגַּיי קוֹמֵי רַבִּי יוֹסֵה. תִּיפְתָּר כְּמָאן דְּאָמַר. עַכּוֹ כְּאֶרֶץ יִשְׂרָאֵל לְגִיטִּין. וַאֲפִילוּ תֵימַר. עַכּוֹ כְּאֶרֶץ יִשְׂרָאֵל לְגִיטִּין. שֶׁמָּא לִתְנָאֵי גִיטִּין.

Halakhah 8: "This is your bill of divorce," etc. For what[150]? Rebbi Elazar said, for his house[151]; Rebbi Joḥanan said, for places[152]. The Mishnah supports him who said, for his house: "If he came to Acco[153], and returned, it is invalidated following his condition." Rebbi Ḥaggai said before Rebbi Yose, explain it following him who said that Acco is part of the Land of Israel for bills of divorce[154]. But even if you say that Acco is part of the Land of Israel for bills of divorce, does that mean also for conditions imposed on a bill of divorce[155]?

150 What does "return" mean in the Mishnah?
151 "Return" means that he returns to his wife for marital relations.
152 He already returned if he entered the community of his residence.
153 If we hold that Acco has the status of a foreign country, the part of the Mishnah dealing with Acco is superfluous. The important statement of the Mishnah then is that he has to return to his wife to invalidate the bill of divorce, following R. Eleazar.
154 Mishnah 1:2, Note 77.
155 Conditions have to be interpreted following common use, not in legal jargon. For everybody, Acco is a border town of the Land.

(49a line 38) וְאָסוּר לְהִתְיַיחֵד עִמָּהּ מִכְּבָר שֶׁמָּא יַעֲבוֹר מִכְּנֶגֶד פָּנֶיהָ ל יוֹם וְנִמְצָא גִיטָּהּ גָּדוֹל מִבְּנָהּ.

He is forbidden to be alone with her immediately, for maybe he shall not visit her for thirty days and then her bill of divorce would be older than her child[156].

[156] The condition was an indeterminate period of thirty days, not "from today". If the husband impregnated his wife after delivering the bill of divorce and later absented himself for 30 days, the record will show that the woman was divorced more than 9 months before the birth of her child. While this has no influence on the duties of the father towards his child, it will damage the child's reputation.

(fol. 48c) **משנה י:** אִם לֹא בָּאתִי מִכָּאן וְעַד שְׁנֵים עָשָׂר חֹדֶשׁ כִּתְבוּ גֵט וּתְנוּ לְאִשְׁתִּי כָּתְבוּ גֵט בְּתוֹךְ שְׁנֵים עָשָׂר חֹדֶשׁ וְנָתְנוּ בְּתוֹךְ שְׁנֵים עָשָׂר חֹדֶשׁ אֵינוֹ גֵט. כִּתְבוּ וּתְנוּ גֵט לְאִשְׁתִּי אִם לֹא בָּאתִי מִכָּאן וְעַד שְׁנֵים עָשָׂר חֹדֶשׁ כָּתְבוּ גֵט בְּתוֹךְ שְׁנֵים עָשָׂר חֹדֶשׁ וְנָתְנוּ לְאַחַר שְׁנֵים עָשָׂר חֹדֶשׁ אֵינוֹ גֵט. רַבִּי יוֹסֵי אוֹמֵר כָּזֶה גֵט. כָּתְבוּ לְאַחַר שְׁנֵים עָשָׂר חֹדֶשׁ וְנָתְנוּ לְאַחַר שְׁנֵים עָשָׂר חֹדֶשׁ וָמֵת אִם הַגֵּט קָדַם לַמִּיתָה הֲרֵי זֶה גֵט וְאִם הַמִּיתָה קָדְמָה לַגֵּט אֵינוֹ גֵט. וְאִם אֵינוֹ יָדוּעַ זוֹ הִיא שֶׁאָמְרוּ מְגוֹרֶשֶׁת וְאֵינָהּ מְגוֹרֶשֶׁת.

Mishnah 10: "If I should not return within twelve months from today write a bill of divorce and deliver to my wife;" if they wrote a bill of divorce within twelve months and delivered it within[157] twelve months, it is no bill of divorce. "Write a bill of divorce and deliver to my wife if I should not return within twelve months from today;" if they wrote a bill of divorce within twelve months and delivered it after twelve months, it is no bill of divorce; Rebbi Yose says, this is an example of a bill of divorce[158]. If they wrote after twelve months and delivered after twelve months but he had died, if the bill of divorce preceded the death it is a bill of divorce but if the death preceded the bill of divorce it is no bill of divorce. If it is not known, it is a case where they say, she is divorced and not divorced[159].

157 This text is supported by a number of Mishnah mss. but all known Babli mss. read "*after* 12 months". In any case the bill is invalid since the instructions of the husband were not followed to the letter.

158 R. Yose holds that the instructions of the husband were followed exactly since he mentioned "writing" before he mentioned a date. The opposing rabbis hold that the instruction may be interpreted to mean that no bill of divorce should exist before the end of 12 months.

159 The widow or divorcee can sue the heirs only for sums due to both widow and divorcee.

(49a line 39) **הלכה י:** אִם לֹא בָּאתִי מִכָּן וְעַד שְׁנֵים עָשָׂר חֹדֶשׁ כול׳. מַה טַעֲמָא דְרִבִּי יוֹסֵי. בְּגִין דְּאַקְדִּים כְּתִיבָה. וְהָא אַקְדִּים נְתִינָה. וְאַתּוּן אֲמְרִין. אֵינוֹ גֵט.

Halakhah 10: "If I should not return within twelve months from today," etc. What is the reason of Rebbi Yose? Because he mentioned writing earlier[158]. But did he not also mention delivering earlier, and you say that it is no bill of divorce[160]?

160 The question is not answered since it is obvious that the second sentence cannot be read as authorizing delivery before 12 months have elapsed.

(49a line 41) רִבִּי חִייָה רוֹבָה בָּעָא קוֹמֵי רִבִּי. הֲרֵי זֶה גִּיטָּיךְ לְאַחַר הֶחָג. אָמַר לֵיהּ. כָּל ל׳ יוֹם שֶׁלְּאַחַר הֶחָג כִּלְאַחַר הֶחָג הֵן. רִבִּי בִּיבוֹן בַּר חִייָה בָּעָא קוֹמֵי רִבִּי זְעִירָא. הֲרֵי גִיטֵּיךְ עֶרֶב הַפֶּסַח. וַאֲפִילוּ כְּמָאן דְּאָמַר. כָּל ל׳ שֶׁלְּאַחַר הֶחָג כִּלְאַחַר הֶחָג הֵן. כָּל ל׳ שֶׁלִּפְנֵי הַפֶּסַח אֵינוֹ כִלְאַחַר הַפֶּסַח. רִבִּי זְעִירָא בָּעָא קוֹמֵי רִבִּי יָסָא. אָמַר. קוֹנָם יַיִן שֶׁאֲנִי טוֹעֵם בְּמוֹצָאֵי שַׁבָּת. אָמַר לֵיהּ. בְּמוֹצָאֵי

שַׁבָּת אָסוּר. עֶרֶב שַׁבָּת מוּתָּר. יָמִים שֶׁבֵּינְתַּיִים צְרִיכָה. וְהָכָא מוֹצָאֵי שַׁבָּת הֲרֵי זֶה גֵּט. עֶרֶב שַׁבָּת אֵינוֹ גֵט. יָמִים שֶׁבֵּינְתַּיִים צְרִיכָה.

The Elder Rebbi Hiyya asked before Rebbi: "This is your bill of divorce after the holiday.[161]" He said to him, all of 30 days after the holiday are called "after the holiday"[162]. Rebbi Bivon bar Hiyya asked before Rebbi Ze'ira: "This is your bill of divorce on Passover eve"? Even a person who says that all of 30 days after the holiday are called "after the holiday" will agree that 30 days before Passover are not like "after Passover"[163]. Rebbi Ze'ira asked before Rebbi Yasa: If somebody said, a *qonam*[164] that I shall not taste wine at the end of the Sabbath? He said to him, after the end of the Sabbath he is forbidden, Sabbath eve he is permitted, the days in between are problematic[165]. And so it is here, after the end of the Sabbath it is a bill of divorce[166], Sabbath eve it is no bill of divorce, but the days in between are problematic.

161 If the language "after the holiday" (or possibly, after the holiday of Tabernacles") was used in connection with a bill of divorce; either that the bill should be valid if the husband did not return "after the holiday" or that the bill should be written and delivered "after the holiday", what is the interpretation of this term?

162 The Babli, 77a, accepts this only as Rebbi's private opinion which is not followed in practice.

163 A reference to "Eve of Passover" means the 14th of Nisan and nothing else.

164 A formula of "a vow of deprivation", cf. Introduction to Tractate *Nedarim*, p. 422.

165 The night following the Sabbath is certainly called "after the Sabbath". The following Friday is certainly not called "after the Sabbath". The days in between are questionable. In the Babli, 77a, Sunday, Monday, and Tuesday are called "after the Sabbath", Wednesday, Thursday, and Friday are called "before the Sabbath".

166 This refers to a condition imposed on a bill of divorce, cf. Note 161.

הזורק פרק שמיני

(fol. 49a) **משנה א:** הַזּוֹרֵק גֵּט לְאִשְׁתּוֹ וְהִיא בְתוֹךְ בֵּיתָהּ אוֹ בְתוֹךְ חֲצֵירָהּ הֲרֵי זוֹ מְגוֹרֶשֶׁת. זְרָקוֹ לָהּ בְּתוֹךְ בֵּיתוֹ אוֹ בְתוֹךְ חֲצֵירוֹ אֲפִילוּ הוּא עִמָּהּ בַּמִּטָּה אֵינָהּ מְגוֹרֶשֶׁת. לְתוֹךְ חֵיקָהּ אוֹ לְתוֹךְ קָלָתָהּ הֲרֵי זוֹ מְגוֹרֶשֶׁת.

If somebody throws a bill of divorce to his wife while she is in her own house or her own courtyard, she is divorced[1]. If he threw it to her inside his house or his courtyard, even if he was together with her in a bed, she is not divorced[2]. Into her bosom or her wool basket[3], she is divorced[2].

1 The verse *Deut.* 24:1 requires the bill of divorce to be delivered "into her hand". Legally, "hand" means "possession" (as in Latin and many other languages). Since anything lying in somebody's real estate is in his possession, delivery of the bill into the wife's real estate is legal delivery.

2 If the wife is in his real estate, only delivery into her hand or her personal belongings (the folds of her garment or her wool basket) is legal delivery.

3 Greek κάλαθος "wicker-basket", e. g., basket for wool.

(49b line 32) **הלכה א:** הַזּוֹרֵק גֵּט לְאִשְׁתּוֹ כול׳. וְכָתַב וְנָתַן בְּיָדָהּ. אֵין לִי אֶלָּא בְיָדָהּ. בְּגִינָּתָהּ בַּחֲצֵירָהּ מְנַיִין. תַּלְמוּד לוֹמַר. וְנָתַן. וְנָתַן. עַד כְּדוֹן כְּרִבִּי יִשְׁמָעֵאל. כְּרִבִּי עֲקִיבָה. תַּנֵּי רִבִּי יִשְׁמָעֵאל. וְיָקַח אֵת כָּל־אַרְצוֹ מִיָּדוֹ וְעַד אַרְנוֹן. וְכִי מִיָּדוֹ לָקַח. אֶלָּא מַהוּ מִיָּדוֹ. מֵרְשׁוּתוֹ.

Halakhah 1: "If somebody throws a bill of divorce to his wife," etc. "He shall write," "he shall deliver into her hand." Not only into her hand;

from where also into her garden or into her courtyard? The verse says "he shall deliver, he shall deliver."4 Is this following Rebbi Ismael? It is following Rebbi Aqiba. It was stated in the name of Rebbi Ismael5, "he took all his land from his hand, up to the Arnon." Did he take it out of his hand? What means "from his hand"? From his possession.

4 A shortened version of this argument is in the Babli, 77b. The argument follows R. Aqiba, who derives rules from every word which could be considered not absolutely necessary. Since "he shall deliver" is mentioned both in *Deut.* 24:1 and 24:3, he concludes that any legal delivery is acceptable.

5 R. Ismael holds that "the Torah speaks in everybody's language." Therefore, if "hand" is to be interpreted as "possession", a verse has to be found in which this sense is documented. This is *Num.* 21:26 which notes that Sihon the Amorite "took all the land from the Moabite king's hand". Since land cannot be grasped in one's hand, "hand" must mean "possession". (A hint of this argument is in *Sifry Deut.* 269. The Babli, *Baba Meṣi'a* 56b, following only R. Aqiba, accepts the interpretation of "hand" as "possession" only in extraordinary cases.)

(49b line 35) וְגִינָתָהּ וַחֲצֵירָהּ אֵינָן מְשׁוּעְבָּדִים לָאִישׁ לַאֲכִילַת פֵּרוֹת. רִבִּי יְהוֹשֻׁעַ בְשֵׁם רִבִּי יַנַּאי. עַד שֶׁיִּכְתּוֹב לָהּ. דִּין וּדְבָרִים אֵין לִי בְנִכְסַיִיךְ. רִבִּי יִצְחָק בַּר חֲקוּלְיָה בְשֵׁם רִבִּי הוֹשַׁעְיָה. אֲפִילוּ לֹא כָתַב לָהּ. דִּין וּדְבָרִים אֵין לִי בְנִכְסַיִיךְ. וְאַתְיָיא דְּרִבִּי יַנַּאי כְּרַבָּנִין וּדְרִבִּי הוֹשַׁעְיָה כְּרִבִּי מֵאִיר. דְּרִבִּי יַנַּאי כְּרַבָּנִין. דְּרַבָּנִין אָמְרִין. עַל יְדֵי שֶׁיַּד הָעֶבֶד כְּיַד רַבּוֹ הוּא זָכָה גִיטוֹ מִיָּדוֹ. וְגִינָתָהּ וַחֲצֵירָהּ הוֹאִיל וְהֵן מְשׁוּעְבָּדִים לָאִישׁ לַאֲכִילַת פֵּרוֹת. עַד שֶׁיִּכְתּוֹב לָהּ. דִּין וּדְבָרִים אֵין לִי בְנִכְסַיִיךְ. וְקַשְׁיָא עַל דְּרַבָּנִין. הוּא יַד הָעֶבֶד כְּיַד רַבּוֹ וְהוּא זָכָה גִיטוֹ. וּדְרִבִּי הוֹשַׁעְיָה כְּרִבִּי מֵאִיר. דְּרִבִּי מֵאִיר אוֹמֵר. עַל יְדֵי שֶׁאֵין הָאִשָּׁה כְּיַד בַּעֲלָהּ הוּא זָכְתָה גִיטָהּ מִיָּדוֹ. וְגִינָתָהּ וַחֲצֵירָהּ אַף עַל פִּי שֶׁאֵין מְשׁוּעְבָּדִים לָאִישׁ לַאֲכִילַת פֵּרוֹת אֲפִילוּ לֹא כָתַב לָהּ. דִּין וּדְבָרִים אֵין לִי בְנִכְסַיִיךְ. נָפְלוּ

לוֹ נְכָסִים וְלָהּ. אֲפִילוּ כָתַב כְּמִי שֶׁלֹא כָתַב. הָיָה נָשׂוּי אֶת בַּת אָחִיו. אֲפִילוּ כָתַב כְּמִי שֶׁלֹּא כָתַב. נָתַן לָהּ אַחֵר מַתָּנָה. וְאָמַר לָהּ. עַל מְנָת שֶׁלֹּא יְהֵא לְבַעֲלָהּ רְשׁוּת בָּהֶן אֶלָּא מַה שֶׁאַתְּ נוֹשֵׂאת וְנוֹתֶנֶת בְּפִיךְ. אֲפִילוּ לֹא כָתַב לָהּ כְּמִי שֶׁכָּתַב.

But are her garden and her courtyard not subject to her husband's having the usufruct[6]? Rebbi Joshua[7] in the name of Rebbi Yannai: Only if he writes to her, "I have nothing to do with your properties[8]." Rebbi Isaac bar Ḥaqulah in the name of Rebbi Hoshaiah: Even if he did not write to her, "I have nothing to do with your properties.[9]" It turns out that Rebbi Yannai follows the rabbis and Rebbi Hoshaiah follows Rebbi Meïr[10]. Rebbi Yannai follows the rabbis, for the rabbis say, even though the slave's hand is his master's hand, he can acquire his document of manumission from [his master's] hand[11]. But her garden and her courtyard are subject to her husband's having the usufruct unless he writes to her, "I have nothing to do with your properties." It is difficult for the rabbis: since the slave's hand is his master's hand, how can he acquire his document of manumission from [his master's] hand[12]? Rebbi Hoshaiah follows Rebbi Meïr, for Rebbi Meïr said since the wife's hand is not her husband's hand, she can acquire her bill of divorce from her husband. Her garden and her courtyard will not be subject to her husband[13], even if he has the usufruct, even if he did not write to her, "I have nothing to do with your properties." If he inherited properties together with her, even if he wrote it is as if he did not write; [for example] if he had married his brother's daughter, even if he wrote it is as if he did not write[14]. If another person gave her a gift and told her, on condition that your husband have no rights to it, but it is for you to trade on your own account, then even if he did not write it is as if he wrote[15].

6   In the absence of a contract to the contrary, the wife's dowry, brought into the marriage, becomes the husband's property as *mortmain* subject to his obligation to restitute the full value at the termination of the marriage. Property coming to the wife during the marriage is *paraphernalia* property about which the husband assumes the duty of administration and from which he has the usufruct. In any case, it is impossible to say that (in the absence of a contract of separation of properties) the wife's properties were in her actual possession during her marriage. Cf. *Yebamot* 7:1, Note 1.

7   No R. Joshua is known among Amoraïm. One has to read with Tosaphot (*s.v.* מה, 77b): R. Joḥanan.

8   Cf. Mishnah *Ketubot* 9:1 (Notes 1-4) about the different formulations of separation of properties.

9   In the words of the Babli, 77a: In a divorce, her bill of divorce and her entering into full possession of her properties are simultaneous. Even if the husband had the administration of the properties when he dispatched the bill of divorce, the moment the latter landed on his wife's property he has lost the administration, and all property rights revert to his ex-wife.

10   In the Babli (*Qiddušin* 23b), the attributions are switched: R. Meïr holds that neither slave nor wife have powers of acquisition separate from husband or master, and the rabbis disagree.

11   While anything the slave acquires automatically becomes his master's property, the master by delivering the bill of manumission empowers the slave to own property, in particular, himself.

12   This is a rhetorical question; the answer was already given, cf. Note 11.

13   The husband possibly is the administrator but not the owner.

14   The right to joint property can be renounced only by transfer of property rights, not by a disclaimer.

15   If the husband never had any rights of administration, he does not have to disclaim them. It is a recognized way of giving property to one's daughter to shield it from the son-in-law; Mishnah *Nedarim* 11:8 (Notes 69,70).

(49b line 50) רִבִּי יִרְמְיָה בָּעֵי. זָרְקוֹ לָהּ בְּחָצֵר שֶׁאֵינָהּ שֶׁלְּשְׁנֵיהֶן מָהוּ. רִבִּי אָחָא בְּשֵׁם רִבִּי חֲנִינָה. צְרִיכָה לְרַבָּנִין. אָמַר רִבִּי אָבִין. מַחֲלוֹקֶת רַב וְרִבִּי חִייָה רוֹבָה. דָּמַר רִבִּי שְׁמוּאֵל רִבִּי זְעִירָה רַב חִייָה בַּר אַשִׁי בְּשֵׁם רַב. אֵין מְשִׁיכָה קוֹנָה בְּחָצֵר שֶׁאֵינָהּ שֶׁלְּשְׁנֵיהֶן. וְתַגֵּי רִבִּי חִייָה וּפָלִיג. אֵימָתַי אָמְרוּ. הַמִּטַּלְטְלִין נִיקְנִין בִּמְשִׁיכָה. בִּרְשׁוּת הָרַבִּים אוֹ בְחָצֵר שֶׁאֵינָהּ שֶׁלְּשְׁנֵיהֶן. אֲבָל בִּרְשׁוּת הַלּוֹקֵחַ כֵּיוָן שֶׁקִּיבֵּל עָלָיו בִּרְשׁוּת הַמּוֹכֵר זָכָה. לֹא קָנָה אֶלָּא עַד שָׁעָה שֶׁיַגְבִּיהַּ אוֹ עַד שָׁעָה שֶׁיִּמְשׁוֹךְ וְיוֹצֵא חוּץ מֵרְשׁוּת הַבְּעָלִים. בִּרְשׁוּת זֶה שֶׁהָיוּ מוּפְקָדִים אֶצְלוֹ לֹא קָנָה עַד שֶׁיְּזַכֵּהוּ בָהֶן אוֹ עַד שֶׁיַּשְׂכִּיר לוֹ אֶת מְקוֹמוֹ.

6 ברשות המוכר זכה. לא קנה | ק קנה. ברשות המוכר לא קנה

Rebbi Jeremiah asked: If he threw it to her in a courtyard which belongs to neither of them, what is the rule[16]? Rebbi Aḥa in the name of Rebbi Ḥanina: That is a problem for the rabbis. [17]Rebbi Abin said, it is a disagreement between Rav and the Elder Rebbi Ḥiyya, for Rebbi Samuel, Rebbi Ze'ira, Rav Ḥiyya bar Ashi said in the name of Rav: Drawing close does not acquire in a courtyard which belongs to neither of them[18]. But Rebbi Ḥiyya stated in disagreement: "Under which circumstances did they say that movables are acquired by drawing close? In the public domain or in a courtyard which belongs to neither of them. But in the buyer's domain he acquired the moment he accepted it[19]. In the seller's domain he does not acquire unless either he lifts it up or moves it out of its prior owner's domain. In a domain where it was deposited[20] he does not acquire unless he either is explicitly empowered or he leases its place.[21]"

16 If the bill of divorce is deposited in a private domain which belongs neither to the husband nor to the wife, can the wife legally acquire the document by lifting it up or drawing it close to her so that it could be lifted up. In the public domain this is possible as explained in Mishnah 2.

17 This is also referred to in *Qiddušin* 1:4 (60b l. 32). The text of

the following Tosephta (attributed to the Elder R. Ḥiyya) is slightly garbled here; it is translated following the text of *Qiddušin* (and its parallels in Babli *Baba batra* 85a, Tosephta *Baba batra* 5:2).

18   Mishnah *Qiddušin* 1:4 states that "movables can only be acquired by being moved" (unless they are acquired together with real estate.) It is a peculiarity of rabbinic law (for which no biblical tradition is claimed) that transfer of money does not transfer ownership of the commodity bought. Delivery is effected and responsibility for the merchandise is transferred from the seller to the buyer uniquely by an act of acquisition by the buyer, which in theory should be actual moving of the merchandise.

19   Since "a person's courtyard acquires for him" (cf. Note 1.)

20   The merchandise was deposited with a third person. Then the owner of the property may grant the buyer the right (with or without payment) to use his property for the acquisition. Without an explicit grant, the merchandise can be acquired only by actual removal from the premises.

21   For Rav, a divorce document can be delivered on another person's property only by direct delivery. For R. Ḥiyya, the delivery can be indirect as long as no party has an interest in the property. The Babli, *Baba batra* 85a, recognizes only R. Ḥiyya's position.

(49b line 58) עוּלָּא בַּר יִשְׁמָעֵאל אָמַר. לֹא עָלְתָה עַל דַּעְתּוֹ לִזְכּוֹת בְּקַלְתָהּ. הַגַּע עַצְמְךָ שֶׁהָיְתָה קַלְתָהּ שֶׁלְזָהָב. כָּל־שֶׁכֵּן לֹא עָלְתָה עַל דַּעְתּוֹ לִזְכּוֹת בְּקַלְתָהּ. רִבִּי יוֹחָנָן אָמַר. וּבִלְבַד בְּמִשְׁתַּמֵּשׁ בָּהּ. אָמַר רִבִּי יוֹסֵי. וּבִלְבַד בְּמִשְׁתַּמֶּשֶׁת בָּהּ בְּאוֹתָהּ שָׁעָה. רֵישׁ לָקִישׁ אָמַר. בִּקְשׁוּרָה לָהּ. אָמַר רִבִּי יוֹסֵי. וּבְמַגְבַּהַת מַחְמָתָהּ. תַּנֵּי רִבִּי הוֹשַׁעְיָה וּמְסַייֵעַ לְרִבִּי יוֹחָנָן. אֲפִילוּ זְרָקוֹ לָהּ בְּתוֹךְ הַמָּלוֹשׁ שֶׁלָּהּ הֲרֵי זוֹ מְגוֹרֶשֶׁת.

Ulla bar Ismael said, he never thought to have a right to her wool basket[22]. Think of it, if her wool basket was of gold? Certainly he never thought to have a right to her wool basket. Rebbi Joḥanan said, only if it is being used[23]. Rebbi Yose said, only if she is using it at that moment[24].

Rebbi Simeon ben Laqish said, if it is tied to her; Rebbi Yose said, if she lifts it for her purpose[25]. Rebbi Hoshaiah stated in support of Rebbi Johanan: Even if he threw it into her *maloš*[26] she is divorced.

22 He explains why the wife is divorced if the husband throws the bill of divorce into her wool basket in his house. According to the Tosephta quoted in the preceding paragraph, the wife should not be able to acquire anything on the husband's premises without bodily removing it from the premises. It is now stated that this excludes the wife's personal things.

23 If she is using the wool basket at the moment, it is part of her outfit. If the husband puts the bill of divorce into one of her bags which is not being used, it is no delivery.

24 R. Yose only makes R. Johanan's statement clear.

25 Similar statements of the parties involved are in the Babli, 78a.

26 This *hapax* is unexplained; the hypothetical meaning "baking trough" from לוש is adopted by the classical commentaries. {Perhaps explain as Greek μαλλός, ὁ "flock of wool, tress", as contents of her κάλαθος (Note 3) (E. G.). In Galilean speech, no difference existed between שׂ, שׁ and ס.}

(fol. 49a) **משנה ב:** אָמַר לָהּ כִּינְסִי שְׁטַר חוֹב זֶה אוֹ שֶׁמְּצָאַתּוּ מֵאֲחוֹרָיו קוֹרְאָה וַהֲרֵי הוּא גִיטָּהּ אֵינוֹ גֵט עַד שֶׁיֹּאמַר לָהּ הֵא גִיטֵּיךְ. נָתַן בְּיָדָהּ וְהִיא יְשֵׁנָה נִיעוֹרָה קוֹרְאָה וַהֲרֵי הוּא גִיטָהּ אֵינוֹ גֵט עַד שֶׁיֹּאמַר לָהּ הֵא גִיטֵּיךְ. הָיְתָה עוֹמֶדֶת בִּרְשׁוּת הָרַבִּים וּזְרָקוֹ לָהּ קָרוֹב לָהּ מְגוֹרֶשֶׁת קָרוֹב לוֹ אֵינָהּ מְגוֹרֶשֶׁת מֶחֱצָה לְמֶחֱצָה מְגוֹרֶשֶׁת וְאֵינָהּ מְגוֹרֶשֶׁת.

Mishnah 2: If he said to her, "take this bond," or she found it behind his back, she read it and it turned out to be her bill of divorce, it is no bill of divorce until he says to her "this is your bill of divorce". If he put it into her hand while she was asleep, after she awoke she read it and it turned out to be her bill of divorce, it is no bill of divorce until he says to her "this is your bill of divorce". If she was standing in the public domain when he threw it to her and it landed close to her it is a bill of divorce, close to him it is no bill of divorce, half and half she is divorced and not divorced.

(49b line 64) **הלכה ב:** אָמַר לָהּ כִּינְסִי שְׁטָר חוֹב זֶה כול'. אָמַר רִבִּי יוֹחָנָן. דְּרִבִּי שִׁמְעוֹן בֶּן אֶלְעָזָר הִיא. דְּרִבִּי שִׁמְעוֹן בֶּן אֶלְעָזָר אוֹמֵר. לְעוֹלָם אֵינוֹ גֵט עַד שֶׁיֹּאמַר לָהּ בִּשְׁעַת מַתָּנָה. הֵא גִיטֵּיךְ.

Halakhah 2: "If he said to her, 'take this bond,'" etc. Rebbi Joḥanan says, this follows Rebbi Eleazar ben Simeon, since Rebbi Eleazar ben Simeon says it never is a bill of divorce unless he says at the moment of delivery: "this is your bill of divorce.[27]"

27 The Babli (78a, Tosephta 6:1), quotes a disagreement between Rebbi, who accepts the husband's declaration even after delivery of the bill, and R. Eleazar ben Simeon, who requires a repeat delivery if the declaration was not made at the moment of delivery. In *Sifry Deut*. 269, the opinion of R. Eleazar ben Simeon is quoted anonymously and referred to the verse *Deut*. 24:1 about the bill of divorce "... hands it over to her and sends her out of his house;" meaning that handing the bill to his wife and making it clear that she is divorced must be simultaneous.

(49b line 66) כַּמָּה הוּא קָרוֹב. רַב אָמַר. אַרְבַּע אַמּוֹת. אָמַר רִבִּי אִלַּאי הַיּוֹרֵשׁ. אַרְבַּע אַמּוֹת. רִבִּי לְעָזָר בְּשֵׁם רִבִּי יוֹחָנָן בְּשֵׁם רִבִּי יַנַּאי. כִּפִישׁוּט יָדַיִּים. וְתַגִּינָן. בִּפְישׁוּט יָדַיִם. רִבִּי בָא רִבִּי יִרְמִיָה בְּשֵׁם רַב. בִּפְישׁוּט יָדַיִם. מַחְלְפָה שִׁיטָתֵיהּ דְּרַב. תַּמָּן הוּא אָמַר. אַרְבַּע אַמּוֹת. וְהָכָא הוּא אָמַר אָכֵן. כָּאן לַהֲלָכָה כָּאן לְמַעֲשֶׂה. תַּנֵּי רִבִּי לְעָזָר. אֲפִילוּ קָרוֹב לָזֶה מִלְזוֹ וּבָא הַכֶּלֶב וּנְטָלוֹ

אֵינָהּ מְגוֹרֶשֶׁת. שְׁמוּאֵל כְּהָדָא דְּרִבִּי לָעָזָר וּפְלִיג. הַמְחַוְונָר בְּכוּלָּן עַד שֶׁיִּתְּנֶנָּה לְתוֹךְ יָדָהּ. הָיָה פּוֹשֵׁט יָדַיִים בֵּינוֹ לְבֵינָהּ. שִׁמְעוֹן בַּר בָּא בְּשֵׁם רִבִּי יוֹחָנָן. קָרוֹב לָהּ מִלּוֹ מְגוֹרֶשֶׁת. לוֹ מִלָּהּ אֵינָהּ מְגוֹרֶשֶׁת. מֶחֱצָה לְמֶחֱצָה מְגוֹרֶשֶׁת וְאֵינָהּ מְגוֹרֶשֶׁת. אַבָּא בַּר רַב יִרְמְיָה אָמַר. כָּל־הֵן דְּתַנִּינָן מְגוֹרֶשֶׁת וְאֵינָהּ מְגוֹרֶשֶׁת. מְזוֹנוֹת מִשֶּׁלּוֹ.

How close is "near"[28]? Rav said, four cubits[29]. Rebbi Ilai the heir said, four cubits. Rebbi Eleazar in the name of Rebbi Joḥanan in the name of Rebbi Yannai: Stretching out hands, and we have stated: "stretching out hands.[30]" Rebbi Abba, Rebbi Jeremiah[31], in the name of Rav: Stretching out hands. The argument of Rav is inverted; there, he says four cubits and here he says so? There in theory[32], here in practice[33]. "Rebbi Eleazar stated: Even if it was closer to her than to him but a dog came and took it away, she is not divorced.[34]" Samuel agrees with Rebbi Eleazar and disagrees. The clearest way is that he puts it into her hand. If there was room for stretching out hands between him and her, Simeon bar Abba in the name of Rebbi Joḥanan [states]: If it was closer to her than to him she is divorced[35], closer to him than to her she is not divorced, half and half she is divorced and not divorced. Abba bar Rav Jeremiah said: In all cases in which we have stated "divorced and not divorced", support is on him[36].

28   This starts the discussion of the last part of the Mishnah.

29   A person standing in the public domain acquires anything movable that is within a circle of four cubits (about 2.2 m) of him if (1) it is his intent to acquire and (2) no other person is present in that circle; cf. *Yebamot* 3:9, Note 120.

30   The bill of divorce is legally delivered only if the wife can pick it up by stretching out her hands without moving her feet. (It seems that this includes the possibility that she has to

kneel down to reach the document.)

31   He is Rav's colleague who in the Babli is called Rav Jeremiah.

32   The principle explained in Note 29 is generally accepted in money matters. For example, if one finds something in the street, he can claim it for himself and sue anybody who would snatch it away from him if the two conditions of acquisition are met. The Babli, 79a/b, goes to great lengths to uphold the principle; its arguments are irrelevant for the understanding of the Yerushalmi.

33   In practice, a divorce is definitive only if the document was picked up by the wife. The Babli emphatically agrees in the names of Samuel and Rav Ashi, 79b.

34   Tosephta 6:1. The sources are divided on whether to read Eliezer or Eleazar. In the Tosephta, R. Eleazar disagrees with the restriction of the distance to four cubits; this is not mentioned in the Yerushalmi. The corresponding text in the Babli, 79b, is noncommittal in the matter.

35   Even if he was standing within 4 cubits of her when he threw the bill to her, which would prevent her from acquiring ownerless property.

36   Since she cannot remarry unless she receives a new, clean bill of divorce, for all consequences in civil law she remains married.

(fol. 49a) **מִשְׁנָה ג:** וְכֵן לְעִנְיָן הַקִּידּוּשִׁין וּלְעִנְיָן הַחוֹב. אָמַר לוֹ זְרוֹק לִי חוֹבִי וּזְרָקוֹ לוֹ קָרוֹב לַמַּלְוֶה זָכָה הַלּוֶֹה קָרוֹב לַלּוֶֹה הַלּוֶֹה חַיָּיב. מֶחֱצָה לְמֶחֱצָה שְׁנֵיהֶן יַחֲלוֹקוּ. הָיְתָה עוֹמֶדֶת בְּרֹאשׁ הַגַּג וּזְרָקוֹ לָהּ כֵּיוָן שֶׁהִגִּיעַ לַאֲוִיר הַגַּג הֲרֵי זוֹ מְגוֹרֶשֶׁת. הוּא מִלְמַעֲלָן וְהִיא מִלְמַטָּן וּזְרָקוֹ לָהּ כֵּיוָן שֶׁיָּצָא מֵרְשׁוּת הַגַּג נִמְחַק אוֹ נִשְׂרַף הֲרֵי זוֹ מְגוֹרֶשֶׁת.

Mishnah 3: The same applies for preliminary marriages[37] and for [liquidation of] debts. If he[38] said to him, throw to me[39] what you owe me and he threw it close to the lender[40], the borrower is acquitted, close to the borrower, the borrower remains obligated, in the middle both of them must share it[41]. If she was standing on top of her roof and he threw it to her[42], as soon as it reached the roof's airspace[43] she is divorced. If he was on top and she below[44], once it left the domain of the roof she is divorced even if it was blotted out or burned.

37 Cf. Mishnah *Yebamot* 3:9, Note 120.

38 The creditor (who is explicitly mentioned in most Mishnah and Babli mss.)

39 In the public domain.

40 The borrower threw it in the public domain close to the lender. The borrower is free even if the creditor is unable to pick up the money.

41 If the money is lost, the borrower and the creditor each have to cover half the loss.

42 The flat roof has the same standing as a courtyard; delivery to the roof is legal delivery (Mishnah 1).

43 Even if the wife never could pick it up since, as explained in the next sentence, it might have landed in a puddle and become illegible or landed in a fire and be destroyed.

44 In her own domain.

(49c line 1) **הלכה ג:** וְכֵן לְעִנְיָין הַקִּידּוּשִׁין כול'. רֵישׁ לָקִישׁ בְּשֵׁם אַבָּא כֹּהֵן בַּר דְּלָא אס[45] זָכָה בִּמְצִיאָה בְּתוֹךְ אַרְבַּע אַמּוֹת. מַה טַעַם. הִנֵּה בְעָנְיִי הֲכִינוֹתִי לְבֵית יְ" זָהָב כִּכָּרִים מֵאָה אֶלֶף וְכֶסֶף אֶלֶף אֲלָפִים כִּכָּרִים וְלַנְּחוֹשֶׁת וְלַבַּרְזֶל אֵין מִשְׁקָל כִּי לָרוֹב הֲכִינוֹתִי וְעֵצִים וַאֲבָנִים הֲכִינוֹתִי וַעֲלֵיהֶם תּוֹסִיף.

1 ריש לקיש | פ שמעון בן לקיש   2 בר דלא | פ בר דליא   אם | פ אדם   במציאה | פ לחבירו במציאה   הנה | פ ואני   4 הכינותי | פ היה

Halakhah 3: "The same applies for preliminary marriages", etc. [46]Rebbi Simeon ben Laqish in the name of Abba Cohen Bar Dalaia: A person acquires a find within four cubits of himself. What is the reason? (*1Chr.* 22:14) "Look, in my poverty I prepared for the House of the Eternal 100'000 *kikkar* of gold, 1'000'000 *kikkar* of silver, bronze and iron unweighed because it was so much; I prepared wood and stones, and you should add to them."

| 45 This has to be read אדם with the text in *Peah*. | 46 The following is from *Peah* 4:2, Notes 30-58. (Variant readings פ). |

(49c line 5) אָמַר רִבִּי יוֹנָה אָמַר רַב הוֹשַׁעְיָה בָּעֵי. מַה אֲנַן קַיָּימִין. אִם בְּתוֹךְ אַרְבַּע אַמּוֹת עָשִׁיר הוּא. אִם חוּץ לְאַרְבַּע אַמּוֹת יֵשׁ אָדָם מַקְדִּישׁ דָּבָר שֶׁאֵינוֹ שֶׁלוֹ. קַיַּמְנוּהָ בְּמַקְדִּישׁ רִאשׁוֹן רִאשׁוֹן.

1 אמ׳ ר׳ יונה אמ׳ | פ ר׳ יונה אמ׳   אנן | פ נן   2 חוץ | פ בחוץ   יש | פ ויש   3 קיימנוה | פ וקיימנוה

Rebbi Jonah said that Rebbi Hoshaiah asked: What are we talking about? If this was within four cubits from him, he was rich. If it was outside of four cubits, may anybody dedicate anything that is not his? We confirmed it if he dedicated it piece by piece.

(49c line 8) אָמַר רִבִּי אָבוּן. מַהוּ בְעוֹנְיִי. שֶׁאֵין עֲשִׁירוּת בִּפְנֵי מִי שֶׁאָמַר וְהָיָה הָעוֹלָם. דָּבָר אַחֵר. הִנֵּה בְעוֹנְיִי. שֶׁהָיָה מִתְעַנֶּה וּמַקְדִּישׁ סְעוּדָתוֹ לַשָּׁמַיִם.

1 אבון | פ אבין   בפני | פ לפני   2 הנה בעונייי | פ בעיניי. בעינוי

Rebbi Abun said, what means "in my poverty?" That there is no wealth before Him Who commanded and the world came into existence! Another explanation: בְּעוֹנְיִי "in my deprivation," because he fasted and donated the price of his meal to Heaven.

(49c line 10) הָתִיב רַב יַעֲקֹב בַּר אִידִי קוֹמֵי רֵישׁ לָקִישׁ. וְהָתַנִּינָן. רָאָה אֶת הַמְצִיאָה וְנָפַל לוֹ עָלֶיהָ וּבָא אַחֵר וְהֶחֱזִיק בָּהּ. זֶה שֶׁהֶחֱזִיק בָּהּ זָכָה בָהּ. תִּיפְתָּר שֶׁלֹּא אָמַר. יִזְכּוּ לִי אַרְבַּע אַמּוֹת. וְהָתַנִּינָן. נָפַל לוֹ עָלֶיהָ וּפָרַס טַלִּיתוֹ עָלֶיהָ מַעֲבִירִין אוֹתוֹ הֵימֶנָּה. עוֹד הִיא בְּשֶׁלֹּא אָמַר יִזְכּוּ לִי אַרְבַּע אַמּוֹת. וְהָא תַנֵּי רִבִּי חִיָּיא. שְׁנַיִם שֶׁהָיוּ מִתְבַּתְּשִׁין עַל הָעוֹמֶר וּבָא אַחֵר וַחֲטָפוֹ. זֶה שֶׁחֲטָפוֹ זָכָה בוֹ. עוֹד הֵם בְּשֶׁלֹּא אָמְרוּ. יִזְכּוּ לָנוּ אַרְבַּע אַמּוֹת.

HALAKHAH 3

1 רב | פ ר'   קומי | פ בשם   ריש לקיש | פ ר' שמעון בן לקיש   2 תיפתר | פ אמ' ליה.
תיפתר   3 שלא | פ בשלא   אמות | פ אמות שלי (corrector's addition)   והתנינן | פ
והתני   4 הימינו | פ ממנו   עוד | פ אמ' ליה. עוד   אמות | פ אמות שלי (corrector's
addition)   והא תני | פ והתני   5 מתבתשין | פ מתכתשין   אחר | פ עני אחר   זה
שחטפו | פ מלפניהן   6 עוד הם | פ אמ' ליה. עוד היא   אמרו יזכו לנו | פ אמר יזכו לי
אמות | פ אמות שלי

Rebbi Jacob bar Idi objected before Rebbi Simeon ben Laqish. Did we not state: (Mishnah *Baba Meẓi'a* 1:4) "If somebody saw a find and fell on it, when another person came and grabbed it, he who grabbed it had the rights to it?" He answered him: Explain it if the first one did not say that his four cubits should acquire it for him. But did we not state: "If he fell on it or spread his talith on it, one removes him from it?" He said to him, that is the same, if he did not say that his four cubits should acquire it for him. But did not Rebbi Ḥiyya state: (Tosephta *Peah* 2:2) "If two were pushing one another because of a sheaf and another person came and grabbed it from before them, the one who grabbed is entitled to it. He said to him, it is the same, they did not say that our four cubits should acquire it for us.

(49c line 16) רִבִּי יָסָא בְשֵׁם רִבִּי יוֹחָנָן. זוֹ בְגִיטִּין מַה שֶׁאֵין כֵּן בְּמַתָּנָה. רוּבָּהּ דְּרִבִּי יוֹחָנָן וְרוּבָּהּ דְּרֵישׁ לָקִישׁ. רוּבָּהּ דְּרִבִּי יוֹחָנָן. מַה אִם מְצִיאָה שֶׁאֵינוֹ זוֹכֶה בָּהּ מִדַּעַת אַחֵר הֲרֵי הוּא זוֹכֶה בְּתוֹךְ אַרְבַּע אַמּוֹת. מַתָּנָה שֶׁהוּא זוֹכֶה בָּהּ מִדַּעַת אַחֵר לֹא כָּל־שֶׁכֵּן. רוּבָּהּ דְּרֵישׁ לָקִישׁ. מַה אִם מַתָּנָה שֶׁאִם זָכָה בָּהּ בְּתוֹךְ אַרְבַּע אַמּוֹת הֲרֵי הוּא זוֹכֶה מִדַּעַת אַחֵר. מְצִיאָה שֶׁהוּא זוֹכֶה בָּהּ בְּתוֹךְ אַרְבַּע אַמּוֹת לֹא כָּל־שֶׁכֵּן.

ר' יסא בשם | פ אמ' ר' יסא אמ'   2 דריש לקיש | פ דר' שמעון בן לקיש   3 זוכה | פ
זוכה בה   4 דריש לקיש | פ דר' שמעון בן לקיש   מתנה שאם | פ מתנה שאינה   5
זוכה | פ זוכה בה

Rebbi Yasa said in the name of Rebbi Joḥanan: That refers to divorce documents, but it does not apply to a gift. Rebbi Joḥanan adds something, Rebbi Simeon ben Laqish adds something. Rebbi Joḥanan adds something. Since a find which cannot be acquired by the knowledge of another person can be acquired within four cubits, should this rule not apply *a fortiori* to a gift that is acquired by the knowledge of another person? Rebbi Simeon ben Laqish adds something. Since a gift which could only be acquired within four cubits by the knowledge of another person, should this not *a fortiori* apply to a find?

(49c line 22) הָתִיב רִבִּי זְעִירָא קוֹמֵי רִבִּי יָסָא. וְהָא תַגִּינָן. וְכֵן לְעִנְיָן קִידּוּשִׁין. אָמַר לֵיהּ. הוּא גִיטִּין הוּא קִידּוּשִׁין. וְהָא תַגִּינָן. וְכֵן לְעִנְיָן הַחוֹב. אָמַר לֵיהּ. שֶׁכֵּן אִם אָמַר לוֹ. זוֹרְקֵהוּ לַיָּם וִיהֵא מָחוּל לָךְ. מָחוּל לוֹ. מֵעַתָּה אֲפִילוּ קָרוֹב לְלֹוֶה זָכָה הַלֹּוֶה. וְתַגִּינָן. קָרוֹב לַלֹּוֶה הַלֹּוֶה חַיָּיב. שֶׁכֵּן אִם אָמַר לֵיהּ. זוֹרְקֵיהוּ עַד שֶׁיִּיכָּנֵס לִרְשׁוּתוֹ. וַעֲדַיִין לֹא נִכְנַס לִרְשׁוּתוֹ. אָמַר רִבִּי אָבִין כָּל־אִילֵּין מְתִיבָתָה דַּהֲוָה רִבִּי זְעִירָא מֵשִׁיב קוֹמֵי רִבִּי יָסָא. וְרֵישׁ לָקִישׁ מוֹתִיב קוֹמֵי רִבִּי יוֹחָנָן וְהוּא מְקַבֵּל מִינַּייהוּ פָּתַר לֵיהּ כְּאִילֵּין פִּיתָרְיָיתָא.

1 והא תנינן | פ והתנינן קידושין | פ הקידושין   2 הוא | פ היא (2 times)   והא תנינן | פ והתנינן   3 לו (corrector) | פ ליה   זורקיהו | פ זרקיהו   4 ללווה | פ ללוה (2 times)   זורקיהו | פ זרקיהו   לרשותו | פ לרשותי   5 לרשותו | פ ברשותו   אבין | פ אבהו   6 מתיבתא | פ תתובתא   משיב | פ מותיב   ריש לקיש | פ ר' שמעון בן לקיש   7 והא מקבל מינייהו | פ מקבל מיניה   כאילין | פ באילין   פיתרייתא | פ פיתריא

Rebbi Zeïra objected before Rebbi Yasa: But did we not state: The same applies to marriage? He answered him, divorce documents and marriage contracts have the same rules. But did we not state: The same applies to debt? He said to him, because if he said to him: Throw it into the sea and your debt will be forgiven, it would be forgiven. But if that is true, even if it fell down close to the debtor, the debtor should have the benefit! But we have stated, if it falls down close to the debtor, the debtor is still obligated. For he said to him, throw it so that it will enter my domain, but it did not yet enter his domain. Rebbi Abbahu said, all those objections that Rebbi Zeïra raised before Rebbi Yasa, Rebbi Simeon ben Laqish raised before Rebbi Joḥanan. Did he accept them from him? He solved them with those same solutions.

(49c line 29) רִבִּי אָבִין בְּשֵׁם חִזְקִיָּה. נִשְׂכָּר הַלִּבְלָר שֵׁינִי.

Rebbi Abin in the name of Ḥizqiah: The second scribe earns money[47].

47 Even though the Mishnah stated that the woman is divorced if the bill reached the airspace of her property, the practice explained in Note 33 forces the parties to have a second document written since otherwise the woman could not remarry and, consequently, the husband could not escape his obligation to support her. {The corrector added a word: נשכר הלבלר שיני שנו "they taught that the second scribe earns money". The attempts of the classical commentators to replace שיני by שנו are most unconvincing.}

(49c line 30) אָמַר רִבִּי אֶלְעָזָר. מַתְנִוּיִין בְּגַג שֶׁיֵּשׁ לוֹ מַעֲקֶה וְהוּא שֶׁיָּרַד לָאֲוִיר מַעֲקֶה. וְשֶׁאֵין לוֹ מַעֲקֶה וְהוּא שֶׁיָּרַד לָאֲוִיר שְׁלֹשָׁה שֶׁהֵן סְמוּכִין לַגַּג. שֶׁכָּל־שְׁלֹשָׁה שֶׁהֵן סְמוּכִין לַגַּג כַּגַּג הֵן. רִבִּי יַעֲקֹב בַּר אָחָא רִבִּי בָּא בַּר הַמְנוּנָא בְּשֵׁם רַב אָדָא בַּר אֲחַוָה. לְעִנְייָן שַׁבָּת. שֶׁכָּל־שְׁלֹשָׁה שֶׁהֵן סְמוּכִין לִמְחִיצָה כִּמְחִיצָה הֵן. אָמַר רִבִּי יָסָא. דְּלָא דַמְיָא. גִּיטִּין מִלְמַעְלָן וְשַׁבָּת מִלְּמַטָּן. גִּיטִּין אֲפִילוּ לֹא נָח. שַׁבָּת עַד שֶׁיָּנוּחַ. רִבִּי אִמִּי בְּשֵׁם רִבִּי יוֹחָנָן. וְהוּא שֶׁיָּרַד לָאֲוִיר מְחִיצוֹת. רִבִּי אִימִּי בְּעָא קוֹמֵי רִבִּי יוֹחָנָן. מַתְנִיתָא דְרִבִּי. דְּרִבִּי עֲבַד מְחִיצָה כְּמַמָּשׁוֹ. אָמַר לֵיהּ. דְּבָרֵי הַכֹּל הִיא הָכָא דְגִיטִּין. וְיָתִיבִינֵיהּ. רִבִּי אוֹמֵר. מְקוּרָה. וְאַתְּ אוֹמֶרֶת. אֵינָהּ מְקוּרָה. מַה בֵּין גִּיטִּין וּמַה בֵּין שַׁבָּת. אָמַר רִבִּי

אַבָּא. בְּשַׁבָּת כְּתִיב לֹא תַעֲשֶׂה מְלָאכָה. נַעֲשֵׂית הִיא מֵאֵילֶיהָ. בְּרַם הָכָא וְנָתַן בְּיָדָהּ. בִּרְשׁוּתָהּ.

Rebbi Eleazar said, the Mishnah speaks of a roof with a parapet when it descended lower than the parapet[48], or one without a parapet when it descended lower than within three handbreadths of the roof, since anything within three handbreadths of the roof is as if it were part of the roof[49]. Rebbi Jacob bar Aḥa, Rebbi Abba bar Hamnuna in the name of Rav Ada bar Aḥawa: This refers to the rules of the Sabbath, where anything within three handbreadths of a partition is considered part of the partition[50]. Rebbi Yasa said, they are not comparable, for bills of divorce are about the top, the rules of the Sabbath about the below[51]. For bills of divorce even if it never came to rest[52], for the Sabbath only if it rested[53]. Rebbi Immi in the name of Rebbi Joḥanan: Only if it descended to within the partitions[54]. Rebbi Immi asked before Rebbi Joḥanan: Does the Mishnah follow Rebbi, since Rebbi considers partitions as solidly filled up[55]? He said to him, here in the matter of bills of divorce it is everybody's opinion[56]. Could one not object that Rebbi said, if it is roofed? And you say, it is not roofed?[57] What is the difference between bills of divorce and the Sabbath? Rebbi Abba said, about the Sabbath it is written: "You shall not do any work;" it may make itself automatically[58]. But here "he shall deliver into her hand," into her domain.

48   The Mishnah in which the bill of divorce is considered as delivered if it arrived at the wife's roof must consider a roof shielded from the wind by a parapet (which by biblical standard must be at least 10 handbreadths high; *Deut.* 22:8).

49   Any opening which is less than 3 handbreadths wide can be disregarded. [In the terminology of the Babli, this is called לָבוּד "glued (to the wall or the ground)", *Šabbat* 97a,

Erubin 16b.] This explanation is also quoted in *Erubin* 10 (26b l. 39).

50   It is forbidden on the Sabbath to move anything from a private (enclosed) domain to the public domain. The corresponding rules have nothing to do with property rights.

51   The bill of divorce is delivered as soon as it enters the roof space defined by the parapet from the top; the rules of "gluing" a hanging wall to the ground refer to the three handbreadths closest to the ground.

52   As the Mishnah explains, even if the bill was burned in a fire on the top, the delivery is valid.

53   In the rules of the Sabbath, moving an object has three stages: Lifting the object from a state of rest, transporting it from one domain to another, and depositing it (Mishnah *Šabbat* 1:1). If any of the three stages is missing, the biblical law was not violated. Therefore, if a document was moved from one domain to another (as from the husband's courtyard to the wife's roof) and burned while still flying, it was delivered as a bill of divorce but not moved by the laws of the Sabbath. (Cf. *Kilaim* 1:9, Note 188).

54   This refers to the last sentence in the Mishnah. If the husband throws the bill from his roof to her courtyard, it is possible to say that the bill was delivered the moment it cleared the roof only if the walls of the wife's courtyard are higher than the husband's roof. Otherwise it would be delivered only if the bill fell below the level of the courtyard walls. (The same argument is quoted in Samuel's name in the Babli, 79a.)

55   Rebbi considers it a violation of the Sabbath if the object was brought within the walls of the domain for which it was intended; he does not require it actually to come to rest (*Šabbat* 1:1 2c l. 63, 11:1 12c l. 59; Babli 4a, 5a, *Giṭṭin* 79a).

56 The Babli agrees, 79a, that the delivery of bills of divorce is governed by the rules of property rights, not those of the Sabbath.

57   This refers to Mishnah and Halakhah *Šabbat* 11:1: "If somebody throws an object from a private domain to the public domain or from the public domain to a private domain, he is guilty. From a private to a private domain across the public domain, R. Aqiba declares him guilty but the Sages declare him not prosecutable." It is then explained that throwing from the public to a private domain is prosecutable only if the object came to rest. On that it is noted that Rebbi

does not require it to come to rest (only to be received within the walls), but R. Abba bar Huna in the name of Rav said that "Rebbi did only find him guilty if the private domain was roofed." It is noted there that R. Johanan objected to the latter statement, which explains that no answer is given to the question raised.

58 As long as it was not intended that the object should come to rest by the force of the thrower (but it was moved along by some mechanical contraption not directly controlled by the thrower), no violation of the Sabbath occured. But for delivery of a bill of divorce, it is the fact of delivery rather than its mode which counts.

(fol. 49a) **משנה ד:** בֵּית שַׁמַּאי אוֹמְרִים פּוֹטֵר אָדָם אֶת אִשְׁתּוֹ בְּגֵט יָשָׁן וּבֵית הִלֵּל אוֹסְרִין. וְאֵי זֶהוּ גֵּט יָשָׁן כָּל שֶׁנִּתְיַיחֵד עִמָּהּ אַחַר שֶׁכְּתָבוֹ לָהּ.

Mishnah 4: The House of Shammai say, a man may send away his wife with an old bill of divorce, but the House of Hillel forbid it[59]. And what is an old bill of divorce? If he was again alone with her after he wrote it for her.

59 In Mishnah 9:11, the House of Shammai forbid divorce except for adultery (whether or not it is provable in court). Therefore, the House of Shammai can assume that the parties hate one another and will not sleep together. But the House of Hillel, who permit divorce for any (or no) reason, must be afraid that the wife could become pregnant after the bill was written and this would put her child in an untenable position. In any case, everybody agrees that the bill of divorce is valid in biblical law.

(49c line 41) **הלכה ד:** בֵּית שַׁמַּי אוֹמְרִים כול׳. רַב יְהוּדָה בְּשֵׁם שְׁמוּאֵל. וְכוּלָּן אִם נִשְׂאוּ לֹא תֵצֵא. שֶׁלֹּא לְהוֹצִיא לִיזָּה עַל בָּנֶיהָ.

Halakhah 4: "The House of Shammai say," etc. Rav Jehudah in the name of Samuel: And any one of them if she was married should not leave, in order not to cause talk about her children[60].

60 Since the bill of divorce is valid in biblical law, there is no reason to punish any woman who remarries based on such a bill. The court has no reason to force her to leave the new husband. The Babli, 79b, agrees and even notes that if the first husband is unavailable to give a corrected bill, the court will instruct the woman to remarry on the basis of the old bill.

(49c line 43) אָנָן תַּנִּינָן. מֵאַחַר שֶׁכְּתָבוֹ לָהּ. אִית תַּנָּיֵי תַנֵּי. מֵאַחַר שֶׁנְּתָנוֹ לָהּ. מָאן דְּאָמַר. מֵאַחַר שֶׁכְּתָבוֹ לָהּ. מְסַיֵּיעַ לְבֵית שַׁמַּי. מָאן דְּאָמַר. מֵאַחַר שֶׁנְּתָנוֹ לָהּ. מְסַיֵּיעַ לְבֵית הִלֵּל.

We stated: "After he wrote it for her." Some Tannaïm state "after he delivered it to her." He who says "after he delivered it to her" supports the House of Shammai[61]; he who says "after he wrote it for her" supports the House of Hillel[62].

61 This refers to the House of Shammai in Mishnah 11: "If a person divorced his wife and stayed with her in a hostelry, she does not need a second bill of divorce from him," since after a divorce for adultery we do not assume that the husband would sleep with his ex-wife.

62 They always expect a man and a woman to take any occasion to sleep together if they were once married.

(fol. 49a) **משנה ה**: כָּתַב לְשֵׁם מַלְכוּת שֶׁאֵינָהּ הוֹגֶנֶת לְשֵׁם מַלְכוּת מָדַי וּלְשֵׁם מַלְכוּת יָוָן לְבִנְיַין הַבַּיִת וּלְחוּרְבַּן הַבַּיִת. הָיָה בַּמִּזְרָח וְכָתַב בַּמַּעֲרָב בַּמַּעֲרָב

וְכָתַב בַּמִּזְרָח תֵּצֵא מִזֶּה וּמִזֶּה וּצְרִיכָה גֵּט מִזֶּה וּמִזֶּה. אֵין לָהּ לֹא כְתוּבָּה וְלֹא פֵּירוֹת וְלֹא מְזוֹנוֹת וְלֹא בְלָאוֹת עַל זֶה וְעַל זֶה וְאִם נָטְלָה מִזֶּה וּמִזֶּה תַּחֲזִיר וְהַוְּלָד מַמְזֵר מִזֶּה וּמִזֶּה. לֹא זֶה וְזֶה מִטַּמְּאִין לָהּ וְלֹא זֶה וְזֶה זַכָּאִין לֹא בִמְצִיאָתָהּ וְלֹא בְמַעֲשֵׂה יָדֶיהָ וְלֹא בַהֲפָרַת נְדָרֶיהָ. הָיְתָה בַת יִשְׂרָאֵל נִפְסְלָה מִן הַכְּהוּנָּה בַת לֵוִי מִן הַמַּעֲשֵׂר וּבַת כֹּהֵן מִן הַתְּרוּמָה. אֵין יוֹרְשָׁיו שֶׁלָּזֶה וְשֶׁלָּזֶה יוֹרְשִׁין כְּתוּבָּתָהּ. מֵתוּ אָחִיו שֶׁלָּזֶה וְאָחִיו שֶׁלָּזֶה חוֹלְצִין וְלֹא מְיַבְּמִין. שִׁינָּה שְׁמוֹ וּשְׁמָהּ שֵׁם עִירוֹ וְשֵׁם עִירָהּ תֵּצֵא מִזֶּה וּמִזֶּה וְכָל־הַדְּרָכִים הָאֵילוּ בָהּ.

Mishnah 5: If he wrote in the name of an inappropriate government[63], in the name of the government of Media[64] or the government of Greece[65], from the construction of the Temple or the destruction of the Temple[66]; if he was in the West and wrote "in the East" or in the East and wrote "in the West"[67], she needs a bill of divorce from both of them[68], she has neither *ketubah* nor usufruct nor used clothing from either of them, and if she took anything she must return it. Any child from either of the men is a bastard; neither of them may defile himself for her. Neither man has any claim on what she finds or earns, or on invalidation of her vows. If she was the daughter of an Israel, she is disabled from priesthood, the daughter of a Levite from tithe, the daughter of a Cohen from heave. The heirs of neither man inherit her *ketubah*. If they died, the brothers of both of them perform *ḥaliṣah* but not levirate. If he changed his or her name or the name of his or her city[69] she shall be divorced from both of them and all the indicated consequences apply to her.

63 If the document was dated by the regnal years of a king who did not rule over the place at which the bill was written.

64 The government of Media had ceased with Cyrus, many centuries earlier. An astronomer like Ptolemy could base his computations (during the reign of Antoninus Pius) on the era of the Assyrian king Nabonassar, but a

legal document had to refer to the years of the Princeps in Rome or the Parthian, later the Persian king in Babylonia.

65 Probably this refers to any one of the successors of Alexander.

66 This way of dating probably was proscribed by the Roman government.

67 If the place of writing the document was described incorrectly.

68 The situation of a woman remarrying based on an invalid bill of divorce is identical with that of a woman wrongly informed of the death of her husband who remarried based on that information; cf. Mishnah *Yebamot* 10:1, Notes 3-6.

69 As noted in the Halakhah, only this section of the Mishnah represents practice; it has given rise to an enormous literature dealing with the correct spelling of Jewish names of persons and places; cf. the Introductions to E. and H. Guggenheimer, *Jewish Family Names and Their Origins, An Etymological Dictionary*, Ktav Publishing 1992; *Etymologisches Lexikon der jüdischen Familiennamen*, K. G. Saur 1996.

(49c line 45) **הלכה ה:** כָּתַב לְשֵׁם מַלְכוּת שֶׁאֵינָהּ הוֹגֶנֶת. לְשֵׁם מַלְכוּת מָדַי כול׳.
רִבִּי יוֹחָנָן בְּשֵׁם רִבִּי יַנַּאי. עָשׂוּ אֶת הַוּוֹלָד מַמְזֵר מִפְּנֵי הַסַּכָּנָה. רַב הוּנָא בְּשֵׁם
רַב. כָּל־הָדָא פִּירְקָא דְּרִבִּי מֵאִיר. חוּץ מִשֵּׁינָה שְׁמוֹ וּשְׁמָהּ שֵׁם עִירוֹ וְשֵׁם עִירָהּ.
רִבִּי מָנָא בְּעָא קוֹמֵי רִבִּי יָסָא. אַף הַמְגָרֵשׁ. אָמַר לֵיהּ. לֵית פִּירְקָא דִידְכוֹן
אֶלָּא דִידָן.

Halakhah 5: "If he wrote in the name of an inappropriate government, in the name of the government of Media," etc. Rebbi Joḥanan in the name of Rebbi Yannai: They declared the child a bastard because of the danger[70]. Rav Huna in the name of Rav: This entire Chapter is Rebbi Meïr's[71] except for "if he changed his or her name or the name of his or her city." Rebbi Mana asked before Rebbi Yasa: Also "if somebody divorced his wife"[72]? He said to him, not your Chapter but our Chapter[73].

70   There is no biblical reason why a bill of divorce should be invalid as long as it is possible to identify its date. The only reason that people are made afraid of the consequences of incorrect dating is to avoid repressive measures by the Roman government. The Babli agrees, 80a.

71   None of the rules which require a double divorce are practice except that which forbids changing the names of the parties or their places of residence. The Babli agrees implicitly by labelling the rules as R. Meïr's.

72   The following Chapter 9.

73   Only the rules in Chapter 8 which require a double divorce.

משנה ו: כָּל־הָעֲרָיוֹת שֶׁאָמְרוּ צָרוֹתֵיהֶן מוּתָּרוֹת הָלְכוּ הַצָּרוֹת הָאֵילוּ וְנִישְׂאוּ וְנִמְצְאוּ אֵילוּ אַיְלוֹנִיּוֹת תֵּצֵא מִזֶּה וּמִזֶּה וְכָל־הַדְּרָכִים הָאֵילוּ בָּהּ. (fol. 49b)

Mishnah 6: Referring to all the close relatives about whom they said that their co-wives are permitted, if any of the co-wives went and married otherwise but the relatives turned out to be she-rams, she shall be divorced from both of them and all the aforementioned consequences apply to her[74].

משנה ז: הַכּוֹנֵס אֶת יְבִמְתּוֹ וְהָלְכָה צָרָתָהּ וְנִישֵּׂאת לְאַחֵר וְנִמְצְאָה זֹאת שֶׁהִיא אַיְלוֹנִית תֵּצֵא מִזֶּה וּמִזֶּה וְכָל־הַדְּרָכִים הָאֵילוּ בָּהּ.

Mishnah 7: If somebody married his sister-in-law while her co-wife went and married somebody else, if the sister-in-law turns out to be a she-ram, the co-wife shall be divorced from both of them and all the aforementioned consequences apply to her[74].

74   A "she-ram" is an infertile woman lacking secondary sex characteristics. Her marriage is considered non-existent by biblical standards. It is the basic tenet of the House of Hillel that if a man dies

without issue and any of his wives is forbidden to any of his brothers, all of his wives are forbidden to all the brothers and are free to marry outside the family without further ceremony (cf. Mishnah *Yebamot* 1:1). If the relative turns out to be a she-ram, who cannot be married, the release of the other wives turns out to have been erroneous and their new marriages incestuous for those who hold that the outside marriage of a candidate for levirate marriage is incestuous (which is an opinion of R. Aqiba rejected by his successors.)

(49c line 50) **הלכה ז:** הַכּוֹנֵס אֶת יְבִמְתּוֹ כול׳. לֹא הָיְתָה צְרִיכָה לְהִינָּשֵׂא אֶלָּא לְהִתְיַיבֵּם. וְזוֹ הִיא יְבָמָה שֶׁנִּיסֵּית בְּלֹא חֲלִיצָה. רִבִּי יִרְמְיָה אָמַר. זֶה חוֹלֵץ וְזֶה מְקַיֵּים. רִבִּי יְהוּדָה בֶּן פָּזִי בְשֵׁם רִבִּי יוֹחָנָן. תֵּצֵא. רִבִּי יוֹסֵי שָׁאַל לְרִבִּי פִּינְחָס. הֵיךְ רִבִּי סָבַר. אָמַר לֵיהּ. כְּרִבִּי יִרְמְיָה. אָמַר לֵיהּ. חֲזוֹר בָּךְ. דְּלָא כֵן אֲנִי כוֹתֵב עָלָךְ זָקֵן מַמְרֵא. אָמַר רִבִּי זְבִידָא. מַתְנִיתָא מְסַייְעָא לְרִבִּי יוֹחָנָן. תֵּצֵא מִזֶּה וּמִזֶּה וּשְׁלֹשָׁה עָשָׂר דְּבָרִים בָּהּ. כְּדִבְרֵי רִבִּי מֵאִיר שֶׁאָמַר מִשּׁוּם רִבִּי עֲקִיבָה. וַחֲכָמִים אוֹמְרִים. אֵין מַמְזֵר מִיְּבָמָה. הָא לָצֵאת תֵּצֵא.

2 וזו היא יבמה שניסית | י והוא יבמה שניששאת   3 יהודה בן פזי | י יודה בר פזי   - | י ר׳ יוסי בשם ר׳ הילא. תצא   שאל | י שאיל   4 ר׳ סבר | י סבר ר׳   5 עלך | י עליך   7 עקיבה | י עקיבה רבו   מיבמה | י ביבמה. | י ביבמה. לא אמר אלא אין ממזר מיבמה.

Halakhah 7: "If somebody married his sister-in-law," etc. [75]If she should not have married but entered levirate, this is the case of a sister-in-law who married without *ḥaliṣah*. Rebbi Jeremiah said, this man performs *ḥaliṣah*, the other one keeps her. Rebbi Jehudah ben Pazi in the name of Rebbi Joḥanan: She must leave. Rebbi Yose asked Rebbi Phineas, how does the rabbi hold? He said, with Rebbi Jeremiah. He said to him, change your mind, for otherwise I shall publicly call you a rebellious Elder. Rebbi Zevidah said, a *baraita* supports Rebbi Joḥanan: "She must leave both of them and the thirteen items apply to her, following Rebbi Meïr who said it in the name of Rebbi Aqibah. But the Sages say, there is no bastard from a sister-in-law." Therefore she must leave.

75   This text is *Yebamot* 10:5, Notes 116-121.

(fol. 49b) **משנה ח:** כָּתַב הַסּוֹפֵר וְטָעָה וְנָתַן גֵּט לָאִשָּׁה וְשׁוֹבָר לָאִישׁ וְנָתְנוּ זֶה לָזֶה וּלְאַחַר הַזְּמַן הֲרֵי הַגֵּט יוֹצֵא מִיַּד הָאִישׁ וְהַשּׁוֹבָר מִיַּד הָאִשָּׁה תֵּצֵא מִזֶּה וּמִזֶּה וְכָל־הַדְּרָכִים הָאֵילוּ בָהּ.

Mishnah 8: If the scribe wrote[76] and then in error handed the bill of divorce to the woman and the receipt to the man and they exchanged them, then later the bill of divorce is found with the man and the receipt with the woman[77], she shall be divorced from both of them and all the indicated consequences apply to her.

משנה ט: רִבִּי אֱלִיעֶזֶר אוֹמֵר אִם לְאַלְתָּר יָצָא אֵין זֶה גֵט אִם לְאַחַר זְמָן יָצָא הֲרֵי זֶה גֵט. שֶׁלֹּא הַכֹּל מִן הָרִאשׁוֹן לְאַבֵּד זְכוּתוֹ שֶׁלַּשֵּׁנִי.

Mishnah 9: Rebbi Eliezer[78] says: If it was found out immediately, this is no bill of divorce. If it was found out later[79], it is a bill of divorce since the first cannot destroy the rights of the second.

76   In the Babylonian sources more in detail: "If the scribe wrote a bill of divorce for the husband and a receipt for the wife and then ..." The husband has the money ready to pay the *ketubah* immediately and the wife will hand him the receipt if she obtains the money with the bill of divorce.

77   Who had remarried in the meantime, thinking that she was divorced when in fact she was not divorced since she handed the bill of

divorce to her husband instead of receiving it from him. One has to assume that both husband and wife were illiterate.

78 Mishnah and Babli sources are divided on whether to read Eliezer or Eleazar; the Halakhah later reads "Eleazar".

79 After the wife had remarried one suspects the first husband to have obtained the bill of divorce illegally to cause trouble.

(49c line 57) **הלכה ח:** כָּתַב הַסּוֹפֵר וְטָעָה כול׳. מָה אֲנָן קַיָּימִין. אִם בְּשֶׁטָּעָה. אַף רִבִּי לְעָזָר מוֹדֶה. עִם בְּשֶׁלֹּא טָעָה. אוֹף רַבָּנָן מוֹדֵיי. אֶלָּא כֵן אֲנָן קַיָּימִין בִּסְתָם. רִבִּי אֶלְעָזָר חָשַׁשׁ שֶׁמָּא לֹא טָעָה. וְרַבָּנָן חוֹשְׁשִׁין שֶׁמָּא טָעָה.

Halakhah 8: "If the scribe wrote," etc. Where do we hold? If he made a mistake, even Rebbi Eleazar agrees[80]. If he made no error, even the rabbis agree[81]. But we must hold that it was unexplained[82]. Rebbi Eleazar suspects that possibly he made no mistake; the rabbis suspect that possibly he did make a mistake.

80 The scribe agrees that he made a mistake, R. Eleazar agrees that no divorce took place.

81 If the scribe denies making a mistake, the rabbis also have to assume that the bill of divorce in the hand of the first husband is fraudulent.

82 The scribe does not remember or is not available to be asked.

(49c line 60) רִבִּי אֶלְעָזָר אוֹמֵר אִם עַל אֲתָר יָצָא אֵינוֹ גֵט. וְאִם לְאַחַר זְמָן יָצָא הֲרֵי זֶה גֵט. שֶׁלֹּא הַכֹּל מִן הָרִאשׁוֹן לְאַבֵּד זְכוּת שֶׁל שֵׁינִי. אֵיזֶהוּ עַל אֲתָר. רִבִּי זְעִירָא אוֹמֵר. עַד שֶׁלֹּא נִתְאָרְסָה וְנִתְאָרְסָה. רִבִּי יִצְחָק בֶּן חֲקוּלָה אָמַר. עַד שֶׁלֹּא נִיסֵּית וְנִיסֵּית. מַתְנִיתָא מְסַייְעָא לְרִבִּי זְעִירָא. לֹא הַכֹּל מִן הָרִאשׁוֹן לְאַבֵּד זְכוּתוֹ מִן הַשֵּׁינִי.

"Rebbi Eleazar says: If it was found out immediately, this is no bill of divorce. If it was found out later, it is a bill of divorce since the first cannot destroy the rights of the second." What is immediately? Rebbi Ze'ira says, before she was preliminarily married, or when she was preliminarily married. Rebbi Isaac ben Ḥaqula said, before she was definitively married, or when she was definitively married[82]. The Mishnah supports Rebbi Ze'ira: "Since the first cannot destroy the rights of the second[83]."

82 The Babli, 80b, considers only this possibility in addition to the obvious interpretation that "immediately" means while they are still in the process of settling the monetary claims arising from the divorce.

83 The second husband acquires his rights to the bride by the preliminary marriage.

משנה י: כָּתַב לְגָרֵשׁ אֶת אִשְׁתּוֹ וְנִמְלַךְ בֵּית שַׁמַּאי אוֹמְרִים פְּסָלָהּ מִן הַכְּהוּנָּה. וּבֵית הִלֵּל אוֹמְרִים אַף עַל פִּי שֶׁנְּתָנוֹ לָהּ עַל תְּנַאי וְלֹא נַעֲשָׂה הַתְּנַאי לֹא פְּסָלָהּ מִן הַכְּהוּנָּה. (fol. 49b)

Mishnah 10: If he wrote a bill to divorce his wife and then changed his mind, the House of Shammai say, he disabled her from the priesthood[84]. But the House of Hillel say, even if he handed her [the bill of divorce] and attached a condition, if the condition was not satisfied he did not disable her from the priesthood[85].

84 A priest is forbidden to marry a divorcee (*Lev.* 21:7). The House of Shammai forbid a woman to her priestly husband if the bill of divorce was written, even if it never was delivered.

85 As long as the divorce was not effective, the priestly husband can take his wife back.

(49c line 65) **הלכה י:** כָּתַב לְגָרֵשׁ אֶת אִשְׁתּוֹ וְנִמְלַךְ כול'. רִבִּי יוֹחָנָן בְּשֵׁם רִבִּי יַנַּאי. אֵין בָּהּ מִשּׁוּם יִיחוּס כְּהוּנָה וְאֵין בֵּית דִּין מְזַחֲמִין אוֹתָהּ. אָתָא עוֹבְדָא קוֹמֵי רִבִּי חִיָּיה רוֹבָה וַעֲבַד כְּבֵית הִלֵּל. אָמַר לֵיהּ רַב. מָה רָאִיתָ לְהַכְנִיס עַצְמְךָ לְמִיסְפֵּק הַזֶּה הַמְרוּבָּה. אָמַר לֵיהּ. רִבִּי יִשְׁמָעֵאל בֵּירִבִּי יוֹסֵי הֲוָה עִמִּי וְקָרָא עֲלֵיהוֹן טוֹבִים הַשְּׁנַיִם מִן הָאֶחָד.

Halakhah 10: "If he wrote a bill to divorce his wife and then changed his mind," etc. Rebbi Johanan in the name of Rebbi Yannai: There is no problem because of the purity of the priestly line and the court will not denigrate her[86]. There came a case before the Elder Rebbi Hiyya and he acted following the House of Hillel. Rav asked him, why did you bring yourself into this great doubt? He answered, Rebbi Ismael ben Rebbi Yose[87] was with me. He quoted about them: "Two are better than one.[88]"

86 If a woman became a widow who had been given a bill of divorce but who was not divorced because the condition attached to the divorce was not fulfilled, the court will not intervene if she marries a Cohen.

87 The greatest authority of his time.

88 Eccl. 4:9.

(49c line 70) הַמְסַלֶּדֶת בִּבְנָהּ. בֵּית שַׁמַּי פּוֹסְלִין וּבֵית הִלֵּל מַכְשִׁירִין. שְׁתֵּי נָשִׁים שֶׁהָיוּ מְסַלְּדוֹת זוֹ אֶת זוֹ. בֵּית שַׁמַּי פּוֹסְלִין וּבֵית הִלֵּל מַכְשִׁירִין.

"A woman who engages in sex play[89] with her son, the House of Shammai disqualify, the House of Hillel qualify." Two women who mutually engage in sex play, the House of Shammai disqualify, the House of Hillel qualify[90].

89 This meaning of the root סלד (usually "to jump") is conjectural, similar to the corresponding root סלל (Biblical "to build a road") in the Babylonian parallels [Šabbat 65a, Yebamot 76a, Sanhedrin 69b; Tosephta

Soṭah 5:7 (ms. Erfurt סלסל "to adorn")]. The text is more explicit in Tosephta *Soṭah* 5:7 (Vienna ms.): "If a woman engages in sex play with her son who touches her genitals, the House of Shammai disqualify from the priesthood, the House of Hillel qualify." The son must be less than 9 years of age for his sex play to be dismissed as meaningless (cf. *Yebamot* 10:13-14). {Also compare the Latin verb *salio, -ui*, "to jump; leap, cover", also said of copulation of animals (E. G.).}

90 In the Babli, *Yebamot* 76a, the opinion that lesbian activity disqualifies a woman from marrying a priest is dismissed as not conforming to 1 practice; lesbian activity is classified as "simply indecent". Maimonides (*Issure Bi'ah* 21:8-9) duly notes that lesbian activity cannot qualify as sexual but then based on a aggadic statement in *Sifra* (*Aḥare Parašah* 9(8)), which defines "the acts of Egypt" (*Lev.* 18:3) as same-sex marriages and polyandry, authorizes rabbinic punishment for lesbian activities, which is nowhere to be found in Talmudic sources. This is copied in *Šulḥan 'Arukh Even Ha'ezer* 20:2. These rules probably owe more to Islamic and Christian influences (*Romans* 1:26) than to strictly Rabbinic rules.

(fol. 49b) **משנה יא:** הַמְגָרֵשׁ אֶת אִשְׁתּוֹ וְלָנָה עִמּוֹ בְּפוּנְדָּקֵי בֵּית שַׁמַּאי אוֹמְרִים אֵינָהּ צְרִיכָה מִמֶּנּוּ גֵט שֵׁנִי וּבֵית הִלֵּל אוֹמְרִים צְרִיכָה הֵימֶנּוּ גֵט שֵׁנִי. אֵימָתַי בִּזְמַן שֶׁנִּתְגָּרְשָׁה מִן הַנִּישׂוּאִין. וּמוֹדִין בְּנִתְגָּרְשָׁה מִן הָאֵירוּסִין שֶׁאֵינָהּ צְרִיכָה מִמֶּנּוּ גֵט שֵׁנִי מִפְּנֵי שֶׁאֵין לִבּוֹ גַּס בָּהּ. כְּנָסָהּ בְּגֵט קֵרֵחַ תֵּצֵא מִזֶּה וּמִזֶּה וְכָל הַדְּרָכִים הָאֵילוּ בָהּ.

Mishnah 11: If somebody divorced his wife but she stayed with him in a hostelry[91], the House of Shammai say that she does not need a second bill of divorce from him, but the House of Hillel say that she needs a second bill of divorce from him[92]. When? If she was divorced after definitive marriage. But they agree that if she was divorced after preliminary marriage, she does not need a second bill of divorce from him since he was not intimate with her[93]. If somebody married her based on a bald bill of divorce[94], she shall be divorced from both of them and all the indicated consequences apply to her.

91 Greek πανδοκεῖον.
92 The reasons are explained in Note 59.
93 They will not sleep with one another as a matter of course.
94 A "bald" document is an irregular "knotted" document. In a usual, "simple" document, the witnesses sign on the document after the text. In a "knotted" document, the scribe will write a few lines, then these are folded, sewn together, fixed with a knot, and a witness signs on the verso. The document is valid if the number of ties equals the number of witnesses on the verso. A "bald" document has less witnesses than ties and is invalid. A woman who remarries on the basis of an invalid bill of divorce commits adultery. The rules of "knotted" documents are discussed in Halakhah 12.

(49c line 72) **הלכה יא:** הַמְגָרֵשׁ אֶת אִשְׁתּוֹ וְלָנָה עִמּוֹ כול'. אָמַר רִבִּי מָנָא. בֵּית שַׁמַּי כְּדַעְתְּהוֹן וּבֵית הֵלֵּל כְּדַעְתְּהוֹן. בֵּית שַׁמַּי דְּאִינּוּן אָמְרִין. פּוֹטֵר אָדָם אֶת אִשְׁתּוֹ בְּגֵט יָשָׁן. אִינּוּן אִינּוּן דְּאָמְרִין. אֵינָהּ צְרִיכָה מִמֶּנּוּ גֵט שֵׁנִי. אָמַר רִבִּי יוֹסֵי בַּר בּוּן. בֵּית שַׁמַּי כְּדַעְתְּהוֹן וּבֵית הֵלֵּל כְּדַעְתְּהוֹן. בֵּית שַׁמַּי דְּאִינּוּן אָמְרִין. לֹא יְגָרֵשׁ אָדָם אֶת אִשְׁתּוֹ אֶלָּא אִם כֵּן מָצָא בָהּ עֶרְוָה אִינּוּן דְּאָמְרִין. מְזוֹהֶמֶת הִיא מִלְּפָנָיו וְאֵינוֹ חָשׁוּד עָלֶיהָ. לְפִיכָךְ אֵינָהּ צְרִיכָה מִמֶּנּוּ גֵט שֵׁנִי. בֵּית הֵלֵּל דְּאִינּוּן אָמְרִין. אֲפִילוּ הִקְדִיחָה תַבְשִׁילוֹ. אִינּוּן אִינּוּן דְּאָמְרִין. אֵינָהּ מְזוֹהֶמֶת מִלְּפָנָיו וְהוּא חָשׁוּד עָלֶיהָ. לְפִיכָךְ צְרִיכָה מִמֶּנּוּ גֵּט שֵׁנִי.

Halakhah 11: "If somebody divorced his wife but she stayed with him," etc. Rebbi Mana said, the House of Shammai are consistent and the House of Hillel are consistent. Since the House of Shammai say that "a man may send away his wife with an old bill of divorce," they say that she does not need a second bill of divorce from him. Rebbi Yose ben Rebbi Abun said, the House of Shammai are consistent and the House of Hillel are consistent. Since the House of Shammai say that "a man shall not divorce his wife unless he found in her a matter of immorality[95]," thy say that she is dirty in his eyes and he is not suspected of having relations with her, therefore she does not need a second bill of divorce from him.. Since the House of Hillel say, "even if she spoiled his food[95]", they say that she is not dirty in his eyes, he is suspected of having relations with her, and she needs a second bill of divorce from him[59,96].

95 Mishnah 9:11.
96 Babylonian sources (Babli 81b, Tosephta 6:9) hold that the House of Hillel require a second bill of divorce only if it was known that the divorced couple shared a bedroom in the hotel. This is not the position of the Yerushalmi.

(49d line 5) הַמְגָרֵשׁ אֶת אִשְׁתּוֹ לֹא תָדוּר עִמּוֹ לֹא בְאוֹתָהּ חָצֵר וְלֹא בְאוֹתוֹ מָקוֹם. אִם הָיְתָה חָצֵר שֶׁלְאִשָּׁה הָאִישׁ מְפַנֶּה. וְשֶׁלְאִישׁ אִשָּׁה מְפַנָּה. שֶׁלִשְׁנֵיהֶן מִי מְפַנֶּה מִפְּנֵי מִי. אִשָּׁה מִפְּנֵי אִישׁ. וְאִם יְכוֹלִין הֵן זֶה פּוֹתֵחַ לְכָאן וְזֶה פּוֹתֵחַ לְכָאן. בַּמֶּה דְבָרִים אֲמוּרִים. בִּזְמַן שֶׁנִּשְּׂאוּ. הָא לֹא נִישְׂאוּ לֹא. וּבְכוֹהֶנֶת אֲפִילוּ לֹא נִישְׂאוּ. וְהָאֲרוּסָה שֶׁבִּיהוּדָה כִּנְשׂוּאָה הִיא. הַחוֹלֵץ לִיבִמְתּוֹ אַף עַל פִּי שֶׁעָשָׂה מַאֲמָר הֲרֵי זֶה לֹא יְפַנֶּה. שֶׁאֵין מַאֲמָר קוֹנֶה קִנְיָן גָּמוּר.

[97]If somebody divorces his wife she should not live in the same courtyard or the same place[98]. If the courtyard was the wife's property, the husband has to move out, if the husband's, the wife has to move out. If it was common property, who has to move because of whom? The woman because of the man, unless they can manage to have separate exits[99]. When has this been said? If they were definitively married, not if

they were not definitively married[100]. But the wife of a Cohen if she was not definitively married[101], as well as the status of a preliminarily married woman in Jehudah[102], is that of one definitively married. Nobody has to move if a person gives *halîṣah* to his sister-in-law even if he had "bespoken[103]" her since "bespeaking" does not fully acquire.

97 A similar text is in *Semaḥot* 2:14, a different formulation is in the Babli (*Ketubot* 27b/28a).

98 *Or zarua'* (*Yibbum waḥalîṣah* #618) reads מבוי "dead-end-street" in place of מקום. This is the language of the Babli.

99 In the interpretation of *Or zarua'*, if they can build a wall dividing the property, each section having its own entrance door from the courtyard.

100 Preliminarily married couples are not supposed to have slept together; they are not suspected to do so after divorce.

101 Since she is biblically prohibited to her preliminary ex-husband.

102 She was unchaperoned together with her preliminary husband and presumed to have slept with him; Mishnah *Ketubot* 1:5.

103 The imitation of preliminary marriage before levirate marriage; cf. Mishnah *Yebamot* 2:1, Note 6. This is a rabbinic formality; if the couple had relations, they would be biblically married and the marriage could only be terminated by a bill of divorce. The act of *halîṣah* guarantees that they never were intimate and the precautions enacted for divorced couples do not apply to them.

(fol. 49b) **משנה יב:** גֵּט קֵרֵחַ הַכֹּל מַשְׁלִימִים עָלָיו כְּדִבְרֵי בֶּן נַנָּס. רַבִּי עֲקִיבָה אוֹמֵר אֵין מַשְׁלִימִין עָלָיו אֶלָּא קְרוֹבִים הָרְאוּיִין לְהָעִיד בְּמָקוֹם אַחֵר. אֵי זֶהוּ גֵּט קֵרֵחַ. כָּל־שֶׁקְּשָׁרָיו מְרוּבִּין מֵעֵידָיו.

Mishnah 12: Anybody can supplement a bald document[104] following the words of Ben Nanas[105]. Rebbi Aqiba says, one supplements the signatures only by relatives who would be able to testify under other circumstances[106]. What is a bald document? One whose knots are more than its signatures.

104 I.e., supply the additional signatures needed to make the document valid.

105 If the first signatures are those of valid witnesses, the remaining slots can be filled by the signatures of people who are inadmissible as witnesses either because they are relatives of one of the parties or because they have been declared untrustworthy by a court decree (Mishnah *Sanhedrin* 3:3-4).

106 He agrees that relatives can sign but he holds that people barred because of disreputable or criminal behavior cannot.

(49d line 12) **הלכה יב:** גֵּט קֵרֵחַ הַכֹּל מַשְׁלִימִין עָלָיו כול׳. וּמְנַיִין לְגֵט הַמְקוּשָּׁר. אָמַר רִבִּי אִימִּי. כְּתִיב וָאֶקַּח אֶת סֵפֶר וגו׳. וְאֶת זֶה הַמְקוּשָּׁר. וְאֶת הַגָּלוּי. זֶה הַפָּשׁוּט שֶׁבַּמְקוּשָּׁר. וְאֶת הַמִּצְוָה וְאֶת הַחוּקִּים. חוּקִּים וּמִצְוֹת בֵּין זֶה לָזֶה. שֶׁזֶּה בִשְׁנַיִם וְזֶה בִשְׁלֹשָׁה. זֶה מִתּוֹכוֹ וְזֶה מֵאַחוֹרָיו. רִבִּי בָּא בְשֵׁם רַב יְהוּדָה. פָּשׁוּט עֵדָיו לְרוֹחְבּוֹ. מְקוּשָּׁר עֵידָיו לְאוֹרְכּוֹ. אָמַר רִבִּי אִידִי. בֵּין קֶשֶׁר לְקֶשֶׁר הָעֵדִים חוֹתְמִין וּבִלְבַד מִלְּמַעֲלָן. וְחָשׁ לוֹמַר שֶׁמָּא סִייֵּף. סָבַר רַב נַחְמָן לְמֵימַר. לְעוֹלָם אֵין הָעֵדִים חוֹתְמִין בּוֹ מִלְּמַטָּן עַד שֶׁיִּקְרְאוּ בוֹ לְמַעֲלָן. אֲנִי פְלוֹנִי בֶּן פְלוֹנִי מְקַבֵּל עָלַי כָּל־מַה שֶׁכָּתוּב בּוֹ מִלְּמַעֲלָן. וְחָשׁ לוֹמַר שֶׁמָּא מָחַק וְחָזַר וְזִייֵּף. סָבַר רַב הוּנָא. מְקוּבָּל עָלַי מְקוּבָּל עָלַי שְׁנֵי פְעָמִים פּוֹסֵל בָּהּ. חָשׁ לוֹמַר שֶׁמָּא כָּתַב דְּבָרִים אֲחֵרִים וְחָזַר וּמָחַק וְזִייֵּף. סָבַר רַב הוּנָא. מָחַק פָּסוּל אֲפִילוּ קַייָם.

Halakhah 12: "Anybody can supplement a bald document," etc. [107]From where that a document can be knotted[108]? Rebbi Immi said, it is written: "I took the document,[109]" etc. "And [the sealed]", that is the knotted [document]. "And the open," that is the simple, part of the knotted[110]. "And the orders and the rules"; orders and rules differ between these, for one is with two [witnesses], the other with three[111]; one in it, the other on its back[112]. Rebbi Abba in the name of Rav Jehudah, on a simple document, the witnesses sign parallel[113], on a knotted one the witnesses sign lengthwise[114]. Rebbi Idi said, the witnesses sign between any two knots, but it must be on top[115]. But should one not be afraid that maybe he falsifies[116]? Rav Naḥman[117] wanted to argue that witnesses never sign below unless they first read before them: "I X son of Y accept everything written above." But should one not be afraid that he erased and changed to falsify? Rav Huna is of the opinion that two times "I accept" makes it invalid[118]. But should one not be afraid that he erased and changed to falsify? Does Rav Huna not consider that he might write another text, erase and change to falsify? Rav Huna is of the opinion that an erasure makes invalid even if the correction is certified[119].

107 A closely related text, but from another editorial tradition, is in *Baba batra* 10:1.

108 The basic use for "knotted" documents was for real estate transactions, probably to hide the financial data from public knowledge. Such a document was certainly impossible in Egypt, where all real estate transactions had to be filed with the State registrar. Its validity in rabbinic tradition is given a biblical basis. It seems from the discussion in Babli *Baba batra* 10 that the use of "knotted" documents was a Palestinian peculiarity (such documents have been found in the Judean desert.)

109 *Jer.* 32:11: "I took the document of acquisition, the sealed one, the orders and rules, and the public one." The verse clearly states that a sealed document is the main object, accompanied by a public document.

110 The text of the document, whose formulation is identical whether sealed or public.

111 A public document needs two witnesses, a sealed (knotted) one at least three.

112 A public document is signed by the witnesses on the recto of the sheet, starting exactly one line after the end

of the text. A sealed document is signed on the verso, between the folds. (According to Rashi (Commentary to *Baba batra* 10:1), the document was written with wide spaces between the lines, was signed by witnesses between the lines, and then was folded and sewn so that the document text was hidden but the signatures appeared on the outside. It seems impossible to accept this explanation for the Yerushalmi text. (Cf. H. Albeck's commentary to *Baba batra* 10:1).)

113 They simply sign on the lines after the body of the document, parallel to the lines used by the scribe.

114 In this opinion, the witnesses sign in the back at a right angle to the scribe's text, starting in the back of the last line of the document. Only the text covered by witnesses' signatures in the back is certified.

115 He disagrees with the preceding description and requires that the witnesses sign in the back parallel to the text written by the scribe, as described in Note 94.

116 How can the witnesses be sure that the writer of the document will not falsify the document after they affixed their signatures? For a public document there is no problem since anything following the signatures has to be disregarded. For a sealed document with signatures at a right angle there is no problem since any text not covered by the signatures at the back has to be disregarded. But if the signatures are affixed while the document is being written, where are the guarantees?

117 In *Baba batra*: Rav Huna. This seems to be the correct attribution, confirmed in the sequel.

118 A sealed document containing two different clauses of acceptation is considered fraudulent and not enforceable in court.

119 An erasure in a sealed document is unacceptable even if confirmed as such by signatures. In the Babli, *Baba batra* 161b, R. Johanan accepts an erasure in a sealed document if it carries a note: "This is a correction".

(49d line 23) אָמַר רִבִּי יוֹחָנָן. לֵית בָּהּ תֵּצֵא. אָמַר רִבִּי אִימִּי. כַּמָּה קוּפִין דְּעוֹבְדָא הֲוָה עָלִיל קוֹמֵי רִבִּי יוֹחָנָן וְקוֹמֵי רֵישׁ לָקִישׁ וְאִינּוּן אָמְרִין. פּוּק וְשַׁלֵּם כְּרִבִּי עֲקִיבָה.

Rebbi Joḥanan said: There is no "she shall be divorced". Rebbi Immi said, several boxes of cases came before Rebbi Joḥanan and Rebbi Simeon ben Laqish and they said, go and complete following Rebbi Aqiba[120].

120 They disagree with the last statement in Mishnah 11 and permit the belated signing by relatives who otherwise are in good standing.

(49d line 25) אָמַר רִבִּי יוֹחָנָן. מַתְנִיתָא בִּמְחוּסָר עֵד אֶחָד וּבִלְבַד מִשְּׁלֹשָׁה וּלְמַעֲלָן. שְׁנַיִם וּשְׁלֹשָׁה לְמַעֲלָן פָּסוּל. וְאֶחָד מִשְּׁלֹשָׁה וּלְמַטָּה כָּשֵׁר. רִבִּי מָנָא בָּעֵי. עַד כְּדוֹן בִּרְצוּפִין. הָיוּ מְסוּרָגִין. כַּיי דָמַר. נַעֲשִׂין כְּמַרְחֶק עֵדוּת. שֶׁלֹא בָאוּ אֶלָּא בְּהֶכְשֵׁירוֹ שֶׁלַּגֵּט. וְכָא כָאן. הָיוּ תִשְׁעָה. מַתִּיר שְׁנַיִם וּמְחַתֵּם שְׁנָיִם. אוֹ אֵין שְׁנֵי הָעֵדִים בְּגֵט הַמְקוּשָּׁר כְּלוּם. הָיוּ חֲמִשָּׁה. פְּשִׁיטָה שֶׁהוּא מַתִּיר אֶחָד וּמְחַתֵּם אֶחָד. נִמְצֵאתָ אוֹמֵר. הַתָּרָתוֹ מַתִּירָתוֹ. וּכְרִבִּי חֲנַנְיָה בֶּן גַּמְלִיאֵל. דְּרִבִּי חֲנַנְיָה בֶּן גַּמְלִיאֵל אוֹמֵר. הַתּוֹרֵף כָּשֵׁר. שֶׁאֲפִילוּ קוֹשֵׁר וְאַחַר כָּךְ חוֹתֵם. הָדָא דְתֵימַר בְּשֶׁקוֹשֵׁר כּוּלְּהֶם וְאַחַר כָּךְ חָתְמוּ שְׁלֹשָׁה הָרִאשׁוֹנִים. אֲבָל אִם קוֹשֵׁר שְׁלֹשָׁה הָרִאשׁוֹנִים וְחוֹתֵם אֲפִילוּ מְקַשֵּׁר וּמְחַתֵּם כַּמָּה כָּשֵׁר. הִילְכְתָא. גֵּט הַמְקוּשָּׁר בְּקֶשֶׁר וְאַחַר כָּךְ מְחַתֵּם. הָיָה מְקַשֵּׁר רִאשׁוֹן רִאשׁוֹן וּמְחַתְּמָן. פְּשִׁיטָה רִאשׁוֹן וְשֵׁינִי לֹא נִמְצְאוּ חֲתוּמִין בְּגֵט הַמְקוּשָּׁר.

Rebbi Joḥanan said, the Mishnah applies if one witness is missing, but only if there are three or more[121]. Two or three[122] at the beginning is invalid, one below the three is valid. Rebbi Mana asked: That is, if they are continuous. If they are with interruptions[123]? As one says, they are considered like testimony at a distance, they only serve to certify the testimony. And so it is here[124]. If there were nine, can he untie two and have two sign? Or are two witnesses on a knotted document nothing[125]? If there were five, it is obvious that he unties one and has it signed[126]. It turns out that his untying permits it following Rebbi Ḥananiah ben

Gamliel, for Rebbi Ḥananiah ben Gamliel says, the essential part is what validates[127], even if he ties and signs after that. That is, if he ties all knots and after that the first three [witnesses] did sign. But if he tied the first three[128] and had them signed, even if he makes many ties and lets many[129] sign it is valid. Practice is that a knotted document is first knotted and then signed. If he made the first knots and had them signed right away, it is obvious that the first two did not sign the knotted document[130].

121 This disagreement between ben Nanas and R. Aqiba about the required qualifications of the witnesses refers to the case that only one additional signature is required in addition to the three statutory ones.

122 Any number of irregular witnesses at the beginning is invalid for everybody.

123 If the three statutory witnesses did not sign together but each one signed for a separate knot, with space in between.

124 Cf. Chapter 1, Note 117.

125 The text is difficult to understand since a document with 9 knots needs an additional 6 signatures. One must assume that some additional signatures already are on the document and the question is directed against R. Joḥanan: Why should it not be possible to let two unqualified witnesses sign since the validation of a knotted document needs three witnesses in any case (Mishnah *Baba batra* 10:3).

126 In fact, there must be two knots untied and confirmed on the verso by two different signatures; only one of them was accepted by R. Joḥanan.

127 Cf. Chapter 3, Note 68. If the text which contains the identities of the parties and their obligations is certified by signatures on the verso for knotted contracts or at the end for open contracts, the contracts are valid. If prepared forms are not certified for sealed contracts it does not impinge on the validity of the contract for R. Ḥananiah ben Gamliel.

128 Which contain the essential data and are certified by three witnesses as required for sealed contracts according to all sources.

129 Unqualified relatives.

130 Since a "knotted" sealed document is validated only by three witnesses, the first two do not combine for validation.

(49d line 36) מָה אֲנָן קַיָּימִין. אִם בְּשֶׁקְּשָׁרוֹ וַחֲתָמוֹ מִבִּפְנִים. כָּל־עַמָּא מוֹדֵיי שֶׁהוּא יָכוֹל לַעֲשׂוֹת פָּשׁוּט. אִם בְּשֶׁקְּשָׁרוֹ וַחֲתָמוֹ מִבַּחוּץ כָּל־עַמָּא מוֹדֵיי שֶׁאֵינוֹ יָכוֹל לַעֲשׂוֹתוֹ פָּשׁוּט. אֶלָּא כֵּן אֲנָן קַיָּימִין בְּשֶׁקְּשָׁרוֹ מִבִּפְנִים וְאַחַר כָּךְ חֲתָמוֹ מִבַּחוּץ. בְּדָא רִבִּי חֲנִינָא בֶן גַּמְלִיאֵל אוֹמֵר. יָכוֹל הוּא לַעֲשׂוֹתוֹ פָּשׁוּט. וְרַבָּנִין אָמְרִין שֶׁאֵינוֹ יָכוֹל לַעֲשׂוֹתוֹ פָּשׁוּט. הֵשִׁיב רִבִּי עַל דִּבְרֵי חֲנַנְיָא בֶן גַּמְלִיאֵל. גּוּפוֹ שֶׁלַּגֵּט. אִם בְּשֶׁקּוֹשְׁרוֹ וַחוֹתָמוֹ מִבַּחוּץ. כָּל־עַמָּא מוֹדֵיי שֶׁאֵינוֹ יָכוֹל לַעֲשׂוֹתוֹ פָּשׁוּט. אֶלָּא כֵּן אֲנָן קַיָּימִין בְּשֶׁקְּשָׁרוֹ מִבִּפְנִים וְאַחַר כָּךְ חֲתָמוֹ מִבַּחוּץ. בְּרַם רִבִּי חֲנַנְיָא בֶן גַּמְלִיאֵל אוֹמֵר. יָכוֹל הוּא לַעֲשׂוֹתוֹ פָּשׁוּט. וְרַבָּנִין אָמְרִין. אֵין יָכוֹל לַעֲשׂוֹתוֹ פָּשׁוּט. הֵשִׁיב רִבִּי עַל דִּבְרֵי רִבִּי חֲנַנְיָא בֶן גַּמְלִיאֵל. גּוּפוֹ שֶׁלַּגֵּט מוֹכִיחַ עָלָיו אִם פָּשׁוּט הוּא אִם אֵינוֹ פָּשׁוּט. אֵי זֶהוּ גּוּפוֹ שֶׁלַּגֵּט. אָמַר רִבִּי בָּא. כַּיֵּי דָמַר רַב הוּנָא. לְעוֹלָם אֵין הָעֵדִים חוֹתְמִין בּוֹ מִלְּמַטָּה עַד שֶׁיִּקְרְאוּ בּוֹ מִלְּמַעֲלָן. אֲנִי פְלוֹנִי בֶּן פְלוֹנִי מְקוּבָּל עָלַי כָּל־מַה שֶּׁכָּתוּב בּוֹ לְמַעֲלָן. וְהָא תַנֵּי. טוֹפֶס שְׁטָרוֹת כֵּן הוּא. אָמַר רִבִּי מָנָא. טוֹפֶס שְׁטָרוֹת מְקוּשָּׁרִין כָּךְ הוּא. אָמַר רִבִּי אָבִין. אֲפִילוּ תֵּימַר הוּא פָּשׁוּט הוּא מְקוּשָּׁר. מְקוּשָּׁר הוּא מְעֻכָּב פָּשׁוּט אֵינוֹ מְעֻכָּב. רִבִּי אָחָא אָמַר. בְּמוֹסִיף עַל הַהֲלָכָה. פָּשׁוּט בִּשְׁנַיִם וּמִנְהָג בִּשְׁלֹשָׁה. עוֹשִׂין אוֹתוֹ בִּשְׁלֹשָׁה. מְקוּשָּׁר מֵאֲחוֹרָיו מִנְהָג מִתּוֹכוֹ וּמֵאֲחוֹרָיו. עוֹשִׂין אוֹתוֹ מִתּוֹכוֹ וּמֵאֲחוֹרָיו.

Where do we hold[131]? If he knotted and signed it inside, everybody agrees that it can be made simple[132]. If he knotted and signed it outside, everybody agrees that it cannot be made simple[133]. But we must deal with the case that he knotted it from the inside and then signed it on the outside[134]; in that case Rebbi Ḥananiah ben Gamliel said that it can be made simple but the rabbis say, it cannot be made simple. [135]{Rebbi objected to the statement of Ḥananiah ben Gamliel: "The body of the document." If he knotted and signed it outside, everybody agrees that it cannot be made simple. But we must deal with the case that he knotted it from the inside and then signed it on the outside; in that case Rebbi Hananiah ben Gamliel said that it can be made simple, but the rabbis say, it cannot be made simple.} Rebbi objected to the statement of Rebbi Hananiah ben Gamliel: The body[136] of the document shows whether it is simple or not simple. What is the body of the document? Rebbi Abba said, as Rav Huna said, witnesses never sign below unless they first read before them: "I X son of Y accept everything written above.[137]" But did we not state: "That is the formula of a document"?[138] Rebbi Mana said, that is the formula of a knotted document. Rebbi Abin said, even if you say it is the same for knotted and simple, for a knotted document it is a necessity, for a simple one it is not a necessity[139]. Rebbi Aha said, if one adds to practice[140]. A simple document [is witnessed] by two persons. If common usage is to have three, one makes it with three. A knotted document is signed on its back. If common usage is to sign it inside and out, one signs it inside and out.

131 This paragraph is out of context here; it refers to Mishnah *Baba batra* 10:1 where R. Hananiah ben Gamliel states that a knotted document can be converted into a simple one if its witnesses sign on the document side.

132 If the document was signed before it was sewn, it is a regular open document. The rules of sealed documents do not apply.

133 If the signatures are on the back of the document, the text itself is left without witnesses; as an open document is would be worthless.

134 As the text stands, it is unintelligible. Mishnah *Baba batra* 10:1 implies that "knotted from the inside" means "had it signed on the inside and then sewed it and had it signed again on the outside", where R. Hanania ben Gamliel holds that it can be used either way; but the opposing

faction holds that once three validating signatures were on the back, the document can only be unsealed in court to be enforced.

135   The text in braces is a first, incomplete version of the following, which the scribe forgot to delete.

136   In the Babli, *Baba batra* 164a/b, Rebbi is stating that the methods of computation of regnal years in open and sealed documents are different. Since sealed documents were not used in Babylonia, this argument seems irrelevant.

137   Since on a sealed document the witnesses start signing once there is space for three signatures, it follows that at the top of the document one has the identification of the person to whom the document refers together with any obligation incurred by that person. In an open document, the main point has to be repeated at the end of the text to make clear what the witnesses certify. In a sealed document, the place of the signatures on the verso of the main part is the certification.

138   Rav Huna's text is required for all documents, whether open or sealed.

139   It is possible to write both sealed and open documents following the same formula. However, a sealed document whose three certifying signatures are not in the back of the text containing the name of the debtor and the exact nature of his obligation is invalid; an open document is valid if only it contains all the necessary information and two signatures. If a sealed document also contains two signatures inside, there is no reason not to follow R. Ḥananiah ben Gamliel.

140   A sealed document minimally valid cannot be turned into an open document. However, at places where the common practice requires more than the minimum, there may be reason to permit turning the sealed into an open document.

(49d line 50) תַּנִּיתָהּ הָכָא וְתַנִּינָתָהּ תַּמָּן כָּשֵׁר. הֲוֵי צְרִיכָה מִיתְנַיָּיא תַּמָּן. אִילוּ תַנִּינָתָהּ הָכָא וְלֹא תַנִּינָתָהּ תַּמָּן הֲוִינָן אָמְרִין. הָכָא עַל שֶׁהוּא חוֹמֶר בָּעֲרָיוֹת פָּסוּל. תַּמָּן עַל יְדֵי שֶׁאֵינוֹ חוֹמֶר בָּעֲרָיוֹת כָּשֵׁר. הֲוֵי צְרִיכָה מִיתְנַיָּיא תַּמָּן. אוֹ אִילוּ מִיתְנַיָּיא תַּמָּן וְלֹא מַתְנִינָן הָכָא הֲוִינָן אָמְרִין. תַּמָּן עַל יְדֵי שֶׁהוּא גוֹבֶה בּוֹ פָּסוּל. וְהָכָא עַל יְדֵי שֶׁאֵינוֹ גוֹבֶה בּוֹ כָּשֵׁר. הֲוֵי צְרִיכָה מִיתְנַיָּיא הָכָא וְצוֹרְכָה מִתְנַיָּיא תַּמָּן.

The condition of validity is stated here and was stated there[141]. It was necessary to state it there. If it had been stated here but not there, we would have said that here it is invalid because of the restrictions connected with adultery but there, since no restrictions connected with adultery are involved, it would be valid. Or if it had been stated there but not here, we would have said that there it is invalid since one comes to collect money based on that document but here, where one does not collect money, it would be valid. Therefore, it was necessary both to state it here and to state it there.

141 Both in *Gittin* 8:12 and in *Baba batra* 10:1 one finds rules about sealed documents. These rules do not overlap. The rules about the bald document are not found in *Baba batra*, the requirement of three witnesses is not in *Gittin*. One would have expected an argument why the rules of one tractate, dealing with divorce documents, also apply to the other, dealing with deeds of real estate and mortgages. For some reason, this seemed obvious to the editors of the Yerushalmi.

המגרש פרק תשיעי

(fol. 49d) **משנה א:** הַמְגָרֵשׁ אֶת אִשְׁתּוֹ וְאָמַר לָהּ הֲרֵי אַתְּ מוּתֶּרֶת לְכָל־אָדָם אֶלָּא לְאִישׁ פְּלוֹנִי רִבִּי אֱלִיעֶזֶר מַתִּיר וַחֲכָמִים אוֹסְרִין. כֵּיצַד יַעֲשֶׂה. יִטְּלֶינּוּ מִמֶּנָּה וְיַחֲזוֹר וְיִתְּנֶנּוּ לָהּ וְיֹאמַר לָהּ הֲרֵי אַתְּ מוּתֶּרֶת לְכָל־אָדָם. אִם כְּתָבוֹ בְּתוֹכוֹ אַף עַל פִּי שֶׁחָזַר וּמְחָקוֹ פָּסוּל.

Mishnah 1: If somebody in divorcing his wife says to her: Herewith you are permitted to any man except Mr. X, Rebbi Eliezer permits[1] but the Sages prohibit. What should he do? He should take the document back from her and deliver it again while saying, herewith you are permitted to any man. If he had written the condition[2] in the document it would be invalid even if he had later erased it.

1   He permits the wife to remarry; the Sages prohibit since they reject the possibility of a divorce which permits control of the divorced wife by the former husband.

2   Which restricts the divorcee in the choice of her future husband.

(50a line 41) **הלכה א:** הַמְגָרֵשׁ אֶת אִשְׁתּוֹ כול׳. אָמַר רִבִּי אִילַי. טַעֲמָא דְּרִבִּי אֱלִיעֶזֶר. וְיָצְאָה מִבֵּיתוֹ וְהָלְכָה וְהָיְתָה לְאִישׁ אַחֵר. אֲפִילוּ לֹא הִתִּירָהּ אֶלָּא לְאָדָם אַחֵר. שְׁמוּעָתָא רוּבָהּ מִמַּתְנִיתָא. מַתְנִיתָא אָמְרָה בְּשֶׁהוּתְּרָה לְכָל וְאָסְרָהּ לְאָדָם אַחֵר. שְׁמוּעָתָא אָמְרָה בְּשֶׁאֲסָרָהּ לַכֹּל וְהִתִּירָהּ לְאָדָם אַחֵר. מַה טַעֲמָא דְּרִבִּי אֱלִיעֶזֶר. מִיתָה מַתֶּרֶת וְגֵט מַתִּיר. מַה מִיתָה מַתֶּרֶת וּמְחֶצָה אַף הַגֵּט מַתִּיר וּמְחֶצָה. מַה טַעֲמוֹן דְּרַבָּנִין. וְיָצְאָה מִבֵּיתוֹ וְהָלְכָה וְהָיְתָה לְאִישׁ אַחֵר. הִקִּישׁ הֲוָיָיתָהּ לִיצִיאָה. מַה הַמִּיתָה[3] יְצִיאָתָהּ אֵין לָהּ יְצִיאָה אֵצֶל אַחֵר. אַף הֲוָיָיתָהּ אֵין לָהּ הֲוָיָיה אֵצֶל אַחֵר.

Halakhah 1: "If somebody in divorcing his wife," etc. Rebbi Ilai[4] said, the reason of Rebbi Eliezer: "She left his house, went, and became another man's[5]", even if he did permit her only to one other man. This argument proves more than the Mishnah[6]! The Mishnah said if she was permitted to all but forbidden to one other man; the argument is that he forbade her to all but permitted her only to one other man. What is the reason of Rebbi Eliezer? Death permits and divorce permits. Since death permits only partially[7], so the bill of divorce permits only partially[8]. What is the reason of the rabbis? "She left his house, went, and became another man's"; it brackets marriage and divorce. Since her divorce is without participation of a third party, so her marriage must be without participation of a third party[9].

3   This word is a scribal error.

4   In the Babli (82b) this is ascribed to R. Yannai. There, the objection is that "she became another man's" could be interpreted as "she became *any* other man's".

5   *Deut.* 24:2.

6   By the mathematical principle *qui nimium probat nihil probat*, R. Ilai's argument proves nothing.

7   The pool of possible marriage partners available to a widow is smaller than the pool which was available to the same woman before her marriage since she is forbidden any close relatives of her deceased husband.

8   Since the divorce does not remove the incest prohibitions, it seems possible that the husband can add prohibitions of his own.

9   If the former husband could impose marriage restrictions on his former wife, her remarriage would be subject to the former husband's edict. This would create a kind of polyandry.

(50a line 49) לְאַחַר מִיתָתוֹ שֶׁלְּרַבִּי אֱלִיעֶזֶר נִכְנְסוּ אַרְבָּעָה זְקֵינִים לְהָשִׁיב עַל דְּבָרָיו שֶׁלְּרַבִּי אֱלִיעֶזֶר. רבִּי אֶלְעָזָר בֶּן עֲזַרְיָה וְרבִּי יוֹסֵי הַגָּלִילִי וְרבִּי טַרְפוֹן

וְרִבִּי עֲקִיבָה. אָמַר לָהֶן רִבִּי יְהוֹשֻׁעַ. אֵין אַתֶּם מְשִׁיבִין אֶת הָאֲרִי לְאַחַר מִיתָה. הֵשִׁיב רִבִּי טַרְפוֹן. הֲרֵי שֶׁאָמַר לָהּ. הֲרֵי אַתְּ מוּתֶּרֶת לְכָל־אָדָם חוּץ מִפְּלוֹנִי. וְהָלְכָה וְנִישֵּׂאת. מֵת בְּלֹא בָנִים הֵיאַךְ זֹאת מִתְיַבֶּמֶת. לֹא נִמְצָא מַתְנֶה עַל הַכָּתוּב בַּתּוֹרָה. וְכָל־הַמַּתְנֶה עַל מַה שֶׁכָּתוּב בַּתּוֹרָה תְּנָאוֹ בָּטֵל. מֵעַתָּה לֹא יִשָּׂא בַּת אָחִיו שֶׁלֹּא יַתְנֶה עַל הַכָּתוּב בַּתּוֹרָה. אָמַר רִבִּי יוֹסֵי בֵּירִבִּי בּוּן. סָבְרָא טַעְמָא. תַּמָּן הַתּוֹרָה אֲסָרְתָהּ עָלָיו. בְּרַם הָכָא הוּא אֲסָרָהּ עָלָיו. הָתִיב רִבִּי חֲנַנְיָה בְּשֵׁם רִבִּי פִינְחָס. נִיתְנֵי שֵׁשׁ עֶשְׂרֵה נָשִׁים כְּרִבִּי אֱלִיעֶזֶר. אָמַר רִבִּי מָנָא. כְּבָר אִיתְּמַר טַעְמָא. תַּמָּן הַתּוֹרָה אֲסָרָהּ עָלָיו. בְּרַם הָכָא הוּא אֲסָרָהּ עָלָיו. רִבִּי יִרְמְיָה בָּעֵי. הֲרֵי שֶׁאָמַר לָהּ. הֲרֵי אַתְּ מוּתֶּרֶת לְכָל־אָדָם חוּץ מִפְּלוֹנִי. וְהָלְכָה וְנִיסֵּית לְאָחִיו וּמֵת בְּלֹא בָנִים. הֵיאַךְ זֶה מַתִּיר מַה שֶׁאָסַר הָרִאשׁוֹן. מִילְּתֵיהּ אֲמָרָהּ. שְׁמִיתַת וְגֵירוּשִׁין וּמַתִּירִין בָּזֶה מַה שֶׁאָסַר הָרִאשׁוֹן. אָמַר רִבִּי יִרְמְיָה. לֹא אָמַר אֶלָּא שְׁמִיתַת וְגֵירוּשִׁין. הָא נִישׁוּאִין לֹא.

[10] After Rebbi Eliezer's death, four Elders assembled to object to Rebbi Eliezer's words: Rebbi Eleazar ben Azariah, Rebbi Yose the Galilean, Rebbi Tarphon, and Rebbi Aqiba. Rebbi Joshua told them, one does not contradict the lion after his death[11]. Rebbi Tarphon objected: If he said to her, you are permitted to any man except Mr. X; she went and married [the latter's brother who][12] died childless; how can she contract the levirate marriage[13]? Does it not turn out that he[14] stipulated against what is written in the Torah, and anybody's condition contradicting what is written in the Torah is invalid. Then nobody should be permitted to marry his brother's daughter, lest he come to stipulate against what is written in the Torah[15]. Rebbi Yose ben Rebbi Abun said, one understands the reason. There, the Torah forbade her to him[16]. But here, he forbids to him[17]! Rebbi Ḥananiah objected in the name of Rebbi Phineas: Should one not state "sixteen women" following Rebbi Eliezer[18]? Rebbi Mana

said, the reason was already explained: there, the Torah forbade her to him. But here, he forbids to him[17]! Rebbi Jeremiah[19] asked: If he said to her, you are permitted to any man except Mr. X; she went and married the latter's brother who died childless, how can the latter permit what the first forbade[20]? His words imply that death and divorce permit what the first [husband] prohibited[21]. Rebbi Jeremiah said, he said only death and divorce; therefore, not marriage[22].

10 Different versions of the following discussions are in the Babli, 83a/b, Tosephta 7:1-5, *Sifry Deut.* 269.

11 He rejects all the following arguments (as does the Babli, except an argument attributed to R. Eleazar ben Azariah not mentioned in the Yerushalmi.)

12 Missing in the text; to be added from the parallel attributed to R. Jeremiah.

13 If the prohibited man was the only brother of the deceased husband, the widow should have to marry him but she is prohibited by the former husband's stipulation. In the Babylonian sources (Note 10) the conclusion is stated explicitly that "this is no cutting loose" (referring to the bill of divorce which in *Deut.* 24:1 is called "scroll of cutting loose" the wife from the husband's power. This really refers to the rabbis' argument, Note 9.)

14 The first husband would in effect stipulate that his ex-wife cannot fulfill the commandment of the levirate marriage.

15 If the uncle married to the niece died childless, the widow clearly is forbidden to marry her own father in levirate. But the possibility of a marriage of the niece to the uncle is one of the doctrines of Pharisaic Judaism, in contrast to the Sadducees (cf. Introduction to Tractate *Yebamot*.)

16 In fact, the greater part of Tractate *Yebamot* is devoted to cases where levirate marriage is impossible.

17 The first husband forbids levirate marriage to the brother of the second husband.

18 Mishnah *Yebamot* 1:1 enumerates 15 categories of women who are forbidden levirate and, in the opinion of the House of Hillel, automatically free their co-wives from

levirate. According to R. Eliezer, should one not add the woman who married the brother of a man forbidden to her by divorce stipulation?

19   It seems that this has to read "R. Simeon ben Eleazar" (Tosephta 7:5).

20   This is a *non sequitur*. It seems that one has to read with the Tosephta: "She went and married an unrelated person who then divorced her unconditionally", i. e., the second husband by his divorce annulled the condition of the first divorce.

21   The condition "except Mr. X" according to R. Eliezer refers only to the next marriage of the divorcee. If the divorcee married according to the stipulation and then the second marriage is dissolved either by divorce or by the husband's death, the widow or divorcee is free to marry anybody she wishes. The Babli agrees with this interpretation, 83a, which shows that R. Tarphon's objection cannot be sustained.

22   R. Eliezer, who declares the divorce valid, will insist that the first remarriage satisfy the first husband's condition.

(50a line 64) אָמַר רַבִּי יוֹסֵי הַגְּלִילִי. מָצִינוּ בַּתּוֹרָה. הָאָסוּר לָזֶה מוּתָּר לָזֶה וְהַמּוּתָּר לָזֶה אָסוּר לָזֶה. אָסוּר לְאֶחָד אָסוּר לְכָל־אָדָם מוּתָּר לְאֶחָד מוּתָּר לְכָל־אָדָם. הֵשִׁיב רַבִּי עֲקִיבָא. הֲרֵי שֶׁהָיְתָה זֶה שֶׁנֶּאֶסְרָה עָלָיו כֹּהֵן וּמֵת הַמְגָרֵשׁ לֹא נִמְצֵאת אַלְמָנָה לוֹ וּגְרוּשָׁה לְכָל־אֶחָיו הַכֹּהֲנִים. וְכִי בַּמֶּה הֶחֱמִירָה תוֹרָה. בִּגְרוּשָׁה אוֹ בָאַלְמָנָה. הֶחֱמִירָה הַתּוֹרָה בִּגְרוּשָׁה יוֹתֵר מִן הָאַלְמָנָה. וּמָה אִם גְּרוּשָׁה חֲמוּרָה לַכֹּל לֹא נֶאֶסְרָה מִמַּה שֶּׁהוּתָּר בָּהּ מִצַּד גֵּירוּשִׁין שֶׁבָּהּ. אַלְמָנָה קַלָּה אֵינוֹ דִין שֶׁתֵּיאָסֵר מִמַּה שֶּׁהוּתָּר לָהּ מִצַּד אֵשֶׁת אִישׁ שֶׁבָּהּ. אֲפִילוּ אֶצְלוֹ נָגְעוּ בּוֹ גֵּירוּשִׁין. וּמָה אַלְמָנָה וּגְרוּשָׁה נֶאֶסְרָה מִמַּה שֶּׁהוּתָּר לָהּ מִצַּד אֵשֶׁת אִישׁ שֶׁבָּהּ. גֵּירוּשִׁין חֲמוּרִין לֹא כָּל־שֶׁכֵּן שֶׁתֵּיאָסֵר מִמַּה שֶּׁהוּתָּר לָהּ מִצַּד גֵּירוּשִׁין שֶׁבָּהּ.

Rebbi Yose the Galilean said: Do we find in the Torah that what is forbidden to one is permitted to the other and what is permitted to one is forbidden for the other? Forbidden to one she is forbidden to everybody;

permitted to one is permitted to everybody[23]. Rebbi Aqiba objected: If the one to whom she was prohibited was a Cohen and the divorcer died, would she not be considered a widow for him but a divorcee for all his clan of Cohanim[24]? Where was the Torah more restrictive, for a divorcee or for a widow[25]? The Torah was more restrictive for a divorcee than for a widow. But since a divorcee, where one is more restrictive in all aspects, does not become forbidden with respect to what was permitted by her divorce[26], would it be logical that the widow should be forbidden from what was permitted her from her aspect of married woman[27]? Even him did the divorce touch[28]. Since both a widow and a divorcee were forbidden[29] even if her aspect of married woman was permitted, with restrictive divorce certainly she should be forbidden even in the aspect[30] that was permitted by her divorce.

23 His argument is the same in the Babylonian sources (Note 10). It is difficult to accept the statement at face value.

24 The situation would be paradoxical in that the divorcee would be forbidden to all Cohanim (*Lev.* 21:7) except the Cohen to whom she was forbidden since for him she is a widow who is forbidden only to the High Priest. (One might ask why a man would forbid his divorcee to a Cohen since she is forbidden to him anyhow.)

25 The lengthy amplification refers to the prior case that the person whom the divorcee could not marry was a Cohen, forbidden to her in any case.

26 As a married woman she was forbidden to everybody except her husband; as a divorcee she is permitted to most men.

27 This is an involved argument repeating the paradoxical situation described in Note 24.

28 The arguments of Notes 24, 27 are to be rejected. A divorcee who cannot be married is still a divorcee; the argument of R. Aqiba is invalid.

29 To the High Priest.

30 Forbidden to the rank-and-file Cohen. The sentence is an amplification of the argument of Note 28.

(50a line 75) דָּבָר אַחֵר. הֲרֵי שֶׁאָמַר לָהּ. הֲרֵי אַתְּ מוּתֶּרֶת לְכָל־אָדָם חוּץ מִפְּלוֹנִי. וְהָלְכָה וְנִיסֵּית לְאַחֵר וְיָלְדָה מִמֶּנּוּ בָּנִים. וּמֵת וְהָלְכָה וְנִיסֵּית לְאוֹתוֹ לֹא נִמְצְאוּ בָנֶיהָ מִן הָאַחֲרוֹן מַמְזֵירִין. מִילְתֵיהּ אָמְרָה שֶׁאֵין גֵּירוּשִׁין מַתִּירִין מַה שֶׁאָסַר הָרִאשׁוֹן. אָמַר רִבִּי שַׁמַּי. מָצִינוּ אִשָּׁה בַּתְּחִילָּה אֵין חַיָּיבִין עָלֶיהָ מִשּׁוּם עֶרְוָה וּבַסּוֹף חַיָּיבִין עָלֶיהָ מִשּׁוּם עֶרְוָה. אָמַר לֵיהּ רִבִּי מָנָא. לְמָה זֶה דוֹמֶה. לְאֶחָד שֶׁאָמַר לְאִשְׁתּוֹ. הֲרֵי זֶה גִיטֵּיךְ עַל מְנָת שֶׁתִּבָּעֲלִי לְאִישׁ פְּלוֹנִי. בַּתְּחִילָּה הוּא אָסוּר לִבְעוֹל. עָבַר וּבָעַל הוּתָּר הַגֵּט לְמַפְרֵעַ.

Another argument[31]: "Assume that he said to her, 'you are permitted to every man except Mr. X;' she went and married another and had children by him. Then her [second] husband died[32]; she went and married Mr. X. Will not her children by her second husband become bastards[33]?" His argument implies that divorce does not permit what the first husband had forbidden[34]. Rebbi Shammai said, do we find that a woman was not originally forbidden to a man because of adultery and then retroactively became forbidden as adulterous[35]? Rebbi Mana said to him, to what can you compare this? To one who told his wife, "this is your bill of divorce on condition that you sleep with Mr. X." At the start, he is forbidden to have sexual relations with her. If he transgressed and slept with her, the divorce was retroactively validated[36].

31   In the Babli, 83a, this argument also is attributed to R. Aqiba.

32   In the Babli: "died or divorced her." This is implied by the sequel here also.

33   The third marriage violates the conditions of the first divorce. If the first divorce is invalidated, the second marriage retroactively becomes adulterous and the children bastards. The argument does not disprove R. Eliezer's position; it shows that from a practical point of view, that position should not be tolerated.

34   Contrary to what was asserted in the name of R. Eliezer (Note 21), a

later divorce or widowhood does not eliminate the conditions of the first divorce.

35   He doubts that anybody can agree that the second husband, who contracted his marriage within the parameters of the first divorce, can become an adulterer without his knowledge by an action of the wife after his death or after a divorce.

36   Even according to the Babli which holds that any expression "on condition that" means "from today, on condition that", Mr. X is barred from marrying the divorcee as long as he had not slept with her since she is not yet divorced and, therefore, unable to contract any marriage. Therefore, when he goes to bed with the divorcee, it is an adulterous act. But at the moment of penetration, the condition of the divorce is satisfied and the aspect of adultery has disappeared. This is just the opposite of the situation which caused discomfort to R. Shammai. (Rashba, *Novellae ad* 84a.)

(50b line 6) אָמַר רִבִּי יוֹחָנָן. הֲלָכָה כְּרִבִּי שִׁמְעוֹן בֶּן אֶלְעָזָר הִיא. דְּרִבִּי שִׁמְעוֹן בֶּן אֶלְעָזָר אָמַר. לְעוֹלָם אֵינוֹ גֵט עַד שֶׁיֹּאמַר בִּשְׁעַת מַתָּנָה. הֲרֵי זֶה גִיטֵּיךְ. רִבִּי יַעֲקֹב בַּר אָחָא בְשֵׁם רִבִּי יַנַּאי. אַף רֵיחַ פְּסוּל אֵין בָּהּ. כַּהֲנָא אָמַר. זֹאת אוֹמֶרֶת לֹא חָשׁוּ. אִין תֵּימַר חָשׁוּ. עַד שֶׁהוּא בְיָדָהּ דְּאָמַר לָהּ. הֲרֵי אַתְּ מוּתֶּרֶת לְכָל־אָדָם. אָמַר רִבִּי אָחָא. זֹאת אוֹמֶרֶת שֶׁחָשׁוּ. אִין תֵּימַר לֹא חָשׁוּ. כָּל־מַה שֶּׁבְּיָדוֹ לְגָרֵשׁ יְגָרֵשׁ.

Rebbi Johanan said[37], the practice follows Rebbi Simeon ben Eleazar, since Rebbi Simeon ben Eleazar said[38] it never is a bill of divorce unless he declares at the moment of delivery: "This is your bill of divorce." Rebbi Jacob bar Aha in the name of Rebbi Yannai: There is not even a hint of invalidity on her[39]. Cahana said, this implies that they did not worry[40]. If they did worry, might he not have said "you are permitted to any man" when it was still in her hand[41]? Rebbi Aha said, his implies that they did worry[42]. If they did not worry, could he not divorce by any power he has to divorce[43]?

37 Here starts the discussion of the statement by the Mishnah, that the husband cannot simply annul the condition he had imposed but has to take the bill back and bodily deliver it while declaring his ex-wife free to marry any man she chooses.

38 Chapter 8, Note 27; Babli 78a.

39 An imperfect bill of divorce will nevertheless make the woman a divorcee according to the rules of the priesthood. Only a bill which clearly is null and void does not have this consequence (and if the woman became a widow before a corrected version could be delivered to her, she would be able to marry a Cohen.) In Yerushalmi language, the invalid bill implies no "hint of invalidity" *for the woman*. In Babli terminology (86b), there is "no hint of a bill of divorce" *on the document* (רֵיחַ הַגֵּט אֵין בּוֹ).

40 The Tanna of the Mishnah accepts the statement of R. Yannai that the document delivered with the exclusion of a possible marriage partner is null and void. (In the Babli, 84b, R. Joḥanan in the name of Cahana adopts the position here described as R. Aḥa's.)

41 If the delivery were valid to disqualify the woman from marrying a Cohen, it also should be valid for a full divorce upon a public disclaimer by the husband of the condition imposed.

42 The Tanna of the Mishnah must reject the statement of R. Yannai. The Babli agrees, 84b.

43 He also rejects the determination of R. Joḥanan that the Mishnah follows R. Simeon ben Eleazar. The fact that the Mishnah requires the husband to retake possession of the bill after the wife already had it in her hand means that the wife already had acquired the bill, became forbidden to a Cohen, and, therefore, a simple statement by the husband would be invalid. (Rashi's explanation, 84b).

(50b line 12) אָמַר רִבִּי זְעִירָא. תַּנֵּי שִׁילָא בַּר בִּינָה. כָּל־שֶׁאִילּוּ בִתְנָיי עַל מְנָת פָּסוּל. כָּל־שֶׁאִילּוּ נְתָנוֹ עַל מְנָת פָּסוּל.

Rebbi Ze'ira said: Shila bar Binah stated: Anything which is invalid containing a condition if delivered on condition is also invalid[44].

44 This refers to the last statement in the Mishnah, that the condition written in the bill of divorce invalidates the bill. It is stated as a general principle that any condition, which written in the bill will invalidate it, also invalidates if not written but imposed orally at the time of the delivery. (The Babli, 84b, takes the opposite track: A written condition invalidates if and only if it invalidates if imposed orally. The Babli invalidates any condition formulated using the term "except" but validates every "on condition that". This is foreign to the Yerushalmi.)

משנה ב: הֲרֵי אַתְּ מוּתֶּרֶת לְכָל־אָדָם אֶלָּא לְאַבָּא וּלְאָבִיךְ לְאָחִי (fol. 49d) וּלְאָחִיךְ לָעֶבֶד לְנָכְרִי וּלְכָל־מִי שֶׁאֵין לָהּ קִידּוּשִׁין עָלָיו כָּשֵׁר. הֲרֵי אַתְּ מוּתֶּרֶת לְכָל־אָדָם אֶלָּא אַלְמָנָה לְכֹהֵן גָּדוֹל גְּרוּשָׁה וַחֲלוּצָה לְכֹהֵן הֶדְיוֹט מַמְזֶרֶת וּנְתִינָה לְיִשְׂרָאֵל בַּת יִשְׂרָאֵל לְנָתִין וּלְמַמְזֵר וּלְכָל־מִי שֶׁיֵּשׁ לָהּ עָלָיו קִידּוּשִׁין אֲפִילוּ בַעֲבֵירָה פָּסוּל.

Mishnah 2: "You are permitted to any man except to my father and your father, to my brother and your brother, to a slave, a Gentile," or anybody she is unable to contract a preliminary marriage with[45], it is valid. "You are permitted to any man except as a widow to the High Priest, a divorcee or one having received ḥaliṣah to a common priest, a bastard or a Gibeonite girl to an Israel, the daughter of an Israel to a a bastard or a Gibeonite[46]," or anybody she could contract a preliminary marriage with even if it is sinful[47], it is invalid[48].

45 An unmarried woman can contract preliminary marriage with any Jewish man except those connections forbidden as incestuous relations which are deadly sins. Marriage is also impossible with Gentiles and slaves. A divorce stipulation which forbids no marriage possible under the law is

empty.

46 All these are subsumed under "holiness prohibitions", enumerated in Mishnah *Yebamot* 2:4.

47 Including common law "commandment prohibitions," Mishnah *Yebamot* 2:4.

48 Since for the rabbis who oppose R. Eliezer, any bill of divorce is invalid if it restricts the pool of legal marriage partners of the divorcee.

(50b line 13) **הלכה ב:** הֲרֵי אַתְּ מוּתֶּרֶת לְכָל־אָדָם כול׳. לֵית כָּאן סָפֵק גֵּירוּשִׁין אֶלָּא גֵירוּשִׁין מַמָּשׁ. כֵּיצַד סְפֵק קִידּוּשִׁין. כַּיֵּי דְּתַנִּינָן תַּמָּן. זָרַק לָהּ קִידּוּשִׁין. סָפֵק קָרוֹב לָהּ סָפֵק קָרוֹב לוֹ. זֶהוּ סְפֵק קִידּוּשִׁין. וְהָכָא הוּא זָרַק לָהּ גִּיטָהּ. סָפֵק קָרוֹב לוֹ סָפֵק קָרוֹב לָהּ. זֶהוּ סְפֵק גֵּירוּשִׁין.

2 אלא גירושין ממש | י ממש   כיי דתנינן תמן | י -   3 קידושין | י קידושיה   לה | י לו
4 לו | י לה   הוא זרק | י זרק

Halakhah 2: "You are permitted to any man," etc. There really is no questionable divorce here. What are questionable *qiddušin*? As we have stated there: If he threw the betrothal gift to her and there is a doubt whether it fell closer to him or to her, those are questionable *qiddušin*. And here, if he threw the divorce document to her and there is a doubt whether it fell closer to him or to her, that is a questionable divorce.

49 The entire Halakhah is copied from *Yebamot* 3:9, Notes 122-136 (י). It is inserted here at the wrong place since its topic is Mishnah 4, as explained in detail in *Yebamot*. The text here was copied negligently.

(50b line 17) רִבִּי יוֹחָנָן בְּשֵׁם רִבִּי חֲלַפְתָּא דְמָן חוּט. וְכוּלָּן אִם נִיסֵּית לֹא תֵצֵא. שֶׁלֹּא לְהוֹצִיא לִיזָה עַל בָּנֶיהָ. בִּתּוֹ שֶׁנִּיסֵּית לַשּׁוּק בְּגֵט זֶה לֹא תֵצֵא. כְּדֵי לִיזּוּק צָרָתָהּ לְאָבִיהָ. צָרָתָהּ שֶׁנִּישֵּׂאת לַשּׁוּק בְּגֵט זֶה תֵצֵא. בִּתּוֹ שֶׁנִּישֵּׂאת לְאָחִיו אֲפִילוּ לְאָבִיהָ לֹא תֵצֵא.

1 חוח | י הוה   ניסית | י נישאת בו   2 ניסית | י נישאת   3 ליזוק | י לזוק   בגט זה
תצא. צרתה שנישאת לאחיו | י שנישאת לאחיו

Rebbi Joḥanan in the name of Rebbi Ḥalaphta from Haifa: Any who were married on the basis of such a document should not leave[126] in order not to give a bad reputation to her children. His daughter who was married outside on the basis of such a document should not leave in order to damage her co-wife to her father. Her co-wife who was married outside on the basis of such a document has to leave. His daughter who married his brother [on the basis of such a document has to leave. Her co-wife who was married to her brother][50] on the basis of such a document, or even to her father, should not leave..

50   Necessary text added from *Yebamot*, missing here.

(50b line 21) תַּנֵּי שְׁלֹשָׁה שְׁטָרוֹת הַלָּלוּ גּוֹבָה מִבְּנֵי חוֹרִין וְאֵינוֹ גּוֹבָה מִן הַמְשׁוּעְבָּדִים. אָמַר רִבִּי בָּא. הָדָא דְּתֵימַר בְּשֶׁלֹא הוּחְזַק שְׁטָר בְּיַד הַמַּלְוָה. [אֲבָל הוּחְזַק הַשְּׁטָר בְּיַד הַמַּלְוָה גּוֹבָה. רִבִּי יוֹסֵה בָּעֵי. אִם שֶׁלֹא הוּחְזַק הַשְּׁטָר בְּיַד הַמַּלְוָה][50] אֲפִילוּ מִבְּנֵי חוֹרִין אֵינוֹ גּוֹבָה. אֶלָּא כֵּן אָנָן קַיָּימִין בְּשֶׁהוּחְזַק הַשְּׁטָר בְּיַד הַמַּלְוָה. וְלָמָּה אֵינוֹ גּוֹבָה. רִבִּי בִּיסְנָא אָמַר. מִפְּנֵי קֵינוֹנְיָא. רִבִּי אָבִינָא אָמַר. מִפְּנֵי פָּסוּל. וְהָכָא מִפְּנֵי שֶׁהוּא פָּסוּל. הָתִיב רִבִּי אָבִין. עַד כְּדוֹן בְּשָׁלְוָה הַזָּקֵן. שִׁיעְבֵּד הַזָּקֵן. אִית לָךְ מֵימָר מִפְּנֵי קֵינוֹנְיָא. לֹא מִפְּנֵי שֶׁהוּא פָּסוּל. הָתִיב רִבִּי אָבוּן. וְהָתַנֵּי אַף בְּגִיטֵּי נָשִׁים. אִית לָךְ מֵימָר מִפְּנֵי קֵינוֹנְיָא. לֹא מִפְּנֵי שֶׁהוּא פָּסוּל. וְהָכָה מִפְּנֵי שֶׁהוּא פָּסוּל.

2 שטר | י בשטר   4 אינו גובה | י לא יגבה   5 ר' ביסנא אמ' | י אמ' ר' ביסנא קינוניא | י קוינונייא   6 אבינא | י אבון   פסול. והכא מפני שהוא פסול. התיב ר' אבין | י שהוא פסול   7 שיעבד | י ושיעבד   אית לך | י לווה הזקן ושיעבד הבן. אית לך קינוניא | י קוינונייא   8 התיב | י אמר   והתני | י והא תני   נשים | י נשים כן

It was stated: [A claim based on] any of these three types of documents can be collected only from unincumbered property, not from mortgaged property. Rebbi Abba said, that means, if the document in the hand of the lender has not been confirmed. [But if the document in the hand of the lender has been confirmed, he may collect. Rebbi Yose asked: If the document in the hand of the lender has not been confirmed,]⁵⁰ he should not be able to collect even from unincumbered property! But one must deal with a document confirmed in the hand of the lender. And why can he not collect? Rebbi Bisna said, because of action in partnership. Rebbi Abina said, because it is invalid And here, because it is invalid.. Rebbi Abin asked, so far, if the old man took the loan [and the old man mortgaged. But if the old man took the loan and the son mortgaged,]⁵⁰ can you say because of a conspiracy? No, because it is invalid. Rebbi Abun asked, was it not stated: The same holds for bills of divorce? Can you say there, because of action in partnership? No, because it is invalid. And here, because it is invalid.

(fol. 49d) **משנה ג:** גוּפוֹ שֶׁלַגֵּט הֲרֵי אַתְּ מוּתֶּרֶת לְכָל־אָדָם. רִבִּי יְהוּדָה אוֹמֵר וְדֵן דְּיִהְוֵי לִיכִי מִינַּאי סֵפֶר תֵּירוּכִין וְאִיגֶּרֶת שִׁיבּוּקִין לִמְהָךְ לְהִתְנַסְבָא לְכָל־גְּבַר דְּתִצְבַּיִין. גוּפוֹ שֶׁלַגֵּט שִׁיחְרוּר. הֲרֵי אַתְּ בֶּן חוֹרִין הֲרֵי אַתְּ לְעַצְמָךְ.

Mishnah 3: The essence⁵¹ of the bill of divorce: You are herewith permitted to any man. Rebbi Jehudah says: This shall be for you from me a divorce scroll and a letter of abandonment, to enable you to marry any man you desire. The essence of the bill of manumission: You are a free person, you are on your own.

51   The required text.

(50b line 28) **הלכה ג:** גּוּפוֹ שֶׁלַגֵּט הֲרֵי אַתְּ מוּתֶּרֶת לְכָל־אָדָם כול'. רִבִּי אֲחָא אָמַר. כְּרִיתוּת לֹא הִתְפִּיסָה הַתּוֹרָה שֵׁם כְּרִיתוּת אֶלָּא עֶרְוָה שֶׁיֵּשׁ בָּהּ הֲוָיָיה.

Halakhah 3: "The essence of the bill of divorce: You are herewith permitted to any man," etc. Rebbi Aḥa said: "Cutting off", the Torah did not choose the term "cutting off" except to refer to a person with whom a marriage is possible[52].

52 This really refers to Mishnah 2 and explains why the prohibition of impossible relations does not invalidate the bill of divorce. The bill is called "a scroll of cutting off" in *Deut.* 24:1,3. If marriage was not possible, it cannot be dissolved.

(50b line 30) אָמַר רִבִּי מָנָא. וּבִלְחוּד דְּלָא יֵימַר. וְדִין. רִבִּי מָנָא בָּעֵי. הֲרֵי אַתְּ בִּרְשׁוּת עַצְמָךְ. אָמַר רִבִּי יוֹסֵי בֵּירִבִּי בּוּן. צָרִיךְ שֶׁיֹּאמַר. הֲרֵי אַתְּ בֶּן חוֹרִין. הֲרֵי אַתְּ שֶׁלְּעַצְמָךְ. מַתְנִיתָא אָמְרָה כֵן. הֲרֵי אַתְּ בֶּן חוֹרִין הֲרֵי אַתְּ שֶׁלְּעַצְמָךְ.

Rebbi Mana said: He has to be careful not to say "וְדִין".[53] Rebbi Mana asked: "You are on your own"[54]? Rebbi Yose ben Rebbi Abun said, one must say: "You are a free person, you are on your own.[55]" The Mishnah said so: "You are a free person, you are on your own."

53 While the usual spelling of "this" is דֵּין, in the divorce document the spelling must be defective so it cannot be read as וְדִין "by law" implying that the husband would not consider a divorce unless forced by some law. This would invalidate the divorce. The Babli, 85b, has a long list of similar spelling rules.

54 Is that an acceptable formula for a divorce? The obvious negative answer is not given.

55 In a bill of manumission, both expressions are required. The Mishnah (with a very slight change in wording) supports this by stating both expressions in parallel, not connected by "or".

משנה ד: שְׁלֹשָׁה גִטִּין פְּסוּלִין וְאִם נִשֵּׂאת הַוָּלָד כָּשֵׁר. כָּתַב בִּכְתָב (fol. 49d) יָדוֹ וְאֵין עָלָיו עֵדִים יֵשׁ עָלָיו עֵדִים וְאֵין בּוֹ זְמַן יֵשׁ בּוֹ זְמַן וְאֵין בּוֹ אֶלָּא עֵד אֶחָד. הֲרֵי אֵילוּ שְׁלֹשָׁה גִטִּין פְּסוּלִין וְאִם נִשֵּׂאת הַוָּלָד כָּשֵׁר.

Mishnah 4: Three kinds of bills of divorce are invalid[56], but if she married, the child is legitimate: If he wrote in his own handwriting but it was not signed by witnesses[57]; it was signed by witnesses but is not dated[58]; it is dated but only one witness signed it[59]. These are three invalid kinds of bills of divorce, but if she married, the child is legitimate.

56   They are invalid only because they violate customary rules, not because of biblical precepts. The woman is forbidden to remarry on the strength of such a bill, but if she did marry, the second marriage and its offspring are legitimate.

57   The witnesses which validate the divorce are those present at the delivery. For the document itself, one can apply the principle valid for I.O.U's: "The signature of the debtor is worth 100 witnesses."

58   According to all opinions, the dating of a bill of divorce is a rabbinic requirement (cf. Chapter 2, Note 32, Chapter 4, Note 64).

59   Even if the document was in the husband's handwriting, one witness alone is not sufficient to let the divorcee remarry without trouble.

(50b line 34) **הלכה ד:** שְׁלֹשָׁה גִטִּין פְּסוּלִין כול׳. רִבִּי יוֹחָנָן בְּשֵׁם רִבִּי יַנַּאי. וְכוּלָּן בִּכְתָב יָדָיִם. רִבִּי לְעָזָר שָׁאַל. עֵדִים יֵשׁ כָּאן. בִּכְתָב יָדַיִם מָה אֲנִי צָרִיךְ. רַב יִרְמְיָה בְּשֵׁם רַב. וְכוּלְּהֶם בִּכְתָב יָדַיִם חוּץ מִשְּׁעֵדָיו עַמּוֹ. אָמַר רַב הַמְנוּנָא. הַלָּלוּ חוֹבֵיהוֹן עַל גַּרְמֵיהוֹן. דְּאִינּוּן שֶׁקִּיבְּלוּ עֲלֵיהֶן לְשַׁקֵּר לַחְתּוֹם בְּגֵט שֶׁאֵין בּוֹ זְמַן.

Halakhah 4: "Three kinds of bills of divorce are invalid," etc. Rebbi Joḥanan in the name of Rebbi Yannai: All in handwriting[60]. Rebbi Eleazar asked: There are witnesses; why do I need handwriting[61]? Rav

Jeremiah in the name of Rav: All in handwriting except if its witnesses are with it[62]. Rav Hamnuna said, they testified to their own sin since they agreed to lie by signing on an undated bill of divorce[63].

60 The bill can only be used in an emergency if it was in the husband's handwriting in all three cases.

61 He questions why the middle case of a signed but undated bill needs to be the husband's autograph to be valid. He is reported in the same sense in the Babli, 86b.

62 Supporting R. Eleazar. A similar statement is in the Babli, 86a/b. Samuel's opinion, that the husband's autograph is needed only in the first case, has no parallel in the Yerushalmi.

63 He supports R. Johanan. The witnesses who signed the undated document impeach themselves; their testimony can be accepted only in an emergency.

(50b line 38) רִבִּי בָּא בַּר הַמְנוּנָא רַב אָדָא בַּר אָחָא בְּשֵׁם רַב. דְּרִבִּי מֵאִיר הִיא. מָה חָמִית מֵימַר כֵּן. אָמַר רִבִּי מָנָא. בְּגִין דְּאָמַר רַב הוּנָא בְּשֵׁם רַב. כָּל־הֲהֵין פִּירְקָא דְּרִבִּי מֵאִיר חוּץ מִשִּׁינָּה שְׁמוֹ וּשְׁמָהּ שֵׁם עִירוֹ וְשֵׁם עִירָהּ. דְּלָא תֵיסְבּוֹר מֵימַר. קַיָּימֵיהּ דְּרִבִּי מֵאִיר הִיא תַּנְיָנַיֵּיהּ דְּרַבָּנָן. לְפוּם כֵּן צָרִיךְ מֵימַר. דְּרִבִּי מֵאִיר הִיא. אָמַר רִבִּי יוֹסֵי. בְּגִין דְּרַב וּשְׁמוּאֵל תְּרֵיהוֹן אָמְרִין. הֲלָכָה כְּרִבִּי לְעָזָר. דְּלָא תֵיסְבּוֹר מֵימַר אוֹף הָכָא. לְפוּם כֵּן צָרִיךְ מֵימַר. דְּרִבִּי מֵאִיר הִיא.

Rebbi Abba bar Hamnuna, Rav Ada bar Aha[64] in the name of Rav: This is Rebbi Meïr's[65]. Why did you have to say this? Rebbi Mana said, since Rav Huna said in the name of Rav[66]: "This entire Chapter is Rebbi Meïr's except for 'if he changed his or her name or the name of his or her city.'" You should not come to say that the first is Rebbi Meïr's, the second the rabbis'[67]. Therefore it is necessary to say that this is Rebbi Meïr's. Rebbi Yose said[68], since Rav and Samuel both say that practice follows Rebbi Eleazar, that you should not be led to say the same here. Therefore it is necessary to say that this is Rebbi Meïr's.

64 These names are not known from any other source. It seems that one should read: Rebbi Aḥa, Rav Hamnuna, Rav Ada bar Ahawa.

65 The Babli agrees, 86a.

66 Chapter 8:5, Note 71.

67 One should not think that only Chapter 8, Mishnah 5 ff. follows R. Meïr but all of Chapter 9 follows the rabbis opposing R. Meïr (who are represented by R. Eleazar in Mishnah 9:5) who hold that all bills of divorce are validated by the witnesses to the delivery, not the signatures on the bill.

68 The explanation of R. Mana is far-fetched.

(fol. 50a) **משנה ה:** רִבִּי אֶלְעָזָר אוֹמֵר אַף עַל פִּי שָׁאֵין עָלָיו עֵדִים אֶלָּא שֶׁנְּתָנוֹ לָהּ בִּפְנֵי עֵדִים כָּשֵׁר וְגוֹבָה מִנְּכָסִים מְשׁוּעְבָּדִים. שָׁאֵין הָעֵדִים חוֹתְמִין עַל הַגֵּט אֶלָּא מִפְּנֵי תִּיקּוּן הָעוֹלָם.

Mishnah 5: Rebbi Eleazar says, it[69] is valid even if there are no signatures of witnesses on it if only he delivered it in the presence of witnesses; and she can use it to collect from encumbered property[70]. For the witnesses sign on the bill of divorce only for the public good[71].

69 One of the irregular bills of divorce mentioned in the preceding Mishnah.

70 The testimony of the witnesses to the delivery will enable the divorcee to request the court to foreclose property if the husband is unwilling or unable to pay her *ketubah*. Cf. Mishnah 4:3.

71 The public good is that the divorcee is much less likely to become a burden on public charity if her claims on her ex-husband are documented rather than dependent on the testimony of witnesses who may or may not be available to testify.

(50b line 45) **הלכה ה:** רִבִּי אֶלְעָזָר אוֹמֵר אַף עַל פִּי שָׁאֵין עָלָיו עֵדִים כול׳. רַב וּשְׁמוּאֵל תְּרֵיהוֹן אָמְרִין. הֲלָכָה כְּרִבִּי לְעָזָר. רִבִּי יוֹחָנָן בְּשֵׁם רִבִּי יַנַּאי. דִּבְרֵי

חֲכָמִים פָּסוּל. אָתָא עוֹבְדָא קוֹמֵי רִבִּי יוֹחָנָן בְּכוֹהֶנֶת וּבָעָא לְמֶיעֲבַד כְּהָדָא
דְרִבִּי יַנַּאי. כַּד שְׁמָעוֹן דְּרַב וּשְׁמוּאֵל פְּלִיגִין. אָתָא קוֹמוֹי אֲפִילוּ יִשְׂרָאֵל. וְשָׁמַע
מִינָהּ. רִבִּי יְהוֹשֻׁעַ בֶּן לֵוִי אָמַר. דִּבְרֵי הַכֹּל. כָּשֵׁר. וְהָא רִבִּי אֶלְעָזָר אָמַר. כָּשֵׁר.
וְרַבָּנָן אָמְרִין. פָּסוּל. מַה בֵּינַיְהוּ. רִבִּי אֶלְעָזָר אָמַר. כָּשֵׁר וְגוֹבָה מִנְּכָסִין
מְשׁוּעֲבָדִין. וְרַבָּנָן אָמְרִין. פָּסוּל וְגוֹבָה מִנְּכָסִין בְּנֵי חוֹרִין.

Halakah 5: "Rebbi Eleazar says, it is valid even if there are no signatures of witnesses on it," etc. Rav and Samuel both say that practice follows Rebbi Eleazar. Rebbi Johanan in the name of Rebbi Yannai: The words of the Sages: It is invalid. There came a case before Rebbi Johanan about a Cohen's wife and he wanted to act on Rebbi Yannai's statement[72] when it was heard that Rav and Samuel disagreed. There came before him [another case] involving an Israel, and he listened to that[73]. Rebbi Joshua ben Levi said, in the opinion of everybody it is valid. But did not Rebbi Eleazar say, it is valid[74], and the rabbis say, it is invalid? What is their disagreement? Rebbi Eleazar said, it is valid and she can collect from encumbered property[75]. The rabbis said, it is invalid and she can collect only from unencumbered property[76].

72 He wanted to declare the bill of divorce as nonexistent and permit the divorcee to return to her Cohen husband.

73 He accepted the unsigned bill of divorce as valid and empowered the wife to collect her *ketubah*.

74 If a name is attached to the statement it proves that it cannot be a unanimous opinion. The opposing, unnamed, rabbis must hold that the bill is invalid.

75 If the husband is unable to pay her *ketubah* and if he sold real estate during the marriage, the wife's lien on that real estate was not broken by the sale and she can foreclose from the buyer.

76 The bill of divorce is not usable in money matters; the divorcee's claim does not have the status of a prior mortgage, which can also be enforced

against the innocent buyer, but that of an undocumented loan which on the testimony of witnesses can be enforced against the debtor (in this case, the ex-husband) but not against a buyer of real property (who could not have discovered the existence of the debt by a title search.)

(fol. 50a) **משנה ו:** שְׁנַיִם שֶׁשִּׁלְחוּ שְׁנֵי גִיטִּין שָׁוִין וְנִתְעָרְבוּ נוֹתֵן שְׁנֵיהֶן לְזוֹ וּשְׁנֵיהֶן לְזוֹ. לְפִיכָךְ אִם אָבַד אֶחָד מֵהֶן הֲרֵי הַשֵּׁנִי בָּטֵל.

Mishnah 6: If two men sent two identical bills of divorce[77] which became mixed up[78], one delivers both to both women. Therefore, if one of them was lost, the second became unusable.

77 Two men, both called X ben Y, living in the same town, divorce their wives, both called Z bat U, living in the same town.

78 They were written be the same scribe and entrusted to the same agent.

(50b line 53) **הלכה ו:** שְׁנַיִם שֶׁשִּׁלְחוּ שְׁנֵי גִיטִּין שָׁוִין כול'. רִבִּי אֶלְעָזָר בֵּירִבִּי יוֹסֵי בְּעָא קוֹמֵי רִבִּי יוֹסֵי. כְּמָה דְאַתְּ אָמַר. גֵּט אַחַר גֵּט פָּסוּל בִּשְׁתֵּי נָשִׁים. וְדִכְוָותָהּ וְהוּא שְׁנֵי גִיטִּין פְּסוּלִין בִּשְׁתֵּי נָשִׁים. אָמַר לֵיהּ. וְכֵינִי. אָמַר לֵיהּ. וְהָא תַנִּינָן. שְׁנַיִם שֶׁשִּׁלְחוּ שְׁנֵי גִיטִּין שָׁוִין וְנִתְעָרְבוּ נוֹתֵן שְׁנֵיהֶן לְזוֹ וּשְׁנֵיהֶן לְזוֹ. תַּמָּן זֶה כְרוּת לִשְׁמָהּ וְזֶה כְרוּת לִשְׁמָהּ. תַּעֲרוֹבֶת הִיא שֶׁגָּרְמָה. בְּרַם הָכָא לֹא זֶה כְרוּת לִשְׁמָהּ וְלֹא זֶה כְרוּת לִשְׁמָהּ. מִכֵּיוָן שֶׁנְּתָנוֹ לָהּ יֵעָשֶׂה כְמִי שֶׁכְּרוּת לִשְׁמָהּ מִשָּׁעָה רִאשׁוֹנָה.

Halakhah 6: "If two men sent two identical bills of divorce," etc. Rebbi Eleazar ben Rebbi Yose asked before Rebbi Yose: Just as you say that a bill of divorce after a bill of divorce is invalid in the case of two wives[79], similarly two bills of divorce should be invalid for two women.

He answered, that is correct. He said to him, but did we not state: "If two men sent two identical bills of divorce and they became mixed up, one delivers both to both women"? There[80], each of the bills was written in the name of the respective wife; the mix-up caused the problem. But here[81], neither one was written as divorce in her name; when it was delivered, could it be considered as divorce in her name from the start?

79 This refers to Halakhah 3:1, where a man has two wives with identical names. If he writes two bills of divorce without specifying to whom it applies, he can divorce neither of his wives, not even if he delivers both bills to both of them.

80 "There" is here, in the case of Mishnah 9:6.

81 The question raised, which refers to Mishnah 3:1.

משנה ז: חֲמִשָּׁה שֶׁכָּתְבוּ כְּלָל בְּתוֹךְ הַגֵּט אִישׁ פְּלוֹנִי מְגָרֵשׁ פְּלוֹנִית (fol. 50a) וּפְלוֹנִי לִפְלוֹנִית וְהָעֵדִים מִלְּמַטָּן כּוּלָּן כְּשֵׁירִין וְיִנָּתֵן לְכָל־אַחַת וְאַחַת. הָיָה כּוֹתֵב טוֹפֶס לְכָל־אַחַת וְאַחַת וְהָעֵדִים מִלְּמַטָּן אֶת שֶׁהָעֵדִים נִיקְרִין עִמּוֹ כָּשֵׁר.

Mishnah 7: If five wrote collectively a bill of divorce[82], the man A divorces B and C D[83] and the witnesses sign at the end, all are valid and [the bill] shall be delivered to each of them. If one wrote the text separately for each of them and the witnesses sign at the end, [only] the one with which the witnesses are read is valid[84].

82 There is only one text; at the point where the names of the persons involed are to be declared, five different couples are mentioned.

83 The Halakhah will point out that the verb "to divorce" is not repeated.

84 Since the witnesses sign at the

end of the last text, that text is certified. The other texts are not certified and, therefore, invalid.

הלכה ז: (50b line 60) חֲמִשָּׁה שֶׁכְּתָבוּ כְּלָל בְּגֵט כּוֹל׳. אָמַר רִבִּי יוֹחָנָן בְּשֵׁם רִבִּי יַנַּאי. וְשׁוֹאֵל אֲנִי בְשָׁלוֹם פְּלוֹנִי. חֲזָקָה עַל הַכֹּל חָתַם. שׁוֹאֵל אֲנִי בְשָׁלוֹם פְּלוֹנִי. לֹא חָתַם אֶלָּא עַל שְׁאִילַת שָׁלוֹם בִּלְבָד. רִישׁ לָקִישׁ אָמַר. אֲפִילוּ אָמַר. שׁוֹאֵל אֲנִי בְשָׁלוֹם פְּלוֹנִי. חֲזָקָה עַל כֹּל חָתַם. אֵי זֶהוּ כְלָלוֹ שֶׁלְּרִבִּי יוֹחָנָן. אִישׁ פְּלוֹנִי מְגָרֵשׁ אֶת פְּלוֹנִית וּפְלוֹנִי לִפְלוֹנִית. אֵי זֶהוּ כְלָלוֹ שֶׁלְּרֵישׁ לָקִישׁ. אָנוּ פְלוֹנִי וּפְלוֹנִי מְגָרְשִׁין אֶת נָשׁוֹתֵינוּ מִמְּקוֹם פְּלוֹנִי. אָמַר רִבִּי זְעִירָא. מוֹדֶה רִבִּי יוֹחָנָן שֶׁאִם הִזְכִּיר גֵּירוּשִׁין לְכָל־אַחַת וְאַחַת שֶׁהוּא צָרִיךְ טוֹפֵס וְעֵדִים לְכָל־אַחַת וְאַחַת. חַיְילֵיהּ דְּרִבִּי יוֹחָנָן מִן הָדָא. שֶׁאֵינִי נֶהֱנֶה לָזֶה וְלָזֶה קָרְבָּן. צְרִיכִין פֶּתַח לְכָל־אַחַת וְאַחַת. אָמַר רִבִּי יוֹסֵי. מַתְנִיתָא מְסַייְעָא לְרִבִּי יוֹחָנָן. הָיָה כוֹתֵב טוֹפֵס לְכָל־אַחַת וְאַחַת וְהָעֵדִים מִלְּמַטָּן. אֶת שֶׁהָעֵדִים נִקְרִין עִמּוֹ כָּשֵׁר. שְׁמוּאֵל אָמַר. פְּרָטוֹ שֶׁלְּרִבִּי מֵאִיר כְּלָלוֹ שֶׁלְּרִבִּי יְהוּדָה וּפְרָטוֹ שֶׁלְּרִבִּי יְהוּדָה כְּלָלוֹ שֶׁלְּרִבִּי מֵאִיר. אָמַר שְׁמוּאֵל בְּשֵׁם רִבִּי זְעִירָא. מִילֵּיהוֹן דְּרַבָּנִין אָמְרִין שֶׁאֵין פְּרָטוֹ שֶׁלְּרִבִּי מֵאִיר כְּלָלוֹ שֶׁלְּרִבִּי יְהוּדָה וּפְרָטוֹ שֶׁלְּרִבִּי יְהוּדָה כְּלָלוֹ שֶׁלְּרִבִּי מֵאִיר. דָּמַר רִבִּי יוֹחָנָן בְּשֵׁם רִבִּי יַנַּאי. וְשׁוֹאֵל אֲנִי בְשָׁלוֹם פְּלוֹנִי. חֲזָקָה עַל הַכֹּל חָתַם. שׁוֹאֵל אֲנִי בְשָׁלוֹם פְּלוֹנִי. לֹא חָתַם אֶלָּא עַל שְׁאִילַת שָׁלוֹם בִּלְבָד. אִם אוֹמֵר אַתְּ. פְּרָטוֹ שֶׁלְּרִבִּי מֵאִיר כְּלָלוֹ שֶׁלְּרִבִּי יְהוּדָה. אֲפִילוּ אָמַר. וְשׁוֹאֵל אֲנִי בְשָׁלוֹם פְּלוֹנִי. חֲזָקָה עַל הַכֹּל חָתַם. מַאי כְדוֹן. אָמַר רִבִּי יוֹסֵי. מַתְנִיתָא אָמְרָה כֵן שֶׁאֵין פְּרָטוֹ שֶׁלְּרִבִּי יְהוּדָה כְּלָלוֹ שֶׁלְּרִבִּי מֵאִיר. דְּתַנִּינָן תַּמָּן. רִבִּי מֵאִיר אוֹמֵר. אֲפִילוּ אָמַר. חִטָּה וּשְׂעוֹרָה וְכוּסֶּמֶת. חַייָב עַל כָּל־אַחַת. וְלֵית בַּר נַשׁ אֲמַר אֲפִילוּ אֶלָּא דוּ מוֹדֶה עַל קַדְמַייָתָא. מַאי כְדוֹן. אָמַר רִבִּי חֲנִינָה. עַל דַּעְתֵּיהּ דְּרִבִּי מֵאִיר בֵּין שֶׁאָמַר. חִטָּה וּשְׂעוֹרָה וְכוּסֶּמֶת. כְּלָל וּפְרָט הוּא. אִם אָמַר. חִיטִּין שְׂעוֹרִין כּוּסְמִין. כְּלָל שֶׁאֵין בּוֹ פְרָט.

2 על הכל | ש לכל   3 על שאילת | ש בשאילת   בלבד | ש -   אפי' אמי' | ש -   4 על כל | ש לכל   כללו שלר' יוחנן | ש כלל. ר' יוחנן אמ'.   5 את פלנית | ש פלנית

לפלנית | ש פלנית   כללו שלריש לקיש | ש כלל. ריש לקיש אמ'   6 את נשותינו | ש
נשינו   זעירא | ש זירא   7 שהו צריך טופס | ש שצריך ליתן טופס   אחת ואחת | ש
אחד ואחד   8 מן הדא | ש מהדא   לזה ולזה קרבן | ש לזה לזה קרבן לזה קרבן   9
לכל אחת ואחת | ש לכל אחד ואחד   מסייעא | ש מסייעה   10 טופס לכל אחת ואחת
והעדים מלמטן | ש טפוס לכל אחד ואחד ועדים למטה   נקרין | ש ניקרין   11 פרטו
שלר' מאיר | ש פרט ר' מאיר   כללו שלר' יהודה | ש כלל לר' יהודה   פרט ר' יהודה | ש
ופרטו שלר' יהודה   כללו שלר' מאיר | ש כלל לר' מאיר   12 אמ' שמואל | ש ר' שמואל
זעירא | ש זירא   דרבנין | ש דרבנן   13 ופרטו של ר' יהודה כללו של ר' מאיר)
(corrector's addition | ש -   15ועל הכל | ש לכל   על שאילת שלום בלבד | ש בשאילת
שלום   16 פרטו שלר' מאיר | ש פרט ר' מאיר   כללו שלר' יהודה | ש כלל לר' יהודה
אפי' אמי' | ש אמ'   ושואל | ש שואל   17ועל הכל | ש לכל   מאי כדון | ש -   18
אמרה כן | ש אמרה   דתנינן תמן | ש דתנינן   19על כל אחת | ש בכל אחת ואחת   20
בר נש | ש איניש   דו מודה | ש מכלל דמודה   על קדמייתא | ש בקדמיתא   מאי כדון | ש
-    חנינה | ש חיננא   21 חיטה ושעורה וכוסמת | ש חיטין ושעורין וכוסמין.   בין שאמ'.
חיטין שעורין כוסמין   22 אם אמר | ש על דעת' דר' יהודה אם אמ'. חיטין ושעורין
וכוסמין

Halakhah 7: "Five who wrote collectively a bill of divorce," etc. [85]Rebbi Joḥanan said in the name of Rebbi Yannai: "And I am greeting X," one can assume that he signed regarding everything[86]; "I am greeting X," he signed only for the greeting. Rebbi Simeon ben Laqish said, even if he said "I am greeting X," one can assume that he signed regarding everything[87]. What means "collectively" for Rebbi Joḥanan[88]? X divorces Y and Z U. What means "collectively" for Rebbi Simeon ben Laqish? We, X and Z, divorce our wives at place A[89]. Rebbi Ze'ira said, Rebbi Joḥanan agrees that if he mentions divorce for each one separately he needs a text and witnesses for each one separately[90]. The strength of Rebbi Joḥanan is from the following: "'That I shall not benefit, a *qorbān* for this one or that one'; each single one needs a separate opening[91]." Rebbi Yose said, the Mishnah supports Rebbi Joḥanan: "If he wrote a separate text[92] for each of them and the witnesses signed at the end, [only] the one with which the witnesses are read is valid." Samuel said, the detailed statement for Rebbi Meïr is the general statement for Rebbi Jehudah and the detailed statement for Rebbi Jehudah is the general statement for Rebbi Meïr[93]. [Rebbi][94] Samuel said in the name of Rebbi Ze'ira, the words of the rabbis show that the detailed statement for Rebbi Meïr is not the general statement for Rebbi Jehudah and the detailed statement for Rebbi Jehudah is not the general statement for Rebbi Meïr, since Rebbi Johanan said in the name of Rebbi Yannai: "and I am greeting X," one can assume that he signed regarding everything; "I am greeting X," he signed only for the greeting. If you would say that the detailed statement for Rebbi Meïr is the general statement for Rebbi Jehudah, even if he said "and I am greeting X," can one assume that he signed regarding everything[95]? How is this[96]? Rebbi Yose said, a Mishnah implies that the detailed statement for Rebbi Jehudah is not the general statement for Rebbi Meïr, as we have stated there[97]: "Rebbi Meïr says, even 'wheat, and barley, and spelt' makes him guilty for each one separately", but nobody says "even" unless he refers to an earlier statement[98]. How is this[96]? Rebbi Hanina said, in Rebbi Meïr's opinion, [whether][99] he said "wheat, and barley, and spelt", [or "wheat, barley, spelt] is a general statement and particulars[100]. [In Rebbi Jehudah's opinion,] if he said, "wheat grains, barley grains, and spelt grains", it is a general statement without particulars[101].

85 A parallel is in Šebuot 5:5; the readings there are noted ⱽ.

86 If a witness to any contract, including a bill of divorce, signs and appends a greeting and formulates the greeting as a sentence standing alone,

his signature cannot be counted as testimony. But if he writes: "*and* I am greeting", he makes clear that his signature refers to the entire document. The same statement (R. Abbahu in the name of R. Johanan) is in the Babli, 87a.

87 This opinion is not mentioned in the Babli.

88 Referring to the Mishnah. How must a collective bill of divorce be formulated to be valid?

89 This statement is ambiguous since no further details are given about R. Simeon ben Laqish's opinion. It is obvious from Halakhah 3:1 that a text which mentions men and women separately, "we X and Z divorce our wives Y and U" is biblically invalid since (a) one cannot divorce two women with one statement and (b) it is not clear which woman was married to which man. One has to assume that the text was something like: "we X and Z divorce our wives, X Y and Z U," with mention of place and date.

90 If the language is "X divorces Y and Z divorces U", there can be no collective bill of divorce. It still can be written on one sheet but it must spell out in full that X divorces Y and frees her to marry any man she choses, Z divorces U and frees her to marry any man she choses, and each statement has to be separately validated by two witnesses.

91 Mishnah *Nedarim* 9:7. The quote is incorrect. The Mishnah states that if each vow separately is declared as *qorban*, it will have to be annulled separately. One has to read: "a *qorbān* for this one, a *qorbān for* that one". This Mishnah supports R. Ze'ira's interpretation of R. Johanan's position.

92 And using a separate sentence containing the verb "to divorce" for each couple represents a separate text for each divorce.

93 The same statement is in *Šebuot* 5:5 (36c l. 4), Babli 38a. It refers to Mishnah *Šebuot* 5:5: "Give me my wheat, and barley, and spelt, (expressed in the plural) which you are holding!" "An oath that I am holding nothing of yours", he is guilty only once (if he swore falsely). "An oath that I am not holding any wheat, or barley, or spelt (expressed in the plural) of yours", he is guilty for every statement. Rebbi Meïr says, even if he said "wheat, or barley, or spelt (expressed in the collective singular)", he is guilty for every statement. In a *baraita* (Babli *Šebuot* 38a, *Qiddušin* 25a; quoted in Yerushalmi *Qiddušin* 2:1, 62b l. 76) R. Meïr states that for a general statement

in a false oath he is guilty only once, for a detailed statement he is guilty for every particular item. R. Jehudah notes that if a person is sued simultaneously by several people (Mishnah *Šebuot* 5:3) and he falsely swears that he owes "not to you, nor to you, nor to you", he is guilty for every single statement. Samuel notes that what is a general statement for one may be a detailed statement for another.

94 From the text in *Šebuot*. The *Giṭṭin* text cannot be correct since the first generation Samuel cannot quote the fourth generation R. Ze'ira.

95 Since in the *baraita*, R. Jehudah is mentioned as differing from R. Meïr, the question arises whether for R. Meïr there is a difference between a denial of a debt "to you, to you, to you" and "to you, and to you, and to you". In the first case, there might be three denials, in the second case, there is only one. The implications for R. Jehudah would be the opposite.

96 As the parallel shows, this interjection should be deleted.

97 Mishnah *Šebuot* 5:5. The omission of חמן "there" in the parallel text is appropriate.

98 Which must have been "wheat, barley, spelt" without connectives.

99 The necessary inserted text is from *Šebuot*.

100 Since there are three particulars, he is obligated for three separate purificatioon offerings.

101 It is one connected statement which, if false, constitutes one sin.

(fol. 50a) **משנה ח:** שְׁנֵי גִיטִין שֶׁכְּתָבָן זֶה בְּצַד זֶה וּשְׁנֵי עֵדִים עִבְרִים בָּאִים מִתַּחַת זֶה לְתַחַת זֶה וּשְׁנַיִם עֵדִים יְוָנִים בָּאִים מִתַּחַת זֶה לְתַחַת זֶה. אֶת שֶׁהָעֵדִים הָרִאשׁוֹנִים נִקְרִין עִמּוֹ כָּשֵׁר. עֵד אֶחָד עִבְרִי וְעֵד אֶחָד יְוָנִי עֵד אֶחָד יְוָנִי וְעֵד אֶחָד עִבְרִי בָּאִין מִתַּחַת זֶה לְתַחַת זֶה שְׁנֵיהֶן פְּסוּלִין.

Mishnah 8: If he wrote two bills of divorce side by side and two Hebrew-writing witnesses signed from one column to the next, and two Greek-writing witnesses signed from one column to the next, the one whose witnesses are read with it is valid. If one Hebrew- and one Greek-writing witness are under each of them, reaching from one column to the other, all are invalid[102].

102   The scribe wrote two bills of divorce in two parallel columns. When the witnesses came to sign, they used the space under both columns. Then only the bill whose witnesses sign directly under it is valid since for the other bill the first witness is at least two lines too far away to be counted. The additional complication is that the Hebrew text starts at the right but the Greek text on the left. For example:

bill	bill
	יצחק בן אברהם
	משה בן עמרם
Ενως υἱὸς Σηθ	
Σημ υἱὸς Νωε	

In this case, if the first two signatures apply to the bill on the right hand side, that bill is valid. If they applied to the bill at the left, both bills would be invalid since the bill is read from the left but the signatures from the right. If each bill carries two signatures, one to be read from the right, the other from the left:

bill	bill
	יצחק בן אברהם
Ενως υἱὸς Σηθ	
	משה בן עמרם
Σημ υἱὸς Νωε	

no bill can be read with its signatures and both are invalid. If both Hebrew signatures belong to one bill and both Greek to the other, both bills are still invalid since the second signature is only on the fourth line.

(50c line 9) **הלכה ח:** שְׁנֵי גִיטִּין שֶׁכְּתָבָן זֶה בְּצַד זֶה כול׳. הִרְחִיק אֶת הָעֵדִים מִן הַכְּתָב. מְקוֹם שְׁנֵי שִׁיטִין פָּסוּל. פָּחוֹת מִכֵּן כָּשֵׁר. שִׁמְעוֹן בַּר בָּא בְּשֵׁם רִבִּי יוֹחָנָן. חָלָק מְקוֹם שְׁנֵי שִׁיטִין לְעִנְיָין אֶחָד. אֲפִילוּ כָּל־שֶׁהוּא פָּסוּל. אָמַר רִבִּי שְׁמוּאֵל בַּר רַב יִצְחָק. מַתְנִיתָא אֲמָרָה כֵן. עֵד אֶחָד עִבְרִי וְעֵד אֶחָד יְוָנִי עֵד אֶחָד יְוָנִי וְעֵד אֶחָד עִבְרִי בָּאִין מִתַּחַת זֶה לְתַחַת זֶה שְׁנֵיהֶן פְּסוּלִין. וְעִבְרִי גַּבֵּי יְוָנִי לֹא כְעִנְיָין אֶחָד הוּא. אָמַר רִבִּי מָנָא. הִתְחִיל בְּסוֹף שְׁתַּיִם וְגָמַר בְּסוֹף

אַרְבַּע כָּשֵׁר. כַּמָּה יְהוּ הָעֵדִים רְחוֹקִין מִן הַכְּתָב. כְּדֵי שֶׁיְּהוּ נִקְרִין עִמּוֹ. דִּבְרֵי רבִּי. רבִּי שִׁמְעוֹן בֶּן אֶלְעָזָר אוֹמֵר. מְלֹא שִׁיטָה. רבִּי דּוֹסְתַּאי בֵּירבִּי יַנַּאי אוֹמֵר. בלא חֲתִימַת יַד הָעֵדִים. בְּאֵי זֶה כְתָב מְשָׁעֲרִין. רבִּי יוֹסֵי בֵּירבִּי שַׁבְּתַי. מְלֹא חֲתִימַת יַד הָעֵדִים. רבִּי אַבָּהוּ בְשֵׁם רבִּי יִצְחָק בַּר חֲקוֹלָא כְּדֵי לך ולד. רבִּי יִרְמְיָה בָּעֵי קוֹמֵי רבִּי זְעֵירָא. חֲתִימַת יוֹסֵי בֶּן יַנַּאי כַּחֲתִימַת שָׁאוּל בֶּן בָּרוּךְ. אֲמַר לֵיהּ. לָכֵן צְרִיכָה. חֲתִימַת יוֹסֵי בֶּן יַנַּאי כַּחֲתִימַת שָׁאוּל בֶּן בָּרוּךְ.

2 בא | **ב** ווא   3 אחד | **ב** אחר   פסול | **ב** -   5 עד אחד עברי ועד אחד יווני באין מתחת זה לתחת זה שניהן פסולין | **ב** -   ועברי | **ב** עברי   6 כעניין אחד | **ב** בעינן אחר אמר ר' מנא. התחיל בסוף שתים וגמר בסוף ארבע כשר | **ב** -   7 רחוקין | **ב** רחוקים נקרין | **ב** מקרין   8 דוסתאי ביר' ינאי | **ב** דוסתא בן יהודה או'   9 בלא | **ב** מלא   ר' יסא ביר' שבתי | **ב** ר' יסא בשם ר' שובתי   10 ר' אבהו בשם ר' יצחק בר חקולא | **ב** רב ירמיה בשם רב   כדי | **ב** משערין אותו עד כדי

Halakhah 8: "If he wrote two bills of divorce side by side," etc. [103]"It is invalid if the witnesses are separated from the text by the width of two lines; less than that it is valid"[104]. [105]Simeon bar Abba in the name of Rebbi Joḥanan: An empty space of two lines in a text about one subject[106] makes invalid in any case. Rebbi Samuel bar Rav Isaac said: The Mishnah says so: "One Hebrew- and one Greek-writing witness are under each of them, reaching from one column to the other, are all invalid." Is not Hebrew combined with Greek one item[107]? Rebbi Mana said, if he started at the end of the second line and ended at the fourth line, it is valid[108]. [109]"How far from the text should the witnesses sign? That they can be read with it, the words of Rebbi. Rebbi Simeon ben Eleazar says, one full line. Rebbi Dositheos ben Yannai[110] says, the width of the witnesses' handwriting." What kind of writing does one use to estimate? Rebbi Yasa ben Rebbi Sabbatai[111] says, the width of the witnesses' handwriting[112]. Rebbi Abbahu in the name of Rebbi Isaac ben

Ḥaqula: Corresponding to לך ולך[113]. Rebbi Jeremiah asked before Rebbi Ze'ira: Does the signature of Yose ben Yannai have equal weight with the signature of Shaul ben Barukh[114]? He said to him: For that it is needed, that the signature of Yose ben Yannai has equal weight with the signature of Shaul ben Barukh[115].

103 There is a parallel in *Baba batra* 10:1, noted ב. Even though this is evidently from a different edition, the text (except for the last two lines) is close enough to be considered identical. The text is Tosephta 7:11 (Babli *Baba batra* 162b).

104 The witnesses cannot sign directly after the text since then they would not appear as witnesses. In commercial contracts, the distance cannot be two full lines since then the holder of the document could insert a line of text at the end after the signing. Since a commercial contract is invalid if the witnesses are too far from the text, the same standard is applied for bills of divorce and manumission.

105 A corresponding rule holds for lacunae in the text: Chapter 3:2, Notes 68, 69.

106 The text in *Baba batra* reads: "Another subject". The parallel in 3:2 shows that this is an editorial difference, not a scribal error.

107 In *Baba batra*: "Is Hebrew relative to Greek not another subject?" The text here is preferable since for a single bill on a sheet of paper it is perfectly acceptable to have one witness sign in Hebrew and the other in Greek or Roman letters. The bills are invalid only because the signatures would be separated by more than one line, not because they are in different alphabets (cf. *Tosephta kiFshutah Gittin* p. 910).

108 If the first witness does not start to sign at the start of the second line but towards its end, extending his signature to the third line and forcing the second witness to write his patronymic on the fourth line, the document is valid since it cannot be adulterated.

109 Tosephta 7:11-12; an extended version is quoted in *Baba batra*.

110 In *Baba batra* erroneously: Dositheos ben Jehudah.

111 In *Baba batra* correctly: R. Yasa *in the name of* R. Sabbatai.

112 In *Baba batra*: The largest of the writing of the scribe or one of the

witnesses. This seems to be from the editors of *Neziqin*; the text here implies that the two lines are judged by the larger of the signatures. The Babli, *Baba batra* 163a, explicitly states that the handwriting of the scribe is irrelevant.

113   The empty line must be large enough as to accomodate separately the height of ל and the bottom of ך. The Babli agrees, *Baba batra* 163a.

114   It seems that it was acceptable if ב~ was written for "son of". In that case, "Yose ben Yannai" had no lengths above and below the line, but "Shaul ben Barukh" had both.

115   In judging a document, the actual signatures count, not theoretical distances. It might be that "Yose ben Yannai" uses up more space than "Shaul ben Barukh".

(50c line 23) שְׁטָר שֶׁיֵּשׁ בּוֹ מַחַק אוֹ תְלוּת. מְגוּפוֹ פָּסוּל. שֶׁלֹּא מְגוּפוֹ כָּשֵׁר. וְאִם הֶחֱזִירוֹ מִלְּמַטָּה אֲפִילוּ מְגוּפוֹ כָּשֵׁר. רִבִּי יוֹנָה וְרִבִּי יוֹסֵי תְּרֵיהוֹן אָמְרִין. צָרִיךְ לְהַחֲזִיר שְׁתֵּי שִׁיטִין מְקוֹם הַכְּתָב. רִבִּי זְעִירָא בְשֵׁם רַב. צָרִיךְ לְהַזְכִּיר עִנְיָינוּ שֶׁלַּגֵּט עִמּוֹ. רִבִּי בָּא בְשֵׁם רַב. לֹא הִזְכִּיר עִנְיָינוּ שֶׁלַּגֵּט עִמּוֹ. מִחְלְפָה שִׁיטָתֵיהּ דְּרִבִּי בָּא. תַּמָּן אָמַר רִבִּי בָּא בְשֵׁם רַב יִרְמְיָה. עֵדִים פְּסוּלִין אֵינָן נַעֲשִׂין כְּהַרְחֵק עֵדוּת. שֶׁלֹּא בָאוּ אֶלָּא לְהַכְשִׁירוֹ שֶׁלַּגֵּט. וְהָכָא הוּא אָמַר הָכֵין. תַּמָּן בְּשֵׁם רִבִּי יִרְמְיָה. הָכָא בְשֵׁם רַב.

A document which has an erasure or insertion in its main part[116] is invalid; in the routine matter it is valid; but if it was mentioned later[117] it is valid even in the main part. Rebbi Jonah and Rebbi Yose both say, one has to mention it at least in the second line before the end of the text. Rebbi Ze'ira in the name of Rav: One has to mention the essence of the document with it[118]. Rebbi Abba in the name of Rav: If one did not mention the essence of the document with it[119]. The argument of Rebbi Abba seems inverted. There, Rebbi Ba said in the name of Rav Jeremiah: Disqualified witnesses do not constitute remote testimony since they came only to support the document's validity[120]. And here, he says so[121]? There, in the name of Rebbi Jeremiah, here in the name of Rav.

116 Where the parties are identified and the sums of money specified.

117 Reference is made to the erasure or the addition before the last line of text.

118 In justifying erasure or addition, the purpose has to be stated.

119 This sentence is incomplete. The following discussion shows that one has to add: "it is invalid."

120 If the first lines after the contract text were filled with the signatures of people invited for reasons other than testimony and the real witnesses sign only later, one validates the document even though the real signatures start more than one line after the text.

121 If the essence of the document is not stated at the acknowledgment of a correction, the document is invalid.

(50c line 31) קָרָא עִרְעֵר עַל חֲתִימַת יְדֵי הָעֵדִים. וְעַל חֲתִימַת יְדֵי הַדַּיָּינִין. רִבִּי בָּא בְשֵׁם רַב יְהוּדָה. שֶׁכֵּן אִם רָצָא לְקַייְמוֹ בִּכְתַב יַד הָעֵדִים מְקוּיָּים. בִּכְתַב יַד הַדַּייָנִין מְקוּיָּים. אֲנִי אוֹמֵר. אֲפִילוּ בְעֵד אֶחָד מִדַּייָן אֶחָד מְקוּיָּים. יָהַב רְשׁוּ לְכָתוֹבָא שֶׁיִּכְתּוֹב וְלַחֲתִימַיָּיא שֶׁיַּחְתִּימוּן. רִבִּי בָּא בְשֵׁם רַב יִרְמְיָה. צְרִיכִין הָעֵדִים לִכְתּוֹב. הַמִּלְוָה הַזֹּאת מֵאֶחָד בְּנִיסָן הוּא וְאָנוּ אִיחַרְנוּ זְמַנּוֹ. רִבִּי זְעִירָא בְשֵׁם רַב הַמְנוּנָא. אֲשָׂרַת הַדַּייָנִין אֲפִילוּ רְחוֹקָה כַּמָּה כָּשֵׁר. אָמַר רִבִּי מָנָא. וְיָאוּת. שֶׁכֵּן אִם רָצָא לְקַייְמוֹ אֲפִילוּ בִּכְתַב אֶחָד מְקַייֵּם. רַב אָמַר. צְרִיכִין הַדַּייָנִין לִכְתּוֹב. אִישַׁרְנוּהִי בְּמַעֲמַד פְּלוֹנִי וּפְלוֹנִי. לָמָה. כְּדֵי שֶׁלֹּא יְהוּ מְצוּיִּין לְהַזִּים. מֵעַתָּה אֲפִילוּ בְּאֵי זֶה יוֹם וּבְאֵי זֶה שָׁעָה וּבְאֵי זֶה מָקוֹם. גְּזַר דִּין נְפַק מִקוֹמֵי רַב וְלֹא הֲוָה כָּתוּב כָּךְ. אָמַר רִבִּי חַגַּיי. צְרִיכִין הַדַּייָנִים מַכִּירִין אֶת הַנִּידּוֹנִין. מַעֲשָׂה הָיָה וְזִייְּפוּ.

If somebody contests the signature of the witnesses or the signature of the judges[122]. Rebbi Abba in the name of Rav Jehudah: If he wants to certify it from the handwriting of the witnesses it is certified, from the handwriting of the judges it is certified[123]; I am saying[124] that even from one witness and one judge it is certified. If he gave permission to the scribe to write and to the witnesses to sign, Rebbi Abba in the name of

Rav Jeremiah: The witnesses have to write: "This loan is from the first of Nisan but we wrote at a later date."[125] Rebbi Ze'ira in the name of Rav Hamnuna: The confirmation of the judges is valid even if it is at some distance[126]. Rebbi Mana said, is that correct? Could he then not certify from one handwriting[127]? Rav said: The judges have to write: We certified this in the presence of X and Y. Why? So they can be convicted of perjury[128]. But then also on which date, at which time, at which place? A judgment was given before Rav and this was not written[129]. Rebbi Haggai said: The judges have to know the parties. It happened that they falsified[130].

122 A debtor whose property is attached following a decree of a court in another jurisdiction claims that the document is counterfeit and the signatures of the witnesses and the judges are fake.

123 The creditor can prove the document genuine either by proving the validity of the signatures of the witnesses or that of the judges.

124 R. Abba adds that only two signatures have to be verified; they can also be those of one witness and one judge.

125 The debtor told the scribe and witnesses to execute a document of indebtedness. If it was not written on the same day, the fact has to be noted on the document even though a postdated document is valid (only a predated one is invalid). The Babli, *Baba batra* 170b, confirms the statement but notes that it is not enforced.

126 Judicial confirmation of the genuineness of a document does not have to be written immediately below the signatures of the witnesses; it can be anywhere on the document. The Babli, *Baba batra* 163b, forbids *any* space between signatures and confirmation, not even one line.

127 R. Mana's argument is that of the Babli: If there is an empty space, the creditor could insert text in between and create a fake document with genuine signatures.

128 The root זמם, used to describe perjury, really means "to devise (a plot)". It is used in *Deut.* 19:16-21 to

characterize the perjurer. In Talmudic theory, a wrong testimony is not usually perjured testimony; it is up to the court to judge the credibility of the witnesses. Perjury is impossible testimony, i. e., the witnesses pretend to have seen things they could not have seen since they were not present at the place at the time indicated. This leads to the notion that the validity of a document could be tested only if the exact time and place of the signing were indicated in the document.

129 It was executed by the signatures of the judges alone.

130 A case of identity theft, where the signatures of the witnesses and the judges were all genuine but the presumed debtor gave a false identity, so that an innocent third party was hit with a decree of payment.

(fol. 50a) **משנה ט:** שִׁיֵּיר מִקְצָת הַגֵּט וּכְתָבוֹ בַּדַּף הַשֵּׁנִי וְהָעֵדִים מִלְּמַטָּן כָּשֵׁר. חָתְמוּ עֵדִים בְּרֹאשׁ הַדַּף מִן הַצַּד אוֹ מֵאֲחוֹרָיו בְּגֵט פָּשׁוּט פָּסוּל. הִקִּיף רֹאשׁוֹ שֶׁלָּזֶה בְּצַד רֹאשׁוֹ שֶׁלָּזֶה וְהָעֵדִים בָּאֶמְצַע שְׁנֵיהֶם פְּסוּלִין. רֹאשׁוֹ שֶׁלָּזֶה בְּצַד סוֹפוֹ שֶׁלָּזֶה וְהָעֵדִים מִלְּמַטָּן אֶת שֶׁהָעֵדִים נִקְרִין בְּסוֹפוֹ כָּשֵׁר.

Mishnah 9: It is valid if some of the text remained and was written in the second column[135], with the witnesses signing below. If the witnesses signed on top of the page, or at the sides[136], or on the other side for a simple document[137], it is invalid. If [two bills of divorce] start at the same place[138] and the witnesses are in the middle, both are invalid. If the start of one bill is next to the end of the other and the witnesses are at the end, the bill whose witnesses are read with the end is valid.

135 The scribe folded the sheet so that it formed two columns. He then used both columns for the text. The witnesses then signed at the end. (The Babli, 88a, points out that this is valid only if the parchment or paper was

folded, not if the two columns were glued together since they originally might have been parts of two different documents.)

136 The signatures are disregarded unless they are affixed at the end of the document, exactly one line from the end of the text.

137 In contrast to a sealed document.

138 Two bills written on the same sheet, one from the middle to the bottom, the other from the middle to the top. The signatures do not belong to either text.

(50c line 43) **הלכה ט:** שִׁיֵּיר מִקְצָת הַגֵּט כול׳. מָהוּ שִׁיֵּיר. אָמַר רִבִּי יוֹסֵי בַּר בִּיבוֹן. כְּגוֹן קַיָּים שָׁרִיר וּבָרוּר.

Halakhah 9: "If some of the text remained," etc. What does "remained" mean? Rebbi Yose ben Rebbi Baibon said, e. g., "true, valid, and clear[139]."

139 The expression "remained" implies that most of the text was in the first column. It is now asserted that the document is valid even if only the last line is written in the second column, in which the husband asserts that the contents of the bill conform to his wishes. (The Babylonian formulary has only the words "valid and true".) Cf. M.A. Friedman, *Jewish Marriage in Palestine* (Tel Aviv 1980) Vol. 1, p. 478, Note 112.

(50c line 44) וְגֵט פָּסוּל פָּשׁוּט בִּמְקוּשָׁר כָּשֵׁר וּבִלְבַד מֵאֲחוֹרָיו.

And what is invalid for a simple document is valid for a "knotted" one if it is on the back[140].

140 Cf. Chapter 8:12 for the rules of simple and sealed (knotted) documents.

(fol. 50a) **משנה י:** גֵּט שֶׁכְּתָבוֹ עִבְרִית וְעֵדָיו יְוָנִית יְוָנִית יְוָנִית וְעֵדָיו עִבְרִית עֵד אֶחָד עִבְרִי וְעֵד אֶחָד יְוָנִי כָּתַב הַסּוֹפֵר וָעֵד כָּשֵׁר. אִישׁ פְּלוֹנִי עֵד כָּשֵׁר. בֶּן אִישׁ פְּלוֹנִי עֵד כָּשֵׁר. אִישׁ פְּלוֹנִי בֶּן אִישׁ פְּלוֹנִי וְלֹא כָתַב עֵד כָּשֵׁר. כָּתַב חֲנִיכָתוֹ וַחֲנִיכָתָהּ כָּשֵׁר. כָּךְ הָיוּ נְקִיֵּי הַדַּעַת בִּירוּשָׁלֵם כּוֹתְבִין. גֵּט מְעוּשֶׂה בְּיִשְׂרָאֵל כָּשֵׁר וּבְגוֹיִים פָּסוּל. וְהַגּוֹיִים חוֹבְטִין אוֹתוֹ וְאוֹמְרִים לוֹ עֲשֵׂה מַה שֶּׁיִּשְׂרָאֵל אוֹמְרִים לָךְ.

Mishnah 10: A bill of divorce written in Hebrew with its witnesses signing in Greek, written in Greek with its witnesses signing in Hebrew, or one witness signing in Hebrew and one in Greek[141], or the scribe wrote with one witness, is valid. "X, witness" is valid. "The son of Y, witness" is valid[142]. "X the son of Y", but he did not write "witness", is valid. If he wrote his or her surname[143], it is valid; that is how the punctilious in Jerusalem used to write. A forced bill of divorce among Jews is valid[144], from Gentiles it is invalid[145]; but the Gentiles may whip him and tell him, do what the Jews tell you[146].

141 If there is only one document to be certified, it makes no difference if one signature is read from the right and the other from the left.

142 If the signature was recognizable as that of a certain person, the exact wording of the signature is irrelevant.

143 The family name (in addition to the proper name but without the patronymic), in a society where family names were not common.

144 In a case where the marriage is valid but sinful.

145 If the wife's family pays Gentiles to beat up the husband or the Gentile ruler to jail the husband until he agrees to a divorce (documented in many cases from Medieval Spain), the resulting divorce is invalid.

146 If the rabbinic court asks the Gentile court to act on its behalf, the resulting divorce is valid.

(50c line 45) **הלכה י׳:** רַב אָמַר. הַדַּיָּינִין חוֹתְמִין אַף עַל פִּי שֶׁאֵינָן יוֹדְעִין לִקְרוֹת. אֲבָל אֵין הָעֵדִים חוֹתְמִין אֶלָא אִם כֵּן הָיוּ יוֹדְעִין לִקְרוֹת. אָמַר. יָבוֹא אֵלַי אִם עָשִׂיתִי מִיָּמָי. אָמַר רִבִּי חַגַּיי קוֹמֵי רִבִּי יוֹסֵי. לֹא בָא קוֹמֵי רַב כְּתָב יְוָנִי מִיָּמוֹי וְקִייְמָהּ בְּחוֹתְמָיו. מַתְנִיתָא פְּלִיגָא עַל רַב. גֵּט שֶׁכְּתָבוֹ עִבְרִית וְעֵדָיו יְוָנִית. יְוָנִית וְעֵדָיו עִבְרִית. עֵד אֶחָד עִבְרִי וְעֵד אֶחָד יְוָנִי. כָּשֵׁר. פָּתַר לָהּ כְּשֶׁהָיוּ יוֹדְעִין לִקְרוֹת וְלֹא הָיוּ יוֹדְעִין לַחְתּוֹם. וְאִם הָיוּ יוֹדְעִין אֶת שְׁנֵיהֶן יַחְתְּמוּ בְּאֵי זֶה מֵהֶן שֶׁיִּרְצוּ.

Halakhah 10: [147]Rav said: Judges may sign even if they cannot read, but no witnesses may sign unless they know how to read[148]. He said, such should come over me[149] if I ever acted thus[150]. Rebbi Haggai said before Rebbi Yose: Did no Greek document come before Rav that he could confirm it by its signatures[151]? The Mishnah disagrees with Rav: "A bill of divorce written in Hebrew with its witnesses signing in Greek, written in Greek with its witnesses signing in Hebrew, or one witness signing in Hebrew and one in Greek, is valid[152]." He explains that they knew how to read but not how to sign; or if they knew both [languages], they could sign in either one of their choice.

147 In the ms., Halakhah 10 starts only at 50d, line 12.

148 If judges sign the document, they only certify that it was presented to them and they attest to the genuineness of the signatures. Therefore, judges who do not know Greek can certify Aramaic signatures on a Greek document. But the witnesses testify to the genuineness of the document and they may be called to testify about its meaning; they are prohibited from signing unless they can read and understand it. In the Babli, *Ketubot* 109a/b, the rule is attributed to R. Hiyya, Rav's uncle.

149 An oath; the speaker invokes all kinds of bad things which should happen to him if he ever did what he denies doing.

150 He never acted on what he permitted in theory.

151 Since Rav exercised jurisdiction only in Babylonia, it is quite possible than no Greek document ever came before him.

152 Does this not mean that the witness signing in Greek did not know Hebrew and vice-versa?

(50d line 5) אָמַר רִבִּי אֶלְעָזָר. דִּבְרֵי הַכֹּל הִיא. אָמַר רִבִּי יוֹחָנָן. דְּרִבִּי יְהוּדָה הִיא. אָמַר רִבִּי יוֹסֵי. לֹא בְעֵית מַדְעְתּוֹ דְּרִבִּי יוֹחָנָן פְּלִיג. בְּשִׁיטָתוֹ הֱשִׁיבְהוּ. לְאוֹרְכּוֹ. דּוּ אָמַר בְּשֵׁם רִבִּי זְעִירָא. מִכֵּיוָן שֶׁאֵינוֹ מָצוּי לְזַוֵויג וְלֹא זִיוֵּוג. כֵּינֵי מַתְנִיתָא. כָּתַב סוֹפֵר וָעֵד כָּשֵׁר. אִישׁ פְּלוֹנִי כָּשֵׁר. בֶּן אִישׁ פְּלוֹנִי כָּשֵׁר. אִישׁ פְּלוֹנִי בֶּן אִישׁ פְּלוֹנִי וְלֹא כָתַב עֵד כָּשֵׁר. כָּתַב חֲנִיכָתוֹ וַחֲנִיכָתָהּ פָּסוּל. רִבִּי אַבָּהוּ בְּשֵׁם רִבִּי יוֹחָנָן. אֲפִילוּ כָתַב אֵינוּ. כָּשֵׁר. רִבִּי אַבָּהוּ כָתַב אל״ף. רַב חִסְדָּא כָּתַב סמ״ך. שְׁמוּאֵל כָּתַב חָרוּתָא.

Rebbi Eleazar said, it is everybody's opinion[153]. Rebbi Johanan said, it is Rebbi Jehudah's[154]. Rebbi Yose said, you should not infer that the opinion of Rebbi Johanan is that he differs, but he answered him following his argument. Lengthwise[155]. That is what he said in the name of Rebbi Ze'ira: Since pairing is infrequent, there was no pairing. So is the Mishnah: "If the scribe wrote with one witness, is it valid[156]. "X" is valid. "The son of Y" is valid[142]. "X the son of Y" but he did not write "witness", is valid[157]. If he wrote his or her surname, it is invalid[158]. Rebbi Abbahu in the name of Rebbi Johanan, even if he wrote "he is it[159]", it is valid. Rebbi Abbahu wrote א. Rav Hisda wrote ס.[160] Samuel wrote a palm branch.

153 The Mishnah which lets the witnesses sign in any way they choose, if only their signatures are characteristic for them.

154 Who in Mishnah 3 requires a lengthy text.

155 Mishnah 9 speaks of the case that the sheet containing the bill was folded lengthwise, with the two columns then in parallel. This may be

ascribed to R. Jehudah who in Mishnah 3 requires that the text be very specific in detailing the divorce.

The *editio princeps* reads instead of לאורכו two words לא רבו and takes it together with the next statement: לא רבו דו אמא : "Was it not his teacher who said", viz., one supports R. Yose, who is quoted in Chapter 3, Note 66, that his teacher R. Jeremiah quoted his own teacher R. Ze'ira to the effect that one does not have to worry that two men, both called X ben Y, divorce their wives, both called A bat B, at the same place on the same day. Therefore, one does not have to worry either that a person whose characteristic signature consists only of one word be taken for another person.

156 J. N. Epstein (² מבוא לנוסח המשנה, p. 476-477) notes that in most documents from the Genizah, at the end the scribe appended his own name. The Mishnah admits this declaration as testimony to the genuineness of the document. This is rejected by the Babli, 88a, in the name of R. Jeremiah. Cf. M.A. Friedman, *Jewish Marriage in Palestine* Vol. 1, p. 489.

157 In the revised version, no witness has to declare that he signs as a witness; his signature at the correct place automatically justifies it.

158 Evrybody, including J. N. Epstein, considers this as a scribal error for "valid". But it might mean that the family name alone, without a proper name, is invalid.

159 Reading אֵינוֹ for הֲנוּ. This is acceptable as a signature as long as it was written in a characteristic way that would be difficult to counterfeit, more or less in the tradition of Sephardic rabbinical signatures through the ages.

160 Probably in a very convoluted manner. In the Babli, 87b, a number of rabbis are mentioned who wrote their names in the form of a picture: R. Ḥanina a palm branch, Rav a beehive, Rabba bar Rav Huna a sail (the latter was imitated in the 18th. Cent. by R. H. Y. D. Azulay.)

(50d line 12) כָּךְ הָיוּ נְקִיֵּי הַדַּעַת בִּירוּשָׁלֵם כּוֹתְבִין. גֵּט מְעוּשָּׂה בְּיִשְׂרָאֵל כָּשֵׁר וּבַגּוֹיִם פָּסוּל כּוֹל׳. שְׁמוּאֵל אָמַר. פָּסוּל וּפוֹסֵל בִּכְהוּנָה. שְׁמוּאֵל אָמַר. אֵין מְעַשִּׂין אֶלָּא לִפְסוּלִין. שְׁמוּאֵל אָמַר. אֵין מְעַשִּׂין אֶלָּא אַלְמָנָה לְכֹהֵן גָּדוֹל גְּרוּשָׁה וַחֲלוּצָה לְכֹהֵן הֶדְיוֹט. וְהָתַנִּינָן שְׁנִיּוֹת. לָא בְגִין אָמַר שְׁמוּאֵל. וְהָתַנִּינָן הַמַּדִּיר אֶת אִשְׁתּוֹ מִלֵּיהַנּוֹת לוֹ. עַד שְׁלֹשִׁים יוֹם יַעֲמִיד פַּרְנָס. יוֹתֵר מִכֵּן יוֹצִיא וְיִתֵּן כְּתוּבָּה. שָׁמַעְנוּ שֶׁהוּא מוֹצִיא. שָׁמַעְנוּ שֶׁכּוֹפִין.

2 בכהונה | • לכהונה. ומר שמואל אכרזון בקרוייכון   3 לפסולין | • פוסלין   אלמנה | •
כגון אלמנה   4 והתנינן | • והא תנינן (2 times)   5 מכן | • מיכן   6 שכופין | •
כופין

"That is how the punctilious in Jerusalem used to write. A forced bill of divorce among Jews is valid, from Gentiles it is invalid". [161]Samuel said, it is invalid and disqualifies from the priesthood. Samuel said, one does not force, only disqualify. Samuel said, one does not force except for example a widow married to a High Priest, a divorcee or one freed by *ḥaliṣah* in the case of a simple priest. But did we not state: "Secondarily forbidden"? Did he not say "for example"? But did we not state: "A person who by a vow forbids his wife to have any usufruct from him for up to 30 days shall appoint a caretaker; after 30 days he shall divorce her and pay *ketubah*"! We heard that he shall divorce; did we hear that one forces him?

161   This paragraph is from *Yebamot* 9:5 (•) Notes 40-46.

(50d line 19) רַב יִרְמְיָה בְּשֵׁם רַב. יִשְׂרָאֵל שֶׁעִיסּוּ כְּמַעֲשֵׂה גוֹיִם פָּסוּל. וּבָאוֹמֵר. אֵינִי זָן וּמְפַרְנֵס. תַּנֵּי רִבִּי חִייָה. וְגוֹיִם שֶׁעִיסּוּ כְּמַעֲשֵׂה יִשְׂרָאֵל כָּשֵׁר. אֲפִילוּ אָמַר. אֵינִי זָן וּמְפַרְנֵס. אָמַר רִבִּי יוֹסֵי. מַתְנִיתָא אָמְרָה כֵן. וְהַגּוֹיִים אוֹמְרִים לוֹ וְחוֹבְטִין אוֹתוֹ וְאוֹמְרִים לוֹ. עֲשֵׂה מַה שֶׁיִּשְׂרָאֵל אוֹמְרִים לָךְ. רַב חִייָה בַּר אַשִׁי בְּשֵׁם אִיסִי. הָאוֹמֵר. אֵינִי זָן וּמְפַרְנֵס. כּוֹפִין אוֹתוֹ לְהוֹצִיא. רִבִּי יִרְמְיָה בָּעֵי קוֹמֵי רִבִּי אַבָּהוּ. וְכוֹפִין. אָמַר לֵיהּ. וְאַדַּיִין אַתְּ לָיֵי. אִם מִפְּנֵי רֵיחַ רַע כּוֹפִין לֹא כָל־שֶׁכֵּן מִפְּנֵי חַיֵּי נֶפֶשׁ. אָתָא רִבִּי חִזְקִיָּה רִבִּי יַעֲקֹב בַּר אָחָא רִבִּי יָסָא בְּשֵׁם רִבִּי יוֹחָנָן. הָאוֹמֵר. אֵינִי זָן וְאֵינִי מְפַרְנֵס. אוֹמְרִים לוֹ. אוֹ זָן אוֹ פַרְנֵס אוֹ פְּטוֹר.

Rav Jeremiah in the name of Rav: Jews who forced in the manner of Gentiles make invalid[162], even if he says, I shall not feed nor provide. Rebbi Ḥiyya stated: Gentiles who forced in the manner of Jews are valid, even if he says, I shall not feed nor provide[163]. Rebbi Yose said, the Mishnah says this: "Gentiles may tell him[164], whip him, and tell him, do what the Jews tell you to do." Rav Ḥiyya bar Ashi in the name of Issy[165]: If somebody says: "I shall not feed nor provide", one forces him to divorce. Rebbi Jeremiah asked before Rebbi Abbahu: Does one force? He said to him, do you still have doubts? If one forces because of a foul smell[166], so much more because of sustenance! Rebbi Ḥizqiah, Rebbi Jacob bar Aḥa, Rebbi Yasa came in the name of Rebbi Joḥanan: If somebody says: "I shall not feed and I shall not provide", one tells him: Either feed and provide, or divorce.

162 In the interpretation of Tosaphot (88b *s.v.* ובגוים, *Baba batra* 48a *s.v.* גט) if the forcing was executed under the supervision of a Gentile court or a Gentile ruler.

163 If the forcing is under the supervision of a rabbinic court, the divorce is valid even if the marriage is completely legitimate because the husband has no right to mistreat his wife in any way.

164 This addition probably is a scribal error.

165 The Babli agrees in the name of Rav (*Ketubot* 77a). Samuel holds that the husband has to be forced to pay but Rav asserts that one cannot require the wife "to live in the same basket with a snake" and the court has to force a divorce.

166 Mishnah *Ketubot* 7:10.

(fol. 50a) **משנה יא:** יָצָא שְׁמָהּ בָּעִיר מְקוּדֶּשֶׁת הֲרֵי זוֹ מְקוּדֶּשֶׁת. מְגוֹרֶשֶׁת הֲרֵי זוֹ מְגוֹרֶשֶׁת. וּבִלְבַד שֶׁלֹּא יְהֵא שָׁם אֲמַתְלָא. וְאֵיזוֹ הִיא אֲמַתְלָא. גֵּירֵשׁ אִישׁ פְּלוֹנִי אֶת אִשְׁתּוֹ עַל תְּנַאי זָרַק לָהּ קִידּוּשִׁין סָפֵק קָרוֹב לָהּ סָפֵק קָרוֹב לוֹ זוֹ הִיא אֲמַתְלָא. בֵּית שַׁמַּאי אוֹמְרִים לֹא יְגָרֵשׁ אָדָם אֶת אִשְׁתּוֹ אֶלָּא אִם כֵּן מָצָא בָהּ עֶרְוָה שֶׁנֶּאֱמַר כִּי מָצָא בָהּ עֶרְוַת דָּבָר. וּבֵית הִלֵּל אוֹמְרִים אֲפִילוּ הִקְדִּיחָה תַבְשִׁילוֹ שֶׁנֶּאֱמַר כִּי מָצָא בָהּ עֶרְוַת דָּבָר. רְבִּי עֲקִיבָה אוֹמֵר אֲפִילוּ מָצָא אַחֶרֶת נָאָה מִמֶּנָּה שֶׁנֶּאֱמַר וְהָיָה אִם לֹא תִמְצָא חֵן בְּעֵינָיו וגו'.

Mishnah 11: If it became public knowledge in town that she was preliminarily married, she is preliminarily married[167]; divorced, she is divorced[168], except if there was an excuse. What would be an excuse? Mr. X divorced his wife conditionally[169], or he threw valuables for preliminary marriage to her and it was doubtful whether it was closer to her than to him[170]; that is an excuse. The House of Shammai say, a person should not divorce his wife unless he found her immoral, as it was said[171]: "For he found with her a matter of nakedness[172]." But the House of Hillel say, even if she spoiled his dish, as it was said: "For he found with her a bad thing[173]." Rebbi Aqiba said, even if he found another more beautiful than her, as it was said: "It will be if she does not appear pleasing in his eyes[171,174], etc."

167 If she had been unmarried, she cannot marry another man without receiving a divorce from the one to whom she is betrothed in the eyes of the public.

168 And could not marry a Cohen even if previously unmarried.

169 And the condition was not satisfied.

170 A doubt whether a doubtful marriage was concluded has to be dismissed as irrelevant.

171 *Deut.* 24:1.

172 If the husband had proof of her infidelity, he would by law be obligated to divorce her (cf. *Soṭah* 1:1,

Notes 13,14). In the absence of proof, the House of Shammai counsel him to divorce her. This probably is also the interpretation to be given to *Matth.* 19:9 and is the basis of the disapproval of marrying a divorcee expressed in *Sifry Deut.* 270.

173 The Houses of Shammai and Hillel explain the same verse. The House of Shammai read עֶרְוַת דָּבָר as if it were (in rabbinic Hebrew) דְּבַר עֶרְוָה "a matter of nakedness (immorality)". The House of Hillel read the construct state עֶרְוַת as a modifier of דָּבָר "thing": an undesirable thing; e.g., being a bad cook.

174 Even if she is beautiful in an objective way, but not beautiful *in his eyes*, he may divorce her. In his opinion (adopted in practice), a divorcee may be completely blameless.

הלכה יא: יָצָא שְׁמָהּ בָּעִיר מְקוּדֶּשֶׁת הֲרֵי זוֹ מְקוּדֶּשֶׁת. רִבִּי יָסָא בְּשֵׁם רִבִּי יוֹחָנָן. נֵירוֹת דּוֹלְקִין וְשִׂיחוֹת בְּנֵי אָדָם מְשִׂיחִין. הֲתִיב רִבִּי זְעִירָא קוֹמֵי רִבִּי יָסָא. וְהָא תַּנִּינָן. יָצָא שְׁמָהּ בָּעִיר מְקוּדֶּשֶׁת הֲרֵי זוֹ מְקוּדֶּשֶׁת. מְגוֹרֶשֶׁת הֲרֵי זוֹ מְגוֹרֶשֶׁת. אִית לָהּ מֵימַר נֵירוֹת דּוֹלְקִין. לֹא שִׂיחוֹת בְּנֵי אָדָם מְסִיחִין. וְהָכָא שִׂיחוֹת בְּנֵי אָדָם מְשִׂיחִין. רִבִּי יָסָא בְּשֵׁם רִבִּי יוֹחָנָן. נִבְדַּק הַשֵּׁם וְנִמְצָא מִפִּי נָשִׁים מִפִּי קְטַנִּים בָּטֵל הַשֵּׁם. רַב אָמַר. לֹא הִתִּירוּ בָהּ אֶלָּא עֵד מִפִּי עֵד בִּלְבָד. (50d line 28)

Halakhah 11: "If it became public knowledge in town that she was preliminarily married, she is preliminarily married". Rebbi Yasa in the name of Rebbi Johanan: If lights are burning and people talk[175]. Rebbi Ze'ira objected before Rebbi Yasa: But did we not state: "If it became public knowledge in town that she was preliminarily married, she is preliminarily married; divorced, she is divorced"? Can you say that lights are burning[176]? No, people talk. So here also, people talk[177]. Rebbi Yasa in the name of Rebbi Johanan: If the title was checked and found to be from the mouth of women or minors, the title is abolished[178]. Rav said, they permitted only in case of a hearsay witness[179].

175 A person can be held married only if there was a marriage celebration and people talk about it. The same opinion is attributed to R. Joḥanan in the Babli, 89a.

176 Since the Mishnah treats divorce as parallel to marriage and usually people do not make divorce parties, no celebration can be required.

177 Likewise for marriage, no testimony about festivities is required.

178 The court cannot act (to require a divorce or to prohibit marriage to a Cohen) unless it is informed by people able to appear as formal witnesses in court.

179 Rav disagrees with R. Joḥanan. If a formal proof were required, the Mishnah would be unnecessary. Therefore, only a determination of facts is needed, and women can be asked about facts. He agrees only that if the information was by hearsay and its source cannot be located, it has to be disregarded. In the Babli, 89a, Rav holds that if the source was located but cannot be asked because the informant left, one accepts the rumor as true.

(50d line 35) וְהָא תַנֵּי. בֵּית שַׁמַּאי אוֹמְרִים. אֵין לִי אֶלָּא הַיּוֹצֵא מִשּׁוּם עֶרְוָה בִּלְבַד. מְנַיִין הַיּוֹצְאָה וְרֹאשָׁהּ פָּרוּעַ צְדָדֶיהָ פְרוּמִים וּזְרוֹעוֹתֶיהָ חֲלוּצוֹת. תַּלְמוּד לוֹמַר כִּי מָצָא בָהּ עֶרְוַת דָּבָר. מַה מְקַייְמִין דְּבֵית שַׁמַּי. שֶׁלֹּא תֹאמַר הַיּוֹצֵא מִשּׁוּם עֶרְוָה אָסוּר. מִשּׁוּם דָּבָר אַחֵר מוּתֶּרֶת. אָמַר רִבִּי שִׁילָא דִכְפַר תָּמַרְתָּא. קִרְייָא מַקְשֵׁי עַל דְּבֵית שַׁמַּי. לֹא יוּכַל בַּעֲלָהּ הָרִאשׁוֹן אֲשֶׁר שְׁלְחָהּ לָשׁוּב לְקַחְתָּהּ. מַה אֲנָן מְקַייְמִין. אִם לְאוֹסְרָהּ עָלָיו כְּבָר הִיא אֲסוּרָה לוֹ. אֶלָּא כֵן אֲנָן קַייָמִין. לִיתֵּן עָלָיו בְּלֹא תַעֲשֶׂה.

[180]Was it not stated in the name of the House of Shammai: Not only that the woman must leave because of incest; from where that she must leave if her head's [hair] is loose, if the side seams of her dress are open, or her arms stripped bare? The verse says, "for he found in her a matter of nakedness." How can the House of Shammai confirm this[181]? Lest you say that one divorced because of immorality is forbidden, for another

cause she would be permitted[182]. Rebbi Shila from Kefar-Tamarta said: The verse is difficult for the House of Shammai: "Her first husband, who had sent her away, cannot afterwards retake her.[183]" Where do we hold? If to forbid her to him, is she not already forbidden to him[184]? But we must hold, to burden him with a prohibition[185].

180 *Soṭah* 1:1, Notes 13,14.
181 In the Mishnah, the House of Shammai admit only adultery as cause of divorce. In the *baraita*, they admit all kinds of lewd behavior.
182 Could be remarried by her first husband after having had a second husband.
183 *Deut.* 24:4.
184 If she committed adultery, she is automatically forbidden to her husband, even if she does not remarry. The prohibition to remarry the first husband after a remarriage seems to be unnecessary for the House of Shammai.
185 In remarrying her, the first husband would commit two sins in one act (cf. Tosaphot 90a, *s.v.* מה).

(50d line 42) כְּתִיב וְהַדָּוָה בְּנִדָּתָהּ וְהַזָּב אֶת זוֹבוֹ. זְקֵנִים הָרִאשׁוֹנִים הָיוּ אוֹמְרִים. תְּהֵא בְּנִדָּתָהּ. לֹא תִכְחוֹל וְלֹא תִפְקוֹס עַד שֶׁתָּבוֹא בַּמַּיִם. אָמַר לָהֶן רִבִּי עֲקִיבָה. מִשָּׁם רְאָיָיה. אִם אַתְּ אוֹמֵר כֵּן אוֹף הִיא עַצְמָהּ מְבִיאָה לִידֵי כְּעִירוּת וְהוּא נוֹתֵן אֶת עֵינָיו בָּהּ לְגָרְשָׁהּ. וְאָתְיָיא דְזְקֵנִים כְּבֵית שַׁמַּי וּדְרִבִּי עֲקִיבָה כְּבֵית הִלֵּל.

It is written[186]: "And the unwell in her menstruation and the sufferer from gonorrhea in his flow." The earlier Elders used to say, "she shall be in her menstruation[187]", she shall not use *kohl* nor any make-up until she comes into water. Rebbi Aqiba said to them: Is that a reason? If you say so, she makes herself ugly and he starts thinking to divorce her. It turns out that the Elders follow the House of Shammai[188] and Rebbi Aqiba the House of Hillel[189].

186 *Lev.* 15:33. The same argument in the Babli, *Šabbat* 64b, *Sifra Meṣora' Pereq* 9(12).

187 *Lev.* 15:19.

188 Since she cannot be divorced, it does not matter how she looks.

189 In the Mishnah, R. Aqiba does not disagree with the House of Hillel; he simply takes their argument to its logical conclusion.

Introduction to Tractate Nazir

The verb נזר "to vow as *nazir*" denotes a specialization of the related verb נדר (Arabic نذر) "to vow"; in a sense, Tractate *Nazir* is an appendix to Tractate *Nedarim*. The rules of the *nazir* vow are detailed in *Num.* 6:1-21. The person who executes a vow of *nazir* is forbidden grapes, wine, and any food derived from the vine; he has to let his hair grow, and is forbidden any contact with corpses. In addition, one finds that Samson was designated a *nazir* by an angel before his birth. Since he never made the vow himself, the rules of *nazir* cannot directly be applied to such a person. It seems that only the prohibition of a haircut and wine applies to a "Samson *nazir*". In Second Temple times, the vow of *nazir* was extremely popular. Philo (*The Special Laws I*, 247-254), following the Septuagint, calls the vow of *nazir* "the Great Vow." Since the *nazir* needs a cleansing ceremony in the Temple, the vow for all practical purposes disappeared with the destruction of the Second Temple. A *nazir* vow today can only mean a life-long abstention from grapes and wine and from haircuts.

The first two Chapters are parallel to the first Chapters of *Nedarim* and deal with valid and invalid ways to make the vow. Without specification of the duration of the vow, it is presumed to be for thirty days; the rules for longer periods or permanent status are also discussed. The second

Chapter discusses mainly indirect statements which have the force of a vow.

The third Chapter starts the discussion of the detailed rules which characterize the *nazir*; in particular the rules for terminating the vow by a haircut and the involuntary interruption of the vow by contamination with the impurity of the dead.

The fourth Chapter starts with conditional vows and then turns to the vows of women and the power of the husband to dissolve them, the power of a father to impose the status of *nazir* on his underage son, and rules covering the obligatory sacrifices at the end of the *nazir* period.

The fifth Chapter contains a discussion of all kinds of vows whose validity is in question.

The sixth Chapter concludes the first part of the Tractate by a discussion of the prohibitions imposed upon the *nazir* and the sacrifices to be offered at the conclusion of his period of *nezirut*.

The last three Chapters are devoted to the rules of impurity of the dead (*Num.* 19); major parts are discussions of Mishnaiot from *Ahilut* rather than from *Nazir*. A major theoretical preoccupation are the rules concerning burial of an abandoned corpse, which has precedence over the restrictions imposed on a *nazir* or a Cohen. The last Chapter also notes that Gentiles, while in general they can make vows under rabbinic rules, cannot obtain the status of *nazir*. It also contains a collection of otherwise disconnected rules whose common interest is that *prima facie* evidence is accepted as long as it is not disproved. The Tractate ends with an aggadic statement that Samuel was a *nazir*.

כל כינויי נזירות פרק ראשון

(fol. 51a) **משנה א:** כָּל־כִּנּוּיֵי נְזִירוּת כַּנְּזִירוּת. הָאוֹמֵר אֱהֵא הֲרֵי זֶה נָזִיר אוֹ אֱהֵא נָוֶה נָזִיר. נָזִיק נָזִיחַ פָּזִיחַ הֲרֵי זֶה נָזִיר. הֲרֵינִי כָּזֶה הֲרֵינִי מְסַלְסֵל הֲרֵינִי מְכַלְכֵּל הֲרֵי עָלַי לְשַׁלַּח פֶּרַע הֲרֵי זֶה נָזִיר. הֲרֵי עָלַי צִיפֳּרִים רִבִּי מֵאִיר אוֹמֵר נָזִיר וַחֲכָמִים אוֹמְרִים אֵינוֹ נָזִיר.

Mishnah 1: All substitute names[1] for *nazir* vows are like *nazir* vows. If somebody says "I shall be" he is a *nazir*[2], "I shall be beautiful", he is a *nazir*[2]; *naziq, naziah, paziah*[3], he is a *nazir*. "I shall be like this one"[2], "I shall tend my hair," "I shall groom my hair". "I shall be obligated to grow my hair", he is a *nazir*. "I have to bring birds", Rebbi Meïr says, he is a *nazir*[4], but the Sages say, he is not a *nazir*[5].

1   Num. 6:2 reads: "A man or a woman who clearly intend to vow the vow of a *nazir*, to become a *nazir* for the Eternal." This makes it clear that making a vow of *nazir*, like any other vow, is implicitly an invocation of God's name. The speaking of any vow therefore is an invocation of God's name and this should be avoided; cf. *Nedarim* 1:1, Note 1. In this the vow of *nazir* is not different from any other vow.

2   But only if stated in the presence of a *nazir*, when it can be interpreted as "I shall be like him".

3   Names invented to avoid spelling out "*nazir*"; Mishnah *Nedarim* 1:2. Some of these words have meaning in Arabic: نزق "to be quick (or irritable)", نزح "to be far away".

4   The required sacrifice for a *nazir* who became impure, Num. 6:10.

5   It is not reasonable to assume that a person vows to be a *nazir* with the expectation to break the rules, even if unintentionally.

הלכה א: כָּל־כִּנּוּיֵי נְזִירוֹת כַּנְּזִירוּת כול׳. כְּתִיב אִישׁ כִּי יִדּוֹר נֶדֶר. מַה תַּלְמוּד לוֹמַר נֶדֶר. אֶלָּא מִיכָּן שֶׁכִּינּוּיֵי נְדָרִים כַּנְּדָרִים. אוֹ הִשָּׁבַע. מַה תַּלְמוּד לוֹמַר שְׁבוּעָה. אֶלָּא מִיכָּן שֶׁבִּיטוּיֵי שְׁבוּעָה כַּשְּׁבוּעָה. גְּרַשׁ רֹאשָׁהּ דִּנְדָרִים קַדְמִיתָא עַד דְּמָטֵי אַשְׁכַּח תַּנֵּי רִבִּי יִשְׁמָעֵאל. נֶדֶר נָזִיר לְהַזִּיר. מִיכָּן שֶׁאָדָם קוֹבֵעַ עָלָיו נְזִירוּת בְּתוֹךְ יְמֵי נְזִירוּתוֹ.

Halakhah 1: "All substitute names[1] for *nazir* vows are like *nazir* vows," etc. "All substitute names for vows are like vows," etc. It is written[12] "Any person who vows," why does the verse say "a vow"? From here that substitute names for vows are like vows. "Or he swears," why does the verse say "an oath"? From here that substitute names for oaths are like oaths. One reads that[6] at the start of the first Chapter of Nedarim, up to: Rebbi Ismael stated: "any person who vows a vow of *nazir*". From there that a person can obligate himself as *nazir* while he currently is a *nazir*.

6   The text is quoted from *Nedarim* 1:1, Notes 12-22.

(51a, line 46) תַּנֵּי. כָּל־כִּנּוּיֵי נְזִירוּת כַּנְּזִירוּת וְלוֹקִין עֲלֵיהֶן. אַף עַל גַּב דְּרִבִּי יוֹחָנָן אָמַר. אֵין לוֹקִין עַל הָאִיסָרוֹת. מוֹדֶה הוּא הָכָא שֶׁהוּא לוֹקֶה. אַף עַל גַּב דְּרִבִּי שִׁמְעוֹן אָמַר. אֵינוֹ מֵבִיא קָרְבָּן. מוֹדֶה הוּא הָכָא שֶׁהוּא לוֹקֶה. אַף עַל גַּב דְּרִבִּי יוּדָה אָמַר. סְפֵק נְזִירוּת מוּתָּר. מוֹדֶה הוּא הָכָא שֶׁהוּא לוֹקֶה. מָה נָן קַיָּימִין. אִם בְּמִתְכַּוֵּון לֵיזוֹר. אֲפִילוּ אָמַר. שֶׁאַזְכִּיר פַּת אֱהֵא נָזִיר. נָזִיר. אִם בְּשֶׁאֵינוֹ מִתְכַּוֵּון לֵיזוֹר. אַף עַל גַּב שֶׁהוֹצִיא נְזִירוּת מִפִּיו לֹא יְהֵא נָזִיר. כָּךְ אִם הָיָה קוֹרֵא בַּתּוֹרָה וְהִזְכִּיר נָזִיר נָזִיק. אֶלָּא כִּי נָן קַיָּימִין. בְּאוֹמֵר. אֶחָד מִכָּל־הַלְּשׁוֹנוֹת הַלָּלוּ נָזַרְתִּי. אִם תּוֹפֵשׂ אֶחָד מֵהֶן נְזִירוּת תָּחוּל עָלָיו נְזִירוּת. אָמַר לוֹ. שְׁמוֹר וְשָׁמַעְתָּ.

It was stated: "All substitute names for *nazir* vows are like *nazir* vows, and one whips because of them." Even though Rebbi Johanan said, one does not whip for prohibitions[7], he agrees in this case that he is whipped[8].

Even though Rebbi Simeon said, he does not bring a sacrifice[9], he agrees in this case that he be whipped[10]. Even though Rebbi Jehudah said, a questionable *nazir* vow is permitted[11], he agrees in this case that he be whipped[10]. Where do we hold? If he has the intention of becoming a *nazir*, even if he only said, I shall be a *nazir* if I mention bread, he is a *nazir*. Similarly, if he had no intention of becoming a *nazir*, even if he mentioned *nazir*, he is no *nazir*; for example if he was reading the Torah and mentioned *nazir, naziq*. But we hold about one who says, I declared my vow of *nazir* by any of these expressions. If one of them is a valid expression of a vow of *nazir*[12], it will fall on him, otherwise, will the vow of *nazir* not fall on him? One tells him: keep the discipline[13].

7 *Nedarim* 1:1, Note 36.

8 If somebody makes a vow using unapproved language and does not keep it, he cannot be accused of transgressing a biblical prohibition. But if he refers, if only obliquely, to the biblical laws of the *nazir*, such an infringement is punishable by law.

9 In Mishnah 5:7, R. Simeon holds that for a questionable vow of *nazir* one cannot bring a sacrifice since the Temple does not accept questionable sacrifices.

10 Since the vow is not questionable.

11 In Halakhah 4:6; based on *Num.* 6:2.

12 From the list mentioned in the Mishnah.

13 *Deut.* 12:28; if he had the intention of becoming a *nazir*, even if he did not use exactly the prescribed language. The same expression is used in the Babli, *Menaḥot* 81b, regarding a person who makes an irregular vow of a sacrifice.

(51a, line 56) אֲהָא. שִׁמְעוֹן בַּר בָּא בְשֵׁם רִבִּי יוֹחָנָן. בְּשָׁרָאָה נְזִירִין עוֹבְרִין. וְאָמַר נָוֶה מָהוּ. וְזֶה מַלְעִיג עֲלֵיהוֹן. אוֹ אֲהָא כְּמוֹתָן. רִבִּי יוֹסֵי בֵּירְבִּי בּוּן בְּשֵׁם שְׁמוּאֵל. הַלְוַאי אֲהָא כְּמוֹתָן.

"I shall be". Simeon bar Abba in the name of Rebbi Joḥanan: When he saw *nezirim* pass by[14]. If he said "beautiful", what is the rule? Does he ridicule them or [does he mean] "I shall be like them"? Rebbi Yose ben Rebbi Abun in the name of Samuel[15]: Certainly, I shall be like them.

14   There is no vow of *nazir* without an implicit or explicit reference to the institution of *nazir*. The reference may be to a *nazir* passing by.

15   In the Babli, 2b, Samuel takes the position attributed to R. Yose ben Ḥanina in the next paragraph.

(51a, line 58) אוֹ אֶהֵא נָוֶה. נָזִיר. מָה אֲנָן קַיָּימִין. אִם כְּשֶׁאָמַר נָוֶה. הָדָא הִיא קַדְמָיָיתָא. אִם בְּתָפוּס בִּשְׂעָרוֹ. וְהָתַנִּינָן. הֲרֵינִי כָּזֶה. וּמִדְּרַבִּי יוֹסֵי בְּרַבִּי חֲנִינָה. אִם בְּתָפוּס בִּשְׂעָרוֹ וְהוּא אָמַר. הֲרֵינִי כָּזֶה. אֶלָּא כִּי נָן קַיָּימִין בְּאוֹמֵר. אֵין נָאֶה כָּזֶה.

"Or I shall be beautiful". Where do we hold? If he said "beautiful", is that not the previous case? When he grabs his hair, is that not what we have stated: "I shall be like this one", following Rebbi Yose ben Ḥanina who holds that "I shall be like this one" refers to the case that he is grabbing his hair[16]. But we must hold that he says, "there is nothing more beautiful than this"[17].

16   Cf. Note 23.
17   In that case, we assume that he himself wants to be as beautiful and let his hair grow.

(51a, line 62) נָזִיק נָזִיחַ פָּזִיק. אָמַר רִבִּי יוֹחָנָן. לְשׁוֹנוֹת שֶׁבֵּירְרוּ לָהֶן רִאשׁוֹנִים אֵין רְשׁוּת לִבִירְיָיה לְהוֹסִיף עֲלֵיהֶן. וְהָא תַנֵּי רִבִּי חִייָה. רָזִיחַ הָזִיח. אָמַר רִבִּי שִׁילָא. לְשׁוֹנוֹת שֶׁבֵּיררוּ לָהֶן מִשְׁנִיּוֹת אֵין רְשׁוּת לִבִירְיָיה לְהוֹסִיף עֲלֵיהֶן. וְהָתַנֵּי בַּר קַפָּרָא. חֶרֶס. לֹא חַסְפָּא. אָמַר רִבִּי זְעִירָא. לְשׁוֹן גָּבוֹהַּ הוּא. הָאוֹמֵר לַחֶרֶס וְלֹא יִזְרַח וְגוֹ'. אָמַר רִבִּי שִׁמְעוֹן בֶּן לָקִישׁ. לְשׁוֹן אוּמּוֹת הָעוֹלָם הוּא. כְּגוֹן אִילֵין גֵּיוָותַי הוּא. דִּינוּן קָרְיֵי לְחַסְפָּא כַסְפָּא. אָמַר רִבִּי יוֹסֵי. נִרְאִין דְּבָרִים בִּמְקוֹמוֹת אֲחֵרִים. אֲבָל בְּמָקוֹם שֶׁקּוֹרְאִין לְנָזִיר נָזִיק אָנוּ אוֹמְרִים. נָזִיר פְּסִילִים אֵינוֹ נָזִיר.

4 חספא | ג חספא היא   5 וגו' | ג -   אמ' ר' | ג בן לקיש אמ'   אומות העולם | ג אומות
6 ניוותי | ג ניוותאי   קריי | ג קריין   7 דברים | ג הדברים   8 אנו אומ' | ג כן אני
אומ'   אינו | ג לא יהא

"*Naziq, naziaḥ, paziq*". Rebbi Joḥanan said, these are expressions chosen by earlier generations and nobody has the right to add to them. But did not Rebbi Ḥiyya state: *raziaḥ, haziaḥ*? Rebbi Shila said, also to expressions chosen by earlier secondary ones nobody has the right to add. [18]But did not Bar Qappara state *ḥeres*? Rebbi Ze'ira said, that is a name relating to the High One: "If He commands the sun: would it not shine?". Rebbi Simeon ben Laqish said, these are Gentile words, like those Nabateans who say *khaspa* for *ḥaspa*. Rebbi Yose said, it is reasonable in other places, but in a place where the *nazir* is called *naziq*, do I say that a *nazir* of people with speech defects should not be a *nazir*?

18 From here to the end of the paragraph the text is from *Nedarim* 1:2, Notes 115-120 (ג).

(51a, line 69) תַּנֵּי. בֵּית שַׁמַּי אוֹמְרִים. בֵּין כִּנּוּיִים בֵּין כִּנּוּיֵי כִינּוּיִים אֲסוּרִין. וּבֵית הִלֵּל אוֹמְרִים. כִּינּוּיִין אֲסוּרִין. כִּנּוּיֵי כִינּוּיִין מוּתָּרִין. הֵיי דֵן אִינּוּן כִּנּוּיֵי כִינּוּיִין. אָמַר רִבִּי בָּא בַּר זַבְדָּא. מְנַצַּקָא מְנַזִּיקְנָא מְפַחֲזָנָא. אָמַר רִבִּי יוֹסֵי. אֵין אִילּוּ כִּנּוּיֵי כִינּוּיִין. כִּינּוּיִין מַמָּשׁ אִינּוּן. אִילּוּ הָאוֹמֵר. מְנַדַּרְנָא. שְׁמָא אֵינוֹ נָזִיר. אֶלָּא מנזדנא כְּאוֹמֵר מְפַחֲזָנָא. אִילֵּין אִינּוּן כִּנּוּיֵי כִינּוּיִין עַל דַּעְתֵּיהּ דְּרִבִּי יוֹסֵי. הָדָא הִיא דְתַנִּינָן. הֲרֵי עָלַי צִיפָּרִין רִבִּי מֵאִיר אוֹמֵר. נָזִיר. וַחֲכָמִים אוֹמְרִים אֵינוֹ נָזִיר. אָמַר רִבִּי יוֹחָנָן. מִשּׁוּם כִּנּוּיֵי כִינּוּיִין. עַד דִּי שַׁעֲרֵיהּ כְּנִישְׁרִין רָבָא וְטִיפְרוֹהִי כְּצִיפּוֹרִין.

It was stated: "The House of Shammai say, both substitute names and substitutes of substitutes are forbidden[19]. But the House of Hillel say, substitute names are forbidden, substitutes of substitutes are permitted." What are substitutes of substitutes? Rebbi Abba bar Zavda said, *menazaqa, menaziqna, mefaḥazna*[20]. Rebbi Yose said, these are not substitutes of substitutes, they are really substitute names, for is somebody who said *menadarna* not a *nazir*? But one who says *menadarna*[21] is like one who said *mefaḥazna*. Following Rebbi Yose, these are substitutes of substitutes, as we have stated: "'I have to bring birds', Rebbi Meïr says, he is a *nazir*, but the Sages say, he is not a *nazir*." Rebbi Joḥanan said, because of substitutes of substitutes: [22]"Until his hair became mighty as an eagle's and his fingernails like those of birds."

19   Tosephta *Nazir* 1:1 (cf. also 1:2); Babli *Nedarim* 10b. The expression "forbidden" refers to "vows of prohibition" rather than to vows of *nazir*.

20   *Pi'el* forms of the accepted roots בזק, פזח.

21   Since Galilean rabbinic Hebrew mostly replaces *qal* by *pi'el* (such as מְהַלֵּךְ for הוֹלֵךְ), an unusual *pi'el* form for נדר "to make a vow" (and equally, for נזר "to vow to be a *nazir*") is valid speech.

The form מנזדנא used here makes no sense; most probably one has to read מְנַזְּרְנָא as in the preceding sentence.

22   Dan. 4:30. This establishes a proverbial connection between long hair and a mention of birds.

(51b, line 1) הֲרֵינִי כָזֶה. אָמַר רִבִּי יוֹסֵי בַּר חֲנִינָה. בְּתָפוּשׂ בְּשַׂעֲרוֹ וְהוּא אָמַר. הֲרֵינִי כָזֶה. הֲרֵינִי מְסַלְסֵל הֲרֵינִי מְכַלְכֵּל. בְּאוֹמֵר. הֲרֵינִי מִן הַמְסַלְסְלִין וּמִן הַמְכַלְכְּלִין. הֲרֵינִי מְסַלְסֵל וּמְכַלְכֵּל. בְּאוֹמֵר. לֹא אֲסַלְסֵל וְלֹא אֲכַלְכֵּל פָּחוֹת מִשְּׁלֹשִׁים אֶלָּא שְׁלֹשִׁים. הֲרֵי עָלַי שֶׁלֹּא אֲסַלְסֵל שֶׁלֹּא אֲכַלְכֵּל. בְּאוֹמֵר לֹא אֲסַלְסֵל וְלֹא אֲכַלְכֵּל יוֹתֵר עַל שְׁלֹשִׁים אֶלָּא שְׁלֹשִׁים. הֲרֵי עָלַי לְשַׁלַּח פֶּרַע הֲרֵי אֲנִי מְסַלְסֵל מְכַלְכֵּל. הֲרֵי עָלַי שֶׁלֹּא אֲסַלְסֵל וְשֶׁלֹּא אֲכַלְכֵּל מֵהֲרֵי עָלַי לְשַׁלַּח פֶּרַע.

"I shall be like this one"; Rebbi Yose bar Ḥanina said, if he grabs [a *nazir's*] hair and says, "I shall be like this one."[23] "I shall tend my hair, I shall groom my hair". If he says, I shall be of those who have to tend or grow their hair[24]. "I shall tend my hair and I shall groom my hair", if he says I shall neither tend nor grow my hair for less than thirty [days], he means thirty[25]. "It shall be my obligation neither to tend nor to grow my hair," if he says, it shall be my obligation neither to tend nor to grow my hair more than thirty [days], he means thirty. "I shall be obligated to grow my hair", means "I shall tend my hair, I shall groom my hair". Or "It shall be my obligation neither to tend nor to groom my hair, but to let it grow wildly[26]."

23 In the Babli, Samuel admits the possibility that a *nazir* was standing nearby and the person making the vow pointed to him.

24 Since in popular speech a *nazir* is characterized by his long hair, saying that one wants to be "of those who grow their hair" is a clear vow of *nazir*.

25 Mishnah 1:3 states that an unspecified period of *nezirut* is 30 days. Therefore, mentioning 30 days in a statement regarding hair is a statement of *nezirut*.

26 For the standard 30 days.

(51b, line 8) הֲרֵי עָלַי צִיפּוֹרִין. רִבִּי מֵאִיר אוֹמֵר. נָזִיר. וַחֲכָמִים אוֹמְרִים. אֵינוֹ נָזִיר. אָמַר רִבִּי יוֹחָנָן. מִשּׁוּם כִּינּוּיֵי כִינּוּיִין. עַד דִּי שַׂעֲרֵיהּ כְּנִשְׁרִין רָבָא וְטִיפְרוֹהִי כְצִפֳּרִין. רִבִּי שִׁמְעוֹן בֶּן לָקִישׁ אָמַר. מִשּׁוּם נָזִיר טָמֵא מֵבִיא עוֹף. וְכִי צִיפּוֹרִין הוּא מֵבִיא. תּוֹרִין וּבְנֵי יוֹנָה הוּא מֵבִיא. אִית תַּנּוּיֵי תַנֵּי. כָּל־עוֹף טָהוֹר קָרוּי צִיפּוֹרִין. וְאִית תַּנָּיֵי תַנֵּי. כָּל־עוֹף בֵּין טָמֵא בֵּין טָהוֹר קָרוּי צִיפּוֹרִין. מָן דָּמַר. כָּל־עוֹף טָהוֹר קָרוּי צִיפּוֹרִין. כָּל־צִפּוֹר טָהוֹר תֹּאכֵלוּ. וּמָן דָּמַר. כָּל־עוֹף בֵּין טָמֵא בֵּין טָהוֹר קָרוּי צִיפּוֹרִין. אֱמוֹר לְצִפּוֹר כָּל־כָּנָף. מַה טַעֲמָא דְרַבָּנִין. נַעֲשָׂה כְּמִתְנַדֵּב צִיפּוֹרִין לְבֶדֶק הַבַּיִת. מַאי טַעֲמָא דְרִבִּי מֵאִיר. נַעֲשָׂה כְּמִתְנַדֵּב אָשָׁם לְבֶדֶק הַבַּיִת. מַה נָפַק מִבֵּינֵיהוֹן. אָמַר. הֲרֵי עָלַי אָשָׁם. עַל דַּעְתֵּיהּ דְּרִבִּי מֵאִיר. מֵאַחַר שֶׁאֵינָן מִתְנַדְּבִין אָשָׁם לְבֶדֶק הַבַּיִת נָזִיר. עַל דַּעְתִּין דְּרַבָּנִין מֵאַחַר שֶׁנָּזִיר טָמֵא מֵבִיא אָשָׁם נָזִיר.

"'I have to bring birds', Rebbi Meïr says, he is a *nazir*, but the Sages say, he is not a *nazir*." Rebbi Joḥanan said, because of substitutes of substitutes: "Until his hair became mighty as an eagle's and his fingernails like those of birds.[22]" Rebbi Simeon ben Laqish said, because an impure *nazir* brings birds[27]. Does he bring birds[28]? He brings turtledoves or young pigeons. There are some Tannaïm who state that all pure birds are called צפור, and there are some Tannaïm who state that all birds, whether pure or impure, are called צפור. He who says that all pure birds are called צפור, "you may eat any pure bird.[29]" He who says that all birds, whether pure or impure, are called צפור, "say to any winged bird[30]." What is the rabbi's reason? He is like somebody offering birds for the upkeep of the Temple[31]. What is Rebbi Meïr's reason? He is like somebody offering a reparation sacrifice for the upkeep of the Temple[32]. What is the difference between them? If somebody says, "I take upon myself to bring a reparation sacrifice." In the opinion of Rebbi Meïr he is a *nazir* since one cannot bring a reparation sacrifice for the upkeep of the Temple. In the opinion of the rabbis he is a *nazir* since an impure *nazir* brings a reparation sacrifice[33].

27 *Num.* 6:10. But no pure person would entertain the idea of becoming a *nazir* if he expects to become impure since that could extend his period of *nezirut* indefinitely.

28 Many people use צִפּוֹר only for wild birds.

29 *Deut.* 14:11. In Scripture, צפור is feminine.

30 *Ez.* 39:14.

31 The expression הֲרֵי עָלַי "I have to bring" is a regular form of a vow, which in Temple times implied a gift to the Temple. A single bird can be offered as a voluntary sacrifice (*Lev.* 1:14-17) but a couple can be given only as an obligatory sacrifice, i. e., a reparation or a purification sacrifice. These can never be given voluntarily, as result of a vow. Since the vow was formulated for *birds*, not *a bird*, it is concluded that the birds have to be given to the Temple for its upkeep, to be sold to persons needing them for obligatory sacrifices, with the proceeds given to the Temple treasury.

32 This is an impossibility; an obligatory sacrifice cannot be given

voluntarily and it has to be offered on the altar, not sold for the Temple's benefit. Therefore, the vow has to be interpreted as a wish to be in a situation in which one has to bring a reparation sacrifice to the Temple. The only reparation sacrifices which depend on the person's initiative are either the possible sacrifice of the impure *nazir* or those required of the person guilty of larceny (*Lev.* 5:14-16, 21-26). Since it is impossible to think that a person should want to commit larceny for religious purposes, the state of *nazir* is the only alternative.

33   Since in this formulation there is no difference between the rabbis and R. Meïr, all commentaries read "he is *not* a *nazir*"; since no person would accept *nezirut* with the prospect of an indefinite duration unless he spells this out clearly at the start, the vow is invalid because it is unrealistic. If one keeps the original wording, the rabbis and R. Meïr agree not only on the result but also on the reasoning behind it.

(fol. 51a) **משנה ב:** הֲרֵינִי מִן הַחַרְצַנִּים וּמִן הַזַּגִּים וּמִן הַתִּגְלַחַת וּמִן הַטּוּמְאָה הֲרֵי זֶה נָזִיר. וְכָל־דִּיקְדּוּקֵי נְזִירוּת עָלָיו. הֲרֵינִי כְּשִׁמְשׁוֹן בֶּן מָנוֹחַ. כְּבַעַל דְּלִילָה. כְּמִי שֶׁעָקַר דַּלְתוֹת עַזָּה. כְּמִי שֶׁנִּיקְּרוּ פְּלִשְׁתִּים אֶת עֵינָיו הֲרֵי זֶה נְזִיר שִׁמְשׁוֹן. מַה בֵּין נְזִיר עוֹלָם לִנְזִיר שִׁמְשׁוֹן. נְזִיר עוֹלָם הִכְבִּיד אֶת שְׂעָרוֹ מֵיקֵל בַּתַּעַר וּמֵבִיא שָׁלֹשׁ בְּהֵמוֹת וְאִם נִיטְמָא מֵבִיא קָרְבַּן טוּמְאָה. נְזִיר שִׁמְשׁוֹן הִכְבִּיד אֶת שְׂעָרוֹ אֵינוֹ מֵיקֵל וְאִם נִיטְמָא אֵינוֹ מֵבִיא קָרְבַּן טוּמְאָה.

Mishnah 2: "I am off grape kernels[34]," or "off grape skin," or "off hair shaving," or "off impurity"; he is a *nazir* and all rules of *nezirut* apply to him. "I am like Samson ben Manoah, like Dalilah's husband, like the one who lifted the gates of Gaza, like the one blinded by the Philistines," he is a Samson-*nazir*[35]. What is the difference between a *nazir* in perpetuity[36] and a Samson-*nazir*? If the hair of a *nazir* in perpetuity becomes heavy, he shaves it off with a knife and brings three animals[37]; if he becomes impure, he brings a sacrifice of impurity. If the hair of a Samson-*nazir* becomes heavy, he does not shave; if he becomes impure, he does not bring a sacrifice of impurity.

34   This uses the expression of the verse *Num.* 6:4: "During the period of his vow, he may eat nothing which can be made from wine-grapes, neither kernels nor skin." Anybody who prohibits to himself anything characteristically forbidden to a *nazir* makes a vow of *nazir* (unless explicitly disawoved in the same breath) and is subject to all its rules.

35   A Samson-*nazir* follows the rules not of *Num.* 6 but of *Jud.* 13:1,5,14: His vow is life-long; he is forbidden wine and any intoxicating drink, and cannot shear his hair. He does not have to avoid the impurity of the dead.

36   A person who made a vow to follow the rules of *Num.* 6 for the rest of his life.

37   He celebrates the end of a *nazir* period, as prescribed in *Num.* 6:13-20, except that at the end of the ceremony he cannot drink wine but immediately starts the next period. The frequency of his shaving is a matter of dispute in the Halakhah.

(51b, line 20) **הלכה ב:** הֲרֵינִי נָזִיר מִן הַחַרְצַנִּים כול'. כֵּינִי מַתְנִיתָא. אוֹ מִן הַחַרְצַנִּין אוֹ מִן הַזַּגִּין אוֹ מִתְגַּלַּחַת אוֹ מִטּוּמְאָה. אִם אָמַר בְּכוּלָּן נָזִיר. כְּרִבִּי יְהוּדָה עַד שֶׁיַּזְכִּיר וָיִם. בְּרַם לְרִבִּי מֵאִיר אֲפִילוּ לֹא הִזְכִּיר וָיִם.

Halakhah 2: "I am a *nazir*[38] off grape kernels," etc. So is the Mishnah: "either off grape kernels," or "off grape skin," or "off hair shaving," or "off impurity"[39]. If he mentioned *nazir* with any one of them, following Rebbi Jehudah only if he mentioned "and", but following Rebbi Meïr even if he did not mention "and"[40].

38   This is the reading of the Mishnah in the Babli and most Mishnah mss.

39   He is a *nazir* if only one of the expressions mentioned were used. One should not translate: "I am off grape kernels and off grape skin and off hair shaving and off impurity", implying

that he only is a *nazir* if he recited the entire catalogue. In the Babli, 3b, the latter is the opinion of R. Simeon.

40 The disagreement between them was explained in *Giṭṭin* 9:7, Notes 85-101, mainly in Notes 93-95. According to R. Jehudah, if he makes a vow to become a *nazir* and then adds "and forbidden kernels, and forbidden skins, and forbidden haircuts, and forbidden impurity", each "and" implies a new vow for an additional period of *nezirut*. According to R. Meïr, just reciting the catalogue adds a new obligation for each item listed, even if the items are not connected by "and".

(51b, line 24) הֲרֵינִי נָזִיר וְנָזִיר. נָזִיר שְׁתַּיִם. דַּהֲוָה יָכִיל מֵימַר. הֲרֵינִי נָזִיר. הֲרֵינִי נָזִיר נָזִיר. שְׁתַּיִם. הֲרֵינִי נָזִיר אַחַת וּשְׁתָּשׁוּב. נָזִיר אַרְבַּע. אָמַר רִבִּי יוֹסֵי בֵּירִבִּי בּוּן. כָּהֶם שְׁמוֹנָה. כְּמוֹתָם שֵׁשׁ עֶשְׂרֵה. כמוכוס. טְטַרְגוֹן אַרְבַּע. טְרִיגוֹן שָׁלֹשׁ. דִּיגוֹן שְׁתַּיִם.

"I am a *nazir* and a *nazir*;" he is two times a *nazir*, for he could have said, ""I am a *nazir*." "I am a *nazir, nazir*," two. "I am a *nazir*, once, and repeated," he is four times a *nazir*[41]. Rebbi Yose ben Rebbi Abun said, "as they", eight. "Like they," sixteen[42]. Following Symmachos[43]: "*Tetragon*, four; *trigon*, three; *digon*, two."

41 Since he will be twice a *nazir* if he said "I am a *nazir*, once" by the preceding argument, the repetition would apply to all that precedes it.

42 This refers to the preceding statement. If one starts with a 4-fold obligation, any repetition doubles the number.

43 The text כמוכוס is corrupt. One has to read with Tosephta 1:1 (Babli 8b): סימכוס or סומכוס, סמכוס. Tosephta 1:2: If he says, I am a *tetragon nazir*, he is a *nazir* four times, דיגין three times, דריגון (*sic!*) two times.

The problem of identifying the numerals is complicated by Babli (8b, *Baba batra* 164b): Symmachos says, *hen* is 1, *digon* 2, *trigon* 3, *tetragon* 4, *pentagon* 5. The rabbis have stated: A circular house, or one *digon, trigon, pentagon*, is not subject to the laws of leprosy of houses (*Lev.* 14:33-53); a house built *tetragon* is subject to those laws. (A text similar to the last sentence is in Tosefta *Nega'im* 6:3; Mishnah *Nega'im* 12:1 mentions only a round house and a *trigon* house.) In *Baba batra*, the word *digon* is further determined by the note that of the two consuls (*Archontes*), the one who is not eponymous is called *archon digon* (in the interpretation of the commentary ascribed to R. Gershom, a person "appointed *archon* for the second time".)

Under the influence of the Babli, the dictionaries, starting with the 11th Cent. *Arukh*, have identified the words *digon, trigon, tetragon* used by Symmachos with the same words used in the Tosephta of *Nega'im*. Now it is clear that in the latter Tosephta, *trigon* corresponds to τρίγωνος "triangular", *tetragon* is τετράγωνος "quadrilateral, square", and *pentagon* to πεντάγωνος "pentagonal". In spherical geometry, there exists a notion of *digon*, but this cannot be traced back earlier than the 17th Cent.; it is a notion foreign to the spirit of Greek mathematics. S. Lieberman (*Tosefta kiFshutah Nazir* p. 504) has recognized correctly that a word δίγωνον does not exist in classical or Byzantine Greek. Therefore, the talmudic *digon* cannot be translated "bi-angular". The word is more likely to be δίγονος "double, twin", which certainly makes sense in the statements about *nazir* and *archon* (*archon digon* "associate *archon*"). In parallel, the words *trigon* and *tetragon* used for the *nazir*'s vow have well documented non-geometric meanings τρίγονος "threefold", τετράγονος "fourfold".

There only remains the problem of explaining the word *digon* used in Tosephta *Nega'im*. It cannot mean "bi-angle" since a house with only two corners automatically must have curved walls and is excluded as a "round house". Since "house" (at least in the Babli) as a rule means "one-room house", it could be that the Tosephta excludes multi-room dwellings from the laws of the leprous house, referring here also to δίγονος.

(51b, line 26) הֲרֵינִי. יָד לַנְזִירוּת. הֲרֵי עָלַי. יָד לְקָרְבָּן. רַבִּי לְעָזָר בְּשֵׁם רַבִּי הוֹשַׁעְיָה. תּוֹפְשִׂין אוֹתוֹ מִשּׁוּם יָד לְקָרְבָּן. רִבִּי בּוּן בַּר חִייָה בָּעֵי. אָמַר. לֹא אוֹכַל לָךְ. תּוֹפְשִׂין אוֹתוֹ מִשּׁוּם יָד לִשְׁבוּעָה. אָמַר רַבִּי יוֹסֵי. אוֹרְחֵיהּ דְּבַר נָשָׁא מֵימַר. שְׁבוּעָה לֹא אוֹכַל לָךְ. דִּלְמָא לֹאוֹכַל לָךְ שְׁבוּעָה. אָמַר רַבִּי מַתַּנְיָיה. אוֹרְחֵיהּ דְּבַר נָשָׁא מֵימַר. קָנְתָה דְכוּלְבָּהּ. דִּילְמָא כּוּלְבָּהּ דְּקָנְתָה.

2 משום | ג משם   אמר | ג אם אמר   3 תופשין | ג תופסין   משום | ג משם   יוסי | ג
יוסה   נשא | ג נש   4 שבועה לא אוכל לך. דילמא לאוכל לך שבועה. אמר רבי
מתנייה. אורחיה דבר נשא מימר | ג -   5 דכולבה | ג דכולכה   כולבה | ג כולכה

"I am" is a handle[44] for *nezirut*, "I am obligated" is a handle for *qorbān*[45]. [46]Rebbi Eleazar in the name of Rebbi Hoshaiah: one catches him because of a handle for *qorbān*. Rebbi Abun bar Ḥiyya asked, if he said, I shall not eat from you, does one catch him because of a handle of an oath? Rebbi Yose said, [47]people usually say "an oath that I shall not eat from yours;" do they ever say "that I shall not eat from yours, an oath"? Rebbi Mattaniah said, people usually say "handle of an axe"; do they ever say "axe of a handle"?

44   As explained in *Nedarim* 1:1, Note 67, a *handle* of a vow is an expression of a vow used in disregard of the formal rules of vows.

45   Not that he vowed a sacrifice but that it should be forbidden to him as if it were a sacrifice; cf. Introduction to Tractate *Nedarim*.

46   From here on, a parallel to the text is in *Nedarim* 1:1, Notes 75-77.

47   In *Nedarim*, the text between people ... people is missing.

(51b, line 31) לֹא נָזַרְתִּי. מוּתָּר. כְּבָר הֲוֵיתִי נָזִיר. הֲרֵי זֶה אָסוּר. רִבִּי בּוּן בַּר חִייָה בְּשֵׁם רִבִּי אֲבִינָא רִבִּי אִימִּי בְּשֵׁם רִבִּי יוֹסֵי בַּר חֲנִינָה. הָאוֹמֵר. הֲרֵינִי מִיץ שֶׁלְּעָרְלָה. לֹא אָמַר כְּלוּם. חֲבֶרַיָּיא אָמְרִין. מַחֲלוֹקֶת כְּרִבִּי שִׁמְעוֹן. דְּתַנִּינָן תַּמָּן. שְׁבוּעָה שֶׁלֹּא אוֹכַל. וְאָכַל נְבֵילוֹת וּטְרֵיפוֹת שְׁקָצִים וּרְמָשִׂים. חַיָּיב. וְרִבִּי שִׁמְעוֹן פּוֹטֵר. אָמַר רִבִּי זְעִירָא. בְּכוֹלֵל נֶחְלָקוּ. אֲבָל בְּפוֹרֵט כָּל-עַמָּא מוֹדוּי שֶׁאֵין שְׁבוּעוֹת חָלוֹת עַל אִיסָּרִין. וְכָאן בְּכוֹלֵל אֲנָן קַייָמִין. אָמַר רִבִּי יוּדָן. כָּאן בִּנְדָרִים כָּאן בִּשְׁבוּעוֹת. נְדָרִים חָלִין עַל אִיסּוּרִין וְאֵין שְׁבוּעוֹת חָלוֹת עַל הָאִיסָּרִין.

"I did not vow as a *nazir*," he is permitted[48]. "I already had been a *nazir*," he is forbidden[49]. Rebbi Abun bar Ḥiyya in the name of Rebbi Avina, Rebbi Immi in the name of Rebbi Yose bar Ḥanina: If somebody says, I am like *'orlah* juice⁵⁰, he did not say anything⁵¹. The colleagues say, that follows Rebbi Simeon in a disagreement. As we have stated there⁵²: "If somebody said, an oath that I shall not eat, but he ate carcass or torn meat, abominations or crawling things, he is guilty. But Rebbi Simeon declares him free from prosecution⁵³." Rebbi Ze'ira said, they disagree if it is an inclusive statement⁵⁴. But if it is a detailed statement⁵⁵, everybody agrees that no oath can be applied to prohibitions. And here, we consider an inclusive statement. Rebbi Yudan said, one is about vows, the other about oaths. Vows can be applied to prohibitions but no oaths can be applied to prohibitions⁵⁶.

48 If somebody used one of the languages classified as referring to *nazir* but immediately puts in a disclaimer, he is free from all rules of *nazir*.

49 This is not a disclaimer since a person who had been a *nazir* might want to be a *nazir* for a second time.

50 Juice from the fruits of a tree less than three full years old. All parts of the fruit, including the juice, are forbidden for any usufruct; cf. *Introduction* to Tractate *'Orlah*.

51 Even though חֲרֵינִי was declared "a handle for *nezirut*," if somebody declares that *'orlah* juice is forbidden to him he is not a *nazir* since *'orlah* juice is forbidden to any Jew.

52 Mishnah *Šebuot* 3:5.

53 For transgressing his oath, but naturally he can be prosecuted for eating prohibited food.

54 If somebody makes an oath which prohibits to him both things originally permitted and those prohibited by biblical law, the rabbis hold that an oath partially valid is valid and any infringement can be prosecuted. But R. Simeon holds that the oath exists only as far as things originally permitted are concerned; for the rest it is non-existent since "he already was sworn to it at Mount Sinai".

55 If the oath only contains a list of items prohibited anyway. In *Šebuot* (3:3; Babli 22b, 23b) this is a matter of dispute and is asserted only by R. Johanan (supported in the Babli by Rav and Samuel) but denied by R. Simeon ben Laqish.

56 Cf. *Nedarim* 2:2, Note 30.

(51b, line 39) כְּשֵׁם שֶׁכִּינּוּיֵי נְזִירוּת כַּנְּזִירוּת כֵּן כִּינּוּיֵי שִׁמְשׁוֹן כְּשִׁמְשׁוֹן. הֵיי דֵין אִינּוּן כִּינּוּיֵי שִׁמְשׁוֹן. אָמַר רִבִּי אֲבִינָא. שִׁמְשׁוֹךְ שִׁמְשׁוֹר שִׁמְשׁוֹץ.

"Just as substitute names for *nazir* vows are like *nazir* vows, so substitute names for Samson [vows] are like Samson [vows]."[57] What are substitute names for Samson [vows]? Rebbi Avina said, Šimšok, Šimšor, Šimšoṣ.

57 Tosephta 1:5.

(51b, line 40) מַן הָכָא הִכְבִּיד שְׂעָרוֹ. רִבִּי. דָּמַר רִבִּי יִרְמְיָה מִשּׁוּם רִבִּי אָמִי. דִּבְרֵי רִבִּי. נָזִיר עוֹלָם מְגַלֵּחַ אֶחָד לִשְׁנֵים עָשָׂר חוֹדֶשׁ. דִּבְרֵי חֲכָמִים. פְּעָמִים שֶׁהוּא מְגַלֵּחַ אַחַת לִשְׁלֹשִׁים יוֹם פְּעָמִים שֶׁהוּא מְגַלֵּחַ אַחַת לִשְׁנֵים עָשָׂר חוֹדֶשׁ. רִבִּי הִילָא בְּשֵׁם רִבִּי אַסִּי. אָמְרָה כֵן. הֲרֵינִי נָזִיר כִּשְׂעַר רֹאשִׁי וְכַעֲפַר הָאָרֶץ וְכַחוֹל הַיָּם. הֲרֵי זֶה נְזִיר עוֹלָם וּמְגַלֵּחַ אַחַת לִשְׁלֹשִׁים יוֹם. רִבִּי אוֹמֵר. אֵין זֶה מְגַלֵּחַ אַחַת לִשְׁלֹשִׁים יוֹם. אֶלָּא אַחַת לִשְׁנֵים עָשָׂר חוֹדֶשׁ. וְאֵי זֶהוּ שֶׁמְּגַלֵּחַ אַחַת לִשְׁלֹשִׁים יוֹם. הָאוֹמֵר. הֲרֵי עָלַי נְזִירוּת בִּשְׂעָרוֹת רֹאשִׁי וּבַעֲפַר הָאָרֶץ וּבְחוֹל הַיָּם. אָמַר רִבִּי זְעִירָא. בִּסְתָמָם חֲלוּקִין. מַה נָּן קַייָמִין. אִם בְּאוֹמֵר. מְלֹא שְׂעָרִי. כָּל־עַמָּא מוֹדוּיֵי שֶׁמְּגַלֵּחַ אַחַת לִשְׁלֹשִׁים יוֹם. אִם בְּאוֹמֵר. כְּמִינְיָין שְׂעָרוֹת רֹאשִׁי. כָּל־עַמָּא מוֹדוּיֵי שֶׁמְּגַלֵּחַ לְאַחַר שְׁנֵים עָשָׂר חוֹדֶשׁ. אֶלָּא כִּי נָן קַייָמִין. בְּאוֹמֵר. בְּשֵׂיעָר. רִבִּי אוֹמֵר. מְלֹא רֹאשִׁי. וְרַבָּנִין אָמְרִין. בְּאוֹמֵר. כְּמִינְיָין שְׂעָרוֹת רֹאשִׁי. וְכָאן לָמָּה לָמָּה אֵין הָאִישׁ נוֹדֵר. שֶׁאֵינוֹ אֶלָּא כִּמְזָרֵז עַצְמוֹ מִן הָאִיסּוּרִין. וְעוֹד מִן הָדָא. הוֹסִיף רִבִּי יוּדָה. אִם אָמַר. כְּמִלַּקְטֵי קַיִץ וְכִשְׁבִּבְלֵי שְׁמִיטָה וְכַכּוֹכָבִים שֶׁבָּרָקִיעַ. הֲרֵי זֶה נְזִיר עוֹלָם וּמְגַלֵּחַ אֶחָד לִשְׁלֹשִׁים יוֹם. אִין תֵּימַר רִבִּי יְהוּדָה כְּרַבָּנָן. כְּרִבִּי הוּא הוֹסִיף רִבִּי יוּדָה. אַבְשָׁלוֹם נְזִיר עוֹלָם הֲוָה וּמְגַלֵּחַ אַחַת לִשְׁנֵים עָשָׂר חוֹדֶשׁ. מַאי טַעְמָא. מִשּׁוּם נְזִירוּת. וְיֵידָא אָמְרָה עַל רַבָּנִין שֶׁהוּא מְגַלֵּחַ אַחַת לִשְׁלֹשִׁים יוֹם. הָדָא הִיא דְּתַנִּינָן. הֲרֵינִי נָזִיר מְלֹא הַבַּיִת אוֹ מְלֹא הַקּוּפָה. בּוֹדְקִין אוֹתוֹ. וְתַנֵּי עֲלָהּ. שֶׁהוּא מְגַלֵּחַ אַחַת לִשְׁלֹשִׁים יוֹם. וְהָא אָמְרַת. שֶׁהוּא מְגַלֵּחַ אֶחָד לִשְׁנֵים עָשָׂר חוֹדֶשׁ.

From here[58], "if his hair became heavy": Rebbi[59]. For Rebbi Jeremiah said in the name of Rebbi Immi: The words of Rebbi: A *nazir* in perpetuity shaves once in twelve months. The words of the Sages: A *nazir* in perpetuity sometimes shaves every thirty days[60], sometimes once in twelve months. Rebbi Hila in the name of Rebbi Assi[61]: It says so[62]: [63]"I am a *nazir* like the hair on my head, like the dust of the earth, or like the sand of the sea. He is a *nazir* in perpetuity and shaves every thirty days. Rebbi says, this one does not shave every thirty days," but once in twelve months. "Who is one who shaves every thirty days? If he says, I am obligated for *nezirut* like the hair on my head, like the dust of the earth, or like the sand of the sea.[64]" Rebbi Ze'ira said, they differ if it was not made explicit. Where do we hold? If he says, "the fullness of my hair", everybody agrees that he shaves once every thirty days. If he says, "the number of the hairs on my head," everybody agrees that he shaves after twelve months[65]. But we must hold that he says "like hair". Rebbi says, "the fullness of my hair". But the rabbis say, he means "the number of the hairs on my head."[66] And here, why? Why did the man not make the vow? He only encourages himself to avoid prohibitions[67]. In addition, from the following: [68]"Rebbi Jehudah added: If he said, like that which is collected in the fig harvest, or like sheaves in a Sabbatical year, or like stars in the sky, he is a *nazir* in perpetuity and shaves every thirty days." Could you say that Rebbi Jehudah follows the rabbis? He holds with Rebbi, as Rebbi Jehudah added: [69]"Absalom was a *nazir* in perpetuity and shaved every twelve months." What is the reason? Because of *nezirut*. But that would mean for the rabbis that he shaved every thirty days; that is what we have stated: [70]"I am a *nazir* the house full, or a chest full. One checks him out.[71]" It was stated on that: He shaves every thirty days. But here he said, he shaved every twelve months[72].

58   Possibly one should read מִן הֲדָא "from the following." One starts the discussion of the *nazir* in perpetuity.

59   The Mishnah, which states that a *nazir* in perpetuity can bring the required sacrifices in order to shave his hair only if it really is heavy, follows Rebbi.

60   As stated in Mishnah 3, this is the minimum period for a vow of *nazir* and is automatically assumed to be the period intended if nothing else is specified.

61   This is an intrusion of a Babylonian text added by the corrector. His name in the Yerushalmi usually is: R. Yasa.

62   Perhaps one should read: מתניתא אמרה כן "The Mishnah said so."

63   Mishnah 1:4.

64   Rebbi agrees that an unspecified period of *nezirut* is 30 days. He requires the vow to state that the person making the vow intends a multitude of vows (each one implying a major expense for three sacrifices). But a reference to the hair on his head is for him a reference to a big tuft of hair, just as a reference to the dust of the earth is to a mound of earth. The Sages hold that the language used implies a reference to a multitude of separate things (hairs, dust particles, sand grains).

65   It seems that the text is corrupt and the statements should be interchanged. If he says "the fulness of my head", he refers to the growth on his head as one entity, implying an indefinite duration of his vow but no obligation for any particular Temple ceremony. He *may* shave his hair after 12 months, provided he offers the three prescribed sacrifices. But if he refers to the "number of hairs on his head", he refers to a very great number of separate *neziriot*, and he can fulfill his obligation only by always offering his sacrifices at the earliest possible moment, after 30 days. He *must* shave every 30 days.

66   This confirms the correction made in the preceding Note.

67   While it is clear that for the rabbis he may shave after 30 days, it is not clear whether he is obligated for more than one period. Maybe he is not a *nazir* in perpetuity.

68   Babli 8b, Tosephta 1:3. In these sources: כהלקטי קיץ וכשבילי שמיטה "the heaps of figs and the pathways of the Sabbatical" (when everybody is permitted to enter any field at any time.)

69   In the Babli, 4b, the statement is attributed to Rebbi. In Tosephta *Soṭah* 3:16: R. Jehudah the Prince (= Rebbi). In *Mekhilta deR. Ismael*, *Širah* 2: R.

Jehudah; *Mekhilta deR. Simeon ben Iohai*, p. 75: R. Jehudah the Prince. The Yerushalmi rejects the attribution to Rebbi. Since R. Jehudah admits that a *nazir* in perpetuity shaves only once a year, he must agree with Rebbi.

70   Mishnah 2:5.

71   One has to ask him what he meant before deciding his status.

72   Since it was stated that for the rabbis of Mishnah 5, he shaves every 30 days even if he vowed *nezirut* in perpetuity, it follows that R. Ze'ira could not be correct when he stated that the rabbis agree that "the fullness of my hair" implies even for the rabbis that he only shaves every 12 months since there is no visible difference between "the fullness of my hair" and "a chest full".

(51b, line 61) מָנָה ו' חֳדָשִׁים וְנִיטְמָא מוֹנֶה עַד ו' חֳדָשִׁים אוֹ חוֹזֵר וּמוֹנֶה י"ב חוֹדֶשׁ. הִשְׁלִים נְזִירוּתוֹ וְלֹא הִסְפִּיק לְגַלֵּחַ עַד שֶׁעָבְרוּ עָלָיו שְׁנַיִם שְׁלֹשָׁה יָמִים וְנִיטְמָא. רִבִּי מָנִי בָּעֵי. מִכֵּיוָן שֶׁלֹּא קִידֵּשׁ שְׂעָרוֹ בְּרַם מִי מַתִּירוֹ לְגַלֵּחַ. הֲרֵינִי נָזִיר לְאַחַר ב' יָמִים. נְזִיר עוֹלָם נָזִיר מִכְּבָר. מֵאַחַר שֶׁיֵּשׁ בְּיָדוֹ לְגַלֵּחַ נָזִיר. הֲרֵינִי נָזִיר לְאַחַר ב' יוֹם. נְזִיר עוֹלָם נָזִיר מִכְּבָר. מֵאַחַר שֶׁיֵּשׁ בְּיָדוֹ לְגַלֵּחַ נָזִיר. אוֹ מֵאַחַר שֶׁאִילּוּ נִיטְמָא וְאֵין לוֹ מֵהֵיכָן לִסְתּוֹר אֵינוֹ נָזִיר.

If he had counted six months when he became impure[73], does he count another six months or does he start anew counting twelve months? If he completed his term as *nazir* but did not manage to shave until two or three days had passed when he became impure[74]. Rebbi Mani asked: Since he did not sanctify his hair, but what permits him to shave[75]? "I am a *nazir* after two days, already a *nazir* in perpetuity." Since he may shave, he is a *nazir*[76]. "I am a *nazir* after [20][77] days, already a *nazir* in perpetuity." Since he may shave, is he a *nazir*, or since if he became impure he has no time to cancel, is he no *nazir*?[78]

73   A regular *nazir* has to start his *nezirut* anew after he underwent the purification ritual (*Num.* 6:12). But a *nazir* in perpetuity has nothing to count; the rules of the regular *nazir* are no help in answering the question.

74   It is obvious that he has to undergo the purification rite and then

start his *nezirut* again, Mishnah 3:4.

75   It seems that this sentence contains a scribal error and the text should be corrected as in the *editio princeps*: מִכֵּיוָן שֶׁלֹא קִידֵּשׁ שְׂעָרוֹ בְּדָם מִי מַתִּירוֹ לְגַלֵּחַ "Since he did not sanctify his hair *by blood* (i. e., by the prescribed triple sacrifice) what permits him to shave?

76   He made two vows, the second to become activated after the first was terminated. There is no reason why not both of them should be valid.

77   Reading כ "20" instead of ב "2" (as in the parallel in the Babli, 14a) with the standard commentaries. Not only is "20" required by the context but also the reading "2" would require ב ימים as against the collective ב יום.

78   In this case, one has to assume that he set a date for the start of his *nezirut* in perpetuity. The question is whether the introductory *nezirut* represents a valid vow. If the dates are chosen so that the *nezirut* in perpetuity starts immediately after the end of the regular *nazir* period, he would be able to fulfill all conditions of that period, which include shaving his head and burning the hair under the well-being offering. But if he should become impure during that time and has to start again, he would not be able at the end of the period to shave his head, and, therefore, could not fulfill the requirements for the triple sacrifice at that time. This might invalidate the first vow. No answer is given; the problem is to be resolved in the future if sacrifices are renewed in a rebuilt Temple. Similarly, the problem remains open in the Babli, 14a.

(51b, line 68) הֲרֵינִי נָזִיר לְאַחַר לֹ יוֹם. נְזִיר שִׁמְשׁוֹן נָזִיר מִכְּבָר. אָמַר רִבִּי חִינָנָא. מִסְתַּבְּרָא שֶׁתִּדְחֶה נְזִירוּת תּוֹרָה לִנְזִירוּת שִׁמְשׁוֹן. מַה טַעֲמָא. כֵּן יַעֲשֶׂה עַל תּוֹרַת נִזְרוֹ. אֶת שֶׁנְּזִירוּתוֹ תּוֹרָה. יָצָאת נְזִירוּת שִׁמְשׁוֹן שֶׁאֵינָהּ תּוֹרָה.

"I am a *nazir* after 30 days, but already a Samson-*nazir*." Rebbi Ḥinena said, it is reasonable that the Torah *nezirut* should preëmpt the Samson-*nezirut*[79]. What is the reason? "Thus he shall proceed, following the Torah of his *nazir* vow;[80]" if his *nazir* vow follows the Torah. This excludes Samson-*nezirut* which is not from the Torah[81].

79   He keeps the regular *nezirut*, including its shaving, as if the Samson-*nezirut* did not exist.

80   *Num.* 6:21.

81   But from the prophets; it is valid as a common usage, not as a biblical precept.

(51b, line 71) נִיטְמָא. אֵינוֹ מֵבִיא קָרְבַּן טוּמְאָה. לֹא אָמַר אֶלָּא אֵינוֹ מֵבִיא קָרְבַּן טוּמְאָה. הָא לִלְקוֹת לוֹקֶה. מַתְנִיתָא דְרִבִּי יוּדָה. דְּתַנֵּי בְשֵׁם רִבִּי יוּדָה. נְזִיר שִׁמְשׁוֹן מְטַמֵּא לַמֵּתִים. שֶׁכֵּן הָיָה שִׁמְשׁוֹן עַצְמוֹ מִיטַּמֵּא לַמֵּתִים. רִבִּי שִׁמְעוֹן אוֹמֵר. אָמַר. כְּשִׁמְשׁוֹן. לֹא אָמַר כְּלוּם. שֶׁלֹּא חָלָה נְזִירוּתוֹ מִפִּיו עָלָיו. מַאי טַעֲמָא. כְּפִי נִזְרוֹ. אֶת שֶׁנְּזִירוּתוֹ חָלָה מִפִּיו עָלָיו. יָצָא נְזִירוּת שִׁמְשׁוֹן שֶׁלֹּא חָלָה מִפִּיו עָלָיו אֶלָּא מִפִּי הַדִּיבֵּר. מַאי טַעֲמָא. כִּי נְזִיר אֱלֹהִים יִהְיֶה הַנַּעַר מִן הַבָּטֶן.

[82]"If he becomes impure, he does not bring a sacrifice of impurity." He only said, "he does not bring a sacrifice of impurity." But is he whipped[83]? The Mishnah follows Rebbi Jehudah, as it was stated in the name of Rebbi Jehudah[84]: A Samson-*nazir* makes himself impure for the dead, since Samson himself was making himself impure for the dead. Rebbi Simeon says, if somebody said, "as Samson", he did not say anything, since the quality of *nazir* was not brought on by his mouth[85]. What is the reason? "By the word of his *nazir*-vow"[86]. Any whose quality of *nazir* was brought on by his mouth; this excludes Samson-*nezirut* which was not brought on by his mouth but by the Word. What is the reason? "For the lad will be God's *nazir* from the womb.[87]"

82   Here starts the discussion of the rules of the Samson-*nazir*.

83   For intentionally violating the commandment of purity of a *nazir*.

84   Babli 4b, Tosephta 1:5. The Babli explains that the sentence about the Samson-*nazir* is formulated in parallel to the sentence about the *nazir* in perpetuity who is forbidden to become impure.

85   In the interpretation of the Babli, 4b, R. Simeon negates the possibility for anybody to validly vow to be a Samson-*nazir*.

86   *Num.* 6:21. In the Biblical text: כְּפִי נִדְרוֹ "by the mouth of his vow".

87   *Jud.* 13:5.

משנה ג: סְתָם נְזִירוּת שְׁלֹשִׁים יוֹם. אָמַר הֲרֵינִי נָזִיר אַחַת גְּדוֹלָה (fol. 51a)
הֲרֵינִי נָזִיר אַחַת קְטַנָּה אֲפִילוּ מִכָּאן וְעַד סוֹף הָעוֹלָם נָזִיר שְׁלֹשִׁים יוֹם. הֲרֵינִי
נָזִיר יוֹם אֶחָד הֲרֵינִי נָזִיר שָׁעָה אַחַת הֲרֵינִי נָזִיר אַחַת וּמֶחֱצָה הֲרֵי זֶה נָזִיר
שְׁתַּיִם. הֲרֵינִי נָזִיר שְׁלֹשִׁים יוֹם וְשָׁעָה אַחַת נָזִיר שְׁלֹשִׁים וְאֶחָד יוֹם שֶׁאֵין נוֹזְרִין
לְשָׁעוֹת.

Mishnah 3: An unspecified *nezirut* is for thirty days[88]. If he said, I shall be a *nazir* once large, I shall be a *nazir* once small, even from here to the end of the world[89], he is a *nazir* for 30 days. I shall be a nazir [and][90] one day, I shall be a nazir [and] one hour, I shall be a nazir one and a half times, he is a *nazir* two times[91]. I am a *nazir* for thirty days and one hour, he is a *nazir* for 31 days since a *nazir* vow cannot be made for hours[92].

88 If no particular time-frame was indicated at the time the vow was made, the vow automatically extends to 30 days, which is the minimum possible for the duration of such a vow..

89 All these expressions relate to surface area, not time measurements; they are irrelevant for a vow of *nazir*. From Mishnah 6 (cf. Note 106) it is clear that he said "I shall be *nazir* once from here to the end of the world."

90 This is the reading of the Babli and all Mishnah mss.; it is required by the context.

91 Since the original vow was not specified in time, it is for 30 days. If then something is added for a specific time (≤ 30 days), the second vow automatically is extended to the full 30 days.

92 Since the verse (*Num.* 6:13) speaks of "fulfilling the *days* of his *nazir* vow." Since he said "30 days and . . . ", he has to bring the three sacrifices after 30 days, shave, and observe a second period of thirty days. But if he said "30+x days", he observes 30+x days and only then brings the sacrifices.

הלכה ג: סְתָם נְזִירוּת שְׁלֹשִׁים יוֹם כול'. בַּר קַפָּרָה אָמַר יְהִיוּ (51c, line 2)
תַּלְתִּין. רִבִּי שְׁמוּאֵל בַּר נַחְמָן בְּשֵׁם רִבִּי יְהוֹנָתָן. כְּנֶגֶד כֹּט פְּעָמִים שֶׁכָּתוּב

בַּתּוֹרָה בְּפָרָשַׁת נָזִיר נֶדֶר נָזִיר לְהַזִּיר. וְהָא תַּלְתֵּין אִינּוּן. אָמַר רִבִּי יוֹסֵי בֵּירִבִּי בּוּן. אַחֵר לְחִידּוּשׁוֹ יָצָא. עַל דַּעְתֵּיהּ דְּבַר קַפָּרָא אִם גִּילַּח יוֹם ל׳ לֹא יָצָא. עַל דַּעְתֵּיהּ דְּרִבִּי יוֹחָנָן אִם גִּילַּח יוֹם ל׳ יָצָא. וְאִית דְּבָעֵי נִישְׁמְעִינָהּ מִן הָכָא. גַּדֵּל פֶּרַע שְׂעַר רֹאשׁוֹ. כַּמָּה הוּא גִּידּוּל שֵׂיעָר. ל׳ יוֹם. וְאִית דְּבָעֵי נִישְׁמְעִינָהּ מִן הָכָא. וּבָכְתָה אֶת אָבִיהָ וְאֶת אִמָּהּ יֶרַח יָמִים. מַה יָּמִים שֶׁנֶּאֱמַר לְהַלָּן שְׁלֹשִׁים אַף יָמִים שֶׁנֶּאֱמַר כָּאן. וְאִית דְּבָעֵי נִישְׁמְעִינָהּ מִן הָכָא. וְהַיָּמִים הָרִאשׁוֹנִים יִפְּלוּ כִּי טָמֵא נִזְרוֹ. יָמִים שֶׁהוּתָּרוּ. שֶׁהִתִּירָן מֹשֶׁה וּבֵית דִּינוֹ. וְאֵין פָּחוֹת מִל׳. וְאִית דְּבָעֵי נִישְׁמְעִינָהּ מִן הָכָא. עַד מְלֹאת הַיָּמִים. וְכַמָּה הֵן יָמִים מְלֵיאִין. ל׳ יוֹם. מֵעַתָּה אִם גִּילַּח יוֹם ל׳ לֹא יָצָא. אָמַר רִבִּי יִצְחָק בַּר אֶלְעָזָר. יָמִים יָמָם כְּתִיב. חָסֵר יוּ״ד.

Halakhah 3: "An unspecified *nezirut* is for thirty days," etc. Bar Qappara said "ι'ε'ι'ε'" is thirty[93]. Rebbi Samuel bar Rav Naḥman in the name of Rebbi Jonathan: Corresponding to the 29 times that in the Chapter about the *nazir* in the Torah is written "vow, *nazir*, to vow as *nazir*"[94]. Are they not 30[95]? Rebbi Yose ben Rebbi Abun said, one has to be removed for its definition[96]. In the opinion of Bar Qappara, if he shaved on the 30th day, he did not fulfill his obligation. In the opinion of Rebbi Joḥanan[97], if he shaved on the 30th day, he fulfilled his obligation[98]. Some want to understand it from here: "To let his head's hair grow wildly.[99]" How much is a hair growth[100]? 30 days. Some want to understand it from here: "She shall cry for her father and her mother the days of a month[101]." Since "days" mentioned there are 30, so also "days" mentioned here. Some want to understand it from here: [102]"The prior days shall fall, for his *nezirut* is impure." The days which became permitted, which Moses and his court had permitted[103], and that is no less than 30 days. Some want to understand it from here: "Until the days are fulfilled[99]". How much are full days[104]? 30 days. Then if he shaved on the 30th day, he did not fulfill his obligation! Rebbi Isaac bar Eleazar said, "days" are written defectively יָמָם, with a letter י missing[105].

93   Num. 6:5: "Until the fulfillment of the days he shall be holy". Since the verse mentions "the fulfillment of the days", it must refer to a fixed number; but none is indicated. The number is found by interpreting "he shall be" יהיה in the Alexandrian numbering system using letters as numbers. Since י (ι) = 10, ה (ε) = 5, the sum is 2·10+2·5 = 30. (In the Babli, 5a and *Sanhedrin* 22b, this is attributed to Rav Mattanah; in *Sifry Deut.* 25 it is a gloss.)

94   In Chapter 6, 6 times in v. 21, 4 times in v. 2, 3 each in vv. 5,12,16, 2 each in vv. 13,19, and once in vv. 3,4,6,8,9,20. In the Babli, 5a, this passage is attributed to bar Pada.

95   If one counts the related word נֶזֶר in v. 7.

96   Before rules of the *nazir* can be explained, the notion of *nazir* has to be defined.

97   This should read: "R. Jonathan" since it refers to the statement of R. Samuel bar Nahman. (However, in the Babli, *Sanhedrin* 22b, R. Samuel bar Nahman reports a similar statement in the name of R. Johanan.)

98   Since the obligation is 29 days, the 30th day automatically is the day of celebration.

99   *Num.* 6:5.

100   The scribe wrote first: "How much is wild hair?" This might be the better reading.

101   *Deut.* 21:13. The argument is based on the doctrine of uniqueness of lexemes, *viz.*, that a word used in the Torah has one and only one meaning: A meaning established in one place can be transferred to any other. Cf. *Berakhot* 1:1, Note 70.

102   *Num.* 6:12.

103   Moses had forbidden Aaron and his sons to let their hair grow in mourning for Nadab and Abihu (*Lev.* 10:6), which otherwise they would have done for the customary period of 30 days (cf. *Num.* 20:29, *Deut.* 34:8).

104   From one full moon to the next.

105   Therefore, there can be a day missing in the count, as there may be only 29 days from one full moon to the next.

(51c, line 15) תַּמָּן תַּנִּינָן. הָאוֹמֵר. הֲרֵינִי נָזִיר מִיכָּן וְעַד מָקוֹם פְּלוֹנִי. וְכָא הוּא אָמַר אָכֵין. שַׁנְיָיא הִיא דְּמַר. אַחַת.

There[106], we have stated: "I am a *nazir* from here to place X", and here, he says so? There is a difference, for he said "once".

106 Mishnah 1:6. He is a *nazir* for the greater number of 30 days or the days one needs to get to place X. Why is the person who is a *nazir* to the end of the world not a *nazir* in perpetuity? Cf. Note 89. The same explanation is in the Babli, 7a.

(51c, line 17) רַב אָמַר. הֲרֵינִי נָזִיר ל' יוֹם וְיוֹם אֶחָד. נָזִיר שְׁתַּיִם. דַּהֲוָא יְכִיל מֵימַר. שְׁלֹשִׁים וְאֶחָד יוֹם. מַתְנִיתָא פְלִיגָא עַל רַב. הֲרֵינִי נָזִיר יוֹם אֶחָד. הֲרֵינִי נָזִיר שָׁעָה אַחַת. הֲרֵינִי נָזִיר אַחַת וּמֶחֱצָה. הֲרֵי זֶה נָזִיר שְׁתַּיִם. מָה הֲוָה לֵיהּ לְמֵימַר. ל' וְאַחַת שָׁעָה. מַתְנִיתָא פְלִיגָא עַל רַבָּנִין. לֹא נֶחְלְקוּ רִבִּי יִשְׁמָעֵאל וְרִבִּי עֲקִיבָה עַל הָאוֹמֵר. הֲרֵינִי נָזִיר ל' יוֹם וְיוֹם אֶחָד. שֶׁאֵינוֹ נָזִיר אֶלָּא אַחַת. וְעַל מַה נֶּחְלְקוּ. עַל הָאוֹמֵר. הֲרֵינִי נָזִיר ל' יוֹם וְעוֹד יוֹם אֶחָד. שֶׁרִבִּי יִשְׁמָעֵאל אָמַר. נָזִיר שְׁתַּיִם. וְרִבִּי עֲקִיבָה אָמַר. נָזִיר אַחַת.

Rav said: "I am a *nazir* for 30 days and one day[107]," he is a *nazir* twice since he could have said "31 days". The Mishnah disagrees with Rav: "I shall be a nazir [and][90] one day, I shall be a nazir [and] one hour, I shall be a nazir one and a half times, he is a *nazir* two times." What could he have said, "30, and an hour"[108]? A *baraita* disagrees with the rabbis[109]: Rebbi Ismael and Rebbi Aqiba did not disagree about one who said, "I am a *nazir* 30 days and one day," that he is a *nazir* only once. Where do they disagree? About one who said, "I am a *nazir* 30 days and in addition one day," where Rebbi Ismael said, he is a *nazir* twice[110], but Rebbi Aqiba said, he is a *nazir* only once[111].

107 In contrast to the Mishnah (Note 90), where *nazir* was not mentioned and, therefore, the addition was something new, here *nazir* is mentioned and it is not clear whether the addition is a new vow.

108 The argument of Rav is disproved from the second part of the sentence, referring to the man who says that he shall be *nazir* "and an hour". Since the Mishnah says that if he said "for 30 days and one hour" he is a *nazir* for 31 days and the mention of "days" does not finish the sentence; each

sentence has to be analyzed to determine as to which expressions are covered by *nazir*.

109 It seems that this must read "Rav", since no rabbis are mentioned in this context.

110 Since "in addition" introduces a second vow.

111 While in speech, "and in addition" may introduce a new clause, in elementary arithmetic וְעוֹד simply means "+". Since one deals with numbers, the usage in arithmetic is decisive.

משנה ד: הֲרֵינִי נָזִיר כִּשְׂעַר רֹאשִׁי וְכַעֲפַר הָאָרֶץ וְכַחוֹל הַיָּם. הֲרֵי זֶה (fol. 51a) נָזִיר עוֹלָם וּמְגַלֵּחַ אַחַת לִשְׁלֹשִׁים יוֹם. רַבִּי אוֹמֵר. אֵין זֶה מְגַלֵּחַ אֶחָד לִשְׁלֹשִׁים יוֹם. וְאֵי זֶהוּ שֶׁמְּגַלֵּחַ אַחַת לִשְׁלֹשִׁים יוֹם. הָאוֹמֵר. הֲרֵי עָלַי נְזִירוּת כִּשְׂעַר רֹאשִׁי וְכַעֲפַר הָאָרֶץ וְכַחוֹל הַיָּם.

Mishnah 4: "I am a *nazir* like the hair on my head, like the dust of the earth, or like the sand of the sea." He is a *nazir* in perpetuity and shaves every thirty days. Rebbi says, this one does not shave every thirty days. Who is one who shaves every thirty days? If he says, "I am obligated for *nezirut* like the hair on my head, like the dust of the earth, or like the sand of the sea[64]."

משנה ה: הֲרֵינִי נָזִיר מְלֹא הַבַּיִת אוֹ מְלֹא הַקּוּפָּה בּוֹדְקִין אוֹתוֹ. אִם אָמַר אַחַת גְּדוֹלָה נָזַרְתִּי נָזִיר שְׁלֹשִׁים יוֹם. וְאִם אָמַר סְתָם נָזַרְתִּי רוֹאִין אֶת הַקּוּפָּה כְּאִילּוּ מְלֵיאָה חַרְדָּל וְנָזִיר כָּל־יָמָיו.

Mishnah 5: "I am a *nazir* a house full[112], or a chest full." One checks him out. If he said, I made one large vow of *nazir*, he is a *nazir* for 30 days. But if he said, I made an unspecified vow of *nazir*, one considers the chest as filled with mustard seed and he is a *nazir* all his days[113].

(51c, line 25) **הלכה ד:** הָאוֹמֵר. הֲרֵי עָלַי נְזִירוּת כּוֹל׳. אָמַר רִבִּי מַנִּי. מְטִילִין אוֹתוֹ לְחוּמָרִין. כַּתְּחִילָה רוֹאִין אוֹתָהּ כְּאִילוּ מְלֵיאָה אֶתְרוֹגִין. וְאַחַר כָּךְ רִמּוֹנִים. וְאַחַר כָּךְ אֱגוֹזִים. וְאַחַר כָּךְ פּוֹנדקרין.[114] וְאַחַר כָּךְ פִּילְפָּלִין. וְאַחַר כָּךְ שׁוּמְשְׁמִין. וְאַחַר כָּךְ חַרְדָּל.

Halakhah 4: If somebody says, I am obligated as *nazir*, etc. Rebbi Manni said, one increases the severity[115]. At the start one looks at it as if full of *etrogim*, after that pomegranates, after that walnuts, after that filberts, after that pepper kernels, after that sesame seeds, after that mustard seed.

112 In *Arukh*, s. v. פונדק, the reading is מלא חבית "an amphora full".

113 And obligated for a triple sacrifice every 30 days. Cf. Note 64.

114 In *Arukh*, s. v. פונדק, the reading is פונדק. This is the basis of the translation, from the Greek κάρυον Ποντικόν "Pontic nut, filbert".

115 This belongs to Mishnah 5. In asking the person making the vow, one starts suggesting that he imagined the box (or amphora) full of citrus fruit. If he denies this, one continues with pomegranates, then walnuts, etc., going from larger items such as etrogim to smaller and finally minuscule fruits, such as mustard seeds, to increase the number of pieces contained in the same amphora, as a simile of increasing the number of *neziriot*, ending with practically limitless number.

(51c, line 28) רִבִּי יוֹסֵי בֵּירִבִּי בּוּן בְּשֵׁם רַב. הַנּוֹתֵן תִּקְנָה לִנְזִירוּתוֹ אֵין מַתִּירִין אוֹתוֹ לְגַלֵּחַ. וְתַנֵּי כֵן. הֲרֵינִי נָזִיר כָּל־יָמָיי. הֲרֵי אֲנִי נָזִיר עוֹלָם מֵאָה שָׁנָה וּמָאתַיִים שָׁנָה. אֵין זֶה נְזִיר עוֹלָם.

Rebbi Yose ben Rebbi Abun in the name of Rav: If somebody sets a term to his state of *nazir*, one does not allow him to shave[116]. And it was stated thus[117]: "I am a *nazir* all my days, I am a *nazir* in perpetuity[118]; 100 years, or 200 years, he is not a *nazir* in perpetuity[119]."

116 But he has only one period of *nezirut*, at the end of which he brings his sacrifices and shaves, and this even if the term he indicated probably exceeds his lifetime.

117 Tosephta 1:4. A similar text (1'000 instead of 200) in the Babli (7a,8b) 7.

118 By an error of the corrector, "he is a *nazir* in perpetuity" is missing here; it does appear in the parallels.

119 He is a *nazir* for 100 or 200 years, not obligated for any sacrifices but not allowed to shave in the meantime.

(fol. 51a) **משנה ו:** הֲרֵינִי נָזִיר מִיכָּן וְעַד מָקוֹם פְּלוֹנִי. אוֹמְדִין כַּמָּה יָמִים מִיכָּן וְעַד מָקוֹם פְּלוֹנִי. אִם פָּחוֹת מִשְּׁלֹשִׁים יוֹם נָזִיר שְׁלֹשִׁים יוֹם וְאִם לָאו נָזִיר כְּמִנְיַן הַיָּמִים.

Mishnah 6: "I am a *nazir* from here to place X." One estimates how many days it is from here to place X. If less than thirty days, he is a *nazir* for 30 days, otherwise for the count of the days.

משנה ז: הֲרֵינִי נָזִיר כְּמִנְיַן יְמוֹת הַשָּׁנָה. מוֹנֶה נְזִירוּת כְּמִנְיַן יְמוֹת הַשָּׁנָה. אָמַר רִבִּי יְהוּדָה מַעֲשֶׂה הָיָה כֵּיוָן שֶׁהִשְׁלִים מֵת.

Mishnah 7: "I am a *nazir* according to the count of the days of the year, he counts *nezirut* in the count of the days of a year. Rebbi Jehudah said, this happened, and after he had finished, he died.

(51c, line 31) **הלכה ו:** הֲרֵינִי נָזִיר מִכָּאן עַד מָקוֹם פְּלוֹנִי וכו'. מָה נָן קַיָּימִין. אִם כְּמִנְיַן יְמוֹת הַחַמָּה. שִׁשָּׁה נְזִירִיּוֹת כְּמִנְיַן יְמוֹת הַחַמָּה. וְאִם כְּמִנְיַן יְמוֹת הַלְּבָנָה. שְׁנֵי נְזִירִיּוֹת כְּמִנְיַן יְמוֹת הַלְּבָנָה. אִם כְּמִנְיַן יְמוֹת הַשָּׁנָה צְרִיכָה.

Halakhah 6: ""I am a *nazir* from here to place X," etc. Where do we hold? If in the count of a solar year, 365 *neziriot* following the count of a solar year. If in the count of a lunar year, 354 *neziriot* following the count of a lunar year. But "the count of the days of a year" is problematic[120].

120 Since he could have in mind either an actual Julianic year of 365 or 366 days, or an actual Jewish lunar-solar year which according to the calendar in current use is between 353 and 385 days (with somewhat greater variations in the Mishnaic calendar, described in the appendix to the author's *Seder Olam*, Northvale 1998.) In the Babli, 8b, and the Tosephta, 1:3, the cases of solar and lunar years are stated as a *baraita*. The formulation of the Yerushalmi Mishnah, referring simply to "a year" is not found in any of these parallel sources.

(51c, line 34) תַּנֵּי בְשֵׁם רִבִּי יוּדָה. רָאוּי הָיָה זֶה לְמִיתָה אֶלָּא שֶׁתָּלָה לוֹ נְזִירוּתוֹ.

It was stated in the name of Rebbi Jehudah: This man was destined for death, only his *nezirut* suspended it.

At this point, the scribe of the ms. wrote

גרש ההלכתא קדמייתא דרישא דנדרים עד מטי סופא דהילכתא

"One reads here from the the first Halakhah at the start of Nedarim until the end of the Halakhah."

This was deleted by the corrector who prepared the ms. for the printer and inserted the text (*Nedarim* 1:1, Notes 93-102). The differences in readings are due to the corrector who probably was influenced by his training in the Babylonian Talmud. The main *baraita*, the story of Simeon the Just, also appears in the Tosephta, 4:7; Babli, 4b, *Nedarim* 9b; *Sifry Naśo* 12; *Num. rabba* 10(7).

מַתְנִיתָא דְּרִבִּי יוּדָה. חֲסִידִים הָרִאשׁוֹנִים מִתְאַוִּין לְהָבִיא קָרְבַּן חַטָּאת. וְלֹא הָיָה הַמָּקוֹם מַסְפִּיק עַל יָדָם חֵטְא וְהָיוּ נוֹדְרִים בְּנָזִיר בִּשְׁבִיל לְהָבִיא קָרְבַּן חַטָּאת. רִבִּי שִׁמְעוֹן אוֹמֵר. חוֹטָאִים הָיוּ שֶׁהָיוּ נוֹדְרִים בְּנָזִיר. שֶׁנֶּאֱמַר וְכִפֶּר

עָלָיו מֵאֲשֶׁר חָטָא עַל הַנָּפֶשׁ. חָטָא זֶה עַל עַצְמוֹ שֶׁמָּנַע עַצְמוֹ מִן הַיַּיִן. וְאַתְיָא דְשִׁמְעוֹן הַצַּדִּיק בְּרַבִּי שִׁמְעוֹן. דְּתַנֵּי. אָמַר שִׁמְעוֹן הַצַּדִּיק. מִיָּמַי לֹא אָכַלְתִּי אָשָׁם נָזִיר אֶלָּא פַּעַם אֶחָד. שָׁעֲלַת אֶחָד אֵלַי מִדָּרוֹם וּרְאִיתִיהוּ דְּמוּת יְפֵה עֵינַיִם וְטוֹב רוֹאִי קְווּצוֹתָיו תַּלְתַּלִּים. וְאָמַרְתִּי לוֹ. בְּנִי. מַה רָאִיתָ לְהַשְׁחִית אֶת הַשֵּׂעָר הַנָּאֶה הַזֶּה. נִימָא לִי. רַבִּי. רוֹעֶה הָיִיתִי בְעִירִי. וְהָלַכְתִּי לְמַלְּאוֹת אֶת הַנִּיאָב מַיִם. וְרָאִיתִי אֶת הַבּוּבִיָּא שֶׁלִּי בְּתוֹךְ הַמַּיִם. וּפָחַז יִצְרִי עָלַי וּבִיקֵּשׁ לְאַבְּדֵינִי מִן הָעוֹלָם. אָמַרְתִּי לוֹ. רָשָׁע. אַתָּה מִפְחֵד בַּדָּבָר שֶׁאֵינוֹ שֶׁלָּךְ. עָלַי לְהַקְדִּישָׁךְ לַשָּׁמַיִם. וְחִבַּקְתִּיו וְנָשַׁקְתִּיו עַל רֹאשׁוֹ וְאָמַרְתִּי לוֹ. בְּנִי. כְּמוֹתָךְ יִרְבּוּ עוֹשֵׂי רְצוֹן הַמָּקוֹם בְּיִשְׂרָאֵל. עָלֶיךָ הַכָּתוּב אוֹמֵר אִישׁ אוֹ אִשָּׁה כִּי יַפְלִא לִנְדּוֹר נֶדֶר נָזִיר לְהַזִּיר לַיי׳. רַבִּי מָנָא בָּעֵי. לָמָּה לִי כְּשִׁמְעוֹן הַצַּדִּיק אֲפִילוּ כְּרַבִּי שִׁמְעוֹן. לֹא אָכַל שִׁמְעוֹן הַצַּדִּיק חַטַּאת חֵלֶב מִיָּמָיו. לֹא אָכַל שִׁמְעוֹן הַצַּדִּיק חַטַּאת דָּם מִיָּמָיו. סָבַר שִׁמְעוֹן. בְּנֵי אָדָם מִתּוֹךְ הַקְפָּדָתָן הֵן נוֹדְרִין. מִכֵּיוָן שֶׁנּוֹדְרִין מִתּוֹךְ הַקְפָּדָן סוֹפוֹ לִתְהוֹת. וּמִכֵּיוָן שֶׁהוּא תוֹהֶא נַעֲשָׂה קָרְבְּנוֹתָיו כְּשׁוֹחֵט חוּלִּין בָּעֲזָרָה. וְזֶה מִתּוֹךְ יִישׁוּב נָדַר. וּפִיו וְלִבּוֹ שָׁוִין.

1 - | דתני בשם ר' יודה.   2 על ידם חטא | בידם חט   4 חטא | חט   עצמו | נפשו
5 בר' | כר'   מימי | מימיי   פעם אחד | אחד   6 שעלת אחד עלי | פעם אחד עלה אלי אדם   וראיתיהו | וראיתיו   7 דמות יפה עינים וטוב רואי קווצותיו תלתלים | אדמוני עם יפא עינים וטוב רואי וקווצותיו מסודרות תילים תילים   8 השער | השיער   נימא | ונם   9 הייתי | הייתי   הניאב | השואב   10 הבוביא | הבובייה   11 מפחד | מפחז   12 וחבקתיו ונשקתיו על ראשו | והרכנתי בראשי   16 שמעון | שמעון הצדיק   הקפדתן | הקפדה   17 הקפדן | הקפדה   18 ומכיון | מכיון   נעשה | נעשו

The Mishnah follows Rebbi Jehudah *since it was stated in the name of Rebbi Jehudah*, the ancient pious ones desired to bring a purification offering, but the Omnipresent did not let a sin happen to them; so they made a vow of *nazir* in order to be able to bring a purification offering. Rebbi Simeon says, they became sinners because they made a vow of *nazir*, for it was said: "He shall atone for himself for what he sinned about the person," that one sinned against his own person because he barred himself from [drinking] wine. It turns out that the position of Simeon the

Just parallels Rebbi Simeon. As it was stated: Simeon the Just said, I never ate the reparation offering of a *nazir* except once. Once a man came to me from the South, I saw that he was handsome, with beautiful eyes and good looks, and his hair in waves. I said to him, my son, what induced you to cut off that beautiful hair? He said to me: Rabbi, I was a shepherd in my village and I went to fill the water vessel with water when I saw my mirror image in the water and my instinct rushed over me and tried to remove me from the World[98]. I said to it, wicked! You are rushing me to something which is not yours; it is upon me to sanctify you to Heaven! I embraced him, kissed him on his head and said, my son, there should be many more in Israel who fulfill the Omnipresent's will like you. About you the verse says, "man or woman, if he clearly articulates vowing a vow of *nazir,* to be a *nazir* for the Eternal." Rebbi Mana asked: Why following Simeon the Just, even following Rebbi Simeon? Did Simeon the Just never eat a purification offering for suet? Did Simeon the Just never eat a purification offering for blood? Simeon the Just holds that people make a vow while they are upset. Since they make the vow while they are upset, in the end, they wonder. But if he wonders, his sacrifices become similar to one of those who slaughtered profane animals in the Temple courtyard. But this one made a well thought-out dedication, when his mouth and his thoughts were in unison.

הריני נזיר פרק שני

(fol. 51c) **משנה א:** הֲרֵינִי נָזִיר מִן הַגְּרוֹגְרוֹת וּמִן הַדְּבֵילָה בֵּית שַׁמַּאי אוֹמְרִים נָזִיר וּבֵית הִלֵּל אוֹמְרִים אֵינוֹ נָזִיר. אָמַר רִבִּי יְהוּדָה אַף כְּשֶׁאָמְרוּ בֵית שַׁמַּאי לֹא אָמְרוּ אֶלָּא בְאוֹמֵר הֲרֵי הֵן עָלַי קָרְבָּן.

Mishnah 1: "I shall be a *nazir* [abstaining] from dried figs and fig cake[1]," the House of Shammai say, he is a *nazir*[2], but the House of Hillel say, he is no *nazir*[3]. Rebbi Jehudah said, when the House of Shammai expressed an opinion, it was about one who said, they are *qorban* for me[4].

1 Figs and all their derivatives are permitted to a *nazir*.

2 If he said "I shall be a *nazir*", he became a *nazir*. The qualification he appended is irrelevant. (In the Babli, 9a, this argument is attributed to R. Meïr, who thinks that "people do not say nonsensical things.")

3 Since a *nazir* is permitted figs, his statement makes no sense and nobody can become a *nazir* by a nonsensical statement since *Num.* 6:2 requires that the vow of *nezirut* be "clearly stated."

4 He disputes the Mishnah; nobody can become a *nazir* by vowing to abstain from figs and fig products. But anybody can make a vow to abstain from figs by declaring them *qorban* for himself (cf. Introduction to Tractate *Nedarim*.)

(51d line 19) **הלכה א:** הֲרֵינִי נָזִיר מִן הַגְּרוֹגְרוֹת כול'. אָמַר רִבִּי יוֹחָנָן. טַעֲמָא דְבֵית שַׁמַּי מִשּׁוּם שֶׁהוֹצִיא נְזִירוּת מִפִּיו. רִבִּי שִׁמְעוֹן בֶּן לָקִישׁ אָמַר. מִשּׁוּם כִּינּוּיֵי כִינּוּיִין. אָמַר רִבִּי יוּדָה בֶּן פָּזִי. קִרְייָא מְסַייֵע לְרִבִּי שִׁמְעוֹן בֶּן לָקִישׁ. כֹּה אָמַר לִי כַּאֲשֶׁר יִמָּצֵא הַתִּירוֹשׁ בָּאֶשְׁכּוֹל וגו'. תּוֹרָה קָרָאת לָאֶשְׁכּוֹל תִּירוֹשׁ. וּבְנֵי אָדָם קוֹרִין לַגְּרוֹגֶרֶת תִּירוֹשׁ. מִשּׁוּם כִּינּוּיִין. מַה נָּפַק מִבֵּינֵיהוֹן.

אָמַר. הֲרֵינִי נָזִיר מִן הַגְּרוֹגְרוֹת וּמִן הַדְּבֵילָה. עַל דַּעְתֵּיהּ דְּרִבִּי יוֹחָנָן נָזִיר. עַל דַּעְתֵּיהּ דְּרִבִּי שִׁמְעוֹן בֶּן לָקִישׁ אֵינוֹ נָזִיר. הֲרֵינִי נָזִיר מִן הַכִּכָּר. עַל דַּעְתֵּיהּ דְּרִבִּי יוֹחָנָן נָזִיר. עַל דַּעְתֵּיהּ דְּרִבִּי שִׁמְעוֹן אֵינוֹ נָזִיר. מִן הַכִּכָּר. לֹא אָמַר כְּלוּם. רִבִּי עוּקְבָא בָּעָא קוֹמֵי רִבִּי מָנָא. מִחְלְפָה שִׁיטָתֵיהּ דְּרִבִּי שִׁמְעוֹן בֶּן לָקִישׁ. דִּתְנִינָן תַּמָּן. הֲרֵי עָלַי מִנְחָה מִן הַשְּׂעוֹרִין. יָבִיא מִן הַחִטִּים. וָמַר רִבִּי אַבָּהוּ בְּשֵׁם רִבִּי שִׁמְעוֹן בֶּן לָקִישׁ. שֶׁהוֹצִיא מִנְחָה מִתּוֹךְ פִּיו. וְכָא הוּא אָמַר אָכֵן. אִית לֵיהּ הָכֵין וְאִית לֵיהּ הָכֵין. אִית לֵיהּ מִשּׁוּם שֶׁהוֹצִיא נְזִירוּת מִפִּיו. וְאִית לֵיהּ מִשּׁוּם כִּינּוּיֵי כִינּוּיִין. תֵּדַע לָךְ שֶׁהוּא כֵן. דִּתְנִינָן. אָמַר. אָמְרָה פָרָה זוֹ. כְּלוּם אָמְרָת. לֹא מִשּׁוּם שֶׁהוֹצִיא נְזִירוּת מִתּוֹךְ פִּיו. וְכָא. מִשּׁוּם שֶׁהוֹצִיא נְזִירוּת מִתּוֹךְ פִּיו.

Halakhah 1: "I shall be a *nazir* [abstaining] from dried figs and fig cake," etc. Rebbi Joḥanan said, the reason of the House of Shammai: because he mentioned the state of *nazir*[2]. Rebbi Simeon ben Laqish said, because of substitutes of substitutes[5]. Rebbi Jehudah ben Pazi said, a verse supports Rebbi Simeon ben Laqish: "So says the Eternal, as cider is found in the grape bunch, etc[6]." The Torah called a grape bunch "cider". And people call a dried fig cider, because of substitutes of substitutes. What is the difference between them? If he said, "I shall be a *nazir* [abstaining] from dried figs and fig cake." In Rebbi Joḥanan's opinion he is a *nazir*, in Rebbi Simeon's opinion he is not a *nazir*[7]. "I shall be a *nazir* [abstaining] from a loaf of bread," in Rebbi Joḥanan's opinion he is a *nazir*, in Rebbi Simeon ben Laqish's opinion he is not a *nazir*[8]. "From a loaf of bread," he did not say anything[9]. Rebbi Uqba asked before Rebbi Mana: The opinion of Rebbi Simeon ben Laqish seems to be inverted, as we have stated there[10]: "'I take upon myself the obligation to bring a flour offering from barley.' He shall bring from wheat." And Rebbi Abbahu said in the name of Rebbi Simeon ben Laqish, because he mentioned "flour offering.[11]" And here, he says so? He accepts one and he accepts the other. He accepts[12] because he mentioned the state of *nazir*, and he accepts because of substitutes of substitutes. You should know that it is so since we have stated[13]: "If he said, the cow said." She did not say anything; it is because he mentioned the state of *nazir*, and here he mentioned the state of *nazir*.

5   Since the House of Shammai accept very far-fetched comparisons and substitutes for a vow of *nezirut*; cf. Chapter 1, Note 19. In the Tosephta, 2:1, this is explicitly given as the reason of the House of Shammai. The Tosephta must have been unknown to the editors of the Yerushalmi.

6   *Is.* 65:8.

7   This is difficult since the House of Shammai declare in the Mishnah that he is a *nazir* and the entire discussion only proceeds according to the House of Shammai. One has to assume that the person making the vow was asked what he understood by "dried figs." If he answered, dried figs, R. Simeon ben Laqish cannot consider this as substitutes of substitutes, but for R. Johanan he still pronounced the word *nazir*. (This interpretation is that of *Tosaphot Menahot* 103a, *s.v.* הריני in the name of Rabbenu Tam.)

8   A loaf of bread is not a grape derivative by any stretch of the imagination.

9   Since the word *nazir* was not used. One has to assume that the expression הֲרֵינִי was used, since הֲרֵי עָלַי כִּכָּר would be a vow to abstain from bread as *qorban* (Chapter 1, Notes 44-45).

10   Mishnah *Menahot* 12:3. A voluntary flour offering is prescribed as an offering of fine wheat flour. Barley is prescribed only for some purification offerings which cannot be voluntary.

11   One would have expected R. Simeon ben Laqish to hold that the vow of the offering was invalid since it was impossible. In the Babli, 9b, his opinion is quoted as generally accepted.

12   He does not dispute the reason given by R. Johanan but only adds a second reason.

13   Mishnah 2:3. This discussion now also proceeds according to the House of Hillel.

(51d line 33) כָּל־הַלְשׁוֹנוֹת מְשַׁמְּשִׁין לְשׁוֹן נְזִירוּת חוּץ מִלְשׁוֹן קָרְבָּן. כָּל־הַלְשׁוֹנוֹת מְשַׁמְּשִׁין לְשׁוֹן קָרְבָּן חוּץ מִלְשׁוֹן נְזִירוּת. אָמַר לָאֶשְׁכּל. [כָּלוּי]14 אֲנִי מִמָּךְ. פָּרוּשׁ אֲנִי מִמָּךְ. מָנוּעַ אֲנִי מִמֶּנּוּ. הֲרֵינִי נָזִיר מִמֶּנּוּ. הֲרֵי זֶה נָזִיר. הֲרֵי עָלַי קָרְבָּן. לֹא אֲסָרוֹ עָלָיו אֶלָּא לְשֵׁם קָרְבָּן. אָמַר לַכִּכָּר. כָּלוּי אֲנִי מִמֶּנּוּ. פָּרוּשׁ אֲנִי מִמֶּנּוּ. מָנוּעַ אֲנִי מִמֶּנּוּ. הֲרֵי הוּא עָלַי קָרְבָּן. לֹא אֲסָרוֹ עָלָיו אֶלָּא לְשֵׁם קָרְבָּן. הֲרֵינִי נָזִיר מִמֶּנּוּ. הֲרֵי הוּא נָזִיר. אָהֵן מָנוּעַ מְשַׁמֵּשׁ לְשׁוֹן נְזִירוּת וּלְשׁוֹן קָרְבָּן. אָהֵן אֶשְׁכּוֹל אִית בֵּיהּ נְזִירוּת וְאִית בֵּיהּ קָרְבָּן. אָמַר לָאֶשְׁכּוֹל. כָּלוּי אֲנִי מִמֶּנּוּ. בָּא לְאוֹכְלוֹ אָמַר לוֹ. לְדָמִים קָדוֹשׁ. פריו15 וּבָא לְאוֹכְלוֹ אָמַר לוֹ. לֹא נָזִיר אַתָּה.

Any expressions can be used for *nezirut*[16] except the expression *qorban*. Any expressions can be used for *qorban*[16] except the expression *nezirut*. If he said about a bunch of grapes, "I am locked away from you, I am separated from you, I am prevented from you, I am *nazir* from you," he is a *nazir*. "It is for me *qorban*," he only forbade it for himself as *qorban*[17]. If he said about a loaf of bread, "I am locked away from it, I am separated from it, I am prevented from it, it is *qorban* for me," he only forbade it for himself as *qorban*.[18] "I am *nazir* from it," he is a *nazir*[19]. "Prevented" implies both *nezirut* and *qorban*. If somebody said about a bunch of grapes, "I am prevented from it," if he wanted to eat it, one tells him, is it not holy for its money's worth? If he redeemed it, one tells him, are you not a *nazir*[20]?

14 From the *editio princeps*. The scribe deleted an inappropriate word שכן "since" but both he and the corrector failed to replace it.

15 Commentators read this as פָּדָיו "if he redeemed it." This reading is accepted in the translation.

16 If otherwise they are appropriate.

17 He cannot use any of the grapes of the bunch but is permitted any other grapes in the world. If he said, "grapes are *qorban* for me," he is forbidden all grapes and their derivates but is not a

nazir.

18 Since nothing connected with a loaf of bread has any relation with the rules of *nazir*, any restriction must be interpretated as a vow of *qorban*.

19 Because he used the word *nazir*, not because of any connection with the loaf.

20 An ambiguous vow has to be interpreted restrictively in all respects. If the vow could be interpreted as *qorban* or *nazir*, it is both (and, in fact, is a triple vow since *qorban* may mean either a prohibition "as if it were a *qorban*" or an offering to the Temple.) Therefore, when the bunch of grapes was redeemed and its value given to the Temple, the person making the vow still cannot eat it since he might be a *nazir* (even though one vow cannot be both *qorban* and *nazir*.)

(51d line 42) כָּל־הַלְּשׁוֹנוֹת מְשַׁמְּשִׁין לְשׁוֹן חִילוּל חוּץ מִלְּשׁוֹן תְּמוּרָה. כָּל־הַלְּשׁוֹנוֹת מְשַׁמְּשִׁין לְשׁוֹן תְּמוּרָה חוּץ מִלְּשׁוֹן חִילוּל. אָמַר לְקָדְשֵׁי מִזְבֵּחַ. הֲרֵי זֶה תַּחַת זֶה. תְּמוּרַת זוֹ. חֲלִיפֵי זוֹ. הֲרֵי זוֹ תְּמוּרָה. זוֹ מְחוּלֶּלֶת עַל זוֹ. אֵינָהּ תְּמוּרָה. אָמַר לְקָדְשֵׁי בֶדֶק הַבַּיִת. הֲרֵי זוֹ תַּחַת זוֹ. חֲלִיפֵי זוֹ. נִתְפְּשָׂה בְדָמִים. תְּמוּרַת זוֹ. לֹא נִתְפְּשָׂה בְדָמִים. תַּנֵּי רִבִּי הוֹשַׁעְיָה. חֲלִיפֵי זוֹ. תְּמוּרַת זוֹ. לֹא אָמַר כְּלוּם. אָהֵן מְשַׁמֵּשׁ לְשׁוֹן חִילוּל וּלְשׁוֹן תְּמוּרָה. אִילֵּין קָדְשֵׁי מִזְבֵּחַ אִית בָּהּוֹ חִילוּל וְאִית בָּהוֹ תְּמוּרָה. קָדְשֵׁי בֶדֶק הַבַּיִת שֶׁקָּדַם שֶׁקִּדְּשָׁן אֶת מוּמוֹ הֲרֵי זוֹ תַּחַת זוֹ. בָּא לְהַקְרִיב תְּמִימָה אוֹמְרִים לוֹ. לְדָמִים קָדְשָׁה. בָּא לוֹכַל בַּעַל מוּם אוֹמְרִים לוֹ. לִתְמוּרָה קָדְשָׁה. וְהָיָה הוּא וּתְמוּרָתוֹ יִהְיֶה קוֹדֶשׁ. אָמַר רִבִּי יִצְחָק בַּר לְעָזָר. מִכֵּיוָן שֶׁהוּא יוֹדֵעַ שֶׁכָּל־הַמֵּימַר לוֹקֶה אַף הוּא לֹא עָלַת עַל דַּעְתּוֹ לְהָמִיר.

Any expressions can be used for redemption except the expression "exchange"[21]. Any expressions can be used for exchange except the expression "redemption." If he said about dedications to the altar: "this one is for that one, exchange for that one, barter for that one," it is an exchange[22]. "This is redeemed for that one," it is no exchange[23]. If he said about dedications for the upkeep of the Temple: "this one is for that one, barter for that one," its money's worth is engaged[24]. "Exchange for that one," he did not say anything[25]. The other [expressions] serve for redemption and exchange. Dedications to the altar are subject both to redemption and to exchange. [Animals] dedicated for the upkeep of the Temple[26] who were dedicated before developing a defect, "this one is for that one," if he wants to sacrifice a perfect animal, one tells him that its sanctity is for its money's worth. If he wants to eat it after it developed a blemish, one tells him that it is holy as exchange[27]: "Itself and its exchange shall be holy[28]." Rebbi Isaac ben Eleazar said, since he knows that anybody who exchanges is whipped, it never occured to him to exchange[29].

21 Animals dedicated for use on the altar acquire what is called קְדֻשַּׁת הַגּוּף "bodily sanctity." An animal used for the altar must be without blemish. Such an animal cannot be redeemed. It also should not be exchanged for another unblemished animal (Lev. 27:10). While any attempt to redeem the animal while unblemished, i. e., to subtract it to profane status, is simply impossible, the substitution of one unblemished animal for another, while sinful, nevertheless is possible and results in both animals being dedicated to the altar. If an altar animal develops a blemish, its bodily sanctity is reduced to קְדֻשַּׁת דָּמִים "holiness of monetary value." The animal must be redeemed, i. e., its sanctity transferred to the money paid for it, and the money then used to buy a replacement animal.

In this case, a substitution is impossible; there is no shortcut to avoid the redemption process.

Anything donated to the Temple treasury has only קְדֻשַּׁת דָּמִים from the start; it can be redeemed but not substituted.

22 Sinful but valid.

23 If an unblemished animal was offered as exchange for an unblemished altar animal but the language of redemption was used, the transaction is void; the animal offered remains profane.

24 The object originally given to the Temple has been redeemed by the object offered as redemption (provided that the monetary value of the thing given in redemption was stated; Mishnah Temurah 5:5).

25 Since תְּמוּרָה is impossible for

anything but unblemished animals dedicated as sacrifices.

26 This text is impossible since objects dedicated for the upkeep of the Temple are not subject to exchange but only to redemption. Unblemished animals may not be offered for the upkeep of the Temple; they automatically would be offered to the altar. Therefore, a "dedication for the upkeep of the Temple whose dedication preceded its defect" is an altar animal which developed a blemish and, therefore, has the reduced status of קָדְשַׁת דָּמִים and can be redeemed. Blemished animals cannot be dedicated to the altar; any such dedication is invalid.

27 If an animal originally destined for the altar but later disqualified was redeemed not by money but by the offering of an unblemished animal and use of a term which can be interpreted to mean either redemption or substitution, the original animal is redeemed but the other animal is both a substitute and a redemption. It cannot be sacrificed since it is a redemption; one cannot wait until it develops a blemish with age because it is a substitution. It must be redeemed to eliminate the "holiness of monetary value" and then be sacrificed on the altar.

28 *Lev.* 27:10.

29 He objects to the construction of a case in which an expression was used that might mean both redemption and substitution. Since redemption is required but substitution is sinful, it is obvious that only redemption was intended.

(51d line 54) כָּל־הַלְּשׁוֹנוֹת מְשַׁמְּשִׁין לְשׁוֹן עֲרָכִין חוּץ מִלְּשׁוֹן דָּמִים. כָּל־הַלְּשׁוֹנוֹת מְשַׁמְּשִׁין לְשׁוֹן דָּמִים חוּץ מִלְּשׁוֹן עֲרָכִין. אָמַר לְאָדָם. עִילּוּיִין עָלַי. סִידּוּרוֹ עָלַי. שׁוּמוֹ עָלַי. עֶרְכּוֹ עָלַי. נוֹתֵן אֶת עֶרְכּוֹ. דָּמָיו עָלַי. נוֹתֵן אֶת דָּמָיו. אָהֵן שׁוּם מְשַׁמֵּשׁ לְשׁוֹן עֲרָכִים וּלְשׁוֹן דָּמִים. אָהֵן אָדָם אִית בֵּיהּ עֲרָכִים וְאִית בֵּיהּ דָּמִים. אָמַר לְאָדָם. שׁוּמוֹ עָלַי. אִם הָיָה נָאֶה נוֹתֵן אֶת דָּמָיו. אִם הָיָה כָּאוּר נוֹתֵן אֶת עֶרְכּוֹ.

Any expressions can be used for valuation[30] except the expression "money's worth". Any expressions can be used for money's worth except the expression "valuation." If he said about a human, "I shall pay his cost, I shall pay his settlement, I shall pay his estimate, I shall pay his valuation," he has to pay his valuation³¹. "I shall pay his money's worth," he has to pay his money's worth. "Estimate" is used as an expression both for valuation and money's worth. A human has both valuation and money's worth. If he said about a human, "I shall pay his estimate," if he was good looking, he pays his money's worth; if he was ugly, he pays his valuation³².

30 "Valuation" is the sum fixed for vows in which a person promises to pay his or another person's valuation to the Temple (*Lev.* 27:1-8). The valuation depends on age and gender; it is fixed by the Biblical text (assuming a known ratio of the Biblical *šeqel* to the local currency.) "Money's worth" of a person is the value he would fetch if sold as a slave. This worth can be promised by a vow, but not by a valuation.

31 If an expression is ambiguous but "paying the valuation" is one of the meanings, in the absence of a definite indication to the contrary that is the legal meaning.

32 In every case, he pays the larger sum.

(51d line 59) בֵּית שַׁמַּי אוֹמְרִים. נָדוּר וְנָזוּר. וּבֵית הִלֵּל אוֹמְרִים. אֵינוֹ נָדוּר וְאֵינוֹ נָזוּר.

The House of Shammai say, he is bound by a vow and is a *nazir*, but the House of Hillel say, he is neither bound by a vow nor is he a *nazir*³³.

33 This refers to the Mishnah. The person made an inappropriate vow of *nazir*, referring to food permitted to a *nazir*. The House of Shammai hold that he is forbidden all kinds of dried figs because of his vow, and he is a *nazir* since he used the word *nazir*. The House of Hillel hold that an inappropriate choice of words invalidates both vow and *nezirut*. This rejects R. Jehudah's interpretation.

The parallel in the Babli, 9b, shows that this is a *baraita*. There, it is given in two versions (of which the Yerushalmi text is a combination). In one, the House of Shammai say, he is bound by a vow and is a *nazir*, but the House of Hillel say, he is bound by a vow but not a *nazir*. In the other, the House of Shammai say, he is bound by a vow but not a *nazir*, but the House of Hillel say, he is neither bound by a vow nor is he a *nazir*.

(fol. 51c) **משנה ב:** אָמַר אָמְרָה פָרָה זוֹ הֲרֵינִי נְזִירָה אִם עוֹמֶדֶת אָנִי. אָמַר הַדֶּלֶת הַזֶּה הֲרֵינִי נָזִיר אִם נִפְתָּח אָנִי. בֵּית שַׁמַּאי אוֹמְרִים נָזִיר וּבֵית הִלֵּל אוֹמְרִים אֵינוֹ נָזִיר. אָמַר רִבִּי יְהוּדָה אַף כְּשֶׁאָמְרוּ בֵּית שַׁמַּאי לֹא אָמְרוּ אֶלָּא בְּאוֹמֵר הֲרֵי פָרָה זוֹ קָרְבָּן אִם עוֹמֶדֶת הִיא.

Mishnah 2: If he said: "this cow said, I shall be a *nezirah* if I be standing up,[34]" or "this door said, I shall be a *nazir* if I be open," the House of Shammai say, he is a *nazir*, but the House of Hillel say, he is no *nazir*. Rebbi Jehudah said, when the House of Shammai expressed an opinion, it was only about one who said, this cow shall be *qorban* for me if she gets up[35].

34 The rancher has trouble to make the cow get on her feet; he says, it seems to me that the cow made a vow to be *nezirah* if she be standing up. For the House of Shammai, he used the word *nazir*; for the House of Hillel what he said was meaningless.

35 Then the cow is forbidden to him as *qorban*, but he is no *nazir*.

(51d line 60) **הלכה ב:** אָמַר אָמְרָה פָרָה זוֹ כול'. רָאָה גוֹי עוֹבֵר אָמַר. רָאוּ מָה אָמַר הַגּוֹי הַזֶּה. הֲרֵי זֶה נָזִיר. הֲוָה דָּמַר. מֵאַחַר שֶׁאֵין גּוֹיִם נוֹזְרִין נָזִיר. לֹא אָמַר. נִשְׁמְעִינָן מִן הָדָא. אָמַר. אָמְרָה פָרָה זֶה. כְּלוּם אָמַרְתְּ. אֶלָּא מִשּׁוּם שֶׁהוֹצִיא נְזִירוּת מִפִּיו. וְכָא שֶׁהוֹצִיא נְזִירוּת מִתּוֹךְ פִּיו. רָאָה יִשְׂרָאֵל עוֹבֵר אָמַר. רְאוּ מָה אָמַר יִשְׂרָאֵל זֶה. הֲרֵי זֶה נָזִיר. לֹא אָמַר. מֵאַחַר שֶׁיִּשְׂרָאֵל נוֹזְרִין נָזִיר. הֲוָה דָּמַר אֲפִילוּ כֵן בְּנָזִיר אוֹ אֵינוֹ אֶלָּא כְּשׁוֹנֶה דְּבָרוֹ. כָּךְ אֲנִי אוֹמֵר. הָיָה קוֹרֵא בַּתּוֹרָה וְהִזְכִּיר נָזִיר נָזִיק.

Halakhah 2: "If he said: 'this cow said,'" etc. If he saw a Gentile passing by and said, "look what this Gentile said.³⁶" Then he is a *nazir*. Does this mean that he is a *nazir* because Gentiles cannot make a vow of *nazir*³⁷? He has not said anything! Let us hear from the following: "If he said: 'this cow said'". You said this only because he spoke the word *nezirut*. And here, he spoke the word *nezirut*³⁴. If he saw a Jew passing by and said, "look what this Jew said.³⁸" Then he is a *nazir*. He³⁹ had not said anything. Does this mean that he is a *nazir* because Jews make a vow of *nazir*? Should we say that nevertheless he is a *nazir* or is he studying the case? So I am saying, "for example, if he was reading the Torah and mentioned *nazir, naziq*.⁴⁰"

36   It is understood that he said: "look what this Gentile said, I shall be a *nazir*."

37   Mishnah 9:1. Therefore, any vow of *nazir* must be the Jew's.

38   He attributed to him a vow of *nazir*.

39   The passer-by.

40   Chapter 1, after Note 10. Since in that case he is not a *nazir*, he cannot be a *nazir* in the present case.

(51d line 68) אִישׁ מָהוּ לְהַתְפִּישׂ לוֹ נְזִירוּת בִּלְשׁוֹן אִשָּׁה. תַּמָּן אָמְרִין. הָא נְזִירָה אִי עֲבַר. אִשָּׁה מָהוּ לְהַתְפִּישׂ לָהּ נְזִירוּת בִּלְשׁוֹן אִישׁ. אָמַר רִבִּי יוֹסֵי. כָּל־עַצְמוֹ אֵינוֹ קָרוּי נְזִירוּת אֶלָּא בִּלְשׁוֹן אִישׁ. אוֹ אִשָּׁה כִּי יַפְלִיא לִנְדּוֹר נֶדֶר.

Can a man be taken to *nezirut* by language appropriate for a woman⁴¹? There, they say, "a *nezirah* was passing by⁴²". Can a man be taken to *nezirut* by masculine language? Rebbi Yose said, the notion of *nezirut* is defined in the masculine: "... or a woman if he clearly makes a vow.⁴³"

41   Probably one should translate: "a vow formulated in the feminine"; but the explanation given "there" (in Babylonia) then does not quite fit.

42   Reading with *editio princeps* איעבר "passed by" (m.) for אי עבר "did

not pass". This refers to the case discussed in Halakhah 1:1 (Notes 2,23) that a person points to a *nazir* and indicates that he wants to be like him. It is admitted that he can point to a female.

43   *Num.* 6:2: "A man or a woman, if he clearly makes a vow". Since a verb referring both to a male and a female is used in the masculine by traditional grammatical rules, he infers that the masculine can be used in all cases.

(51d line 71) עַד שֶׁתַּעֲמוֹד הַפָּרָה עַד שֶׁתִּפְתַּח הַדֶּלֶת. נִשְׁמְעִינָהּ מִן הָדָא. בֵּית שַׁמַּי אוֹמְרִים. כּוּלָּן נְזִירִין. וּבֵית הִלֵּל אוֹמְרִים. אֵינָן נְזִירִין אֶלָּא מִי שֶׁלֹּא נִתְקַיְּימוּ דְּבָרָיו. כֵּינִי מַתְנִיתָא. מִי שֶׁלֹּא נִתְקַיְּימוּ דְּבָרָיו. לָשׁוֹן הֶפֶר הוּא. דְּלָה מִלָּה קָבְרַת בְּרָהּ. אֲפִילוּ לֹא עָמְדָה הַפָּרָה. אֲפִילוּ לֹא נִפְתַּח הַדֶּלֶת.

Unless the cow stood up, unless the door was opened[44]? Let us hear from the following[45]: "The House of Shammai say, they are all *nezirim*. But the House of Hillel say, only those are *nezirim* whose words turned out not to be true." So is the Mishnah[46]: "Whose words turned out not to be true;" it is formulated in the opposite, as not to say that she should not bury her son. Even if the cow did not stand up, even if the door was not opened[47].

44   Under which circumstances will the House of Shammai insist that the maker of the vow is a *nazir*? If the cow does stand up or if she never stands up?

45   Mishnah 5:6: "If people dispute facts; A says that he will be *nazir* if a fact is true, B says that he will be *nazir* if it is not true, C says that he will be *nazir* if both A and B are wrong. The House of Shammai say, . . ."

46   The text is garbled here (and somewhat garbled in Halakhah 6:6): "So is the Mishnah: 'Whose words turned out to be true;' it is formulated in the opposite, so as not to bury her son." The rancher's statement, that his cow said, "I shall be a *nezirah* if I be standing up", for the House of Shammai has to be interpreted as a vow of *nazir* if the cow *never* stands up, since the cow standing up is the desired outcome; just as a woman who is afraid her son might die will formulate it saying her

son certainly will not die. (It is possible to read a similar interpretation into the text of the Babli, 10b.)

47   For the House of Shammai, he is a *nazir* in any case.

(52a line 1) בֵּית שַׁמַּאי אוֹמְרִים. נָדוּר וְנָזוּר. וּבֵית הִלֵּל אוֹמְרִים. אֵינוֹ נָדוּר וְאֵינוֹ נָזוּר.

The House of Shammai say, he is bound by a vow and is a *nazir*, but the House of Hillel say, he is neither bound by a vow nor is he a *nazir*[33].

(fol. 51c) **משנה ג:** מָזְגוּ לוֹ אֶת הַכּוֹס אָמַר הֲרֵינִי נָזִיר מִמֶּמּוּ הֲרֵי זֶה נָזִיר. מַעֲשֶׂה בְאִשָּׁה אַחַת שֶׁהָיְתָה שְׁכּוֹרָה. מָזְגוּ לָהּ אֶת הַכּוֹס וְאָמְרָה הֲרֵינִי נְזִירָה מִמֶּמּוּ אָמְרוּ חֲכָמִים לֹא נִתְכַּוְונָה אֶלָּא כְלוֹמַר הֲרֵי הוּא עָלַי קָרְבָּן.

Mishnah 3: If a cup of wine was prepared[48] for somebody who then said, "I am a *nazir* [abstaining] from it", he is a *nazir*[49]. It happened that a cup of wine was prepared for a woman who already was drunk, when she said, "I am a *nazir* [abstaining] from it". The Sages said that she only intended to say, "it shall be *qorban* for me.[50]"

48   Mixed with water.

49   Since *nezirut* cannot be partial. Once he mentions *nezirut* for one cup of wine, he is forbidden all wine, all grapes, all haircuts, and any impurity of the dead.

50   Since she was drunk, she certainly did not want to forbid all wine to herself, but only that particular cup which was too much for her.

(fol. 51c) **משנה ד:** הֲרֵינִי נָזִיר עַל מְנָת שֶׁאֱהֵא שׁוֹתֶה בַּיַּיִן וּמִיטַּמֵּא לַמֵּתִים הֲרֵי זֶה נָזִיר וְאָסוּר בְּכוּלָּן. יוֹדֵעַ אֲנִי שֶׁיֵּשׁ נְזִירִים אֲבָל אֵינִי יוֹדֵעַ שֶׁהַנָּזִיר אָסוּר בַּיַּיִן הֲרֵי זֶה אָסוּר בַּיַּיִן וְרִבִּי שִׁמְעוֹן מַתִּיר. יוֹדֵעַ אֲנִי שֶׁהַנָּזִיר אָסוּר בַּיַּיִן אֲבָל סָבוּר הָיִיתִי שֶׁחֲכָמִים מַתִּירִין לִי מִפְּנֵי שֶׁאֵינִי יָכוֹל לִחְיוֹת בְּלֹא יַיִן אוֹ מִפְּנֵי שֶׁאֲנִי קוֹבֵר אֶת הַמֵּתִים הֲרֵי זֶה מוּתָּר וְרִבִּי שִׁמְעוֹן אוֹסֵר.

Mishnah 4: "I am a *nazir* on condition that I may drink wine or become impure for the dead," he is a *nazir* and forbidden everything⁵¹. "I knew that there are *nezirim* but I did not know that wine is forbidden to the *nazir*⁵²"; wine is forbidden to him, but Rebbi Simeon permits⁵³. "I knew that wine was forbidden to the *nazir* but I thought that the Sages would permit me because I cannot live without wine, or because I am an undertaker;" he is permitted but Rebbi Simeon forbids⁵⁴.

51 Since *nezirut* is defined in the Torah and any stipulation contradicting a biblical law is void (*Ketubot* 9:1, Note 5).

52 A person who declared himself a *nazir*, and when told that wine was forbidden to him declares that at the moment of the vow he was ignorant of its implications.

53 Because the vow was made in error and such a vow is excluded by the requirement that the vow be clearly enunciated (*Num.* 6:2).

54 For the majority, the vow is in error; for R. Simeon it is a frivolous vow.

(52a line 2) **הלכה ג**: מָזְגוּ לוֹ אֶת הַכּוֹס כול׳. מַתְנִיתָא בְּשֶׁאֵינוֹ יָכוֹל. אֲבָל אִם יָכוֹל הָדָא דְתַנִּינָן. מַעֲשֶׂה בְאִשָּׁה אַחַת שֶׁהָיְתָה שְׁכּוֹרֶת. מָזְגוּ לָהּ אֶת הַכּוֹס. אָמְרָה. הֲרֵינִי נְזִירָה מִמֶּנּוּ. וְאָמְרוּ חֲכָמִים. לֹא נִתְכַּוְונָה אֶלָּא כְלוֹמַר. הֲרֵי הוּא עָלַי קָרְבָּן. רִבִּי יִרְמְיָה בְּשֵׁם רִבִּי זְעִירָה. אֲפִילוּ לְשׁוֹן קָרְבָּן אֵינוֹ. לָמָּה. שֶׁאֵינוֹ קוֹבֵעַ עָלָיו לֹא נְזִירוּת בִּלְשׁוֹן קָרְבָּן וְלֹא קָרְבָּן בִּלְשׁוֹן נְזִירוּת.

Halakhah 3: "If a cup of wine was prepared," etc. The Mishnah applies if he is not used to it⁵⁵; but if he is used to it, that is what we have stated: "It happened that a cup of wine was prepared for a woman who already was drunk when she said, "I am a *nazir* [abstaining] from it". The Sages said that she only intended to say, "it shall be *qorban* for me." Rebbi Jeremiah in the name of Rebbi Ze'ira: It is not even an expression of *qorban*. Why? Because one can neither use an expression of *nezirut* for *qorban* nor an expression of *qorban* for *nezirut*⁵⁶.

55 The first part, in which the person who declares himself *nazir* for one cup is actually a *nazir* applies only to people who are not used to getting drunk.

56 As explained in Halakhah 1, Note 16.

(52a line 7) מַתְנִיתָא דְּרִבִּי מֵאִיר. דְּרִבִּי מֵאִיר אוֹמֵר. צָרִיךְ לִכְפּוֹל תמן. דִּבְרֵי הַכֹּל הִיא. אָמַר לוֹ. שְׁמוֹר וְשָׁמַעְתָּ. מַתְנִיתָא דְּרִבִּי מֵאִיר וְרִבִּי יְהוּדָה בֶּן תֵּימָא. דְּתַנֵּי. הֲרֵי זֶה גִיטֵּיךְ עַל מְנָת שֶׁלֹּא תִפְרְחִי בָאֲוֵיר. שֶׁלֹּא תַעַבְרִי אֶת הַיָּם הַגָּדוֹל בְּרַגְלַיִיךְ. הֲרֵי זֶה גֵט. עַל מְנָת שֶׁתִּפְרְחִי בָאֲוֵיר. עַל מְנָת שֶׁתַּעַבְרִי הַיָּם הַגָּדוֹל בְּרַגְלַיִיךְ. אֵינוֹ גֵט. רִבִּי יְהוּדָה בֶּן תֵּימָא אוֹמֵר. גֵּט. אָמַר רִבִּי זְעִירָא. תֵּדַע לָךְ שֶׁעִילָּה הָיָה רוֹצֶה לְגָרְשָׁהּ. שֶׁתְּלָאָהּ בִּדְבָרִים שֶׁאֵינָהּ יְכוֹלָה לַעֲמוֹד. מַה טַעֲמָא דְּרִבִּי יוּדָה בֶּן תֵּימָא. מִכֵּיוָן שֶׁתְּלָאָהּ בִּדְבָרִים שֶׁאֵינָהּ יְכוֹלָה לַעֲמוֹד כְּמִי שֶׁנִּתְקַיֵּים הַתְּנַאי בַּגֵּט הוּא.

The Mishnah follows Rebbi Meïr, since Rebbi Meïr says, one has to double one's stipulation[57]. It follows everybody's opinion[58]; one tells him: Watch and keep discipline[59]. The Mishnah follows Rebbi Meïr[60] or Rebbi Jehudah ben Tema[61], as it was stated[62]: "This is your bill of divorce, on condition that you not fly in the air, that you not cross the Sea on your feet, that is a bill of divorce. On condition that you fly in the air, that you cross the Sea on your feet, that is no bill of divorce; Rebbi Jehudah ben Tema said, it is a bill of divorce." Rebbi Ze'ira said, you should realize that he seeks a subterfuge for the bill of divorce[63], since he attached conditions that cannot be satisfied. What is Rebbi Jehudah ben Tema's reason? Since he attached conditions that cannot be satisfied, it is as if the condition attached to the bill of divorce were satisfied[64].

57 Mishnah *Qiddušin* 3:3. A legal stipulation must follow the example of the stipulation between Moses and the tribes of Gad and Reuben (*Num.* 32), which covers both the positive (if they fulfill the stipulation, they will acquire the land in Transjordan), and the negative (if they fail to fulfill the

stipulation, they will be given land in Cisjordan). Since in Mishnah 4 the person declaring himself a *nazir* failed to state that if he could not be a *nazir* on his terms, he would not be a *nazir*, his stipulation is invalid and he is a *nazir*.

58   The waiving of any stipulation in violation of biblical law (Note 51) does not depend on R. Meïr's opinion.

59   *Deut.* 12:28; a poetic formulation of the principle of Note 51.

60   As explained in Note 57.

61   Who holds that an impossible condition is considered nonexistent. Since a stipulation against biblical law is impossible, the condition mentioned in the first sentence of Mishnah 4 is considered nonexistent.

62   Tosephta *Giṭṭin* 5:12; Babli *Giṭṭin* 84a.

63   He thinks that he can doubly hurt his wife, by preventing her to remarry and not paying her *ketubah*, since he may claim that he is waiting for her to satisfy the stipulation. By declaring the stipulation invalid, the court will permit her to remarry and force him to pay.

64   In Tosephta and Babli: R. Jehudah ben Tema states as a principle that any stipulation which cannot be satisfied is only intended as a delaying tactic.

(52a line 15) מַתְנִיתָא דְּרִבִּי שִׁמְעוֹן. דְּרִבִּי שִׁמְעוֹן פּוֹטֵר. שֶׁלֹּא הִתְנַדֵּב כְּדֶרֶךְ הַמִּתְנַדְּבִים. וְאָמַר רִבִּי יְהוֹשֻׁעַ בֶּן לֵוִי. שַׁנְיָיא הִיא. שֶׁשִּׁיֵּיר תִּגְלַחַת. רִבִּי יִרְמְיָה בָּעֵי. אִם בְּשֶׁשִּׁיֵּיר תִּגְלַחַת אָמוּר דְּבָתְרָהּ. הֲרֵי זֶה אָסוּר וְרִבִּי שִׁמְעוֹן מַתִּיר. הֲרֵי שֶׁשִּׁיֵּיר תִּגְלַחַת טוּמְאָה רִבִּי שִׁמְעוֹן פּוֹטֵר. שַׁנְיָיא הִיא. מִשּׁוּם פְּתִיחַת נֶדֶר. אִם מִשּׁוּם פְּתִיחַת נֶדֶר אָמוּר דְּבָתְרָהּ. הֲרֵי זֶה מוּתָּר וְרִבִּי שִׁמְעוֹן אוֹסֵר. רִבִּי שִׁמְעוֹן אוֹמֵר. אֵינוֹ פְּתִיחַת נֶדֶר. וְרַבָּנִין אָמְרִין. פְּתִיחַת נֶדֶר הוּא. לָמָּה. מִפְּנֵי שֶׁהוּא תוֹלֶה נִדְרוֹ בְּחַיָּיו. נִיחָא לִשְׁתּוֹת יַיִן. לְטַמֵּא לַמֵּתִים. אוּמָּנוּתוֹ קוֹבֵר מֵתִים.

Does the Mishnah follow Rebbi Simeon[65]? For "Rebbi Simeon declares him free, because his offering was not according to the way of offerers.[66]" And Rebbi Joshua ben Levi said, there is a difference because he reserved shaving[67]. Rebbi Jeremiah asked: If it is because he reserved shaving, does not the following state "it is forbidden to him, but Rebbi Simeon permits." Did he not reserve shaving [and] impurity but Rebbi Simeon frees him[68]? There is a difference, because of an opening for the vow[69]. If it was because of an opening for the vow, does not the following state "he is permitted but Rebbi Simeon forbids"? Rebbi Simeon does not recognize it as an opening for the vow but the rabbis recognize it as an opening for the vow. Why? Because he connects his vow with his life[70]. One understands, to drink wine. The defile oneself for the dead? It is his profession to bury the dead[71].

65   Since R. Simeon is quoted as disagreeing in two of the three cases quoted in Mishnah 4, does one have to assume that he agrees in the first case?

66   Mishnah *Menaḥot* 12:3. If somebody vows an offering of barley flour (which cannot be a voluntary offering), the rabbis require him to bring an offering of wheat flour but "R. Simeon declares him free, because his offering was not according to the way of offerers." One should assume that R. Simeon declares a person who wants to be *nazir* on condition that he may drink wine as "offering not according to the way of offerers." Why does he not disagree in the first case?

67   Since the person making the vow did not stipulate that he may shave, the vow is valid for the prohibition of shaving and a partially valid vow is valid.

68   The vow is partially valid; why is it not valid?

69   Since he bases his vow on an argument which will automatically grant him a revocation of the vow (cf. *Nedarim* Chapter 9), the vow is automatically revoked. In the Babli, 11b, this argument is attributed to Rav Assi. In the Tosephta, 2:3, it is explicitly attributed to R. Simeon.

70   If he needs wine for medical purposes, the use of wine must be permitted to him.

71   The only person who can have a vow of *nazir* annulled because he has to defile himself for the dead is the undertaker.

(fol. 51c) **משנה ה:** הֲרֵינִי נָזִיר וְעָלַי לְגַלַּח נָזִיר וְשָׁמַע חֲבֵירוֹ וְאָמַר וַאֲנִי עָלַי לְגַלַּח נָזִיר אִם הָיוּ פִקְחִין מְגַלְּחִין זֶה אֶת זֶה וְאִם לָאו מְגַלְּחִין לִנְזִירִים אֲחֵרִים.

Mishnah 5: "I shall be a *nazir* and obligate myself to shave[72] a *nazir*," if another heard him and said: "I also shall be and I obligate myself to shave another *nazir*," if they are clever, they will shave one another[73]; otherwise they have to shave other *nezirim*.

72 "To shave a *nazir*" means to pay for the three required sacrifices which enable a *nazir* to shave his head. It seems that most *nezirim* were poor and depended on charity to pay for their sacrifices; cf. *Berakhot* 7:3, Notes 78-89.

73 They will have fulfilled their vows without added expenditure.

(52a line 22) **הלכה ה:** הֲרֵינִי נָזִיר וְעָלַי לְגַלַּח נָזִיר כול'. אָהֵן וַאֲנִי מַה מִתְעַבֵּד לֵיהּ. וַאֲנִי עַל כָּל־דִּיבּוּרוֹ אוֹ וַאֲנִי עַל חֲצִי דִיבּוּרוֹ. אֵין תַּעַבְדִינָהּ וַאֲנִי עַל כָּל־דִּיבּוּרוֹ אָמַר. וַאֲנִי נָזִיר. אֵין תַּעַבְדִינָהּ וַאֲנִי עַל חֲצִי דִיבּוּרוֹ וְאָמַר. הֲרֵינִי נָזִיר. תַּנֵּי דְבֵית רִבִּי. וַאֲנִי עַל כָּל־דִּיבּוּרוֹ. אָמַר רִבִּי יוֹסֵה. הָדָא אָמְרָה. אַחַר שֶׁאָמַר. הֲרֵינִי נָזִיר מֵאָה יוֹם. וְשָׁמַע חֲבֵירוֹ וְאָמַר. וַאֲנִי. זֶה נָזִיר מֵאָה יוֹם וְזֶה נָזִיר לִשְׁלֹשִׁים יוֹם. עַד שֶׁיֹּאמַר. הֲרֵינִי כְמוֹתוֹ. הֲרֵינִי כַיּוֹצֵא בוֹ. תַּנֵּי רִבִּי חִייָה. הֲרֵי עָלַי לְגַלַּח חֲצִי. וְחָזַר וְאָמַר. הֲרֵינִי נָזִיר. אִם גִּילַּח יוֹם שְׁלֹשִׁים יָצָא. אָמַר רִבִּי יוֹסֵה. מַתְנִיתָהּ אָמְרָה כֵן. הֲרֵינִי נָזִיר וְעָלַי לְגַלַּח נָזִיר. וְשָׁמַע חֲבֵירוֹ וְאָמַר וַאֲנִי. וְאָמַר וְעָלַי לְגַלַּח נָזִיר. אִם הָיוּ פִקְחִין מְגַלְּחִין זֶה אֶת זֶה. הָא לְעַצְמָן לֹא. מִפְּנֵי שֶׁאָמַר. הֲרֵינִי נָזִיר וְעָלַי לְגַלַּח נָזִיר. אֲבָל אָמַר. הֲרֵי עָלַי לְגַלַּח חֲצִי נָזִיר. וְחָזַר וְאָמַר. הֲרֵינִי נָזִיר. אִם גִּילַּח לְעַצְמוֹ יָצָא. נִיחָא שֵׁינִי לְגַלַּח אֶת הָרִאשׁוֹן. רִאשׁוֹן מְגַלֵּחַ אֶת הַשֵּׁינִי. רִבִּי יוֹסֵי בְשֵׁם רִבִּי זְעִירָא. זֹאת אוֹמֶרֶת שֶׁאָדָם קוֹבֵעַ עָלָיו קָרְבָּן נָזִיר וְעָתִיד לֵיזוֹר. רִבִּי חִינָּנָא בְשֵׁם רִבִּי זְעִירָא אָמַר תָּלַת. הָדָא אָמְרָה. אִם גִּילַּח עַצְמוֹ יָצָא. הָדָא אָמְרָה. שֶׁאָדָם קוֹבֵעַ לַחֲבֵירוֹ קָרְבָּן נְזִירוּת לֵיזוֹר. הָדָא אָמְרָה. שֶׁאָדָם קוֹבֵעַ לַחֲבֵירוֹ קָרְבָּן נְזִירוּת שֶׁלֹּא מִדַּעְתּוֹ. אֲבָל אֵינוֹ מַפְרִישׁוֹ שֶׁלֹּא מִדַּעְתּוֹ.

Halakhah 5: "I shall be a *nazir* and obligate myself to shave a *nazir*," etc. This "I also", what do you subsume under it? Does "I also" refer to the entire sentence[74], or does "I also" only refer to part of the sentence[75]? If "I also" refers to the entire sentence, he says "I also am a *nazir*[76]." If "I also" only refers to part of the sentence, he said "I am a *nazir*." It was stated in the House of Rebbi: "'I also' refers to the entire sentence[77]." Rebbi Yose said, this implies that if some person said, I am a *nazir* for 100 days, and another person heard him and said, "I also"; the first one is a *nazir* for 100 days, the other is a *nazir* for 30 days[78] unless he says, "I am like him, I am the same as he is." Rebbi Hiyya stated: "I am obligated to shave half [a *nazir*]. Then he said, I am a *nazir*. If he shaved after 30 days he has fulfilled his obligation[79]." Rebbi Yose said, the Mishnah implies this: "'I shall be a *nazir* and obligate myself to shave a *nazir*,' if another heard him and said: 'I also shall be and I obligate myself to shave another *nazir*,' if they are clever, they will shave one another." But not themselves[80]. Because he said, "I shall be a *nazir* and obligate myself to shave a *nazir*". But if he said, "I obligate myself to shave half a *nazir*[81]" and then he said, "I shall be a *nazir*," if he shaved himself he has acquitted himself of his obligation[79]. One understands that the second one can shave the first, but can the first shave the second[82]? Rebbi Yose in the name of Rebbi Ze'ira: This means that a person can take upon himself the sacrifice of a *nazir* who only in the future will make his vow[83]. Rebbi Hinena in the name of Rebbi Ze'ira inferred three [statements]: It implies that if he shaved himself he acquitted himself. It implies that a person obligates himself for another's *nezirut* sacrifices of a future vow. It implies that a person chooses another's *nezirut* sacrifices without the other's knowledge. But he cannot dedicate [the animals] without the other's knowledge[84].

74   In that case, the second person by saying "I also" would accept the obligations of being a *nazir* and of paying for another person's sacrifices. If then he adds a vow to pay for another person's sacrifices, he should be held liable for two sets of sacrifices.

75   One has to assume that it refers only to the first obligation pronounced by the first person.

76   And he has to pay for another person's sacrifices.

77   The Babli, 11b, proves from the wording of the Mishnah that "I also" only refers to the first obligation pronounced by the first person.

78   Since without further specification, "I also" only refers to the obligation of *nazir*, not to the added term.

79   Since the obligation to pay for a set of sacrifices precedes his own vow of *nazir*, he can fulfill his obligation by applying the sacrifices to himself.

80   Since the vow of *nazir* implies the obligation of the sacrifices, a later vow to pay for sacrifices establishes a separate obligation; it cannot be used retroactively for his own obligation.

81   Cf. Mishnah 6.

82   By the preceding argument, a vow to pay for sacrifices can be used for later vows of *nazir*, not for earlier ones.

83   It really is used in the inverse direction. If somebody makes a vow to pay for sacrifices, it does not matter whether or not the sacrifices were already due at the moment the vow was made. It is only for one's own sacrifices that the order in which the vows were made does matter.

84   Since an animal cannot be brought to the Temple without having been dedicated, and the dedication has to be for a specific obligation, the *nazir* whose sacrifices are paid for must be informed of the dedication for it to be valid. The same statement is in *Pesaḥim* 8:1(35d l.13), but is denied in the Babli, *Nedarim* 36a.

(52a line 39) רִבִּי מָנָא בָּעֵי קוֹמֵי רִבִּי יוּדָן. אָמַר. הֲרֵי עָלַי קָרְבַּן נָזִיר. וְעָתִיד לִיזוֹר בְּשָׁעָה שֶׁנָּזַר סְתָם. מְנַלַּח בֵּין נָזִיר שֶׁכְּבָר נָזִיר בֵּין נָזִיר שֶׁעָתִיד לִיזוֹר. פֵּירֵשׁ. יָבֹא כְהָדָא. רִבִּי לֵוִי בֶן חַיָּיתָה בָעֵי. כָּתַב לָהּ. דִּין וּדְבָרִים אֵין לִי בִּנְכָסַיָּיךְ הָעֲתִידִין לִיפּוֹל לָךְ. מָה הֵן. וְיֵשׁ אָדָם מַתְנֶה עַל דָּבָר שֶׁלֹּא בָא לָעוֹלָם.

Rebbi Mana asked before Rebbi Yudan: If he said "I am obligated for the sacrifices of a *nazir*," might he[85] make the vow of *nazir* in the future?

If he made the vow without explaining[86], he may shave any *nazir*, whether he already made the vow or whether he would make it in the future. If he explained[87]? It can be compared to the following, as Rebbi Levi ben Ḥayyata asked: If he wrote to her[88], "I shall have nothing to do with the properties which you might inherit in the future." May a person make a condition on things not yet in existence[89]?

85 The person B whose sacrifices A just has vowed to pay.

86 A did not put any condition on his vow; when he comes to pay for it, he simply pays for any needy *nazir* whose sacrifices are due on that day.

87 May he specify that his vow is valid only for a *nazir* who was not yet a *nazir* at the time of his vow?

88 A husband, who normally would have the administration of his wife's property, writes a disclaimer to his wife in which he renounces all interest in her property. The details of this question are given in *Ketubot* 9:1, Notes 22-23.

89 Since Talmudic law does not admit futures contracts on produce which does not yet exist, there can be no valid vow for obligations that do not yet exist.

משנה ו: הֲרֵי עָלַי לְגַלֵּחַ חֲצִי נָזִיר וְשָׁמַע חֲבֵירוֹ וְאָמַר וַאֲנִי עָלַי לְגַלֵּחַ חֲצִי נָזִיר זֶה מְגַלֵּחַ נָזִיר שָׁלֵם וְזֶה מְגַלֵּחַ נָזִיר שָׁלֵם דִּבְרֵי רִבִּי מֵאִיר. וַחֲכָמִים אוֹמְרִים זֶה מְגַלֵּחַ חֲצִי נָזִיר וְזֶה מְגַלֵּחַ חֲצִי נָזִיר. (fol. 51c)

Mishnah 6: "I am taking upon myself to shave half a *nazir*," and his neighbor heard it and said, "I also am taking upon myself to shave half a *nazir*," each one of them shaves an entire *nazir*, the words of Rebbi Meïr[90]. But the Sages say, each of them shaves half a *nazir*[91].

90 Since the sacrifices of a *nazir* must either be brought whole or not at all; the vow for half the sacrifices

(which would be 1½ animals) is impossible. Since he made the vow, it has to be interpreted as a vow for a whole set of animals.

91 The vow simply was for paying half the expenses of one *nazir*.

(52a line 44) **הלכה ו:** הֲרֵי עָלַי לְגַלֵּחַ חֲצִי נָזִיר כול׳. רִבִּי אַבָּהוּ בְּשֵׁם רִבִּי יוֹחָנָן וְרַב חִסְדָּא תְּרַוֵּיהוֹן אֲמְרִין. בִּסְתָּם חֲלוּקִין. מַה מְקַיְּימִין. אִם בְּאוֹמֵר. כָּל־חֲצִי רֹאשׁ. כָּל־עַמָּא מוֹדוֹי שֶׁהוּא מְגַלֵּחַ נָזִיר שָׁלֵם. אִם בְּאוֹמֵר. חֲצִי חוֹבָה. כָּל־עַמָּא מוֹדֵיי שֶׁהוּא מְגַלֵּחַ חֲצִי נָזִיר. אֶלָּא כֵּן אֲנָן קַיְּימִין בְּאוֹמֵר. חֲצִי. רִבִּי מֵאִיר אוֹמֵר בְּאוֹמֵר. חֲצִי רֹאשׁ. וְרַבָּנִין אֲמְרִין. בְּאוֹמֵר חֲצִי חוֹבָה. אָמַר רִבִּי יוּדָן. אַשְׁכַּח אָמַר קַלֵּת וְחוּמְרַת. עַל דַּעְתֵּיהּ דְּרִבִּי מֵאִיר דּוּ אָמַר. חֲצִי רֹאשׁ. מֵבִיא קָרְבָּן אֶחָד. שֶׁכֵּן הַנָּזִיר מְגַלֵּחַ עָלָיו קָרְבָּן שָׁלֵם. עַל דַּעְתּוֹן דְּרַבָּנִין דְּאִינּוּן אֲמְרִין. חֲצִי חוֹבָה. מֵבִיא קָרְבָּן וּמֶחֱצָה חֲצִי חוֹבַת יָחִיד.

Halakhah 6: "I am taking upon myself to shave half a *nazir*," etc. Rebbi Abbahu in the name of Rebbi Johanan and Rav Hisda both say that they disagree if it was not spelled out. What are we dealing with? If he said, every half head[92], everybody agrees that he completely shaves a *nazir*. If he says, half of the obligation, everybody agrees that he shaves half a *nazir*. But we are dealing with the case that he says: "half". Rebbi Meïr says, as if he said half a head, but the rabbis said, as if he said, half of the obligation. Rebbi Yudan said, it turns our that leniency is a restriction. In the opinion of Rebbi Meïr who said, as if he had said half a head, he brings one sacrifice since the *nazir* can shave on one sacrifice[93]. In the opinion of the rabbis who said, half of the obligation, he has to pay for a sacrifice and a half, half of the obligation of a person.

92 If he vows half of every animal, he has to give three animals since half an animal is no sacrifice.

93 Mishnah 6:7 states that a *nazir* can shave even if he brings only one sacrifice. (Note that the vow is interpreted as meaning "half a head", not "every half head").

משנה ז: הֲרֵינִי נָזִיר כְּשֶׁיִּהְיֶה לִי בֵן וְנוֹלַד לוֹ בֵן הֲרֵי זֶה נָזִיר. בַּת טוּמְטוּם וְאַנְדְּרוֹגִינוֹס אֵינוֹ נָזִיר. אִם אָמַר כְּשֶׁאֶרְאֶה לִי וָלָד אֲפִילוּ נוֹלַד לוֹ בַּת טוּמְטוּם וְאַנְדְּרוֹגִינוֹס הֲרֵי זֶה נָזִיר. (fol. 51d)

Mishnah 7: "I shall be a *nazir* if I have a son," when a son is born to him, he is a *nazir*; if a daughter, a sexless[94], or a hermaphrodite[95], he is not a *nazir*. If he said, "when I see a child of mine," even if a daughter, a sexless, or a hermaphrodite were born to him he is a *nazir*.

94   He has neither penis nor vagina.
95   He has both penis and vagina.
         Cf. Mishnah *Yebamot* 8:6; Notes 224-237; *Niddah* 1:1, Notes 27,28.

הלכה ז: הֲרֵינִי נָזִיר כְּשֶׁיִּהְיֶה לִי בֵן כול׳. בַּת לֹא כְּלוּם. טוּמְטוּם וְאַנְדְּרוֹגִינוֹס צְרִיכָה. (52a line 52)

Halakhah 7: "I shall be a *nazir* if I have a son," etc. A daughter counts for nothing, a sexless or a hermaphrodite are questionable[96].

96   This refers to the first part of the Mishnah. If the vow was conditional, a daughter certainly does not count as a son, but a sexless or a hermaphrodite might be crypto-males. This creates a problem only for R. Simeon who in the Mishnah holds that a vow of *nazir* whose validity is in doubt must be kept. There is no problem for the majority who hold that a vow of *nazir* whose validity is in doubt is void. The Babli, 13a, disagrees and accepts the Mishnah as everybody's opinion.

משנה ח: הִפִּילָה אִשְׁתּוֹ אֵינוֹ נָזִיר. רִבִּי שִׁמְעוֹן אוֹמֵר אִם אָמַר אִם הָיָה בֶּן קַיָּימָא הֲרֵינִי נָזִיר חוֹבָה וְאִם לָאו הֲרֵינִי נְזִיר נְדָבָה. חָזְרָה וְיָלְדָה הֲרֵי זֶה נָזִיר. רִבִּי שִׁמְעוֹן אוֹמֵר יֹאמַר אִם הָרִאשׁוֹן בֶּן קַיָּימָא הָרִאשׁוֹנָה חוֹבָה וְזוֹ נְדָבָה וְאִם לָאו הָרִאשׁוֹנָה נְדָבָה וְזוֹ חוֹבָה. (fol. 51d)

Mishnah 8: If his wife[97] had a miscarriage, he is not a *nazir*. Rebbi Simeon says, he should say: If it was a viable child, I am a *nazir* as an obligation, if not, I am a *nazir* voluntarily[98]. If afterwards she had a child, he is a *nazir*[99]. Rebbi Simeon says, he should say: If the earlier one was a viable child, I earlier was a *nazir* as an obligation, and now I am a *nazir* voluntarily; otherwise, I earlier was a *nazir* voluntarily, and now I am a *nazir* as an obligation.

97 For whom he made the vow described in Mishnah 7.
98 He holds that a vow of *nezirut* in doubt must be kept.

99 Since according to the anonymous majority he did not observe *nezirut* after the stillbirth.

(52a line 53) **הלכה ח**: הִפִּילָה אִשְׁתּוֹ אֵינוֹ נָזִיר כול'. וְחָשׁ לוֹמַר שֶׁמָּא בֶּן קַיָּימָה הוּא. אָמַר רבי יוֹחָנָן. דְּרבי יוּדָה הִיא. דְּרבי יוּדָה אָמַר. סְפֵק נְזִירוּת מוּתָּר. אָמַר לֵיהּ. לֹא אָמַר רבי יוּדָה אֶלָּא לְבַסּוֹף. אֲבָל לְכַתְּחִילָה אוֹף רבי יוּדָה מוֹדֵי. אֵי זֶהוּ בַּתְּחִילָה וְאֵי זֶהוּ בַסּוֹף. אָמַר רבי שְׁמוּאֵל בַּר רַב יִצְחָק. כָּל־עַמָּא מוֹדֵי. אֵינִי יוֹדֵעַ אִם נָזַרְתִּי וְאִם לֹא נָזַרְתִּי. אָהֵן הוּא בַּתְּחִילָה. אִם מ' וְאִם נ'. אָהֵן הוּא בַסּוֹף. רבי יוֹסֵי בְּירבי בּוּן אָמַר. אִיתְפַּלְגוּן רבי חִייָה בַּר בָּא וְרבי שְׁמוּאֵל בַּר רַב יִצְחָק. כָּל־עַמָּא מוֹדֵי. אֵינִי יוֹדֵעַ אִם נָזַרְתִּי וְאִם לֹא נָזַרְתִּי. אָהֵן הוּא בַּתְּחִילָה. אִם מ' וְאִם נ'. הֲהֵנּוּ בַסּוֹף. מָה פְּלִיגִין. אִם אַחַת אִם שְׁתַּיִם. רבי חִייָה בַּר בָּא עֲבַד לֵיהּ כְּבַסּוֹף. רבי שְׁמוּאֵל עֲבַד לֵיהּ כְּבַתְּחִילָה. רבי מָנָא. אִם אַחַת אִם שְׁתַּיִם צְרִיכָה לְרבי שְׁמוּאֵל בַּר רַב יִצְחָק. הוּא כְּבַתְּחִילָה הוּא כְּבַסּוֹף.

Halakhah 8: "If his wife had a miscarriage," etc. Should one not be afraid that he might have been viable? Rebbi Johanan said, [the Mishnah] is Rebbi Jehudah's, since Rebbi Jehudah said, any doubt of *nezirut* is permitted[100]. It was said to him that Rebbi Jehudah said so only for the end; but for the start even Rebbi Jehudah will agree[101]. What is beginning and what is end? Rebbi Samuel ben Rav Isaac said, everybody agrees that "I do not know whether I made a vow of *nazir* or not," is at the beginning, "whether it was for 30 or 50 days", is at the end[102]. Rebbi Yose ben Rebbu Abun said: Rebbi Ḥiyya bar Abba and Rebbi Samuel ben Rav Isaac disagreed: Everybody agrees that "I do not know whether I made a vow of *nazir* or not," is at the beginning, "whether it was for 30 or 50 days", is at the end. Where do they disagree? If it was once or twice[103]. Rebbi Ḥiyya bar Abba considered it the end, Rebbi Samuel considered it the beginning. Rebbi Mana: The problem for Rebbi Samuel ben Rav Isaac about one or two times is whether it is the beginning or the end[104].

100 Tosephta 2:8: "'I shall be a *nazir* if I have a son,' and there was a son born to him but it is doubtful whether he is viable or not. R. Jehudah frees him since a doubt of *nezirut* is permitted. R. Simeon obligates him since a doubt of *nezirut* is forbidden."

101 That a vow of *nazir* has to be kept.

102 Since a vow of *nazir* had to precede the statement of duration.

103 Whether he vowed one or two periods of *nezirut*.

104 In his opinion, R. Ḥiyya bar Abba had no problem with this case.

משנה ט: הֲרֵינִי נָזִיר וְנָזִיר כְּשֶׁיִּהְיֶה לִי בֵן הִתְחִיל מוֹנֶה אֶת שֶׁלּוֹ וְאַחַר כָּךְ נוֹלַד לוֹ בֵן מַשְׁלִים אֶת שֶׁלּוֹ אַחַר כָּךְ מוֹנֶה אֶת שֶׁל בְּנוֹ. הֲרֵינִי נָזִיר כְּשֶׁיְּהֵא לִי בֵן וְנָזִיר הִתְחִיל מוֹנֶה אֶת שֶׁלּוֹ וְאַחַר כָּךְ נוֹלַד לוֹ בֵן מַנִּיחַ אֶת שֶׁלּוֹ וּמוֹנֶה אֶת שֶׁל בְּנוֹ וְאַחַר כָּךְ מַשְׁלִים אֶת שֶׁלּוֹ. (fol. 51d)

Mishnah 9: "I am a *nazir* and a *nazir* when a son is born to me." If he started counting for himself when a son was born to him, he finishes his own[105] and then counts for his son. "I am a *nazir* when a son is born to me, and a *nazir*." If he had started counting for himself when a son was born to him he interrupts his own, counts for his son[105], and then finishes for himself[106].

105 Then he brings his sacrifices and shaves.

106 Since it is after shaving, he has to complete 30 days.

(52a line 53) **הלכה ט:** הֲרֵינִי נָזִיר וְנָזִיר כְּשֶׁיִּהְיֶה לִי בֵן כול'. רבי יוסי בָּעֵי. אָמַר. הֲרֵינִי נָזִיר לִשְׁלֹשִׁים יוֹם אִילּוּ וְלִשְׁלֹשִׁים יוֹם אִילּוּ. אָמַר רבי זְעִירָא קוֹמֵי רבי מָנָא. וְלֹא מַתְנִיתָא הִיא. מַנִּיחַ אֶת שֶׁלּוֹ וּמוֹנֶה אֶת שֶׁלִּבְנוֹ. לֹא אֲפִילוּ אִשְׁתּוֹ יוֹשֶׁבֶת עַל הַמַּשְׁבֵּר. אָמַר לֵיהּ. נְזִירוּתוֹ לִנְזִירוֹת בְּנוֹ לֹא דַמְיָא. אֶלָּא אָמַר. הֲרֵינִי נָזִיר מִכְּבָר וְנָזִיר לְאַחַר עֶשְׂרִים יוֹם. רבי לֶעְזָר וְרבי יוסי בֶּן חֲנִינָה תְּרֵיהוֹן אָמְרִין. הִשְׁלִים נְזִירוּתוֹ לְעוֹלָם אֵין נְזִירוּת בְּנוֹ חָלָה עָלָיו עַד שֶׁתְּהֵא קָרְבַּן מְגַלֵּחַ. נָזִיר שֶׁנִּיטְמָא. מַחְלְפָה שִׁיטָתֵיהּ דְּרבי יוסי בֶּן חֲנִינָה. תַּמָּן הוּא אָמַר. טָמֵא מֵת שֶׁנָּזַר שְׁבִיעִי שֶׁלּוֹ עוֹלֶה מִן הַמִּנְיָן. נָזִיר שֶׁנִּיטְמָא אֵין שְׁבִיעִי שֶׁלּוֹ עוֹלֶה מִן הַמִּנְיָן. וְכָא לֹא כִטְמֵא מֵת שֶׁנָּזַר הוּא. וְלֹא טָמֵא מֵת שֶׁנָּזַר שְׁבִיעִי שֶׁלּוֹ עוֹלֶה מִן הַמִּנְיָן. שֶׁהוּא זָקוּק לוֹ לְהָבִיא קָרְבָּן טוּמְאָה. וְלֹא נָזִיר שֶׁנִּיטְמָא אֵין שְׁבִיעִי שֶׁלּוֹ עוֹלֶה לוֹ מִן הַמִּנְיָן. שֶׁאֵינוֹ זָקוּק לְהָבִיא קָרְבָּן טוּמְאָה. וְכָא הוֹאִיל וְהוּא זָקוּק לְהָבִיא קָרְבָּן טוּמְאָה הַשְּׁבִיעִי שֶׁלּוֹ עוֹלֶה מִן הַמִּנְיָן.

Halakhah 9: ""I am a *nazir* and a *nazir* when a son is born to me," etc. Rebbi Yose asked: If he said, "I am a *nazir* for these 30 days and those 30 days.[107]" Rebbi Ze'ira said before Rebbi Mana: Is that not the Mishnah? "He interrupts his own, counts for his son, and then finishes for himself." Not even if his wife is in the process of giving birth[108]? He said to him, his *nezirut* is not comparable to his son's *nezirut*[109], but to the case that he said, "I am already a *nazir* and a *nazir* after twenty days.[110]" Rebbi Eleazar and Rebbi Yose ben Ḥanina both say: If he finished his *nezirut*, his son's *nezirut* cannot start for him before he was shaving with a sacrifice. About a *nazir* who became impure, the opinions of Rebbi Yose ben Hanina seem contradictory. There, he says, if a person impure by the impurity of the dead made a vow of *nazir*, his seventh day is counted[111]. If a *nazir* becomes impure, his seventh day is not counted[112]. In our case[113], is he not like a person impure by the impurity of the dead, who made a vow of *nazir*? And is not the seventh day counted for a person impure by the impurity of the dead, who made a vow of *nazir*? Would this obligate him to bring a sacrifice for his impurity? But if a *nazir* who becomes impure, his seventh day is not counted; does it not obligate him to bring a sacrifice for his impurity? And here, because he is obligated to bring a sacrifice (of impurity)[114], the seventh day is [not][115] counted for him.

107 Since he vows twice for the same period of time, may he observe his *nezirut* for 30 days and then bring two sets of sacrifices to fulfill both vows?

108 If he made any of the vows described in the Mishnah while his wife was in labor, the Mishnah still requires him to first observe *nezirut* for his son and only then his own even though they might start on the same day.

109 In the case of the Mishnah, the two periods cannot start together since it is possible that his wife's labor be prolonged and there is a 50% chance that the child will be a girl.

110 Where he has to start the second period of *nezirut* not after 20 days but after 30 days and after he acquitted himself of his obligatory sacrifices.

111 If the person was purified by water containing some ashes of the Red Cow on the 3rd and 7th days of his impurity, he immerses himself in water on the 7th day and is pure (*Num.* 19). There is no reason why he cannot start a period of *nezirut* on that same day. Quoted in the Babli, 17a, 18a.

112 It is a biblical decree that he has to bring a sacrifice on the 8th day and start counting anew from that day (*Num.* 6:10).

113 Of the father expecting a baby boy. His vow is a new one, not a continuation of an old one as in the case of the impure *nazir*.

114 The text is corrupt: He is obligated to bring a sacrifice for the end of his first *nezirut*, but it is not a sacrifice for impurity.

115 The text is corrupt: The count of the new *nezirut* cannot start before he has acquitted himself of his prior obligations; therefore the 30th day of his *nezirut*, which corresponds to the 7th day of impurity, cannot be counted.

(52b line 1) שִׁמְעוֹן בַּר אַבָּא בְּשֵׁם רִבִּי יוֹחָנָן. נִיטְמָא בִנְזִירוּת בְּנוֹ וְהִתְרוּ בּוֹ מִשׁוּם נְזִירוּתוֹ לוֹקֶה. הִפְרִישׁ קָרְבְּנוֹתָיו קָדָשׁוּ. לֹא חָשִׁין לְהָא דְתַנֵּי רִבִּי חִייָה. קָרְבָּנוֹ לַיֿי עַל נִזְרוֹ. שֶׁיִקְדּוֹם נִזְרוֹ לְקָרְבָּנוֹ. לֹא שֶׁיִקְדּוֹם קָרְבָּנוֹ לְנִזְרוֹ.

Simeon bar Abba in the name of Rebbi Johanan: If he polluted himself during his son's *nezirut* but was warned because of his own *nezirut*, he is whipped[116]. If he dedicated his sacrifices, they are sanctified[117]. One does not consider what Rebbi Hiyya stated: "His sacrifice to the Eternal for his *nezirut*,[118]" i. e., his vow of *nazir* should precede his sacrifice, rather than that his sacrifice precede his vow of *nazir*.

116 Since a *nazir* is forbidden by biblical law to pollute himself with the impurity of the dead (*Num.* 6:6-7), if he pollutes himself intentionally and his criminal intent was ascertained because he was warned by two witnesses not to pollute himself and he did it anyway, he is punished in criminal law. In order to lead to prosecution, the warning must correctly state the law which might be broken.

117 In the Babli, 14a, in a different context, R. Johanan holds that his two *neziriot* are only one extended vow. There, it is disputed by R. Simeon ben Laqish.

118 *Num.* 6:21. Tosephta 2:6, Halakhah 3:2 (52c l. 37), *Šebuot* 4:4 (35c l. 58) {*Num. rabba* 10:42}. In the parallel sources, the statement is accepted as practice.

(52b line 5) רִבִּי יוּדָה בָּעָא קוֹמֵי רִבִּי יוֹסֵי. וְתִקְדּוֹם נְזִירוּתוֹ לִנְזִירוּת בְּנוֹ. לֹא כֵן אָמַר רִבִּי אַבָּהוּ בְּשֵׁם רִבִּי יוֹחָנָן. הֲרֵי זֶה עוֹלָה לְאַחַר ל׳ יוֹם. מְכָרָהּ בְּתוֹךְ ל׳ יוֹם מְכוּרָה וְהַקְדִּישָׁהּ קָדֵשָׁה. אָמַר. לֹא בָאוֹמֵר. הֲרֵי זוֹ. דִּילְמָא בָאוֹמֵר. הֲרֵי עָלַי. וְהָאוֹמֵר. הֲרֵי אֲנִי. כָּאוֹמֵר. הֲרֵי עָלַי.

Rebbi Judah asked before Rebbi Yose: Why should his *nezirut* not precede that of his son[119]? Did not Rebbi Abbahu say in the name of Rebbi Johanan: "This animal shall be dedicated as elevation sacrifice after 30 days." If he sold it within the thirty days, it is sold; its dedication sanctifies[120]. He said, is that not, if one said "This". Perhaps if he said: "I have the obligation[121]"? But the one who says, "I am", is like one who says, "I have the obligation."

119 This refers to the second part of the Mishnah. If he had started his own *nezirut* when his son was born, why should he not finish his own and only then start the *nezirut* honoring his son's birth?

120 If the animal dedicated as one kind of sacrifice after 30 days was dedicated and used for another sacrifice within this period, it is perfectly legal since the prior dedication was inactive in the intervening period. (Quoted in *Qiddušin* 3:1, 63c l. 42.)

121 If a person dedicates an animal saying: "this animal is dedicated", and anything happens to the animal before it is sacrificed, the owner does not have to look for a replacement. But if he says, "it is my obligation to bring", he has to bring the dedicated animal and, if anything happens to it, the owner must provide a replacement. Therefore, if the animal was dedicated after 30 days but no longer exists, no replacement is due. But a vow of *nazir* is personal and has to be dealt with under the rules of personal responsibility.

(52b line 9) תַּנֵּי רִבִּי חִייָה. נָזִיר לְאַחַר עֶשְׂרִים יוֹם נָזִיר מֵעַכְשָׁיו לְמֵאָה יוֹם. הֲרֵי זֶה מוֹנֶה עֶשְׂרִים יוֹם וּמַפְסִיק וְחוֹזֵר וּמוֹנֶה עוֹד ל׳ יוֹם וְחוֹזֵר וּמוֹנֶה עוֹד שְׁמוֹנִים כְּדֵי לְהַשְׁלִים נְזִירוּתוֹ הָרִאשׁוֹנָה.

Rebbi Hiyya stated: "*Nazir* after twenty days and *nazir* 100 days from now on." He counts twenty days, interrupts and counts another 30 days, and counts another 80 to complete his first *nezirut*[122].

122 Tosephta 2:10, Babli 14a. A person makes a vow to be a *nazir* after 30 days and simultaneously makes a vow immediately to be a *nazir* for 100

days. Then he starts his immediate *nezirut* for 20 days, continues to count the 30 days of his other *nezirut*, brings his sacrifices and shaves, and counts the remaining 80 days of his immediate *nezirut* and brings the second set of sacrifices. Since the continuation of the interrupted *nezirut* is for more than 30 days, it is a valid *nezirut* and he does lose the initial 20 days.

(fol. 51d) **משנה י:** הֲרֵינִי נָזִיר כְּשֶׁיִּהְא לִי בֵן וְנָזִיר מֵאָה יוֹם. נוֹלַד לוֹ בֵן עַד שִׁבְעִים לֹא יַפְסִיד כְּלוּם. לְאַחַר שִׁבְעִים סוֹתֵר שִׁבְעִים שֶׁאֵין תִּגְלַחַת פָּחוֹת מִשְּׁלשִׁים יוֹם.

Mishnah 10: "I shall be a *nazir* if a son is born[123] to me and a *nazir* for 100 days.[124]" If a son is born to him in less than 70 [days], he should not lose anything[125]. After 70 [days], he reduces to 70 since no shaving is for less than 30 days[126].

123 An unspecified term, i. e., 30 days.

124 He starts this *nezirut* immediately.

125 As explained in Note 122, he starts his *nezirut*, after his son's birth he starts counting 30 days, brings his sacrifices and shaves, and then finishes the count of the days missing for the vow of 100 days.

126 If less than 30 days were left in his count of 100, he must observe *nezirut* for 30 days after his celebration for his son.

(52b line 11) **הלכה י:** הֲרֵינִי נָזִיר כְּשֶׁיִּהְא לִי בֵן כול'. פְּשִׁיטָא שֶׁבְּסוֹף הַיּוֹם עוֹלֶה לוֹ כְּכוּלּוֹ. תְּחִילַת הַיּוֹם מָהוּ שֶׁיַּעֲלֶה לוֹ כְּכוּלּוֹ. וְלֹא מַתְנִיתָא הִיא. לְאַחַר שִׁבְעִים סוֹתֵר שִׁבְעִים. לֹא אֲפִילוּ מִקְצָת. הָדָא אֳמָרָה. שֶׁתְּחִילַת הַיּוֹם עוֹלָה לוֹ כְּכוּלּוֹ.

Halakhah 10: ""I shall be a *nazir* if a son is born to me," etc. It is obvious that the end of a day is counted as a full [day][127]. Is the start of a day counted as a full day[128]? Is that not the Mishnah: "after 70 [days], he reduces to 70," not even a part[129]? This implies that the start of a day is counted as a full day.

127 If the son was born towards the end of a day, that day counts as day 1 of the son's *nezirut* which by Mishnah 9 starts automatically at the moment of birth.

128 If the son was born during daytime and the father started the day as *nazir* on his own count, does the day also count as a full day for the father?

129 If part of the day is not counted as a full day then if the son was born on the 71st day, no day would be lost. Since the Mishnah says that even in this case, a day is lost, it implies that without this rule the 71st day would count for both *neziriot*. Therefore, the 70th day counts for both. In the Babli, 15a, this a statement attributed to Rav.

(52b line 15) נוֹלַד בְּיוֹם שְׁמוֹנִים סוֹתֵר עֲשָׂרָה. נוֹלַד בְּיוֹם תִּשְׁעִים סוֹתֵר עֶשְׂרִים. הִשְׁלִים נְזִירוּתוּ וּבָא לְהַשְׁלִים נְזִירוּת בְּנוֹ. נִיטְמָא בְּתוֹךְ עֲשָׂרָה יָמִים הָרִאשׁוֹנִים סוֹתֵר הַכֹּל. בְּתוֹךְ עֲשָׂרִים יָמִים הָאַחֲרוֹנִים. רִבִּי בָּא בְשֵׁם רַב וְרִבִּי יוֹחָנָן תְּרֵיהוֹן אֱמְרִין. סוֹתֵר שְׁלֹשִׁים. רִבִּי שְׁמוּאֵל אָמַר. אֵינוֹ סוֹתֵר אֶלָּא שֶׁבַע. שְׁמוּאֵל בַּר בָּא בְעָא קוֹמֵי רִבִּי יָסָא. מִיסְבַּר סָבַר רִבִּי יוֹחָנָן. סְתִירַת תַּעַר כִּסְתִירַת מַמָּשׁ. אָמַר רִבִּי זְעִירָא. אֵין יִסְבּוֹר רִבִּי יוֹחָנָן. סְתִירַת תַּעַר כִּסְתִירַת מַמָּשׁ. לָמָּה לִי לְמֵימַר. סוֹתֵר לִשְׁלֹשִׁים יוֹם. וְיִסְתּוֹר הַכֹּל. אָמַר רִבִּי אָבִין בַּר חִייָה קוֹמֵי רִבִּי זְעִירָא. תִּיפְתּוֹר שֶׁנּוֹלַד בְּיוֹם שֶׁאֵינוֹ רָאוּי לְהָבִיא קָרְבָּן. הַגַּע עַצְמָךְ שֶׁנּוֹלַד בַּלַּיְלָה הֲרֵי אֵינוֹ רָאוּי לְהָבִיא קָרְבָּן. רָאוּי הוּא. לַיְלָה הוּא שֶׁגָּרַם. הַגַּע עַצְמָךְ הֲרֵי שֶׁנּוֹלַד בַּשַׁבָּת הֲרֵי אֵינוֹ רָאוּי לְהָבִיא קָרְבָּן. רָאוּי. שַׁבָּת הִיא שֶׁגָּרְמָה. הִשְׁלִים נְזִירוּתוּ וְלֹא הִסְפִּיק לְגַלֵּחַ עַד שֶׁנּוֹלַד בַּשַׁבָּת הֲרֵי אֵינוֹ רָאוּי לְהָבִיא קָרְבָּן. רָאוּי. שַׁבָּת הִיא שֶׁגָּרְמָה. הִשְׁלִים נְזִירוּתוּ וְלֹא הִסְפִּיק לְגַלֵּחַ עַד שֶׁנּוֹלַד הַבֵּן. מְגַלֵּחַ תִּגְלַחַת אַחַת לִשְׁתֵּיהֶן. הִפְרִישׁ קָרְבְּנוֹתָיו וְלֹא הִסְפִּיק לְגַלֵּחַ עַד שֶׁנּוֹלַד הַבֵּן. תַּמָּן אָמְרִין. מְגַלֵּחַ תִּגְלַחַת אַחַת עַל שְׁתֵּיהֶן. רִבִּי יוֹחָנָן אָמַר. מְגַלֵּחַ וְחוֹזֵר וּמְגַלֵּחַ. מַתְנִיתָא פְּלִיגָא עַל רִבִּי יוֹחָנָן. שָׁאֲלוּ אֶת רִבִּי שִׁמְעוֹן בֶּן יוֹחַי. הֲרֵי שֶׁהָיָה נָזִיר וּמְצוֹרָע מָהוּ שֶׁיְּגַלַּח תִּגְלַחַת אַחַת וְתַעֲלֶה

לוֹ לִנְזִירוּתוֹ וּלְצָרַעְתּוֹ. אָמַר לָהֶן. אִילוּ זֶה מְגַלֵּחַ לְהַעֲבָרַת שֵׂיעָר. יָפֶה הָיִיתָ אוֹמֵר. אֶלָּא שֶׁהַנָּזִיר מְגַלֵּחַ לְהַעֲבִיר שֵׂיעָר וּמְצוֹרָע מְגַלֵּחַ לְגִידּוּל שֵׂיעָר. אָמְרוּ לוֹ. לֹא תַעֲלֶה לוֹ יְמֵי גָמְרוֹ. לֹא תַעֲלֶה לוֹ יְמֵי סְפִירוֹ. שְׁנֵיהֶן מְגַלְּחִין לְהַעֲבָרַת שֵׂיעָר. אָמְרוּ לוֹ. אִילוּ זֶה מְגַלֵּחַ לִפְנֵי זְרִיקַת דָּמִים וְזֶה מְגַלֵּחַ לִפְנֵי זְרִיקַת דָּמִים יָפֶה הָיִיתָ אוֹמֵר. אֶלָּא שֶׁהַנָּזִיר מְגַלֵּחַ לִפְנֵי זְרִיקַת דָּמִים וּמְצוֹרָע מְגַלֵּחַ לְאַחַר זְרִיקַת דָּמִים. אָמְרוּ לוֹ. לֹא תַעֲלֶה לוֹ יְמֵי גָמְרוֹ. לֹא תַעֲלֶה לוֹ יְמֵי סְפִירוֹ. שְׁנֵיהֶן מְגַלְּחִין לִפְנֵי זְרִיקַת דָּמִים. אָמַר לָהֶן. אִילוּ זֶה מְגַלֵּחַ לִפְנֵי בִיאַת הַמַּיִם וְזֶה מְגַלֵּחַ לִפְנֵי בִיאַת הַמַּיִם יָפֶה הָיִיתָ אוֹמֵר. אֶלָּא שֶׁהַנָּזִיר מְגַלֵּחַ לִפְנֵי בִיאַת הַמַּיִם וּמְצוֹרָע מְגַלֵּחַ לְאַחַר בִּיאַת הַמַּיִם. אָמְרוּ לוֹ. תֵּקֵן הַדָּבָר. לֹא תַעֲלֶה לוֹ יְמֵי גָמְרוֹ לֹא תַעֲלֶה לוֹ יְמֵי סְפִירוֹ. לֹא תַעֲלֶה לוֹ לְטָהֵר לֹא תַעֲלֶה לוֹ לְטַמֵּא. הֲרֵי שֶׁהָיָה נָזִיר וּמְצוֹרָע. אֲבָל אִם הָיָה נָזִיר וְנָזִיר מְגַלֵּחַ תִּגְלַחַת אַחַת עַל שְׁתֵּיהֶם. מָה עֲבַד לָהּ רִבִּי יוֹחָנָן. פָּתַר לָהּ. חֲלוּקִים הֵן עַל רִבִּי שִׁמְעוֹן בֶּן יוֹחַי.

If he was born on the eightieth day, he eliminates ten[130]. If he was born on the ninetieth day, he eliminates twenty. If he finished his *nezirut* and came to complete his son's *nezirut* and became impure within the first ten days, he eliminates everything[131]. Within the last twenty days? Rebbi Abba in the name of Rab and Rebbi Johanan both say, he eliminates thirty[132]. Rebbi Samuel said, he eliminates seven only[133]. Samuel bar Abba asked before Rebbi Yose: Does Rebbi Johanan think that eliminating by a shaving knife is identical with substantial eliminating[134]? Rebbi Ze'ira said, if Rebbi Johanan thought that eliminating by a shaving knife is identical to substantial eliminating, why would he say that he eliminates thirty[135]? Should he not invalidate everything? Rebbi Abin bar Hiyya said before Rebbi Ze'ira: Explain it if he was born on a day unsuitable to bring a sacrifice[136]. Think of it, if he was born in the night[137], is that not unsuitable to bring a sacrifice? It is suitable; the night caused it. Think of it, if he was born on the Sabbath, is that not unsuitable to bring a sacrifice[138]? It is suitable; the Sabbath caused it. If he had finished his *nezirut* but did not manage to shave when [the son] was born on the Sabbath, is that not unsuitable to bring a sacrifice? It is suitable; the Sabbath caused it. If he had finished his *nezirut* but did not manage to shave before his son was born[139], he celebrates one shaving for both. If he had dedicated his sacrifices but did not manage to shave before his son was born. There[140], they say that he celebrates one shaving for both. Rebbi Joḥanan said, he shaves and then shaves a second time. A *baraita* disagrees with Rebbi Joḥanan: [141]"They asked[142] Rebbi Simeon ben Ioḥai: Assume that he was both a *nazir* and a sufferer from scale disease[143], may he shave once and have it counted for his *nezirut* and his scale disease? He said to them: If he shaved[144] to remove hair, you would be correct. But the *nazir* shaves to remove hair whereas the sufferer from scale disease shaves[145] to have hair grow. They said to him, if it cannot be counted for the days of his completeness[146], should it not be counted for the days of his count[147]? Both of them shave to remove hair. (They said to him[148]. If both of them shaved before the sprinkling of the blood, you would be correct. But the *nazir* shaves before the sprinkling of the blood and the sufferer from scale disease shaves after the sprinkling of the blood! They said to him, if it cannot be counted for the days of his completeness, should it not be counted for the days of his count? Both of them shave before the sprinkling of the blood!)[149] He said to them, if both shaved before they immerse themselves in water, you would be correct. But the *nazir* shaves before he immerses himself in water and the sufferer from scale disease shaves after he immerses himself in water[150]. They said to him, the matter is settled. It cannot be counted for the days of his completeness, it cannot be counted for the days of his count. It cannot be counted for purification; it cannot be counted for impurity[151]. That is, if he was a *nazir* and sufferer from scale disease. But if he was a *nazir* and *nazir*, he may shave once for both.[152"] What does Rebbi Johanan do with this? He explains that they disagree with Rebbi Simeon ben Laqish[153].

130   Since only the first 70 days of the father's first *nezirut* are counted, the last 10 are disregarded. (A gloss in Tosaphot 13b, *s.v.* לאחר has a different explanation.)

131   If the son was born on the 90th day of his *nezirut* and he starts counting his son's days, as long as his 100 days are not completed, any impurity of the dead will invalidate all his *nezirut* (Mishnah 3:4). If the impurity occurs after he has counted 100 days, his days are immunized; the question is only what happens to the days he counts for his son.

132   He has to keep 30 days in purity for his son and afterwards another thirty to finish his *nezirut* as prescribed in the Mishnah.

133   Of his own completed count, only the seven days of impurity of the dead are invalidated, following R. Eliezer (Mishnah 3:3).

134   The *nazir* is forbidden to shave. If he shaves anyway, he loses 30 days of his count (Mishnah 6:5). But impurity of his body, called here "substantial", invalidates everything from the start.

135   Obviously, if the *nazir* for 100 days becomes impure (being defiled by a corpse) at any time before he has completed his count, he has to start a new count.

136   Everybody agrees that a defiled *nazir* has to start anew if he was defiled before he could have offered his sacrifices. Could one think of a situation where he had finished his count and still could not have offered sacrifices? The answer is negative.

137   No sacrifice can be offered in the night. *Megillah* 3:5,6 (73c l. 8,10), Babli 20b, *Sifra Ṣaw Pereq* 18(7), based on *Lev.* 7:38.

138   The only sacrifices possible on the Sabbath are those which are explicitly commanded for that day.

139   And automatically his new *nezirut* starts on the day of the birth. He now cannot bring the sacrifices for thr prior *nezirut* since this would involve shaving his hair.

140   In Babylonia, they hold that not the dedication but rather the actual Temple ceremony determines the end

of his *nezirut*.

141   Tosephta 5:2, Babli 60b, *Sifry Num.* 38 (best *Sifry* text in *Yalqut Šim'ony Num.* #709).

142   In *Sifry*, the persons who ask are R. Eleazar ben Šamua' and R. Johanan the Alexandrian.

143   While suffering from the disease, he is impure. The ritual of purification (*Lev.* 14) requires the healed patient to shave all his hair after a preliminary ceremony (14:8), undergo a week of quarantine, shave again, including even his eyebrows (14:9), and offer his sacrifices the next day (14:10). The only impurity forbidden to the *nazir* is the impurity of corpses; therefore, it is quite possible for a sufferer from scale disease to be a *nazir* (even though such a person could never shave before he is healed since he cannot enter the Temple precinct.)

144   Probably, the text of Tosephta and *Sifry* is better: "If each of them shaved ...". In the Babli: "If both of them shaved to grow or both of them to remove."

145   After the preliminary ceremony, he shaves to have his hair grow to be shorn after a week.

146   The impurity of the sufferer from scale disease varies with his status. It is a minor impurity as long as the diagnosis of his sickness is only tentative (*Lev.* 13, *passim*), it is severe while his diagnosis is complete (*Lev.* 13:45,46), and it is minor again during his quarantine in the process of purification. What Yerushalmi, Tosephta, and *Sifry* call גמרו "his completeness (of diagnosis)", the Babli calls חֲלוּטוֹ "his absoluteness".

147   Of his quarantine, after which he has to shave again. (But then he shaves after 7 days, not at least 30 days as required for a *nazir*.)

148   This must read: He said to them (as in Tosephta and *Sifry*).

149   The passage in parentheses is hopelessly corrupt. It is missing in Tosephta and *Sifry*. One should read with the Babli: "But the nazir shaves *after* the sprinkling of the blood and the sufferer from scale disease shaves *before* the sprinkling of the blood." The *nazir* shaves after the sacrifices have been brought (*Num.* 6:18) while the person healed from scale disease shaves the day before he brings his sacrifices. The problem is that the students declare that both the *nazir* and the sufferer from scale disease in his preliminary purification shave *before* the sprinkling of the blood; this seems to presuppose the uncorrected reading in the preceding sentence. The only way to make sense of the statement is

also to emend this sentence: "Both of them shave *after* the sprinkling of the blood," and to refer to the blood of the bird used in the preliminary ceremony of the sufferer from scale disease (*Lev.* 14:7).

150   One has to read (with the parallel sources): "But the nazir shaves *after* he immerses himself in water and the sufferer from scale disease shaves *before* he immerses himself in water." The *nazir* shaves in the Temple, therefore he had to immerse himself in water to be able to enter the Temple. The sufferer from scale disease is required to shave before he immerses himself (*Lev.* 14:9).

151   Probably one should read with Tosephta and Sifry: תַּקִּין הַדָּבָר. ל'א עוֹלָה בִּימֵי גָמְרוֹ עוֹלָה בִּימֵי סְפִירוֹ. ל'א עוֹלָה בְּטָהֵר עוֹלָה בְּטָמֵא. "It does not count in the days of his completeness; it counts in the days of his count. It does not count if [the *nazir*] is pure; it counts if he is impure." The impure *nazir* shaves on the seventh day of his purification; this may be before he immerses himself. He has to shave before he brings his sacrifice on the eighth day. Therefore, a healed sufferer from scale disease who also is an impure *nazir* may combine his first shaving for his healing together with the shaving for his impure *nezirut*.

152   This sentence, which is not in any of the other sources, supports the Babylonians and contradicts R. Johanan.

153   Since the *baraita* is declared to be R. Simeon ben Laqish's personal opinion, it is a minority opinion which does not represent practice.

מי שאמר פרק שלישי

משנה א: מִי שֶׁאָמַר הֲרֵינִי נָזִיר מְגַלֵּחַ יוֹם שְׁלֹשִׁים וְאֶחָד. וְאִם גִּילַּח (fol. 52b) יוֹם שְׁלֹשִׁים יָצָא. הֲרֵינִי נָזִיר שְׁלֹשִׁים יוֹם אִם גִּילַּח יוֹם שְׁלֹשִׁים לֹא יָצָא.

Mishnah 1: If somebody said, "I am a *nazir*," he shaves on the 31st day, but if he shaved on the 30th day, he has fulfilled his obligation[1]. "I am a *nazir* for 30 days[2]," if he shaved on the 30th day, he did not fulfill his obligation.

1   An unspecified *nezirut* is 30 days (Mishnah 1:3), and part of a day is counted as a full day (Chapter 2, Note 127).

2   If he spelled out "30 days", it has to be interpreted as meaning "30 full days".

הלכה א: מִי שֶׁאָמַר הֲרֵינִי נָזִיר כול׳. הָדָא מְסַייְעָא לְבַר קַפָּרָא. (52c line 7) אִם גִּילַּח יוֹם ל׳ לֹא יָצָא. הָדָא מְסַייְעָא לְרִבִּי יוֹנָתָן. אִם גִּילַּח יוֹם ל׳ יָצָא. הָא תַרְתֵּיי. לֵית הִיא אֶלָּא חֲדָא. זוֹ עֵדוּת. יוֹדְעִין הָיוּ שֶׁהוּא אָסוּר לְגַלֵּחַ אֶלָּא שֶׁהֵן סְבוּרִין אִם גִּילַּח יוֹם שְׁלֹשִׁים לֹא יָצָא. בָּא לְהָעִיד אִם גִּילַּח יוֹם שְׁלֹשִׁים יָצָא.

Halakhah 1: "If somebody said, "I am a *nazir*," etc. This supports Bar Qappara[3], that if he shaved on the 30th day, he did not fulfill his obligation. This supports Rebbi Jonathan[4], that if he shaved on the 30th day, he did fulfill his obligation. Both of them[5]? It is only one opinion, "this testimony[6]". They knew that it was forbidden to shave on the 30th; they thought that if he shaved on the 30th day, he did not fulfill his obligation. He came to testify that if he shaved on the 30th day, he fulfilled his obligation.

3   Chapter 1:3, Note 93.
4   Chapter 1:3, Note 94.
5   One anonymous Mishnah cannot represent two contradictory opinions.
6   Mishnah 2. R. Pappaias testified that a person who vowed two *neziriot* and shaved for the first on the thirtieth day may shave the second time on the 60th day (since the 30th day is counted for both; cf. Note 1.) Since the testimony is formulated conditionally, "if he shaved on the 30th day", not as an absolute statement, "he shaves on the 30th and 60th days", it follows that shaving on the 30th day is irregular. The Mishnah follows neither Bar Qappara nor R. Jonathan but the practice proclaimed by R. Pappaios.

(52c line 11) רִבִּי אִימִּי הֲוָה לֵיהּ עוֹבְדָא וְגִילַּח יוֹם ל׳. וַהֲוָה לֵיהּ עוֹבְדָא וְגִילַּח יוֹם לֹא. אָמַר רִבִּי זְרִיקָא. מִן מַתְנִיתָא יְלִיף לָהּ רִבִּי אִימִּי. דְּתָנִינָן תַּמָּן. מִי שֶׁנָּזַר שְׁתֵּי נְזִירִיּוֹת מְגַלֵּחַ אֶת הָרִאשׁוֹנָה יוֹם שְׁלֹשִׁים וְאֶחָד וְהַשְּׁנִייָה יוֹם שִׁשִּׁים וְאֶחָד. אָמַר רִבִּי יוֹסֵי. תַּמָּן לְשֶׁעָבַר וָכָא לְכַתְּחִילָּה. רִבִּי יִרְמְיָה הוֹרֵי לְרִבִּי יִצְחָק עֲטוֹשִׁיָּא וְאִית דְּאָמְרֵי לְרַב חִייָה בַּר רַב יִצְחָק עֲטוֹשִׁיָּא לְגַלֵּחַ יוֹם ל׳ מִן מַתְנִיתָא. שְׁמוֹנָה יָמִים. בָּטְלוּ מִמֶּנּוּ גְּזֵירַת שְׁלֹשִׁים. הִיא שְׁמִינִית הִיא יוֹם ל׳. אָמַר רִבִּי יוֹסֵי. שַׁנְיָיא הִיא תַּמָּן שֶׁמִּפְּנֵי כְבוֹד הָרֶגֶל הִתִּירוּ. תֵּדַע לָךְ. דָּמַר רִבִּי חֶלְבּוֹ בַּר חוּנָה בְּשֵׁם רִבִּי יוֹחָנָן. חָל יוֹם שְׁמוֹנָה שֶׁלּוֹ לִהְיוֹת בַּשַּׁבָּת מְגַלֵּחַ עֶרֶב שַׁבָּת. אִין תֵּימַר. שֶׁלֹּא מִפְּנֵי כְבוֹד הָרֶגֶל הִתִּירוּ. מֵעַתָּה אֲפִילוּ חָל יוֹם ל׳ שֶׁלּוֹ לִהְיוֹת בַּשַּׁבָּת מְגַלֵּחַ בְּעֶרֶב שַׁבָּת. וְעוֹד מִן הָדָא דְּאָמַר רִבִּי יוֹחָנָן. עַל כָּל־הַמֵּתִים כּוּלָּן שׁוֹלֵל לְאַחַר שִׁבְעָה וּמְאַחֶה לְאַחַר שְׁלֹשִׁים. וְיִשְׁלוֹל יוֹם ז׳ וִיאַחֶה יוֹם ל׳. אָמַר רִבִּי חַגַּי. דִּי הוּא שְׁמוּעֲתָא כֵן וּשְׁמוּעָתָא כֵן.

Something happened[7] to Rebbi Immi and he shaved on the 30th day, and something happened to Rebbi Immi and he shaved on the 31st day[8]. Rebbi Zeriqa said, Rebbi Immi learned this from the Mishnah, as we have stated there[9]: "If somebody vowed two *neziriot*, he shaves for the first on the 31st day, for the second on the 61st day[10]." Rebbi Yose said, there when it happened, here from the start[11]. Rebbi Jeremiah instructed Rebbi Isaac Aṭoshia, and some say, Rav Ḥiyya bar Rav Isaac Aṭoshia, to shave on the 30th day, following the Mishnah[12]: "Eight days, the decree of 30 days is waived for him." The eighth has the same status as the 30th day[13]. Rebbi Yose said, there is a difference; there they permitted in order to honor the holiday. You should know this, since Rebbi Ḥelbo bar Ḥuna said in the name of Rebbi Joḥanan: If his eighth day falls on the Sabbath, he shaves Sabbath eve. If you say that they did not permit in order to honor the holiday, then even if his 30th day falls on the Sabbath, he should shave Sabbath eve[14]. In addition, from what Rebbi Joḥanan had said[15]: "For all deceased[16] he stitches together after seven days and mends after 30." Why should he not stitch on the seventh day and mend on the 30th day? Rebbi Ḥaggai said, this has been transmitted in this way and that has been transmitted in that way[16].

7 A close relative died. By rabbinic convention, the mourner cannot leave his house for the first seven days after burial; he does not shave for thirty days. R. Immi considered the 30 days' period of the *nazir* as a paradigm for the 30 day period of the mourner.

8 He was inconsistent in his actions.

9 Mishnah 2.

10 The argument is from the part of the Mishnah which is not quoted: "But if he shaved for the first on the 30th day, he shaves for the second on the 60th" (cf. Note 6).

11 R. Yose criticizes R. Immi. The Mishnah requires the *nazir* to shave on his 31st day; it only legitimizes shaving on the 30th after the fact. But R. Immi shaved on the 30th on his own initiative. R. Zeriqa seems to hold that what is acceptable after the fact in biblical rules is permitted from the start in rabbinic usage.

12 *Mo'ed qaṭan* 3:5. "If somebody buried his relative three days before a holiday, the seven-day rule is waived for him. Eight days, the 30 day rule is waived for him, as they said: Sabbath is counted but does not interrupt, holidays interrupt but do not count." If somebody was mourning for three days before the holiday, he does not have to continue the intense mourning period after the holiday; he continues with the remainder of the 30-day period. Similarly, if he was keeping at least one day of mourning after the seven-day period, the holiday cancels the

remainder of the 30-day mourning period. (The Babli, *Mo'ed qatan* 19b, reduces the 8 day period to 7 since "part of a day is like a whole day" and the 30-day period starts on the seventh.)

13   The argument here goes as follows: If the 8th day of mourning was holiday eve, the mourner can shave in the afternoon in preparation for the holiday. The time elapsed from dawn to the afternoon is counted as a full day for him. Therefore, the person who shaves on the 30th day can nevertheless count the entire 30th day as being part of his mourning period.

14   Nobody allows the mourner to shave on the 29th day. (Quoted by Tosaphot *Mo'ed qatan* 19b, *s. v.* הלכה).

15   *Mo'ed qatan* 3:5 (82b l. 10), 3:8 (83d l. 23); Babli 22b.

16   Except for father and mother.

The first sign of mourning required is to tear one's garment. For the seven-day period, the mourner is required to wear the torn garment. He can stitch together the tear *after* the end of the seven-day period (after 30 days for father or mother) and invisibly mend it *after* thirty days (never mending invisibly for father or mother.) Why does one not allow stitching or mending on the last day of a period if "part of the day is counted as a whole day"?

16   Since one tradition is in the name of R. Johanan himself (meaning that the exact formulation is R. Johanan's) but the other is R. Helbo bar Huna's formulation of a ruling which R. Johanan had given, there is no proof that R. Johanan had meant to negate that part of the day is counted as a full day in all respects.

(fol. 52b) **משנה ב:** מִי שֶׁנָּזַר שְׁתֵּי נְזִירִיּוֹת מְגַלֵּחַ אֶת הָרִאשׁוֹנָה יוֹם שְׁלֹשִׁים וְאֶחָד וְהַשְּׁנִיָּיה יוֹם שִׁשִּׁים וְאֶחָד. וְאִם גִּילַּח אֶת הָרִאשׁוֹנָה יוֹם שְׁלֹשִׁים מְגַלֵּחַ אֶת הַשְּׁנִיָּיה יוֹם שִׁשִּׁים וְאִם גִּילַּח יוֹם שִׁשִּׁים חָסֵר אֶחָד יָצָא. וְזוֹ עֵדוּת הֵעִיד רִבִּי פַּפְּיַיס עַל מִי שֶׁנָּזַר שְׁתֵּי נְזִירִיּוֹת שֶׁאִם גִּילַּח אֶת הָרִאשׁוֹנָה יוֹם שְׁלֹשִׁים מְגַלֵּחַ אֶת הַשְּׁנִיָּיה יוֹם שִׁשִּׁים וְאִם גִּילַּח יוֹם שִׁשִּׁים חָסֵר אֶחָד יָצָא שֶׁיּוֹם שְׁלֹשִׁים עוֹלֶה לוֹ מִן הַמִּנְיָין.

Mishnah 2: If somebody vowed two *neziriot*, he shaves for the first on the 31st day, for the second on the 61st day[17], but if he shaved for the first on the 30th day, he shaves for the second on the 60th, and if he shaved on the day before the 60th[18], he has fulfilled his obligation. The following testimony did Rebbi Pappaias give[19]: if somebody vowed two *neziriot*, he shaves for the first on the 31st day, for the second on the 61st day, but if he shaved for the first on the 30th day, he shaves for the second on the 60th, and if he shaved on the day before the 60th, he has fulfilled his obligation since the 30th day is counted for him.

17   In all cases in this Mishnah, "part of a day is counted as an entire day" and the last day of a period is at the same time the first of the next period, whether the period be 30 or 31 days.

18   Compare Latin usage to replace 19 by 20-1, etc.

19   Any "testimony" mentioned in the Mishnah was given in Yabneh and accepted by the Synhedrion.

(52c line 25) **הלכה ב:** מִי שֶׁנָּזַר שְׁתֵּי נְזִירִיּוֹת כול'. הִשְׁלִים נְזִירוּתוֹ הָרִאשׁוֹנָה וּבָא לְהִישָּׁעֵן עַל הַשְּׁנִיָּיה. לֹא מָצְאוּ פֶתַח לָרִאשׁוֹנָה עַד שֶׁמָּצְאוּ פֶתַח לַשְּׁנִיָּיה. עָלַת לוֹ שְׁנִיָּיה רִאשׁוֹנָה. מַה נָן קַיָּימִין. אִם בְּאוֹמֵר. הֲרֵינִי נָזִיר שְׁתַּיִם. גֶּדֶר שֶׁבָּטַל מַחֲצִיתוֹ בָּטַל אֶת כּוּלּוֹ. אִם בְּאוֹמֵר. הֲרֵינִי נָזִיר ל יוֹם אִילוּ ל יוֹם אִילוּ. לֹא בְדָא עָלַת לוֹ שְׁנִיָּיה רִאשׁוֹנָה. אֶלָּא כִּי נָן קַיָּימִין בְּאוֹמֵר. הֲרֵינִי נָזִיר וְנָזִיר. בְּאוֹמֵר. אֵילוּ לִנְזִירוּת. אֲבָל אִם אָמַר. אֵילוּ לִנְזִירוּתִי וְאֵילוּ לִנְזִירוּת אַחֶרֶת לֹא בְדָא עָלַת לוֹ שְׁנִיָּיה רִאשׁוֹנָה. אָמַר רַבִּי לָעֶזָר. הִשְׁלִים נְזִירוּתוֹ לָרִאשׁוֹנָה. מִיכֵּן שֶׁהֵבִיא קָרְבָּן וְגִילַּח עָלַת לוֹ רִאשׁוֹנָה שְׁנִיָּיה. רַבִּי יַעֲקֹב בַּר אָחָא פְּקִיד לַחֲבֵרַיָּיא. אִין שְׁמַעְתּוּן מִילָּה מֵרַבִּי אֶלְעָזָר הֲווֹן יָדְעִין דְּרַבִּי יוֹחָנָן פְּלִיג. עַד שֶׁיָּבִיא כָּל־קָרְבְּנוֹתָיו. כְּרַבָּנִין. בְּרַם כְּרַבִּי שִׁמְעוֹן אֲפִילוּ לֹא הֵבִיא אֶלָּא קָרְבָּן אֶחָד. הִפְרִישׁ שְׁתֵּיהֶן כְּאַחַת אֵין בְּיָדוֹ אֶלָּא אַחַת. הִפְרִישָׁהּ זוֹ בִּפְנֵי עַצְמָהּ וְזוֹ בִּפְנֵי עַצְמָהּ אוֹ שֶׁהֵבִיא שְׁלִיזוֹ בְּזוֹ וְשֶׁלְּזוֹ בְּזוֹ לֹא יָצָא. הָא לְקַדֵּשׁ קֶדְשָׁה. לֹא כֵן

תַּנֵּי רִבִּי חִייָה. קָרְבָּנוּ לַיי עַל נִזְרוֹ. שֶׁיִּקְדּוֹם נִזְרוֹ לְקָרְבָּנוֹ וְלֹא שֶׁיִּקְדּוֹם קָרְבָּנוֹ לְנִזְרוֹ. שַׁנְיָיא הִיא שֶׁעוֹמֵד בִּנְזִירוּתוֹ. נִיחָא שְׁנִייָה רִאשׁוֹנָה. רִאשׁוֹנָה שְׁנִייָה. אָמַר רִבִּי יוּדָה. וְהָדָא מְסַייְעָא לְרִבִּי אֶלְעָזָר. לֹא כֵן רִבִּי יַעֲקֹב בַּר אָחָא מְפַקֵּד לַחֲבֵרַיָּיא. אִין שְׁמַעְתּוּן מִילָּה מֵרִבִּי אֶלְעָזָר הָווּן יָדְעִין דְּרִבִּי יוֹחָנָן פְּלִיג. עַד שֶׁיָּבִיא כָּל־קָרְבְּנוֹתָיו. וְסָבְרִין מֵימַר כְּרַבָּנִין. וְכָא כְּרִבִּי שִׁמְעוֹן אֲנָן קַייָמִין. רִבִּי חִינָנָא בְשֵׁם רִבִּי פִינְחָס. תִּיפְתָּר בִּנְזִירוּתוֹ וּבְנִזִירוּתוֹ שֶׁל בְּנוֹ. בְּדָא עָלַת לוֹ שְׁנִייָה רִאשׁוֹנָה. אָמַר רִבִּי יוֹסֵי בֵּירִבִּי בּוּן. לֹא כֵן סָבְרָן מֵימַר בָּאוֹמֵר. הֲרֵינִי נָזִיר. בְּדִין הָיָה שֶׁלֹּא יְהֵא נָזִיר אֶלָּא אַחַת. אַתְּ הוּא שֶׁהֶחֱמַרְתָּה עָלָיו שֶׁיְּהֵא נָזִיר שְׁתַּיִם. לֹא דַיֶּיךְ שֶׁהֶחֱמַרְתָּ עָלָיו שֶׁיְּהֵא נָזִיר שְׁתַּיִם אֶלָּא שֶׁאַתְּ אוֹמֵר. אֵין בְּיָדוֹ כְּלוּם.

Halakhah 2: "If somebody vowed two *neziriot*," etc. If he finished his first period of *nezirut* and started to lean[20] on the second, when they did not find an opening for the first while they found an opening for the second[21], the second can be used for the first[22]. Where do we hold? If he said, "I am a *nazir* twice," a vow which is partially annulled is totally annulled[23]. If he said, "I am a *nazir* for these 30 days and those 30 days," in this case the second cannot be used for the first[24]. But we must hold that he said, "I am a *nazir* and *nazir*." If he said, "these are for *nezirut*.[25]" But if he said, "these are for my *nezirut*; those are for the other *nezirut*," in this case the second cannot be used for the first[24]. Rebbi Eleazar said, if he finished the first *nezirut*, as soon as he brought a sacrifice and shaved, the first is credited for the second[26]. Rebbi Jacob bar Aḥa commanded the colleagues: If you hear anything formulated by Rebbi Eleazar, you should know that Rebbi Joḥanan disagrees[27]: not unless he brings all his sacrifices, following the rabbis; but following Rebbi Simeon even if he brings only one sacrifice[28]. If he dedicated both together, he has only one in his hand[29]. If he dedicated each of them separately or[30] brought each of them for the other, he did not acquit himself [of his obligation]. This means that as far as holiness goes, they became holy[31]. But did not Rebbi Hiyya state[32]: "His sacrifice to the Eternal for his *nezirut*," i. e., that his vow of *nazir* should precede his sacrifice, rather than that his sacrifice precede his vow of *nazir*. It is different, because he still is in *nezirut*[33]. One understands the second for the first[34]. The first for the second[35]? Rebbi Jehudah said, this supports Rebbi Eleazar. But did not Rebbi Jacob bar Aha command the colleagues: If you hear anything formulated by Rebbi Eleazar, you should know that Rebbi Johanan disagrees; not unless he brings all his sacrifices. They wanted to say, following the rabbis. But here, we hold with Rebbi Simeon[36]. Rebbi Hinena in the name of Rebbi Phineas: Explain it for his *nezirut* and the *nezirut* he pledged for his son. In that, the second can be used for the first[37]. Rebbi Yose ben Rebbi Abun said, did we not argue about one who said, "I am a *nazir*"[38]? He really should be a *nazir* only once. You were severe with him and obligated him to be a *nazir* twice. Is it not enough that you were severe with him and obligated him to be a *nazir* twice, that now you say, he has nothing in his hands?

20 The expression "to lean on" for "going to start" is found only here.

21 Since *nezirut* presupposes a vow, any *nezirut* can be eliminated by an Elder who finds "an opening" to declare the vow invalid; cf. *Nedarim*, Introduction, p. 422; Chapter 3:1, Notes 6-9; Chapter 9:1.

22 If he had sacrifices prepared for the second *nezirut* but none for the first, those of the second may be used for the first.

23 Mishnah *Nedarim* 9:6. In this case, no sacrifice is due since there is no *nezirut*; if he wishes, he can shave without formality.

24 If he made two separate vows, rather than one vow covering separate periods, the sacrifices are not transferable since they are dedicated for separate vows.

25 He refers to the vow but not to the particular instance mentioned in the vow. Then the sacrifice can be

brought for any obligation implied by the vow.

26   R. Eleazar deals with the opposite case. He made the double vow, finished the first period, brought a sacrifice, and then went to ask an Elder about his vow. If the first *nezirut* was annulled, he can count the *nezirut* he kept as second *nezirut* and be freed from his obligation. This is essentially stated in Tosephta 2:15 (quoted in the Babli, *Nedarim* 17b, *Šebuot* 27b): "If somebody vowed two *neziriot*, finished the first one but did not bring his sacrifices, went to an Elder to ask to annul his first [*nezirut*], the second *nezirut* is fulfilled by the first."

27   Since R. Eleazar was R. Johanan's student, if he felt impelled to formulate a statement by himself, not referring to R. Johanan, it is safe to assume that R. Johanan disagreed.

28   R. Johanan does not disagree with the main thrust of R. Eleazar's statement, that the *nezirut* can be counted as the one covered by his vow, but he objects to the formulation referring to "a sacrifice", which implies that a *nazir* can shave and drink wine after one sacrifice. This is R. Simeon's opinion in Mishnah 6:11. R. Johanan insists that all three sacrifices be brought in order to be valid; this is the opinion of the anonymous majority which in R. Johanan's opinion always defines practice (cf. *Yebamot* 4:11, Note 177).

29   This refers to a different situation, Tosephta 2:15: "If somebody vowed two *neziriot*, finished both of them, and brought the sacrifices for both of them together, he has only one in his hand." Since the sacrifices of a *nazir* presuppose a period of at least 30 days for the growth of his hair, it is impossible for one person to bring sacrifices for multiple periods of *nezirut* together. He has to be *nazir* for another 30 days and bring another set of sacrifices.

30   This must read "and"; then the text becomes the last sentence in Tosephta 2:15.

31   If one of the *neziriot* was dissolved by an Elder, why should the sacrifice attached to it be holy? If the vow was in error, the dedication is in error.

32   Chapter 2:9, Note 118.

33   The argument of R. Hiyya is not applicable to our case. It is clear that a person cannot dedicate animals to satisfy a future vow of *nazir* since that would be "stipulating about non-existence" (Chapter 2:5, Note 89). But in the present case, the vow exists.

34   The case treated at the start of the Halakhah.

35   The case discussed by R. Eleazar. Does the argument of R. Hiyya not apply in this case, when the dedication of the sacrifice for the first period preceded the start of the second.

36   Since the disagreement between R. Eleazar and R. Johanan only refers to the disagreement between R. Simeon and the rabbis, it is clear that R. Eleazar follows R. Simeon and the second period substituted for the first both in time and in sacrifices.

37   He rejects the previous explanation and restricts the possibility of substituting the second period for the first to the case that both are occasioned by the birth of a son, one period for himself and one for his son's birth. In this case, it was stated in Chapter 2:9 (Note 118) that R. Hiyya's argument is disregarded; both *neziriot* combined constitute one vow.

38   It had been decided that the substitution of sacrifices was possible only for the person who said, "I am a *nazir* and *nazir*." It would be a reasonable interpretation to say that the second "and *nazir*" was said for emphasis rather than duplication. Therefore, the second *nezirut* is a rabbinic obligation, not an original vow, and there should be no discussion of legalistic niceties in this case.

(fol. 52b) **משנה ג:** מִי שֶׁאָמַר הֲרֵינִי נָזִיר נִטְמָא יוֹם שְׁלֹשִׁים סָתַר אֶת הַכֹּל. רַבִּי אֱלִיעֶזֶר אוֹמֵר. אֵינוֹ סוֹתֵר אֶלָּא שִׁבְעָה. הֲרֵינִי נָזִיר שְׁלֹשִׁים יוֹם נִטְמָא יוֹם שְׁלֹשִׁים סָתַר אֶת הַכֹּל.

Mishnah 3: If somebody says, "I am a *nazir*" and became impure on the 30th day[39], he invalidated everything[40]; Rebbi Eliezer says, he invalidated only seven[41]. "I am a *nazir* for 30 days," if he became impure on the 30th day, he invalidated everything[42].

39   Before he offered his sacrifices.

40   He has to wait 7 days to cleanse himself from the impurity of the dead, shave, bring the sacrifices prescribed for the impure *nazir*, and be a *nazir* another 30 days in purity.

41   Since he could have brought the sacrifices on the 30th day, he has to

wait 7 days to cleanse himself from the impurity of the dead, shave, bring the sacrifices prescribed for the impure *nazir*, wait another 7 days to have some hair to shave, and then brings his 3 sacrifices and shaves in purity.

42 R. Eliezer agrees that he has to start anew since he must wait until the 31st day to bring his sacrifices.

(52c line 49) **הלכה ג:** מִי שֶׁאָמַר הֲרֵינִי נָזִיר כול׳. רַבִּי אַבָּהוּ בְּשֵׁם רַבִּי יוֹחָנָן. מִמְצוֹרָע לָמַד רַבִּי אֱלִיעֶזֶר. שֶׁכֵּן מָצִינוּ בֵּין תִּגְלַחַת וְתִגְלַחַת שִׁבְעָה. וְלָמָּה לֹא יְלִיף מִנָּזִיר טָמֵא. מְצוֹרָע מְגַלֵּחַ וְחוֹזֵר וּמְגַלֵּחַ. נָזִיר טָמֵא אֵינוֹ מְגַלֵּחַ וְחוֹזֵר וּמְגַלֵּחַ. רַבָּנִין דְּקַיְסָרִין אֲמָרִין. בְּפֵירוּשׁ פְּלִיגִין. רַבִּי יוֹחָנָן אָמַר. מִמְּצוֹרָע לָמַד רַבִּי אֱלִיעֶזֶר. רַבִּי אֶלְעָזָר אוֹמֵר. מִנָּזִיר טָמֵא לָמַד רַבִּי לִיעֶזֶר. וְהָא רַבִּי אֱלִיעֶזֶר מַה שְׁנָה בֵּין נָזִיר שֶׁנָּזַר סְתָם לְנָזִיר שֶׁפִּירֵשׁ. בְּשָׁעָה שֶׁנָּזַר סְתָם מֵירֵט אֵינוֹ סוֹתֵר וְהַשְּׁבִיעִי שֶׁלּוֹ עוֹלֶה לוֹ מִן הַמִּנְיָין. וּבְשָׁעָה שֶׁפִּירֵשׁ אִם הָיָה מוֹרֵט סוֹתֵר וְאֵין הַשְּׁבִיעִי שֶׁלּוֹ עוֹלֶה לוֹ מִן הַמִּנְיָין.

Halakhah 3: "If somebody says, 'I am a *nazir*'," etc. Rebbi Abbahu in the name of Rebbi Joḥanan: Rebbi Eliezer learned from the sufferer from skin disease, for whom we find seven days between shaving and shaving[43]. Why does he not learn from the impure *nazir*? The sufferer from skin disease shaves repeatedly; the impure *nazir* does not shave repeatedly. The rabbis from Caesarea say, they disagree explicitly: Rebbi Joḥanan said, Rebbi Eliezer learned from the sufferer from skin disease; Rebbi Eleazar says, Rebbi Eliezer learned from the impure *nazir*[44]. What difference does it make for Rebbi Eliezer whether the vow for *nazir* was implicit rather than explicit[45]? If the vow for *nazir* was implicit, he does not invalidate if he tears his hair out[46], and his seventh day[47] is counted for him; if the vow for *nazir* was explicit[48], he invalidates if he tears his hair out and his seventh day is not counted for him.

43 Cf. Chapter 2:10, Note 143.

44 Who shaves after 7 days, *Num.* 6:9.

45 Whether he says "I am a *nazir*" and it is understood that he will be a *nazir* for 30 days, or he says "I am a *nazir* for 30 days"?

46 *Num.* 6:5 spells out first a prohibition, "a shaving knife shall not touch his head", followed by a positive commandment "he shall let the hair of his head grow wildly." If the order had been inverted, it would have been clear that only shaving with a knife was forbidden. Now that the commandment of letting the hair grow is separated from the prohibition of using a knife, the majority opinion (*Sifry Num.* 25; Tosephta 4:3; Halakhah 6:2, Babli 39b) holds that removing any hair is forbidden and the simultaneous removal of any two hairs during the period of *nezirut* invalidates the *nezirut* and requires a fresh start. Only on the 30th day, tearing out a hair has no consequences since *Num.* 6:5 also states: "until the days are completed he shall be holy," and on the 30th day of the implicit vow they are completed.

47 If he became impure by the impurity of the dead, he has to shave on the 7th day itself.

48 Then his days were not yet completed when he became impure.

משנה ד: הֲרֵינִי נָזִיר מֵאָה יוֹם נִיטְמָא יוֹם מֵאָה סָתַר אֶת הַכֹּל וְרִבִּי אֱלִיעֶזֶר אוֹמֵר לֹא סָתַר אֶלָּא שְׁלֹשִׁים. נִיטְמָא יוֹם מֵאָה וְאֶחָד סָתַר שְׁלֹשִׁים יוֹם. רִבִּי אֱלִיעֶזֶר אוֹמֵר לֹא סָתַר אֶלָּא שִׁבְעָה. (fol. 52b)

Mishnah 4: "I am a *nazir* for 100 days," if he became impure on day 100 he invalidated everything but Rebbi Eliezer said, he invalidated only 30[49]. If he became impure on day 101, he invalidated 30; Rebbi Eliezer said, he invalidated only seven[41].

47 Even though he may offer his sacrifices only on day 101, the 100th day is "the day of completion" of his vow; if he shaves for his impurity, he only has to keep the days of an implicit vow.

הלכה ד: הֲרֵינִי נָזִיר מֵאָה יוֹם כול׳. רִבִּי זְעִירָא בְּשֵׁם רִבִּי שִׁמְעוֹן (52c line 57) בֶּן לָקִישׁ. טַעֲמָא דְּרִבִּי אֱלִיעֶזֶר. זֹאת תּוֹרַת הַנָּזִיר בְּיוֹם מְלֹאת. הַמִּטַּמֵּא בְּיוֹם מְלֹאת נוֹתְנִין לוֹ תּוֹרַת נָזִיר. שְׁמוּאֵל בַּר בָּא בָּעָא קוֹמֵי רִבִּי זְעִירָא. נִיטְמָא בְּאוֹתָן הַיָּמִים מַה הֵן נִיתָּן לְתוֹרַת נָזִיר. אָמַר רִבִּי שַׁמַּיי. מִכֵּיוָן דְּתֵימַר. נִיתָּק לְתוֹרָתוֹ שֶׁלְּנָזִיר כְּמִטַּמֵּא בְּיוֹם מְלֹאת. וְהַמִּטַּמֵּא בְּיוֹם מְלֹאת אֵין שְׁבִיעִי עוֹלֶה לוֹ מִן הַמִּנְיָין. רִבִּי מָנָא בָּעֵי. אִם מִטַּמֵּא בְּתוֹךְ מְלֹאת לָמָּה לִי סוֹתֵר ל׳ יוֹם. לֹא יִסְתּוֹר אֶלָּא ז׳. אֶלָּא בְּמִטַּמֵּא לְאַחַר מְלֹאת שְׁבִיעִי שֶׁלּוֹ עוֹלֶה לוֹ מִן הַמִּנְיָין.

Halakhah 4: ""I am a *nazir* for 100 days," etc. Rebbi Ze'ira in the name of Rebbi Simeon ben Laqish: The reason of Rebbi Eliezer: "This is the teaching for the *nazir* on the day of his fulfilling;[48]" if he becomes impure on the day of his fulfilling, one gives him the teaching for the *nazir*[49]. Samuel bar Abba asked before Rebbi Ze'ira: If he becomes impure in those days[50], what is their status, to be given the teaching for the *nazir*? Rebbi Shammai said, he is obligated by the teaching for the *nazir* if he becomes impure on the day of his fulfilling, and for one who becomes impure on the day of his fulfilling the seventh day is not counted[51]. Rebbi Mana asked: If he becomes impure at fulfilling, why should he invalidate 30, should he not invalidate only seven[52]? But if somebody became impure after fulfilling[53], the seventh day is counted for him.

48 Num. 6:13.

49 And the implicit vow of a *nazir* runs for 30 days.

50 If he became impure on the last day of his *nezirut*; according to R. Eliezer, how many days does he lose if he becomes impure again while keeping the 30 days of *nezirut*.

51 The problem arises only if he becomes impure on the 30th day since before it is obvious that he has to start anew. If he is considered to have finished his *nezirut*, then the 7th day of purification can also be the day he brings his sacrifices since "part of the day is counted as an entire day"

(Halakhah 2:10, Note 129). But if he is under the rules of the *nazir* who shaves on the 7th but brings his sacrifice only on the 8th (*Num.* 6:9,10), the 7th day obviously cannot be the day on which he can conclude his *nezirut*.

52   Since the entire argument follows R. Eliezer, why does he make a difference between the cases of Mishnaiot 3 and 4?

53   If he becomes impure on day 101, R. Eliezer will apply his ruling of Mishnah 3.

(fol. 52b) **משנה ה:** מִי שֶׁנָּזַר וְהוּא בְּבֵית הַקְּבָרוֹת אֲפִילוּ הָיָה שָׁם שְׁלֹשִׁים יוֹם אֵין עוֹלִין לוֹ מִן הַמִּנְיָן וְאֵינוֹ מֵבִיא קָרְבַּן טוּמְאָה. יָצָא וְנִכְנַס עוֹלִין לוֹ מִן הַמִּנְיָן וּמֵבִיא קָרְבַּן טוּמְאָה. רִבִּי אֱלִיעֶזֶר אוֹמֵר לֹא בוֹ בַיּוֹם שֶׁנֶּאֱמַר וְהַיָּמִים הָרִאשׁוֹנִים יִפְּלוּ עַד שֶׁיִּהְיוּ לוֹ יָמִים רִאשׁוֹנִים.

Mishnah 5: If somebody made a vow of *nazir* while he was in a cemetery[54], even if he stayed there for thirty days, they are not counted and he does not bring a sacrifice for impurity[55]. If he left and re-entered, they are counted and he has to bring a sacrifice for impurity[56]. Rebbi Eliezer said, not on that day, since it is said: "The earlier days fall away[57]," until he has earlier days.

54   Since a *nazir* may not be in a cemetery, in one opinion the vow cannot be activated until he leaves the cemetery; in the other opinion the vow is activated but the days cannot be counted since the *nazir* is not pure (Babli 16b).

55   The vow is activated the moment he leaves the cemetery. While the *nazir* is forbidden to defile himself by the impurity of the dead, it is not forbidden to vow to be a *nazir* while one is impure. He has to untergo the seven-day purification ritual; these days are counted as regular days of *nezirut*.

56   The special sacrifices prescribed for the *nazir* who became impure, *Num.* 6:10-11.

57   *Num.* 6:12. Since a plural

(52c line 65) **הלכה ה:** מִי שֶׁנָּזַר וְהוּא בְּבֵית הַקְּבָרוֹת כול'. נָזַר וְהוּא בֵּין הַקְּבָרוֹת. רִבִּי יוֹחָנָן אָמַר. מַתְרִין בּוֹ עַל הַיַּיִן וְעַל הַתִּגְלַחַת. רִבִּי שִׁמְעוֹן בֶּן לָקִישׁ אָמַר. מֵאַחַר שֶׁאֵין מַתְרִין בּוֹ עַל הַטּוּמְאָה אֵין מַתְרִין בּוֹ עַל הַיַּיִן וְעַל הַתִּגְלַחַת. מִחְלְפָה שִׁיטָתֵיהּ דְּרִבִּי יוֹחָנָן. תַּמָּן הוּא אָמַר. מַתְרִין בּוֹ עַל הַיַּיִן וְעַל הַטּוּמְאָה וְעַל הַתִּגְלַחַת. וְכָא הוּא אָמַר אָכֵן. רַבָּנִין דְּקַיְסָרִין. עַל כּוּלָּהּ פְּלִיגִין. דְּרִבִּי יוֹחָנָן אָמַר. מַתְרִין בּוֹ עַל הַיַּיִן וְעַל הַתִּגְלַחַת. רִבִּי שִׁמְעוֹן בֶּן לָקִישׁ אָמַר. מֵאַחַר שֶׁאֵין מַתְרִין בּוֹ עַל הַטּוּמְאָה אֵין מַתְרִין בּוֹ לֹא עַל הַיַּיִן וְלֹא עַל הַתִּגְלַחַת.

Halakhah 5: "If somebody made a vow of *nazir* while he was in a cemetery," etc. If he made the vow while he was among grave sites[58], Rebbi Joḥanan said, one warns him about wine and shaving[59]. Rebbi Simeon ben Laqish said, since one cannot warn him because of impurity, one does not warn him about wine and shaving[60]. The argument of Rebbi Joḥanan seems inverted. There[61], he says, one warns him about wine, impurity, and shaving. And here, he says so? The rabbis from Caesarea: They disagree about the whole, for Rebbi Joḥanan said, one warns him about wine and shaving[62]. Rebbi Simeon ben Laqish said, since one cannot warn him because of impurity, one does not warn him either about wine or about shaving.

58 He is not in an open cemetery but in a graveyard consisting of burial caves. A cave forms a "tent"; the impurity of the dead is transmitted by the tent even without any touching (*Num.* 19:14). But in the open space before the caves, no impurity is transmitted; it is possible there to start a vow of *nazir*. It is assumed that the person making the vow participated in a burial and is impure at the moment of the vow.

59 It is impossible to require that he be pure from the moment of the

vow, since he is impure. R. Joḥanan holds that in all other respects the vow is valid immediately.

60 For him, the vow is suspended until the *nazir* has undergone the ritual of purification; once he is pure he can be punished for drinking wine or shaving.

61 Halakhah 6:4. The text there consists simply of a referral to the present Halakhah. *A nazir* who does not observe the rules of *nezirut* has to be warned and can be punished for every infringement. There, R. Joḥanan requires that even a *nazir* who comes to drink wine has to be warned about wine, impurity, and shaving. Then it should be impossible to punish a *nazir* for infringing the rules of wine and shaving, if he is not punishable for impurity.

62 It is understood: because from the start one also warns him about impurity.

(52c line 72) עוֹדֵינוּ שָׁם. רַבִּי יוֹחָנָן אָמַר. מַתְרִין עַל הַכֹּל כְּדֵי פְּרִישָׁה וּפְרִישָׁה וְהוּא לוֹקֶה. רַבִּי לְעָזָר אוֹמֵר. אֵינוֹ מְקַבֵּל עַד שֶׁיִּפְרוֹשׁ וְיַחֲזוֹר. אָמַר רַבִּי בָּא. כָּךְ הָיָה מֵשִׁיב רַבִּי יוֹחָנָן אֶת רַבִּי לְעָזָר. וְהָא כְּתִיב לֹא יָבוֹא וְלֹא יִטַּמָּא. אָמַר לֵיהּ. שֶׁאִם הִתְרוּ בוֹ מִשּׁוּם וְלֹא יָבוֹא לוֹקֶה. מִשּׁוּם לֹא יִטַּמָּא אֵינוֹ לוֹקֶה. אָמַר רַבִּי הִילָא. מֵהִשְׁתַּחֲוָיָה לָמַד רַבִּי יוֹחָנָן. דְּתַנִּינָן תַּמָּן. הִשְׁתַּחֲוָה אוֹ שֶׁשָּׁהָה כְּדֵי הִשְׁתַּחֲוָיָה. אָמַר רַבִּי מַתַּנְיָיה. הַוְיָנָן סָבְרִין מֵימַר. מָה פְלִיגִין. בְּמַכּוֹת. הָא קָרְבָּן לֹא. מִן מָה דָמַר רַבִּי הִילָא. מֵהִשְׁתַּחֲוָיָה לָמַד רַבִּי יוֹחָנָן. הָדָא אֲמָרָה. הִיא בַּמַּכּוֹת הִיא בַּקָּרְבָּן. מַתְנִיתָא פְלִיגָא עַל רַבִּי יוֹחָנָן. נָזִיר שֶׁהָיָה שׁוֹתֶה יַיִן כָּל־הַיּוֹם אֵינוֹ חַיָּיב אֶלָּא אַחַת. פָּתַר לָהּ שֶׁאֵין בֵּית הַבְּלִיעָה פָּנוּי. מַתְנִיתָא פְלִיגָא עַל רַבִּי יוֹחָנָן. הָיָה מִטַּמֵּא לְמֵת כָּל־הַיּוֹם אֵינוֹ חַיָּיב אֶלָּא אַחַת. פָּתַר לָהּ בְּשׁוּהֵא עַל כָּל־פְּרִישָׁה וּפְרִישָׁה וְהוּא לוֹקֶה. מַתְנִיתָא פְלִיגָא עַל רַבִּי יוֹחָנָן. כֹּהֵן שֶׁעוֹמֵד בְּבֵית הַקְּבָרוֹת וְהוֹשִׁיטוּ לוֹ מֵת אַחֵר יָכוֹל יְקַבֵּל. תַּלְמוּד לוֹמַר יִטַּמָּא בַעַל בְּעַצְמוֹ. הֲרֵי שֶׁקִּיבֵּל יָכוֹל יְהֵא חַיָּיב. תַּלְמוּד לוֹמַר לְהֵחַלּוֹ. אֶת שֶׁהוּא מוֹסִיף חִילּוּל עַל חִילּוּלוֹ. יָצָא זֶה שֶׁאֵינוֹ מוֹסִיף חִילּוּל עַל חִילּוּלוֹ. אָמַר רַבִּי זְעִירָא אָמַר רַבִּי יוֹחָנָן. לְהֵחַלּוֹ. יָצָא זֶה שֶׁאֵינוֹ מוֹסִיף חִילּוּל עַל חִילּוּלוֹ. שֶׁלֹּא יֹאמַר. הוֹאִיל וְנִיטְמֵאתִי עַל אַבָּא אֲלַקֵּט עַצְמוֹת פְּלוֹנִי בְּיָדִי. לְהֵחַלּוֹ. בִּשְׁעַת מִיתָה. רַבִּי אוֹמֵר. אַף בְּמוֹתָן. רַבִּי שִׁמְעוֹן בֶּן לָקִישׁ

אָמַר. מַחֲלוֹקֶת בֵּינֵיהֶן. וְאָתְיָיא דְּרִבִּי שִׁמְעוֹן בַּר וָוא כְּרִבִּי שִׁמְעוֹן בֶּן לָקִישׁ. שִׁמְעוֹן בַּר וָוא מִי דְמָךְ הֲוָה אֲמַר. הָא נְפִיקָא מִיכָּא וְהָא נְפִיקָא מִיכָּא.

If he is still there[63], Rebbi Joḥanan said, one warns him about everything for every possible leaving,[64] and he is whipped. Rebbi Eleazar said, he does not accept [warning] unless he leaves[65] and returns. Rebbi Abba said: So did Rebbi Joḥanan answer Rebbi Eleazar: Is it not written, "he shall not come" and "he may not defile himself"[66]? He said to him, if they warned him because of "he shall not come", he is whipped; because of "he shall not defile himself" he is not whipped[67]. Rebbi Hila said, Rebbi Joḥanan learned from prostrating, as we have stated there[68]: "If he prostrated himself or stayed there long enough to prostrate himself." Rebbi Mattaniah said, we thought that was where they do disagree? About lashes, but not about a sacrifice. Since Rebbi Hila said, Rebbi Joḥanan learned from prostrating[69], that means that lashes and sacrifices are one and the same. A Mishnah disagrees with Rebbi Joḥanan: "A *nazir* who drank wine the entire day is guilty only once.[70]" He explains it, that his throat was never empty[71]. A Mishnah disagrees with Rebbi Joḥanan: "If he was defiling himself for the dead the entire day, he is guilty only once[70]." He explains it about one who waits before every leaving, who is whipped[72]. A *baraita* disagrees with Rebbi Joḥanan: If a Cohen was standing in a cemetery[73] and they were handing another corpse to him, could he accept? The verse says, "the husband shall be defiled for his family[74]." If he accepted it, I could think that he was guilty. The verse says, "to be profaned". One who adds impurity to the impurity; that excludes him who does not add impurity to his impurity[75]. Rebbi Ze'ira said, Rebbi Neḥemiah said, "to be profaned", that excludes him who does not add impurity to his impurity, lest he say, because I became defiled for my father I may go and collect the bones of X. "To be profaned", at the time of death; Rebbi said, also "in their death.⁷⁶" Rebbi Simeon ben Laqish said, they disagree⁷⁷. It follows that Rebbi Simeon bar Abba follows Rebbi Simeon ben Laqish. When Simeon bar Abba was dying, he said, this should be taken out here, that should be taken out there⁷⁸.

63   Here starts the discussion of the Mishnah. What is the situation of the person who vowed in the cemetery to be a *nazir*.

64   R. Johanan holds that the vow becomes effective the moment it is uttered. Then the *nazir* is informed that he has to leave the cemetery immediately (and refrain from wine and shaving). If he does not obey, he can be repeatedly warned and the disregard of every warning is a new, punishable offence.

65   He holds that the vow becomes effective only when the *nazir* leaves the cemetery. Then also the warning becomes relevant for him and he can be punished if he returns to the cemetery.

66   If *Num.* 6:6, there is a general prohibition, "to any dead person he shall not come." In v. 7, there is a particular prohibition; for close relatives "he may not be defiled." R. Johanan interprets this to mean: even in a case where he does not defile himself, because he was defiled before he made the vow, he violates the separate prohibition of v. 6.

67   He reads the verses as they are written. The *nazir* can be warned, and is whipped, for an active *coming* to corpses. But nobody can be whipped for a prohibition formulated in the passive voice.

68   Mishnah *Šebuot* 2:3. A person who comes to the Temple precinct and belatedly remembers that he is impure, has to leave immediately. If he tarries long enough for an act of prostration, he is punished.

69   Where the main thrust of the entire Chapter in the Mishnah is the obligation to bring a sacrifice to purify himself from the inadvertent sin.

70   Mishnah 6:4. This presupposes that he was warned only once.

71   If the *nazir* actually never stopped drinking the entire day, he could not have been warned more than once. The Mishnah is irrelevant for the statement that separate warnings imply separate punishments.

72   He explains the Mishnah, if there was only one warning. But if he was warned repeatedly, each action

represents a new offense. (Whether tarrying plays a role in this case remains an open question in the Babli, *Šebuot* 17a.)

73   Legitimately, when burying a close relative.

74   *Lev.* 21:4. The verse really reads: "The husband shall *not* be defiled for his family, to be profaned," meaning that the Cohen cannot defile himself for a wife he was forbidden to marry. This implies that he can be defiled only for the benefit of his legal family.

75   If he already is impure, touching another corpse does not change his status. (In the Babli, the Babylonian authorities disagree, 42b.)

76   *Num.* 6:7 prohibits the *nazir* from being defiled for his close relatives "in their death", meaning that he does not have to leave the house when they lie dying, but only after they are dead. The same *baraita* is quoted in the Babli, 43a.

77   The authorities disagreeing with Rebbi require the *nazir* to leave the house when they lie dying.

78   To avoid that vessels become impure at his death.

(52d line 16) יָצָא וְנִכְנַס. רִבִּי טַרְפוֹן פּוֹטֵר וְרִבִּי עֲקִיבָה מְחַיֵּיב. אָמַר לוֹ רִבִּי טַרְפוֹן. וְכִי מַה הוֹסִיף זֶה חִילּוּל עַל חִילּוּלוֹ. אָמַר רִבִּי עֲקִיבָה. בְּשָׁעָה שֶׁהָיָה שָׁם טָמֵא טוּמְאַת שִׁבְעָה. פֵּירַשׁ טָמֵא טוּמְאַת עֶרֶב. יָצָא וְנִכְנַס טָמֵא טוּמְאַת עֶרֶב. אָמַר לוֹ רִבִּי טַרְפוֹן. עֲקִיבָה. כָּל־הַפּוֹרֵשׁ מִמְּךָ כְּפוֹרֵשׁ מֵחַיָּיו.

If he left and re-entered[79], Rebbi Ṭarphon frees him from prosecution, Rebbi Aqiba declares him guilty. Rebbi Ṭarphon said to him, what did this one add to his desecration[80]? Rebbi Aqiba said, as long as he was there, he was defiling himself by the impurity of seven days[81]. When he left, he was defiling himself by the impurity of evening[82]. When he re-entered, defiling himself by the impurity of (evening)[83]. Rebbi Ṭarphon told him, Aqiba! Any who leaves you is as if he left his life.

79   He left the cemetery and then re-entered as *nazir*.

80   Since he already was defiled when he made his vow, how can he be prosecuted for defiling himself?

81   As long as he was in contact with a corpse or forming a "tent" over it and he touched another person, that

person becomes impure and has to undergo the 7 day ritual.

82   If one who is impure by the impurity of the dead touches another person, that person becomes impure in a derivative way. He has to immerse himself in water and becomes pure at sundown.

83   This is clearly a scribal (corrector's) error and must read: "the impurity of 7 days." In the cemetery, he at least acquires the capability of transmitting the impurity of 7 days. Therefore, his status of impurity has changed; he can be prosecuted.

(52d line 20) רַב אָמַר. יָצָא מוֹנֶה לִנְזִירוּת בְּטָהֳרָה. נִכְנַס בַּשְּׁבִיעִי שֶׁלוֹ מֵבִיא קָרְבַּן טוּמְאָה בּוֹ בַיּוֹם. רִבִּי לִיעֶזֶר אוֹמֵר. לֹא בּוֹ בַיּוֹם. כַּהֲנָא בְּעָא קוֹמֵי רַב. וְאֵין טָעוּן הַזָּיָיה חֲמִישִׁי וּשְׁבִיעִי. אֲמַר לֵיהּ. תּוֹרָה קָרְאָת לַפּוֹרֵשׁ מִן הַקֶּבֶר טָהוֹר. אַחֲרֵי טָהֳרָתוֹ שִׁבְעַת יָמִים יִסְפְּרוּ לוֹ. שְׁמוּאֵל אָמַר. יָצָא וְהִזָּה שָׁנָה וְטָבַל. נִכְנַס בּוֹ בַיּוֹם מֵבִיא קָרְבַּן טוּמְאָה בּוֹ בַיּוֹם. רִבִּי אֱלִיעֶזֶר אוֹמֵר. לֹא בּוֹ בַיּוֹם.

Rav said, when he has left, he counts his *nezirut* in purity[84]. If he entered again on his seventh day, he brings a sacrifice of impurity for that day; Rebbi Eliezer said, not for that day[85]. Cahana asked before Rav: Does he not need the sprinkling of the third and seventh[86]? He answered him, the Torah called "pure" the one who leaves the grave: "After his purity, seven days shall be counted for him.[87]" Samuel said, after he left, sprinkled, and repeated, immersed himself, and entered again on that day, he brings a sacrifice of impurity for that day; Rebbi Eliezer said, not for that day[88].

84   The person who vowed in the cemetery to be a *nazir* and who will be impure for the next 7 days does nevertheless count his valid days of *nezirut* from the moment he leaves the cemetery.

85   If he entered the cemetery again on the day he regained his purity, he is considered a *nazir* who became impure on the first day of his *nezirut*, obligated for a sacrifice according to the rabbis but not R. Eliezer.

86 The purification rite prescribed in *Num.* 19: Being sprinkled with water containing some of the ashes of the Red Cow on the 3rd and 7th day, and immersing himself on the 7th. He becomes pure only after immersion.

87 *Ez.* 44:26; one would have expected: "Seven days shall be counted until his purity." Even though this is a verse by a prophet and therefore without legal standing, it can be applied to show usage.

88 Samuel disagrees with Rav; the rules of purity start only on day seven, after the completion of the purification. In the Babli, 19a, Rav agrees with Samuel.

(52d line 26) עוּלָא בַּר יִשְׁמָעֵאל אָמַר. מַה צְּרִיכָה לֵיהּ. בְּנָזִיר טָמֵא. אֲבָל בְּנָזִיר טָהוֹר אַף רִבִּי אֱלִיעֶזֶר מוֹדֵי אֲפִילוּ אֵין לוֹ מֵהֵיכָן לְהַפִּיל. שְׁמוּאֵל בַּר אַבָּא בָּעֵי. יוֹם אֶחָד לִנְזִירוּתוֹ וְיוֹם אֶחָד לִנְזִירוּת בְּנוֹ מַהוּ שֶׁיִּצְטָרְפוּ. מַה נָן קַייָמִין. אִם בְּשֶׁנּוֹלַד בְּנוֹ הַיּוֹם וּמָחָר נִכְנָס הֲרֵי יֵשׁ לוֹ לִנְזִירוּתוֹ שְׁנֵי יָמִים. וְאִם בְּשֶׁנּוֹלַד בְּנוֹ לְמָחָר וְנִכְנָס לְמָחָר הֲרֵי יֵשׁ לוֹ לִנְזִירוּת בְּנוֹ שְׁנֵי יָמִים. אָמַר רִבִּי מָנָא. תִּיפְתָּר בֵּין הַשְּׁמָשׁוֹת. אָמַר רִבִּי אָבִין. אֲפִילוּ תֵּימַר בַּחֲצִי הַיּוֹם. לֹא כֵן סַבְרִינָן מֵימַר. תְּחִילַת הַיּוֹם עוֹלָה לוֹ. סוֹף הַיּוֹם לִבְנוֹ.

Ulla bar Ismael said, what is his problem[89]? Of an impure *nazir*. But for a pure *nazir,* even Rebbi Eliezer agrees if he has nothing to omit. Samuel bar Abba asked: May one day of his *nezirut* and one day of *nezirut* for his son be combined[90]? Where do we hold? If his son was born today and tomorrow he enters, he has two days for his[91] *nezirut.* If his son was born the next day and he enters the next day, he has two days for his son's[92] *nezirut!* Rebbi Mana said, explain it at twilight[93]. Rebbi Abin said, even if you say in the middle of the day, did we not intend to say that the start of the day is counted for him, the end of the day is counted for his son[94]?

89 He refers to the statement of R. Eliezer in the Mishnah. R. Eliezer requires at least two days of *nezirut* only from a *nazir* who made his vow in

impurity. If the vow was made in purity, he agrees that even if he becomes impure on the first day, he is required to bring a sacrifice.

90 In the case described in Mishnah 3:9: He started his own *nezirut*; at the son's birth his count is interrupted automatically and his son's begins.

91 This must read: His son's. The remainder of the day of birth and the start of the next day are counted as two days; if he becomes impure he has to bring a sacrifice even if we reject the interpretation of Ulla bar Ismael.

92 This must read: His own.

93 Then the entire first day is the father's only.

94 As explained in Halakhah 3:10, the first part of the day of birth is counted as a full day for the father's *nezirut*; the second part, after the birth, is counted as a full day for the *nezirut* on account of the son. It is not unreasonable to expect that for R. Eliezer the day also is counted as two.

(52d line 33) אָמַר רִבִּי יוֹסֵי. מַה צְרִיכָה לֵיהּ. בְּנָזִיר טָהוֹר. אֲבָל בְּנָזִיר טָמֵא פְּשִׁיטָא לֵיהּ שֶׁאֵין מִצְטָרְפִין. אָמַר רִבִּי מָנָא קוֹמֵי רִבִּי יוֹסֵי. לֹא כָּל־שֶׁכֵּן הוּא. וּמַה יָּמִים שֶׁאֵין עוֹלִין לֹא בִּנְזִירוּתוֹ וְלֹא בִנְזִירוּת בְּנוֹ אַתְּ אוֹמֵר. מִצְטָרְפִין. יָמִים שֶׁהֵן עוֹלִין בִּנְזִירוּתוֹ וּבִנְזִירוּת בְּנוֹ אֵינוֹ דִין שֶׁיִּצְטָרְפוּ. אָמַר רִבִּי מָנָא. תַּמָּן אֵינוֹ רָאוּי לְקַבֵּל הַתְרָייָה. בְּרַם הָכָא רָאוּי לְקַבֵּל הַתְרָייָה. רִבִּי בּוּן בַּר חִייָה בָּעֵי. כַּמָּה דְּתֵימַר תַּמָּן עַל דְּרִבִּי אֱלִיעֶזֶר בַּתְּחִילָּה וְהוּא שֶׁיְּהֵא לוֹ מֵהֵיכָן לְהַפִּיל. וּבַסּוֹף אַף עַל פִּי שֶׁאֵין לוֹ מֵאֵיכָן לְהַפִּיל. אָמַר רִבִּי זְעִירָא קוֹמֵי רִבִּי מָנָא. וְלֹא מַתְנִיתָא הִיא. נִיטְמָא יוֹם אֶחָד וּמֵאָה סוֹתֵר שְׁלֹשִׁים. וְרִבִּי אֱלִיעֶזֶר אוֹמֵר. לֹא סוֹתֵר אֶלָּא שִׁבְעָה. אָמַר לֵיהּ. שָׁמַעְנוּ שֶׁהוּא סוֹתֵר. שָׁמַעְנוּ שֶׁמֵּבִיא קָרְבַּן טוּמְאָה.

Rebbi Yose said, what is his problem[89]? Of a pure *nazir*. But for an impure *nazir*, it is obvious to him that they cannot[95] be combined. Rebbi Mana said before Rebbi Yose: Is that not an argument of "so much more"? Since for days which are counted neither for his nor for his son's *nezirut*[96], you say that they are combined, days which are counted for his and for his son's *nezirut*, it would only be logical that they should be combined! Rebbi Mana[97] said, there[98] he is not in a state to receive a warning, but here[99] he is in a state to receive a warning. Rebbi Abun bar Ḥiyya asked: Since you say there about Rebbi Eliezer, at the start only if he has something to omit; at the end even if he has nothing to omit[100]? Rebbi Ze'ira said before Rebbi Mana, is that not a Mishnah? "If he became impure on day 101, he invalidated 30; Rebbi Eliezer said, he invalidated only seven[101]." He said, we hear that he invalidates; did we hear that he brings a sacrifice?

95 From R. Mana's argument, it seems that one has to read שֶׁהֵן "they are" instead of שֶׁאֵין "they cannot". If the Italian scribe wrote from dictation, he would not hear the difference between the two words.

96 The days of impurity.

97 The reading "R. Mana" should be confirmed as *lectio difficilior*. It is not unique that a person who raises a difficulty should answer it himself.

98 If he is impure, he cannot be warned not to become impure. It does not matter in which *nezirut* he is at the moment.

99 If he is pure, the person who warns him not to become impure must deliver separate warnings depending on him being a *nazir* for himself or for his son. Therefore it is not automatic that the days may be combined.

100 *Sifry Num.* 30 on *Num.* 6:12: "The earlier days fall away," can be said only if there are later days. If he made a vow to be a *nazir* for 100 days and became impure on day 101, one would expect R. Eliezer to rule that no sacrifice for impurity is due.

101 Since he has to keep another 7 days even for R. Eliezer, R. Abun bar Ḥiyya's question should become moot.

משנה ו: מִי שֶׁנָּזַר נְזִירוֹת הַרְבֵּה הִשְׁלִים נְזִירוּתוֹ וְאַחַר כָּךְ בָּא לָאָרֶץ בֵּית שַׁמַּאי אוֹמְרִים נָזִיר שְׁלֹשִׁים יוֹם. וּבֵית הִלֵּל אוֹמְרִים נָזִיר בַּתְּחִילָּה. מַעֲשֶׂה בְהֵילְנֵי הַמַּלְכָּה שֶׁהָלַךְ בְּנָהּ לַמִּלְחָמָה וְאָמְרָה אִם יָבֹא בְנִי מִן הַמִּלְחָמָה (fol. 52b)

אֱהֵא נְזִירָה שֶׁבַע שָׁנִים וּבָא בְנָהּ מִן הַמִּלְחָמָה וְהָיְתָה נְזִירָה שֶׁבַע שָׁנִים. וּבְסוֹף שֶׁבַע שָׁנִים עָלַת לָאָרֶץ וְהוֹרוּהָ בֵית הִלֵּל שֶׁתְּהֵא נְזִירָה עוֹד שֶׁבַע שָׁנִים אֲחֵרוֹת. וּבְסוֹף שֶׁבַע שָׁנִים נִיטְמֵאת וְנִמְצֵאת נְזִירָה עֶשְׂרִים וְאַחַת שָׁנָה. אָמַר רִבִּי יְהוּדָה לֹא הָיְתָה נְזִירָה אֶלָּא אַרְבַּע עֶשְׂרֵה שָׁנָה.

Mishnah 6: If somebody vowed[102] a lengthy *nezirut*, finished his *nezirut*, and then came to the Land, the House of Shammai say, he is a *nazir* for 30 days[103], but the House of Hillel say, he is a *nazir* from the start. It happened to Queen Helena[104] that her son went to war and she said, if my son returns from the war, I shall be a *nezirah* for seven years. Her son returned from war and she was a *nezirah* for seven years. At the end of seven years, she came to the Land[105], and the House of Hillel instructed her to be a *nezirah* for another seven years. At the end of seven years she became impure and was *nezirah* for a total of 21 years. Rebbi Jehudah said, she was a *nezirah* only for fourteen years[106].

102 Somewhere in the diaspora. Then he should have come to the Land immediately since outside he is automatically impure in the impurity of "the land of the Gentiles" which has aspects of the impurity of corpses.

103 The minimum needed for *nezirut* in genuine purity which permits the *nazir* to offer his sacrifices.

104 Of Adiabene.

105 According to Josephus, she arrived about 43 C.E.

106 Since R. Ilai, R. Jehudah's father, was a student of R. Eliezer who followed the House of Shammai, R. Jehudah tells us that Helene followed the House of Shammai, became impure at the end of 30 days, and had to restart her original *nezirut*.

(52d line 42) **הלכה ו:** מִי שֶׁנָּזַר וכו'. רִבִּי יוֹסֵי בֵּירִבִּי בּוּן אָמַר. אִיתְפַּלְגוּן רִבִּי חִייָה בַּר יוֹסֵף וְרִבִּי יוֹחָנָן. חַד אָמַר. רִבִּי יוּדָה כְּבֵית שַׁמַּי. וְחָרְנָה אָמַר. סָבַר רִבִּי יוּדָה. שֶׁלֹּא נִטְמֵאת כָּל־עִיקָּר. אִין תֵּימַר. רִבִּי יוּדָה כְּבֵית שַׁמַּי. וְתַנֵּי לֵ יוֹם וי"ד שָׁנָה. לָא תַנִּינָן מַתְנֵי חֲדָשִׁים גַּבֵּי שָׁנִים.

Halakhah 6: "If somebody vowed," etc. Rebbi Yose ben Rebbi Abun said, Rebbi Ḥiyya bar Joseph and Rebbi Joḥanan disagreed. One said, Rebbi Jehudah follows the House of Shammai. But the other said, Rebbi Jehudah thinks that she never became impure. If you say, Rebbi Jehudah follows the House of Shammai, should he not have stated 30 days and forteen years? One does not state months while reporting years[107].

107 The Babli disagrees, 20a.

(fol. 52b) **משנה ז**: מִי שֶׁהָיוּ שְׁתֵּי כִּתֵּי עֵדִים מְעִידוֹת אוֹתוֹ. אֵילוּ מְעִידִין שֶׁנָּזַר שְׁתַּיִם וְאֵילוּ מְעִידִין שֶׁנָּזַר חָמֵשׁ. בֵּית שַׁמַּאי אוֹמְרִים נֶחְלְקָה הָעֵדוּת וְאֵין כָּאן נְזִירוּת. וּבֵית הִלֵּל אוֹמְרִים יֵשׁ בִּכְלָל חָמֵשׁ שְׁתַּיִם שֶׁיְּהֵא נָזִיר שְׁתָּיִם.

Mishnah 7: If two groups of witnesses were testifying against a person, one group say that he vowed *nazir* two times, the others say that he vowed *nazir* five times. The House of Shammai say, the testimony is split[108] and there is no *nezirut* here. But the House of Hillel say, five contains two[109]; he should be a *nazir* twice.

108 Following the rules of criminal procedure by which contradictory testimony has to be disregarded.

109 Following the rules of civil procedure. If one group testifies that A owes 500 while the other group testifies that he owes 200, he has to pay 200. An identical Mishnah is *Idiut* 4:11.

(52d line 46) **הלכה ז**: מִי שֶׁהָיוּ שְׁתֵּי כִּתֵּי עֵדִים וכו'. רַב אָמַר. בְּכוֹלֵל נֶחְלְקוּ. אֲבָל בְּפוֹרֵט כָּל־עַמָּא מוֹדֵיי. יֵשׁ בִּכְלָל חָמֵשׁ שְׁתַּיִם שֶׁיְּהֵא נָזִיר שְׁתָּיִם. רִבִּי יוֹחָנָן אָמַר. בְּמוֹנֶה נֶחְלְקוּ. אֲבָל בְּכוֹלֵל כָּל־עַמָּא מוֹדֵיי. נֶחְלְקָה הָעֵדוּת אֵין כָּאן נְזִירוּת. הֵיי דֵין נוּ כוֹלֵל. וְהֵיי דֵין נוּ מוֹנֶה. כּוֹלֵל. אָהֵן אוֹמֵר. תַּרְתֵּיי.

וְאָהֵן דָּמַר. חָמֵשׁ. מוֹנָה. אָהֵן אָמַר. חֲדָא תַּרְתֵּי. וְאָהֵן אָמַר. תְּלַת אַרְבַּע
חָמֵשׁ. רַב אָמַר. הִכְחֵשׁ עֵדוּת בְּתוֹךְ עֵדוּת לֹא בָּטְלָה עֵדוּת. וְרַבִּי יוֹחָנָן אָמַר.
הִכְחֵשׁ עֵדוּת בְּתוֹךְ עֵדוּת בָּטְלָה עֵדוּת. דִּבְרֵי הַכֹּל מַכְחֵשׁ עֵדוּת לְאַחַר עֵדוּת לֹא
בָּטְלָה. אָמַר רַבִּי יוֹחָנָן כְּדַעְתֵּיהּ. דָּמַר רַבִּי בָּא רַבִּי חִיָּיה בְּשֵׁם רַבִּי יוֹחָנָן.
הוּחְזַק מָמוֹנָהּ. זֶה אוֹמֵר. מִן הַכִּיס מוֹנֶה. וְזֶה אוֹמֵר. מִן הַצְּרוֹר מוֹנֶה. הִכְחֵשׁ
עֵדוּת בְּתוֹךְ עֵדוּת אַף רַב מוֹדֶה שֶׁבָּטְלָה הָעֵדוּת. מַה פְלִיגִין. בְּשֶׁהָיוּ שְׁנֵי כִּיתֵּי
עֵדִים. אֵילוּ אוֹמְרִים. מִן הַכִּיס מָנֶה. וְאֵילוּ אוֹמְרִים. מִן הַצְּרוֹר מָנֶה. הִכְחֵשׁ
עֵדוּת בְּתוֹךְ עֵדוּת בָּטְלָה הָעֵדוּת. וּכְרַב לֹא בָּטְלָה הָעֵדוּת. זֶה אוֹמֵר. בְּמַקֵּל
הֲרָגוֹ. וְזֶה אוֹמֵר. בְּסַיִף הֲרָגוֹ. הִכְחֵשׁ עֵדוּת בְּתוֹךְ עֵדוּת אוֹף רַב מוֹדֶה שֶׁבָּטְלָה
עֵדוּת. מַה פְלִיגִין. כְּשֶׁהָיוּ שְׁנֵי כִּתּוֹת עֵדִים. אֵילוּ אוֹמְרִים. בְּמַקֵּל הֲרָגוֹ.
וְאֵילוּ אוֹמְרִים. בְּסַיִף הֲרָגוֹ. הִכְחֵשׁ עֵדוּת בְּתוֹךְ עֵדוּת בָּטְלָה הָעֵדוּת. וּכְרַב
לֹא בָּטְלָה הָעֵדוּת. אֵילוּ אוֹמְרִים. לַדָּרוֹם פָּנָה. וְאֵילוּ אוֹמְרִים. לַצָּפוֹן פָּנָה.
כָּל־עַמָּא מוֹדוּ. הִכְחֵשׁ עֵדוּת בְּתוֹךְ עֵדוּת לֹא בָּטְלָה עֵדוּת. חַיְילֵיהּ דְּרַב מִן
הָדָא. רַבִּי יוּדָה וְרַבִּי שִׁמְעוֹן אוֹמְרִין. הוֹאִיל וְזוֹ וְזוֹ מוֹדוֹת שֶׁאֵינוֹ קַיָּים הֲרֵי
אִילּוּ יִנָּשְׂאוּ. וְלֹא שָׁמִיעַ דָּמַר רַבִּי לָעְזָר. מוֹדֶה רַבִּי לִיעְזֶר בְּעֵדִים. מַה בֵּין
עֵדִים מַה בֵּין צָרָה. לֹא חָשְׁשׁוּ דְּבַר צָרָה אֵצֶל חֲבֵירָתָהּ כְּלוּם. מַתְנִיתָא פְלִיגָא
עַל רַב. אֶחָד חֲקִירוֹת וְאֶחָד בְּדִיקוֹת בִּזְמָן שֶׁהֵן מַכְחִישׁוֹת זוֹ אֶת זוֹ עֵדוּתָן
בְּטֵלָה. אָמַר רַבִּי מָנָא. פָּתַר לָהּ רַב עַד בְּעַד. אָמַר רַבִּי אָבִין. וַאֲפִילוּ תֵּימַר
כַּת בְּכַת. שַׁנְיָיא הִיא דִּינֵי נְפָשׁוֹת. דִּכְתִיב צֶדֶק צֶדֶק תִּרְדּוֹף.

1 בכלל | **יס** בכלל 2 בפורט | **יס** בפרט יש | **י** שיש מודיי שיש בכלל חמש שתים שיהא נזיר שתים | **ס** מודו נחלקה העדות ר' | **ס** ור' 3 ר' יוחנן אמ' | **י** אמ' ר' יוחנן במונה | **י** בזמנה בכולל | **י** בכלל נחלקה | **י** נחלקת מודיי נחלקה העדות אין כאן נזירות | **ס** מודו שיש חמש שתים 4 היי די נו כולל היי די נו | **יס** הידינו כלל והידינו כולל | **י** כלל אהן או' | **י** ההן אמ' תרתיי | **ס** תרתי ואהן דמר | **י** והחנן אמ' **ס** ואהן אמ' 5 אהן | **י** ההן (2 times) תרתיי | **ס** תרתי ארבע חמש | **י** ארבע וחמש **ס** ארבעי רב אמ' | **י** רב אידי 6 הכחיש | **יס** הכחיש הכחש | **יס** הכחיש עדות | **יס** העדות 7 מכחש | **יס** הכחיש בטלה | **יס** בטלה העדות 8 אמ' ר' יוחנן כדעתיה | **י** ר' יוחנן כדעתיה **ס** חייליה דר' יוחנן מהדא 9 ממונה | **יס** המונה זה או' | **י** זה אמ' מונה | **ס** מנה הכחש | **יס** הכחיש 10 אף | **י** ואף **ס** אוף 11 אילו אומ' | **ס** אחת אומרת מנה | **יס** מונה (2 times) ואילו אומ' | **ס** ואחת אומרת מן הצרור | **ס** מצרור

הכחש | **ס** הכחיש 12 **בטלה** | **י** בטל   העדות | **ס** עדות   זה אומ' | **י** אילו אומ'. בתוך חיקו המה. ואילו אומ'. בתוך פונדתו המה.   דברי הכל. הכחיש עדות לאחר עידות לא בטלה עדות.   זה אמ' **ס** אחת אומרת. לתוך חיקו מנה. ואחת אומרת. לתוך פונדתו מנה.   דברי הכל הכחיש עדות בתוך עדות לא בטלה עדות.   אחד או' במקל | **ס** בסייף 13   וזה | **ס** ואחד   בסייף | **ס** במקל   זה אמ' | **י** זה אומ' **ס** ואחד או'   הכחש | **י** הכחיש אוף | **יס** בטלה העדות ואף 14 כיתות | **יס** כיתי   אילו אומ' | **י** אלו אומ' **ס** אחת אומרת   במקל הרגו | **ס** בסייף 15 ואילו אומ' | **י** ואילו אמ' **ס** ואחת אומרת   בסייף הרגו | **ס** במקל   הכחש | **י** הכחיש   העדות | **ס** עדות 16 אילו אומ' | **ס** אחת אומרת לדרום פנה | **י** בדרום פנה **ס** לצפון נטה   ואילו אומ' | **ס** ואחת אומרת   לצפון | **י** בצפון **ס** לדרום 17 כל עמא מודו | **ס** דברי הכל   הכחש | **יס** הכחיש   בתוך | **יס** לאחר 18 מן הדא | **ס** מהדא דתנינן תמן   ר' יודה ור' שמעון | **י** ר' שמעון ור' יודה **ס** ר' שמעון ור' יודן   הרי אילו | **י** לא **ס** - 19 ר' ליעזר | **י** ר' יודה ור' שמעון ור' יהודה ור' שמעון 20 חששו דבר | **יס** עשו דברי   כלום | **ס** כלום. אמ' ר' יוחנן. אין אמרה ר' לעזר מיני שמעה ואמרה. 21 הן מכחישות | **י** הן מכחישין **ס** שמכחישין 22 אמ' ר' מנא | **ס** מה עבד לה רב. אמ' ר' מנא 23 דיני | **י** בדיני **ס** לדיני   דכת' | **י** -

Halakhah 7: "If two groups of witnesses," etc. [110]Rav said, they differ in the overall testimony. But in detail, everybody agrees that five contains two, and that he has to be a *nazir* for two periods. Rebbi Joḥanan said, they differ in counting. But in an overall testimony, everybody agrees that the testimonies contradict one another and there is no *nezirut*. What is overall and what is counting? Overall, this one says two, the other one says five. Counting, this one says one, two, the other one says three, four, five. Rav said, if testimony was contradictory in its essence, the testimony is not void. Rebbi Joḥanan said, if testimony was contradictory in itself, the testimony is void. In the opinion of everybody, if testimony was contradictory in some aspects that belong after the fact, the testimony is not void. Rebbi Joḥanan is consistent in what he said, since Rebbi Abba, Rebbi Ḥiyya, said in the name of Rebbi Joḥanan, if it was agreed that he counted but one [witness] said, he counted from a wallet and the other said, he counted from a bundle, that contradicts the essence of the testimony, and Rav will agree that the testimony is void. Where do they disagree? If there were two groups of witnesses, these say he counted from a wallet and the others say he counted from a bundle. That contradicts the essence of the testimony, the testimony is void, but according to Rav, the testimony is not void. If one [witness] said, he killed him with a mace, the other [witness] said, he killed him with a sword, that contradicts the essence of the testimony; the testimony is void and Rav will agree that the testimony is void. Where do they disagree? If there were two groups of witnesses, these say he killed him with a mace and the others say, he killed him with a sword. That contradicts the essence of the testimony; the testimony is void, but according to Rav, the testimony is not void. If these say, he ran away to the South and those say, he ran away to the North, everybody agrees that the testimony was contradictory in some aspects that refer [to][111] the facts, the testimony is not void. The strength of Rav comes from the following: "Rebbi Jehudah and Rebbi Simeon say, since both agree that he is not alive they can remarry." He did nor hear that Rebbi Eleazar said, Rebbi Eliezer[112] concedes in the case of witnesses. What is the difference between witnesses and the co-wife? They do not consider the co-wife's words compared to that of her companion. A Mishnah disagrees with Rav: "Both in investigations and in cross examinations, if they contradict one another their testimony is void." Rebbi Mana said, Rav will explain that as referring to single witness against single witness. Rebbi Abun said, even if you say groups and groups. There is a difference in criminal cases, as it is written: "Justice, justice you shall pursue".

110 Parallels are in *Yebamot* 15:5 (י), Notes 115-134, and *Sanhedrin* 5:2 (ט).
111 Read: "after"; cf. the variant readings.
112 Read: "R. Simeon and R. Jehudah"; cf. the variant readings.

(52d line 70) תַּנֵּי. לֹא נֶחְלְקוּ רִבִּי יִשְׁמָעֵאל וְרִבִּי עֲקִיבָה עַל מִי שֶׁהָיוּ שְׁתֵּי כִיתֵּי עֵדִים מְעִידִין אוֹתוֹ שֶׁיְּהֵא נָזִיר כַּקַּל שֶׁבָּהֶן. וְעַל מָה נֶחְלְקוּ. עַל שְׁנֵי עֵדִים. שֶׁבֵּית שַׁמַּי אוֹמְרִים. נֶחְלְקָה הָעֵדוּת וְאֵין נְזִירוּת. וּבֵית הִלֵּל אוֹמְרִים. יֵשׁ בִּכְלָל חָמֵשׁ שְׁתַּיִם. שֶׁיְּהֵא נָזִיר שְׁתַּיִם.

It was stated[113]: "Rebbi Ismael and Rebbi Aqiba do not disagree about a person about whom two groups of witnesses testify, that he should be *nazir* according to the minimal testimony. Where do they disagree? About two witnesses, where the House of Shammai say, the testimony is split[108] and there is no *nezirut*, but the House of Hillel say, five contains two and he shall be a *nazir* twice.[109]"

113 An alternative text of the Mishnah. In Babylonian sources (Babli 20a, Tosephta 3:1): "R. Ismael, son of R. Johanan ben Baroqa, says, the Houses of Shammai and Hillel do not disagree about . . ." The text shows that this is the correct version.

מי שאמר בתרא פרק רביעי

(fol. 53a) **משנה א:** מִי שֶׁאָמַר הֲרֵינִי נָזִיר וְשָׁמַע חֲבֵירוֹ וְאָמַר וַאֲנִי וַאֲנִי וַאֲנִי כּוּלָּן נְזִירִין. הוּתַּר הָרִאשׁוֹן הוּתְּרוּ כוּלָּן הוּתַּר הָאַחֲרוֹן הָאַחֲרוֹן מוּתָּר וְכוּלָּן אֲסוּרִין. הֲרֵינִי נָזִיר וְשָׁמַע חֲבֵירוֹ וְאָמַר פִּי כְפִיו וּשְׂעָרִי כִּשְׂעָרוֹ הֲרֵי זֶה נָזִיר. הֲרֵינִי נָזִיר וְשָׁמְעָה אִשְׁתּוֹ וְאָמְרָה וַאֲנִי מֵיפֵר אֶת שֶׁלָּהּ וְשֶׁלּוֹ קַיָּים. הֲרֵינִי נְזִירָה וְשָׁמַע בַּעֲלָהּ וְאָמַר וַאֲנִי אֵינוֹ יָכוֹל לְהָפֵר.

Mishnah 1: If somebody said "I am a *nazir*" and another person heard it and said, "and so am I", "and so am I", "and so am I",[1] all of them are *nezirim*. If the first one was permitted, all are permitted[2]; if the last was permitted, the last is permitted and all others forbidden[3]. "I am a *nazir*" and another person heard it and said, "my mouth is as his mouth and my hair as his hair," he is a *nazir*. "I am a *nazir*" and his wife heard it and said, "and so am I", he can dissolve hers[4] but his vow remains. "I am a *nezirah*" and her husband heard it and said, "and so am I", he cannot dissolve[5].

[1] A_1 declares to be a *nazir*, A_2 hears A_1 and says "so am I", A_3 hears A_2 and says "so am I", A_4 hears A_3 and says "so am I".

[2] If the first went to an Elder who dissolved his vow, the others did refer to a non-existent vow; their vows are non-existent. Cf. Mishnah *Nedarim* 9:7.

[3] In general, if A_i had his vow dissolved, automatically all vows of persons A_j, $j > i$, are dissolved.

[4] Even though the initiative is his, it does not limit his power to dissolve his wife's vows (cf. *Nedarim* Chapter 10).

[5] Nobody can dissolve his own vow. If he could dissolve his wife's vow, his own would be dissolved, as explained in the second sentence of this Mishnah.

(53a line 40) **הלכה א:** מִי שֶׁאָמַר. הֲרֵינִי נָזִיר. וְשָׁמַע חֲבֵירוֹ וְאָמַר. וַאֲנִי כול'. כֵּן הִיא מַתְנִיתָא. וַאֲנִי וַאֲנִי. מָאן תַּנָּא וָוִים. רִבִּי יוּדָה. בְּרַם כְּרִבִּי מֵאִיר. אֲנִי אֲנִי. מַתְנִיתָא שֶׁהָיוּ כוּלְּהֶם בְּתוֹךְ כְּדֵי דִיבּוּרוֹ שֶׁלָּרִאשׁוֹן. תַּנֵּי. הוּתַּר הָאֶמְצָעִי. מִמֶּנּוּ וּלְמַטָּן מוּתָּר. מִמֶּנּוּ וּלְמַעְלָן אָסוּר. מַתְנִיתָא אֲפִילוּ אֵין כּוּלְּהֶם בְּתוֹךְ כְּדֵי דִיבּוּרוֹ שֶׁלָּרִאשׁוֹן אֶלָּא בְּתוֹךְ דִיבּוּרוֹ שֶׁלָּזֶה וְזֶה בְּתוֹךְ דִיבּוּרוֹ שֶׁלָּזֶה. כַּמָּה הוּא כְּדֵי דִיבּוּרוֹ. רִבִּי סִימוֹן בְּשֵׁם רִבִּי יְהוֹשֻׁעַ בֶּן לֵוִי. כְּדֵי שְׁאִילַת שָׁלוֹם בֵּין אָדָם לַחֲבֵירוֹ. אַבָּא בַּר בַּר חָנָה בְּשֵׁם רִבִּי יוֹחָנָן. כְּדֵי שְׁאִילַת שָׁלוֹם בֵּין הָרַב לַתַּלְמִיד וְיֹאמַר לוֹ. שָׁלוֹם עָלֶיךָ רִבִּי.

Halakhah 1: "If somebody said 'I am a *nazir*' and another person heard it and said, 'and so am I'," etc. So is the Mishnah: "and so am I", "and so am I"[6]. Who is the Tanna of conjunctions? Rebbi Jehudah[7]. But following Rebbi Meïr, "I am," "I am". Does the Mishnah require that all of them follow immediately after the speaking of the first[8]? It was stated[9]: If the middle one was permitted, all following him are permitted, all preceding him are forbidden[10]. The Mishnah applies even if not all of them follow immediately after the speaking of the first, but each one follows immediately after the speaking of the preceding person[11]. What means "to follow immediately after the speaking"? [12]Rebbi Simon in the name of Rebbi Joshua ben Levi: The time needed for greeting between two people. Abba bar bar Hana in the name of Rebbi Johanan: The time needed for greeting between teacher and student, that he say to him, "peace upon you, my master."

6   This version has only two people responding, with most of the Babli and some Mishnah mss. The paragraph is discussed in detail by J. N. Epstein, ²מבוא לנוסח המשנה, p. 477-479.

7   He holds that there is a connection between the statements only if they are formulated as conjunctions; cf. Chapter 1:2, Note 40, *Gittin* 9:7, Notes 85-101.

8   If the number of additional *nezirim* is reduced to 2, is that because

both A_2 and A_3 refer to the original vow, not that A_3 refers to that of A_2? In that case, there would not be time for three additional people to express their vow if the rule at the end of the paragraph be followed.

9   The same *baraita* is quoted in the Babli, 21a, for the same conclusion.

10   This is only possible if A_{i+1} refers to A_i's vow, not to A_1's. Therefore, the original text of the Mishnah is correct and essential.

11   This is explicit in Tosephta 3:2: "If somebody said 'I am a *nazir*' and another said 'so am I' but not immediately after him, the first is forbidden but the second is permitted."

12   *Berakhot* 2:1 (Notes 50-52), *Mo'ed qatan* 3:7 (83c l. 37). Babli 20b, *Makkot* 6a, *Baba qama* 73b, *Šebuot* 32a. In the Babli, the longer version has an additional word: "peace upon you, my teacher and master."

(53a line 48) אֶחָד שֶׁאָמַר. הֲרֵינִי נָזִיר מֵאָה יוֹם. וְשָׁמַע חֲבֵירוֹ וְאָמַר. וַאֲנִי מֵאָה יוֹם. וְחָזַר וְאָמַר. וַאֲנִי. נַעֲשָׂה עִיקָּר טְפֵילָה. אֶחָד שֶׁאָמַר. הֲרֵינִי נָזִיר. וְאָמַר. אֲנִי. בְּתוֹךְ דִּיבּוּרוֹ שֶׁלָּרִאשׁוֹן. וְשָׁמַע חֲבֵירוֹ וְאָמַר. וַאֲנִי. בְּתוֹךְ כְּדֵי דִיבּוּרוֹ שֶׁלַּשֵּׁינִי. הוּתַּר הָרִאשׁוֹן הוּתַּר הַשֵּׁינִי. הוּתַּר הַשֵּׁינִי לֹא הוּתַּר הַשְּׁלִישִׁי. אֶחָד שֶׁאָמַר. הֲרֵינִי נָזִיר שְׁתַּיִם. וְשָׁמְעוּ שְׁנַיִם וְאָמְרוּ. וְאָנוּ. נְזִירִין שְׁתַּיִם אוֹ כָּל־אֶחָד וְאֶחָד שְׁתַּיִם. הוּא הוּתַּר הוּתְּרוּ הֵן. לֹא הוּתַּר הוּא. שְׁנַיִם שֶׁאָמְרוּ. הֲרֵי אָנוּ נְזִירִין. וְשָׁמַע אֶחָד וְאָמַר. וַאֲנִי. תַּחַת שְׁנֵיהֶן נָזֵר אוֹ תַחַת כָּל־אֶחָד וְאֶחָד נָזֵר. הוּתְּרוּ הֵן הַיּוֹם הוּא. הוּתַּר הֵן לֹא הוּתְּרוּ הֵן.

If one said, "I am a *nazir* for 100 days, and another heard it and said, "so am I for 100 days", and repeated[13] and said, "so am I", the main [statement] becomes an accessory.

If one said, "I am a *nazir*;" somebody said "and I" following immediately the first, another heard it and said, "so am I" following immediately the second. If the first became permitted, so does the second[14]. If the second became permitted, the third was not permitted[15].

If one said, "I am a *nazir* twice," and two people heard it and said, "so are we", are they two *nezirim* or is each of them a *nazir* twice?[16] If he was permitted, they were permitted. [17]He was not permitted.

If two said, "we are *nezirim*," another heard it and said, "so am I," did he make a vow regarding both of them[18] or did he make a vow parallel to each of them?[16] If they were permitted, [he][19] was permitted; if [he][20] was permitted, they were not permitted.

13   It is not clear who is speaking, whether the second is making an additional vow or the first is repeating after the second. In the first case, if the first had his vow permitted, the second was not permitted; the "main vow", his hitching on to the first person's, becomes an accessory to the second vow which needs separate permission. In the second case, the first vow of the first person (the "main") cannot become permitted unless the Elder also permits the secondary vow (the "accessory".)

14   And the third.

15   The Tanna of this *baraita* disagrees with the argument of the preceding section and holds that, since the vow of the second is predicated on the first, the third also depends on the first but not on the third. Therefore, if the first vow is annulled, all are annulled; if any other vow is annulled, that alone is annulled but nothing else.

16   The question is not answered. The answer is obvious both for R. Jehudah and for R. Simeon (Chapter 2, Note 100; Tosephta 2:8).

17   It seems that a sentence is missing: "If he was permitted, they did not become permitted."

18   Then he would have vowed two *neziriot*.

19   Reading הוּתַּר "he was permitted" for incomprehensible הַיּוֹם "today".

20   Reading הוּא "he" for הֵן "they".

(53a line 56) פִּי מִן הַיַּיִן. רֹאשִׁי מִן הַתִּגְלַחַת. יָדִי מִן הַטּוּמְאָה. רַגְלִי מִן הַטּוּמְאָה. רֹאשִׁי נָזִיר. כְּבֵידִי נְזִירָה. נָזִיר. הִילּוּכִי נָזִיר דִּיבּוּרִי נָזִיר. לֹא אָמַר כְּלוּם. לָמָּה. שֶׁהִתְפִּיס אֶת הַנֶּדֶר בְּדָבָר שֶׁהַנְּשָׁמָה תְלוּיָה בוֹ. נֶדֶר, נֶדֶר. מַה נֶּדֶר שֶׁנֶּאֱמַר לְהַלָּן דָּבָר שֶׁהַנְּשָׁמָה תְלוּיָה בוֹ. אַף נֶדֶר שֶׁנֶּאֱמַר כָּאן דָּבָר שֶׁהַנְּשָׁמָה תְלוּיָה בוֹ.

"My mouth [shall be *nazir*] from wine[21], my head from shaving, my hand from impurity, my foot from impurity; my head shall be *nazir*; my liver shall be *nezirah*,[22]" he is a *nazir*. "My walking shall be *nazir*; my talking shall be *nazir*"; he did not say anything. Why? Because he referred the vow to something on which life depends. "Vow, vow[23]." Just as "vow" mentioned there refers to something on which life depends, so "vow" mentioned here refers to something on which life depends.

21   This refers to the Mishnah, where one person says "my mouth shall be like his mouth." Somewhere it must have been mentioned that the mouth is the organ to which wine is forbidden. Similarly, if head or foot are mentioned, reference must be to the corresponding taboo imposed on the *nazir*. Then it is a valid vow of *nazir* by Mishnah 1:2.

22   This is a separate set of rules. If somebody says, my *x* shall be *nazir*, he is a *nazir* as long as *x* is a body part necessary for survival (Babli 21b, Tosephta 3:3).

23   One invokes the rule of *gezerah šawah*, "equal cut" (cf. *Berakhot* 1:1, Note 70; *Nedarim* 1:1, Note 18, 1:4, Note 159.) The *nazir* starts his obligation with a vow, mentioned "here" (*Num.* 6:2). Another personal obligation accepted by a vow is that of paying "the valuation of living persons", mentioned "there", (*Lev.* 27:2). In a different formulation, the argument is in *Sifra Behuqqotay Parašah* 3(6).

(fol. 53a) **משנה ב:** הֲרֵינִי נָזִיר וְאַתְּ וְאָמְרָה אָמֵן מֵפֵר אֶת שֶׁלָּהּ וְשֶׁלּוֹ בָּטֵל. הֲרֵינִי נְזִירָה וְאַתָּה וְאָמַר אָמֵן אֵינוֹ יָכוֹל לְהָפֵר.

Mishnah 2: "I am a *nazir*, and you[24]?" If she said "amen", he may dissolve hers[25], and his is void[26]. "I am *nezirah*, and you[27]?" If he said "amen"[28], he cannot dissolve.

24   The husband makes a vow and invites his wife to join him. As the Halakhah explains, he makes his vow conditional on her concurrence.

25   By asking her, he did not waive his privilege of dissolving her vows.

26 Since his vow is conditional on hers, his disappears with hers. "Void" is also the reading of Maimonides (in his Mishnah Commentary and his Code, *Nedarim* 13:14), against the Babli in Mishnah and Gemara which reads "confirmed". Y. Qafeḥ in his edition of Maimonides's Commentary notes (in his grandfather's name) that the disagreement between Rav Jehudah and Abbai in the Babli (22b) may be based on different readings in the Mishnah.

27 The wife makes a vow and invites her husband to join her.

28 By this act, not only did he become a *nazir* but he confirmed her vow and, therefore, lost his power of dissolution.

(53a line 61) **הלכה ב**: הֲרֵינִי נָזִיר וְאַתְּ כול׳. הוּתָּר הוּא הִיא הוּתְּרָה. הוּתְּרָה הִיא הוּא לֹא הוּתָּר.

Halakhah 2: "I am a *nazir*, and you," etc. If he was permitted, she is permitted[29]. If she was permitted, he is not permitted.

29 This must refer to Mishnah 1, the case that the wife says "and so am I". Then her vow is dependent on his; if his vow is declared non-existent, so is hers. But in Mishnah 2, saying "amen" makes her vow independent of his; if his vow were permitted, hers would still exist.

(53a line 62) מַה הֵן וַאֲנִי. מָה אַתְּ עֲבַד לָהּ. בְּאָמֵן וְקַיָּים לָךְ. אוֹ יָפָה עָשִׂית. דְּחִיָּיא רוּבָּא וְרִבִּי הוֹשַׁעְיָה רוּבָּא. תַּנֵּי. הָאִשָּׁה שֶׁנָּזְרָה בְּנָזִיר וְשָׁמַע בַּעֲלָהּ וְאָמַר לָהּ. מָה רָאִית שֶׁתִּזּוֹרִי. מַדּוּעַ עָשִׂית שֶׁנָּזַרְתְּ. וְלֹא הָיִיתִי רוֹצֶה שֶׁתִּזּוֹרִי. אֵין כַּאן נֶדֶר אֵין כַּאן שְׁבוּעָה. לֹא אָמַר כְּלוּם. אֲבָל אִם אָמַר. יָפָה עָשִׂית שֶׁנָּזַרְתְּ. וְכָךְ הָיִיתִי רוֹצֶה שֶׁתִּזּוֹרִי. וְאִילּוּ לֹא נָזַרְתְּ הָיִיתִי מַזִּירָךְ. תַּנֵּי רִבִּי חִייָה. כּוּלְּהֶם אֵינוֹ יָכוֹל לְהָפֵר. תַּנֵּי רִבִּי הוֹשַׁעְיָה. כּוּלְּהֶם יָכוֹל לְהָפֵר. עַד שֶׁיֹּאמַר בְּאָמֵן וְקַיָּים לִיךְ עוֹד אֵינוֹ יָכוֹל לְהָפֵר.

What about, "and so am I[30]," how do you treat this? As "amen, it is confirmed for you,[31]" or "you did well[32]"? The elder [Rebbi] Ḥiyya and the elder Rebbi Hoshaia. It is stated: If a woman made a vow to be a *nazir*; her husband heard and said to her, "why did you make a vow of *nazir*? What did you do to make a vow of *nazir*? I would not like that you made a vow of *nazir*! There is neither vow nor oath here;" he did not say anything³³. But if he said, "you did well that you did make a vow of *nazir*; I liked that you did make a vow of *nazir*; if you had not made a vow of *nazir* I would have told you to make one", Rebbi Ḥiyya stated on this, in all of these cases he cannot dissolve³⁴. But Rebbi Hoshaia stated: In all these cases, he can dissolve unless he said "amen" or "it is confirmed for you", then he can no longer dissolve.

30   The last case in Mishnah 1, if the husband says "so am I" to his wife's vow.

31   Then he confirmed his wife's vow. The confirmation of a wife's vow by her husband is irrevocable.

32   This is talk, not confirmation.

33   The only language which the husband is empowered to use is that of dissolution, הפרה. Any other language is invalid; cf. *Nedarim* 10:10, Note 95 (Babli *Nedarim* 77b).

34   In his opinion, confirmation of a vow is not restrictedr to a fixed formula, but dissolution would be.

(53a line 69) הוּתְרָה הִיא הוּתָּר הוּא. הוּתָּר הוּא לֹא הוּתְרָה הִיא. רְבִּי אַבָּהוּ בְּשֵׁם רִבִּי יוֹחָנָן מִפְּנֵי שֶׁהוּא כְּתוּלֶה נִדְרוֹ בָהּ. בְּאוֹמֵר עַל מְנָת וְאַתְּ.

If she is permitted, he is permitted³⁵. If he is permitted, she is not permitted³⁶. Rebbi Abbahu in the name of Rebbi Joḥanan: Because he makes his vow conditional on hers, if he says, on condition that you [accept]³⁷.

35   This now refers to the first sentence in Mishnah 2 and explains why his vow disappears with hers. The explanation is that given by Abbai in the Babli, 22b.

36   Since her vow was an independent act.

37   But if the Mishnah is taken as

formulated, that the husband's vow is absolute and the wife is only invited to participate, if she has her vow revoked by an Elder, his vow is not touched.

(53a line 70) רִבִּי אַבָּהוּ בְשֵׁם רִבִּי יוֹחָנָן. הַבַּעַל שֶׁאָמַר. אֵין כָּאן נֶדֶר אֵין כָּאן שְׁבוּעָה. לֹא אָמַר כְּלוּם. זָקֵן שֶׁאָמַר. מוּפָר לִיךְ בָּטֵל לִיךְ. לֹא אָמַר כְּלוּם. אֶלָּא זֶה כְהִילְכָתוֹ וְזֶה כְהִילְכָתוֹ. הַבַּעַל אוֹמֵר. מוּפָר לִיךְ בָּטֵל לִיךְ. וְזָקֵן אוֹמֵר. אֵין כָּאן נֶדֶר אֵין כָּאן שְׁבוּעָה.

1 זקן | וזקן   3 או' | אמ'   וזקן | והזקן

[38]Rebbi Abbahu in the name of Rebbi Joḥanan: The husband who said "there is no vow, there is no oath," did not say anything. Also the Elder who said "it is dissolved for you, it is voided for you," did not say anything. But everybody has to follow his own rules. The husband says "it is dissolved for you, it is voided for you," and the Elder says, "there is no vow, there is no oath".

38   Text from *Nedarim* 10:10, Note 95.

(fol. 53a) **משנה ג**: הָאִשָּׁה שֶׁנֶּדְרָה בַנָּזִיר וְהָיְתָה שׁוֹתָה בַיַּיִן וּמִיטַּמָּא לַמֵּתִים הֲרֵי זוֹ סוֹפֶגֶת אֶת הָאַרְבָּעִים. הֵיפֵר לָהּ בַּעֲלָהּ וְהִיא לֹא יָדְעָה שֶׁהֵיפֵר לָהּ בַּעֲלָהּ וְהָיְתָה שׁוֹתָה בַיַּיִן וּמִיטַּמָּא לַמֵּתִים אֵינָהּ סוֹפֶגֶת אֶת הָאַרְבָּעִים. רִבִּי יְהוּדָה אוֹמֵר אִם אֵינָהּ סוֹפֶגֶת אֶת הָאַרְבָּעִים תִּסְפוֹג מַכַּת מַרְדּוּת.

Mishnah 3: If a woman had made a vow of *nazir* but drank wine or defiled herself for the dead, she receives forty [lashes][39]. If her husband had dissolved her vow but she did not know that he had dissolved her vow[40] when she drank wine or defiled herself for the dead, she does not receive forty [lashes][41]. Rebbi Jehudah said, if she does not receive forty, let her receive blows of rebelliousness[42].

39 Since she violates biblical prohibitions, is duly warned by two witnesses, and persists in her action, she is subject to the biblical punishment of at most 39 lashes.

40 Since the husband can dissolve his wife's vows in her absence.

41 While there was criminal intent, there was no crime committed. The husband had legitimized her actions.

42 Rabbinic punishment, usually reserved for transgression of rabbinic rules.

(53a line 75) **הלכה ג**: הָאִשָּׁה שֶׁנָּדְרָה בַנָּזִיר כול'. מַלְקוּת תּוֹרָה אַרְבָּעִים חָסֵר אַחַת. אוֹמְדִין אוֹתוֹ. אִם יֵשׁ מַלְקִין אוֹתוֹ וְאִם לָאו אֵין מַלְקִין אוֹתוֹ. מַכּוֹת מַרְדּוּת חוֹבְטִין אוֹתוֹ עַד שֶׁיְּקַבֵּל אוֹ עַד שֶׁתֵּצֵא נַפְשׁוֹ.

Halakhah 3: "If a woman had made a vow of *nazir*," etc. Biblical whippings are 39 lashes[43]. One evaluates him; if he can stand it, one whips him, if not, one does not whip him. Blows of rebelliousness: one strikes him until he accepts[44] or until he dies.

43 Mishnah *Makkot* 3:10.

44 To follow rabbinic rules.

(53b line 2) כְּתִיב וַיְיָ יִסְלַח לָהּ. מַגִּיד שֶׁטְּעוּנָה סְלִיחָה. כְּשֶׁהָיָה רִבִּי יַעֲקֹב מַגִּיעַ לְפָסוּק זֶה הָיָה אוֹמֵר. מִי שֶׁנִּתְכַּוֵּון שֶׁיַּעֲלֶה בְיָדוֹ בְּשַׂר חֲזִיר וְעָלָה בְיָדוֹ בְּשַׂר כְּשֵׁירָה צָרִיךְ כַּפָּרָה. הַמִּתְכַּוֵּין שֶׁיַּעֲלֶה בְיָדוֹ בְּשַׂר חֲזִיר וְעָלָה בְיָדוֹ בְּשַׂר חֲזִיר עַל אַחַת כַּמָּה וְכַמָּה.

It is written: "The Eternal will forgive her[45]." This tells that she needs forgiveness. When Rebbi Jacob came to this verse, he used to say: If somebody needs atonement having intended to get pig's meat but happened to get kosher [animal's] meat, so much more one who had the intent to get pig's meat and got pig's meat.

45 Num. 30:6,9,13. The verses refer to girls or women whose vows are dissolved by father or husband. The verses assume that they felt impelled to make vows for some hidden guilt. In the Babli, 23a, the verse is interpreted

to refer only to the case of the woman violating her vow, not knowing that it had been dissolved. The speaker there and in Tosephta 3:14 is R. Aqiba.

(53b line 5) תַּנֵּי. הָאִשָּׁה שֶׁנְּדְרָה בְּנָזִיר וְשָׁמְעָה חֲבֶירְתָּהּ וְאָמְרָה. וַאֲנִי. וְשָׁמַע בַּעֲלָהּ שֶׁלָּרִאשׁוֹנָה וְאָמַר. מוּתָּר לֵיךְ. הָרִאשׁוֹנָה מוּתֶּרֶת וְהַשְּׁנִיָּיה אֲסוּרָה. רִבִּי שִׁמְעוֹן אוֹמֵר. אִם אָמְרָה. לֹא נִתְכַּוַּנְתִּי אֶלָּא לִהְיוֹת כְּמוֹתָהּ וְכַיּוֹצֵא בָהּ. אַף הַשְּׁנִיָּיה מוּתֶּרֶת.

It was stated[46]: "A woman made a vow as *nazir* and her friend heard it and said, 'so am I;' if the first's husband heard and told her, 'it is permitted to you,' the first one is permitted but the second forbidden[47]. Rebbi Simeon says, if she said, my intention was only to be like her, in her state, the second also is permitted."

46 Tosephta 3:10; Babli 22a.

47 The Babli explains that in contrast to an Elder, who has the power to retroactively annul a vow from the start, the husband can only annul his wife's vow from the moment he heard about it. Therefore, for the second woman, the reference was to a valid vow and she is a *nezirah*.

(53b line 9) תַּמָּן תַּנִּינָן. רִבִּי לְעָזָר אוֹמֵר. עַד שֶׁיֹּאמַר שְׁבוּעָה בָּאַחֲרוֹנָה. רִבִּי שִׁמְעוֹן אוֹמֵר. עַד שֶׁיֹּאמַר שְׁבוּעָה עַל כָּל־אַחַת וְאַחַת. אָמַר רִבִּי יוֹחָנָן. נִמְצָא שֶׁאֵין בְּיָדוֹ חִטִּים פָּטוּר עַל הַשְּׁאָר. אָמַר רִבִּי אַבָּא. אוֹף רִבִּי יוּדָה מוֹדֶה בָהּ. נִמְצָא שֶׁאֵין בְּיָדוֹ חִטִּין מָהוּ שֶׁתָּחוּל עָלָיו שְׁאָר הַמִּינִין. חֲבֶרַיָּיא אָמְרִין. לֹא חָלָה. רִבִּי זְעִירָא אָמַר. חָלָה. אָמַר רִבִּי יַעֲקֹב בַּר אָחָא. מַתְנִיתָא מְסַיְּיעָא לַחֲבֶרַיָּיא. הָאִשָּׁה שֶׁנְּדְרָה בְּנָזִיר וְשָׁמְעָה חֲבֶירְתָּהּ וְאָמְרָה. וַאֲנִי. וְשָׁמַע בַּעַל הָרִאשׁוֹנָה וְהֵיפֶר לָהּ. הָרִאשׁוֹנָה מוּתֶּרֶת וְהַשְּׁנִיָּיה אֲסוּרָה. רִבִּי שִׁמְעוֹן אוֹמֵר. אִם אָמְרָה. לֹא נִתְכַּוַּנְתִּי אֶלָּא לִהְיוֹת כְּמוֹתָהּ וְכַיּוֹצֵא בָהּ. אַף הַשְּׁנִיָּיה מוּתֶּרֶת. מִפְּנֵי שֶׁאָמְרָה. לִהְיוֹת כְּמוֹתָהּ וְכַיּוֹצֵא בָהּ. הָא אִם לֹא אָמְרָה. לִהְיוֹת כְּמוֹתָהּ וְכַיּוֹצֵא בָהּ. הָרִאשׁוֹנָה מוּתֶּרֶת וְהַשְּׁנִיָּיה אֲסוּרָה. מָה אִם תַּמָּן שֶׁאֵין שָׁם עִיקַּר נְזִירוּת אַתְּ אוֹמֵר. חָלָה. כָּאן שֶׁיֵּשׁ כָּאן עִיקַּר שְׁבוּעָה לֹא כָל־שֶׁכֵּן. מַהוּ דְּאָמַר

רִבִּי יוֹחָנָן. דִּבְרֵי רִבִּי שִׁמְעוֹן נִמְצָא שֶׁאֵין בְּיָדוֹ חִטִּין וּפָטוּר עַל הַשְּׁאָר. בְּמַתְפִּישׂ. בְּאוֹמֵר. שְׁעוֹרִין יְהוּ כְּחִיטִּין. כּוּסְמִין יְהוּ כְּחִיטִּין.

2 נמצא | דברי ר' שמעון נמצא   3 על השאר | בשאר   אבא | בא   יודה | יסא   4 שאין | שיש   שאר | שבועה בשאר   אמרין | אמרי   5 זעירא | זירא   מסייעא | מסייע   6 לחבריא | למה דאמרי חברייא   האשה שנדרה בנזיר | אשה שאמרה. הריני נזירה   7 ר' שמעון או' | -   8 אלא להיות | להיות אלא   וכיוצא בה | -   אף השנייה מותרת | שתיהן מותרות   9 להיות | לא נתכוונתי אלא להיות   11 נזירות | שבועה   כל שכן | כל שכן שתחול   מהו | ומאי דא   13 על השאר | בשאר   במתפיש | במתפיס

There, we have stated[48]: "Rebbi Eleazar says, only if he mentions 'oath' at the end. Rebbi Simeon says, only if he mentions 'oath' for every item." [49]Rebbi Joḥanan said, [Rebbi Simeon implies][50] if it turns out that he had no wheat, he is not prosecutable for the rest[51]. Rebbi Abba said, even Rebbi Jehudah will agree with this[52]. If it turns out that he had no wheat, does [the oath] refer to the other kinds? The colleagues said, it does not[53]; Rebbi Ze'ira said, it does. Rebbi Jacob bar Aḥa said, the *baraita* supports the colleagues: "A woman made a vow as *nazir* and her friend heard it and said, 'so am I;' if the first's husband heard and told her, 'it is permitted to you,' the first one is permitted and the second forbidden. Rebbi Simeon says, if she said, my intention was only to be like her, in her state, the second also is permitted." Because she said "to be like her, in her state;" therefore, if she did not say "to be like her, in her state," the first is permitted and the second forbidden[54]. Since there, where there was no original *nezirut*, you say it applies, here, where there was an original oath, not so much more[55]? When Rebbi Joḥanan said, Rebbi Simeon implies that if it turns out that he had no wheat, he is not prosecutable for the rest, if he attaches[56]: If he says, [my obligation for] barley shall be like that for wheat; [my obligation for] spelt shall be like that for wheat.

48 Mishnah Šebuot 5:3: "If 5 people claim a deposit which he holds for them and he swears that he holds nothing of theirs, and this was false, he can be prosecuted for one perjury. But if he said, an oath that I hold nothing of yours, and of yours, etc. (using the singular in each case), he can be prosecuted for 5 perjuries. R. Eleazer says, [he can be prosecuted for 5 perjuries] only if he mentioned 'oath' at the end (to make it clear that he meant an oath for each of them singly.) R. Simeon says, only if he mentioned an oath in every case," i. e., an oath that I hold nothing of yours, and an oath that I hold nothing of yours, etc.

The following Mishnah 5:4 deals with the case that one claimant demands from him wheat, barley, and spelt which he holds, and he swears falsely that he holds nothing, he is prosecuted for one perjury. But if he swears that he holds neither wheat, nor barley, nor spelt, he is prosecuted for each item separately; R. Meïr says, even if he swore that he did not have wheat, barley, spelt. For this part of the Mishnah, cf. *Ketubot* 13:4, Notes 79-86.

49 From here to the end of the Halakhah, a parallel text is in *Šebuot* 5:4 (36b l. 46).

50 The parallel text and the quote later in this paragraph show that the text in parentheses belongs here.

51 Since in the preceding Mishnah, R. Simeon held that the "oath" only referred to the first item on the list; if there was no perjury for the first item, there was no perjury. (The Babli agrees, *Menaḥot* 103a.) As long as he did not say, "an oath for barley, and an oath for spelt", he cannot be prosecuted for lying about these items.

52 It is established in *Šebuot* that R. Jehudah is the anonymous Tanna of these Mishnaiot. He agrees that no prosecution is possible if the oath regarding the first item of the list was true.

53 When she said, "so am I", she only referred to the first woman in her present state, as *nezirah*, without further thought. This supports the colleagues' interpretation.

54 Interpreting R. Simeon's opinion, they hold that any vow or oath only refers to the item mentioned as its object.

55 The argument of R. Jacob bar Aḥa is rejected. If an accessory vow is interpreted maximally, an original oath cannot be intepreted minimally.

56 He explicitly attaches the second and third items to the first. Then it is clear that he cannot be prosecuted for perjury if he swore correctly on the first item.

פְּשִׁיטָא דָא מִילְתָא. לֹא הֵיפֵר לָהּ בַּעֲלָהּ שֶׁלָּרִאשׁוֹנָה וְעָבְרָה עַל (53b line 23)
נִדְרָהּ לוֹקָה. שְׁנִייָה מָהוּ שֶׁתִּלְקֶה. אָמַר רִבִּי יוֹסֵה. מֵאַחַר שֶׁזּוֹ לוֹקָה זוֹ לוֹקָה.
אָמַר רִבִּי לָא. רִבִּי שִׁמְעוֹן הִיא. וְתֵיעָשֶׂה שְׁנִייָה כְּאוֹמֶרֶת. הֲרֵינִי נְזִירָה לְאַחַר
עֶשְׂרִים יוֹם. רִבִּי שִׁמְעוֹן כְּדַעְתֵּיהּ. רִבִּי שִׁמְעוֹן פּוֹטֵר. שֶׁלֹּא נִתְנַדֵּב כְּדֶרֶךְ
הַמִּתְנַדְּבִין.

1 בעלה שלראשונה | בעל הראשונה   ועברה על נדרה | ועמדה בנדרה   2 שתלקה | -
יוסה | יוסי   3 ר' לא. ר' שמעון היא | ר' יודן. ותניי בית דין הוא.   לאחר עשרים יום | ל
יום   4 כדעתיה | כדעתיה דאמ'   שלא נתנדב כדרך המתנדבין | במגבה הדבר תלוי

The following is obvious: If her husband did not dissolve for the first [woman] and she transgressed her vow, she is whipped. Can the second be whipped[57]? Rebbi Yose said, since one is whipped, the other also is whipped. Rebbi La said, this[58] follows Rebbi Simeon. Can the second not be considered like one who said, I am a *nezirah* after twenty days[59]? Rebbi Simeon follows his own opinion; for Rebbi Simeon declares him free, because his offering was not according to the custom of offerers.[60]

57   If the second woman stated that "my intention was only to be like her, in her state," and the first violated her vow and now cannot be a *nezirah* while she undergoes the purification rite, when the second also violated her vow.
58   R. Yose's statement.
59   That the vow should count again after the first woman was purified.
60   Mishnah *Menaḥot* 12:3 (formulated in the masculine), cf. Halakhah 2:4, Note 66. There does not exist an intermittent vow of *nazir*; if the second woman's vow was valid, it remains valid.

מִשְׁנָה ד: הָאִשָּׁה שֶׁנָּדְרָה בַנָּזִיר הִפְרִישָׁה אֶת בְּהֶמְתָּהּ וְאַחַר כָּךְ הֵיפֵר (fol. 53a)
לָהּ בַּעֲלָהּ אִם שֶׁלּוֹ הָיְתָה בְּהֵמָה תֵּצֵא וְתִרְאֶה בָעֵדֶר. וְאִם מִשֶּׁלָּהּ הָיְתָה בְּהֵמָה
הַחַטָּאת תָּמוּת וְהָעוֹלָה תִּיקָּרֵב עוֹלָה וּשְׁלָמִים יִקְרְבוּ שְׁלָמִים וְנֶאֱכָלִין לְיוֹם

אֶחָד וְאֵינָן טְעוּנִין לֶחֶם. הָיוּ לָהּ מָעוֹת סְתוּמִים יִפְּלוּ לִנְדָבָה. מָעוֹת מְפוֹרָשִׁים דְּמֵי חַטָּאת יֵלְכוּ לְיָם הַמֶּלַח לֹא נֶהֱנִין וְלֹא מוֹעֲלִין. דְּמֵי עוֹלָה יָבִיאוּ עוֹלָה וּמוֹעֲלִין בָּהֶן. דְּמֵי שְׁלָמִים יָבִיאוּ שְׁלָמִים וְנֶאֱכָלִין לְיוֹם אֶחָד וְאֵינָן טְעוּנִין לֶחֶם.

Mishnah 4: A woman who had made a vow of *nazir* and designated her animal[61] when her husband dissolved her vow, if the animal was his, it leaves and grazes with the herd[62]. But if the animal was hers[63], the purification offering shall die[64], the elevation offering shall be brought as an elevation offering[65], the well-being offering as a well-being offering[66], to be eaten on one day; it does not need bread. If she had money not designated[67], it should be given as a donation[68]. If the monies were designated, the value of the purification offering shall be thrown into the Dead Sea[69]; one may not use it[70] but there can be no larceny[71]. For the value of the elevation offering, they shall bring an elevation offering; it is subject to the law of larceny. For the value of the well-being offering, they shall bring a well-being offering, to be eaten on one day; it does not need bread[72].

61 Really three animals for her prescribed sacrifice.

62 Since one cannot dedicate anybody else's property, the animals are not dedicated.

63 If the spouses had signed a contract of separation of properties by which the husband renounced his right of administration and usufruct. Then the wife can dedicate her property without asking the husband's consent.

64 Since an animal designated as purification offering can never be redeemed.

65 Since elevation offerings can be brought as voluntary gifts; *Lev.* 1.

66 Most well-being offerings are voluntary gifts. But those are eaten during two days and the intervening night (*Lev.* 7:16) while the *nazir's* well-being offering follows the rules of thanksgiving offerings which may be eaten only during one day and the following night (*Lev.* 7:15). The *nazir's*

offering also needs an accompanying gift of bread, similar to the thanksgiving offering. But since the woman is no *nezirah* after the husband's dissolution of her vow, the bread cannot be offered. (The bread is baked on the day it is offered; since the husband has to dissolve the vow before it has run its course, there is no dedicated bread.)

67   Money put aside for her sacrifices, without specifying which money should be used for which animal.

68   Given to the special Temple account, to be used for elevation sacrifices if the altar otherwise would be vacant.

69   Where it will be quickly dissolved by the chemicals in the water. "Throwing something into the Dead Sea" means: "making sure it cannot be used."

70   Since it is designated for a sacrifice.

71   Since the sacrifice cannot be offered, misappropriation of the money cannot be prosecuted; the rules of *Lev.* 5:14-16 cannot be applied.

72   Well-being sacrifices remain the property of the offerer; they may be *sancta*, but are not "The Eternal's *Sancta*", never subject to the rules of *Lev.* 5:14-16.

(54b line 27) **הלכה ד:** הָאשָׁה שֶׁנֶּדְרָה בַנָּזִיר כול׳. הָא לִיקַדֵּשׁ קָדְשָׁה. אֶלָּא בְּשֶׁנְתָן לָהּ אַחֵר מַתָּנָה וְאָמַר לָהּ. עַל מְנָת שֶׁלֹּא יְהֵא לְבַעֲלֵיךְ רְשׁוּת בָּהֶן. שָׁלַהּ הֵן. אָמַר רִבִּי מַתַּנְיָיה. בְּמִשְׁלַטֶת עַל נְכָסָיו. וְאִם בָּא לִמְחוֹת לֹא קָדְשָׁה. וְאִם לָאו קָדְשָׁה.

Halakhah 4: "A woman who had made a vow of *nazir*," etc. Does this mean it became holy by dedication[73]? But if a third person gave her a gift and said, on condition that your husband have no right of disposition over it[74], then it is hers. Rebbi Mattaniah said, if he gave her power over his properties[75]. If he comes to protest, it did not become holy; otherwise, it became holy.

73   Since in the absence of a contract to the opposite, all property of the wife's is administered by her husband, how can the wife dedicate animals for her sacrifices without asking her husband to do it for her?

74 This is one scenario in which the husband has no say in what she does. (Cf. *Nedarim* 11:8, Notes 69-70; Babli 24b.)	to sign for everything concerning their properties. In this case, she is able to dedicate the animals but he retains veto power. In the scenario described in Note 63, he has no veto power.
75 The husband gives her the right	

(54b line 30) תַּמָּן אַתְּ מוֹצֵא אוֹמֵר. תִּרְעֶה בָּעֵדֶר. וְכָא אַתְּ אָמַר אָכֵן. תַּמָּן הַזָּקֵן עוֹקֵר אֶת הַנֶּדֶר מֵעִיקָרוֹ. בְּרַם הָכָא אֵינוֹ עוֹקֵר אֶלָּא מִיכָּן וְלַבָּא.

There[76], you find it possible to say, "it should go grazing", and here, you say so? There, the Elder eliminates the vow from the start; here, he[77] eliminates only from that moment onwards.

76 Mishnah 5:3: If an Elder annuls the vow for which animals already had been reserved, the animals are profane. Why are the wife's animals not profane if her husband dissolves her vow?	77 The husband. In the Babli, 19a, the question of the reach of the husband's action remains unanswered. Only for the Elder, the Babli agrees, *Ketubot* 74b.

(54b line 32) מִי מֵיפֵר אֶת שֶׁעָלֶיהָ. אָמַר רִבִּי יוֹסֵי בֶּן חֲנִינָה. גְּזֵירַת הַכָּתוּב הִיא. הֵפֵר אֶת נִדְרָהּ. הֵפֵר אֶת מַה שֶּׁעָלֶיהָ. מִי שֶׁהוּא הֵיפֵר נִדְרָהּ הוּא מֵיפֵר מַה שֶּׁעָלֶיהָ.

Who dissolves her obligations[78]? Rebbi Yose ben Hanina said, it is a decree of Scripture: "He dissolved her vow;" he dissolved her obligation[79]. The one who dissolved her vow dissolved her obligation.

78 It is agreed that *Num.* 30 gives the husband the right to dissolve his wife's vows. But where is it written that the husband can eliminate the sacrifices which are implied by his	wife's vow? 79 *Num.* 30:9: "If on the day of his hearing he stops her and dissolves her vow [and] obligations."

(54b line 34) תַּנֵּי. אֵין טְעוּנִין לֹא לֶחֶם וְלֹא זְרוֹעַ. רִבִּי בּוּן בַּר חִייָה בָּעֵי. שְׁלָמִים בָּאִין לְאַחַר מִיתָה. (בְּרֵיהּ דְּרִבִּי שִׁמְעוֹן)[80] מָהוּ שֶׁיִּטְעֲנוּ לֶחֶם. חָזַר וְאָמַר. וְכֵן בַּחַיִּים. לֹא עַל הַבַּטָּלָה הֵן בָּאִין. אַתְּ אָמַר. טְעוּנִין לֶחֶם. וְכָא טְעוּנִין לֶחֶם. אָמַר רִבִּי יוֹסֵה. פְּשִׁיטָה לְרִבִּי בּוּן בַּר חִייָה בִּשְׁלָמִים הַבָּאִין לְאַחַר הֲפָרָה שֶׁאֵין טְעוּנִין לֶחֶם. מַה בֵּין מִיתָה מַה בֵּין הֲפָרָה. מִיתָה כְּבָר נִרְאוּ לְהִיטָּעֵן לֶחֶם. הֲפָרָה לֹא נִרְאוּ לְהִיטָּעֵן לֶחֶם. תַּנֵּי. אָשָׁם לְאַחַר הֲפָרָה. אֵין אָשָׁם לְאַחַר מִיתָה. מֵתָה אֵין אֲשָׁמָהּ קָרֵב. שֶׁאֵין לָךְ אָשָׁם קָרֵב לְאַחַר מִיתָה. הֵיפֵר לָהּ אֲשָׁמָהּ קָרֵב. שֶׁאֵין לָךְ אָשָׁם בָּא עַל הַבַּטָּלָה כָּזֶה.

It was stated: They[81] need neither bread nor foreleg. Rebbi Abun bar Ḥiyya asked: Do well-being sacrifices which are brought after death[82] need bread? He turned around and said, is it not the same during his lifetime, do they not come for nothing[83]? You say, they need bread, and here they need bread. Rebbi Yose said, it is obvious for Rebbi Abun bar Ḥiyya that well-being sacrifices which are brought after dissolution do not need bread[84]. What is the difference between death and dissolution? In the case of death, they already were prepared to need bread; In the case of dissolution, they never were prepared to need bread[85]. It was stated: There is a reparation sacrifice after dissolution[86]; there is no reparation sacrifice after death[87]. If she died, her reparation sacrifice is not offered, since there is no reparation sacrifice after death. If he dissolved for her, her reparation sacrifice is offered since that reparation sacrifice does not come for nothing.

80 These three words seem not to belong anywhere in this paragraph; they are not translated.

81 The sacrifices offered after a vow of *nazir* was dissolved. The Mishnah mentions that no bread is offered; it is a logical consequence that the officiating Cohen does not receive a foreleg from the goat offered as well-being sacrifice since *Num.* 6:19 makes the gift of the foreleg dependent on the gift of bread.

82 If the estate of a deceased person included animals dedicated for well-being sacrifices, the heirs have to offer these animals in the Temple.

83 A person made a vow for sacrifices and afterwards dedicated certain animals to satisfy his vow. If then these animals were lost or ran away, he dedicated other animals and offered them; when afterwards the original animals are found, they have to be sacrificed; this is "for nothing" since the vow already was fulfilled.

84 Since this is stated in our Mishnah. The question is why did R. Abun bar Ḥiyya not conclude (with the Babli, 24b) from the Mishnah that well-being sacrifices after the dedicator's death do not need bread?

85 In the case of animals dedicated to fulfill a vow of well-being offerings, they can immediately be brought to the Temple and offered. But a well-being offering for a vow of *nazir* cannot be brought before the period of the vow has expired; before that time the dedication is potential, rather than actual.

86 If the wife became impure before her vow was annulled, she incurred the obligation of a reparation sacrifice. If the husband then dissolves her vow, the obligation is not dissolved since his action is not retroactive (Note 77).

87 Reparation sacrifices are parallel to purification sacrifices (*Lev.* 7:7). Since purification sacrifices after death are impossible, so are reparation sacrifices.

(54b line 43) תַּמָּן תַּנִּינָן. מוֹתַר נְזִירִים לַנְּזִירִים. מוֹתַר נָזִיר לִנְדָבָה. אָמַר רַב חִסְדָּא. וְהוּא שֶׁקְּרָבָה חַטָּאתוֹ בַּסּוֹף. וְאִם קָרְבוּ שְׁלָמָיו בַּסּוֹף מוֹתְרוֹ שְׁלָמִים. אָמַר רִבִּי זְעִירָא. אֲפִילוּ קָרְבוּ שְׁלָמָיו לְבַסּוֹף הֲלָכָה אַחַת הִיא בַּנָּזִיר שֶׁתְּהֵא מוֹתְרוֹ נְדָבָה. מַתְנִיתָא מְסַיְּיעָה לְדֵין וּמַתְנִיתָא מְסַיְּיעָה לְדֵין. מַתְנִיתָא מְסַיְּיעָה לְרִבִּי זְעִירָא. אֵילוּ הֵן מָעוֹת סְתוּמִין. כָּל־שֶׁדְּמֵי חַטָּאוֹת מֵתוֹת מְעוֹרָבוֹת בָּהֶן. וַאֲפִילוּ הִפְרִישׁ דְּמֵי חַטָּאוֹת מֵתוֹת מְתוֹכָן מָעוֹת סְתוּמִין הֵן. מַתְנִיתָא מְסַיְּיעָא לְרַב חִסְדָּא. אֵילוּ לְחַטָּאתִי וְהַשְּׁאָר לִנְזִירוּתִי. וָמֵת. מוֹעֲלִין בְּכוּלָּן וְאֵינָן מוֹעֲלִין בְּמִקְצָתָן. וְלֹא אָמַר. וְאִם מֵת יִפְּלוּ נְדָבָה.

There, we have stated[88]: "Leftovers for *nezirim* are for *nezirim*; what is left over from a *nazir* is for donation[89]." Rav Ḥisda said, only if his purification offering was presented last. But if his well-being offering was presented last, what is left over is for a well-being offering⁹⁰. Rebbi Ze'ira said, even if his well-being offering was presented last, it is a general rule for a *nazir* that his leftover be for donation⁹¹. A *baraita* supports one and a *baraita* supports the other. A *baraita* supports Rebbi Ze'ira: "The following are undesignated monies: any which contain money for purification offerings that should die. Even if he designated money for purification offerings that should die, it remains undesignated.⁹²" A *baraita* supports Rav Ḥisda: "This is for my purification offering and the rest for my *nezirut*⁹³. Then he died. One commits larceny with all of them but not with part of them⁹⁴."⁹⁵ It does not say, when he died it should be given for donation.

88 Mishnah *Šeqalim* 2:6.

89 If moneys were collected to help indigent *nezirim* with the expenses of their sacrifices but not all was used, the remainder has to be kept in trust to be used in the future for the same purpose. But if a person dedicated his own money for his sacrifices and had money left over, that should go to the account for offerings (Note 68).

90 Mishnah *Šeqalim* 2:6 also states that leftovers of monies for purification offerings go to the offerings account, but leftovers for well-being offerings must be used for well-being offerings.

91 Overriding the general rules of Mishnah *Šeqalim* 2:6. In the Babli, 25a, this rule is attributed to R. Joḥanan (and, therefore, declared to be practice to be followed.)

92 This refers to Mishnah *Me'ilah* 3:2 which decrees that money left over from unspecified funds set aside for *nazir*'s sacrifices must be given to the Temple's offering account. Such money can be used for elevation or well-being offerings only if absolutely no money of purification offerings is mixed in (since one has to avoid the danger that the value of purification offerings be totally lost if anything goes wrong with that kind of sacrifice.)

93 The required elevation and well-being offerings.

94 Since well-being offerings are not subject to larceny by its owner, misappropriation cannot be prosecuted unless one can prove that money for elevation offerings is involved.

95 A different version of this *baraita* is in the Babli, 26b; Tosephta *Me'ilah* 1:10.

(54b line 51) אָמַר רַב חִסְדָּא. מוֹתַר לֶחֶם נָזִיר יִרְקַב. אָמַר רִבִּי יוֹסֵי. וְיָאוּת. לְהַקְרִיבוֹ בִּפְנֵי עַצְמוֹ אֵי אַתָּה יָכוֹל. שֶׁאֵין לָךְ אָשָׁם קָרֵב בִּפְנֵי עַצְמוֹ. לְהַקְרִיבוֹ עִם נְזִירוּת אַחֶרֶת אֵין אַתְּ יָכוֹל. שֶׁאֵין לָךְ נְזִירוּת בָּאָה עַל לֶחֶם. לְפוּם כֵּן צָרַךְ לוֹמַר. מוֹתַר לֶחֶם נָזִיר יִרְקַב. סָבְרִין מֵימַר. הוּא מוֹתַר לַחְמוֹ הוּא מוֹתַר נְסָכָיו. אָמַר רִבִּי יוֹסֵי בֵּירִבִּי בּוּן. מוֹתַר נְסָכָיו קָדְשֵׁי קָדָשִׁים אִינּוּן יִפְּלוּ לִנְדָבָה. עַל דַּעְתֵּיהּ דְּרִבִּי יוֹסֵי בֵּירִבִּי בּוּן. שְׁמוּאֵל וְרַב חִסְדָּא וְרִבִּי אֶלְעָזָר שְׁלָשְׁתָּן אָמְרוּ דָבָר אֶחָד. רַב חִסְדָּא. הָהֵן דְּהָכָא. שְׁמוּאֵל. דָּמַר רִבִּי יוֹסֵי. עַד תַּמָּן שָׁמְעַת קָל רַב יְהוּדָה שָׁאַל לְרַבֵּינוּ שְׁמוּאֵל. הִפְרִישׁ שִׁקְלוֹ וָמֵת. אָמַר לֵיהּ. יִפְּלוּ לִנְדָבָה. מוֹתַר עֲשִׂירִית הָאֵיפָה שֶׁלּוֹ. רִבִּי יוֹחָנָן אָמַר. יוֹלִיכֵם לְיָם הַמֶּלַח. רִבִּי לָעְזָר אוֹמֵר. יִפְּלוּ בִנְדָבָה.

Rav Hisda said, a *nazir*'s leftover bread shall be left to decay. Rebbi Yose said, that is correct. You cannot sacrifice it by itself since (reparation sacrifices)[96] cannot be brought alone. You cannot sacrifice it together with another *nazir*'s since no *nazir* sacrifices without bread[97]. Therefore, it was necessary to say that a *nazir*'s leftover bread shall be left to decay. They wanted to say, the same rule applies to his leftover bread as to his leftover wine offering[98]. Rebbi Yose ben Rebbi Abun said, his leftover wine offering is most holy; it should be given to donation accounts[99]. In the opinion of Rebbi Yose ben Rebbi Abun, Samuel, Rav Hisda, and Rebbi Eleazar, all three said the same. Rav Hisda, as quoted here[100]. Samuel, as Rebbi Yasa[101] said, when I still was there[102], I heard the voice of Rav Jehudah asking our teacher Samuel: If he designated his *sheqel* and died? He said, it should be given as donation[103]. The leftover of his tenth of an *epha*[104]: Rebbi Johanan said, he should bring it to the Dead Sea; Rebbi Eleazar said, it should be given as donation[105].

96 Instead of אָשָׁם "reparation sacrifice" one has to read לֶחֶם "bread". While there are all kinds of offerings of flour and baked goods (*Lev.* 2), no offering of bread alone is authorized.

97 Also, nowhere do we find a procedure to redeem sacrificial bread.

98 Required in *Num.* 6:15, following the rules of *Num.* 15:1-16.

99 Since all leftovers of sacrifices characterized as "most holy" are to be given to the donation account of the Temple (Mishnah *Šeqalim* 2:5).

100 About wine offerings, in the interpretation of R. Yose ben R. Abun.

101 For historical reasons, one has to read ר׳ יסא instead of ר׳ יוסי

102 In Babylonia.

103 But leftover money to be used for the Temple tax of a living person is profane (Mishnah *Šeqalim* 2:5).

104 To buy the required flour offering belonging to a purification offering.

105 Mishnah (Mishnah *Šeqalim* 2:5).

(54b line 61) רִבִּי בָּא בְשֵׁם רַב. מָעוֹת סְתוּמִין. אֵין בְּהֵמָה סְתוּמָה. אָמַר רַב שֵׁשֶׁת. וְתַנֵּי כֵן. יָכוֹל לֹא יֵצֵא בְקָרְבָּן אָבִיו שֶׁהִפְרִישׁ מִן הַקַּלָּה לַחֲמוּרָה וּמִן הַחֲמוּרָה לַקַּלָּה וּמִן הַקַּלָּה לַקַּלָּה וּמִן הַחֲמוּרָה לַחֲמוּרָה. שֶׁכֵּן אֵינוֹ מְגַלֵּחַ עַל בְּהֵמַת אָבִיו נְזִירוֹת. אֲבָל יֵצֵא בְקָרְבָּן אָבִיו בְּמָעוֹת שֶׁהִפְרִישׁ מִן הַקַּלָּה לַחֲמוּרָה וּמִן הַחֲמוּרָה לַקַּלָּה וּמִן הַקַּלָּה לַקַּלָּה וּמִן הַחֲמוּרָה לַחֲמוּרָה. שֶׁכֵּן הוּא מְגַלֵּחַ עַל מָעוֹת נְזִירוּת. בְּזְמַן שֶׁהֵן סְתוּמִין לֹא בִזְמַן שֶׁהֵן מְפוֹרָשִׁין. תַּלְמוּד לוֹמַר קָרְבָּנוֹ. בְּקָרְבָּנוֹ הוּא יוֹצֵא. אֵינוֹ יוֹצֵא בְקָרְבָּנוֹ שֶׁלְּאָבִיו. כְּשֶׁהוּא אֵצֶל הַמָּעוֹת הוּא מַזְכִּיר סְתוּמִין.

Rebbi Abba in the name of Rav: Money can be non-designated, no animal can be non-designated[106]. Rav Sheshet said, it was stated thus: [107]"I might think that one could not satisfy his obligation with his father's sacrifice, with an animal which he dedicated, whether from a minor sin for a major sin[108], or from a major sin for a minor sin, or from a minor sin for a minor sin, or from a major sin for a major sin, since he cannot shave for his *nezirut* with his father's animal; but he could satisfy his obligation with his father's sacrifice, with money he dedicated, whether from a minor sin for a major sin, or from a major sin for a minor sin, or from a minor sin for a minor sin, or from a major sin for a major sin, since he can shave on money for his *nezirut*, any time it is not designated, but not if it is designated. The verse says[109] '*his* sacrifice', he can only satisfy his obligation with his sacrifice, not with his father's sacrifice." Talking about money, one mentions "not designated".[110]

106   Money can be used to buy any animal; an animal usually defines the sacrifice for which it can be used: A female exclusively for a purification offering, a young male for an elevation offering, an older animal for a well-being offering. The same argument is in the Babli, 26b.

107   *Sifra Wayyiqra II Parašah* 6(2), Babli 27b, *Keritut* 27b.

108   A minor sin is one not punished either by divine exstirpation or by capital punishment. The latter are major sins. Since all purification offerings are the same, if it were possible to use one's father's designated purification offering for oneself, it would not matter for which sin his father designated the animal.

109   For purification offerings, *Lev.* 4:29,32. For the *nazir*, *Num.* 6:14. The mention of *his* sacrifice in *Lev.* 4:32 is redundant; this is given as motivation for the restrictive interpretation of all three verses.

110   But non-designated animals are not mentioned. This is Rav Sheshet's support for Rebbi Abba's statement.

(54b line 70) בְּהֵמָה אֵין עָלֶיהָ הִילְכוֹת סְתוּמִין כַּתְּחִילָה. יֵשׁ עָלֶיהָ הִילְכוֹת סְתוּמִין בַּסוֹף. מָעוֹת יֵשׁ עֲלֵיהֶן הִילְכוֹת סְתוּמִין בַּתְּחִילָה. וְאֵין עֲלֵיהֶן הִילְכוֹת סְתוּמִין בַּסוֹף. מָעוֹת יֵשׁ עָלֶיהָ הִילְכוֹת סְתוּמִין בַּתְּחִילָה. דְּתַנִּינָן. הָיוּ לָהּ מָעוֹת סְתוּמִין יִפְּלוּ לִנְדָבָה. בְּהֵמָה יֵשׁ עָלֶיהָ הִילְכוֹת סְתוּמִין בַּסוֹף. דִּתְנַן. רַבָּן שִׁמְעוֹן בֶּן גַּמְלִיאֵל אוֹמֵר. הֵבִיא שָׁלֹשׁ בְּהֵמוֹת וְלֹא פֵּירֵשׁ. יֵשׁ עֲלֵיהֶן הִילְכוֹת סְתוּמִין בַּתְּחִילָה. דִּתְנַן. אֵילוּ לְחַטָּאתִי וּשְׁאָר לִשְׁאָר נְזִירוּתִי. וָמֵת. מוֹעֲלִין בְּכוּלָּן וְאֵין מוֹעֲלִין בְּמִקְצָתָן. אֵין עֲלֵיהֶן הִילְכוֹת סְתוּמִין בַּסוֹף. כְּשֶׁהֵבִיא מָעוֹת וְחִילְּלָן עַל בְּהֵמָה. הִפְרִישׁ חֲמוֹר כְּמַפְרִישׁ מָעוֹת. הִפְרִישׁ שׁוֹר. רִבִּי יוֹסֵי בֵּירִבִּי בּוּן רִבִּי חִייָה בַּר לוּלְייָנִי תְּרֵיהוֹן אֱמְרִין בְּשֵׁם שַׁמַּאי. חַד אֲמַר. כְּמַפְרִישׁ מָעוֹת. וְחַד אֲמַר. כְּמַפְרִישׁ בְּהֵמָה.

An animal is not subject to the rules of the non-designated at the beginning[111], but it is subject to the rules of the non-designated at the end[112]. Money is subject to the rules of the non-designated at the beginning, but it is not subject to the rules of the non-designated at the end[113]. Money is subject to the rules of the non-designated at the beginning, as we have stated: "If he had money not designated, it should be given as donation." An animal is subject to the rules of the non-designated at the end[114], as we have stated: "Rabban Simeon ben Gamliel says, if he brought three animals but did not explain.[115]" They are subject to the rules of the non-designated at the beginning,[116] as we have stated[117]: "'These are for my purification offering, the remainder is for the rest of my *nezirut'*, when he died. One commits larceny about all but one cannot commit larceny about a part[118]." It is not subject[119] to the rules of the non-designated at the end, when he brought money and redeemed it for an animal. If he designated a donkey[120], it is as if he designated money. If he designated an ox[121], Rebbi Yose ben Rebbi Abun and Rebbi Ḥiyya ben Julianus, both speak in Shammai's name. One says, he is like one who designates money; the other says, he is like one who designates an animal[122].

111   Cf. Note 106.

112   If an animal develops a defect and can no longer be offered on the altar, it must be redeemed and the redemption money may be used for any type of offering.

113   Cf. Note 121.

114   As written, this is a *non sequitur*. It seems that one has to read: An animal is *not* subject to the rules of the non-designated at the *beginning*.

115   Mishnah 6:12. If somebody brings his three animals to the Temple without specification, the officiating priests do not have to ask him to designate the animals for specific offerings since the situation is clear, cf. Note 106.

116   This must read: *Money* is *not* subject to the rules of the non-

designated at the *end*.

117 Tosephta *Me'ilah* 1:10. The text there is more complete: "'These are for my purification offering, the remainder is for the rest of my *nezirut*', when he died. *The money's worth of the purification offering shall be thrown into the Dead Sea; one may not use it but there can be no larceny. The remainder may be used for either elevation or well-being offerings.* One commits larceny about all but one cannot commit larceny about a part."

If the moneys were under the rules of the non-designated, any surplus would have to be used for donation, i. e., to buy elevation offerings. Since it may also be used for well-being offerings, it is not subject to these rules.

118 Since no money destined for well-being offerings can be misappropriated by its owner.

119 One has to read: "An animal is subject", cf. Note 112.

120 An animal unfit as sacrifice is simply representing its money's worth.

121 A sacrificial animal in general, but not for a *nazir* who is required to offer one female and one male sheep, and one male goat. The Babli rules that the animal must be treated as a sacrifice unless it be blemished, when it follows the rules of money (27b).

122 It cannot be redeemed unless it develops a blemish; *Lev.* 27:10.

(fol. 53a) **משנה ה:** נִזְרַק עָלֶיהָ אֶחָד מִן הַדָּמִים אֵינוֹ יָכוֹל לְהָפֵר. רַבִּי עֲקִיבָה אוֹמֵר אֲפִילוּ נִשְׁחֲטָה עָלֶיהָ אַחַת מִכָּל־הַבְּהֵמוֹת אֵינוֹ יָכוֹל לְהָפֵר. בַּמֶּה דְּבָרִים אֲמוּרִים בְּתִגְלַחַת הַטַּהֲרָה אֲבָל בְּתִגְלַחַת הַטּוּמְאָה יָפֵר שֶׁהוּא יָכוֹל לוֹמַר אִי אֶיפְשִׁי בְּאִשָּׁה מְנֻוֶּלֶת. רַבִּי אוֹמֵר אַף בְּתִגְלַחַת הַטַּהֲרָה יָפֵר שֶׁהוּא יָכוֹל לוֹמַר אִי אֶיפְשִׁי בְּאִשָּׁה מְגוּלַּחַת.

Mishnah 5: If one of the bloods was sprinkled for her[123], he cannot dissolve. Rebbi Aqiba says, even if one of the animals was slaughtered for her, he cannot dissolve. When has this been said? If she shaves in purity. But if she shaves in impurity[124] he may dissolve since he can say, I cannot stand an unseemly wife[125]. Rebbi says, he may dissolve even if she shaves in purity, since he can say, I cannot stand a shorn wife[126].

123 The essence of any sacrifice is that its blood should be sprinkled on the walls of the altar. Once at least one of the sacrifices was presented, the *nezirut* is completed. The husband cannot dissolve a vow which no longer is active.

124 And then has to start anew.

125 Since as a *nezirah* she is forbidden to comb her hair, lest she tear one out.

126 While she could wear a wig after shearing off her hair, the Babli (28b) explains that the husband can object to her wearing a wig, which is difficult to keep clean. Therefore, a vow which will cause his wife to have to wear a wig is one which causes pain to the husband and is one which he may dissolve (Mishnah *Nedarim* 11:1).

(54b line 27) **הלכה ה:** נִזְרַק עָלֶיהָ אֶחָד מִן הַדָּמִים כול׳. מֵיפֵר לָהּ מִפְּנֵי שַׂעֲרָהּ. רִבִּי יוֹסֵי בֵּירִבִּי בּוּן בְּשֵׁם רִבִּי יֹסֵא בֶּן חֲנִינָה. גְּזֵירַת הַכָּתוּב הוּא. הֵפֵר נְדָרֶיהָ. הֵיפֵר מַה שֶּׁעָלֶיהָ. בְּשָׁעָה שֶׁהוּא מֵיפֵר נְדָרֶיהָ מֵיפֵר מַה שֶּׁעָלֶיהָ. אָמַר רִבִּי לָעְזָר דְּרִבִּי שִׁמְעוֹן הִיא. אָמַר רִבִּי יוֹחָנָן. דִּבְרֵי הַכֹּל הִיא. מִשֶּׁנִּיתַּק מְלֹא תַעֲשֶׂה לַעֲשֵׂה. רַבָּנִין אָמְרִין. וְאַחַר יִשְׁתֶּה הַנָּזִיר יָיִן. אַחַר כָּל־הַמַּעֲשִׂים הַלָּלוּ. רִבִּי שִׁמְעוֹן אוֹמֵר. אֲפִילוּ אַחַר מַעֲשֶׂה יְחִידִי. אָמַר חִזְקִיָּה. מַתְנִיתָא מְסַיְּיעָא לְרִבִּי בֵּבַי. בַּמֶּה דְבָרִים אֲמוּרִים בְּתִגְלַחַת הַטַּהֲרָה. אֲבָל בְּתִגְלַחַת הַטּוּמְאָה יָפֵר. שֶׁהוּא יָכוֹל לוֹמַר אֵי אֶיפְשִׁי בְּאִשָּׁה מְנֻוֶּולֶת. הָא תִגְלַחַת טַהֲרָה אֵינָהּ מְנַוֶּולֶת. מָאן דְּאִית לֵיהּ תִגְלַחַת אֵינָהּ מְנַוֶּולֶת. לֹא רִבִּי שִׁמְעוֹן. אָמַר רִבִּי יוֹסֵי בַּר אָבוּן. אוֹף רִבִּי דִכְוָותָהּ. רִבִּי אוֹמֵר. אַף בְּתִגְלַחַת יָפֵר. שֶׁהוּא יָכוֹל לוֹמַר. אֵי אֶיפְשִׁי בְּאִשָּׁה מְגוּלַחַת. וְיֵימַר. אֵי אֶיפְשִׁי בְּאִשָּׁה מְנֻוֶּלֶת וּמְגוּלַחַת. אָמַר רִבִּי יוֹחָנָן. לֹא אָמַר רִבִּי יוּדָה אֶלָּא בַחַטָּאת. שֶׁחַטָּאת פְּסוּלָה שֶׁלֹּא לִשְׁמָהּ. מֵעַתָּה אֲפִילוּ בַחַיִּים אֵינָהּ נִמְסֶרֶת לַגָּבוֹהַּ אֶלָּא בִשְׁחִיטָה.

Halakhah 5: "If one of the bloods was sprinkled for her," etc. He dissolves for her because of her hair[126]. Rebbi Yose ben Rebbi Abun in the name of Rebbi Yose ben Ḥanina: It is a decision of Scripture: "He dissolved her vows," he dissolves what is on her[127]. Whenever he dissolves her vow, he dissolves what is on her. Rebbi Eleazar said, it[128] follows Rebbi Simeon. Rebbi Joḥanan said, it is everybody's opinion, after she was transferred from the prohibition to the positive commandment[129]. The rabbis say, "afterwards, the *nazir* shall drink wine," after all these actions[130]. Rebbi Simeon says, even after a single action[131]. Ḥizqiah said, the Mishnah supports Rebbi (Bevai)[132]. "When has this been said? If she shaves in purity. But if she shaves in impurity, he may dissolve since he can say, I cannot stand an unseemly wife." Therefore, shaving in purity does not make her unseemly. Who holds that shaving does not make unseemly[133]? Rebbi Simeon. Rebbi Yose bar Abun said, even Rebbi thinks so: "Rebbi says, he may dissolve even if she shaves [in purity], since he can say, I cannot stand a shorn wife." Should he not say, I cannot stand an unseemly and shorn wife[134]? Rebbi Joḥanan said, Rebbi (Jehudah)[135] said that only for the purification sacrifice, since a purification sacrifice would be invalid if not in her name[136]. That means, as long as it is alive it is surrendered to Heaven only by slaughter[137].

127 He disagrees and holds that living with a shorn wife imposes no hardship on the husband and, therefore, the general rules of vows do not permit the husband to dissolve his wife's vow of *nazir*. But he finds a special dispensation which empowers the husband to dissolve his wife's vow of *nazir*. The verse, (*Num.* 30:9) is slightly misquoted; instead of הפר נדריה it should be והפר את נדרה. As in most cases, the argument is from the part of the verse which is not quoted: "But if on the day on which her husband hears it, he prevents her, and *dissolves her vow which is on her* . . ." This gives the husband the power to dissolve any vow she makes regarding what is on her; i. e., her hair. (In *Sifry Num.* 153, the verse is interpreted to mean that the husband has a say only over vows which are *on her*, i. e., after she made them. A preëmptive dissolution is invalid just as the Mishnah here states that a dissolution after the end of the period is invalid.)

128 The Mishnah, which considers the *nezirut* completed once the blood of a single animal was sprinkled on the altar in the final ceremony.

129 From the moment when she starts the final ceremony, she is no

longer forbidden to shave her hair but ordered to shave the hair and burn it in the fire under the well-being sacrifices. Since shaving the hair cannot be prohibited and required at the same time, the *nezirut* is completed according to everybody.

130   Cf. Mishnah 6:9. In their opinion, the *nazir* may shave only after the conclusion of the entire ceremony.

131   Mishnah 6:12; cf. Note 128.

132   Read: Eleazar.

133   Therefore "unseemly" cannot mean "shaven"; it must refer to the fact that she cannot drink wine. Since R. Simeon allows the *nazir* to drink wine after the offering of one animal, before he shaves, he asserts that shaving and not drinking wine are separate matters.

134   Therefore, the argument that the husband suffers if his wife does not drink wine is applicable only if her vow was not completed and she shaves in impurity.

135   Read: Aqiba; the reference is to the Mishnah.

136   If the husband were able to dissolve his wife's *nezirut* after the slaughter of her purification offering, that offering would become invalid and would have to be burned outside the Temple precinct. Both elevation and well-being offerings may be used if the original intent became void.

137   Even though we say (Mishnah *Qiddušin* 1:6) that "a promise to Heaven is like a delivery to a person", an animal dedicated as purification offering becomes Heaven's property only by its slaughter, in contrast to all other sacrifices for which the dedication also equals delivery.

משנה ו: הָאִישׁ מַדִּיר אֶת בְּנוֹ בַּנָּזִיר וְאֵין הָאִשָּׁה מַדֶּרֶת אֶת בְּנָהּ (fol. 53a) בַּנָּזִיר. כֵּיצַד גִּילַּח אוֹ שֶׁגִּילְּחוּהוּ קְרוֹבִים. מִיחָה אוֹ שֶׁמִּיחוּהוּ קְרוֹבִים. הָיְתָה לוֹ בְהֵמָה מְפוֹרֶשֶׁת הַחַטָּאת תָּמוּת. וְהָעוֹלָה תִּקְרַב עוֹלָה. וְהַשְּׁלָמִים יִקְרְבוּ שְׁלָמִים וְנֶאֱכָלִין לְיוֹם אֶחָד וְאֵינָן טְעוּנִין לֶחֶם. הָיוּ לוֹ מָעוֹת סְתוּמִים יִפְּלוּ לִנְדָבָה. מָעוֹת מְפוֹרָשִׁין דְּמֵי חַטָּאת יֵלְכוּ לְיָם הַמֶּלַח לֹא נֶהֱנִין וְלֹא מוֹעֲלִין. דְּמֵי עוֹלָה יָבוֹאוּ עוֹלָה וּמוֹעֲלִין בָּהֶן. דְּמֵי שְׁלָמִים יָבִיא שְׁלָמִים וְנֶאֱכָלִין לְיוֹם אֶחָד וְאֵינָן טְעוּנִין לֶחֶם.

Mishnah 6: A man can declare his son[138] a *nazir* but a woman cannot declare her son a *nazir*[139]. How is this? If he shaved him or relatives shaved him[140]; if he protested or relatives protested[141], if he had designated animals, the purification offering shall die; the elevation offering shall be brought as elevation offering; the well-being offering shall be brought as elevation offering; it may be eaten for one day and does not need bread. If he had money not designated, it should be given as donation. If the monies were designated, the money's worth of the purification offering shall be thrown into the Dead Sea; one may not use it but there can be no larceny. For the value of the elevation offering, he shall bring an elevation offering; it is subject to the law of larceny. For the value of the well-being offering, he shall bring a well-being offering, to be eaten on one day; it does not need bread.

138 His underage son. Why a father should have such power is a matter of disagreement in the Babli, 28b/29a.

139 Since rabbinic law knows no *materna potestas*.

140 If either the son or some relatives provided the sacrifices required while the father already had dedicated either animals or the monies needed for them.

141 If either the son or relatives protested the father's action, the child's *nezirut* is voided. If the father already had dedicated either animals or the monies needed for them, they have to be treated according to the rules detailed in Mishnah 4 in the case of the woman who had prepared her sacrifices when her vow was dissolved by her husband.

משנה ז: הָאִישׁ מְגַלֵּחַ עַל נְזִירוּת אָבִיו וְאֵין הָאִשָּׁה מְגַלַּחַת עַל נְזִירוּת (fol. 53a) אָבִיהָ. כֵּיצַד מִי שֶׁהָיָה אָבִיו נָזִיר וְהִפְרִישׁ מָעוֹת סְתוּמִים עַל נְזִירוּתוֹ וּמֵת וְאָמַר הֲרֵינִי נָזִיר עַל מְנָת שֶׁאֲגַלַּח עַל מָעוֹת אַבָּא. אָמַר רִבִּי יוֹסֵי הֲרֵי אִילוּ יִפְּלוּ לִנְדָבָה אֵין זֶה מְגַלֵּחַ עַל נְזִירוּת אָבִיו. אֵיזֶהוּ מְגַלֵּחַ עַל נְזִירוּת אָבִיו. מִי שֶׁהָיָה הוּא וְאָבִיו נְזִירִים וְהִפְרִישׁ אָבִיו מָעוֹת סְתוּמִים לִנְזִירוּתוֹ וָמֵת זֶהוּ שֶׁמְגַלֵּחַ עַל נְזִירוּת אָבִיו.

Mishnah 7: A man may shave on the basis of his father's *nezirut*, but a woman may not shave on the basis of her father's *nezirut*. How is this? If his father was a *nazir* and had set aside unspecified money for his *nezirut* when he died, and he said, I am a *nazir* on condition that I may shave on my father's money, Rebbi Yose said, the money shall be given as donation, for he cannot shave on his father's money. Who may shave based on his father's *nezirut*? If both he and his father were *nezirim* and his father had set aside unspecified money for his *nezirut* when he died; this one shaves on his father's *nezirut*.

(54c line 19) **הלכה ו:** הָאִישׁ מַדִּיר וכו'. אִישׁ. אֵין לִי אֶלָּא אִישׁ. אִשָּׁה מְנַיָּין. תַּלְמוּד לוֹמַר. צָרוּעַ. בֵּין אִישׁ בֵּין אִשָּׁה בֵּין קָטָן. אִם כֵּן לָמָּה נֶאֱמַר אִישׁ. לְעִנְיָן שֶׁלְּמַטָּן. הָאִישׁ פּוֹרֵעַ וּפוֹרֵם. אֵין הָאִשָּׁה פּוֹרַעַת וּפוֹרֶמֶת.

Halakhah 6: "A man can declare his son a *nazir*," etc. [142]"A man". This refers not only to a man; from where for a woman? The verse says, "afflicted with skin disease," whether man, woman, or minor. If it is so, why is "a man" written? For the next theme, "a man is dishevelled and has open seams, no woman is dishevelled and has open seams."

[142] Since the Mishnah deals with a difference between a man and a woman, it quotes another difference, regarding people afflicted with skin disease. The text is from *Soṭah* 3:9, Note 228.

(54c line 21) הָאִישׁ מַדִּיר וְהָאִישׁ מְגַלֵּחַ. רִבִּי יוֹחָנָן בְּשֵׁם רִבִּי מֵאִיר. כֹּד דְּבָרִים מְקוּלֵּי בֵית שַׁמַּי וּמֵחוּמְרֵי בֵית הִלֵּל וְזֶה אֶחָד מֵהֶן. בֵּית שַׁמַּי אוֹמְרִים. אֵין הָאִישׁ מַדִּיר אֶת בְּנוֹ בַּנָּזִיר. וּבֵית הִלֵּל אוֹמְרִים. מַדִּיר בְּנוֹ בַּנָּזִיר. תַּנֵּי בְנִיזְרֵי מְרֵחֶם. אִית דְּבָעֵי מֵימַר. עַד שֶׁיָּבִיא שְׁתֵּי שְׂעָרוֹת. אִית דְּבָעֵי מֵימַר. עַד שֶׁיָּבוֹא לְעוֹנַת נְדָרִים. הַכֹּל מוֹדִין שֶׁאִם יָבוֹא לְעוֹנַת נְדָרִים שֶׁאֵינוֹ מַזִּירוֹ.

HALAKHAH 6

A man can declare a *nazir*, and a man can shave[143]. Rebbi Joḥanan in the name of Rebbi Meïr: [144]In 24 matters are the House of Shammai lenient but the House of Hillel stringent, and this is one of them: The House of Shammai say, a man cannot declare his son to be a *nazir* but the House of Hillel say, a man can declare his son to be a *nazir*. It was stated about those who are *nazir* from the womb[145]. Some want to say, until he grows two pubic hairs[146]. Some want to say, until he reaches the time of vows[147]. Everybody agrees that he can no longer declare him a *nazir* once he reaches the time of vows[148].

143 A man can declare his son to be a *nazir*, and the son can shave on the offerings which his father brings for him.

144 Tosephta *Idiut* 2:2.

145 This sentence seems to be incomplete.

146 I. e., the father can declare his son to be a *nazir* until the latter reaches adulthood.

147 Mishnah *Niddah* 5:6: "The vows of a girl 11 years and one day of age or a boy 12 years and one day of age are checked." If they know what they are doing, their vows are valid.

148 Once a boy's own vows are valid, his father can no longer make vows for him. In the Babli, 29b/30a, the matter remains undecided.

(54c line 27) גִּילַּח אוֹ שֶׁגִּילְּחוּהוּ קְרוֹבִים. מִיחָה אוֹ שֶׁמִּיחוּהוּ קְרוֹבִים בְּכָל־לָשׁוֹנוֹת כְּמִי שֶׁמִּיחָה. יָשַׁב לוֹ לִפְנֵי הַסַּפָּר כְּמִי שֶׁלֹּא מִיחָה. קָרוֹב מַהוּ שֶׁיִּמְחֶה.

"If he shaved him or relatives shaved him; if he protested or relatives protested," in any language it is a valid protest[149]. If he sat before a barber[150], it is not a protest; may a relative protest[151]?

149 No particular language is prescribed for these protests.

150 The protest must be verbal; a silent action does not count.

534   NAZIR CHAPTER FOUR

| 151   If the child sits in a barber's chair, may a relative protest for him? | The question needs no answer since the relative can protest anywhere. |

(54c line 29) מָהוּ שֶׁתָּחוּל עָלָיו נְזִירוּתוֹ וּנְזִירוּת אָבִיו כְּאַחַת. מַעֲשֶׂה בְּרַבִּי חֲנִינָה בֶּן חֲנִינָה שֶׁהִדִּירוֹ אָבִיו וְהָיָה רַבָּן שִׁמְעוֹן בֶּן גַּמְלִיאֵל בּוֹדְקוֹ אִם הֵבִיא שְׁתֵּי שְׂעָרוֹת. אָמַר לוֹ. מִפְּנֵי מָה אַתָּה בּוֹדְקֵינִי. אִם נְזִירוּת אַבָּא עָלַי הֲרֵינִי נָזִיר וְאִם לָאו הֲרֵינִי נָזִיר מִכְּבָר. עָמַד רַבָּן גַּמְלִיאֵל וּנְשָׁקוֹ עַל רֹאשׁוֹ וְאָמַר לוֹ. בָּטוּחַ אֲנִי שֶׁאֵי אַתְּ יוֹצֵא מִן הַזִּיקְנָה עַד שֶׁתּוֹרֶה הוֹרָאוֹת בְּיִשְׂרָאֵל. אָמַר רִבִּי אֶלְעָזָר בַּר צָדוֹק. אֲנִי רְאִיתִיו יוֹשֵׁב וְדוֹרֵשׁ בְּיַבְנֶה.

May his own vow of *nazir* and that of his father fall on him together[152]? [153]It happened that Rebbi Ḥanina ben Ḥanina[154]'s father made him a *nazir* and Rebbi Simeon ben Gamliel[155] checked him whether he had grown two pubic hairs. He said to him, why are you checking me? If my father's *nezirut* is on me, I am a *nazir*; otherwise, I declare being a *nazir*. Rabban Gamliel stood up and kissed him on his head and said, I am sure that you will not die from old age before you taught instruction in Israel. Rebbi Eleazar bar Ṣadoq[156] said, I saw him sitting and explaining in Jabneh.

152   If he is between childhood and adulthood and it is not clear which vow would apply. The positive answer is given by the story.

153   Parallels are in the Babli, 29b, and Tosephta *Niddah* 5:15.

154   In the Tosephta, Ḥananiah ben Ḥananiah. In the Babli, R. Ḥaninah.

155   In both other sources, Rabban Gamliel. Since the story presupposes the existence of the Temple, Rabban Simeon ben Gamliel would have to be the president of the revolutionary government in the war against the Romans, Rabban Gamliel his father.

156   A Tanna of the first generation at Jabneh.

(54c line 35) רִבִּי אָחָא רִבִּי אִימִּי אָמַר. רִבִּי יוֹסֵי בֶּן חֲנִינָה שָׁאַל. מְלִיקַת הָעוֹף שֶׁלּוֹ מָהוּ שֶׁתֵּיאָכֵל. עַד דְּאַתְּ מַקְשֵׁי לָהּ לִמְלִיקַת הָעוֹף קְשִׁיתָהּ לִשְׁחִיטַת הָעוֹף.

תַּמָּן סָפֵק אֶחָד. וְכָא שְׁתֵּי סְפֵיקוֹת. אָמַר רִבִּי מָנִי. וַאֲפִילוּ הָכָא סָפֵק אֶחָד הוּא. כְּהָדָא דְתַנֵּי. הַנּוֹחֵר וְהַמְעַקֵּר אֵין בּוֹ מִשּׁוּם שְׁחִיטַת חוּלִּין בָּעֲזָרָה. רַבָּנִין דְּקַיְסָרִין בְּשֵׁם רִבִּי יוֹסֵי בֶּן חֲנִינָה. אֲפִילוּ סָפֵק אֶחָד אֵינוֹ. כְּמַאן דְּאָמַר. אֵין שְׁחִיטַת הָעוֹף מְחוּוֶּרֶת מִדְּבַר תּוֹרָה. וַיִּשְׁטְחוּ לָהֶם שָׁטוֹחַ. וַיִּשְׁטְחוּ לָהֶם שָׁחוּט.

Rebbi Aḥa: Rebbi Immi said that Rebbi Yose ben Ḥanina asked: May his bird be eaten when its neck was broken[157]? Instead of asking about a bird whose neck was broken, why do you not ask about a slaughtered bird[158]? There is one doubt, here are two doubts[159]. Rebbi Mani said, here also it is one doubt, as it was stated: One who perforates or tears out is not guilty because of profane slaughter in the Temple courtyard[160]. The rabbis of Caesarea in the name of Rebbi Yose ben Ḥanina: There is not even one doubt, following him who says that slaughtering birds is not clear from the Torah[161]: "They spread them a spread,"[162] they spread out slaughtered [birds].

157 If the child who was declared *nazir* by his father became impure, his father has to bring a couple of birds for him. Both birds (pigeons or turtle doves) are killed by having their necks broken by the Cohen's thumbnail (*Lev.* 5:8). The meat of one of them, offered as purification sacrifice, should be eaten by the priests. If the boy's vow is valid in biblical law, there is no problem. But if it is valid only rabbinically, then the priest who eats this meat commits two sins, since (a) he slaughters in the Temple what is not a legitimate sacrifice and (b) he eats meat forbidden outside the Temple precinct since it was not ritually slaughtered.

In the Babli, 29a, R. Joḥanan holds that the vow is biblically valid; there are no problems. R. Simeon ben Laqish holds that the vow is rabbinic; his position is that articulated by R. Mani in this paragraph.

158 Since it is forbidden to bring profane animals into the Temple precinct, one could ask not about birds, but about the animals required for the *nazir* who finishes his term in purity, whether his purification offering could

be eaten by the priests.

159   The sacrifices of the pure underage *nazir* have only the problem of the validity of his vow in biblical law. The sacrifice of the impure in addition has the problem that the consumption of meat from a bird whose neck was broken is forbidden to everybody except priests in the Temple in the line of duty.

160   It is forbidden to ritually slaughter profane animals in the Temple precinct. If the animals are killed in other ways than by slaughter, that prohibition was not violated (other prohibitions may have been violated). Cf. Babli *Ḥulin* 86a. There remains only the problem of eating the meat; the irregular slaughter in the Temple precinct is not an infraction.

161   Ritual slaughter of four-legged animals is clearly prescribed in the Torah. In the desert, all non-sacrificial slaughter was forbidden, *Lev.* 17:1-7. When the Israelites entered the Land, profane slaughter was permitted, *Deut.* 12:21. Profane slaughter has to be executed "as I commanded you", i. e., by the method of slaughter used in the Tabernacle. In all of *Lev.*, slaughter is described by the verb שׁחט, Arabic حط "to cut the throat". According to this argument, birds should be killed by breaking their neck, rather than by cutting their throat.

162   *Num.* 11:32, speaking of the quail. In *Sifry Num.* 98, the metathesis שׁחט - שׁטח is attributed to R. Jehudah.

(54c line 42) עַד כְּדוֹן בְּשָׁוִין. הוּא נָזִיר אַחַת וּבְנוֹ נָזִיר שְׁתַּיִם. הוּא וּבְנוֹ נָזִיר אַחַת. הוּא נָזִיר טָהוֹר וּבְנוֹ נָזִיר טָמֵא. הוּא נָזִיר טָמֵא וּבְנוֹ נָזִיר טָהוֹר.

So far, if they are equal. If he was *nazir* once, his son *nazir* twice? He and his son *nazir* once, [but] he was a pure *nazir*, his son an impure *nazir*, [or] he an impure *nazir*, his son a pure *nazir*163?

163   Here starts the discussion of Mishnah 7. As explained in the next paragraph, R. Yose requires that the son's vow precede the father's dedication. How would R. Yose deal with the case that the vow of the son's second *nezirut* precedes the father's dedication but the actual realization of the vow starts only after the father's death? Both for the anonymous Tanna, who allows the son unrestricted access to his father's dedicated money, and for R. Yose, the question arises whether the money can be used for a sacrifice

for which it was not intended (money for the offerings in purity for the reparation offering of the impure or vice versa)? The questions are not answered, neither here nor in the Babli (30b).

(54c line 44) מַאי טַעֲמָא דְּרִבִּי יוֹסֵי. קָרְבָּנוֹ לַיִי עַל נִזְרוֹ. שֶׁיִּקְדּוֹם קָרְבָּנוֹ לְנִזְרוֹ. וְלֹא שֶׁיִּקְדּוֹם נִזְרוֹ לְקָרְבָּנוֹ. הֲווֹן בְּעָיֵי מֵימַר. רִבִּי יְהוּדָה יוֹדֵי לְרִבִּי יוֹסֵי. אַשְׁכְּחֵיהּ אָמַר. לֹא דוּ מוֹדֵי לְדוֹ וְלֹא דוּ מוֹדֵי לְדוֹ.

What is Rebbi Yose's reason[164]? "His offering to the Eternal for his vow"[165], that (his sacrifice precede his vow)[166] but not (that his vow precede his sacrifice). They wanted to say that Rebbi Jehudah[167] would agree with Rebbi Yose. It was found said that neither of them agrees with the other.

164 That the son's vow must precede the father's dedication.
165 *Num.* 6:21.
166 The two parentheses have to be interchanged. The correct text is copied in *Num. rabba* 10(42), *Yalqut* #709.
167 In the Tosephta, 3:18, it is explained that R. Jehudah and R. Meïr hold that any unspecified money in the estate can be used by the son for a future *nezirut* (but specified money has to be treated by the rules of Mishnah 6.) The opinion of R. Yose is shared by R. Eleazar (ben Shamua) and R. Simeon (ben Iohai). The problems with the text of Tosephta and Babli are treated at length by S. Lieberman (*Tosefta ki-Fshutah* p. 537-538).

The Yerushalmi does not treat the anomaly that, by tradition, the daughter cannot use the father's dedicated money even if she is the only heir (Babli 30a/b).

בית שמאי פרק חמישי

(fol. 53c) **משנה א:** בֵּית שַׁמַּאי אוֹמְרִים הֶקְדֵּשׁ טָעוּת הֶקְדֵּשׁ וּבֵית הִלֵּל אוֹמְרִים אֵינוֹ הֶקְדֵּשׁ. כֵּיצַד אָמַר שׁוֹר שָׁחוֹר שֶׁיֵּצֵא מִבֵּיתִי רִאשׁוֹן הֲרֵי הוּא הֶקְדֵּשׁ וְיָצָא לָבָן בֵּית שַׁמַּאי אוֹמְרִים הֶקְדֵּשׁ וּבֵית הִלֵּל אוֹמְרִים אֵינוֹ הֶקְדֵּשׁ.

Mishnah 1: The house of Shammai say, dedication in error is dedication, but the House of Hillel say, dedication in error is not dedication. How? If one said, the black ox which comes out of my house first shall be dedicated, and a white one came out; the house of Shammai say, it is dedicated[1], but the House of Hillel say, it is not dedicated.

משנה ב: דִּינָר זָהָב שֶׁיַּעֲלֶה בְיָדִי רִאשׁוֹן הֲרֵי הוּא הֶקְדֵּשׁ וְעָלָה שֶׁלְּכֶסֶף בֵּית שַׁמַּאי אוֹמְרִים הֶקְדֵּשׁ וּבֵית הִלֵּל אוֹמְרִים אֵינוֹ הֶקְדֵּשׁ.

Mishnah 2: The gold denar which first comes into my hand shall be dedicated, but it was a silver one; the house of Shammai say, it is dedicated, but the House of Hillel say, it is not dedicated.

משנה ג: חָבִית שֶׁלְּיַיִן שֶׁתִּעֲלֶה בְיָדִי רִאשׁוֹנָה הֲרֵי הִיא הֶקְדֵּשׁ וְעָלְתָה שֶׁלְּשֶׁמֶן בֵּית שַׁמַּאי אוֹמְרִים הֶקְדֵּשׁ וּבֵית הִלֵּל אוֹמְרִים אֵינוֹ הֶקְדֵּשׁ.

Mishnah 3: The wine amphora which first comes into my hand shall be dedicated, but it was a one of oil; the house of Shammai say, it is dedicated, but the House of Hillel say, it is not dedicated[2].

1   We assume that he simply wanted to dedicate one of his animals as a sacrifice and since most of his animals were black, he mentioned black. If he had said explicitly, "the first ox which comes out of my house shall be dedicated *if* it be black," the House of Shammai will agree that there is no dedication. Since oxen are possible as sacrifices, the dedication

mentioned here is dedication as sacrifice.

2   Even though all three Mishnaiot illustrate the same principle, the statements imply that the positions of the Houses of Hillel and Shammai apply to all kinds of dedications. Mishnah 1 exemplifies dedications for the altar, Mishnah 2 money donations, and Mishnah 3 things which could be brought to the altar as accessories but never are sacrifices on their own. The three Mishnaiot are an introduction to the *nazir* vow made in error treated in Mishnah 4.

(53d line 16) **הלכה א**: בֵּית שַׁמַּי אוֹמְרִים הֶקְדֵּשׁ טָעוּת הֶקְדֵּשׁ כּוֹל׳. תַּמָּן תַּנִּינָן. הַמִּתְכַּוֵּן לוֹמַר תְּרוּמָה וְאָמַר מַעֲשֵׂר. מַעֲשֵׂר וְאָמַר תְּרוּמָה. עוֹלָה וְאָמַר שְׁלָמִים. שְׁלָמִים וְאָמַר עוֹלָה. אָמַר רְבִּי יִרְמְיָה. בָּא לוֹמַר חוּלִין וְאָמַר עוֹלָה. קַדְשָׁהּ. אָמַר רְבִּי יוֹסֵי. בְּמִתְכַּוֵּין לְהַקְדִּישׁ אֲנָן קַיָּימִין אֶלָּא שֶׁהוּא טוֹעֶה מִשּׁוּם דָּבָר אַחֵר.³ הִיא מַתְנִיתָא מַה הִיא. עַל דַּעְתֵּיהּ דְּרְבִּי יִרְמְיָה בְּמַחְלוֹקֶת. עַל דַּעְתֵּיהּ דְּרְבִּי יוֹסֵי דִּבְרֵי הַכֹּל.

3 אמ׳ | ואמ׳   ואמ׳ | אמ׳   4 להקדש | להקדיש   שהוא טועה משום | שטעה מחמת
5 אחת | אחר   היא | והדא

Halakhah 8: "The House of Shammai say, dedication in error is dedication." There⁴, we have stated: " If somebody intends to say heave but says tithe, tithe but says heave, fire offering but says well-being offering, well-being offering but says fire offering." Rebbi Jeremiah said, if he intends to say "profane" and says "fire sacrifice", he dedicated it. Rebbi Yose said, we consider only whether he intended to dedicate but erred because of something else. What is the status of this Mishnah? In the opinion of Rebbi Jeremiah it is in dispute, in the opinion of Rebbi Yose it is everybody's opinion.

3   Read אַחֵר see the reading in *Terumot*.

4   Mishnah *Terumot* 3:8. The following two paragraphs are Halakhah *Terumot* 3:8, explained there in Notes 85 - 92.

(53d line 21) בִּשְׂפָתַיִם. לֹא בַּלֵּב. יָכוֹל שֶׁאֲנִי מוֹצִיא אֶת הַגּוֹמֵר בַּלֵּב. תַּלְמוּד לוֹמַר לְבַטֵּא. וּשְׁמוּאֵל אָמַר. הַגּוֹמֵר בְּלֵב אֵינוֹ חַיָּיב עַד שֶׁיּוֹצִיא בִשְׂפָתָיו. וְהָתַנֵּי. כֹּל נְדִיב לֵב. זֶה הַגּוֹמֵר בַּלֵּב. אַתָּה אוֹמֵר. זֶה הַגּוֹמֵר בַּלֵּב. אוֹ אֵינוֹ אֶלָּא הַמּוֹצִיא בִשְׂפָתָיו. כְּשֶׁהוּא אוֹמֵר מוֹצָא שְׂפָתֶיךָ תִּשְׁמוֹר וְעָשִׂיתָ הֲרֵי מוֹצָא בִשְׂפָתָיו אָמוּר. הָא מַה אֲנִי מְקַיֵּים כֹּל נְדִיב לֵב. זֶה הַגּוֹמֵר בַּלֵּב. מָאן דָּמַר שְׁמוּאֵל לְקָרְבָּן.

1 בשפתים | תני. בשפתים לא | ולא 2 בלב | בלבו 4 ועשית | - 5 מאן דמר | מה דאמר

"With his lips but not in his mind." I could think that I exclude him who decides in his mind; the verse says (*Lev.* 5:4): "To articulate". But Samuel said, he who decides in his mind is not obligated until he pronounces with his lips. But did we not state: "(*Ex.* 35:5) Everyone who volunteers in his mind," that is he who decides in his mind. You say, that is he who decides in his mind, but maybe that is he who pronounces with his lips? When he says (*Deut.* 23:24): "What comes out from your lips you have to keep," that speaks about him who pronounces with his lips. Therefore, how can I confirm "every one who volunteers in his mind?" That is he who decides in his mind. What Samuel said refers to a sacrifice.

(53d line 21) תַּמָּן תְּנִינָן. הַמְכַנֵּס מָעוֹת וְאָמַר. הֲרֵי אֵילִי לִשְׁקָלִי. בֵּית שַׁמַּי אוֹמְרִים. מוֹתָרָן נְדָבָה. וּבֵית הִלֵּל אוֹמְרִים. מוֹתָרָן חוּלִין. שֶׁאָבִיא מֵהֶן שְׁקָלִי. שָׁוִין שֶׁמּוֹתָרָן חוּלִין. אֵילוּ לְחַטָּאתִי. שָׁוִין שֶׁמּוֹתְרֵיהֶן נְדָבָה. מֵהֶן חַטָּאתִי. שָׁוִין שֶׁמּוֹתְרֵיהֶן חוּלִין. רִבִּי יוֹסֵי בְּשֵׁם רִבִּי אֶלְעָזָר. מַה פְלִיגִין. בִּמְכַנֵּס פְּרוּטְרוֹט. אֲבָל בְּאוֹמֵר. אֵילוּ. כָּל-עַמָּא מוֹדֵיי שֶׁהַמּוֹתָר נְדָבָה. רִבִּי חִזְקִיָּה רִבִּי בִּיבִי בְּשֵׁם רִבִּי לָעְזָר. מַה פְלִיגִין. בִּמְכַנֵּס פְּרוּטְרוֹט. אֲבָל בְּאוֹמֵר. אֵילוּ. כָּל-עַמָּא מוֹדֵיי שֶׁהַמּוֹתָר חוּלִין. אָמַר רִבִּי חִזְקִיָה. מַתְנִיתָא מְסַיְּיעָא לְרִבִּי בִּיבַי. אָמַר רִבִּי שִׁמְעוֹן. מַה בֵּין שְׁקָלִים לַחַטָּאת. אֶלָּא שֶׁהַשְּׁקָלִים יֵשׁ לָהֶן קִצְבָּה. מָה נָן קַיָּימִין. אִם בְּאוֹמֵר. שֶׁאָבִיא מֵהֶן שְׁקָלִים. כָּל-עַמָּא מוֹדֵיי

שֶׁהַמּוֹתָר נְדָבָה. אִם בָּאוֹמֵר. שֶׁאָבִיא מֵהֶן חַטָּאתִי. כָּל־עַמָּא מוֹדֵיי שֶׁהַמּוֹתָר חוּלִין. אֶלָּא כֵּן אֲנָן קַיָּימִין בָּאוֹמֵר. אֵילוּ. שְׁקָלִים עַל יְדֵי שֶׁקִּצְבָּתָן מִן הַתּוֹרָה מוֹתָרָן חוּלִין. חַטָּאת עַל יְדֵי שֶׁאֵין קִצְבָּתָן מִן הַתּוֹרָה מוֹתָרָהּ נְדָבָה. מָה עֲבַד לָהּ רִבִּי יוֹסֵי. פָּתַר לָהּ בִּמְכַנֵּס פְּרוֹטְרוֹט כְּבֵית הִלֵּל.

4 ר׳ יוסי בשם ר׳ אלעזר | ר׳ יוסה בשם ר׳ לעזר   5 אילו | אילו לשקלי   7 אמ׳ | דתנן אמ׳   9 קצבה | קצבה ולחטאת אין להן קצבה   נן | אנן   9 שקלים | שקלי   10 נדבה | חולין   11 חולין | נדבה   שקצבתן | שקצוותן   13 ר׳ יוסי | ר׳ שמעון בן לקיש

There[6], we have stated: "If somebody collects coins and says, 'these are for my Temple tax[15],' the House of Shammai say, the excess should be given as a donation[7], but the House of Hillel say, the excess is profane[8]. 'That I shall be able to pay my Temple tax,' they agree that the excess is profane[9]. 'These [monies] are for my purification offering', they agree that the excess is profane.[10]" [11]Rebbi Yose in the name of Rebbi Eleazar: When do they disagree? If he collects little by little[12]. But if he says "these[13]," everybody agrees that the excess should be given as a donation. Rebbi Ḥizqiah, Rebbi Bevai in the name of Rebbi Eleazar: When do they disagree? If he collects little by little. But if he says "these," everybody agrees that the excess is profane. Rebbi Ḥizqiah said, the Mishnah[14] supports Rebbi Bevai: "Rebbi Simeon says, what is the difference between Temple tax and purification sacrifices? Only that the Temple tax is a fixed amount[15]." Where do we hold? If he says, "that I shall use it for the Temple tax," everybody agrees that the excess should be given as a donation[16]. If he says, "that I shall use it for my purification offering," everybody agrees that the excess is profane[17]. But we are considering one who says "these[18]." Since the Temple tax has a fixed rate from the Torah, the excess is profane. Since purification offerings do not have a fixed rate from the Torah, the excess should be given as a donation[19]. How does

Rebbi Yose handle this? He explains it if he collects little by little[20], following the House of Hillel.

5 In the Babli's version: R. Simeon. While this is a possible text, the version of *Nazir* is preferable.

6 Mishnah *Šeqalim* 2:3.

7 They hold that the entire amount was dedicated even if only part can be used for the purpose stated.

8 Explained in Mishnah 2:4; Note 13.

9 The formulation makes it clear that the amount in excess of the required tax is not dedicated.

10 The text is shortened so much as to be unintelligible. The Mishnah reads: "'These are for a purification sacrifice,' they agree that the excess should be a donation (cf. Chapter 4, Note 90). 'That I shall be able to bring a purification sacrifice,' the excess is profane (Note 8)."

11 From here to the end of the next paragraph, the text is Halakhah *Šeqalim* 2:3. The Yerushalmi text reproduced in the Babli (*editio princeps*) is too closely adapted to Babylonian spelling to be useful for variant readings.

12 He starts a cache of small coins with the declared intention of collecting money for either his future Temple tax or purification sacrifice.

13 He declares that all his coins shall be dedicated to the stated purpose. The House of Hillel will agree that everything is dedicated and if it cannot be used for the stated purpose, it should be given to the Temple's donation account.

14 *Šeqalim* 2:4.

15 Half a biblical *šeqel* (*Ex.* 30:13). While the relation of the biblical *šeqel* to currency in circulation may have varied from time to time, at the beginning of the tax season the amount was clearly stated and known to everybody (Mishnah *Šeqalim* 2:4). Therefore, nobody who mentions the Temple tax will intend to dedicate more than the stated amount. In contrast, a purification sacrifice can be a sheep or a goat (*Lev.* 4), in special circumstances also a couple of birds or a flour offering (*Lev.* 5).

16 Read with the *Šeqalim* text: "Is profane" (as explained in Note 13).

17 Read with the *Šeqalim* text: "Should be given as a donation" (as explained in Note 13).

18 The monies are already collected; he declares them dedicated for a given purpose.

19 Cf. Chapter 4, Note 90.

20 The argument of R. Simeon applies only if the stated intent is to collect money for the Temple tax, not if the declaration is made on monies already available. In the latter case, R. Simeon may agree that the excess is earmarked for donation.

(53d line 40) הִפְרִישׁ שִׁקְלוֹ. סָבוּר הוּא שֶׁהוּא חַיָּיב וְנִמְצָא שֶׁאֵינוֹ חַיָּיב. לֹא קָדַשׁ. הִפְרִישׁ שְׁנַיִם. סָבוּר שֶׁחַיָּיב שְׁנַיִם וְנִמְצָא שֶׁאֵינוֹ חַיָּיב אֶלָּא אַחַת. אוֹתוֹ הַשֵּׁינִי מָה אַתְּ עֲבַד לֵיהּ. סָבַר שֶׁהוּא חַיָּיב וְנִמְצָא שֶׁאֵינוֹ חַיָּיב. בְּאוֹמֵר. אִילוּ. הִפְרִישׁ חַטָּאתוֹ. סָבוּר שֶׁהוּא חַיָּיב וְנִמְצָא שֶׁאֵינוֹ חַיָּיב. לֹא קָדְשָׁה. הִפְרִישׁ שְׁתַּיִם. סָבוּר שֶׁהוּא חַיָּיב שְׁתַּיִם וְנִמְצָא שֶׁאֵינוֹ חַיָּיב אֶלָּא אַחַת. אוֹתָהּ הַשְּׁנִיָּיה מָה אַתְּ עֲבַד לָהּ. סָבוּר שֶׁחַיָּיב וְנִמְצָא שֶׁאֵינוֹ חַיָּיב. אוֹ בְאוֹמֵר. אִילוּ.

1 הפריש שקלו. סבור הוא | המפריש שקלו וסבור 2 הפריש | המפריש אחת | אחד 3 סבר | כסבור 4 הפריש (The entire sentence was deleted by the scribe himself.) | נשמעינה מן הדא. הפריש 5 סבור | וסבור 6 סבור שחייב ונמצא שאינו חייב. או באו'. אילו. | אלא רועה. הכא נמי אלו לנדבה היאך אתה או' אילו (Insertion by the corrector. *nammē* is pure Babylonian Aramaic.

If somebody put aside his Temple tax in the belief that he owed it and it turned out that he did not owe[21], it was not dedicated[22]. If he put aside two in the belief that he owed twice and it turned out that he owed only once, how do you treat the second[23]? If he believed that he owed it and it turned out that he did not owe[24], [or as] if he said: "these"[25]? [26]If somebody put aside a purification sacrifice in the belief that he owed it and it turned out that he did not owe, it was not dedicated. If he put aside two in the belief that he owed two and it turned out that he owed only one, how do you treat the second? As if he believed that he owed it and it turned out that he did not owe, or as if he had said "these"[27]?

21 After the dedication he remembered that he already had paid.

22 In the next paragraph, it will be determined that this is the opinion of the House of Hillel.

23 In the first case, the entire

dedication was in error; it is invalid. But in the second case, there is a valid dedication. In order to be able to speak of a second, the amounts must have been dedicated one after the other. But if two animals were dedicated simultaneously, it is clear that a choice of one over the other in this case would be an act of retroactive validation, which is not accepted in biblical law; both coins certainly remain dedicated.

24   In that case, the dedication is removed as being made in error.

25   Referring to R. Yose's opinion in the preceding paragraph, implying that the money should be donated to the Temple.

26   In *Šeqalim*, this is introduced with a referral clause, "let us hear from the following." That clause is correctly missing in the present text since the argument from *Šeqalim* is not presented here.

27   By contrast, in *Šeqalim* it is stated that the dedication is not removed automatically, that the second animal has to be sent to graze until it develops a defect or becomes too old to be an acceptable sacrifice. The implied conclusion seems to be that the redemption money for that animal is a donation to the Temple.

(53d line 46) תַּמָּן תַּנִּינָן. הָאוֹמֵר. הֲרֵי עָלַי בַּמַּחֲבַת. וְהֵבִיא בַּמַּרְחֶשֶׁת. בַּמַּרְחֶשֶׁת. וְהֵבִיא בַּמַּחֲבַת. רִבִּי יוֹסֵי בְּשֵׁם רִבִּי שִׁמְעוֹן בֶּן לָקִישׁ. דְּבֵית שַׁמַּי הִיא. דְּבֵית שַׁמַּי אוֹמְרִים. הֶקְדֵּשׁ טָעוּת הֶקְדֵּשׁ. רִבִּי זְעִירָה בְּעָא קוֹמֵי רִבִּי יוֹסֵי. וְלָמָּה לֵי נָן פְּתִרִין לָהּ דִּבְרֵי הַכֹּל בְּאוֹמֵר בַּמַּחֲבַת אֲמַרְתִּי. אֲבָל אִם אָמַר. הֲרֵי עָלַי בַּמַּחֲבַת. וְחָזַר וְאָמַר. בַּמַּרְחֶשֶׁת. יָצָא. אָתָא רִבִּי חֲנִינָא וְרִבִּי יָסָא בְּשֵׁם רִבִּי יוֹחָנָן. דִּבְרֵי הַכֹּל הִיא. רִבִּי יִרְמְיָה בָּעֵי. אָמַר. הֲרֵי עָלַי אוֹ בַּמַּחֲבַת אוֹ בַּמַּרְחֶשֶׁת. וְחָזַר וְאָמַר. בַּמַּחֲבַת. וְחָזַר וְאָמַר. בַּמַּרְחֶשֶׁת. רִבִּי יוּדָה בַּר פָּזִי בְּשֵׁם רִבִּי אָחָא רִבִּי חָמָא בְּשֵׁם רִבִּי יוֹסֵי. קוֹבְעָן אֲפִילוּ בְּפֶה. סָבְרִין מֵימַר. אֲפִילוּ יָמִים טוֹבִים קוֹבְעִין. אֲפִילוּ כֵלִים קוֹבְעִין.

There[28], we have stated: "If somebody says, 'I undertake [to bring] on a pan[29]' and he brought in a deep vessel[30], in a deep vessel and he brought on a pan.[31]" Rebbi Yose in the name of Rebbi Simeon ben Laqish: This is the House of Shammai's[32], since the House of Shammai say, "dedication in error is dedication." Rebbi Ze'ira asked before Rebbi Yose[33]: Why do we not explain it according to everybody, if he said, "I said, on a pan"?[34] But if he said, "I undertake [to bring] on a pan," and then he changed his mind[35] and said, "in a deep vessel", he fulfilled his duty. Rebbi Ḥanina[36] and Rebbi Yasa came in the name of Rebbi Joḥanan: it is everybody's opinion. Rebbi Jeremiah asked: If he said, "I undertake [to bring] on a pan or in a deep vessel," turned around[35] and said, "on a pan", and turned around and said, "in a deep vessel"?[37] Rebbi Jehudah bar Pazi in the name of Rebbi Aḥa, Rebbi Ḥama in the name of Rebbi Yose: He determines even orally[38]. They thought to say, even holidays determine[39], even vessels determine[40].

28 Mishnah *Menaḥot* 12:2.
29 A cereal offering fried in oil on a flat clay pan, *Lev.* 2:5-6.
30 A cereal offering cooked in boiling oil in a deep clay vessel, *Lev.* 2:7.
31 "What he brought is acceptable but he did not fulfill his vow."
32 Why should a flour offering be acceptable if it was not properly dedicated? Since it is forbidden to bring profane food into the Temple precinct (*Deut.* 12:26), the House of Hillel should hold that an offering which does not fulfill the specification of the donor's vow has to be rejected by the officiating priests. But for the House of Shammai, who hold that a dedication is always valid, even if made in error, the nonconforming

offering is not profane.
33 Since R. Yose was R. Ze'ira's student's student, one has to read: R. Yasa (Assi).
34 If the person who made the vow agrees that the present offering does not satisfy his vow, there is no reason why it should not be accepted as a separate offering.
35 Immediately.
36 It seems that one has to read "R. Ḥinena".
37 Since he demonstrates that he did not make up his mind, do we hold him to his last statement or can he satisfy his vow with any of the kinds mentioned as possibilities?
38 This is an independent statement. From the Mishnah in *Menaḥot* it follows that the donor's

statement determines the kind of cereal sacrifice he is required to bring, even if as yet he owes no flour.

39   If he vows the sacrifice for a holiday, he cannot satisfy his vow on a workday.

40   If he vowed a cereal sacrifice without specifying its kind and then put the flour into one of the acceptable vessels without saying a word, the vessel determines the kind of offering he vowed and he cannot change it any longer.

(53d line 57) תַּמָּן תַּנִּינָן. רְבִּי יוֹסֵי בֵּירְבִּי יוּדָה אוֹמֵר. עָשָׂה שׁוֹגֵג כְּמֵזִיד בִּתְמוּרָה. וְלֹא עָשָׂה שׁוֹגֵג כְּמֵזִיד בְּמוּקְדָּשִׁין. חִזְקִיָּה אָמַר. לְשׁוֹגֵג בְּלֹא תַעֲשֶׂה וּלְמֵמִיר בְּלֹא תַעֲשֶׂה. אֲבָל אִם בָּא לוֹמַר חוּלִּין וְאָמַר עוֹלָה. קֶדְשָׁה. אָמַר רִבִּי יוֹחָנָן. בָּא לוֹמַר חוּלִּין וְאָמַר עוֹלָה. קֶדְשָׁה. אֲבָל אִם בָּא לוֹמַר עוֹלָה וְאָמַר חוּלִּין לֹא קֶדְשָׁה. וַתְיָיא דְּרִבִּי יוֹחָנָן כְּרִבִּי יוֹסֵי בֵּירְבִּי יוּדָה בִּתְמוּרָה כפרתה[41] דְרִבִּי יִרְמְיָה עַל דְּבֵית שַׁמַּי בְּמוּקְדָּשִׁין. עַל דַּעְתֵּיהּ דְּרִבִּי יוֹחָנָן נִיחָא. עָשָׂה שׁוֹגֵג כְּמֵזִיד בִּתְמוּרָה. וְלֹא עָשָׂה שׁוֹגֵג כְּמֵזִיד בְּמוּקְדָּשִׁין. בְּמַקְדִּישׁ בְּכוֹר. וּמִי קָדַשׁ. לֹא כֵן אָמַר רִבִּי חִיָּיה וְרִבִּי אָחָא רִבִּי יָסָא בְּשֵׁם רִבִּי יוֹחָנָן. הִקְדִּישׁ בְּכוֹר וְעוֹלָה לַמִּזְבֵּחַ אֲפִילוּ לְדָמִים לֹא קָדַשׁ. הִקְדִּישׁ בַּעַל מוּם לַמִּזְבֵּחַ אֲפִילוּ בִּתְמוּרָה לֹא קֶדְשָׁה. אֶלָּא הַמַּקְדִּישׁ בַּעַל מוּם עוֹבֵר. וּמְחוּבָּר הוּא לְמַכּוֹת. אָמַר רִבִּי יוּדָן אָבוֹי דְּרִבִּי מַתַּנְיָה. תִּיפְתָּר בְּמַקַדֵּשׁ תְּמִימִים לְבֶדֶק הַבַּיִת.

There[42], we have stated: "Rebbi Yose ben Rebbi Jehudah says, He[43] made error equal to intent for substitution, but not for sacrifices." Ḥizqiah said, in error: a prohibition, the one who substitutes: a prohibition[44]. If he wants to say "profane" but said "an elevation sacrifice", it is sanctified[45]. If he wants to say "an elevation sacrifice" but said "profane", it is not sanctified. It follows that Rebbi Joḥanan, interpreting Rebbi Yose ben Rebbi Jehudah, parallels Rebbi Jeremiah's explanation[46] regarding the House of Shammai on sacrifices. In Rebbi Joḥanan's opinion, may one understand that "He made error equal to intent for substitution, but not for sacrifices," if somebody dedicates a firstling?[47] Can it be dedicated?

Did not Rebbi Ḥiyya, Rebbi Aḥa, and Rebbi Yasa say in the name of Rebbi Joḥanan: If somebody dedicated a firstling and it was brought to the altar, it is not sanctified even for its money's worth[48]. If somebody dedicated a blemished animal for the altar, even as a substitute it is not sanctified[49]. But if somebody dedicated an animal with a temporary blemish. Is that consistent[50] with whipping[51]? Rebbi Yudan, Rebbi Mattaniah's father, said, explain it if he gave unblemished animals for the upkeep of the Temple[52].

41   Read: כְּפִתְרָהּ "as explanation".
42   Mishnah *Temurah* 2:3.
43   God, in instituting the rules of *Lev.* 27:10 ff.
44   He explains the Mishnah. Once an animal has been dedicated, it cannot be exchanged for another animal as long as it did not develop a blemish (*Lev.* 27:10). A person who intentionally violates this prohibition is whipped. It is asserted that a person who unintentionally violates the prohibition is also whipped (see the next paragraph). But a dedication in error is not a dedication for the House of Hillel.
45   While for vows one requires that "his heart and mouth be in unison", for Temple dedications only the pronouncement counts (*Deut.* 23:24).
46   In the first paragraph of this Halakhah (*Terumot* 3:8, Note 86).
47   This is a question for Ḥizqiah. Without his comment, we would have

read the Mishnah in *Temurah* to state that substitution in error is substitution, dedication in error is not dedication. But he insists that for R. Yose ben R. Jehudah, substitution in error is criminally punishable. Now everybody agrees that dedication in error is not punishable, but where do we find that intentional dedication should be punishable, to justify R. Yose ben R. Jehudah's formulation? The answer is that the dedication of a firstling (which must be given to a Cohen) for any other sacrifice is forbidden (*Lev.* 27:26) and, therefore, should be subject to criminal prosecution.

48   The firstling is sanctified at birth and never becomes the rancher's property. The rancher has to raise the calf or lamb for 30 days and then is obligated to deliver it to a Cohen. Since nobody can dedicate what is not his, any dedication of a firstling by the rancher is void, not only invalid. In the

case described, any Cohen can come and take the firstling from the altar and eat it (since only the blood of a firstling is given to the altar but nothing of its meat). There can be no prosecution for a nonexisting act.

49   The example of dedication of a blemished animal cannot be used as illustration of R. Yose ben Jehudah's statement. A blemished animal cannot be dedicated; therefore, it neither can become a substitute sacrifice. The rules of substitutions and dedications are identical for blemished animals.

50   (Logically) connected. This technical term appears as מְחַוֵּר "whitish, clear" in the Babli, pointing to differences in the pronunciation of ב, β in Galilee and ב in Babylonia. Cf. H. Guggenheimer, *Die Aussprache des "Bet" in talmudischer Zeit*, Bulletin, Verband jüdischer Lehrer und Kantoren der Schweiz Nr. 21, 1977, pp. 4-5.

51   Since a temporary blemish does not permanently disqualify the animal from the altar, the dedication cannot be a crime. Again, there is no difference between dedication and substitution; R. Yose ben R. Jehudah cannot refer to this case.

52   Donating unblemished cattle, sheep, or goats for the upkeep of the Temple clearly violates the injunction of *Lev.* 27:9 to reserve such animals for the altar. However, that rule is formulated as an obligation, not as a prohibition and, therefore, involves no prosecutable offense. In the next paragraph it is established that R. Jehudah and his son found a biblical source which allows one to find a prohibition in *Lev.* 27:9. The rule of R. Yose ben Jehudah is valid only for him and his father, not for most other Sages.

(53d line 71) רִבִּי יוֹסֵי בֵּירִבִּי יוּדָה בְּשִׁיטַת אָבִיו. הִקְדִּישׁ תְּמִימִים לְבֶדֶק הַבַּיִת עוֹבֵר בַּעֲשֵׂה. מְנַיִין בְּלֹא תַעֲשֶׂה. תַּלְמוּד לוֹמַר וַיְדַבֵּר יי אֶל מֹשֶׁה לֵּאמוֹר. לָאו אָמוּר. דְּבְרֵי רִבִּי יוּדָה. רִבִּי הֲוָה יְתִיב מַתְנֵי בְּפָרָשַׁת אֵין מְמִירִין בִּבְכוֹר וְחוֹלִין אֲבוֹי דְּבַר פְּדָיָיה. חַמְתֵּיהּ רִבִּי. אָמַר. אֲנָא יָדַע מָה אֲנָא אָמַר כְּדוֹן אֲנָא מֵימַר וַיְדַבֵּר יי אֶל מֹשֶׁה לֵּאמוֹר. לֹא יֵימַר דִּבְרֵי רִבִּי יוּדָה. וּכְתִיב כֵּן. דָּמַר רִבִּי אִמִּי בְּשֵׁם רִבִּי יוֹחָנָן. גּוֹרְעִין לִדְרוֹשׁ מִתְּחִילַת הַפָּרָשָׁה לְסוֹפָהּ. רִבִּי חֲנִינָה בְּשֵׁם רִבִּי יִרְמְיָה. וַאֲפִילוּ בְּאֶמְצַע הַתֵּיבָה. וְיָצַקְתָּ עָלֶיהָ שֶׁמֶן מִנְחָה הִיא. וְיָצַקְתָּ מִשְּׁמֶן מִשְׁחָה. לְרַבּוֹת כָּל־הַמְּנָחוֹת לִיצִיקָה.

7 מתחילת הפרשה | ס מתחילתה   לסופה | ה עד סופה   חנינה | ה חנניה   7 התיבה |
ה תיבה   שמן מנחה היא | ס שמן   משמן משחה | ס שמן מנחה   8 כל | ס את כל

Rebbi Yose ben Rebbi Jehudah follows his father's method: If somebody dedicated unblemished animals for the upkeep of the Temple, he violates a positive commandment[53]. Why also a prohibition? The verse says: "The Eternal spoke to Moses לאמר"[54]: a prohibition was pronounced[55], the words of Rebbi Jehudah. Rebbi was sitting and studying the rule that "a firstling cannot be substituted" when Bar Pedaiah's father was passing by. Rebbi saw him, and said, do I know what I should say here, "the Eternal spoke to Moses לאמר," could one explain the words of Rebbi Jehudah? Is it written thus? [56]It follows what Rebbi Immi said in the name of Rebbi Joḥanan: For interpretation, one removes from its beginning to its end. Rebbi Ḥanina in the name of Rebbi Jeremiah: Even a middle word[57]. "You have to pour oil on." You have to pour oil on a flour offering, to subject all flour offerings to pouring.

53 Lev. 27:9.

54 Lev. 27:1. It is assumed that this heading applies also to the paragraph Lev. 27:9-34 since v. 9 starts with a connecting ו.

55 "He said 'no'". The underlying pronunciation of לאמר cannot be recovered from the indications given here.

56 Soṭah 5:1 (ט), explained there in Notes 8-10, Horaiot 1:3 (ה).

57 In the application here, the word is split by duplication of a letter, לא אמר as לאמר.

(53d line 76) תַּמָּן תַּנִּינַן. שׁוֹם הַיְתוֹמִין שְׁלֹשִׁים יוֹם. שׁוֹם הֶקְדֵּשׁ שְׁלֹשִׁים יוֹם. וּמַכְרִיזִין בַּבּוֹקֶר וּבָעֶרֶב. אָמַר רְבִּי מָנָא. רְבִּי לִיעֶזֶר חָשֵׁשׁ עַל הָעֲרָמָה. רְבִּי יְהוֹשֻׁעַ לֹא חָשַׁשׁ עַל הָעֲרָמָה. אָמַר רְבִּי יוֹסֵי בֵּירְבִּי בּוּן. אַתְיָא דְּרְבִּי אֱלִיעֶזֶר כְּבֵית שַׁמַּי וּדְרְבִּי יְהוֹשֻׁעַ כְּבֵית הִלֵּל. דְּרְבִּי אֱלִיעֶזֶר כְּבֵית שַׁמַּי. דְּבֵית שַׁמַּי אוֹמְרִים. אָדָם נִשְׁאָל עַל הֶקְדֵּישׁוֹ. וְהוּא דַהֲוָה אָמַר. אֵינוֹ צָרִיךְ לְהַדִּיר הֲנָייָה. וּדְרְבִּי יְהוֹשֻׁעַ כְּבֵית הִלֵּל. דְּבֵית הִלֵּל אוֹמְרִים. אֵין אָדָם נִשְׁאָל עַל הֶקְדֵּישׁוֹ.

וְהוּא דַהֲוָה אָמַר. צָרִיךְ לְהַדִיר הֲנָיָיה. מַה נַפְשָׁךְ. תְּהֵא בוֹ הָאִישׁ הַזֶּה שֶׁיִּשְׁאַל עַל הֲנָיָיתוֹ. מוֹדֶה רִבִּי יְהוֹשֻׁעַ בְּעָרֵב שֶׁהוּא צָרִיךְ לְהַדִיר הֲנָיָיה. מָה אָמַר רִבִּי יְהוֹשֻׁעַ בְּמַתָּנָה. מִכֵּיוָן שֶׁהוּא נוֹתֵן מַתָּנָה בְּעַיִן יָפָה אֵינוֹ צָרִיךְ לְהַדִיר הֲנָיָיה. אוֹ מֵאַחַר שֶׁהוֹרַע כּוֹחוֹ וְהוּא חוֹזֵר בּוֹ צָרִיךְ לְהַדִיר הֲנָיָיה. נִישְׁמְעִינָהּ מִן הָדָא. קְרִיבְתֵּיהּ דְּרִבִּי חַגַּיי הֲוָה בַּעַל חַיָּיב קַרְטֵס. אָתָא מָרֵי חוֹבָא וְטָרַף. אָתָא עוֹבְדָא קוֹמֵי דְרִבִּי אָחָא. אָמַר. צָרִיךְ לְהַדִיר הֲנָיָיה. רִבִּי יוֹסֵי אָמַר. אֵין צָרִיךְ לְהַדִיר הֲנָיָיה. אָמְרִין חֲבֵרַיָּיא קוֹמֵי רִבִּי אָחָא רִבִּי יוֹסֵי. יָאוֹת אָמַר רִבִּי אָחָא. דְּאִין חָזַר הוּא עֲלֵיהּ לֹא אָתָא מָרֵי חוֹבָא וְטָרַף. אָמַר לוֹן רִבִּי יוֹסֵי. עַבְדָא לוֹן תַּכְשִׁיטִין עַבְדָּא לוֹן פָּרָה פְרָנוֹן. אָמַר רִבִּי חַגַּיי. מֹשֶׁה. יָאוֹת אָמַר רִבִּי יוֹסֵי. וּנְפַק עוֹבְדָא כְּרִבִּי אָחָא.

There, we have stated[58]: "The public sale of orphans' property[59] goes on for 30 days, the public sale of Temple property[60] goes on for 30 days, and they are publicly announced mornings and evenings." Rebbi Mana said, Rebbi Eliezer is afraid of trickery[61], Rebbi Joshua is not afraid of trickery. Rebbi Yose ben Rebbi Abun said, Rebbi Eliezer follows the House of Shammai and Rebbi Joshua the House of Hillel[62]. Rebbi Eliezer follows the House of Shammai, since the House of Shammai say, a person may ask about his dedication; could he say that he does not have to vow usufruct?[63] Rebbi Joshua follows the House of Hillel, since the House of Hillel say, a person may not ask about his dedication; could he say that he has to vow usufruct[64]? In any case, could not a man ask about his vow of usufruct?[65] Rebbi Joshua agrees that a guarantor must execute a vow of usufruct[66]. What does Rebbi Joshua say about a gift? Since he gives voluntarily, he does not have to vow usufruct, or since [the recipient's] power is small and [the donor] may change his mind, does he have to vow usufruct? Let us hear from the following: The husband of a relative of Rebbi Ḥaggai owed on a document[67]. The creditor came and foreclosed. The case[68] came before Rebbi Aḥa, who said, he[69] owes a vow of usufruct. Rebbi Yose said, he does not have to vow usufruct. The colleagues said before Rebbi Aḥa [and] Rebbi Yose: Does Rebbi Aḥa say it correctly? Since if he takes her back, does not the creditor come and foreclose[70]? Rebbi Yose said to them, she turns it into jewelry or keeps it as additions to her dowry[71]. Rebbi Ḥaggai said, by Moses! Rebbi Yose says it correctly. It was executed following Rebbi Aḥa[72].

58 Mishnah *Arakhin* 6:1. The argument refers to the part of the Mishnah which is not quoted: "The public sale of orphans' property goes on for 30 days, the public sale of Temple property goes on for 30 days, and one publicly announces mornings and evenings. If somebody dedicates his property while the lien if favor of a wife's *ketubah* was in effect, Rebbi Eliezer says, if he would divorce her, he has to make her vow not to have any usufruct from him; Rebbi Joshua says, it is not necessary. Similarly, Rabban Simeon ben Gamliel says regarding a guarantor of a woman's *ketubah* whose husband divorces her, that he shall make him execute a vow of usufruct lest he could plot against his property and take his wife back."

59 The administrator of an estate whose beneficiaries are underage can sell real estate to satisfy claims against the estate only under supervision by the court. There has to be a 30 day public notice of the land being up for sale; at the end of the period the parcel is sold to the highest bidder.

60 Sale of real estate donated to the Temple.

61 If the wife has to vow not to have any future usufruct from her past husband in order to collect her *ketubah* from the Temple, she cannot remarry him. R. Eliezer suspects that a husband who donates his property to the Temple might want to get it back by divorcing his wife, waiting until she has collected her *ketubah*, then remarrying her and receiving the *ketubah* money as dowry.

62 He disagrees with R. Mana and holds that their differences are systemic. This is the only opinion quoted in the Babli, *'Arakhin* 23a.

63 This text seems to be corrupt. Since in our Mishnah, the House of Shammai hold that dedication in error is valid, it is clear that they must hold that a vow of dedication cannot be abrogated by an Elder (cf. *Nedarim*, Introduction p. 422, Chapter 9).

Therefore, the text must read: דְּבֵית שַׁמַּי אוֹמְרִים. אֵין אָדָם נִשְׁאָל עַל הֶקְדֵּשׁוֹ. וְהוּא דַהֲוָה אָמַר. אֵינוּ צָרִיךְ לְהַדִּיר הֲנָיָיה. וּדְרִבִּי יְהוֹשֻׁעַ כְּבֵית הִלֵּל. דְּבֵית הִלֵּל אוֹמְרִים. אָדָם נִשְׁאָל עַל הֶקְדֵּשׁוֹ. וְהוּא דַהֲוָה אָמַר. צָרִיךְ לְהַדִּיר הֲנָיָיה. "Rebbi Eliezer follows the House of Shammai, since the House of Shammai say, a person may *not* ask about his dedication; could he say that he does not have to vow ususfruct? Rebbi Joshua follows the House of Hillel, since the House of Hillel say, a person *may ask* about his dedication; could he say that he has to vow usufruct?" The "vow of usufruct" is a vow never to have any usufruct from the person designated in the vow.

64   Since he could ask an Elder about his vow, he does not need any tricks.

65   R. Eliezer should agree that a man who cannot have his dedication annulled may try to have his vow of usufruct annulled.

66   R. Joshua will agree that the husband of a woman whose *ketubah* is collected from a third party has to promise never to take her back. It is not that the guarantor has to vow; he has to ask the divorcing couple for their vows.

67   Greek χάρτης, Latin *charta*, "papyrus, roll of papyrus".

68   After the foreclosure, the husband divorced his wife and she went to court to foreclose on the foreclosed parcel since the lien of her *ketubah* preceded the creditor's loan document.

69   The husband owes a vow of usufruct which will forbid him to remarry his wife in order to permit the wife to collect her *ketubah*.

70   If the husband should remarry his divorcee, would not her property become the husband's property as dowry, and could not the creditor then foreclose it for his claim? It seems that the creditor loses nothing if there is no vow.

71   Cf. *Ketubot* 5:10, Note 218. Before the marriage, they sign a stipulation that the husband shall have no rights to the property. Then the creditor would be left without recourse.

72   In this and similar cases, the husband has to deliver a vow which forbids him any future usufruct from his divorcee.

(54a line 16) תַּמָּן אַתְּ אָמַר. תֵּצֵא וְתִרְעֶה בָעֵדֶר. וְכָא אַתְּ אָמַר אָכֵין. אָמַר רִבִּי יוֹסֵי בְּרִבִּי בּוּן. תַּמָּן לִנְזִירוּתוֹ נִשְׁאַל. מִכּוֹחַ נְזִירוּת יָצְאוּ קָרְבְּנוֹתָיו לַחוּלִין.

There[73], you say: "It shall leave and graze with the herd." And here, you say so[74]? Rebbi Yose ben Rebbi Abun said, there he asked about his vow of *nazir*. Because of the vow of *nazir*[75] did his sacrifices become profane.

---

[73] Mishnah 4. If a person makes a vow of *nazir*, designates an animal as his sacrifice at completion, and then asks about his vow and has it annulled, the animal becomes profane.

[74] Should not the House of Shammai hold that the animal must remain dedicated if it was designated even in error?

[75] There never was a direct dedication of the animal, only a designation as *nazir* sacrifice. If there is no *nazir*, there is no sacrifice. The Babli rejects this argument and holds (9a) either that for the House of Shammai there can be no dissolution of a vow of *nazir* because there can be no dissolution of a dedication, or (32a) for the House of Hillel substitutions can be revoked.

(54a line 18) רִבִּי יִרְמְיָה בְּשֵׁם רִבִּי חוּנָה רִבִּי חִזְקִיָּה רִבִּי אָחָא בְּשֵׁם רִבִּי יוֹחָנָן. כָּל־עַמָּא מוֹדֵיי שֶׁאֵין נִשְׁאַל עַל תְּמוּרָתוֹ. מַה פְּלִיגִין. בְּהֶקְדֵּישׁוֹ. שֶׁבֵּית שַׁמַּי אוֹמְרִים. כְּשֵׁם שֶׁאֵין אָדָם נִשְׁאַל עַל תְּמוּרָתוֹ כָּךְ אֵין נִשְׁאַל עַל הֶקְדֵּישׁוֹ. בֵּית הִלֵּל אוֹמְרִים. אָדָם נִשְׁאַל עַל הֶקְדֵּישׁוֹ וְאֵין נִשְׁאַל עַל תְּמוּרָתוֹ.

Rebbi Jeremiah in the name of Rebbi Huna; Rebbi Ḥizqiah, Rebbi Aḥa, in the name of Rebbi Joḥanan: Everybody agrees that nobody can ask about his substitution[75,76]. Where do they disagree? About his dedication; for the House of Shammai say, since a person cannot ask about his substitution, he cannot ask about his dedication, but the House of Hillel say, a person can ask about his dedication but not about his substitution[77].

---

[76] No Elder has the power to annul a (forbidden) substitution.

[77] It is difficult to read *Lev.* 27:10 according to the House of Hillel but the interpretation is confirmed by the Babli, 31a.

(54a line 22) בִּי שִׁמְעוֹן בֶּן לָקִישׁ בְּשֵׁם בַּר קַפָּרָא. אִם תּוֹפְשׂוֹ מִשָּׁם שׁוֹר מִשָּׁם רִאשׁוֹן. שׁוֹר שָׁחוֹר שֶׁיֵּצֵא מִבַּיִת רִאשׁוֹן. וְיָצָא לָבָן וְיָצְאוּ שְׁחוֹרִין אַחֲרָיו. אַתְּ תּוֹפְשׂוֹ מִשּׁוּם רֹאשׁ לַשְּׁחוֹרִים. שׁוֹר לָבָן שֶׁיֵּצֵא מִבֵּיתִי רִאשׁוֹן. וְיָצָא שָׁחוֹר וְיָצְאוּ לְבָנִים אַחֲרָיו. אַתְּ תּוֹפְשׂוֹ מִשּׁוּם רֹאשׁ לַלְּבָנִים. שׁוֹר שֶׁעָמַד עַל הָאֵבוּס. וְנִמְצָא רָבוּץ. רָבוּץ. וְנִמְצָא עוֹמֵד. יְהֵא בָהּ כְּהָדָא דְּאָמַר רִבִּי אַבָּהוּ בְּשֵׁם רִבִּי יוֹחָנָן. נִתְכַּוֵּון לִתְרוֹם כְּרִי חִיטִּין וְתָרַם שְׂעוֹרִים. בַּלַּיְלָה לֹא עָשָׂה כְּלוּם. בַּיּוֹם מַה שֶּׁעָשָׂה עָשׂוּי. שְׁחַמְתִּית. וְנִמְצֵאת אַגְרוֹן. אֲפִילוּ בַּיּוֹם לֹא עָשָׂה כְּלוּם. אַיִל. לֹא כְלוּם. עֵגֶל. אִין. דִּכְתִיב וְעֵגֶל בֶּן בָּקָר לְחַטָּאת. כֶּבֶשׂ. לֹא כְלוּם. סְלָעִים. לֹא כְלוּם. פְּרוֹטְרוֹט. לֹא כְלוּם. דִּינַר זָהָב. קָדַשׁ.

Rebbi Simeon ben Laqish in the name of Bar Qappara: You catch him at the mention of "ox", at the mention of "first"[78]. "The black ox which comes out of my house first," if a white one came out and the black followed him, you catch him because he is the leader of the black ones. "The white ox which comes out of my house first," if a black one came out and the white followed him, you catch him because he is the leader of the white ones. "The ox which stands at the manger" and it was lying down, "lying down" and it was standing, should be like what Rebbi Abbahu said in the name of Rebbi Johanan: If he wanted to give heave from wheat and he gave from barley, during nighttime he did not do anything, during daytime, what he did is done[79]. Brown grain and it turned out to be white[80], even during daytime he did not do anything. "A ram" is nothing[81]. "A calf" yes, since it is written: "A calf of cattle as purification offering." "A sheep" is nothing. "Tetradrachmas" is nothing. "Change" is nothing[82]. "A gold denar"[83] was sanctified.

78   He denies that the reason of the House of Shammai be a comparison with the rules of substitutions but holds that they interpret any statement of dedication for the maximum benefit of the Temple (similar to the position of Rav Papa in the Babli, 32a).

79   Since at night he could not see

what he did, we have to take his word as expressing his intent. Therefore, the heave designated during nighttime is not sanctified. But during daytime, his action overrides his words and the heave from barley is sanctified. Similarly, the House of Shammai will sanctify the ox if the dedication was made under circumstances in which his action can override his words.

80 For the spelling and definition of these words, cf. *Peah* 2:5, Notes 85-86. אגרו, אגדו is human food, שחמתית שמחית usually is animal feed.

81 If he dedicated some kind of cattle but the animal coming out of his house was a goat or sheep, even the House of Shammai will agree that there was no dedication.

83 This refers to Mishnah 2. If he dedicated the first "denar" which he takes out of his wallet, the House of Shammai will agree that if he takes out only small change, none of which carries the denomination "denar", it is not dedicated. Also tetradrachmas are never called "denar". {*Denar* might mean "money" or "coin" in general. Denominations in late provincial usage may not correspond to standard values.}

84 Even though an unspecified "denar" in normal speech means "silver denar", the House of Hillel might agree that in a dedication it does apply to an aureus, a gold denar (in honest coin worth 25 silver denars) even though it is always referred to as "gold denar", not simply "denar".

משנה ד: מִי שֶׁנָּדַר בְּנָזִיר וְנִשְׁאַל לַחֲכָמִים וְאָסְרוּ מוֹנֶה מֵשָׁעָה שֶׁנָּדַר. (fol. 53c) נִשְׁאַל לַחֲכָמִים וְהִתִּירוּ הָיְתָה לוֹ בְהֵמָה מוּפְרֶשֶׁת תֵּצֵא וְתִרְעֶה בָעֵדֶר. אָמְרוּ בֵית הִלֵּל לְבֵית שַׁמַּאי אֵין אַתֶּם מוֹדִין בָּזֶה שֶׁהוּא הֶקְדֵּשׁ טָעוּת שֶׁתֵּצֵא וְתִרְעֶה בָעֵדֶר. אָמְרוּ לָהֶן בֵּית שַׁמַּאי אִי אַתֶּם מוֹדִין בְּמִי שֶׁטָּעָה וְקָרָא לַתְּשִׁיעִי עֲשִׂירִי וְלָעֲשִׂירִי תְּשִׁיעִי וּלְאַחַד עָשָׂר עֲשִׂירִי שֶׁהוּא מְקוּדָּשׁ. אָמְרוּ לָהֶן בֵּית הִלֵּל לֹא הַשֵּׁבֶט קִידְּשׁוֹ. וּמָה אִילוּ טָעָה וְהִנִּיחַ אֶת הַשֵּׁבֶט עַל הַשְּׁמִינִי וְעַל שְׁנֵים עָשָׂר שֶׁמָּא עָשָׂה כְלוּם. אֶלָּא כָּתוּב שֶׁקִּידֵּשׁ אֶת הָעֲשִׂירִי הוּא קִידֵּשׁ אֶת הַתְּשִׁיעִי וְאֶת אַחַד עָשָׂר.

Mishnah 4: A person who made a vow of *nazir,* asked the Sages and they forbade, counts from the moment of his vow[85]. If he asked the Sages and they permitted, if he had an animal designated, it leaves and grazes with the herd[73]. The house of Hillel said to the House of Shammai: Do you not agree that this is dedication in error, it leaves and grazes in the herd[86]? The House of Shammai anwered, do you not agree that if somebody erred and designated the ninth as the tenth, or the tenth as ninth, or the eleventh as tenth, it is sanctified[87]? The House of Hillel anwered, not the staff sanctified it, for if he erred and put his staff on the eighth or the twelfth, did he do anything? But the verse which sanctified the tenth sanctified the ninth and the eleventh[88].

85   He regretted his vow. When the vow was confirmed, the time of his regret is also counted.

86   Therefore, the principle announced in Mishnah 1 does not always apply.

87   Mishnah *Bekhorot* 9:8. Every tenth newborn animal of cattle, sheep, and goats has to be brought as sacrifice (*Lev.* 27:31). The sacrifice is eaten by the rancher and his family; the priests have no part in it. The verse requires that the animals be counted with a staff and the tenth be designated. If the rancher erred between 9, 10, 11, all animals involved are sanctified. But if the error was by a count of more than one, there is no dedication and the animals remain profane.

88   *Lev.* 27:31, interpreted in the Halakhah, the Babli *Bekhorot* 61a, and *Sifra Behuqqotay Pereq* 13(2).

(54a line 31) **הלכה ד**: מִי שֶׁנָּדַר בַּנָּזִיר כוֹל׳. תַּנֵּי. בֵּית שַׁמַּי אוֹמְרִים. מִשָּׁעָה שֶׁנִּשְׁאַל. וּבֵית הִלֵּל אוֹמְרִים. מִשָּׁעָה שֶׁנָּדַר. מַה נָן קַיָּימִין. אִם בְּשֶׁגִּילְגֵּל בְּנִזְרוֹ. כָּל־עַמָּא מוֹדֵיי מִשָּׁעָה שֶׁנִּשְׁאַל. אִם בְּשֶׁלֹּא גִּילְגֵּל בְּנִזְרוֹ. כָּל־עַמָּא מוֹדֵיי מִשָּׁעָה שֶׁנָּדַר. אֶלָּא כִּי נָן קַיָּימִין בְּשֶׁעָתִיד לִישָּׁאֵל. בֵּית שַׁמַּי אוֹמְרִים. מִכֵּיוָן שֶׁעָתִיד לִישָּׁאֵל מְנַלְגֵּל הוּא. וּבֵית הִלֵּל אוֹמְרִים. אִילּוּ גִילְגֵּל לֹא הָיָה נִשְׁאָל. הֲרֵי שֶׁנָּדַר וְהָיָה מְנַלְגֵּל בְּנִזְרוֹ אֵין נִשְׁאָלִין לוֹ אֶלָּא אִם כֵּן נָהַג בָּהֶן בְּאִיסּוּר כַּיָּמִים שֶׁנָּהַג

בָּהֶן בְּהֵיתֵר. דִּבְרֵי רִבִּי יוּדָה. אָמַר רִבִּי יָסָא. בַּמֶּה דְבָרִים אֲמוּרִים. בְּנִזְרוֹ מְרוּבֶּה. אֲבָל בְּנִזְרוֹ מְמוּעָט דַּייוֹ שְׁלֹשִׁים יוֹם. וּמַה בֵּין נִזְרוֹ מְרוּבֶּה לְנִזְרוֹ מְמוּעָט. אֶלָּא אָכֵן הוּא. בַּמֶּה דְבָרִים אֲמוּרִים. בִּזְמַן שֶׁגִּילְגֵּל בְּנִזְרוֹ זְמַן מְרוּבֶּה. אֲבָל גִּילְגֵּל בְּנִזְרוֹ זְמַן מְמוּעָט דַּייוֹ שְׁלֹשִׁים יוֹם. מַה נָן קַייְמִין. בְּשֶׁגִּילְגֵּל בְּטוּמְאָה כָּל־עַמָּא מוֹדֵיי שֶׁסָּתַר הַכֹּל. אִם בְּשֶׁלֹּא גִילְגֵּל בְּתִגְלַחַת כָּל־עַמָּא מוֹדֵיי שֶׁלֹּא סָתַר אֶלָּא ל יוֹם. אֶלָּא כֵּן אָנָן קַייְמִין בְּשֶׁגִּילְגֵּל בַּיַּיִן. בְּעוֹמֵד בְּתוֹךְ נְזִירוּתוֹ. אֲבָל בְּעוֹמֵד לְאַחַר נְזִירוּתוֹ אַכֹּל סָתַר.

Halakhah 4: "A person who made a vow of *nazir*," etc. It was stated[89]: The House of Shammai say, from the moment he asked; but the House of Hillel say, from the moment he vowed. Where do we hold? If he scoffed[90] at his vow, everybody agrees from the moment he asked[91]. If he did not scoff at his vow, everybody agrees from the moment he vowed. But we have to deal with one who is going to ask. The House of Shammai say, since he decided to ask, he is now scoffing. But the House of Hillel say, if he were scoffing, he would not ask. If he made a vow of *nazir* and scoffed at his vow, one does not let him ask about it unless he kept its prohibitions for the number of days he did not keep the prohibitions, the words of Rebbi Jehudah. Rebbi Yasa said, when has this been said? If he vowed a lengthy period[92]. But if he vowed a short period, thirty days are sufficient for him. What is the difference between a lengthy and a short period[93]? But it must be: When has this been said? If he scoffed at his vow for a lengthy period. But if he scoffed at his vow for a short period, thirty days are sufficient for him[94]. Where are we holding? If he scoffed in impurity, everybody agrees that he invalidated everything[95]. If he scoffed in shaving, everybody agrees that he invalidated only 30 days[96]. But we must deal with the case that he scoffed with wine[97]. That is, if he is still within his period of *nazir*. But after his period of *nazir*, he invalidated everything[98].

89   Tosephta 3:19, referring to the first sentence of the Mishnah.

90   For לגלג = גלגל cf. *Peah* 1:1, Note 178 (*Berakhot* 6:3, Note 130).

91   If he did not keep his vow, the time elapsed cannot be counted. The questions to be raised here are treated at the end of the paragraph.

92   More than 30 days.

93   In any case, one requires that he keep his vow the number of days for which he vowed.

94   The minimum of a *nazir* vow.

95   Since the impurity of the dead invalidates a vow of *nazir* by biblical decree.

96   Since the *nazir* for many periods shaves every thirty days, Mishnah 1:4.

97   This is forbidden for the *nazir*; he is whipped if his transgression is observed by two witnesses after due warning. Biblical law contains no instructions which would require him to continue his vow for additional days. R. Jehudah's rule which requires him to continue for an additional time, equal to that in which he disregarded the prohibition of wine, is purely rabbinical.

98   It follows from R. Jehudah's rule that he has to start anew if he disregarded the prohibition of wine during the entire prior period of his vow.

(54a line 45) תַּמָּן תַּנִינָן. קָרָא לַתְּשִׁיעִי עֲשִׂירִי וְלַעֲשִׂירִי תְּשִׁיעִי וּלְאַחַד עָשָׂר עֲשִׂירִי. שְׁלָשְׁתָּן מְקוּדָּשִׁין. הַתְּשִׁיעִי נֶאֱכַל בְּמוּמוֹ וְהָעֲשִׂירִי מַעֲשֵׂר וְאַחַד עָשָׂר קָרֵב שְׁלָמִים. יִהְיֶה קֹדֶשׁ. מְלַמֵּד שֶׁהַקְּדוּשָׁה חָלָה עַל הַתְּשִׁיעִי וְעַל אַחַד עָשָׂר. יָכוֹל יִקְרְבוּ שְׁנֵיהֶן. תַּלְמוּד לוֹמַר בָּקָר. בָּקָר לָרַבּוֹת אַחַד עָשָׂר. בֶּן בָּקָר לְהוֹצִיא אֶת הַתְּשִׁיעִי. מָה רָאִיתָ לְרַבּוֹת אַחַד עָשָׂר וּלְהוֹצִיא תְּשִׁיעִי. אַחַר שֶׁרִיבָּה הַכָּתוּב מִיעֵט. שֶׁתִּימְצָא אוֹמֵר. אֵימָתַי הַקּוֹדֶשׁ עוֹשֶׂה תְמוּרָה לְפָנָיו אוֹ לְאַחֲרָיו. הֱוֵי אוֹמֵר. לְאַחֲרָיו. מַרְבֶּה אֲנִי אַחַד עָשָׂר שֶׁהוּא אַחַר הַקְּדוּשָׁה. וּמוֹצִיא אֲנִי אֶת הַתְּשִׁיעִי שֶׁהוּא לִפְנֵי הַקְּדוּשָׁה.

There[99], we have stated: "If he called the ninth tenth, and the tenth ninth, and the eleventh tenth, all three are sanctified. The ninth may be eaten when it develops a defect[100], the tenth is tithe, the eleventh is brought as well-being sacrifice[101]." "It shall be holy"[102], this teaches that holiness falls on the ninth and the eleventh. [103]I could think that both of them should be sacrificed, the verse says "cattle"[104], "cattle" to include the eleventh. "From the cattle"[105], to exclude the ninth. What reason do you have to include the eleventh and to exclude the ninth? After the verse included, it excluded. You can argue, when are sanctified [animals] subject to substitution[106]? Before[107] or after? One has to say, afterwards. I am including the eleventh which is after sanctification and I am excluding the ninth which is before sanctification.

99 Mishnah *Bekhorot* 9:8. This starts the discussion of the rules of animal tithes (Note 87).

100 As explained later in this paragraph, the ninth is holy but is not dedicated as a sacrifice. Therefore, it is barred from becoming a sacrifice. The owner has to wait until it develops a blemish (which will be automatic with age); then it can be redeemed and eaten under the rules of profane slaughter.

101 It is holy and a sacrifice, but not tithe. Therefore, the priest's parts are due from it.

102 *Lev.* 27:32: "About tithes of cattle and flocks, anything which passes under the staff, the tenth shall be holy for the Eternal." Since the determination of which animal is the tenth is not automatic, any which either is the tenth or is designated as the tenth by the rancher's staff is holy.

103 Babli *Bekhorot* 61a, *Sifra Wayyiqra Pereq* 16(4).

104 *Lev.* 3:1, speaking of well-being sacrifices.

105 In all situations, the expression מן "*from*" is interpreted to mean: "Not all." It is then a problem of rabbinic interpretation to determine which kinds are excluded. Since the expression "*from* the cattle" mentioned in *Lev.* 1:3 was used to exclude animals used for sinful purposes [*Sifra Wayyiqra Parsheta* 2(7)], the expression used here can be taken to apply to other situations.

106 Substitutions of tithe animals are mentioned in *Lev.* 27:33.

107 There can be no substitution for an animal which has not yet been designated as sacrifice since that would be a purely profane operation.

(54a line 54) עַד כְּדוֹן כְּסָבוּר בּוֹ שֶׁהוּא עֲשִׂירִי וְקָרוּי עֲשִׂירִי. הָיָה יוֹדֵעַ בּוֹ שֶׁהוּא תְּשִׁיעִי וְקַרְיָין עֲשִׂירִי. חֲבְרַיָּיה אָמְרִין. קָדַשׁ. רִבִּי יוּדָן אָמַר. לֹא קָדַשׁ. מַתְנִיתָא מְסַיְּיעָא לַחֲבְרַיָּיה. אָמְרוּ בֵית הִלֵּל לְבֵית שַׁמַּי. אֵין אַתֶּם מוֹדִין. שֶׁתֵּצֵא וְתִרְעֶה בָעֵדֶר. אָמְרוּ לָהֶן בֵּית שַׁמַּי. אֵי אַתֶּם מוֹדִין בְּמִי שֶׁטָעָה וְקָרָא לַתְּשִׁיעִי עֲשִׂירִי וְלַעֲשִׂירִי תְּשִׁיעִי וּלְאֶחָד עָשָׂר עֲשִׂירִי שֶׁהוּא מְקוּדָּשׁ. וְאֵינָן מְקַבְּלִין מִינְהוֹן. דְּלֹא כֵן יְתִיבוּנוֹן. מָה אַתֶּם מְשִׁיבִין אוֹתָנוּ מִן דָּבָר שֶׁהָיָה קָדוֹשׁ שֶׁלֹא בְטָעוּת עַל דָּבָר שֶׁהוּא קָדוֹשׁ בֵּין בְּטָעוּת בֵּין שֶׁלֹא בְטָעוּת. כַּיי דְּמַר רִבִּי אַמִּי. עֲשִׁירֵי הֲווֹ בִתְשׁוּבָה. אוֹ יֵיבָא כַּיי דְּמַר רִבִּי נָסָא. כְּאֵינָשׁ דְּאִית לֵיהּ תְּרֵין טַעֲמִין וּמָתִיב חַד מִנְהוֹן.

So far, if he thought that it was the tenth which he called "tenth". If he knew that it was the ninth and called it "tenth"? The colleagues say, it is sanctified. Rebbi Yudan said, it is not sanctified[108]. The Mishnah supports the colleagues: "The House of Hillel said to the House of Shammai: Do you not agree that it leaves and grazes with the herd? The House of Shammai anwered them, do you not agree that if somebody erred and designated the ninth as the tenth, or the tenth as ninth, or the eleventh as tenth, it is sanctified." And they do not accept it! Otherwise, they could have answered: Why do you answer us from something which is sanctified only if not in [willful] error about something which will be sanctified both in error and not in error! As Rebbi Immi said, they were rich in answer[109], or as Rebbi Nasa said, like somebody who has two reasons and he responds by giving one of them.

108 In the Babli, 32a, the different opinions are quoted in the name of Babylonian authorities.

109 The Talmudim never exhaust all possible arguments but quote only one. The text is better in *Pesaḥim* 6:2 (32b): עֲשִׁירִין הֲווֹ בִתְשׁוּבוֹת.

משנה ה: מִי שֶׁנָּזַר בַּנָּזִיר וְהָלַךְ לְהָבִיא אֶת בְּהֶמְתּוֹ וּמְצָאָהּ שֶׁנִּגְנְבָה (fol. 53c)
אִם עַד שֶׁלֹּא נִגְנְבָה בְהֶמְתּוֹ נָזַר הֲרֵי זֶה נָזִיר. וְאִם מִשֶּׁנִּגְנְבָה בְהֶמְתּוֹ נָזַר אֵינוֹ
נָזִיר. זוֹ טָעוּת טָעָה נַחוּם אִישׁ הַמָּדִי כְּשֶׁעָלוּ נְזִירִין מִן הַגּוֹלָה וּמָצְאוּ בֵית
הַמִּקְדָּשׁ חָרֵב אָמַר לָהֶם נַחוּם אִישׁ הַמָּדִי אִילּוּ הֱיִיתֶם יוֹדְעִים שֶׁבֵּית הַמִּקְדָּשׁ
עָתִיד לִיחָרֵב נוֹזְרִין הֱיִיתֶם. אָמְרוּ לוֹ לָאו וְהִתִּירָן נַחוּם אִישׁ הַמָּדִי. וּכְשֶׁבָּא
דָבָר אֵצֶל חֲכָמִים אָמְרוּ כָּל־שֶׁנָּזַר עַד שֶׁלֹּא חָרַב בֵּית הַמִּקְדָּשׁ נָזִיר וּמִשֶּׁחָרַב
בֵּית הַמִּקְדָּשׁ אֵינוֹ נָזִיר.

Mishnah 5: A person vowed to be a *nazir* and went to bring his animal[110] when he found that it was stolen; if he vowed before the animal was stolen he is a *nazir*, after the animal was stolen he is not a *nazir*[111]. This error was made by Naḥum from Media: When *nezirim* came from the Diaspora[112] and found that the Temple had been destroyed, Naḥum from Media asked them: If you had known that the Temple would be destroyed, would you have made a vow of *nazir*[113]? They said to him, no, and Naḥum from Media permitted them. When the case came before the Sages they said, anyone who made his vow before the Temple was destroyed is a *nazir*, after the Temple was destroyed he is not a *nazir*.

110   And from the start it was his intention to use this animal as his sacrifice at the end of the period of *nezirut*.

111   Since the vow was made in error.

112   The Parthian empire, which was not touched by the Jewish revolt.

113   The question was legitimate for R. Eliezer (Mishnah *Nedarim* 9:2) who admits that people may ask to annul a vow because of unforeseeable circumstances, but the anonymous majority forbid this kind of question.

(54a line 63) **הלכה ה**: מִי שֶׁנָּזַר בַּנָּזִיר וְהָלַךְ לְהָבִיא אֶת בְּהֶמְתּוֹ כול׳. מָה אָנָן
קַיָּימִין. אִם בְּשֶׁרָאָה בְהֶמָה עוֹבֶרֶת בַּשּׁוּק וְאָמַר. הֲרֵינִי נָזִיר עַל בְּהֵמָה זֹאת
שֶׁעֲבָרָה. אֲפִילוּ מִשֶּׁנִּגְנְבָה בְהֶמָה נָזִיר. אִם כִּסְבוּר שֶׁיֵּשׁ לוֹ וְנִמְצָא שֶׁאֵין לוֹ. כָּךְ
אָנוּ אוֹמְרִים. הָיָה עָשִׁיר וְהֶעֱנִי תִּפָּקַע מִמֶּנּוּ נְזִירוּתוֹ. אֶלָּא אָכֵן אֲנַן קַיָּימִין.

בָּאוֹמֵר. הֲרֵינִי נָזִיר עַל בְּהֵמָה שֶׁיֵּשׁ לִי בְתוֹךְ הַבַּיִת. וְהָלַךְ וּמְצָאָהּ שֶׁנִּגְנְבָה. אִם עַד שֶׁלֹּא נִגְנְבָה הַבְּהֵמָה נָזַר הֲרֵי זֶה נָזִיר. אִם מִשֶּׁנִּגְנְבָה הַבְּהֵמָה נָזַר אֵין זֶה נָזִיר. תַּלְמִידוֹהִי דְּרִבִּי חִייָה בַּר לוּלְיָינָא אֲמְרִין. רִבִּי יוּדָה שָׁאֵל. הֶחֱזִירוּהָ הַגַּנָּבִים בַּלַּיְלָה. לְמַפְרֵעַ חָזַר עָלָיו נְזִירוּתוֹ אוֹ מִכָּן וָלְבָא.

Halakhah 5: "If a person vowed to be a *nazir* and went to bring his animal," etc. Where do we hold? If he saw an animal passing on the market and said, I am a *nazir* on that animal which passed by, he is a *nazir* even if the animal was stolen[114]. If he thought that he had one and it turned out that he did not, would we say if he was rich and became poor, the *nezirut* would be invalidated? But we must hold that he said, I am a *nazir* on the animal I have at home, then went and found it stolen. If he vowed before the animal was stolen he is a *nazir*, after the animal was stolen he is not a *nazir*. The students of Rebbi Ḥiyya bar Julianus say: Rebbi Jehudah asked: If the thieves returned it in the night, did his *nezirut* return to him retroactively[115] or for the future[116]?

114 Since the animal was not his and he could not be sure that the owners would sell it to him, his vow was not dependent on that animal (unless he would spell out that he would not be a *nazir* unless the animal was sold to him).

115 From the moment of his vow.

116 He has to start anew from the moment the animal was returned. No answer is given.

(54a line 72) זוֹ טָעוּת טָעָה נַחוּם אִישׁ הַמָּדִי. מַה טָעָה. שֶׁפָּתַח לָהֶם בְּנוֹלָד. אָמַר לָהֶם נַחוּם אִישׁ הַמָּדִי. אִילוּ הָיִיתֶם יוֹדְעִין שֶׁבֵּית הַמִּקְדָּשׁ עָתִיד לִיחָרֵב נוֹדְרִין הָיִיתֶם. אָמַר רִבִּי זְעִירָא. הֲוָה צָרִיךְ מֵימַר לוֹן. לֹא הָיִיתֶם יוֹדְעִין שֶׁכְּבָר נִתְנַבְּאוּ הַנְּבִיאִים לָכֶם שֶׁבֵּית הַמִּקְדָּשׁ עָתִיד לִיחָרֵב. לֹא הֲוַות כְּנוֹלָד. אָמַר לוֹן רִבִּי הִילָא. עוֹד הוּא כְּנוֹלָד. יָכְלִין הֲווֹן מֵימַר. יָדְעִין הֲוֵינָן. אֶלָּא הֲוֵינָן סָבְרִין דְּמִילַיָּיא רְחִיקִין. הֶחָזוֹן אֲשֶׁר הוּא חוֹזֶה לְיָמִים רַבִּים.

1 איש - (2 times) | להם | להן (2 times) 3 הייתם | הייתם להיות נזירין זעירא |
זעורה הוה | הכין הוה לא הייתם יודעין שכבר נתנאו הנביאים לכם שבית המקדש
עתיד ליחרב | לא הייתם יודעין שניבאו לכם נביאים הראשונים בזמן שבית המקדש קיים
שעתיד ליחרב 4 הוות | הוה 5 אמ' לון ר' הילא | אמ' ר' הילא כנולד | בנולד
6 הויין | דהויין 7 לימים רבים | לימים רבים ולעיתים רחוקות

[117]"That was the error of Nahum from Media." What was his error? That he found for them an opening due to changed circumstances. "Nahum from Media said to them: 'Would you have made a vow to become *nezirim* if you had known that the Temple would be destroyed at some future time?'" Rebbi Ze'ira said, the following he should have said to them: Did you not know that the prophets already had prophesied that eventually the Temple would be destroyed? Then there are no changed circumstances. Rebbi Hila said, still it is changed circumstances. They could have said to him, we knew it, but it seemed to us that this referred to the distant future: "The vision he sees is for many years."

117 *Nedarim* 9:2, Notes 48-49.

(54b line 2) תַּנֵּי. שְׁלֹשׁ מֵאוֹת נְזִירִין עָלוּ בִּימֵי שִׁמְעוֹן בֶּן שָׁטַח. מֵאָה וַחֲמִשִּׁים מָצְאוּ לָהֶן פֶּתַח. וּמֵאָה וַחֲמִשִּׁים לֹא מָצְאוּ לָהֶן פֶּתַח. אָתָא גַּבֵּי יַנַּאי מַלְכָּא. אֲמַר לֵיהּ. אִית הָכָא תְּלַת מְאוֹוָן נְזִירִין בְּעֵיי תְּשַׁע מְאוֹוָן קָרְבָּנִין. הַב אַתְּ פַּלְגָּא מִן דִּידָךְ וַאֲנָא פַּלְגָּא מִן דִּידִי. שָׁלַח לֵיהּ אַרְבַּע מְאָה וְחַמְשִׁין. אֲזַל לִשְׁנָא בִּישָׁא אֲמַר לֵיהּ. לָא יְהַב מִדִּידֵיהּ כְּלוּם. שָׁמַע יַנַּאי מַלְכָּא וְכָעַס. שָׁמַע שִׁמְעוֹן בֶּן שָׁטַח וְעָרַק. לְבָתַר יוֹמִין סַלְקִין בְּנֵי נָשׁ רַבְרְבִין מִמַּלְכוּתָא דְפָרֵס. אָמְרוּ לֵיהּ. נְהִירִין הֲוֵינָן דַּהֲוָה הָכָא חַד גַּבְרָא סָב וַהֲוָה אָמַר קוֹמֵינָן מִילִּין דְּחָכְמָה. תַּנֵּי לוֹן עוּבְדָא. אָמְרוּ לוֹן שְׁלַח וְאַייְתִיתֵיהּ. שָׁלַח יְהַב לֵיהּ מִילָה וְאַייְתִיתֵיהּ. אָתָא יְתַב לֵיהּ בֵּין מַלְכָּא לְמַלְכְּתָא. אֲמַר לֵיהּ. לָמָּה אַפְלֵיתָה בִּי. אֲמַר לֵיהּ אֲנָא לָא אַפְלֵיתִי בָךְ. אַתְּ מִמָּמוֹנָךְ וַאֲנָא מִן אוֹרַייָתִי. דִּכְתִיב כִּי בְּצֵל הַחָכְמָה בְּצֵל הַכֶּסֶף. אֲמַר לֵיהּ. וְלָמָּה עֲרַקְתְּ. אֲמַר לֵיהּ. שְׁמָעִית דְּמָרִי כְּעַס עָלַי וְקַיֵּימִית

הָדֵין קְרָא חֲבִי כִּמְעַט רֶגַע עַד יַעֲבָר זָעַם. וּקְרָא עֲלוֹי. וְיִתְרוֹן דַּעַת הַחָכְמָה תְּחַיֶּה בְעָלֶיהָ. אֲמַר לֵיהּ. וְלָמָּה יָתְבַתְּ בֵּין מַלְכָּא לְמַלְכְּתָא. אֲמַר לֵיהּ. בְּסִיפְרָא דְּבַר סִירָא כְּתִיב. סַלְסְלֶיהָ וּתְרוֹמְמֶךָּ וּבֵין נְגִידִים תּוֹשִׁיבֶךָ. אֲמַר לֵיהּ. הַב כַּסָּא וְנִיבְרִיךְ. יָבוֹן לֵיהּ כַּסָּא וְאָמַר. נְבָרֵךְ עַל הַמָּזוֹן שֶׁאָכַל יַנַּאי וַחֲבֵירָיו. אֲמַר לֵיהּ. וּמָה נֵימוֹר. עַל הַמָּזוֹן שֶׁלֹּא אָכַלְנוּ. אֲמַר. יֵיבוּן לֵיהּ וְיֵיכוֹל. יָבוֹן לֵיהּ וְאָכַל. וְאָמַר. נְבָרֵךְ עַל הַמָּזוֹן שֶׁאֲכַלְנוּ. אֲמַר רִבִּי יוֹחָנָן. חֲלוּקִין עַל שִׁמְעוֹן בֶּן שָׁטַח. רִבִּי יִרְמְיָה אֲמַר. עַל הָרִאשׁוֹנָה. רִבִּי בָּא אֲמַר עַל הַשְּׁנִיָּיה. מֵחֲלָפָא שִׁיטָתֵיהּ דְּרִבִּי יִרְמְיָה. תַּמָּן צְרִיכָה לֵיהּ וָכָא פְּשִׁיטָא לֵיהּ. הֵן דִּצְרִיכָא לֵיהּ כְּרַבָּנָן. הֵן דִּפְשִׁיטָא לֵיהּ כְּרַבָּן שִׁמְעוֹן בֶּן גַּמְלִיאֵל. דְּתַנֵּי. עָלָה הֵיסֵב וְטִבֵּל עִמָּהֶן אַף עַל פִּי שֶׁלֹּא אָכַל עִמָּהֶן כְּזַיִת דָּגָן מְזַמְּנִין דִּבְרֵי חֲכָמִים. רִבִּי יַעֲקֹב בַּר אָחָא בְּשֵׁם רִבִּי יוֹחָנָן. לְעוֹלָם אֵין מְזַמְּנִין עָלָיו עַד שֶׁיֹּאכַל כְּזַיִת דָּגָן. דְּתַנֵּי. שְׁנַיִם בְּפַת וְאֶחָד בַּיָּרָק מְזַמְּנִין. מַתְנִיתָה דְּרַבָּן שִׁמְעוֹן בֶּן גַּמְלִיאֵל.

1 שמעון | ר' שמעון   מצאו | מצא (2 times)   מאוון | מאה (2 times)   3   הב | אלא יהב   5 אמר | ומר   מדידה | מן דידיה   שמע | דחל   6 לבתר | בתר   סלקין | סלקון ממלכותא דפרס | מן מלכותא דפרס גבי ינאי מלכא   אמרו ליה | מן דיתבין אכלין אמרין ליה   7 הוינן דהוה חד גברא סב והוה אמר קומינן | אנן דהוה הכא חד גבר סב והוה אמר קומין   8 אמרו לון | אמרין ליה   והב ליה מילה | ויהב בי מילא   אייתיתיה | -   9 אתא יתיב | ואתא ויתיב   אפלית | אפלייַת   11 אפליתי | אפליית   13 קרא | קרייא   14 בר סירא | בן סירא   15 אמ' ליה. הב כסא ונבריך | אמ'. הבו ליה כסא דלבריך   יבון ליה כסא ומר | נסב כסא ומר   ינאי | יניי   אס' ליה | אמ' ליה. עד כדון את בקשיותך. אמ' ליה.   17נימור | נאמ'   ייבון | הבון   יבון | יהבו   אמעון | ר' שמעון   20 תמן | התם   וכא | וכה   21 דתני | תני   וטבל | ואכל   22 עמהן | -   דתני | תני בפת | פת   23 בירק | ירק   דרבן | כרבן

¹¹⁸It has been stated: 300 *nezirim* came in the days of Rebbi Simeon ben Shetaḥ. For 150 of them he found an opening, for 150 of them he did not find an opening. He came to king Yannai and said to him: There are here 300 *nezirim* who need 900 sacrifices. You should give half of them from your side, I shall give half from my side. The king sent him 450 animals. An informer went around and said that the other one had not

given anything from his own money. King Yannai heard about it and got angry. Simeon ben Shetah heard and fled. After some time, important people from the Persian empire came to king Yannai. They said to him: We remember that there was an old man who gave us a rabbinic discourse. They said to him, send and bring him! He sent and gave him his word; he came and sat between king and queen. He said to him, why did you trick me? He said, I did not trick you; you with your money and I with my learning, as it is written (*Eccl.* 7:12) "In the shadow of wisdom, in the shadow of money." He said to him, why did you disappear? He said to him, I heard that my lord was angry with me and I wanted to fulfill the verse (*Is.* 26:20) "Hide a little bit until the rage passes;" he used about himself (*Eccl.* 7:12): "Knowledge is an advantage, wisdom lets its possessor live." He said to him, why did you sit between king and queen? He said to him, it is written in the book of Ben Sirach: "Esteem it and it will raise you and seat you among princes." He said, bring him a cup that he may recite Grace. They brought him a cup and he said: "Let us give praise for the food that Yannai and his company ate." He said to him, what should I say, "for the food that we did not eat?" He said, bring him something that he may eat. They brought, he ate and recited: "For the food that we ate."

119Rebbi Yohanan said, his colleagues disagree with Simeon ben Shetah. Rebbi Jeremiah said, about the first action; Rebbi Abba said, about the second action. Rebbi Jeremiah seems to contradict himself! There he wondered about it and here it is obvious for him! He wondered following the Sages; it is obvious to him following Rabban Simeon ben Gamliel. We have stated about this: If one came, was lying on a couch, and dipped with them, even if he did not eat grain the volume of an olive one 'invites' with him, the words of the Sages. Rebbi Jacob bar Aha in the name of

Rebbi Yoḥanan: One never 'invites' anyone unless he has eaten grain the volume of an olive. But did we not formulate, "two [eating] bread and one [eating] vegetable, then one 'invites'?" This *baraita* follows Rabban Simeon ben Gamliel.

118 *Berakhot* 7:2, Notes 79-90.
119 This paragraph has no place here, it refers to the discussion in *Berakhot*.

(fol. 53c) **משנה ו:** הָיוּ מְהַלְּכִין בַּדֶּרֶךְ וְאֶחָד בָּא כְּנֶגְדָּן אָמַר אֶחָד מֵהֶן הֲרֵינִי נָזִיר שֶׁזֶּה אִישׁ פְּלוֹנִי. וְאֶחָד אָמַר הֲרֵינִי נָזִיר שֶׁאֵינוֹ הוּא. הֲרֵינִי נָזִיר שֶׁאֶחָד מִכֶּם נָזִיר שֶׁאֵין אֶחָד מִכֶּם נָזִיר שֶׁשְּׁנֵיכֶם נְזִירִין שֶׁכּוּלְּכֶם נְזִירִין. בֵּית שַׁמַּאי אוֹמְרִים כּוּלָּן נְזִירִין. וּבֵית הִלֵּל אוֹמְרִים אֵינוֹ נָזִיר אֶלָּא מִי שֶׁלֹּא נִתְקַיְּימוּ דְּבָרָיו. וְרִבִּי טַרְפוֹן אוֹמֵר אֵין אֶחָד מֵהֶן נָזִיר.

Mishnah 6: If they were walking on the road and a person came towards them when one said, "I am a *nazir* unless he is Mr. X", and another said, "I am a *nazir* if it is not he"; "I am a *nazir* unless one of you is a *nazir*", "unless both of you are *nezirim*", "unless all of you are *nezirim*". The House of Shammai say, they are all *nezirim*[120], but the House of Hillel say, only those whose assertions prove wrong are *nezirim*. Rebbi Țarphon said, none of them is a *nazir*[121].

(fol. 53d) **משנה ז:** הִרְתִּיעַ לַאֲחוֹרָיו אֵינוֹ נָזִיר. רִבִּי שִׁמְעוֹן אוֹמֵר אִם הָיָה כִּדְבָרַי הֲרֵינִי נָזִיר חוֹבָה. וְאִם לָאו הֲרֵינִי נָזִיר נְדָבָה. רָאָה אֶת הַכּוֹי וְאָמַר הֲרֵינִי נָזִיר שֶׁזֶּה חַיָּה הֲרֵינִי נָזִיר שֶׁאֵין זֶה חַיָּה. הֲרֵינִי נָזִיר שֶׁזֶּה בְּהֵמָה הֲרֵינִי נָזִיר שֶׁאֵין זֶה בְּהֵמָה. הֲרֵינִי נָזִיר שֶׁזֶּה חַיָּה וּבְהֵמָה. הֲרֵינִי נָזִיר שֶׁאֵין זֶה לֹא חַיָּה וְלֹא בְהֵמָה. הֲרֵינִי נָזִיר שֶׁאֶחָד מִכֶּם נָזִיר שֶׁאֵין אֶחָד מִכֶּם נָזִיר שֶׁשְּׁנֵיכֶם נְזִירִין הֲרֵי כּוּלָּם נְזִירִין.

Mishnah 7: If he suddenly returned, no one is a *nazir*[122]. Rebbi Simeon says, one[123] should say: If it was as I said, I am a *nazir* by obligation, otherwise I am a *nazir* voluntarily.

If one saw a *koy*[124] and said, "I am a *nazir* if this is a wild animal", "I am a *nazir* if this is not a wild animal"[125], "I am a *nazir* if this is a domestic animal", "I am a *nazir* if this is a not a domestic animal", "I am a *nazir* if this is a wild and domestic animal", "I am a *nazir* if this is neither a wild nor a domestic animal", "I am a *nazir* if one of you is a *nazir*", "if one of you is not a *nazir*", "if both of you are *nezirim*", then all of them are *nezirim*.

120 By their rule, anybody who said "I am a *nazir*" is a *nazir*, even if his condition was not satisfied.

121 Since *Num*. 6:2 requires that a vow of *nazir* be clearly expressed, but these people did mention *nazir* only to emphasize their statements, there is no valid vow.

122 This is a continuation of the previous Mishnah. The object of the disagreement of the travelers suddenly disappears and it is not possible to determine who is right and who is wrong, who should be a *nazir* and who should not.

123 Everyone whose vow is in doubt. On the one hand, not to fulfill one's vow is a grave sin; on the other hand, the sacrifices at the end of the period of *nezirut* can be offered only if they are due, otherwise the animals would be sinful profane offerings in the Temple. Therefore, it is necessary to offer a new vow which takes care of all possibilities.

124 An animal neither wild nor domesticated, which partially follows the rules of both kinds (Mishnah *Bikkurim* 2:9 ff., Note 154).

125 These are statements by different prople walking together. Since all assertions are more or less true, all persons involved are *nezirim*.

(54b line 27) **הלכה ו**: הָיוּ מְהַלְּכִין בַּדֶּרֶךְ כול'. כֵּינֵי מַתְנִיתָא. מִי שֶׁנִּתְקַיְימוּ דְּבָרִים. לָשׁוֹן הָפוּךְ הוּא. דְּלָא קַבְרָה בְּרָהּ.

Halakhah 6: "If they were walking on the road," etc. Should the Mishnah not read: "whose assertions are correct"?[126] It is language of opposites, "that she did not bury her son."[127]

[126] If Mishnah 6 is translated strictly literally, it reads: "I am a *nazir* if he is Mr. X", and another said, "I am a *nazir* if he is not"; "I am a *nazir* if one of you is a *nazir*", "if both of you are *nezirim*", "if all of you are *nezirim*". In that case, the House of Hillel should state that the ones whose statements are correct are *nezirim*.

[127] One does not want to express anything negative. A woman who is afraid for the life of her son will assert that she will not bury her son. A different explanation of the paragraph is given by J. N. Epstein, מבוא לנוסח המשנה² pp. 332-335, more in accordance with the Babli (32b-33a).

(54b line 29) תַּנֵּי. רִבִּי יוּדָה אוֹמֵר מִשּׁוּם רִבִּי טַרְפוֹן. אֵין אֶחָד מֵהֶן נָזִיר. שֶׁאֵין נְזִירוּת אֶלָּא עַל הַתְרָיָיה. הָדָא הִיא דְרִבִּי יוּדָה אָמַר. סְפֵק נְזִירוּת מוּתָּר.

It was stated: "Rebbi Jehudah said in the name of Rebbi Ṭarphon: None of them is a *nazir* since *nezirut* exists only by warning."[128] That is what Rebbi Jehudah said, "doubtful *nezirut* is permitted.[129]"

[128] In the Babylonian sources, Babli 34a, Tosephta 3:19, "*nezirut* exists only by הפלאה 'clear statement'". The meaning is the same here; a legal warning for a breach of the vow could only be issued if the vow was clearly stated.

[129] Mishnah *Ṭahorot* 4:12.

(54b line 31) מַה נָן קַייָמִין. אִם בְּשֶׁזֶה אוֹמֵר. רְאוּבֵן. וְזֶה אוֹמֵר. שִׁמְעוֹן. מַה נַפְשָׁךְ. רְאוּבֵן הוּא נָזִיר הוּא. שִׁמְעוֹן הוּא נָזִיר הוּא. אֶלָּא כִּי נָן קַייָמִין. בְּשֶׁזֶה אוֹמֵר. רְאוּבֵן. וְזֶה אוֹמֵר. שִׁמְעוֹן. הִרְתִּיעַ לַאֲחוֹרָיו אֵינוֹ לֹא רְאוּבֵן וְלֹא שִׁמְעוֹן אֵינוֹ נָזִיר.

[130]Where do we hold? If one says, Reuben, and the other says, Simeon, as you take it, if he is Reuben, one is a *nazir*, if he is Simeon, one is a

nazir. But we must hold that one says, Reuben, and the other says, Simeon. He suddenly disappeared, he was neither Reuben nor Simeon; nobody is a *nazir*.

הָדָא הִיא דְּרִבִּי שִׁמְעוֹן אוֹמֵר. אֵינוֹ מֵבִיא קָרְבָּן עַד שֶׁיִּהְיֶה.

That is what Rebbi Simeon said, he cannot bring a sacrifice unless it exists[131].

130 Here starts the discussion of Mishnah 7.
131 The statement of R. Simeon parallels his own in Mishnah 2:8, regarding the man who vowed to be nazir if his wife bore a son and she had a miscarriage.

(54b line 35) תַּנֵּי. וְכוּלָּן מוֹנִין תִּשְׁעָה נְזִירִיּוֹת. וְהָא אִינּוּן עֲשָׂר. אִי אֶפְשָׁר שֶׁלֹּא נִתְקַיְימוּ דִּבְרֵי אֶחָד מֵהֶן. אָמַר רִבִּי יָסָא. דְּבֵית שַׁמַּי הִיא. דְּבֵית שַׁמַּי אוֹמְרִים. הֶקְדֵּשׁ טָעוּת הֶקְדֵּשׁ.

It was stated[132]: "All of them count nine *neziriot*". Are they not ten?[133] It is impossible that the words of any of them should not be correct. Rebbi Yasa said, this[134] is the House of Shammai's, since the House of Shammai say, dedication in error is dedication.

132 In the Tosephta, 3:19, this refers to people who meet a hermaphrodite and quarrel whether or not he is a man, a woman, or a man and a woman. In the Babli, 34a, there is a question whether to read "9 *neziriot*", or "9 *nezirim*". The formulation of the Mishnah in the Yerushalmi clearly speaks of only two people who dispute and pile vow onto vow.
133 The questioner has a slightly different reading in the Mishnah which exhausts all logical possibilities: Wild animal or not, domestic or not, wild and domestic or not, neither wild nor domestic, one or none or both *nezirim*.
134 The Tosephta which counts 9 possibilities.

שלשה מינין פרק ששי

(fol. 54b) **משנה א:** שְׁלֹשָׁה מִינִין אֲסוּרִין בַּנָּזִיר הַטּוּמְאָה וְהַתִּגְלַחַת וְהַיּוֹצֵא מִן הַגֶּפֶן. וְכָל־הַיּוֹצֵא מִן הַגֶּפֶן מִצְטָרְפִין זֶה עִם זֶה וְאֵינוֹ חַיָּיב עַד שֶׁיֹּאכַל מִן הָעֲנָבִים כַּזַּיִת. מִשְׁנָה רִאשׁוֹנָה עַד שֶׁיִּשְׁתֶּה רְבִיעִית יָיִן. רִבִּי עֲקִיבָה אוֹמֵר אֲפִילוּ שָׁרָה פִּיתּוֹ בַּיַּיִן וְיֵשׁ בָּהּ כְּדֵי לְצָרֵף כַּזַּיִת חַיָּיב.

Mishnah 1: Three kinds are forbidden for the *nazir*: Impurity, shaving, and anything coming from the vine. Everything coming from the vine is added together[1]. He is only guilty when he eats grapes in the volume of an olive; according to the early Mishnah if he drinks a *quartarius* of wine[2]. Rebbi Aqiba says, even if he dipped his bread in wine for a total volume[3] of an olive, he is guilty.

1   The verse prohibiting "anything coming from the vine" to the *nazir* makes it clear that the most minute amount is forbidden. But a *nazir* cannot cleanse himself by a purification sacrifice (or, if duly warned by two witnesses, cannot be criminally prosecuted for desecrating his holy status) unless he consumed more than the legal minimum. For most matters of food, the legal minimum is the size of an average olive used for the production of oil (cf. H. Guggenheimer, *The Scholar's Haggadah*, Northvale 1995, pp. 326-328). For beverages, the standard is the *revi'it*, defininied by the Mishnah (*Kelim* 17:11) as Roman *quartarius*, 133 ml (*loc. cit.* pp. 212-213).

2   Or eats an amount of grapes from which a *quartarius* of juice could be extracted.

3   The bread plus the wine absorbed in it.

(54c line 25) **הלכה א:** שְׁלֹשָׁה מִינִין אֲסוּרִין בַּנָּזִיר כוּל׳. הַטּוּמְאָה. דִּכְתִיב כָּל־יְמֵי הַזִּירוֹ לַיְיָ עַל נֶפֶשׁ מֵת לֹא יָבֹא. תִּגְלַחַת. דִּכְתִיב כָּל־יְמֵי נֶדֶר נִזְרוֹ תַּעַר לֹא יַעֲבוֹר עַל רֹאשׁוֹ. הַיּוֹצֵא מִן הַגֶּפֶן. דִּכְתִיב כָּל־יְמֵי נִזְרוֹ מִכֹּל אֲשֶׁר יֵעָשֶׂה מִגֶּפֶן הַיַּיִן וגו׳.

Halakhah 1: "Three kinds are forbidden for the *nazir*," etc. Impurity, as it is written[4]: "During all the days he vowed to the Eternal he shall not come close to a human corpse." Shaving, as it is written[5]: "During all the days of his *nazir* vow, a shaving knife shall not come onto his head." Anything from the vine, as it is written[6]: "During all the days of his vow, of anything coming from the wine-vine [he shall not eat.]"

4   Lev. 6:6.   5   Lev. 6:5.   6   Lev. 6:4.

(54c line 28) תַּנֵּי רַב זַכַּיי קוֹמֵי רִבִּי יוֹחָנָן. זִיבַּח וְקִיטֵּר נִיסֵּךְ בְּהֶעֱלֵם אֶחָד חַיָּיב עַל כָּל־אַחַת וְאַחַת. אָמַר לֵיהּ רִבִּי יוֹחָנָן. בַּבְלַיָּיא. עָבַרְתְּ בְּיָדָךְ תְּלָתָא נְהָרִין וְאִתְּבָּרַת. וְאֵינוֹ חַיָּיב אֶלָּא אַחַת. עַד דְּלָא יַתְבְּרִינָהּ בְּיָדֵהּ יֵשׁ כָּאן אַחַת וְאֵין כָּאן הִנֵּה. מָאן דְּתָבְרָהּ בְּיָדֵהּ יֵשׁ כָּאן הִנֵּה וְאֵין כָּאן אַחַת. רִבִּי בָּא בַּר מָמָל בְּעָא קוֹמֵי רִבִּי זְעִירָא. וִיהֵא חַיָּיב עַל כָּל־אַחַת. כַּמָּה דְּתֵימַר בַּשַּׁבָּת. לֹא תַעֲשֶׂה כָּל־מְלָאכָה כְּלָל. לֹא תְבַעֲרוּ אֵשׁ בְּכָל־מוֹשְׁבוֹתֵיכֶם פְּרָט. וַהֲלֹא הַבְעָרָה בִּכְלָל הָיָה וְיָצָא מִן הַכְּלָל לְלַמֵּד. מַה הַבְעָרָה מְיוּחֶדֶת מַעֲשֶׂה יְחִידִים וְחַיָּיבִין עָלֶיהָ בִּפְנֵי עַצְמָהּ אַף כָּל־מַעֲשֶׂה וּמַעֲשֶׂה שֶׁיֵּשׁ בּוֹ לְחַיֵּיב עָלָיו בִּפְנֵי עַצְמוֹ. וְכָא. לֹא תַעַבְדֵם. כְּלָל. לֹא תִשְׁתַּחֲוֶה פְּרָט. וַהֲלֹא הִשְׁתַּחֲוָיָה בִּכְלָל הָיָה וְלָמָּה יָצָאת מִן הַכְּלָל. לְלַמֵּד. לוֹמַר לָךְ. מַה הִשְׁתַּחֲוָיָה מְיוּחֶדֶת מַעֲשֶׂה יְחִידִים וְחַיָּיבִין עָלֶיהָ בִּפְנֵי עַצְמָהּ אַף כָּל־מַעֲשֶׂה וּמַעֲשֶׂה שֶׁיֵּשׁ בָּהּ לְחַיֵּיב עָלָיו בִּפְנֵי עַצְמוֹ. אָמַר לָהּ. בַּשַּׁבָּת כָּלַל בְּמָקוֹם אֶחָד וּפָרַט בְּמָקוֹם אַחֵר. וּבַעֲבוֹדָה זָרָה כְּלָל שֶׁהוּא בְּצַד הַפְּרָט. אָמַר לֵיהּ. וְהָכְתִיב לֹא תִשְׁתַּחֲוֶה לְאֵל אַחֵר. הֲרֵי שֶׁכָּלַל בְּמָקוֹם אֶחָד וּפָרַט בְּמָקוֹם אַחֵר. אָמַר לֵיהּ. מִכֵּיוָן שֶׁאֵין אַתְּ לָמֵד מֵעִידוֹ אֲפִילוּ מִמָּקוֹם אַחֵר אִי אַתְּ לָמֵד. חֲבֵרַיָּיא אָמְרֵי. לֹא שַׁנְיָיא הִיא. בֵּין שֶׁכָּלַל בְּמָקוֹם אֶחָד וּפָרַט בְּמָקוֹם אַחֵר בֵּין שֶׁכָּלַל וּפָרַט בְּמָקוֹם אֶחָד כְּלָל

וּפְרָט הוּא. בַּשַּׁבָּת כְּלָל וְאַחַר כָּךְ פְּרָט. וּבַעֲבוֹדָה זָרָה פְּרָט וְאַחַר כָּךְ כְּלָל.
רִבִּי יוֹסֵי אוֹמֵר. לֹא שַׁנְיָיא. בֵּין שֶׁכְּלָל בְּמָקוֹם אֶחָד וּפְרָט בְּמָקוֹם אַחֵר בֵּין
שֶׁכְּלָל וּפְרָט בְּמָקוֹם אֶחָד כְּלָל וּפְרָט הִיא. בַּשַּׁבָּת כְּלָל בַּעֲבוֹדָתָהּ וּפְרָט
בַּעֲבוֹדָתָהּ. וּבַעֲבוֹדָה זָרָה כְּלָל בַּעֲבוֹדָתָהּ וּפְרָט לִמְלֶאכֶת הַגָּבוֹהַּ.

1 תני | תנא א:תני   זכיי | זכאי   וקיטר ניסך | קיטר וניסך   3 ואתברת | ואיתברת
דלא | לא   ואין | אינו   בידה | בידיה   (2 times)   5 ר׳ זעירא | דר׳ זעירא   בשבת | גבי
שבת   7 היה ויצא | הייתה ויצאת   יחידים | יחידי   8 וכא | אף הכא   9
תשתחוה | תשתחווה להם   היה | היתה   10 לומר לך | -   יחידים | יחידי   12 לך |
ליה   12 אחר | אחר. זובח לאלקים יחרם   14 שכלל | כלל   אחד | אחר   למד |
לומד   15 ממקום אחר אי | במקום אחד   היא | -   17 ובע״ז | בע״ז   18 אומ׳ |
אמ׳   בין שכלל במקום אחד ופרט במקום אחר בין שכלל ופרט במקום אחד | בין שכלל
ואחר כך פרט. בין שפרט ואחר כך כלל. בין שכלל ופרט וכלל   20 למלאכת | במלאכות

[7]Rav Zakkai stated before Rebbi Joḥanan: If somebody sacrificed, burned incense, and poured a libation in one forgetting[8], he is guilty for each action separately[9]. Rebbi Joḥanan told him, Babylonian! You crossed three rivers with your hands[10] and were broken. He is guilty only once! [11]{Before he broke[12] in his hand there is "one" but not "those"; after he broke in his hand there are "those" but not "one".} Rebbi Abba bar Mamal asked before Rebbi Ze'ira: Should he not be guilty for each action separately? As you say for the Sabbath: "Do not perform any work[13]," principle. "Do not light fire in any of your dwelling places,[14]" a detail. Was not lighting fire subsumed under the principle, but it is mentioned separately from this principle! Since lighting fire is special in that it is the work of a single individual[15] and one would be guilty for it alone, so everything for which alone one is guilty[16]. Also here[17]: "Do not worship them,[18]" a principle. "Do not prostrate yourself,[18]" a detail. Was not prostrating itself included in the principle and why was it mentioned separately? To infer, to tell you that prostrating oneself is special in that it is the work of a single individual and one would be guilty for it alone,

so everything for which alone one is guilty[16]. He answered[19]: For the Sabbath, he mentioned the principle at one place and the details at another place. For idol worship, the principle is found close to the detail[20]. He retorted: Is it not witten: "Do not prostrate yourself before another power"[21]? He did not state the principle and the detail at the same spot! He said, since you do not infer anything from it close up, you cannot infer anything from afar[22]. The colleagues say, it makes no difference; whether He gave the principle at one place and the detail at another, or gave principle and detail at the same place, it is a matter of principle and detail. For the Sabbath, He first gave the principle and then the detail. For idolatry, He gave the detail and only later the principle[23]. Rebbi Yose said, it makes no difference whether [24][He first gave the principle and then the detail or He gave the detail and only later the principle, or He gave principle, detail, and principle[25]]; it is a matter of principle and detail. For the Sabbath, He gave a general prohibition of work, followed by details; for idolatry, He was indeterminate regarding its worship but detailed the worship of Heaven[26].

7 This paragraph and the next are from Šabbat 7:2 (9c, l. 11 ff.), as will be seen in the commentary. The variant readings refer to that text. The introductory section is from Šabbat 7:1 (9a, l. 20-24), the one variant in spelling there is noted by :א.

Mishnah Šabbat 7:2 states that on the Sabbath, 39 different activities are forbidden. This means that a person who violates the Sabbath unintentionally may be liable for up to 39 purification sacrifices. The question then appears whether in other cases multiple sacrifices also are necessary.

8 He committed idolatry but forgot that sacrificing, burning incense, and pouring libations are forbidden as idolatrous actions, or he was conscious that these acts are part of idolatry but forgot that idolatry was forbidden.

9 In the Babli, Šabbat 72a, Sanhedrin 62a, the positions of R. Joḥanan and R. Zakkai are switched.

10   Tigris, Euphrates, and Jordan.

11   The sentences in braces are unintelligible here; they refer to and are quoted from a discussion in *Šabbat* 7:1 (fol. 9a) which deals with the introductory sentence to the chapter of purification offerings, *Lev.* 4:2: "Speak to the Children of Israel, saying: If a person sins unintentionally against any commandments of the Eternal that are not to be broken, and did *from any one, from those.*" This implies that sometimes a purification offering is due for violating *one* prohibition, and sometimes one sacrifice is valid for a number *of those.* In general, the answer depends on what was unintentional. If a person does not know that today is Sabbath, for all he does wrong he owes one sacrifice. If he knows that it is Sabbath but forgot what is forbidden, he owes one sacrifice for each category of forbidden work. The problem is first whether this principle also applies to idolatry, the sacrifice for which is not described in *Lev.* 4 but in *Num.* 15:22-26, and second what is the status of the details enumerated in the Second Commandment, in particular why a detail, "do not prostrate yourself before them" is mentioned before the principle "do not serve them".

12   The reference to "breaking" here is a continuation of R. Johanan's criticism of Rav Zakkai (who in the Babli is Rebbi Zakkai): If the Second Commandment is considered a unit, there are no "those" to be applied to idolatry. If all activities mentioned are separate rules, how can one bring only one sacrifice?

13   *Ex.* 20:10.

14   *Ex.* 35:3.

15   A forbidden action on the Sabbath which is executed only by the common effort of several people is not prosecutable.

16   Needs a separate sacrifice. This is an application of the 9th hermeneutical principle of R. Ismael: Any detail which was subsumed under a principle but is mentioned separately in order to instruct, was not mentioned for itself but to explain the entire principle [*Sifra Introduction* 2; *Pereq* 1(1)]. In the text this is called "principle and detail", which in the technical language of the Babli refers to the completely different rule No. 5 [*Sifra Introduction* (1,7)]. In *Mekhilta dR. Ismael* p. 347 the argument is attributed to R. Jonathan (who in the Babli, *Šabbat* 70a, appears as R. Nathan.)

Whether there is a connection between rules 5 and 9 is left open in the Babli, *Baba qama* 85a, decided in the negative in *Menaḥot* 55b. Menahem Cahana, in an exhaustive study of the problem (קווים לתולדות התפתחותה של מידת כלל ופרט בתקופת התנאים p. 173-216 in: Studies in Talmudic and Midrashic Literature in Memory of Tirzah Lifshitz) holds that the original Tannaïtic theory knew only of two principles, one which corresponded to the later (Babli, Sifra, Sifry) rules entitled "principle and detail", "detail and principle", "principle and detail and principle"; the other one referring to all rules which in Babylonian formulation start with "any detail which was subsumed under a principle". His arguments support the thesis of the present commentary that Mekhilta, Sifra, Sifry (and Tosephta) in our hands are essentially Babylonian editions.

17   Regarding idolatry.
18   *Ex.* 20:5.
19   R. Ze'ira, answering R. Abba bar Mamal. The translation follows the text in *Šabbat*.
20   In the same sentence. If "prostrating" had been mentioned after "serving", the 5th hermeneutical principle would imply that the two notions are identical in intent. As the verse stands, it cannot be interpreted as "principle and detail".
21   *Ex.* 34:14.
22   Since 34:14 does not teach anything not contained in *Ex.* 20:5.
23   Therefore, the 9th principle does not apply to idolatry since the detail does not follow after the principle.
24   Text from *Šabbat*.
25   This really is the case for the Second Comandment.
26   The prohibition refers to performing for idolatry any ceremony commanded for the worship of Heaven. The case of R. Zakkai really has no connection with the argument about the status of the mention of prostrating oneself in the Second Commandment.

(54c line 51) אָמַר רבִּי מָנָא. הַבְעָרָה שֶׁלֹּא לְצוֹרֶךְ יָצָאת. הִשְׁתַּחֲוָיָה לְצוֹרֶךְ יָצָאת. לְלַמֵּד עַל עַצְמָהּ שֶׁאֵינָהּ מַעֲשֶׂה. וְתִייָא כְהָדָא דְתַנֵּי חִזְקִיָּה. זֹבֵחַ לָאֱלֹהִים יָחֳרָם. יָצְאָת זְבִיחָה לְלַמֵּד עַל הַכֹּל. הִשְׁתַּחֲוָיָה לְלַמֵּד עַל עַצְמָהּ שֶׁאֵינָהּ מַעֲשֶׂה. אוֹ חָלָף. דָּבָר שֶׁהוּא מַעֲשֶׂה מְלַמֵּד. דָּבָר שֶׁאֵינוֹ מַעֲשֶׂה אֵינוֹ מְלַמֵּד. אָמַר רבִּי יִרְמְיָה. הַבְעָרָה לְצוֹרֶךְ יָצָאת. לְלַמֵּד עַל בָּתֵּי דִינִין שֶׁלֹּא יְהוּ יוֹשְׁבִין בַּשַּׁבָּת. מַה טַעֲמָא. נֶאֱמַר כָּאן בְּכָל־מוֹשְׁבוֹתֵיכֶם. וְנֶאֱמַר לְהַלָּן וְהָיוּ אֵלֶּה לְחוּקַת עוֹלָם לְדוֹרוֹתֵיכֶם בְּכָל־מוֹשְׁבוֹתֵיכֶם. מַה מוֹשָׁבוֹת שֶׁנֶּאֱמַר לְהַלָּן

בָּתֵּי דִינִין. אַף מוֹשָׁבוֹת שֶׁנֶּאֱמַר כָּאן בְּבָתֵּי דִינִין הַכָּתוּב מְדַבֵּר. אָמַר רִבִּי שְׁמוּאֵל בַּר אָבְדּוּמָא. מִכֵּיוָן דְּתֵימַר. לְצוֹרֶךְ יָצָאת. כְּמִי שֶׁיָּצָאת שֶׁלֹּא לְצוֹרֶךְ. וְדָבָר שֶׁיָּצָא שֶׁלֹּא לְצוֹרֶךְ מְלַמֵּד.

2 ותייא כהדא | אתיא כההיא   3 לאלהים | לאלקים²⁷   על עצמה | ללמד על עצמה
5 אמ' | דמר   5 דיניין | דינים   6 יושביין | דנין   מה | ומה   7 לחוקת עולם
לדורותיכם | לחקת משפט לדרתיכם   מושבות | מושבותיכם (2 times)

Rebbi Mana said, lighting fire was mentioned unnecessarily²⁸; prostrating oneself was mentioned by necessity to explain about itself since it is not work²⁹. This follows what Ḥizqiah stated: "He who sacrifices to powers shall be banned³⁰." Sacrificing was mentioned separately to teach about everything³¹, prostrating oneself to explain about itself since it is not work. Rebbi Jeremiah said, lighting fire was mentioned by necessity, to teach that courts should not sit on the Sabbath³². What is the reason? It says here, "in all your settlements" and it says there, "these should be rules of law for your generations, in all your settlements³³." Since "settlements" mentioned there refers to courts, "settlements" referred to here also refers to courts. Rebbi Samuel bar Eudaimon said, even if you say that it was mentioned by necessity, it is as if it were mentioned unnecessarily³⁴, and anything mentioned unnecessarily teaches.

27 The sentence about Ḥizqiah's statement was added by the corrector of the Venice edition. כההיא is Babli style for Yerushalmi כהדא, only a relatively modern author would think of using the form אלקים (to avoid profane use of God's name) for pagan deities.

28 Since the prohibition of making fire is implied in the Fourth Commandment in any reasonable interpretation. Therefore, making fire is a detail which can be used to characterize *all* work forbidden on the Sabbath.

29 Nothing is changed or produced by prostrating oneself; it is not obvious that it should be forbidden under any

circumstances.

30 *Ex.* 22:19. This explains the punishment for idolatrous acts forbidden in the Second Commandment. This is the interpretation in all of talmudic literature (Babli *Sanhedrin* 60b, *Mekhilta dR. Ismael* p. 310, *dR. Simeon ben Iohai* p. 210.) {Nowhere in rabbinic literature does one find the more obvious explanation of *Ex.* 22:19: "Anyone sacrificing to *the Elohim* (God as Creator, Ruler of the physical world) shall be banned, only to YHWH (God the Merciful and Dispenser of Grace) alone." In all of *Lev.* and *Num.*, there is never any mention of a sacrifice to *Elohim*.}

31 Since punishment for sacrificing is spelled out separately, any punishment for an act of idolatry must be given separately by the 9th rule, supporting R. Zakkai against R. Johanan.

32 In the Babli, *Yebamot* 6b, this is a Tannaïtic statement from the school of R. Ismael, appended to an argument also quoted in *Mekhilta dR. Ismael*, ויקהל.

33 *Num.* 35:29. The quote is correct in *Šabbat*.

34 Since the argument is based on *Num.* 35:29, not on *Ex.* 22:19, the latter verse can be used in an application of the 9th rule.

(54c line 61) וָכָא חַרְצָנִין וְזַגִין בִּכְלָל הָיוּ וְיָצְאוּ מִן הַכְּלָל. וִיחַלְקוּ וְלֹא יִצְטָרְפוּ. אֶלָּא תַּמָּן כְּלָל בְּמָקוֹם אֶחָד וּפְרָט בְּמָקוֹם אַחֵר. וָכָא כְּלָל וּפְרָט בְּמָקוֹם אֶחָד. וְהָא חַבְרַיָּיא אָמְרִי. לֹא שַׁנְיָיא. בֵּין כְּלָל וְאַחַר כָּךְ פְּרָט בֵּין שֶׁפְּרָט וְאַחַר כָּךְ כְּלָל. בֵּין שֶׁכְּלָל וְאַחַר כָּךְ כְּלָל וְאַחַר כָּךְ פְּרָט. וָכָא כְּלָל וְאַחַר כָּךְ פְּרָט. וְהָא רִבִּי יוֹסֵי אָמַר. לֹא שַׁנְיָיה. בֵּין כְּלָל וְאַחַר כָּךְ פְּרָט וְאַחַר כָּךְ כְּלָל. כְּלָל וּפְרָט הוּא. תַּמָּן שֶׁלֹּא לְצוֹרֶךְ יָצְאוּ. וְלָמָּא יָצָאוּ. לְמַעֵט הֶעָלִים וְהַלּוּלָבִים. וְהָא תַנֵּי מִשּׁוּם רִבִּי אֱלִיעֶזֶר. מִכָּל־אֲשֶׁר יֵעָשֶׂה מִגֶּפֶן הַיַּיִן מֵחַרְצַנִּים וְעַד זָג לֹא יֹאכֵל. אַף הֶעָלִים וְהַלּוּלָבִים בְּמַשְׁמַע. תַּמָּן לְצוֹרֶךְ נִכְלְלוּ. בְּרַם הָכָא שֶׁלֹּא לְצוֹרֶךְ נִכְלְלוּ. וְלָמָּה. לצירוכין.

But here, skins and seeds were understood in the principle, and were listed separately[35]. Should they not be separate rather than common? But there[36], the principle is at one place and the details are at another place. But did not the colleagues say: It makes no difference: Whether he stated the principle and then a detail or the detail and after that the principle. And here, he stated the principle and then a detail. But did not Rebbi Yose say, there is no difference whether He gave principle, detail, and principle, it is the principle and then a detail, it is counted as the principle and then a detail. There, the detail was not necessary. Why were they detailed? To exclude leaves and twigs[37]. But was it not stated in the name of Rebbi Eliezer[38]: "From anything coming from the wine-vine, from skins to seeds, he shall not eat;" leaves and twigs are also understood. There[39], they are mentioned for a need, but here, they are mentioned without need. Why? For additions[40].

35 In *Num.* 6:4, it is started that a *nazir* is forbidden "everything coming from the vine", followed by "skins and seeds". Since skins and seeds of grapes come from the vine, this is "principle and detail" and the question arises why the Mishnah prescribes that all that comes from the vine be counted together; should not every kind be counted separately?

36 The rules of the Sabbath.

37 Which may not be directly edible. But vine leaves are used in cooking, supporting R. Eliezer.

38 Babli 34b, *Sifry Num.* #24; rejected in the Babli.

39 While this paragraph is not found in *Šabbat*, it seems to have originated there since "there" is here, the discussion of the rules of *nazir*, but "here" is *Šabbat*, the discussion of the mention of making fire. In the case of the *nazir*, everything that comes from the vine is added together (one minimum quantity, one sacrifice) since everything mentioned (including in v. 3 wine, liquor, vinegar, grapes and raisins) is necessary as explained in *Sifry Num.* #23-24.

40 Reading לְצֵירוּפִין for לצירוכין of the text.

(54c line 71) אַזְהָרָה לָאוֹכֵל נְבֵילוֹת מְנַיִין. לֹא תֹאכְלוּ כָל־נְבֵילָה. עַד כְּדוֹן נְבֵילָה. טְרֵיפָה מְנַיִין. אָמַר רבי יוֹחָנָן. נְבֵילָה וְכָל־נְבֵילָה. לְרַבּוֹת הַטְּרֵיפָה. הָאוֹכֵל אֵבֶר מִן הַחַי מִטְּרֵיפָה. רבי יָסָא אָמַר. אִיתְפְּלְגוּן רבי יוֹחָנָן וְרבי

שִׁמְעוֹן בֶּן לָקִישׁ. רִבִּי יוֹחָנָן אָמַר. חַיָּיב שְׁתַּיִם. רִבִּי שִׁמְעוֹן בֶּן לָקִישׁ אָמַר. אֵינוֹ חַיָּיב אֶלָּא אַחַת. מַה טַעֲמָא דְּרִבִּי יוֹחָנָן. לֹא תֹאכַל כָּל־נְבֵילָה. וְלֹא תֹאכַל הַנֶּפֶשׁ עִם הַבָּשָׂר. מַה טַעֲמָא דְּרִבִּי שִׁמְעוֹן בֶּן לָקִישׁ. אָמְרֵי חֲבֵרִין קוֹמֵי רִבִּי יוֹסֵי. אַתְיָיא דְּרִבִּי שִׁמְעוֹן בֶּן לָקִישׁ כְּהָדָא דְּתַגֵּי רִבִּי אֱלִיעֶזֶר בֶּן יַעֲקֹב. וּבָשָׂר בַּשָּׂדֶה טְרֵיפָה לֹא תֹאכֵלוּ. אַל תְּהֵא תוֹלֵשׁ וְאוֹכֵל מִן הַבְּהֵמָה כְּדֶרֶךְ שֶׁאַתָּה תוֹלֵשׁ מֵהַקַּרְקַע וְאוֹכֵל. מַה טַעֲמָא דְּרִבִּי שִׁמְעוֹן בֶּן לָקִישׁ. חֲבֶרַייָה קוֹמֵי רִבִּי יוֹסֵי. רִבִּי שִׁמְעוֹן בֶּן לָקִישׁ לֹא סָבַר בִּטְרֵיפָה כְּרִבִּי יוֹחָנָן. אֵין יִסְבּוּר כֵּן שֶׁיְּהֵא חַיָּיב שְׁתַּיִם. אָמַר לוֹן. אֲפִילוּ דְּיִסְבּוּר כֵּן לֹא יְהֵא חַיָּיב אֶלָּא אַחַת. שְׁנִייָא הִיא שֶׁחָזַר וְכָלַל. הֲתִיבוּן. חֵלֶב לֹא תֹאכֵלוּ. וְדָם לֹא תֹאכֵלוּ. וּכְתִיב כָּל־חֵלֶב וְכָל־דָּם לֹא תֹאכֵלוּ. מֵעַתָּה מִכֵּיוָן שֶׁחָזַר וְכָלַל לֹא יְהֵא חַיָּיב אֶלָּא אַחַת. אָמַר לוֹן. אִילּוּ הָיָה כָּתוּב חֵלֶב וְדָם יָאוּת. לֵית כְּתִיב אֶלָּא כָּל־חֵלֶב וְכָל־דָּם. לְחַיֵּיב עַל זֶה בִּפְנֵי עַצְמוֹ וְעַל זֶה בִּפְנֵי עַצְמוֹ. וְהָא כְּתִיב וְכָל־מִשְׁרַת עֲנָבִים לֹא יִשְׁתֶּה. וּכְתִיב מֵחַרְצַנִּים וְעַד זָג לֹא יֹאכֵל. מֵעַתָּה מִכֵּיוָן שֶׁחָזַר וְכָלַל לֹא יְהֵא חַיָּיב אֶלָּא אַחַת. אָמַר לוֹן. אִילּוּ הָיָה כָּתוּב מֵחַרְצַנִּים וְזָג יָאוּת. לֵית כְּתִיב אֶלָּא מֵחַרְצַנִּים וְעַד זָג. לְחַיֵּיב עַל זֶה בִּפְנֵי עַצְמוֹ וְעַל זֶה בִּפְנֵי עַצְמוֹ.

Warning[41] for one who eats carcass meat, from where? "You shall not eat any carcass meat.[42]" That covers carcass meat; from a "torn"[43] animal from where? Rebbi Joḥanan said, "carcass meat" and "any carcass meat", to include the "torn" animal[44]. If somebody eats flesh from a living animal which is "torn", Rebbi Yasa said, Rebbi Joḥanan and Rebbi Simeon ben Laqish disagree. Rebbi Joḥanan said, he is guilty twice, Rebbi Simeon ben Laqish said, he is guilty only once. What is the reason of Rebbi Joḥanan? "You shall not eat any carcass meat[42];" "you shall not eat of life with the flesh[45,46]." What is the reason of Rebbi Simeon ben Laqish? The colleagues said before Rebbi Yose: The assertion of Rebbi Simeon ben Laqish parallels what Rebbi Eliezer ben Jacob stated: "'Flesh torn on the field you shall not eat'[47], you shall not tear from an animal and eat in the way you tear from the ground[48] and eat." What is the reason of Rebbi

Simeon ben Laqish? The colleagues before Rebbi Yose: Rebbi Simeon ben Laqish does not hold with Rebbi Johanan about the "torn" animal; if he did hold with him, one should be twice guilty. He said to them, even if he held with him, one should be guilty only once. There is a difference, because He repeated it and combined it[49]. They objected: "Suet you shall not eat,[50]" "and blood you shall not eat,[51]" and it is written: "Any suet and any blood you shall not eat.[52]" Then because He repeated it and combined it, one should be guilty only once! He said to them, if it were written "suet and blood", you would be correct. But it is written "*any* suet and *any* blood," to declare him guilty for each case separately. But it is not written: "Anything soaked with grapes he shall not drink[53]," and it is written, "from skins to seeds he shall not eat[54]." Then because He repeated it and combined it, one should be guilty only once![55] He said to them, if it were written "skins and seeds", you would be correct. But it is written "skins *unto*[56] seeds," to declare him guilty for each case separately.

41   An infraction of a biblical law is prosecutable only if the prohibition is mentioned at least twice in the text, once as "warning" to spell out the prohibition and once to specify the punishment for infraction. If no punishment is specified, whipping is intended; nevertheless, the second mention is necessary. Cf. *Yebamot* 11:1, Note 47.

42   *Deut.* 14:21.

43   *Terephah* is a technical term, originally meaning an animal which cannot survive an attack by a predator. The meaning has been extended to include all animals who cannot survive for any length of time, including dangerously sick animals and those born with severe birth defects. (As a practical matter, slaughtered animals have to be inspected for signs of tuberculosis, which would prohibit the meat for human consumption.)

44   The verse must forbid more than carcass meat, otherwise the mention of "all" was superfluous. The argument is reported as tannaitic in *Sifry Deut.* 104.

45   *Deut.* 12:23. It is forbidden to eat limbs torn from a living animal. (In

rabbinic interpretation, this is the prohibition imposed on all mankind by *Gen.* 9:4: "But meat in whose blood is life you shall not eat", meat taken when life is still carried by the blood.)

46   The argument is that in one act one may transgress two prohibitions referring to two distict verses as warnings and, therefore, be subject to distinct punishments. In the Babli, *Hulin* 102b/103a, the difference between the interpretations of R. Johanan and R. Simeon ben Laqish boils down to the question whether "flesh from a living animal" and "limbs from a living animal" are different prohibitions following distinct rules. (For the problems raised by the competition of laws, cf. *Terumot* 7:1, Notes 6 ff.)

47   *Ex.* 22:30. In this interpretation, the verse forbids flesh or limbs torn from an animal (and also supports R. Johanan's interpretation of *Deut.* 14:21.) A similar formulation, also in the name of R. Eliezer ben Jacob, is in *Mekhilta dR. Simeon ben Iohai*, p. 214.

48   Vegetables.

49   It is impossible to say that *Ex.* 22:30 does not contain a prohibition of meat from "torn" animals, since this is the obvious meaning of the text. But since following R. Eliezer ben Jacob, the verse also prohibits flesh torn from living animals, there is no separate "warning" for eating meat from "torn" animals. The offender can be prosecuted either on basis of *Deut.* 14:21 or of *Ex.* 22:30, but not of both together. (Since in the desert, consumption of any non-sacrificial meat of domesticated animals was forbidden, *Lev.* 17:4, the mention of carcass meat would have been out of place in *Ex.* 22.)

50   *Lev.* 7:24.

51   *Lev.* 7:26.

52   *Lev.* 3:17.

53   *Num.* 6:3.

54   *Num.* 6:4.

55   But Mishnah 6:2 will state that the *nazir* can be punished separately for each item on the list.

56   A redundant word, not really required by the context.

(54d line 15) רִבִּי אוֹמֵר לַחֲבֵרַיָּיא. הֲווֹ יָדְעִין דְּאִתְפַּלְגוּן רִבִּי יוֹחָנָן וְרִבִּי שִׁמְעוֹן בֶּן לָקִישׁ. אֶבֶר מִן הַחַי שְׁחָלְקוֹ וַאֲכָלוֹ. דִּבְרֵי הַכֹּל פָּטוּר. מַה פְּלִיגִין. בְּשֶׁחָלְקוֹ בְּפִיו וַאֲכָלוֹ. רִבִּי יוֹחָנָן עָבַד פִּיו כִּלְפָנִים. רִבִּי שִׁמְעוֹן בֶּן לָקִישׁ עָבַד פִּיו כִּלְחוּץ. אָמְרִין לֵיהּ. אַתְּ מָה אֲמַר. אֲמַר לוֹן. אֲנָא אָמְרִי לְכוֹן. הָרֵי עוֹלָם פְּלִיגִין

וְאַתּוּן אָמְרִין אָמְרִין אָכֵן. אֵין כֵּנִי אֲפִילוּ חִלְקוֹ בַּחוּץ וַאֲכָלוֹ יְהֵא חַיָּיב. לָמָּה. דֶּרֶךְ אֲכִילָה הִיא. נְמָלָה שֶׁחִלְּקָהּ בְּפִיו וַאֲכָלָהּ. תַּפְלוּגְתָּא דְּרַבִּי יוֹחָנָן וְרַבִּי שִׁמְעוֹן בֶּן לָקִישׁ. רִבִּי מַיְישָׁא שָׁאַל לְרַבִּי זְעִירָה. עֲנָבָה שֶׁחִלְּקָהּ בְּפִיו וַאֲכָלָהּ. תַּפְלוּגְתָּא דְּרַבִּי יוֹחָנָן וְרַבִּי שִׁמְעוֹן בֶּן לָקִישׁ. אָמַר לֵיהּ. תַּמָּן דָּבָר שֶׁיֵּשׁ בּוֹ אִיסוּר וְטוּמְאָה. מָקוֹם שֶׁבָּטְלָה טוּמְאָתוֹ בָּטְלָה אִיסּוּרוֹ. בְּרַם הָכָא יֵשׁ כָּאן אִיסּוּר וְאֵין כָּאן טוּמְאָה. רִבִּי בָּא בְּרַבִּי מָמָל בָּעֵי. כְּזַיִת מַצָּה שֶׁחִלְּקוֹ בְּפִיו וַאֲכָלוּ. תַּפְלוּגְתָּא דְּרַבִּי יוֹחָנָן וְרַבִּי שִׁמְעוֹן בֶּן לָקִישׁ. אָמַר רִבִּי יוֹסֵי בֵּירַבִּי בּוּן. בְּכָל־מָקוֹם לֹא נֶהֱנָה חִיכּוֹ כְּזַיִת. רַבָּנִין דְּקַיְסָרִין אָמְרֵי. רִבִּי נִיסָא שָׁאַל. פְּרֵידִים שֶׁלְּרִימּוֹן שֶׁלְּעָרְלָה שֶׁחִלְּקוֹ בְּפִיו וַאֲכָלוֹ. תַּפְלוּגְתָּא דְּרַבִּי יוֹחָנָן וְרַבִּי שִׁמְעוֹן בֶּן לָקִישׁ. מָה אֲנָן קַיָּימִין. אִי מִשּׁוּם מַשְׁקֶה. כְּבַר תַּנִּינָן. אֵין מְטַמֵּא מִשֵּׁם מַשְׁקֶה אֶלָּא הַיּוֹצֵא מִן הַזֵּיתִים וּמִן הָעֲנָבִים. רַבָּנִין דְּקַיְסָרִין אָמְרִין. תִּיפְתָּר שֶׁבְּלָעָן.

Rebbi [Yose][57] said to the colleagues: You should know that Rebbi Johanan and Rebbi Simeon ben Laqish disagree: If somebody split a limb from a living animal and ate it, everybody agrees that he is free from prosecution[58]. Where do they disagree? If he split it in his mouth before he ate it. Rebbi Johanan considers his mouth as inside, Rebbi Simeon ben Laqish considers his mouth as outside[59]. They asked him, what do you say? He answered them, I informed you that mighty mountains disagree, and you ask this? If it is so, even if he split it outside and then ate, he should be guilty! Why? That is how one eats[60]. If somebody split an ant in his mouth[61] and ate it, that is the disagreement of Rebbi Johanan and Rebbi Simeon ben Laqish[62]. Rebbi Maisha asked Rebbi Ze'ira: If he[63] split a grape in his mouth and ate it, is that the disagreement of Rebbi Johanan and Rebbi Simeon ben Laqish? He answered, there[64] it is something for which there is a prohibition and impurity. In a circumstance in which its impurity disappeard, its prohibition disappeared. But here is a prohibition and no impurity[65]. Rebbi Abba ben Rebbi

Mamal asked: If he split an olive-sized bit of *mazzah*[66] in his mouth and ate it, is that the disagreement of Rebbi Johanan and Rebbi Simeon ben Laqish? Rebbi Yose ben Rebbi Abun said, in the other cases, his palate did not enjoy an olive sized bit[67]. The rabbis of Caesarea said that Rebbi Nisa asked: If he split in his mouth pomegranate berries[68] which are *'orlah*[69] and ate them, is that the disagreement of Rebbi Johanan and Rebbi Simeon ben Laqish? Where do we hold? If because of fluids, we already did state: "Nothing makes impure as a drink except what comes from olives and grapes.[70]" The rabbis of Caesarea said, explain it if he swallowed them[71].

57 Missing in ms. and *editio princeps*; needed by the context and historical considerations.

58 He has an olive-sized piece of flesh taken from a living animal and splits it in two. Neither piece has the minimum size that would make prosecution possible. He eats both pieces in one meal. As Rashi explains in *Hulin* 103b (*s.v.* מה): "In general, undersized parts of forbidden food consumed in the same meal are added together (Babli *Yoma* 80b). But the prohibition of limbs from a living animal is particular since in general inedible sinews and bones (of carcass and "torn" meat) are not forbidden food. By contrast, here one would be guilty since there is no limb without sinews and bones. One may say that its rules are separate and if one eats it in one piece one is guilty, since this is the normal way of eating, but not in minute pieces."

59 In the interpretation of the Babli, for R. Johanan the prohibition is triggered by the palate's enjoyment, for R. Simeon ben Laqish by the act of swallowing.

60 In the Babli, *Hulin* 103b, this is R. Eleazar's opinion. The configuration of the food is irrelevant.

61 Since an ant is a complete creature, it is forbidden food (*Lev.* 11:41) irrespective of size (cf. *Berakhot* 6:1, Note 17). In the Babli, *Makkot* 16b, eating an ant is counted as violating up to five prohibitions simultaneously.

62 According to R. Simeon ben Laqish, what he did is forbidden but not prosecutable.

63 A *nazir*, who can be criminally

prosecuted for eating an olive's volume of grapes.

64   A limb taken from a living animal causes impurity (*Ahilut* 2:1); similarly, crawling animals are called "impure". An entire crawling animal is always impure. But all parts of such an animal cut into pieces smaller than lentils are pure.

65   R. Simeon ben Laqish will agree that for the *nazir* only the total amount consumed is relevant.

66   In the first night of Passover, when there is a biblical commandment to eat *mazzah* (in the minimal amount of one olive's size); *Ex.* 12:18.

67   Here also, R. Simeon ben Laqish will agree with R. Johanan.

68   The berries of the pomegranate, each containing a single seed. Such a berry is a creature (cf. *Berakhot* 6:1, Note 18).

69   Harvested before the tree is three years old, when all usufruct is forbidden.

70   Mishnah *Terumot* 11:3. Therefore, the pomegranate berries are food and follow the rules of food.

71   A pomegranate berry is much smaller than an olive. It is agreed that eating a whole berry of *'orlah* can be prosecuted since it means eating a complete creature. But if the berry is eaten after being split into two parts, one might assume that R. Johanan will agree with R. Simeon ben Laqish that one cannot be prosecuted.

(54d line 31) טְרֵיפָה שֶׁעֲשָׂאָהּ נְבֵילָה. רִבִּי יָסָא בַּר בְּרַתֵּיהּ דְּרִבִּי יָסָא בְּשֵׁם רִבִּי יִרְמְיָה. אִיתְפַּלְגוּן רִבִּי יוֹחָנָן וְרִבִּי שִׁמְעוֹן בֶּן לָקִישׁ. רִבִּי יוֹחָנָן אוֹמֵר. חַייָב שְׁתַּיִם. וְרִבִּי שִׁמְעוֹן בֶּן לָקִישׁ אָמַר. אֵינוּ חַייָב אֶלָּא אַחַת. אָמַר רִבִּי אֶלְעָזָר בֵּירִבִּי יוֹסֵי קוֹמֵי רִבִּי יוֹסֵי. וְדָא מְסַייְיעָא לְרִבִּי יוֹחָנָן. וְכָל־נֶפֶשׁ אֲשֶׁר תֹּאכַל כָּל־נְבֵילָה. מַה תַּלְמוּד לוֹמַר וּטְרֵיפָה. אִם טְרֵיפָה חַיָה וַהֲלֹא כְּבָר נֶאֱמַר נְבֵילָה. אִם טְרֵיפָה מֵתָה הֲרֵי הִיא בִּכְלַל נְבֵילָה. וְיֵימַר נְבֵילָה הִיא. רִבִּי אַבָּהוּ בְּשֵׁם רִבִּי יוֹסֵי בֶּן חֲנִינָה. טַעֲמָא דְּרִבִּי יוֹסֵי לֹא תְשַׁקְּצוּ אֶת נַפְשׁוֹתֵיכֶם בַּבְּהֵמָה וּבָעוֹף. וַהֲלֹא אֵין מְטַמֵּא אֶלָּא שְׁמוֹנָה שְׁרָצִים בִּלְבָד. אֶלָּא כְּשִׁיעוּר טוּמְאוֹתֵיהֶן כָּךְ הוּא שִׁיעוּר אֲכִילָתָן. הָתִיב רִבִּי אֶלְעָזָר. הֲרֵי אֵיבָרֵי בְּהֵמָה טְהוֹרִין מְטַמְּאִין כָּל־שֶׁהֵן וַאֲכִילָתָן כְּזַיִת. וְקַבְּלָהּ. מַהוּ וְקַבְּלָהּ. כְּאִינַשׁ דַּאֲמַר. בַּעַל דִּינָא קַבְּלֵיהּ. חִייָה בַּר בָּא אָמַר. לֹא כָּל־נְבֵילָה. הַתּוֹרָה הִשְׁווֹת

כָּל־הָאֲכִילוֹת שֶׁבַּתּוֹרָה כְּאַחַת. הָתִיב רִבִּי חֲנִינָה. הֲרֵי שְׁמוֹנָה שְׁרָצִים מְטַמְּאִין בְּכָעֲדָשָׁה וַאֲכִילָתָן כְּזַיִת בֵּין לְדָם בֵּין לְבָשָׂר.

A "torn" [creature] that was turned into a carcass[72]. Rebbi Yasa, the son of Rebbi Yasa's daughter, in the name of Rebbi Jeremiah: Rebbi Joḥanan and Rebbi Simeon ben Laqish disagree. Rebbi Joḥanan says, he is guilty twice; Rebbi Simeon ben Laqish said, he is guilty only once. Rebbi Eleazar ben Rebbi Yose said before Rebbi Yose, the following[73] supports Rebbi Joḥanan: "'Any person who would eat any carcass meat[74],' why does the verse say 'and torn'? If a 'torn' animal can survive, was 'carcass meat' mentioned before[75]? If a 'torn' animal must die, is it not included in 'carcass meat'"[76]? Should he not say, it is carcass meat? Rebbi Abbahu in the name of Rebbi Yose ben Ḥanina: The reason of Rebbi Yose[77]: "Do not defile yourself by animals and birds[78]," but only the Eight Reptiles impart impurity! But the measure of their impurities is the measure of their uses as food[79]. Rebbi Eleazar objected[80]: May not the limbs of pure animals impart impurity in the most minute amount[81] but as food only in the volume of an olive? He accepted it. What is meant by "he accepted it"? Like a person who said, the opponent accepted it. Ḥiyya bar Abba said: "You shall not [eat] any carcass meat." The Torah identified all eating together. Rebbi Ḥanina objected: Is not the impurity of the Eight Reptiles in the size of a lentil, but as food in the volume of an olive, whether for blood or for meat[82]?

72 If a "torn" animal was not slaughtered according to the rules, is the meat forbidden under one or two statutes?

73 Sifra Aḥare Pereq 11(8).

74 Lev. 17:15.

75 No animal is ritually impure while alive. [Even the "impure" animals forbidden as food (Lev. 11:26, Deut. 14:9) are ritually pure while alive.] If a "torn" animal can survive and was ritually slaughtered, it does

not become impure.

76   If a "torn" animal must die in the short run, it simply becomes impure as a carcass. The mention of "torn" in the verse seems superfluous; it can only be justified as adding another prohibition. (In *Sifra*, the argument is inverted to prove that a "torn" animal, if ritually slaughtered, is not impure even as it is forbidden food.)

77   Who seems to accept his son's argument.

78   The argument refers to the part of the verse, *Lev.* 20:25, which is not quoted: "Do not defile yourself by animals and birds, and anything which crawls on the ground, which I separated for you as impure." Now anything crawling on the ground (and in the water) is forbidden as food, but impurity caused by dead bodies is restricted to mammals, birds, and the Eight Reptiles enumerated in *Lev.* 11:29-30.

79   Since even in biblical usage, mammals and birds acceptable as food are called "pure" (*Gen.* 8:20). By inference, non-kosher animals are called "impure" even while alive and technically pure.

80   To R. Abbahu.

81   Mishnah *Ahilut* 1:7.

82   In the Babli, *Me'ilah* 15b, R. Yose ben R. Ḥanina states, as explanation of his inference (Note 78) that eating parts of any of the Eight Reptiles is prosecutable in amounts the size of a lentil (Maimonides *Ma'akhalot asurot* 2:7). The identity of the rules for blood and flesh of these reptiles is Mishnah *Me'ilah* 4:3, for the rules of impurity *Sifra Šemini Parašah* 5(2), *Pereq* 7(6).

(54d line 44) רִבִּי שְׁמוּאֵל בַּר סוֹסַרְטִי בָּעֵי. מֵעַתָּה הָאוֹכֵל אֵבֶר מִן הַחַי מִן הַטְּהוֹרִין יְהֵא חַיָּיב שְׁתַּיִם. מִשּׁוּם לֹא תֹאכְלוּ כָּל־נְבֵילָה וּמִשּׁוּם לֹא תֹאכַל הַנֶּפֶשׁ עִם הַבָּשָׂר. וּמְשִׁיבִין טְהוֹרִין עַל הַטְּמֵאִים. וְכִי רִבִּי אֱלִיעֶזֶר לֹא הֵשִׁיב טְהוֹרִין עַל הַטְּמֵאִים. מֵעַתָּה הָאוֹכֵל אֵבֶר מִן הַחַי מִן הַטְּמֵאִין יְהֵא חַיָּיב שָׁלֹשׁ. מִשּׁוּם לֹא תֹאכַל כָּל־נְבֵילָה וּמִשּׁוּם לֹא תֹאכַל הַנֶּפֶשׁ עִם הַבָּשָׂר וּמִשּׁוּם וּמִבְּשָׂרָם לֹא תֹאכֵלוּ. רִבִּי אַבָּהוּ בְּשֵׁם רִבִּי יוֹסֵי בֶּן חֲנִינָה. אָכַל חֲמִשָּׁה נְמָלִים כְּאַחַת בְּהֶעֱלֵם אֶחָד חַיָּיב עַל כָּל־אַחַת וְאַחַת מִשּׁוּם בִּירִיָּיה. רְסָסָן וַאֲכָלָן אֵינוֹ חַיָּיב אֶלָּא אַחַת. וְהוּא שֶׁיְּהֵא בָּהֶן כְּזַיִת. אָכַל מִן הָרִיסּוּסִין וְיֵשׁ בָּהֶן כְּזַיִת חַיָּיב. אָכַל מִן הָרִיסּוּסִין כְּזַיִת וּנְמָלָה חַיָּיב שְׁתַּיִם. אֵין כֵּינִי אָכַל מִן הָרִיסּוּסִין

פָּחוֹת מִכְּזַיִת וְהִשְׁלִים לָהֶם נְמָלָה חַיָּב שְׁתַּיִם. אֵין כֵּינִי אָכַל נְמָלָה שֶׁיֵּשׁ בָּהּ כְּזַיִת חַיָּב שְׁתַּיִם. אַף בְּצֵירוּפֵי נָזִיר כֵּן. אָכַל מִן הַצֵּירוּפִין וְיֵשׁ בָּהֶן כְּזַיִת חַיָּב. אָכַל מִן הַצֵּירוּפִין כְּזַיִת וַעֲנָבָה חַיָּב שְׁתַּיִם. אֵין כֵּינִי אָכַל עֲנָבָה שֶׁיֵּשׁ בָּהּ כְּזַיִת חַיָּב שְׁתַּיִם. רִבִּי אַבָּהוּ בְשֵׁם רִבִּי יוֹחָנָן. כָּל־הָאִיסוּרִין מִצְטָרְפִין לִלְקוֹת עֲלֵיהֶן כְּזַיִת וּנְמָלָה חַיָּב שְׁתַּיִם. אֵין כֵּינִי אָכַל מִן הָאִיסוּרִין פָּחוֹת מִכְּזַיִת וְהִשְׁלִים לָהֶן נְמָלָה חַיָּב שְׁתַּיִם. אֵין כֵּינִי אָכַל נְמָלָה שֶׁיֵּשׁ בָּהּ כְּזַיִת חַיָּב שְׁתַּיִם.

Rebbi Samuel bar Sosarti asked: Then one who eats a limb from a kosher living animal should be guilty on two counts[83], because of "you shall not eat any carcass meat[42,84];" and because of "you shall not eat of life with the flesh[45]." Does one argue from kosher abour non-kosher animals? But did not Rebbi Eleazar argue[80] from kosher about non-kosher animals? Then one who eats a limb from a non-kosher living animal should be guilty on three counts, because of "you shall not eat any carcass meat[42];" and because of "you shall not eat of life with the flesh[45]"; and because of "you shall not eat from their flesh.[85]" Rebbi Abbahu in the name of Rebbi Yose ben Ḥanina: If somebody ate five ants together, in one forgetting[86], he is guilty for each one separately because of "creature"[61]. If he fragmented and ate them, he is guilty only once, if together they amount to the volume of an olive. If he ate of the fragments in the volume of an olive, he is guilty; if he ate of the fragments in the volume of an olive and an ant, he is guilty twice[87]. If this is correct, then if he ate of the fragments less than the volume of an olive and an ant completed the volume of an olive, is he guilty twice[88]? If this is correct, if the ate an ant the size of an olive, is he guilty twice? The same rule applies to combinations[89] of a *nazir*. If he ate of the combinations in the volume of an olive, he is guilty. If he ate of the combinations in the volume of an olive and a grape berry, is he guilty twice[90]? If this is correct, then if he ate a grape berry for the volume of an olive, is he guilty twice? Rebbi Abbahu in the name of Rebbi Joḥanan: All [food] prohibitions combine together[91] to be whipped for the volume of an olive, but for an ant one is guilty twice. Then if he ate prohibited food and an ant completed the volume of an olive, he is guilty twice. Then if he ate an ant the volume of an olive, he is guilty twice.

83   He argues against R. Joḥanan who stated that one who eats a limb from a "torn" animal violates two laws at the same time. Why should the verses quoted not apply to a completely healthy kosher animal?

84   Since the impurity of limbs from a living animal is identical with the impurity of carcasses, and by the argument of R. Yose ben Ḥanina food prohibitions follow impurity.

85   *Lev.* 11:8. The verse also connects food prohibition and impurity: "you shall not eat from their flesh nor touch their carcasses". The prohibition of touching applies to people intending to enter the holy precinct.

86   Even though all sins of the same kind incurred while one was oblivious of the prohibition can be atoned for by one purification sacrifice, each creature is in a category by itself.

87   The same argument, applied to the Babli's opinion (Note 62), is in the Babli *Makkot* 16b.

88   Since the ant it counted for itself, can it be counted with the volume filled by the forbidden pieces?

89   As enumerated in Mishnah 2, combining wine, vinegar, leaves, husks, pomace, etc.

90   For eating the volume of an olive from the produce of the vine he violates *Num.* 6:4; for the single intact grape berry he violates *Num.* 6:3.

91   In the Babli, *'Avodah zarah* 66a, this is a tannaitic statement derived from *Deut.* 14:3.

(54d line 61) רִבִּי אַבָּהוּ בְשֵׁם רִבִּי יוֹחָנָן. וּלְאִיסוּר מְשַׁעֲרִין אוֹתוֹ כְּאִילוּ בַּבָּצָל כְּאִילוּ בַּקְּפָלוֹט. וְאָתְיָיא כַּיי דָמַר רִבִּי אַבָּהוּ בְשֵׁם רִבִּי יוֹסֵי בֶּן חֲנִינָה. נְבֵילָה שֶׁבִּיטְלָהּ בִּשְׁחוּטָה בָּטֵל מַגָּעָהּ דְּבַר תּוֹרָה.

ולאיסור | כל האיסורין   כאילו בצל כאילו קפלוט | כילו בצל כילו קפלוט

Rebbi Abbahu in the name of Rebbi Joḥanan: One estimates [food] prohibitions as if they concerned onions or leeks[92]. This parallels what

Rebbi Abbahu said in the name of Rebbi Yose ben Ḥanina: If carcass meat disappeared among slaughtered meat[93], its [impurity by] touch has disappeared by biblical law.

92   Cf. *Terumot* 10:1, Notes 10-11.

93   A piece of carcass meat is mixed up with slaughtered meat, and if the volume of the carcass meat were filled by onions and leeks one could not taste the onions after cooking, then the impurity of carcass meat also has disappeared (in the opinion of the Babli, *Bekhorot* 23a, only the impurity transmitted by touch has disappeared, not the impurity tranmitted by carrying without touching, *Lev.* 11:40.)

(54d line 64) רִבִּי אַבָּהוּ בְשֵׁם רִבִּי יוֹחָנָן. כָּל־נוֹתְנֵי טְעָמִים אֵין לוֹקִין עֲלֵיהֶן עַד שֶׁיִּטְעוֹם טַעַם מַמָּשׁוֹ שֶׁלְאִיסּוּר. הוֹתִיב רִבִּי חִייָא בַּר יוֹסֵף קוֹמֵי רִבִּי יוֹחָנָן. הֲרֵי בָשָׂר בְּחָלָב וְלֹא טָעַם טַעַם מַמָּשׁוֹ שֶׁלְאִיסּוּר. וְאַתְּ אָמַר. לוֹקֶה. וְקִבְּלָהּ. וְאָמַר רִבִּי בּוּן בַּר חִייָה קוֹמֵי רִבִּי זְעִירָה. מַאי וְקִבְּלָהּ. כְּאִינָּשׁ דְּאָמַר. בַּעַל דִּינָא קִבְּלֵיהּ.

2 הותיב | התיב   חייא בר יוסף | חמא בר יוסי   3 ולא טעם טעם | הרי לא טעם
ואמ' ר' בון בר חייה קומי ר' זעיר'. מאי | מהו   4 דאמ'. בעל | דשמע מיליה דבעל
5 קבליה | קבלה

[94]Rebbi Abbahu in the name of Rebbi Joḥanan: One does not whip for anything imparting taste until he tasted the forbidden thing itself. Rebbi Ḥiya bar Yosef objected before Rebbi Joḥanan: Take, for example, meat in milk, where he did not taste the forbidden thing itself and you say that he is whipped! He accepted that. What is meant by: he accepted that? Rebbi Ḥiya bar Abun said before Rebbi Ze'ira: Like a person who listens to the argument of the opposing party he accepted it.

94   This and the next paragraph are from *'Orlah* 2:6 (Notes 136-152).

(54d line 68) רִבִּי אַבָּהוּ בְשֵׁם רִבִּי יוֹחָנָן. כָּל־נוֹתְנֵי טְעָמִים אֵין לוֹקִין עֲלֵיהֶן חוּץ מִנּוֹתְנֵי טְעָמִים שֶׁלְּנָזִיר. וְנָזִיר אֲפִילוּ לֹא טָעַם טַעַם מַמָּשׁוּ שֶׁלְּאִיסּוּר. אָמַר רִבִּי בָּא בַר מָמָל. כָּל־נוֹתְנֵי טְעָמִים אֵין אִיסּוּר וְהֶיתֵּר מִצְטָרְפִין. וְהַנָּזִיר אִיסּוּר וְהֶיתֵּר מִצְטָרְפִין. מַתְנִיתָא מְסַייְעָה לְדֵין וּמַתְנִיתָא מְסַייְעָה לְדֵין. מַתְנִיתָא מְסַייְעָה לְרִבִּי זְעִירָא. כְּזַיִת יַיִן שֶׁנָּפַל לִקְדֵירָה וְאָכַל מִמֶּנָּה כְּזַיִת פָּטוּר עַד שֶׁיֹּאכַל כּוּלָּהּ. עַל דַּעְתֵּיהּ דְּרִבִּי בָּא בַר מָמָל מִכֵּיוָן שֶׁאָכַל מִמֶּנָּה כְּזַיִת יְהֵא חַייָב. מַתְנִיתָא מְסַייְעָה לְרִבִּי בָּא בַר מָמָל. מִמַּשְׁמַע שֶׁנֶּאֱמַר וְכָל־מִשְׁרַת עֲנָבִים לֹא יִשְׁתֶּה וַעֲנָבִים לַחִים וִיבֵשִׁים לֹא יֹאכֵל. וְכִי מָה הִנִּיחַ הַכָּתוּב שֶׁלֹּא אָמְרוּ. אֶלָּא לְפִי שֶׁנֶּאֱמַר מִכֹּל אֲשֶׁר יֵעָשֶׂה מִגֶּפֶן הַיַּיִן מֵחַרְצַנִּים וְעַד זָג לֹא יֹאכֵל. וּכְתִיב מִיַּיִן וְשֵׁכָר יַזִּיר. מַה תַּלְמוּד לוֹמַר וְכָל־מִשְׁרַת עֲנָבִים לֹא יִשְׁתֶּה. אֶלָּא שֶׁאִם שָׁרָה עֲנָבִים בַּמַּיִם וְשָׁרָה פִיתּוֹ בָּהֶן וְיֵשׁ בָּהֶן כְּדֵי לְצָרֵף כְּזַיִת חַייָב. מִיכָּן אַתָּה דָן לְכָל־הָאִיסּוּרִין שֶׁבַּתּוֹרָה. וּמַה הַיּוֹצֵא מִן הַגֶּפֶן שֶׁאֵין אִיסּוּרוֹ אִיסּוּר עוֹלָם וְאֵין אִיסּוּרוֹ אִיסּוּר הֲנָייָה וְיֵשׁ לוֹ הֶיתֵּר אַחַר אִיסּוּרוֹ עָשָׂה בוֹ טַעַם כְּעִיקָּר. שְׁאָר אִיסּוּרִין שֶׁבַּתּוֹרָה שֶׁאִיסּוּרָן אִיסּוּר עוֹלָם וְאִיסּוּרָן אִיסּוּר הֲנָייָה וְאֵין לָהֶן הֶיתֵּר אַחַר אִיסּוּרָן דִּין הוּא שֶׁנַּעֲשֶׂה בָּהֶן אֶת טַעַם כְּעִיקָּר. מִכָּן לָמְדוּ חֲכָמִים לְכָל־נוֹתְנֵי טְעָמִים שֶׁהֵן אֲסוּרִין. וְקַשְׁיָא עַל דְּרִבִּי זְעִירָא. בְּכָל־אֲתָר אַתְּ אָמַר. עַד שֶׁיִּטְעוֹם וָכָא אַתְּ אָמַר. אֲפִילוּ לֹא טָעַם.

2 טעמים | טעם   ונזיר | ובנזיר   3 והנזיר | ובנזיר   4 מסייעה | מסייעא (3 times)
5 יאכל | אכל   6 כולה | את כולה   7 יהא חייב | חייב   מסייעה | מסייעא   8 וענבים לחים ויבישים לא יאכל | -   10 וכתי' | -   11 במים | -   12 מיכן | ומיכן   היוצא | אם היוצא   13 הנייה | הנאה   14 איסורין | כל האיסורין   15 דין הוא | אינו דין   טעם | הטעם   16 לכל | כל   שהן | שיהו   17 את אמ' | אמ'   וכא | וכה

Rebbi Abbahu in the name of Rebbi Joḥanan: One does not whip for anything imparting taste except imparting taste for the *nazir*. [Rebbi Zeʿira said, one does not whip for anything imparting taste until he tasted the forbidden thing itself]⁹⁵ except the *nazir* even if he did not taste the forbidden thing itself. Rebbi Abba bar Mamal said, for food imparting taste what is forbidden and what is permitted is not combined, but for the *nazir* forbidden and permitted do combine. A *baraita* supports one and a *baraita* supports the other. A *baraita* supports Rebbi Ze'ira: If wine in the volume of an olive fell into a dish and he ate from it, he cannot be prosecuted unless he ate the entire dish. In the opinion of Rebbi Abba bar Mamal, if he ate the volume of an olive from it he is guilty. A *baraita* supports Rebbi Abba bar Mamal: "What do we understand when it is said (*Num.* 6:3): 'Anything in which grapes were soaked he shall not eat, and fresh or dried grape berries he shall not eat'? What did the verse leave out that was not said? But since it was said (*Num.* 6:4): 'anything made from the wine-vine, from grape skins to seeds he should not eat;' (*Num.* 6:3) 'from wine and liquor he shall abstain.' Why does the verse say 'anything in which grapes were soaked he should not eat'? It means that if he soaked grapes and then soaked his bread in that, if it adds up to the volume of an olive, he is guilty. From here you argue about all prohibitions of the Torah. Since for all that comes from the vine, whose prohibition is neither permanent, nor a prohibition of usufruct, and whose prohibition can be lifted, He made taste like the thing itself; it is logical that for every prohibition of the Torah which is permanent, is a prohibition of usufruct, whose prohibition cannot be lifted, taste is treated like the thing itself. From here, the Sages inferred that everything imparting taste is forbidden." This is difficult for Rebbi Ze'ira: you say everywhere "unless he tasted[152]", and here you say, "even if he did not taste."

95 Missing here, added from the text in *'Orlah* since it is required by the following text.

(55a line 12) מִשְׁנָה רִאשׁוֹנָה עַד שֶׁיִּשְׁתֶּה רְבִיעִית יַיִן. דַּהֲווֹן דָּרְשִׁין שֵׁכָר. מַה שֵּׁכָר שֶׁנֶּאֱמַר לְהַלָּן רְבִיעִית אַף כָּאן רְבִיעִית. חָזְרוּ לוֹמַר. לֹא יֹאכַל. לֹא יִשְׁתֶּה. מַה אֲכִילָה כְזַיִת אַף שְׁתִיָּיה כְּזַיִת.

"According to the early Mishnah if he drinks a *quartarius* of wine." They did explain "liquor". Since "liquor" mentioned there[96] means a *quartarius*, so "liquor" mentioned here also means a *quartarius*. They changed to say "he shall not eat, he shall not drink."[97] Since eating is defined by an olive's size so drinking is by an olive's size.

96 *Lev.* 10:9, the prohibition for a priest to enter the holy precinct after he drank "wine or liquor"; *Sifra Šemini Parašah* 1(1). In the Babli, *Keritut* 13a, the rules of priests are deduced from those of the *nazir*.

97 *Num.* 6:3. Since both expressions appear in the same verse, they should conform to the same standard. Since the volume of an average olive is much smaller than a *quartarius*, the smaller standard in applicable in both cases.

(55a line 15) רִבִּי עֲקִיבָה אוֹמֵר אֲפִילוּ שָׁרָה פִיתּוֹ בַיַּיִן וְיֶשׁ בָּהּ כְּדֵי לְצָרֵף כַּזַּיִת חַייָב. אָמַר רִבִּי חֲנַנְיָה. וְהוּא דִשְׁרָיֵיהּ בִּכְזַיִת יַיִן. רִבִּי אִימִּי בְּשֵׁם רִבִּי יוֹחָנָן. כּוֹס מָזוּג מִשּׁוּם מִשְׁרָה לוֹקִין עָלָיו. הָדָא דְאַתְּ אָמַר בְּשֶׁלֹּא הִתְרוּ בוֹ מִשּׁוּם מִשְׁרָה. אֲבָל אִם הִתְרוּ בוֹ מִשּׁוּם מִשְׁרָה לֹא בְדָא. כְּתִיב וְכָל־מִשְׁרַת עֲנָבִים לֹא יִשְׁתֶּה. אֵין לִי אֶלָּא מִשְׁרַת עֲנָבִים. מִשְׁרַת חַרְצַנִּים מְנַיִין. תַּלְמוּד לוֹמַר מִשְׁרַת וְכָל־מִשְׁרַת. לְרַבּוֹת כָּל הַמִּשְׁרִיּוֹת לְמִשְׁרָה. מִשְׁרַת יַיִן בְּיַיִן מִצְטָרְפִין. מִשְׁרַת עֲנָבִים בַּעֲנָבִים מִצְטָרְפִין. מִשְׁרַת עֲנָבִים בְּיַיִן מַהוּ שֶׁיִּצְטָרְפוּ. אֲבָל חֲצִי זַיִת יַיִן וַחֲצִי זַיִת מִשְׁרָה זֶה בִּפְנֵי עַצְמוֹ אֵינוֹ חַייָב. זֶה בִּפְנֵי עַצְמוֹ וְזֶה בִּפְנֵי עַצְמוֹ פָּטוּר. מִפְּנֵי שֶׁצֵּירֵף חַייָב. אָכַל כְּזַיִת יַיִן וּכְזַיִת זַיִת מִשְׁרָה אֵינוֹ חַייָב אֶלָּא אַחַת. זֶה בִּפְנֵי עַצְמוֹ וְזֶה בִּפְנֵי עַצְמוֹ חַייָב שְׁתַּיִם. מִפְּנֵי שֶׁצֵּירֵף לֹא יְהֵא חַייָב אֶלָּא אַחַת.

"Rebbi Aqiba says, even if he dipped his bread in wine for a total volume[3] of an olive, he is guilty." Rebbi Ḥanania said, only if he dipped in an olive-sized volume of wine. Rebbi Immi in the name of Rebbi

Johanan: For a mixed cup[98] one whips because of soaking. That is, if they did (not)[99] warn because of soaking. But if they warned because of soaking, this does not apply. It is written: "He shall not drink anything soaked in grapes[100]." Not only soaking grapes, from where soaking grape skins? The verse says "soaked, anything soaked," that all kinds of soaking are counted[101]. Mixed wine combines with pure wine[102]. Soaking water of grapes combines with grapes. Do soaked grapes and wine combine? If one ate half an olive's volume of wine and half an olive's volume of soaking water, is he not guilty[103]. Separately[104], he is not prosecutable. Because he combined, he is guilty. If he ate (*sic!*) an olive's volume of wine and an olive's volume of soaking water, he is guilty only once. Separately, he is guilty twice. Because he combined, he should be guilty only once[105].

---

98 One third wine mixed with two thirds water.

99 This word seems to be an error. It seems that R. Immi stated that if the *nazir* drank wine mixed with water when was he warned not to drink wine, he is whipped for drinking wine, but if he was warned not to drink anything soaked with the fruit of the vine, he is whipped for that. The next sentence then should read לֹא הִתְרוּ "did not warn" instead of הִתְרוּ "warned".

100 *Num.* 6:3.

101 Cf. Note 44.

102 Half an olive's volume pure wine and half an olive mixed wine result in an olive of forbidden drink for the *nazir*.

103 The context shows that this sentence is interrogatory.

104 Drinking the two parts at different times.

105 This is quite obvious; it is stated only as contrast to the preceding case, in which combining made things worse.

משנה ב: וְחַיָּב עַל הַיַּיִן בִּפְנֵי עַצְמוֹ וְעַל הָעֲנָבִים בִּפְנֵי עַצְמָן וְעַל (fol. 54b) הַחַרְצַנִּים בִּפְנֵי עַצְמָן וְעַל הַזַּגִּים בִּפְנֵי עַצְמָן. רִבִּי לֶעְזָר בֶּן עֲזַרְיָה אוֹמֵר אֵינוֹ חַיָּב עַד שֶׁיֹּאכַל שְׁנֵי חַרְצַנִּים וְזַגִּין. אֵילוּ הֵן הַחַרְצַנִּים וְאֵילוּ הֵן הַזַּגִּים. הַחַרְצַנִּים אֵילוּ הַחִיצוֹנִים הַזַּגִּים אֵילוּ הַפְּנִימִיִּין דִּבְרֵי רִבִּי יְהוּדָה. רִבִּי יוֹסֵי אוֹמֵר שֶׁלֹּא תִטְעֶה כְּזוּג שֶׁלַּבְּהֵמָה הַחִיצוֹן זוּג וְהַפְּנִימִי עִינְבּוֹל.

Mishnah 2: One is guilty for wine separately, for grapes separately, for grape skins separately, for seeds separately[106]. Rebbi Eleazar ben Azariah says, he is guilty only if he eats two חרצנים and their זגים[107]. What are חרצנים and what זגים[108]? חרצנים are the outer skins, זגים the inner (seeds), the words of Rebbi Jehudah. Rebbi Yose said, that you should make no mistake[109], like an animal's bell, the outer shell is זוג, the inner the clapper.

106   All types of produce of the vine enumerated in the verses represent separate prohibitions; cf. Note 35.
107   Since a plural implies a minimum of 2.
108   Both expressions are unexplained *hapax legomena*.

109   He disagrees with R. Jehudah and defines חרצן as seed, זג as skin (cf. Arabic زج "to be transparent"). The interpretation of R. Yose is accepted in the Babli (39a) and Targum Onkelos. Targum Yerushalmi follows R. Jehudah.

הלכה ב: וְחַיָּב עַל הַיַּיִן בִּפְנֵי עַצְמוֹ וְעַל הָעֲנָבִים בִּפְנֵי עַצְמָן כול'. (55a line 26) כְּתִיב וַעֲנָבִים לַחִים וִיבֵישִׁים לֹא יֹאכֵל. מִמַּשְׁמַע שֶׁנֶּאֱמַר עֲנָבִים אֵין אָנוּ יוֹדְעִין שֶׁהֵן לַחִין. מַה תַּלְמוּד לוֹמַר עֲנָבִים לַחִים וִיבֵישִׁים. לְחַיֵּיב עַל זֶה בִּפְנֵי עַצְמוֹ וְעַל זֶה בִּפְנֵי עַצְמוֹ. וְאַתְיָיא כְּהָדָא דְּתַנֵּי חִזְקִיָּה. מָה אִם בְּמָקוֹם שֶׁלֹּא עָשָׂה פְּסוֹלֶת פְּרִי כִפְרִי עָשָׂה לַחִים כִּיבֵישִׁין. כָּאן שֶׁעָשָׂה פְּסוֹלֶת פְּרִי כִפְרִי אֵינוֹ דִין שֶׁנַּעֲשָׂה לַחִין כִּיבֵשִׁין. תַּלְמוּד לוֹמַר לַחִים וִיבֵישִׁים. לְחַיֵּיב עַל זֶה בִּפְנֵי עַצְמוֹ וְעַל זֶה בִּפְנֵי עַצְמוֹ. וְאַתְיָיא כַּהֲהִיא דְּאָמַר רִבִּי הִילָא. לֹא יַחֲבֹל רֵחַיִם וָרָכֶב. מִמַּשְׁמַע שֶׁנֶּאֱמַר רֶכֶב אֵין אָנוּ יוֹדְעִין שֶׁהָרֵחַיִם בִּכְלָל. מַה תַּלְמוּד לוֹמַר רֵחַיִם וָרֶכֶב. לְחַיֵּיב עַל זֶה בִּפְנֵי עַצְמוֹ וְעַל זֶה בִּפְנֵי עַצְמוֹ.

Halakhah 2: "One is guilty for wine separately, for grapes separately," etc. It is written[110]: "Also grapes, fresh or dried, he shall not eat." One understands, since it said "grapes", do we not know that they are fresh[111]? Why does the verse say, "grapes, fresh or dried"? To declare guilty for either one separately. This parallels what Ḥizqiah stated: Since at a place where He did not treat the waste of fruits like fruits[112], He treated fresh and dried equally, here, where He treated the waste of fruits like fruits, would it not be logical that we treat fresh and dried equally? The verse said, "fresh or dried", to declare guilty for either one separately. This parallels what Rebbi Hila said: "One may not impound the movable and the fixed part of a flour-mill.[113]" One understands, since it said "the fixed part", do we not know that the entire mill is understood? Why does the verse say, "the movable and the fixed part"? To declare guilty for either part separately[114].

110   *Num.* 6:3.
111   Since raisins are called צִמוּקִים.
112   The biblical rules of *'orlah*, the prohibition of fruits for the first three years of a fruit tree, do not extend to branches, leaves, or flowers (Mishnah *'Orlah* 1:7).
113   *Deut.* 24:6.
114   In *Sifry Deut.* 272, the conclusion arrived at here is taken as the obvious meaning of the verse.

(55a line 36) לַחִים לְרַבּוֹת אֶת הַבּוֹסֶר. לַחִים לְרַבּוֹת אֶת הַסְּמָדַר. מַתְנִיתָא דְרָבִּי יוֹסֵי. דְּרָבִּי יוֹסֵי אָמַר. סְמָדַר אָסוּר בַּנָּזִיר מִפְּנֵי שֶׁהוּא פְּרִי. יֵשׁ אוֹכֵל אֶשְׁכּוֹל וְחַיָּיב מִשּׁוּם עֲנָבִים לַחִים וִיבֵישִׁים וְחַרְצַנִּים וְזַגִּין. שְׁרִיָּין לְשֵׁם מִשְׁרָה. סְחָטוֹ לְשֵׁם יַיִן. וְהִתְרוּ בּוֹ מִשּׁוּם מִכָּל־אֲשֶׁר יֵצֵא מִגֶּפֶן הַיַּיִן. וגו'.

"Fresh", to include unripe berries.[115] "Fresh", to include the flower. The *baraita* follows Rebbi Yose, since Rebbi Yose said, the flower is forbidden for the *nazir* because it is a fruit[116]. It is possible to eat a bunch of grapes and to be guilty in reference to "grapes, fresh or dried, he shall not eat.[117]" If he soaked it for soaking, pressed it for wine, and they warned him about "anything that comes from the wine-vine"[118], etc.

115   *Sifry Num.* 23.

116   Cf. Mishnah *'Orlah* 1:6, Note 182 (Babli *Berakhot* 36b). Probably the reference is to the bottom of the flower, from which the fruit develops.

117   If some grapes in the bunch dried on the stem.

118   *Jud.* 13:14, as substitute of *Num.*

6:4. If the *nazir* took a bunch of grapes some of which where dried up, soaked it in water to fill the raisins with water as one does to prepare raisin wine, and then presses the bunch for its juice, and drinks after being duly warned, he can be convicted of four simultaneous crimes.

(55a line 41) אָמַר רִבִּי בָּא בַּר אָחָא. טַעֲמָא דְּרִבִּי לְעָזָר בֶּן עֲזַרְיָה מִשּׁוּם בִּירְיָה. וְתַנֵּי. חַרְצַנִּים וְזַגִּין. לְהָבִיא אֶת הַשָּׁלֹשׁ שֶׁבֵּינְתַיִים. וְהָא תַנֵּי בְשֵׁם רִבִּי לְעָזָר. מִכָּל־אֲשֶׁר יֵעָשֶׂה מִגֶּפֶן הַיַּיִן. אַף הֶעָלִין וְהַלּוּלָבִין בְּמַשְׁמַע. רִבִּי לִיעֶזֶר כְּרִבִּי יִשְׁמָעֵאל. דְּרִבִּי יִשְׁמָעֵאל אָמַר. כְּלָל וּפְרָט הַכֹּל בִּכְלָל. וּכְדָרְבָהּ מִן דְּרִבִּי יִשְׁמָעֵאל אָמַר. אֲפִילוּ כְּלָל וּפְרָט הַכֹּל בִּכְלָל. לְאֵי זֶה דָּבָר נֶאֱמַר חַרְצַנִּין וְזַגִּין. לְהָבִיא הַשָּׁלֹשׁ שֶׁבֵּינְתַיִים.

Rebbi Abba bar Aha said: The reason of Rebbi Eleazar ben Azariah is because of a creature[119]. But it was stated: "Skins and seeds," to include the third [kind] between them[120]. But was it not stated in the name of Rebbi Eliezer[38]: "From anything made from the wine-vine", leaves and twigs are also understood? Rebbi Eliezer parallels Rebbi Ismael, since Rebbi Ismael said, [if you have] a principle and a detail, everything is included in the principle[121]. And more than that, since Rebbi Ismael said, with a principle and a detail, everything is included in the principle; why are "skins and seeds" said? To include the third [kind] in between[122].

119 Even if skin and the seed inside do not fill the volume of an olive, the *nazir* who eats them is guilty for eating a complete creature.

120 The flesh of the fruit. Since one speaks of skins and seeds as separate from the grape berry, one speaks of the husks left after pressing. Therefore, the "third" is what is left of the flesh after all juice has been squeezed out.

121 In the Babylonian sources (35a; *Sifra Introduction* 7), R. Ismael's hermeneutical rule 5 is stated as: If the detail precedes the general statement, the general statement receives the maximal extension. If the general statement precedes the detail, the extension of the general statement is defined by the detail. This interpretation must be rejected by the Yerushalmi since *Num.* 6:4 contains first a general statement (all that comes from the vine) and then a detail (skins and seeds). The discussion disregards that v. 3 contains a list of details only.

122 Previously (Note 56), the expression "from skins unto seeds" was meant to imply that the *nazir* is guilty separately for skins and for seeds. This was derived from the additional word *unto*. Here, the argument refers to the mention of skins and seeds themselves, which does not seem to add anything to "everything coming from the vine." For a different formulation, cf. *Sifry Num.* 24.

(55a line 46) מַה טַעֲמָא דְּרִבִּי יוֹסֵי. אָכַל חֲצִי זַיִת חַרְצַנִּים וְזָגִּין מֵעֲנָבָה אַחַת. עַל דַּעְתֵּיהּ דְּרִבִּי לְעָזָר בֶּן עֲזַרְיָה חַיָּיב. עַל דַּעְתֵּיהּ דְּרַבָּנִין פָּטוּר. מַה טַעֲמָא דְּרִבִּי יוּדָה. אָכַל כְּזַיִת חַרְצַנִּים וְזָגִּין מִשְּׁתֵּי עֲנָבוֹת. עַל דַּעְתֵּיהּ דְּרִבִּי לְעָזָר בֶּן עֲזַרְיָה אֵינוֹ חַיָּיב אֶלָּא אַחַת. עַל דַּעְתֵּיהּ דְּרַבָּנִין חַיָּיב שְׁתַּיִם. אָמַר רִבִּי אָבוּן אָתְיָיא דְּרִבִּי לְעָזָר בֶּן עֲזַרְיָה כְּרִבִּי יוֹסֵי. אִין תֵּימַר כְּרִבִּי יוּדָה אָכַל כְּזַיִת שְׁנֵי זוֹגִין וְחַרְצַנִּין.

What is Rebbi Yose's reason[123]? If one ate half the volume of an olive of seeds and peels from one grape berry, in Rebbi Eleazar ben Azariah's opinion he is guilty[124], in the rabbis' opinion he is not prosecutable. What is Rebbi Jehudah's reason? If he ate the volume of an olive of peels and seeds from two grape berries, in Rebbi Eleazar ben Azariah's opinion he is guilty only once[125], in the rabbis' opinion he is guilty twice. Rebbi Abun said, it turns out that Rebbi Eleazar ben Azariah holds with Rebbi Jehudah, if he ate the volume of an olive of two זגים and their חרצנים[126]?

123 R. Yose clearly must think that his interpretation of the words is linguistically correct. The question is, what are the legal implications of his definition; how would he rule differently from R. Jehudah?

124 If a single berry was squeezed dry but two seeds and the skin were left, for R. Eleazar ben Azariah this would represent a creature and the *nazir* who eats them would be guilty. For the rabbis, anything less than the volume of an olive cannot lead to a conviction. But for R. Jehudah, two חרצנים means skins from two berries; there is no creature and the *nazir* is not prosecutable..

125 According to R. Jehudah, R. Eleazar ben Azariah's requirement that the *nazir* must eat two חרצנים to be guilty means that even if each grape berry has the size of an olive, he must eat two of them to become guilty. For the rabbis, eating a single berry the size of an olive is a punishable offense.

126 He holds that the statement of R. Eleazar ben Azariah cannot be reconciled with the opinion of R. Jehudah since then he should have switched the mention of חרצן and זג as explained in Note 124.

(fol. 54b) **מִשְׁנָה ג:** סְתָם נְזִירוּת שְׁלֹשִׁים יוֹם. גִּילַּח אוֹ שֶׁגִּילְּחוּהוּ לִיסְטִין סוֹתֵר שְׁלֹשִׁים. נָזִיר שֶׁגִּילַּח בֵּין בְּזוּג בֵּין בַּתַּעַר אוֹ שֶׁסִּיפְסֵף כָּל־שֶׁהוּא חַיָּיב. נָזִיר חוֹפֵף וּמְפַסְפֵּס אֲבָל לֹא סוֹרֵק. רִבִּי יִשְׁמָעֵאל אוֹמֵר לֹא יָחוֹף בָּאֲדָמָה מִפְּנֵי שֶׁהִיא מַשֶּׁרֶת אֶת הַשֵּׂיעָר.

Mishnah 3: An unspecified *nezirut* is thirty days[127]. If he shaved, or robbers shaved him[128], he starts again for thirty[129]. A *nazir* who shaved any [hair], whether with scissors or razor knife, or cropped[130], is guilty. A *nazir* may wash his head and separate his hair but may not comb. Rebbi Ismael says, he cannot wash his hair with powder because that removes hair.

127 Repeated from Mishnah 1:3.
128 Forcibly.
129 He counts a minimum of 30 days after his shaving before he can bring his sacrifices since no *nazir* can shave after less than 30 days.
130 *Arukh*: ספסף, "tearing off part of the hair, cropping," with the root remaining in the scalp, contrasting רט "tearing or falling out completely". (Compare Arabic سفاف "to sift"). The commentary from the school of Rashi and Maimonides explain: "tore out."

(55a line 52) **הלכה ג:** סְתָם נְזִירוּת ל' יוֹם כול'. כְּתִיב תַּעַר לֹא יַעֲבֹר עַל רֹאשׁוֹ. הָא עָבַר חַיָּיב. גִּדֵּל פֶּרַע שְׂעַר רֹאשׁוֹ. כַּמָּה הוּא גִּידּוּל שֵׂיעָר. ל' יוֹם. עַד כְּדוֹן נָזִיר טָמֵא. נָזִיר טָהוֹר. וְגִלַּח רֹאשׁוֹ בְּיוֹם טָהֳרָתוֹ. מַה תַּלְמוּד לוֹמַר בַּיּוֹם הַשְּׁבִיעִי יְגַלַּח אֶת כָּל־שְׂעָרוֹ. מִיכָּן שֶׁהוּא חוֹזֵר וּמְגַלֵּחַ. וְגִילַּח. כּוּלּוֹ וְלֹא מִקְצָתוֹ. מִיכָּן שֶׁאִם שִׁייֵר שְׁתֵּי שְׂעָרוֹת לֹא אָמַר¹³¹ כְּלוּם. תַּעַר לֹא יַעֲבֹר עַל רֹאשׁוֹ. אֵין לִי אֶלָּא תַּעַר. מְנַיִין לְרַבּוֹת אֶת הַמְסַפְסֵף וְאֶת הַמְסָפְּרִים כְּבַתַּעַר. תַּלְמוּד לוֹמַר לֹא יַעֲבֹור עַל רֹאשׁוֹ. אֵין לִי אֶלָּא תַּעַר. כָּל הַמַּעֲבִירִין בְּמַשְׁמָע. מִיכָּן שֶׁאֵינוֹ סוֹתֵר בּוֹ אֶלָּא¹³² בִּלְבַד.

Halakhah 3: "An unspecified *nezirut* is thirty days," etc. [133]It is written: "A shaving knife shall not pass over his head[134];" therefore, if it did pass, he is guilty[135]. "His head's hair grows wildly;" how much means growing hair? 30 days[136]. {That refers to an impure *nazir*. A pure *nazir*? "He has to shave his head on the day be becomes pure." Why does the verse say: "On the seventh day he shall shave all his hair"? That shows that he shaves a second time.}[137] "He shaves,"[138] all, not in part[139]. From here that if he left two hairs, he [did] nothing. "A shaving knife shall not pass over his head.[134]" Not only a shaving knife, from where to treat a cropper and scissors like a shaving knife? The verse says, "shall not pass over his head." That means not only a shaving knife; all methods of removal are understood. From here that he starts again only for a [shaving knife][140].

131 Clearly, this should read עָשָׂה "did" instead of אָמַר "said".

132 A word is missing, which can be conjectured to be תַּעַר, see the commentary to this sentence.

133 The text of the first two paragraphs of this Halakhah is in rather bad shape.

134 *Num.* 6:5.

135 *He* is guilty if *it* passed: even if the *nazir* is passive. (In the Babli, 44a, and *Sifry Num.* 25, the sentence is interpreted to make the shaver equally guilty with the shaved.)

136 Chapter 1, Notes 99,100.

137 The text in braces is corrupt as it stands. The proposals for emendations create a new text; it seems better to try to understand the text as it is.

The verses quoted up to this point do not mention an impure *nazir*; it is possible to read with the classical commentaries: "That refers to a pure *nazir*. An impure *nazir*? 'He has to shave his head on the day be becomes pure' (*Num.* 6:9)." This presupposes that a pure *nazir* who shaves has to start anew; why does an impure *nazir*, who anyhow has to start anew for a minimum of 30 days, add to his period of *nezirut* if he tears out a hair?

The following quote, *Lev.* 14:9, and its accompanying text have nothing to do with the *nazir* but refer to the convalescent sufferer from skin disease. He has to shave a second time, 7 days after the shaving ordered in v. 8.

138 *Num.* 6:9 (the impure *nazir*), 6:18 (the pure *nazir*).

139 This is a *non sequitur*. In all other sources, the rule for the *nazir* is determined in comparison with the recovered sufferer from skin disease (Note 137) and the Levites when inducted into the service of the Tabernacle (*Num.* 8:7). In both cases, the verse emphasizes the necessity to shave *all* hair, meaning that no two hairs can be left standing [Babli 32a; Mishnah *Nega'im* 14:4; *Sifra Meṣora' Pereq* 2(6)].

140 Part of the last sentence is missing here but can be recovered from the Babli, 39b, and *Sifry Num.* 25, where a text parallel to that extending the prohibition from a shaving knife to anything that shaves is attributed to R. Joshia; but R. Jonathan states that "the verse speaks of a shaving knife. Therefore, if he tore out, cropped, or went to the barber, he cannot be whipped."

Since the wording of R. Joshia's text in the Yerushalmi differs from the Babli/Sifry text, for R. Jonathan's opinion only the meaning, but not the text, can be recovered.

(55a line 61) רִבִּי בָּא בַּר מָמָל וְרִבִּי אִילָא בְּעוֹן קוֹמֵי רִבִּי יָסָא. לֹא יִסְתְּרוּ בוֹ שְׁלֹשִׁים אֲבָל יִסְתְּרוּ בוֹ שִׁבְעָה. לֹא. בְּשֶׁאֵינוֹ סוֹתֵר בּוֹ לֹא שִׁבְעָה וְלֹא שְׁלֹשִׁים. אִין תֵּימַר. לֹא יִסְתְּרוּ בוֹ שְׁלֹשִׁים. מַה בֵּין נָזִיר טָהוֹר מַה בֵּין נָזִיר טָמֵא. תַּנֵּי קַל וְחוֹמֶר בְּנָזִיר טָהוֹר. תַּנֵּי קַל וְחוֹמֶר בְּנָזִיר טָמֵא. קַל בְּנָזִיר טָהוֹר שֶׁאֵינוֹ סוֹתֵר אֶלָּא שְׁלֹשִׁים. וְחוֹמֶר שֶׁהוּא סוֹתֵר בּוֹ שִׁבְעָה. אִין תֵּימַר. לֹא יִסְתְּרוּ בוֹ שְׁלֹשִׁים. מַה שָּׁנֵי בֵּין נָזִיר טָהוֹר מַה בֵּין נָזִיר טָמֵא. קַל בְּנָזִיר טָמֵא שֶׁבְּכוּלָּן סוֹתְרִין בּוֹ. וְחוֹמֶר שֶׁהוּא סוֹתֵר בּוֹ שִׁבְעָה. אִין תֵּימַר. לֹא יִסְתְּרוּ בוֹ שְׁלֹשִׁים. מַה שָּׁנֵי בֵּין נָזִיר טָהוֹר לְנָזִיר טָמֵא. אִית דְּבָעֵי מֵימַר. מַה שָּׁנֵי בֵּין בְּמִסְפָּרַיִם לְבְתַעַר וְנָזִיר טָהוֹר כְּרִבִּי אֱלִיעֶזֶר.

Rebbi Abba bar Mamal and Rebbi Ila asked before Rebbi Yasa: They should not start again for thirty, but should start again for seven[141]! No, should they restart neither for seven nor for thirty[142]? If you say, they should not start again for thirty, what is the difference between a pure and an impure *nazir*[143]? "One has stated a leniency and a restriction for a pure *nazir*; one has stated a leniency and a restriction for an impure *nazir*. A leniency for a pure *nazir* that he restart only for thirty; a restriction that he restart for seven[144]. If you say, he should restart for thirty, what is the difference between a pure and an impure *nazir*?[145] A leniency for an impure *nazir* that all cases make him restart; a restriction that he restarts for seven[146]." Should he not restart for thirty? If you say, he should restart for thirty, what is the difference between a pure and an impure *nazir*[147]? Some want to say, what is the difference between scissors and a shaving knife for a pure *nazir* following Rebbi Eliezer[148]?

141 Since the person healed of skin disease shaves both after the initial ceremony (*Lev.* 14:8) and seven days afterwards (v. 9), it follows that seven days are sufficient to justify another shaving. Since shaving by means other than a knife is forbidden for the *nazir* only by implication, it seems reasonable to require only a 7 days' growth for a *nazir* who removed hair

not by a knife.

142   According to R. Jonathan (Note 140), shaving other than by a knife should not have any consequence.

143   The *baraita* to be quoted states that the exact duration of the period to restart the growth of hair is different for a pure *nazir* who shaves and an impure *nazir* who is forced to shave.

144   This text makes no sense. It seems that it must read with Tosephta 4:3: "He restarts only if shaved by a knife (most of his head); a restriction that he restart for 30 days."

145   This sentence has to be deleted; it belongs to the discussion after the *baraita* is quoted in its entirety.

146   In this sentence, "leniency" and "restriction" have to be switched. At the required shaving of the impure *nazir*, "knife" is not mentioned; everybody agrees that all methods of shaving are equally valid.

147   And the *baraita* clearly stated that the time lost is different for the two kinds of *nazir*.

148   Who in Mishnah 3:4 requires the *nazir* who fulfilled his time but shaved before he brought his sacrifice only to wait another seven days. He certainly must agree with R. Jonathan that if the *nazir* did not use a knife he does not have to wait at all.

(55a line 71) תַּמָּן תַּנִּינָן. שְׁלֹשָׁה מְגַלְּחִין וְתִגְלַחְתָּן מִצְוָה. הַנָּזִיר וְהַמְצוֹרָע וְהַלְוִיִּם. וְכוּלָּן שֶׁגִּילְּחוּ שֶׁלֹּא בְתַעַר אוֹ שֶׁשִּׁיְּירוּ שְׁתֵּי שְׂעָרוֹת לֹא עָשׂוּ כְלוּם. אָמַר רִבִּי אֶלְעָזָר. מַתְנִיתָא בְּנָזִיר טָמֵא. אֲבָל בְּנָזִיר טָהוֹר כֵּיוָן שֶׁגִּילַּח רוֹב רֹאשׁוֹ אֲפִילוּ שֶׁלֹּא בְתַעַר יָצָא. רִבִּי אָמִי כְּהָדָא דְּרִבִּי אֶלְעָזָר (בֶּן עֲזַרְיָה) בָּעֵי. כָּל־עַצְמוֹ אֵינוֹ קָרוּי תַּעַר אֶלָּא בְּנָזִיר טָהוֹר. תַּעַר לֹא יַעֲבֹר עַל רֹאשׁוֹ עַד מְלֹאת הַיָּמִים. הָא אִם הִשְׁלִים צָרִיךְ תַּעַר. דִּילְמָא לֹא אִיתְאֲמָרַת אֶלָּא בְּנָזִיר טָמֵא בִּשְׁתֵּי שְׂעָרוֹת. אָמַר רִבִּי יוֹסֵי לְרִבִּי יַעֲקֹב בַּר אָחָא. נְהִיר אַתְּ דַּהֲוֵיתוֹן קַיָּימִין בְּנָזִיר וְאָמְרִינָן. לֹא שַׁנְיָיא בֵּין מִסְפָּרַיִם לַבְּתַעַר. וְאָמַר רִבִּי לְעָזָר. מַתְנִיתָא בְּנָזִיר טָמֵא. נָזִיר טָהוֹר לָמָּה לֹא. נָזִיר טָהוֹר מְגַלֵּחַ אַחַר זְרִיקָה. כֵּיוָן שֶׁקָּדַשׁ שַׁלְמָה נְזִירוּ. בְּרַם. כְּנָשׁוּר הוּא.

There, we have stated[149]: "Three categories of people shave and their shaving is a commandment: the *nazir*, the sufferer from skin disease, and the Levites. All these, if they shaved not with a knife or left two hairs, did not do anything." Rebbi Eleazar said: The Mishnah [speaks] about an impure *nazir*. But a pure *nazir*, once he shaved most of his head, even if not with a knife, has acquitted himself [of his obligation]. Rebbi Immi, following Rebbi Eleazar (ben Azariah)[150], asked: The only place where a knife is mentioned is about a pure *nazir*: "A shaving knife shall not pass over his head until the days are fulfilled.[151]" Therefore, after he fulfilled them he needs a knife! Perhaps it was said only about an impure *nazir* with regard to two hairs[152]. Rebbi Yose[153] said to Rebbi Jacob bar Aḥa: Do you remember when we were studying *Nazir*, we said that there was no difference between scissors and a knife, and Rebbi Eleazar said: The Mishnah [speaks] about an impure *nazir*! Why not about a pure *nazir*? The pure *nazir* shaves after the blood was sprinkled[154]. When that was sanctified, his vow was completed. But it[155] is as if fallen out.

149   Mishnah *Nega'im* 14:4; quoted Babli 40a; cf. Note 139.

150   Since the author of the remark is R. Eleazar ben Pada, the words in parenthesis have to be deleted.

151   *Num.* 6:5.

152   The impure *nazir* cannot restart his vow if he left two hairs uncut. But the requirement of a knife also applies to a pure *nazir*.

153   In the Babli, 42a, the remark is attributed to R. Yose ben Ḥanina. Since R. Jacob bar Aḥa was a colleague of R. Yasa and a teacher of R. Yose, it seems that one has to read "Yasa" instead of "Yose"; the attribution of the Babli is impossible.

154   For all sacrifices, the sprinkling of the blood on the walls of the altar fulfills the purpose of the sacrifice; nothing that happens afterwards can invalidate the sacrifice.

155   The hair of the *nazir*'s head.

(55b line 6) אַתְּ אָמַר בְּנָזִיר טָהוֹר רוֹב רֹאשׁוֹ מְעַכֵּב בּוֹ. גִּילַּח שְׁלִישׁוֹ. לֹא הִסְפִּיק לְגַלְּחוֹ עַד שֶׁגָּדַל כּוּלוֹ. מְגַלֵּחַ הַשְּׁאָר וְדַיּוֹ אוֹ צָרִיךְ לְגַלֵּחַ אֶת כּוּלוֹ. אַתְּ אָמַר בְּנָזִיר טָמֵא שְׁתֵּי שְׂעָרוֹת מְעַכְּבוֹת בּוֹ שְׁתֵּי שְׂעָרוֹת סוֹתְרוֹת בּוֹ. וְדִכְוָתָהּ בְּנָזִיר טָהוֹר שְׁתֵּי שְׂעָרוֹת מְעַכְּבוֹת בּוֹ שְׁתֵּי שְׂעָרוֹת סוֹתְרוֹת בּוֹ. אָמַר רִבִּי יוֹסֵי

בְּירַבִּי בּוּן. וְכֵן הִיא. וְתַנֵּי כֵן. רִבִּי שִׁמְעוֹן בֶּן יְהוּדָה אוֹמֵר מִשֵּׁם רִבִּי שִׁמְעוֹן. כְּשֵׁם שֶׁשְׁתֵּי שְׂעָרוֹת מְעַכְּבוֹת בּוֹ כָּךְ שְׁתֵּי שְׂעָרוֹת סוֹתְרוֹת בּוֹ.

You say about a pure *nazir* that most of his hair hinders him[156]. If he shaved a third but did not manage to finish until everything grew again: Is it sufficient that he shave the remainder or does he have to shave everything?[157] You say about an impure *nazir* that two hairs hinder[152] or two hairs make him start again. Similarly, for a pure *nazir*, do two hairs hinder him or two hairs make him start again? Rebbi Yose ben Rebbi Abun said, so it is, and it was stated[158]: "Rebbi Simeon ben Jehudah said in the name of Rebbi Simeon, just as two hairs hinder him, so two hairs cause him to start again."

156 If he shaved less than 50% of his head's hair, he has not lived up to the conditions of his vow.

157 The question is not answered, being unrealistic.

158 Tosephta 4:3; Babli 40a.

(55b line 12) רִבִּי יִרְמְיָה בָּעֵי. וְגִילַּח אֶת כּוּלוֹ וְשִׁייֵר בּוֹ שְׁתֵּי שְׂעָרוֹת וְהָיָה בָהֶן כְּדֵי לָכוּף רֹאשׁוֹ לְעִיקָּרוֹ שְׁתֵּי פְעָמִים וְגִילַּח פַּעַם אַחַת. מֵאַחַר שֶׁגִּילַּח כְּדֵי סִימָן יָצָא אוֹ מֵאַחַר שֶׁשִׁייֵר כְּדֵי סִימָן לֹא יָצָא.

Rebbi Jeremiah asked: If he shaved everything but left two hairs which were long enough each to bend its end to its root[159] twice; he shaved to reduce it to one[160]. Since he cut the required length, has he fulfilled his obligation, or because he omitted what was required, did he not fulfill his obligation?

159 A hair is considered cut if it cannot be bent so that its head touches its root.

160 He cut all hairs to below the limit except two which he cut exactly to the limit. R. Jeremiah in general holds that the rules only state that the condition is fulfilled if the limit is not reached and violated if the limit is exceeded but at the exact limit nothing has been decided; cf. Babli *Baba batra* 22b, a position rejected in general.

(55b line 16) רִבִּי אִילָא אָמַר קוֹמֵי רִבִּי יוֹסֵי. לְמַלְקוּת אַחַת. לְעִיכּוּב שְׁתַּיִם. לִסְתִירָה שָׁלֹשׁ. מַתְנִיתָא פְּלִיגָא עַל רִבִּי יוֹסֵי. וְהוּא שֶׁסִּיפְסֵף כָּל־שֶׁהוּא חַייָב. אָמַר רִבִּי אַבָּא בַּר מָמָל. פָּתַר לֵיהּ רִבִּי יָסָא כָּל־שֶׁהוּא מִזֶּה וְכָל־שֶׁהוּא מִזֶּה. מַתְנִיתָא פְּלִיגָא עַל שְׁמוּאֵל. יֵשׁ תּוֹלֵשׁ שְׁתֵּי שְׂעָרוֹת חַייָב עֲלֵיהֶן מִשֵּׁם אַרְבָּעָה לָוִין. מִשֵּׁם נָזִיר מִשֵּׁם מְצוֹרָע מִשֵּׁם יוֹם טוֹב מִשֵּׁם מַקִּיף. לַוִּין אַתִּינָן מִיתְנֵי. אֲבָל לַמַּלְקוּת לוֹקִין אֲפִילוּ עַל אַחַת.

Rebbi Ila said before Rebbi Yose[161]: For whipping one, for hindering two, to start again three[162]. A *baraita* disagrees with Rebbi Yose[161]: "If he cropped any[163], he is guilty." Rebbi Abba bar Mamal said, Rebbi Yasa explains it by a little bit from each one[164]. A *baraita* disagrees with Samuel[165]: A person may tear out two hairs and have violated four prohibitions[166]: As a *nazir*, as a sufferer from sking disease, on a holiday, because of jaw stripping[167]. We have enumerated the prohibitions; but with regard to whippings, one even whips for one[168].

161 Here also one has to read: Yasa.

162 A *nazir* who cut one hair can be whipped. If he was impure and failed to cut two hairs, he cannot re-start his *nezirut*; if he was pure and failed to cut two hairs, he did not fulfill his vow. If he is pure and cut three hairs, he has to keep a minimum of 30 days of *nezirut* after that.

163 He did not even cut one entire hair.

164 Cropping many hairs is not comparable to cutting one hair.

165 The mention of Samuel instead of R. Hila seems to be a scribal error.

166 The scribe did not quite understand his text. He wrote ללוים "for the Levites" insteat of לוים, לאוים "prohibitions", literally "no's".

167 If a person who is both a *nazir* and a sufferer from skin disease (who has to grow his hair, *Lev.* 13:45) shaves his sideburns on a holiday, he violates 4 prohibitions with one act. Since shaving on a holiday is prosecutable only if he shaves a minimum of two hairs, R. Hila's assertion that one can be whipped for shaving a single hair is put into question.

168 Things may be prohibited even if they cannot be prosecuted.

(55b line 22) אִית תַּנָּיֵי תַנֵּי. מְפַסְפְּסִין בִּקְלִיקִין. וְאִית תַּנָּיֵי תַנֵּי. אֵין מְפַסְפְּסִין. אָמַר רַב חִסְדָּא. מָאן דְּאָמַר מְפַסְפְּסִין. בִּבְרִיא. מָאן דְּאָמַר אֵין מְפַסְפְּסִין. בְּתַשׁ.

Some *Tannaïm* state: "One separates matted hair[169]." Some *Tannaïm* state: "One does not separate." Rav Ḥisda said, the one who states that one separates, for healthy [hair]; the one who states that one does not separate, for weak [hair].

[169] קליקין is usually explained as κιλίκιον, τό "coarse cloth (of Cilician goat's hair); covering used by soldiers and seamen", but in this case (and the related one in Mishnah *Miqwa'ot* 9:2) one might refer to Latin *culcita, culcitra,* "sack filled with feathers, wool, or hair; cushion, mattress" (E. G.).

(fol. 54b) **משנה ד:** נָזִיר שֶׁהָיָה שׁוֹתֶה בַּיַּיִן כָּל־הַיּוֹם אֵינוֹ חַיָּיב אֶלָּא אַחַת. אָמְרוּ לוֹ אַל תִּשְׁתֶּה אַל תִּשְׁתֶּה וְהוּא שׁוֹתֶה חַיָּיב עַל כָּל־אַחַת וְאַחַת.

Mishnah 4: A *nazir* who was drinking wine all day long is guilty only once. If he was told "do not drink, do not drink" and he did drink, he is guilty for each single infraction[170].

משנה ה: הָיָה מְגַלֵּחַ כָּל־הַיּוֹם אֵינוֹ חַיָּיב אֶלָּא אַחַת. אָמְרוּ לוֹ אַל תְּגַלַּח אַל תְּגַלַּח וְהוּא מְגַלֵּחַ חַיָּיב עַל כָּל־אַחַת וְאַחַת.

Mishnah 5: One who shaved all day long is guilty only once. If he was told "do not shave, do not shave" and he did shave, he is guilty for each single infraction.

משנה ו: הָיָה מִיטַּמֵּא לַמֵּתִים כָּל־הַיּוֹם אֵינוֹ חַיָּיב אֶלָּא אַחַת. אָמְרוּ לוֹ אַל תִּיטַּמֵּא אַל תִּיטַּמֵּא וְהוּא מִיטַּמֵּא חַיָּיב עַל כָּל־אַחַת וְאַחַת.

Mishnah 6: One who defiled himself for the dead all day long is guilty only once. If he was told "do not defile yourself, do not defile yourself" and he did defile himself, he is guilty for each single infraction.

170 If he was duly warned once by two witnesses, he can be prosecuted and punished for one offense.

If he was repeatedly warned and flouted each warning, he can be prosecuted for disregarding each warning separately. The same rules apply for all three prohibitions imposed on a *nazir*.

(55b line 24) **הלכה ד:** נָזִיר שֶׁהָיָה שׁוֹתֶה בַּיַּיִן כּוֹל׳. נָזִיר וְהוּא בְּבֵית הַקְּבָרוֹת. רִבִּי יוֹחָנָן אָמַר. מַתְרִין בּוֹ עַל הַיַּיִן וְעַל הַתִּגְלַחַת. רִבִּי שִׁמְעוֹן בֶּן לָקִישׁ אוֹמֵר. מֵאַחַר שֶׁאֵין מַתְרִין בּוֹ עַל הַטּוּמְאָה אֵין מַתְרִין בּוֹ עַל הַיַּיִן וְעַל הַתִּגְלַחַת. גָּרַשׁ כּוּלָּהּ הִילְכְתָא בְּפֶרֶק ג.

1 נזיר | נזר   2 אומר | אמר

Halakhah 4: "A *nazir* who drank wine," etc. A *nazir* while he was in a cemetery: Rebbi Joḥanan said, one warns him about wine and shaving. Rebbi Simeon ben Laqish said, since one cannot warn him because of impurity, one does not warn him about wine and shaving. One reads all this in the Third Chapter[171].

171 Halakhah 3:5, Notes 58 ff.

(55b line 28) **הלכה ה:** הָיוּ לְפָנָיו צְלוֹחִיּוֹת שְׁתַּיִם. אַחַת שְׁלָמִים וְאַחַת שְׁלָיָין. נָטַל וְשָׁתָה אוֹתָהּ שְׁלָמִים. אָמְרוּ לוֹ. הֲוֵי יוֹדֵעַ מִשֶּׁאַתְּ שׁוֹתֶה שְׁלָמִים אַתְּ שׁוֹתֶה שְׁלָיָין וְיֵשׁ בָּהּ י׳ זֵיתִים. וְאַתָּה מִתְחַיֵּיב י׳ מַלְקִיּוֹת. אֵינוֹ מְקַבֵּל הַתְרָיָיה בְּדַעַת הַזֹּאת. אֲבָל אִם צְלוֹחִית אַחַת שְׁלָיָין וְהִתְחִיל לִשְׁתּוֹת בָּהּ. אָמְרוּ לוֹ. תְּהֵא יוֹדֵעַ אִם תִּשְׁתֶּה אֶת כּוּלָּהּ יֵשׁ בָּהּ עֲשָׂרָה זֵיתִים וְהִתְחַיָּיב עֲשָׂרָה מַלְקִיּוֹת. מְקַבֵּל הַתְרָיָיה בְּדַעַת הַזֹּאת.

Halakhah 5: If before him were two bottles, one of water and one of wine. He took and emptied the water bottle. They said to him, you should know that after you drank the water, if you then drink the wine, since its volume corresponds to ten olives you will be subject to ten whippings; he does not accept warning in this way[172]. But if it was a wine bottle and he started drinking from it when they said to him, you should know that if you then drink it all, since its volume corresponds to ten olives you will be subject to ten whippings; he accepts warning in this way.

172 Since he did not touch the wine bottle yet and gave no indication that he would take it, the warning is purely preventive. In order to be used in criminal prosecution, the warning must be given when the person to whom it is directed seems likely to violate the law.

הלכה ו: הָיוּ לְפָנָיו שְׁנֵי שַׁפּוּדִין. אַחַת שֶׁלִּשְׁחוּטָה וְאַחַת שֶׁלִּנְבֵילָה. (55b line 34) נָטַל לֶאֱכוֹל אוֹתָהּ שֶׁלִּשְׁחוּטָה. אָמְרוּ לוֹ. תְּהֵא יוֹדֵעַ מַה שֶׁאַתָּה אוֹכֵל שֶׁלִּשְׁחוּטָה. אִם אַתְּ אוֹכֵל אֶת הַנְּבֵילָה וְיֵשׁ בָּהּ י׳ זֵיתִים וְאַתָּה מִתְחַיֵּיב עָלֶיהָ עֲשָׂרָה מַלְקִיּוֹת. אֵינוּ מְקַבֵּל הַתְרָיָיה בְּדַעַת הַזֹּאת. אֲבָל אִם הָיָה שַׁפּוּד אֶחָד שֶׁלִּנְבֵילָה. הִתְחִיל לֶאֱכוֹל בָּהּ. אָמְרוּ לוֹ. תְּהֵא יוֹדֵעַ מִשֶּׁאַתְּ אוֹכֵל כּוּלוֹ וְיֵשׁ בָּהּ עֲשָׂרָה זֵיתִים וְאַתָּה מִתְחַיֵּיב י׳ מַלְקִיּוֹת. מְקַבֵּל הַתְרָיָיה בְּדַעַת הַזֹּאת.

Halakhah 6: If before him were two roasting spits, one with slaughtered meat and one with carcass meat. He took and ate the slaughtered meat. They said to him, you should know that after you ate the slaughtered meat, if you then ate the carcass meat, since its volume corresponds to ten olives you will be subject to ten whippings; he does not accept warning in this way[172]. But if there was a roasting spit of carcass meat and he started eating from it when they said to him, you should know that if you then ate it all, since its volume corresponds to ten olives you will be subject to ten whippings; he accepts warning in this way.

משנה ז: (fol. 54b) שְׁלֹשָׁה מִינִים אֲסוּרִין בַּנָּזִיר הַטּוּמְאָה וְהַתִּגְלַחַת וְהַיּוֹצֵא מִן הַגֶּפֶן. חוֹמֶר בַּטּוּמְאָה וּבַתִּגְלַחַת מִבַּיּוֹצֵא מִן הַגֶּפֶן שֶׁהַטּוּמְאָה וְהַתִּגְלַחַת סוֹתְרִים וְהַיּוֹצֵא מִן הַגֶּפֶן אֵינוֹ סוֹתֵר. חוֹמֶר בַּיּוֹצֵא מִן הַגֶּפֶן מִבַּטּוּמְאָה וּמִבַּתִּגְלַחַת שֶׁהַיּוֹצֵא מִן הַגֶּפֶן לֹא הוּתַר מִכְּלָלוֹ וְהַטּוּמְאָה וְהַתִּגְלַחַת הוּתְרוּ מִכְּלָלָן בְּתִגְלַחַת מִצְוָה וּבְמֵת מִצְוָה. וְחוֹמֶר בַּטּוּמְאָה מִן הַתִּגְלַחַת שֶׁהַטּוּמְאָה סוֹתֶרֶת אֶת הַכֹּל וְחַיָּיבִין עָלֶיהָ קָרְבָּן וְהַתִּגְלַחַת אֵינָהּ סוֹתֶרֶת אֶלָּא עַד שְׁלֹשִׁים יוֹם וְאֵין חַיָּיבִין עָלֶיהָ קָרְבָּן.

Mishnah 7: Three kinds are forbidden for the *nazir*: Impurity, shaving, and consuming produce of the vine[173]. Impurity and shaving are more severe than the prohibition of produce of the vine since impurity and shaving require him to start again, but produce of the vine does not require him to start again. The prohibition of produce of the vine is more severe than impurity and shaving since produce of the vine is never permitted but impurity and shaving are permitted for a commanded shaving[174] and a corpse of obligation[175]. Impurity is more severe than shaving since for impurity he has to start again from the beginning and is obligated for a sacrifice, but for shaving he has to start again for at most 30 days and is not obligated for a sacrifice.

173 Repeated from Mishnah 6:1.

174 If a sufferer from skin disease is a *nazir* when he is healed, his vow does not preclude the required shavings for his rehabilitation.

175 Any person, even a *nazir* or a High Priest, who comes upon an unattended corpse, has to defile himself and bring the dead to burial. The rules of the commanded burial are detailed in the next Chapter.

הלכה ז: (55b line 42) הַטּוּמְאָה. דִּכְתִיב כָּל־יְמֵי הַזִּירוֹ לַיְיָ עַל נֶפֶשׁ מֵת לֹא יָבֹא. תִּגְלַחַת. דִּכְתִיב כָּל־יְמֵי נֶדֶר נִזְרוֹ תַּעַר לֹא יַעֲבוֹר עַל רֹאשׁוֹ. הַיּוֹצֵא מִן הַגֶּפֶן. דִּכְתִיב כָּל־יְמֵי נִזְרוֹ מִכֹּל אֲשֶׁר יֵעָשֶׂה מִגֶּפֶן הַיַּיִן וגו'.

Halakhah 7: [176]Impurity, as it is written: "During all the days he vowed to the Eternal he shall not come close to a human corpse." Shaving, as it is written: "During all the days of his *nazir* vow, a shaving knife shall not come onto his head." Anything from the vine, as it is written: "During all the days of his vow, of anything coming from the wine-vine [he shall not eat.]"

176   Halakhah 6:1, Notes 4-6.

(55b line 45) חוֹמֶר בַּטוּמְאָה וּבַתִּגְלַחַת מִבַּיוֹצֵא מִן הַגֶּפֶן. הַטוּמְאָה. דִּכְתִיב כָּל־יְמֵי הַזִּירוֹ לַיָי. וְהַתִּגְלַחַת. דִּכְתִיב וְהַיָמִים הָרִאשׁוֹנִים יִפְּלוּ כִּי טָמֵא נִזְרוֹ.

"Impurity and shaving are more severe than produce of the vine." Impurity, as it is written: "All the days he vowed to the Eternal." And shaving, as it is written: "The earlier days fall away[177], for his vow in impure.[178]"

177   Cf. Halakhah 3:5, Note 57.

178   This verse proves that the impure *nazir* has to start again from the beginning. One is tempted, with the classical commentators, to move this verse to the previous sentence and find an appropriate verse for shaving. The problem is that no biblical verse requires the shaved *nazir* to start counting anew, as explained in Halakhah 3. The reference is to an argument, reproduced *in extenso* in the Babli 44a and *Sifry Num.* 31, shortened in *Num. rabba* 10(34), on exactly the quoted verse, *Num.* 6:12: "For his vow is impure', impurity requires him to start from the beginning, shaving does not require him to start from the beginning, but he has to repeat 30 days."

(55b line 47) חוֹמֶר בַּיוֹצֵא מִן הַגֶּפֶן מִבַּטּוּמְאָה וּמִבַּתִּגְלַחַת. הֲווֹן בָּעֵיי מֵימַר בְּאַרְבַּע כּוֹסוֹת (שְׁלֵמִים אוֹ) שְׁלֵיָין. אֲבָל אִם אָמַר. שְׁבוּעָה שֶׁאֶשְׁתֶּה וְנָזִיר אֶשְׁתֶּה אָתָא לְמֵימַר לֹא יִשְׁתֶּה.

"The produce of the vine is more severe than impurity and shaving." They wanted to say, for the Four Cups (of water or)[179] wine[180]. But if he said, "a vow that I shall drink and be a *nazir*", "that I shall drink" comes to say that he will not drink[181].

179 This clearly is a scribal error.

180 The 4 cups of wine one is required to drink in the *Seder* night (cf. H. Guggenheimer, *The Scholar's Haggadah*, pp. 185-191.) Since this is a rabbinic (or in any case, post-biblical) requirement, it cannot eliminate a biblical prohibition. (In the opinion of the Babli, 3b/4a, the *nazir* may drink wine for the Sabbath *qidduš* since the Fourth Commandment to sanctify the Sabbath cannot be pushed aside by the vow of the *nazir*. This fact is irrelevant here since impurity and shaving can be imposed on the *nazir* after his vow, but the Sabbath wine is his duty before the vow. The Yerushalmi clearly holds that *qidduš* can be recited over bread; wine is not absolutely necessary.)

181 Since in an oath formula, the positive stands for the negative.

(55b line 47) הוּתַּר בְּתִגְלַחַת מִצְוָה. לֹא סוֹף דָּבָר לִיתֵּן סִימָן לְנִגְעוֹ. אֶלָּא לִיתֵּן סִימָן לְנִתְקוֹ וְלֵידַע אִם פָּשָׂה אִם לֹא פָּשָׂה. וּבְמֵת מִצְוָה. הָדָא הִיא דְתַנִּינָן. הָיוּ מְהַלְּכִין בַּדֶּרֶךְ וּמָצְאוּ מֵת מִצְוָה.

He is permitted commanded shavings. Not only to signify his skin disease[181] but also to signify his scall, to know whether it spread or did not spread[182]. "And a corpse of obligation." That is what we have stated: "If they were walking and came upon a corpse of obligation.[183]"

181 The healing of his skin disease, *Lev.* 14:8,9.

182 The shavings needed for diagnostic purposes, *Lev.* 13:33

183 Mishnah 7:1.

(55b line 53) חוֹמֶר בַּטּוּמְאָה מִן הַתִּגְלַחַת. הַטּוּמְאָה. דִּכְתִיב וְהַיָּמִים הָרִאשׁוֹנִים יִפְּלוּ. וְהֵבִיא כֶּבֶשׂ בֶּן שְׁנָתוֹ לְאָשָׁם. חוֹמֶר בַּתִּגְלַחַת שֶׁעָשָׂה בָהּ הַמְגֻלָּח כְּמִתְגַּלֵּחַ. וְהַטָּמֵא לֹא עָשָׂה בָהּ הַמְטַמֵּא כְּמִיטַּמֵּא.

"Impurity is more severe than shaving." Impurity, as it is written: "The earlier days fall away," "and he shall bring a yearling sheep as a reparation offering[184]." Shaving is more severe because He made the shaver equal to the shaved[185], but in impurity He did not make the defiler equal to the defiled[186].

184 *Num.* 6:12.

185 The person who shaves a *nazir* can be criminally prosecuted. Babli 44a, *Sifry Num.* 25, Tosephta 4:4.

186 A person who causes a *nazir* to be defiled by the impurity of the dead cannot be prosecuted.

(fol. 54b) **משנה ח:** תִּגְלַחַת הַטּוּמְאָה כֵּיצַד הָיָה מַזֶּה בַּשְּׁלִישִׁי וּבַשְּׁבִיעִי וּמְגַלֵּחַ בַּשְּׁבִיעִי וּמֵבִיא קָרְבְּנוֹתָיו בַּשְּׁמִינִי. וְאִם גִּילַח בַּשְּׁמִינִי מֵבִיא קָרְבְּנוֹתָיו בּוֹ בַיּוֹם דִּבְרֵי רִבִּי עֲקִיבָה. אָמַר לוֹ רִבִּי טַרְפוֹן מַה בֵּין זֶה לִמְצוֹרָע. אָמַר לוֹ זֶה טַהֲרָתוֹ תְּלוּיָה בְיָמָיו וּמְצוֹרָע טַהֲרָתוֹ תְּלוּיָה בְתִגְלַחְתּוֹ. אֵינוֹ מֵבִיא קָרְבְּנוֹתָיו אֶלָּא אִם כֵּן הָיָה מְעוֹרָב שֶׁמֶשׁ.

Mishnah 8: What is shaving in impurity? He was sprinkled on the third and seventh [days][187], shaves on the seventh, and brings his sacrifices on the eighth[188]. If he shaved on the eighth, he may bring his sacrifices[189] on the same day, the words of Rebbi Aqiba. Rebbi Ṭarphon asked him, what is the difference between this one and the sufferer from skin disease[190]? He told him, the purification of this one is bound to his days[188], but the purification of the sufferer from skin disease is bound to his shaving[191]. He cannot bring his sacrifices unless the sun had set for him[192].

187 Since the only impurity which defiles the *nazir* is the impurity of the dead, he must have water with ashes from the Red Cow sprinkled on him on the 3rd and 7th days of his impurity (*Num.* 19).

188 As prescribed in *Num.* 6:9,10.

189 Two birds (*Num.* 6:10) and a sheep (*Num.* 6:12).

190 Mishnah *Nega'im* 14:3 states that the person healed from skin disease can bring his sacrifices only after the sundown following his immersion in a *miqweh*. According to R. Aqiba [readings of Tosaphot, 44b *s.v.* א״ל, Maimonides (Commentary *ad loc.*; *Meḥusere Kappara* 4:2); see the readings in *Sifra Meṣora' Pereq* 2(7); another reading in the Commentary attributed to Rashi] this implies that he has to bring his sacrifices on the 9th if he shaved on the 8th.

191 *Lev.* 14:9 prescribes the immersion of the sufferer from skin disease *after* his shaving but *Num.* 6:9 requires the impure *nazir* to shave "on the day of his purity", i. e., after the second sprinkling and his immersion.

192 It is a general principle that immersion in water makes ritually pure only for profane places or food; for *sancta* only the following sundown brings purity, *Lev.* 22:7; cf. *Soṭah* 5:2, Note 42.

(55b line 55) **הלכה ח:** כְּתִיב וְהִזִּיר לַיי אֶת יְמֵי נִזְרוֹ. מִיּוֹם הֲבָאַת קָרְבְּנוֹתָיו. דִּבְרֵי רִבִּי. רִבִּי יוֹסֵי בֵּירִבִּי יְהוּדָה אוֹמֵר. מִשְׁעַת תִּגְלַחְתּוֹ. רִבִּי זְעִירָא בְּשֵׁם רַב הוֹשַׁעְיָה רִבִּי חִייָה בְּשֵׁם רִבִּי יוֹחָנָן. מַה פְּלִיגִין. בְּשֶׁגִּילַח בַּשְּׁבִיעִי וְהֵבִיא קָרְבְּנוֹתָיו בַּשְּׁמִינִי. אֲבָל אִם גִּילַח בַּשְּׁמִינִי וְהֵבִיא קָרְבְּנוֹתָיו בּוֹ בַיּוֹם כָּל־עַמָּא מוֹדֶה בְּיוֹם הֲבָאַת קָרְבְּנוֹתָיו. אָמַר רִבִּי יוֹסֵי. וְהוּא שֶׁטָּבַל בַּשְּׁבִיעִי. אֲבָל אִם טָבַל בַּשְּׁמִינִי נַעֲשָׂה שְׁבִיעִי שְׁמִינִי וּשְׁמִינִי שְׁבִיעִי. וְאֵינוֹ מוֹנֶה אֶלָּא מִן הַשְּׁבִיעִי בִּלְבָד. נִיטְמָא וְחָזַר וְנִיטְמָא מֵבִיא קָרְבָּן עַל כָּל־אֶחָד וְאֶחָד. אָמַר רִבִּי זְעִירָה. כְּרִבִּי יוֹסֵי בֵּירִבִּי יוּדָה. בְּרַם כְּרִבִּי חַיי דָא הוּא עוֹמֵד בִּנְזִירוּת בְּטוּמְאָה. אָמַר רִבִּי אִילָא. מַה פְּלִיגִין. לִמְנוֹת לִנְזִירוּת בְּטַהֲרָה. וְהִזִּיר לַיי אֶת יְמֵי נִזְרוֹ וְהֵבִיא. אָמַר רִבִּי. עַד שֶׁיְּהֵבִיא מַמָּשׁ. רִבִּי יוֹסֵי בֵּירִבִּי יְהוּדָה אוֹמֵר. אֲפִילוּ נִרְאָה לְהָבִיא. קָרְבַּן טוּמְאָה קָל־עַמָּא מוֹדוֹי שֶׁמֵּבִיא קָרְבַּן טוּמְאָה. וְתַנֵּי כֵן. נִיטְמָא בַּשְּׁבִיעִי וְחָזַר וְנִיטְמָא בַּשְּׁמִינִי מֵבִיא קָרְבָּן לְכָל־אֶחָד וְאֶחָד. עַל דַּעְתֵּיהּ דְּרִבִּי זְעִירָא כְּרִבִּי נִדְחָה קָרְבָּן רִאשׁוֹן וּמֵבִיא קָרְבָּן שֵׁנִי. עַל דַּעְתֵּיהּ דְּרִבִּי יוֹסֵי

בְּירְבִּי יְהוּדָה לֹא נִדְחָה. עַל דַּעְתֵּיהּ דְּרִבִּי הִילָא דְּבְרֵי הַכֹּל לֹא נִדְחָה וּמֵבִיא אַחֵר.

Halakhah 8: It is written: "He has to vow to the Eternal the days of his *nezirut*,[193]" from the day he brings his sacrifices, the words of Rebbi. Rebbi Yose ben Rebbi Jehudah says, from the time of his shaving[194]. Rebbi Ze'ira in the name of Rav Hoshaia, Rebbi Ḥiyya in the name of Rebbi Joḥanan: Where do they disagree? If he shaved on the seventh and brought his sacrifices on the eighth. But if he shaved on the eighth and brought his sacrifices on the same day, everybody agrees on the day he brings his sacrifices. Rebbi Yose said, that is, if he immersed himself on the seventh. But if he immersed himself on the eighth, the eighth takes the place of the seventh[195] and the seventh of the eighth[196]; he counts only from that "seventh"[197]. If he became impure and impure again[198], he brings a sacrifice for each occurrence. Rebbi Ze'ira said, that statement follows Rebbi Yose ben Rebbi Jehudah[199], but following Rebbi this person still stays in impure *nezirut*[200]. Rebbi Hila said, where do they disagree? To count *nezirut* in purity[201]. "He has to vow to the Eternal the days of his *nezirut* and bring." Rebbi said, until he actually brought. Rebbi Yose ben Rebbi Jehudah says, even if he was enabled to bring the sacrifice for impurity. Everybody agrees that he brings a sacrifice for impurity. It was stated thus: If he became impure on the seventh, and again impure on the eighth, he brings a sacrifice for each occurrence. In Rebbi Ze'ira's opinion[193,194], following Rebbi the first sacrifice is superseded and he brings the second; following Rebbi Yose ben Rebbi Jehudah it was not superseded. In Rebbi Hila's opinion[201], everybody agrees that nothing is superseded and he brings another.

193 *Num.* 6:12. The requirement to renew his vow is written between the mention of the sacrifice of two birds and that of the sheep. The verse seems to refer to the eighth day, the day of his sacrifices.

194 I. e., after he immersed himself and is pure for profane purposes. Since he is no longer impure, there is no reason for him not to be a fully functioning *nazir*.

In the Babli, 18b/19a, the verse quoted is brought as support for the majority opinion, that a resumption of the status of *nazir* only depends on his shaving, here attributed to R. Yose ben R. Jehudah, while the opinion of Rebbi, that a resumption of the status of *nazir* depends of his reparation offering, is quoted there in the name of R. Johanan ben Baroqa. This implies that the Yerushalmi prefers the opinion of Rebbi, the Babli that of R. Yose ben R. Yehudah.

195 Since he cannot enter the holy precinct before sundown.

196 I. e., the eighth is not different in status from the seventh.

197 For Rebbi from the 9th, for R. Yose ben R. Yehudah from the 8th.

198 He became impure after he went to the *miqweh* on the 7th day but before he brought his sacrifices on the 8th; cf. Tosephta 4:8; Babli 18b.

199 In the Babli, 18b, 52a, "R. Eliezer". Rebbi's opinion is referred to as that "of the rabbis" in the Babli.

200 Since only the reparation offering eliminates his disability as *nazir*.

201 Only for the count. Rebbi will agree that if he immersed himself on the 7th, any impurity he incurs after that is a new impurity even if he could not yet start counting the days of his *nezirut*.

משנה ט: תִּגְלַחַת הַטַּהֲרָה כֵּיצַד. הָיָה מֵבִיא שָׁלֹשׁ בְּהֵמוֹת חַטָּאת (fol. 54b) עוֹלָה וּשְׁלָמִים וְשׁוֹחֵט אֶת הַשְּׁלָמִים וּמְגַלֵּחַ עֲלֵיהֶן דִּבְרֵי רִבִּי יְהוּדָה. רִבִּי אֶלְעָזָר אוֹמֵר לֹא הָיָה מְגַלֵּחַ אֶלָּא עַל הַחַטָּאת שֶׁהַחַטָּאת קוֹדֶמֶת בְּכָל־מָקוֹם. וְאִם גִּילַּח עַל אֶחָד מִשְּׁלָשְׁתָּן יָצָא.

Mishnah 9: What is shaving in purity? He brings three animals[202], a purification sacrifice, an elevation sacrifice, and a well-being sacrifice. He slaughters the well-being sacrifice ands shaves for it[203], the words of Rebbi Jehudah. Rebbi Eleazar[204] says, he only should shave for the purification sacrifice since that has precedence everywhere[205], but if he shaved for any of the three, he satisfied his obligation.

202   Num. 6:14.
203   Since shaving is mentioned in v. 18, after the slaughter of the well-being offering in v. 17.
204   In some Mishnah mss., "R. Eliezer".
205   In the case of the *nazir*, v. 16; in other cases of a common offering of purification and elevation offerings, Lev. 5:8.

(55b line 71) **הלכה ט:** רִבִּי יְהוֹשֻׁעַ בֶּן לֵוִי אָמַר. וְאֶת הָאַיִל יַעֲשֶׂה וגו'. מַה תַּלְמוּד לוֹמַר יַעֲשֶׂה. הַקְדִּים בּוֹ מַעֲשֶׂה. הָתִיב רִבִּי חִינְנָא קוֹמֵי רִבִּי מָנָא. וְהָא כְּתִיב וְעָשָׂה הַכֹּהֵן אֶת מִנְחָתוֹ וְאֶת נִסְכּוֹ. מֵעַתָּה יַעֲשֶׂה הַקְדִּים בּוֹ מַעֲשֶׂה. מַאי כְדוֹן. אָתָא רִבִּי חִינְנָא בְּשֵׁם רִבִּי יְהוֹשֻׁעַ בֶּן לֵוִי. שֶׁאִם גִּילַח עַל אַחַת מִשְּׁלָשְׁתָּן יָצָא. רִבִּי זְעִירָא בְּעָא קוֹמֵי רִבִּי מָנָא. מָאן תַּנָּא. כָּל־הַחַטָּאוֹת שֶׁבַּתּוֹרָה קוֹדְמוֹת לָאֲשָׁמוֹת. רִבִּי אֶלְעָזָר אָמַר. דִּבְרֵי הַכֹּל הִיא. כָּל־הַחַטָּאוֹת שֶׁבַּתּוֹרָה קוֹדְמוֹת לָאֲשָׁמוֹת.

Halakhah 9: Rebbi Joshua ben Levi said: "The ram he shall offer, etc.[206]" Why does the verse say, "he shall offer"? Start the procedure with it[207]. Rebbi Hinena objected before Rebbi Mana[208]: But is it not written: "He shall offer his flour offering and his libation[206]"? Should he not start with them? How is that? Rebbi Hinena in the name of Rebbi Joshua ben Levi: If he shaved for any of the three, he satisfied his obligation[209]. Rebbi Ze'ira asked before Rebbi Mana: Who is the Tanna of: "All purification offerings in the Torah precede the reparation offerings"? Rebbi Eleazar said, it is everybody's opinion, "all purification offerings in the Torah precede the reparation offerings.[210]"

206 *Num.* 6:17.

207 In *Sifry zuṭa* 17, this argument is tannaïtic and attributed to R. Jehudah. It seems that he contrasts the imperfect used for sacrificing the well-being offering with the perfect used for the other offerings, to indicate beginning of an action. In the Babli and *Sifry Num. 35*, the preferred treatment of the well-being offering is deduced from v. 18.

208 The R. Mana quoted in this Halakhah is neither R. Mana I, of the first, nor R. Mana II, of the fifth generation. Either there exists a third, otherwise unknown, Amora of this name or "Mana" is erroneous for "Yasa", or "Ze'ira" is erroneous for "Ezra".

209 Flour offerings and libations are mentioned last in v. 17. They accompany both the well-being offering (v. 17) and the elevation offering, mentioned in v. 16 together with the purification offering which needs neither flour nor wine. It is inferred that the order of the sacrifices is irrelevant.

210 Mishnah *Zebaḥim* 10:5. No reparation offering is due from the pure *nazir*.

(fol. 54b) **משנה י:** רַבָּן שִׁמְעוֹן בֶּן גַּמְלִיאֵל אוֹמֵר הֵבִיא שָׁלֹשׁ בְּהֵמוֹת וְלֹא פֵּרֵשׁ הָרְאוּיָה לַחַטָּאת תִּיקָרֵב חַטָּאת. לָעוֹלָה תִּיקָרֵב עוֹלָה. לַשְּׁלָמִים תִּיקָרֵב שְׁלָמִים. הָיָה נוֹטֵל שְׂעַר רֹאשׁ נִזְרוֹ וּמְשַׁלֵּחַ תַּחַת הַדּוּד וְאִם גִּילַח בַּמְּדִינָה הָיָה מְשַׁלֵּחַ תַּחַת הַדּוּד. בַּמֶּה דְבָרִים אֲמוּרִים בְּתִגְלַחַת הַטַּהֲרָה אֲבָל בְּתִגְלַחַת הַטּוּמְאָה לֹא הָיָה מְשַׁלֵּחַ תַּחַת הַדּוּד. רִבִּי מֵאִיר אוֹמֵר. הַכֹּל מְשַׁלְּחִין תַּחַת הַדּוּד חוּץ מִן הַטָּמֵא שֶׁבַּמְּדִינָה בִּלְבָד.

Mishnah 10: Rabban Simeon ben Gamliel says, if he brought three animals but did not specify[211], the one proper for the purification offering shall be brought as purification offering, for the elevation offering shall be brought as elevation offering, for the well-being offering shall be brought as well-being offering. He took the hair shorn from his *nazir* head and sent it under the cooking pot[212]; even if he shaved in the countryside[213] he sent it under the cooking pot. When has this been said? If he shaved in purity. But if he shaved in impurity, he does not send it under the cooking pot[214]. Rebbi Meïr says, all send under the cooking pot except the impure in the countryside.

211 No sacrifice can be offered unless it was sanctified by dedication. In general, the dedication must specify for which sacrifice the animal will be used. But for a *nazir*, dedication "for the *nazir*'s sacrifices" is sufficient since the purification offering requires a female sheep, the elevation offering a male sheep, and the well-being offering a male goat.

212 In general, any sacrificial meat permitted for human consumption can be eaten as desired, cooked, roasted, or scalded. Only for the well-being offering of the *nazir* does the verse prescribe cooking; *Num.* 6:19. The hair is "sent" since the *nazir* shaves outside the holy precinct but the well-being offering must be cooked inside (vv. 19-20).

213 If he sends money so that the sacrifices should be offered on his behalf while he remains outside of Jerusalem, his hair has to be burned.

214 His hair has to be buried; Mishnah *Temurah* 7:4.

(55c line 2) **הלכה י:** הָווֹן בָּעֵי מֵימַר. בְּשָׁלֹא פֵּירֵשׁ. הָא בְּתוֹךְ בֵּיתוֹ פֵּירֵשׁ. אָמְרִין. אֲפִילוּ בְּתוֹךְ בֵּיתוֹ פֵּירֵשׁ לֹא. לָמָּה. בְּהֵמָה עָלֶיהָ הֲלָכוֹת סְתוּמוֹת כַּתְּחִילָה.

Halakhah 10: They wanted to say, if he did not specify, but in his house he did specify[215]. They said, even in his house he need not specify. Why? The animal which at the start has the rules of the indeterminate[216].

215 He did not dedicate specifically but when he selected the animals he specified.

216 An animal has to be dedicated specifically only if there can be a doubt for what it will be used. For a *nazir*, no doubt is possible.

(55c line 5) רִבִּי יוֹסֵי בֵּירִבִּי בּוּן בְּשֵׁם רַב. טוֹבְלוֹ בָּרוֹטֶב. מַה טַעֲמָא. וְנָתַן עַל הָאֵשׁ. אַף הַזֶּבַח יְהֵא בָאֵשׁ.

Rebbi Yose ben Rebbi Abun in the name of Rav: He puts it into the sauce[217]. What is the reason? "He puts it into the fire,[218]" the sacrifice also into the fire.

217 Babli 45b [*Num. rabba* 6(39), as tannaïtic text. One takes from the sauce in which the well-being offering is cooked, wets the hair with it, and puts it into the fire.

218 *Num.* 6:18.

(55c line 6) תַּנֵּי. הַכֹּל מְשַׁלְחִין תַּחַת הַדּוּד חוּץ מִן הַטָּמֵא שֶׁבַּגְּבוּלִין. הַטָּהוֹר שֶׁבַּמִּקְדָּשׁ תַּחַת הַדּוּד שֶׁלְּאָשָׁם מֵבִיא. דִּבְרֵי רִבִּי מֵאִיר. רִבִּי יוּדָה אוֹמֵר. הַטָּהוֹר כָּךְ וְכָךְ מֵבִיא הַטָּמֵא כָּךְ וְכָךְ אֵינוֹ מֵבִיא. וַחֲכָמִים אוֹמְרִים. הַטָּמֵא שֶׁבַּמִּקְדָּשׁ וְהַטָּהוֹר שֶׁבַּגְּבוּלִין אֵינוֹ מֵבִיא. אֵין לָךְ מְשַׁלֵּחַ תַּחַת הַדּוּד אֶלָּא הַמְגַלֵּחַ בְּטַהֲרָה. פֶּתַח אוֹהֶל מוֹעֵד. רִבִּי מֵאִיר אוֹמֵר. עַד שֶׁיְּהֵא רָאוּי וְסָמוּךְ. וְרַבָּנִין אָמְרִין. רָאוּי אַף עַל פִּי שֶׁאֵינוֹ סָמוּךְ. סָמוּךְ אַף עַל פִּי שֶׁאֵינוֹ רָאוּי.

It was stated[219]: "All send under the cooking pot except the impure in the countryside. The pure[220] in the Temple brings it under the cooking-pot of the reparation sacrifice, the words of Rebbi Meïr. Rebbi Jehudah says, the pure brings in any case, the impure does not bring in any case. But the Sages say, neither the impure in the Temple nor the pure in the countryside bring. Nobody sends under the cooking-pot except the one who shaves in purity." "Outside the door of the Tent of Meeting.[218]" Rebbi Meïr[221] says, only if he is proper and near; but the rabbis[221] say, proper even if not near, near even if not proper.

219 Slightly different text in the Babli, 45b, Tosephta 4:6.
220 This "pure" refers to a *nazir* who was impure, had to bring a reparation offering for his impurity, but now is pure after having been sprinkled with the ashes of the Red Cow and been immersed in a *miqweh*.

221 Obviously, the attributions have to be switched. The rabbis allow burning only if the *nazir* is pure at the Temple gate; Rebbi Meïr allows it if either he is pure or at the Temple gate.

(fol. 54c) **משנה יא:** הָיָה מְבַשֵּׁל אֶת הַשְּׁלָמִים אוֹ שׁוֹלְקָן וְכֹהֵן נוֹטֵל אֶת הַזְּרוֹעַ בְּשֵׁלָה מִן הָאַיִל. וְחַלַּת מַצָּה אַחַת מִן הַסַּל וּרְקִיק מַצָּה אֶחָד וְנוֹתֵן עַל כַּפֵּי הַנָּזִיר וּמְנִיפָן וְאַחַר כָּךְ הוּתַּר הַנָּזִיר לִשְׁתּוֹת בַּיַּיִן וְלִיטַּמֵּא לַמֵּתִים. רַבִּי שִׁמְעוֹן אוֹמֵר כֵּיוָן שֶׁנִּזְרַק עָלָיו אֶחָד מִן הַדָּמִים הוּתַּר הַנָּזִיר לִשְׁתּוֹת בַּיַּיִן וּלְהִיטַּמֵּא לַמֵּתִים.

Mishnah 11: He cooked the well-being offering or scalded[222] it. A Cohen takes the cooked fore-leg of the ram, one unleavened loaf from the basket, and one unleavened thin bread, places it on the *nazir*'s hands and waves it[223]. Afterwards the *nazir* is permitted to drink wine and to defile himself with the dead. Rebbi Simeon says, when one of the bloods was sprinkled, the *nazir* is permitted to drink wine and to defile himself with the dead[224].

222 Cf. *Nedarim* 6:1, Note 1.
223 *Num.* 6:19-20.
224 In v. 20, the note that the *nazir* is now permitted to drink wine is an appendix to the text which deals exclusively with the Cohen, not the *nazir*. Therefore, it remains unclear whether the *nazir* is permitted only after all ceremonies or after the start of the ceremonies, when one of the sacrifices was validated by having its blood sprinkled on the walls of the altar [*Num. rabba* 6(41)].

(55c line 13) **הלכה יא:** מַתְנִיתָא אֲמָרָה. הַשָּׁלוּק קָרוּי מְבוּשָּׁל. דְּתַנִינָן. הָיָה מְבַשֵּׁל הַשְּׁלָמִים אוֹ שׁוֹלְקָן. וְקַרְיָיא אֲמָרָה שֶׁהַצְּלִי קָרוּי מְבוּשָּׁל. דִּכְתִיב וַיְבַשְּׁלוּ אֶת הַפֶּסַח בָּאֵשׁ. אִין תֵּימַר שֶׁלֹּא כַהֲלָכָה. רִבִּי יוֹנָה בּוֹצְרָיָיה אָמַר

כְּמִשְׁפָּט. וּמַתְנִיתָא אָמְרָה שֶׁהַשָּׁלוּק קָרוּי מְבוּשָּׁל. וְהָתַנִינָן. הַנּוֹדֵר מִן הַמְבוּשָּׁל מוּתָּר בַּצָּלִי וּבַשָּׁלוּק. אָמַר רִבִּי יוֹחָנָן. הָלְכוּ בַּנְּדָרִים אַחַר לְשׁוֹן בְּנֵי אָדָם. אָמַר רִבִּי יֹאשִׁיָּה. הָלְכוּ בַּנְּדָרִים אַחַר לְשׁוֹן תּוֹרָה. מַה נָפִיק מִבֵּינֵיהוֹן. קוֹנָם יַיִן שֶׁאֵינִי טוֹעֵם בֶּחָג. עַל דַּעְתֵּיהּ דְּרִבִּי יוֹחָנָן אָסוּר בְּיוֹם טוֹב הָאַחֲרוֹן. עַל דַּעְתֵּיהּ דְּרִבִּי יֹאשִׁיָּה מוּתָּר. אַף רִבִּי אוֹשַׁעְיָה מוֹדֶה שֶׁהוּא אָסוּר. לֹא אָמַר רִבִּי יֹאשִׁיָּה אֶלָּא לְחוּמְרִין.

1 השלוק | שהשלוק   2 השלמים | את השלמים   שולקן | שולק   אמרה שהצלי | שהצלוי   דכתיב | -   3 באש | וגו'   בוצרייה | בוצרייא   4 ומתניתא | מתניתא   והא תנינן | וקרייא אמר שהצלוי קרוי מבושל. והתנינן   8 אושי' | יאשיה   שהוא אסור | שאסור

Halakhah 11: [225]A Mishnah states that scalding is called cooking, as we have stated: "If he cooked the well-being offering or scalded it[7]." A verse [states] that "roasted" is called "cooked": "They cooked the *pesaḥ*", etc. If you say, against the rules, Rebbi Jonah from Bostra said, "as is the rule". A Mishnah states that scalded is called cooked: "Is one who makes a vow to abstain from cooked food permitted roasted and scalded food"? Rebbi Joḥanan said, in matters of vows one follows common usage. Rebbi Joshia said, in matters of vows one follows biblical usage. What is the difference between them? 'A *qônām* that I shall not taste wine on Tabernacles.' In the opinion of Rebbi Joḥanan he is forbidden on the last day of the holiday. In the opinion of Rebbi Joshia, is he permitted? Rebbi Joshia also agrees that he is prohibited. Rebbi Joshia said it only for restrictions.

(55c line 24) רִבִּי חִייָה בַּר בָּא אָמַר. רִבִּי יוֹחָנָן אָכַל חֲלִיטָא וְאָמַר. לֹא טְעָמִית מָזוֹן בְּהָדֵין יוֹמָא. וְהָתַנִינָן. הַנּוֹדֵר מִן הַמָּזוֹן מוּתָּר בְּמַיִם וּבְמֶלַח. פָּתַר לָהּ כְּרִבִּי יֹאשִׁיָּה דְּאָמַר. הִילְכוּ בַּנְּדָרִים אַחַר לְשׁוֹן הַתּוֹרָה. מְנַיִין שֶׁכָּל־הַדְּבָרִים קְרוּיִין מָזוֹן. אָמַר רִבִּי אָחָא בַּר עוּלָא. וְעֶשֶׂר אֲתוֹנוֹת נוֹשְׂאוֹת בַּר וְלֶחֶם וּמָזוֹן וגו'. מַה תַּלְמוּד לוֹמַר וּמָזוֹן. אֶלָּא מִכָּן שֶׁכָּל־הַדְּבָרִים קְרוּיִין מָזוֹן.

2 בהדין | בהדא   והתנינן | והא תנינן   3 התורה | תורה   מניין | ומניין   4 אמ' ר'
אחא בר עולא | ר' אחא בר עולא אמ'   5 וגו' | -

Rebbi Ḥiyya bar Abba said, Rebbi Joḥanan ate bake-meats and said, I did not taste food on that day. But did we not state: "He who made a vow not to eat food is permitted water and salt"? Explain it following Rebbi Joshia, who said, in matters of vows one follows biblical usage. And from where that everything is called food? Rebbi Aḥa bar Ulla said: "And ten female donkeys carrying grain, bread, and food, etc." Why does the verse say, "and food"? From here that everything is called food.

225   The following two paragraphs are from *Nedarim* 6:1, Notes 6-14.

(55c line 29) כְּתִיב וְלָקַח הַכֹּהֵן אֶת הַזְּרֹעַ בְּשֵׁלָה מִן הָאַיִל. אִי בְּשֵׁילָה יָכוֹל בִּפְנֵי עַצְמָהּ. תַּלְמוּד לוֹמַר מִן הָאַיִל. הָא כֵּיצַד. חוֹתְכָהּ עַד שֶׁהוּא מַנִּיחַ בָּהּ כִּשְׂעוֹרָה. וְלֹא הַקּוֹדֶשׁ בּוֹלֵעַ מִן הַחוֹל וְלֹא הַחוֹל בּוֹלֵעַ מִן הַקּוֹדֶשׁ.

It is written: "The Cohen takes the cooked fore-leg of the ram.[226]" If cooked, I could think separately[227]. The verse says, "from the ram". How is this? He cuts it off so that only a barley grain's width remains. Does not the sanctified absorb from the profane, or the profane from the sanctified?[228].

226   *Num.* 6:19.
227   Since the fore-leg becomes the property of the Cohen and will be forbidden to lay people, its holiness is greater than the remainder of the well-being offering which is consumed by the *nazir* and his family. The obvious question is whether it is permissible to cook meat of different degrees of holiness together, which is answered in the following paragraphs.
228   The question is answered in the following paragraphs which are paralleled in *'Orlah* 1:4, Notes 137-154. The readings from there are noted ע.

(55c line 32) חִילְפַּיי שָׁאַל לְרַבִּי יוֹחָנָן וּלְרַבִּי שִׁמְעוֹן בֶּן לָקִישׁ. טֶבֶל מַהוּ שֶׁיְּיוּסַר בְּיוֹתֵר מִמָּאתַיִם. אָמְרוּ לֵיהּ. אֵין טֶבֶל בְּיוֹתֵר מִמָּאתַיִם. וְהָא תַגִּינָן. כָּל־הַמְחַמֵּץ וְהַמְתַבֵּל וְהַמְדַמֵּעַ. אֵין תֵּימַר לְמֵאָה וּלְמָאתַיִם. אֲפִילוּ לֹא חִימֵּץ אֲפִילוּ לֹא טִיבֵּל. אֶלָּא בָּעֲנָבִים אֲנָן קַיָּימִין. רִבִּי יוֹסֵי בְּשֵׁם רִבִּי יוֹחָנָן. בְּשֶׁלֹא צִימְּקוּ אֲבָל אִם צִימְּקוּ יֵשׁ טֶבֶל בְּיוֹתֵר מִמָּאתַיִם. רִבִּי חִיָּיה בְּשֵׁם רִבִּי יוֹחָנָן. בְּשֶׁלֹא בִּישְּׁלוֹ. אֲבָל אִם בִּישְּׁלוֹ יֵשׁ טֶבֶל בְּיוֹתֵר מִמָּאתַיִם.

1 שמעון בן לקיש | ע שמעון   טבל | ע תבל (4 times)   שיוסר | ע שייאסר   3 ולמאתים | ע מאתים   4 טיבל | ע תיבל   צימקו | ע צמקו (2 times)

Hilfai asked Rebbi Johanan and Rebbi Simeon ben Laqish, do condiments forbid with more than 200? They said to him, condiments are not in more than 200. But did we not state: "Anything which sours, flavors, or creates *dema'*?" If you say about 100 or 200, even if it does not sour, flavor, or create *dema'*! But we deal with grapes. Rebbi Assi in the name of Rebbi Johanan, if they were not raisins, but if they were raisins they are condiments in more than 200. Rebbi Hiyya in the name of Rebbi Johanan, if they were not cooked, but if they were cooked they are condiments in more than 200.

(55c line 38) רִבִּי יָסָא וְרִבִּי יְהוֹשֻׁעַ בֶּן לֵוִי בְּשֵׁם בַּר פְּדָיָיה. כָּל־נוֹתְנֵי טְעָמִים אֶחָד מִמֵּאָה. רִבִּי חִיָּיה בְּשֵׁם רִבִּי הוֹשַׁעְיָה בֶּן לֵוִי בְּשֵׁם בַּר פְּדָיָיה. כָּל־נוֹתְנֵי טְעָמִים אֶחָד מִשִּׁשִּׁים. אָמַר רִבִּי שְׁמוּאֵל בַּר רַב יִצְחָק לְרִבִּי חִיָּיה בַּר אַבָּא. הָא רִבִּי יָסָא פְּלִיג עֲלָךְ. וְהָא מַתְנִיתָא פְּלִיגָא עַל תְּרֵיכוֹן. כָּל־הַמְחַמֵּץ מְטַבֵּל מְחַמֵּעַ. אֵין תֵּימַר לְמֵאָה מִמָּאתַיִם. אֲפִילוּ לֹא חִימֵּץ אֲפִילוּ לֹא טִיבֵּל. אֶלָּא בְּיוֹתֵר אֲנָן קַיָּימִין. אָמַר רִבִּי יִרְמְיָה. תִּיפְתָּר בָּשָׂר בְּבָשָׂר. אָמַר רִבִּי יוֹסֵי. הוּא בָּשָׂר בְּבָשָׂר הוּא שְׁאָר כָּל־הָאִיסּוּרִין. רִבִּי אַבָּהוּ בְּשֵׁם רִבִּי יוֹחָנָן. וּלְאִיסּוּר מְשַׁעֲרִין אוֹתוֹ כִּילוּ בָּעַל כִּלּוֹ קְפָלוֹט.

1 יסא | ע יוסי   ור' | ע בשם ר'   פדייה | ע פדיה   כל נותני | ע נותני   2 ר' חייה בשם ר' יושעיה בן לוי בשם בר פדיה. כל־ | ע - 229   3 אבא | ע בא   4 יסא | ע יוסי עלך | ע -   והא מתניתא | ע ומתניתא   מטבל מחמע | ע המתבל והמדמע   5 ממאתים

ע מאתים | טיבל | ע תיבל   6 הוא | ע היא (2 times)   7 ר' אבהו | ע דאמ' ר' אבהו ולאיסור | ע כל האיסורין   8 כילו בָּצָל כילו קפלוט | ע כילו כן

Rebbi Yasa in the name of Rebbi Joshua ben Levi in the name of Bar Pedaiah: All sources of flavor one in a hundred. Rebbi Ḥiyya in the name of Rebbi Joshua ben Levi in the name of Bar Pedaiah: All sources of flavor one in sixty. Rebbi Samuel ben Rav Isaac said to Rebbi Ḥiyya bar Abba: Rebbi Yasa disagrees with you and the Mishnah disagrees with both of you: "Anything which sours, flavors, or creates *dema'*? If you say about 100 or 200, even if it does not sour, flavor, or create *dema'*[230]! Therefore, we hold even more. Rebbi Jeremiah said, explain it for meat in meat. Rebbi Yose said, meat in meat is the same as all other prohibitions since Rebbi Abbahu said in the name of Rebbi Joḥanan, one estimates as if they were onion or leeks[92].

229 The missing text is in the Rome ms. of *'Orlah*.

230 Translation of the text in *'Orlah*. Here: "Make leavened".

(55c line 47) מַיי כְדוֹן. אָהֵן אָמַר. נוֹתְנֵי טְעָמִים אֶחָד מִמֵּאָה. וְאָהֵן אָמַר נוֹתְנֵי טְעָמִים אֶחָד מִשִּׁשִּׁים. וּשְׁנֵיהֶן לְמֵידִין מֵאִיל נָזִיר. מָאן דְּאָמַר. נוֹתְנֵי טְעָמִים אֶחָד מִמֵּאָה. אַתְּ עוֹשֶׂה אֶת הַזְּרוֹעַ אֶחָד מִמֵּאָה לָאַיִל. וּמָאן דְּאָמַר. נוֹתְנֵי טְעָמִים אֶחָד מִשִּׁשִּׁים. אַתְּ עוֹשֶׂה הַזְּרוֹעַ אֶחָד מִשִּׁשִּׁים לָאַיִל. מָאן דְּאָמַר. נוֹתְנֵי טְעָמִים אֶחָד מִמֵּאָה. אַתְּ מוֹצִיא אֶת הַזְּרוֹעַ הָעֲצָמוֹת. וּמָאן דְּאָמַר נוֹתְנֵי טְעָמִים אֶחָד מִשִּׁשִּׁים. אֵין אַתְּ מוֹצִיא אֶת הַזְּרוֹעַ מִן הָעֲצָמוֹת. וּכְשֵׁם שֶׁאַתְּ מוֹצִיא אֶת הָעֲצָמוֹת מִן הַזְּרוֹעַ כָּךְ אַתְּ מוֹצִיא מִן הָאַיִל. לֵית יְכִיל. דְּתַנֵּי אֵין טִנּוֹפֶת שֶׁלַּתְּרוּמָה מִצְטָרֶפֶת עִם הַתְּרוּמָה לְהַעֲלוֹת אֶת הַחוּלִין. אֲבָל טִנּוֹפֶת שֶׁלְּחוּלִין מִצְטָרֶפֶת עִם הַחוּלִין לְהַעֲלוֹת אֶת הַתְּרוּמָה. רִבִּי בִּיבִי בָּעֵי. טִינּוֹפֶת שֶׁלַּתְּרוּמָה מָהוּ שֶׁתִּצְטָרֵף עִם הַחוּלִין לְהַעֲלוֹת אֶת הַתְּרוּמָה. מִן מַה דְּאָמַר רַב חוּנָא. קְלִיפֵי אִיסּוּר מִצְטָרְפִין לְהַתִּיר. הָדָא אָמְרָה טִינּוֹפֶת שֶׁל תְּרוּמָה מִצְטָרֶפֶת עִם הַחוּלִין לְהַעֲלוֹת אֶת הַתְּרוּמָה.

HALAKHAH 11

1 אהן | ע ההן   ואהן | ע והן   3 ממאה | ע מששים   (2 times)   4 נותני טעמים אחד |
ע אחד   מששים | ע ממאה (2 times)   5 נותני טעמים אחד | ע אחד (2 times)   את
הזרוע העצמות | ע העצמות מן הזרוע   6 את הזרוע מן העצמות | ע את העצמות מן
הזרוע   7 את מוציא | ע הוציאם   8 התרומה | ת תרומה   להעלות | עת לאסור
את | ת על   9 שתצטרף | ת שתצרף   11 מצטרפין | ע מצטרפות   להתיר | עת להיתר
12 עם החולין | ע לחולין

How is this? One says, all sources of flavor by one in 100; the other says, all sources of flavor by one in 60. For him who says all sources of taste by one in 100, you take the foreleg as one in 100 of the ram. For him who says all sources of taste by one in 60, you take the foreleg as one in 60 of the ram. For him who says one in 100, you remove the bones from the foreleg. But if you remove the bones from the foreleg, remove them from the ram! This you cannot do, as it was stated: [230]"The waste of heave does not combine with heave to forbid[231] the profane, but the waste of profane combines with the profane to lift the heave." Rebbi Vivian asked: Does the waste of heave combine with profane to lift the heave? Since Rav Huna said, the husks of what is forbidden combine to permit; that means waste of heave combines with profane to lift the heave.

230 This text is also from *Terumot* 5:9, Notes 103-108. The readings from there are noted **ת**.

231 The translation follows *Terumot* and *'Orlah*; the text here, "to lift", makes no sense.

(55c line 60) תַּנֵּי רִבִּי חִזְקִיָּה. כָּל־מַה שֶׁאָסַרְתִּי לָךְ מִמָּקוֹם אַחֵר הִתַּרְתִּי לָךְ כָּאן. לְפִי שֶׁבְּכָל־מָקוֹם מֵאָה אָסוּר. מֵאָה וְעוֹד מוּתָּר. וְכָא אֲפִילוּ מֵאָה מוּתָּר.

1 חזקיה | ע חייה   2 שבכל מקום | ע שבכל   אסור | ע איסור   וכא | ע ברם הכא

Rebbi Hizqiah[232] stated: All I forbade to you at other places I permitted to you here. Since everywhere 100 is a prohibition, more than 100 is permitted, but here even 100 is permitted.

232 The reading "Ḥiyya" probably is correct since Ḥizqiah, the collector of *baraitot* and son of R. Ḥiyya (the Elder) has no title.

(55c line 63) רַב אָמַר. תְּנוּפָה מְעַכֶּבֶת בַּנָּזִיר. וְהָתַנֵּי. תּוֹרַת הַנָּזִיר. בֵּין שֶׁיֵּשׁ לוֹ כְנָפַיִם בֵּין שֶׁאֵין לוֹ כְנָפַיִם. דְּאָמַר רַב. בְּנָזִיר שֶׁיֵּשׁ לוֹ. וְתַנֵּי כֵן. הָרָאוּי לִתְנוּפָה תְּנוּפָה מְעַכֶּבֶת בּוֹ. וְשֶׁאֵין רָאוּי לִתְנוּפָה אֵין תְּנוּפָה מְעַכֶּבֶת בּוֹ. שְׁמוּאֵל אָמַר. שִׁיעוּר מְעַכֶּבֶת בַּנָּזִיר. כִּתְנוּפוֹת וְכִבְהוֹנוֹת שֶׁלַּמְצוֹרָע. וְהָתַנֵּי. תּוֹרַת הַמְצוֹרָע. בֵּין שֶׁיֵּשׁ לוֹ בְהוֹנוֹת בֵּין שֶׁאֵין לוֹ בְהוֹנוֹת. פָּתַר לָהּ כְּרִבִּי אֱלִיעֶזֶר דְּאָמַר. נוֹתֵן עַל מְקוֹמָן.

Rav said, waving stops the *nazir*[233]. But did we not state: "The teachings for the *nazir*,[234]" whether or not he has wings[235]? What Rav says, if he does, as it was stated thus: For somebody able to wave, waving stops him; for somebody unable to wave, waving does not stop him. Samuel says, measure[236] stops a *nazir*, as for the waves and thumbs of a sufferer from skin disease[237]. But did we not state: "The teachings for the sufferer from skin disease,[238]" whether or not he has thumbs? He explains it following Rebbi Eliezer who said, he puts it on their place[239].

233 The *nazir* is not permitted to drink wine or become impure unless he perfomed the waving of his well-being sacrifice. This is also quoted in the Babli, 46a/b, but is rejected there as practice.

234 Num. 6:21.

235 Tosephta 1:5, Babli 46b. "The teaching of the *nazir*" must be applicable to everybody, whether he has arms and hands ("wings") or not. But since the wavings have to be given "on the *nazir*'s hands", how can they be absolutely required if the *nazir* has no hands?

236 It is unclear what this means. Most authors emend "measure" to "waving".

237 The poor sufferer from skin disease must wave his reparation offering (*Lev.* 14:24); every healed sufferer from skin disease must receive blood and oil on his right thumb and great toe (*Lev.* 14:14,17,25,28).

238 *Lev.* 14:2.

239 Mishnah *Nega'im* 14:9; *Sifra*

Meṣora' Pereq 3(11); quoted similarly in the Babli Yoma 61b (cf. Diqduqe Soferim Yoma p. 171 Note נ). In Babli Nazir, 47b, (with a different editorial history) R. Eliezer holds that he cannot ever be purified; R. Simeon is quoted parallel to R. Eliezer in the other sources.

(fol. 54c) **משנה יב:** גִּילַח עַל הַזֶּבַח וְנִמְצָא פָּסוּל תִּגְלַחְתּוֹ פְּסוּלָה וּזְבָחָיו לֹא עָלוּ לוֹ. גִּילַח עַל הַחַטָּאת שֶׁלֹּא לִשְׁמָהּ וְאַחַר כָּךְ הֵבִיא קָרְבְּנוֹתָיו לִשְׁמָן תִּגְלַחְתּוֹ פְּסוּלָה וְקָרְבְּנוֹתָיו לֹא עָלוּ לוֹ. גִּילַח עַל הָעוֹלָה וְעַל הַשְּׁלָמִים שֶׁלֹּא לִשְׁמָן וְאַחַר כָּךְ הֵבִיא קָרְבְּנוֹתָיו לִשְׁמָן תִּגְלַחְתּוֹ פְּסוּלָה וּזְבָחָיו לֹא עָלוּ לוֹ. רִבִּי שִׁמְעוֹן אוֹמֵר אוֹתוֹ הַזֶּבַח לֹא עָלָה לוֹ אֲבָל שְׁאָר הַזְּבָחִים עָלוּ לוֹ. וְאִם גִּילַח עַל שְׁלָשְׁתָּן וְנִמְצָא אֶחָד מֵהֶן כָּשֵׁר תִּגְלַחְתּוֹ כְּשֵׁירָה וְיָבִיא שְׁאָר הַזְּבָחִים.

Mishnah 12: If he shaved for one of the sacrifices and it turned out to be invalid, his shaving is invalid[240] and his sacrifices are not counted for him. If he shaved for the purification offering not in its name[241] but brought the other sacrifices in their names, his shaving is invalid and his sacrifices are not counted for him[242]. If he shaved for the elevation or well-being offerings not in their names[243] but then brought his sacrifices[244] in their names, his shaving is invalid and his sacrifices are not counted for him. Rebbi Simeon says, that sacrifice is not counted for him but the others are counted for him[245]. But if he shaved for all three[246] and one of them is valid, his shaving is valid and he has to repeat the other sacrifices.

240 And he has to wait another 30 days to regrow his hair.

241 A purification offering must be slaughtered explicitly for that purpose;

Lev. 4:33.

242 Elevation and well-being offerings are valid and can be brought to the altar. But since the *nazir* is

required to bring all three sacrifices together, this Tanna holds that they cannot be counted as fulfilling his obligation.

243 These are valid sacrifices even if slaughtered for the wrong purpose "but are not counted for their owners to relieve them of their obligations" (Mishnah *Zebaḥim* 1:1).

244 The remaining two.

245 Except for the purification offering not slaughtered for its purpose which is disqualified by biblical law.

246 Without specifying for which one he shaved; cf. Mishnah 9.

(fol. 54c) **משנה יג:** מִי שֶׁנִּזְרַק עָלָיו אֶחָד מִן הַדָּמִים וְנִיטְמָא רִבִּי אֱלִיעֶזֶר אוֹמֵר סוֹתֵר אֶת הַכֹּל. וַחֲכָמִים אוֹמְרִים יָבִיא שְׁאָר קָרְבְּנוֹתָיו וְיִטְהַר. אָמְרוּ לוֹ מַעֲשֶׂה בְמִרְיָם הַתַּדְמוּרִית שֶׁנִּזְרַק עָלֶיהָ אֶחָד מִן הַדָּמִים וְאָמְרוּ לָהּ בִּתָּהּ שֶׁהִיא מְסֻכֶּנֶת וְהָלְכָה וּמְצָאַתָהּ שֶׁמֵּתָה וְאָמְרוּ חֲכָמִים תָּבִיא שְׁאָר קָרְבְּנוֹתֶיהָ וְתִטְהַר.

Mishnah 13: If one of the bloods had been sprinkled for him[247] when he became impure, Rebbi Eliezer says, he has to repeat everything[248]. But the Sages say, he shall bring his remaining sacrifices once he became pure again[249]. They told him, it happened with Miriam the Palmyrene, that one of the bloods had been sprinkled for her when she was informed that her daughter was dying; she went and found her dead[250]; then the Sages said, she shall bring her remaining sacrifices once she becomes pure again[251].

247 Sprinkling its blood on the walls of the altar makes any sacrifice irrevocably valid.

248 Not the *nezirut*, but all his sacrifices since he holds, against the Sages, that the sacrifices cannot be brought separately (cf. Mishnah 8:4).

249 And can enter the Temple precinct.

250 And defiled herself for her daughter.

251 Tosephta 4:10.

(55c line 69) **הלכה יב:** עָלַת לוֹ וּלְתִגְלַחְתּוֹ. אִין תֵּימַר. לֹא עָלַת לוֹ וּלְתִגְלַחְתּוֹ. אֲפִילוּ זְבָחָיו לֹא עָלוּ לוֹ. רִבִּי יוֹחָנָן בָּעֵי. מָהוּ עַל שַׁלְמֵי חֲגִיגָה לְגַלֵּחַ כְּרִבִּי שִׁמְעוֹן. וְלֹא מַתְנִיתָא הִיא. רִבִּי שִׁמְעוֹן אוֹמֵר אוֹתוֹ הַזֶּבַח לֹא עָלָה לוֹ אֲבָל

שְׁאָר כָּל־הַזְּבָחִין עָלוּ לוֹ. וַאֲפִילוּ שְׁחָטָן לֹא כְּשַׁלְמֵי נְדָבָה הֵן. הֲדָא אֲמְרָה. שֶׁהוּא מְגַלֵּחַ עַל שַׁלְמֵי נְדָבָה כְּרִבִּי שִׁמְעוֹן. רִבִּי יוֹסֵי בַּר אָבוּן אָמַר. רַב אָדָא בַּר אֲחָה וְרִבִּי יוֹחָנָן. רַב אָדָא בַּר אֲחָוָה צְרִיכָא לֵיהּ. וְרִבִּי יוֹחָנָן פְּשִׁיטָא לֵיהּ.

Halakhah 12: Is it counted for him and his shaving[252]? If you would say that it is not counted for him and his shaving, then his sacrifices count for nothing. Rebbi Johanan asked: Following Rebbi Simeon, may he shave for his holiday well-being offerings[253]? Is that not the Mishnah? "Rebbi Simeon says, that sacrifice is not counted for him but the others are counted for him." When he slaughtered them[254] are they not like voluntary well-being offerings[255]? This means that he may shave for voluntary well-being offerings following Rebbi Simeon. Rebbi Yose bar Abun said[256], Rav Ada bar Ahawa and Rebbi Johanan. For Rav Ada bar Ahawa it is problematic[257], but for Rebbi Johanan it is obvious.

252 If a *nazir* shaved for an improper sacrifice when afterwards he brought two proper sacrifices, R. Simeon said that the two proper sacrifices are counted for him. But if the shaving were improper, he would have to wait another 30 days and bring a new set of sacrifices, and there would be no way in which the earlier sacrifices could be counted for him. It is proved that for R. Simeon, shaving is valid as long as one sacrifice was valid.

253 He shaves on a holiday and brings with him not only the three obligatory sacrifices of a *nazir* but additional sacrifices for the holiday.

254 The well-being or elevation offerings which are acceptable as gifts to the altar if slaughtered without indicating the kind of sacrifices they should be.

255 In rabbinic terminology, a sacrifice corresponds to a *vow* (נדר) if a person engages himself for a certain kind of sacrifice. Then if the animal chosen to satisfy the vow becomes unusable for any reason, the vower has to provide a replacement animal. A voluntary gift (נדבה) is an animal dedicated as sacrifice. If it becomes unusable for any reason, the owner does not have to provide a replacement. Well-being and elevation sacrifices slaughtered for the wrong

purpose or no purpose fall under the category of voluntary gifts.
256   He corrects the tradition: the person who asks is R. Ada bar Aḥawa, not R. Joḥanan.
257   But in the Babli, 46b, he is quoted as proving the statement attributed here to R. Joḥanan.

(55c line 75) מִחְלְפָא שִׁיטָתֵיהּ דְּרִבִּי אֱלִיעֶזֶר. תַּמָּן הוּא אוֹמֵר. לֹא סָתַר אֶלָּא שְׁלֹשִׁים. וָכָא הוּא אָמַר אָכֵן. רִבִּי יוֹחָנָן אָמַר. סוֹתֵר כָּל קָרְבְּנוֹתָיו.   פְּשִׁיטָא דָא בְלֹא נִיטְמָא כָּשֵׁר. לֹא בְדָא כָשֵׁר וְאַחַר כָּךְ נִיטְמָא. אָמַר רִבִּי חִינְנָא. וְלֹא רִבִּי אֱלִיעֶזֶר הִיא. וְרִבִּי אֱלִיעֶזֶר שַׁמּוּתִי הוּא. דְּתַנֵּי. נָזִיר וּמִירֵט. בֵּית שַׁמַּי אוֹמְרִים. צָרִיךְ לְהַעֲבִיר תַּעַר עַל רֹאשׁוֹ. בֵּית הִלֵּל אוֹמְרִים. אֵין צָרִיךְ לְהַעֲבִיר תַּעַר עַל רֹאשׁוֹ.

The argument of Rebbi Eliezer seems inverted. There[258], he says: "he has to repeat only for 30," and here, he says so[259]? Rebbi Joḥanan says, he has to repeat all his sacrifices[248]. It is obvious, if it would have been valid without him becoming impure, then why is it not valid if later he becomes impure[260]? Rebbi Ḥinena said, is that not Rebbi Eliezer's? And Rebbi Eliezer follows the Shammaites, as it was stated[261]: Concerning a *nazir* who lost all his hair, the House of Shammai say, he has to move a shaving knife over his head; the House of Hillel say, he does not need to move a shaving knife over his head.

258   Mishnah 3:4.
259   If he becomes incapacitated, he has to repeat only for 30 days. If his sacrifice becomes invalid, why should he have to start everything anew?
260   Why should R. Eliezer not agree that once part of the ceremony was performed correctly, he can replace any missing part?
261   Babli 46b (in different formulation), *Yoma* 61b; Tosephta 1:6. As the Babli explains, the House of Shammai require him to shave, but since he cannot shave he never can terminate his *nezirut*.

כֵּן הִיא מַתְנִיתָא. יִטְהַר וְיָבִיא שְׁאָר קָרְבְּנוֹתָיו. כֵּן הִיא מַתְנִיתָא.(55c line 75) תִּטְהַר וְתָבִיא שְׁאָר קָרְבָּנָהּ.

So is the Mishnah[262]: He shall become pure again and then bring his remaining sacrifices. So is the Mishnah: She shall become pure again and then bring her remaining sacrifices.

262 The Mishnah is formulated with a temporal inversion. The action to become pure must precede the offering of his or her sacrifices.

כהן גדול פרק שביעי

(fol. 55d) **משנה א:** כֹּהֵן גָּדוֹל וְנָזִיר אֵינָן מִיטַּמְאִין בִּקְרוֹבֵיהֶן. הָיוּ מְהַלְּכִין בַּדֶּרֶךְ וּמָצְאוּ מֵת מִצְוָה רִבִּי אֱלִיעֶזֶר אוֹמֵר יִטַּמָּא כֹּהֵן גָּדוֹל וְאַל יִטַּמָּא נָזִיר. וַחֲכָמִים אוֹמְרִים יִטַּמָּא נָזִיר וְאַל יִטַּמָּא כֹּהֵן גָּדוֹל. אָמַר לָהֶן רִבִּי אֱלִיעֶזֶר יִטַּמָּא כֹּהֵן שֶׁאֵינוֹ מֵבִיא קָרְבָּן עַל טֻמְאָתוֹ וְאַל יִטַּמָּא נָזִיר שֶׁמֵּבִיא קָרְבָּן עַל טֻמְאָתוֹ. אָמְרוּ לוֹ יִטַּמָּא נָזִיר שֶׁקְּדוּשָׁתוֹ קְדוּשַׁת שָׁעָה וְאַל יִטַּמָּא כֹּהֵן שֶׁקְּדוּשָׁתוֹ קְדוּשַׁת עוֹלָם.

Mishnah 1: The High Priest and the *nazir* do not defile themselves for their relatives[1]. If they were walking on a road and found a corpse of obligation, Rebbi Eliezer says, the High Priest[2] shall defile himself but the *nazir* shall not defile himself. But the Sages say, the *nazir* shall defile himself but the High Priest shall not defile himself. Rebbi Eliezer said to them, the Priest shall defile himself, who does not bring a sacrifice for his defilement, but the *nazir* shall not defile himself, who has to bring a sacrifice for his defilement. They told him, the *nazir* shall defile himself, whose holiness is temporary, but the Priest shall not defile himself, whose holiness is permanent.

1 The High Priest is forbidden to defile himself even for father or mother, *Lev.* 21:11; the same holds for the *nazir*, *Num.* 6:7. In the Babli and many Mishnah mss. (but not in Maimonides's autograph) there is an additional clause: "but they have to defile themselves for a corpse of obligation", i. e., an abandoned corpse of whose burial nobody is taking care. The first person finding the body has to bury him.

2 Even the High Priest, and certainly a common priest. Similarly,

the Sages require that the *nazir* defile himself but not a common priest if they stumble on the corpse together.

(55d line 48) **הלכה א:** כֹּהֵן גָּדוֹל וְנָזִיר כול'. כְּתִיב וְעַל כָּל־נַפְשׁוֹת מֵת לֹא יָבוֹא. מָה אֲנָן קַיָּימִין. אִם לְאוֹסְרָן עַל הָרְחוֹקִים הֲרֵי הוּא בִּכְלַל כֹּהֵן הֶדְיוֹט. אֶלָּא אִם אֵינוֹ עִנְיָין לָרְחוֹקִים תְּנֵיהוּ עִנְיָין לַקְּרוֹבִים. כְּתִיב וְעַל כָּל־נַפְשׁוֹת וְאַתְּ אָמַר אָכֵן. אָמַר רִבִּי חִיָּיה בַּר גַּמְדָא. מִיכָּן אִיסּוּר אַחַר אִיסּוּר בַּתּוֹרָה. אֶלָּא לְהַתִּיר מֵת מִצְוָה. אִית דְּבָעֵי נִישְׁמְעִינָהּ מִן הָדָא. לֹא יִטַּמָּא בַּעַל בְּעַמָּיו. אֵינוֹ מִיטַּמָּא. מִיטַּמָּא הוּא לְמֵת מִצְוָה. אִית דְּבָעֵי מִישְׁמְעִינָהּ מִן הָכָא. לְהֵחַלּוֹ. לְהֵחַלּוֹ אֵינוֹ מִיטַּמָּא. אֲבָל מִיטַּמָּא הוּא עַל מֵת מִצְוָה.

Halakhah 1: "The High Priest and the *nazir*," etc. It is written: "He shall not go close to a dead body.[3]" Where do we hold? If to forbid non-relatives, is he not also under the rules of a simple priest[4]? If it cannot refer to non-relatives, refer it to relatives. It is written: "Not to go close to a dead body," and you say so? Rebbi Ḥiyya bar Gamda said, from here repeated prohibitions in the Torah[5]. But it is to permit the corpse of obligation[6]. Some understand it from the following: "[7]The man shall not defile himself, in the midst of his people" he may not defile himself[8]. But he defiles himself for a corpse of obligation. Some understand it from the following: "[7]To profane himself." He may not defile himself to profane himself; he defiles himself for a corpse of obligation.

3 *Lev.* 21:11, speaking of the High Priest. A parallel argument in the Babli, 47b.

4 A common priest is forbidden to defile himself for any dead person other than close relatives, *Lev.* 21:1-3.

5 In his opinion, the High Priest who defiles himself for a corpse violates two identical prohibitions.

6 This follows the rule that "an exclusion on top of an exclusion means an inclusion." Since in general a Cohen is forbidden to defile himself for the dead, the repetition of the prohibition for the High Priest indicates an obligation to defile himself in some

cases. Since father and mother, for whom defilement is commanded to the common priest, are forbidden to the High Priest, the corpse for whom the High Priest (and by implication, any priest) has to defile himself is a non-relative, the corpse of obligation.

7   Lev. 21:4.

8   If other Jews are present who may bury the dead, he may not defile himself. By implication, if he is alone, he must defile himself.

(55d line 55) אִית דְּבָעֵי מִישְׁמְעִינָהּ מִן הָדָא. כִּי קִלְלַת אֱלֹהִים תָּלוּי. אֶת שֶׁהוּא מוּזְהָר עַל קִלְלַת הַשֵּׁם מוּזְהָר הוּא עַל מֵת מִצְוָה. וְשֶׁאֵינוֹ מוּזְהָר עַל קִלְלַת הַשֵּׁם אֵינוֹ מוּזְהָר עַל מֵת מִצְוָה. הֲתִיבוּן. הֲרֵי גוֹיִם. אִילוּ שְׁמִיתָתָן בִּתְלִיָּיה. יָצָא זֶה שֶׁמִּיתָתוֹ בַּסַּיִיף. קָבוֹר. מִצְוַת עֲשֵׂה. מְנַיִין אַתְּ מַרְבֶּה סַיִיף שֶׁנֶּהֱרַג בּוֹ. עֵץ שֶׁנִּתְלָה בּוֹ. סוּדָר שֶׁנֶּחֱנַק בּוֹ. מַה תַּלְמוּד לוֹמַר תִּקְבְּרֶנּוּ. יָכוֹל יִקְבְּרוּ עַצְמוֹ. תַּלְמוּד לוֹמַר כִּי קָבוֹר תִּקְבְּרֶנּוּ. קְבוּרָה לוֹ וּלְעֵצוֹ וּלְאַבְנוֹ. הָא כֵּיצַד. מַעֲמִיק שְׁלֹשָׁה כְּדֵי שֶׁלֹּא תַעֲלֵם הַמַּחֲרִישָׁה. תִּקְבְּרֶנּוּ. כּוּלוֹ וְלֹא מִקְצָתוֹ. תִּקְבְּרֶנּוּ. מִיכָּן שֶׁאִם שִׁיֵּיר מִמֶּנּוּ לֹא עָשָׂה כְּלוּם. שֶׁנֶּאֱמַר כִּי קָבוֹר תִּקְבְּרֶנּוּ. מִיכָּן שֶׁאֵין נַעֲשָׂה מֵת מִצְוָה עַד שֶׁיְּהֵא רֹאשׁוֹ וְרוּבּוֹ.

Some want to derive it from the following: "For a hanged person is blasphemy.[9]" Anybody warned about blasphemy is warned about a corpse of obligation. Anybody not warned about blasphemy is not warned about a corpse of obligation[10]. They objected, are there not Gentiles[11]? Those executed by hanging, this exludes those executed by the sword[12]. "Bury!" A positive commandment[13]. From where do you add the sword he was killed with, the gallows on which he was hanged, the towel with which he was strangled? Why does the verse say, "you shall bury him"? I could think he alone is buried; the verse says "bury, you shall bury him", a burial for him, and his gallows, and his stone[14]. How does one do it? One digs down three [handbreadths], so the plough shall not unearth him. "You shall bury him", whole and not partially. "You shall bury him", from here that if he left anything [unburied], he did not do anything, for it is said "bury, you shall bury him". From here that it is not a corpse of obligation unless it consists of his head with most of the body.

9   Deut. 21:23: "You may not leave his corpse on the gallows overnight, but bury, you shall bury him on that day, for a hanged person is blasphemy ..."

10   This means that the details of the rules for burials apply only to Jews to whom the details of the rules of blasphemy apply.

11   The prohibition of blasphemy is part of the "natural law" given to Adam and Noah (Tosephta 'Avodah zarah 9:4, Babli Sanhedrin 56a/b).

12   The only method of execution recognized for Gentiles, Babli Sanhedrin 57a.

13   This is a shortened version of the explanation in Sifry Deut. 220: "You may not leave his corpse on the gallows overnight," a prohibition, "but bury!", a positive commandment. A biblical commandment which is both positive and negative is the strongest of all commandments and will supersede opposing simple positive or simple negative commandments (Babli Yom Tob 8b, severely restricted in Yebamot 3b/4a) if written in the same verse (Yerushalmi Yom Tob 1:3, Hallah 2:1, Note 10, unrestricted).

14   Quoted in the Babli, Sanhedrin 45b.

(55d line 65) תַּנֵּי רִבִּי יָסָא קוֹמֵי רִבִּי יוֹחָנָן. כְּשֵׁם שֶׁאָדָם מִיטַּמֵּא לְמֵת מִצְוָה כָּךְ אָדָם מִיטַּמֵּא עַל אֵבֶר מֵת מִצְוָה. אָמַר לֵיהּ רִבִּי יוֹחָנָן. וְיֵשׁ כֵּן זוֹ. רִבִּי יַעֲקֹב בַּר אָחָא בְּשֵׁם רִבִּי זְעִירָא. בְּחוֹזֵר תִּיפְתָּר. תַּנֵּי. רִבִּי יוֹסֵי אוֹמֵר. אֵין אָדָם מִיטַּמֵּא עַל אֵבֶר מִן הַחַי מֵאָבִיו אֲבָל אָדָם מִיטַּמֵּא עַל עֶצֶם כִּשְׂעוֹרָה מֵאָבִיו. רִבִּי יוּדָה אוֹמֵר. כְּשֵׁם שֶׁאָדָם מִיטַּמֵּא עַל עֶצֶם כִּשְׂעוֹרָה מֵאָבִיו כָּךְ מִיטַּמֵּא עַל אֵבֶר מִן הַחַי מֵאָבִיו. מַעֲשֶׂה בְּיוֹסֵי בֶּן פַּכְסָס שֶׁעָלַת עַל רַגְלוֹ נוֹמִי וְנִכְנַס הָרוֹפֵא לְחוֹתְכָהּ. אָמַר לוֹ. כְּשֶׁתַּנִּיחַ בּוֹ כְחוּט הַשְּׂעָרָה הוֹדִיעֵנִי. חֲתָכָהּ וְהִנִּיחַ בָּהּ כְּחוּט הַשְּׂעָרָה וְהוֹדִיעוֹ. קָרָא לִנְחוּנְיָיה בְּנוֹ אָמַר לוֹ. נְחוּנְיָיה בְּנִי. עַד כָּאן הָיִיתָה חַיָּיב לִיטַּפֵּל בִּי. מִיכָּן וְאֵילַךְ צֵא. שֶׁאֵין אָדָם מִיטַּמֵּא עַל אֵבֶר מִן הַחַי מֵאָבִיו. וּכְשֶׁבָּא דָּבָר אֵצֶל חֲכָמִים אָמְרוּ. עַל זֶה נֶאֱמַר יֵשׁ צַדִּיק אוֹבֵד בְּצִדְקוֹ. הַצַּדִּיק אוֹבֵד וְצִדְקוֹ עִמּוֹ.

Rebbi Yasa stated before Rebbi Johanan: Just as one defiles himself for a corpse of obligation, so one defiles himself for a limb of a corpse of obligation[15]. Rebbi Johanan answered him: Is that so? Rebbi Jacob bar Aha in the name of Rebbi Ze'ira: Explain it if he returns[16]. It was stated: Rebbi Yose said, nobody has to defile himself for a limb from his living father, but one has to defile himself for bone the size of a barley corn from his father. Rebbi Jehudah says, just as one has to defile himself for bone the size of a barley corn from his father, so one has to defile himself for a limb from his living father[17]. [18]"It happened that Yose ben Paxas developed a growth[19] on his foot. When the surgeon came to remove it, he told him to inform him when only a hair's breadth was left[20]. He[21] cut until only a hair's breadth was left, and informed him. He[22] addressed his son Onias and told him, Onias my son, up to now you had to care for me, but leave now since nobody has to defile himself for a limb from his living father[23]. When this came before the Sages, they said, about him it was said: "It happens that a just man is lost in his merit[24];" the just is lost and his merit accompanies him.

15 This contradicts the preceding statement.

16 If a Cohen was burying a corpse of obligation and later found another limb of the same corpse, he may bury the limb since he already is impure and the prohibition of *Lev.* 21:1 refers only to him *becoming* impure, not to what he does once he is impure. In the Babli, 43b, this is a tannaïtic statement ascribed to R. Jehudah.

17 *Semahot* 4:27. In the Babylonian sources, Babli 43b, *Sifra Emor Introduction* 13, R. Jehudah represents the opinion ascribed here to R. Yose, while R. Yose denies that a Cohen defiles himself for a piece of his father's bone. The reason given is *Lev.* 21:3 (speaking of the Cohen's unmarried sister): "For her he has to defile himself," interpreted as "for her body, but not for her body parts."

18 *Sifra Emor Introduction* 14. *Semahot* 4:28 (יוסף פסס), *Yalqut Qohelet*

976 (יוסף הכהן). It is clear from the story that one speaks of a priestly family.
19 Greek νομή "cancerous growth".
20 Connecting the growth to his body.
21 The surgeon.
22 Yose ben Paxas.
23 Since the growth, once separated from his body, is impure in the impurity of the dead (Mishnah *Ahilut* 2:1).
24 *Eccl.* 7:15. The implication is that practice follows R. Yose.

(56a line 1) אֵי זֶהוּ מֵת מִצְוָה. כָּל־שֶׁהוּא צָוֵחַ וְאֵין בְּנֵי הָעִיר בָּאִים. בָּאוּ בְּנֵי הָעִיר הֲרֵי זֶה מוֹשֵׁךְ אֶת יָדוֹ. עַד הֵיכָן. עַד כְּדֵי נוֹשְׂאֵי הַמִּטָּה וְחִילוּפֵיהֶן וְחִילוּפֵי חִילוּפֵיהֶן. בְּשֶׁאֵינָן צְרִיכִין לוֹ. אֲבָל אִם הָיוּ צְרִיכִין לוֹ לֹא בְדָא. בְּשֶׁאֵינָן מַכִּירִין אוֹתוֹ. אֲבָל אִם הָיוּ מַכִּירִין אוֹתוֹ לֹא בְדָא. בְּשֶׁאֵין כְּבוֹדוֹ. אֲבָל אִם הָיָה כְבוֹדוֹ אָכֵן לֹא בְדָא. וְהַנָּשִׂיא כְבוֹדוֹ לָכֵן.

What is a corpse of obligation? Anyone for whom he shouts and nobody comes[25]. If the villagers come, he refrains[26]. How many? For the carriers of the bier, their replacements, and the replacements of their replacements[27]. If he is not needed; but if he is needed, it is different[28]. If [the deceased] is not recognized[29]. But if he is recognized, it is different. If it is not according to his honor; but if it is according to his honor, it is different[30]. For the Patriarch it is his honor.

25 In the Babli (43b, *Yebamot* 89b, *Erubin* 17b): "Anyone who has nobody to bury him; if he calls and others answer him it is not a corpse of obligation." The Yerushalmi version is in *Semahot* 4:29.
26 Cohen or *nazir* refrain from defiling themselves.
27 In *Semahot* 4:30: Carriers of the bier and grave diggers.
28 If the dead cannot have a decent burial without the help of *nazir* or Cohen, the latter have to defile themselves.
29 If the deceased is not recognized by the locals; if he is recognized the *nazir* or Cohen is precluded from defiling himself.
30 This is the introduction to the following paragraphs. If the prestige of the deceased is so great that priests have to defile themselve for his burial,

it is obvious that the *nazir* or Cohen who stumbles on his body also has to defile himself.

(56a line 6) וּמַהוּ שֶׁיִּטָּמֵא כֹּהֵן לִכְבוֹד הַנָּשִׂיא. כַּד דָּמַךְ רִבִּי יוּדָן נְשִׂיָיא אַכְרִיז רִבִּי יַנַּאי וְאָמַר. אֵין כְּהוּנָּה הַיּוֹם. כַּד דָּמַךְ רִבִּי יוּדָן נְשִׂיָיא בַּר בְּרֵיהּ דְּרִבִּי יוּדָן נְשִׂיָיא דָּחַף רִבִּי חִייָה לְרִבִּי זְעִירָא בַּר בָּא בִּכְנִישְׁתָּא דְגוּפְנָה דְצִיפּוֹרִין וּמְסָאֲבֵיהּ. כַּד דָּמְכַת יְהוּדִינַיי אֲחָתֵיהּ דְּרִבִּי יוּדָן נְשִׂיָיא שָׁלַח רִבִּי חֲנִינָה בָּתַר רִבִּי מָנָא וְלָא סְלַק. אָמַר לֵיהּ. אִם בְּחַיֵּיהֶן אֵין מִיטַּמִּין לָהֶן כָּל־שֶׁכֵּן בְּמִיתָתָן. אָמַר רִבִּי נַסָּא בְּמִיתָתָן עָשׂוּ אוֹתָן כְּמֵת מִצְוָה.

1 נשייא | נשיאה   2 ואמר | ומר   יודן | יודה   3 יודן | יודה   ר' חייה לר' זעירא בר בא | ר' חייא בר אבא לר' זעירא   ומסאביה | וסאביה   4 יהודיניי | נהוראי יודן | יהודה   5 סלק | סליק   מיטמין | מיטמאין

[31]May a Cohen defile himself for the Patriarch? When Rebbi Judah the Prince died, Rebbi Yannai proclaimed and said: "There is no priesthood today." When Rebbi Judah the Prince, grandson of Rebbi Judah the Prince, died, Rebbi Hiyya bar Abba did push Rebbi Zeïra[32] in the Gufna synagogue of Sepphoris and defiled him. When Yehudinai, the sister of Rebbi Judah the Prince, died, Rebbi Hanina sent for Rebbi Mana but the latter did not come. He said to him, if one does not defile himself for them during their lifetime, so much less in their death. Rebbi Nassa said, in their death they treated them like a corpse of obligation.

31 The same text is in *Berakhot* 3:1, Notes 95-101. The following paragraphs (to 56a, line 68) are from the same source, Notes 64-120.

32 The *Berakhot* text clearly is the correct one.

(56a line 12) מַהוּ שֶׁיִּטָּמֵא לִכְבוֹד רַבּוֹ. רִבִּי יַנַּאי זְעִירָא דְּמַךְ חָמוּי. הוּא הֲוָה חָמוּי הוּא הֲוָה רַבֵּיהּ. שָׁאַל לְרִבִּי יוֹסֵי וְאָסַר לֵיהּ. שָׁמַע רִבִּי חָמָא וְאָמַר. יִטָּמְאוּ לוֹ תַלְמִידָיו. נִטְמְאוּ לוֹ תַלְמִידָיו וְאָכְלוּ בָשָׂר וְשָׁתוּ יַיִן. אָמַר לוֹן רִבִּי

מָנָא. חֲדָא מִן תַּרְתֵּי לָא פְלָטָה לְכוֹן. אִם אֲבֵילִים אַתֶּם לָמָה אֲכַלְתֶּם בָּשָׂר וּשְׁתִיתֶם יַיִן. וְאִם אֵין אַתֶּם אֲבֵילִים לָמָה נִטְמֵאתֶם.

1 מהו | כהן מהו   2 הוא | והוא   חמא | אחא   ואמ' | ומר   3 נטמאו | ר' יוסי נטמאו   4 פלטה | פלטת   ושתיתם | ולמה שתיתם   5 אבילים | מתאבלין

May a Cohen defile himself for the honor of his teacher? The father-in-law of Rebbi Yannai the Younger died. He was both his father-in-law and his teacher. He asked Rebbi Yose who forbade it. Rebbi Ḥama (?) heard it and said: His students should defile themselves for him. The students [of Rebbi Yose][33] defiled themselves for him but ate meat and drank wine. Rebbi Mana told them: One of two things you cannot escape. If you are mourners, why did you eat meat and drink wine; if you are not mourners, why did you defile yourselves?

33   From the text in *Berakhot*, required by the context.

(56a line 17) מַהוּ שֶׁיִּטָּמֵא אָדָם לְתַלְמוּד תּוֹרָה. רִבִּי יוֹסֵי הֲוָה יָתִיב וּמַתְנֵי וְאָעַל מִיתָא. מָן דְּיָתַב לֵיהּ לֹא אָמַר כְּלוּם וּמָן דְּנָפַק לֵיהּ לֹא אָמַר לֵיהּ וְלֹא כְלוּם.

1 אדם | כהן   לתלמוד | לכבוד[34]   ומתני | מתני   2 דיתב | דנפיק ליה   אמ' | אמ' ליה   דנפק | דיתב   ולא כלום | כלום

May a Cohen defile himself for the study of Torah? Rebbi Yose was sitting and teaching when a dead body was brought in. He did not say anything either to those who remained sitting or to those who left.

34   The Rome ms. parallels the text in *Nazir*.

(56a line 19) רִבִּי נִיחוּמִי בְּרֵיהּ דְּרִבִּי חִייָה בַּר אַבָּא אָמַר. אַבָּא לֹא הֲוָה עֲבִיר תְּחוֹת כִּפְתָּא דְקֵיסָרִין. וְרִבִּי אַמִּי עֲבַר. רִבִּי חִזְקִיָּה רִבִּי כֹּהֵן וְרִבִּי יַעֲקֹב בַּר אָחָא הֲווֹן מְטַיְילִין בִּפְלַטְיָא דְקַיסָרִין. הִגִּיעוּ לְכִיפָה וּפֵירֵשׁ רִבִּי כֹּהֵן. הִגִּיעוּ

לְמָקוֹם טַהֲרָה וְחָזַר אֶצְלָן. אָמַר לוֹן. בַּמֶּה הֲוִיתוּן עֲסָקִין. אָמַר רִבִּי חִזְקִיָּה לְרִבִּי יַעֲקֹב בַּר אָחָא. לֹא תֵימָא לֵיהּ כְּלוּם. אִין דְּפָרַשׁ לֵיהּ דְּבָאֵשׁ שֶׁמִּיטָּמֵא לְתַלְמוּד תּוֹרָה לָא יָדְעִין. וְאִין מִשּׁוּם דַּהֲוָה סַיְיסָן לָא יָדְעִין.

1 ניחומי | ניחומיה   חייה   עביר | עבור   2 כפתא | כפתה   עבר | - ר' כהן |
ור' כהן   3 הוון | הוו   בפלטיא דקיסרין | באילין פלטיותא דציפורי   4 הויתון | -
5 תימא | תימור   דפרש ליה דבאש שמיטמא | משום דבאיש ליה דפרש שמטמא   6
סייסן | נוייסן

Rebbi Niḥumi the son of Rebbi Ḥiyya bar Abba said: My father did not walk under the arch of Caesarea. Rebbi Ammi walked. Rebbi Ḥizqiah, Rebbi Cohen and Rebbi Jacob bar Aḥa went walking in the streets of Caesarea. They came to the arch and Rebbi Cohen left. They reached a place of purity and he returned to them. He asked them: "What were you discussing?" Rebbi Ḥizqiah said to Rebbi Jacob bar Aḥa: "Do not tell him anything!" We do not know whether it was because he was angry that he left since one defiles oneself for words of Torah or whether it was because he was haughty.

(56a line 25) תַּנֵּי. מִיטַּמֵּא הוּא כֹהֵן וְיוֹצֵא חוּצָה לָאָרֶץ לְדִינֵי מָמוֹנוֹת וְדִינֵי נְפָשׁוֹת וּלְקִידּוּשׁ הַחוֹדֶשׁ וּלְעִיבּוּר הַשָּׁנָה וּלְהַצִּיל מִן הַגּוֹי וְלִלְמוֹד תּוֹרָה וְלָשֵׂאת אִשָּׁה. רִבִּי יוּדָה אוֹמֵר. אִם יֶשׁ לוֹ מֵאַיִן לִלְמוֹד אַל יִטָּמֵא. רִבִּי יוֹסֵי אוֹמֵר. אֲפִילוּ יֵשׁ לוֹ מֵאַיִן לִלְמוֹד יִטָּמֵא. שֶׁלֹּא מֵהַכֹּל אָדָם זוֹכֶה לִלְמוֹד. אָמְרוּ עָלָיו עַל רִבִּי יוֹסֵף הַכֹּהֵן שֶׁהָיָה יוֹצֵא אַחַר רַבּוֹ וּמִטַּמֵּא אַחַר רַבּוֹ לְצַיְּידָן. אֲבָל אָמְרוּ. אַל יֵצֵא כֹהֵן לְחוּץ לָאָרֶץ אֶלָּא אִם כֵּן הִבְטִיחוּ לוֹ אִשָּׁה.

1 מיטמא | מטמא   הוא כהן | הכהן   ודיני | ולדיני   2 השנה | שנה   ולהציל | להציל
הגוי ואפי' ליטור יוצא ועוה עליה   ולשאת | ולישא   3 מאיין | מאיכן   4
מאיין | מאיכן   ללמוד | ללמוד תורה   מהכל | מכל   5 ר' | -   יוצא | מיטמא ויוצא
ציידן | צידן

It is stated: A Cohen may defile himself by leaving the Land for civil and criminal suits, for the consecration of the New Moon and intercalation of a year, to redeem a field from a Gentile, to study Torah, and to marry a wife. Rebbi Judah says, if he has a place to study, he should not defile himself. Rebbi Yose says, even if he has a place to study, he may defile himself, since a man may not have the luck to learn from every teacher. They said about Joseph the Cohen that he followed his teacher and defiled himself following his teacher to Sidon. In truth, they said a priest should not go abroad unless one promised him a wife.

(56a line 32) מַהוּ שֶׁיִּטָּמֵא כֹהֵן גָּדוֹל לִנְשִׂיאוּת כַּפַּיִם. גַּבִּילָה אֲחוּי דְרִבִּי בָּא בַּר כֹּהֵן אָמַר קוֹמֵי רִבִּי יוֹסֵה בְּשֵׁם רִבִּי אָחָא. מְטַמֵּא הוּא כֹהֵן לִנְשִׂיאוּת כַּפַּיִם. שָׁמַע רִבִּי אָחָא וְאָמַר. אֲנָא לָא אֲמָרִית לֵיהּ כְּלוּם. חָזַר וָמַר. אוֹ דִילְמָא לָא שָׁמַע מִינִּי אֶלָּא כְיַי דָמַר רִבִּי יוּדָה בַּר פָּזִי בְּשֵׁם רִבִּי אֱלִיעֶזֶר. כָּל־כֹּהֵן שֶׁעוֹמֵד בַּכְּנֶסֶת וְאֵינוֹ נוֹשֵׂא אֶת כַּפָּיו עוֹבֵר בַּעֲשֵׂה. וְסָבַר מֵימַר שֶׁמִּצְוַת עֲשֵׂה דוֹחָה לְמִצְוַת לֹא תַעֲשֶׂה. אֲנָא לָא אֲמָרִי לֵיהּ. אַייְתוּנֵיהּ וַאֲנָא מַלְקֵי לֵיהּ.

1 גדול | - ‎ נשיאות | נשיאת ‎ גבילה | מגבילה ‎ בא | אבא ‎ 2 יוסה | יוסי ‎ הוא | - ‎ נשיאות | נשיאת ‎ 3 ואמ׳ | ומר ‎ ומר ואמ׳ ‎ 4 בר | בן ‎ אליעזר | אלעזר ‎ שעומד | שהוא עומד ‎ 5 בכנסת | בבית הכנסת ‎ 6 אמרי ליה | אמרית ליה כלום ‎ מלקי ליה | אלקוניה

May a (High) Priest defile himself for the lifting of hands? Gabilah, the brother of Rebbi Abba bar Cohen said before Rebbi Yose in the name of Rebbi Aḥa: A Cohen defiles himself for the lifting of hands. Rebbi Aḥa heard it and said: I never told him anything. On second thoughts he said, maybe he heard from me what Rebbi Jehudah ben Pazi said in the name of Rebbi Eleazar: Every Cohen who stays in the synagogue and does not lift his hands transgresses a positive commandment, and he wanted to say that a positive commandment supersedes a negative commandment. I never told him anything. Bring him in and I will flog him!

(56a line 38) רִבִּי אַבָּהוּ הֲוָה יָתִיב מַתְנֵי בִּכְנִישְׁתָּא מְדַרְתָּא דְקֵיסָרִין וַהֲוָה תַמָּן מֵיתָא. הִגִּיעַ עוֹנַת נְשִׂיאוּת כַּפַּיִם. לָא שָׁאֲלוֹן לֵיהּ. עֲנָתָא דְמֵיכְלָא אָתָא וְשָׁאֲלוֹן לֵיהּ. אָמַר לוֹן. עַל נְשִׂיאוּת כַּפַּיִם לָא שְׁאַלְתּוּן לִי וְעַל מֵיכְלָא שְׁאִילְתּוּן יָתִי. כַּד שָׁמְעִין כֵּן הֲוָה כָּל־חַד וְחַד מִנְּהוֹן שָׁמַט גַּרְמֵיהּ וַעֲרָק.

1 מדרתא | מדדתא   דקיסרין | בקיסרין   2 הגיע עונת נשיאות | אתת ענתא דנשיאות לא ולא   ענתא | אתת ענתא   אתא | -   3 שאלתון | שאילתון   ועל מיכלא | ולמיכלא   4 כד שמעין | כיון דשמעון   מינהון שמט | שבק

Rebbi Abbahu was sitting teaching in the fortified synagogue in Caesarea; there was a coffin there. There came the time for lifting the hands and they did not ask him. There came the time for eating and they asked him. He said to them: For the lifting of hands you did not ask me, for eating you are asking me? When they heard this, each one was taking himself away and fled.

(56a line 43) אָמַר רִבִּי יַנַּאי. מִיטַּמֵּא כֹהֵן לִרְאוֹת הַמֶּלֶךְ. כַּד סָלַק דּוּקְלֵינוּס מַלְכָּא לְהָכָא חָמוֹן לְרִבִּי חִייָה מִיפְסַע עַל קִבְרַיָּא דְצוֹר בְּגִין מֵיחְמִינֵיהּ. רִבִּי חִזְקִיָּה רִבִּי יִרְמִיָּה וְרִבִּי חִייָה בְּשֵׁם רִבִּי יוֹחָנָן. מִצְוָה לִרְאוֹת גְּדוֹלֵי מַלְכֻיוֹת. לִכְשֶׁתָּבוֹא מַלְכוּת בֵּית דָּוִד יְהֵא יוֹדֵעַ לְהַפְרִישׁ בֵּין מַלְכוּת לְמַלְכוּת.

1 מיטמא | מטמא   המלך | את המלך   סלק דוקלינוס | סליק דוקליטיינוס   2 חייה | חייא בר אבא   קברייא | קבריה   3 ר' ירמיה ור' חייה | ור' ירמיה

Rebbi Yannai said: A Cohen defiles himself in order to see the King. When King Diocletian visited here, Rebbi Ḥiyya bar Abba was seen stepping over graves at Tyre in order to see him. Rebbi Ḥizqiah and Rebbi Jeremiah in the name of Rebbi Joḥanan: There is an obligation to see great persons of government, so that when the kingdom of the dynasty of David will return one will know how to distinguish one government from the other.

(56a line 47)מַהוּ שֶׁיִּטָּמֵא לִכְבוֹד אָבִיו וְאִמּוֹ. רִבִּי יָסָא שָׁמַע דְּאָתַת אִימֵּיהּ
לְבוֹצְרָה. אָתָא וְשָׁאַל לְרִבִּי יוֹחָנָן. מָהוּ לָצֵאת. אָמַר לֵיהּ. מִפְּנֵי סַכָּנַת דְּרָכִים
צֵא. וְאִם בִּשְׁבִיל כְּבוֹד אִמָּךְ אֵינִי יוֹדֵעַ. אָמַר רַב שְׁמוּאֵל בַּר רַב יִצְחָק עוֹד
הִיא צְרִיכָה לְרִבִּי יוֹחָנָן. אַטְרַח עֲלוֹי וְאָמַר. גָּמַרְתָּ לָצֵאת תָּבוֹא בְשָׁלוֹם. שָׁמַע
רִבִּי אֶלְעָזָר וְאָמַר. אֵין רְשׁוּת גְּדוֹלָה מִזֹּאת.

1 לכבוד | כהן לכבוד   2 ושאל | שאל   מפני | אין מפני   3 ואם בשביל כבוד אמך |
אין משום כבוד אביו ואמו   3 רב | ר'   4 לר' יוחנן | -   אטרח | אטרח ר' יוחנן
ואמ' | ומר (2 times)   גמרת | אם גמרת   5 מזאת | מזו

May [a Cohen] defile himself in honor of his father and mother? Rebbi Yasa heard that his mother had come to Bostra. He went and asked Rebbi Yoḥanan, may I leave? He said to him, if it is because of danger on the road, leave. If it is in order to honor your mother, I do not know. Rebbi Samuel bar Rav Isaac said, Rebbi Yoḥanan still needs to answer. He importuned him, so he said: Since you decided to go, return in peace. Rebbi Eleazar heard this and said: there is no greater permission than that.

(56a line 52) מַהוּ שֶׁיִּטָּמֵא אָדָם לִכְבוֹד הָרַבִּים. תַּנֵּי הָיוּ שְׁנֵי דְרָכִים מַתְאִימוֹת.
אַחַת רְחוֹקָה וּטְהוֹרָה וְאַחַת קְרוֹבָה וּטְמֵיאָה. אִם הָיוּ הָרַבִּים הוֹלְכִין בָּרְחוֹקָה
הוֹלֵךְ עִמָּהֶן. וְאִם לָאו הוֹלֵךְ בַּקְּרוֹבָה מִפְּנֵי כְבוֹד הָרַבִּים. עַד כְּדוֹן בְּטוּמְאָה
שֶׁהוּא מִדִּבְרֵיהֶן. וַאֲפִילוּ בְטוּמְאָה שֶׁהִיא מִדְּבַר תּוֹרָה. מִן מַה דְּאָמַר רִבִּי
זְעִירָא. גָּדוֹל כְּבוֹד הַבְּרִיּוֹת שֶׁדּוֹחָה לְמִצְוָה בְּלֹא תַעֲשֶׂה שָׁעָה אַחַת. הָדָא
אָמְרָה וַאֲפִילוּ טוּמְאָה שֶׁהָיָה מִדְּבַר תּוֹרָה.

1 אדם | כהן   שני | שתי   3 עמהן | ברחוקה   ואם לאו | אם לאו   4 שהוא
מדבריהן | שלדבריהם   ואפי' | אפי'   שהוא | שהיא   מדבר | מדברי   דאמ' | דמר   5
כבוד הבריות שדוחה למצוה | הוא כבוד הבריות שהוא דוחה מצוה   הדא | אדא   6
ואפי' טומאה שהיה | אפי' בטומאה שהיא

May a (person) [Cohen] defile himself in honor of the public? It is stated: When there are two acceptable roads, one long and pure, the other one short and impure: If the public was walking on the long one, he goes on the long one; otherwise, he goes on the short one in honor of the public. That refers to impurity by their words; also for impurity that is from the words of the Torah? From what Rebbi Zeïra said, so great is the honor of the public that it temporarily pushes aside a prohibition, that means even impurity that is from the words of the Torah.

(56a line 58) רִבִּי יוֹנָה רִבִּי יוֹסֵי גְלִילָיָא בְשֵׁם רִבִּי יוֹסֵי בֶּן חֲנִינָא. אֵין שׁוֹאֲלִין הֲלָכוֹת לִפְנֵי מִיטָתוֹ שֶׁלְּמֵת. וְהָא רִבִּי יוֹחָנָן שָׁאַל לְרִבִּי יַנַּיי קוֹמֵי עַרְסֵיהּ דְּרִבִּי שִׁמְעוֹן בֶּן יוֹצָדָק. הִקְדִּישׁ עוֹלָתוֹ לְבֶדֶק הַבַּיִת. וַהֲוָה מְגִיב לֵיהּ. אָמַר. כַּד הֲוָה מַסְקִין לֵיהּ לְסִדְרָא. וְהָא רִבִּי יִרְמְיָה שָׁאַל לְרִבִּי זְעִירָא קוֹמֵי עַרְסֵיהּ דְּרִבִּי שִׁמְעוֹן וּדְרִבִּי שְׁמוּאֵל בַּר רַב יִצְחָק והוא מְגִיב לֵיהּ. אָמַר. כַּד הֲוָה רָחִיק הֲוָה מְגִיב לֵיהּ. כַּד הֲוָה קָרִיב לָא הֲוָה מְגִיב לֵיהּ.

1 יוסי בן | יסא בר'   2 ינייי | ינאי   3 שמעון שמואל   והוה | והוא   אמ' | נימר הוה מסקין | הוה רחיק או כד הוון מסקין   4 זעירא | זעורא   דר' שמעון ו | -   5 אמ' | נימר

Rebbi Jonah, Rebbi Yose the Galilean, in the name of Rebbi Yose ben Ḥanina: One does not ask rulings on practice before the bier of a deceased. But Rebbi Yoḥanan asked Rebbi Yannai before the bier of Rebbi Simeon ben Yoẓadaq about him who dedicated his elevation sacrifice for the upkeep of the Sanctuary, and he answered him! Let us say when they were bringing him to the study hall. But Rebbi Jeremiah asked Rebbi Zeïra before the bier of (Rebbi Simeon and) Rebbi Samuel bar Rav Isaac! Let us say that he answered him when he was far away; when he was close he did not answer him.

(56a line 64) תַּנֵּי הַכַּתָּפִים אֲסוּרִים בִּנְעִילַת הַסַּנְדָּל שֶׁמָּא יִפְסֹק סַנְדָּלוֹ שֶׁלְּאֶחָד מֵהֶן וְנִמְצָא מִתְעַכֵּב מִן הַמִּצְוֹת.

1 אסורים | אסורין   יפסק | יפסוק   2 המצות | המצוה

It is stated: The carriers may not wear sandals lest a shoelace of one of them break so he would be prevented from performing a good deed.

(56a line 66) רִבִּי זְעִירָא שְׁמַע בְּדִיבּוּרֵיהּ. אָתוֹן בָּעֵיי מִיזְקְפוּנֵיהּ וְאַשְׁכְּחוּנֵיהּ אִיעֲנֵי. אָמְרוּ לֵיהּ. מַהוּ אָכֵן. אָמַר לוֹן. לְהֵן דְּתַגִּינָן וְהַחַי יִתֵּן אֶל לִבּוֹ.

1 שמע | שרע   בדיבוריה | בדיבורא   בעיי מיזקפוניה | בעיין מיזקפניה   2 אכן | כן לחן דתנינן | לכן דאתינן על שם

Rebbi Zeïra bent down during a eulogy. They wanted to straighten him up and found that he tarried. They said to him, what is this? He said to them, because we will go there, following (*Eccl.* 7:2): "Let the one who is alive take it to heart."

(56a line 68) הַמּוֹצֵא מֵת מִצְוָה הֲרֵי זֶה מִיטַּפֵּל בּוֹ וְקוֹבְרוֹ בִּמְקוֹמוֹ. אֵימָתַי. בִּזְמַן שֶׁמְּצָאוֹ חוּץ לַתְּחוּם. אֲבָל אִם מְצָאוֹ בְּתוֹךְ הַתְּחוּם הֲרֵי זֶה מֵבִיאוֹ בִּמְקוֹם הַקְּבָרוֹת וְקוֹבְרוֹ.

If somebody finds a corpse of obligation, he has to take care of it and bury it at its place[35]. When is that? If he finds it outside the town limits[36]. But if he found it inside the town limits, he brings it to the cemetary to bury it.

35 The definition of "its place" is given in the paragraph after the next.
36 Outside of 2000 cubits from the built-up domain of a village, or the city walls.

(56a line 70) אָמַר רִבִּי עֲקִיבָה. כָּךְ הָיְתָה תְּחִילַּת תַּשְׁמִישִׁי לִפְנֵי חֲכָמִים. פַּעַם אַחַת הָיִיתִי מְהַלֵּךְ בַּדֶּרֶךְ וּמָצָאתִי מֵת מִצְוָה וְנִיטְפַּלְתִּי בּוֹ כְּאַרְבַּעַת מִיל עַד שֶׁהֲבֵאתִיו לִמְקוֹם הַקְּבָרוֹת וּקְבַרְתִּיו. וּכְשֶׁבָּאתִי אֵצֶל רִבִּי אֱלִיעֶזֶר וְאֵצֶל רִבִּי יְהוֹשֻׁעַ אָמַרְתִּי לָהֶם אֶת הַדָּבָר. אָמְרוּ לִי. עַל כָּל־פְּסִיעָה וּפְסִיעָה שֶׁהָיִיתָ פּוֹסֵעַ מַעֲלִין עָלֶיךָ כְּאִילּוּ שָׁפַכְתָּ דָּמִים. אָמַרְתִּי. אִם בְּשָׁעָה שֶׁנִּתְכַּוַּונְתִּי לִזְכוּת

נִתְחַיַּבְתִּי. בְּשָׁעָה שֶׁלֹּא נִתְכַּוַּנְתִּי לִזְכוּת עַל אַחַת כַּמָּה וְכַמָּה. בְּאוֹתָהּ שָׁעָה לֹא זָזְתִּי מִלְּשַׁמֵּשׁ חֲכָמִים. הוּא הָיָה אוֹמֵר. דְּלָא שִׁימֵּשׁ חֲכִימַיָּא קְטָלָא חַיָּיב.

[37]Rebbi Aqiba said, the start of my practice before the Sages was the following. Once I was on the road when I found a corpse of obligation; I carried it about four *mil* to a cemetery and buried it. When I came to Rebbi Eliezer and Rebbi Joshua and told them, they said to me that every step that you walked is counted against you as if you were shedding blood[38]. I said, if I became guilty when I intended to acquire merit, how much worse is it if I do not intend to acquire merit. From that time on I did not interrupt practicing before Sages. He used to say, anybody who did not practice before Sages deserves the death penalty.

37 *Semaḥot* 4:34; *Derekh Ereṣ zuṭa* 8. Quoted *Tosaphot Ketubot* 17a, *Megillah* 29a, s.v. מבטלין.

38 Since the corpse was removed from its natural place of burial.

(56b line 2) מֵת מִצְוָה קָנָה מְקוֹמוֹ אַרְבַּע אַמּוֹת אֲפִילוּ שָׂדֶה מָלֵא כּוּרְכְּמִין. שַׁעַל מְנָת כֵּן הִנְחִיל יְהוֹשֻׁעַ לְיִשְׂרָאֵל אֶת הָאָרֶץ. אֵימָתַי. בַּזְּמַן שֶׁמְּצָאוֹ בַּשָּׂדֶה. אֲבָל אִם מְצָאוֹ בַּדֶּרֶךְ קוֹבְרוֹ אוֹ לִימִין הַדֶּרֶךְ אוֹ לִשְׂמֹאל הַדֶּרֶךְ. שְׂדֵה בוּר וּשְׂדֵה נִיר. קוֹבְרוֹ בִּשְׂדֵה בוּר. שְׂדֵה נִיר וּשְׂדֵה זֶרַע. קוֹבְרִין אוֹתוֹ בִּשְׂדֵה נִיר. שְׂדֵה כֶּרֶם וּשְׂדֵה זֶרַע. קוֹבְרוֹ בִּשְׂדֵה זֶרַע. שְׂדֵה כֶּרֶם וּשְׂדֵה אִילָן. אִית תַּנָּיֵי תַּנֵּי. קוֹבְרוֹ בִּשְׂדֵה כֶּרֶם. אִית תַּנָּיֵי תַּנֵּי. קוֹבְרוֹ בִּשְׂדֵה אִילָן. מָאן דְּאָמַר. קוֹבְרוֹ בִּשְׂדֵה כֶּרֶם. אֲבָל בִּשְׂדֵה אִילָן לֹא מִפְּנֵי אֹהֶל הַמֵּת. מָאן דְּאָמַר. בִּשְׂדֵה אִילָן. אֲבָל בִּשְׂדֵה כֶּרֶם לֹא מִפְּנֵי הֶכְשֵׁר בְּצִירָה. הֶחְלִיף. רִבִּי אִימִּי בְּשֵׁם רִבִּי שִׁמְעוֹן בֶּן לָקִישׁ. עוֹבֵר מִשּׁוּם לֹא תְּטַמֵּא אֶת אַדְמָתְךָ. הָיוּ שְׁתֵּיהֶן בּוּר. שְׁתֵּיהֶן נִיר. שְׁתֵּיהֶן זֶרַע. קוֹבֵר בְּאֵי זֶה שֶׁיִּרְצֶה.

The corpse of obligation acquired its place, four cubits[39] even in a field of saffron, for on this condition did Joshua distribute the Land to Israel[40]. When is this? If he found it in the field. But if he found it on the road, he buries it either to the right or to the left of the road[41]. A fallow and a ploughed field, he buries it in the fallow field[42]. A ploughed and a sown field, he buries it in the ploughed field. A vineyard and a sown field, he buries it in the sown field. A vineyard and an orchard, some Tannaïm state, he buries it in the vineyard; some Tannaïm state, he buries it in the orchard. He who says, he buries it in the vineyard but not in the orchard, because of a tent over the corpse[43]. He who says, he buries it in the orchard but not in the vineyard because of the preparation of the grape harvest[44]. If he switched, Rebbi Immi said in the name of Rebbi Simeon ben Laqish: He transgressed "do not defile your land[45]." If both were fallow, or ploughed, or sown, he buries in the one he chooses.

39 A square of land, four cubits in each direction, can be taken to dig the grave without requesting permission from the owner, who has no claim to compensation.

40 Therefore, these rules do not apply outside the Land. The list of reservations for public use attributed to Joshua is in *Baba batra* 5:1, Babli *Baba qama* 80b-82a; cf. *Kilaim* 2:5, Note 73.

41 Use of the road is public use; use of land for burial of a corpse of obligation is public use. The later use cannot displace the prior. The Babli, *Eruvin* 17b, explains this *baraita* away, assuming that the corpse was lying across the narrow roadway and encroaching on the fields on either side. According to Rashi, the corpse may be moved to protect passing Cohanim from the impurity of the dead.

42 If the corpse was found on the road between two fields.

43 If a grave is is the shade of a tree, the entire canopy of the tree forms a "tent" over the grave; any person passing under the tree becomes impure by the impurity of the dead (*Num.* 19:14).

44 Since wine-grapes collected in a basket at harvest time will be wet from the juice of some squashed grapes, they are "prepared" for impurity (cf. *Demay* 2:3, Note 141), and a grave in a vineyard makes its entire harvest irreparably impure.

45 *Deut.* 21:23.

כֹּהֵן וְלֵוִי יִטַּמֵּא לֵוִי. לֵוִי וְיִשְׂרָאֵל יִטַּמֵּא יִשְׂרָאֵל. וְלֹא הוּא לֵוִי(56b line 13) הוּא יִשְׂרָאֵל. אָמַר רִבִּי אָבִין. בִּשְׁעַת דּוּכָן שָׁנִינוּ. מוֹדִין חֲכָמִים לְרִבִּי אֱלִיעֶזֶר בְּכֹהֵן גָּדוֹל וְנָזִיר שֶׁיִּטַּמֵּא נָזִיר וְאַל יִטַּמֵּא כֹהֵן גָּדוֹל. וּמוֹדֶה רִבִּי אֱלִיעֶזֶר לַחֲכָמִים בְּכֹהֵן גָּדוֹל וְנָזִיר שֶׁיִּטַּמֵּא נָזִיר וְאַל יִטַּמֵּא כֹהֵן גָּדוֹל. הַגַּע עַצְמָךְ שֶׁהִקְדִּישׁוֹ אָבִיו מֵרֶחֶם. זוֹ תוֹרָה וְזוֹ אֵינָהּ תּוֹרָה. רִבִּי הוּנָא בְּשֵׁם רַב יוֹסֵף. אַתְיָא דְרִבִּי אֱלִיעֶזֶר כְּבֵית שַׁמַּי. דְּבֵית שַׁמַּי אוֹמְרִים. תָּדִיר וּמְקוּדָּשׁ תָּדִיר קוֹדֵם. כֵּן רִבִּי אֱלִיעֶזֶר אוֹמֵר. תָּדִיר וּמְקוּדָּשׁ תָּדִיר קוֹדֵם. נְזִיר שְׁלֹשִׁים וּנְזִיר מֵאָה. יִטַּמֵּא נְזִיר שְׁלֹשִׁים. נְזִיר מֵאָה וּנְזִיר עוֹלָם. יִטַּמֵּא נְזִיר מֵאָה. נְזִיר עוֹלָם וּנְזִיר נְזִירוֹת. אִית תַּנָּיֵי תַנּוּ. יִטַּמֵּא נְזִיר עוֹלָם. וְאִית תַּנָּיֵי תַנּוּ. יִטַּמֵּא נְזִיר נְזִירוֹת. מָאן דְּאָמַר. יִטַּמֵּא נְזִיר עוֹלָם. הָא נְזִיר נְזִירוֹת לֹא. מִפְּנֵי שֶׁתִּגְלַחְתּוֹ מְרוּבָּה. מָאן דְּאָמַר. יִטַּמֵּא נְזִיר נְזִירוֹת. וּנְזִיר עוֹלָם לֹא. מִפְּנֵי שֶׁקָּרְבְּנוֹתָיו מְרוּבִּין. הֲחֵלִיף. יָיבָא כְּהָדָא דְּאָמַר רִבִּי אִמִּי בְּשֵׁם רִבִּי שִׁמְעוֹן בֶּן לָקִישׁ. עוֹבֵר מִשּׁוּם לֹא תְטַמֵּא אֶת אַדְמָתְךָ. וְכָא כֵן.

A Cohen and a Levite, the Levite shall defile himself[46]. A Levite and an Israel, the Israel shall defile himself. No, is not the Levite like the Israel[47]? Rebbi Abin said, it was taught in the time of the platform[48]. The Sages agree with Rebbi Eliezer that between a High Priest and a *nazir*, the *nazir* shall defile himself but not the High Priest[49]. Rebbi Eliezer agrees with the Sages that between a High Priest and a *nazir*, the *nazir* shall defile himself but not the High Priest[50]. Think of it, if his father sanctified him from birth[51]. The one[52] is from the Torah, the other is not from the Torah[53]. Rebbi Huna in the name of Rav Joseph: Rebbi Eliezer parallels the House of Shammai. As the House of Shammai say, between holy and frequent the holy has precedence[54], so Rebbi Eliezer says, between holy and frequent the holy has precedence[55]. A *nazir* for 30 days and a *nazir* for 100, the *nazir* for 30 days shall defile himself. A *nazir* for 100 days and a *nazir* forever, the *nazir* for 100 days shall defile himself. A *nazir* forever[56], and a *nazir* of *neziriot*[57], some Tannaïm state, the *nazir* forever shall defile himself; but some Tannaïm state, the *nazir* of *neziriot* shall defile himself. He who says, the *nazir* forever shall defile himself but not the *nazir* of *neziriot*, since he[58] shaves more frequently. He who says, the *nazir* of *neziriot* shall defile himself but not the *nazir* forever, since he brings more sacrifices[59]. If he switched, it should be as Rebbi Immi said in the name of Rebbi Simeon ben Laqish: He transgressed "do not defile your land[45]." Here it is the same.

46 Since a Levite is not forbidden to defile himself.

47 In matters of impurity, the Levite has no more obligations than the Israel.

48 The platform in the Temple for the levitic singers. If the Levite was engaged in the Temple service, he must be careful not to become disabled by impurity.

49 This is the position of the Sages in the Mishnah.

50 R. Eliezer holds to his position in the Mishnah only for a common priest, not the High Priest.

51 Like Samson or Samuel. The reference is to the argument of the Sages that the *nazir* has to defile himself because his holiness is temporary. If the *nazir* is *nazir* from birth, that argument does not hold but the formulation of the Sages in the first sentence of the Mishnah does not admit of any exception.

52 The holiness of the Cohen.

53 The possibility of a *nazir* from birth is only given in the Prophets.

54 In Mishnah *Berakhot* 8:1, the House of Shammai require that on Friday nights, the benediction for the Sanctification of the Sabbath (the holy) precede the benediction for the wine (the frequent).

55 For him, the *nazir* who must bring a sacrifice for his defilement is holier than the Cohen who brings no sacrifice.

56 He cuts his hair (but does not shave it off) once a year and brings three sacrifices; Halakhah 1:2.

57 Similar to one described in Mishnah 1:4; from the argument it seems that the *nazir* referred to here has vowed many periods of more than one year.

58 The *nazir* forever shall defile himself since he never shaves.

59 If the basic period of the *nazir* of *neziriot* is more than one year, the *nazir* forever brings more sacrifices.

משנה ב: (fol. 55d) עַל אֵילוּ הַטֻּמְאוֹת הַנָּזִיר מְגַלֵּחַ. עַל הַמֵּת וְעַל כְּזַיִת מִן הַמֵּת וְעַל כְּזַיִת נֶצֶל וְעַל מְלֹא תַרְוָד רָקָב עַל הַשִּׁזְרָה וְעַל הַגּוּלְגּוֹלֶת וְעַל אֵבֶר מִן הַמֵּת וְעַל אֵבֶר מִן הַחַי שֶׁיֵּשׁ עֲלֵיהֶם בָּשָׂר כָּרָאוּי וְעַל חֲצִי קַב עֲצָמוֹת וְעַל חֲצִי לוֹג דָּם וְעַל מַגָּעָן וְעַל מַשָּׂאָן וְעַל אֲהִילָן. וְעַל עֶצֶם כִּשְׂעוֹרָה וְעַל מַגָּעוֹ וְעַל מַשָּׂאוֹ וְעַל אֲהִילוֹ עַל אֵילוּ הַנָּזִיר מְגַלֵּחַ וּמַזֶּה בַּשְּׁלִישִׁי וּבַשְּׁבִיעִי וְסוֹתֵר אֶת הַקּוֹדְמִים וְאֵינוֹ מַתְחִיל לִמְנוֹת עַד שֶׁיִּטְהַר וְיָבִיא אֶת קָרְבְּנוֹתָיו.

Mishnah 2: The *nazir* shaves for the following impurities: For a corpse, for flesh in the volume of an olive of a corpse, and for the volume of an olive of decayed matter from a corpse[60], and for a spoonful of decay, for the spine and for the skull[61], for a limb from a corpse or a limb from the living on which there is sufficient flesh[62], for half a *qab*[63] of bones, and for half a *log*[63] of blood, if they are touched, or carried[64], or under a tent[43]. Also for a bone in the volume of a barley grain if it is touched, or carried, (or under a tent.)[65] For these, the *nazir* shaves, he sprinkles on the third and seventh [days], he disregards the preceding days and starts to count only after he purifies himself and brings all his sacrifices.

60 Either decaying flesh or fluid from the corpse. If it is decayed so that it looks like dust it is counted as decay and follows the standard of the spoonful (under certain conditions). It is implied that all impurities enumerated in the Mishnah are biblical in nature.

61 Even if no flesh is left.

62 "Sufficient flesh" is enough left on a limb connected to a living body that it could heal.

63 A *qab* is 4 *log* or 2.13 liter.

64 Even if the carrier does not touch the cause of impurity.

65 The last clause, which originally was also in Babli mss., is a scribal error since only half a *qab* of bones transmits impurity in a tent but less than that transmits impurity only by touch or carrying, not in a tent (Tosaphot 49b, *s. v.* על משאו).

הלכה ב: עַל אֵילּוּ הַטֻּמְאוֹת הַנָּזִיר מְגַלֵּחַ כוּל'. חַד סָב שָׁאַל מֵרבִּי (56b line 26)
יוֹחָנָן. כְּזַיִת מִן הַמֵּת מְטַמֵּא. כּוּלוֹ לֹא כָל־שֶׁכֵּן. אָמַר לוֹ. לְהָבִיא אֶת הַנֶּפֶל
שֶׁאֵין בּוֹ כְּזַיִת. חָזַר וְשָׁאַל. אֵבֶר מִן הַמֵּת מְטַמֵּא. לֹא כָל־שֶׁכֵּן כּוּלוֹ. אָמַר לוֹ.
לְהָבִיא אֶת הַנֶּפֶל שֶׁלֹּא קָרְשׁוּ אֵיבָרָיו. אָמַר רִבִּי יוֹסֵי. חֲכִים הוּא הָהֵן סַבָּא
דְּלָא חֲכִים מַשְׁאִיל. מִכֵּיוָן דְּשָׁאַל לְקַדְמִיתָא לָא הֲוָה צָרִיךְ מִישָׁאַל תִּינְיָיתָא.
וְאִיבָּעֵי מִישָׁאוֹל תַּרְתֵּיהוֹן שָׁאַל תִּינְיָיתָא וַחֲזַר מִישָׁאַל קַדְמִיתָא. תַּלְמִידוֹי
דְּרִבִּי יוֹסֵי בֶּן חֲלַפְתָּא שָׁאֲלוּן תִּינְיָיתָא וְלָא שָׁאֲלוּן קַדְמִיתָא. דְּהָא פְּשִׁיטָא לוֹן.
מִכֵּיוָן שֶׁאֵין בּוֹ כְּזַיִת דָּבָר בָּרִיא הוּא שֶׁלֹּא קָרְשׁוּ אֵיבָרָיו. אָמַר רִבִּי מָנָא בַּר
חִזְקִיָּה. נְהִיר אַתְּ דַּהֲוָה רִבִּי יַעֲקֹב בַּר אֲחָא קָאִים הָכָא. וְאַף תַּרְתֵּין שְׁאֵילָתָא
דְּהֵן סַבָּא בָּאֲהִילוּת לְהָדָא מִילָּא לֹא. שֶׁהַנָּזִיר מְגַלֵּחַ עֲלֵיהֶן. וְעוֹד מִן הָדָא
דְּאָמַר רִבִּי יוֹחָנָן. הָיִיתִי סָבוּר שֶׁאֵין הַנְּפָלִים תּוֹרָה. מִמַּה שֶּׁהוּא מוֹשִׁיב אֶת
אִימָּן יְמֵי טוֹהַר. הָדָא אֲמָרָה. שֶׁהַנְּפָלִים תּוֹרָה.

Halakhah 2: "The *nazir* shaves for the following impurities," etc. An old man asked Rebbi Joḥanan[66]: If the volume of an olive from a corpse makes impure, then certainly all of it also[67]? He said to him, to include the stillbirth which did not reach the volume of an olive[68]. He continued to ask: If a limb of a corpse makes impure, then certainly all of it also? He said to him, to include the stillbirth whose limbs did not yet jell[69]. Rebbi Yose said, was that old man wise? His questions were not wise since after he asked the first question, it was not necessary to ask the second. If he wanted to ask both, he should have asked the second and after that the first[70]. The students of Rebbi Yose ben Ḥalaphta[71] asked the second but did not ask the first because it was obvious for them that if he did not reach the volume of an olive it is certain that his limbs did not yet jell. Rebbi Mana bar[72] Ḥizqiah said, do you remember when Rebbi Jacob bar Aḥa was here, were not both questions by that old man [asked] about *Ahilut*[72] that the *nazir* shaves for them[74]? In addition, from what Rebbi Joḥanan said, I thought that the stillbirths were not Torah[75]. But since he makes his mother sit days of purity[76], it is implied that [the rules of] stillbirths are Torah.

66 In the Babli, 49b/50b, the entire discussion is tannaïtic: Symmachos, a student of R. Meïr, asked R. Jehudah.

67 The formulation of the Mishnah is redundant. If one *kezayit* of a corpse induces the impurity of the dead, why is it necessary to say that a complete corpse induces the impurity?

68 As explained in Mishnaiot *Niddah* 3:3 ff.

69 No limb has a recognizable shape.

70 If the fetus does not fill the volume of an olive, it is to be assumed that its limbs are not recognizable. If its limbs are not recognizable, the body still might be larger than the volume of an olive.

71 He is "R. Yose" the Tanna; in the Babli, he gives the explanations ascribed in the Yerushalmi to R. Johanan.

72 There is no "R. Mana bar Hizqiah" mentioned otherwise in the entire talmudic/midrashic literature. Moreover, it is not mentioned who his partner was. Therefore, it is reasonable to follow all commentators and emend בר to לר׳ and read: "R. Mana (II) said to R. Hizqiah."

73 The parallel Mishnah *Ahilut* 2:1, to which both questions also apply.

74 R. Yose's criticism of the old man is unjustified since it would not be inconsistent with either Mishnah to hold that a corpse induces biblical impurity but a small part of the corpse only rabbinic impurity. In that case, the double mention in the Mishnah would be justified and, as noted in the sequel, R. Johanan once held this opinion.

75 It is generally accepted that a termination of pregnancy within 40 days of conception is simply a failed conception, not an abortion, since there is no human fetus (*Niddah* 3:5, Note 135). The status of the fetus between the 41st day and delivery is never defined in the biblical text.

76 Mishnaiot *Niddah* 3:3-5 state that if there was a miscarriage and the sex of the fetus cannot be determined, the mother has to observe 14 days of impurity (for a girl) but the next 26 days are days of purity during which no genital discharge will make her impure (*Niddah* 3:2, Note 14). Since normally any genital discharge induces the seven-day impurity of menstruation in a woman, the rules of Tractate *Niddah* imply that the impurity of a

stillbirth is biblical. If the impurity were rabbinic, it could not imply immunity (by necessity biblical) from impurity.

(56b line 39) תַּנֵּי. רִבִּי שִׁמְעוֹן בֶּן יוֹחַי אוֹמֵר. מִפְּנֵי מָה אָמְרוּ. הַשֶּׁרֶץ מְטַמֵּא בְּכָעֲדָשָׁה. מִפְּנֵי שֶׁהַשֶּׁרֶץ תְּחִילַת בְּרִייָתוֹ בְּכָעֲדָשָׁה. רִבִּי יוּדָן בָּעֵי. הַמֵּת יְטַמֵּא פָּחוֹת מִכְּזַיִת. דְּאָמַר רִבִּי יוֹחָנָן. לְהָבִיא אֶת הַנֵּפֶל שֶׁאֵין בּוֹ כְזַיִת. וּנְבֵילָה מְטַמָּא כְאָפוּן. דְּאָמַר רִבִּי חֲנִינָה. אֲנִי רָאִיתִי עֵגֶל כְּאָפוּן בְּשִׁפִיר. מַאי כְדוֹן. מִדְרָשׁוֹת אֱמִינָא. דְּרוֹשׁ וְקַבֵּל שָׂכָר.

It was stated: Rebbi Simeon bar Iohai says, why did they say that a crawling animal[77] the size of a lentil makes impure? Because the start of the creation of a crawling animal is the size of a lentil[78]. Rebbi Yudan asked: Should not a corpse bring impurity even if it is less than the volume of an olive, for did not Rebbi Johanan say, "to include the stillbirth which did not reach the volume of an olive"[79]? And a carcass[80] the size of a pea should cause impurity[81], for Rebbi Hanina said, I saw a calf the size of a pea in a placenta! How is that? I say, [these are] sermons. Preach and receive reward[82].

77 Enumerated in *Lev.* 11:29-30.

78 In the Babli, 52a and *Niddah* 56a, the parallel is an anonymous tannaïtic statement, deriving the power of tradition to determine the amount which induces impurity from the change in wording from בהם in *Lev.* 11:31 to מהם in 11:32. Since that change is required by the meaning of the verses, the Babli's source is the school of R. Aqiba.

79 This in itself is an irrelevant question since R. Johanan makes it clear, here and elsewhere, that the minimal size requirements do not apply to fully formed creatures (cf. *Berakhot* 6:1, Note17; Babli *Nazir* 51b).

80 From an otherwise kosher animal but which dies without being slaughtered.

81 When in fact the unchallenged tradition is that a minimum volume of an olive is required.

82 But rules of practice should never be derived from sermons.

(56b line 44) אֵי זֶהוּ נֶצֶל. בָּשָׂר הַמֵּת שֶׁנָּתוּק וְהַמּוֹחַל שֶׁקָּרַשׁ. הָא עוֹדֵהוּ מָחוּי לֹא. לֹא כֵן אָמַר רִבִּי חֲנִינָה בְּשֵׁם רִבִּי. חֶלְבּוֹ הַמֵּת שֶׁהִתִּיכוֹ הֲרֵי זֶה טָמֵא. חֲתָכוֹ וְהִתִּיכוֹ הֲרֵי זֶה טָהוֹר. רִבִּי יוּדָן וְרִבִּי יוֹסֵי. חַד אָמַר. לְהוֹצִיא מֵי בָשָׂר שֶׁבּוֹ. וְחָרְנָה אָמַר. שְׂאִים יִקְרַשׁ וִיהֵא בוֹ כְּזַיִת יְהֵא מְטַמֵּא מָחוּי.

What is decayed matter? Flesh of the corpse which was separated[83] and fluid that coagulated. Therefore not when it[84] is still mashed? Did not Rebbi Ḥanina say in the name of Rebbi: [85]Fat from a corpse[86] which was melted remains impure; if he cut it[87] and then melted it, it is pure[88]. Rebbi Yudan and Rebbi Yose, one says to exclude the fluid in the flesh[89]; the other says that if it will fill the volume of an olive when congealed, it will be impure when still mashed[90].

83   This text does not make much sense. The parallel in the Babli, 50a, reads בָּשָׂר הַמֵּת שֶׁקָּרַשׁ וְהַמּוֹחַל שֶׁהִרְתִּיחַ, "Flesh of the corpse that coagulated and fluid that was heated." A gloss in the *Arukh* (s. v. נצל) explains: "A stillbirth whose flesh coagulated but did not firm." The quote from the Yerushalmi reads in the *Arukh*: בָּשָׂר הַמֵּת שֶׁנֻּצַּל וְהַמּוֹחַל שֶׁקָּרַשׁ which can also be translated as: "Flesh of the corpse which was separated and fluid that coagulated", the difference being that נצל means "to separate" in an abstract sense, as in *Gen*. 31:16 where Rachel and Leah congratulate themselves that God had *separated* Laban's property from him and *transferred* it to them, while נתק means bodily separation, "tearing apart." The suggestion by M. Margalit and J. Sussman to read נתוך instead of נתוק has no basis. It is remarkable that Tosephta *Ahilut* (2:3, quoted later in our text) goes into the details of the rules of decay but except for a fleeting reference to our Mishnah (*Ahilut* 4:5) never mentions נֶצֶל If the text is taken as it stands, one might define *nĕṣel* as "fibers from the corpse and fluid that coagulated."

84   The blood in an intermediate state between fluidity and coagulation. It is unreasonable to assume that the blood should be impure as fluid and as fully coagulated matter, but not in an intermediate state.

85   The text is paralleled in the Babli, 50a, and Tosephta *Ahilut* 4:3. In the latter, a Babylonian scribe or compiler systematically wrote חתך for

החך, היתיך (as noted by D. Pardo).

86 The text is a contamination of two versions. "The fat of a corpse" may either be חֶלְבּוֹ שֶׁל הַמֵּת or חֵלֶב הַמֵּת.

87 The fat was cut in pieces smaller than olive size. Either this was done outside a "tent" (because all body parts of a corpse under one "tent" are joined together by the "tent"; Tosephta *Ahilut* 4:4), or small pieces of fat from two different corpses are fused together by heating. The resulting olive-sized piece is not impure since "connection by a human is not counted" (Tosephta *Ahilut* 4:3).

88 Then the question is, if the state of the material does not matter, why should the mashed state matter?

89 Any fluid which is not blood but oozes from a corpse is impure only if it became solid in an olive-sized piece.

90 An exactly olive-sized piece of colloidal material will be pure since in solid form it will have shrunk.

(56b line 49) תָּנֵינָן. רִבִּי יוֹסֵי אוֹמֵר. בְּשַׂר הַמֵּת שֶׁיָּבַשׁ וְאֵינוֹ יָכוֹל לְהַשְׁרוֹת וְלַחֲזוֹר כְּמוֹת שֶׁהָיָה טָהוֹר. מַאי טַעֲמָא דְּרִבִּי יוֹסֵי. וְלֹא מִן הַנְּבֵילָה לָמַד. מִן הַנְּבֵילָה מַה נְּבֵילָה אִם יָבְשָׁה טְהוֹרָה אַף הַמֵּת אִם יָבַשׁ יְהֵא טָהוֹר. רִבִּי אַמִּי בָּעֵי. אִי מָה הַנְּבֵילָה אִם נִסְרְחָה טְהוֹרָה אַף הַמֵּת אִם נִסְרַח יְהֵא טָהוֹר. מֵעַתָּה אֵין נֶצֶל כְּרִבִּי יוֹסֵי. אַשְׁכַּח תַּנֵּי בְּשֵׁם רִבִּי יוֹסֵי. יֵשׁ נֶצֶל. חַבְרַיָּיא בָּעוּן קוֹמֵי רִבִּי יוֹסֵי. אִי מָה הַנְּבֵילָה אֵין לָהּ רָקָב אַף הַמֵּת אֵין לוֹ רָקָב. אָמַר לוֹן. לֹא לָמַד הַמֵּת מִן הַנְּבֵילָה לַעֲצָמוֹת אֶלָּא לְבָשָׂר. אֵין רָקָב לְבָשָׂר יֵשׁ רָקָב לַעֲצָמוֹת. כְּהָדָא דְּתַנֵּי בַּר קַפָּרָא וּרְקַב עֲצָמוֹת קִנְאָה. רִבִּי יַנַּאי אָמַר. אוֹ בְקָבָר. אֲפִילוּ נָגַע בְּקֶבֶר אָדָם הָרִאשׁוֹן. חַבְרַיָּיא אָמְרִין. מְסָרֵס קְרִיָּיה. אוֹ בְקָבָר. אוֹ בְרָקָב הוּא. תַּנֵּי בַּר קַפָּרָא אוֹמֵר. אוֹ בְקָבָר. אוֹ בְרָקָב.

We have stated[91]: "Rebbi Yose said, dried flesh from a corpse which even if soaked[92] will not return to its former status is pure[93]. What is Rebbi Yose's reason? Did he not infer this from a carcass? From a carcass, since a dried carcass is pure[94], so also a dried corpse should be pure. Rebbi Immi asked: Since a foul-smelling carcass is pure[95], would a foul-smelling corpse also be pure? Then there can be no decayed matter for Rebbi Yose! It was found stated in Rebbi Yose's name that there was decayed matter[93]. The colleagues asked before Rebbi Yose: Since a carcass has no decay[96], so a corpse should have no decay! He told them that he inferred from an animal only for the flesh, not for the bones. There is no decay from flesh[97], there is decay from bones, as Bar Qappara stated, "decay of bones is jealousy[98]." Rebbi Yannai said, "or a grave[99]", even if one touched the first Adam's grave. The colleagues say, he[100] transposes the verse: "or a grave *qbr*" means "or decay *rqb*". Bar Qappara stated, "or a grave *qbr*", "or decay *rqb*".

91 Mishnah *Niddah* 7:1.

92 The Babli, *Niddah* 56a, explains soaking 24 hours in lukewarm water.

93 In the Babli, *Niddah* 56a, this is qualified to mean that there is no impurity of flesh, but there is impurity of decay (requiring a spoonful for impurity.)

94 Babli, *Niddah* 56a.

95 Babli, *Bekhorot* 23b. The argument is based on *Deut.* 14:21 which requires the animal carcass to be given to the non-Jewish resident or sold to the stranger. It is inferred that once a carcass can no longer be given away or sold, it has lost its legal standing as carcass. This corresponds to the rule, expounded at length in Tractate *Kelim*, that impure objects become pure once they have lost any commercial value.

96 By the argument of Note 95, a decaying animal carcass has no commercial value and, therefore, is pure. "No decay" means "no impurity classified under the heading of 'decay'".

97 The argument of the colleagues is well taken; R. Yose accepts the impurity of human decay only for decaying bone material, not for decayed flesh.

98 *Prov.* 14:30.

99 *Num.* 19:20. This is a new statement. Touching a grave induces the impurity of the dead irrespective of the age of the grave and the person buried while in the opinion of R. Simeon ben Iohai only a Jewish corpse induces the impurity of a "tent" (Babli *Yebamot* 61a.) The Babli concurs (*loc. cit.*). R. Yannai's statement is attributed in the Babli, 54a, to his student R. Simeon ben Laqish.

100 As confirmed by a fragment of *baraita*, Bar Qappara holds that any root may represent all 6 permutations of its letters. This cannot be classified as a derivation; it is a hint.)

(56b line 59) אָמַר רִבִּי יוּדָה בֶּן פָּזִי. מְלֹא תַרְוָוד אֶחָד נָטַל הַקָּדוֹשׁ בָּרוּךְ הוּא מִמְּקוֹם הַמִּזְבֵּחַ וּבָרָא בוֹ אָדָם הָרִאשׁוֹן. אָמַר. הַלְוַאי יִיבָּרֵא מִמְּקוֹם הַמִּזְבֵּחַ וּתְהֵא לוֹ עֲמִידָה. הָדָא הוּא דִכְתִיב וַיִּיצֶר יי אֱלֹהִים אֶת הָאָדָם עָפָר מִן הָאֲדָמָה וּכְתִיב מִזְבַּח אֲדָמָה תַעֲשֶׂה לִי. מָה אֲדָמָה שֶׁנֶּאֱמַר לְהַלָּן מִזְבֵּחַ אַף כָּאן מִזְבֵּחַ. וְהָיוּ יָמָיו מֵאָה וְעֶשְׂרִים שָׁנָה. קָרוֹב לְאֶלֶף שָׁנָה חָיָה אָדָם הָרִאשׁוֹן וְאַתְּ אָמַר וְהָיוּ יָמָיו מֵאָה וְעֶשְׂרִים שָׁנָה. אֶלָּא לְקַמֹ שָׁנָה הוּא חוֹזֵר לְמִלֹא תַרְוָוד אֶחָד רָקָב. וְקַשְׁיָא. עוֹג מֶלֶךְ הַבָּשָׁן מֵאָה וְעֶשְׂרִים שָׁנָה. וְתִינוֹק בֶּן יוֹמוֹ מֵאָה וְעֶשְׂרִים שָׁנָה. עוֹג מְלֹא תַרְוָוד רָקָב. וְתִינוֹק בֶּן יוֹמוֹ מְלֹא תַרְוָוד רָקָב. מְלֹא תַרְוָוד רָקָב שֶׁאָמְרוּ יֶשְׁנוֹ מִקִּישְׁרֵי אֶצְבְּעוֹתָיו וּלְמַעֲלָה. דִּבְרֵי רִבִּי מֵאִיר. וַחֲכָמִים אוֹמְרִים. מְלֹא הַיָּד הַגְּדוֹלָה. רִבִּי זְעִירָא רִבִּי חִייָה בְּשֵׁם רִבִּי מְחַוֵּי הָדָא דְּרִבִּי מֵאִיר הָכֵין וְהָדָא דְּרַבָּנָן הָכֵין.

Rebbi Jehudah ben Pazi said, the Holy One, praise to Him, took a spoonful from the place of the altar and created Adam from it. He said, he shall have been created from the place of the altar so that he should be able to stand up[101]. That is what is written: "The Eternal Omnipotent formed Adam the first of dust from the earth[102]", and it is written: "You shall build for me an altar of earth[103]." Since "earth" there means an altar, here also [it means] an altar. "His days should be a hundred and twenty years.[104]" Adam the first lived close to a thousand years and you say, "his days should be a hundred and twenty years"! But after 120 years he returns to be a spoonful of decay. That is difficult. For Og, the king of Bashan, 120 years, and for a newborn baby 120 years? Og [becomes] a spoonful of decay, and a newborn baby becomes a spoonful of decay. "[105]The spoonful of decay which they mentioned is from his finger joints and upwards, the words of Rebbi Meïr, but the Sages say, from a fully developed hand." Rebbi Ze'ira, Rebbi Ḥiyya in the name of Rebbi was illustrating that of Rebbi Meïr one way, that of the rabbis in another way.

101 *Gen. rabba* 14(9), R. Berekhiah and R. Ḥelbo in the name of R. Samuel ben Naḥman. The altar, with definite article, is the altar in the Temple courtyard in Jerusalem which by tradition [*Gen. rabba* 34(8)] is the altar used by Adam, Noah, and Abraham.	103 *Ex.* 20:24.
	104 *Gen.* 6:3.
	105 Tosephta *Ahilut* 2:2; *Kelim Baba Meṣi'a* 7:1, as legal principle independent of the story of 120 years. Quoted in the Babli, 50b, but there the rabbis derive the decay from the body of the hand, without the fingers.
102 *Gen.* 2:7.	

(56b line 70) אֵי זֶהוּ מֵת שֶׁיֵּשׁ לוֹ רָקָב. הַנִּקְבָּר עָרוֹם בְּאָרוֹן שֶׁלְשַׁיִּישׁ אוֹ עַל גַּבֵּי רִצְפָה אוֹ עַל גַּבֵּי טַבְלָה שֶׁלְשַׁיִּישׁ. אֲבָל אִם נִקְבַּר בִּכְסוּתוֹ עַל אָרוֹן שֶׁלְעֵץ אוֹ עַל גַּבֵּי טַבְלָה שֶׁלְעֵץ אֵין זֶה רָקָב. זֶהוּ עֲפַר קְבָרוֹת וְצָרִיךְ מְלֹא תַרְוָד וְעוֹד. רִבִּי יוֹחָנָן אָמַר. נִקְבַּר עִמּוֹ אֲפִילוּ גִילְגְּלִין קָטָן אֵין זֶה רָקָב. רִבִּי יָסָא בְשֵׁם רִבִּי יוֹחָנָן. שְׁנֵי מֵתִים שֶׁקְּבָרָן זֶה בְצַד זֶה. זֶה נַעֲשָׂה גִילְגְּלִין לָזֶה וְזֶה נַעֲשָׂה גִילְגְּלִין לָזֶה. מַה נַּפְשָׁךְ. גִּילְגְּלִין לָזֶה וְלֹא לָזֶה. הֵתִיב אַבָּא בַּר נָתָן. הַגַּע עַצְמָהּ שֶׁהֵבִיא חֲצִי תַרְוָד רָקָב מִזֶּה וַחֲצִי תַרְוָד רָקָב מִזֶּה וְעִירְבָן זֶה בָזֶה. וַהֲוָה עַיְּינָן. וְאִיתְחֲמֵי גָּחִיךְ וְאִיקְפַּד עֲלוֹי וָמִית. אָמַר רִבִּי יוֹסָא. הָא אֲזִיל גַּבְרָא וְלָא שְׁמַעִינָן מִינָהּ כְּלוּם. מַאי כְדוֹן. תַּמָּן אֵין כָּל־אֶחָד רָאוּי לְמַלֵּא תַּרְוָד רָקָב. בְּרַם הָכָא כָּל־אֶחָד וְאֶחָד רָאוּי לִמְלוֹא תַּרְוָד רָקָב.

"Which corpse has decay[106]? One who was buried naked in a marble coffin, or on a stone floor, or on a marble table. But if he was buried in a wooden casket or on a woooden plank; that is not decay but graves' dust and needs somewhat more than a spoonful."[107] Rebbi Joḥanan said, if even the smallest attachment was buried with him, there is no decay[108]. Rebbi Yasa in the name of Rebbi Joḥanan: Of two corpses which were buried together, each one becomes an attachment for the other[109]. This[110] is automatic; could one alone be an attachment to another? Abba bar Nathan[111] objected: Think of it, that somebody brought half a spoonful from one and half a spoonful from the other! He[112] was considering it when he[113] was seen laughing; he[112] was offended by him and he[113] died. Rebbi Yose[114] said, there this man is gone and we did hear nothing about it[115]. What about it? There, neither of them will produce a spoonful of decayed matter, but here, each of them can generate a spoonful of decay[116].

106 Obviously, every corpse will eventually produce decayed matter. What is meant here is, under which circumstances does one apply the rules of "decay" which induces impurity by the spoonful, and when the rules of "grave dust" which requires more than a spoonful (*Ahilut* Mishnah 2:2, Tosephta 2:3.)

107 Tosephta *Ahilut* 2:3; quoted in the Babli *Nazir* 51a, *Niddah* 27b.

108 But graves' dust. In the Babli, 51a, this is implied by a statement of Ulla.

109 Babli 51a.

110 That there is symmetry between both corpses.

111 In the Babli, 51a, a Rav Nathan states that decay combined from two corpses induces impurity.

112 R. Yasa.

113 Abba bar Nathan.

114 Two generations later.

115 Whether decay from two corpses combines to induce impurity.

116 If two corpses are buried in a common grave, neither of them can produce decay by R. Joḥanan's definition. But pure decay from two distinct corpses can be combined.

(56c line 6) נֶחְתְּכָה רַגְלוֹ. מֵאַרְכּוּבָה וּלְמַעְלָה אֵין לוֹ רָקָב. מֵאַרְכּוּבָה וּלְמַטָּה יֵשׁ לוֹ רָקָב. נִקְבְּרָה עִמּוֹ. מֵאַרְכּוּבָה וּלְמַטָּן הִיא נַעֲשֵׂית לוֹ גִילְגְּלִין. מֵאַרְכּוּבָה וּלְמַעְלָן אֵין נַעֲשֵׂית לוֹ גִילְגְּלִין. חֲבֶרַיָּיא בְּעוּ קוֹמֵי רִבִּי שְׁמוּאֵל בַּר אַבְדּוּמָא. קָשַׁר גִּילְגְּלִין מִן הָאַרְכּוּבָה וּלְמַטָּן. וְאָמַר לוֹן. אִין כֵּינִי אֲפִילוּ לֹא נֶחְתְּכָה אֶרְאֶה אוֹתָהּ כְּאִילוּ הִיא חֲתוּכָה וְתֵיעָשֶׂה לוֹ גִילְגְּלִין. מִכֵּיוָן שֶׁהִיא מְחוּבֶּרֶת לוֹ כּוּלּוֹ גּוּף אֶחָד הוּא. חָסַר מַהוּ שֶׁיִּהְיֶה לוֹ רָקָב. נִישְׁמְעִינָהּ מִן הָדָא. חָסַר אֵין לוֹ רָקָב וְאֵין לוֹ תְּפִישַׂת קֶבֶר וְאֵין לוֹ שְׁכוּנַת קְבָרוֹת. רִבִּי יוֹחָנָן בָּעֵי. כַּמָּה יֶחְסַר וְלֹא יִהְיֶה לוֹ רָקָב. יָבֹא כַּיי דְּתַנִּינָן תַּמָּן. כְּדֵי שֶׁיִּינָּטֵל מִן הַחַי וְיָמוּת. וְכָא כֵן. הַגַּע עַצְמָךְ שֶׁנִּיקַּב וְשָׁתוּ הֲרֵי אֵינוֹ חָסֵר וְאֵינוֹ חַיָּה. לֵית לָךְ אֶלָּא

כְּחָדָא. נֶחְתְּכָה רַגְלוֹ. מִן הָאַרְכּוּבָה וּלְמַטָּה יֶשׁ לוֹ רָקָב. מִן הָאַרְכּוּבָה וּלְמַעֲלָן אֵין לוֹ רָקָב. נִקְבְּרָה עִמּוֹ. מִן הָאַרְכּוּבָה וּלְמַטָּן נַעֲשֵׂית לוֹ גִילְגְּלִין. מִן הָאַרְכּוּבָה וּלְמַעֲלָן אֵינָהּ נַעֲשֵׂית לוֹ גִילְגְּלִין.

If his foot was cut off, from above the joint[117] there is no "decay"[118], from below the joint there is "decay". If it[119] was buried together with him, from below the joint it becomes an attachment to him[120], from above the joint it does not become an attachment to him. The colleagues asked before Rebbi Samuel ben Eudaimon: If he bound from below the joint as attachment? He said to them, if it were so[121], even if it was not cut I should consider it as if cut and it should be an attachment! Since it is connected to him, it forms one body. If there is something missing, can it have "decay"? Let us hear from the following: If it is imcomplete, there is no "decay", it does not require the surrounding earth, and it is not part of a row of graves[122]. Rebbi Johanan asked, how much must be missing that it have no "decay"? Might it follow what we have stated there[123]: "That he will die if it was removed." Is it the same here? Think of it, if the esophagus was perforated, nothing was missing but he could not survive. You have only the following: If his foot was cut off, from below the joint there is "decay", from above the joint there is no "decay". If it was buried together with him, from below the joint it becomes an attachment to him, from above the joint it does not become an attachment to him.

117 Since there is no Yerushalmi extant to Tractate *Hulin*, it is impossible to know exactly what is meant. Mishnah *Hulin* 6:4 states that an animal, one of whose legs was cut above the ארכובה, is unfit for consumption since it could not survive. There is no unanimity as to which leg joint is meant, the knee or the ankle. In the language of the Babli, both are called ארכובה (root רכב by metathesis from biblical ברך) and are distinguished

by appropriate adjectives. It is reasonable to identify ארכובה here as the ankle, but this is far from certain.

118 The corpse is missing a limb; the rules of "decay" do not apply.

119 The amputated limb.

120 Since he could have survived the amputation, the part taken becomes an attachment. But if the part amputated is so large that by the medical standards of the day the patient could not have survived, the amputated leg is part of the corpse if buried together with it.

121 If the amputated limb was sewn back to the corpse, if it were considered a separate part then any limb could be considered separate and there never would be a complete corpse. The Babli, 63b, does not require sewing but holds that a grave makes a complete corpse whole even if it was brought to the grave in pieces.

122 This is also quoted in the Babli, 51b.

It is stated in Mishnah 9:3 that a person who finds an unattended corpse must bury it together with all *surrounding earth* which might have soaked up his blood. This is now qualified to apply only to complete corpses.

If one finds three graves next to one another they form a cemetery which may not be disturbed. The rules governing possible removal of graves are detailed in Halakhah 9:3. The rules are restricted here to graves containing complete corpses.

123 Mishnah *Ahilut* 2:3. In the list of body parts of a corpse which cause impurity by touch and carrying but not in a "tent" appears an incomplete skull. The skull is considered incomplete by the House of Shammai if it exhibits a hole made by a surgeon's drill, but by the House of Hillel only if the missing piece was large enough so "that he would die if it was removed."

(56c line 20) נְפָלִים מָהוּ שֶׁיְּהֵא לָהֶן רָקָב. מָאן דָּמַר. דָּמָן מְטַמֵּא בִּרְבִיעִית. יֵשׁ לָהֶן רָקָב. וּמָאן דָּמַר. אֵין דָּמָן מְטַמֵּא בִּרְבִיעִית. אֵין לָהֶן רָקָב. נִשְׁמְעִינָהּ מִן הָדָא. עָפָר תְּלוּלִיּוֹת לָמָּה הוּא טָמֵא. מִפְּנֵי שֶׁהַנַּשִׁים קוֹבְרוֹת שָׁם נִפְלֵיהֶן. אָמַר רִבִּי יוּדָן אָבוֹי דְּרִבִּי מַתַּנְיָיה. לֹא מִסְתַּבְּרָה דְלֹא דְּמוּכֵי שָׁחִין קוֹבְרִין שָׁם אֵיבָרֵיהֶן. אִית לָךְ מֵימַר מִשָּׁם רָקָב לֹא מִשָּׁם מַגַּע כִּשְׂעוֹרָה. וְהָא תַנֵּי. נָטַל מִמֶּנּוּ עָפָר וּסְמָכוֹ לוֹ טָהוֹר. תִּיפְתָּר כְּהָדֵין תַּנָּיָיא דְתַנֵּי. עֲקָרוֹ מִמְּקוֹמוֹ טָמֵא. רַבָּן שִׁמְעוֹן בֶּן גַּמְלִיאֵל מְטַהֵר.

Do stillbirths generate "decay"? For him who says that their blood induces impurity by a *quartarius*[124], they generate "decay"; for him who says that their blood does not induce impurity by a *quartarius*, do they generate "decay"? Let us hear from the following: [125]"Why is the dust from small heaps impure? Because women bury there their stillbirths." Rebbi Yudan, the father of Rebbi Mattaniah, said: Would it not be reasonable otherwise, that lepers bury their limbs there?[126] You must say that it is because of "decay", not because a bone the size of a lentil, since it was stated[127]: "If he took some dust from it and replaced it, [the small heap] is pure." Explain it following Tannaïm, as it was stated: If one removed it[128], it remains impure; Rabban Simeon ben Gamliel declares it pure.

124   For him a fetus is human; a stillbirth follows all rules of human corpses.

125   Tosephta *Ahilut* 16:1: "Small heaps close to a town or to a road, whether new or old, are impure since women bury there their stillbirths and lepers their limbs. Far away, new ones are pure, old ones impure; I am saying that there had been a road nearby."

126   Obviously, the Tosephta in this formulation was unknown to the editors of the Yerushalmi. The full Tosephta text is paraphrased in the Babli, *Ketubot* 20b.

127   If some decay is replaced by pure dust from another place, the latter becomes an attachment and by the rules of the previous paragraph, the earth lost its character of "decay". But if the impurity were caused by a human bone, its impurity would be original biblical impurity; the new dust would have become impure immediately as a "tent" over the bone. Therefore, the second opinion expressed in the first part of the Tosephta is inconsistent with the rule stated at the end.

128   If the entire little heap was levelled (without there appearing any bones in it), it remains impure if one assumes that some bone is buried below the levelled surface; it is pure if one assumes that it consisted only of "decay".

אָמַר רִבִּי שִׁמְעוֹן בֶּן אֶלְעָזָר. וְיָרְדוּ בְשִׁיטַת רִבִּי שִׁמְעוֹן. דְּתַנֵּי. (56c line 27)
הַשִּׁזְרָה וְהַגּוּלְגּוֹלֶת אֲפִילוּ מְכוּתָּתִין אֲפִילוּ מְפוּרְקִין טָמֵא. שֶׁהַקֶּבֶר מְצָרְפָן מִשּׁוּם אָדָם בָּאוֹהֶל.

Rebbi Simeon ben Eleazar said[129], it was formulated following Rebbi Simeon, as it was stated: [130]The spine and the skull are impure even if crushed, even disconnected, because the grave unites them as "a human in a tent"[131].

129 This name attribution cannot be correct since R. Simeon ben Eleazar was a Tanna, student of R. Meïr. A statement of his appears in Tosephta *Ahilut* 2:6, denying that people with a trepanned skull can survive a winter. Probably one has to read: R. Eleazar said.

130 This refers to the Mishnah and explains why spine and skull were mentioned separately when "half a *qab* of bones" is also mentioned and both a skull and a spine fill the required volume of about 1 liter. A similar (anonymous) text is in Tosephta *Ahilut* 2:5: "A spine of which bones were removed is pure even if its outline still exists; But in a grave it is impure, even if broken, even if crushed, since the grave unites them."

131 *Num.* 19:14.

(56c line 29) מַתְנִיתָא דְּרִבִּי לָעֶזֶר בֶּן עֲזַרְיָה. דְּתַנֵּי. אָמַר רִבִּי שִׁמְעוֹן בֶּן אֶלְעָזָר. בָּרִאשׁוֹנָה הָיוּ בָתֵּי דִינִין חֲלוּקִין. מִקְצָתָן אוֹמְרִין. רְבִיעִית דָּם רוֹבַע עֲצָמוֹת. מִקְצָתָן אוֹמְרִין. חֲצִי לוֹג דָּם חֲצִי לוֹג עֲצָמוֹת. לִנְזִירוּת וּלְטוּמְאַת מִקְדָּשׁ וְקָדָשָׁיו. רִבִּי יַעֲקֹב בַּר אִידִי בְּשֵׁם רִבִּי שִׁמְעוֹן. מִדְרָשׁ אֲמָרוּהָ מִפִּי חַגַּי זְכַרְיָה וּמַלְאָכִי.

The Mishnah follows Rebbi Eleazar ben Azariah[132], as it was stated[133]: "Rebbi Simeon ben Eleazar said, earlier the courts were divided; some said, a *quartarius* of blood, a quarter bones; some said, half a *log* of blood, a half a *log* of bones, for *nezirut* and the impurity of the Sanctuary and its sacred offerings." Rebbi Jacob bar Idi in the name of Rebbi Simeon[134]:

They said this[135] as explanation from the mouths of Ḥaggai, Zachariah, and Malachi.

132 Probably both "Eleazar ben Azariah" and "Simeon ben Eleazar" should read simply "Eleazar".

133 Tosephta *Ahilut* 4:13: "Rebbi Eleazar said, earlier the Elders were divided; some said, a *quartarius* of blood, a quarter (*qab*) of bones; some said, half a *qab* of bones and half a log of blood. The later court said: a *quartarius* of blood, a quarter (*qab*) of bones for heave and sacrifices, a half a *qab* of bones and half a log of blood for the *nazir* and the Temple." It is difficult to correct the Yerushalmi text by the Tosephta since our text clearly puts Temple and sacrifices in the same category. In a parallel text to the Tosephta in the Babli, 53a, the speaker is R. Eliezer. Instead of "Temple" (meaning "access to the Temple"), he formulates the equivalent, "people who come for the Passover sacrifice".

134 R. Simeon ben Laqish.

135 The determination of the minimum amounts inducing impurity was the result of prophetic inspiration, rathet than of logical derivation. In the Babli, *loc. cit.*, this is a statement of R. Jacob bar Idi himself.

משנה ג: אֲבָל הַסְּכָכוֹת וְהַפְּרָעוֹת וּבֵית הַפְּרָס וְאֶרֶץ הָעַמִּים וְהַגּוֹלֵל (fol. 55d) וְהַדּוֹפֵק וּרְבִיעִית דָּם וְאֹהֶל וְרוֹבַע עֲצָמוֹת וְכֵלִים הַנּוֹגְעִים בַּמֵּת וִימֵי סְפוֹרוֹ וִימֵי גָמְרוֹ עַל אֵילוּ אֵין הַנָּזִיר מְגַלֵּחַ וּמַזֶּה בַּשְּׁלִישִׁי וּבַשְּׁבִיעִי וְאֵינוֹ סוֹתֵר אֶת הַקּוֹדְמִין הִתְחִיל מוֹנֶה מִיָּד וְקָרְבָּן אֵין לוֹ. בֶּאֱמֶת יְמֵי הַזָּב וְהַזָּבָה וִימֵי הֶסְגֵּירוֹ שֶׁלַּמְצוֹרָע הֲרֵי אֵילוּ עוֹלִין לוֹ.

Mishnah 3: But for overhanging branches[136], or protuberances[137], or broken fields[138], or Gentile territory[139], or the cave door, or its frame[140], or a *quartarius* of blood[141], or a tent[142], or a quarter (*qab*) of bones[141], or objects that touched the corpse[143], or the days of his counting or his being absolute[144], the *nazir* does not shave[145] but sprinkles on the third and seventh days[146], does not disregard the preceding[147], starts counting immediately, and has no sacrifice. In truth[148], the days of a male or female sufferer from flux[149] and the days of quarantine of the sufferer from skin disease are counted for him.

136   If the *nazir* walks under a tree under which a grave is suspected.

137   Standing out from a building or a fence and it is suspected that a grave may be buried underneath.

138   "The house of the broken-off piece" is a field which contained a grave ploughed under. Not only is the suspected place of the grave impure by biblical standards but the entire field is rabbinically impure since the plough might have caught a bone and transported it to another part of the field.

139   Which is rabbinically impure even in the Holy Land.

140   גּוֹלֵל "the roller" is a large circular stone which closes the entrance to a burial cave. דּוֹפֵק "the knocker" is the frame which keeps the roller in place. The expressions were later transferred to burial in the earth, where "the roller" became the stone plate covering the grave and "the knocker" the stone frame on which it rests. Cf. Note 142.

141   One-half of the amount which induces biblical impurity.

142   Everything inside a tent in which there is a corpse is impure (*Num.* 19:14). The tent confines the impurity; outside of the tent everything is pure. The impurity of a person touching a tent (or a "roller" or a "knocker") from the outside is purely rabbinical. But cf. Note 164.

143   An object inside a tent in which there is a corpse is a source of original impurity. But an object touching a corpse under the open sky becomes impure in a derivative way. Anybody touching such an object becomes impure in a secondary way which in most cases is only rabbinical; cf. *Demay* 2:3, Note 137.

144   This refers to the sufferer from skin disease. The *nazir* is enjoined from becoming impure by the impurity of the dead; in general, impurity generated by the *nazir*'s own body has no influence on his status as *nazir*. "The days of his counting" are the eight days which the healed sufferer from skin disease has to observe between the preliminary and the final expiation ceremonies. These days do not

interfere with his status as *nazir* but they cannot count since he has to shave *all* his hair on the first and seventh days. "The days of his being absolute" is the time in which the sufferer is declared to be certainly impure. Then he is required not to shave his hair (*Lev.* 13:45); nevertheless, these days do not count towards the fulfillment of his vow.

145   If his impurity is caused by a corpse and either is rabbinical or questionable.

146   *Num.* 19:12.

147   The time he is in any state of impurity caused by the dead, whether rabbinical or questionable, cannot be counted towards fulfillment of his vow of *nazir*. But the preceding and following days count and after purification he simply completes the count; he does not start anew.

148   This expression is a label for an old, pre-Mishnaic, rule.

149   *Lev.* 15. As explained in Note 144, this impurity generated by the *nazir*'s own body has no influence on his state of *nezirut*. "The days of quarantine" are those in which the possible sufferer from skin disease is put under observation before his final status is determined (*Lev.* 13:4,5,21,26, 31).

(56c line 34) **הלכה ג:** אֲבָל הַסְּכָכוֹת וְהַפְּרָעוֹת כּוּל'. בֵּנְתַיִּים מָהוּ. רִבִּי יוֹחָנָן אָמַר. בֵּיינְתַיִּים לְהָקֵל. רִבִּי שִׁמְעוֹן בֶּן לָקִישׁ אָמַר. בֵּנְתַיִּים לְהַחֲמִיר. מָהוּ בֵּינְתַיִּים. זֶה אֵבָר מִן הַמֵּת וְאֵבָר מִן הַחַי שֶׁאֵין עֲלֵיהֶן בָּשָׂר כְּרָאוּי. רִבִּי יוֹסֵי בָּעֵי. מִנְיָין עֶצֶם כִּשְׂעוֹרָה. לֹא מִן הָדֵין קִרְיָיא אוֹ בְעֶצֶם אָדָם. הָכָא אַתְּ עֲבַד לָהּ כִּשְׂעוֹרָה. וְהָכָא אַתְּ עֲבַד לָהּ פָּחוֹת מִכִּשְׂעוֹרָה. תַּנֵּי רִבִּי שְׁמוּאֵל בַּר אַבְדוּמָא. בַּחֲלָל. כָּל־שֶׁהוּא חָלָל. בַּחֲלָל. זֶה אֵבָר מִן הַמֵּת וְאֵבָר מִן הַחַי שֶׁאֵין עֲלֵיהֶם בָּשָׂר כְּרָאוּי.

Halakhah 3: "But for overhanging branches, or protuberances," etc. What is the status of the undistributed middle[150]? Rebbi Joḥanan said, the undistributed middle is judged leniently[151]. Rebbi Simeon ben Laqish said, the undistributed middle is judged restrictively[152]. What is the undistributed middle? That is a limb from a corpse or a limb from a living body which is not sufficiently[62] covered by flesh[153]. Rebbi Yose asked[154]: From where [do we infer that] a bone [induces impurity in the size of] a barley grain? Not from that verse, "or a person's bone[155]"? Here you require a barley grain, there you do not require a barley grain[156]! Rebbi Samuel bar Eudaimon stated: "A slain one", anything from a slain person[157], that is a limb from a corpse or a limb from a living body which is not sufficiently covered by flesh.

150 Mishnah 2 spells out for which biblical impurities the *nazir* has to shave; the implication is that for anything less he does not have to shave. Mishnah 3 has a list of rabbinic impurities for which the *nazir* does not have to shave; the implication is that for anything more he has to shave. We are left without instructions for cases which fall in between.

151 Anything not covered by Mishnah 2 is not biblical; the *nazir* is prevented from shaving.

152 Anything not exempted by Mishnah 3 requires shaving and a new start. The Babli, 53b, reports the same opinions, limited to the case taken here as illustration.

153 Mishnah *Ahilut* 1:8 spells out that such a limb induces impurity by touch or carrying but not in a tent.

154 He questions R. Simeon ben Laqish's position.

155 *Num.* 19:16. In v. 18, only "bone" is mentioned but not "human". This is interpreted in *Sifry Num.* #127,129 to cover bones coming from both living or dead persons; cf. Babli 54a, Targum Pseudo-Jonathan *Num.* 19:16,18.

156 For a bare bone, everybody agrees that a barley grain represents the minimum size which induces impurity. According to R. Simeon ben Laqish, a bone fragment with some flesh is not subject to a legal minimum.

157 Without a minimum; *Sifry Num.* #127.

(56c line 41) אָמַר רִבִּי יוֹחָנָן. סְכָכוֹת וּפְרָעוֹת תּוֹרָה הֵן אֵצֶל תְּרוּמָה וְאֵין הַנָּזִיר מְגַלֵּחַ. רִבִּי יִרְמְיָה בָּעֵי. אִם לִשְׂרוֹף. אֲפִילוּ עַל סְפֵק דִּבְרֵיהֶן שׂוֹרְפִין. אִם לְלָקוֹת. תַּנֵּי רִבִּי צַיְידָנָיָיה קוֹמֵי רִבִּי יִרְמְיָה וּפְלִיג עַל רִבִּי יִרְמְיָה. כָּל־טוּמְאָה מִן הַמֵּת שֶׁהַנָּזִיר מְגַלֵּחַ חַיָּיבִין עָלֶיהָ עַל בִּיאַת הַמִּקְדָּשׁ. וְכָל־טוּמְאָה מִן הַמֵּת שֶׁאֵין הַנָּזִיר מְגַלֵּחַ עָלֶיהָ אֵין חַיָּיבִין עָלֶיהָ עַל בִּיאַת הַמִּקְדָּשׁ.

Rebbi Johanan said, overhanging branches and protuberances are biblical for heave[158] even though the *nazir* does not shave. Rebbi Jeremiah asked[159], if to burn it, one burns even for a rabbinic doubt; maybe to whip[160]? Rebbi [Yose][161] from Sidon stated before Rebbi Jeremiah and disagrees with Rebbi Jeremiah: "For any impurity deriving from a corpse for which a *nazir* shaves one is guilty if entering the Sanctuary, but any impurity deriving from a corpse for which a *nazir* does not shave one is not guilty if entering the Sanctuary.[162]"

158 If heave was transported under overhanging branches or protuberances which might cover a grave, it becomes impure and forbidden as food; it must be burned.

159 Is there any practical difference whether the impurity imputed to the heave is biblical or rabbinical?

160 Implying that a person can be whipped for exposing heave to the impurity induced by overhanging branches or protuberances.

161 Missing in the text; identified in Halakhah 4 (Note 219).

162 Mishnah 4. If entering the Temple is not prosecutable, neither is exposing heave to this impurity.

(56c line 46) אָמַר רִבִּי יוֹחָנָן. רוֹבְדֵי אִילָן שֶׁיֵּשׁ בָּהֶן אַרְבָּעָה עַל אַרְבָּעָה הַנָּזִיר מְגַלֵּחַ. רִבִּי יוֹסֵי אָמַר רִבִּי יוֹחָנָן. יָדוֹ אַחַת בְּצַד זוֹ וְיָדוֹ אַחַת בְּרוֹבָד אֵין הַנָּזִיר מְגַלֵּחַ. רִבִּי יוֹסֵי בָּעֵי. אִם חוֹצֵץ הוּא בִּפְנֵי הַטּוּמְאָה יָחוּץ בִּפְנֵי טַהֳרָה. אִם אֵינוֹ חוֹצֵץ הוּא בִּפְנֵי טוּמְאָה אַל יָחוּץ בִּפְנֵי טַהֳרָה. אָמַר רִבִּי יוֹחָנָן. הַמֵּת בַּבַּיִת וְהַנָּזִיר תַּחַת הַמִּיטָה נָזִיר מְגַלֵּחַ. כָּל־שֶׁכֵּן הַמֵּת תַּחַת הַמִּיטָה וְהַנָּזִיר בַּבַּיִת אֵינוֹ מְגַלֵּחַ. אָמַר רִבִּי יוֹחָנָן. הַמֵּת וְהַנָּזִיר תַּחַת כַּרְעֵי הַמִּיטָה תַּחַת מְעִי הַגָּמָל תַּחַת מְעִי הַמַּשְׁקוֹף תַּחַת מְלְתָּרִיּוֹת אֵין הַנָּזִיר מְגַלֵּחַ. וְלֹא כָל־דָּבָר שֶׁנִּרְאֶה לְהָגֵן. שָׁמַע חִזְקִיָּה וְאָמַר. טְהָרוּ מֵתִים. אָמַר רִבִּי יוֹחָנָן. הַמֵּת בַּבַּיִת וְהַנָּזִיר בִּטְרִיקְלִין נָזִיר מְגַלֵּחַ. כָּל־שֶׁכֵּן הַמֵּת בִּטְרִיקְלִין וְהַנָּזִיר בַּבַּיִת שֶׁהַנָּזִיר מְגַלֵּחַ. רִבִּי מָנָא בָּעֵי. אִם אֹהֶל לָחוּץ יְהֵא אֹהֶל לְהַמְשִׁיךְ. אִם אֵינוֹ אֹהֶל לְהַמְשִׁיךְ תִּיפְקַע טוּמְאָה. אָמַר רִבִּי יוֹחָנָן. טוּמְאָה מֶחֱצִי כוֹתֶל וְלַחוּץ הַנָּזִיר

מְגַלֵּחַ. אָמַר רִבִּי יֹאשִׁיָּה. טוּמְאָה טְמוּנָה בַּקַּרְקַע שֶׁלַּבַּיִת נָזִיר מְגַלֵּחַ. רִבִּי יַעֲקֹב בַּר אָחָא בְּשֵׁם רִבִּי יֹאשִׁיָּה. רוֹב בִּנְיָינוֹ וְרוֹב מִנְיָינוֹ שֶׁלְּמֵת אֵין הַנָּזִיר מְגַלֵּחַ.

Rebbi Johanan said, layers of a tree which cover four-by-four [handbreadths]: the *nazir* shaves[163]. Rebbi Yose, Rebbi Johanan said, if one of his hands is on the other side and one hand is in the layer, the *nazir* does not shave[164].

Rebbi Yose asked: If it separates from impurity it also should separate from purity; if it does not separate from impurity, it should not separate from purity[165]. Rebbi Johanan said, if the corpse is in the bedroom and the *nazir* under the bed, the *nazir* shaves[166]. Certainly if the corpse is under the bed and the *nazir* in the bedroom, does the *nazir* not shave[167]? Rebbi Johanan said, if the corpse and the *nazir* are under the bed frame[168], under the belly of a camel[169], under the width of a gate, under the gutters[170], the *nazir* does not shave, nor for anything which is there for protection[171]. Hizqiah heard it and said, they purified the dead[172]!

Rebbi Johanan said, if the corpse is in the anteroom and the *nazir* in the dining hall, the *nazir* shaves; certainly if the corpse is in the dining hall and the *nazir* in the anteroom, the *nazir* shaves[173]. Rebbi Mana asked, if it is a tent to separate it should be a tent to draw along; if it is not a tent to draw along, the impurity should disappear[174]!

Rebbi Johanan said, if the impurity is under the outer half of the wall, the *nazir* shaves[175]. Rebbi Joshia said, if impurity is hidden in the ground[176] of the house, the *nazir* shaves. Rebbi Jacob bar Aha in the name of Rebbi Joshia: The *nazir* does not shave for most of the skeleton[177] or most of the bones[178].

163 If a tree has a thick crown which forms a roof over an area of at least 4 by 4 handbreadths so that the sky is not visible, and impurity derived from a corpse is under this roof; a *nazir* which passes under the tree is in a "tent" together with the impurity and has to shave.

164 If the *nazir* stands outside the tree and only one of his hands is in the crown, he does not become impure by the "tent" formed by the tree. In general, the roof of a "tent" covering an impurity shields anything above it from impurity. The only exception is טוּמְאָה רְצוּצָה "squeezed impurity": If the roof of the tent is less that a handbreadth above the impurity, it does not shield but the impurity rises up to the sky and below into the ground (Mishnah *Ahilut* 7:1, 14:7).

165 This question is directed towards Mishnah *Ahilut* 6:1 which states that "humans and objects form tents to make impure but not to make pure." In the Mishnah, R. Eliezer disagrees and holds that any roof which brings impurity shields everything above it from impurity. R. Yose notes that the position of R. Eliezer is the only rational one.

166 Since a bed can be moved, it is an object and brings impurity, even if the *nazir* is more than one handbreadth below the bottom of the bed.

167 Even if the bed is one handbreadth above the corpse it does not form a "tent" to protect the *nazir*. The ceiling of the room is the "tent" and everything below it is impure.

168 Not in a room, and the frame is not holding bedding. This is a situation similar to that of standing under the gutters attached to a building.

169 A moving "tent" which only transmits rabbinic impurity.

170 Greek μέλαθρον "roof-tree, beam, roof".

171 But not for dwelling.

172 Since Ḥizqiah was R. Joḥanan's teacher, practice cannot follow R. Joḥanan.

173 This now refers to Mishnah *Ahilut* 4:3: "If [impurity] was in the entrance with the door open, the house is pure; if it was in the house, everything in the house is impure, *since it is the way of impurity to leave but not to enter*." If the dining hall had no windows (or its windows were narrow slits through which no corpse could be transported), so that the only way out was through the door of the anteroom, it is obvious that everybody in the anteroom was biblically impure if the corpse was in the dining hall. If the corpse was in the outer room, it still was on the same floor in the same

building as the *nazir*, who would be made biblically impure by the "tent", the ceiling of his room.

174 As explained in the preceding Note, the second case is the more natural and should have been mentioned first. In the formulation given, should one not ask whether in the first case the *nazir* was not biblically impure since impurity is supposed to leave?

175 This is a commentary on Mishnah *Ahilut* 6:3. If the wall of a house is rather thick and the "squeezed" impurity (Note 165) is under the inner part of the wall, the house is impure but anybody standing on the roof is pure since the roof intercepts the impurity. But if the "squeezed" impurity (Note 165) is under the outer part of the wall, the house is pure but anybody standing on the wall is impure since a roof does not intercept a "squeezed" impurity. R. Joḥanan asserts that this rule is biblical.

176 The definition of "squeezed" impurity.

177 The spine and skull (assuming they do not amount to half a *qab*); cf. Babli 53a.

178 125 bones (assuming they do not amount to half a *qab*); Mishnah *Ahilut* 2:1.

(56c line 60) בֶּאֱמֶת. דְּאָמַר רִבִּי אֱלִיעֶזֶר. כָּל־מָקוֹם שֶׁשָּׁנִינוּ. בֶּאֱמֶת. הֲלָכָה לְמֹשֶׁה מִסִּינַי.

"In truth;" Rebbi Eliezer[179] said that every place where they stated "in truth," refers to practice going back to Moses on Mount Sinai.

178 This reading is found also in *Šabbat* 10:4 (12c, l. 46). But in the other occurences in the Yerushalmi, *Šabbat* 1 (3b l. 69), *Kilaim* 2:2 Note 36, *Terumot* 2:1 Note 16, the name is "Eleazar" (Lazar). In the Babli the quote is anonymous in *Šabbat* 92b; it appears in the name of R. Eleazar in *Baba meṣi'a* 60a.

(56c line 61) יִפְּלוּ כִּי טָמֵא נְזָרוֹ. מִיכָּן שֶׁטְּמֵאִים נוֹפְלִין. וְיִסְתּוֹר. אֵין לָךְ סוֹתֵר אֶלָּא יְמֵי הַמֵּת בִּלְבַד. וְלֹא יַעֲלוּ. מָה אִם יָמִים שֶׁעוֹשִׂין מִשְׁכָּב וּמוֹשָׁב אַתְּ אוֹמֵר. עוֹלִין. יָמִים שֶׁאֵין עוֹשִׂין מִשְׁכָּב וּמוֹשָׁב אֵינוֹ דִין שֶׁיַּעֲלוּ. מַה חָמִית מֵימַר שֶׁאֵין עוֹלִין. אָמַר רִבִּי [] בְּשֵׁם רִבִּי שִׁמְעוֹן בֶּן לָקִישׁ. גַּדֵּל פֶּרַע שְׂעַר

רֹאשׁוֹ. יָמִים שֶׁלְּגִידוּל שֵׂיעָר עוֹלִין. יָמִים שֶׁלְהַעֲבָרַת שֵׂיעָר אֵין עוֹלִין. עַד כְּדוֹן בִּימֵת סְפִירוֹ. בִּימֵי גְמָרוֹ. רִבִּי יוֹחָנָן בְּשֵׁם רִבִּי יַנַּאי. אַל נָא תְהִי כַמֵּת. מַה יְמֵי הַמֵּת אֵין עוֹלִין אַף יְמֵי הֶסְגֵּר אֵין עוֹלִין. חַד בֵּי רַב אָמַר הָדָא דְרִבִּי יוֹחָנָן קוֹמֵי רִבִּי שִׁמְעוֹן בֶּן לָקִישׁ וְלֹא קִיבֵּל עֲלוֹי. אָמַר לֵיהּ. הָכָא אַתְּ עֲבַד לָהּ הֶסְגֵּר. וְהָכָא אַתְּ עֲבַד לָהּ הֶחְלֵט. לֵית יְכִיל. דְּאָמַר רִבִּי יוֹחָנָן בְּשֵׁם רִבִּי יַנַּאי. אַל נָא תְהִי כַמֵּת. תִּסְגֵּר. מַה יְמֵי הַמֵּת שִׁבְעָה. אַף יְמֵי הֶסְגֵּר שִׁבְעָה.

"They shall fall away, for his vow of *nazir* is impure.[179]" From here that the days of impurity fall away[180]. Then should he invalidate[181]? He invalidates only the days of [impurity of] the dead[182]. Why should they not be counted? If you say that days in which he causes [impurity to] couch and seat are counted, days in which he does not cause [impurity to] couch and seat are certainly counted[183]! What did you see to say that they are not counted? Rebbi [][184] said in the name of Rebbi Simeon ben Laqish: "For a wild growth of his head's hair"[185]. Days of hair growth are counted, days preparing for shaving[186] are not counted. So far in his days of counting; in the days of his definite status? Rebbi Johanan in the name of Rebbi Yannai: "Please do not let her be like a corpse[187]." Since the days of a corpse are not counted, the days of quarantine are not counted. A student quoted this saying of Rebbi Johanan's before Rebbi Simeon ben Laqish, who did not accept it. He said to him: Here, you call it quarantine, but there, you want to call it absolute; you cannot do that. For Rebbi Johanan said in the name of Rebbi Simeon ben Laqish: "Please do not let her be like a corpse; let her be quarantined[188]." Just as the days of the dead are seven, so the days of quarantine are seven[189].

179 *Num.* 6:12.

180 The days of certified skin disease cannot count as days of *nezirut* even though the sufferer from skin disease is also required to let his hair grow.

181 The Mishnah states that a *nazir* who develops skin disease simply waits

until he is healed and then finishes his count. Why does he not start anew as in the case of impurity of the dead?

182   The biblical law is quite clear that only the impurity of the dead makes him lose the earlier days of his count.

183   Mishnah *Kelim* 1:4 states that the impurity of the sufferer from skin disease is more severe than the impurity of the female sufferer from flux. For the latter, it is stated explicitly (*Lev.* 15:26) that any couch and any seat used by her becomes a source of original impurity. No direct biblical source exists for declaring the sufferer from skin disease to cause this kind of impurity; it is derived indirectly in *Sifra Meṣora' Parashah* 2(6). This derivation is accepted at face value by Maimonides both in his Mishnah Commentary (*Kelim* 1:4) and in his Code (*Tum'at Ṣara'at* 10:11). The commentators of the Babli (Rashi, *Pesaḥim* 67b s. v. זו, Ravad, Commentary to *Sifra*) have difficulties in accepting the *Sifra* since it seems to contradict the Babli *Pesaḥim* 67b, but a student of the Yerushalmi does not have to consider this, in particular since Ravad does not object to Maimonides's ruling in his Code. For impurity there is no difference between a sufferer from skin disease in quarantine and one positively declared infirm (Mishnah *Megillah* 1:7, *Nega'im* 8:8).

The argument given here refers to Mishnah *Nega'im* 14:2 which states that the healed sufferer from skin disease in his days of counting, between the preliminary and the definitive purification, is free from all severe impurities and does not cause more impurity than a dead reptile (the slightest of impurities, Mishnah *Kelim* 1:1). It does not seem to make any sense to accept the days of the severely impure quarantined but not to accept the slightly impure counting sufferer from skin disease (cf. Note 144).

184   There are no sources which would permit filling in the lacuna.

185   *Num.* 6:5.

186   For the final purification of the sufferer from skin disease.

187   *Num.* 12:12, speaking of Miriam who was punished for calumniating Moses by becoming a clear sufferer from skin disease (v. 10), not a case of quarantine.

188   *Num.* 12:14.

189   While the case of Miriam was clearly not one of quarantine, the verse treats it as such by (1) calling her exclusion from the camp "quarantine" and (2) exempting her from the cleansing ritual which is required of

the absolute sufferer but not the quarantined (Mishnah *Megillah* 1:8, *Nega'im* 8:8). The verse cannot be applied to the absolute sufferer.

(fol. 55d) **משנה ד:** רִבִּי אֶלְעָזָר אָמַר מִשּׁוּם רִבִּי יְהוֹשֻׁעַ כָּל־טוּמְאָה מִן הַמֵּת שֶׁהַנָּזִיר מְגַלֵּחַ עָלֶיהָ חַיָּיבִין עָלֶיהָ עַל בִּיאַת מִקְדָּשׁ. וְכָל־טוּמְאָה מִן הַמֵּת שֶׁאֵין הַנָּזִיר מְגַלֵּחַ עָלֶיהָ אֵין חַיָּיבִין עָלֶיהָ עַל בִּיאַת הַמִּקְדָּשׁ. אָמַר רִבִּי מֵאִיר לֹא תְהֵא זוֹ קַלָּה מִן הַשֶּׁרֶץ. אָמַר רבי עֲקִיבָה דַּנְתִּי לִפְנֵי רִבִּי אֶלִיעֶזֶר מָה אִם עֶצֶם כַּשְּׂעוֹרָה שֶׁאֵינוֹ מְטַמֵּא אֶת הָאָדָם בָּאוֹהֶל הַנָּזִיר מְגַלֵּחַ עַל מַגָּעוֹ וְעַל מַשָּׂאוֹ. רְבִיעִית דָּם שֶׁהוּא מְטַמֵּא אֶת הָאָדָם בָּאוֹהֶל אֵינוֹ דִין שֶׁיְּהֵא הַנָּזִיר מְגַלֵּחַ עַל מַגָּעָהּ וְעַל מַשָּׂאָהּ. אָמַר לִי מַה זֶה עֲקִיבָה. אֵין דָּנִין כָּאן מִקַּל וָחוֹמֶר. וּכְשֶׁבָּאתִי וְהִרְצֵאתִי אֶת הַדְּבָרִים לִפְנֵי רִבִּי יְהוֹשֻׁעַ אָמַר לִי יָפֶה אָמַרְתָּ אֶלָּא כָּךְ אָמְרוּ הֲלָכָה.

Mishnah 4: Rebbi Eleazar said in the name of Rebbi Joshua: For any impurity caused by a corpse for which the *nazir* shaves[190], one is guilty if entering the Sanctuary, but for any impurity caused by a corpse for which the *nazir* does not shave[191], one is not guilty if entering the Sanctuary. Rebbi Meïr said, this should not be less than the impurity of a dead reptile[192]! Rebbi Aqiba said, I argued before Rebbi Eliezer: If for a barley-grain sized bone, which does not cause impurity to a human in a tent[193], a *nazir* shaves if he touches or carries it[190], should it not be logical that for a *quartarius* of blood, which causes impurity to a human in a tent[194], a *nazir* should have to shave if he touches or carries it? He said to me, what is that, Aqiba? This is not a place for an argument *de minore ad majus*! When I came and expounded that before Rebbi Joshua, he said to me, you have a good argument, but that is what they said was practice[195].

190 Explained in Mishnah 2.
191 Explained in Mishnah 3. In Mishnah *Parah* 11:4 the formulation is: "For any impurity which requires immersion in water by biblical decree, one is guilty if entering the Sanctuary, but for any impurity which does not require immersion in water by biblical decree, one is not guilty if entering the Sanctuary."
192 Which requires immersion in water by biblical decree, *Lev.* 11:31, and a person is guilty if he enters the Sanctuary when impure, *Lev.* 5:2.
193 Mishnah *Ahilut* 2:1.
194 Mishnah *Ahilut* 2:2. The *nazir* does not shave, Mishnah 3.
195 "Practice" here means an old tradition, whose origin can no longer be ascertained and which cannot be overruled. The relationship of this kind of practice to the interpretation of biblical verses is not amenable to logical analysis.

(56c line 72) **הלכה ד:** רִבִּי אֶלְעָזָר אָמַר בְּשֵׁם רִבִּי יְהוֹשֻׁעַ כול'. תַּמָּן תַּנִּינָן. שְׁנַיִם טְמֵאִין בַּמֵּת. אֶחָד טָמֵא טוּמְאַת שִׁבְעָה וְאֶחָד טָמֵא טוּמְאַת טְמֵיאֵי עֶרֶב. שְׁלֹשָׁה טְמֵאִים בַּמֵּת. שְׁנַיִם טְמֵאִים טוּמְאַת שִׁבְעָה וְאֶחָד טָמֵא טוּמְאַת עֶרֶב. אַרְבָּעָה טְמֵאִים בַּמֵּת. שְׁלֹשָׁה טְמֵאִים טוּמְאַת שִׁבְעָה וְאֶחָד טָמֵא טוּמְאַת עֶרֶב. כֵּיצַד שְׁנֵי בְנֵי אָדָם. הַנּוֹגְעִין בַּמֵּת טְמֵאִים טוּמְאַת שִׁבְעָה. וְאָדָם הַנּוֹגֵעַ בּוֹ טָמֵא טוּמְאַת עֶרֶב כול'. רִבִּי יוֹחָנָן בְּשֵׁם רִבִּי יַנַּאי. וְכוּלְּהוֹן תּוֹרָה הֵן אֵצֶל תְּרוּמָה. אֲבָל עַל בִּיאַת הַמִּקְדָּשׁ אֵינוֹ חַייָב אֶלָּא עַל שֵׁנִי שֶׁנָּגַע בָּרִאשׁוֹן. מַה טַעַם. וְאִישׁ אֲשֶׁר יִטְמָא וְלֹא יִתְחַטָּא. הַטָּעוּן חִיטּוּי חַייָב עַל בִּיאַת מִקְדָּשׁ וְשֶׁאֵין טָעוּן חִיטּוּי אֵינוֹ חַייָב עַל בִּיאַת הַמִּקְדָּשׁ. הֲתִיבוֹן. הֲרֵי אָדָם הַנּוֹגֵעַ בַּכֵּלִים וְנוֹגְעִין בַּמֵּת טָעוּן חִיטּוּי וְהוּא שֵׁנִי. אָמַר רִבִּי אָבִין בַּר חִייָה. בְּטוּמְאַת אִישׁ בְּאִישׁ לֹא בְטוּמְאַת אִישׁ בְּכֵלִים. מִילְּתֵיהּ דְּרִבִּי אָבִין בַּר חִייָה אֵינוֹ חַייָב אֶלָּא הָרִאשׁוֹן בִּלְבַד. מֵאַחַר שֶׁאִילּוּ אָדָם בְּאָדָם אֵינוֹ חַייָב אֶלָּא הָרִאשׁוֹן בִּלְבַד. וְכָא אֵינוֹ חַייָב אֶלָּא הָרִאשׁוֹן בִּלְבַד. אָמַר רִבִּי יוֹסֵי. וְהוּא שֶׁטָּבַל. אֲבָל אִם לֹא טָבַל הָדָא הִיא דְרִבִּי. דְּרִבִּי אָמַר. כָּל־הַטְּמֵאִים בְּטוּמְאָתָן עַד שֶׁיָּבוֹאוּ בַמַּיִם.

Halakhah 4: "Rebbi Eleazar said in the name of Rebbi Joshua," etc. There[196], we have stated: "Two are impure from the dead, one is impure for seven days and one is impure by the impurity of evening[197]. Three are impure from the dead, two are impure for seven days and one is impure until nightfall[198]. Four are impure from the dead, three are impure for seven days and one is impure until nightfall[199]. How is it for two? Any person who touches a corpse is impure for seven days; a person who touches him is impure until nightfall," etc. Rebbi Joḥanan in the name of Rebbi Yannai: All are biblically [impure] for heave[200], but for entering the Sanctuary only the second impure who touched the first impure. What is the reason? "A person who would be impure and did not purify himself[201];" anybody needing purification is guilty for entering the Sanctuary; anybody not needing purification is not guilty for entering the Sanctuary. They objected: But a person who touches objects which touched a corpse needs purification, but is he the second[202]? Rebbi Abin bar Ḥiyya said, for impurity of a person from a person[203], not for impurity of a person from objects. The statement of Rebbi Abin bar Ḥiyya [implies that] only the first is guilty[204]. Since [for impurity of] a person from a person only the first is guilty, so here the first is guilty. Rebbi Yose said, only if he immersed himself. That is a statement of Rebbi, since Rebbi said, all impure persons remain impure until the are immersed in water[205].

196 Mishnah *Ahilut* 1:1.

197 As explained at the end of the Mishnah, a person touching a corpse becomes a source of original impurity. A second person touching the first becomes impure in the first degree. The first is subject to the rules of *Num.* 19, the second can cleanse himself by immersion in water; then he will become pure in all respects at sundown (*Lev.* 22:7). For degrees of impurity, cf. *Demay* 2:3, Note 137.

198 Explained in Mishnah *Ahilut* 1:2: An object touching the corpse becomes impure like the corpse itself (*Sifry Num.* 130). A second object touches the first; it becomes a source of original impurity; both need the ritual

of *Num.* 19. A third object or a human touching the second object becomes impure in the first degree and can become pure at sundown.

199 Explained in Mishnah *Ahilut* 1:3: An object which touches the corpse becomes impure like the corpse itself. A human touches the first object, becoming a source of original impurity; a second object touches the human, also becoming a source of original impurity. A third object or a human touching the second object becomes impure in the first degree and can become pure at sundown.

200 Not only for heave but also for sacrifices: anything with a status of sanctity. But for profane food, humans, or objects, anything touching a corpse becomes a source of original impurity; the person touching it or him becomes impure in the first degree. In biblical law, no human can become impure by derivative impurity. No person touching anything more than once removed from the corpse can become biblically impure.

201 *Num.* 19:20: "This person will be extirpated from the congregation, for he desecrated the Eternal's Sanctuary".

202 A person who touched objects which touched objects which touched the corpse is a third in line who is impure by biblical standards and guilty if he enters the Sanctuary unpurified.

203 The statement of R. Joḥanan refers to impurity of a person induced by a person.

204 Anybody needing the ritual of *Num.* 19 but entering the Sanctuary without it is guilty of a deadly sin, as stated in *Num.* 19:20. The person only impure in the first degree, not subject to this ritual, is guilty of a sin but not a deadly one. As explained in Note 199, if the impurity is transmitted by an object, the human may be the second in the sequence.

205 The person impure in the first degree may still commit a deadly sin by entering the Sanctuary (*Lev.* 22:3) without immersing himself in water. But if he enters (or eats sanctified food) between immersion and sundown, he commits a minor sin (*Lev.* 22:7).

(56d line 12) אָמַר רְבִּי אִילָא. הוּא עַצְמוֹ שֶׁנָּגַע בְּמֵת חַיָּיב. אָמְרָהּ וְאָמַר טַעֲמָהּ. אֲשֶׁר יִטְמָא. בְּטוּמְאַת אִישׁ הוּא. וְהוּא שְׁלִישִׁי. כִּדְאָמַר רִבִּי אָבוּן בַּר חִיָּיה. בְּטוּמְאַת אִישׁ בְּאִישׁ אָדָם חַיָּיב עַל טוּמְאַת מִקְדָּשׁ. הֲתִיבוּן. הֲרֵי כֵלִים נוֹגְעִין בְּמֵת וְאָדָם בַּכֵּלִים וְכֵלִים בָּאָדָם. בְּטוּמְאַת אִישׁ בְּאִישׁ וְלֹא בְטוּמְאַת אָדָם

בְּכֵלִים. רַבִּי זְרִיקָא בְּשֵׁם רַב הַמְנוּנָא. תַּנָּיֵי תַּמָּן פְּלִיג עַל רַבִּי אִילָא. כְּלִי שֶׁחֶצְיוֹ מִן הָאֲדָמָה הַחֶלְמָה וְחֶצְיוֹ מִן הַגְּלָלִים אֵין חַיָּיבִין עָלָיו עַל בִּיאַת הַמִּקְדָּשׁ. מִפְּנֵי שֶׁחֶצְיָיו מִן הָאֲדָמָה וְחֶצְיוֹ מִן הַגְּלָלִים. אֲבָל אִם הָיָה כולו מִן הָאֲדָמָה חַיָּיב. מָנוֹ חַיָּיב. לֹא הַנּוֹגֵעַ. לֹא שֵׁינִי שֶׁנָּגַע בָּרִאשׁוֹן הוּא. אָמַר רַבִּי פִּינְחָס קוֹמֵי רַבִּי יוֹסֵי. תִּיפְתָּר בְּשֶׁזְּרָקוֹ. אָמַר לֵיהּ. אֵין בְּשֶׁזְּרָקוֹ. בְּדָא תַּנֵּי. עַל רְחִיצַת גּוּפוֹ עָנוּשׁ כָּרֵת וְעַל כִּיבּוּס בְּגָדָיו בְּאַרְבָּעִים. מִשָּׁם מַכְנִיס כֵּלִים טְמֵאִים בַּמִּקְדָּשׁ. אָמַר רַבִּי לְעֶזָר בֵּירִבִּי יוֹסֵי קוֹמֵי רַבִּי יוֹסֵי. אוֹף אֲנָן תַּנִּינָן. הָדָא מְסַייְעָא לְהָדֵין תַּנָּיָיא קַדְמָיָא דְּתַנֵּי. רַבִּי אֶלְעָזָר אָמַר מִשּׁוּם רַבִּי יְהוֹשֻׁעַ. כָּל־טוּמְאָה מִן הַמֵּת שֶׁהַנָּזִיר מְגַלֵּחַ עָלֶיהָ חַיָּיבִין עָלֶיהָ עַל בִּיאַת מִקְדָּשׁ. וְכָל־טוּמְאָה מִן הַמֵּת שֶׁאֵין הַנָּזִיר מְגַלֵּחַ עָלֶיהָ אֵין חַיָּיבִין עָלֶיהָ עַל בִּיאַת הַמִּקְדָּשׁ. רִאשׁוֹן שֶׁהַנָּזִיר מְגַלֵּחַ עָלָיו חַיָּיבִין עָלָיו עַל בִּיאַת מִקְדָּשׁ. שֵׁינִי שֶׁאֵין הַנָּזִיר מְגַלֵּחַ עָלָיו אֵין חַיָּיבִין עָלָיו עַל בִּיאַת הַמִּקְדָּשׁ. אָמַר רַבִּי יוֹחָנָן. לַטּוּמְאוֹת הַפּוֹרְשׁוֹת מִן הַמֵּת נִצְרְכָה. רְבִיעִית דָּם רוֹבַע עֲצָמוֹת שֶׁאֵין הַנָּזִיר מְגַלֵּחַ עֲלֵיהֶן אֵין חַיָּיב עֲלֵיהֶן עַל בִּיאַת מִקְדָּשׁ. חֲצִי לוֹג דָּם וַחֲצִי קַב עֲצָמוֹת שֶׁהַנָּזִיר מְגַלֵּחַ עֲלֵיהֶן חַיָּיבִין עֲלֵיהֶן עַל בִּיאַת הַמִּקְדָּשׁ. אָמַר רַבִּי יִרְמְיָה. הָוִינָן סַבְרִין מֵימַר. מַה פְּלִיגֵי. לְקָרְבָּן. אֲבָל לְמַלְקוּת לוֹקִין אֲפִילוּ עַל הַשְּׁלִישִׁי אֲפִילוּ עַל הָרְבִיעִי. תַּנֵּי רַבִּי יוֹסֵי צַיְידָּנָיָיה קוֹמֵי רַבִּי יִרְמְיָה וּפְלִיג עֲלֵיהּ רַבִּי יִרְמְיָה. כָּל־טוּמְאָה מִן הַמֵּת שֶׁהַנָּזִיר מְגַלֵּחַ עָלֶיהָ חַיָּיבִין עָלֶיהָ עַל בִּיאַת הַמִּקְדָּשׁ. וְכָל־טוּמְאָה מִן הַמֵּת שֶׁאֵין הַנָּזִיר מְגַלֵּחַ עָלֶיהָ אֵין חַיָּיבִין עָלֶיהָ עַל בִּיאַת הַמִּקְדָּשׁ. אָמַר רַבִּי יוֹסֵי בֵּירִבִּי בּוּן רַבִּי יַנַּאי רַבִּי יוֹחָנָן. לַטֻּמְאוֹת הַפּוֹרְשׁוֹת מִן הַמֵּת נִצְרְכָה. רְבִיעִית דָּם רוֹבַע עֲצָמוֹת שֶׁאֵין הַנָּזִיר מְגַלֵּחַ עֲלֵיהֶן אֵין חַיָּיבִין עֲלֵיהֶן. חֲצִי לוֹג דָּם וַחֲצִי קַב עֲצָמוֹת שֶׁהַנָּזִיר מְגַלֵּחַ עֲלֵיהֶן לוֹקִין עֲלֵיהֶן.

Rebbi Illa said: He himself, who touched the corpse, is guilty[206]. He said it and gave its reason: "who became impure[201]," that refers to the impurity of a human. But is there not a third[207]? As Rebbi Abun bar Ḥiyya said, for impurity of a person from a person a man is guilty for impurity in the Sanctuary[208]. They objected: If objects touch the corpse, a human the objects, and objects the human[197]. For impurity of a person from a person, not for impurity of a person from objects[208]. Rebbi Zeriqa in the name of Rav Hamnuna: The Tanna there[209] disagrees with Rebbi Illa: "For an object made half of cement-earth[210] and half of dung[211] one is not guilty for coming to the Sanctuary[212]" Because it is half of earth and half of dung; but if it were totally of earth, one would be guilty. Who is guilty? Not the one who touches it? Is he not the second who touches the first[213]? Rebbi Phineas said before Rebbi Yose: Explain it if he threw it[214]. He answered him, about him who threw it we stated: For washing his body he is subject to extirpation, for washing his garments to the forty[215]. Rebbi Eleazar ben Rebbi Yose said before Rebbi Yose, do we not have the Mishnah in support of that first Tanna[216], as is stated: "Rebbi Eleazar said in the name of Rebbi Joshua: For any impurity caused by a corpse for which the *nazir* shaves, one is guilty if entering the Sanctuary, but for any impurity caused by a corpse for which the *nazir* does not shave, one is not guilty if entering the Sanctuary." For the first, for which the *nazir* shaves, one is guilty if entering the Sanctuary; for the second, for which the *nazir* does not shave, one is not guilty if entering the Sanctuary. Rebbi Johanan said[217], it is needed from what comes from the corpse: For a *quartarius* of blood or a quarter *qab* of bones, for which the *nazir* does not shave, one is not guilty if entering the Sanctuary; for half a *log* of blood and half a *qab* of bones, for which the *nazir* shaves, one is guilty if entering the Sanctuary. Rebbi Jeremiah said, we were of the opinion that they disagree about a sacrifice, but one whips even the third, even the fourth[218]. Rebbi Yose from Sidon stated before Rebbi Jeremiah in opposition to Rebbi Jeremiah[219]: "For any impurity caused by a corpse for which the *nazir* shaves, one is guilty if entering the Sanctuary, but for any impurity caused by a corpse for which the *nazir* does not shave, one is not guilty if entering the Sanctuary." Rebbi Yose ben Rebbi Abun said, Rebbi Yannai, Rebbi Johanan[220]: It is needed from what comes from the corpse: For a *quartarius* of blood or a quarter *qab* of bones, for which the *nazir* does not shave, one is not guilty; for half a *log* of blood and half a *qab* of bones, for which the *nazir* shaves, one is guilty.

206 He holds that a deadly sin is only committted if a person impure by contact from body to body is entering the Sanctuary, not if the impurity was transmitted by contact with an object as explained in Notes 197,198.

207 How could it be that a person needs purification by the rites of *Num.* 19 and not be guilty entering the Sanctuary unpurified?

208 The verse does not deal with the impurity transmitted by objects; its status remains indeterminate.

209 Tosephta *Kelim Baba Meṣi'a* 1:5 says the same in different words.

210 Probably clay is meant; earth of a consistency from which objects can be made. Clay objects are the paradigm of objects which can become impure; they cannot be purified except by being broken.

211 Objects made of dried camel or cow dung cannot become impure.

212 If such an object was brought to the Sanctuary after being exposed to impurity, no sin was committed.

213 Since an object cannot be guilty, the human who touches it must be guilty. This contradicts both R. Ila and R. Abin bar Ḥiyya.

214 Somebody threw an impure clay object into the Sanctuary grounds. Then there is no question of a human entering the holy precinct.

215 A person is impure in original impurity who transmits impurity to his garments. If he enters the Sanctuary while impure, he commits a deadly sin with his body. But at the same time, he carries his impure garments into the holy precinct. This is a separate offense, punishable by 39 (= 40-1) lashes. The implication is that a person throwing an impure object into the Sanctuary is whipped but not subject to Divine extirpation.

216 R. Ila, an Amora.

217 R. Johanan holds that the entire discussion up to this point is based on a false premise. It is clear to him that anybody impure in at least the first degree is forbidden access to the

Sanctuary on penalty of extirpation. R. Joshua's statement only deals with the impurity generated by the corpse. Such impurity prohibits the person contaminated by it (or any of its derivatives up to the level of first degree impurity) from entering the Sanctuary if and only if it forces the *nazir* to shave.

218   He tries to salvage the opinions of R. Illa and R. Abin ben Ḥiyya, that everybody would agree that any person entering the Sanctuary in impurity commits a sin; the question would only be about a sacrifice for an unintended infraction. But for wilful transgression, the Mishnah in *Ahilut* is quite clear that it is punishable even for the third and fourth person.

219   He confirms the interpretation given in Note 217.

220   The order of the last two names has to be inverted: R. Yose ben R. Bun said in the name of R. Joḥanan who heard it from R. Yannai.

שני נזירין פרק שמיני

משנה א: (fol. 56d) שְׁנֵי נְזִירִין שֶׁאָמַר לָהֶן אֶחָד רָאִיתִי אֶחָד מִכֶּם שֶׁנִּיטְמָא וְאֵינִי יוֹדֵעַ אֵי זֶה מִכֶּם מְבִיאִין קָרְבַּן טוּמְאָה וְקָרְבַּן טַהֲרָה וְאוֹמֵר אִם אֲנִי הוּא הַטָּמֵא קָרְבַּן טוּמְאָה שֶׁלִּי וְקָרְבַּן טַהֲרָה שֶׁלָּךְ. וְאִם אֲנִי הוּא הַטָּהוֹר קָרְבַּן טַהֲרָה שֶׁלִּי וְקָרְבַּן טוּמְאָה שֶׁלָּךְ. וְסוֹפְרִין שְׁלֹשִׁים יוֹם וּמְבִיאִין קָרְבַּן טַהֲרָה. (משנה ב) וְאוֹמֵר אִם אֲנִי הוּא טָמֵא קָרְבַּן טוּמְאָה שֶׁלִּי וְקָרְבַּן טַהֲרָה שֶׁלָּךְ. וְזֶה קָרְבַּן טַהֲרָתִי. וְאִם אֲנִי הוּא הַטָּהוֹר קָרְבַּן טַהֲרָה שֶׁלִּי וְקָרְבַּן טוּמְאָה שֶׁלָּךְ. וְזֶה קָרְבַּן טַהֲרָתָךְ.

Mishnah 1: If a person said to two *nezirim*: I saw one of you becoming impure but I do not know which one of you it was, they bring[1] one sacrifice of impurity[2] and one of purity[3]. One of them says, if I am impure, the sacrifice of impurity is mine and that of purity is yours; otherwise the sacrifice of purity is mine and that of impurity is yours. Then they count another thirty days[4] and bring one sacrifice of purity; (Mishnah 2) one of them says, if I was impure, the sacrifice of impurity was mine and that of purity was yours, hence this is my sacrifice of purity; otherwise the sacrifice of purity was mine and that of impurity was yours, hence this is your sacrifice of purity.

1 They purify themselves from the impurity of the dead and at the end of their period of *nezirut* they shave and bring the sacrifices in common.

2 Two birds and a sheep.

3 A male and a female sheep and a ram.

4 Assuming that both had vowed the standard period of 30 days. Otherwise they would have to repeat the longer of the respective periods of *nezirut*.

(fol. 56d) **שנה ב:** מֵת אֶחָד מֵהֶן אָמַר רִבִּי יְהוֹשֻׁעַ יְבַקֵּשׁ אֶחָד מִן הַשּׁוּק וְיִדּוֹר כְּנֶגְדּוֹ נָזִיר וְאוֹמֵר אִם טָמֵא הָיִיתִי הֲרֵי אַתָּה נָזִיר מִיָּד וְאִם טָהוֹר הָיִיתִי הֲרֵי אַתָּה נָזִיר אַחַר שְׁלֹשִׁים יוֹם. וְסוֹפְרִים שְׁלֹשִׁים יוֹם וּמְבִיאִין קָרְבַּן טוּמְאָה וְקָרְבַּן טַהֲרָה. (משנה ג) וְאוֹמֵר אִם אֲנִי הוּא הַטָּמֵא קָרְבַּן טוּמְאָה שֶׁלִּי וְקָרְבַּן טַהֲרָה שֶׁלָּךְ וְאִם אֲנִי הוּא הַטָּהוֹר קָרְבַּן טַהֲרָה שֶׁלִּי וְקָרְבַּן טוּמְאָה בְּסָפֵק. וְסוֹפְרִים שְׁלֹשִׁים יוֹם וּמְבִיאִין קָרְבַּן טַהֲרָה. (משנה ד) וְאוֹמֵר אִם אֲנִי הוּא טָמֵא קָרְבַּן טוּמְאָה שֶׁלִּי וְקָרְבַּן טַהֲרָה שֶׁלָּךְ וְזֶה קָרְבַּן טַהֲרָתִי וְאִם אֲנִי הוּא טָהוֹר קָרְבַּן טַהֲרָה שֶׁלִּי וְקָרְבַּן טוּמְאָה בְּסָפֵק וְזֶה קָרְבַּן טַהֲרָתָהּ.

Mishnah 2: If one of them died[5], Rebbi Joshua said, he should seek out a person from the general public who would make a vow of *nazir* corresponding to his needs and say: If I was impure, you are a *nazir* immediately[6], but if I was pure, you are a *nazir* after 30 days. They count 30 days and bring one sacrifice of impurity and one of purity (Mishnah 3) and he says: If I am impure, the sacrifice of impurity is mine and that of purity is yours; otherwise the sacrifice of purity is mine and that of impurity is questionable[7]. Then they count another thirty days, bring one sacrifice of purity (Mishnah 4) and he says: If I was impure, the sacrifice of impurity was mine and that of purity was yours, hence this is my sacrifice of purity; otherwise the sacrifice of purity was mine and that of impurity was questionable; hence this is your sacrifice of purity.

5   Then the survivor is in danger of never being able to conclude his *nezirut* since, not knowing which sacrifice to bring, he can bring neither.

6   And the sacrifice of purity will be yours.

7   The sacrifice of impurity consists of two birds. The one offered as elevation sacrifice can be given as obligation, if there was impurity, or as voluntary gift, if there was none. The bird offered as purification sacrifice cannot be eaten by the priests; after its blood was used, it has to be burned outside the Temple precinct (Mishnah *Temurah* 7:6).

משנה ד: (fol. 56d) אָמַר לוֹ בֶּן זוֹמָא וּמִי שׁוֹמֵעַ לוֹ שֶׁיִּדּוֹר כְּנֶגְדּוֹ. אֶלָּא מֵבִיא חַטֵּאת הָעוֹף וְעוֹלַת בְּהֵמָה וְאוֹמֵר אִם טָמֵא הָיִיתִי הַחַטָּאת מֵחוֹבָתִי וְהָעוֹלָה נְדָבָה. וְאִם טָהוֹר הָיִיתִי הָעוֹלָה מֵחוֹבָתִי וְהַחַטָּאת בְּסָפֵק וְסוֹפֵר שְׁלֹשִׁים יוֹם וּמֵבִיא קָרְבַּן טוּמְאָה וְקָרְבָּן קָרְבַּן טַהֲרָה. (משנה ה) וְאוֹמֵר אִם טָמֵא הָיִיתִי הָעוֹלָה רִאשׁוֹנָה נְדָבָה וְזוֹ חוֹבָה. וְאִם טָהוֹר הָיִיתִי הָעוֹלָה רִאשׁוֹנָה חוֹבָה וְזוֹ נְדָבָה וְזֶה שְׁאָר קָרְבָּנִי. אָמַר רִבִּי יְהוֹשֻׁעַ נִמְצָא זֶה מֵבִיא קָרְבְּנוֹתָיו חֲצָיִים. אֲבָל הוֹדוּ חֲכָמִים לְדִבְרֵי בֶן זוֹמָא.

Mishnah 4: Ben Zoma said to him, who would accommodate him to make a vow of *nazir* corresponding to his needs? But he brings a bird as purification offering and an animal as elevation offering and says: If I was impure, the purification offering is for my obligation[8] and the elevation offering is voluntary[9]. But if I was pure, the elevation offering is for my obligation and the purification offering is questionable. Then he counts 30 days and brings one sacrifice (of impurity and one)[10] of purity[3] (Mishnah 5) and says: If I was impure, the first elevation offering was voluntary and the one now is for my obligation. But if I was pure, the first elevation offering was for my obligation and now I am bringing the remainder of my sacrifices. Rebbi Joshua said, then it turns out that he brings his sacrifices piecemeal[11]! But the Sages accepted the words of Ben Zoma[12].

8   While this offering is incomplete, it is sufficient to let him shave and restart his *nezirut*.

9   Of all kinds of offerings required from a pure or impure *nazir*, only the elevation offering can be voluntary.

10   The clause in parenthesis is obviously false; it is missing in the Babli and the independent Mishnah mss.

11   If he was pure, he brings the first offering 30 days before the other two, but the verse (*Num.* 6:14) calls all three sacrifices together "his sacrifice" in the singular, meaning that they have to be offered together.

12   As the only reasonable solution to an intractable problem.

(57a line 1) **הלכה א:** שְׁנֵי נְזִירִין שֶׁאָמַר לָהֶן אֶחָד כול'. וְלֹא סוֹף דָּבָר כְּשֶׁאָמַר לָהֶן אֶחָד. רָאִיתִי אֶת אֶחָד מִכֶּם שֶׁנִּיטְמָא וְאֵינִי יוֹדֵעַ אֵי זֶה מִכֶּם. אֶלָּא אֲפִילוּ אָמַר לָהֶם. רָאִיתִי אֶחָד מִכֶּם שֶׁנָּזַר וְאֵינִי יוֹדֵעַ אֵי זֶה מִכֶּם. שְׁנֵיהֶן נוֹהֲגִין נְזִירוּת עַל פִּיו. בְּשֶׁאֵינָן מַכְחִישִׁין אוֹתוֹ. אֲבָל אִם מַכְחִישִׁין אוֹתוֹ לֹא בְדָא. הָיוּ שְׁנֵיהֶם מַכְחִישִׁין. יָבֹא כְהָדָא. עֵד אוֹמֵר. נִיטְמָא. וְהוּא אוֹמֵר. לֹא נִיטְמֵאתִי. טָהוֹר. שְׁנַיִם אוֹמְרִים. נִיטְמֵאתָ. וְהוּא אוֹמֵר. לֹא נִיטְמֵאתִי. שְׁנֵיהֶן נֶאֱמָנִין מִמֶּנּוּ. דִּבְרֵי רִבִּי מֵאִיר. וַחֲכָמִים אוֹמְרִים. הוּא נֶאֱמָן עַל יְדֵי עַצְמוֹ. רַב יְהוּדָה בְּשֵׁם רַב. כֵּינִי מַתְנִיתָא. רִבִּי מֵאִיר מְטַמֵּא. רִבִּי יְהוּדָה וַחֲכָמִים מְטָהֲרִין. אָמַר רִבִּי יוֹחָנָן. כֵּינִי מַתְנִיתָא. רִבִּי מֵאִיר מְטַמֵּא וְרִבִּי יְהוּדָה מְטָהֵר. מִילֵּיהוֹן דְּרַבָּנִין מְסַייְעִין לְרִבִּי יוֹחָנָן. דְּאָמַר רִבִּי גוּרְיוֹן בְּשֵׁם רִבִּי יוֹסֵי בֶּן חֲנִינָה. לֹא אָמַר רִבִּי יוּדָה אֶלָּא בְטוּמְאָה יְשָׁנָה. שֶׁיָּכוֹל לוֹמַר. נִיטְמֵאתִי וְטָהַרְתִּי. וְתַנֵּי. כֵּן הַדָּבָר עַל אֲכִילַת חֵלֶב. הוּא הַדָּבָר עַל בִּיאַת הַמִּקְדָּשׁ. וְיוֹדוּן לֵיהּ בְּטוּמְאָה. מִפְּנֵי טוּמְאַת נָזִיר. שֶׁאֵין אוֹמְרִים לוֹ. אֵיכָן הוּא קָרְבָּנְךָ שֶׁהֲבֵאתָ. וְיוֹדוּן לֵיהּ בִּתְרוּמָה. עַד כָּאן קַשִּׁי רִבִּי חֲנִינָה.

Halakhah 1: "If a person said to two *nezirim*," etc. Not only if he said to one of them, "I saw one of you becoming impure but I do not know which one of you it was,[13]" but even if he said, "I saw one of you vowing to be a *nazir* but I do not know which one of you it was," both of them have to follow the rules of *nazir* because of his testimony. If they do not contradict him[14]. But if they contradict him, this does not apply[15]. If both of them[16] contradict, it parallels the following: "If one witness says, he became impure, but he says, I did not become impure, he is pure. If two witnesses say, he became impure, but he says, I did not become impure, the two are believed more than he is, the words of Rebbi Meïr. But the Sages say, everybody is believed about himself.[17]" Rav Jehudah in the name of Rav: So is the Mishnah: Rebbi Meïr declares impure, Rebbi Jehudah and the Sages declare pure[18]. Rebbi Joḥanan said, so is the Mishnah: Rebbi Meïr declares impure, Rebbi Jehudah declares pure[19].

The rabbis' words support Rebbi Joḥanan, since Rebbi Gurion said in the name of Rebbi Yose ben Ḥanina: Rebbi Jehudah said this only about an old impurity, for he can say to them, I had been impure but I purified myself[20], and we have stated: The same holds for eating suet; the same holds for entering the Sanctuary[21]. Should they not accept his position for impurity? Because of the impurity of a *nazir*[22], could they not say, where is the sacrifice which you brought? Then should they not accept his position for heave[23]? So far the questions of Rebbi Ḥanina.

13   In this case it can really happen that the witness knew of a "tent" impurity unknown to the *nezirim*.

14   In matters of ritual law, the uncontested testimony of a single witness is valid.

15   A contested testimony of a single witness is worthless, not even admissible as supporting evidence.

16   It seems that the text, שניהם, is an error for שְׁנַיִם, "two [witnesses]." The concurrent testimony of two witnesses must be believed by biblical standards.

17   Mishnah *Ṭaharot* 5:9.

18   In this matter of the standing of two witnesses, the Sages fully accept the position of R. Jehudah.

19   But the Sages disagree with R. Jehudah; the Mishnah should have mentioned R. Jehudah and not the Sages. In his interpretation, the Sages follow R. Jehudah in accepting the statement of a person accused of a sin even against two witnesses but not in cases of impurity.

20   If at least one evening has passed since the possible impurity and the person in question denies that he was impure, we read from his disclaimer that he admits having incurred impurity but eliminated it quickly by immersion in a *miqweh*.

21   A single witness can force a person to bring a purification sacrifice for committing a sin. But since for an intentional sin, no purification sacrifice is possible, the person accused of committing the sin can always assert that he committed the sin intentionally and, therefore, cannot bring a sacrifice. Then he also must be believed if he asserts that he did not commit the sin (Babli *Keritut* 12a). (Talmudic law does not accept confessions since testimony of relatives is excluded and "everybody is related to himself." Therefore, the person asserting that he

intentionally committed the sin attributed to him by a single witness, cannot be prosecuted.)

22 The *nazir* brings a sacrifice for becoming impure by the impurity of the dead whether incurred willingly or involuntarily. The sacrifice is a public act; he cannot claim to have purified himself in private.

23 If an unauthorized person is accused of eating heave, he can always claim to have done it intentionally; so he does not have to pay the 25% fine (Mishnah *Terumot* 7:1).

(57a line 16) רִבִּי מָנָא שָׁמַע לָהּ מִן דְּבַתְרָהּ. אָמְרוּ לוֹ. אִם יִרְצֶה לוֹמַר. מֵזִיד הָיִיתִי. בְּשִׁפְחָה הָרוּפָה מָה אִית לָךְ. שׁוֹגֵג חַיָּיב מֵזִיד חַיָּיב. שֶׁיָּכוֹל לוֹמַר לוֹ. הֵיעַרְתִּי אֲבָל לֹא גָמַרְתִּי. כַּיֵי דְּאָמַר רִבִּי שִׁמְעוֹן בֶּן לָקִישׁ. נֶאֱנַסְתִּי מִפְּנֵי כְשָׁפִים שֶׁעָשְׂתָה לִי. בִּנְזִירוּת מָה אִית לָךְ. שׁוֹגֵג חַיָּיב מֵזִיד חַיָּיב אָנוּס חַיָּיב. בְּפֶתַע לְרַבּוֹת הַשׁוֹגֵג. בְּפֶתַע לְרַבּוֹת הַמֵּזִיד. תְּנַאי הָיָה בְלִיבִּי. לִכְשֶׁאֶטָּמֵא תִיפָּקַע נְזִירוּתִי מִמֶּנִּי תָחוּל עָלַי נְזִירוּת אַחֶרֶת. מִכָּל־מָקוֹם לֹא נִתְחַיֵּיב בִּנְזִירוּת עַד עַכְשָׁיו. תְּנַאי הָיָה בְלִיבִּי. לִכְשֶׁאֶטָּמֵא תִפָּקַע נְזִירוּתִי מִמֶּנִּי תָחוּל עָלַי נְזִירוּת אַחֶרֶת.[24] מָה אִית לָךְ. שׁוֹגֵג חַיָּיב מֵזִיד חַיָּיב. תְּנֵי בִדְבָרִים אֵין תְּנַאי בִּשְׁבִיעִית.[24] וְאָתְיָיא כַּיֵי דְּמַר רִבִּי בָּא רַב יְהוּדָה. בְּשׁוֹגֵג בְּקָרְבָּנָהּ בְּמֵזִיד בְּקָרְבָּנָהּ. אֲבָל אִם אָמַר. סָבוּר הָיִיתִי שֶׁאֵין זוֹ שְׁבוּעָה. פָּטוּר. הָא כָּל־אִילֵּין מִילַּיָּיא לֹא מָצֵי תְּנָיֵיהּ. וְכָא מָצֵי תְּנָיֵיהּ.

Rebbi Mana understood it[25] from the following[26]: "They told him, if he wishes, he says that he did it intentionally." What can he say for an assigned slave girl[27]? In error[28], he is obligated; intentionally[29], he is obligated! He can tell him, I touched her but did not finish[30], or as Rebbi Simeon ben Laqish said, I was forced to it by the spell she put on me[31]. For a *nazir*[32] what can you say? In error, he is obligated; intentionally, he is obligated; forced, he is obligated! "Suddenly", to include in error, "suddenly", to include intentionally[33]. "There was a condition in my mind that if I should become impure, my *nezirut* should burst away from me and a new *nezirut* would fall on me"; in any case he was not obligated to be a *nazir* until now[34]. ("There was a condition in my mind that if I should become impure, my *nezirut* should burst away from me and a new *nezirut* would fall on me"; in any case he was not obligated to be a *nazir* until now.)[35] What do you have in case of an oath[36]? In error, he is obligated; intentionally, he is obligated[37]! A condition may apply to words[38]; there is no condition for oaths! It follows what Rebbi Abba said, Rav Jehudah: For error, its sacrifice, for intention, its sacrifice. But if he said, I thought that this was no oath, he is free[39]. Therefore, all these subjects cannot be stated, but the following can be stated[40].

24 Read: שְׁבוּעוֹת (already corrected in *editio princeps*).

25 That the Sages and R. Jehudah do not agree about the weight of a person's disclaimer as against two witnesses to his actions.

26 Mishnah *Keritut* 3:1.

27 *Lev.* 19:20-22, the case of a man sleeping with a slave girl assigned as a future wife to another free man. As long as the girl is not totally freed, she cannot marry the man to whom she is assigned. Therefore, her relations with another man are not adultery. A reparation offering is required from the man. This is one of the few cases in which a sacrifice is possible for deliberate sin.

28 If in the dark he thought that she was his wife.

29 This is the case treated by the verse. If he denies the accusation by two witnesses, one cannot take his denial as assertion that he did it but already had remedied the situation.

30 This is a first explanation: A sacrifice is due only if there was an ejaculation of semen (*v.* 20). If he took the slave girl to bed but stopped before there was an ejaculation, no sacrifice is due.

31 He disclaims responsibility by reason of temporary insanity caused by the girl's charms. This is enough to support his disclaimer against even two witnesses.

32 Exposed to the impurity of the dead; the case of the Mishnah.

33 This is proof that the *nazir* must bring his sacrifices even if forced. The reference is to *Num.* 6:9. In all other sources, *Sifry Num.* 28 [= *Num. rabba* 10(31)], Babli *Keritut* 9a, the inference is from the double expression "if a

person should die near him *suddenly, unexpectedly . . .*" "Suddenly" is taken to refer to accidental impurity, "unexpectedly" to outside force (*Sifry*) or outside force and intention (Babli).

34   Since the vow of *nezirut* could have been formulated in a way that eliminates the possibility of a sacrifice for impurity, the testimony of the witnesses can be explained away.

35   A case of dittography.

36   If two witnesses tell a person that he owes a sacrifice because he has violated an oath imposed on him by other people (*Lev.* 5:1,4). How can he be believed if he denies the accusation?

37   Mishnah *Keritut* 2:2.

38   If he undertakes anything, he may add conditions. If others (usually a court of law) impose an oath on him, he swears according to their understanding, rather than his own.

39   Here, there may be a case in which no sacrifice can be demanded if the interested party denies their obligation.

40   In all cases discussed so far, the Sages cannot disagree with R. Jehudah; that is possible only in the cases dealt with in the next paragraph.

(57a line 26) מַה דְּרַבִּי יוֹסֵי אָמַר. פְּלוֹנִי אָכַל חֵלֶב וְהִתְרֵיתִי בּוֹ. אֵינוֹ לוֹקֶה. אָמַר לוֹ אֶחָד. נָזִיר. וְהָיָה נוֹהֵג בִּנְזִירוּת עַל פִּיו. וְשָׁתָה יַיִן וְנִיטְמָא לַמֵּתִים וְהִתְרוּ בּוֹ שְׁנַיִם לוֹקֶה. עִיקַר עֵידוּתוֹ לֹא בְּעֵד אֶחָד הוּא. מַה דְּרַבִּי מָנָא אָמַר. פְּלוֹנִית כּוֹהֶנֶת וְזִינָת וּבָא עָלֶיהָ בַּעֲלָהּ כֹּהֵן וְהִתְרֵיתִי בּוֹ. אֵינוֹ לוֹקֶה. נִסְתְּרָה בִּפְנֵי שְׁנַיִם. אָמַר אֶחָד מֵהֶם. אֲנִי רְאִיתִיהָ שֶׁנִּיטְמֵאת. וּבָא עָלֶיהָ בַּעֲלָהּ. וְהִתְרוּ בּוֹ שְׁנַיִם לוֹקֶה. וְעִיקַר עֵידוּתוֹ לֹא בְּעֵד אֶחָד.

1 מה | ממה ל   יוסי | יוסה ג   והתריתי | והתרו ל   - | אמ' לו אחד. חלב הוא והתרו בו שנים. לוקה. ועיקר עידותו לא בעד אחד הוא. ממה דר' יודה או'. פל' נזיר וניטמא. התריתי בו. אינו לוקה ל   והיה נוהג נזירות על פיו. אכל חלב והתרו בו ל . . ה. עיקר עדותו לא בעד אחד היא. מה דר' יודן אמר פלוני נזיר וניטמא והיתריתי בו אינו לוקה ג   2 נזיר | נזיר אתה ל   ושתה | שתה גל   3 והתרו | התרו ל   עיקר | ועיקר ל   עידותו | עידותי ל   נזירותו ג   הוא | היא ג   4 כהן | ובעלה כהן ל הכהן ג   והתריתי | והיתריתי ל   5 מהם | - ל   - | עליה בעלה גל   עליה עליה כהן ל בעלה כהן ג   6 ועיקר | עיקר גל   הוא | היא ג

[41]From what Rebbi Yose said, "X ate suet, and they warned him," he is not whipped. If one person said to him, you are a *nazir*, and based on this testimony he behaved like a *nazir*, when then he drank wine or became impure in the impurity of the dead, if two warned him, he is whipped. Is not the main testimony given by a single witness?

From what Rebbi Mana said, "X is the wife of a Cohen and whored; her husband, a Cohen, then had relations with her but I had warned him;" he is [not] whipped. If she went to a secluded place in the presence of two, and one said, I saw her that she became impure; when her husband, the Cohen, had relations with her but two had warned him, he is whipped. Is not the main testimony given by a single witness?

41 From *Soṭah* 6:2, Notes 34-42. The readings from the Leiden ms. in *Soṭah* are noted ל, those from a Genizah text א. The sentence which really refers to the discussion here is missing in the text; the scribe omitted from the first אמר לו אחד to the next occurrence; cf. *Soṭah* p. 252.

(57a line 32) וּמְבִיאִין קָרְבַּן טוּמְאָה וְקָרְבַּן טַהֲרָה. הָדָא בְּעוֹמֵד בְּסוֹף שְׁלֹשִׁים. אֲבָל בְּעוֹמֵד בְּתוֹךְ שְׁלֹשִׁים מַמְתִּינִין לוֹ עַל שְׁלֹשִׁים. בְּשֶׁהָיָה זֶה נְזִיר שְׁלֹשִׁים וְזֶה נְזִיר שְׁלֹשִׁים. אֲבָל אִם הָיָה זֶה נְזִיר שְׁלֹשִׁים וְזֶה נְזִיר מֵאָה מַמְתִּינִין לוֹ עַד מֵאָה. רִבִּי יַעֲקֹב דְּרוֹמָיָא בָּעָא קוֹמֵי רִבִּי יוֹסֵי. נִיטְמָא בְּאוֹתָן הַיָּמִים מָה הֵן. אָמַר לוֹ. כְּמִי שֶׁחֲבֵירוֹ מְבַקֵּשׁ לוֹ מֵאֶחָד מִן הַשּׁוּק.

"They bring one sacrifice of impurity and one of purity." That is, if they are at the end of thirty days[42]. But if one is in the middle of thirty days, one has to wait till the end of thirty days. If both of them were *nezirim* for thirty days. But if one was a *nazir* for thirty and the other a *nazir* for 100, one has to wait for 100. Rebbi Jacob the Southerner asked before Rebbi Yose: If one of them became impure during these days, what is the rule? He said to him, like one who has to seek out a person from the general public[43].

42 The Mishnah seems to indicate that immediately after being informed of the impurity, the *nezirim* bring the sacrifices. This impression is rectified here; the first set of sacrifices is due only if both have satisfied the terms of their original vows.

43 The *nazir* who is not impure without a doubt observes the rules (either following R. Yose or Ben Zoma) for a person possibly impure whose companion *nazir* has died (Mishnaiot 2-4).

(57a line 36) שָׁתָה יַיִן בְּתוֹךְ ל יוֹם הָרִאשׁוֹנִים אֵינוֹ לוֹקֶה. בְּתוֹךְ ל יוֹם הָאַחֲרוֹנִים לוֹקֶה. הַבָּא מִן הַשׁוּק אֵינוֹ לוֹקֶה לֹא עַל הַשְּׁנַיִים וְלֹא עַל הָאַחֲרוֹנִים. עַד כְּדוֹן בְּשֶׁהִתְרוּ בוֹ עַל זֶה בִּפְנֵי עַצְמוֹ וְעַל זֶה בִּפְנֵי עַצְמוֹ. הִתְרוּ בוֹ עַל שְׁנֵיהֶן כְּאֶחָד. פְּלוּגְתָּא דְרִבִּי יוֹחָנָן וְרִבִּי שִׁמְעוֹן בֶּן לָקִישׁ. דְּאִיתְפַּלְגוֹן בִּשְׁנֵי יָמִים טוֹבִים שֶׁלַּגָּלֻיּוֹת. רִבִּי יוֹחָנָן אָמַר. מְקַבְּלִין הַתְרָיָיה עַל סָפֵק. רִבִּי שִׁמְעוֹן בֶּן לָקִישׁ אָמַר. אֵין מְקַבְּלִין הַתְרָיָיה עַל סָפֵק.

If he drank wine within the first 30 days, he is (not) whipped; within the last 30 days, he is [] whipped[44]. The one coming from the general population cannot be whipped, either for the (second) or the last period[45]. So far, if he was warned separately for each period[46]. If they warned him for both together[47] this is the disagreement[48] between Rebbi Johanan and Rebbi Simeon ben Laqish who disagreed about the two days of holiday in the diaspora[49]. Rebbi Johanan said, one accepts warning in case of a doubt; Rebbi Simeon ben Laqish said, one does not accept warning in case of a doubt[50].

44 Here begins the discussion of Mishaniot 2 ff. The scribe (or the text he copied from) switched the places of "whipped" and "not whipped". If one of the *nezirim* died, the other certainly has to finish the period of his vow and then has to start a second period because he might have been impure and the *nezirut* of part of his first period might have been invalid. Since the first period was in fulfillment of his vow of *nazir*, any transgression is prosecutable. But since he keeps the second period only because of a doubt,

even if there are two witnesses both to his vow of *nazir* and to his drinking wine, a prosecutor could not prove that a crime certainly had been commited. Nobody can be found guilty by a human court if the crime was not proven.

45   Since his *nezirut* in both periods is conditional, the certainty of his crime is not provable.

46   Even if the crime was proven, a conviction is possible only if criminal intent was proven by two witnesses who testify that the perpetrator was warned of the criminality of his undertaking; cf. *Kilaim* 8:1, Note 9.

47   It is clear that either the first or the second period of *nezirut* are in fulfillment of his vow, even if it is not known which period counts in biblical law. If the *nazir* was warned for both during his first period after it was determined that he had to keep a second period, and he drank wine during both periods, the fact of the crime has been established. (The separate problem, that the accused might have forgotten the warning if it preceded the action by a long time, is not considered here.)

48   פלוגתא is the Babylonian form for Galilean חפלוגתא.

49   Before the publication of the computed calendar, communities which could not be informed by messengers about the determination of the first days of the months of Nisan and Tishri, kept two days of holidays to account for possible variations in the dates. Since each day was only one of a possible two, no work on the holidays could be prosecutable unless the warning was given for both days, the infraction occured on both days, and this kind of long-term conditional warning was accepted in court. [After the publication of the calendar computations, the first day of a holiday is of biblical character; the second day is of purely rabbinic character and is kept only because the algorithm was published on condition that its users continue to keep the second day (*Eruvin* 3:10 21c l. 24; Babli *Beṣah* 4b).]

50   *Yebamot* 11:7 (Note 171), *Pesaḥim* 5:4 (32s l. 5); Babli *Makkot* 16a.

(57a line 41) נָזַרְתִּי וְאֵינִי יוֹדֵעַ מַה נָזַרְתִּי אִם לְעַכְשָׁיו אִם לְאַחַר זְמָן. אָמְרוּ לוֹ. זוֹ לְעַכְשָׁיו וְזוֹ לְאַחַר זְמָן. שָׁתָה יַיִן בְּתוֹךְ ל׳ יוֹם הָרִאשׁוֹנִים לוֹקֶה. בְּתוֹךְ ל׳ יוֹם הָאַחֲרוֹנִים אֵינוֹ לוֹקֶה. וְחָשׁ לוֹמַר שֶׁמָּא הָרִאשׁוֹנִים בְּתוֹךְ נְזִירוּתוֹ וְהָאַחֲרוֹנִים

לְאַחַר נְזִירוּתוֹ. כָּל יְמֵי נִזְרוֹ. לַעֲשׂוֹת יָמִים שֶׁלְּאַחַר מְלֹאת כִּבְתוֹךְ מְלֹאת לְיַיִן לְטוּמְאָה וּלְתִגְלַחַת.

"I made a vow of *nazir* but I forgot whether it was for now or for a later date[51]." They told him, this [warning] is for now, and that for the later date. If he drank wine within the first 30 days, he is [] whipped; within the last 30 days, he is (not) whipped[52]. Should one not say that the first days may be within the period of his vow, the later ones are after the period of his vow[53]? "All days of his status as *nazir*,[54]" to make the days after he finished his term like the days before he finished his term with respect to wine, impurity, and shaving.

51   From the context it seems that he vowed a standard 30 day *nezirut* but does not remember whether it was to begin immediately or after 30 days. Then he has to keep 60 days and bring one set of sacrifices after 60 days.

52   Here again, the statements are switched. He cannot be convicted during the first 30 days since it cannot be proven that he is obligated during these days.

53   How can he be convicted for drinking wine during the second 30 days when it cannot be proven that these were intended by his vow (unless he drank during both periods)?

54   *Num.* 6:4. As spelled out in v. 20, the *nazir* is forbidden to drink wine until he has brought his sacrifices. Since he did not bring sacrifices after the first 30 days, during the second 30 days he certainly is guilty, either because of his vow of the second 30 days or as an extension of his vow of the first 30 days for which the sacrifice was not yet offered.

(57a line 46) וְיָבִיא קָרְבְּנוֹתָיו חֲצָיִים. שֶׁלֹּא תִנְעוֹל תְּשׁוּבָה מִבֵּית הַוַּעַד.

Why can he not bring his sacrifices one by one? Not to preclude answers in the house of study[55].

55   This refers to the objection R. Joshua voiced to the method proposed by Ben Zoma. There is no reason why the sacrifices could not be brought at different times; R. Joshua offered his objection as a training exercise to his

students, lest they accept any statement without subjecting it to criticism and also that they should not be afraid to propose hypothetical answers which could be disproved by analysis.

(57a line 47) צִיבּוּר שֶׁנִּיטְמָא בִּסְפֵק רְשׁוּת הַיָּחִיד בַּפֶּסַח. רִבִּי הוֹשַׁעְיָה אָמַר. יִדְחֶה לַפֶּסַח שֵׁינִי. רִבִּי יוֹחָנָן אָמַר. מְשַׁלְּחִין אוֹתוֹ דֶּרֶךְ רְחוֹקָה. וְאַתְיָיא כַּיי דְּאָמַר רִבִּי יוֹחָנָן. גִּיטְמָא טוּמְאַת הַתְּהוֹם מְשַׁלְּחִין אוֹתוֹ דֶּרֶךְ רְחוֹקָה. נָזִיר שֶׁנִּיטְמָא בִּסְפֵק רְשׁוּת הַיָּחִיד בַּפֶּסַח. רִבִּי יוֹחָנָן אָמַר. יֵעָשֶׂה כִסְפֵיקָן. וְרִבִּי הוֹשַׁעְיָה אָמַר. יֵעָשֶׂה בְטוּמְאָה. אַף רִבִּי הוֹשַׁעְיָה רַבָּה מוֹדֵי שֶׁיַּעֲשׂוּ בִּסְפֵיקָן. לֹא אָמַר רִבִּי הוֹשַׁעְיָה אֶלָּא לְחוּמְרִין.

[56](The community) [A person] who became impure by a doubt relating to a private domain[57] on Passover[58]. Rebbi Hoshaia said, he should be pushed to the Second Passover[59]. Rebbi Johanan said, one sends him on a far journey[60]. This follows what Rebbi Johanan said, if he became impure by the impurity of the abyss[61], one sends him on a far journey. (A *nazir*) [The community] who became impure by a doubt relating to a private domain on Passover[62]. Rebbi Johanan said, it should be presented in their doubt; Rebbi Hoshaia said, it should be made in impurity[63]. The great Rebbi Hoshaia also agrees that it should be presented in their doubt; what Rebbi Hoshaia said referrred only to restrictions.

56 This paragraph presents textual difficulties. Since the following paragraph makes sense only in *Pesaḥim* 8:8, the present paragraph also must be parallel *Pesaḥim* 8:8 (36b l. 43 ff.) But the text there is quite different from the text here; they are not versions of a common original. In the text, the words "the community" and "a (single) person" have switched places. In *Pesaḥim*, different questions are asked, and the comparison is between "the community" and "a *nazir*", which would make better sense here.

57 It is a general principle that doubts about impurity are resolved by treating doubts in a private domain as certain impurity, in a public domain as certain purity (cf. *Soṭah* 1:2, Note 88). The rule becomes ineffective if the

doubt arises in a domain whose status is in doubt.

58   The 14th of Nisan, the day on which the *Pesaḥ* sacrifice has to be slaughtered in the afternoon.

59   The 14th of Iyyar, instituted for someone who either was impure or "on a far journey" on the 14th of Nisan (*Num.* 9:9-14). R. Hoshaia treats him as certainly impure; he can stay near the Temple precinct and nevertheless celebrate the "Second Passover".

60   For R. Joḥanan the case remains one of doubt. If he stayed near the Temple precinct, he could celebrate neither the first (not being pure) nor the second (not being impure) Passover. Therefore, one sends him away so he can celebrate the Second Passover under a different qualification.

61   In *Pesaḥim*, this is called "the impurity of a broken field" (cf. Mishnah 7:3, Note 138); it applies to all impurities rabbinic in character. If the person incurs the impurity during the 14th of Nisan, he cannot offer the First Passover because he becomes pure after immersion in a *miqweh* only at sundown. He cannot offer the Second Passover because he was not biblically impure on the 14th of Nisan. He has to leave Jerusalem to be sufficiently "far away" in the afternoon of the 14th of Nisan.

62   The Second Passover was instituted only for individuals; if the majority of the people were impure, the Passover sacrifice was offered in impurity (Mishnah *Pesaḥim* 7:4,6).

63   Since the community offers the First Passover in impurity, the difference between the two opinions is only that for R. Joḥanan the pure minority offers its sacrifices in purity whereas it seems that for R. Hoshaia the minority is obligated to follow the majority. This interpretation is rejected in the next sentence so that there remains no material difference between the two statements.

(57a line 52) רִבִּי יוֹחָנָן אָמַר בְּשֵׁם רִבִּי בְּנָיָיה. יִשְׂרָאֵל עָרֵל מַזִּין עָלָיו. שֶׁכֵּן מָצִינוּ שֶׁקִּיבְּלוּ אֲבוֹתֵינוּ בַּמִּדְבָּר הַזָּיַית עֲרֵלִים. אָמַר רַב חִסְדָּא. אַתְיָיא כְּמַאן דְּאָמַר. בִּיאָ מָלוּ. בְּרַם כְּמַאן דְּאָמַר. בַּעֲשִׂירִי מָלוּ. לֹא מָנוּ הַזָּיַית עֲרֵלִים. אָמַר רִבִּי אָבִין. מִכָּל־מָקוֹם לֹא מָנוּ הַזָּיַית עֲרֵלִים. רִבִּי אֶלְעָזָר בְּשֵׁם רִבִּי חֲנִינָה. מַעֲשָׂה בְּכֹהֵן עָרֵל שֶׁהוּזָּה וְהוּכְשְׁרוּ הַזָּיוֹתָיו. תַּנֵּי. רִבִּי אֱלִיעֶזֶר בֶּן יַעֲקֹב אוֹמֵר. אִיסְטְרָטִיּוֹת וְשׁוֹמְרֵי צִירִים הָיוּ בִּירוּשָׁלַיִם וְטָבְלוּ וְאָכְלוּ פִּסְחֵיהֶם לָעֶרֶב.

1 אמר | - | 2 מצינו | מצאנו הזיית | הזייה אתייא | אתיא 3 ביא | באחד עשר
מנו | קיבלו הזיית | הזייה 4 אבין | אבון הזיית | להזייה אלעזר | לעזר 5
שהוזה | שהיזה תני | וכן תני 6 איסטרטיות | איסרטיוטות ישומרי צירים | היו
שומרין צירין פסחיהם | פסחיהון

[64]Rebbi Joḥanan in the name of Rebbi Benaiah: One sprinkles on an uncircumcised Jew[65], for we find that our forefathers in the desert[66] received sprinkling when uncircumcised. Rav Ḥisda said, following him who said that they circumcised on the eleventh[67]. But for him who said that they circumcised on the tenth, they did not count sprinkling when uncircumcised. Rebbi Abin said, did they not have to count for sprinkling when uncircumcised in any case[68]? Rebbi Eleazar in the name of Rebbi Ḥanina: It happened that an uncircumcised Cohen was sprinkled[69] and the sprinklings were declared valid. It was stated: Rebbi Eliezer ben Jacob says, there were soldiers[70] and gate keepers in Jerusalem who immersed themselves and ate their Passover sacrifices in the evening[71].

64   The parallel text is in *Pesaḥim* 8:8 (36b, l. 55ff.) It belongs there and has no direct connections with the topics discussed here. A parallel discussion is in the Babli, *Yebamot* 71b.

65   The person impure by the impurity of the dead has to be sprinkled with water containing ashes of the Red Cow on the third and the seventh day of his impurity (*Num.* 19). The uncircumcised is barred from the Passover sacrifice (*Ex.* 12:48). It is asserted that the uncircumcised can purify himself from the impurity and, being circumcised later, participate in the Passover celebration.

66   Not in the desert, but after crossing the Jordan on the 10th of Nisan (*Jos.* 4:19). They were then circumcised (*Jos.* 5:2-8) and celebrated Passover on the 14th (*Jos.* 5:10).

67   If they were circumcised on the 11th they had to be sprinkled on the 10th, when they still were uncircumcised, in order to become pure on the 14th.

68   Rav Ḥisda's argument has to be rejected since if sprinkling on an uncircumcised person is ineffective, the underlying counting (of the third,

seventh days) also must be ineffective. But for the Passover on the 14th, the counting had to start on the 7th, when according to the biblical text everybody (except Joshua, Caleb, and possibly Levites and/or Priests) were uncircumcised. He will hold that the first Passover in Canaan was held in impurity. This argument, represented in the Babli, *loc. cit.*, by Mar Zuṭra, there is rejected by Rav Ashi.

69   In *Pesaḥim*: "he sprinkled" (active verb form).

70   Greek στρατιώτης.

71   They were Gentiles who converted to Judaism, were circumcised on the 14th of Nisan, immersed themselves in a *miqweh* and participated in Passover, not needing cleansing by sprinkling following the House of Shammai (Mishnah *Pesaḥim* 8:8).

משנה ו: נָזִיר שֶׁהָיָה טָמֵא בְּסָפֵק וּמוּחְלָט בְּסָפֵק וּמוּחְלָט אוֹכֵל בַּקֳּדָשִׁים אַחַר (fol. 56d) שִׁשִּׁים יוֹם. וְשׁוֹתֶה בַּיַּיִן וּמִיטַּמֵּא לַמֵּתִים אַחַר מֵאָה וְעֶשְׂרִים יוֹם שֶׁתִּגְלַחַת הַנֶּגַע דּוֹחָא תִגְלַחַת הַנָּזִיר בִּזְמַן שֶׁהִיא וַדַּאי אֲבָל בִּזְמַן שֶׁהִיא סָפֵק אֵינָהּ דּוֹחָה.

Mishnah 6: A *nazir* who was doubtfully impure and doubtfully definitely [suffering from skin disease][72] may eat sacrificial meat after 60 days[73] and drink wine and become impure by the dead after 120 days[74], since the shaving for skin disease supersedes the shaving of the *nazir* when it is certain, but when it is in doubt it does not supersede.

72   A person who has completed the 30 days of his *nazir* vow but is not sure whether or not he became impure from the impurity of the dead in his period of *nezirut*. Also, he was recently healed from skin disease. The sufferer from skin disease is called "definitively suffering from the disease" only if the conditions for impurity apply and he was declared impure *by a Cohen* (*Lev.* 13:8,11,20,22,25,27,30,44). A definitively suffering person has to be cleansed by the ritual of *Lev.* 14:1-32 which includes repeated shavings of all his hair. In the case treated in the Mishnah, the person was in a group where one was declared definitively

affected, but the Cohen does not remember whom in particular he declared impure.

73   After he was healed from skin disease, purified from his impurity, and has completed the 30 days of his vow, he shaves the first time for his rehabilitation from skin disease. He cannot do it before he has completed the 30 days since he might be a pure *nazir* for whom it is forbidden to shave for a possible impurity of skin disease, as explained at the end of the Mishnah. He then should count seven days and shave a second time, but he cannot do that since he might have been impure and the shaving was not for his skin disease but for his impurity. Therefore, he can shave a second time and finish his purification from skin disease after an additional *nazir* period

of 30 days; then he is able to partake of sacrificial meat.

74   He cannot drink wine after 60 days since he might have been definitively sick but pure from the impurity of the dead; the period of his impurity as a sufferer from skin disease is not counted for his *nezirut* (Halakhah 7:3), which he has to keep for another 30 days. He cannot drink wine after 90 days since he might have been both definitively sick and impure from the impurity of the dead; his three shavings take care of the impurities both of skin disease and of the impure *nazir*; he has satisfied his obligations after 120 days and four shavings. The details of the required procedures and sacrifices are explained in the Halakhah.

(57a line 57) **הלכה ב:** אֵי זֶהוּ מוּחְלָט מִסָּפֵק. שְׁנַיִם שֶׁבָּאוּ אֶצְלוֹ וְהֶחֱלִיט אֶת אֶחָד מֵהֶן וְלֹא הִסְפִּיק לְהַחֲלִיט אֶת הַשֵּׁינִי עַד שֶׁנֶּחְלְפוּ לוֹ. זֶהוּ מוּחְלָט בְּסָפֵק. הֲדָא הִיא דְתַנֵּי רִבִּי חִיָּיה. סְפֵק נָזִיר טָמֵא סְפֵק נָזִיר טָהוֹר אָבָל נָזִיר וַדַּאי הָיָה. סְפֵק מְצוֹרָע טָמֵא סְפֵק מְצוֹרָע טָהוֹר אָבָל מְצוֹרָע וַדַּאי הָיָה. אוֹכֵל בַּקֳּדָשִׁים אַחַר ט' יוֹם. וְשׁוֹתֶה יַיִן וּמִיטַּמֵּא לַמֵּתִים אַחַר ק' כ' יָמִים. כֵּיצַד. אָמְרוּ לוֹ. נָזִיר טָמֵא אַתָּה. צֵא וּמְנֵה שִׁבְעָה וְהַזֶּה וְשָׁנָה וְגִילַּח וְהֵבִיא. מָנָה שִׁבְעָה וְרָצָה לְגַלֵּחַ. אָמְרוּ לוֹ. נָזִיר טָמֵא. צֵא וּמְנֵה שִׁבְעָה וְהַשְׁלִימָן לִשְׁלֹשִׁים. מָנָה שְׁלֹשִׁים וְרָצָה לְגַלֵּחַ. אָמְרוּ לוֹ. נָזִיר טָהוֹר אַתָּה. וְאֵין נָזִיר טָהוֹר מְגַלֵּחַ עַל מִינֵי דָמִים. הֲרֵי זֶה מֵבִיא עוֹלָה וּמְגַלֵּחַ עָלֶיהָ. חַטַּאת הָעוֹף וּמַתְנֶה עָלֶיהָ. וְאוֹמֵר. אִם טָמֵא הָיִיתִי. הַחַטָּאת מֵחוֹבָתִי וְהָעוֹלָה נְדָבָה. אִם טָהוֹר. הָעוֹלָה

מְחוֹבָתִי וְהַחַטָּאת סָפֵק. מְגַלֵּחַ אֶת רֹאשׁוֹ וְאֶת זְקָנָיו וְאֶת גַּבּוֹת עֵינָיו כְּדֶרֶךְ שֶׁמְצוֹרָע מְגַלֵּחַ.

Halakhah 2: Who is doubtfully definitely [suffering]? Two who came to him[75]. He declared one of them definitively affected but before he could declare the second one definitively affected, they were changed for him[76]. That is a doubtfully definitely [suffering person]. This is the one about whom Rebbi Ḥiyya stated[77]: A *nazir*, in doubt whether impure or pure, but certainly he was a *nazir*. A sufferer from skin disease, in doubt whether impure or pure, but certainly he was a sufferer from skin disease. He eats from sacrificial meat after 60 days, drinks wine and defiles himself for the dead after 120 days. How is that? One said to him, you are an impure *nazir*, go count seven [days]. He sprinkled, repeated, shaved, and brought[78]. He then counted seven [days] and wanted to shave. One said to him, impure *nazir*, go count seven [days] and continue for 30. He counted 30 [days] and wanted to shave. One said to him, you are a pure *nazir*; does not a pure *nazir* shave on kinds of blood[79]? He brings an elevation offering and shaves on it, a bird purification offering and stipulates, saying: "If I was impure, the purification offering is my obligation and the elevation offering is voluntary. If I was pure, the elevation offering is my obligation and the purification offering is in doubt.'" He shaves his head, his beard, and his eyebrows in the way the sufferer from skin disease shaves[80].

75 To a Cohen knowledgeable in the diagnosis of skin disease.

76 Since he does no longer recognize them, he cannot declare the second one definitively impure, even though he realizes that both of them satisfy all criteria of impurity, since the Cohen may not see two cases together (Mishnah *Nega'im* 3:1), and by now both are healed (cf. S. Lieberman, *Tosefta kiFshutah Nezirut* p. 563.)

77 Tosephta *Nazir* 6:1. (Cf.

Tosaphot *Zebaḥim* 76a, *Menaḥot* 105a, *Niddah* 70a, all s.v. למחרת.)

78 The offerings of two birds required from the impure *nazir*. The sentence can also be interpreted as imperative: Go count seven [days], sprinkle, repeat (on day 7), shave (on day 7), and bring! The Erfurt text of the Tosephta is self-contradictory; it is partially vocalized חַיזֶה ושנה וגילח, the consonantal text is in the imperfect, the punctuation in the imperative.

79 He cannot shave without an appropriate sacrifice. In the Tosephta, the sentence is declarative: וְאֵין נָזִיר טָהוֹר מְגַלֵּחַ אֶלָּא עַל הַדָּמִים "a pure *nazir* shaves only on a bloody sacrifice".

80 Lev. 14:9.

(57a line 69) **הלכה ג:** כֵּיצַד עוֹשִׂין לוֹ לְהַחֲמִיר. מֵבִיא שְׁתֵּי צִיפּוֹרֵי דְרוֹר. שׁוֹחֵט אֶחָד מֵהֶן עַל כְּלִי חֶרֶשׂ עַל מַיִם חַיִּים. חוֹפֵר וְקוֹבְרָהּ בְּפָנָיו וְאָסוּרָה בַהֲנָיָיה. וְגִילַח רֹאשׁוֹ וּזְקָנוֹ וְגַבּוֹת עֵינָיו כְּדֶרֶךְ שֶׁמְּצוֹרָעִין מְגַלְּחִין אוֹתָהּ. וּמוֹנִין שְׁלֹשִׁים יוֹם וּמֵבִיא עוֹלַת בְּהֵמָה אַחֶרֶת וּמַתְנֶה עָלֶיהָ וְאוֹמֵר. וְאִם טָמֵא הָיִיתִי הָעוֹלָה הָרִאשׁוֹנָה נְדָבָה אוֹ חוֹבָה וְהַחַטָּאת מְחוֹבָתִי. אִם טָהוֹר הָיִיתִי הָעוֹלָה הָרִאשׁוֹנָה חוֹבָה אוֹ נְדָבָה וְהַחַטָּאת סָפֵק. מְגַלֵּחַ רֹאשׁוֹ וּזְקָנוֹ וְגַבּוֹת עֵינָיו כְּדֶרֶךְ שֶׁמְּצוֹרָע מְגַלֵּחַ.

Halakhah 3: [77]How does one deal with him in a restrictive way? He brings two swallows and slaughters one of them over a clay vessel filled from running water; one digs und buries it, for it is forbidden for usufruct[81]. He shaves his head, beard, and eyebrows in the way the sufferers from skin disease do. He counts 30 days and brings another animal as elevation offering, saying: "If I was impure, the first elevation offering was voluntary and this one[82] is obligatory, and the purification offering is my obligation. If I was pure, the first elevation offering was my obligation, this one[82] is voluntary, and the purification offering is in doubt.[7]" He shaves his head, his beard, and his eyebrows in the way the sufferer from skin disease shaves[80].

81 Mishnah *Nega'im* 14:1 (*Lev.* 14:4-5).

82 This translation follows the Tosephta text. In ms. and *editio princeps* at both places אוֹ "or" instead of וְזֶה "and this one".

(57a line 75) **הלכה ד:** רַבִּי שִׁמְעוֹן אוֹמֵר. לְמָחֳרָת הוּא מֵבִיא אֲשָׁמוֹ וְלוֹג שֶׁמֶן עַל גַּבָּיו וּמַתָּנָה עָלָיו וְאוֹמֵר. אִם טָמֵא הָיִיתִי הֲרֵי הִיא חוֹבָתִי וְאִם לָאו הֲרֵי הוּא סְפֵיקִי. וְיִשְׁחוֹט בַּצָּפוֹן וְטָעוּן מַתַּן בְּהוֹנוֹת וְנֶאֱכַל לְזִכְרֵי כְהוּנָה בְּכָל־מָקוֹם לְיוֹם וָלַיְלָה עַד חֲצוֹת. אֲבָל חֲכָמִים הוֹדוּ לְרַבִּי שִׁמְעוֹן שֶׁהוּא מֵבִיא אֶת הַקֳּדָשִׁים לְבֵית הַפְּסוּל.

Halakhah 4: [757]Rebbi Simeon said: On the next day[83], he brings his reparation sacrifice[84] and a *log*[85] of oil with it and says: If I was impure, this is my obligatory offering, otherwise it is my doubtful offering[86]. He slaughters in the North[87], it needs giving on the thumbs[88], and it is eaten by male Cohanim at any place[89] during the day and the following night until midnight. But the Sages did [not][90] agree with Rebbi Simeon because he causes sacrifices to become invalid[91].

83 As required in the purification ritual for the sufferer from skin disease, *Lev.* 14:10.

84 The healed person has to bring three sacrifices (*Lev.* 14:10,21-22), but only the sheep as reparation sacrifice is needed in the purification ceremony.

85 A *log* is .533 l.

84 This text cannot be accepted; it makes no sense and contradicts the last statement in the Halakhah. The text should be replaced by the corresponding one in the Tosephta: וְאִם לָאו הֲרֵי זֶה שַׁלְמֵי נְדָבָה "otherwise, it should be a voluntary well-being offering". It is impossible to bring a reparation offering except for an obligation but a well-being offering is voluntary in almost all cases.

87 Since a reparation offering is "most holy", it must be slaughtered to the North of the altar (*Lev.* 7:2). The Tosephta adds that the sacrifice also needs the obligatory gifts accompanying a well-being offering.

88 Blood of the sacrifice and oil from the flask have to be put on the convalescent's right earlobe, right thumb, and right great toe (*Lev.* 14:14,17).

89 Any place within the Temple precinct; *Lev.* 7:6, Mishnah *Zebaḥim* 5:5).

90 Text of the Tosephta, required by the context.

91 Well-being sacrifices may be eaten by all pure Israelites for two days and the intervening night, reparation sacrifices only by priests and only for a day and half a night. There is a likelyhood that some of the meat of the reparation sacrifice will become invalid after midnight; it has to be burned outside the Temple precinct. This is an alienation from the original purpose and has to be avoided.

(57b line 4) **הלכה ה:** הֵבִיא חַטָּאת בְּהֵמָה אֵינוֹ יָכוֹל שֶׁאֵין לוֹ חַטָּאת בְּהֵמָה. חַטָּאת הָעוֹף אֵינוֹ יָכוֹל שֶׁהֲרֵי עָשִׁיר שֶׁהֵבִיא קָרְבָּן עָנִי לֹא יָצָא. כֵּיצַד יַעֲשֶׂה. יִכְתּוֹב נְכָסָיו לְאַחֵר וְיָבִיא קָרְבָּן עָנִי. נִמְצָא עָשִׁיר מֵבִיא חַטָּאת עוֹף. וּמַתְנֶה עָלֶיהָ וְאוֹמֵר. אִם טָמֵא הָיִיתִי הֲרֵי הִיא חוֹבָתִי. וְאִם לָאו הֲרֵי הוּא סָפֵק.

Halakhah 5: [77]He cannot bring an animal as purification sacrifice since he does not have the right to an animal purification sacrifice[92]. He cannot bring a bird as purification sacrifice[93] since a rich person who brought the sacrifices prescribed for a poor person did not fulfill his obligation[94]. What can he do? He shall write his property over to another person[95] and bring the sacrifices prescribed for a poor person; this enables the rich person to bring a bird as a purification sacrifice. He stipulates and says: If I was impure, that is my obligation. Otherwise, this is in doubt[7].

92 The Tosephta is more explicit: "Because an animal purification sacrifice cannot be offered in case of doubt."

93 The offering of the poor person healed from skin disease, *Lev.* 14:22.

94 Mishnah *Nega'im* 14:12.

95 Then he is poor.

הלכה ו: (57b line 9) אוֹכֵל בַּקֳּדָשִׁים מִיָּד. לִשְׁתּוֹת יַיִן וְלִיטַּמֵּא לַמֵּתִים אֵינוֹ יָכוֹל. שֶׁאֵין נְזִירוּתוֹ עוֹלָה לוֹ מִתּוֹךְ צָרַעְתּוֹ.

Halakhah 6: [77]He may eat sacrificial meat immediately. He cannot drink wine or defile himself for the dead since his *nezirut* is not counted during the days of his [impurity of] skin disease[74].

הלכה ז: מוֹנֶה שְׁלֹשִׁים יוֹם וּמֵבִיא קָרְבְּנוֹתָיו שְׁלָמִין וּמַתְנָה עֲלֵיהֶן וְאוֹמֵר. אִם טָמֵא הָיִיתִי הָעוֹלָה הָרִאשׁוֹנָה חוֹבָה וְזוֹ נְדָבָה. וְאִם טָהוֹר הָיִיתִי הָעוֹלָה הָרִאשׁוֹנָה נְדָבָה וְזוֹ חוֹבָה. וְהַחַטָּאת סָפֵק. וּמְגַלֵּחַ רֹאשׁוֹ וּזְקָנוֹ וְגַבּוֹת עֵינָיו כול'.

Halakhah 7: He counts another 30 days and brings all his sacrifices, stipulates, and says: If I was impure, the first elevation offering was obligatory and this one is voluntary. But if I was pure, the first elevation offering was voluntary and this one is obligatory. The purification offering is in doubt. He shaves his head, beard, and eyebrows, etc.[96].

96 It is difficult to make sense of this text (which has no parallel in the Tosephta). The last sentence is certainly out of place since the ceremonies at the end of 60 days disposed of all possible impurities of the sufferer from skin disease. He cannot bring the entire set of sacrifices of the pure *nazir* before 120 days, as explained in Note 74. In addition, since an impure *nazir* has to bring a bird as elevation offering, rather than a four-legged animal, it is clear that after 120 days the declaration must read: "If I was impure, the first elevation offering *was voluntary and this one is obligatory*. But if I was pure, the first elevation offering *was obligatory and this one is voluntary*." It seems that a paragraph is missing, describing the offering after 90 days (which is parallel to the one after 30 days for the person who might have been impure by the impurity of the dead, Mishnah 3) and that the duly corrected present paragraph describes the sacrifices after 120 days.

(57b line 14) **הלכה ח:** כֵּיצַד עוֹשִׂין לוֹ כְּדִבְרֵי בֶן זוֹמָא. הֲרֵי זֶה מֵבִיא עוֹלַת בְּהֵמָה וּמְגַלֵּחַ עָלֶיהָ חַטָּאת הָעוֹף וּמַתְנֶה עָלֶיהָ וְאוֹמֵר. אִם טָמֵא הָיִיתִי הַחַטָּאת מֵחוֹבָתִי וְהָעוֹלָה נְדָבָה. אִם טָהוֹר הָיִיתִי הָעוֹלָה מֵחוֹבָתִי וְחַטָּאת סָפֵק. מְגַלֵּחַ עָלֶיהָ רֹאשׁוֹ וּזְקָנוֹ וְגַבּוֹת עֵינָיו כול'.

הלכה ט: שׁוֹתֶה יַיִן וּמִיטַּמֵּא לַמֵּתִים מִיָּד. בַּמֶּה דְבָרִים אֲמוּרִים. בִּזְמַן שֶׁנָּזַר מִתּוֹךְ יְמֵי נְזִירוּתוֹ. אֲבָל אִם נָזַר מִתּוֹךְ יְמֵי צָרַעְתּוֹ אוֹכֵל בַּקֳּדָשִׁים אֲפִילוּ לְאַחַר שְׁתֵּי שָׁנִים. שׁוֹתֶה בַיַּיִן וּמִיטַּמֵּא לַמֵּתִים אַחַר ד' שָׁנִים.

Halakhah 8: [97]How does one treat him according to Ben Zoma? He brings an animal elevation offering and shaves for it, a bird as purification offering, stipulates, and says: "If I was impure, the purification offering is for my obligation and the elevation offering is voluntary. If I was pure, the elevation offering is for my obligation and the purification offering is in doubt." He shaves his head, beard, and eyebrows, etc.[98]

Halakhah 9: He may drink wine and defile himself for the dead immediately[99]. When has this been said? If he made the vow of *nazir* as a *nazir*, but if he made the vow of *nazir* as a sufferer from skin disease he might eat sacrificial meat after two years, drink wine, and defile himself for the dead after four years[97,99].

97 This text is hopelessly garbled. It seems that the original text was close to the Tosephta:

כֵּיצַד תַּעֲשֶׂה לוֹ כְּדִבְרֵי בֶן זוֹמָא. סוֹפֵר שְׁלֹשִׁים יוֹם וּמֵבִיא עוֹלַת בְּהֵמָה וּמְגַלֵּחַ וּמֵבִיא חַטַּאת הָעוֹף וּמַתְנֶה עָלֶיהָ וְאוֹמֵר אִם טָמֵא אֲנִי חַטָּאת מֵחוֹבָתִי וְעוֹלָה נְדָבָה אִם טָהוֹר אֲנִי עוֹלָה מֵחוֹבָתִי וְחַטָּאת סָפֵק. וְסוֹפֵר שְׁלֹשִׁים יוֹם וּמֵבִיא קָרְבְּנוֹתָיו שְׁלָמִים וּמֵבִיא עוֹלַת בְּהֵמָה וּמַתְנֶה עָלֶיהָ וְאוֹמֵר אִם טָמֵא אֲנִי עוֹלָה הָרִאשׁוֹנָה חוֹבָה וְזוֹ נְדָבָה וְחַטַּאת הָעוֹף מֵחוֹבָתִי. אִם טָהוֹר אֲנִי עוֹלָה הָרִאשׁוֹנָה נְדָבָה וְזוֹ חוֹבָה וְחַטַּאת הָעוֹף סְפֵיקִי וְשׁוֹתֶה יַיִן וּמִטַּמֵּא לַמֵּתִים מִיָּד. בַּמֶּה דְבָרִים אֲמוּרִים בִּזְמַן שֶׁנָּזַר שְׁלֹשִׁים יוֹם אֲבָל נָזַר שְׁנֵים עָשָׂר חֹדֶשׁ אוֹכֵל בַּקֳּדָשִׁים לְאַחַר שְׁתֵּי שָׁנִים. וְשׁוֹתֶה יַיִן וּמִיטַּמֵּא לַמֵּתִים אַחַר אַרְבַּע שָׁנִים.

How does one treat him according to Ben Zoma[a]? He counts 30 days, brings an animal elevation offering and shaves[b], a bird as purification offering[c], stipulates, and says: "If I was impure, the purification offering is for my obligation and the elevation offering is voluntary. If I was pure, the elevation offering is for my obligation and the purification offering is in doubt." Then he counts 30 days, brings the completion of his sacrifices[d] and an animal elevation offering, stipulates, and says: [e]"If I was impure, the prior purification offering was voluntary, the present one is obligatory, and the bird purification offering is obligatory. If I was pure, the prior elevation offering was obligatory and the present one voluntary; the purification offering is in doubt." [f]He immediately drinks wine and defiles himself for the dead. When had this been said? If the vow of *nazir* was for 30 days. But if his vow was for 12 months, he eats sacrificial meat after two years, drinks wine, and defiles himself for the dead after four years.

[a] Ben Zoma disagrees with R. Simeon and holds that the healed sufferer from skin disease can cleanse himself by the bird purification sacrifice of the poor, without a reparation sacrifice. The Tosephta text also is defective, since Ben Zoma also agrees that complete purification is possible only after four periods. The original statement also must have contained four parts, not two as in the current text.

[b] As Tosaphot explains in *Zebaḥim* 76a, it is assumed that he already cleansed himself from the impurity of the dead by sprinkling. This shaving is valid if he was not impure from skin disease; it is useless if he was impure from skin disease since then it was not done in the correct framework and *nezirut* is not counted during his skin disease impurity.

[c] After another 30 days.

[d] The well-being offering of the pure *nazir*. He cannot bring the animal purification offering since this may not be offered in cases of doubt. Naturally, he also shaves for this sacrifice, and he has to stipulate that all sacrifices are either voluntary or in doubt in case he was already completely purified by the prior shavings

[e] This text is from the Vienna ms. and the *editio princeps*. The Erfurt ms. reads "If I was impure, the prior purification offering was *obligatory*, the present one is *voluntary*, and the bird purification offering is obligatory. If I was pure, the prior elevation offering was *voluntary* and the present one *obligatory*; the purification offering is in doubt." It seems that the two texts are not variations of one

another (which would make the Erfurt text obviously erroneous) but residues of two different paragraphs of the original four-part text.

f The forth period; its sacrifices and declarations are missing.

98 This sentence is out of place here.

99 There is a possibility that the original text underlying the Halakhah was not that of the Tosephta but referred to the situation mentioned by R. Ze'ira in the next Halakhah.

(57b line 21) **הלכה י:** אָמַר רִבִּי יוֹחָנָן. זוֹ דִּבְרֵי בֶּן זוֹמָא. אֲבָל דִּבְרֵי חֲכָמִים. לְעוֹלָם הוּא בַּחֲלִיטוֹ עַד שֶׁיָּנִיף הָאָשָׁם. רִבִּי יִרְמְיָה בָּעֵי. שֶׁיָּנִיף הָאדם יְהֵא זֶה בַּחֲלִיטוֹ. אָמַר לֵיהּ רִבִּי יוֹסֵי. לָמָּה לֹא. מָצִינוּ כַּמָּה אֲשָׁמוֹת דּוֹחִין מִפְּנֵי הַסְּפֵיקוֹת. דְּתַנִּינָן תַּמָּן. אָשָׁם שֶׁנִּתְעָרֵב בִּשְׁלָמִים. רִבִּי שִׁמְעוֹן אוֹמֵר. שְׁנֵיהֶם יִשָּׁחֲטוּ בַצָּפוֹן וְיֵאָכְלוּ כַחוֹמֶר שֶׁבָּהֶן. אָמְרוּ לוֹ. אֵין מְבִיאִין אֶת הַקֳּדָשִׁים לְבֵית הַפְּסוּל.

Halakhah 10: Rebbi Johanan said, these are Ben Zoma's words, but the words of the Sages: Forever is he definitively [impure] until he heave[100] the reparation sacrifice[101]. Rebbi Jeremiah asked: Why is he definitively [impure] until he heave the reparation sacrifice[102]? Rebbi Yose said to him, why not? We find several reparation sacrifices which are pushed aside because of doubts! As we have stated there[103]: "If a reparation sacrifice was mixed up with a well-being sacrifice, Rebbi Simeon says that both should be slaughtered in the North and eaten following the more restrictive rules. They said to him, one does not cause sacrifices to become invalid[91].

100 *Lev.* 14:12,24.

101 The entire purification of the convalescent from skin disease is by the blood of the reparation sacrifice and the olive oil; the other sacrifices are dependent on the reparation sacrifice; cf. Mishnah *Nega'im* 14:11.

102 This would imply that the *nazir* who may be impure from the dead and may be definitively impure from skin disease can never cleanse himself for sacrificial meat since R. Simeon's

approach was rejected. The purification of the convalescent in all other respects only depends on the ceremonies described in *Lev.* 14:1-9, which do not require any sacrifice (Mishnah *Nega'im* 14:3; Maimonides *Tum'at Ṣara'at* 11:2).

103 Mishnah *Zebaḥim* 8:3. The animals should be put out to graze until they develop a blemish, when they can be sold and the money used for new sacrifices. In the meantime, the owners of the sacrifices can fulfill their obligations only by offering substitute animals.

(57b line 26) רִבִּי יַעֲקֹב דְּרוֹמָיָא בְּעָא קוֹמֵי רִבִּי יוֹסֵי. וְיַעֲשׂוּ לוֹ תַקָּנָה לְיֵינוֹ. אָמַר לֵיהּ. וְגִלַּח הַנָּזִיר פֶּתַח אֹהֶל מוֹעֵד. הָרָאוּי לָבוֹא אֶל פֶּתַח אֹהֶל מוֹעֵד. יָצָא זֶה שֶׁאֵינוֹ רָאוּי לָבוֹא אֶל פֶּתַח אֹהֶל מוֹעֵד.

Rebbi Jacob the Southerner asked before Rebbi Yose: Could they not arrange something for his wine[104]? He said to him, "the *nazir* shaves at the gate of the Tent of Meeting[105];" if he is able to appear at the gate of the Tent of Meeting. This excludes him who is unable to appear at the gate of the Tent of Meeting.

104 Why does the *nazir* have to wait until the problems arising from the skin disease are resolved, which in the best case takes 2 periods of *nezirut* and in the worst forever? Why can he not shave twice within eight days to remove the impurity of skin disease (for profane purposes and heave) and then proceed directly to resolve the problem of *nezirut*?

105 *Num.* 6:18. The *nazir* cannot proceed to liquidate his vow as long as he is barred from holy places. (Cf. also Note 110).

(57b line 28) שְׂעָרוֹ מָהוּ. רִבִּי יַעֲקֹב בַּר אָחָא. אִיתְפַּלְגוּן רִבִּי יוֹחָנָן וְרִבִּי שִׁמְעוֹן בֶּן לָקִישׁ. רִבִּי יוֹחָנָן אָמַר. שְׂעָרוֹ אָסוּר. רִבִּי שִׁמְעוֹן בֶּן לָקִישׁ אָמַר. שְׂעָרוֹ מוּתָּר. רִבִּי זְעִירָה בָּעֵי. בִּמְצוֹרָע שֶׁנָּזַר פְּלִיגִין. אוֹ בְנָזִיר שֶׁנִּצְטָרַע פְּלִיגִין. אִין תֵּימַר. בִּמְצוֹרָע שֶׁנָּזַר פְּלִיגִין. הָא בְנָזִיר שֶׁנִּצְטָרַע דִּבְרֵי הַכֹּל הוּא אָסוּר. אִין תֵּימַר. בְּנָזִיר שֶׁנִּצְטָרַע פְּלִיגִין. הָא בִמְצוֹרָע שֶׁנָּזַר דִּבְרֵי הַכֹּל מוּתָּר. רִבִּי יִרְמְיָה פְּשִׁיטָא לֵיהּ בִּמְצוֹרָע שֶׁנָּזַר פְּלִיגִין. הָא בְנָזִיר שֶׁנִּצְטָרַע דִּבְרֵי הַכֹּל מוּתָּר.

What is the status of his hair[106]? Rebbi Jacob bar Aḥa: Rebbi Joḥanan and Rebbi Simeon ben Laqish disagreed. Rebbi Joḥanan said, his hair is forbidden; Rebbi Simeon ben Laqish said, his hair is permitted. Rebbi Zeʻira asked: Do they disagree about a sufferer from skin disease who made a vow of *nazir* or do they disagree about a *nazir* who became a sufferer from skin disease? If you say that they disagree about a sufferer from skin disease who made a vow of *nazir*, then for a *nazir* who became a sufferer from skin disease everybody agrees that it is forbidden[107]. If you say that they disagree about a *nazir* who became a sufferer from skin disease, then for a sufferer from skin disease who made a vow of *nazir* everybody agrees that it is permitted[108]. For Rebbi Jeremiah it was obvious that they disagreed about a sufferer from skin disease who made a vow of *nazir*. Therefore, for a *nazir* who became a sufferer from skin disease everybody agrees that it is permitted[109]

106   The shavings of a *nazir* are forbidden for usufruct; they must be burned within the Temple precinct (*Num.* 6:18). But nothing is prescribed for the shavings of the convalescent sufferer from skin disease; therefore, these are permitted for usufruct.

107   Since his hair was forbidden already before he contracted the disease.

108   Any shavings for his convalescence are subject to the rules of skin disease.

109   For consistency, one should read here: "forbidden."

(57b line 35) תִּגְלַחַת מִצְוָה מָהוּ שֶׁתִּדְחֶה לְתִגְלַחַת הָרְשׁוּת. נִישְׁמְעִינָהּ מִן הָדָא. וּמְגַלֵּחַ רֹאשׁוֹ וּזְקָנוֹ וְגַבּוֹת עֵינָיו כְּדֶרֶךְ שֶׁמְּצוֹרָעִין מְגַלְּחִין. וְחָשׁ לוֹמַר. שֶׁמָּא תִּגְלַחַת מִצְוָה הָיִיתָ. רִבִּי זְעִירָא בְּשֵׁם רִבִּי יוּדָן. מַתְנִיתָא אֲמָרָה כֵן. שֶׁרִבִּי שִׁמְעוֹן אוֹמֵר. כֵּיוָן שֶׁנִּזְרַק עָלָיו אֶחָד מִן הַדָּמִים הוּתַּר הַנָּזִיר לִשְׁתּוֹת יַיִן וְלִיטַּמֵּא לַמֵּתִים. וְאֵינוֹ אָסוּר אֶלָּא מִשּׁוּם בַּל תַּשְׁחֵת. שְׁמוּאֵל בַּר אַבָּא אֲמַר. תִּיפְתַּר בְּסָרִיס. וְהָא תַּגִּינָן זָקֵן. אִית לָךְ מֵימַר סָרִיס. לֵית לָךְ אֶלָּא כִּדְאָמַר

רִבִּי יַעֲקֹב בְּשֵׁם רִבִּי יוֹחָנָן. נְטָלָן מִלְמַטָּן לְמַעֲלָן אָסוּר. רִבִּי יוֹסֵי בַּר אָבִין אָמַר. לֹא שַׁנְיָיא. הִיא לְמַטָן לְמַעֲלָן הִיא לְמַעֲלָה לְמַטָן.

Does the obligatory shaving push aside the rules of voluntary shaving[110]? Let us hear from the following[111]: "He shaves his head, his beard, and his eyebrows in the way sufferers from skin disease shave." But there one could say, maybe it was an obligatory shaving. [112]Rebbi Ze'ira in the name of Rebbi Yudan: The Mishnah says so; "for Rebbi Simeon says, when one of the bloods was sprinkled, the *nazir* is permitted to drink wine and to defile himself with the dead." Is he not forbidden because of "do not destroy"? Samuel bar Abba[113] said, explain it if he was a eunuch[114]. But did we not state "the beard"? How can you say, a eunuch? You have only what Rebbi Jacob said in the name of Rebbi Johanan: If he removed it from bottom to top it is forbidden[115]. Rebbi Yose bar Abin said, there is no difference between bottom to top or top to bottom[116].

110 *Lev.* 19:27 forbids to "shear off the corners of your head and to destroy the corners of your beard." The *nazir* must shave his entire head, including its corners; the sufferer from skin disease must shave off all his hair, including corners of head and beard. There is no question that a person certainly impure, either from a corpse in the case of the *nazir*, or being declared impure as a sufferer from skin disease, must shave as required. The problem is only how far a shaving because of doubt really pushes aside the general rules about forbidden shaving.

111 Halakhah 4, speaking of a case of double doubt.

112 It seems that this text does not belong here. It belongs to the paragraph before the last (Notes 102, 103), where R. Ze'ira notes that the *nazir* cannot begin counting for his vow unless he is able to enter the Temple precinct. He brings an additional proof from Mishnah 6:11, which notes that permission to drink wine is given to the *nazir* if and only if one of his sacrifices was offered in the Temple, whether he shaved or not.

Therefore, his proceedings as *nazir* cannot be based on the shavings as a convalescent alone, disregarding his required sacrifice. There can be no shortcut.

113   It seems that reference is made not to R. Samuel bar Abba, the student of R. Joḥanan, but to Samuel (bar Abba bar Abba) the Babylonian who in the Babli, 57b, restricts the applicability of the rules of shavings to women and minors, to whom *Lev.* 19:27 does not apply.

114   Since we are speaking of a person who certainly had made a vow of *nazir*, there can be no question that he is entitled to shear "the corners of his head"; the only problem is to shave "the corners of his beard" when it is not clear that it is really required. If the person in question has no beard, there is no problem.

115   By implication it would not be forbidden if the head was shaved totally before the beard was.

116   The preceding statement is rejected. It follows that *Lev.* 19:27 forbids to "shear off the corners of your head and to destroy the corners of your beard" but not to shave off *all* hair on the head and *all* hair on the chin in case of need.

(57b line 43) טָמֵא בְסָפֵק מוּחְלָט וַדַּאי אוֹכֵל קֳדָשִׁים לְאַחַר שִׁשִּׁים יוֹם וְשׁוֹתֶה יַיִן וּמִיטַמֵּא לַמֵּתִים לְאַחַר מֵאָה וְעֶשְׂרִים יוֹם. טָמֵא וַדַּאי מוּחְלָט בְּסָפֵק אוֹכֵל בְּקֳדָשִׁים לְאַחַר עֶשְׂרִים יוֹם וְשׁוֹתֶה יַיִן וּמִיטַמֵּא לַמֵּתִים לְאַחַר מ"ד יוֹם. טָמֵא וַדַּאי מוּחְלָט וַדַּאי אוֹכֵל בְּקֳדָשִׁים לְאַחַר שְׁמוֹנַת יָמִים שׁוֹתֶה בַּיַּיִן וּמִיטַמֵּא לַמֵּתִים לְאַחַר מ"ד יוֹם.

[117]"If he was doubtfully impure and certainly definitely [suffering from skin disease], he eats from sacrificial meat after 60 days, drinks wine and defiles himself for the dead after 120 days. If he was certainly impure and doubtfully definitely [suffering from skin disease], he eats from sacrificial meat after 20 days, drinks wine and defiles himself for the dead after 44 days. If he was certainly impure and certainly definitely [suffering from skin disease], he eats from sacrificial meat after eight days, drinks wine and defiles himself for the dead after 44 days."

117   Tosephta 6:1, Babli 60b. The text as it stands here is mostly unintelligible; the correct numbers are given in Tosephta 6/Babli:

טָמֵא בְסָפֵק וּמוּחְלָט בְּוַדַּאי אוֹכֵל בַּקֳדָשִׁים לְאַחַר שְׁמוֹנָה יָמִים שׁוֹתֶה יַיִן וּמִיטַּמֵּא לַמֵּתִים לְאַחַר שִׁשִּׁים וְשִׁבְעָה יוֹם. טָמֵא בְוַדַּאי וּמוּחְלָט בְּסָפֵק אוֹכֵל בַּקֳדָשִׁים לְאַחַר שְׁלֹשִׁים וְשִׁבְעָה יוֹם שׁוֹתֶה יַיִן וּמִטַּמֵּא לַמֵּתִים לְאַחַר שִׁבְעִים וְאַרְבַּע יוֹם. טָמֵא בְוַדַּאי וּמוּחְלָט בְּוַדַּאי אוֹכֵל בַּקֳדָשִׁים לְאַחַר שְׁמוֹנָה יָמִים וְשׁוֹתֶה בַּיַּיִן וּמִיטַּמֵּא לְאַחַר אַרְבָּעִים וְאַרְבָּעָה יוֹם.

If he was doubtfully impure and certainly definitely [suffering from skin disease], he eats from sacrificial meat after *8 days*[a], drinks wine and defiles himself for the dead after *67 days*[b]. If he was certainly impure and doubtfully definitely [suffering from skin disease], he eats from sacrificial meat after *37 days*[c], drinks wine and defiles himself for the dead after *74* days. If he was certainly impure and certainly definitely [suffering from skin disease], he eats from sacrificial meat after eight days[a], drinks wine and defiles himself for the dead after 44 days[d].

[a] The eight days of purification of the sufferer from skin disease.

[b] The sixty days for two periods of *nezirut* plus seven days of the sufferer from skin disease which do not count for his *nezirut*.

[c] He waits 7 days and shaves, both for his impurity of the dead and since he might have been impure with skin disease. He then keeps 30 days of *nezirut* in purity and shaves. This shaving certainly counts for the second shaving of the sufferer from skin disease; afterwards he may eat sacrificial meat. Since the thirty days would not count for his *nezirut* if he actually was a sufferer from skin disease, he keeps another 7 days for his impurity of the dead followed by 30 days of *nezirut* in purity, shaves, and is permitted wine.

[d] Seven days of the convalescent sufferer from skin disease, seven days of the person defiled by the impurity of the dead, and 30 days of pure *nezirut*.

(57b line 48) אָמַר רִבִּי אַבָּמָרִי אֲחוֹי דְּרִבִּי יוֹסֵי. זֹאת אוֹמֶרֶת שֶׁהַתַּעַר סוֹתֵר בְּנָזִיר טָמֵא שִׁבְעָא.

Rebbi Abbamari, the brother of Rebbi Yose said, this shows that the shaving knife destroys seven for an impure *nazir*[118].

118 This shows that the Tosephta/Babli text is also understood here. In no case are the seven days counting for the convalescent counted for the *nazir*.

הגויים אין להם פרק תשיעי

(fol. 57b) **משנה א:** הַגּוֹיִם אֵין לָהֶן נְזִירוּת. נָשִׁים וַעֲבָדִים יֵשׁ לָהֶן נְזִירוּת. חוֹמֶר בַּנָּשִׁים מִבַּעֲבָדִים שֶׁהוּא כּוֹפֶף אֶת עַבְדּוֹ וְאֵינוֹ כוֹפֶף אֶת אִשְׁתּוֹ. חוֹמֶר בָּעֲבָדִים מִבַּנָּשִׁים שֶׁהוּא מֵיפֵר נִדְרֵי אִשְׁתּוֹ וְאֵינוֹ מֵיפֵר נִדְרֵי עַבְדּוֹ. הֵיפֵר לְאִשְׁתּוֹ הֵיפֵר עוֹלָמִית. הֵיפֵר לְעַבְדּוֹ יָצָא לְחֵירוּת הַשְׁלִים נְזִירוּתוֹ. עָבַר מִכְּנֶגֶד פָּנָיו רִבִּי מֵאִיר אוֹמֵר לֹא יִשְׁתֶּה. וְרִבִּי יוֹסֵי אוֹמֵר יִשְׁתֶּה.

Mishnah 1: Gentiles cannot take a vow as *nazir*[1]. Women and slaves[2] can take a vow as *nazir*. A man's power is restricted for his wives more than for his slaves since he can force his slave[3] but he cannot force his wife. His power is restricted for his slaves more than for his wives since he can dissolve his wife's vows[4] but not his slave's vows[5]. If he dissolved his wife's, they are eternally dissolved. If he dissolved his slave's, once the slave gains his freedom he has to fulfill his *nezirut*. If [the slave][6] is not in the presence of his master, Rebbi Meïr says, he cannot drink[7], but Rebbi Yose says, he may drink.

1 As explained in the Halakhah, Gentiles may vow under Jewish law. Only the special vow of *nazir* is restricted to Jews.

2 Who had been circumcised and become Jewish by immersion in a *miqweh*. When manumitted, such a slave will be a full member of the Jewish community. While still in servile status, he is obligated to follow all rules imposed on women.

3 If the slave makes any vow which inconveniences his master, the latter can veto the execution of the vow as long as the slave is under his authority.

4 *Nedarim* Chapters 10,11.

5 If the master vetoed the implementation of his slave's vow, that vow becomes dormant but not

cancelled. Once the master's authority is lifted, the vow is automatically activated, as explained in the next sentence.

6   Who made a vow of *nazir* against his master's wishes.

7   Wine. Similarly, R. Meïr will hold that the slave may not defile himself for the dead without specific instruction by his master.

(57c line 9) **הלכה א:** הַגּוֹיִם אֵין לָהֶן נְזִירוּת כול'. בְּנֵי יִשְׂרָאֵל נוֹדְרִין בַּנָּזִיר וְאֵין הַגּוֹיִם נוֹדְרִין בַּנָּזִיר. כְּמָה דְאַתְּ אָמַר. אִישׁ. מַה תַּלְמוּד לוֹמַר אִישׁ. לְהָבִיא הַגּוֹיִם שֶׁנּוֹדְרִין נְדָרִים וּנְדָבוֹת כְּיִשְׂרָאֵל. אֱמוֹר אַף הָכָא כֵן. שַׁנְיָיא הִיא. דִּכְתִיב וְכִפֶּר עָלָיו. אֶת שֶׁיֵּשׁ לוֹ כַּפָּרָה. יָצְאוּ גוֹיִם שֶׁאֵין לָהֶן כַּפָּרָה.

Halakhah 1: "Gentiles cannot vow as *nazir*," etc. Israelites can vow as *nazir*, Gentiles cannot vow as *nazir*. [8]Since you say, "a man", why does the verse mention "a man"[9]? To include Gentiles, who make vows and offer voluntary gifts like Israelites! Why should one not say the same here[10]? There is a difference, for it is written "He shall atone for him.[11]" This refers to one to whom atonement applies. It excludes Gentiles, to whom atonement does not apply.

8   *Sifra Emor Parašah* 7(2); Babli *Menaḥot* 72b. The reference is to *Lev.* 22:18: "Every man of the House of Israel, and of the sojourners in Israel, who would bring their sacrifices for all their vows and all their gifts, to present them to the Eternal as elevation offerings." In the same Chapter, v. 25 makes it clear that what is acceptable from the Israelite is accptable from the Gentile both as vow (in which a person engages himself to dedicate an animal) and a gift (in which a person dedicates an animal, in which case he does not have to supply a replacement if anything should happen to the animal before it could be sacrificed.)

9   "Every person" is in Hebrew אִישׁ אִישׁ "man, man". The repetition has to be explained.

10   *Num.* 6:2 reads: "A man or a woman, if he makes a clear vow of *nazir* to the Eternal." "Man" should include Gentiles by the preceding argument.

11   *Num.* 6:11. Since Gentiles are not subject to the rules of impurity, the rituals of purification cannot apply to them.

HALAKHAH 1

(57c line 13) תַּמָּן תַּנִּינָן. הַנָּכְרִי. רַבִּי מֵאִיר אוֹמֵר. נֶעֱרָךְ אֲבָל לֹא מַעֲרִיךְ. רַבִּי יְהוּדָה אוֹמֵר. מַעֲרִיךְ אֲבָל לֹא נֶעֱרָךְ. וְזֶה וְזֶה מוֹדִין שֶׁהֵן נוֹדְרִין וְנִדָּרִין. רַבִּי יִרְמְיָה בָּעֵי. מָאן דְּאָמַר תַּמָּן מַעֲרִיךְ. וְהָכָא מַזִּיר. מָאן דְּאָמַר נֶעֱרָךְ. הָכָא נִזּוֹר. מַזִּיר הֵיךְ אֵיפְשָׁר. יִשְׂרָאֵל מַזִּיר אֶת הַגּוֹי. וְשָׁמַע הוּא לֵיהּ. אֶלָּא בְּשֶׁאָמַר יִשְׂרָאֵל. הֲרֵינִי נָזִיר. וְשָׁמַע הַגּוֹי וְאָמַר. מַה שֶּׁאָמַר זֶה עָלַי. אֵינוֹ אֶלָּא כְפוֹרֵעַ חוֹב. נִזּוֹר הֵיךְ אֵיפְשָׁר. גּוֹי מַזִּיר אֶת יִשְׂרָאֵל. יִשְׂרָאֵל לְיִשְׂרָאֵל אֵינוֹ מַזִּיר וְגוֹי מַזִּיר אֶת יִשְׂרָאֵל. אֶלָּא בְּשֶׁאָמַר הַגּוֹי. הֲרֵינִי נָזִיר. וְשָׁמַע יִשְׂרָאֵל וְאָמַר. מַה שֶּׁאָמַר זֶה עָלַי. מַה מִיעַטְתָּ בּוֹ. יִשְׂרָאֵל בְּבַל יָחֵל וְאֵין הַגּוֹי בְּבַל יָחֵל. אָמַר רִבִּי יוֹנָה. יִשְׂרָאֵל יֵשׁ לָהֶן הֵיתֵר חָכָם. גּוֹיִם אֵין לָהֶן הֵיתֵר חָכָם. אָמַר רִבִּי יוֹסֵי. יִשְׂרָאֵל צְרִיכִין הֵיתֵר חָכָם וְהַגּוֹיִם אֵין צְרִיכִין הֵיתֵר חָכָם. וְאָתְיָיא דְרִבִּי יוֹנָה כְּדִרְבִּי אַבָּהוּ. חֲדָא גוֹיָה אָתַת לְגַבֵּי רִבִּי אַבָּהוּ. אָמַר לַאֲבִימִי בַּר טוֹבִי. פּוּק וּפְתַח לָהּ בְּנוֹלָד. וּדְרִבִּי יוֹנָה כְּרִבִּי אָחָא. דְּאָמַר. הוּא לָבָן הוּא כּוּשַׁן רִשְׁעָתַיִם. וְלָמָּה נִקְרָא שְׁמוֹ כּוּשַׁן רִשְׁעָתַיִם. שֶׁעָשָׂה שְׁתֵּי רְשָׁעִיּוֹת. אַחַת שֶׁחִילֵּל אֶת הַשְּׁבוּעָה וְאַחַת שֶׁשִּׁיעְבַּד בְּיִשְׂרָאֵל שְׁמוֹנֶה שָׁנָה.

There[12], we have stated: "The Non-Jew, Rebbi Meïr says, is evaluated but does not evaluate[13]; Rebbi Jehudah says, he evaluates but is not evaluated. Both agree that they make vows and are objects of vows[14]." Rebbi Jeremiah asked: For him who says there that he evaluates, here can he declare a *nazir*? For him who says there that he is evaluated, here can he be declared a *nazir*[15]? How would it be possible for him to [be declared a *nazir*][16]? A Israelite can declare a Gentile to be a *nazir*[17]. Would he listen to him[18]? But the Israelite said, "I am a *nazir*," the Gentile heard it and said, "I am responsible for what this one said." It is only as if he paid a debt[19]. How would it be possible for him to [declare a *nazir*][16]? A Gentile can declare an Israelite to be *nazir*[17]. Since an Israelite cannot declare [another] Israelite to be a *nazir*, a Gentile cannot declare an Israelite to be a *nazir*[18]. But it must be that the Gentile said, "I am a *nazir*", the Israelite heard it and said, "I am taking upon me what this one said.[20]" What did you exclude from him[21]? An Israelite is subject to "not to desecrate"[22], a Gentile is not subject to "not to desecrate". Rebbi Jonah said, Israelites can be relieved by a Sage[23], Gentiles cannot be relieved by a Sage[24]. Rebbi Yose said, Israelites need a Sage to be relieved, Gentiles do not need a Sage to be relieved[25]. It follows that Rebbi (Jonah) [Yose] follows Rebbi Abbahu. A Gentile woman came before Rebbi Abbahu, who said to Abime bar Tobi: Go and find her an opening by unforeseen circumstances[26]. And Rebbi Jonah follows Rebbi Aha, who said that Laban was *Kushan-Riš'ataim*. Why was he called "Kushan the doubly bad"? Because he committed two evils. One that he desecrated his oath, the other that he subjugated Israel for eight years[27].

12   Mishnah *'Arakhin* 1:2.

13   This refers to *Lev.* 27:1-8, where "evaluation" amounts are specified to be offered to the Sanctuary for persons of specified age and sex. According to R. Meïr, a Jew may vow to pay a Gentile's evaluation but a Gentile cannot make such a vow. According to R. Jehudah, a Gentile may vow to pay a Jew's valuation but a Jew cannot offer to pay the Gentile's evaluation.

14   Both Jew and Gentile may make a vow to pay to the Sanctuary the amount another person would fetch were he to be sold on the slave market.

15   The texts used to introduce a vow of evaluation (*Lev.* 27:2) and a vow of *nazir* (*Num.* 6:2) are completely parallel. It is to be assumed that the rules derived from the texts are also parallel; if a Gentile can cause an obligation of payment of an evaluation, he also can cause an obligation of *nazir*; if a Gentile can be the object of an obligation of payment of an evaluation, he also can be the object of an obligation of *nazir*.

16   The context requires to read ניזור for מזיר and vice-versa.

17   Tentative answer.

18   Rejection of the tentative answer.

19   The Gentile may well vow to the Jew's obligatory sacrifices since by biblical law, Gentiles' sacrifices are accepted. But this does not make the Gentile a *nazir*.

20   Since the Gentile's vow is invalid, so is the Jew's.

21   This now is R. Jeremiah's real

question. Since it was shown that the power to evaluate is not related to the power to vow for *nazir*, the question arises whether in general the power of Gentiles to make vows is equal to that of Jews or not.

22   *Num.* 30:3; *Sifry zuṭa* 30:2. Since a Gentile is not subject to biblical laws other than those given to Adam and Noah, he cannot be held responsible if he "desecrates his word," i. e., does not keep his vow.

23   An Elder can annul the vow; cf. Tractate *Nedarim*, Introduction and Chapter 9.

24   Since Gentiles are not subject to the Law, they cannot profit from the Law. He will hold that Gentiles, whose informal marriages have biblical sanction, never can be divorced; cf. *Qiddušin* 1:2, Notes 33 ff.

25   Since Gentiles are not subject to the Law, they do not need the Law. He will hold that since Gentiles are not under the biblical obligation of formal marriage, they never need a divorce but can validly terminate a companionship through unilateral action by either one of the parties.

26   Which is forbidden to Jews, Mishnah *Nedarim* 9:2. He ordered the lady's vow to be dissolved to give her peace of mind, not because it would have been necessary.

27   Babli *Sanhedrin* 105b, as tannaïtic text. The story would make Laban live more than 300 years.

(57c line 28) וְיִכּוֹף אֶת אִשְׁתּוֹ. לֹא כֵן אָמַר רִבִּי הוּנָא. הֲנָיָיתִי עָלָיךְ. כּוֹפָה וּמְשַׁמְּשָׁתוֹ. הֲנָיָיתָךְ עָלַי. הֲרֵי זֶה יָפֵר. שַׁנְיָיא הִיא שֶׁהִיא הֲנָיָיתוֹ וַהֲנָיָיתָהּ. וְלֹא יִכּוֹף אֶת עַבְדוֹ. שַׁנְיָיא הִיא. דִּכְתִיב כִּי נֵזֶר אֱלֹהָיו עַל רֹאשׁוֹ. אֶת שֶׁאֵין לוֹ אָדוֹן אַחֵר. יָצָא עֶבֶד שֶׁיֵּשׁ לוֹ אָדוֹן אַחֵר. הָיָה יָכוֹל לִמְחוֹת עַל דְּבַר רַבּוֹ. אוֹמֵר לוֹ. הֲלָכָה הִיא. שְׁמַע לְדִבְרֵי רַבָּךְ. כְּפָפוֹ רַבּוֹ וְנִיטְמָא מָהוּ שֶׁיָּבִיא קָרְבָּן טוּמְאָה. וְכִי נָזִיר הוּא. לֹא אַתְּ הוּא שֶׁגְּזַרְתָּהּ עָלָיו שֶׁיִּטַּמֵּא. אַתְּ אָמַר. מֵבִיא קָרְבָּן טוּמְאָה. וְכָא מֵבִיא קָרְבָּן טוּמְאָה. כְּפָפוֹ רַבּוֹ וְנִיטְמָא מָהוּ שֶׁיִּסְתּוֹר. וְכִי נָזִיר הוּא. אֶלָּא אַתְּ אַתְּ הוּא שֶׁגְּזַרְתָּ עָלָיו שֶׁיִּטַּמֵּא. אַתְּ אוֹמֵר. סוֹתֵר. וְכָא סוֹתֵר.

[28]Why can he not force his wife? Did not Rebbi Huna say, [if she vowed] any benefit from me [shall be forbidden] to you, he forces her and sleeps with her. Any benefit from you [shall be forbidden] to me, he has

to dissolve. There is a difference because it is a benefit for him and her. He should not be able to force his slave! There is a difference, "because his God's crown is on his head[29]," a person who has no other master. This excludes the slave who has another master[30]. If he comes to protest his master's word, one says to him: this is practice[31], obey your master's orders! If his master pushed him and he became impure, does he have to bring a sacrifice of impurity? Is he a *nazir*, did not you decide for him that he should become impure[32]? You say, he brings a sacrifice of impurity; could he bring here a sacrifice of impurity? Does he annul? Is he a *nazir*, did not you decide for him that he should become impure? You say, he annuls; could he here annul[33]?

28 The argument about the wife's vow is from *Nedarim* 11:1, Notes 23-25.
29 *Num.* 6:7.
30 The master has the power to force the slave to disregard the vow. The slave in obeying his master does not commit any sin.
31 He has to follow his master's command.
32 If his master's action invalidates the slave's vow, there is no valid vow of *nazir*. The status of the slave reverts to profane; the slave is not responsible for the lifting of the status of *nazir* from him. If there were anything sinful in this action, it would be the master's responsibility.
33 Argument and meaning are completely parallel to the preceding.

(57c line 37) פְּשִׁיטָא דָא מִילְתָא. נִיטְמָא וְאַחַר כָּךְ יָצָא לְחֵירוּת מֵבִיא קָרְבַּן טוּמְאָה. מָהוּ. שֶׁכְּפָפוֹ רַבּוֹ אוֹ בְשָׁלֹא כְפָפוֹ רַבּוֹ. אִין תֵּימַר בְּשֶׁכְּפָפוֹ. מֵבִיא קָרְבַּן טוּמְאָה. אִין תֵּימַר בְּשָׁלֹא כְפָפוֹ. רַבּוֹ יַשְׁלֵם כָּל־זְמַן שֶׁהוּא תַחְתָּיו. אָמַר רִבִּי יוֹסֵי. בְּשֶׁכְּפָפוֹ רַבּוֹ אֲנָן קַייָמִין. שֶׁלֹּא תֹאמַר. הוֹאִיל וְיָצָא לְחֵירוּת תִּפְקַע מִמֶּנּוּ נְזִירוּת בְּטוּמְאָה. לְפוּם כֵּן צָרַךְ מֵימַר. מוֹנֶה לִנְזִירוּת בְּטוּמְאָה.

The following is obvious: If he became impure and then was manumitted, he brings a sacrifice of impurity. When is that, if his master forced him or if his master did not force him[34]? If you say that he forced him, how can be bring a sacrifice of impurity[35]? If you say he did not force him, should he not count for his master as long as he still is in the latter's power[36]? Rebbi Yose said, we are dealing with the case that his master forced him. You should not say that because he was manumitted, the *nezirut* in impurity was lifted from him[37]. Therefore, it was necessary to say that he counts *nezirut* in impurity[38].

34 What was the cause of the slave's impurity?

35 It was shown in the preceding paragraph that no sacrifice is due.

36 If the slave made a vow of *nazir* for a specified period, he should be able to count that period as long as he did not violate its terms by his own will.

37 Even if the slave was manumitted during his *nezirut*, the days he was impure because of his master's command are counted. The rules of *nezirut* of free men apply to him only from the moment of his manumission.

38 This is explained somewhat more fully in the Tosephta (6:6): "If [the slave] became impure and was manumitted, he counts from the time he became impure." In contrast to the free person, the 7 days he counts for his purification by means of the ashes of the Red Cow are counted as days of *nezirut*.

(57c line 43) אָמַר רִבִּי יוֹסֵי. עֶבֶד שֶׁאָמַר. הֲרֵינִי נָזִיר לִכְשֶׁאֵצֵא לְחֵירוּת. כּוֹפוֹ לִנְזִירוּת. עֶבֶד כּוֹפוֹ לִנְזִירוּת וְאֵינוֹ כוֹפֶה לֹא לִנְדָרִים וְלֹא לִשְׁבוּעוֹת. רִבִּי יִרְמְיָה בְּעָא קוֹמֵי רִבִּי זְעִירָא. כְּפָפוֹ רַבּוֹ וְנִיטְמָא מַהוּ שֶׁיִּלְקֶה. אוֹ אֵינוֹ אֶלָּא הֲלָכָה. מָה אֲנָן קַייָמִין. אִם בְּשֶׁנְּזִירָתוֹ תּוֹרָה וַהֲלָכָה יֵשׁ לָכוּף לוֹקֶה. אִם בְּשָׁאֵילוּ וְאֵילוּ מִדִּבְרֵיהֶן לֹא יַלְקֶה. אָמַר רִבִּי מָנָא. לוֹקִין עַל הֲלָכָה. אֶלָּא אָכֵן הוּא. אִם בְּשֶׁנְּזִירָתוֹ הֲלָכָה וַהֲלָכָה יֵשׁ לָכוּף וְלוֹקֶה. אִם בְּשָׁאֵילוּ וְאֵילוּ מִדִּבְרֵיהֶן לֹא יַלְקֶה.

[39]"Rebbi Yose said, if a slave said, 'I shall be a *nazir* when manumitted,' his master forces him in matters of *nezirut*[40]. [The master] can force a

slave in matters of *nezirut*; he does not have to force him in matters either of vows or of oaths[41]." Rebbi Jeremiah asked before Rebbi Ze'ira: If his master forced him and he became impure, is he to be whipped? Or is that only practice? Where do we hold? If his *nezirut* has biblical status and by practice one may force, he is whipped. If both are rabbinical, he is not whipped. Rebbi Mana said, does one whip for practice? But it must be the following: If his *nezirut* is practice and by practice one may force, he is whipped. If both are rabbinical, he is not whipped[42].

39 Tosephta 6:6; Babli 62b.

40 Without having any influence on the status of the vow.

41 Since the slave is not his own master, he has no power to forbid anything to himself by vow or oath (explanation of the Babli, 62b).

42 The question of R. Mana shows that two sentences have to be switched. Instead of נזירתו תורה one has to read נזירותו הלכה and vice-versa.

The first version of the argument of R. Jeremiah goes as follows: If the power of the slave to enter into a state of *nazir* is the same as the power of the master to force him to disregard his vow, and both have status of "practice", i. e., have quasi-biblical status as part of Judaism as organized by Ezra and his contemporaries, in the absence of a special practice exempting the slave, the latter should be held liable for infractions of his vow even if he was forced. But if the power of the slave to vow as *nazir* be rabbinical, then there can be no biblical punishment for infraction. On this R. Mana notes that quasi-biblical status is not biblical status, and biblical punishment for non-biblical infractions (*Deut*. 25:4) is impossible.

Therefore, the question is rephrased: If the power of the slave to enter into a state of *nazir* is biblical but the power of the master to force him to disregard his vow is only from practice, should the slave not be subject to prosecution for infringing his vow? The question is not to be taken seriously; it rather points out a logical inconsistency between the rule which allows the slave to become a *nazir* and the rule which allows the master to override, but not abolish, that vow.

(57c line 50) כְּפָפוֹ רַבּוֹ לְדָבָר אֶחָד מָהוּ שֶׁיִּכּוֹף אוֹתוֹ לְכָל־הַדְּבָרִים. בָּאנוּ לְמַחֲלוֹקֶת רִבִּי מֵאִיר וְרִבִּי יוֹסֵי. עָבַר מִכְּנֶגֶד פָּנָיו. רִבִּי מֵאִיר אוֹמֵר. לֹא יִשְׁתֶּה. רִבִּי יוֹסֵי אוֹמֵר. יִשְׁתֶּה. מָה אֲנָן קַיָּימִין. אִם בְּשֶׁאָמַר. בֵּין בְּפָנַיי בֵּין שֶׁלֹּא בְפָנַיי שְׁתֵה. אוֹף רִבִּי מֵאִיר מוֹדֶה. אִם בָּאוֹמֵר. בְּפָנַיי שְׁתֵה שֶׁלֹּא בְפָנַיי אַל תִּשְׁתֶּה. אוֹף רִבִּי יוֹסֵי מוֹדֶה. אֶלָּא כֵן אֲנָן קַיָּימִין בָּאוֹמֵר שְׁתֵה. רִבִּי מֵאִיר אוֹמֵר. בְּפָנַיי שְׁתֵה שֶׁלֹּא בְפָנַיי אַל תִּשְׁתֶּה. רִבִּי יוֹסֵי אוֹמֵר. בְּאוֹמֵר. בֵּין בְּפָנַיי בֵּין שֶׁלֹּא בְפָנַיי שְׁתֵה.

If his master forced him in one respect, did he force him in all respects[43]? We came to the disagreement between Rebbi Meïr and Rebbi Yose: "If [the slave] is not in the presence of his master, Rebbi Meïr says, he cannot drink, but Rebbi Yose says, he may drink." Where do we hold? If he told him, drink whether in my presence or not in my presence, even Rebbi Meïr will agree. If he told him, drink in my presence, do not drink in my absence, even Rebbi Yose will agree. But we hold in the case that he tells him: "drink!" Rebbi Meïr says, [it means] drink in my presence, do not drink in my absence[44]. Rebbi Yose says, [it is] as if he said, drink whether in my presence or not in my presence.

43 *Nezirut* has three aspects: Growing hair, abstention from the fruit of the vine, and avoidance of the impurity of the dead. If the master objected to one aspect, does he reject the others automatically?

44 Therefore, R. Meïr must hold that objection to one aspect does not imply anything for the others, while R. Yose holds that an objection to one aspect is interpreted as objection to all of them unless specified otherwise by the master.

(fol. 57b) **משנה ב:** נָזִיר שֶׁגִּלַּח וְנוֹדַע לוֹ שֶׁהוּא טָמֵא. אִם טוּמְאָה יְדוּעָה סוֹתֵר וְאִם טוּמְאַת הַתְּהוֹם אֵינוֹ סוֹתֵר. אִם עַד שֶׁלֹּא גִילַּח בֵּין כָּךְ וּבֵין כָּךְ סוֹתֵר. כֵּיצַד. יָרַד לִטְבּוֹל בַּמְּעָרָה וְנִמְצָא מֵת צָף עַל פִּי הַמְּעָרָה טָמֵא. נִמְצָא מְשׁוּקָּע בְּקַרְקַע הַמְּעָרָה יָרַד לְהָקֵר טָהוֹר לִיטַּהֵר מִטּוּמְאַת הַמֵּת טָמֵא שֶׁחֶזְקַת הַטָּמֵא טָמֵא וְחֶזְקַת הַטָּהוֹר טָהוֹר שֶׁרַגְלַיִם לַדָּבָר.

Mishnah 2: If a *nazir* was informed that he was impure after he had shaved[45] and it was a known impurity he cancels[46], but if it was impurity of the abyss[47] he does not cancel. If it was before he shaved, he cancels in any case. How is that? If he went to immerse himself in a cave[48] where a corpse was floating at the entrance, he is impure[49]. If it was found buried in the ground and he went there to refresh himself[50], he is pure, but to purify himself from the impurity of the dead he is impure[51] since the presumptive state of the impure is impure and the presumptive state of the pure is pure, for it is not unsubstantiated[52].

45   After he had finished his *nezirut* and has reverted to profane status.

46   He has to repeat the entire period of *nezirut*.

47   If the source of impurity was only detected after he had shaved in purity.

48   A *miqweh* in a cave. It seems that in the Judean and Galilean hills practically all *miqwaot* were in caves.

49   Even if there is a doubt whether the corpse already was there when he immersed himself, or if the corpse was there whether it floated outside the cave (when it would have transmitted impurity only by touch) or was inside (where the cave created the impurity of a "tent" and everybody under the "tent" became impure.)

50   And did not take sufficient care about his purity.

51   In any case of probable impurity caused by a buried corpse one continues in the prior state.

52   Since his prior state is known but his actual state in doubt, the certainly known is preferred to the doubtful.

(57c line 57) **הלכה ב:** אָמַר רִבִּי יוֹחָנָן. מָאן תַּנָא אִם גִּילַח וְאִם לֹא גִילַח. רִבִּי אֱלִיעֶזֶר. בְּרַם כְּרַבָּנִין עַד שֶׁלֹּא נִזְרַק הַדָּם עָלָיו. עוּלָּא בַּר יִשְׁמָעֵאל בְּשֵׁם רִבִּי לָעְזָר. טַעֲמָא דְרִבִּי אֱלִיעֶזֶר. וְגִילַּח הַנָּזִיר אֶת שְׂעַר רֹאשׁ נִזְרוֹ. הַתּוֹרָה תָלַת לִנְזִירוּתוֹ בִּשְׂעָרוֹ.

Halakhah 2: Rebbi Johanan said, who is the Tanna of "when he had shaved, before he shaved"[53]? Rebbi Eliezer! But for the rabbis it would be before the blood was sprinkled for him[54]. Ulla bar Ismael in the name of Rebbi Eleazar: What is Rebbi Eliezer's reason? "The *nazir* shall shave the hair of his crowned head.[55]" The Torah made his *nezirut* dependent on his hair.

53 That the final act of *nezirut* which returns the *nazir* to normal life is shaving.

54 Mishnah 6:13: The Sages say that a person who became impure after one kind of sacrificial blood was sprinkled on the altar for him can bring his remaining sacrifices after he was purified but does not have to start anew.

55 This is a telescoped version of *Num*: 6:18: "The *nazir* shall shave his *crowned head* at the door of the Tent of Meeting, take the *hair of his crowned head* and put it in the fire under the well-being sacrifice."

(57c line 60) הִשְׁלִים לִנְזִירוּתוֹ לֹא הִסְפִּיק לְגַלֵּחַ עַד שֶׁנּוֹדַע לוֹ בִּסְפֵק קֶבֶר הַתְּהוֹם סוֹתֵר. הִפְרִישׁ קָרְבְּנוֹתָיו וְלֹא הִסְפִּיק לְגַלֵּחַ עַד שֶׁנִּתְוַוֹדַע לוֹ קֶבֶר הַתְּהוֹם. אָמַר רִבִּי זְעִירָא קוֹמֵי רִבִּי מָנָא. וְלֹא מַתְנִיתָא הִיא. וְלֹא הוּא גִילַּח הוּא לֹא גִילַּח כְּרִבִּי לִיעֶזֶר. הוּא עַד שֶׁלֹּא נִזְרַק הַדָּם עָלָיו הוּא מִשֶּׁנִּזְרַק הַדָּם עָלָיו כְּרַבָּנִין.

If he completed his *nezirut* but did not manage to shave before he was informed about a possible case of a grave in the abyss, he cancels. If he designated his sacrifices but did not manage to shave before he was informed about a grave in the abyss[56]? Rebbi Ze'ira said before Rebbi Mana: Is that not the Mishnah? Whether he shaved or did not shave following Rebbi Eliezer, or whether it happened before or after blood was sprinkled according to the rabbis[57]!

56 Can designating the sacrifices be considered as liquidation of the status of *nazir* to free the person from repeating in case of a possible impurity from a hidden source?

57 The Mishnah makes it quite clear that only shaving (according to R. Eliezer) or sprinkling of blood (according to the rabbis) is counted; dedicating the sacrifices does not mean anything in this respect.

(57c line 64) מְנַיִין לִסְפֵק קֶבֶר הַתְּהוֹם. רְבִּי יַעֲקֹב בַּר אָחָא בְּשֵׁם רַבָּנָן. אוֹ בְדֶרֶךְ רְחוֹקָה לָכֶם. מַה לָכֶם בְּגָלוּי. אַף כָּל־דָּבָר שֶׁהוּא בְגָלוּי. יָצָא קֶבֶר הַתְּהוֹם שֶׁאֵינוֹ בְגָלוּי.

From where about a doubtful case of a grave in the abyss? Rebbi Jacob bar Aḥa in the name of the rabbis: "Or on a far trip for you.[58]" What is open for you, including everything in the open. This excludes the case of a grave in the abyss which is not open[59].

58 *Num.* 9:10, detailing the rules of "Second Passover" for people impure or absent on the 14th of Nisan.

59 This and the following paragraphs are copied from *Pesaḥim* 7:7. In the present paragraph, the main text is missing. Both for the person going to celebrate the Passover sacrifice and the *nazir* who finished his term, the impurity caused by a doubtful case of a grave in the abyss is disregarded. In view of the central role of purity in everything connected with the Sanctuary, it is obvious that some biblical justification has to be found for the rule. In the case of Passover, the argument notes that the verse could have stated that a person "on a far trip" was required to celebrate the Second Passover. The addition "for you" seems to be superfluous. It is interpreted to mean just as the road is open to the wanderer, so the impurity has to be in the open for the impure person. The same argument is in the Babli, *Pesaḥim* 81b.

What is missing here is the argument for the *nazir* who had finished his term. In *Pesaḥim* 7:7 (34c bottom), R. Johanan in the name of R. Yannai quotes *Num.* 6:9: "If a person dies suddenly *on him*", and explains the expression "over him" to indicate that it has to be in the open:

עַד כְּדוֹן עוֹשֵׂי פֶסַח. נָזִיר מְנַיין. רִבִּי יוֹחָנָן בְּשֵׁם רִבִּי [יַנַּאי] וְכִי יָמוּת מֵת עָלָיו. מַה עָלָיו שֶׁהוּא בְּגָלוּי. אַף כָּל־דָּבָר שֶׁהוּא בְגָלוּי. יָצָא קֶבֶר הַתְּהוֹם שֶׁאֵינוֹ בְּגָלוּי.

So far for the people celebrating Passover. From where the *nazir*? Rebbi Johanan in the name of Rebbi [Yannai]: "If a person dies suddenly on him". Since on him it is in the open, so everything in the open. This eliminates the grave in the abyss which is not in the open.

(57c line 66) צִיבּוּר בְּגָלוּי שֶׁנִּיטְמָא בִּסְפֵק קֶבֶר הַתְּהוֹם מָהוּ שֶׁיִּרְצֶה עָלָיו הַצִּיץ. קַל וָחוֹמֶר. וּמָה אִם יָחִיד שֶׁהוֹרָעָתָהּ כּוֹחוֹ בְּטוּמְאָה יְדוּעָה. יִיפִּיתָה כּוֹחוֹ בְּקֶבֶר הַתְּהוֹם. צִיבּוּר שֶׁיִּפִּיתָה כּוֹחוֹ בְּטוּמְאָה יְדוּעָה אֵינוֹ דִין שֶׁתִּיַּיפֶה כּוֹחוֹ בְּקֶבֶר הַתְּהוֹם. קַל שֶׁאַתְּ מֵיקַל בְּיָחִיד אַתְּ מַחֲמִיר בַּצִּיבּוּר. קַל שֶׁאַתָּה מֵיקַל בְּיָחִיד שֶׁאִם נִתְוַוּדַע לוֹ לְאַחַר זְרִיקָה יֵעָשֶׂה כְּמִי שֶׁנִּיטְמָא לִפְנֵי זְרִיקָה. בִּשְׁבִיל שֶׁיּאכַל הַבָּשָׂר. קַל שֶׁאַתְּ מֵיקַל בְּנָזִיר טָהוֹר אַתְּ מַחֲמִיר בְּנָזִיר טָמֵא. קַל שֶׁאַתְּ מֵיקַל בְּנָזִיר טָהוֹר שֶׁאִם נִתְוַוּדַע לוֹ לְאַחַר זְרִיקָה יֵעָשֶׂה כְּמִי שֶׁנִּיטְמָא לְאַחַר זְרִיקָה בִּשְׁבִיל שֶׁיָּבִיא קָרְבָּן טוּמְאָה. אַתְּ מַחֲמִיר בְּנָזִיר טָמֵא שֶׁאִם נוֹדַע לוֹ לְאַחַר זְרִיקָה יֵעָשֶׂה כְּמִי שֶׁנִּיטְמָא וְחָזַר וְנִיטְמָא בִּשְׁבִיל שֶׁיָּבִיא קָרְבָּן טוּמְאָה עַל כָּל־אֶחָד וְאֶחָד. כְּהָדָא דְתַנֵּי. נִיטְמָא וְחָזַר וְנִיטְמָא מֵבִיא קָרְבָּן עַל כָּל־אֶחָד וְאֶחָד. עוֹבֵר שֶׁלְּפֶּסַח מָהוּ שֶׁיִּרְצֶה עָלָיו הַצִּיץ. קַל וָחוֹמֶר. מָה אִם הַבְּעָלִים שֶׁהוֹרָעָתָהּ כּוֹחָן בְּזָקֵן וְחוֹלֶה יִיפִּיתָה כּוֹחָן בְּקֶבֶר הַתְּהוֹם. עוֹבֵר שֶׁיִּיפִּיתָה כּוֹחוֹ בְּזָקֵן וְחוֹלֶה אֵינוֹ דִין שֶׁתִּיַּיפֶה כּוֹחוֹ בְּקֶבֶר הַתְּהוֹם. לֹא. אִם אָמַרְתְּ בַּבְּעָלִים שֶׁהוֹרָעָתָהּ כּוֹחָן בִּשְׁאָר כָּל־טֻמְאוֹת שֶׁבַּשָּׁנָה. תֹאמַר בְּעוֹבֵר שֶׁהוֹרָעָתָהּ כּוֹחוֹ בִּשְׁאָר כָּל־הַטֻּמְאוֹת שֶׁבַּשָּׁנָה. הוֹאִיל וְהוֹרָעָתָהּ כּוֹחוֹ בִּשְׁאָר כָּל־הַטֻּמְאוֹת שֶׁבַּשָּׁנָה הוֹרַע כּוֹחוֹ בְּטָמֵא מֵת בַּפֶּסַח. מַאי כְדוֹן. לָכֶם. בֵּין לוֹ בֵּין לְעוֹבֵר שֶׁלּוֹ. עַד כְּדוֹן עוֹשֵׂי פֶסַח. נָזִיר מְנַיין. רִבִּי יוֹסֵי בֵּי רִבִּי בּוּן בְּשֵׁם רַב חִסְדָּא. הֲוֵינָן סָבְרִין מֵימַר. עָלָיו. לֹא עַל הָעוֹבֵר שֶׁלּוֹ. מִן מַה דְתַנֵּי. הוּא נָזִיר הוּא עוֹשֶׂה פֶסַח. הָדָא אָמְרָה. מַה דְנָפַל לְדֵין נָפַל לְדֵין.

1 בגלוי | - | קבר | - | הציץ | את הציץ | 2 ומה | מה | יחיד | היחיד | שהורעתה | שהורעת 3 בקבר | בספק קבר | שיפיתה | שייפיתה | שתייפה | שייפיתה | 4 בקבר | בספק קבר | שאתה | שאת | 5 לאחר | לפני | יעשה | ייעשה | לפני זריקה | לאחר זריקה בשביל שלא ידחה לפסח שיני | 6-5 בשביל שיאכל הבשר | את מחמיר עליו בציבור. שאם נתוודע לו לאחר זריקה ייעשה כמי שניטמא לפני זריקה בשביל שלא יאכל הבשר | 6 קל שאת מיקל בנזיר טהור את מחמיר בנזיר טמא | - | 7 לאחר | לפני יעשה | ייעשה | 8 בשביל | שלא שיביא | יביא נודע | נתוודע | 9 בשביל שיביא | מביא | 10 על כל | לכל דתני | דתנא ניטמא וחזר וניטמא | נטמא וחזר ונטמא קרבן | קרבן טומאה | 11 עובר | עובד הציץ | את הציץ מה | ומה | 12 וחולה | ובחולה בקבר | בספק קבר עובר | עובד | 13 וחולה | ובחולה בקבר | בספק קבר 14 שהורעתה | שייפיתה בעובר | בעובד | 16 שבשנה | שלכל השנה הורע | תורע מאי | מיי לכם | ר' נהמן בשם ר' מנא. לכם | 17 לעובר | לעובד ר' יוסי ביר' בון | ר' יוסה | 18 העובר | העובד הוא | היא | 19 הוא | היא

[60]If the public became publicly[61] impure in a doubtful case of a grave in the abyss, does the diadem make it acceptable[62]? It is a conclusion *de minore ad maius.* Since in the case of a single person, whose position you clarified to his disadvantage in the case of known impurity[63], you clarified to his advantage in the case of a grave in the abyss[64], it should be only logical that for the public, whose position you clarified to its advantage in the case of known impurity, you should clarify it to its advantage in the case of a grave in the abyss. A leniency which you apply to a single person you treat as a restriction for the public[65]. A leniency which you apply to a single person, so that if it became known to him *after* sprinkling he should be treated as if he became impure before sprinkling, that he should eat the meat[66]. The leniency which you apply to the pure *nazir* is a restriction for the impure *nazir*[67]. The leniency which you apply to the pure *nazir, so* that if it became known to him after sprinkling he is treated as impure after sprinkling, that he should bring a sacrifice of impurity[68]. You treat it as a restriction for the impure *nazir*, that if it became known to him after sprinkling he is treated as somebody

repeatedly becoming impure so that he has to bring a sacrifice of impurity for each single case[69]. As it was stated: If he repeatedly became impure, he has to bring a sacrifice for each single case[70]. If somebody is officiating[71] for the Passover sacrifice, does the diadem make it acceptable? It is a conclusion *de minore ad maius*. Since for the owners [of the Passover sacrifice] whose position you clarified to their disadvantage in the case of the infirm and the aged[72], you clarified to their advantage in the case of a grave in the abyss, it should be only logical that for the officiating, whose position you clarified to his advantage in the case of the infirm and the aged, you should clarify it to his advantage in the case of a grave in the abyss. No. For the owners [of sacrifices] you clarify to their disadvantage[73] in the case of impurity during the rest of the year; you also say for the officiating that you clarify their position to their disadvantage in the case of impurity during the rest of the year. Since you clarify their position to their disadvantage in the case of impurity during the rest of the year, you also clarify their position to their disadvantage in the case of the impurity of the dead on Passover. How is it really? "For you[58]", whether for him or for the one officiating for him. So far for the people celebrating Passover. From where the *nazir*? Rebbi Yose ben Rebbi Abun in the name of Rav Ḥisda: We thought, "on him[74]", not on the one officiating for him. Since we stated that the same rules apply to the *nazir* and to those celebrating Passover, it means that what holds for the one holds for the other[75].

60 While the text in *Pesaḥim* 7:7 is not without its problems, it is clear that the text there has to be taken as the source; the copyist here neither understood nor proofread what he wrote.

61 The word is [correctly] missing in *Pesaḥim*; a case of doubtful impurity in the public domain is always resolved by a presumption of purity (*Soṭah* 1:2,

Note 88).

62   About the diadem worn by the High Priest, *Ex.* 28:38 states: "It shall be on Aaron's forehead; Aaron shall carry the iniquity of the sacrificial gifts which the Children of Israel will dedicate, all their holy gifts; it shall always be on his forehead, *to be accepted for them* before the Eternal." The action of the diadem, to make somewhat questionable sacrifices, e. g., those offered while using one of the legal fictions that may be used to overlook possible impurities, is therefore called "to make it acceptable."

63   A single person impure on the 14th of Nisan is required to celebrate the Second Passover on the 14th of Iyar while if the majority of the people are impure on the 14th of Nisan the congregation celebrate Passover in impurity. In this respect the standing of a single person clearly is inferior to that of the majority of the people.

64   If a doubt (mentioned explicitly in *Pesaḥim*, understood here) arises about a "grave of the abyss" in a private domain, it is treated as if it were in the public domain (Note 61).

65   This disproves the previous argument. The rules of impurity for private persons and for the majority of the people are not comparable.

66   This text does not make any sense. The correct text is in *Pesaḥim*: "A leniency which you apply to a single person, viz., that if it became known to him *before* sprinkling he should be treated as if he became impure *after* sprinkling, so that he should *not be pushed to the Second Passover. You treat that as restriction for the public, that if it became known to them after sprinkling it should be treated as if they became impure before sprinkling, that* the meat should *not* be eaten."

The first statement is derived from Mishnah *Pesaḥim* 7:7: "For a *nazir* and one who celebrates Passover who became impure in the impurity of the abyss, the diadem makes it acceptable." The private person being involved in a possible impurity caused by a grave of the abyss never has to celebrate the Second Passover.

The second statement refers to Mishnaiot *Pesaḥim* 7:4-5. If the public are impure, the Passover sacrifice is slaughtered and eaten in impurity. But if it was slaughtered as pure and then it became impure or became known to be impure, it cannot be eaten.

67   This is a kind of headline for the following argument, rather than a case of dittography.

68   The intelligible text is in

Pesaḥim: "The leniency which you apply to the pure *nazir*, viz., that if it became known to him *before* sprinkling he is treated as impure after sprinkling, so that he should *not* bring a sacrifice of impurity." This is the statement of the Mishnah here, following the rabbis.

69   But if the impure *nazir* became aware of the second impurity before he offered his sacrifice of impurity, he has to bring only one sacrifice.

70   Halakhah 6:8, Note 198.

71   The *Nazir* text has עוֹבֵר "the passer-by" instead of עוֹבֵד "the officiating [priest]" *passim*.

72   The Passover sacrifice has to be slaughtered in the name of those who will be eating it, its "subscribers" (Mishnah *Pesaḥim* 5:3, *Ex.* 12:4). An old person and an infirm one who cannot eat meat in the volume of an olive may not subscribe to the Passover sacrifice, but as long as they do not exhibit a disability which disqualifies them (*Lev.* 21:18-20), old or infirm priests may serve in the Temple.

73   The correct reading "advantage" is in *Pesaḥim*. An impure person (including a *nazir* not impure by the impurity of the dead) can send his sacrifices (other than the Passover sacrifice) to the Temple by a pure agent, but an impure priest cannot officiate, irrespective of the nature of his impurity.

74   *Num.* 6:9: "If a person suddenly dies *on him*." In *Sifry Num.* 28, the expression "if a person dies" is interpreted as stating a fact, not a suspicion. This is used to clear the *nazir* from any suspected, unproven impurity from the dead.

75   Babli *Pesaḥim* 80b.

(57d line 12) אֵי זֶה הוּא קֶבֶר הַתְּהוֹם. הַמֵּת שֶׁנִּקְבַּר בְּקַשׁ וּבְתֶבֶן וּבְעָפָר וּבִצְרוֹרוֹת. אֲבָל אִם נִקְבַּר בַּמַּיִם וּבָאֲפִילָה וּבִנְקִיקֵי הַסְּלָעִים אֵינוֹ עוֹשֶׂה קֶבֶר הַתְּהוֹם. כְּלָלוֹ שֶׁלְּדָבָר. כָּל־שֶׁאַתְּ יָכוֹל לְפַנּוֹתוֹ עוֹשֶׂה קֶבֶר הַתְּהוֹם. וְכָל־שֶׁאֵי אַתָּה יָכוֹל לְפַנּוֹתוֹ אֵינוֹ עוֹשֶׂה קֶבֶר הַתְּהוֹם. וְקַשׁ וְתֶבֶן אֵין אַתְּ יָכוֹל לְפַנּוֹתוֹ. מַתְנִיתָא דְלָא כְרִבִּי יוֹסֵי. דְּרִבִּי יוֹסֵי אוֹמֵר. תֶּבֶן וּבִטְּלוֹ בָטֵל. רִבִּי יוֹסֵי בֵּירִבִּי בּוּן בְּשֵׁם רַב חִסְדָּא. דִּבְרֵי הַכֹּל הִיא. מַה דְּאָמַר רִבִּי יוֹסֵי בְּשֶׁבְּלָלוֹ בְּעָפָר. יֵשׁ תֶּבֶן שֶׁהוּא כְעָפָר וְעָפָר שֶׁהוּא כְתֶבֶן. תֶּבֶן שֶׁאֵין יָכוֹל לְפַנּוֹתוֹ הֲרֵי הוּא כְעָפָר. וְעָפָר שֶׁאַתְּ יָכוֹל לְפַנּוֹתוֹ הֲרֵי הוּא כְתֶבֶן. דְּבֵי רִבִּי יַנַּאי אָמְרֵי. חִיפָּהוּ מַחֲצָלוֹת בָּטֵל. אִיתָא חֲמֵי. חִיפָּהוּ מַחֲצָלוֹת לֹא בָטֵל. חִיפָּהוּ מַחֲצָלוֹת בָּטֵל. מִילְאָהוּ חָרִיּוֹת צְרִיכָה. רִבִּי זְרִיקָן רִבִּי אַמִּי בְּשֵׁם רֵישׁ לָקִישׁ. אֲפִילוּ רִיק.

1 זה הוא | זהו   התהום | תהום   3 התהום | תהום   שאי | שאין   4 אתה | את
התהום | תהום   5 אומ׳ | אמ׳   ובטלו | וביטלו   6 בשבללו | בשבלל   7 ועפר |
ויש עפר   יכול   עתיד   8 ועפר | עפר   יכול | עתיד   9 חיפהו | מילאהו   10
חריות | חייות   ריש לקיש | ר׳ שמעון בן לקיש   ריק | רק

"What is a grave of the abyss? A corpse buried in stubble, straw, dust, or pebbles[76]. But if it was buried in water, a dark spot, or rock crevasses, it does not create a grave of the abyss[77]." The principle: Any place from where it can be removed creates a grave of the abyss; any place from where it cannot be removed does not create a grave of the abyss[78]. Can stubbles and straw not be removed? Does the Mishnah not follow Rebbi Yose, since Rebbi Yose said, straw said to be disregarded is disregarded[79]. Rebbi Yose ben Rebbi Abun in the name of Rav Ḥisda: It is everybody's opinion. What Rebbi Yose said, if he mixed it with dust[80]. "There is straw which is treated like dust and dust which is treated like straw. Straw not to be removed is like dust; dust to be removed is like straw.[81]" In the House of Rebbi Yannai they said: If he covered it with mats it is disregarded[82]. Come and see: If he [filled][83] it with mats it is not disregarded[84], if he covered it with mats it is disregarded[85]. If he filled it with branches of date palms it is problematic[86]. Rebbi Zeriqan, Rebbi Immi, in the name of Rebbi Simeon ben Laqish: Even thin sheets[87].

76 Tosephta *Zabim* 2:9; quoted in the Babli, 63b and *Pesaḥim* 81b, without further discussion. As explained in the next paragraph, a "grave of the abyss" is that of a person killed by an accident not witnessed by anybody. If one finds a corpse buried under a heap of straw, one has to assume that he suffocated when the straw fell on him. A corpse buried in dust or pebbles probably was the victim of an accident.

77 In this case, the person also probably was the victim of an accident. But since it could have been seen by a passer-by, the competent authorities should have been alerted; this is not an unknown body.

78 Obviously, the clauses in this sentence are switched (here and in *Pesaḥim*). As explained in the preceding notes, one must read: "Any place from where it *cannot* be removed creates a grave of the abyss; any place from where it *can* be removed does not create a grave of the abyss." A corpse whose existence is unknown cannot be removed.

79 This refers to the rules of the tent-impurity caused by a corpse. A "tent" is any covered space in which there is at least one handbreadth of space between the corpse and the roof. If the space is enclosed, the impurity is restricted to the "tent"; anything above the ceiling and below the floor of the "tent" is pure. But if the entire space between floor and ceiling is filled with matter, there is no "tent" and the impurity entends indefinitely above and below the tent space. This is known as טוּמְאָה רְצוּצָה "squeezed impurity" (Mishnah *Ahilut* 15:1,5,6; Halakhah 7:3, Note 164). It is implied in Tosephta *Ahilut* 15:5 that R. Yose restricts "squeezed impurity" to material permanently deposited; but a storage of straw which is to be removed in the future is not counted as filler.

80 Not really "mixed with", but "treated like," as formulated in the Tosephta.

81 Statement of R. Yose in Tosephta *Ahilut* 15:5; quoted in the Babli *Eruvin* 79a. "Straw" stands here for "material to be removed," "dust" for "permanent filling."

82 Straw covered with mats is not considered filling.

83 Reading from *Pesaḥim*, required by the text. In *Nazir*: "covered".

84 Filling the "tent" with mats creates "broken impurity".

85 If the floor is covered with mats, anything below the mats is disregarded concerning impurity.

86 No ruling is available in this case.

87 This translation is tentative, it follows the *Pesaḥim* text, reading רָק. The *Nazir* text reads רִיק, which cannot be רִיק "emptiness", nor רֵיק "empty", nor רוֹק "spittle".

(57d line 23) אֵי זֶה הוּא קֶבֶר הַתְּהוֹם. כָּל־שֶׁאֵין אָדָם זוֹכְרֵהוּ. וְחָשׁ לוֹמַר. שֶׁמָּא אֶחָד בְּסוֹף הָעוֹלָם. בְּחֶזְקַת הַחַי בַּחַיי. תִּיפְתָּר שֶׁמְּצָאוֹ קַמְצוּץ.

1 התחום | התחום   זוכרהו | זוכרו   2 העולם | העולם יודע   בחיי | כחי   קמצוץ | קמציץ

[88]"What is a grave of the abyss? Any which nobody remembers." Should we not be cautious and say, maybe one at the end of the world[89]? And is the permanence of the living not like living[90]? Explain that he was found compressed[91].

88 Tosephta *Zabim* 2:9, quoted Babli *Pesaḥim* 81b.
89 He might know of the grave even if we do not.
90 Cf. *Giṭṭin* 3:3, Notes 81,87. If any person left from here, when that person left he was alive and we have to apply the legal principle of permanence of the *status quo* and consider him permanently alive, disregarding the notion of "unknown grave".
91 Which clearly shows that he was not buried by humans but was the victim of an accident. Since the accident was not noticed when it occurred, there is nobody "at the end of the world" who would know of it.

(57d line 25) תַּנֵּי. אֵין לָךְ עוֹשֶׂה קֶבֶר הַתְּהוֹם אֶלָּא מֵת בִּלְבַד. הָא נְבֵילָה לֹא. קַל וָחוֹמֶר. וּמָה אִם הַמֵּת שֶׁאֵינוֹ עוֹשֶׂה מִשְׁכָּב וּמוֹשָׁב הֲרֵי הוּא עוֹשֶׂה קֶבֶר הַתְּהוֹם. נְבֵילָה שֶׁעוֹשָׂה מִשְׁכָּב וּמוֹשָׁב אֵינוֹ דִין שֶׁתַּעֲשֶׂה קֶבֶר הַתְּהוֹם. לְאֵי זֶה דָבָר נֶאֱמַר. אֵין לָךְ עוֹשֶׂה קֶבֶר הַתְּהוֹם אֶלָּא מֵת בִּלְבַד. לְהוֹצִיא מִשְׁכָּב וּמוֹשָׁב.

1 התתהום | תהום   מת | המת   נבילה | נבלה   2 הרי הוא | -   3 התתהום | תהום שעושה | שהיא עושה   התתהום | תהום   4 עושה | דבר עושה   התהום | תהום   מת | המת

It was stated: "Only a corpse creates a grave of the abyss."[92] Therefore, not a carcass[93]. Would it not be a conclusion *de minore ad majus*? Since a corpse, which does not cause impurity of couch and seat, creates a grave of the abyss, should a carcasss which causes impurity of couch and seat not create a grave of the abyss? Why was it said that only a corpse creates a grave of the abyss? To exclude couch and seat[94].

92 Tosephta *Zabim* 2:9, quoted Babli *Pesaḥim* 80b.
93 Obviously, only a human corpse has a grave that presents problems of

impurity. A buried animal carcass does not produce impurity. Carcasses cause impurity only when touched or carried. The meaning of this sentence can be clarified: Only for the impurity of the dead do we find a rule that sometimes allows one to disregard biblical impurity.

94 This argument, equally found in *Pesaḥim*, does not make any sense. There are several distinct ways to emend the passage to create sense; therefore, no textual emendation is proposed but the meaning can easily be clarified.

A person who is the source of his own impurity (a male or female sufferer from genital discharges) causes *original* impurity to any couch or personal seat he is using (*Lev.* 15:4-6,21-22,26). But any impurity induced on an inanimate object by a corpse is only *derivative*. The argument shows that the rules of the impurity of the dead and impurity produced by a living human body are not comparable: Each kind of impurity has its own severities and leniencies not found in the other.

(57d line 29) רִבִּי יוֹסֵי בֵּירִבִּי בּוּן אָמַר. בַּר פִּיקָה שָׁאַל לְרִבִּי. עַד כְּדוֹן בִּמְעָרָה מְקוּרָה. אֲפִילוּ בִּמְעָרָה שֶׁאֵינָהּ מְקוּרָה. סָבַר בַּר פִּיקָה. אֵין סְפֵק טוּמְאָה צָפָה עַל פְּנֵי הַמַּיִם טָהוֹר. אָמַר לֵיהּ רִבִּי. אֲדַיִין בַּר פִּיקָה עוֹמֵד בְּשְׁטוּתוֹ. אֵין סְפֵק טוּמְאָה צָפָה עַל פְּנֵי הַמַּיִם טָהוֹר אֶלָּא שֶׁרֶץ. אֲבָל בְּמֵת כְּעוֹמֵד הוּא. כְּהָדָא דְתַאנֵי. כָּל־הַנִּזְרָקִין סְפֵיקָן טָהוֹר חוּץ מִכְּזַיִת מִן הַמֵּת הַמַּאֲהִילִין שֶׁהֵן מְטַמְּאִין מִלְמַטָּן לְמַעְלָן.

Rebbi Yose ben Rebbi Abun said that Bar Piqa asked Rebbi: So far in a cave that had a ceiling[95]. Even in a cave without ceiling[96]? Does Bar Piqa think that if there is a doubt regarding floating impurity, it is pure? Rebbi told him, Bar Piqa remains in his stupidity: No case of doubt regarding floating impurity is declared pure except a reptile[97]; but a corpse is like something fixed in place. As it was stated[98]: "Anything thrown[99] is pure in case of a doubt except an olive-sized piece from a corpse, [and] also those covers[100] which induce impurity on bottom and top."

95   This refers to the Mishnah about the person who immersed himself in water in a cave in which a corpse was later found.

96   Is he impure only because of the "tent" impurity induced by the ceiling of the cave or is he impure since he might have touched the corpse without noticing? A "cave without ceiling" seems to be a pond.

97   Or any similar impurity which is removed by immersion in water without delay or further ceremony.

98   The meaning of this *baraita*, formulated differently, is found in Tosephta *Taharot* 5:6-7 and in the Babli, 63b-64a.

99   An impure item thrown over a person and it is not clear whether he or she was touched by the item or not.

100 Those whose impurity is generated by their bodies (Note 93) who cause original impurity to what is below (the couch or seat) and above (the clothing) their persons.

(57d line 35) לֵית הָדָא פְלִיגָא עַל רבִּי יֹאשִׁיָּה. דְּרבִּי יֹאשִׁיָּה אָמַר. טוּמְאָה טְמוּנָה בַּקַּרְקַע שֶׁלַּבַּיִת הַנָּזִיר מְגַלֵּחַ. אָמַר רבִּי יוֹחָנָן. כָּאן מִן הַצַּד וְכָאן מִכְּנֶגְדָּן. רבִּי עֶזְרָה בְּשֵׁם רבִּי יוּדָן אָמַר. וַאֲפִילוּ תֵימַר. כָּאן וְכָאן מִן הַצַּד. וְתֵימַר. כָּאן וְכָאן מִכְּנֶגְדָּן. מָהוּ טָמֵא. טָמֵא וְאֵינוֹ מְגַלֵּחַ.

Does this[101] not disagree with Rebbi Joshia, since Rebbi Joshia said[102], if impurity is hidden in the ground below the house, the *nazir* shaves. Rebbi Johanan said, here on the side, there on place[103]. Rebbi Ezra said in the name of Rebbi Yudan: Even if you say in both cases on the side, in both cases on place. What means "impure"? Impure and he does not shave[104]?

101 Since the Mishnah states that he is impure but not, speaking of a *nazir*, that he has to shave, do we have to read the Mishnah as equating this impurity to those mentioned in Chapter Seven for which the *nazir* does not have to shave?

102 Chapter 7:3, Note 176.

103 The Mishnah deals with a doubt of impurity; R. Joshia speaks of "squeezed impurity", which is certain.

104 The Mishnah has to be read as meaning: "He is impure and, if a *nazir*, has to shave."

(fol. 57b) **משנה ג:** הַמּוֹצֵא מֵת בַּתְּחִילָה מוּשְׁכָּב כְּדַרְכּוֹ נוֹטְלוֹ וְאֶת תְּפוּשָׁתוֹ. מָצָא שְׁנַיִם נוֹטְלָן וְאֶת תְּפוּשָׁתָן. מָצָא שְׁלֹשָׁה אִם יֵשׁ בֵּין זֶה לָזֶה מֵאַרְבַּע אַמּוֹת עַד שְׁמוֹנֶה כִּמְלוֹא הַמִּטָּה וְקוֹבְרֶיהָ הֲרֵי זוֹ שְׁכוּנַת קְבָרוֹת. בּוֹדֵק מִמֶּנּוּ וּלְהַלָּן עֶשְׂרִים אַמָּה. מָצָא אֶחָד בְּסוֹף עֶשְׂרִים אַמָּה בּוֹדֵק הֵימֶנּוּ וּלְהַלָּן עֶשְׂרִים אַמָּה שֶׁרַגְלַיִם לַדָּבָר שֶׁאִילּוּ מִתְּחִילָה מְצָאוֹ נוֹטְלוֹ וְאֶת תְּבוּסָתוֹ.[105]

Mishnah 3: If somebody finds[106] a corpse in original position, lying as usual[107], he takes him and his surroundings[108]. If he finds two, he takes them and their surroundings. If he finds three[109] and between one and the next is a distance of between four and eight cubits, enough for the bier and the people who bury[110], that is a cemetery[111]. He has to check on both sides for another 20 cubits. If he finds a grave at the end of 20 cubits, he has to check another 20 cubits since it is obvious that if this were a new burial ground, one would have taken him and his surroundings there[112].

---

105 An alternative spelling of תְּפוּשָׁתוֹ.

106 Ploughing his field or excavating his property, he finds a grave unknown to him.

107 The position of the bones is that usual in Jewish burials.

108 He can remove the bones and the earth that will have absorbed the decaying flesh. The Mishnah assumes that no sarcophagus was used.

109 Three parallel graves.

110 It is forbidden to step on a grave while burying another person. Therefore, a Jewish cemetery must allow enough space that burials can take place which do not desecrate prior graves.

111 It is forbidden to remove the graves or to use the ground for other purposes.

112 If a series of graves was found which conform to the rules of a cemetery, it must be a cemetery since otherwise the bones would have been removed.

(57d line 39) **הלכה ג:** אֵי זֶהוּ מֵשְׁכָּב כְּדַרְכּוֹ. רַגְלָיו מְפוּשָׁטוֹת וְיָדָיו עַל לִבּוֹ. אֲבָל אִם מְצָאוֹ קַמְצוּץ. אֲנִי אוֹמֵר. גַּל נָפַל עָלָיו וַהֲרָגוֹ. וְהָתַנֵּי. מָצָא שְׁנַיִם

רָאשֵׁיהֶם בְּצַד מַרְגְּלוֹתֵיהֶם נוֹטְלָן וְאֶת תְּפוּסָתָן. סָבְרִין מֵימַר. קַמְצוּץ מָהוּ. רָאשֵׁיהֶם בְּצַד מַרְגְּלוֹתֵיהֶם. אָמַר רִבִּי יִצְחָק בֵּירִבִּי אֶלְעָזָר. כְּגוֹן אִילֵּין נוּנַיָּא צְלָיָיא רֵישֵׁיהּ דְּהֵן גַּבֵּי עוּקְצֵיהּ דְּהֵן עוּקְצֵיהּ דְּהֵן גַּבֵּי רֵישֵׁיהּ דְּהֵן.

Halakhah 3: What means "lying as usual"? His legs straight and his hands over his heart. But if he found him compressed, I am saying that a heap fell on him and killed him. But did we not state: "If he found two with their heads beside their legs, he takes them and their surroundings?"[113] They wanted to say, what means "compressed"? Their heads beside their legs[114]. Rebbi Isaac ben Rebbi Eleazar said, like fried fish, the head of one near the tail of the other and vice versa[115].

113 Babli 65a.
114 A Gentile way of burial.
115 The head of one corpse between the legs of another is not a form of burial but a sign of an accident.

(57d line 44) רִבִּי יִצְחָק בַּר גּוּפְתָּא בְּעָא קוֹמֵי רִבִּי מָנָא. תַּנֵּי אַתְּ אָמַר מְלַקֵּט עֶצֶם עֶצֶם וְהַכֹּל טָהוֹר. וְכָא אַתְּ אָמַר הָכֵין. אָמַר לֵיהּ. אֱמוֹר דְּבַתְרָהּ. אִם הִתְקִינוֹ לְקֶבֶר מִתְּחִילָּה יֵשׁ לוֹ תְּפוּסָה.

Rebbi Isaac bar Gufta asked before Rebbi Mana: In a statement you say, "he collects every single bone and everything is pure[116];" and here, you say so? He answered him, say what comes afterwards: "If he prepared it from the start as a grave, it has surroundings.[117]"

116 Mishnah Ahilut 16:5: "If one removes a grave from his field, he collects every single bone and everything is pure." In contrast, the Mishnah here requires that a certain amount of earth also be removed.

117 Statement of R. Simeon in the same Mishnah. From a cistern used to bury stillbirths or crime victims (incomplete corpses which have no claim to "surroundings") one can remove all bones and it is pure. *But if he prepared the cistern from the start as a temporary grave, it has surroundings* (when the bones are finally removed). This is the case

considered in the Mishnah here, since one speaks of graves parallel to one another, i. e., intended as temporary graves.

(57d line 46) כַּמָּה הִיא תְפוּסַת קֶבֶר. קוֹלֵף ג׳ אֶצְבָּעוֹת עַד מָקוֹם שֶׁהַמּוֹהֵל יוֹרֵד.

How much is the surrounding of a grave? One shaves off three finger-breadths, the place where fluid penetrates[118].

118 In the Babli, 65a, this is a little more explicit: In virgin soil, one takes three finger-breadths. In loose soil, one takes as much as one recognizes that the decomposing flesh penetrated.

(57d line 47) אָמַר רַב חִסְדָּא. הָדָא אָמְרָה. מֵת מִצְוָה מוּתָּר לְפַנּוֹתוֹ. אָמַר רִבִּי זְעִירָא. תִּיפְתָּר שֶׁנִּקְבַּר שֶׁלֹּא בִרְשׁוּת אוֹ שֶׁנִּקְבַּר לִשְׁאֵלָה. וְחָשׁ לוֹמַר שֶׁמָּא מֵת מִצְוָה הִיא. סָבַר רִבִּי זְעִירָא שֶׁאֵין מֵיתֵי מִצְוָה מְצוּיִין. נִמְצֵאתָהּ אוֹמֵר. שְׁלֹשָׁה מִינֵי קְבָרוֹת הֵן. קֶבֶר הַנִּמְצָא מְפַנִּין אוֹתוֹ. פִּינֵּהוּ מְקוֹמוֹ טָמֵא וְאָסוּר בַּהֲנָייָה. קֶבֶר הַיָדוּעַ אֵין מְפַנִּין אוֹתוֹ. פִּינֵּהוּ מְקוֹמוֹ טָהוֹר וּמוּתָּר בַּהֲנָייָה. קֶבֶר שֶׁהוּא מַזִּיק אֶת הָרַבִּים מְפַנִּין אוֹתוֹ. פִּינֵּהוּ מְקוֹמוֹ טָמֵא וְאָסוּר בַּהֲנָייָה. הוֹרָה רִבִּי אַבָּא בַּר כֹּהֵן בִּכְפַר עֲקַבְיָה. מְקוֹמוֹ וּמוּתָּר בַּהֲנָייָה. מַה וּפְלִיג. כָּאן בְּשֶׁקָּדַם הוּא אֶת הָעִיר וְכָאן בְּשֶׁקְּדָמָתוֹ הָעִיר. תַּנֵּי. קֶבֶר שֶׁהֶקִּיפָתוֹ הָעִיר מִשְּׁלֹשׁ רוּחוֹת מְפַנִּין אוֹתוֹ. מִשְּׁתֵּי רוּחוֹת. אִית תַּנֵּיי תַּנֵּי. מְפַנִּין אוֹתוֹ. אִית תַּנֵּיי תַּנֵּי. מְפַנִּין אוֹתוֹ. אֵין תַּנֵּי. אָמַר רַב חִסְדָּא. מָאן דְּאָמַר מְפַנִּין אוֹתוֹ. בְּנָתוּן בְּתוֹךְ שִׁבְעִים אַמָּה וְשִׁירַיִים. מָאן דְּאָמַר אֵין מְפַנִּין אוֹתוֹ. בְּנָתוּן חוּץ לְשִׁבְעִים אַמָּה וְשִׁירַיִים. מָאן דְּאָמַר מְפַנִּין אוֹתוֹ. בְּעָשׂוּי כְּמִין גַּם. מָאן דְּאָמַר אֵין מְפַנִּין אוֹתוֹ. בְּעָשׂוּי כְּמִין הֵיא. כָּל-הַקְּבָרוֹת מִתְפַּנִּין חוּף מִקִּבְרֵי הַמֶּלֶךְ וּמִקִּבְרֵי הַנָּבִיא. אָמְרוּ לוֹ. וַהֲלֹא קִבְרֵי בְּנֵי דָוִד מִתְפַּנִּין וְקִבְרֵי בְּנֵי חוּלְדָּה הָיוּ בִּירוּשָׁלַיִם וְלֹא נָגַע אָדָם בָּהֶן לְפַנּוֹתָן מֵעוֹלָם. אָמַר לָהֶן רִבִּי עֲקִיבָה. מִשָּׁם רְאַייָה. מְחִילָה הָיָה שָׁם וּמִשָּׁם הָיְתָה טוּמְאָה מְקַדֶּדֶת וְיוֹצְאָה לְנַחַל קִדְרוֹן.

Rav Ḥisda said, [the Mishnah] implies that it is permitted to remove a corpse of obligation[119]. Rebbi Zeʿira said, explain it if the burial was unauthorized or subject to question. Should one not be afraid that it might be a corpse of obligation? Rebbi Zeʿira thinks that corpses of obligation are infrequent[120]. [121]"It turns out that there are three kinds of burials. A grave which is found one removes; after removal the place is impure[122] and forbidden for use[123]. A known grave may not be removed; but if it was removed the place is pure and permitted for use[124]. A grave which endangers the public[125] is removed; after removal the place is impure and forbidden for use." Rebbi Abba bar Cohen instructed in Kefar Aqabia[126] that its place is permitted for use. Does he disagree? There if it preceded the village, here if the village preceded it[127]. It was stated: "A grave surrounded by a village on three sides can be removed[128, 129]," on two sides, some Tannaïm state that one removes it, some state that one may not remove it. Rav Ḥisda said, he who says that one removes it, if it is within slightly more than 70 cubits[130]. He who says that one does not remove it, if it is outside slightly more than 70 cubits. He who says that one removes it, if [the village] is built in the form of a Γ[131]. He who says that one does not remove it, if [the village] is built in the form of a ח.[132]
[128]"All kinds of graves may be removed except the graves of a king or a prophet. They said to him, were not the graves of David's sons removed but the graves of the sons of Ḥulda were in Jerusalem and nobody ever touched them to remove them[133]. Rebbi Aqiba told them, is that a proof? A duct was there and the impurity exited from there horizontally into the Qidron valley[134]."

119   Since the Mishnah permits removal of any grave which was found accidentally, it must permit the removal of a "corpse of obligation"

once it is no longer remembered.

120 R. Ze'ira holds that graves of unattended people are such a rarity that their locations remain known over a very long time. If the owner of a parcel finds there a grave of whose existence he was not informed by its prior owner, either it was an illegitimate burial (which may be removed since "nobody can fulfill his obligations with his neighbor's money") or it was a burial with consent of the prior owner done on condition that it might later be removed and the prior owner was under the mistaken impression that it already had been removed. The same interpretation is given in the Babli *Sanhedrin* 47b.

121 Tosephta *Ahilut* 16:9; Tractate *Semaḥot* 14; Babli *Sanhedrin* 47b. To this one may add the versions in Maimonides *Ṭum'at Mēt* 9:5-6 which is essentially identical with the Yerushalmi and the text there of Ravad, which in general follows the Babli. Tractate *Semaḥot* does not give an opinion about impurity; otherwise it follows the Babli. The three texts, Yerushalmi (Y), Babli (B), and Tosephta (T) state that if the grave found accidentally be removed the place is impure (Y), pure (BT); its use is forbidden (YT), permitted (B). The place of a known grave after removal is pure (YT), impure (B); its use is permitted (YT), forbidden (B). The place of a grave removed because of a danger to the public is impure (YT), pure (B); its use is forbidden (YBT) except that Ravad reads here "permitted" in the Babli, a reading contradicting all our other sources for the Babli.

122 In the interpretation of Maimonides, the place is only impure as long as not all earth, including 3 finger-breadths of virgin soil, has been removed. This interpretation shows clearly that he reads here "impure"; there can be no emendation of the text.

123 Since a grave is forbidden for any use by biblical law, a removal cannot change the character of the ground.

124 Since the Tosephta shows that the text here cannot be amended, the only explanation is that a known grave may be removed only if either it was established illegally as a criminal act which cannot deprive the owner of the lawful use of his property, or it was intended as a temporary grave exempt from the biblical rules (Note 120).

125 A grave in a public road is considered a danger to the public.

126 The locality has not been determined; it might designate any place located on a hill (عقبة).

127 If the grave predated the building of the access road to a village, the road should have avoided the place of the grave; it has to be rerouted. But if the grave was dug in an existing public road, it is illegal, not considered a grave, nor protected by the rules.

128 A similar text is in Tractate *Semaḥot* 14.

129 Since it will be a public obstacle.

130 In *Semaḥot*, this is part of the statement of the *baraita*: If a grave is between two parallel rows of houses and the empty space in between is at least the size of a standard field, a *bet se'ah*, it cannot be removed. If the difference is less, it may be removed. The *bet se'ah* is defined as 5'000 square cubits (cf. *Peah* 2:1, Note 31), its edge length is √5000 = 70.71... cubits. This length is the general standard for defining a "built-up area." As long as no two buildings are separated by more than 70.7 cubits, they are part of the same urban area, e. g., for defining the area of free mobility on the Sabbath. Therefore, an empty strip less than 70.7 cubits wide is not open space but a built-up area.

131 Any point within the right angle is accessible from the outside and is considered part of an open field.

132 Since the break in the left hand stroke of the letter ה is a relatively late development, it would be better to designate the shape of the village as ח. In old texts, the left stroke of ח is flush with the end of the horizontal stroke and ends a little higher; the one of ה is slightly to the right of the end of the horizontal stroke and ends exactly at the horizontal stroke. The meaning is that if the grave is between two rows of houses at a distance less than 70.7 cubits, it is within a built-up area where it does not belong.

133 Which is extraordinary since within the urban area of Jerusalem no grave could be tolerated, seeing that a grave is a "squeezed impurity" (Note 79) which causes "tent" impurity to anybody stepping over it and disables him from entering the Temple Mount.

134 If the graves were open to the outside, the impurity was not "squeezed" and there was no induced "tent" impurity over them.

(57d line 65) תַּמָּן תַּנִּינָן. וְעוֹשֶׂה חָצֵר עַל פֶּתַח הַמְעָרָה שֵׁשׁ עַל שֵׁשׁ כִּמְלוֹא הַמִּטָּה. וְהָכָא הוּא אָמַר הָכֵין. תַּמָּן מְלֹא הַמִּטָּה עוֹמֶדֶת. בְּרַם הָכָא מְלוֹא מִיטָה חוֹזֶרֶת. עַד אֵיכָן. עַד כְּדֵי נוֹשְׂאֵי הַמִּיטָה וְחִילּוּפֵיהֶן וְחִילּוּפֵי חִילּוּפֵיהֶן.

There[135], we have stated: "He makes a courtyard[136] in front of the cave six cubits square as a place for the bier." And here, he says so[137]? There for a bier standing, here for the width of a turning bier. How far[138]? For the carriers of the bier, their replacements, and the replacements of their replacements.

135 Mishnah *Baba batra* 6:8, detailing the standards for a builder of burial caves.

136 A flat space outside the cave.

137 Why does the contractor only have to build a space of six cubits square for burial in a cave whereas for burial in the ground one reserves eight cubits on either side? It is to be expected that the minimal standards for a commercial contract are less than those for checking for impurity.

138 This has nothing to do with either commercial contracts or impurity; it defines the persons participating in a funeral and exempt from any other duties while the funeral procession is in progress; Mishnah *Berakhot* 3:1.

(57d line 68) תַּמָּן תַּנִּינָן. כֶּרֶם שֶׁהוּא נָטוּעַ עַד פָּחוֹת מֵאַרְבַּע אַמּוֹת. רִבִּי שִׁמְעוֹן אוֹמֵר. אֵינוֹ כֶרֶם. וַחֲכָמִים אוֹמְרִים כֶּרֶם. וְרוֹאִין אֶת הָאֶמְצָעִיּוֹת כְּאִילוּ אֵינָן. שִׁמְעוֹן בַּר בָּא בְשֵׁם רִבִּי יוֹחָנָן. כְּשֵׁם שֶׁהֵן חוֹלְקִין כָּאן כָּךְ הֵן חוֹלְקִין בִּשְׁכוּנַת קְבָרוֹת. אָמַר רִבִּי יוֹנָה. וְלֹא דַמְיָיא. תַּמָּן יֵשׁ עֲלֵיהֶן שְׁכוּנַת קְבָרוֹת. בְּרַם הָכָא אֵין עֲלֶיהָ שְׁכוּנַת קְבָרוֹת. אָמַר רִבִּי יוֹסֵי. וְלֹא דַמְיָיא. תַּמָּן מְרוּוָחִין וּרְצָפָן בְּמַחְלוֹקֶת. רְצוּפִין וְרִיוְוחָן דִּבְרֵי הַכֹּל. בְּרַם הָכָא מָהוּ פְלִיגִין. בְּשֶׁבָּא וּמְצָאָן רְצוּפִין. רִבִּי שִׁמְעוֹן אוֹמֵר. נָפַל עֲלֵיהֶן וּרְצָפָן. וְרַבָּנָן אָמְרֵי. מְרוּוָחִין הָיוּ וּרְצָפָן.

There, we have stated[139]: "If a vineyard is planted with less that four cubits of space, Rebbi Simeon says that it is no vineyard. But the Sages say that it is a vineyard and one disregards the plants in the middle as if nonexistent." [140]Simeon bar Abba in the name of Rebbi Johanan[32]: Just as they disagree here, they disagree about a graveyard[33]. Rebbi Jonah said, one cannot compare these. There, they form a graveyard; here, they do not form a graveyard. Rebbi Yose said, one cannot compare these. There, if they were spaced apart and one moved them closer together, that is the disagreement. If they were close and one moved them apart, everybody would agree. But here, what is their disagreement? When one found them close together. Rebbi Simeon said, a landslide fell on them and compressed them. But the Sages say, were they spaced apart and somebody brought them close together?"

139   Mishnah *Kilaim* 5:2.
140   *Kilaim* 5:2 (29d l. 54 ff.), full

variant readings and commentary there, Notes 32-40.

(57d line 75) ‏עַד¹⁴¹ כַּמָּה מַטְרִיחִין עָלָיו. רִבִּי יוֹסֵי בְּשֵׁם רִבִּי מִייָשָׁא בַּר יִרְמִיָה.‏
‏עַד מ' אַמָּה. בָּדַק עֶשְׂרִים וּמָצָא בּוֹדֵק עַד עֶשֶׂר. בָּדַק עֶשְׂרִים וּמָצָא בּוֹדֵק עַד‏
‏עֶשֶׂר. אִית תַּנָּיֵי תַּנֵּי. בָּדַק עֶשֶׂר וּמָצָא בּוֹדֵק עַד עֶשֶׂר. בָּדַק עֶשֶׂר וּמָצָא בּוֹדֵק‏
‏עַד עֶשֶׂר.‏

How far does one importune him[142]? Rebbi Yose in the name of Rebbi Miasha bar Jeremiah: Up to 40 cubits. If he checked twenty and found, he checks another ten. If he checked twenty and found, he checks another ten[143]. Some Tannaïm state: If he checked ten and found, he checks another ten. If he checked ten and found, he checks another ten[144].

141   In ms. and *editio princeps* this is the start of Halakhah 4.
142   This refers to the end of Mishnah 3: If there are three parallel graves and one found another grave at the end of 20 cubits, how often does he have to repeat the operation?

143   In this version, he has to check 60 cubits. On either side of the graves he has to check at most 20 cubits. If he found a grave, he has to check 10 more cubits, for a total of $2(20+10) = 60$ cubits.
144   This agrees with the original

statement. He has to check a maximum of 10+10 = 20 cubits on either side for a total of 40.

(fol. 57b) **משנה ד:** כָּל־סְפֵק נְגָעִים בַּתְּחִלָּה טָהוֹר עַד שֶׁלֹּא נִזְקַק לְטוּמְאָה. מִשֶּׁנִּזְקַק לְטוּמְאָה סְפֵיקוֹ טָמֵא. בְּשִׁבְעָה דְרָכִים בּוֹדְקִין אֶת הַזָּב עַד שֶׁלֹּא נִזְקַק לְטוּמְאָה בְּמַאֲכָל בְּמִשְׁתֶּה בְּמַשָּׂא בִּקְפִיצָה בְּחוֹלִי בְּמַרְאֶה וּבְהִירְהוּר. מִשֶּׁנִּזְקַק לְטוּמְאָה אֵין בּוֹדְקִין אוֹתוֹ. אָנְסוֹ וּסְפֵיקוֹ וְשִׁכְבַת זַרְעוֹ טְמֵאִים שֶׁרַגְלַיִם לַדָּבָר.

Mishnah 4: Any person with initially doubtful skin disease is pure as long as he was not declared impure. After he was declared impure, in doubt he is impure[145]. [146]In seven ways does one check the sufferer from a genital discharge before he becomes impure[147]: About eating and drinking[148], carrying a load or jumping[149], sickness, looking, and thought[150]. After he becomes impure one does not check him; his accident, doubtful case, and semen are impure since the matter is not unsubstantiated[151].

---

145 A sufferer from skin disease is impure only after he was declared impure by a Cohen. Once he is impure, he can regain purity only by a ceremony administered by a Cohen. A Cohen may not declare a person impure unless the impurity is clearly demonstrated; he may not cleanse a person declared impure unless that person is clearly healed. The details are given in Mishnah *Nega'im* 5:4-5.

146 The Mishnah is given in great detail in *Zavim* 2:2; it is included here only because it is a "not unsubstantiated" case.

147 The basic source is *Lev.* 15:1-15. After a discharge of semen, a male is impure for the rest of the day (*Lev.* 15:16). For any other discharge, the first time he is pure. After the second discharge within 24 hours he is impure for seven days. However, if there is a

reason to suspect that the discharge was induced by an outside cause, he remains pure since impurity is created by (*Lev.* 15:2) "flow from his flesh", not from any outside cause. After the third discharge, he needs purification by a sacrifice.

148   If he ate or drank excessively.

149   Extraordinary physical exertion, whether professional or for sport.

150   Looking at women might cause an ejaculation as well as thinking of copulation.

151   Once he is suffering from gonorrhea, any discharge is ascribed to his condition rather than to extraneous influences.

(58a line 3) **הלכה ד:** וְטִמֵּא אוֹתוֹ. אֶת הַוַודַּאי הוּא מְטַמֵּא אֵינוּ מְטַמֵּא אֶת הַסָּפֵק. לְעוֹלָם הוּא בְּטוּמְאָתוֹ עַד שֶׁיֵּדַע שֶׁטָּהַר. וְטִיהֲרוֹ. אֶת הַוַודַּאי הוּא מְטַהֵר אֵינוּ מְטַמֵּא אֶת הַסָּפֵק.

Halakhah 4: "He shall declare him impure[152]." The certain case he declares impure, he does not declare the doubtful case impure. Forever he is in his impurity until he is known to be pure. "He shall purify him[153]." The certain case he declares pure, he does not declare the doubtful case impure[154].

152   *Lev.* 13:2. This is the first case of skin disease treated in *Lev.*; it stands for all cases.

153   *Lev.* 13:23. *Sifra Tasria' Parashah* 4(9); Babli 65b.

154   Read: "pure".

(58a line 6) כְּתִיב וְהַדָּוָה בְּנִידָּתָהּ וְהַזָּב אֶת זוֹבוֹ. מַה נִידָּה מְטַמָּא מֵאוֹנְסִים. אַף הַזָּב מְטַמֵּא מֵאוֹנְסִים. מֵעַתָּה אֲפִילוּ מֵרְאִייָה הָרִאשׁוֹנָה. אָמַר רִבִּי זְעִירָא. לִכְשֶׁיֵּיעָשֶׂה כְּנִידָּה.

It is written[155]: "The unwell woman in her separation and the sufferer from flux in his flux." Since the menstruating woman may become impure also by accident, so the sufferer from flux may become impure also by accident[156]. Then even at his first episode[157]? Rebbi Ze'ira said, from the moment he becomes like a menstruating woman[158].

155 *Lev.* 15:33, the final verse of the chapter dealing with impurity caused by the human body.
156 Since the two kinds of impurity are mentioned together.
157 But the Mishnah declares that outside influences are disregarded only after the sufferer from flux is subject to a week-long impurity.
158 Whose impurity always extends for seven days.

(58a line 8) אוֹנְסוֹ. אָמַר רִבִּי אֶלְעָזָר. אוֹנְסוֹ מַמָּשׁ. סְפֵיקוֹ. סָפֵק זוֹב סָפֵק קֶרִי. זוֹבוֹ וְשִׁכְבַת זַרְעוֹ בְּלֹא כָךְ אֵינוֹ מְטַמֵּא. אֶלָּא שֶׁאֵין תּוֹלִין בָּהּ מֵעֵת לָעֵת.

"His accident," Rebbi Eleazar said, his real accident. "His doubtful case," a doubt whether it is flux or ejaculation. Are flux and semen not impure anyhow[159]? But one does not consider it for the 24 hour period[160].

159 But semen is impure only until sundown after immersion in water.
160 If the sufferer is impure for seven days and he has an ejaculation, any further discharge within 24 hours of his prior episode of flux is not considered caused by his sexual activity but will cause him to require a sacrifice for his purification.

(fol. 57b) **משנה ה:** הַמַּכֶּה אֶת חֲבֵירוֹ וַאֲמָדוּהוּ לְמִיתָה הֵיקֵל מִמַּה שֶּׁהָיָה וְאַחַר מִכֵּן הִכְבִּיד וָמֵת חַיָּיב. רִבִּי נְחֶמְיָה אוֹמֵר פָּטוּר שֶׁרַגְלַיִם לַדָּבָר.

Mishnah 5: If somebody injured another person who was judged dying and then this person's state improved[161] but later he died, he is guilty. Rebbi Nehemiah says, he cannot be prosecuted[162] since it is not unsubstantiated.

161 The injured is no longer critical but did not get out of bed, which would be the biblical criterion preventing a prosecution of the attacker for murder (*Ex.* 21:19).
162 If at any moment the victim was judged not critically ill, death could have a cause unrelated to the attack.

(58a line 10) **הלכה ה:** מָנֵי מַתְנִיתָא. רַבִּי נְחֶמְיָה פּוֹטֵר וַחֲכָמִים מְחַיְּיבִין שֶׁרַגְלַיִים לַדָּבָר. רַבָּנִין אֲמְרִין. שְׁנֵי עוֹמְדִין רָבִים עַל עוֹמֵד אֶחָד. רַבִּי נְחֶמְיָה אוֹמֵר. עוֹמֵד הָעֶמְצָעִי רָבָּה עַל שְׁנֵיהֶם. מַה טַעֲמָא דְּרַבִּי נְחֶמְיָה. אִם יָקוּם וְהִתְהַלֵּךְ בַּחוּץ עַל מִשְׁעַנְתּוֹ וְנִקָּה הַמַּכֶּה. וְכִי עָלַת עַל דַּעְתָּךְ שֶׁיְּהֵא זֶה מְהַלֵּךְ בַּשּׁוּק וַהֲלָה נֶהֱרַג עַל יָדָיו. אֶלָּא אֲפִילוּ מֵת מַחֲמַת עֲמָדָה רִאשׁוֹנָה פָּטוּר. מַה טַעֲמוֹן דְּרַבָּנִין. וְלֹא יָמוּת וְנָפַל לְמִשְׁכָּב. וְכִי אֵין אָנוּ יוֹדְעִין שֶׁאִם אֵינוֹ מֵת שֶׁהוּא נוֹפֵל לְמִשְׁכָּב. אֶלָּא בִּשְׁעֲמָדוּהוּ לְמִיתָה. אִם בִּשְׁעֲמָדוּהוּ לְמִיתָה הָדָא הִיא דִּכְתִיב אִם יָקוּם וְהִתְהַלֵּךְ בַּחוּץ עַל מִשְׁעַנְתּוֹ. הָא אִם לֹא קָם חַיָּיב. אֶלָּא בְּשֶׁלֹּא עֲמָדוּהוּ לְמִיתָה. אִם בְּשֶׁלֹּא עֲמָדוּהוּ לְמִיתָה הָדָא הִיא דִּכְתִיב רַק שִׁבְתּוֹ יִתֵּן. רַבִּי אִילָא בְּשֵׁם רַבִּי שִׁמְעוֹן בֶּן לָקִישׁ. חִידוּשׁ מִקְרָא הוּא שֶׁיִּתֵּן. רַבִּי אֲבָהוּ בְּשֵׁם רַבִּי יוֹסֵי בְּיִרְבִּי חֲנִינָה. עָמַד שֶׁלְּטָעוֹת הָיָה. מַה נְּפָק מִבֵּינֵיהוֹן. הֵקַל מִמַּה שֶׁהָיָה. מָאן דְּאָמַר. חִידוּשׁ מִקְרָא הוּא שֶׁיִּתֵּן. אִם נָתַן נָתַן. לֹא נָתַן מִקְרָא שֶׁיִּתֵּן. מַתְנִיתָא מְסַיְּיעָא לְדֵין וּמַתְנִיתָא מְסַיְּיעָא לְדֵין. מַתְנִיתָא מְסַיְּיעָא לְרַבִּי יוֹסֵי בֶּן חֲנִינָה. עֲמָדוּהוּ לְמִיתָה וְחָיָה. מֵאֵימָתַי נוֹתְנִין לוֹ. מִשָּׁעָה שֶׁיַּעֲקֹל. מָאן דְּאָמַר. עוֹמֵד שֶׁלְּטָעוֹת הָיָה. לֹא נָתַן אֵין אוֹמְרִין לוֹ שֶׁיִּתֵּן. נָתַן מַהוּ שֶׁיִּטּוֹל. מְסַיְּיעָא לֵיהּ לְרַבִּי שִׁמְעוֹן בֶּן לָקִישׁ. אֲמָדוּהוּ לְחַיִּים וָמֵת. מֵאֵימָתַי נוֹתְנִין לוֹ. מִשָּׁעָה שֶׁיַּכְבִּיד. אָמַר רַבִּי יוֹסֵי. לֵית כָּאן מִשָּׁעָה שֶׁיַּכְבִּיד אֶלָּא מִשָּׁעָה שֶׁיַּעֲקֹל.

1 מני | כיני   2 עומדין | אמודין   3 שניהם | שניחן   4 עלת | עלתה   5 מחמת עמדה | בעמידה   6 אינו מת | לא ימות   7 שהוא נופל | ונפל   בשעמדוהו | בשלא עמדוהו | בשעמדוהו | בשלא עמדוהו   הדא היא דכת' | בדא כת'   8 משענתו | משעננתו וניקה המכה   9 בשלא עמדוהו | בשעמדוהו (2 times)   הדא היא דכת' | בדא כת'   10 יתן | יתן ורפא ירפא   ר' אילא | ר' הילא   11 ביר' | בן   היה | הייתה   נפק | מפקה   12 הקל | היקל   שהיה | שהיה ואחר כך הכביד ומת חייב. ר' נחמיה פוטר. שרגלים לדבר   אם נתן | נתן   13 מקרא | מהו   14 בן | בר   למתה וחיה | לחיים ומת   נותנין | מונין   15 משעה שיקל | משיכביד ג משיקל   מאן דאמ' | הדא אמרה לא נתן אומרין לו שיתן | ואין תימר. חידוש מקרא הוא שיתן. יתן משעה ראשונה   16 מסייעא | מתניתא מסייעא   ליה לר' | לר'   אמדוהו | עמדוהו   לחיים | למיתה וחיה   17 נותנין | מונין   משעה שיכביד | משהכביד   18 שיקל | הראשונה. הדא אמרה. חידוש מקרא הוא שיתן. ואין תימר. עומד שלטעות היית. נותן עד שעה שימות.

HALAKHAH 5

Halakhah 5: [163]So[164] is the Mishnah: Rebbi Nehemia declares him not prosecutable but the Sages declare him guilty since it is not unsubstantiated[165]. The Sages say, two estimations have precedence over one estimation[166]; Rebbi Nehemiah says, the intermediate estimation has precedence over the two[167]. What is Rebbi Nehemiah's reason? "'If he gets up and walks outside on his cane, the attacker is exonerated[168].' Could you think that this one walks in the market and the other is executed because of him[169]? But even if he died according to the first estimation he cannot be prosecuted[170]."[171] What is the rabbi's reason? "If he does not die but is bedridden[172]." Would we not know that even if he does not die that he will be bedridden[173]? But if they estimated[174] that he would die. If they estimated[174] that he would die, that is what is written: "If he gets up and walks outside on his cane." Therefore, if he does not get up, [the attacker] is guilty. But if they did not estimate[174] that he would die? If they did not estimate[174] that he would die, that is what is written: "But he has to pay for his disability." Rebbi Ila in the name of Rebbi Simeon ben Laqish: It is an extraordinary decree of Scripture that he has to pay[175]. Rebbi Abbahu in the name of Rebbi Yose ben Hanina: It was an erroneous estimation[176]. [177]What is the difference between them? If his state improved. For him who says, it is an extraordinary decree of Scripture that he has to pay; if he paid, he paid. If he did not pay, the verse makes him pay. A *baraita* supports one and a *baraita* supports the other. A *baraita* supports Rebbi Yose ben Hanina: If they estimated that he would die, when does he have to pay him? From the moment he improves. For him who says, it was an erroneous estimation; if he did not pay one does not order him to pay. If he paid, can he take it back? This supports Rebbi Simeon ben Laqish: If they estimated that he would live but he died. From when does one have to pay him? From the moment he turns worse. Rebbi Yose said, it does not say here, "from the moment he turns worse" but "from the moment he turns better."

163   The origin of this and the following paragraphs is in *Sanhedrin* 9:3 (fol. 27a). The first part of our text is almost identical with the text there; the second part is badly garbled and can be understood only from the *Sanhedrin* text. (ג denotes a Genizah reading.)

164   Reading כיני as in *Sanhedrin*, in place of מני "who is the author"?

165   The expression רגלים לדבר "the thing has feet" formulates *prima facie* evidence of guilt, not an argument which prohibits prosecution.

166   Any "estimation" here is a judicial act. If the physician in charge as an officer of the court considered the victim as critically ill both at the beginning and at the end of treatment, this overrides the fact that for some time the victim was taken off the critical list. The attacker can be jailed only if the victim is in danger of his life and there is the possibility that the case may become one of capital crime (*Mekhilta dR. Ismael, Mišpaṭim* 6; Babli *Sanhedrin* 78b, *Ketubot* 33b).

167   Once the victim was taken off the critical list, it is impossible to convict the attacker of premeditated murder.

168   *Ex.* 21:19. Both *Targum Onqelos* and *Mekhilta dR. Ismael* explain משענת not as "cane" but as "health". This meaning seems to be understood here.

169   The verse seems to be superfluous (but its continuation, spelling out the financial obligations of the attacker, is not.)

170   The term "exonerated" is read as "permanently exonerated."

171   Babli *Sanhedrin* 78a/b, *Ketubot* 33b; Tosephta *Baba qama* 9:7; *Mekhilta dR. Simeon bar Ioḥai* pp. 174-175.

172   *Ex.* 21:18.

173   Otherwise there could not be any monetary claim derived from this paragraph. (There could be a claim under rabbinic rules for insult, etc.)

174   In *Sanhedrin*: "estimated" and "did not estimate" are exchanged everywhere. This seems to be the correct version; in v. 18 the imperfect לא יָמוּת is read as "not expected to die", since it does not say לֹא מֵת. But then v. 19 could simply mean that [the attacker] has to pay for disability and medical costs; the long introductory clause therefore refers to another case. For the Sages, the medical prognosis is irrelevant.

175   As a matter of principle, a

person convicted of a crime cannot be made to pay since that would constitute multiple punishment (cf. *Terumot* 7:1, Notes 3-73; *Ketubot* 3:1). Therefore, a verse is needed to force the potential murderer to pay if his victim survives.

176   If the victim survives, it is proof that the first estimation was wrong;
there is no criminal case and the civil case can proceed unhindered.

177   From here on, the sentences have to be re-ordered as indicated by the text in *Sanhedrin* (different text in *Sanhedrin* is in parentheses and *italicized*):

What is the difference between them? If his state improved. For him who says, it is an extraordinary decree of Scripture that he pay, if he paid, he paid. If he did not pay, the verse makes him pay^{178} (*does he have to pay?*).

For him who says, it was an erroneous estimation, if he did not pay one does not order him to pay^{178}. If he paid, can he take it back?

A *baraita* supports one and a *baraita* supports the other. A *baraita* supports Rebbi Yose ben Hanina: If they estimated that he would die, when does he have to pay him? From the moment he improves^{179}. (*It proves that the estimate was wrong.*)

This (*A baraita*) supports Rebbi Simeon ben Laqish: If they estimated that he would live but he died (*die but he lived*). From when does he have to pay him (*count for him*)? From the moment he turns worse^{180}. Rebbi Yose said, it does not say here, "from the moment he turns worse" but "from the moment he turns better.^{181}" (*but from the start. That means, it is an extraordinary decree of Scripture that he pay. But if you say, it was an erroneous estimation, he has to pay until [the victim] dies.*)

178   Even if the victim later dies.

179   But for R. Simeon ben Laqish he has to pay for disability from the moment of the injury.

180   That means, even if he turns worse, since he had to pay from the start by court order. For R. Yose ben Hanina, he never pays once the case has turned into a criminal matter.

181   Then the *baraita* is no support for R. Simeon ben Laqish since R. Yose ben Hanina will agree that the agressor has to pay the victim who is getting better.

הִכָּהוּ עַל יָדוֹ וְצָמְתָה. אָמְרִין אַסָיָיא. אִין מִקְטָעָה הִיא חַיָיה הוּא.(58a line 28) מַהוּ שֶׁיִּתֵּן דְּמֵי הָעֶבֶד. נִשְׁמְעִינָה מִן הָדָא. וְכִי יִנָּצוּ. וְכִי יְרִיבוּן. וַהֲלֹא הִיא מַצּוּת הִיא מְרִיבָה. הִיא מְרִיבָה הִיא מַצּוּת. מַה תַּלְמוּד לוֹמַר וְכִי יִנָּצוּ וְכִי יְרִיבוּן. אֶלָּא לִיתֵּן אֶת הַמִּתְכַּוֵין עַל שֶׁאֵינוֹ מִתְכַּוֵּין וְאֶת שֶׁאֵינוֹ מִתְכַּוֵּין עַל הַמִּתְכַּוֵּין. אִם בְּשֶׁאֵינוֹ מִתְכַּוֵּין הוּא חַיָיב כָּל־שֶׁכֵּן בַּמִּתְכַּוֵּין. אֶלָּא כֵינִי. הִכָּהוּ עַל יָדוֹ וְצָמְתָה. אָמְרִין אַסָיָיא. אִין מִקְטָעָה הִיא חַיָיה הוּא. מַהוּ שֶׁיִּתֵּן דְּמֵי הַיָד. כְּמָה דְּאַתְּ אָמַר תַּמָּן. חִידוּשׁ מִקְרָא הוּא שֶׁיִּתֵּן דְּמֵי הָעֶבֶד. וְכָא חִידוּשׁ מִקְרָא הוּא שֶׁיִּתֵּן דְּמֵי הַיָד.

1 וצמתה | וצבת   היא חייה | ידיה חיי   2 העבד | היד   וכי ינצו | כי ינצו אנשים   ירובון | יריבון אנשים   והלא היא מצות היא מריבה | -   3 וכי ינצו וכי יריבון | כי ינצו כי יריבון כי יריבון כי ינצו   5 - | ניחא את המתכוין על שאינו מתכוין. ואת שאינו מתכוין על המתכוין   חייב | מתחייב   במתכוין | על המתכוין   6 וצמתה | וצבת   היא | ידיה   חייה | חיי   7 דאת | דת   העבד | היד   וכא | ומה

If he hit him on his hand and it withered. The physicians said, if it is amputated he will live. Does he have to pay for the [hand][182]? Let us hear from the following: "If people quarrel[183]," "if people brawl.[184]" Is not quarrel brawl and brawl quarrel? Why does the verse say, "if people quarrel, if people brawl"? To apply the rules of the unintended to the intended and of the intended to the unintended[185]. It must be the following: If he hit him on his hand and it withered. The physicians said, if it is amputated he will live. Does he have to pay for the [hand][182]? Since you say there, it is an extraordinary decree of Scripture that he pay for the hand, so here it is an extraordinary decree of Scripture that he pay for the hand[186].

182 Reading of *Sanhedrin*. The reading here, הָעֶבֶד "the slave" is an obvious misspelling for הָאֵבֶר "the limb". Throughout the Halakhah, the scribe is not sure in his distinction between ע and א.

It is clear that the attacker has to pay for the operation since this is medical treatment. The question is whether he also has to pay for the permanent impairment of the victim's earning power caused by the loss of his hand.

183 *Ex.* 21:22, speaking of the injury to an innocent bystander, the unintended victim of an intended hit. The verse decrees the responsibility of the attacker for pain and impairment of the victim.

184 *Ex.* 21:18, the paragraph under discussion, about the intended victim of an intended hit. The verse decrees the responsibility of the attacker for medical cost and disability.

185 In both cases, all four payments are due from the attacker.

186 Since the attacker has to pay for the operation, he has to pay for the permanent impairment.

(fol. 57b) **משנה ו:** נָזִיר הָיָה שְׁמוּאֵל כְּדִבְרֵי רִבִּי נְהוֹרָיי שֶׁנֶּאֱמַר וּמוֹרָה לֹא יַעֲלֶה עַל רֹאשׁוֹ. נֶאֱמַר בְּשִׁמְשׁוֹן מוֹרָה וְנֶאֱמַר בִּשְׁמוּאֵל מוֹרָה מַה מוֹרָה הָאֲמוּרָה בְּשִׁמְשׁוֹן נָזִיר אַף מוֹרָה הָאֲמוּרָה בִּשְׁמוּאֵל נָזִיר. אָמַר רִבִּי יוֹסֵי וַהֲלֹא אֵין מוֹרָא אֶלָּא שֶׁל בָּשָׂר וָדָם. אָמַר לוֹ רִבִּי נְהוֹרָאי וַהֲלֹא כְּבָר נֶאֱמַר וַיֹּאמֶר שְׁמוּאֵל אֵיךְ אֵלֵךְ וְשָׁמַע שָׁאוּל וַהֲרָגָנִי וּכְבָר הָיָה עָלָיו מוֹרָא שֶׁל בָּשָׂר וָדָם.

Mishnah 6: Samuel was a *nazir* following the words of Rebbi Nahorai, as it is said: "A shaving knife shall not come on his head[187]." It is said about Samson "a shaving knife[188]", and it is said about Samuel "a shaving knife". Since "a shaving knife" mentioned for Samson refers to *nazir*[188], so "a shaving knife" mentioned for Samuel refers to *nazir*. Rebbi Yose said, but fear[189] is only of flesh and blood! Rebbi Nahorai answered him: Was it not said: "Samuel said, how can I go? Will not Saul hear of it and kill me?[190]" The fear[191] of flesh and blood already was on him.

187 *1S.* 1:11.
188 *Jud.* 13:5
189 Reading מוֹרָא (root ירא) "fear" for מוֹרָה (root possibly נער) "shaving

knife".
190 *1S.* 16:2.

191 In most Mishnah mss., the reading here also is מוֹרָה.

הלכה ו: אָמַר רִבִּי יַנַּאי. כְּתִיב וְכָל־הֶהָרִים אֲשֶׁר בַּמַּעְדֵּר יֵעָדֵרוּן לֹא תָבֹא שָׁמָּה יִרְאַת שָׁמִיר וָשָׁיִת. מָה הָדֵין בִּיזָרָא דְּחִיל מִן הָדֵין פַּרְזְלָא. אַף הָדֵין סְעָרָא דְּחִיל מִן הָדֵין פַּרְזְלָא. (58a line 35)

Halakhah 6: Rebbi Yannai said: It is written[192]: "To all the hills which are to be worked by the harrow the fear of worm[193] and snail will not come." Just as the stalk fears the iron, so the hair fears the iron[194].

192 *Is.* 7:25.
193 A rock-splitting worm used by King Solomon to quarry the stones for the Temple without iron implements

(*Soṭah* 9:13/14, Note 219.)

193 For him, מוֹרָה also is derived from the root ירא.

Indices

Index of Biblical Quotations

Gen. 2:7	658	5:1	689	15:1	743		
6:3	658	5:4	540	15:2	744		
8:20	586	5:8	535,616	15:19	408		
9:4	581	5:14	419,518	15:33	408,745		
31:16	654	5:17	311	16:6	309		
		5:22	205	17:1	536		
Ex. 12:18	584	7:6	702	17:15	585		
12:43	152	7:7	521	18:3	352		
19:20	151	7:15	517	19:20	688		
20:5	575	7:16	517	19:27	709,710		
20:10	574	7:24	581	19:36	256		
20:24	658	7:26	581	20:25	586		
21:18	748,751	7:38	473	21:1	633,636		
21:19	745,748	10:9	592	21:3	636		
21:22	751	11:8	588	21:4	493,634		
21:26	154	11:26	585	21:7	86,350		
21:33	185	11:29	586,653	21:11	632,633		
21:35	181,182	11:34	77	21:13	310		
21:36	182	12:8	310	21:28	271		
22:4	183	13:2	744	22:3	677		
22:6	239	13:23	744	22:7	613,677		
22:8	205,206	13:33	611	22:11	219		
22:19	577	13:45	605,666	22:18	714		
22:30	581	14:2	626	22:25	714		
34:14	575	14:4	701	23:40	71		
35:3	574	14:8	474,601,611	25:28	179		
35:5	540	14:9	474,475,600,613, 700	27:1	448,549		
				27:2	508,716		
Lev. 1:2	290	14:10	474,701	27:9	548,549		
1:3	559	14:12	706	27:10	447,527,547, 553		
2:5	545	14:14	626,701	27:19	184		
3:17	581	14:22	702	27:26	547		
4:32	525	14:24	626,706	27:31	556		
4:33	627	14:33	421	27:32	559		

Num. 6:2	411,451,453, 508, 714,716	21:26	326	5:10	696	
		30:3	717			
6:3	581,588,592,593, 595	30:6	512	Jud. 13:1	420	
		30:9	519,529	13:5	430,751	
6:4	420,571,578,581, 588,591,597,693	35:29	577	13:14	596	
6:5	433,486,571,600, 603,673	Deut. 12:21	536	1S. 1:11	751	
		12:23	540	16:2	752	
6:6	467,492,571	12:26	545			
6:7	467,492,493,632 ,718	12:28	413,455	1K. 12:31	40	
		14:3	588			
6:9	488,600,613,688 ,729	14:9	585	2K. 12:6	119	
		14:11	416	17:24	40	
6:10	411,418,466, 88 ,613	14:21	580,581,656			
		15:19	119	Is. 7:25	752	
6:11	614	15:20	119	65.8	443	
6:12	428,488,497,610, 612,613,615,672	15:21	119			
		18:3	119	Jer. 2:20	144	
6:13	420,487	19:16	395	32:11	357	
6:14	525,616,684	19:17	295			
6:15	524	21:13	433	Ez. 39:14	418	
6:17	616,617	21:23	635,647	44:26	495	
6:18	474,600,616, 19, 707,708,723	22:8	340			
		23:24	540,547	Job 5:10	232	
6:19	520,618,620, 622	24:1	1,15,68,71,77,84, 91,94,101,151,171,250, 254,326,332,368, 404	Cant. 2:8	232	
6:20	620					
6:21	429,430,467,537, 626					
		24:2	94	Eccl. 4:9	351	
8:7	600	24:3	16,164,167,326			
9:10	724	24:4	407	Dan. 4:30	416	
11:32	536	24:6	595			
12:12	673	24:11	189	1Chr. 22:14	335	
12:14	673	26:10	179			
15:30	311	31:19	235			
19:12	666	34:8	433	Mark 10:9	4	
19:15	665					
19:16	667			Matth. 19:9	4,405	
19:20	667	Jos. 4:19	696			
20:29	433	5:2	696	Romans 1:26	352	

Index of Talmudical Quotations

Babylonian Talmud

Šabbat 4a	341	69b	109	18b	615		
5a	341	71b	696	19a	519		
64b	408	76a	351,352	20a	503		
65a	351			20b	473,506		
70a	574	Ketubot 17a	646	21a	508		
72a	573	18b	142	22b	509,510		
92b	671	20b	662	24b	519,521		
97a	340	27b	355	25a	522		
		33b	748	25b	523		
Erubin 16b	340	49b	203	26b	525		
17b	637,647	51a	203	27b	525,527		
69b	290	54a	145	28a	528		
79a	731	55a	275	29a	535		
		69a	202,203	29b	534		
Pesaḥim 67b	673	74b	519	30a	537		
80b	729,739	77a	150,403	32a	554,560,600		
81b	730,732	109a	399	34a	568		
				34b	578		
Yoma 55b	310	Nedarim 9b	438	35a	597		
61b	627,630	10b	416	39a	694		
80b	583	17b	483	39b	486,600		
		77b	510	40a	603,604		
Sukkah 41b	72			42a	603		
		Nazir 2b	414	43a	493		
Yom Ṭob 8b	635	3b	421,611	43b	636,637		
		4a	427	44a	600,610,612		
Megillah 28a	235	4b	430,438	45b	619		
29a	646	5a	433	46b	626,630		
		7a	434	47b	627,632		
Mo'ed qaṭan 19b	479	8b	427	49b	650,652		
22b	479	9b	443,448	50a	654		
		11b	456,459	50b	658		
Ḥagigah 10a	151	13b	473	51a	659		
		14a	467,468	51b	653		
Yebamot 3b	635	15a	470	52a	615,653		
6b	577	16b	488	Nazir 54a	667		
43b	637	17a	466	57b	710		
58a	219	18a	466	62b	720		

Nazir 63b	661,730	33b	138	75b	316
65a	736,737	34b	140	76b	299,320
65b	744	35a	145	77a	324,328
		37b	149,150	77b	326,328
Giṭṭin 2a	7	38a	314	78a	15,331,332
2b	7	39a	152,157	78b	23
3a	8,142	41b	151,162,163	79a	334,341
5a	19	42a	154	79b	334,343
5b	15,17	44b	166	80b	350
6a	19,27	45b	169	81a	354
6b	19	46a	171	82b	366
7a	273	46b	175,176	83a	368,371
7b	24	47a	176	84a	455
8a	30	48a	187	84b	15,99,373
9a	34	48b	181,187	86a	380,381
10a	36,37	49a	181	86b	105,373
11b	12,13,248	50b	197	87b	401
13a	46,54	52a	215	88a	396
14a	50,52	52b	211	88b	403
15a	54	53a	212	89a	21,406
15b	59	55a	221,222		
17a	61,63,145	58a	228	Qiddušin 9a	93
17b	63	58b	224,231,235	9b	94
18b	38,59,66	59a	224	21b	254
19a	69,70	60a	241	23a	151
20b	72,74	60b	238	23b	328
21a	76	61b	241	25a	388
21b	79	62b	250	43a	45
22b	81,83	63a	254	43b	161
23a	83,85	63b	251,255,258	44a	263
23b	85,162	65a	267,270	59a	133,304
24a	88	65b	263	75b	40
24b	90,92	66a	103,273,277		
25a	92,93	66b	282,296	Baba qama 7a	185
25b	93	67a	296	7b	190
26a	103,104	67b	283	8a	191
27b	108	70b	290,295	11b	113
28a	108,109	71a	295	30b	160
29a	112,282	71b	282	56b	113
29b	115,151,271	72b	282,299,301	73b	506
30a	119,121	73a	306	80b	647
30b	121	73b	308,309	85a	574
32b	135	74a	312		
33a	137,138	75a	313		

INDEX OF TALMUDICAL QUOTATIONS

Baba meṣiʻa 7a	23	22b	433	103a	443,515
10b	263	27b	483	105a	700
11a	263	32a	506		
14b	197	38a	388	Keritut 9a	688
15b	197			12a	686
16a	199,200	Sanhedrin 22a	4	13a	592
36a	113	22b	433	24b	48
49a	256	45b	635	27b	525
56b	326	47b	739		
60a	671	56a	635	Bekhorot 13b	256
72a	160	60b	577	23a	589
101a	221	62a	573	23b	656
		69b	351		
Baba batra 85a	330	78a	748	ʻArakhin 7b	272
94b	160	105b	717		
96a	128			Temurah 25b	162
121a	54	Makkot 6a	506		
136a	303	16b	588	Meʻilah 15b	586
138a	48				
161b	358	Abodah zarah 37a		Ḥulin 5a	290
162b	392		299	39b	48,280
163a	393	66a	588	44a	273
163b	395			86a	536
164a	82,363	Zebaḥim 12b	290	102b	581
168a	143	76a	700,705	103b	583
175a	54				
175b	274	Menaḥot 72b	714	Niddah 56a	653, 656
Šebuʻot 17a	493	81b	413	70a	700

Jerusalem Talmud

Berakhot 1:1	433		665, 676	6:1	6,24,25,30
2:1	506	3:4	40	9:6	304
3:1	638	4:6	242	10:2	189
4:5	263	4:7	269	10:3	144,147
5:5	235,237	5:9	177	10:5	142
6:1	584,653	Kilaim 1:9	341	Terumot 1:1	208,287,
7:2	566	2:5	647		292
Peah 1:1	558	5:2	742	1:4	138
2:5	555	8:1	692	2:1	671
3:9	192,271,275	Ševiʻit 1:1	179	Terumot 3:1	283
4:2	336	4:3	3,246	3:8	539,547
Demay 2:3	77,647,	5:9	3,243	5:9	625

Terumot 7:1	215,581	11:1	580	2:2	424	
10:1	589	14:1	290	5:4	170	
Ma'aser Šeni 4:4	240	14:2	217	6:1	620,622	
4:7	254	14:3	216	9:2	563	
5:5	234	15:3	203	10:1	260	
Orlah 1:4	622	15:4	8,87	10:10	510,511	
2:6	589	15:5	503	11:1	718	
Hallah 2:1	635	16:6	107,276	11:8	162,519	
		Ketubot 1:5	226	Qiddušin 1:1	93,94	
Šabbat 1:1	299, 341	2:2	34	1:3	86	
3:4	274	2:3	142	1:4	113,329	
7:1	573,574	2:10	111	2:1	45,254,262,388	
7:2	573	4:2	251	2:4	267	
10:4	671	5:5	119,233	3:1	468	
12:5	68	5:10	552	3:2	313,317	
Erubin 3	317	6:1	162	3:3	52	
6	238	6:4	201	4:9	113	
10	341	6:6	201			
Pesaḥim 1:1	36	7:7	144,173	Baba qama 4:5	209	
2:2	159,160	7:9	173	9:1	221	
6:2	560	7:10	142	10:1	273	
7:7	724	9:1	453,460	Baba meṣi'a 1:1	23	
8:8	694,696	9:4	313	1:6	273	
Šeqalim 2:3	542	9:5	112	Baba batra 6:1	128	
Yoma 3:5	142	9:8	143,195	6:9	47,103	
Yom Ṭob 1:3	635	10:5	228	8:8	48	
5:2	4	11:1	54	5:1	647	
Megillah 3:5	473	11:5	11	10:1	357,392	
	Ta'aniot	12:5	192	10:14	314	
Mo'ed qaṭan 1:7	163	15:3	197	Šebuot 3:3	424	
3:5	479	Soṭah 1:1		4:4	469	
3:7	506		308,404,407	5:4	515	
		1:2	694,727	5:5	387,388	
Yebamot 1:1	137, 173	2:5	66	Sanhedrin 1:2	281	
1:2	216	2:6	78	5:2	503	
1:6	40	3:9	532	9:3	748	
3:9	375	4:4	314	Makkot 1:16	11	
4:8	203	5:1	549	Horaiot 1:2	290	
7:1	160,229,328	5:2	613	1:3	549	
9:5	402	6:2	690	Abodah Zarah 2:8		
10:1	27	9:13	752		299	
10:4	34	Nedarim 1:1				
10:5	348		412,413,423	Niddah 3	299	
10:13	352	1:2	415			

Mishnah

Peah 3:9	193	9:2	561,717	9:8	556,559
Demay 7:5	125	9:6	482	Keritut 2:2	689
Kilaim 3:3	742	9:7	388,504	3:1	688
Terumot 3:8	539	11:1	528	Ḥulin 2:7	279
11:3	584	11:8	328	6;4	659
Ma'aśer Šeni 4:7	255	Qiddušin 1:1	317	Temurah 2:3	547
Orlah 1:6	596	1:4	330	5:5	446
1:7	595	1:6	304	7:6	683
Bikkurim 1:2	179, 124	3:1	304	Arakhin 1:2	716
				6:1	551
2:9	567	Baba qama 1:5	209	6:2	183
		4:3	181	6:5	145
Šabbat 1:1	341	9:2	212,221	Me'ilah 3:2	522
11:1	341	Baba meṣi'a 1:4	337	4:3	586
12:5	68	7:8	52		
Pesaḥim 7:4	728	Baba batra 6:3	130	Kelim 1:4	673
7:7	728	6:8	741	17:11	570
Šeqalim 2:4	542	8:7	302	24:13	96
2:5	524	10:1	362,364	Ahilut 1:1	676
2:6	522	10:3	360	1:2	676
Yoma 1:1	309	10:4	141	1:3	677
Megillah 1:8	674	Šebuot 2:3	492	1:7	586
Mo'ed qaṭan 1:7	163	3:5	424	2:1	584,637,652, 675
3:5	478	5:3	515		
		5:5	389	2:2	658,675
Yebamot 1:1	347, 368	6:1	205	2:3	661
		Sanhedrin 3:3	356	4:3	670
2:1	355	Makkot 3:10	512	4:5	654
2:4	375	Idiut 4:11	499	6:1	670
3:9	335	Abodah Zarah 2:9		6:3	671
6:5	173		299	7:1	670
10:1	8,345			15:1	731
15:4	86	Zebaḥim 1:1	628	16:5	736
Ketubot 1:5	355	5:5	702	Nega'im 3:1	699
4:6	309	8:3	707	8:8	674
7:10	46	10:5	6:7	14:1	701
9:1	328	Menaḥot 12:2	545	14:3	707,613
12:5	193	12:3	443,456,516	Nega'im 14:4	603
13:5	317	Bekhorot 2:8	119	14:9	626
Nedarim 1:1	411	4:4	212	14:12	702

760 INDICES

Ṭaharot 3:5	129	9:2	605	3:3	652	
4:12	568	Zabim 2:2	743	3:5	652	
5:9	686	Parah 11:4	675	5:6	533	
Miqwa'ot 2:2	125	Niddah 3:2	652	7:1	656	

Tosephta

Peah 2:2	337	1:8	50	Soṭah 3:16	427
Demay 7:15	120	1:9	50,54	5:5	352
		2:1	15		
Šabbat 11:8	70	2:2	22,61	Baba qama 10:5	221
		2:4	70	9:7	748
Ketubot 8:10	221	2:5	72	10:6	221
12:2	187	2:10	105	Baba batra 8:1	48
Nazir 1:1	416,421,	2:12	111	Sanhedrin 2:11	72
	438	2:13	112	'Abodah zarah 3:6	
1:3	427	3:1	120		169
1:4	437	3:3	138	3:7	169
1:5	425,430,626	3:4	150	3:18	166
1:6	630	3:5	171,173	9:4	635
2:1	443	3:7	207	Idiut 2:2	533
2:3	456	3:8	207		
2:6	467	3:10	226,227	Me'ilah 1:10	523, 527
2:8	464	3:11	228		
2:10	468	4:1	254	Kelim baba meṣi'a 1:5	
2:15	483	4:2	250,254,257		680
3:1	503	4:7	277	1:13	96
3:3	508	4:12	109	3:10	129
3:10	513	4:13	283	Ahilut 2:2	658
3:19	568,569	5:1	291,295	2:3	654,659
4:3	486,604	5:4	308,309	2:5	663
4:4	612	5:5	312	2:6	663
4:6	619	5:6	313,316	4:3	654,655
4:7	438	5:12	455	4:4	655
4:8	615	6:1	15,332	4:13	664
4:10	628	6:2	20	15:5	731
5:2	474	6:4	13	16:1	662
6:1	699,704,711	6:5	140	16:9	739
6:6	719,720	6:9	277,354	Ṭaharot 5:6	732
Giṭṭin 1:1	34	7:5	369	Nega'im 12:1	421
1:6	50	7:11	13,38,72,103, 392	Zabim 2:9	730, 732
1:7	50	Qiddušin 3:3	454	Niddah 5:15	534

Midrashim

Gen. rabba	658	Sifra	78,179,256,290,	Sifry zuṭa	617,717
Num. rabba	438,467,		352,408,473,508,525,	Sifry Deut.	164,189,
	537,610,619,620		559,574,585,586,592,		326,332,386,405,433,580,
Mekhilta dR. Ismael			597,600,613,626,636,		595
	154,181,187,272,427,574,		673,614,744	Tractate Śemaḥot	355,636,
	577,748	Sifry Num.	438,474,		637,646,739,740
Mekhilta dR. Simeon bar			486,497,529,536,578,596,	Targum Onqelos	748
Ioḥai	187,272,428,577,		597,600,610,612,617,667,	Targum Pseudo-Jonathan	
	581,748		676,688		667

Rabbinic Literature

Arukh	97,422,436,654	Nissim Gerondi	139, 265	Sefer Ha'iṭṭur	63,65,80,
Aviezri	50	Or Zarua	355		81,83,108,228,231,271,
Azulay, H.Y.D.	401	Pardo, D.	97,654		283
Maimonides	97,129,	Qafeḥ, Y.	509	Sefer Miṣwot Gadol	
	232,352,509,586,599,613,	Rashba	50,80,198,199,		50,129
	673,707,739		249,277,303,319,372	Šulḥan Arukh	53,352
Margalit, M.	654	Rashi	199,232,271,295,	Yalquṭ Šim'oni	474,537,
Meïri	198,199		358,599,613,673		636
Mordekhay	50	Ravad	673,739	Yosef Ḥabiba	249
Nahmanides	99,100	Rosh	50		

Index of Greek, Latin, and Hebrew Words

ἀναφορά	228			κιλίκιον	606
ἀντίδοσις	168	ἐπίτροπος	206	κορδακικός	285
ἀντίχρησις	168	ἐπίχειρον	168		
ἀποίητος	232			μαλλός	331
ἀρχεῖα, τά	36	ἡγεμών	6	μέλαθρον	670
ἀρχεῖον, τό	36			μῆλον	68
		Ἰουδαϊκός	13		
γλωσσόκομον	106			νάρθηξ	77
γραμμάριον	231	κάλαθος	325	νομή	657
		κάρυον ποντικόν		νόμος	269
δίγονος	422		305		

πεντάγωνος	422	salio	352	הרנירק טיאנום	153
		sicarius	223		
στολίς	312	stola	312	מחובר,מחוור	240,548
στρατιώτης	697			מלוש	331
σύμφωνος, -ον	317	tremis	231		
				סבא	138
τετράγωνος	422	vindicta	154	סיקריקון,סיקריקין	223
τρίγωνος	422	vivus	303	סלד,סלל,סלסל	351
ὕστερος	303			פיגול	207
		איסרטא	303		
ὠνή	168	אנדוכתרי	104,155	ترنگان	71
		אנטוקטא	154		
collare	270	ארכובה	660	فندق	305
cordax, κόρδαξ	285				
culcitra	605	גלגל	556	نزح	411
				نزق	411

Author Index

Albeck, H.	358	Guggenheimer, H.	240,306, 438,548,570,611	Ostersetzer, I.	168
Epstein, J.N.	46,168, 277,401,505	Gulak, A.	223,228	Philo	35,409
				Pineles, H.M.	154
		Joseph II, Emperor	140		
Feldblum, M.S.	180			Sussman, J.	654
Fleischer, H.L.	232				
Friedman, M.A.	13,397	Lieberman, S.	45,50,72, 97,120,224,228,229,233,	Taubenschlag, R.	155,168
Guggenheimer, E. and H.	13,287,345		254,392,422,537,699	Zuckermandel, M.S.	277

Subject Index

Abandonment	151,227	questionable	255
Acco	22	revocation	133,135
legal status	30	silent	254
Acquisition, by property	264	wife's	257,258
on public land	264	Agent, joint	282
power of	328,333	of creditor	50
Admission, partial	205	substitute	112,115,116
Adolescent	259,262	to deliver	250
After Sabbath	324	to receive	250
Agency, for words	282	Animal, crawling	586
Agency, power of	45	impure	585,586

GENERAL INDEX 763

limb of living	583,588
Antipatris	320
Apprentice	233
Arrest, precautionary	748
Asmakhta contract	233
Bill of manumission, text	378
Babylonia, legal status	27
Bar Kokhba, war of	226
Benefit, to unaware	248
Bespeaking	355
Bet se'ah	740
Bill of divorce, autograph	379
bilingual	390
certified	114
conditional	99,100
delivery	15,16,20,42,75
dforclosure	381
indirect delivery	22
loan, undocumented	383
text	378,397
validation	19,59,61
Bird sacrifices	535
Building material, stolen	221
Burial caves	741
Caesarea maritima	24
Calendar, computed	692
Carcass meat	656
Commandment, positive and negative	685
Confession	686
Convert, single	157
Corpse, incomplete	636,650,661, 661,663
of obligation	632,637,645,647
unattended	609
Counting, subtractive	480
Court certification	13
Court, *ad hoc*	135
permanent	135
Creature, complete	584,588,598
Criminal intent	692
Day, part of	470,476,480,496
Days, immunized	473
Dead Sea, throwing into	518
Deaf-mute	216
Deaf-mute	290
Deathbed gift	271
divorce	282,298
Debt, renunciation	53
Debts, in dispute	499
inherited	185
liquidation	182,192
privileged	181
Decrees of Joshua	647
Dedication, as donation	714
as gift	714
in anticipation	483
in error	538,544,547,548
invalid	447
redemption of	184
Defects, invisible	207,212,213
Dema'	207
Demons	276
Denar	555
area	231
money	231
Diadem, of High Priest	728
Divorce document, delivery	333, 339,341
Divorce, and *ketubah*	74
annulled retroactively	171, 174,175
conditional	312,369,371,374,378
consensual	74
date of	346,379
deferred	299,300,305,309,311
forced	20,403
imperfect	373
invalidated	308
multiple	388
no fault	405
of Cohen	92,93
paid	112
payment for	142,143
presumptive	106
public	259
sex after	342,343,354,355
smell of	373
Divorcee	350,370
Document, bald	353
confirmation	395
date	301
knotted	353,357,360
postdated	395
predated	12
public	357
sealed	358,363
signatures	392
simple	353
forms of	56
dating	63,65,101
invalid	103
of marriage	94
retroactive validation	93
Double doubt	404
Double expression	689

Eight Reptiles	586	Idolatry	574
Equal cut	508	Immediately	506
Eruv	234,237	Immersion and sundown	613,677
Estate, claims against	209	Impurity, degrees of	676
claims of	205	derivative	494,665,733
daughters' claim	202	disappearing	589
of minors	551	guilt for	675,677
Evaluation	716	immune objects	680
Expenses, medical	750	in doubt	694,697,706,722
		in public	725,727
False oath	515	leaving	670
Firstling	547	major	667
questionable	119	of blood	664
Food, impure	214	of bones	650,664,667
supervision	299	of broken field	665,695
Foreclosure, from buyer	193	of corpse	696
of pledge	160	of discharge	743,745
Four Cups	611	of fetus	652
		of flux	673
Generally known	21	of garments	680
Geṭ	1	of objects	670,677
Girl, nubile	218,219	of skin disease	673
Gladiator	176	of stalks	76
Glued	340	original	676,677,733
Government, foreign	344	rabbinic	694
Grave	663	squeezed	670,671,731,734,740
common	659	week-long	745
dust	659,662	of vessels	97
in abyss	723,724,728,730,732	prepared	77
in public road	739	Injury, critical	745
knocker	665	Insane	216
removal	738,739		
roller	665	Jubilee	179
site	647	Judge, incompetent	212
surroundings	736		
Graveyard	735,736	Kafr 'Uthnay	36,320
Guardian	207,210	Kefar Ludim	5
		Kefar Simaï	28
Ḥaliṣah	355	Ketubah	194
Hair, removal of	486	Kol Nidre	144
Hand	325	Koy	567
Heave, biblical	138		
future	123	Laban	717
Ḥeger	5	Language, unapproved	413
Hermeneutical rules	574,578,597,633	Lawyers, need for	104
High Priest, unmarried	310	Legal tender	185
Holidays, intermediate	163	Legalese	321
Honest yes	256	Letter numerals	433
Human decay	656,658	Lexemes, uniqueness	433
Husband, legal standing	34	Libation wine	207,215
testimony of	8	Line size	393
		Loan, antichretic	168
		Loan, repaid indirectly	117
Identity theft	396	Lydda	5

GENERAL INDEX

marriage, impossible	374
to niece	368
Manumission,	166
consequences	11
effective date	44
in absentia	157
of pledge	160
partial	162
Marriage, by contract	317,318
celebration	406
deferred	304
incestuous	137
preliminary	308
Mem partitive	559
Metathesis	536
Miqweh, in cave	722
Money, leftover	522
non-designated	527
Mortgage, rabbinic	12
Mortmain	229,230,328
Mourning week	478
Names, Gentile	12
Natural law	635,717
Nazir	409
defiled	492
exiting	724
in diaspora	498
limbless	626
purified	619
relieved	620
sacrifice	627,628
shaved improperly	629
shavings of	708
shaving of	457
Nests	310
Nezirut, completion	709
in perpetuity	429
of child	531
long	437
multiple	427,431,436
partial	452
resumption	615
suspended	666
unspecified	417,427
Nursing, obligatory	314,316
Oath, biblical	205
partially valid	424
Of age, adolescent	262,265
in general	206
real estate transactions	206
Offering account	522

unusual	456
Olive size	570,592
Orlah	424
Overseas trip	320
Ownership	168
transfer of	330
Prozbol	144
Palimpsest	82
Paraphernalia	225,228,231
Paraphernalis	328
Passover, exlusion from	152
in impurity	728
Second	695,724,728
subscriber	729
Pawn	168
Perjury	396
Permanence of status quo	735,736
Permutation	656
Phrygian cap	154
Piggul	207,279
Plural	594
Possession	168
Practice	675
Pregnancy, termination of	652
Priest, at burial	637,644
intoxicated	592
Priestly blessing	237
Prima facie evidence	748
Profane, in Temple	545
Promise to Heaven	520
Property, encumbered	193
not seizable	145
Prothetic Alef	303
Public sale	551
Punishment, multiple	215,749
Purification offering	290,310,311, 517,525,530, 627,683,705
Qab	650
Qorban	441
Quartarius	570,592
Queen Helena	499
Ransoming	148 ff.,164
of slaves	150
Real estate, graded	183,187,190,191
robbed	196,197.199,224
sold to extortionist	225,228,231
wife's	2229,230
Red Cow	213,466,495,613,696,719
Redemption	447
Reparation offering	521
Reqam	5

Rights of the poor	234	sacrificial	279
		while thinking	280
Sabbath prohibitions	573	Slave girl, assigned	688
Sabbath domain	341,342	Slave, as agent	85,86
Sacrifice, at nighttime	473	injured	154
cereal	545	marrying	158
consumption	618	obligations of	164
dedication	618	ownerless	152,157,167
disqualified	447	property of	162
donation	629	resident of Land	166
empty	521	testimony of	308
forced	688	Status, biblical	720
inherited	536	quasi-biblical	720
obligatory	419	*Status quo ante*	108
of impurity	682	Stillbirth	662
of *nazir*	684,698	Stipulation, of Gad and Ruben	454
of purity	682	Substitution	447
sinful	216	in error	547
time limit	702		
unacceptable	222	Temple tax	542
voluntary	701	Tent impurity	489,655,670,662,665
vow of	629	*Terephah*	580
Sacrificial animal, not usable	707	Testimonials	216
Samaritans	35,36,37,39,40	*Tevel*	126
Samson *nazir*	420,430,649	Tithe, animal	556
Samuel, prophet	751	Torah reading, precedence	234
Sanctity, bodily	446	Tosephta, unknown to Talmudim	121
of worth	446	Transgression, composite	583,588
Separation of properties	517	multiple	581,605
Sepphoris	24	warning for	593
Shamir	752	Trapping	241
Shaving	612,618	Trustee, unpaid	313
in doubt	709,710,711		
She-ram	173,346	Uncircumcised	696
Signature, artful	401	Underage girl, emancipation	251
notarized	34	married	265
of illiterate	70	Urban area	740
of judges	399		
of scribe	405	Valuation	448
place of	38,73	*Vectigal*	228
Sin, intentional	311	*Via maris*	320
major	525	Vinegar	128
minor	525,677	Vow formula	418
passive	600	Vow, ambiguous	445
unintentional	574	annulment	513,521
Sins, multiple	407	conditional	462
Skin disease	474,600,601	dissolution	717
diagnosed	673,697,699,743	frivolous	457
expiation	701,702,705,711,743	inappropriate	448
healed	609,613,626,665,698	in error	453
in quarantine	666,673	of drunk	452
Slaughter, for idolatry	279	of Gentile	713
in Temple	536	of sacrifice	459,468
ritual	536	of slave	713,718,719,720,721

GENERAL INDEX

of value	716
opening	482
unclear	568,569
Vows, public	170
Warning, of punishment	490,492
Water canals	318
Welfare fund, borrowing power	123
Well-being offering	517,518,530
Widow's oath	143
Wig	272,528
Wine, trade standards	130
Witness, disqualified	38,356
factual	406
Gentile	42
single	686
Witnesses	686,689
Woman, anchored	137
Word, split	549
Writing materials	70,72
Year, definition	438

www.ingramcontent.com/pod-product-compliance
Lightning Source LLC
Chambersburg PA
CBHW030235240426
43663CB00037B/457